June 11-14, 2018
Yokohama, Japan

Association for
Computing Machinery

Advancing Computing as a Science & Profession

ICMR'18

Proceedings of the 2018 ACM

International Conference on Multimedia Retrieval

Sponsored by:

ACM SIGMM

Supported by:

NEC, Hitachi, NVIDIA, CyberAgent, LIFULL, Mercari, DeNA, Yahoo! Japan, Kayarnori Foundation, The Telecommunicatins Advancement Foundation, SCAT, Yokohama Convention & Visitors Bureau

Association for
Computing Machinery

Advancing Computing as a Science & Profession

The Association for Computing Machinery
2 Penn Plaza, Suite 701
New York, New York 10121-0701

ISBN: 978-1-4503-5046-4 (Digital)

ISBN: 978-1-4503-6152-1 (Print)

Additional copies may be ordered prepaid from:

ACM Order Department
PO Box 30777
New York, NY 10087-0777, USA

Phone: 1-800-342-6626 (USA and Canada)
+1-212-626-0500 (Global)
Fax: +1-212-944-1318
E-mail: acmhelp@acm.org
Hours of Operation: 8:30 am – 4:30 pm ET

Message from the General Chairs

We are delighted to welcome you to the eighth ACM International Conference on Multimedia Retrieval, ACM ICMR 2018, which is held from June 11th to 14th, 2018 in Yokohama, Japan. Welcome to Yokohama, Japan's second most populous city and the symbolic city of its opening to the world.

ACM ICMR is the premier conference and a worldwide event bringing together experts and practitioners in the fields related to multimedia retrieval across academia and industry. The core feature of the conference, which continues this year as in every year, is the outstanding Technical Program chosen through a highly selective review process.

In addition to the Technical Program, this year's conference features a diverse range of activities including Keynote talks, Demonstrations, Special Sessions, a Panel, a Doctoral Symposium, Industrial Talks, and Tutorials. Additionally, Workshops bring focus on new topics for investigation.

In an attempt to continuously improve ACM ICMR and ensure its vibrant role in the multimedia community, we have made a number of enhancements for this year's conference. Among them, it should be noted that the Technical Program Committee decided to remove the distinction of long and short papers and unified them into a single "regular paper" track.

We greatly acknowledge those who have contributed to the success of ACM ICMR 2018. We thank the many paper authors and proposal contributors for the various technical and program components. We thank the large number of volunteers, including the Organizing Committee members and the Technical Program Committee members who worked very hard to create this year's outstanding conference. Every aspect of the conference was aided by the Local Committee members to whom we are very grateful. We thank also ACM and Sheridan Printing for their constant support.

Finally, we thank our official sponsors, ACM and SIGMM, for their sustained help. We also thank our many supporters from Japan who generously sponsored ACM ICMR 2018. They include NEC, Hitachi, NVIDIA, CyberAgent, LIFULL, Mercari, DeNA, and YAHOO! JAPAN. Other generous support were kindly provided by Kayamori Foundation, The Telecommunications Advancement Foundation, SCAT (Support Center for Advanced Telecommunications Technology Research, Foundation), and Yokohama Convention & Visitors Bureau.

Enjoy ACM ICMR 2018!

ACM ICMR 2018 General Chairs

Kiyoharu Aizawa
The University of Tokyo

Shin'ichi Satoh
National Institute of Informatics

Michael Lew
Leiden University

Message from the Technical Program Chairs

We are pleased to introduce you to the Technical Program for the eighth ACM International Conference on Multimedia Retrieval, ACM ICMR 2018, which will take place from June 11 to June 14, 2018 in Yokohama, Japan.

ACM ICMR is the premier conference in the area of multimedia retrieval, offering great opportunities for exchanging leading-edge multimedia retrieval ideas among researchers and practitioners across academia and industry. Multimedia computing, indexing, and retrieval continue to be one of the most exciting and fastest-growing research areas in the field of multimedia technology. The Technical Program of ACM ICMR has gathered outstanding works advancing the field of multimedia retrieval with state-of-the-art technologies, which were selected through a highly selective review process.

From this year, following the success initiated at ACM Multimedia 2017, the conference invited research papers with varying lengths from six to eight pages, plus an additional one page for references. There is no longer the distinction between long and short papers but authors may themselves decide on the appropriate length of the paper. Long and short paper tracks were unified into a single "regular paper" track, and all papers went through the same review process and review period.

This year, ACM ICMR received 179 submissions to the main conference. After a rigorous review process by the program committee members, 68 papers were accepted for presentation including 44 regular papers, 11 special session papers, 8 demo papers, and 5 doctoral symposium papers. Detailed statistics are as follows:

Tracks	*# Submissions*	*# Accepted*	*Acceptance Rate*
Regular	136	44 (Oral: 21, Poster: 23)	32.4% (Oral: 15.4%)
Special Session	23	11 (Oral: 5, Poster: 6)	47.8% (Oral: 21.7%)
Demonstrations	13	8	61.5%
Doctoral Symposium	7	5	71.4%

Regarding regular papers, we aimed to have four reviews for each submission. We have recruited 111 program committee members to contribute their professional reviews to the submission in a double-blind manner. In the end, we received 518 reviews, which equates to 3.8 reviews for each regular submission. We, TPC co-chairs, selected 21 oral papers and 23 poster papers based on the review scores and comments. As a result, we were able to prepare a very strong technical program, although unfortunately we had to reject many good papers.

We greatly acknowledge those who have contributed to the success of ACM ICMR 2018. We thank the many paper authors and Technical Program Committee members who worked very hard to create this year's outstanding program.

ACM ICMR 2018 Technical Program Chairs

Benoit Huet
Eurecom

Qi Tian
The University of Texas at San Antonio

Keiji Yanai
The University of Electro-Communications, Tokyo

Table of Contents

Session: Oral Session 1: Multimedia Retrieval

Session Chair: Qi Tan *(The University of Texas at San Antonio)*

Session: Oral Session 2: Multimedia Content Analysis

Session Chair: Wei-Ta Chu *(National Chung Cheng University)*

Session: Oral Session 3: Multimedia Applications

Session Chair: Wolfgang Hürst *(Utrecht University)*

Session: Oral Session 4: Video Analysis

Session Chair: Koichi Shinoda *(Tokyo Institute of Technology)*

Session: Poster Paper Session

Session Chair: Keiji Yanai *(The University of Electro-Communications, Tokyo)*

Session: Special Session 1: Predicting User Perceptions of Multimedia Content

Session Chair: Claire-Hélène Demarty *(Technicolor)*

ICMR '18 International Conference on Multimedia Retrieval Organization

Conference Co-Chairs: Kiyoharu Aizawa *(The Univ. of Tokyo, Japan)*
Michael Lew *(Leiden Univ., Netherlands)*
Shin'ichi Satoh *(National Inst. of Informatics, Japan)*

Honorary Co-Chairs: Noboru Babaguchi *(Osaka Univ. , Japan)*
Yong Rui *(Lenovo, China)*

Technical Program Co-Chairs: Benoit Huet *(Eurecom, Japan)*
Qi Tian *(The Univ. of Texas at San Antonio, Japan)*
Keiji Yanai *(The Univ. of Electro-Comm., Japan)*

Organizing Co-Chairs: Ichiro Ide *(Nagoya Univ., Japan)*
Toshihiko Yamasaki *(The Univ. of Tokyo, Japan)*

Practitioners Co-Chairs: Go Irie *(Nippon Telegraph & Telephone, Japan)*
Tao Mei *(JD.com, China)*

Doctoral Symposium Co-Chairs: Martha Larson *(Delft Univ. of Tech., Netherlands)*
Takahiro Ogawa *(Hokkaido Univ., Japan)*

Special Session Co-Chairs: Shuqiang Jiang *(Chinese Academy of Sci., China)*
Takahiro Mochizuki *(NHK STRL, Japan)*

Workshop Co-Chairs: Winston Hsu *(National Taiwan Univ., Taiwan)*
Naoko Nitta *(Osaka Univ., Japan)*

Panel Co-Chairs: Chong-Wah Ngo *(City Univ. of Hong Kong, China)*
Vincent Oria *(New Jersey Inst. of Tech., United States)*

Tutorial Co-Chairs: Richang Hong *(Hefei Univ. of Tech., China)*
Balakrishnan Prabhakaran *(The Univ. of Texas at Dallas, United States)*

Demo Co-Chairs: Koichi Shinoda *(Tokyo Inst. of Tech., Japan)*
Zhipeng Wu *(Apple Japan, Japan)*

Publicity Co-Chairs: Alexander Hauptmann *(Carnegie Mellon Univ., United States)*
Chil-Woo Lee *(Chonnam National Univ., Korea)*
Rainer Lienhart *(Univ. of Augsburg, Germany)*
Changsheng Xu *(Chinese Academy of Sci., China)*

Publication Co-Chairs: Yusuke Matsui *(National Inst. of Informatics, Japan)*
Yoshitaka Ushiku *(The Univ. of Tokyo, Japan)*

Finance Chair: Yusuke Uchida *(DeNA, Japan)*

Technical Program Committee: Laurent Amsaleg *(CNRS-IRISA, France)*
Werner Bailer *(JOANNEUM RESEARCH, Austria)*
Olfa Ben-Ahmed *(EURECOM, France)*
Marco Bertini *(Universita' degli Studi di Firenze, Italy)*
K. Selcuk Candan *(Arizona State University, United States)*
Jean Carrive *(French National Audiovisual Institute, France)*
Pablo Cesar *(CWI: Centrum Wiskunde & Informatica, Netherlands)*
Cunjian Chen *(Michigan State University, United States)*
Wen-Huang Cheng *(Academia Sinica, Taiwan)*
Wei-Ta Chu *(National Chung Cheng University, Taiwan)*
Yung-Yu Chuang *(National Taiwan University, Taiwan)*
Matthew Cooper *(FX Palo Alto Lab, Inc., United States)*
Maaike de Boer *(TNO / Radboud University Nijmegen, Netherlands)*
Alberto Del Bimbo *(Universita degli Studi di Firenze, Italy)*
Emmanuel Dellandrea *(LIRIS-Ecole Centrale de Lyon, France)*
Pinar Duygulu *(Hacettepe University, Turkey)*
Koji Eguchi *(Kobe University, Japan)*
Ralph Ewerth *(Leibniz Information Centre for Science and Technology (TIB),* Hannover, Germany)
Jianping Fan *(UNC Charlotte, United States)*
Quanfu Fan *(IBM, United States)*
Giovanni Maria Farinella *(University of Catania, Italy)*
Haiyan Fu *(Dalian University of Technology, China)*
Chuang Gan *(MIT-Watson Lab, China)*
Efstratios Gavves *(University of Amsterdam, Netherlands)*
Xavier Giro-I-Nieto *(Universitat Politècnica de Catalunya, Catalonia/Spain)*
Nikolaos Gkalelis *(ITI, Greece)*
Guillaume Gravier *(CNRS, IRISA, France)*
Cathal Gurrin *(Dublin City University, Ireland)*
Yahong Han *(Tianjin University, China)*
Jonathon Hare *(University of Southampton, United Kingdom)*
Andreas Henrich *(University of Bamberg, Germany)*
Richang Hong *(Hefei University of Technology, China)*
Frank Hopfgartner *(The University of Sheffield, United Kingdom)*
Wolfgang Hürst *(Utrecht University, Netherlands)*
Ichiro Ide *(Nagoya University, Japan)*
Bogdan Ionescu *(University Politehnica of Bucharest, Romania)*
Go Irie *(NTT, Japan)*
Yu-Gang Jiang *(Fudan University, China)*
Alexis Joly *(INRIA, France)*
Gareth Jones *(Dublin City University, Ireland)*
Joemon Jose *(University of Glasgow, United Kingdom)*
Brendan Jou *(Google, United States)*
Mohan Kankanhalli *(National University of Singapore, Singapore)*

Technical Program Committee (continued):

John Kender *(Columbia University, United States)*
Lyndon Kennedy *(FXPAL, United States)*
Akisato Kimura *(NTT, Japan)*
Yiannis Kompatsiaris *(CERTH - ITI, Greece)*
Xirong Li *(Renmin University of China, China)*
Rainer Lienhart *(Universitt Augsburg, Germany)*
Jianquan Liu *(NEC Corporation, Japan)*
Xueliang Liu *(Hefei University of Tech, China)*
Yijuan Lu *(Texas State University, United States)*
Mathias Lux *(Klagenfurt University, Austria)*
Joao Magalhaes *(Universidade NOVA de Lisboa, Portugal)*
Yasushi Makihara *(Osaka University, Japan)*
Yusuke Matsui *(NII, Japan)*
Kevin Mcguinness *(Dublin City University, Ireland)*
Bernard Merialdo *(EURECOM, France)*
Michele Merler *(IBM TJ Watson, United States)*
Pascal Mettes *(University of Amsterdam, Netherlands)*
Vasileios Mezaris *(Informatics and Telematics Institute/ Centre for Research and Technology Hellas, Greece)*
Elaheh Momeni *(University of Vienna - Multimedia Information Systems, Austria)*
Henning Müller *(HES-SO, Switzerland)*
Toru Nakashika *(The University of Electro-Communications, Japan)*
Yuta Nakashima *(Osaka University, Japan)*
Hideki Nakayama *(The University of Tokyo, Japan)*
Chong-Wah Ngo *(City University of Hong Kong, Hong Kong)*
Liqiang Nie *(Shandong University, China)*
Naoko Nitta *(Osaka University, Japan)*
Noel E. O Connor *(Dublin City University, Ireland)*
Takahiro Ogawa *(Hokkaido University, Japan)*
Ryutarou Ohbuchi *(University of Yamanashi, Japan)*
Vincent Oria *(NJIT, United States)*
Symeon Papadopoulos *(Information Technologies Institute, Greece)*
Nikolaos Pappas *(Idiap Research Institute, Switzerland)*
Yuxin Peng *(Peking University, China)*
Balakrishnan Prabhakaran *(The University of Texas at Dallas, USA)*
Georges Quénot *(Laboratoire d'Informatique de Grenoble, CNRS, France)*
Mohammed Abdel-Mgeed M. Salem *(German University in Cairo, GUC, Egypt)*
Maria Luisa Sapino *(Universita' di Torino, Italy)*
Klaus Schöffmann *(Institute of Information Technology, University of Klagenfurt, Austria)*
Fumin Shen *(University of Electronic Science and Technology of China, China)*

Technical Program Committee (continued):

Lidan Shou *(Zhejiang University, China)*
Chiao-Fe Shu *(IBM, United States)*
Mei-Ling Shyu *(University of Miami, United States)*
Mats Sjöberg *(Aalto University, Finland)*
John Smith *(IBM, United States)*
Cees Snoek *(University of Amsterdam, Netherlands)*
Mohammad Soleymani *(University of Geneva, Switzerland)*
Bart Thomee *(Google, United States)*
Xinmei Tian *(University of Science and Technology of China, China)*
Theodora Tsikrika *(Information Technologies Institute, CERTH, Greece)*
Rosario Uceda-Sosa *(IBM, United States)*
Yusuke Uchida *(DeNA Co., Ltd., Japan)*
Yoshitaka Ushiku *(The University of Tokyo, Japan)*
Remco Veltkamp *(Utrecht University, Netherlands)*
Stefanos Vrochidis *(Information Technologies Institute, Greece)*
Xiangyu Wang *(National University of Singapore, Singapore)*
Marcel Worring *(University of Amsterdam, Netherlands)*
Xiao Wu *(Southwest Jiaotong University, China)*
Lingxi Xie *(The Johns Hopkins University, USA)*
Toshihiko Yamasaki *(The University of Tokyo, Japan)*
Yi-Hsuan Yang *(Academia Sinica, Taiwan)*
Guangnan Ye *(Columbia University, United States)*
Jing Zhang *(Beijing University of Technology, China)*
Shiliang Zhang *(Peking University, China)*
Xiaopeng Zhang *(National University of Singapore, Singapore)*
Wengang Zhou *(University of Science and Technology of China, China)*
Xiangdong Zhou *(Fudan University, China)*
Xiaofang Zhou *(The University of Queensland, Australia)*
Yingying Zhu *(Shenzhen university, China)*

Demo Program Committee

Zhongwei Cheng *(Amazon, United States)*
Masaaki Iiyama *(Kyoto University, Japan)*
Nakamasa Inoue *(Tokyo Institute of Technology, Japan)*
Kunio Kashino *(NTT, Japan)*
Lin Ma *(Tencent AI Lab, China)*
Zhe Xue *(BUPT, China)*

Doctoral Symposium Program Committee

Muhammad Atif Tahir *(National University of Computing & Emerging Sciences – Karachi Campus, Pakistan)*
Duc Tien Dang Nguyen *(Dublin City University, Ireland)*
Maria Eskevich *(CLARIN ERIC, Netherlands)*
Ryosuke Harakawa *(Hokkaido University, Japan)*
Yu-Gang Jiang *(Fudan University, China)*
Mathias Lux *(Klagenfurt University, Austria)*
Tomas Piatrik *(Queen Mary University of London, United Kingdom)*
Till Plumbaum *(DAI-Labor, Technische Universität Berlin, Germany, Germany)*
Konstantin Pogorelov *(Simula, Norway)*
Sho Takahashi *(Hokkaido University, Japan)*
Vedran Vukotić *(LAMARK, France)*
Soh Yoshida *(Kansai University, Japan)*

Program Committee of Special Session on Predicting User Perceptions of Multimedia Content

[Organizers]
Yoann Baveye *(Capacities, France)*
Emmanuel Dellandrea *(Ecole Centrale Lyon, France)*
Claire-Helene Demarty *(Technicolor, France)*
Thanh-Toan Do *(University of Adelaide, Australia)*
Ngoc Duong *(Technicolor, France)*
Bogdan Ionescu *(University Politehnica of Bucharest, Romania)*
Mats Sjöberg *(Aalto University, Finland)*

[Program Committee Members]
Xavier Alameda-Pineda *(INRIA, France)*
Mihai Gabriel Constantin *(University POLITEHNICA of Bucharest, Romania)*
Qi Dai *(Microsoft, China)*
Xavier Giro *(Universitat Politecnica de Catalunya, Spain)*
Guillaume Gravier *(CNRS, France)*
Tanaya Guha *(IIT Kanpur, India)*
Benoit Huet *(Eurecom, France)*
Olivier Le Meur *(Irisa, France)*
Nikolaos Pappas *(Idiap, Switzerland)*
Alexey Ozerov *(Technicolor, France)*
Miriam Redi *(Wikimedia Foundation, United Kingdom)*
Yilin Wang *(Arizona State University, United States)*
Gloria Zen *(University of Trento, Italy)*
Sicheng Zhao *(Tsinghua University, China)*
Yoann Baveye *(Capacities, France)*
Emmanuel Dellandrea *(Ecole Centrale Lyon, France)*
Claire-Helene Demarty *(Technicolor, France)*
Thanh-Toan Do *(University of Adelaide, Australia)*
Ngoc Duong *(Technicolor, France)*
Bogdan Ionescu *(University Politehnica of Bucharest, Romania)*
Mats Sjöberg *(Aalto University, Finland)*

Program Committee of Special Session on Large-Scale 3D Multimedia Analysis and Applications	**[Organizers]** Yue Gao *(Tsinghua University, China)* Rongrong Ji *(Xiamen Unviersity, China)* Sicheng Zhao *(University of California, Berkeley, United States)* **[Program Committee Members]** Yuchen Guo *(Tsinghua University, China)* Hong Liu *(Xiamen University, China)* Weizhi Nie *(Tianjin University, China)* Xiaoshuai Sun *(Harbin Institute of Technology, China)* Dong Wang *(Harbin Institute of Technolog, China)* Shengchuan Zhang *(Xiamen University, China)* Yan Zhang *(Harbin Institute of Technology, China)* Sendong Zhao *(UIUC,HIT, United States)*
Program Committee of Special Session on Social-Media Visual Summarization	**[Organizers]** Krishna Chandramouli *(Queen Mary University of London, United Kingdom)* Michael Evans *(BBC, United Kingdom)* Joao Magalhaes *(Universidade NOVA de Lisboa, Portugal)* **[Program Committee Members]** Goncalo Marcelino *(Universidade NOVA de Lisboa, Portugal)*

ICMR 2018 Sponsor & Supporters

Sponsor:

SIGMM

Corporate Supporters (Gold):

\Orchestrating a brighter world
NEC

HITACHI
Inspire the Next

NVIDIA.

Corporate Supporters (Silver):

CA
CyberAgent.

LIFULL

mercari

Corporate Supporters (Bronze):

:DeNA

YAHOO!
JAPAN

Supporters:

SCAT

公益財団法人
電気通信普及財団
The Telecommunications Advancement Foundation

The Ongoing Evolution of Broadcast Technology

Kohji MITANI
Deputy Director of Science & Technology Research Laboratories NHK (Japan Broadcasting Corporation)

ABSTRACT

The media environment of program production, content delivery, and viewing has been changing because of progress in broadcasting and communication technologies and other technologies like IoT, cloud computing, and artificial intelligence (AI). In December 2018, 8K and 4K UHDTV satellite broadcasting will start in Japan, which means that viewers will soon be able to enjoy 8K and 4K programs featuring a wide color gamut and high dynamic range characteristics together with 22.2 multi-channel audio at home. Meanwhile, distribution services for sending content to PCs and smartphones through the Internet have rapidly been spreading and the introduction of the next generation of mobile networks (5G) will accelerate their spread. The coming of such advanced broadcast and broadband technologies and consequent changes in lifestyle will provide broadcasters with a great opportunity for a new stage of development. At NHK Science & Technology Research Laboratories (NHK STRL), we are pursuing a wide range of research with the aim of creating new broadcast services that can provide viewing experiences never before imagined and user experiences more attuned to daily life. To enhance the convenience of television and the value of TV programming, we are developing technology for connecting the TV experience with various activities in everyday life. Extensions to "Hybridcast Connect" will drive applications that link TVs, smartphones, and IoT. They will enable spontaneous consumption of content during everyday activities through various devices around the user. Establishing a new program production workflow with AI, which we call "Smart Production", is one of our most important research topics. We are developing speech and face recognition technologies for making closed captions and metadata efficiently, as well as technologies for automatically converting content into computer-generated sign language, audio descriptions, and simplified Japanese. This presentation introduces these research achievements targeting 2020 and beyond, as well as other broadcasting technology trends including 4K8K UHDTV broadcasting in Japan, 3D imaging, and VR/AR.

ACM Reference Format:
Kohji MITANI. 2018. The Ongoing Evolution of Broadcast Technology. In *ICMR'18: 2018 International Conference on Multimedia Retrieval, June 11–14, 2018, Yokohama, Japan.* ACM, New York, NY, USA, 1 page. https: //doi.org/10.1145/3206025.3210489

ICMR'18, June 11–14, 2018, Yokohama, Japan

ACM ISBN 978-1-4503-5046-4/18/06.
https://doi.org/10.1145/3206025.3210489

BIO

Kohji Mitani joined NHK in 1987. He has contributed to develop 8K-SHV, for a future television system since 1995 at Science & Technology Research Laboratories. Especially he was involved in the development of 8K camera systems as a person in charge. He moved to the headquarters of NHK in 2010 and has belonged to Engineering Administration Department for the development of the practical 8K production and broadcasting system. In 2016, he was appointed to the current position at NHK. He received the Ph.D. degree in 1999, from Kyoto University and the fellow grade of membership from SMPTE in 2010. He is the vice president of the institute of image information and television engineers for 2017-2018 term.

Prototyping for Envisioning the Future

Yamanaka Shunji
Design Engineer / Professor, University of Tokyo
(Interfaculty Initiative in Information Studies/Institute of Industrial Science)

ABSTRACT

As an industrial designer I have worked in collaboration with various researchers and scientists since the beginning of this century. I have made many prototypes showing the possibility of their leading edge technologies, and exhibited them in these years. As the archives of academic documents and papers have became open, and the internet gave public access to the recordings of various experiments being conducted throughout the world, technology in laboratories are now constantly exposed to the public. In this context, prototypes are becoming more important as the medium that bridges between advanced technology and society. Now a prototype is not merely an experimental machine. It is a device created to present user experience in advance, to share the benefits of the technology with many others. The role of a prototype is not limited to just sharing of values within the development team, but goes beyond that: it is a medium used to voice the significance of research and development to society; an inspiration to stimulate future markets; and also a tool to secure development budgets. A prototype is the physical embodiment of speculative story that connects people to technology that has yet to be brought to society. I would like to introduce some of the prototypes we developed and share the future vision they invoke.

ACM Reference Format:

Yamanaka Shunji. 2018. Prototyping for Envisioning the Future. In *ICMR '18: 2018 International Conference on Multimedia Retrieval, June 11–14, 2018, Yokohama, Japan.* ACM, New York, NY, USA, 1 page. https://doi.org/10.1145/3206025.3210490

ICMR '18, June 11–14, 2018, Yokohama, Japan

ACM ISBN 978-1-4503-5046-4/18/06.
https://doi.org/10.1145/3206025.3210490

BIO

As a design engineer, Yamanaka Shunji has designed industrial products ranging from wristwatches to railway carriages, while also developing the technology behind robots and telecommunication systems. He graduated with a BA in Engineering from the University of Tokyo in 1982 and spent five years at the Nissan Motors Design Centre before becoming a freelance industrial designer in 1987. In 1994, he founded his industrial design practice, Leading Edge Design, where he serves as president. From 2008 to 2012 he was a professor at Keio University. He became a professor at the University of Tokyo in 2013. His recent research focuses on re-examining the relationships between humans and man-made objects through projects such as beautiful prosthetics and lifelike robots. Yamanaka Shunji has been awarded numerous honours, including the 2004 Mainichi Design Award (sponsored by the major Japanese newspaper, Mainichi Shimbun), the iF Design Award, and multiple Good Design Awards (backed by the Japan Ministry of Economy, Trade, and Infrastructure). His 2010 work, Tagtype Garage Kit, is part of the New York Museum of Modern ArtâĂŹs permanent collection.

Orion: An Integrated Multimedia Content Moderation System for Web Services

Yusuke Fujisaka
CyberAgent, Inc.

ABSTRACT

Social Networking Services (SNS) depend on user-generated content (UGC). A fraction of UGC is considered spam, such as adult, scam and abusive content. In order to maintain service reliability and avoid criminal activity, content moderation is employed to eliminate spam from SNS. Content moderation consists of manual content-monitoring operations and/or automatic spam-filtering. Detecting a small portion of spam among a large amount of UGC mostly relies on manual operation, thus it requires a large number of human operators and sometimes suffers from human error. In contrast, automatic spam-filtering can be processed with smaller cost, however it is difficult to follow spams' continuously changing trend, and it may declines service experience due to false positives. This presentation introduces an integrated content moderation platform called "Orion", which aims to minimize manual process and maximize detection of spam in UGC data. Orion preserves post history by users and services, which enables calculating the risk level of each user and decide whether monitoring is required. Also, Orion has a scalable API that can perform number of machine-learning based filtering processes, such as DNN (Deep Neural Network) and SVM for text and images that are posted in many SNS systems. We show that Orion improves efficiency of content moderation compared to a fully manual operation.

ACM Reference Format:
Yusuke Fujisaka. 2018. Orion: An Integrated Multimedia Content Moderation System for Web Services. In *ICMR '18: 2018 International Conference on Multimedia Retrieval, June 11–14, 2018, Yokohama, Japan.* ACM, New York, NY, USA, 1 page. https://doi.org/10.1145/3206025.3210491

BIO

Yusuke Fujisaka is a machine learning research-and-development engineer at CyberAgent, Inc. since 2012. He studied computer science and telecommunication, and received B.S. and M.S. of Engineering from the Tokyo Institute of Technology in 2010, 2012, respectively. He currently works to build middleware, integrated platform systems for services provided by the company, with multimedia processing technology including image, audio and video recognition utilizing deep learning and other machine learning techniques.

ICMR '18, June 11–14, 2018, Yokohama, Japan

ACM ISBN 978-1-4503-5046-4/18/06.
https://doi.org/10.1145/3206025.3210491

Industrial Applications of Image Recognition and Retrieval Technologies for Public Safety and IT Services

Tomokazu Murakami
Ph.D, Senior Researcher
Hitachi, Ltd., Research & Development Group, Center for Technology Innovation

ABSTRACT

Hitachi has a wide variety of technologies ranging from systems for infrastructure to IT platforms such as railway management systems, water supply operation systems, manufacturing management systems for factories, surveillance cameras and monitoring systems, rolling stocks, power plants, servers, storages, data centers, and various IT systems for governments and companies. The research and development group of Hitachi is developing video analytics and other media processing techniques and applying them to various products and solutions with business divisions for such as public safety, productivity improvement of factories and other IT applications. In this talk, I would like to introduce some of the products, solutions and research topics in Hitachi which video analytics and image retrieval techniques are applied. These include an image search system for retrieving public registered design graphics, a person detection and tracking function for video surveillance system and our activities and results in TRECVID 2017. In each cases, we integrated our original high speed image search database and deep learning based image recognition technique. Through these use cases, I would like to present how image recognition and retrieval technologies are practically utilized to industrial products and solutions and contributing to the improvement of social welfare.

ACM Reference Format:
Tomokazu Murakami. 2018. Industrial Applications of Image Recognition and Retrieval Technologies for Public Safety and IT Services. In *ICMR '18: 2018 International Conference on Multimedia Retrieval, June 11–14, 2018, Yokohama, Japan.* ACM, New York, NY, USA, 1 page. https://doi.org/10.1145/3206025.3210492

ICMR '18, June 11–14, 2018, Yokohama, Japan

ACM ISBN 978-1-4503-5046-4/18/06.
https://doi.org/10.1145/3206025.3210492

BIO

Tomokazu Murakami is a Senior Researcher of Hitachi, R&D Group, Center for Technology Innovation, currently leading a team of researchers developing video analytics technologies. He has been engaged in research and development of image processing, image coding and image recognition techniques for 20 years and now his team is developing new technologies and solutions for video surveillance and content management systems. He received a Master degree in Information and Communication Engineering and a Ph.D. degree in Information Science and Technology from The University of Tokyo. Dr. Murakami is a member of The Institute of Electronic, Information, and Communication Engineers (IEICE), The Institute of Image Information and Television Engineers (ITE), and The Virtual Reality Society of Japan (VRSJ).

NEC's Object Recognition Technologies and their Industrial Applications

Kota Iwamoto
NEC Corporation

ABSTRACT

Recent advancements in image recognition technologies has enabled image recognition-based systems to be widely used in real world applications. In this talk, I will introduce NEC's image-based object recognition technologies targeted for recognizing various manufactured goods and retail products from a camera, and talk about their industrial applications which we have developed and commercialized. These image-based object recognition technologies enable highly efficient and cost-effective management of goods and products throughout their life-cycle (manufacturing, distribution, retail, and consumption), which otherwise cannot be achieved by human labor or by use of ID tags. Firstly, I will talk about a technology to recognize multiple objects from a single image using feature matching of compact local descriptors, combined with a more recent Deep Learning-based recognition. It enables large number of objects to be recognized at once, which greatly reduces human labor and time for various product inspection and checking works. Using this technology, we have developed and commercialized the product inspection system in warehouses, the planogram recognition system for retail shop shelves, and the self-service POS system for easy-to-use and fast checkout in retail stores. Secondly, I will talk about the "Fingerprint of Things" technology. It enables individual identification of tiny manufactured parts (e.g. bolts and nuts) by identifying images of their unique surface patterns, just like human fingerprints. We have built a prototype of mass-produced parts traceability system, which enables users to easily track down the individual parts using a mobile device. In the talk, I will explain the key issues in realizing these industrial applications of image-based object recognition technologies.

ACM Reference Format:
Kota Iwamoto. 2018. NEC's Object Recognition Technologies and their Industrial Applications. In *ICMR '18: 2018 International Conference on Multimedia Retrieval, June 11–14, 2018, Yokohama, Japan.* ACM, New York, NY, USA, 1 page. https://doi.org/10.1145/3206025.3210493

BIO

Kota Iwamoto is a Principal Researcher of Data Science Research Laboratories, NEC Corporation. He received the B.E. degree and the M.E. degree in Electronics, Information and Communication Engineering from Waseda University in 2001 and 2003, respectively. He joined NEC Corporation in 2003 and since has been engaged in the research and commercialization of image processing, image/video indexing and retrieval, and image recognition technologies. Since 2007, he has also been involved in the ISO/IEC 15938 (known as MPEG-7) standardization and has contributed to the establishment of many international standards as an ISO project editor. He received the Young Scientists' Prize of the Commendation for Science and Technology by the Minister of Education, Culture, Sports, Science and Technology (Japan) in 2012, the Advanced Technology Award "The Prize of Minister of Economy, Trade and Industry" in 2013, the JSPE Takagi Award in 2014, and the IEICE SUEMATSU-Yasuharu Award in 2017.

ICMR '18, June 11–14, 2018, Yokohama, Japan

ACM ISBN 978-1-4503-5046-4/18/06.
https://doi.org/10.1145/3206025.3210493

Promoting Open Innovations in Real Estate Tech: Provision of the LIFULL HOME'S Data Set and Collaborative Studies

Yoji Kiyota, Ph.D.
Principal Investigator, LIFULL Lab, LIFULL Co., Ltd.

ABSTRACT

The LIFULL HOME'S Data Set, which is provided for academic use since November 2015, is being used for research in a variety of fields such as economics, architecture, urban science and so on. In particular, since it contains 83 million object property images and 5.1 million floor plan images, utilization in the computer vision and multimedia field is thriving, and papers using data sets are also adopted at the top conference ICCV 2017 in the image processing field it is. This presentation summarizes the results that have been obtained through the provision of datasets, and shows plans to promote open innovation in the field of real estate technology.

ACM Reference Format:
Yoji Kiyota, Ph.D.. 2018. Promoting Open Innovations in Real Estate Tech: Provision of the LIFULL HOME'S Data Set and Collaborative Studies. In *ICMR '18: 2018 International Conference on Multimedia Retrieval, June 11–14, 2018, Yokohama, Japan.* ACM, New York, NY, USA, 1 page. https://doi.org/10.1145/3206025.3210494

ICMR '18, June 11–14, 2018, Yokohama, Japan

ACM ISBN 978-1-4503-5046-4/18/06.
https://doi.org/10.1145/3206025.3210494

BIO

Yoji Kiyota is a principal investigator at LIFULL Co., Ltd., which operates LIFULL HOME'S, the largest real estate properties listing website in Japan. His research interests include recommender systems, information navigations systems, and applications of natural language processing. From 2004 to 2012, he was engaged in research on information navigation systems for libraries as assistant professor and special lecturer at Information Technology Center, the University of Tokyo. In 2007, he was involved in the foundation of Littel Corporation, a start-up from the University of Tokyo, and worked on developing large-scale data processing technologies. He joined LIFULL in 2011 because of the LIFULL's acquisition of Littel Corporation. In addition to research and development such as recommender systems for real estate information, he is engaged in joint research with universities, and promotion of open innovation through data provision. He is an editorial board of the Japanese Society for Artificial Intelligence (JSAI), and a secretary of the SIG in database systems of the Information Processing Society of Japan. He holds PhD and MS degrees in informatics, and BS degrees in engineering from Kyoto University. Corporate web site: https://lifull.com/en/

Objects, Relationships, and Context in Visual Data

Hanwang Zhang
Nanyang Technological University, Singapore

Qianru Sun
Max-Planck Institute for Informatics, Germany

ABSTRACT

For decades, we are interested in detecting objects and classifying them into a fixed vocabulary of lexicon. With the maturity of these low-level vision solutions, we are hunger for a higher-level representation of the visual data, so as to extract visual knowledge rather than merely bags of visual entities, allowing machines to reason about human-level decision-making and even manipulate the visual data at the pixel-level. In this tutorial, we will introduce a various of machine learning techniques for modeling visual relationships (e.g., subject-predicate-object triplet detection) and contextual generative models (e.g., generating photo-realistic images using conditional generative adversarial networks). In particular, we plan to start from fundamental theories on object detection, relationship detection, generative adversarial networks, to more advanced topics on referring expression visual grounding, pose guided person image generation, and context based image inpainting.

ACM Reference Format:
Hanwang Zhang and Qianru Sun. 2018. Objects, Relationships, and Context in Visual Data. In *ICMR '18: 2018 International Conference on Multimedia Retrieval, June 11–14, 2018, Yokohama, Japan.* ACM, New York, NY, USA, 1 page. https://doi.org/10.1145/3206025.3210496

BIO

Dr. Hanwang Zhang is an Assistant Professor at Nanyang Technological University, Singapore. He was a research scientist at the Department of Computer Science, Columbia University, USA and a senior research fellow at the School of Computing, National University of Singapore, Singapore. He has received the B.Eng (Hons.) degree in computer science from Zhejiang University, Hangzhou, China, in 2009, and the Ph.D. degree in computer science from the National University of Singapore in 2014. His research interest includes computer vision, multimedia, and social media. Dr. Zhang is the recipient of the Best Demo runner-up award in ACM MM 2012, the Best Student Paper award in ACM MM 2013, and the Best Paper Honorable Mention in ACM SIGIR 2016. He is also the winner of Best Ph.D. Thesis Award of School of Computing, National University of Singapore, 2014.

Dr. Qianru Sun is a postdoctoral researcher in the department of Computer Vision and Multimodal Computing, Max-Planck Institute for Informatics, Germany. She holds a PhD degree from the School of Electronics Engineering and Computer Science, Peking University since Jan. 2016. Her research interests include computer vision and pattern recognition. Specific experiences have been made in human action recognition, anomaly event detection in videos, social relation recognition and head image inpainting in social media photos, person image generation for both low-resolution re-identification images and high-resolution fashion photos.

ICMR '18, June 11–14, 2018, Yokohama, Japan

ACM ISBN 978-1-4503-5046-4/18/06.
https://doi.org/10.1145/3206025.3210496

Recommendation Technologies for Multimedia Content

Xiangnan He
National University of Singapore, Singapore

Hanwang Zhang
Nanyang Technological University, Singapore

Tat-Seng Chua
National University of Singapore, Singapore

ABSTRACT

Recommendation systems play a vital role in online information systems and have become a major monetization tool for user-oriented platforms. In recent years, there has been increasing research interest in recommendation technologies in the information retrieval and data mining community, and significant progress has been made owing to the fast development of deep learning. However, in the multimedia community, there has been relatively less attention paid to the development of multimedia recommendation technologies. In this tutorial, we summarize existing research efforts on multimedia recommendation. We first provide an overview on fundamental techniques and recent advances on personalized recommendation for general items. We then summarize existing developments on recommendation technologies for multimedia content. Lastly, we present insight into the challenges and future directions in this emerging and promising area.

ACM Reference Format:

Xiangnan He, Hanwang Zhang, and Tat-Seng Chua. 2018. Recommendation Technologies for Multimedia Content. In *ICMR '18: 2018 International Conference on Multimedia Retrieval, June 11–14, 2018, Yokohama, Japan.* ACM, New York, NY, USA, 1 page. https://doi.org/10.1145/3206025.3210497

BIO

Dr. Xiangnan He is a senior research fellow with School of Computing, National University of Singapore (NUS). He received his Ph.D. in Computer Science from NUS. His research interests span recommender systems, information retrieval, and multi-media processing. He has over 30 publications appeared in several top conferences such as SIGIR, WWW, MM, CIKM, and IJCAI, and journals including TKDE, TOIS, and TMM. His work on recommender systems has received the Best Paper Award Honorable Mention of ACM SIGIR 2016. Moreover, he has served as the PC member for the prestigious conferences including SIGIR, WWW, MM, KDD, WSDM, CIKM, IJCAI, AAAI, and ACL, and the regular reviewer for prestigious journals including TKDE, TOIS, TKDD, TMM etc.

Dr. Hanwang Zhang is an Assistant Professor at Nanyang Technological University, Singapore. He was a research scientist at the Department of Computer Science, Columbia University, USA and a senior research fellow at the School of Computing, National University of Singapore, Singapore. He has received the B.Eng (Hons.) degree in computer science from Zhejiang University, Hangzhou, China, in 2009, and the Ph.D. degree in computer science from the National University of Singapore in 2014. His research interest includes computer vision, multimedia, and social media. Dr. Zhang is the recipient of the Best Demo runner-up award in ACM MM 2012, the Best Student Paper award in ACM MM 2013, and the Best Paper Honorable Mention in ACM SIGIR 2016. He is also the winner of Best Ph.D. Thesis Award of School of Computing, National University of Singapore, 2014.

Dr. Tat-Seng Chua is the KITHCT Chair Professor at the School of Computing, National University of Singapore. He holds a PhD from the University of Leeds, UK. He was the Acting and Founding Dean of the School from 1998-2000. Dr Chua's main research interest is in multimedia information retrieval and social media analytics. In particular, his research focuses on the extraction, retrieval and question-answering (QA) of text and rich media arising from the Web and multiple social networks. He is the co-Director of NExT, a joint Center between NUS and Tsinghua University to develop technologies for live social media search. Dr Chua is the 2015 winner of the prestigious ACM SIGMM award for Outstanding Technical Contributions to Multimedia Computing, Communications and Applications. He is the Chair of steering committee of ACM International Conference on Multimedia Retrieval (ICMR) and Multimedia Modeling (MMM) conference series. Dr Chua is also the General Co-Chair of ACM Multimedia 2005, ACM CIVR (now ACM ICMR) 2005, ACM SIGIR 2008, and ACM Web Science 2015. He serves in the editorial boards of four international journals. Dr. Chua is the co-Founder of two technology startup companies in Singapore.

ICMR '18, June 11–14, 2018, Yokohama, Japan

ACM ISBN 978-1-4503-5046-4/18/06.
https://doi.org/10.1145/3206025.3210497

Multimedia Content Understanding by Learning from Very Few Examples: Recent Progress on Unsupervised, Semi-Supervised and Supervised Deep Learning Approaches

Guo-Jun Qi
University of Central Florida

ABSTRACT

In this tutorial, the speaker will present serval parallel efforts on building deep learning models with very few supervision information, with or without unsupervised data available. In particular, we will discuss in details.

(1) Generative Adverbial Nets (GANs) and their applications to unsupervised feature extractions, semi-supervised learning with few labeled examples and a large amount of unlabeled data. We will discuss the state-of-the-art results that have been achieved by the semi-supervised GANs.
(2) Low-Shot Learning algorithms to train and test models on disjoint sets of tasks. We will discuss the ideas of how to efficiently adapt models to tasks with very few examples. In particular, we will discuss several paradigms of learning-to-learn approaches.
(3) We will also discuss how to transfer models across modalities by leveraging abundant labels from one modality to train a model for other modalities with few labels. We will discuss in details the cross-modal label transfer approach.

ACM Reference Format:
Guo-Jun Qi. 2018. Multimedia Content Understanding by Learning from Very Few Examples: Recent Progress on Unsupervised, Semi-Supervised and Supervised Deep Learning Approaches. In *ICMR '18: 2018 International Conference on Multimedia Retrieval, June 11–14, 2018, Yokohama, Japan.* ACM, New York, NY, USA, 1 page. https://doi.org/10.1145/3206025.3210498

ICMR '18, June 11–14, 2018, Yokohama, Japan

ACM ISBN 978-1-4503-5046-4/18/06.
https://doi.org/10.1145/3206025.3210498

BIO

Dr. Qi is a faculty member in the Department of Computer Science at the University of Central Florida. His research interests include knowledge discovery, analysis and aggregation of big data deluging from a variety of modalities and sources in order to build smart and reliable information and decision-making systems. He aspires to apply my research to solve the practical problems through high quality data processing and analysis in healthcare, sensor and social networks, financial systems and so forth. He was the recipient of one-time Microsoft Fellowship, and twice IBM Fellowships. His research has been sponsored by grants and projects from government agencies and industry collaborators, including NSF, IARPA, Microsoft, IBM, and Adobe. Dr. Qi has published more than 100 papers in a broad range of venues, such as Proceedings of IEEE, IEEE T PAMI, IEEE T KDE, IEEE T Image Processing, ACM SIGKDD, WWW, ICML, ACM MM, CVPR, ICDM, SDM and ICDE. Among them are the best student paper of ICDM 2014, âĂIJthe best ICDE 2013 paperâĂİ by IEEE Transactions on Knowledge and Data Engineering, as well as the best paper (finalist) of ACM Multimedia 2007 (2015). He has served or will serve as a technical program co-chair for MMM 2016 and ACM Multimedia 2020, and an area chair (a senior program committee member) for ICCV, ICPR, ACM SIGKDD, ACM CIKM, as well as ACM Multimedia. He is also serving or has served in the program committees of several academic conferences, including CVPR, ICCV, KDD, WSDM, CIKM, IJCAI, ICMR, ACM Multimedia, ACM/IEEE ASONAM, ICDM, ICIP, and ACL. He is an associate editor for IEEE Transactions on Circuits and Systems for Video Technology (CSVT), as well as a guest/lead editor for the special issue on âĂIJBig Media Data: Understanding, Search, and MiningâĂİ in IEEE Transactions on Big Data, âĂIJDeep Learning for Multimedia ComputingâĂİ in IEEE Transactions on Multimedia, and âĂIJSocial Media Mining and Knowledge DiscoveryâĂİ in Multimedia Systems, Springer. He was also a panelist for the NSF and the United States Department of Energy.

Ranking News-Quality Multimedia

Gonçalo Marcelino
NOVA LINCS
Universidade NOVA de Lisboa
goncalo.bfm@gmail.com

Ricardo Pinto
NOVA LINCS
Universidade NOVA de Lisboa
rjr.pinto@campus.fct.unl.pt

João Magalhães
NOVA LINCS
Universidade NOVA de Lisboa
jmag@fct.unl.pt

ABSTRACT

News editors need to find the photos that best illustrate a news piece and fulfill news-media quality standards, while being pressed to also find the most recent photos of live events. Recently, it became common to use social-media content in the context of news media for its unique value in terms of immediacy and quality. Consequently, the amount of images to be considered and filtered through is now too much to be handled by a person. To aid the news editor in this process, we propose a framework designed to deliver high-quality, news-press type photos to the user. The framework, composed of two parts, is based on a ranking algorithm tuned to rank professional media highly and a visual SPAM detection module designed to filter-out low-quality media. The core ranking algorithm is leveraged by aesthetic, social and deep-learning semantic features. Evaluation showed that the proposed framework is effective at finding high-quality photos (true-positive rate) achieving a retrieval MAP of 64.5% and a classification precision of 70%.

CCS CONCEPTS

- **Information systems → Multimedia information systems**;
- **Computing methodologies → Computer vision tasks**;

KEYWORDS

News photos, News quality, Visual aesthetics, Social-media

ACM Reference Format:

Gonçalo Marcelino, Ricardo Pinto, and João Magalhães. 2018. Ranking News-Quality Multimedia. In *ICMR '18: 2018 International Conference on Multimedia Retrieval, June 11–14, 2018, Yokohama, Japan.* ACM, New York, NY, USA, 9 pages. https://doi.org/10.1145/3206025.3206053

1 INTRODUCTION

Picking images to be used in the context of news media is a difficult and nuanced task, normally attributed to news editors. The process itself is complex and takes into account many variables: the visual quality of the image, how it relates to the news it is supposed to illustrate and how much of the story it conveys by itself, are just some of them [11]. However, with the advent of large scale social media platforms like Twitter, Facebook and Flickr, interesting and appealing images that can illustrate a piece of news are no longer only present in the portfolio of news photographers. User generated content has become a great source of news images as the photographic quality of mobile devices continues to rise. Additionally, social media users document the events they participate in themselves, taking photos that cover many more places and perspectives, than a group of news photographers could ever be able to create. Consequently there is now too much content for a news editor to filter through, as the job of crawling Twitter for photographies as the ones in Figure 1, that capture an event while maintaining high visual quality standards, cannot be attributed to a human.

To aid the news editor in this task, we propose a framework designed to filter and rank event related media according to news professionals standards. We aim at reducing and simplifying the task of the news editor, from choosing an image from a set of thousands, including SPAM and low quality images, to choosing an image from a small set of automatically ranked high quality images.

Figure 1: News-quality photos.

Consequently, our main contribution is the specification of a machine learning based approach for selecting high quality media that can be used to represent a piece of news. To model and quantify the photographic quality that news-editors are looking for, our hypothesis is that one needs to consider the problem across three fundamental dimensions: aesthetics, semantic and social. The argument is that ranking by visual aesthetics alone, is not enough – the sharpness and colorfulness of pictures needs to be complemented by strong and clear semantic content. Also, getting some preliminary human feedback is crucial, hence, social features are also an important element.

Considering these three domains of a photography (visual, semantic and social) is an important step towards the solution of the problem, but one still lacking in the ability to capture its full complexity. First, we need to consider the non-linear decisions that news editors make when assessing the news-quality of a photo. To overcome this challenge, the proposed framework uses Gradient

ICMR '18, June 11–14, 2018, Yokohama, Japan

ACM ISBN 978-1-4503-5046-4/18/06...$15.00
https://doi.org/10.1145/3206025.3206053

Boosted Trees [3] (GBT) that can capture such non-linear relations. Second, since SPAM is a big part of the content present in social media we explicitly tackle the task of SPAM detection, to ensure that low-quality photos such as memes and adverts are not even considered for analysis. We do this by reviewing the textual and visual components of the content under scrutiny. Enforcing this specialized SPAM detection methodology allows us to simplify the task of the filtering and ranking models, as these can be designed to solely work with content that is beyond a basic threshold of quality. Finally, we remove redundant duplicated content from the list of photos presented to the news-editor, ensuring the non-redundancy of the images suggested.

The rest of the paper is organized as follows: Section 2 describes related works that either influenced this work or that can be used to complement it. Section 3 elaborates on the structure of the proposed framework. Section 4 describes the methodologies developed to classify and rank images according to their usability in the context of news media. Section 5 deals with the methods and algorithms used for SPAM detection. Finally, Section 6 scrutinizes the evaluation processes the framework was subjected to, while Section 7 concludes the paper.

2 RELATED WORK

The proposed framework is designed to filter and rank social media content according to news-quality standards. Hence, news illustration is a close problem that addresses some of the same challenges. Marchesotti et al. [16] propose a system to illustrate events, where semantic inferencing and visual analysis processes are combined to automatically find media to illustrate events, in Internet services and platforms. Additionally, Liu and Huet [15] propose a process for finding media related to an event, by leveraging information about the event against content metadata and additional textual information. As a result, one could use these methodologies to find content to be filtered and ranked by the proposed framework.

Although the study of methods for measuring the quality of news pieces, such as the one described in [1], is a fairly popular topic, not much work can be found dedicated to the development of tools to help journalists in their tasks, specially when the task is picking media to illustrate news. Due to this, one may turn to works tackling other content filtering and ranking tasks for context and information. Harper et al. [7] propose an architecture for qualifying content in Q&A dedicated forums like Yahoo! Answers. Although the objectives are different, we take advantage of some of these techniques. Namely we take into account social signals and what is referred to, by the authors, as *intrinsic content quality*, while also making use of the semantic characteristics of the content.

Works on aesthetic assessment were also considered. Although we are not directly interested in finding aesthetic pleasing images, we are aware of the importance of visual quality and aesthetics in news media content. In this context, works such as [4] propose the use of high-level features, like compositional attributes, content of the photography and illumination quality, as a way to assess aesthetic quality. On the other hand, Marchesotti et al. [16] make use of low-level generic features and supervised learning techniques to infer the aesthetic quality of images. Taking both the importance of low and high level features into account, we considered a large set of image features, a subset of them extracted using the tool also employed in [17], making use of visual features of different, but possibly complementary, levels of abstraction.

Finally, and now relating to SPAM detection, both McParlane et al. [19] and Schinas et al. [21] address the problem of automatically detecting images unsuitable for visual summarization tasks, stating the importance of dealing with images such as "memes" and captioned images. Particularly, in [19], the authors also deal with the problem of finding duplicated and near-duplicated images using techniques such as pHash, to avoid presenting the same image to a user twice. Since many of the images by us considered as SPAM fall into the "synthetic images" category (such as digital flyers and some "memes") we also searched for previous work regarding the topic. Even though synthetic image taxonomy is not a field that has received a lot of attention so far, [14], [19] and [24] hint at some low level features that help distinguish synthetic images from photographs, such as color histograms, edge histograms and geometric shape counters. To increase the performance of our synthetic image classifier, we make use of some of these suggested features, proposing our own in the process.

3 FINDING NEWS-QUALITY PICTURES

Our goal is to find news worthy photos that depict real life events. Therefore, we want unedited photographs (unless the editing aims to improve aesthetic quality), representing the viewpoints of peple witnessing the event. Figure 2 illustrates the architecture of the proposed framework. Its main components are:

- **Social-media listener.** We chose Twitter as the source of social-media pictures. This choice is supported by a proven correlation between what is posted on the social network and news media. As an example, [13] shows that over 85% of the topics trending on Twitter are also covered by the news.
- **Visual SPAM filter.** The stream of social media posts are first processed and filtered by a spam detection module. This way, images such as memes, adverts, and images of extremely low resolution, are immediately removed from the pipeline and are never considered in the ranking and classification processes.
- **Visual redundancy.** The content that is not discarded by the Visual SPAM filter is then processed by the duplicate and near-duplicate image detection algorithms.
- **News-quality ranking.** Finally we have a component charged with ranking photos by their news-quality, i.e., a machine learning model, Gradient Boosted Trees, that combines aesthetic, semantic and social criteria to infer how news worthy an image is.

In the following sections, the above components are presented in detail.

4 RANKING BY NEWS-QUALITY

Determining if a picture has news-quality is a complex task that cannot be solved by taking only into account its visual appeal. The picture can, for instance, be visual appealing but severely lacking in interesting content and information. To solve this problem we consider not only the *visual aesthetics* of pictures, but also the *semantic content* and the *social signals* associated with them. Moreover, we

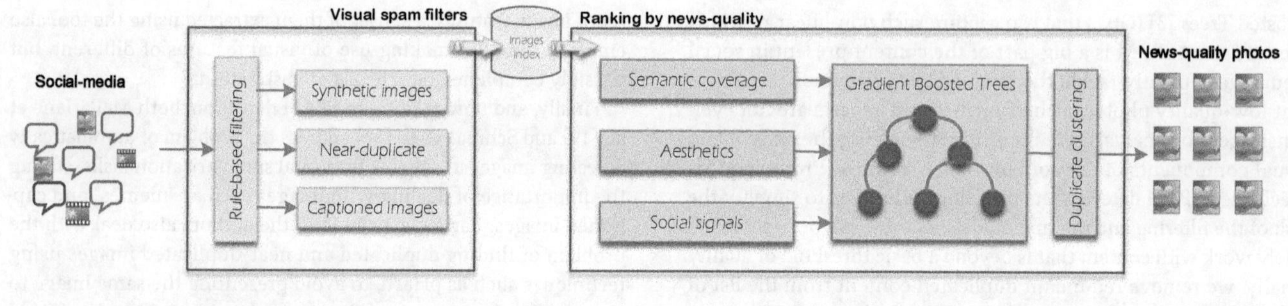

Figure 2: The framework for ranking news-quality pictures in social-media is leveraged by a machine learning algorithm that merges social, visual, semantic and aesthetic evidence.

Table 1: Visual features and respective descriptions

Feature	Description
#Edges	the number of vertical, horizontal and diagonal edges present in an image.
Rule of 1/3	real value representing how much an image complies with the commonly used photography composition rule.
Focus	real value describing how focused an image is.
Entropy	real value measuring an image's entropy.
Faces	the number of human faces present in an image.
Luminance	real value describing an image's brightness.
Simplicity	real value representing how simple an image is in therms of the distribution of its colors.
Area	the width × height of an image in pixels.
Aspect	the height of an image divided by its width.
Orientation	if an image is square or in a portrait or landscape orientation.
Colorfulness	real value describing an image's colorfulness.

argue that there are non-linear pairwise interactions among these distinct sets of features. Due to this, and inspired by the work of [7], we propose to solve the present problem with Gradient Boosted Trees – a tree based machine learning model designed for supervised learning.

Besides being robust to outliers, Gradient Boosted Trees (GBT) are known to work well with categorical and continuous data, which is a critical advantage to solve our problem, where both types of features co-exist. Additionally, GBT also works well with both larger and smaller datasets, which means the ability to train the model with sets of news related media of different sizes. Finally, additional benefits of GBT also include the fact that it performs implicit feature selection, the ability to deal with non-linear relationships in the data as well as capture high-order interactions between features, making it, overall, a very versatile model. These, and other advantages are discussed in greater detail in [6] and [20].

While we also tested other models, such as Linear and Ridge regression models, SVM^{rank} (an instance of SVM^{struct} [10]), Naive Bayes and Logistic regression, in the end, the model that yielded the best performance was GBT.

Table 2: Most common concepts associated with news-worthy and non-news-worthy images ordered by decreasing probability of appearance.

Low quality concepts	Prob.	High quality concepts	Prob.
performance	0.198	product	0.282
performing arts	0.189	fun	0.225
event	0.189	event	0.134
entertainment	0.153	advertising	0.126
fun	0.153	font	0.118
performance art	0.126	girl	0.115
recreation	0.117	facial hair	0.099
dancer	0.108	recreation	0.099
crowd	0.108	stage	0.095
product	0.108	performance	0.092

4.1 Visual quality

Deciding if a photo is news worthy is a very subjective task. Nevertheless, when approaching news media one expects a certain set of characteristics to be present in its visual content, even if only subconsciously. In order to make use of these latent characteristics we extracted a large set of visual features to quantify the visual quality of photos. This large set of features allows GBT to perform implicit feature selection and capture complex feature interactions. These features are presented and described in Table 1, being that the first seven were extracted using the image feature extractor made available[1] by [17] and Colorfulness was extracted through the method proposed in [8]. While the intuition for choosing some of these features might seem obvious, it should be noted that the feature regarding the number of faces present in a photo was chosen as works such as the one presented in [9] show the positive visual impact of the presence of faces in photographies. Additionally, aspect ratio was added as a feature because certain photography equipment is directly associated with a specific image aspect ratio. As an example, DSLR's, cameras normally used in a professional or semi professional setting, normally output images with an aspect ratio of 3:2 [5].

[1] https://github.com/pcpmartins/extractor

4.2 Image concepts

Our initial intuition, was that images that are used to illustrate news pieces have a particular distribution of concepts associated to them. As Table 2 shows, concepts such as *product* are expected to be less frequent in news media images then a concept like *stage*. Using this knowledge, we propose a way to calculate two additional features that take advantage of these trends to improve our filtering and ranking methodologies.

Given two sets, Y containing images known to have news-quality, and N containing images known to not have news-quality, we first calculate Py_i and Pn_i the probability of concept i appearing in the images present in Y and N, respectively. We do this for all concepts extracted from the images in Y and N, that appear in more then one image. When a new image containing the set of concepts C is given as input to the framework, both $\sum_{x \in C} Py_x$ and $\sum_{x \in C} Pn_x$ are calculated so that they can be used by the Gradient Boosted Trees model. These values are the sum of probabilities of each concept belonging to an image that is news worthy and not news worthy, respectively.

Although multiple image concept extraction methodologies are currently available, we choose to use the Google Cloud Vision API for the purpose. We considered a total of 850 unique concepts and, on average, each image was annotated with 7.7 concepts. Table 2 shows the most common concepts associated with the news worthy and non news worthy images present in the social-media photos datset described in Section 6.1.

4.3 Social signals

Given the subjectivity associated with the task of identifying news worthy images, it is important to take into account not only the data extracted directly from the images but also the social signals generated by the users who interacted with the associated social media post, from which the images were extracted. In practice, we consider the following social signals:

- **#RT:** number of retweets associated with the post the image was extracted from;
- **#FL:** the number of followers associated with the user who posted the tweet containing the image;
- **#UN:** the number of times the image is featured in individual posts;
- **#DD:** the number of times a visually near-duplicated image is featured in individual posts.

This information is used as a proxy for the users opinions regarding an image's importance and its entertainment and informative value.

5 VISUAL SPAM AND REDUNDANCY

Images of adverts, captioned images, memes and similar visual content are big portion of the content posted by social-media users which must be filtered by the framework. To solve this problem we propose a method to filter low-quality and redundant visual information, in order to prevent content like the one presented in Figure 3 from being indexed together with valid photos.

We propose a filtering pipeline composed of four distinct parts. The first is the application of a set of simple thresholds well established in literature [18] to features extracted from both the images and posts they were taken from. The second is the usage of a linear model trained to detect synthetic images, to filter images such as digital adverts. The third is the application of OCR technology to subsequently filter out captioned images, such as memes. Finally, the forth part deals with the large number of duplicated images found among social-media content. The pipeline is detailed in the following subsections.

Figure 3: Examples of unwanted images that can be immediately discarded (i.e., logos, adverts and memes).

5.1 Coarse filtering

To filter thumbnails, banners and adverts, we follow the approaches of Mcparlane et al. [19] and McMinn et al. [18], and exclude images extracted from posts that contain more than 3 hashtags, more than 3 mentions or more than 2 URLs. Additionally we also discard small images that, due to their size, are not useful in a news context (i.e., images with less than 200 pixels of width or height).

5.2 Synthetic images detection

Several works on synthetic image detection [14, 24], have shown that some simple low-level features allow to discriminate synthetic images from photographies with great success. We trained a logistic regression model to distinguish synthetic images from real photos using some of the features proposed by [14, 24]: *number of corners, number of vertical and horizontal lines, number of dominant colors, most common color (C1)*, and 3 features derived from the color transitions feature (the measure of color distance between two neighbor pixels).

5.2.1 Color transitions. Color transitions [2] are a common property of real world images. Synthetic images have large portions with very similar colors and limited transitions. Color transitions are calculated as follows: for each pixel px in the image, we compute the color distance in the RGB space, to all its nearest neighbours as

$$d_{color}(px) = \sum_{n=1}^{8}(|r_{px} - r_n| + |g_{px} - g_n| + |b_{px} - b_n|)$$

From this metric, we are able to extract 3 additional features: the fraction f_1 of pixels with a color distance greater than zero, the fraction f_2 of pixels with a color distance greater than 1/4 of the maximum distance, and the ratio between f_2 and f_1. Synthetic images are expected to have a lower value for fraction f_1, as they usually contain large regions with the same exact color. On the other hand, photographic images are expected to have a lower value for fraction f_2 for the same reason stated in section 5.2.2, regarding color gradients.

5.2.2 Most common color. It is expected that, in synthetic images, the most common (exact) color will be more frequent across the entire image, whereas photographies will tend to have their colors divided into slightly different hue, saturation or brightness values, forming a color gradient across regions of the image. Therefore, we work with *the ratio between the number of pixels with the most common color and the total number of pixels in the image* as one of the features used to distinguish both classes of images.

5.2.3 Dominant colors. We hypothesize that photographic images in general have a larger number of *dominant colors* than synthetic images. To calculate this feature, we build a HSV color histogram, subdividing each color space into 8 bins, making up a total of $8^3 = 512$ bins. We then count how many of these bins have a frequency higher than a given threshold. This count corresponds to the *number of dominant colors* feature.

The threshold was determined by iterating different values, choosing the one that minimizes the normalized difference $Norm_{\Delta_{dom}}$ in the following equations:

$$\Delta_{dom} = (\mu_{photo} - \sigma_{photo}) - (\mu_{synth} + \sigma_{synth}) \quad (1)$$

$$Norm_{\Delta_{dom}} = \frac{|\Delta_{dom}|}{\mu_{photo}} + \frac{|\Delta_{dom}|}{\mu_{synth}} \quad (2)$$

where μ_{photo} and μ_{synth} denote the average number of dominant colors in the images belonging to the *photographic* and *synthetic* classes, respectively and, σ_{photo} and σ_{synth}, their standard deviations.

5.2.4 Horizontal and vertical lines. Following the assumption that synthetic images in general have a lot of lines parallel to the frame of the image, we extracted horizontal and vertical lines with the Hough Line Transform, using a minimum threshold of 20 points per line.

5.2.5 Number of corners. The number of corners of an image was extracted with the Harris corner detector. After applying a threshold to the corner filter response image, one obtains the corners of a given image. To find the optimal threshold we used a synthetic images dataset. We calculated this threshold as a fraction of the maximum score in the corner filter response image and attempted to find the percentage for which the *ratio between the mean number of corners in the photo class and the mean number of corners in the synthetic class* was the lowest.

5.3 Captioned images

Images whose main subject is text tend to be unusable in the context of news illustration. Examples of these types of images include highly captioned images like memes. To filter this type of content we apply a simple prepossessing method to all images and then, using Tesseract [22], an Optical Character Recognition Engine, exclude images containing prominent text. Since the preprocessing method involves applying median blur to the images, and since

Figure 4: Example of near-duplicate images. The first is the original image. The second is a cropped version of the first with different contrast.

Tesseract is only able to recognize easily identifiable text, images with small text or text present in the background are correctly left unfiltered by the framework.

5.4 Visual redundancy

Since a lot of images present in social-media are slightly altered versions of their respective originals, we propose a way to find not only duplicated but also near-duplicated images. This is important as it means the ability to filter redundant content before it is presented to the news editor.

5.4.1 Duplicate detection. To access whether two images are exact duplicates of each other we make use of the MD5 hash algorithm. More specifically, we consider two images to be exact duplicates if their respective MD5 hash is the same. Before presenting the results of the ranking and filtering models to the user, all duplicated images are removed.

5.4.2 Near-duplicate detection. To detect near-duplicated images, we employ perceptual hash (pHash)[2] which relies on the lower frequencies of images, ignoring higher frequencies. This algorithm is a simple and fast method for comparing images, hence our choice. Previous work already proved it presents a high performance in the this task [23], regardless if the image is rotated, resized, cropped, exposure compensated or even if small elements are added to it (like a logo or signature).

As a method for assessing if two images are near-duplicates, we calculate the Hamming distance between their pHash codes, which corresponds to the amount of bit positions where those codes differ [12]. For example, if two images represented by 64 bit codes, are separated by a Hamming distance of 5, it means their pHash codes differ in 5 bits. We consider two images to be near-duplicates if the Hamming distance between their pHash values is below 8 as proposed in [19]. An example of two near-duplicate images can be found in Figure 4.

6 EVALUATION

6.1 Datasets

To evaluate the different components of the proposed framework, we used three datasets[3].: (i) social-media content from which we need to retrieve high-quality photos; (ii) newswire photos, used to build the high-quality photos model; and (iii) a visual SPAM dataset to learn to filter low-quality photos.

[2] http://www.phash.org/

[3] Links and features of the used photos are available at http://novasearch.org/datasets/

Table 3: Results of the annotations performed on the news-quality photos dataset according to the question "Could this image have appeared in the New York Times?".

Agreem.	Images	High quality	LQ/HQ ratio
57%	124	58	1.14
71%	129	55	1.35
86%	144	39	2.69
100%	103	17	5.06
78%	500	169	1.96

Social-media photos. We crawled a dataset of 15,439 images from Twitter concerning several real-world concerts and shows that spanned one full month. In order to evaluate the ranking algorithm, we created a small sample of 1,500 photos for results pooling. Ground-truth was obtained through crowdsourcing by resorting to 5 annotators that judged the top-k photos of each baseline.

News-quality photos. To create a robust model that is able to qualify photos acording to their news-quality, we obtained newswire photos from The New York Times and the BBC web sites. We collected a total of 100 newswire photos and added 400 social-media photos, sampled from the previous 15,439 images dataset. This dataset comprises a total of 500 images that were annotated by 7 annotators with respect to their "*news-quality provenance*", as described in the following section. Moreover, the annotation effort allowed us to better understand the specific characteristics of news-quality photos.

Visual SPAM. The detection of visual SPAM requires the detection of different types of images. The NPIC image dataset [24] contains several photographic and synthetic images, including logos, cartoons and CG images. However, NIPC also contains images that are not common in social-media (e.g. oil paintings) and misses images that are common in social-media (e.g. memes and adverts). To more accurately reflect the type of content found on social-media, we combined some of the NIPC images with social-media images. Hence, we created the new NIPC-Twitter dataset consisting of 13,668 images (638 real-world photos and 390 synthetic images from Twitter, and 10,271 real-world photos and 2,369 synthetic images from NPIC) tailored to the detection of visual SPAM in social-media.

6.2 News-quality photos ground-truth

Regarding the 500 image dataset used to train the models, all 500 images were annotated via crowdsourcing by 7 annotators. The annotators were presented with the images and asked the question "*Could this image have appeared in the New York Times?*". Table 3 presents, in an abbreviated manner, the results of the annotation process. Through their answers we can infer the ambiguity of the task, as the 7 annotators only fully agreed on 102 images. As ground truth for the ranking task, 7 quality levels were attributed to each image according to the number of annotators that voted that the image might have appeared in the New York Times. For this task all 500 images were considered and the regression models used in it were trained to match these quality levels. As a ground-truth for the classification task only images where 71% or more of the annotators agreed, were considered. In this case, the image was regarded as having news-quality if the majority of the crowd answered yes to the already mentioned question. The classification models used in the filtering task were trained to match this binary judgment.

Table 4: News-quality filtering task results.

Features	Prec.	Acc.
GBT_V	0.672	0.787
GBT_C	0.555	0.742
GBT_S	0.639	0.834
GBT_F	0.701	0.854

As Table 3 shows, out of all 500 images, only 17 of them were classified as possibly having appeared in the New York Times, by all 7 annotators. Of these 17 images, 14 belong to the set of images extracted from news sources, which shows the ability of the annotators to distinguish news-quality images. In Figure 1 we present four of these images as examples.

6.3 Results and discussion

6.3.1 Modeling news-quality photos. The filtering and ranking models were trained using 70% of the dataset while the results presented next regarding the classification task were measured using the remaining 30%. We tested models where visual (GBT_V), social (GBT_S) and semantic (GBT_C) features were used separately and combined (GBT_F) to understand the impact of the different feature sets. Table 4 shows the results of these tests. The advantage of joining multiple groups of features, to tackle the proposed task, is being able to attain clearly higher precision, nDCG and MAP values in comparison to the models where only one feature group is used. Consequently using only the visual quality, semantics, or social signals associated with an image as criteria for deciding if it has news-quality, equates to having a worst performance in the task overall.

6.3.2 Ranking high-quality social-media photos. The performance of the ranking model was evaluated in an out-of-domain context using the described annotated dataset, created through results pooling. To do so, we first trained 4 distinct models, the first three taking only advantage of visual (GBT_V), social (GBT_S) and semantic (GBT_C) features individually and the forth using all of the three feature sets simultaneously (GBT_F). Each model was then applied to the dataset and the k better ranked images were extracted. These images were, in turn, annotated by 5 annotators again according to the question "*Could this image have appeared in the New York Times?*". Finally, images were classified as news worthy if the majority of the annotators answered yes to the question.

Table 5 shows the precision and nDCG values of the various models tested, while Figure 5 presents their precision-recall curve. By analyzing both these metrics we discover that, overall, the models that performed worst were GBT_V and GBT_S. In turn the model trained only with semantic features, GBT_C, was marginally more successful, specially when retrieving the first half of the relevant images. This shows the importance of semantics in the context of news media. Finally, the complete model (GBT_F) was the one that performed better as it was able to take advantage of the combined strengths of the feature groups used.

Table 5: Results of the performance tests done on the various ranking models.

Features	Prec@30	nDCG@50	MAP
GBT_V	0.833	0.837	0.448
GBT_C	0.833	0.859	0.532
GBT_S	0.733	0.836	0.454
GBT_F	0.967	0.906	0.645

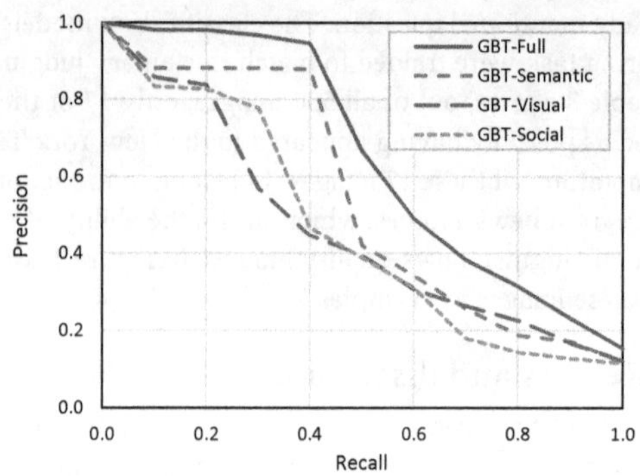

Figure 5: Precision recall curves of the various ranking models.

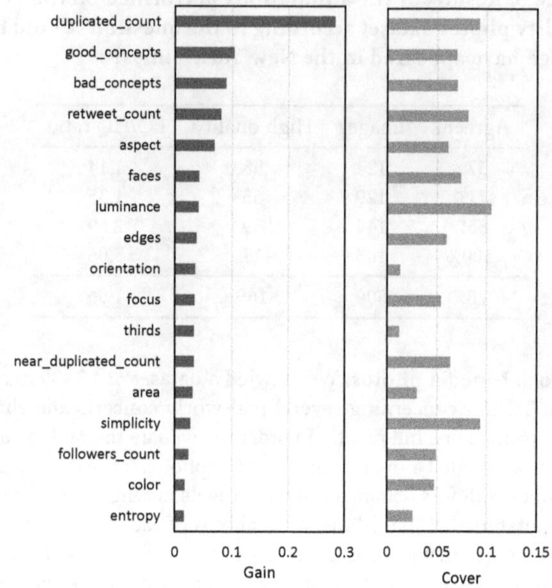

Figure 6: The importance of each feature measured through its gain and cover in the Gradient Boosted Trees regression model.

Table 6: Performance of the photo/synthetic image classifier for several combinations of features.

Best single features (NIPC)	Precision	Recall	F-measure
Luminance	0.72	0.68	0.66
Dom. colors	0.79	0.79	0.79
Ratio C1	0.85	0.81	0.80
Best feature set	**Precision**	**Recall**	**F-measure**
NIPC trained	0.97	0.97	0.97
NIPC-Twitter trained	0.91	0.91	0.91

In Table 7 we exemplify this tendency by examining specific examples of images ranked by each model while identifying, in a broad way, the features that influenced the model's choices. The images GBT_V ranked higher (shown on the left side of the table) are of high visual quality, but the model is unable to ensure the interestingness of the images it presents, the image with the mobile phone being a good example of this problem. GBT_C is able to correctly assert that a photo of a concert is more likely to be used in news media then a selfie. However the model ends up ranking an extremely blurry image as one of the best in the set, when possibly better suited alternatives were available, like the one displayed on its right. In turn, GBT_S ranks images according to social signals, consequently discarding good images that did not gain social traction. The model ranks correctly images that have a lot of social traction but, when this ceases to be the case, the existing social signals stop being enough to distinguish between images. This tendency is not only observable in Table 7 but also in the precision-recall curve, as the model is the worst for recall values higher then 0.6. Lastly GBT_F leverages the benefits of the other models to correct, to a degree, their individual faults. The GBT_F model is still able to distinguish a *selfie* from a photo of a concert but is also able to assure the visual quality of the better ranked images. Additionally the model does not focus singularly on social signals meaning that, although these are considered, an unpopular but visual appealing image, semantically tied to news media, is still ranked high by the model.

Finally, Figure 6 presents, for each visual, social and semantic feature, its associated gain and cover in the context of the GBT_F model. The higher the gain, the more important a feature is in improving the accuracy of the model. Similarly, cover equates to the amount of coverage of a feature when used in the trees. Here, the gain table shows that, although most visual features have a small gain individually, the model comprised only of visual features still retains a decent performance due to the high number of distinct visual features used. Additionally we can find visual, social and semantic features in the top 5 features with more gain, confirming that all feature groups increase, by themselves, the performance of the model.

6.3.3 Filtering low quality photos. To detect synthetic and captioned images, we trained a logistic regression classifier (with L1 penalty and $\lambda = 1.0$). We applied 5-fold cross-validation and trained the model with the dataset from [24]. Features include luminance, edge histograms (with edges grouped into vertical, horizontal, 45 and 135 degrees orientations), dominant colors and corners ratio. After normalizing the size of all images to 240px width and 180px height we tuned different feature parameters. Namely, the domaint

GBT_V	Luminance$^{\uparrow}$, Focus$^{\uparrow}$, Color$^{\uparrow}$	Luminance$^{\uparrow}$, Focus$^{\uparrow}$,	Luminance$^{\downarrow}$, Focus$^{\downarrow}$	Aspect$^{\downarrow}$, Faces$^{\uparrow}$ Focus$^{\downarrow}$ Entropy$^{\downarrow}$

GBT_C	Performing Arts$^{\uparrow}$, Event$^{\uparrow}$, Stage$^{\uparrow}$	Event$^{\uparrow}$, Festival$^{\uparrow}$	(No interesting concepts)	Girl$^{\downarrow}$, Selfie$^{\downarrow}$

GBT_S	#Duplicates$^{\uparrow}$, #Retweets$^{\uparrow}$	#Duplicates$^{\uparrow}$, #Retweets$^{\downarrow}$	#Retweets$^{\uparrow}$ #Duplicates$^{\downarrow}$	#Duplicates$^{\downarrow}$, #Retweets$^{\downarrow}$

GBT_F	Visual$^{\uparrow}$, Social$^{\uparrow}$, Semantic$^{\uparrow}$	Semantic$^{\uparrow}$, Visual$^{\uparrow}$	Social$^{\downarrow}$, Semantic$^{\uparrow}$	Visual$^{\downarrow}$, Social$^{\downarrow}$, Semantic$^{\downarrow}$

Table 7: Examples of images ranked by four distinct models with increasing ranks from left to right.

colors threshold was set to 600 and the ratio between the number of corners in synthetic/natural images was set to 0.1801, for a maximum distance of 20%.

Having extracted multiple featues, we experimented different combinations. Using luminance only, we managed to achieve a decent performance. We hypothesized that dominant colors and the ratio of pixels with the most common color (C1) were also good features that individually could distinguish both classes. Table 6 shows the performance of both these features, which corresponds to our expectation. The C1 feature has an exceptionally good performance for a unidimensional classifier.

Selecting the best set of features, we reach 97% precision on the NIPC dataset. However, as discussed previously, it seems that some of the images found on Twitter fall outside the categories defined by the authors of NPIC and thus we had to retrain the model. The classifier was retrained on the NIPC-Twitter dataset, making it now able to correctly classify as SPAM partially *synthetic* images, that have, for instance, a photography as background (see Figure 3). In the end, the final model trained on the NIPC-Twitter dataset achieved 91% precision on the NPIC dataset.

7 CONCLUSIONS

We proposed a framework designed help news editors by ranking and filtering images extracted from social media, according to their quality in the context of news media. The framework takes advantage of visual, social and semantic feature groups. Using several methods of evaluation we show the importance of having these groups of features tackle the different problems associated with the task:

- Social features can be used as proxies to measure the interestingness and quality of an image but the lack of strong social signals does not directly imply the image is not news worthy.
- Semantic features can be used to discard images that are generally not employed in the context of news media, such as *selfies*, while giving priority to topics covered more often in the news. However, semantic features not only do not ensure the visual quality of images but also may not be of great help with images that have rare concepts associated with them, that the model was not able to interact with in the training phase.
- Finally, visual features can be used to ensure the visual quality of an image but are not enough to ensure the interestingness and quality of the information it provides.

Consequently, the model that performed systematically better during evaluation was the one that leverages simultaneously these three feature groups

Finally, the above results were only possible to achieve in real-world social-media data because we deployed a thorough visual SPAM and redundancy filtering process. SPAM is a big part of the social-media, thus, we combined synthetic image detectors, captioned image filters, near-duplicate removal and other heuristics to clean low-quality data, allowing the ranking and filtering models to work with cleaner data.

Acknowledgements. This work has been partially funded by the CMU Portugal research project GoLocal Ref. CMUP-ERI/TIC/0033/2014, by the H2020 ICT project COGNITUS with the grant agreement No 687605 and by the project NOVA LINCS Ref. UID/CEC/04516/2013.

REFERENCES

[1] Ioannis Arapakis, Filipa Peleja, Berkant Barla Cambazoglu, and Joao Magalhaes. Linguistic benchmarks of online news article quality. In *ACL (1)*, 2016.

[2] Vassilis Athitsos, Michael J Swain, and Charles Frankel. Distinguishing photographs and graphics on the world wide web. In *Content-Based Access of Image and Video Libraries, 1997. Proceedings. IEEE Workshop on*, pages 10–17. IEEE, 1997.

[3] Tianqi Chen and Carlos Guestrin. Xgboost: A scalable tree boosting system. In *Proceedings of the 22nd acm sigkdd international conference on knowledge discovery and data mining*, pages 785–794. ACM, 2016.

[4] Sagnik Dhar, Vicente Ordonez, and Tamara L Berg. High level describable attributes for predicting aesthetics and interestingness. In *Computer Vision and Pattern Recognition (CVPR), 2011 IEEE Conference on*. IEEE, 2011.

[5] Michael Freeman et al. *The Photographer's Eye: Composition and Design for Better Digital Photos*. CRC Press, 2007.

[6] Jerome Friedman, Trevor Hastie, and Robert Tibshirani. *The elements of statistical learning*. Springer series in statistics New York, 2001.

[7] F Maxwell Harper, Daphne Raban, Sheizaf Rafaeli, and Joseph A Konstan. Predictors of answer quality in online q&a sites. In *Proceedings of the SIGCHI Conference on Human Factors in Computing Systems*. ACM, 2008.

[8] David Hasler and Sabine Süsstrunk. Measuring colourfulness in natural images. In *Proc. IST/SPIE Electronic Imaging 2003: Human Vision and Electronic Imaging VIII*, volume 5007, 2003.

[9] Phillip Isola, Devi Parikh, Antonio Torralba, and Aude Oliva. Understanding the intrinsic memorability of images. In *Advances in Neural Information Processing Systems*, 2011.

[10] Thorsten Joachims. Training linear svms in linear time. In *Proceedings of the 12th ACM SIGKDD international conference on Knowledge discovery and data mining*. ACM, 2006.

[11] Kenneth Kobre and Betsy Brill. *Photojournalism: the professionals' approach*, volume 5. Focal Press Burlington, MA, 2004.

[12] Neal Krawetz. Looks like it. http://www.hackerfactor.com/blog/index.php?/archives/432-Looks-Like-It.html. Accessed: 2017-03-23.

[13] Haewoon Kwak, Changhyun Lee, Hosung Park, and Sue Moon. What is twitter, a social network or a news media? In *Proceedings of the 19th International Conference on World Wide Web*, WWW '10, New York, NY, USA, 2010. ACM. ISBN 978-1-60558-799-8. doi: 10.1145/1772690.1772751. URL http://doi.acm.org/10.1145/1772690.1772751.

[14] R Lienhart and A Hartmann. Classifying images on the web automatically. *Journal of Electronic Imaging*, 11(4):445–454, 2002. ISSN 10179909 (ISSN). doi: 10.1117/1.1502259. URL https://www.scopus.com/inward/record.uri?eid=2-s2.0-0036810385{&}partnerID=40{&}md5=072fa45adaab336e2352ad149091bc16.

[15] Xueliang Liu and Benoit Huet. Eventenricher: a novel way to collect media illustrating events. In *Proceedings of the 3rd ACM conference on International conference on multimedia retrieval*. ACM, 2013.

[16] Luca Marchesotti, Florent Perronnin, Diane Larlus, and Gabriela Csurka. Assessing the aesthetic quality of photographs using generic image descriptors. In *Computer Vision (ICCV), 2011 IEEE International Conference on*. IEEE, 2011.

[17] Pedro Martins and Nuno Correia. Semi-automatic video assessment system. In *Proceedings of the 15th International Workshop on Content-Based Multimedia Indexing*, page 33. ACM, 2017.

[18] Andrew J McMinn, Yashar Moshfeghi, and Joemon M Jose. Building a large-scale corpus for evaluating event detection on twitter. In *Proceedings of the 22nd ACM international conference on Information & Knowledge Management*. ACM, 2013.

[19] Philip J Mcparlane, Andrew J Mcminn, and Joemon M Jose. âĂIJ Picture the scene ...âĂİ; Visually Summarising Social Media Events Categories and Subject Descriptors. *Proceedings of the 23rd ACM International Conference on Conference on Information and Knowledge Management*, pages 1459–1468, 2014. doi: 10.1145/2661829.2661923. URL http://dl.acm.org/citation.cfm?id=2661923.

[20] Kevin P Murphy. *Machine learning: a probabilistic perspective*. MIT press, 2012.

[21] Manos Schinas, Symeon Papadopoulos, Yiannis Kompatsiaris, and Pericles A. Mitkas. Visual Event Summarization on Social Media using Topic Modelling and Graph-based Ranking Algorithms. In *Proceedings of the 5th ACM on International Conference on Multimedia Retrieval - ICMR '15*, pages 203–210, New York, New York, USA, jun 2015. ACM Press. ISBN 9781450332743. doi: 10.1145/2671188.2749407. URL http://dl.acm.org/citation.cfm?id=2671188.2749407.

[22] Ray Smith. An overview of the tesseract ocr engine. In *Document Analysis and Recognition, 2007. ICDAR 2007. Ninth International Conference on*, volume 2. IEEE, 2007.

[23] Z Tang, Y Dai, and X Zhang. Perceptual hashing for color images using invariant moments. *Appl. Math*, 2012. URL http://www.naturalspublishing.com/files/published/54515x71g3omq1.pdf.

[24] Fei Wang and Min-yen Kan. NPIC : Hierarchical Synthetic Image Classification Using Image Search and Generic Features. *Work*, pages 473–482, 2006. ISSN 16113349.

Learning Joint Embedding with Multimodal Cues for Cross-Modal Video-Text Retrieval

Niluthpol Chowdhury Mithun
University of California, Riverside, CA
nmithun@ece.ucr.edu

Juncheng Li
Carnegie Mellon University, PA
Bosch Research and Technology Center, PA
junchenl@cs.cmu.edu

Florian Metze
Carnegie Mellon University, PA
fmetze@cs.cmu.edu

Amit K. Roy-Chowdhury
University of California, Riverside, CA
amitrc@ece.ucr.edu

ABSTRACT

Constructing a joint representation invariant across different modalities (e.g., video, language) is of significant importance in many multimedia applications. While there are a number of recent successes in developing effective image-text retrieval methods by learning joint representations, the video-text retrieval task, however, has not been explored to its fullest extent. In this paper, we study how to effectively utilize available multimodal cues from videos for the cross-modal video-text retrieval task. Based on our analysis, we propose a novel framework that simultaneously utilizes multi-modal features (different visual characteristics, audio inputs, and text) by a fusion strategy for efficient retrieval. Furthermore, we explore several loss functions in training the embedding and propose a modified pairwise ranking loss for the task. Experiments on MSVD and MSR-VTT datasets demonstrate that our method achieves significant performance gain compared to the state-of-the-art approaches.

CCS CONCEPTS

• **Information systems → Multimedia and multimodal retrieval**; *Learning to rank*;

KEYWORDS

Video-Text Retrieval, Joint Embedding, Multimodal Cues.

ACM Reference Format:
Niluthpol Chowdhury Mithun, Juncheng Li, Florian Metze, and Amit K. Roy-Chowdhury. 2018. Learning Joint Embedding with Multimodal Cues for Cross-Modal Video-Text Retrieval. In *ICMR '18: 2018 International Conference on Multimedia Retrieval, June 11–14, 2018, Yokohama, Japan.* ACM, New York, NY, USA, 9 pages. https://doi.org/10.1145/3206025.3206064

1 INTRODUCTION

Cross-modal retrieval between visual data and natural language description remains a long-standing challenge in multimedia [12, 41]. Joint visual-semantic embeddings [9, 15, 20, 26, 35] underpin the building of most cross-modal retrieval methods as they can bridge the gap between different modalities. In this joint space, the similarity of different points reflects the semantic closeness between their corresponding original inputs. In this work, we focus on learning effective joint embedding models for the cross-modal video-text retrieval task (See Fig. 1).

ICMR '18, June 11–14, 2018, Yokohama, Japan

ACM ISBN 978-1-4503-5046-4/18/06...$15.00
https://doi.org/10.1145/3206025.3206064

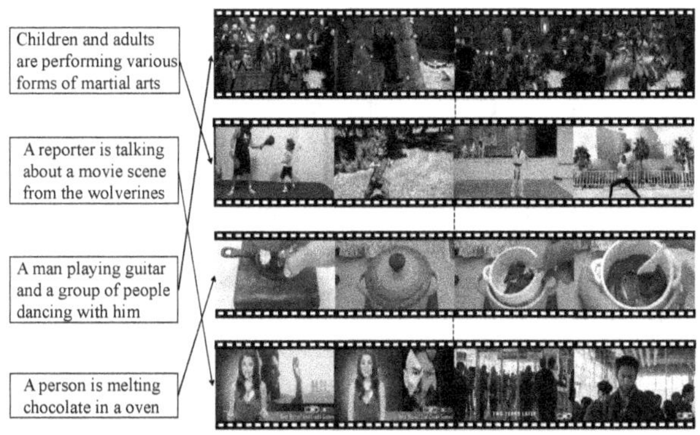

Figure 1: Illustration of Cross-Modal Video-Text retrieval task: given a text query, retrieve and rank videos from the database based on how well they depict the text or vice versa.

Recently, a few methods have been proposed for learning visual-semantic embeddings for the video-language matching task [6, 24, 25, 30, 37]. Most of these existing approaches are very similar to the image-text retrieval methods by design and focus mainly on the loss functions. We observe that simple adaptation of a state-of-the-art image-text embedding method [7] by mean-pooling features from video frames provides a better result than most existing video-text retrieval approaches [6, 24]. Image-text retrieval is a relatively maturefi eld of study, and one might think that directly applying such techniques to video-text retrieval may give optimal performance. However, such methods fail to take advantage of the supplementary information such as the temporal dynamics and sounds, which are already included in the videos. This limits the robustness of the systems; for instance, it may be very difficult to distinguish a video with the caption "a dog is barking" apart from another "a dog is playing" based only on visual appearance. Associating video motion content and sound can give supplementary cues in this scenario and improve the chance of correct prediction. Similarly, to understand a video described by "gunshot broke out at the concert" may require analysis of both visual and audio modalities simultaneously.

Developing a practical system for video-text retrieval without considering most available cues in the video content is unlikely to be comprehensive. However, an inappropriate fusion of complementary features may increase ambiguity and degrade performance. In this regard, we study how to judiciously utilize different cues from videos to develop a successful video-text retrieval system. We propose a novel framework, which is tailored towards achieving high performance in the task of cross-modal video-text retrieval. Compared to the existing methods, our framework fuses four types of feature (object, action, text and, audio) for efficient retrieval. Furthermore, we propose a modified pairwise ranking loss for the retrieval task that emphasizes on hard negatives and relative ranking of positive labels. Our approach shows significant performance improvement compared to previous approaches and baselines.

1.1 Overview of the Proposed Approach

In the cross-modal video-text retrieval task, an embedding network is learned to project video features and text features into the same joint space, and then retrieval is performed by searching the nearest neighbor in the latent space. Utilizing multiple characteristics of video (e.g., objects, actions, place, time) is evidently crucial for efficient retrieval [39] and has become a common practice. In the closely related task of video captioning, dynamic information from video along with static appearance features has been shown to be effective [27, 42]. Methods have been developed to extract features from videos that focus on different characteristics. For example, ResNet feature focuses on identifying objects in the frames, whereas I3D feature focuses on identifying the activities. Since in this work we are looking at videos in general, detecting both objects and activities from the video is very important for higher performance. Therefore, we need to develop a strategy that fuses information from different video features efficiently for the target task.

In this work, we propose to leverage the capability of neural networks to learn a deep representationfi rst and fuse the video features in the latent spaces so that we can develop expert networks focusing on specific subtasks (e.g. detecting activities, detecting objects). We propose to learn two joint video-text embedding networks as shown in Fig. 2. One model learns a joint space (Object-Text Space in Fig. 2) between text features and visual appearance features. Another model learns a joint space (Activity-Text Space in Fig. 2) between text feature and a combination of activity and audio features. Here, Object-Text space is the expert in solving ambiguity between objects in a video, whereas Activity-Text space is the expert in solving ambiguity between actions/events in the video. Given a query sentence, we calculate the sentence's similarity scores with each one of the videos in the entire dataset in both Object-Text and Activity-Text embedding spaces and use the sum of similarity scores forfi nal ranking.

We follow network architecture proposed in [18] that learns the embedding model using a two-branch network using image-text pair. One of the branches in this network takes text feature as input and the other branch takes in a video feature. We propose a modified bi-directional pairwise ranking loss to train the embedding. Inspired by the success of ranking loss proposed in [7] in image-text retrieval task, we emphasize on hard negatives. We also apply a weight-based penalty on the loss according to the relative ranking of the correct match in the retrieved result.

Contributions: The main contributions of this work can be summarized as follows.

• The success of video-text retrieval depends on more robust video understanding. This paper studies how to achieve the goal by utilizing multimodal features from a video (different visual features and audio inputs.).

• Our proposed framework uses action, object, text and audio features by a fusion strategy for efficient retrieval. We also present a modified pairwise loss to better learn the joint embedding.

• We demonstrate a clear improvement over the state-of-the-art methods in the video to text retrieval tasks with the MSR-VTT dataset [36] and MSVD dataset [4].

2 RELATED WORK

Image-Text Retrieval. Recently, there has been significant interest in learning robust visual-semantic embeddings for image-text retrieval [12, 16]. Based on a triplet of object, action and, scene, a method for projecting text and image to a joint space was proposed in early work [8]. Canonical Correlation Analysis (CCA) was used in several previous works for learning joint embeddings for the retrieval task [10, 13, 29, 38]. However, CCA based methods have been reported to be unstable and incur a high memory cost due to the covariance matrix calculation [34].

Most recent works relating to text and image modality are trained with ranking loss [7, 9, 18, 23, 32, 34]. In [9], authors proposed a method for projecting words and visual content to a joint space utilizing ranking loss that applies a penalty when a non-matching word is ranked higher than the matching one. A cross-modal image-text retrieval method has been presented in [18] that utilizes triplet ranking loss to project image feature and RNN based sentence description to a common latent space. Several image-text retrieval methods have adopted a similar approach with slight modifications in input feature representations [23], similarity score calculation [34], or loss function [7]. VSEPP model [7] modified the pair-wise ranking loss based on violations caused by the hard-negatives (i.e., non-matching query closest to each training query) and has been shown to be effective in the retrieval task. For image-sentence matching, a LSTM based network is presented in [14] that recurrently selects pairwise instances from image and sentence descriptions, and aggregates local similarity. In [23], authors proposed a multimodal attention mechanism to attend to sentence fragments and image regions selectively for similarity calculation. Our method complements these works that learns joint image-text embedding using a ranking loss (e.g., [7, 18, 32]). The framework can be applied to most of these approaches for improved video-text retrieval.

Video-Text Retrieval. Most relevant to our work are the methods that relate video and language modalities. Two major tasks in computer vision related to connecting these two modalities are video-text retrieval and video captioning. In this work, we only focus on the retrieval task. Similar to image-text retrieval approaches, most video-text retrieval methods employ a shared subspace. In [37], authors vectorize each subject-verb-object triplet extracted from a given sentence by word2vec model [22] and then aggregate the Subject, Verb, Object (SVO) vector into a sentence level vector using RNN. The video feature vector is obtained by mean pooling over frame-level features. Then a joint embedding is trained using a

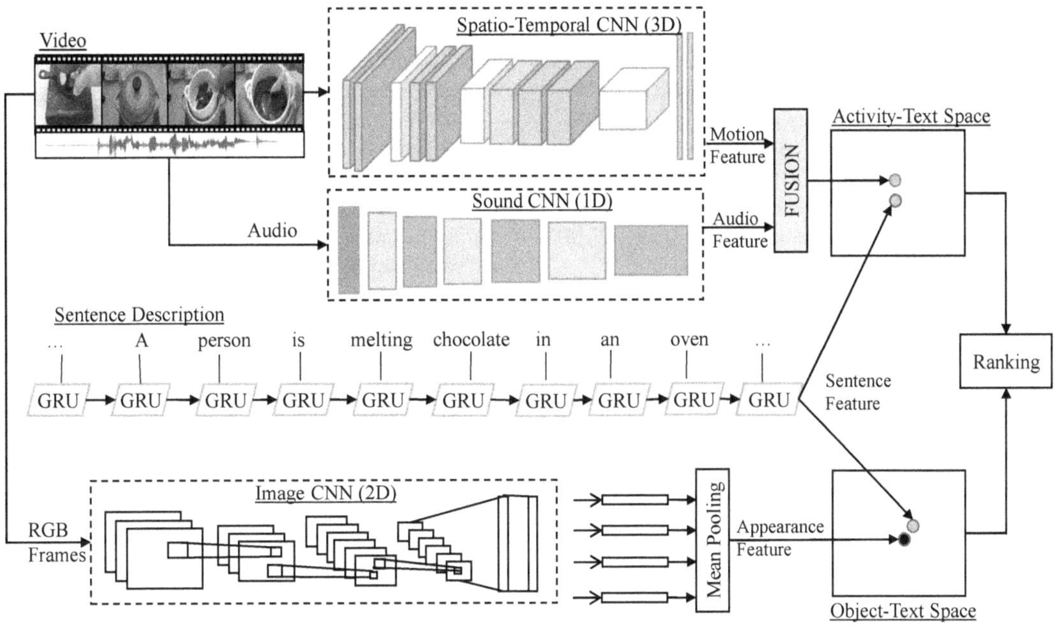

Figure 2: An overview of the proposed retrieval process. Please see Section 1.1 for an overview and Section 3 for details.

least squares loss to project the sentence representation and the video representation into a joint space. Web image search results of input text have been exploited by [24], which focused on word disambiguation. In [33], a stacked GRU is utilized to associate sequence of video frames to a sequence of words. In [25], authors propose an LSTM with visual-semantic embedding method that jointly minimizes a contextual loss to estimate relationships among the words in the sentence and a relevance loss to reflect the distance between video and sentence vectors in the shared space. A method named Word2VisualVec is proposed in [6] for the video to sentence matching task that projects vectorized sentence into visual feature space using mean squared loss. A shared space across image, text and sound modality is proposed in [2] utilizing ranking loss, which can also be applied to video-text retrieval task.

Most of these video-text retrieval approaches are very similar to the image-text retrieval methods by design and fail to utilize video dynamics for retrieval. In contrast to the existing works, our approach is capable of utilizing different visual cues and audio (if available) concurrently for more efficient retrieval.

3 APPROACH

In this section, wefi rst describe the input feature representation for video and text (Section 3.1). Then, we describe the basic framework for learning visual-semantic embedding using pair-wise ranking loss (Section 3.2). Next, we present our modification on the loss function to improve the basic framework to achieve better recall (Section 3.3). Finally. we present the proposed fusion step for video-text matching (Section 3.4).

3.1 Input Feature Representation

Text Feature. For encoding sentences, we use Gated Recurrent Units (GRU) [5]. We set the dimensionality of the joint embedding space, D, to 1024. The dimensionality of the word embeddings that are input to the GRU is 300. Note that the word embedding model and the GRU are trained end-to-end in this work.

Object Feature. For encoding image appearance, we adopt deep pre-trained convolutional neural network (CNN) model trained on ImageNet dataset as the encoder. Specifically, we utilize state-of-the-art 152 layer ResNet model ResNet152 [11]. We extract image features directly from the penultimate fully connected layer. We first rescale the image to 224x224 and feed into CNN as inputs. The dimension of the image embedding is 2048.

Activity Feature. The ResNet CNN can efficiently capture visual concepts in static frames. However, an effective approach to learning temporal dynamics in videos was proposed by inflating a 2-D CNN to a deep 3-D CNN named I3D in [3]. We use I3D model to encode activities in videos. In this work, we utilize the pre-trained RGB-I3D model and extract 1024 dimensional feature utilizing continuous 16 frames of video as the input.

Audio Feature. We believe that by associating audio, we can get important cues to the real-life events, which would help us remove ambiguity in many cases. We extract audio feature using state-of-the-art SoundNet CNN [1], which provides 1024 dimensional feature from audio. Note that, we only utilize the audio sound which is readily available with the videos.

3.2 Learning Joint Embedding

In this section, we describe the basic framework for learning joint embedding based on bi-directional pairwise ranking loss.

Given a video feature representation (e.g., appearance feature, or a combination of action and audio features) $\overline{v}$ ($\overline{v} \in \mathbb{R}^V$), the projection for a video feature on the joint space can be derived as $v = W^{(v)}\overline{v}$ ($v \in \mathbb{R}^D$). In the same way, the projection of input text embedding $\overline{t}(\overline{t} \in \mathbb{R}^T)$ to joint space is $t = W^{(t)}\overline{t}(t \in \mathbb{R}^D)$. Here, $W^{(v)} \in \mathbb{R}^{D \times V}$ is the transformation matrix that projects the video content into the joint embedding and D is the dimensionality of the joint space. Similarly, $W^{(t)} \in \mathbb{R}^{D\times T}$ maps input sentence/caption embedding to the joint space. Given feature representation for words in a sentence, the sentence embedding $\bar{t}$ is found from the hidden state of the GRU. Here, given the feature representation of both videos and corresponding text, the goal is to learn a joint embedding characterized by θ (i.e., $W^{(v)}$, $W^{(t)}$ and GRU weights) such that the video content and semantic content are projected into the joint embedding space. We keep image encoder (e.g., pre-trained CNN)fi xed in this work.

In the embedding space, it is expected that the similarity between a video and text pair to be more reflective of semantic closeness between videos and their corresponding texts. Many prior approaches have utilized pairwise ranking loss for learning joint embedding between visual input and textual input. They minimize a hinge based triplet ranking loss combining bi-directional ranking terms in order to learn to maximize the similarity between a video embedding and corresponding text embedding and minimize similarity to all other non-matching ones. The optimization problem can be written as,

$$\min_{\theta} \sum_{v}\sum_{t^-}[\alpha - S(v,t) + S(v,t^-)]_+ + \sum_{t}\sum_{v^-}[\alpha - S(t,v) + S(t,v^-)]_+ \tag{1}$$

where, $[f]_+ = max(0, f)$. t^- is a non-matching text embedding, and t is the matching text embedding. This is the same for video embedding v. α is the margin value for the pairwise ranking loss. The scoring function $S(v,t)$ is defined as the similarity function to measure the similarity between the videos and text in the joint embedded space. We use cosine similarity as it is easy to compute and shown to be very effective in learning joint embedding [7, 18].

In Eq. (1), in thefi rst term, for each pair (v,t), the sum is taken over all non-matching text embedding t^-. It attempts to ensure that for each visual feature, corresponding/matching text features should be closer than non-matching ones in the joint space. Similarly, the second term attempts to ensure that text embedding that corresponds to the video embedding should be closer in the joint space to each other than non-matching video embeddings.

3.3 Proposed Ranking Loss

Recently, focusing on hard-negatives has been shown to be effective in many embedding tasks [7, 21, 28]. Inspired by this, we focus on hard negatives (i.e., the negative video/text sample closest to a positive/matching (v,t) pair) instead of summing over all negatives in our formulation. For a positive pair (v,t), the hardest negative sample can be identified using $\hat{v} = \arg\max_{v^-} S(t,v^-)$ and $\hat{t} = \arg\max_{t^-} S(v,t^-)$. The optimization problem can be written as following to focus on hard-negatives,

$$\min_{\theta} \sum_{v}[\alpha - S(v,t) + S(v,\hat{t})]_+ + \sum_{t}[\alpha - S(t,v) + S(t,\hat{v})]_+ \tag{2}$$

The loss in Eq. 2 is similar to the loss in Eq. 1 but it is specified in terms of the hardest negatives [7]. We start with the loss function in Eq. 2 and modify the loss function following the idea of weighted ranking [31] to weight the loss based on the relative ranking of positive labels.

$$\min_{\theta} \sum_{v} L(r_v)[\alpha - S(v,t) + S(v,\hat{t})]_+ + \sum_{t} L(r_t)[\alpha - S(t,v) + S(t,\hat{v})]_+ \tag{3}$$

where $L(.)$ is a weighting function for different ranks. For a video embedding v, r_v is the rank of matching sentence t among all compared sentences. Similarly, for a text embedding t, r_t is the rank of matching video embedding v among all compared videos in the batch. We define the weighting function as $L(r) = (1+1/(N-r+1))$, where N is the number of compared videos.

It is very common, in practice, to only compare samples within a mini-batch at each iteration rather than comparing the whole training set for computational efficiency [15, 21, 28]. This is known as semi-hard negative mining [21, 28]. Moreover, selecting the hardest negatives in practice may often lead to a collapsed model and semi-hard negative mining helps to mitigate this issue [21, 28]. We utilize a batch-size of 128 in our experiment.

It is evident from Eq. 3 that the loss applies a weight-based penalty based on the relative ranking of the correct match in retrieved result. If a positive match is ranked top in the list, then $L(.)$ will assign a small weight to the loss and will not cost the loss too much. However, if a positive match is not ranked top, $L(.)$ will assign a much larger weight to the loss, which ultimately try to push the positive matching pair to the top of rank.

3.4 Matching and Ranking

The video-text retrieval task focuses on returning for each query video, a ranked list of the most likely text description from a dataset and vice versa. We believe, we need to understand two main aspects of each video: (1) the salient objects of the video and (2) the action and events in the video. To achieve this, we learn two joint video-text embedding spaces as shown in Fig. 2.

The Object-Text embedding space is the common space where both appearance features and text are mapped to. Hence, this space can link video and sentences focusing on the objects. On the other hand, the Activity-Text embedding space focuses on linking video and language description which emphasizes more on the events in the video. Action features and audio features both provide important cues for understanding different events in a video. We fuse action and audio features by concatenation, and map the concatenated feature and text feature into a common space, namely, the Activity-Text space. If the audio feature is absent from a video, we only use the action feature as the video representation for learning the Activity-Text embeddings. We utilize the same loss functions described in Sec. 3.3 for training both the Object-Text and Activity-Text embedding models.

At the time of retrieval, given a query sentence, we compute the similarity score of the query sentence with each one of the videos in the dataset in both Object-Text and Activity-Text embedding spaces and use a sum of similarity scores for thefi nal ranking. Conversely, given a query video, we calculate its similarity scores with all the sentences in the dataset in both embedding spaces and use a sum of similarity scores forfi nal ranking. It may be desired to use a weighted sum when it is necessary in a task to put more emphasis on one of the facets of the video (objects or captions). In this work, we put equal importance to both facets in ranking.

4 EXPERIMENTS

4.1 Datasets and Evaluation Metric

We present experiments on two benchmark datasets: Microsoft Research Video to Text (MSR-VTT) Dataset [36] and Microsoft Video Description dataset (MSVD) [4] to evaluate the performance of our

Table 1: Video-to-Text and Text-to-Video Retrieval Results on MSR-VTT Dataset.

#	Method	Video-to-Text Retrieval						Text-to-Video Retrieval					
		R@1	*R@5*	*R@10*	*MedR*	*MeanR*	*Recall*	*R@1*	*R@5*	*R@10*	*MedR*	*MeanR*	*Recall*
3.1	VSE-ResNet	7.7	20.3	31.2	28.0	185.8	19.7	5.0	16.4	24.6	47.0	215.1	15.3
	VSEPP ResNet	10.2	25.4	35.1	25.0	228.1	23.5	5.7	17.1	24.8	65.0	300.8	15.8
3.2	ResNet	10.5	26.7	35.9	25.0	266.6	24.4	5.8	17.6	25.2	61.0	296.6	16.2
	Audio	0.4	1.1	1.9	1051	2634.9	1.1	0.2	0.9	1.5	1292	1300	0.8
	I3D	8.4	22.2	32.3	30.3	229.9	21.0	4.6	15.3	22.7	71.0	303.7	14.2
3.3	CON(ResNet-I3D)	9.1	24.6	36.0	23.0	181.4	23.2	5.5	17.6	25.9	51.0	243.4	16.3
	CON(ResNet-I3D-Audio)	9.3	27.8	38.0	22.0	162.3	25.0	5.7	18.4	26.8	48.0	242.5	16.9
3.4	Joint Image-Text-Audio Embedding	8.7	22.4	32.1	31.0	225.8	21.0	4.8	15.3	22.9	73.0	313.6	14.3
3.5	Fusion [ResNet & I3D]	12.3	31.3	42.9	16.0	145.4	28.9	6.8	20.7	29.5	39.0	224.7	19.0
	Fusion [ResNet & CON(I3d-Audio)]	**12.5**	**32.1**	**42.4**	**16.0**	**134.0**	**29.0**	**7.0**	**20.9**	**29.7**	**38.0**	**213.8**	**19.2**

proposed framework. We adopt rank-based metric for quantitative performance evaluation.

MSR-VTT. The MSR-VTT is a large-scale video description dataset. This dataset contains 10,000 video clips. The dataset is split into 6513 videos for training, 2990 videos for testing and 497 videos for the validation set. Each video has 20-sentence descriptions. This is one of the largest video captioning dataset in terms of the quantity of sentences and the size of the vocabulary.

MSVD. The MSVD dataset contains 1970 Youtube clips, and each video is annotated with around 40 sentences. We use only the English descriptions. For a fair comparison, we used the same splits utilized in prior works [33], with 1200 videos for training, 100 videos for validation, and 670 videos for testing. The MSVD dataset is also used in [24] for video-text retrieval task, where they randomly chose 5 ground-truth sentences per video. We use the same setting when we compare with that approach.

Evaluation Metric. We use the standard evaluation criteria used in most prior work on image-text retrieval and video-text retrieval task [6, 18, 24]. We measure rank-based performance by *R@K*, Median Rank(*MedR*) and Mean Rank (*MeanR*). *R@K* (Recall at *K*) calculates the percentage of test samples for which the correct result is found in the top-*K* retrieved points to the query sample. We report results for *R@1*, *R@5* and *R@10*. Median Rank calculates the median of the ground-truth results in the ranking. Similarly, Mean Rank calculates the mean rank of all correct results. We also report the average of *R@1*, *R@5* and *R@10* as Recall in the tables.

4.2 Training Details

We used two GTX 1080 Ti GPUs for this work. We implemented the network using PyTorch following [7]. We start training with a learning rate of 0.002 and keep the learning ratefi xed for 15 epochs. Then the learning rate is lowered by a factor of 10 and the training continued for another 15 epochs. We use a batch-size of 128 in all the experiments. The embedding networks are trained using ADAM optimizer [17]. When the $L2$ norm of the gradients for the entire layer exceeds 2, gradients are clipped. We tried different values for margin α in training and empirically choose α as 0.2. The embedding model was evaluated on the validation set after every epoch. The model with the best sum of recalls on the validation set is chosenfi nally. Our code is publicly available[1].

[1] https://github.com/niluthpol/multimodal_vtt

4.3 Results on MSR-VTT Dataset

We report the result on MSR-VTT dataset [36] in Table 1. We implement several baselines to analyze different components of the proposed approach. To understand the effect of different loss functions, features, effect of feature concatenation and proposed fusion method, we divide the table into 5 rows (1.1-1.5). In row-1.1, we report the results on applying two different variants of pair-wise ranking loss. VSE[18] is based on the basic triplet ranking loss similar to Eq. 1 and VSEPP[7] is based on the loss function that emphasizes on hard-negatives as shown in Eq. 2. Note that, all other reported results in Table. 1 is based on the modified pairwise ranking loss proposed in Eq. 3. In row-1.2, we provide the performance of different features in learning the embedding using the proposed loss. In row-1.3, we present results for embedding learned utilizing video feature that is a direct concatenation of different video features. In row-1.4, we provide the result when a shared representation between image, text and audio modality is learned using proposed loss following the idea in [2] and used for video-text retrieval task. Finally, in row-1.5, we provide the result based on the proposed approach that employs two video-text space for retrieval.

Loss Function. For evaluating the performance of different ranking loss in the task, we can compare results reported in row-1.1 and row-1.2. We can choose only ResNet feature based method from these two rows for a fair comparison. We see that VSEPP loss function and proposed loss function performs significantly better than the traditional VSE loss function in *R@1*, *R@5*, *R@10*, and recall. However, VSE loss function has better performance in terms of mean rank. This phenomenon is expected based on the characteristics of the loss functions. As higher *R@1*, *R@5* and *R@10* are more desirable for a efficient video-text retrieval system than the mean rank, we see that our proposed loss function performs better than other loss functions in this task.

Video Features. We can compare the performance of different video features in learning the embedding using the proposed loss from row-1.2. We observe that ResNet feature and I3D feature performs reasonably well. The performance is very low when only audio feature is used for learning the embedding. It can be expected that the natural sound associated in a video alone does not contain as much information as videos. However, utilizing audio along with other feature provides a boost in performance as shown in row-1.3 and row-1.4.

Table 2: Video-to-Text Retrieval Results on MSVD Dataset. We highlight the proposed method. The methods which has 'Ours' keyword in name are trained with the proposed loss.

Method	*R@1*	*R@5*	*R@10*	*MedR*	*MeanR*	*Recall*
Results Using Partition used by JMET and JMDV						
CCA					245.3	
JMET					208.5	
JMDV					224.1	
W2VV-ResNet	16.3		44.8	14.0	110.2	
VSE-ResNet	15.8	30.2	41.4	12.0	84.8	34.5
VSEPP-ResNet	21.2	43.4	52.2	9.0	79.2	39.0
Ours-ResNet	23.4	45.4	53.0	8.0	75.9	40.6
Ours-I3D	21.3	43.7	53.3	9.0	72.2	39.5
Ours-(ResNet-I3d Fusion)	**31.5**	**51.0**	**61.5**	**5.0**	**41.7**	**48.0**
Results Using Partition used by LJRV						
ST	2.99	10.9	17.5	77.0	241.0	10.5
LJRV	9.85	27.1	38.4	19.0	75.2	25.1
W2VV-ResNet	17.9		49.4	11.0	57.6	
Ours-ResNet	20.9	43.7	54.9	7.0	56.1	39.9
Ours-I3D	17.5	39.6	51.3	10.0	54.8	36.1
Ours-(ResNet-I3d Fusion)	**25.5**	**51.3**	**61.9**	**5.0**	**32.5**	**46.3**

Feature Concatenation for Representing Video. Rather than training multiple video-semantic spaces, one can argue that we can simply concatenate all the available video features and learn a single video-text space using this concatenated video feature [6, 36]. However, we observe from row-1.3 that integrating complementary features by static concatenation based fusion strategy fails to utilize the full potential of different video features for the task. Comparing row-1.2 and row-1.3, we observe that a concatenation of ResNet feature, I3D feature and Audio feature performs even worse than utilizing only ResNet feature in *R@*1. Although we see some improvement in other evaluation metrics, overall the improvement is very limited. We believe that both appearance feature and action feature gets suppressed in such concatenation as they focus on representing different entities of a video.

Learning a Shared Space across Image, Text and Audio. Learning a shared space across image, text and sound modality is proposed for cross-modal retrieval task in [2]. Following the idea, we trained a shared space across image-text-sound modality using the pairwise ranking loss by utilizing image-text and image-sound pairs. The result is reported in row-1.4. We observe that performance in video-text retrieval task degrades after training such an aligned representation across 3 modalities. Training such a shared representation gives thefl exibility to transfer across multiple modalities. Nevertheless, we believe it is not tailored towards achieving high performance in a specific task. Moreover, aligning across 3 modalities is a more computationally difficult task and requires many more examples to train.

Fusion. The best result in Table. 1 is achieved by our proposed fusion approach as shown in row-1.5. We see that the proposed method achieves 19.5% improvement in *R@*1 for text retrieval and 20.68% improvement for video retrieval in *R@*1 compared to ResNet(row-1.2), which is the best among the other methods which use a single embedding space for the retrieval task. In row-1.5, Fusion[Resnet & CON (I3D-Audio)] differs from Fusion[ResNet & I3d] in the feature used in learning the activity-text space. We see that utilizing audio in learning the embedding improves the result slightly. However, as the retrieval performance of individual audio feature is very low (shown in row-1.2), we did not utilize audio-text space separately in fusion as we found it degrade the performance significantly.

Table 3: Text-to-Video Retrieval Results on MSVD Dataset. We highlight the proposed method.

Method	*R@1*	*R@5*	*R@10*	*MedR*	*MeanR*	*Recall*
Results Using Partition used by JMET and JMDV						
CCA					251.3	
JMDV					236.3	
VSE-ResNet	12.3	30.1	42.3	14.0	57.7	30.2
VSEPP-ResNet	15.4	39.6	53.0	9.0	43.8	36.0
Ours-ResNet	16.1	41.1	53.5	9.0	42.7	36.9
Ours-I3D	15.4	39.2	51.4	10.0	43.2	35.3
Ours-(ResNet-I3d Fusion)	**20.3**	**47.8**	**61.1**	**6.0**	**28.3**	**43.1**
Results Using Partition used by LJRV						
ST	2.6	11.6	19.3	51.0	106.0	11.2
LJRV	7.7	23.4	35.0	21.0	49.1	22.0
Ours-ResNet	15.0	40.2	51.9	9.0	45.3	35.7
Ours-I3D	14.6	38.9	51.0	10.0	45.1	34.8
Ours-(ResNet-I3d Fusion)	**20.2**	**47.5**	**60.7**	**6.0**	**29.0**	**42.8**

4.4 Results on MSVD Dataset

We report the results of Video-to-Text retrieval task on MSVD dataset [4] in Table 2 and the results for Text-to-Video retrieval in Table 3. We compare our approach with existing video-text retrieval approaches, CCA[29], ST [19], JMDV [37], LJRV [24], JMET [25], and W2VV [6]. For these approaches, we directly cite scores from respective papers when available. We report score for JMET from [6]. The score of CCA is reported from [37] and the score of ST is reported from [24]. If the score for multiple models is reported, we select the score of the best performing method from the paper. We could not compare with method [40] which focuses on movie retrieval task and results are not available on our experimented datasets. We did not re-implement this method in our setting as their method is based on an ensemble of several models and it is very difficult to exactly emulate the implementation details.

We also implement and compare results with state-of-the-art image-embedding approach VSE[18] and VSEPP[7] using ResNet152 feature as the video feature following publicly available code [7]. Our proposed fusion method is named as Ours-(ResNet-I3D Fusion) in the Table. 2 and Table. 3. Our method utilizes the proposed loss and employs two embedding spaces for calculating similarity between video and text. We use ResNet-152 feature as the appearance feature in training Object-Text space. As the audio is muted in this dataset, we train the Activity-Text space utilizing only I3D feature from videos. To show the impact of only using the proposed loss in retrieval, we also report results based on each of these two embedding space (Ours-ResNet and Ours-I3D) in the tables.

From Table 2 and Table 3, it is evident that our proposed approach performs significantly better than existing ones. The result is improved significantly by utilizing the fusion proposed in this paper that utilizes both the video-text spaces in calculating thefinal ranking. Moreover, utilizing the proposed loss improves the result over previous state-of-the-art methods. It can also be identified that our loss function is not only useful for learning embedding independently, but also it is useful for the proposed fusion.

Figure 3: Examples of 9 test videos from MSVD dataset and the top 1 retrieved captions for Ours-ResNet, Ours-I3D, and the proposed method as shown in Table. 2. The value in brackets is the rank of the highest ranked ground-truth caption. Ground Truth (GT) is a sample from the ground-truth captions. Among the approaches, ResNet and I3D are methods where single video-text space is used for retrieval (ResNet is trained using ResNet feature as video feature and I3D is trained using the I3D feature). We also report result for the proposed fusion approaches where both video-text spaces are used for retrieval.

4.5 Qualitative Results

MSVD Dataset. In Fig. 3, we show examples of few test videos from MSVD dataset and the top 1 retrieved captions for the proposed approach. We also show the retrieval result when only one of the embeddings is used for retrieval. Additionally, we report the rank of the highest ranked ground-truth caption in thefi gure. We can observe from thefi gure that in most of the cases, utilizing cue from both video-text spaces helps to match the correct caption. It can be easily identified from the top-1 retrieved caption that the projection learned between video and text by utilizing appearance feature (ResNet) is significantly different from that learned using Activity feature (I3D). The variation between the rank of the highest matching caption further strengthens this observation. We also cannot claim that one video feature is better than others for this task. ResNet feature performs better than the I3D feature in retrieval for some videos. For other videos, the I3D feature achieves higher performance. However, combining knowledge from two video-text spaces, we have consistently better performance than utilizing one of the features. We see from Fig. 3 that, among 9 videos, the retrieval performance is improved or higher recall is retained for 7 videos. Video-6 and video-9 show two of our failure cases, where utilizing multiple video-text spaces degrades the performance slightly than ResNet in Video-6 and I3D in Video-9.

MSR-VTT Dataset. Similar to Fig. 3, we also show qualitative results for a few test videos from MSR-VTT dataset in Fig. 4. Video 1-6 in Fig. 4 shows a few examples where utilizing cue from both video-text spaces helps to match the correct caption compared to using only one of the video-text space. Moreover, we also see the result was improved after utilizing audio in learning the second video-text space (Activity-text space). We observe this improvement for most of the videos, as we also observe from Table. 1.

Video 7-9 shows some failure cases for our fusion approach in Fig. 4. Video 7 shows a case, where utilizing multiple video-text spaces for retrieval degrades the performance slightly compared to utilizing only one of the video-text space. For Video-8 and video-9 in Fig. 4, we observe that the performance improves after fusion overall, but the performance is better when the audio is not used in learning video-text space. On the other hand, video 1-6 includes cases where utilizing audio helped improving the result. Since we did not exploit the structure of the audio and analyze the structural

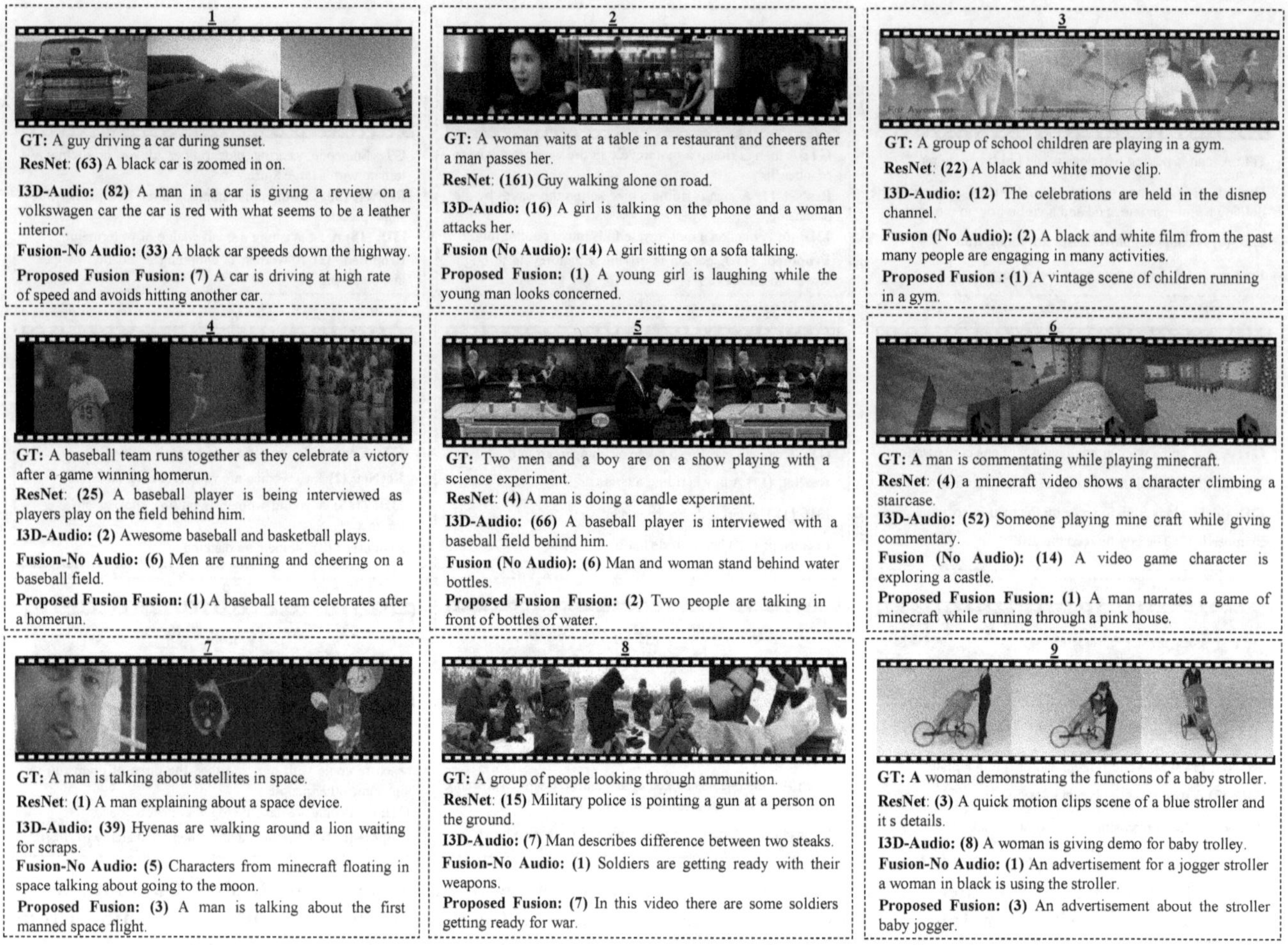

Figure 4: A snapshot of 9 test videos from MSR-VTT dataset with success and failure cases, the top 1 retrieved captions for four approaches based on the proposed loss function and the rank of the highest ranked ground-truth caption inside the bracket. Among the approaches, ResNet and I3D-Audio are methods where single video-text space is used for retrieval (ResNet is trained using ResNet feature as video feature and I3D-Audio is trained using the concatenated I3D feature and Audio feature as video feature). We also report results for two fusion approaches where two video-text spaces are used for retrieval. Both fusion approaches use a object-text space trained with ResNet feature, while in our proposed approach, the activity-text space is trained using audio along with I3D feature. Fusion (No Audio) uses activity-text space that is trained with only I3D feature.

alignment between audio and video, it is difficult to determine whether audio is always helpful. For instance, audio can come from different things (persons, animals or objects) in a video, and it might shift our attention away from the main subject. Moreover, the captions are provided mostly based on the visual aspects. We observe that using audio is crucial in many cases where there is deep semantic relation between visual content and audio (e.g., the audio is from the third person narration of the video, the audio is music or song) and it gives important cues in reducing description ambiguity (e.g., video-2, video-5 and video-6). We see an overall improvement in the quantitative result (Table 1) which also supports our idea of using audio. These failure cases provide future directions of this work focusing on developing more sophisticated algorithms to combine similarity scores from multiple joint spaces and further analyze the role of associated audio for video-text retrieval.

5 CONCLUSIONS

We propose an approach for efficient cross-modal video-text retrieval using joint embeddings by effectively including features from different visual entities and features from audio. We also propose a new loss function that further exploits the multimodal correlation. Experiments on two benchmark datasets demonstrate that our proposed loss function learns better embeddings for the video-text retrieval task than existing ones. Moreover, our overall framework achieves significant performance improvement compared to several state-of-the-art approaches.

Acknowledgement. This work was partially supported by NSF grants IIS-1746031 and CNS-1544969. Juncheng Li was supported by the Bosch Graduate Fellowship to CMU LTI. We thank the anonymous reviewers for insightful suggestions. We would also like to thank Rameswar Panda and Sujoy Paul for helpful comments.

REFERENCES

[1] Yusuf Aytar, Carl Vondrick, and Antonio Torralba. 2016. Soundnet: Learning sound representations from unlabeled video. In *Advances in Neural Information Processing Systems*. 892–900.

[2] Yusuf Aytar, Carl Vondrick, and Antonio Torralba. 2017. See, Hear, and Read: Deep Aligned Representations. *arXiv preprint arXiv:1706.00932* (2017).

[3] Joao Carreira and Andrew Zisserman. 2017. Quo vadis, action recognition? a new model and the kinetics dataset. In *IEEE Conference on Computer Vision and Pattern Recognition*. IEEE, 4724–4733.

[4] David L Chen and William B Dolan. 2011. Collecting highly parallel data for paraphrase evaluation. In *Annual Meeting of the Association for Computational Linguistics: Human Language Technologies-Volume 1*. ACL, 190–200.

[5] Junyoung Chung, Caglar Gulcehre, KyungHyun Cho, and Yoshua Bengio. 2014. Empirical evaluation of gated recurrent neural networks on sequence modeling. *arXiv preprint arXiv:1412.3555* (2014).

[6] Jianfeng Dong, Xirong Li, and Cees GM Snoek. 2016. Word2VisualVec: Image and Video to Sentence Matching by Visual Feature Prediction. *arXiv preprint arXiv:1604.06838* (2016).

[7] Fartash Faghri, David J Fleet, Jamie Ryan Kiros, and Sanja Fidler. 2017. VSE++: Improved Visual-Semantic Embeddings. *arXiv preprint arXiv:1707.05612* (2017).

[8] Ali Farhadi, Mohsen Hejrati, Mohammad Amin Sadeghi, Peter Young, Cyrus Rashtchian, Julia Hockenmaier, and David Forsyth. 2010. Every picture tells a story: Generating sentences from images. In *European Conference on Computer Vision*. Springer, 15–29.

[9] Andrea Frome, Greg S Corrado, Jon Shlens, Samy Bengio, Jeff Dean, Tomas Mikolov, et al. 2013. Devise: A deep visual-semantic embedding model. In *Advances in Neural Information Processing Systems*. 2121–2129.

[10] Yunchao Gong, Qifa Ke, Michael Isard, and Svetlana Lazebnik. 2014. A multi-view embedding space for modeling internet images, tags, and their semantics. *International Journal of Computer Vision* 106, 2 (2014), 210–233.

[11] Kaiming He, Xiangyu Zhang, Shaoqing Ren, and Jian Sun. 2016. Deep residual learning for image recognition. In *IEEE Conference on Computer Vision and Pattern Recognition*. IEEE, 770–778.

[12] Christian Andreas Henning and Ralph Ewerth. 2017. Estimating the information gap between textual and visual representations. In *International Conference on Multimedia Retrieval*. ACM, 14–22.

[13] Micah Hodosh, Peter Young, and Julia Hockenmaier. 2013. Framing image description as a ranking task: Data, models and evaluation metrics. *Journal of Artificial Intelligence Research* 47 (2013), 853–899.

[14] Yan Huang, Wei Wang, and Liang Wang. 2017. Instance-aware image and sentence matching with selective multimodal lstm. In *IEEE Conference on Computer Vision and Pattern Recognition*. IEEE, 2310–2318.

[15] Andrej Karpathy and Li Fei-Fei. 2015. Deep visual-semantic alignments for generating image descriptions. In *IEEE Conference on Computer Vision and Pattern Recognition*. IEEE, 3128–3137.

[16] Andrej Karpathy, Armand Joulin, and Fei Fei F Li. 2014. Deep fragment embeddings for bidirectional image sentence mapping. In *Advances in Neural Information Processing Systems*. 1889–1897.

[17] Diederik Kingma and Jimmy Ba. 2014. Adam: A method for stochastic optimization. *arXiv preprint arXiv:1412.6980* (2014).

[18] Ryan Kiros, Ruslan Salakhutdinov, and Richard S Zemel. 2014. Unifying visual-semantic embeddings with multimodal neural language models. *arXiv preprint arXiv:1411.2539* (2014).

[19] Ryan Kiros, Yukun Zhu, Ruslan R Salakhutdinov, Richard Zemel, Raquel Urtasun, Antonio Torralba, and Sanja Fidler. 2015. Skip-thought vectors. In *Advances in Neural Information Processing Systems*. 3294–3302.

[20] Benjamin Klein, Guy Lev, Gil Sadeh, and Lior Wolf. 2015. Associating neural word embeddings with deep image representations usingfi sher vectors. In *IEEE Conference on Computer Vision and Pattern Recognition*. IEEE, 4437–4446.

[21] R Manmatha, Chao-Yuan Wu, Alexander J Smola, and Philipp Krahenbuhl. 2017. Sampling Matters in Deep Embedding Learning. In *2017 IEEE International Conference on Computer Vision*. IEEE, 2859–2867.

[22] Tomas Mikolov, Kai Chen, Greg Corrado, and Jeffrey Dean. 2013. Efficient estimation of word representations in vector space. *arXiv preprint arXiv:1301.3781* (2013).

[23] Hyeonseob Nam, Jung-Woo Ha, and Jeonghee Kim. 2017. Dual Attention Networks for Multimodal Reasoning and Matching. In *IEEE Conference on Computer Vision and Pattern Recognition*. IEEE, 299–307.

[24] Mayu Otani, Yuta Nakashima, Esa Rahtu, Janne Heikkilä, and Naokazu Yokoya. 2016. Learning joint representations of videos and sentences with web image search. In *European Conference on Computer Vision*. Springer, 651–667.

[25] Yingwei Pan, Tao Mei, Ting Yao, Houqiang Li, and Yong Rui. 2016. Jointly modeling embedding and translation to bridge video and language. In *IEEE Conference on Computer Vision and Pattern Recognition*. IEEE, 4594–4602.

[26] Bryan Plummer, Matthew Brown, and Svetlana Lazebnik. 2017. Enhancing Video Summarization via Vision-Language Embedding. In *IEEE Conference on Computer Vision and Pattern Recognition*. IEEE.

[27] Vasili Ramanishka, Abir Das, Dong Huk Park, Subhashini Venugopalan, Lisa Anne Hendricks, Marcus Rohrbach, and Kate Saenko. 2016. Multimodal video description. In *ACM Multimedia Conference*. ACM, 1092–1096.

[28] Florian Schroff, Dmitry Kalenichenko, and James Philbin. 2015. Facenet: A unified embedding for face recognition and clustering. In *IEEE Conference on Computer Vision and Pattern Recognition*. IEEE, 815–823.

[29] Richard Socher and Li Fei-Fei. 2010. Connecting modalities: Semi-supervised segmentation and annotation of images using unaligned text corpora. In *IEEE Conference on Computer Vision and Pattern Recognition*. IEEE, 966–973.

[30] Atousa Torabi, Niket Tandon, and Leonid Sigal. 2016. Learning language-visual embedding for movie understanding with natural-language. *arXiv preprint arXiv:1609.08124* (2016).

[31] Nicolas Usunier, David Buffoni, and Patrick Gallinari. 2009. Ranking with ordered weighted pairwise classification. In *International Conference on Machine Learning*. ACM, 1057–1064.

[32] Ivan Vendrov, Ryan Kiros, Sanja Fidler, and Raquel Urtasun. 2016. Order-embeddings of images and language. In *International Conference on Learning Representations*.

[33] Subhashini Venugopalan, Marcus Rohrbach, Jeffrey Donahue, Raymond Mooney, Trevor Darrell, and Kate Saenko. 2015. Sequence to sequence-video to text. In *IEEE International Conference on Computer Vision*. IEEE, 4534–4542.

[34] Liwei Wang, Yin Li, Jing Huang, and Svetlana Lazebnik. 2018. Learning two-branch neural networks for image-text matching tasks. *IEEE Transactions on Pattern Analysis and Machine Intelligence* (2018).

[35] Liwei Wang, Yin Li, and Svetlana Lazebnik. 2016. Learning deep structure-preserving image-text embeddings. In *IEEE Conference on Computer Vision and Pattern Recognition*. IEEE, 5005–5013.

[36] Jun Xu, Tao Mei, Ting Yao, and Yong Rui. 2016. Msr-vtt: A large video description dataset for bridging video and language. In *IEEE Conference on Computer Vision and Pattern Recognition*. 5288–5296.

[37] Ran Xu, Caiming Xiong, Wei Chen, and Jason J Corso. 2015. Jointly Modeling Deep Video and Compositional Text to Bridge Vision and Language in a Unified Framework.. In *AAAI*, Vol. 5. 6.

[38] Fei Yan and Krystian Mikolajczyk. 2015. Deep correlation for matching images and text. In *IEEE Conference on Computer Vision and Pattern Recognition*. IEEE, 3441–3450.

[39] Rong Yan, Jun Yang, and Alexander G Hauptmann. 2004. Learning query-class dependent weights in automatic video retrieval. In *ACM Multimedia Conference*. ACM, 548–555.

[40] Youngjae Yu, Hyungjin Ko, Jongwook Choi, and Gunhee Kim. 2017. End-To-End Concept Word Detection for Video Captioning, Retrieval, and Question Answering. In *IEEE Conference on Computer Vision and Pattern Recognition*. IEEE, 3165–3173.

[41] Liang Zhang, Bingpeng Ma, Guorong Li, Qingming Huang, and Qi Tian. 2017. Multi-Networks Joint Learning for Large-Scale Cross-Modal Retrieval. In *ACM Multimedia Conference*. ACM, 907–915.

[42] Xishan Zhang, Ke Gao, Yongdong Zhang, Dongming Zhang, Jintao Li, and Qi Tian. 2017. Task-Driven Dynamic Fusion: Reducing Ambiguity in Video Description. In *IEEE Conference on Computer Vision and Pattern Recognition*. IEEE, 3713–3721.

Class-aware Self-Attention for Audio Event Recognition

Shizhe Chen
Renmin University of China
cszhe1@ruc.edu.cn

Jia Chen
Carnegie Mellon University
jiac@cs.cmu.edu

Qin Jin*
Renmin University of China
qjin@ruc.edu.cn

Alexander Hauptmann
Carnegie Mellon University
alex@cs.cmu.edu

ABSTRACT

Audio event recognition (AER) has been an important research problem with a wide range of applications. However, it is very challenging to develop large scale audio event recognition models. On the one hand, usually there are only "weak" labeled audio training data available, which only contains labels of audio events without temporal boundaries. On the other hand, the distribution of audio events is generally long-tailed, with only a few positive samples for large amounts of audio events. These two issues make it hard to learn discriminative acoustic features to recognize audio events especially for long-tailed events. In this paper, we propose a novel class-aware self-attention mechanism with attention factor sharing to generate discriminative clip-level features for audio event recognition. Since a target audio event only occurs in part of an entire audio clip and its corresponding temporal interval varies, the proposed class-aware self-attention approach learns to highlight relevant temporal intervals and to suppress irrelevant noises at the same time. In order to learn attention patterns effectively for those long-tailed events, we combine both the domain knowledge and data driven strategies to share attention factors in the proposed attention mechanism, which transfers the common knowledge learned from other similar events to the rare events. The proposed attention mechanism is a pluggable component and can be trained end-to-end in the overall AER model. We evaluate our model on a large-scale audio event corpus "Audio Set" with both short-term and long-term acoustic features. The experimental results demonstrate the effectiveness of our model, which improves the overall audio event recognition performance with different acoustic features especially for events with low resources. Moreover, the experiments also show that our proposed model is able to learn new audio events with a few training examples effectively and efficiently without disturbing the previously learned audio events.

*Qin Jin is the corresponding author.

ICMR '18, June 11–14, 2018, Yokohama, Japan

ACM ISBN 978-1-4503-5046-4/18/06...$15.00
https://doi.org/10.1145/3206025.3206067

KEYWORDS

Audio Event Recognition; Class-aware Self-attention; Attention Factor Sharing

ACM Reference Format:
Shizhe Chen, Jia Chen, Qin Jin, and Alexander Hauptmann. 2018. Class-aware Self-Attention for Audio Event Recognition. In *ICMR '18: 2018 International Conference on Multimedia Retrieval, June 11–14, 2018, Yokohama, Japan.* ACM, New York, NY, USA, 9 pages. https://doi.org/10.1145/3206025.3206067

1 INTRODUCTION

Audio is an important type of multimedia data and it contains valuable information such as speeches, emotions, scenes, events and so on, which can be critical for multimedia content analysis for indexing and retrieval. In this paper, we focus on the audio event recognition (AER) task, which aims to detect the existence of different sound events in the audio clip such as bell rings, dog barks, wind blows etc. Audio event recognition has a broad range of applications such as assisting event detection for surveillance videos, content-based indexing and retrieval of multimedia data, wildlife monitoring and so on.

Recently, the collections of large-scale audio event datasets such as DCASE sound event detection dataset [16] and Google Audio Set [8] have greatly promoted current AER research enabling more training data and more number of events. However, there are two main challenges to work with these datasets, which are also common challenges in real world applications. Firstly, the audio clips are usually "weak" labeled which only contain labels of the audio events without the exact temporal boundaries of the event occurrence. Because annotating the event boundaries is quite time-consuming and labor expensive which requires annotators to go back and forth several times in the audio clip to mark appropriate temporal intervals for different events [14]. As shown in the example in Figure 1(a), the audio clip contains multiple audio events such as "speech" and "horse" with each event corresponding to different temporal intervals in the audio clip. However, what we can get from the training data are only the labels of "speech" and "horse" for this audio clip. We do not know when exactly these two events occur in the audio clip. But in order to generate discriminative audio features for the target audio event, it is important to focus on the relevant temporal intervals while suppressing the irrelevant background or other audio event intervals.

Secondly, the number of audio events typically follows the long-tailed distribution, which means that there are large amounts of audio events which have quite low labeled training resources. For example, Figure 1(b) presents the log-scaled audio event distribution

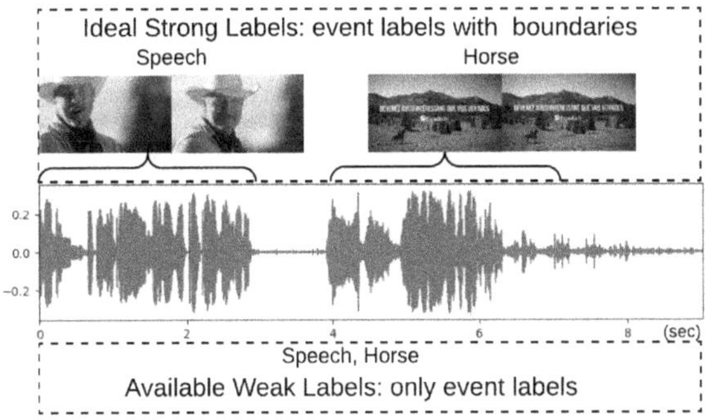

(a) An example in the Audio Set corpus, which represents the weak label challenge: The audio clip is annotated with audio event labels, but the grounded temporal boundaries for each audio event are not annotated. The audio events may occur at different temporal intervals in the audio clip.

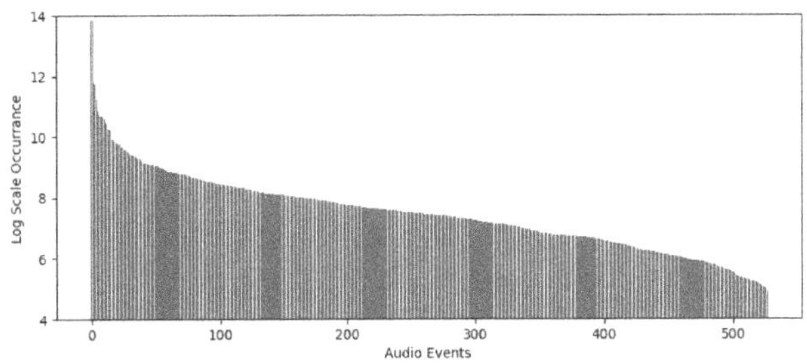

(b) The audio event distribution in the Audio Set corpus, which illustrates the long-tailed distribution challenge: large number of audio events only contain a few positive training data.

Figure 1: The weak label and long-tailed distribution challenges in the audio event recognition task.

in the Audio Set corpus. We can see that the audio event classes are quite unbalanced with the frequent classes such as music and speech containing thousands of times more data than the long-tailed classes such as splinter, creak and so on. However, different audio events might share similar patterns due to the correlation of the audio events. Hence, effective transfer learning approaches are desired to deploy the knowledge learned from audio events with abundant training data to benefit the learning for low-resourced audio events.

In order to address the above two challenges, in this work, we propose a novel class-aware self-attention mechanism with attention factor sharing strategy which follows the general attention-based AER framework. The general attention-based model employs an attention module to construct discriminative clip-level representations for classification. Unlike the mean pooling [6] or global self-attention mechanism [17] used in previous work, which either clutters all the background noise or attends to regions with high relevance without considering the specific audio events, our proposed class-aware self-attention learns to attend to relevant temporal intervals for each audio event via using class-specific attention vector. Thus the generated features for different audio events could be more salient and discriminative. In order to learn the attention patterns effectively for audio events with low-resources, we propose an attention factor sharing approach to transfer the common attention patterns learned in other events. We explore different attention factor sharing strategies including purely based on domain knowledge of audio events correlation, data driven audio event correlation, and the combination of both. The combination strategy is the most effective one from our experimental analysis.

We evaluate our proposed model on a large-scale audio event corpus "Audio Set", which consists of millions of annotated audio clips and 527 different audio events. To demonstrate the robustness of our model, we carry out extensive experiments with two different frame-level acoustic features, including the short-term acoustic features extracted with the state-of-the-art acoustic convolutional neural networks (CNN) [9] and the long-term acoustic features extracted with the recurrent neural networks which could capture the temporal evolution of the events. Consistent experimental results with these two set of features show that the class-aware self-attention mechanism can highlight the event-related temporal intervals and thus generate more discriminative class-aware clip-level features for audio event recognition. The attention factor sharing approach not only reduces the number of parameters to be learned, but also improves the performance especially for low-resourced audio events. We also show that our proposed model is able to learn new audio events using a few training examples effectively and efficiently, which requires low training cost and achieves considerable performance.

The rest of the paper is organized as follows: Section 2 introduces the related works. Section 3 describes our proposed class-aware self-attention based AER system. Section 4 presents the experimental results. Finally Section 5 concludes the paper.

2 RELATED WORKS

Audio Event Recognition (AER): Previous approaches for AER typically consist of three stages [22]. The first stage is to generate low-level acoustic features. The most common low-level features are the hand-crafted features, Mel-Frequency Cepstral Coefficients (MFCCs) [25], which have achieved successful applications in many audio tasks. The recent emergence of the large-scale audio event datasets such as manually annotated Audio Set [8] and weakly-labeled Soundnet [1], enables learning representations from raw wave signals. The acoustic features learned with the Convolution Neural Networks (CNN), which achieve the state-of-the-art performance in vision tasks, have also shown superior performance than traditional MFCC features for audio event recognition.

In the second stage, a clip-level representation is generated based on low-level features. For example, feature encoding methods [6], such as bag-of-audio-words (BoAW) and fisher vector encoding, learn a global vocabulary and compute the distributions of low-level features over the vocabulary as the clip-level features. Inspired by the speaker identification techniques, Gaussian Mixture Models (GMM) supervectors [5] and i-vectors [7] are also explored to generate more event-discriminative features. However, the above methods ignore the long-term context and order of low-level features, which are useful for recognizing the audio events. In order to capture the temporal information, researchers have proposed to use semantically meaningful audio units to build clip-level representation via Hidden Markov Models (HMM) [3, 4] or recurrent neural networks (RNN) [20–22].

Finally, the last stage is to build the multi-label or multi-class classifiers based on clip-level acoustic features to recognize test audio events. Neural networks (NN), support vector machines (SVM) etc. have been explored in the audio event recognition literature [13]. In our work, we focus on the second stage to generate discriminative clip-level feature representations.

Attention Mechanism: The attention-based models are firstly proposed in sequence generation tasks such as machine translation [2], image captioning [23], and video captioning [24] etc. In these tasks, it naturally involves using a query vector, which contains relevant information for generating the next token, to select the relevant parts of the input as additional context features. Two types of attention methods [23] have been proposed for the query-based tasks, namely the hard attention and the soft attention. The hard attention makes a hard selection of which subsets of the input to attend, which is non-differentiable and relies on reinforce algorithms to optimize. The soft attention method adopts the softmax function to make soft decisions on different subsets, so it can be trained by back-propagation and is more widely used in different tasks.

However, for classification problems, it is not natural to involve a query vector. Some previous works, such as Zhou et al. [26], computed the attention score by applying the image-level classification model to image patches via post-processing. Mnih et al. [18] converted the classification task into a recurrent decision making process and the attention mechanism was implemented by a glimpse network to focus on image local contents. Jetley et al. [19] proposed a trainable attention module for image classification, where they used the final global image feature as query to locate low-level image patches. Rather than explicitly constructing the query vector, the self-attention mechanism [15] is proposed to enable attention to be used in cases when there are no extra queries, which computes the attention scores purely based on the self-representation. Our work follows the self-attention scheme, but instead of using one global attention vector to compute the attention score, we propose to use multiple class-specific attention vectors to better characterize the different attention strategies needed for different classes.

3 CLASS-AWARE SELF-ATTENTION BASED AUDIO EVENT RECOGNITION

In this section, we first present the general framework of our audio event recognition (AER) system, which consists of three main components, namely the encoder, attention and prediction modules. We then describe our proposed class-aware self-attention mechanism in the attention module and compare it to the widely used mean pooling and global attention methods. Finally, we introduce our proposed attention factor sharing approach in order to learn the class-aware self-attention more effectively and improve the generalization ability.

3.1 General Attention-based AER Model

The general framework of our attention-based AER system is illustrated in Figure 2, which shows the pipeline for audio event recognition based on different types of individual components. There are mainly three components in the general framework, namely the encoder module, the attention module and the prediction module.

The encoder module takes the input of audio spectrogram derived from raw audios and outputs consecutive frame-level acoustic features $\{h_1, \cdots, h_T\}, h_t \in \mathbb{R}^H$, where T is the number of audio frames and H is the dimension of the feature. The frame-level feature h_t could be the short-term feature that only covers a short-term context such as the MFCC feature [25], the convolutional neural networks (CNN) feature [9] etc., or it can be the long-term feature derived from the recurrent neural networks [10] to capture more context dependencies.

In order to exploit relevant frame-level information to form the fixed-length clip-level feature, the attention module estimates the importance score s_t for each frame feature h_t. The importance scores are then normalized by the softmax function:

$$a_t = \frac{\exp(s_t)}{\sum_{t=1}^{T} \exp(s_t)}, \tag{1}$$

the a_t is used as the probabilistic heatmap. The clip-level acoustic feature $h \in \mathbb{R}^H$ then can be represented as the element-wise weighted average of the frame-level features, which is:

$$h = \sum_{t=1}^{T} a_t h_t. \tag{2}$$

Based on the above clip-level acoustic feature h, the prediction module is trained to automatically predict audio events in the clip. There are wide ranges of prediction models in the literature. Since our main focus in this work is to generate more discriminative clip-level features via the attention module, we use a simple fully connected neural network as our multi-label audio event prediction model as follows:

$$\hat{y}^c = p(y^c|h) = \frac{1}{1 + e^{-(w^c h + b^c)}} \in [0, 1], \tag{3}$$

where $c = 1, \cdots, C$ with C being the total number of audio events, w^c and b^c are parameters to predict the c-th audio event.

The overall model can be trained end-to-end via minimizing the multi-label classification loss as below:

$$L = -\frac{1}{C} \sum_{c=1}^{C} \mathcal{H}(y^c, \hat{y}^c), \tag{4}$$

where y^c is the ground-truth label for the c-th audio event and $\mathcal{H}$ is the cross-entropy function.

3.2 Class-Aware Self-Attentions

In this subsection, we first describe the two commonly used attention approaches, namely the mean pooling and the global self-attention. We then present our proposed class-aware self-attention approach to alleviate limitations in the above two approaches.

3.2.1 *Mean Pooling*

The naive way of generating the clip-level representation is to perform mean-pooling over time on the frame-level features, which assumes that different frames contribute equally to the final clip-level representation with $s_t = 1, t = 1, \cdots, T$. However, such assumption cannot hold on the weakly labeled dataset, where the

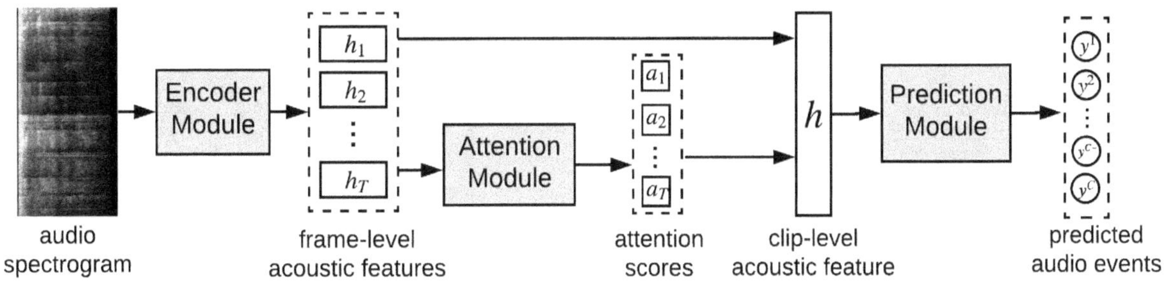

Figure 2: General framework of our attention-based audio event recognition system. The encoder module extracts frame-level acoustic features $h_1, \cdots, h_T$ from the audio spectrogram. Then the attention module estimates the normalized importance scores $a_1, \cdots, a_T$ for frame-level features, which are then used to generate the fixed-length clip-level feature h. Finally the prediction module takes the feature h to predict different audio events.

exact temporal boundaries are not available and not all segments in the clip contain the audio events.

3.2.2 *Global Self-Attention*

The attention mechanism [17] is proposed recently to address the problems of mean-pooling. The importance of different frames is dynamically adjusted according to the frame feature itself, which could be defined in various ways. In this paper, we use the inner product between the global attention vector g and the frame feature h_t as the score of the t-th frame, which is:

$$s_t = \langle g, h_t \rangle. \tag{5}$$

The attention vector $g \in \mathbb{R}^H$ keeps the same to construct clip-level features for different audio events, hence it can be interpreted as learning the general pattern of event relevance of frames. Figure 3(a) illustrates the computation of the global self-attention mechanism.

The global attention mechanism allows the contribution of different frames to change based on the quality of the feature itself. However, it doesn't distinguish whether the frame relates to the desired target audio event or to any other irrelevant events when constructing the clip-level representation.

3.2.3 *Class-Aware Self-Attention*

The motivation of the class-aware self-attention is that different audio events usually happen in different temporal regions, so when predicting different events, we should pay attention to different audio intervals that are relevant to the audio event. Therefore, instead of using the global attention vector g, we utilize a class-aware attention matrix $G = [g^1, \cdots, g^C] \in \mathbb{R}^{H\times C}$, with each column as a class-specific attention vector. The g^c memorizes the specific attention pattern for the c-th audio event to select event-related temporal intervals. As a result, the clip-level representation h becomes a matrix $\mathbb{R}^{H\times C}$ rather than a vector. Each column h^c denotes the c-th audio event relevant clip-level feature, which is calculated similar to the global self-attention mechanism with the attention vector g^c. The computation structure is presented in Figure 3(b).

To be noted, though the clip-level representation is C times huge than that in the global self-attention method, no additional modification is needed for other modules such as the prediction module. The prediction module can reuse the classification weight

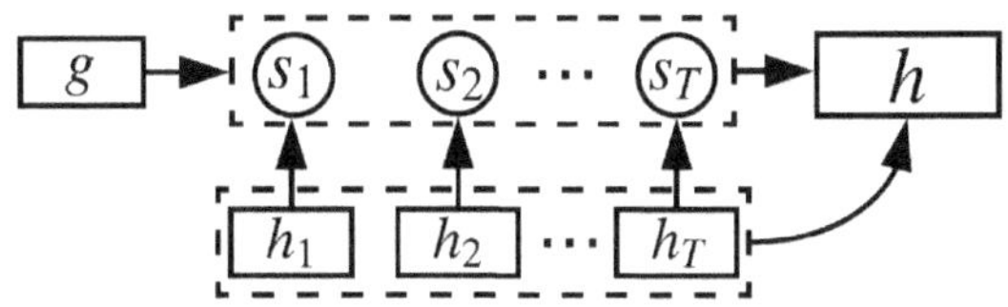

(a) Global self-attention mechanism to generate clip-level representation.

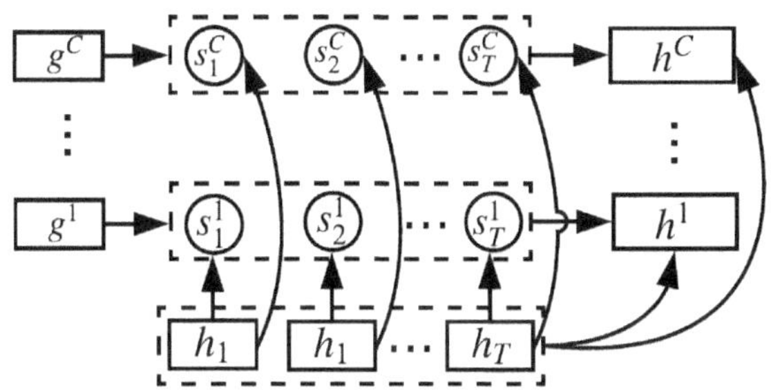

(b) Class-aware self-attention mechanism to generate discriminative clip-level representation for each audio event.

Figure 3: The global and class-aware self-attention mechanisms for audio event recognition.

w^c to predict the corresponding audio event as follows:

$$p(y^c|h^c) = \frac{1}{1 + e^{-(w^c h^c + b^c)}}. \tag{6}$$

Since the clip-level features h^c is more related to the c-th event, it would be more discriminative than the general clip-level feature h to predict the c-th event.

3.3 Attention Factor Sharing

Although class-aware self-attention is of great benefit, the number of parameters in G grows linearly with the number of classes C, which is a great burden when the number of audio events is huge. Furthermore, using independent attention vector g^c for each class might not take full advantage of the useful information in data, because different audio events might have internal correlations and share the similar attention patterns. Therefore, we propose

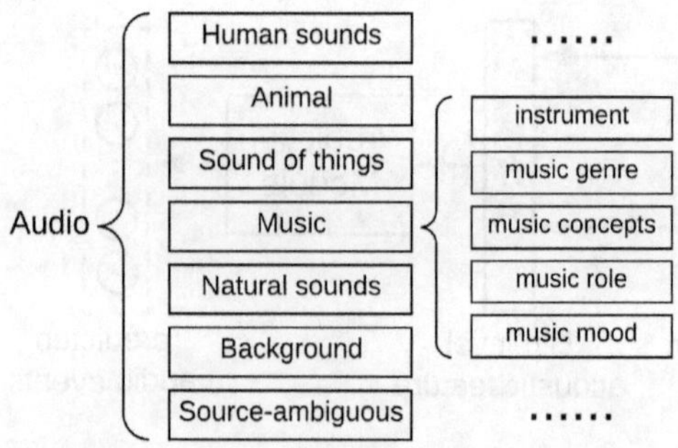

Figure 4: Expert-defined hierarchical ontology of audio events on Audio Set corpus.

the following three attention factor sharing strategies to reduce the number of learned parameters and transfer common attention patterns among different audio events.

3.3.1 *Domain-knowledge based Attention Factor Sharing*

Similar to the hierarchical structures of the Wordnet, domain experts [8] have defined an hierarchical ontology of the audio events as shown in the Figure 4. The audio events are divided into different clusters. The difference between audio events across clusters is bigger than that inside the cluster. Hence, the attention criteria for audio events inside the cluster could be similar. Based on this assumption, instead of training separate attention vectors for each audio event, we train independent attention vectors for each cluster and share the same attention vector for audio events in the same cluster. In this work, we use the seven highest-level clusters as shown in Figure 4. Therefore, we reduce the number of parameters from $H \times C$ to a constant number $H \times 7$ since each audio event can be assigned to one of the clusters. However, this approach heavily depends on the pre-defined audio event clusters. As a result, it might suffer from ill clustering problems, such as unbalanced clusters or inappropriate clusters which group semantic related but acoustically dissimilar audio events together.

3.3.2 *Factorization on Class-aware Attention Matrix*

As mentioned earlier, the attention strategies for different audio events might share some general patterns, while maintain the uniqueness for specific audio events at the same time. Based on this assumption, we propose to factorize the class-aware attention matrix G into two parts:

$$G = UV, \tag{7}$$

where $U \in \mathbb{R}^{H \times F}$, $V \in \mathbb{R}^{F \times C}$, and F is the dimension of the factor. U is shared for all the audio events to capture the common attention pattern, while V encodes the specialty of the attention pattern for each event. Each column of V denoted by v^c can be viewed as the class-aware vector, so the attention vector g^c for the c-th audio event is calculated as follows:

$$g^c = Uv^c. \tag{8}$$

In this way, we force the attention module to learn to separate the universal features and class-related features, which can significantly reduce parameters into $H \times F + F \times C$. Furthermore, for the long-tailed audio events without enough training data to learn the attention vector, the factorization approach transfers the common knowledge from other audio events, so it could alleviate the requirement for the amount of positive training examples. However, the factorization strategy ignores the semantic distance of different audio events.

3.3.3 *Combination of Domain-knowledge and Factorization*

The above two strategies for attention factor sharing are complementary with each other. The domain-knowledge based attention factor sharing strategy utilizes the domain knowledge of the semantic relevance of the audio events, while the matrix factorization directly learns the relevance and specialty in the data from scratch. Therefore, it is worthwhile to combine both strategies in a hierarchical manner. We first separate the audio events into clusters according to ontology, which means that audio events with quite different semantic meanings will not share attention patterns. Then for the audio events inside the same cluster, we adopt the data-driven strategy to factorize the attention matrix.

To be specific, we firstly divide the class-aware attention matrix G into different clusters according to the audio event ontology such as $G_k \in \mathbb{R}^{H \times N_k}$, where N_k is the number of audio events belonging to the cluster k. Then we apply the matrix factorization method on each G_k into the multiplication of U_k and V_k. Therefore, the number of attention parameters are reduced to $\sum_{k=1}^{K} H \times F + F \times N_k$.

Table 1: Number of audios and labels on the training, validation and testing set.

	training	validation	testing
#audios	619,085	7,500	20,280
#labels	1,438,300	20,468	77,122
#label/audio	2.3	2.7	3.8

4 EXPERIMENTS

4.1 Dataset

The Audio Set corpus is a large-scale dataset of manually annotated audio events. It utilizes a expert-defined hierarchical ontology of 527 audio classes to crawl audios from YouTube and results in over 2 millions of 10 second segments. Each segment is labeled with one or more class labels.

Due to bandwidth limitation, we only downloaded the full balanced training set, eval set and about 30% of the unbalanced training set, which include the full 527 audio classes. Therefore, we utilize the full evaluation set as [8] for testing and combine the balanced and unbalanced set as our training set. We separate about 1.2% audios from the training set for validation. The details of our training, validation and testing set are shown in the Table 1.

4.2 Frame-level Acoustic Features

In order to demonstrate the robustness of our proposed approach, we construct two sets of frame-level acoustic features including both the short-term and long-term acoustic features.

Short-term Acoustic Features We utilize the pretrained VGGish network[1] to extract the short-term acoustic features. The audio is first divided into non-overlapping frames with window size 0.96s. Each frame is then transformed into log-mel spectrogram

[1] https://github.com/tensorflow/models/tree/master/research/audioset

Table 2: mAP performance using different attention mechanisms based on short-term and long-term acoustic features.

	short-term	long-term
mean pooling	23.53	30.06
global self-attention	24.29	30.62
class-aware self-attention	25.52	**31.32**

as the input to the VGGish network. We extract activations from the last two fully connected layers with dimensionality of 4096 and 128 respectively and concatenate them as the audio embedding feature. Then we use two hidden layers with hidden size to be 2,048 and 1,024 respectively to reduce the dimensionality of the audio embedding feature. Finally we obtain the short-term acoustic features h_t of dimension 1,024.

Long-term Acoustic Features The short-term CNN based acoustic features only capture the local context less than 1s. In order to capture long-term temporal structure which is important for high-level audio events, we adopt the long short-term memory recurrent neural network (LSTM-RNN) to generate long-term acoustic features using the short-term CNN features as input to LSTM-RNN. We set the LSTM to be one layer with 1024 hidden units so that the parameters in the long-term acoustic feature encoder is comparable with that of the short-term acoustic feature encoder.

4.3 Experimental Results

We use the mean Average Precision (mAP) as our evaluation metric. mAP is the mean over the Average Precision (AP) of each class, which is widely used in previous works [9, 11] for large-scale audio event recognition. We train each model for 25 epochs with batch size of 128. The learning rate is set to be 0.001 and dropout is applied to reduce over-fitting with rate of 0.5. We use the ADAM algorithm [12] to optimize our neural networks.

4.3.1 *Evaluation of Different Attention Mechanisms*

Table 2 presents the performance of different attention mechanisms based on the short-term and long-term acoustic features respectively. We can see that the long-term features significantly outperform the short-term features with different attention mechanisms, which demonstrates that the temporal information is critical for audio event recognition. Mean pooling mechanism performs the worst because it treats all frames equally without considering the features or the predicted classes. By taking the quality of the frame features into consideration, global self-attention mechanism slightly improves over the mean pooling. Our proposed class-aware self-attention mechanism outperforms both the mean pooling and global self-attention mechanism consistently with both the short- and long-term acoustic features, which shows the effectiveness of the class-aware self-attention mechanism.

4.3.2 *Evaluation of Attention Factor Sharing Methods*

In Table 3, we compare the performance of different attention factor sharing strategies. The domain-knowledge based attention factor sharing strategy deteriorates the performance compared to that with no attention factor sharing (using the full attention matrix G), which suggests that it might share too much attention factors for different audio events. However, the matrix factorization strategy

Table 3: mAP performance using different attention factor sharing strategies based on short-term and long-term acoustic features.

	short-term	long-term
class-aware attention (no sharing)	25.52	31.32
domain-knowledge based	24.85	30.94
matrix factorization	26.39	31.50
combination	**26.88**	**31.58**

Table 4: mAP performance of different high-level audio classes using different methods.

	mean pooling	global attn	class-aware attn	class-aware attn sharing
Things	0.3064	0.3192	0.3185	**0.3247**
Natural	0.3031	0.2874	0.2996	**0.3094**
Music	0.3494	0.3555	**0.3662**	0.3645
Human	0.2886	0.2928	0.3029	**0.3058**
Animal	0.3108	0.3196	**0.3213**	**0.3213**
Source -ambiguous	0.1732	0.1706	0.1830	**0.1865**

improves audio event recognition performance consistently with both sets of acoustic features. Since the amount of positive examples for some audio events are very limited, it might be hard to learn the independent attention weights for these event classes. By sharing the correlation among different event labels, rare audio events could benefit from other related events with more data examples. Finally, the combination of domain-knowledge and the matrix factorization strategies achieves the best performance with both long- and short-term features, which demonstrates the complementary of the two strategies.

Table 4 shows the class breakdown mAP performance using different methods. We cluster audio events according to the highest level of the hierarchical ontology in Figure 4, and average the mAP performance of audio events inside the cluster groups. The class-aware self-attention with combination attention factor sharing strategy also achieves the best performance for all different event groups except for the Music group.

4.3.3 *Qualitative Analysis*

In order to evaluate the learned attention patterns for different audio events by our class-aware self-attention model, we visualize the attention scores of different temporal intervals in the audio clips in Figure 5. We can see that our proposed self-attention mechanism could well align the occurrence of audio events to their corresponding temporal intervals. For example, in Figure 5(a), the class-aware self-attention mechanism distinguishes temporal intervals belonging to different audio events such as "music" and "livestock" separately, which is unattainable by the global self-attention mechanism since it does not distinguish different events. In addition, with the attention factor sharing approach, for similar audio events such as "horse" and "whinny", the learned attention patterns also appear to be alike, which suggests that our model is able to effectively exploit the correlations among different audio events.

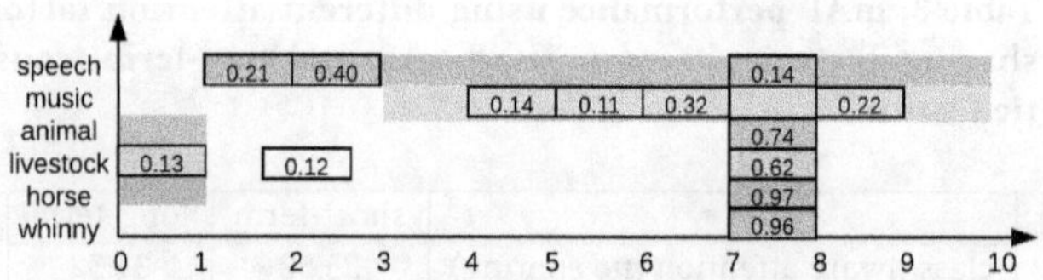

(a) Audio clip "-0jeONf82dE" in the testing set.

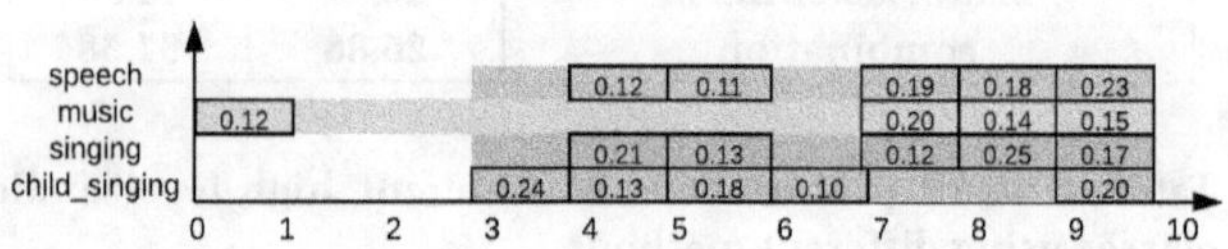

(b) Audio clip "-7TanrCbmME" in the testing set.

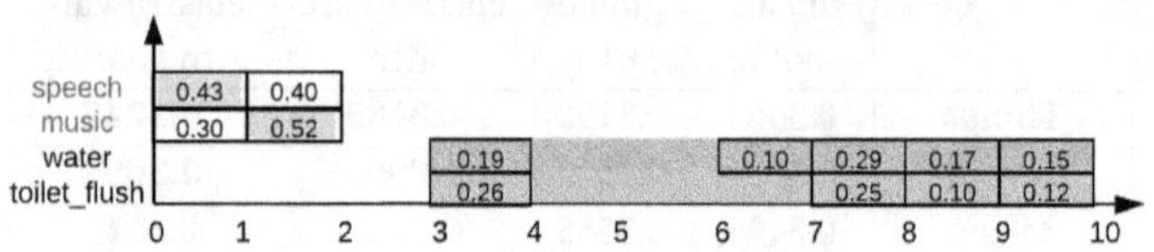

(c) Audio clip "-Gr9P8Abnlk" in the testing set.

Figure 5: Visualization of the predicted attention scores for different temporal intervals in the audio clip. The x-axis represents the temporal evolution with 1 sec per unit. Tags in y-axis are the audio events occurred in the audio clip (black tags are groundtruth annotations while red tags are not annotated labels). The temporal boundries of the audio events are aligned by ourselves, and the numbers in the black boxes are the attention scores above 0.1 predicted by our class-aware self-attention with attention factor sharing model.

We also notice that in the "Audio Set" corpus, though the annotated labels are mostly verified by human annotators and guaranteed to be correct, some correct labels might be missing in the audio clip. For instance, in Figure 5(c) the "speech" and "music" audio events occurred in the audio clip are not annotated as the ground-truth labels. But our proposed method also recognizes the audio events correctly and mark the temporal boundaries of the events in the roughly right location in the audio clip .

In addition to the nice property of class-aware attention, our proposed model also shows effectiveness in dealing with the long-tailed distribution challenge. It can improve the prediction of audio events with low-resources via the attention factor sharing approach. We first divide all audio events into 10 groups according to the occurrence of the audio events, with group 0 representing the rarest audio events and group 9 as the most frequent audio events. Then for each group, we average the relative improvement between the attention factor sharing approach and class-aware attention without sharing model over all events in the group. Results are presented in Figure 6. We can see that the attention factor sharing approach improves the performance for audio events with different occurrence frequencies in general. In particular, the audio events with lower resources benefit more from the attention factor sharing approach than those with abundant training resources, which demonstrates the effectiveness of our attention factor sharing approach.

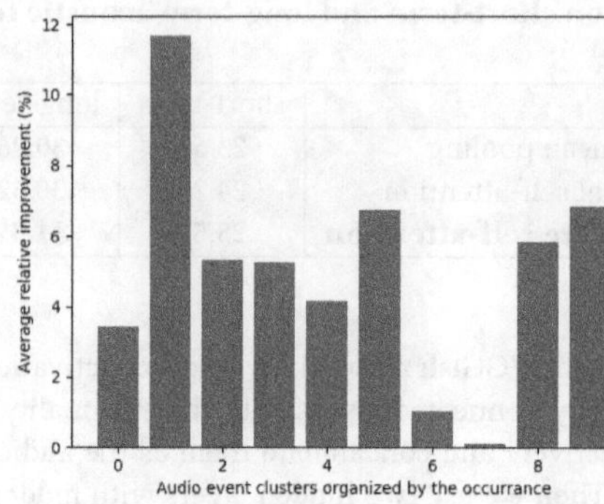

Figure 6: Performance gain from attention factor sharing approach for different audio event groups. Group 0 contains audio events with lowest resources and group 9 contains audio events with the most abundant resources.

4.3.4 *Learning of New Audio Events with Few Examples*

In practice, it is very important for the model to learn new audio events from a handful of examples since it is extremely hard to cover all of the audio events beforehand. Moreover, retraining the whole model from scratch with a few new data exmaples from new audio events is usually inefficient, especially when the model is very big. Therefore, we fix shared components in the pre-trained model and only update new parameters introduced to predict the new audio events, which we call the new audio events learning strategy. Since our proposed class-aware self-attention model learns the commonality and specialty of the attention patterns for different audio events, we argue that it could be much easier for our model to learn new audio events with a few examples than the previous attention models.

We select one rare audio event from each of the seven highest-level event clusters in Figure 4 respectively and set these seven events as new audio events. These seven audio events are listed in Table 5. We then train our model on 520 audio events excluding the above seven audio events. We fix the parameters of the model and add parameters which are specific to predict the new audio events. For the global self-attention model, we fix the encoder, attention module as well as parameters for the other 520 audio events in the prediction module, and add additional parameters in the prediction module to predict the seven new events. For the class-aware self-attention model, we also add attention vectors for the new audio events in the attention module. To be noted, for the attention factor sharing model, we do not update the shared attention factors such as U in the matrix factorization of G, which are considered to contain attention commonality and thus are important to be shared to audio events without enough data to learn. In this way, predictions for other 520 audio events are not influenced, and we only use a few new training examples for the prediction of new audio events.

Table 6 presents the performances of new audio events by three different models, including the global self-attention model, class-aware self-attention model and class-aware self-attention model with attention factor sharing. We can see that the class-aware self-attention and attention factor sharing significantly outperforms the

Table 5: Number of selected new audio events for training and testing.

	chopping_food	sniff	zing	cacophony	hoot	bicycle_bell	thunder
training	120	76	54	91	91	78	1067
testing	49	54	46	51	53	48	51

Table 6: mAP performance of new audio events via different models on the testing set.

	chopping_food	sniff	zing	cacophony	hoot	bicycle_bell	thunder	average
global attention	0.1686	0.2021	0.2316	0.1392	0.2959	0.1407	0.5194	0.2425
class-aware (w/o sharing)	0.1702	0.1996	0.2352	**0.1728**	0.2836	0.1720	**0.5868**	0.2600
class-aware (combination sharing)	**0.2304**	**0.2194**	**0.3086**	0.1430	**0.3178**	**0.2002**	0.5669	**0.2838**
entire model retraining (upper bound)	0.4093	0.3321	0.2444	0.1450	0.4119	0.2318	0.5885	0.3376

global self-attention without much training data in general, which demonstrates the generalization and scalability of our proposed model. We also compare the new audio events learning strategy with the retraining strategy using the class-aware self-attention and attention factor sharing model. The performance of new audio events learning strategy is on par with that of retraining strategy for almost half of the audio events, while the training cost is significantly reduced. Therefore, our class-aware attention with attention factor sharing approach can better balance the training cost and prediction performance when learning new audio events with a few examples.

5 CONCLUSIONS

In this work, we present a novel class-aware self-attention mechanism with attention factor sharing strategy to generate discriminative clip-level feature representations for audio event recognition (AER). Our model addresses two challenges to develop large scale AER models: the weak label challenge and the long-tailed distribution challenge. The weak label challenge refers to fact that the annotated event labels are not grounded with temporal boundaries in the audio clip. To generate discriminative acoustic features from such weak labeled data, we propose the class-aware self-attention approach, which learns to highlight temporal intervals that are more relevant to the audio event and suppress other irrelevant noises. The long-tailed distribution challenge refers to the fact that large amounts of audio events do not have enough training data. In order to learn attention patterns effectively for those long-tailed events, we combine both domain knowledge driven and data driven attention factor sharing strategies in the class-aware self-attention approach, which transfers the common knowledge from other similar event classes. Experimental results on the large-scale Audio Set corpus with two sets of acoustic features show the effectiveness of our proposed solution, which improves the overall audio event recognition performance consistently and can learn new audio events with a few examples effectively and efficiently. In the future, we will further explore the scalability of our approach to unseen audio events with zero examples, and expand our approach for multimodal event recognition.

6 ACKNOWLEDGMENTS

This work was supported by National Natural Science Foundation of China under Grant No. 61772535 and National Key Research and Development Plan under Grant No. 2016YFB1001202. The author Shizhe Chen gratefully acknowledges the financial support from the China Scholarship Council. Any opinions, findings, and conclusions or recommendations expressed in this material are solely those of the authors.

REFERENCES

[1] Yusuf Aytar, Carl Vondrick, and Antonio Torralba. 2016. Soundnet: Learning sound representations from unlabeled video. In *Advances in Neural Information Processing Systems*. 892–900.

[2] Dzmitry Bahdanau, Kyunghyun Cho, and Yoshua Bengio. 2014. Neural machine translation by jointly learning to align and translate. *arXiv preprint arXiv:1409.0473* (2014).

[3] Susanne Burger, Qin Jin, Peter F Schulam, and Florian Metze. 2012. Noisemes: Manual annotation of environmental noise in audio streams. (2012).

[4] Sourish Chaudhuri, Mark Harvilla, and Bhiksha Raj. 2011. Unsupervised Learning of Acoustic Unit Descriptors for Audio Content Representation and Classification.. In *Interspeech*. 2265–2268.

[5] Shizhe Chen, Qin Jin, Xirong Li, Gang Yang, and Jieping Xu. 2014. Speech emotion classification using acoustic features. In *Chinese Spoken Language Processing (ISCSLP), 2014 9th International Symposium on*. IEEE, 579–583.

[6] Shizhe Chen, Xinrui Li, Qin Jin, Shilei Zhang, and Yong Qin. 2016. Video emotion recognition in the wild based on fusion of multimodal features. In *Proceedings of the 18th ACM International Conference on Multimodal Interaction*. ACM, 494–500.

[7] Najim Dehak, Patrick J Kenny, Réda Dehak, Pierre Dumouchel, and Pierre Ouellet. 2011. Front-end factor analysis for speaker verification. *IEEE Transactions on Audio, Speech, and Language Processing* 19, 4 (2011), 788–798.

[8] Jort F Gemmeke, Daniel PW Ellis, Dylan Freedman, Aren Jansen, Wade Lawrence, R Channing Moore, Manoj Plakal, and Marvin Ritter. 2017. Audio Set: An ontology and human-labeled dataset for audio events. In *IEEE ICASSP*.

[9] Shawn Hershey, Sourish Chaudhuri, Daniel PW Ellis, Jort F Gemmeke, Aren Jansen, R Channing Moore, Manoj Plakal, Devin Platt, Rif A Saurous, Bryan Seybold, et al. 2017. CNN architectures for large-scale audio classification. In *Acoustics, Speech and Signal Processing (ICASSP), 2017 IEEE International Conference on*. IEEE, 131–135.

[10] Sepp Hochreiter and Jürgen Schmidhuber. 1997. Long short-term memory. *Neural computation* 9, 8 (1997), 1735–1780.

[11] Aren Jansen, Jort F Gemmeke, Daniel PW Ellis, Xiaofeng Liu, Wade Lawrence, and Dylan Freedman. 2017. Large-scale audio event discovery in one million youtube videos. In *Acoustics, Speech and Signal Processing (ICASSP), 2017 IEEE International Conference on*. IEEE, 786–790.

[12] Diederik P Kingma and Jimmy Ba. 2014. Adam: A method for stochastic optimization. *arXiv preprint arXiv:1412.6980* (2014).

[13] Anurag Kumar and Bhiksha Raj. 2016. Audio event detection using weakly labeled data. In *Proceedings of the 2016 ACM on Multimedia Conference*. ACM, 1038–1047.

[14] Anurag Kumar and Bhiksha Raj. 2017. Deep cnn framework for audio event recognition using weakly labeled web data. *arXiv preprint arXiv:1707.02530* (2017).

[15] Zhouhan Lin, Minwei Feng, Cicero Nogueira dos Santos, Mo Yu, Bing Xiang, Bowen Zhou, and Yoshua Bengio. 2017. A structured self-attentive sentence embedding. *arXiv preprint arXiv:1703.03130* (2017).

[16] Annamaria Mesaros, Toni Heittola, Aleksandr Diment, Benjamin Elizalde, Ankit Shah, Emmanuel Vincent, Bhiksha Raj, and Tuomas Virtanen. 2017. DCASE 2017 challenge setup: Tasks, datasets and baseline system. In *DCASE 2017-Workshop on Detection and Classification of Acoustic Scenes and Events.*

[17] Seyedmahdad Mirsamadi, Emad Barsoum, and Cha Zhang. 2017. Automatic speech emotion recognition using recurrent neural networks with local attention. In *Acoustics, Speech and Signal Processing (ICASSP), 2017 IEEE International Conference on.* IEEE, 2227–2231.

[18] Volodymyr Mnih, Nicolas Heess, Alex Graves, et al. 2014. Recurrent models of visual attention. In *Advances in neural information processing systems.* 2204–2212.

[19] Namhoon Lee Philip Torr Saumya Jetley, Nicholas A. Lord. 2018. Learn to Pay Attention. *International Conference on Learning Representations* (2018). https://openreview.net/forum?id=HyzbhfWRW accepted as poster.

[20] Yun Wang and Florian Metze. 2016. Recurrent Support Vector Machines for Audio-Based Multimedia Event Detection. In *Proceedings of the 2016 ACM on International Conference on Multimedia Retrieval.* ACM, 265–269.

[21] Yun Wang and Florian Metze. 2017. A first attempt at polyphonic sound event detection using connectionist temporal classification. In *Proc. of ICASSP.*

[22] Yun Wang, Leonardo Neves, and Florian Metze. 2016. Audio-based multimedia event detection using deep recurrent neural networks. In *Acoustics, Speech and Signal Processing (ICASSP), 2016 IEEE International Conference on.* IEEE, 2742–2746.

[23] Kelvin Xu, Jimmy Ba, Ryan Kiros, Kyunghyun Cho, Aaron Courville, Ruslan Salakhudinov, Rich Zemel, and Yoshua Bengio. 2015. Show, attend and tell: Neural image caption generation with visual attention. In *International Conference on Machine Learning.* 2048–2057.

[24] Li Yao, Atousa Torabi, Kyunghyun Cho, Nicolas Ballas, Christopher Pal, Hugo Larochelle, and Aaron Courville. 2015. Describing videos by exploiting temporal structure. In *Proceedings of the IEEE international conference on computer vision.* 4507–4515.

[25] Fang Zheng, Guoliang Zhang, and Zhanjiang Song. 2001. Comparison of different implementations of MFCC. *Journal of Computer Science and Technology* 16, 6 (2001), 582–589.

[26] Bolei Zhou, Aditya Khosla, Agata Lapedriza, Aude Oliva, and Antonio Torralba. 2016. Learning deep features for discriminative localization. In *Computer Vision and Pattern Recognition (CVPR), 2016 IEEE Conference on.* IEEE, 2921–2929.

Mining Exoticism from Visual Content with Fusion-based Deep Neural Networks

Andrea Ceroni
L3S Research Center, Leibniz Universität Hannover
ceroni@L3S.de

Chenyang Ma
L3S Research Center, Leibniz Universität Hannover
chenyangma89@gmail.com

Ralph Ewerth
L3S Research Center, Leibniz Universität Hannover
ewerth@l3s.de

ABSTRACT

Exoticism is the charm of the unfamiliar, it often means unusual, mystery, and it can evoke the atmosphere of remote lands. Although it has received interest in different arts, like painting and music, no study has been conducted on understanding exoticism from a computational perspective. To the best of our knowledge, this work is the first to explore the problem of *exoticism–aware image classification*, aiming at automatically measuring the amount of exoticism in images and investigating the significant aspects of the task. The estimation of image exoticism could be applied in fields like advertising and travel suggestion, as well as to increase serendipity and diversity of recommendations and search results. We propose a Fusion-based Deep Neural Network (FDNN) for this task, which combines image representations learned by Deep Neural Networks with visual and semantic hand-crafted features. Comparisons with other Machine Learning models show that our proposed architecture is the best performing one, reaching accuracy over 83% and 91% on two different datasets. Moreover, experiments with classifiers exploiting both visual and semantic features allow to analyze what are the most important aspects for identifying exotic content. Ground truth has been gathered by retrieving exotic and not exotic images through a web search engine by posing queries with exotic and not exotic semantics, and then assessing the exoticism of the retrieved images via a crowdsourcing evaluation. The dataset is publicly released to promote advances in this novel field.

KEYWORDS

Exoticism; Image Classification; Benchmark; Human Computation

1 INTRODUCTION

Exoticism is often defined in art and literature as "the charm of the unfamiliar", the description of one culture for consumption by another one [23]. It often means unusual, excitement, mystery, and it can evoke the atmosphere of remote lands. The perception of exoticism can pertain to a diverse set of things, e.g. animals, buildings, fruits, artifacts, persons of any ethnicity, and depends on how a subject is unfamiliar to a given observer. For instance, the pictures depicted in Figure 1a are likely to be perceived as exotic by most people, but not by persons who live close to those places.

Inline with the definition above, dictionaries (e.g. [1, 2]) assign two main meanings to the term *exotic*: either "something remote, from another part of the world" or "something intriguingly unusual or different". The difference between them is clarified in Figure 1. The pictures in Figure 1a belong to the former meaning, as they depict places that are remote to most people; differently, the objects in Figure 1b are examples of the latter meaning because they are unusual variations of common objects.

ICMR'18, June 11–14, 2018, Yokohama, Japan

ACM ISBN 978-1-4503-5046-4/18/06...$15.00
https://doi.org/10.1145/3206025.3206044

(a) (b)

Figure 1: Two meanings of *exotic*: something remote, from another part of the world (1a) and something unusual (1b).

Although the concept of exoticism has been widely studied and represented in different forms of art, such as painting, music and decorative art [12, 19, 28], to the best of our knowledge, no study has been conducted on understanding and assessing exoticism in a multimedia and computational manner. In this paper, we explore the novel problem of *exoticism–aware image classification* and tackle the following research questions. Is it possible to automatically model the notion of exoticism and identify images with exotic content? What are the most important dimensions in this task? Are there concepts that are more subject to exoticism than others?

Potential applications embrace fields like advertising, travel suggestion, recommender systems, and search-result diversification. Travel agencies or advertising companies could automatically retrieve and incorporate exotic pictures into their travel plans and advertisements [20, 47], or recommend different kind of exotic pictures based on customers' profiles. Furthermore, the exoticism of images could be used as an additional dimension for the diversification of image search results [44, 50] and recommendations [35, 51], as well as to increase their serendipity [4, 10]. This is especially inline with recent research trends in recommender systems [25, 43].

Being exoticism defined as the description of one culture for consumption by another one, it can be subjective and dependent, for example, on people's cultural background and origins. People might perceive pictures of one remote place as exotic, while people who grown there might not. Given the lack of attempts to model exoticism even for single cultures, we start studying its perception from the perspective of one single culture.

The first step consists in gathering a comprehensive ground truth to evaluate any approach to our task. We construct our dataset by first identifying sets of concepts carrying exotic and not exotic connotations and then using them as queries to retrieve related images via a popular web search engine (Google). For instance, for the given concept *animal*, we use both the query *animal* and *exotic animal* to retrieve not exotic and exotic candidate images for it. The actual amount of exoticism within each retrieved image has been subject to human assessment based on crowdsourcing. This evaluation investigates how concepts can incorporate different degrees of exoticism: some are prevalently exotic, some are mostly not exotic, while other can have a more balanced proportion between their exotic and not exotic versions (images). This crowdsourced dataset is publicly released[1] to foster further research on this novel topic.

To classify images as *exotic* or *not exotic*, we propose a Fusion-based Deep Neural Network architecture (FDNN) that combines image representations learned by Deep Neural Networks (DNNs) with visual and semantic hand-crafted features. The intuition is that the general image descriptions of DNNs could be complemented by the most discriminative hand-crafted features for a particular task. We compare our approach with the single components in isolation, namely (i) two DNNs (AlexNet [26] and GoogLeNet [45]) fine–tuned for our task and (ii) visual and semantic features used as input to different classifiers. Also, such features allow to analyze which aspects drive the perception of exoticism the most.

The contributions of this paper are: (1) definition of the problem of *exoticism-aware image classification*; (2) a Fusion-based Deep Neural Network combining deep features with hand-crafted ones, which results to be more effective than baselines using the single components in isolation; (3) a crowdsourcing analysis on how pictures and visual concepts can be subject to different amounts and types of exoticism, along with the release of two datasets for the task; (4) a comparison of different types of features to understand what are the most important aspects in this task.

2 RELATED WORK

The concept of exoticism has been considered in different forms of art, such as painting [12], music [28], decorative art [19], as the depiction of something belonging to a foreign culture. It has been also examined by cultural theorists for studying cultural diversities [40]. However, to the best of our knowledge, no study has been conducted on understanding and assessing exoticism from a multimedia and computational perspective.

The novel topic of exoticism–aware image classification can be positioned among other multimedia content–based tasks, such as computational aesthetics, affective image classification, and attractive photo classification. Computational models of image aesthetics have been widely investigated [33, 48, 53, 54]. These are based on the extraction of low–level features like HSV distribution, colorfulness, textures [48, 53], or more complex composition rules such as rule of thirds, simplicity, balance [33, 54] to classify appealing pictures by mean of supervised Machine Learning. Such combination of low–level visual features and more complex aesthetics rules has been also exploited for classifying emotions triggered by images [30, 57]. We also consider both aesthetics and more low–level visual information for our task. An approach for classifying visual attractiveness has been presented in [39]. A combination of visual (e.g. contrast, saturation, sharpness, colorfulness) and textual (user annotations in Flickr) information is used as features of a linear SVM to classify images as attractive or not. We consider this work for comparison purposes under the assumption that attractiveness might play a role in identifying exotic images. However, we believe that these are two different problems because both exotic and not exotic pictures could exhibit different degrees of attractiveness.

Multicultural aspects have been considered for visual sentiment detection [24, 37]. Jou et al. [24], in particular, investigated how images are used to express affective visual concepts in different languages. They created a multilingual visual sentiment ontology organized hierarchically into adjective-noun pairs carrying different sentiments from different languages, which was used to learn a set of multilingual and sentiment-driven visual concept detectors. Like emotions, also the concept of exoticism is dependent on cultural aspects by definition [23]. However, while approaches for affective and emotion classification from a single cultural perspective have been already investigated [6, 30, 57], this does not hold for exoticism. This is the reason why, in this paper, we start analyzing the perception of exoticism from the perspective of one single culture. Other not visual research on cross–lingual matters has been conducted on information retrieval [18, 42], web search [13], and textual sentiment analysis [5, 34].

[1] https://github.com/xander7/MiningExoticism

3 DATASETS

We use the Web as data source by (i) identifying sets of queries carrying exotic and not exotic interpretations and (ii) performing them into a web search engine to retrieve related images. As mentioned in Section 1, the concept of exoticism depends on cultural aspects by definition and our work, as first one exploring the topic, studies how exoticism is perceived from the viewpoint of one single culture. Under the assumption that a culture can be represented by its language, as recently done by Jou et al. [24] when studying how images are used in different languages to express affective visual concepts, we consider the English language to formulate queries. This implicitly steered the gathering of images towards the collective notion of exoticism based on the content in English handled by the search engine. Nevertheless, the actual amount of exoticism within each retrieved image has been assessed via crowdsourcing (Section 3.3).

We distinguish two datasets: *generic* and *concept–specific*. In the former, exotic and not exotic queries represent high–level and not overlapping concepts, meaning that the difference between the retrieved exotic and not exotic images should be broad. Differently, the latter contains more specific concepts and both exotic and not exotic variants for each of them. The datasets are available[1] to encourage further research on this topic.

3.1 Generic Dataset

The generic dataset is meant to contain a broad separation between exotic and not exotic images, without delving into specific concepts. To do this, we identified two distinct sets of queries, one exotic and one not exotic, which do not semantically overlap and can retrieve images that are clearly exotic or not exotic. The two sets are listed in Table 1. The 10 exotic queries have been manually formulated with the goals of being as general as possible and, of course, carrying the notion of exoticism. The 20 not exotic queries have been picked among the concepts defined as part of the TRECVID 2013 benchmarking activity [36]. The criteria considered to choose them were that a concept should be familiar, clearly not carrying exoticism, and as general as possible. For instance, we ignored concepts like *actor*, *glasses*, *rifle* as too specific, and others like *beach*, *desert*, *forest* as they could retrieve images carrying some amount of exoticism.

Having defined these queries, we used the Google Custom Search API to perform them and retrieve images. We aimed at including at least 20,000 images in the dataset, to come up with a reasonable amount of data suitable for Machine Learning purposes, therefore we retrieved the top–1200 images for exotic queries and the top–600 for not exotic queries (to have a balanced proportion of the two classes). We removed visually duplicate images automatically and irrelevant images (i.e. those wrongly retrieved by the search engine) by manual inspection. To cope with the size decrease when deleting duplicate or irrelevant pictures, we repeated such procedure (ignoring the images previously retrieved) until the constraint of having at least 20,000 images was satisfied. Eventually, the dataset contained a total of 21,757 images (49.3% belonging to exotic queries, 50.7% to not exotic ones). Examples of images retrieved for exotic and not exotic queries are in Figure 2. Note that, due to the kind of performed queries, most of the exotic images within it reflect the first meaning of exoticism among those mentioned in Section 1, namely *something remote*.

3.2 Concept–specific Dataset

The *concept–specific* dataset contains a more fine–grained distinction between exotic and not exotic content, delving into the concept level, where each concept can have both exotic and not exotic images associated

Table 1: Exotic and not exotic queries performed to create the *generic* dataset

Exotic Queries			Not Exotic Queries			
exotic scene	exotic location	exotic place	Airport	Apartments	Bar	Building
exotic view	exotic panorama	exotic landscape	City	Crowd	Factory	Gym
exotic	exoticism	exotic things	Industrial Setting	Office	Road	Room
exotic image			School	Technology	Shopping	Sport
			Streets	Traffic	Urban Scenes	Vehicle

(a) (b)

Figure 2: Examples of exotic images (2a) and not exotic images (2b) in the *generic* dataset.

Figure 3: Exotic (bottom) and not exotic (top) images in the *concept-specific* dataset: each column shows the same concept (animal, flower, hill) but with different amount of exoticism.

to it. Figure 3 shows some examples of this: for the very same "neutral" concept (*animal, flower, hill*), the dataset contains both exotic (bottom row) and not exotic (top row) images.

Again from the concepts of TRECVID 2013 [36], we selected 100 of them as seed to retrieve images. We ignored concepts not suitable for our task, including those representing actions (e.g. *bicycling, cheering, running*) and the abstract ones (e.g. *joy, sadness*). The selected concepts are listed in Table 2. Exotic and not exotic variants of each concept have been created to be used as queries: not exotic variants are the names of the concepts themselves, while exotic variants have the term *exotic* before each concept.

The image retrieval process has been performed as in Section 3.1 for the generic dataset and still has the objective of producing a dataset of at least 20,000 images. While we already ignored those concepts that clearly do not fit to our task, there might be concepts within our set that are less subject to variations of exoticism than others. For instance, concepts like *police* and *gym* might have few exotic images retrieved, while concepts like *whale* and *desert* might have many exotic images retrieved also when querying their not exotic variants. We preferred to keep such concepts in the dataset and analyze this aspect through crowdsourcing (Section 3.3.2). However, to cope in advance with the possible reduction of the dataset due to the exclusion of unsuitable concepts, we collected a bigger amount of pictures for each concept by retrieving the top-200 images for each of the 100 exotic and 100 not exotic variants of each seed concept. After removing duplicates automatically and irrelevant images by manual inspection we got 35,138 images in the dataset (49.6% belonging to exotic queries, 50.4% belonging to not exotic ones). Figure 3 shows examples of the retrieved images, split by concept and amount of exoticism.

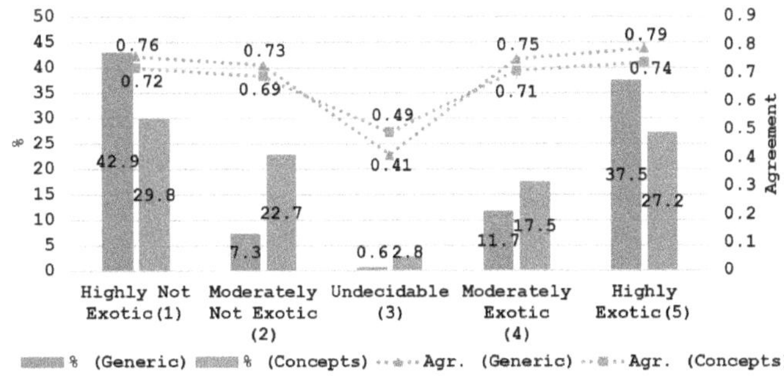

Figure 4: Judgments and annotator agreement in the datasets.

3.3 Crowdsourcing Assessment

Once the images belonging to the generic and concept-specific datasets have been retrieved, they have been subject to a crowdsourcing evaluation to assess their amount and type of exoticism. We first describe the setup of the evaluation and afterward we discuss its results for both the datasets.

We decompose the task of assessing the amount and type of exoticism contained in images into atomic units and deploy them on CrowdFlower, a premier crowdsourcing platform. For each image, workers were given an explanation of the concept of exoticism in terms of the two definitions stated in Section 1 and were asked to specify the degree of exoticism by choosing among 5 possible answers: *highly not exotic, moderately not exotic, undecidable, moderately exotic, highly exotic.* In case of images rated as either moderately or highly exotic, the workers were asked to specify the reason by choosing among the two definitions of *exotic* stated in Section 1, named hereafter *remote* and *unusual* for brevity. Only contributors having English as primary language could participate for sake of coherence with respect to the way the images were retrieved. Moreover, since English is used as primary language in different countries spread over the world, which might have different understandings of what is recognized as exotic, we had to be more selective and we chose to consider only workers located in North America. That is, the resulting ground truth will reflect the perception of exoticism from the North American perspective.

Different precautions were taken to ensure the results quality. First, we employed test questions to detect untrustworthy workers [9], both as a preparatory quiz and during the work mode. In both cases we imposed a minimum accuracy of 80%, otherwise the workers were excluded. Second, we only allowed contributors regarded as *highly performing* to participate. Last, we imposed a minimum duration of 30 seconds for evaluating 10 images. We paid 0.1 USD for successfully evaluating each set of 10 images.

We gathered 5 independent judgments for each image and, based on these, we used the majority vote given by workers for the same image as the aggregated judgment for that image. In case of ties, which were around 1.5%, we assigned an integer value from 1 to 5 to each image with order coherent to the level of exoticism (i.e. 1 to *highly not exotic*, 5 to *highly exotic*) and we considered the judgment closest to the average of all judgments for the same image. These aggregated judgments are the ones considered in Section 4 to define labels. The judgment distribution and inter-annotator agreement (Fleiss' κ computed for each image and then averaged) are reported in Figure 4 and are discussed hereafter for the two datasets separately. We will refer to the judgments using increasing integer values (from 1 for *highly not exotic* to 5 for *highly exotic*) as in the legend of Figure 4.

Table 2: Concepts in the concept-specific dataset. For each concept, both exotic and not exotic queries are generated.

Concepts									
Airplane	Airport	Animal	Bar	Apartment	Beach	Bicycle	Bird	Boat	Dining Room
Building	Bus	Canoe	Car	Chair	Church	City	Classroom	Cows	Crustacean
Dance	Desert	Bridge	Dolphin	Doorway	Dress	Face	Field	Flower	Sea Mammal
Forest	Fruit	Furniture	Glasses	Outdoor	Gym	Helicopter	Highway	Landscape	Religious Building
Insect	Park	Island	Kitchen	Lake	Hill	Mammal	Motorcycle	Mountain	Religious Figures
Office	Gun	Pavilion	Person	Plant	Police	Primate	Horse	Vertebrate	Residential Buildings
River	Road	Rocks	Room	Rowboat	Food	Synagogue	Technology	Ruminant	Shopping Mall
Ski	Sky	Skyscraper	Sofa	Stadium	Streets	Suits	Sunglasses	Waterfront	Sailing Ship
Table	Taxi	Telephones	Tent	Tower	Traffic	Trees	Truck	Underwater	Invertebrate
Scenes	Valleys	Vegetation	Vehicle	Ocean	Pool	Weapons	Whale	Window	Wild Animal

3.3.1 Generic Dataset. The distribution of judgments for the generic dataset shown in Figure 4 is skewed towards the two opposite judgments (1 and 5) but balanced when grouping judgments either referring to not exotic (1+2) and exotic (4+5) content. The inter-annotator agreement is *substantial* [27] for these judgments but it becomes lower for *undecidable* pictures (3), which anyway are only 0.6% of the data and have been discarded. When merging moderate and high judgments into two classes (i.e. 1+2 and 4+5), the agreement becomes $\kappa = 0.87$ and $\kappa = 0.91$ respectively. These facts are inline with the way the dataset has been gathered, aiming at a balanced and broad distinction between exotic and not exotic content. Regarding the reasons of exoticism, 89% of the images rated with either 4 or 5 have been marked as *remote*, which is again due to the nature of the queries used to retrieve exotic images. All the aggregated image ratings were coherent with the queries used to retrieve them, i.e. pictures rated with either 4 or 5 were retrieved by exotic queries while all those rated with either 1 or 2 belonged to not exotic queries. This is also due to the manual inspection of the dataset before launching the crowdsourcing evaluation to remove the images that were wrongly retrieved by the search engine (see Section 3.1). After discarding *undecidable* images, the dataset contains 21,627 images (50,5% rated with 1 or 2, 49.5% with 4 or 5).

3.3.2 Concept-specific Dataset. The ratings distribution for the concept-specific dataset is in Figure 4. The most frequent judgments are again 1 and 5, but in this case the amount of moderate judgments (i.e. 2 and 4) increased. This fact, along with a slightly decreased (but still substantial) inter-annotator agreement, anticipates that the distinction between exotic and not exotic content gets narrower when digging into the concept level. The distribution is slightly unbalanced towards not exotic pictures: 44.7% has been judged as exotic (4+5) and 52.5% as not exotic (1+2), with an inter-annotator agreement of $\kappa = 0.83$ and $\kappa = 0.8$ respectively.

Although we removed irrelevant images retrieved by the search engine (see Section 3.2) before the crowdsourcing evaluation, we observed that part of the evaluated images have not been judged coherently with their seed queries: some of those rated with either 1 or 2 were retrieved using exotic queries and vice-versa. This matter has been already introduced in Section 3.2 and is not due to noisy images or bad quality judgments, but rather to the fact that part of the concepts in our set are lowly subject to variations of exoticism and they remain belonging to one single class. For instance, the *police* concept is mostly unrelated to exoticism and even its exotic query (i.e. *exotic police*) would mostly retrieve not exotic images. While for some of these concepts it might be possible to mitigate the unbalance between their exotic and not exotic samples, merely by searching for additional images belonging to the minority class, we regard such unbalance (driven by the search engine's ranking) as signal of how much a concept is collectively perceived as exotic or not. We deliberately retained such concepts and make them undergo the crowdsourcing evaluation for sake of investigation, because we believe that some of them might not be clearly judgeable as completely exotic or not exotic in advance. Moreover, this aspect is also important for our experiments, as concepts always associated to only one class are not relevant for our learning purposes. The proportion of images retrieved for each neutral concept and judged as exotic (either judgments 4 or 5) or not exotic (either 1 or 2) is shown in the bottom part of Figure 5. The concepts are sorted from left to right based on the percentage of images judged as exotic. We can observe fluctuations of exoticism over the concepts, with around one quarter being lowly exotic (e.g. *classroom, airport*) and a smaller part being highly exotic (e.g. *desert, whale*). The others can exhibit a more variable amount of exoticism and, therefore, have a more balanced proportion between their exotic and not exotic versions, for instance *animal, vegetation, room.* The upper part of Figure 5 shows the distribution of the exoticism types (either *remote* or *unusual*) for each concept. We can observe that exoticism as *unusual* is mostly used for common objects, like *glasses* and *bicycle*, which might look unusual because of, e.g., their shapes or colors (see Figure 1b). Differently, exoticism as *remote* often refers to natural places like *island* and *desert*, but also to artifacts like *dresses* and *doorways* with style belonging to foreign cultures. There are also balanced concepts, like *food* and *animal*.

To experiment with concepts that have a fair balance of exotic and not exotic pictures of each of them in the dataset, we chose to retain those concepts having at least 30% of pictures belonging to one class and at most 70% belonging to the other one for our experiments. This resulted in keeping 73 concepts, which span from *horse* to *ocean* in Figure 5. This filtered dataset contains 23,861 pictures and is still balanced: 48.4% are exotic (either rated 4 or 5) and 51.6% are not exotic (rated 1 or 2).

4 EXOTICISM–AWARE IMAGE CLASSIFICATION

We recall the problem statement and afterward we describe our Fusion-based Deep Neural Network (FDNN), which combines image representations given by a DNN and hand-crafted features. These individual components are described in Sections 4.3 (DNNs) and 4.4 (hand-crafted features).

We do not rely on non visual information, for instance user generated tags or GPS coordinates, because we are interested in how exoticism is recognizable only visually. This also makes our models applicable to a wider range of cases, where such additional information is not available.

4.1 Problem Statement

The problem of exoticism–aware image classification consists in automatically assessing the amount of exoticism contained in a given picture. We refer to the two main definitions of the term *exotic* reported in Section 1 and any picture fulfilling at least one of them is considered as *exotic*. Although images might exhibit different degrees of exoticism, we chose to pose the problem as binary classification to have a clearer distinction between the classes, also coping with disagreement and personal tastes even among individuals of the same culture. We therefore binarized the crowdsourcing judgments described in Section 3 to come up with binary labels: images rated as either highly not exotic or moderately not exotic are regarded as *not exotic*, while those judged as either highly exotic or moderately exotic are considered as *exotic*.

4.2 Fusion-based Deep Neural Network for Exoticism–Aware Image Classification

Image representations learned with DNNs, e.g. AlexNet [26], Clarifai [55], or GoogLeNet [45], have been successfully employed for classification by

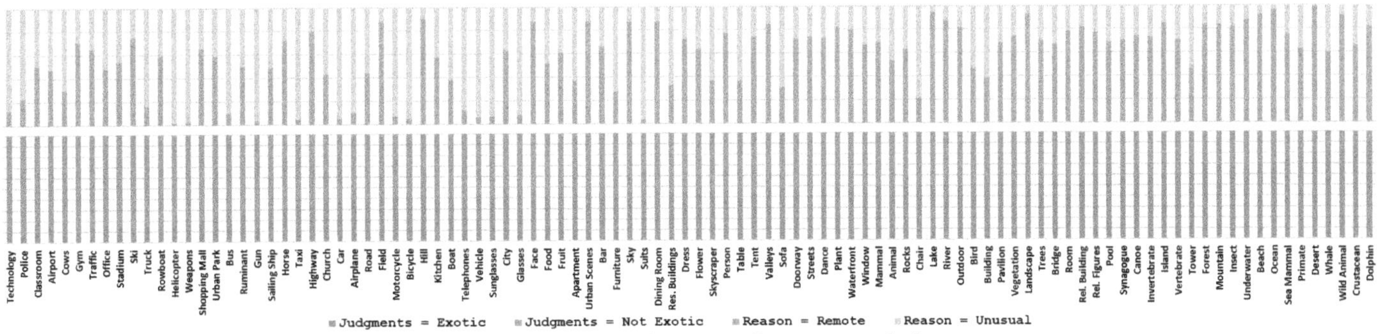

Figure 5: Binarized judgments and reasons of exoticism split by concepts.

fine-tuning the network weights for a more specific task [8, 11, 55, 56]. We want to investigate whether hand-crafted features extracted for a given task can be injected into DNNs to learn a new and more effective image description. The main intuition is that hand-crafted features encoding important and discriminative information for a given problem might complement the representation given by a DNN (even after fine-tuning), which would rather learn a more complementary set of features. Overall, such Fusion-based Deep Neural Network (FDNN) would generate features that are more discriminative than either the hand-crafted or DNN features alone. Also, due to back-propagation, the hand-crafted features could influence the weights of the inner layers in the DNN when fine-tuning.

The architecture of our proposed FDNN is depicted in Figure 6. It is made of two parallel flows, namely a DNN (on the top) and the hand-crafted feature extraction and selection (bottom), which are then fused by a set of fully connected layers. The different DNNs and features used in our work will be described in Sections 4.3 and 4.4, respectively. However, our FDNN architecture can accommodate other implementations as well.

The DNN is assumed to be initialized with weights learned from a general-purpose dataset (see Section 4.3). Its last Softmax layer is removed so that we can use its learned representation as input, named *DNN-F* hereafter, whose type and dimensionality N depends on the employed DNN. Note that *DNN-F* has been drawn outside the bounding box of the DNN only for sake of explanation. In the bottom part is the hand crafted feature extraction, which produces the features described in Section 4.4. Regarding the hand-crafted features, we apply Correlation-based Feature Selection [15] to identify the best set of top-k features for our task, which form the *HC-F* layer in the picture. The value $k = 200$ has been cross-validated as done for the DNN hyper-parameters in Section 4.3 (grid search [50; 500] with steps of 50). The set of best features was identified for each fold only based on its training set (80%-20% training-validation split).

Both *DNN-F* and *HC-F* are followed by a fully connected layer of size N (*DNN-F** and *HC-F**) for uniforming the sizes of the two feature vectors. This is particularly important for *HC-F*, but it would be crucial also for *DNN-F* if the chosen size was different from N. The concatenation $x = [\text{DNN-F}^*, \text{HC-F}^*]$ of these layers is the input of the combination layer C, which has the role of learning to combine the two sets of features into a common representation of size N. Its output is $y_C(x) = h\left(w_C^T x + b_C\right)$, where w_C and b_C are the weights and bias of the layer C, and h is its activation function (ReLU). Eventually, the last softmax layer gives the probabilities of the two classes (*exotic* and *not exotic*).

The described FDNN network is still end-to-end differentiable and, therefore, we randomly initialize the weights of the introduced layers and we fine-tune the whole network weights w based on our dataset (Section 3) by Stochastic Gradient Descent (SGD) to minimize the soft-max loss function ℓ over the training data $\{x_1, y_1\}, ..., \{x_N, y_N\}$: $w = \arg\min_w \frac{1}{N}\sum_{i=1}^{N} \ell(x_i, y_i, w)$, $\ell(\cdot) = -\ln(\frac{e^{s_{y_i}}}{\sum_j e^{s_j}})$, where s_{y_i} is the predicted score $f_{y_i}(x_i, w)$ for a given image x_i and class y_i. The values of

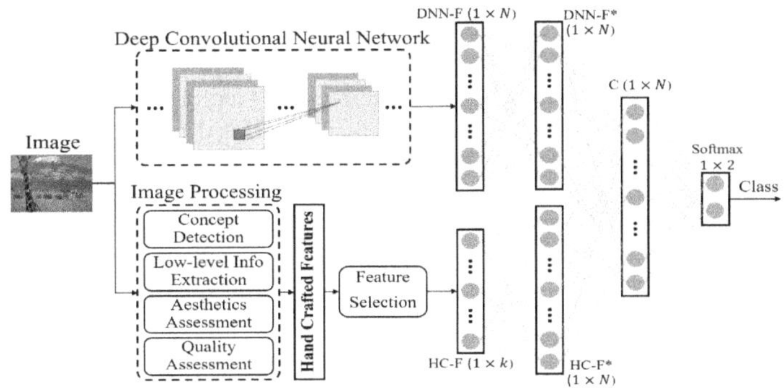

Figure 6: Architecture of our Fusion-based Deep Neural Network, combining deep features with hand-crafted features.

the parameters used for fine-tuning depend on the employed DNN and are given in Section 4.3. Summarizing, by this procedure we end up with a FDNN that is fine-tuned for exoticism-aware image classification and that learns to combine DNN features with hand-crafted ones.

We show how the *HC-F* layer influences the gradient of the DNN parameters [52]. We start the enumeration from the *DNN-F* layer, which gets the index 1. Let $y_j^n = \sum_j w_{ji}^{n-1} h(y_i^{n-1})$. The partial derivative of the loss wrt the outgoing weights of *DNN-F* is $\frac{\partial \ell}{\partial w_{ij}^1} = x_j^D \frac{\partial \ell}{\partial y_i^2}$, where $\frac{\partial \ell}{\partial y_i^2} = (\sum_j w_{ji}^2 \frac{\partial \ell}{\partial y_j^3})\dot{h}(y_i^2)$, $\frac{\partial \ell}{\partial y_j^3} = (\sum_k w_{kj}^3 \frac{\partial \ell}{\partial y_k^4})\dot{h}(y_j^3)$. The layer x^H appears in $\frac{\partial \ell}{\partial y_j^3}$ because $y_k^3 = \sum_j w_{kj}^2 h(y_j^2) + \sum_j w_{kj}^{H^2} h(\sum_i w_{ji}^{H^1} x_i^H)$, where w^{H^1} and w^{H^2} indicate the outgoing weights of the *HC-F* (i.e. x^H) and *HC-F** layers, respectively.

4.3 DNNs for Exoticism-Aware Classification

We experiment the inclusion of two Convolutional Neural Networks in our FDNN, namely AlexNet [26] and GoogLeNet [45], whose weights are learned from the large-scale ImageNet dataset. We chose AlexNet and GoogLeNet because they were the best performing models in the ImageNet Large-Scale Visual Recognition Challenge (ILSVRC) [38] in years 2012 and 2014, respectively, and they have been widely used for image classification in the recent years (e.g. in [8, 11, 31, 56]).

AlexNet consists of 5 convolutional layers (one with 11×11, one with 5×5, three with 3×3 filter sizes), max-pooling layers, and 3 final fully connected layers. Dropout layers are placed after each fully connected layer to prevent overfitting. GoogLeNet is a very deep convolutional neural network, made of 22 layers, where *inception modules* are stacked on top of each other and perform in parallel 1×1, 3×3, 5×5 convolutions, and max-pooling before concatenating the output of such filters into a single output vector becoming the input for the next module. At last, the activations are subject to average-pooling. The output layer of both AlexNet and GoogLeNet is a 1,000-dimensional vector, whose elements correspond to the class predictions for the 1,000 categories defined in

ILSVRC. The inputs are images of size 224×224 and, therefore, all the images in our dataset have been scaled to that size.

As stated in Section 4.2, the employed DNN determines the type and dimensionality of the last DNN layer used in our FDNN: it is a 4096-d Fully Connected layer for AlexNet and a 1024-d Average Pooling for GoogLeNet. The parameter values of the training of the FDNN, which also depend on the actual DNN, are as follows. SGD is performed with momentum of 0.9 and learning rate of 0.01/0.005, reducing it every 30,000/20,000 iterations by a factor of 10, for GoogLeNet/AlexNet respectively. At each iteration, a mini–batch of 100/150 images for GoogLeNet/AlexNet (with balanced proportion of the two classes) is used to approximate the gradient of the loss function (with back-propagation). The learning is executed for 100,000 iterations. These hyperparameters (learning rate, momentum, etc.) have been tuned via 5–fold cross validation, using 20% of the training data of each split for their validation and the remaining for training. As it will be explained in Section 5.1, the networks are evaluated in our experiments by averaging their accuracy over the test sets of each split.

For sake of comparison with our FDNN, we also fine–tuned the weights of the AlexNet and GoogLeNet networks alone, based on our dataset. Their training has been done as in Section 4.2, changing the dimensionality of their last layer from 1,000 to 2 and randomly initializing its weights.

4.4 Hand Crafted Features

We extract semantic and visual features to be incorporated in our FDNN (Section 4.2). Moreover, such features serve for other two purposes: analyzing the importance of the aspects they encode for classifying exoticism (Sections 5.2 and 5.3), and comparing classifiers based on them (Naive Bayes, C4.5 Decision Trees, MLPs, SVMs) with the approaches described before. Again, these models are evaluated via 5–fold cross validation and the parameters cross–validated within each split, using 20% of the training data of the given split for validation and the remaining 80% for training.

4.4.1 Concept Features. Concept Detection might provide discriminative information for the task. There might be concepts appearing more frequently in images with exotic content, while others might be more familiar to the culture for which the model is learned. Also, the joint occurrence of not exotic concepts might result in an exotic image. Consider the third picture in the bottom row of Figure 3, judged as exotic. The image depicts a mountain, which is not necessarily exotic on its own, but it becomes exotic due to the prominent presence of rocky buildings on it.

The approach that we used to extract concepts has been presented in [31] and produces two sets of concepts. The first one is given by a pre–trained GoogLeNet[45] network, using its 1000–dimensional output as concepts scores. The second one is obtained via 346 SVMs as concept detectors for the 346 concepts defined in TRECVID 2013 [36]. The SVMs have been trained on the TRECVID 2013 dataset, comprising 800 hours of video. For training, GoogLeNet was applied on the keyframes and the 1000 output values were used as features for each of the 346 SVMs, which were trained in isolation for each target concept. We can observe from this description that our concept features are not entirely hand crafted since their computation exploits image representations learned via DCNNs.

4.4.2 Low-level Visual Information. Low–level visual information about images might reveal some insights to identify exotic content. For instance, tropical places and animals often exhibit vivid colors while urban scenes might have a prevalence of grayscale colors. Exotic or unusual objects might contain particular textures if compared to the usual ones.

HSV Statistics. We represented pictures in the HSV color space and computed avg, std, min, max for each dimension.

Colors. We extract two kinds of color-related information, namely *colorfulness* and *color names*, to measure the variety and distribution of colors within an image. The former is measured by computing the Earth Mover's Distance (EMD) between the histogram of an image and the histogram having a uniform color distribution (one for each R,G,B channel). For the latter, we used the algorithm in [49] to classify pixels into the 11 basic colors (black, blue, brown, green, gray, orange, pink, purple, red, white, yellow) and we counted the percentage of pixels for each of them.

Tamura Textures. We compute two Tamura features [46] representing textural aspects such as *coarseness* and *directionality*. *Coarseness* is related to texture scales and reflects the size of the largest texture within an image. First, for each image point (x, y), we take the averages over neighborhoods of sizes $2^k \times 2^k$, $A_k(x, y) = \sum_{i=x-2^{k-1}}^{x+2^{k-1}-1} \sum_{j=y-2^{k-1}}^{y+2^{k-1}-1} f(i,j)/2^{2k}$, where $0 \leq k \leq 5$ and $f(i,j)$ is the gray–level at (x, y). Second, for each point (x, y) and for both horizontal and vertical dimensions, we consider the averages computed at not overlapping neighborhoods on opposite sides of (x, y) and compute the difference between them, i.e. $E_k(x, y) = |A_k(x + 2^{k-1}, y) - A_k(x - 2^{k-1}, y)|$ along the horizontal direction. Finally, for each point, we take the best neighborhood size $S_{best}(x, y) = 2^{k_{best}}$ which maximizes E in either direction and we compute the coarseness value for the whole image by averaging $S_{best}(x, y)$ over all the points. Regarding content *directionality*, it is computed in two steps. First, for each point, we take horizontal (Δ_h) and vertical (Δ_v) derivatives and we compute the local edge direction $\theta = tan^{-1}\frac{\Delta_v}{\Delta_h} + \frac{\pi}{2}$. Second, a histogram is built by quantization of the θ values in 16 bins and the overall directionality value is computed by summing the second moments around each peak (peak sharpness) in the histogram [46].

GLCM Textures. A Gray–Level Co–Occurrence Matrix (GLCM) [16] represents how often different combinations of pixel intensities (gray levels) occur in an image and it is a well known mean to extract textural features. Given the normalized GLCM $P(i, j)$ of an image, we compute *correlation* as $\sum_i \sum_j P(i,j) \frac{(i-\mu)(j-\mu)}{\sigma^2}$, *energy* as $\sum_i \sum_j P^2(i,j)$, *homogeneity* as $\sum_i \sum_j \frac{P(i,j)}{1+|i-j|}$ [17], where μ and σ are mean and variance of P.

Dynamics. The presence and slope of lines can be particular of some environments, e.g. usual buildings would have mostly vertical and horizontal lines while more unusual constructions might show more sloping lines. We identify lines by Hough transform and count the number and length statistics of *static* lines (horizontal and vertical) and *slant* lines (we consider a line as static if its slope is within $[-15°; 15°]$ or $[75°; 105°]$).

4.4.3 Aesthetics Features. Image Aesthetics can reflect how an image is well posed, attractive and pleasant to an observer, for instance considering how colors, shapes, and objects are arranged together. Although in principle both exotic and not exotic pictures might have comparable aesthetics characteristics, there might be cases where these features become discriminative. For instance, remote places might have a higher level of *simplicity* than crowded urban scenes.

Rule of Thirds. It consists of splitting the image content in vertical and horizontal thirds and placing the main subjects at their intersections (power points). First, the main subjects are identified by segmenting the image, assigning a saliency score to each pixel according to [3], and computing the saliency of each segment by averaging the scores of the pixels belonging to it. Second, the rule of thirds is measured by aggregating, over all the segments, their sizes A_i, saliencies S_i, and distances D_i to the closest power point: $\frac{1}{\sum_i A_i S_i} \sum_i A_i S_i e^{-\frac{D_i^2}{2\sigma}}$, with $2\sigma = 0.34$ used for distance normalization. Intuitively, main subjects close to power points will make the feature value higher.

Simplicity. We compute two values to represent *simplicity*. For the first, we build the Region of Interest (ROI) map based on saliency (computed as for rule of thirds), we binarize it by setting $ROI(i, j) = 1$ if $S(i, j) >$

αS_{max} ($\alpha = 0.67$) and $ROI(i,j) = 0$ otherwise, and we sum the areas A_i of all the bounding boxes of the not overlapping saliency regions identified in the map $\sum_i \frac{A_i}{img\_size}$ as simplicity value. The second value, regarding simplicity as the "attention distraction of the objects from the background"[29], is calculated by separating subject and background regions and using the color distribution of the background to evaluate simplicity[54]. A histogram h of 4096 bins is generated from the RGB channels of the background (16 levels per channel) and the simplicity value is measured as $\frac{\|S\|}{4096}$, where $S = \{x | h(x) \geq 0.1 \cdot h_{max}\}$.

Contrast. We computed two measures of contrast, defined as the degree of diversity among the components of an image [54]. The first one is the Weber Contrast, which assesses contrast in terms of the diversity of intensity $I(x,y)$ values within the image: $\frac{1}{X \cdot Y} \sum_{x=0}^{X-1} \sum_{y=0}^{Y-1} \frac{I(x,y)-\hat{I}}{\hat{I}}$, where $\hat{I}$ is the average intensity. In order to consider also color contrast, we segment images and use the CIEDE2000 color difference equation [41], which estimates color disparity between each pair of segments based on their average colors and sums them together: $\sum_i \sum_{j=i+1} (1 - d(i,j)) \frac{c(i,j)}{A_i A_j}$, with $d(i,j)$ and $c(i,j)$ being the distance and color dissimilarity between two segments i, j, respectively, and A_i, A_j their sizes.

Intensity Balance. Content balance can transmit equilibrium and calmness to an observer. We assess balance in terms of pixel intensity, computing the Chi-Square difference between two intensity histograms, one for the left-hand and one for the right-hand part of the image.

4.4.4 Quality Features. We consider also image quality mostly for sake of completeness and comparison. However, it is not supposed to be highly discriminative because quality degradation could affect both exotic and not exotic images in similar manners. Based on the method presented in [32], we extract three quality measures, such as blur, darkness, and noise.

5 EXPERIMENTS

5.1 Experimental Setup

Evaluation. We evaluate the classification performances in terms of accuracy, which is a fair indicator given the balanced distribution of the binary classes in our datasets (see Sections 3.3.1 and 3.3.2). The datasets were split via 5-fold cross validation (with label stratification) and the reported values are averaged over the test sets of each split. Statistical significance over the closest less performing model is marked as ▲ ($p < 0.05$).

Baselines. We compare our models with respect to two baselines: the aesthetics assessment method by Yeh et al. [54], which proposes rules of aesthetics to classify and rank amateur pictures in appealing and not appealing, and the approach presented in [39] to classify attractive pictures in folksonomies, exploiting visual content and social feedback. For both methods, we train predictive models based on their datasets, features, and classifiers, and we evaluate them on our datasets. We only extracted visual features among those included in [39] because textual and social information is not assumed to be available in our scenario.

Feature Selection. Correlation-based Feature Selection [15] has been performed to reduce the number of features used by the classifiers of Section 4.4. The top-200 features have been retained when training on the whole set of features, while the top-160 have been kept when training only using the concept features. These values have been identified via cross-validation as done for the k parameter in Section 4.2. We did not apply any feature selection to the other smaller feature sets.

Implementation. The DNNs in Sections 4.2 and 4.3 were implemented and fine-tuned using Caffe[21], while we trained the other feature-based classifiers using the Weka API[14]. The features in Section 4.4 were extracted using OpenCV[7] and OpenIMAJ [22].

Table 3: Accuracy (averaged over folds) of different models on the generic and concept-specific datasets.

	Generic Dataset	Concept-specific Dataset
Baselines		
Yeh et al. [54]	62.31 ± 1.9	56.64 ± 2.0
San Pedro et al. [39]	65.15 ± 1.4	58.24 ± 1.2
Exoticism-aware Models		
NB	73.16 ± 2.0▲	65.09 ± 1.9▲
C45-DT	76.73 ± 1.5▲	67.88 ± 2.1
MLP	79.06 ± 1.3▲	72.12 ± 1.5▲
L-SVM	80.42 ± 1.5	72.59 ± 1.7
RBF-SVM	82.79 ± 1.7▲	75.34 ± 1.6▲
ANEX	87.45 ± 1.4▲	79.02 ± 1.3▲
GNEX	88.05 ± 1.6	79.91 ± 1.7
FDNN-AN	90.68 ± 1.6▲	82.53 ± 1.5▲
FDNN-GN	**91.27 ± 1.5**	**83.40 ± 1.4**

5.2 Generic Analysis

The results of the experiments on both generic and concept-specific dataset are reported in Table 3, within this section we will discuss the ones referring to the former. The accuracy (averaged over folds) is reported for all the models: Naive Bayes (*NB* in short), C4.5 Decision Trees (*C45-DT*), Multilayer Perceptron (*MLP*), Linear SVM (*L-SVM*), SVM with RBF kernels (*RBF-SVM*), the two DCNNs trained by fine-tuning AlexNet (*ANEX*) and GoogLeNet (*GNEX*), and two versions of our Fusion-based Deep Neural Network (Section 4.2), one using AlexNet (*FDNN-AN*) and one using GoogLeNet (*FDNN-GN*) within their architectures. We also report the performances of the two baselines mentioned in Section 5.1, named *Yeh et al.* [54] and *San Pedro et al.* [39], respectively. These names will be used hereafter. Regarding concept features, we removed from the training those explicitly related to the queries that were used to construct the dataset (Table 1), as they could provide unfair information simplifying the task.

All the models trained for exoticism-aware classification significantly outperform the baselines. The relatively low accuracy of the baselines suggests that the task of assessing image aesthetics (*Yeh et al.* [54]) or classifying attractive pictures (*San Pedro et al.* [39]) is different from ours, since also not exotic images could be aesthetically well posed or attractive in general. Also when training *L-SVM* with either *low-level* or *aesthetics* features in isolation (see Table 4), which is our most similar configuration to the setup used in [54] and [39], we obtain better accuracy. The two DCNNs fine-tuned for our task (*ANEX* and *GNEX*) outperform all the classifiers based on hand-crafted features. Nevertheless, it is worth noting that *RBF-SVM* (the best representative among the feature-based classifiers) obtained a decent accuracy, which suggests that fusing DCNNs with the best hand-crafted features for our task could indeed enhance the results. In facts, our *FDNN-AN* and *FDNN-GN*, incorporating AlexNet and GoogLeNet respectively, are more accurate than *ANEX* and *GNEX* fine-tuned alone. The best model is *FDNN-GN* with an average accuracy of 91.27, while *FDNN-AN* had slightly lower but comparable performances.

To understand what are the aspects with highest impact in detecting exotic content, we rely on the different features described in Section 4.4 as they are more intuitive than the image representation learned via Deep Learning. Moreover, while the accuracy of our FDNNs and the pure DCNNs is higher, the one of the best performing classifiers (*RBF-SVM, L-SVM, MLP*) is still fairly good and, therefore, we believe that meaningful insights can be distilled from analyzing their features. For each feature-based classifier, different "versions" have been trained by using each family of features described in Section 4.4 in isolation. The results are listed in Table 4 and we consider only the values referring to the generic dataset for this discussion. The models trained when using only *concept* features are the most accurate, meaning that a semantic understanding of the image content plays an important role in this dataset. Since it has been constructed

Table 4: Averaged accuracy of models trained with different feature subsets, on generic and concept-specific datasets. Significant improvement (▲) of a feature subset is assessed with respect to the closest less performing feature subset for the same classifier.

	Generic Dataset				Concept-specific Dataset			
	Quality	Aesthetics	Low Level	Concepts	Quality	Aesthetics	Low Level	Concepts
NB	54.45 ± 2.3	58.36 ± 1.6	57.97 ± 2.2	72.07 ± 2.1▲	50.51 ± 2.5	53.13 ± 1.5	53.47 ± 2.4	63.22 ± 2.3▲
C45-DT	58.09 ± 1.8	65.91 ± 2.2▲	67.40 ± 2.3	75.46 ± 2.9▲	52.13 ± 2.4	60.68 ± 1.6▲	61.02 ± 1.9	64.54 ± 2.2▲
MLP	59.46 ± 1.9	64.41 ± 1.4▲	70.82 ± 1.2▲	77.32 ± 1.8▲	53.24 ± 1.2	59.25 ± 1.4▲	67.19 ± 1.0▲	68.65 ± 1.6
L-SVM	59.72 ± 1.4	69.01 ± 1.3▲	72.90 ± 1.5▲	78.89 ± 1.8▲	54.17 ± 1.6	62.33 ± 1.3▲	68.83 ± 1.2▲	69.39 ± 1.1
RBF-SVM	60.93 ± 1.8	69.35 ± 2.1▲	75.75 ± 1.6▲	80.26 ± 1.3▲	54.84 ± 1.2	63.71 ± 1.7▲	72.24 ± 1.5▲	72.96 ± 0.9

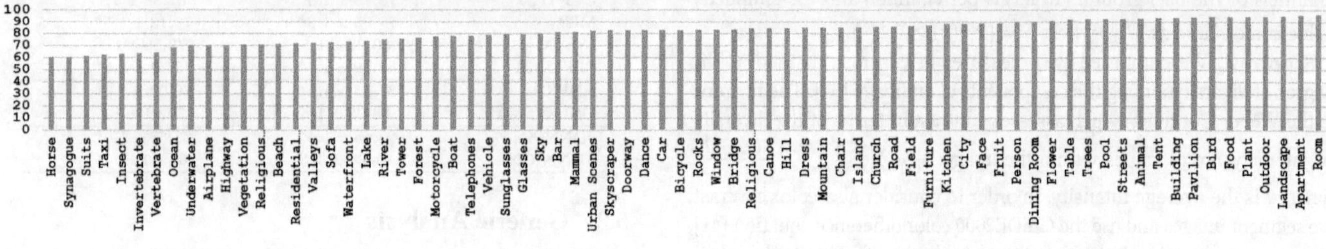

Figure 7: Accuracy of the best performing model (*FDNN-GN*) on the concept-specific dataset, split by concepts.

with the goal of having an ample separation between exotic and not exotic images, using high-level and not overlapping queries to gather images (see Section 3.1), the presence of concept highly related either to exotic or not exotic images is an informative signal for the task. Also, this might be partially due to the fact that concepts features are indirectly based on Deep Learning (see Section 4.4.1). Although the visual features have lower accuracy values, the exploitation of both visual and semantic features (Table 3) does lead to improvements if compared to concept features alone. Among the visual features, the *low-level* information is the most important one for all the classifiers (except Naive Bayes). This confirms the intuition that exotic and not exotic images can exhibit dissimilar visual characteristics such as colors, textures, and pixel distributions. Also *aesthetics*, capturing composition aspects like simplicity, shows fair contributions to the task. Differently, *quality* features had the poorest performances, which can be due to the fact that both exotic and not exotic images can be subject to quality degradation in similar ways, regardless of their class.

5.3 Concept-specific Analysis

We now delve into the concept-level discussing the experiments done on the concept-specific dataset (Section 3.2). Differently from the generic dataset, which contains a broader distinction between exotic and not exotic content, the concept-specific dataset includes exotic and not exotic images referring to the very same concept. This setup can be reasonably expected to be harder, because the difference between an exotic and not exotic exemplar of the same "neutral" concept might be thin and hard to capture automatically in different cases. For sake of evaluation, exotic and not exotic samples of each concept have been evenly distributed among the folds of the cross validation. Differently from the previous evaluation, we did not remove any concept feature from the training since the same concept can appear as exotic and not exotic images.

The accuracy (averaged over folds) on this dataset is reported in Table 3 (right-hand side). It has decreased for all the models, if compared with those obtained on the generic dataset (left-hand side). This confirms that the setup represented by the concept-specific dataset is indeed more difficult than the previous one. Besides the changes in the absolute values, all the observations done in Section 5.2 hold. All the models trained for the task of exoticism-aware classification show better accuracy than the baselines, with the models based on DCNNs being the best ones and followed by *RBF-SVM* among the classifiers relying on feature engineering. Also in this case, the combination of DCNNs with the most effective hand-crafted features for our problem (*FDNN-AN* and *FDNN-GN*) resulted to be more accurate than the two DCNNs fine-tuned alone (*ANEX* and *GNEX*).

Few differences can be noticed when using different subsets of features in isolation to train the models (Table 4). The concept features, while remaining the most accurate ones, are those subject to the highest relative decrease. Conversely, more importance is retained by the visual features, especially the *low level* information. This behavior is more evident for *MLP, L-SVM, RBF-SVM* and it is coherent with the nature of the dataset: since every concept can have both exotic and not exotic samples, the visual information becomes more discriminative for discerning them.

Finally, to show how the difficulty of discriminating between exotic and not exotic examples of the same concept can vary based on the concept itself, we report in Figure 7 the accuracy of the best performing model (*FDNN-GN*) split by concepts. Note that the standard deviation when splitting by concepts becomes higher than the one over folds (Table 3).

6 CONCLUSION

We explored the novel problem of *exoticism-aware image classification* as the task of automatically assessing the amount of exoticism contained in images. As first work aiming at identifying exotic content in images, we experimented with different Machine Learning models encompassing both Deep Learning and classifiers based on hand-crafted features. Our experiments showed that combining generic image representations learned by DCNNs with features that are most discriminative for our task led to the best results. The ground truth was gathered from the Web, subject to a crowdsourcing evaluation, and made publicly available. We also used the extracted features to understand how different aspects contribute to the task. While semantic information (concepts) was the most important one, visual information could enhance the accuracy of the models, especially to distinguish between exotic and not exotic variants of a same concept.

Since we worked on the perception of exoticism from the viewpoint of one single culture, our work can be extended to other cultures to make a comparative analysis among them. Another future work is the inclusion of exoticism as additional dimension for diversifying recommendations and search results, as well as to increase their serendipity.

Acknowledgments This work was funded by the German Research Foundation (DFG) in the context of the SPP 1921 *Intentional Forgetting in Organizations*, project *Managed Forgetting* (NI-1760/1-1).

REFERENCES

[1] Merriam-Webster, Inc.. Merriam-Webster's Dictionary of English Usage. (Merriam-Webster, Inc.).
[2] William Morris, Ed.. The American Heritage Dictionary of the English Language. (William Morris, Ed.).
[3] R. Achanta, S. Hemami, F. Estrada, and S. Susstrunk. 2009. Frequency-tuned salient region detection. In *IEEE CVPR '09*.
[4] P. Adamopoulos and A. Tuzhilin. 2015. On Unexpectedness in Recommender Systems: Or How to Better Expect the Unexpected. *ACM TIST* (2015).
[5] Erik Boiy and Marie-Francine Moens. 2009. A machine learning approach to sentiment analysis in multilingual Web texts. *Information retrieval* (2009).
[6] D. Borth, T. Chen, R. Ji, and S.F. Chang. 2013. Sentibank: large-scale ontology and classifiers for detecting sentiment and emotions in visual content. In *MM'13*.
[7] G. Bradski. 2000. *Dr. Dobb's Journal of Software Tools* (2000).
[8] J. Donahue, Y. Jia, O. Vinyals, J. Hoffman, N. Zhang, E. Tzeng, and T. Darrell. 2014. DeCAF: A Deep Convolutional Activation Feature for Generic Visual Recognition. In *ICML '14*.
[9] Carsten Eickhoff and Arjen P de Vries. 2013. Increasing cheat robustness of crowd-sourcing tasks. *Information retrieval* (2013).
[10] M. Ge, C. Delgado-Battenfeld, and D. Jannach. 2010. Beyond Accuracy: Evaluating Recommender Systems by Coverage and Serendipity. In *RecSys '10*.
[11] R. Girshick, J. Donahue, T. Darrell, and J. Malik. 2014. Rich Feature Hierarchies for Accurate Object Detection and Semantic Segmentation. In *CVPR '14*.
[12] Robert J. Goldwater. 1986. *Primitivism in modern art*. Harvard University Press.
[13] Jorge Gracia, Elena Montiel-Ponsoda, Philipp Cimiano, Asunción Gómez-Pérez, Paul Buitelaar, and John McCrae. 2012. Challenges for the multilingual web of data. *Web Semantics: Science, Services and Agents on the World Wide Web* (2012).
[14] Mark Hall, Eibe Frank, Geoffrey Holmes, Bernhard Pfahringer, Peter Reutemann, and Ian H. Witten. 2009. The WEKA Data Mining Software: An Update. *SIGKDD Explor. Newsl.* (2009).
[15] Mark A Hall. 1999. *Correlation-based feature selection for machine learning*. Ph.D. Dissertation. The University of Waikato.
[16] Robert M Haralick. 1979. Statistical and structural approaches to texture. *Proc. IEEE* 67, 5 (1979).
[17] Peter Howarth and Stefan Rüger. 2004. Evaluation of Texture Features for Content-Based Image Retrieval. In *CIVR '04*.
[18] David A. Hull and Gregory Grefenstette. 1996. Querying Across Languages: A Dictionary-based Approach to Multilingual Information Retrieval. In *SIGIR '96*.
[19] Michael Jacobs. 1995. *The painted voyage: art, travel and exploration 1564-1875*. British Museum Press London.
[20] Olivia H Jenkins. 1999. Understanding and measuring tourist destination images. *International Journal of Tourism Research* (1999).
[21] Yangqing Jia, Evan Shelhamer, Jeff Donahue, Sergey Karayev, Jonathan Long, Ross Girshick, Sergio Guadarrama, and Trevor Darrell. 2014. Caffe: Convolutional Architecture for Fast Feature Embedding. In *ACM MM '14*.
[22] Jonathan Hare, Sina Samangooei, and David Dupplaw. 2011. OpenIMAJ and ImageTerrier: Java Libraries and Tools for Scalable Multimedia Analysis and Indexing of Images. In *MM '11*.
[23] Alden Jones. 2007. This is Not a Cruise. http://archive.fo/TEec. (2007).
[24] B. Jou, T. Chen, N. Pappas, M. Redi, M. Topkara, and S.F. Chang. 2015. Visual Affect Around the World: A Large-scale Multilingual Visual Sentiment Ontology. In *MM '15*.
[25] Marius Kaminskas and Derek Bridge. 2017. Diversity, Serendipity, Novelty, and Coverage: A Survey and Empirical Analysis of Beyond-Accuracy Objectives in Recommender Systems. *ACM Trans. Interact. Intell. Syst.* (2017).
[26] Alex Krizhevsky, Ilya Sutskever, and Geoffrey E Hinton. 2012. ImageNet Classification with Deep Convolutional Neural Networks. In *NIPS '12*.
[27] J. Richard Landis and Gary G. Koch. 1977. The Measurement of Observer Agreement for Categorical Data. *Biometrics* (1977).
[28] Ralph P Locke. 2009. Musical exoticism. *Images and reflections, Cambridge, Cambridge University Pres* (2009).
[29] Yiwen Luo and Xiaoou Tang. 2008. Photo and Video Quality Evaluation: Focusing on the Subject. In *ECCV '08*.
[30] Jana Machajdik and Allan Hanbury. 2010. Affective Image Classification Using Features Inspired by Psychology and Art Theory. In *ACM MM'10*.
[31] F. Markatopoulou, A. Moumtzidou, C. Tzelepis, K. Avgerinakis, N. Gkalelis, S. Vrochidis, V. Mezaris, and I. Kompatsiaris. 2015. ITI-CERTH participation to TRECVID 2015. In *TRECVID 2015 Workshop*.
[32] E. Mavridaki and Vasileios Mezaris. 2014. No-Reference blur assessment in natural images using Fourier transform and spatial pyramids. In *ICIP '14*.
[33] E. Mavridaki and V. Mezaris. 2015. A comprehensive aesthetic quality assessment method for natural images using basic rules of photography. In *IEEE ICIP '15*.
[34] R. Mihalcea, C. Banea, and J. Wiebe. 2007. Learning Multilingual Subjective Language via Cross-Lingual Projections. In *ACL '07*.
[35] T. T. Nguyen, P.M. Hui, F.M. Harper, L. Terveen, and J.A. Konstan. 2014. Exploring the Filter Bubble: The Effect of Using Recommender Systems on Content Diversity. In *WWW'14*.
[36] Paul Over, George Awad, Martial Michel, Jonathan Fiscus, Greg Sanders, Wessel Kraaij, Alan F. Smeaton, and Georges Quéenot. 2013. TRECVID 2013 – An Overview of the Goals, Tasks, Data, Evaluation Mechanisms and Metrics.
[37] N. Pappas, M. Redi, M. Topkara, B. Jou, H. Liu, T. Chen, and S.F. Chang. 2016. Multilingual Visual Sentiment Concept Matching. In *ICMR '16*.
[38] O. Russakovsky, J. Deng, H. Su, J. Krause, S. Satheesh, S. Ma, Z. Huang, A. Karpathy, A. Khosla, M. Bernstein, A.C. Berg, and L. Fei-Fei. 2015. ImageNet Large Scale Visual Recognition Challenge. *IJCV* 115, 3 (2015).
[39] Jose San Pedro and Stefan Siersdorfer. 2009. Ranking and Classifying Attractiveness of Photos in Folksonomies. In *WWW '09*.
[40] Victor Segalen. 2002. *Essay on Exoticism: An Aesthetics of Diversity*. Duke University Press.
[41] G. Sharma, W. Wu, and E. N. Dalal. 2005. The CIEDE2000 color-difference formula: implementation notes, supplementary test data, and mathematical observations. *Color research and application* (2005).
[42] Páraic Sheridan and Jean Paul Ballerini. 1996. Experiments in Multilingual Information Retrieval Using the SPIDER System. In *SIGIR '96*.
[43] Yue Shi, Martha Larson, and Alan Hanjalic. 2014. Collaborative Filtering Beyond the User-Item Matrix: A Survey of the State of the Art and Future Challenges. *ACM Comput. Surv.* (2014).
[44] Kai Song, Yonghong Tian, Wen Gao, and Tiejun Huang. 2006. Diversifying the Image Retrieval Results. In *ACM MM '06*.
[45] C. Szegedy, W. Liu, Y. Jia, P. Sermanet, S. Reed, D. Anguelov, D. Erhan, V. Vanhoucke, and A. Rabinovich. 2015. Going deeper with convolutions. In *CVPR'15*.
[46] H. Tamura, S. Mori, and T. Yamawaki. 1978. Textural Features Corresponding to Visual Perception. *IEEE Transactions on Systems, Man and Cybernetics* (1978).
[47] Nirundon Tapachai and Robert Waryszak. 2000. An examination of the role of beneficial image in tourist destination selection. *Journal of travel research* (2000).
[48] H. Tong, M. Li, H.J. Zhang, J. He, and C. Zhang. 2004. Classification of Digital Photos Taken by Photographers or Home Users. In *PCM '04*.
[49] J. van de Weijer, C. Schmid, and J. Verbeek. 2007. Learning Color Names from Real-World Images. In *IEEE CVPR'07*.
[50] Reinier H. van Leuken, Lluis Garcia, Ximena Olivares, and Roelof van Zwol. 2009. Visual Diversification of Image Search Results. In *WWW '09*.
[51] Saúl Vargas and Pablo Castells. 2011. Rank and Relevance in Novelty and Diversity Metrics for Recommender Systems. In *RecSys '11*.
[52] Shangxuan Wu, Ying-Cong Chen, Xiang Li, An-Cong Wu, Jin-Jie You, and Wei-Shi Zheng. 2016. An enhanced deep feature representation for person re-identification. In *Applications of Computer Vision (WACV), 2016 IEEE Winter Conference on*. 1–8.
[53] Yaowen Wu, Christian Bauckhage, and Christian Thurau. 2010. The good, the bad, and the ugly: Predicting aesthetic image labels. In *ICPR '10*.
[54] Che-Hua Yeh, Yuan-Chen Ho, Brian A. Barsky, and Ming Ouhyoung. Personalized Photograph Ranking and Selection System. In *ACM MM '10*.
[55] Matthew D. Zeiler and Rob Fergus. 2014. Visualizing and Understanding Convolutional Networks. In *ECCV '14*.
[56] Ning Zhang, Jeff Donahue, Ross B. Girshick, and Trevor Darrell. 2014. Part-based R-CNNs for Fine-grained Category Detection. *ECCV '14* (2014).
[57] S. Zhao, Y. Gao, X. Jiang, H. Yao, T.S. Chua, and X. Sun. 2014. Exploring principles-of-art features for image emotion recognition. In *MM '14*.

Modal-adversarial Semantic Learning Network for Extendable Cross-modal Retrieval

Xing Xu
Center for Future Media & School of Computer Science and Engineering
University of Electronic Science and Technology of China
Chengdu, China
xing.xu@uestc.edu.cn

Jingkuan Song
Center for Future Media & School of Computer Science and Engineering
University of Electronic Science and Technology of China
Chengdu, China
jingkuan.song@gmail.com

Huimin Lu
Department of Mechanical and Control Engineering
Kyushu Institute of Technology
Kitakyushu, Japan
dr.huimin.lu@ieee.org

Yang Yang
Center for Future Media & School of Computer Science and Engineering
University of Electronic Science and Technology of China
Chengdu, China
dlyyang@gmail.com

Fumin Shen
Center for Future Media & School of Computer Science and Engineering
University of Electronic Science and Technology of China
Chengdu, China
fumin.shen@gmail.com

Zi Huang
School of Information Technology & Electrical Engineering
The University of Queensland
Brisbane, Australia
huang@itee.uq.edu.au

ABSTRACT

Cross-modal retrieval, e.g., using an image query to search related text and vice-versa, has become a highlighted research topic, to provide flexible retrieval experience across multi-modal data. Existing approaches usually consider the so-called *non-extendable* cross-modal retrieval task. In this task, they learn a common latent subspace from a source set containing labeled instances of image-text pairs and then generate common representation for the instances in a target set to perform cross-modal matching. However, these method may not generalize well when the instances of the target set contains "*unseen*" classes since the instances of both the source and target set are assumed to share the same range of classes in the *non-extensive* cross-modal retrieval task. In this paper, we consider a more practical issue of *extendable* cross-modal retrieval task where instances in source and target set have disjoint classes. We propose a novel framework, termed Modal-adversarial Semantic Learning Network (MASLN), to tackle the limitation of existing methods on this practical task. Specifically, the proposed MASLN consists two subnetworks of cross-modal reconstruction and modal-adversarial semantic learning. The former minimizes the cross-modal distribution discrepancy by reconstructing each modality data mutually, with the guidelines of class embeddings as side information in the reconstruction procedure. The latter generates semantic representation to be indiscriminative for modalities, while to distinguish the modalities from the common representation via an adversarial learning mechanism. The two subnetworks are jointly trained to enhance the cross-modal semantic consistency in the learned common subspace and the knowledge transfer to instances in the target set. Comprehensive experiment on three widely-used multi-modal datasets show its effectiveness and robustness on both *non-extendable* and *extendable* cross-modal retrieval task.

CCS CONCEPTS

• **Computing methodologies → Transfer learning**; *Supervised learning by classification*;

KEYWORDS

Extendable Cross-modal Retrieval, Adversary Learning, Auto-encoder

ACM Reference Format:
Xing Xu, Jingkuan Song, Huimin Lu, Yang Yang, Fumin Shen, and Zi Huang. 2018. Modal-adversarial Semantic Learning Network for Extendable Cross-modal Retrieval. In *ICMR '18: 2018 International Conference on Multimedia Retrieval, June 11–14, 2018, Yokohama, Japan.* ACM, New York, NY, USA, 9 pages. https://doi.org/10.1145/3206025.3206033

1 INTRODUCTION

Over the last decade, multimedia data have been emerging on the Internet and enriching people's life. Consequently, multimedia retrieval has been an essential problem for information retrieval, especially when the multimodal data such as text, image, video, sensors has become the main form of multimedia information. The presence of massive multimodal data on the Internet brings enormous demand for cross-modal retrieval such as using an image query to search related texts or using a text query to search images. Different from traditional single-modal retrieval such as [2][22][39][9][25][24], cross-modal retrieval [8][6][35][34][36][18] allows the modalities of query and retrieval results to be different. Thus it is a challenging problem due to the "heterogeneity gap",

ACM ISBN 978-1-4503-5046-4/18/06...$15.00
https://doi.org/10.1145/3206025.3206033

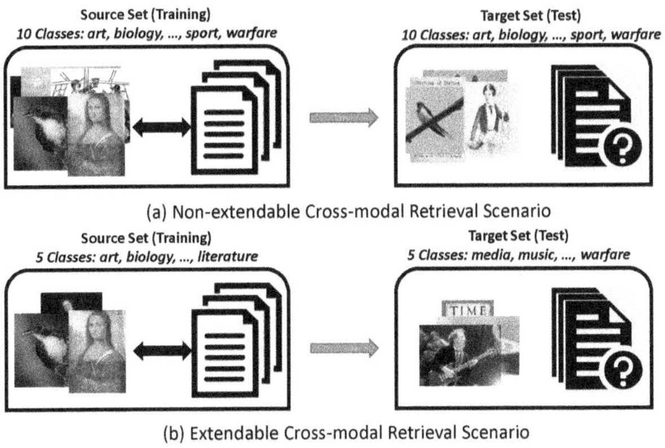

(a) Non-extendable Cross-modal Retrieval Scenario

(b) Extendable Cross-modal Retrieval Scenario

Figure 1: Illustration of different principles: (a) non-extendable cross-modal retrieval, which has been widely adopted in most existing methods; (b) extendable cross-modal retrieval, which is proposed in this work.

which means that the representation forms of different modalities are inconsistent, so cross-modal similarity cannot be directly computed.

To eliminate the "heterogeneity gap", most existing the cross-modal retrieval methods in the literature follow the paradigm of common representation learning. These methods assume that there exists an intermediate common semantic space where data of relevant semantics can be represented as similar "feature" and be close to each other. To learn effective common representations, traditional methods [3][12][28][29][37] mainly take linear projections as basic models, while latest methods [4][16][17] utilize deep neural network (DNN) to capture the nonlinearity of cross-modal correlation, showing superior performance compared with the traditional methods.

Though these methods adopt various schemes to learn linear or nonlinear projections, they follow the same principle to perform cross-modal retrieval. Specifically, in the principle, a collection of instances is required, with each instance is formed by an image-text pair with assigned class label. Then the collection is divided into a *source set* and a *target set*, where each set has disjoint image-text pairs from all classes. A common semantic space is learned from the source set in training phase and then applied on the target set to generate common representations for the instances. Finally, cross-modal similarities of the instances can be measured by the common representations and cross-modal retrieval can be performed. Take the widely used multimodal dataset Wikipedia [21] as example, Figure 1(a) illustrates the principle that is commonly adopted in most existing cross-modal retrieval methods. We call the principle *Non-extendable* cross-modal retrieval. In this case, each instance in the target set belongs to one of the pre-defined classes (10 classes in total) as in the source set. However, this assumption does not always hold in practice, the target set may exhibit various categories that the source set cannot fully cover for the training process.

In this paper, we hold the same viewpoint as [13] that cross-modal retrieval can be extendable, i.e., the learned model from the source set can handle the instances of "unseen" classes in the target set. This new principle is similar as the zero-shot learning (ZSL) in computer vision community. However, ZSL focuses on enabling knowledge transferring in single modal data such as image [31][15][40], while we consider the expansibility of cross-modal learning approaches on multimodal data. Figure 1(b) shows the proposed new principle, which is named *Extendable* cross-modal retrieval. Specifically, in the new principle, the source set and the target set have instances from disjoint classes. For example, the five classes in the source set do not overlap with those in the target set. Models are learned on the source set and directly tested on the target set, evaluating the expansibility of models. Under this principle, the performance of existing cross-modal retrieval approaches degrades drastically (detailed experimental results are showed in Section 4), since they fail to consider the different distributions of instances in the source set and the target set.

To overcome the shortcoming of existing methods on the *extendable* cross-modal retrieval task, we propose modal-adversarial semantic learning network (MASLN), which is an end-to-end architecture with two subnetworks jointly trained to mutually boost and learn cross-modal common representation for the *extendable* cross-modal retrieval task. Figure 2 demonstrates the flowchart of the proposed MASLN, where its main contributions are:

- **Cross-modal reconstruction subnetwork** is proposed to minimize the cross-domain distribution discrepancy with conditional auto-encoder for reconstructing each modality. Different from the existing method [4] uses auto-encoder to reconstructing modality data, here the conditional auto-encoder takes class embeddings as side information in the reconstruction procedure. It helps incorporate the discrimination of classes in the learned common representation, and enables the knowledge transfer from the source set to the target set.
- **Modal-adversarial semantic learning subnetwork** is proposed to generate semantic representation to be indiscriminative for modalities, while to distinguish the modalities from the common representation. These two processes are jointly accomplished in an adversarial training mechanism. It makes the learned common representation discriminative for semantics but indiscriminative for modalities, thus effectively enhances cross-modal semantic consistency to improve retrieval accuracy.

Compared with existing approaches, the proposed MASLN can effectively transfer knowledge from the source set to the target set for addressing the problem of *Extendable* cross-modal retrieval. Extensive experiments compared with several state-of-the-art methods on three widely-used cross-modal datasets show the effectiveness and generality of our MASLN approach, including both the *Non-extensive* and *Extensive* cross-modal retrieval task.

2 RELATED WORK

As introduced in Section 1, cross-modal retrieval is proposed to perform retrieval task across different modalities. The main effort on cross-modal retrieval is to represent data of different modalities with common representation, to eliminate the "heterogeneity gap". Existing methods can be classified into traditional methods and DNN-based methods according to the difference of basic models.

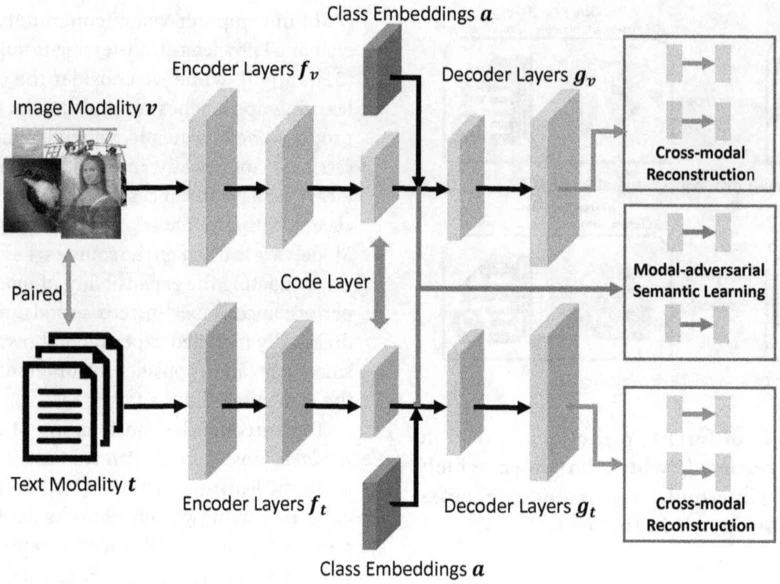

Figure 2: The flowchart of the proposed MASLN, including two subnetworks of cross-modal reconstruction and modal-adversarial semantic learning. The green arrow indicates the reconstruction flow, and the red arrow represents the semantic learning arrow.

Traditional methods mainly learn linear projection to maximize the correlation between the pairwise data of different modalities, which project the feature of different modalities into one common space to generate common representation. The typical methods include canonical correlation analysis (CCA) [21], cross-modal factor analysis (CFA) [12], etc. Recent work [14][16][26][30][32][38] have made great efforts to apply deep neural network (DNN) to cross-modal retrieval, such as Correspondence Auto-encoder (Corr-AE) [4], deep canonical correlation analysis (DCCA) [1], cross-media multiple deep networks (CMDN) [16], adversarial cross-modal retrieval (ACMR) [27] and etc. The advantage of DNN based methods is that it is powerful to model nonlinearity in multimodal data distribution and can incorporate various information into common representation learning.

It is notable that most of these works only perform model training with the cross-modal datasets considering the so-called *non-extendable* cross-modal retrieval task. Besides, a majority of these methods relies on the assigned class labels for instances in training phase, to learn discriminant common subspace. They may not generalize well on the practical case of *extendable* cross-modal retrieval task, where the multi-modal instances are from "unseen" classes that has no overlap with the training instances. Due to the different distributions of the source and target set in the *extendable* cross-modal retrieval task, the performance of the existing methods become inferior as the learned models are weak to enable knowledge transfer in the common subspace. Our MASLN is proposed for addressing the problem of *extendable* cross-modal retrieval task. It take the available class embeddings as side information to reconstruct modality data mutually, which help transfer knowledge, in the common subspace. Besides, it effectively captures the semantic correlation as well as the discrimination of classes in the common subspace via an adversarial learning mechanism, thus effectively enhances cross-modal semantic consistency to improve retrieval accuracy.

3 PROPOSED METHOD

3.1 Problem Formulation

Assume that we have a source set consists of N_s multi-modal instances with image-text pairs, i.e. $O_s = \{o_i\}_{i=1}^{N_s}$, $o_i = (v_i, t_i)$, where $v_i \in \mathbb{R}^m$ is the image feature vector and $t_i \in \mathbb{R}^d$ is the text feature vector for the i-th instance o_i. Here m and d are the dimensionality of image and text feature space, respectively. In addition, a label y_i is also assigned to o_i, $y_i \in \mathcal{Y}_s$, i.e., the class set for O_s. We also have a target set of N_t instances, $O_t = \{o_j\}_{j=1}^{N_t}$, where each instance $o_j = (v_j, t_j)$ has the same format as that in the source set. Differently, each instance o_j in O_t is assigned with a label $y_q \in \mathcal{Y}_t$, where $\mathcal{Y}_t$ is disjoint with $\mathcal{Y}_s$, i.e., $\mathcal{Y}_t \bigcap \mathcal{Y}_s = 0$.

Our goal is to learn a common subspace from the instances in O_s and then apply to generate common representation for the instances in O_t, which is considered as the *extendable* cross-modal retrieval task in this paper. This is different from the widely explored *non-extendable* cross-modal retrieval task in previous methods, where the classes of both source and target set are identical. Inspired by ZSL approaches that leverage side information as intermediate clues for knowledge transfer between source and target set, here we also introduce the word embeddings of classes (called class embeddings) as useful side information in our work. Specifically, the class embeddings are extracted from linguistic knowledge by natural language processing models and used as semantic representations of the classes in both $\mathcal{Y}_s$ and $\mathcal{Y}_t$. For each instance o_i in O_s and

O_t, its class embeddings are denoted as $a_i \in \mathcal{R}^k$, where k is the dimension of the embedding vector.

3.2 Modal-adversarial Semantic Learning Network

As illustrated in Figure 2, the proposed MASLN contains two subnetwork: cross-modal reconstruction subnetwork and modal-adversarial semantic learning subnetwork. The former is to minimize the cross-domain distribution discrepancy by reconstructing each modality data mutually, and the latter is to generate semantic representation to be indiscriminative for modalities, while to distinguish the modalities from the common representation.

3.2.1 Cross-modal Reconstruction Subnetwork. The subnetwork consists of two branches, which are connected by a predefined similarity measure on the hidden code layer. The inputs to each branch are features from one modality and are fed into fully-connected layers, and then they are mutually reconstructed through a conditional auto-encoder, where the class embeddings act as the side information to incorporate discrimination of classes in the code layer and enable knowledge transfer.

Specifically, in the image modality, each training instance v_i is mapped to hidden codes $f_v(v_i;\theta_v)$ by encoder $f_v(\cdot)$, and then reconstructed by $\hat{v}_i = g_v(f_v(v_i), a_i; \theta'_v)$, where θ_v and θ'_v denote the model parameters in encoder and decoder, respectively. Similar process is conduct on the text modality. Note that during the reconstruction procedure, the associated class embedding a_i to sample is concatenated to the representation of the code layer. Therefore, the shared code layer explicitly incorporate the knowledge of class embeddings.

During learning, the two branches are coupled at their code layer using a similarity measure. After learning, the two subnetworks in the Corr-AE exhibit different parameters even if they have the same architecture. As illustrated in Figure 2, the conditional auto-encoder reconstruction not only the input itself, but also input from the other modality. The shared representation space in the code layers of two branches contains information from both modalities. The loss function of any pair of inputs are formulated as follows:

$$L_{rec}(v_i, t_i; \Theta_r) = L_I(v_i, t_i; \Theta_r) + L_T(v_i, t_i; \Theta_r), \tag{1}$$

where

$$\begin{aligned} L_I(v_i, t_i; \Theta_r) &= \|v_i - \hat{v}_i^I\|_2^2 + \|t_i - \hat{t}_i^I\|_2^2, \\ L_T(v_i, t_i; \Theta_r) &= \|v_i - \hat{v}_i^T\|_2^2 + \|t_i - \hat{t}_i^T\|_2^2. \end{aligned} \tag{2}$$

Here $\hat{v}_i^I$ and $\hat{t}_i^I$ are the reconstruction instance from v_i and t_i in the image branch; $\hat{v}_i^T$ and $\hat{t}_i^T$ are the reconstruction instance from v_i and t_i in the text branch. $\|\cdot\|_2$ is the L_2 norm and $\Theta_r = [\theta_v, \theta'_v, \theta_t, \theta'_t]$ denotes the parameters of the encoders and decoders in two branches. By this subnetwork, the reconstruction across different modalities help model the cross-modal correlations, and the usage of class embeddings in reconstruction further enhances the discrimination of the shared code layer and enables knowledge transfer to target data.

3.2.2 Modal-adversarial Semantic Learning Subnetwork. In our work, we introduce this subnetwork to enhance the shared code layer (cross-modal common subspace), which further enables the knowledge transfer on the extandable cross-modal retrieval task. Notably, the abovementioned cross-modal reconstruction subnetwork only exploits pairwise correlation (reconstruction) in the original feature space. Indeed, the high-level semantic consistency is the essential property to associate the source and target domain data, which should be effectively modeled in the shared code layer. For addressing this issue, the modal-adversarial feature learning subnetwork is designed as in Figure 2, which is fed to the shared code layer (common representation layer) to generate common representation. Specifically, it contains three branches to drive the network training, namely *semantic correlation learning*, *semantic discrimination learning* and *modal-adversarial consistency learning.*

Semantic Correlation Learning. This branch exploits cross-modal correlation to jointly transfer knowledge to all modalities. Intuitively, the network outputs of pairwise samples across two modalities should be similar to each other, which aims to align their representations and achieve knowledge sharing. To represent the cross-modal pairwise discrepancy, we adopt Euclidean distance between the specific representation layers of both image and text modalities. The cross-modal pairwise discrepancy are defined as follows:

$$f_{corr}(v_i, t_i) = \|f_v(v_i; \Theta_r) - f_t(t_i; \Theta_r)\|_2^2, \tag{3}$$

where $f_v(\cdot)$ and $f_t(\cdot)$ is the encoders of two modalities that generate representation in the code layer, θ_v and θ_t respectively denote the network parameters. Then we get the semantic correlation loss as

$$L_{corr} = \sum_{i=1}^{N_s} f_{corr}(v_i, t_i). \tag{4}$$

By optimizing loss, the cross-modal pairwise discrepancy can be reduced.

Semantic Discrimination Learning. This branch ensures the cross-modal common representations in the shared code layer to be semantically discriminative. Because the pairwise samples in two modalities share the same common representation, the cross-modal semantic consistency can be ensured under the guidance of supervision information in the target domain. To achieve this goal, we use a fully-connected layer as a common classification layer with softmax loss function. The semantic discrimination loss is defined as follows:

$$L_{dis} = \frac{1}{N_s} \sum_{i=1}^{N_s} (f_{softmax}(v_i, y_i; \Theta_d) + f_{softmax}(t_i, y_i; \Theta_d). \tag{5}$$

Here $f_{softmax}(x, y; \theta)$ is the softmax loss function as:

$$f_{softmax}(x, y, \theta) = \sum_{k=1}^{c} 1\{y = k\} \log[\hat{p}(x, k, \theta)], \tag{6}$$

where y denote the label of sample x, θ contains network parameters and c is the total number of classes. $\hat{p}(x, k, \theta)$ is the softmax probability distribution over c classes of x. By optimizing this loss, we can maximize the classification accuracy jointly for all modalities, which preserves the semantic consistency contained in cross-modal target domain.

Modal-adversarial consistency learning. This branch contains two players: a modality discriminator and a common representation generator. They play a min-max game to maximize the semantic discriminative ability and to minimize the difference of the cross-modal representations simutaneousely in the subnetwork. This procedure is performed under the adversarial training style [5] that have been used in recent work [27][18].

Similar as [27][18], in training stage, each instance is assigned with a one-hot encoding vector to indicate which modality it belongs to, and the modal-adversarial consistency loss is:

$$L_{adv} = \frac{1}{N_s} \sum_{i=1}^{N_s} f_{cross}(z_j, p(z_j); \Theta_a), \tag{7}$$

where $p(\cdot)$ denotes the label indicator, θ_a represents the network parameters, and $f_{cross}(x, p, \theta)$ is the sigmoid cross entropy loss function as in [10]:

$$f_{cross}(x, p, \theta) = p(x)log(\hat{p}(x, \theta)) + [1 - p(x)]log[1 - \hat{p}(x, \theta)]. \tag{8}$$

By maximizing L_{adv}, we can explicitly reduce heterogeneity gap among modalities and enhance the consistency of common representation.

The proposed MASLN is an end-to-end architecture with jointly training the cross-modal reconstruction subnetwork and modal-adversarial semantic learning subnetwork. In the testing stage, each testing instance in target set can be converted the final common representation for extendable retrieval task. With different class embeddings, each testing instance (with feature of one modality given) can obtain different common representation, and the most similar samples can be retrieved when computing pairwise similarity.

3.3 Optimization

We first denote the parameters in cross-modal reconstruction subnetwork as Θ_r, and in modal-adversarial semantic learning subnetwork the parameters are denoted as Θ_d and Θ_a. Then the joint objective function with the loss terms in the two subnetworks can be formulated as

$$\begin{aligned} L(\Theta_r, \Theta_d, \Theta_a) &= L_{rec}(\Theta_r) + L_{corr}(\Theta_r) + \\ & Ł_{dis}(\Theta_r, \Theta_d) - \lambda L_{adv}(\Theta_r, \Theta_a) \end{aligned} \tag{9}$$

where λ is a positive trade-off parameter between the positive and negative loss function in the adversarial training stage. Our goal is to find the model parameters in the min-max optimization process via an adversarial training style, as

$$(\hat{\Theta_r}, \hat{\Theta_d}) = \arg\min L(\Theta_r, \Theta_d, \hat{\Theta_a}), \tag{10}$$

$$(\hat{\Theta_a}) = \arg\max L(\hat{\Theta_r}, \hat{\Theta_d}, \Theta_a). \tag{11}$$

Based on Eq. 10 and Eq. 11, we can update the parameter as follows:

$$\Theta_r \leftarrow \Theta_r - \mu(\frac{L_{rec}}{\partial\Theta_r} + \frac{L_{cor}}{\partial\Theta_r}), \tag{12}$$

$$\Theta_d \leftarrow \Theta_d - \mu(\frac{L_{dis}}{\partial\Theta_d}), \tag{13}$$

$$\Theta_a \leftarrow \Theta_a - \mu(\frac{L_{adv}}{\partial\Theta_a}). \tag{14}$$

In the above update rules, μ denote the learning rate, and these rules can be realized by stochastic gradient descent (SGD) algorithm. In this way, we can optimize these loss functions and perform knowledge transfer to cross-modal in training stage, to get effective cross-modal common representation.

4 EXPERIMENT

4.1 Experimental Setup

Datasets and Features. We conduct experiments on 3 widely-used cross-modal datasets, named Wikipedia [21], Pascal Sentence [20] and NUS-WIDE-10k [4], which have been well explored in the literature [16][10][13][11][27]. The detailed information of the three datasets are as follows: 1) Wikipedia consists of 2,866 image/text pairs, and each pair is labeled by one of its 10 categories; 2) Pascal Sentence contains 1,000 images which are evenly categorized into 20 categories, and each image has 5 corresponding sentences which makes up one document. 3) NUS-WIDE-10K has totally 10,000 image/text pairs selected evenly from the 10 largest categories of the original NUS-WIDE dataset.

As image feature extracted from convolutional neural network (CNN) has shown strong ability and been widely used for image representation, so we also use CNN image feature for all datasets in the experiment. Specifically, the adopted CNN feature has 4,096 dimensions extracted by the fc7 layer of VGGNet [23] for all compared methods on 3 datasets. Similar as the previous work [16][17][27], we use 1,000 dimensional bag of words (BOW) vector as text feature for Wikipedia dataset and 3,000 dimensional BOW vector for the other two datasets. For word embeddings of classes, each class name is mapped to a 300 dimensional vector in the word space learned by the skip- gram model [19] using a text corpus containing 4.6M Wikipedia pages.

Retrieval Tasks. Follows the protocol proposed in [13], we conduct two types of cross-modal retrieval tasks on all datasets as follows:

- Non-extendable (**non-XTD**) retrieval, which is the traditional cross-modal retrieval task including two sub-tasks: image-to-text (Img2Txt) and text-to-image (Txt2Img). The non-XTD retrieval task divides each dataset of image-text pairs into a source set for training and a target set for testing. Note that , both the source set and the target set include all the classes in the dataset. Therefore, we use the original data split of each dataset as the source/target set for non-XTD retrieval task, i.e., 2,173/693 for Wikipedia, 800/200 for Pascal Sentence and 8,000/2,000 for NUS-WIDE-10K, respectively.
- Extendable (**XTD**) retrieval. In this task, we still split each dataset to a source set and a target set. Different from non-XTD retrieval, here it is required that there is no class overlap between the source and target set. Thus, for each dataset, we take the pairs of one half classes as the source set and those of the other half classes as the target set. To balance the influences of the different class splits, we also shuffle the classes before making split, and perform the experiment K ($K = 5$) times on each dataset. The performances are averaged over the K times to get the final performance.

Details of Network. In the cross-modal reconstruction subnetwork, the details of layers and dimensions of each layer are as follows: we use a four fully connected layers with dimensions $[2048, 1024, 512, 50]$ for image feature transform and a three fully connected layers with dimensions $[1024, 512, 50]$ for text feature branch, where the dimension of the code layer is set to 50. The activation function is set to $tanh$ function after each layer. For the discrimination and modality classifiers, we use a two-layer network with dimensions $[50, 100, 2]$. While training our model we notice that a strong modality classifier on the contrary can worsen the performance. To alleviate this, we update the modality classifiers less often then the feature transforms, which is commonly used scheme in GANs [7][5]. Adam optimizer with a learning rate of $\mu = 0.0001$ is used for training each subnetwork, with the mini-bath size as 128. We set the parameters λ to 0.02 on all datasets for adversarial training.

Compared Methods and Evaluation Metric. We compare our proposed MASLN with seven state-of-the-art methods in the experiment, including three traditional cross-modal retrieval methods, namely CCA [21], CCA-3V [6], LCFS [29]; and four deep learning based methods, namely Corr-AE [4], Deep-SM [33], CMDH [16], MHTN[11] and ACMR [27]. We use the source codes released by the authors of the compared methods to make fair comparison. Specifically, we first learn the projections or deep models for all the methods, and then convert the testing data into the common representation by the learned projections or deep models. Finally, cross-modal retrieval is performed by computing the cosine similarities of pairwise instances with common representations.

To evaluate the retrieval performance of all methods fairly, we adopt the widely-used mean average precision (MAP) score as the evaluation metric. The MAP score is the mean value of calculated average precision (AP) on each query, which jointly considers the overall ranking information and precision. To overcome this shortage, In addition, we also use the metric of cumulative matching characteristics (CMC) curve proposed in [13] to provide insights of the retrieval results. The CMC curve is a fine-grained metric that computes the first match in the top-r ranks in the retrieved list for a query. Therefore, it is a good complementary metric for MAP and provides different aspect to assess the retrieval performance.

4.2 Results on Non-XTD Retrieval Task

We first evaluate our proposed method and the compared baselines on the Non-XTD retrieval task. Table 1 shows the experimental results of MAP scores of our MASLN approach as well as the compared baselines on three datasets. On all the datasets, our proposed MHTN achieves the highest average MAP scores on all retrieval tasks. On Wikipedia dataset, the highest average MAP score of compared methods is obtained by ACMR, and an inspiring accuracy improvement is obtained by the proposed MASLN from 0.546 to 0.567. On Pascal Sentence and NUS-WIDE-10k dataset, MASLN keeps its advantage and achieves the highest average MAP score of 0.545 and 0.551, respectively. In particular, the improvement on the Txt2Img task is more remarkable than that on the Img2Txt task. It is notable that the proposed MASLN outperforms the DNN based methods Corr-AE, MHTN and ACMR that also capture pairwise correlation. The reason is that MASLN additionally takes the class embeddings as side information to enhance the correspondence of pairwise instances with class information during cross-modal reconstruction, thus obtaining more effective common representations in the code layer. Moreover, MASLN also use the adversarial learning mechanism as MHTN and ACMR, and still outperforms the two methods. It indicates that the adversarial learning helps the proposed MASLN to learn more compact common representations that is invariant across different modalities.

4.3 Results on XTD Retrieval Task

We then investigate the proposed MASLN and the compared methods for the XTD retrieval task. The MAP scores of all methods on three dataset are presented in Table 2. The XTD retrieval task indeed is more challenging than the non-XTD retrieval task, since the target set of each dataset is not observed during training. Compared with the scores of all method on the Non-XTD task in Table 1, here in Table 2 the scores of all method decrease seriously. For example, the best method among the compared baselines, i.e., ACMR, the average MAP scores for the Non-XTD task on three datasets are 0.567, 0.545, 0.551, respectively, while for the Non-XTD task, the scores drop to 0.299, 0.263, 0.282, respectively. Similar considerable performance drop can be observed on the other baselines, as well as our proposed MASLN. This is reasonable because the distributions of the target set are different from the source set, thus trained models of all methods may not well reflect the pairwise correlations of target set in the learned common representation. Nevertheless, our proposed MASLN still gains significant improvements on all dataset for the XTD retrieval task. We attribute the advantage of the MASLN to the usage of class embeddings during cross-modal reconstruction, as the class embeddings are incorporated to the code layers of the AE in each modality and reduce the disparities between the distributions of the source and the target set when generating the common representation in the learned subspace.

Furthermore, we set the top-rank number r from 1 to 15, and plot the CMC curves of the proposed method and several compared baselines on three dataset for the XTD task in Figure 3. We can observe that our proposed MASLN keeps the highest matching rating at different levels of top ranked list. Specifically, the matching rate increases when r becomes larger, and when r is small (e.g, $r = 1, 2, \ldots, 5$), the matching rate of MASLN is significantly better than the compared baselines. Therefore, it indicates that MASLN can obtain more effective common representations for target set, which benefits the XTD retrieval performance.

4.4 Further Analysis on MASLN

4.4.1 Visualization of Learned Common Representation. We further investigate the effectiveness of the cross-modal representations learned by our MASLN. In particular, for each of the image and text modality, we randomly choose the common representation of 1000 instances in the source and target set to form a total of 2000 samples containing images and texts. We then use t-SNE to visualize the distribution of these samples. Fig. 4 shows the t-SNE embedding for the data distribution of Wikipedia dataset on pre-defined 10 classes. We can see that with the guideless of the class embeddings, the learned common representations of both image and text modalities form discriminant clusters in the common subspace, where the instances with the same classes is in the same cluster. This indicates that the proposed MASLN is effective to close the statistical gaps between different modalities and capture the correlations of different modalities in the aligned cluster.

4.4.2 Effects of Class Embeddings in MASLN. As discussed in above subsection, using class embeddings is helpful for the proposed

Table 1: The Non-XTD retrieval comparison in terms of MAP on three datasets. The best results on each dataset are highlighted in bold font.

Methods	Wikipedia			Pascal Sentences			NUSWIDE-10k		
	Img2Txt	Txt2Img	Avg.	Img2Txt	Txt2Img	Avg.	Img2Txt	Txt2Img	Avg.
CCA [21]	0.267	0.222	0.245	0.363	0.219	0.291	0.189	0.188	0.189
CCA-3V [6]	0.437	0.383	0.41	0.416	0.332	0.374	0.272	0.293	0.283
LCFS [29]	0.455	0.398	0.427	0.442	0.357	0.400	0.383	0.346	0.365
Corr-AE [4]	0.402	0.395	0.398	0.489	0.444	0.467	0.366	0.417	0.392
Deep-SM [33]	0.478	0.422	0.45	0.511	0.482	0.497	0.389	0.496	0.443
CMDH [16]	0.488	0.427	0.458	0.534	0.534	0.534	0.492	0.515	0.504
MHTN [11]	0.514	0.444	0.479	0.496	0.500	0.498	0.520	0.534	0.527
ACMR [27]	0.619	0.489	0.546	0.535	0.543	0.539	0.544	0.538	0.541
MASLN	**0.623**	**0.499**	**0.561**	**0.544**	**0.547**	**0.545**	**0.550**	**0.552**	**0.551**

Table 2: The XTD retrieval comparison in terms of MAP on three datasets. The best results on each dataset are highlighted in bold font.

Methods	Wikipedia			Pascal Sentences			NUSWIDE-10k		
	Img2Txt	Txt2Img	Avg.	Img2Txt	Txt2Img	Avg.	Img2Txt	Txt2Img	Avg.
CCA [21]	0.183	0.172	0.178	0.144	0.112	0.128	0.102	0.11	0.106
CCA-3V [6]	0.262	0.196	0.229	0.176	0.125	0.151	0.114	0.125	0.120
LCFS [29]	0.285	0.203	0.244	0.195	0.178	0.187	0.243	0.236	0.240
Corr-AE [4]	0.274	0.212	0.243	0.235	0.196	0.2155	0.258	0.264	0.261
Deep-SM [33]	0.295	0.233	0.264	0.241	0.213	0.227	0.259	0.257	0.258
CMDH [16]	0.302	0.252	0.277	0.256	0.227	0.242	0.272	0.265	0.269
MHTN [11]	0.316	0.247	0.282	0.269	0.243	0.256	0.279	0.261	0.270
ACMR [27]	0.322	0.276	0.299	0.272	0.253	0.263	0.286	0.278	0.282
MASLN	**0.331**	**0.287**	**0.309**	**0.281**	**0.261**	**0.271**	**0.291**	**0.284**	**0.287**

Table 3: The XTD retrieval performance of the MASLN$_{cls}$ without class embeddings, comparing with the full MASLN and the ACMR methods.

Methods	Wikipedia			Pascal Sentences		
	Img2Txt	Txt2Img	Avg.	Img2Txt	Txt2Img	Avg.
ACMR	0.322	0.276	0.299	0.272	0.253	0.263
MASLN	0.331	0.287	0.309	0.281	0.261	0.271
MASLN$_{cls}$	0.319	0.284	0.302	0.274	0.258	0.266

MASLN to enhance the correspondence of pairwise correlation with class information in the cross-modal reconstruction subnetwork. Intuitively, when omitting the input of class embeddings, the proposed MASLN will degrade to a basic model of ACMR that captures the pairwise correlations and performs semantic learning under the adversarial mechanism. We denote MASLN$_{cls}$ as MASLN without class embeddings and investigate the contribution of using class embeddings in MASLN. The optimization procedure of MASLN$_{cls}$ is similar to MASLN. Table 3 shows the performance of MASLN$_{cls}$ and the full MASLN and ACMR methods for the XTD retrieval task on Wikipedia dataset and Pascal Sentence dataset. It can be observed that MASLN$_{cls}$ is inferior to the full MASLN on the two datasets, showing the effectiveness of using class embeddings in the full MASLN to learn more effective and domain-invariant common representations. In addition, MASLN$_{cls}$ performs on par with the ACMR, as it has similar network architecture as ACMR when ignoring the class embeddings.

5 CONCLUSION

In this paper, we proposed a novel Modal-adversarial Semantic Learning Network (MASLN) for the practical issue of *extendable* cross-modal retrieval task. The proposed MASLN is an end-to-end architecture with two subnetworks: 1) the cross-modal reconstruction subnetwork minimizes the cross-domain distribution discrepancy with conditional auto-encoder for reconstructing each modality mutually; 2) the modal-adversarial semantic learning subnetwork utilizes an adversarial training mechanism to generates semantic representation that are indiscriminative for modalities, while distinguishable from the common representation of different modalities. The extensive experiments on both *non-extendable* and *extendable* cross-modal retrieval tasks validated the superiority of

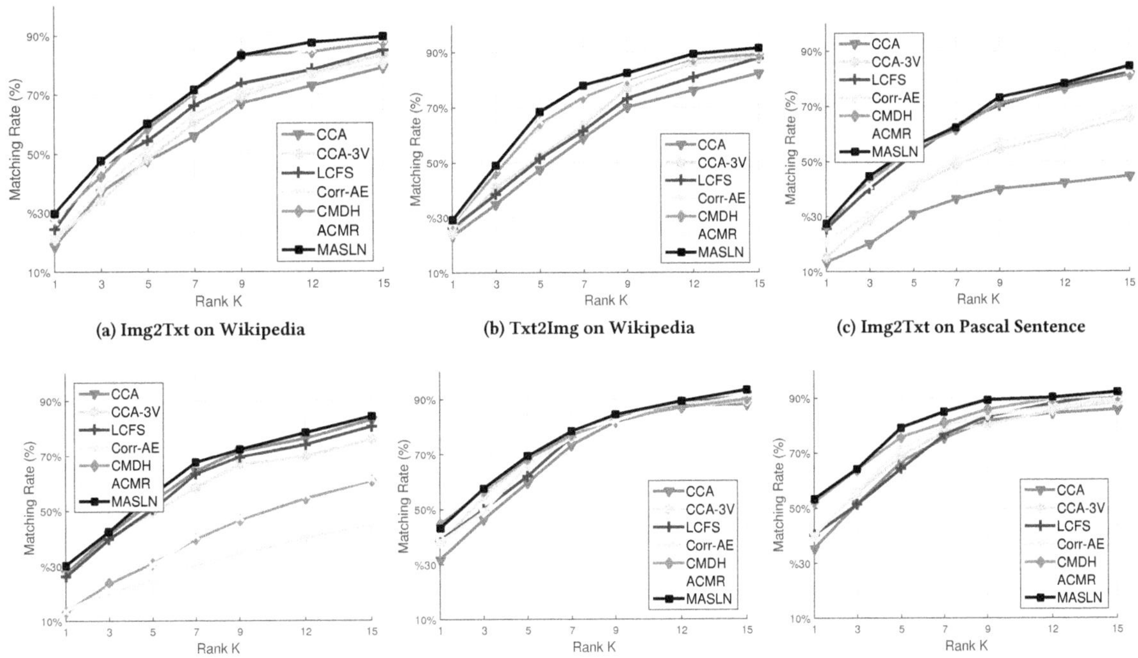

(a) Img2Txt on Wikipedia (b) Txt2Img on Wikipedia (c) Img2Txt on Pascal Sentence

(d) Txt2Img on Pascal Sentence (e) Img2Txt on NUS-WIDE-10K (f) Txt2Img on NUS-WIDE-10K

Figure 3: The CMC curves of the proposed MASLN and the compared baselines on all datasets for the XTD task. The curves are plotted on two subtasks: Img2Txt and Txt2Img.

(a) Distribution of image modality (b) Distribution of text modality

Figure 4: t-SNE visualization for the chosen data in Wikipedia dataset. Clusters with different color belongs to different classes.

the proposed MASLN on learning more effective common subspace and enabling knowledge transfer to target set labeled with "unseen" classes.

ACKNOWLEDGMENTS

The work in this paper is partially supported by NSFC grants 61602089, 61772116, 61572108, 61632007; LEADER of MEXT-Japan (16809746), The Telecommunications Foundation, NII and NICT.

REFERENCES

[1] G. Andrew, R. Arora, J. Bilmes, and K. Livescu. 2013. Deep Canonical Correlation Analysis.. In *ICML*. 1247–1255.
[2] Lin Chen, Dong Xu, Ivor Wai-Hung Tsang, and Xuelong Li. 2014. Spectral Embedded Hashing for Scalable Image Retrieval. *IEEE Trans. Cybernetics* 44, 7 (2014), 1180–1190.
[3] J. Costa Pereira, E. Coviello, G. Doyle, N. Rasiwasia, G. Lanckriet, R. Levy, and N. Vasconcelos. 2014. On the role of Correlation and Abstraction in Cross-Modal Multimedia Retrieval. *TPAMI* 36, 3 (2014), 521–535.
[4] F. Feng, X. Wang, and R. Li. 2014. Cross-modal retrieval with correspondence autoencoder.. In *ACM MM*. 7–16.
[5] Y. Ganin and V. S. Lempitsky. 2015. Unsupervised Domain Adaptation by Backpropagation.. In *ICML*. 1180–1189.
[6] Y. Gong, Q. Ke, M. Isard, and S. Lazebnik. 2014. A multi-view embedding space for modeling internet images, tags, and their semantics. *IJCV* 106, 2 (2014), 210–233.
[7] I. Goodfellow, J. Pouget-Abadie, M. Mirza, B. Xu, D. Warde-Farley, S. Ozair, A. Courville, and Y. Bengio. 2014. Generative Adversarial Nets. In *NIPS*. 2672–2680.
[8] D. Hardoon, S. Szedmak, and J. Shawe-Taylor. 2004. Canonical correlation analysis: An overview with application to learning methods. *Neural computation* 16, 12 (2004), 2639–2664.
[9] Mengqiu Hu, Yang Yang, Fumin Shen, Ning Xie, and Heng Tao Shen. 2018. Hashing with Angular Reconstructive Embeddings. *IEEE Transactions on Image Processing* 27, 2 (2018), 545–555.
[10] Xin Huang, Yuxin Peng, and Mingkuan Yuan. 2017. Cross-modal Common Representation Learning by Hybrid Transfer Network. In *Proceedings of the Twenty-Sixth International Joint Conference on Artificial Intelligence, IJCAI 2017, Melbourne, Australia, August 19-25, 2017.* 1893–1900.
[11] Xin Huang, Yuxin Peng, and Mingkuan Yuan. 2017. MHTN: Modal-adversarial Hybrid Transfer Network for Cross-modal Retrieval. *CoRR* abs/1708.04308 (2017).
[12] D. Li, N. Dimitrova, M. Li, and I. K. Sethi. 2003. Multimedia content processing through cross-modal association. In *ACM MM*. 604–611.
[13] Ruoyu Liu, Yao Zhao, Liang Zheng, Shikui Wei, and Yi Yang. 2017. A New Evaluation Protocol and Benchmarking Results for Extendable Cross-media Retrieval. *CoRR* abs/1703.03567 (2017).
[14] J. Ngiam, A. Khosla, M. Kim, J. Nam, H. Lee, and A. Ng. 2011. Multimodal deep learning. In *ICML*. 689–696.
[15] Mohammad Norouzi, Tomas Mikolov, Samy Bengio, Yoram Singer, Jonathon Shlens, Andrea Frome, Greg Corrado, and Jeffrey Dean. 2013. Zero-Shot Learning by Convex Combination of Semantic Embeddings. (2013), 410–418.
[16] Y. Peng, X. Huang, and J. Qi. 2016. Cross-media shared representation by hierarchical learning with multiple deep networks. In *IJCAI*. 3846–C3853.
[17] Y. Peng, J. Qi, X. Huang, and Yuan Y. 2017. CCL: Cross-modal Correlation Learning with Multi-grained Fusion by Hierarchical Network. (2017). arXiv:1704.02116

[18] Yuxin Peng, Jinwei Qi, and Yuxin Yuan. 2017. CM-GANs: Cross-modal Generative Adversarial Networks for Common Representation Learning. *CoRR* abs/1710.05106 (2017).

[19] J. Pennington, R. Socher, and C. Manning. 2014. GloVe: Global Vectors for Word Representation. In *EMNLP*. 1532–1543.

[20] C. Rashtchian, M. Young, P. Hodosh, and J. Hockenmaier. 2010. Collecting Image Annotations Using Amazon's Mechanical Turk. In *NAACL HLT 2010 Workshop on Creating Speech and Language Data with Amazon's Mechanical Turk*.

[21] N. Rasiwasia, J. Costa Pereira, E. Coviello, G. Doyle, G. Lanckriet, R. Levy, and N. Vasconcelos. 2010. A new approach to cross-modal multimedia retrieval.. In *ACM MM*. 251–260.

[22] Fumin Shen, Yang Yang, Li Liu, Wei Liu, and Heng Tao Shen Dacheng Tao. 2017. Asymmetric Binary Coding for Image Search. *IEEE Transactions on Multimedia* (2017). https://doi.org/10.1109/TMM.2017.2699863 doi:10.1109/TMM.2017.2699863.

[23] K. Simonyan and A. Zisserman. 2014. Very Deep Convolutional Networks for Large-Scale Image Recognition. *CoRR* abs/1409.1556 (2014).

[24] Jingkuan Song, Tao He, Lianli Gao, Xing Xu, Alan Hajalic, and Heng Tao Shen. 2018. Binary Generative Adversarial Networks for Image Retrieval. *AAAI*.

[25] Jingkuan Song, Tao He, Lianli Gao, Xing Xu, and Heng Tao Shen. 2018. Deep Region Hashing for Efficient Large-scale Instance Search from Images. *AAAI*.

[26] N. Srivastava and R. Salakhutdinov. 2012. Learning representations for multimodal data with deep belief nets. In *ICML Workshop*.

[27] Bokun Wang, Yang Yang, Xing Xu, Alan Hanjalic, and Heng Tao Shen. 2017. Adversarial Cross-Modal Retrieval. In *ACM MM*. 154–162.

[28] K. Wang, R. He, L. Wang, W. Wang, and T. Tan. 2011. Joint Feature Selection and Subspace Learning for Cross-Modal Retrieval. *TPAMI* 38, 10 (2011), 2010–2023.

[29] K. Wang, R. He, W. Wang, L. Wang, and T. Tan. 2013. Learning coupled feature spaces for cross-modal matching. In *ICCV*. 2088–2095.

[30] L. Wang, Y. Li, and S. Lazebnik. 2016. Learning Deep Structure-Preserving Image-Text Embeddings. In *CVPR*. 5005–5013.

[31] Qian Wang and Ke Chen. 2017. Zero-Shot Visual Recognition via Bidirectional Latent Embedding. 124, 3 (2017), 356–383.

[32] W. Wang, R. Arora, K. Livescu, and J. Bilmes. 2015. On deep multi-view representation learning. In *ICML*. 1083–1092.

[33] Yunchao Wei, Yao Zhao, Canyi Lu, Shikui Wei, Luoqi Liu, Zhenfeng Zhu, and Shuicheng Yan. 2017. Cross-Modal Retrieval With CNN Visual Features: A New Baseline. *IEEE Trans. Cybernetics* 47, 2 (2017), 449–460.

[34] Xing Xu, Li He, Huimin Lu, Lianli Gao, and Yanli Ji. 2018. Deep Adversarial Metric Learning for Cross-Modal Retrieval. *World Wide Web* (2018). https://doi.org/10.1007/s11280-018-0541-x

[35] Xing Xu, Fumin Shen, Yang Yang, Heng Tao Shen, Li He, and Jingkuan Song. 2016. Cross-modal Retrieval with Label Completion. In *Proceedings of the 2016 ACM on Multimedia Conference (MM '16)*. 302–306.

[36] Xing Xu, Fumin Shen, Yang Yang, Heng Tao Shen, and Xuelong Li. 2017. Learning Discriminative Binary Codes for Large-scale Cross-modal Retrieval. *IEEE Trans. Image Processing* 26, 5 (2017), 2494–2507.

[37] X. Xu, Y. Yang, A. Shimada, R. Taniguchi, and L. He. 2015. Semi-supervised coupled dictionary learning for cross-modal retrieval in internet images and texts.. In *ACM MM*. 847–850.

[38] F. Yan and K. Mikolajczyk. 2015. Deep correlation for matching images and text. In *CVPR*. 3441–3450.

[39] Yang Yang, Fumin Shen, Heng Tao Shen, Hanxi Li, and Xuelong Li. 2015. Robust discrete spectral hashing for large-scale image semantic indexing. *IEEE Transactions on Big Data* 1, 4 (2015), 162–171.

[40] Li Zhang, Tao Xiang, and Shaogang Gong. 2017. Learning a Deep Embedding Model for Zero-Shot Learning. In *CVPR*. 3010–3019.

Cross-Modal Retrieval Using Deep De-correlated Subspace Ranking Hashing

Kevin Joslyn
University of Central Florida
Orlando, Florida
KevinJoslyn@knights.ucf.edu

Kai Li
University of Central Florida
Orlando, Florida
kaili@cs.ucf.edu

Kien A. Hua
University of Central Florida
Orlando, Florida
kienhua@cs.ucf.edu

ABSTRACT

Cross-modal hashing has become a popular research topic in recent years due to the efficiency of storing and retrieving high-dimensional multimodal data represented by compact binary codes. While most cross-modal hash functions use binary space partitioning functions (e.g. the *sign* function), our method uses ranking-based hashing, which is based on numerically stable and scale-invariant rank correlation measures. In this paper, we propose a novel deep learning architecture called Deep De-correlated Subspace Ranking Hashing (DDSRH) that uses feature-ranking methods to determine the hash codes for the image and text modalities in a common hamming space. Specifically, DDSRH learns a set of de-correlated nonlinear subspaces on which to project the original features, so that the hash code can be determined by the relative ordering of projected feature values in a given optimized subspace. The network relies upon a pre-trained deep feature learning network for each modality, and a hashing network responsible for optimizing the hash codes based on the known similarity of the training image-text pairs. Our proposed method includes both architectural and mathematical techniques designed specifically for ranking-based hashing in order to achieve de-correlation between the bits, bit balancing, and quantization. Finally, through extensive experimental studies on two widely-used multimodal datasets, we show that the combination of these techniques can achieve state-of-the-art performance on several benchmarks.

CCS CONCEPTS

• **Information systems → Multimedia and multimodal retrieval**; *Learning to rank*; *Top-k retrieval in databases*; • **Computing methodologies** → Neural networks;

KEYWORDS

Multimodal retrieval; cross-modal hashing; image and text retrieval

ACM Reference Format:
Kevin Joslyn, Kai Li, and Kien A. Hua. 2018. Cross-Modal Retrieval Using Deep De-correlated Subspace Ranking Hashing. In *ICMR '18: 2018 International Conference on Multimedia Retrieval, June 11–14, 2018, Yokohama, Japan.* ACM, New York, NY, USA, 9 pages. https://doi.org/10.1145/3206025.3206066

ACM ISBN 978-1-4503-5046-4/18/06...$15.00
https://doi.org/10.1145/3206025.3206066

1 INTRODUCTION

The prevalence of digital and social media in modern society has created a world that is dominated by multimedia. For billions of people around the globe, images, stories, social posts and even videos are just a query and a click away. A relatively new but already popular research area inspired by the fresh abundance of multimedia is cross-modal hashing for multimodal retrieval. The problem is defined as follows: given a query from a certain modality (such as image or text), the goal is to retrieve relevant results from a database of another modality. Typical examples of cross-modal retrieval are using text to retrieve relevant images or vice versa (e.g. Google image search).

The K-nearest neighbors (kNN) problem is a classic problem that involves retrieving the k database items that are most similar to the query. The main issue with kNN is the high computational costs that can be attributed to the curse of dimensionality, especially when dealing with multimedia such as high-dimensional images and videos. In order to avoid making costly comparisons among examples in the original feature space, hashing for similarity search has become a popular dimensionality reduction technique. Through hashing, examples can be compared much more efficiently in a discrete (rather than continuous) hamming space of a much lower dimensionality.

Locality Sensitive Hashing (LSH) [10] introduced the concept of hashing for similarity search. Initially, methods in the LSH family relied on choosing random hyperplanes to separate the data points, where each hyperplane accounts for one hash bit and the hash bit is determined according to which side of the hyperplane the data point belongs. LSH is an example of a *data-independent* hashing method, since the hash function depends on randomization rather than the actual data. *Data-dependent* hashing methods are now the more common variety- these methods use either supervised or unsupervised learning algorithms to learn meaningful hash functions that are tailored to the data.

The problem of cross-modal retrieval is especially complex because it requires the comparison of two objects that exist in entirely different feature spaces. Thus, cross-modal hashing solutions must either determine an effective mapping from one modality to the other modalities, or a mapping from each modality to a common hamming space. In this work, we focus on the latter approach. Most cross-modal hashing methods generate hash codes by discretizing a continuous output space, most commonly by using the *sign* function to create a binary code. Instead, this work is motivated by the ideas introduced in [16], called *Linear Subspace Ranking Hashing* (LSRH). The idea is to learn a unique K-dimensional linear subspace for each hash "bit", such that we may generate a K-ary hash code. To determine each hash bit, the original data point is projected onto the corresponding K-dimensional subspace, and the hash bit is set equal to the index of the dimension with the maximum projection.

Although LSRH has achieved competitive performance on a number of cross-modal retrieval benchmarks, there are several limitations that need to be addressed. First, the use of strictly linear subspaces prevents the optimality that may be achieved by exploiting the nonlinearities of deep neural networks. Second, there is no explicit way for LSRH to make sure that multiple hash bits are uncorrelated, and it has to rely on boosting to implicitly reduce the code redundancy. Third, the hash codes generated by LSRH are not balanced, which can cause an underutilization of the available information capacity of an L- bit hash code. Finally, LSRH has no unified method for feature representation across modalities or datasets. The use of hand-crafted features (1) undermines the generalizability of the model, and (2) neglects the potential of supervised deep learning for feature representation that has proven to be powerful in many recent hierarchical deep learning methods [3–5, 12, 24].

In this paper, we introduce a novel deep neural network architecture for cross-modal hashing called Deep De-correlated Subspace Ranking Hashing (DDSRH) that addresses the above limitations of LSRH. First, by making use of deep neural networks, DDSRH is able to learn ranking subspaces that are more optimal due to their nonlinearity. We address correlation between the bits (i.e. bit redundancy) by abandoning the typical fully-connected model in favor of fully-connected sub-layers, with one sub-layer for each K–ary hash bit. Next, we counter the effects of unbalanced bit distributions by introducing a regularization term designed to encourage bit balance. A second regularization term is also added to improve the quantization performance of the model, which actually competes with the bit balance term in an effort to achieve an optimal balance of the terms. Finally, we create a unified feature representation by employing pre-trained image and text feature extractors to precede the hashing network and feed it with meaningful features that have benefited from supervised deep learning.

In this paper, we describe each of the aforementioned components in detail and evaluate the effectiveness of each technique by using each one in isolation and in combination with the others (see Section 4.3, Ablation Study.) We show that the overall model not only greatly outperforms LSRH, but furthermore achieves state-of-the-art results on two widely used datasets for cross-modal retrieval.

In summary, the major contributions of this paper are as follows:

- We propose a novel deep neural network architecture that is the first to use de-correlated nonlinear subspace ranking hashing for cross-modal retrieval.
- We introduce novel de-correlation, bit balancing, and quantization techniques that are specifically designed for hashing using subspace ranking, and evaluate the performance gains obtained by using each technique.
- We demonstrate through several experiments that DDSRH obtains state-of-the-art performance on two widely used datasets for cross-modal retrieval.

The remainder of the paper is organized in the following manner. Section 2 discusses related work, including both linear and nonlinear/deep cross-modal hashing methods. Section 3 describes our method in detail, including the architecture of the neural network and loss function formulation. Section 4 discusses the experiments and results, and Section 5 concludes the work.

2 RELATED WORK

The earliest work on cross-modal hashing was Cross-Modal Similarity Sensitive Hashing (CMSSH) [2], which uses boosting to sequentially learn linear hash functions for each modality. Other early cross-modal hashing methods include Cross-View Hashing (CVH) [15] and Co-Regularized Hashing (CRH) [28]. Since these pioneering works, cross-modal hashing research has split into several directions, summarized here.

Some methods, including Collective Matrix Factorization Hashing (CMFH) [8] and Latent Semantic Sparse Hashing (LSSH) [29] use matrix factorization methods to learn hash functions that bridge the modalities. Other methods were designed with scalability considerations at the forefront, including Inter-media hashing (IMH) [22], Semantic Correlation Maximization (SCM) [27], and Semantic Topic Multimodal Hashing (STMH) [23]. Quantized Correlation Hashing (QCH) [25] and Composite Correlation Quantization (CCQ) [19] are examples of methods that use quantization techniques for cross-modal hashing.

An emerging category of cross-modal hashing algorithms uses a two-stage learning framework that separates binary code learning from hash function learning. In the first stage, the binary codes for each training instance are discretely optimized by minimizing a loss function based on the similarity of the instances. In the second stage, the hash functions are learned for each modality by treating each of the optimized bits as a classification problem. Semantics-Preserving Hashing (SePH) [18] is a well-known approach that first learns the hash codes by minimizing the KL-divergence between the cross-modal similarity distribution and the hash code distribution. SePH then uses logistic regression to learn the hash functions for each modality. Label Preserving Multimedia Hashing (LPMH) [17] introduces a general loss function and optional bit balancing term to be used for the hash code learning, and it makes use of boosted decision trees for the hash function learning stage. Semantic Neighbor Graph Hashing (SNGH) [13] introduces a semantic neighbor graph to guide the hash code learning by introducing a fine-grained similarity metric based on the neighborhood structure of the graph and the semantic similarity of the instances.

Another increasingly popular direction for cross-modal hashing algorithms involves deep learning. Masci et al. [20] were the first to use parallel neural networks for cross-modal hashing. The general structure, involving one neural network for the text modality and a parallel network for the image modality, has been imitated and modified by more recent works, including the proposed DDSRH. Of these similar works, Deep Cross-Modal Hashing [12] was the first method to use deep neural networks to learn features and hash codes simultaneously. During each training iteration, similar image-text pairs are given the same hash code while just the image or the text feature parameters are learned. In the third step of each iteration, the image and text feature parameters are held constant while the hash codes are learned. Correlation Hashing Network (CHN) [3] was the first network to consider cosine max-margin loss for deep hashing methods, as well as quantization max-margin loss, which acts as a regularizer. Note that rather than learning feature and hash codes simultaneously, CHN pre-trains an image feature extractor and a text feature extractor, both of which become components of the final model. Our proposed method follows this same approach. Collective Deep Quantization (CDQ) [4] is the successor to CHN. The main difference is the use of a collective quantization "codebook" that is shared across modalities, which was seen to improve the quantizability of the deep representations and quality of the resulting hash codes.

One drawback of all of the aforementioned methods is that they are all dependent on exact feature values, which makes them arguably more susceptible to noise and variations. By contrast, our method belongs to a relatively new class of hash functions based on ranking operations, which are closely related to rank correlation measures. These techniques in particular are known to be robust against noise and variations [16, 26]. Even so, ranking-based hashing for cross-modal retrieval remains a very understudied area. Linear Subspace Ranking Hashing (LSRH) [16] was the first method to use ranking-based hash functions for the cross-modal retrieval problem. Inspired by Winner-Take-All (WTA) Hash [26] and Minwise Hash [1], LSRH generates K-ary hash bits that correspond to the maximum feature dimension for each feature subspace. Rather than using randomized subspaces in the original feature space like WTA and MinHash, LSRH learns optimal subspaces in a new feature space by using boosting for each linear hash function. To date, LSRH remains the only work of its kind to use ranking-based methods for cross-modal hashing, and it serves as the basis for this work.

In summary, the proposed DDSRH bridges the gap between the deep learning and ranking-based categories of cross-modal hashing algorithms, incorporating the core advantages of both. The following section explains the proposed method in detail.

3 DEEP DE-CORRELATED SUBSPACE RANKING HASHING

3.1 Problem Definition

Let $\mathcal{D}_\mathcal{X} = \mathrm{X} = \{\mathbf{x}_i\}_{i=1}^{N_\mathcal{X}}$ and $\mathcal{D}_\mathcal{Y} = \mathrm{Y} = \{\mathbf{y}_j\}_{j=1}^{N_\mathcal{Y}}$ be datasets of the image and text modalities, respectively, where $\mathbf{x}_i \in \mathcal{D}_\mathcal{X}$ is a $d_\mathcal{X}$-dimensional image and $\mathbf{y}_j \in \mathcal{D}_\mathcal{Y}$ is a $d_\mathcal{Y}$-dimensional text (set of tags). We also define $\mathrm{S} = \{s_{ij}\} \in \{0,1\}^{N_\mathcal{X} \times N_\mathcal{Y}}$ to be a set of similarity labels, where $s_{ij} = 1$ if $\mathbf{x}_i$ is similar to $\mathbf{y}_j$ (by belonging to the same concept), and 0 otherwise. The goal is to learn two sets of hash functions $H_* = \{h_*^{(l)}\}_{l=1}^{L}$, one for each modality, to transform the input images and texts into a common K-ary Hamming space, such that similar image-text pairs are hashed to codes that are close together in Hamming space while dissimilar image-text pairs are hashed to codes that are far apart. In this paper, * is a placeholder for the modality when we need not refer to one modality specifically (thus it can refer to modality $\mathcal{X}$ or $\mathcal{Y}$), and likewise Z_* refers to either dataset X or Y. Finally, $\mathbf{W}_*$ represents the learned parameters for the given modality.

In the following sections, K refers to the number of subspace dimensions we seek to optimize, resulting in a K-ary hash code. L refers to the number of K-ary digits in a hash code, while $L_B = L \times \lceil \log_2 K \rceil$ is the number of binary bits used to represent the code. N refers to the number of examples in question (for example, training instances) The softmax function is denoted by $\sigma(x)$.

3.2 Ranking-Based Hashing

We consider a different category of ranking-based hash functions other than the well-studied sign or thresholding-based functions. Formally, the ranking-based hash function is defined as follows:

$$\begin{aligned} h(\mathbf{z}_*; \mathbf{W}_*) &= \underset{\mathbf{h}}{\operatorname{argmax}}\, \mathbf{h}^T \phi(\mathbf{z}_*; \mathbf{W}_*) \\ \text{s.t. } \mathbf{h} &\in \{0,1\}^K, \mathbf{1}^T\mathbf{h} = 1 \end{aligned} \tag{1}$$

where $\mathbf{z}_* \in \mathcal{D}_*$ is the input sample (text or image) and $\phi(\mathbf{z}_*)$ is an embedding of the input. Note that the 1-of-K constraint ensures that there is only a single 1 in the output hash code corresponding to the maximum entry of the embedded data point, while the remaining entries are 0s. Therefore, one instance of the above hash function encodes a K-ary hash code corresponding to the maximum index of data embeddings. To obtain a length-L hash code, one needs to apply the hash function to L different embeddings.

Hash functions based on ranking operations are closely related to rank correlation measures which are known to be robust against noise and variations [16, 26]. In fact, as long as the implicit ordering of embedded features remains the same, the hash code will not change.

Note that the hash functions used in LSRH and WTA are special cases of the above hash function. LSRH defines each embedding function as $\phi(\mathbf{z}_*; \mathbf{W}_*) = \mathbf{W}_*^T \mathbf{z}_*$, where $\mathbf{W}_* \in \mathbb{R}^{K \times d_*}$ defines a K-dimensional linear subspace used to rank the projected features. On the other hand, WTA's embedding function can be realized by using the same embedding function but setting the columns of $\mathbf{W}_*$ equal to columns randomly selected from a $d_* \times d_*$ identity matrix [16].

3.3 DDSRH

From (1), note that both LSRH and WTA use linear embedding functions for ϕ. DDSRH instead uses a nonlinear embedding function ϕ that can be used to reveal more discriminative nonlinear ranking structures that cannot be exposed in linear subspaces. We accomplish this by designing a deep neural network architecture to learn the nonlinear ranking subspaces. Such a design allows us to take advantage of both rank correlation measures and deep learning structures to learn the most discriminative ranking-based hash functions.

DDSRH also makes use of novel de-correlation, bit balancing and quantization approaches that are designed specifically for the K-ary encoding scheme and the subspace ranking problem. By comparison, LSRH does not consider bit balancing or quantization loss, and it has to rely upon boosting for bit de-correlation rather than explicit bit de-correlation which is made possible with DDSRH. In the following subsection, we introduce the objective function and its components, which are responsible for ensuring cross-modal similarity, bit balancing, and quantization. We leave bit de-correlation to section 3.8 because it is an architectural modification rather than a term in the objective function.

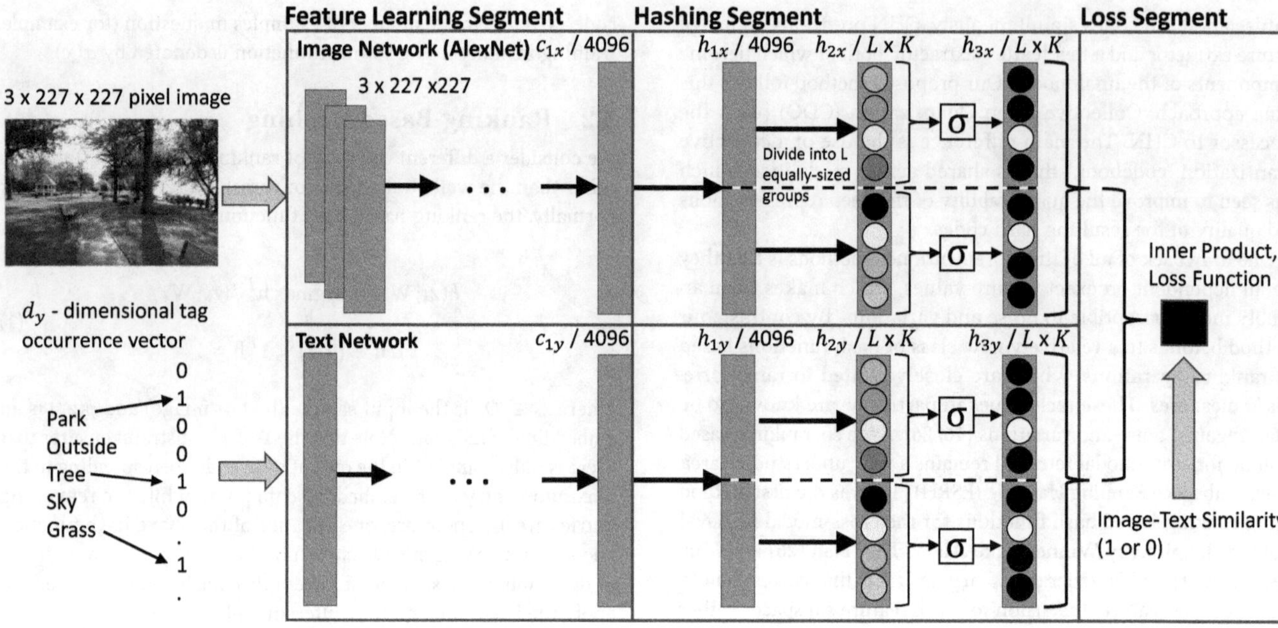

Figure 1: Full Network structure for deep cross-modal hashing. The network consists of three segments: the feature learning segment, the hashing segment, and the loss segment. Inputs to the network are given by the wide arrows, while solid black arrows indicate fully-connected layers or groups. Layers are given a label (e.g. $h_{1\mathcal{X}}$) and a dimension. The softmax function is given by σ, and is applied to groups of neurons of size K. Neuron values are depicted in grayscale, with black indicating low values and white indicating high values (relative to the group). Assuming that the first neuron in each group is at index 0, the corresponding hash code for both the image and the text would be the quaternary code 21.

3.4 Objective Function

The objective function has three components: a cross-modal similarity loss term, a bit balancing term, and a quantization loss term.

3.4.1 Cross-Modal Similarity. Each cross-modal training pair is given a binary similarity label s_{ij} that defines whether the pair is similar or not similar. Incorporating the ranking hash function h from (1), we define the loss term for a single training pair as

$$l(\mathbf{x}_i, \mathbf{y}_j) = \left(\frac{1}{L}\mathbf{b}_{i\mathcal{X}}^T \mathbf{b}_{j\mathcal{Y}} - s_{ij}\right)^2, \tag{2}$$

where $\mathbf{b}_{i\mathcal{X}}, \mathbf{b}_{j\mathcal{Y}} \in \{0,1\}^{LK} = [h^1(\cdot)^T\ h^2(\cdot)^T\ ..\ h^L(\cdot)^T]^T$ are the vectorized hash codes for image $\mathbf{x}_i$ and text $\mathbf{y}_j$ respectively, and $h^l(\cdot)$ denotes $h^l(\mathbf{x}_i; \mathbf{W}_\mathcal{X})$ for images and $h^l(\mathbf{y}_j; \mathbf{W}_\mathcal{Y})$ for texts respectively. Note that although the length of the hash code is represented as $L \times K$ bits only for mathematical convenience, the actual binary code length is only $L \times \log_2 K$.

We can interpret (2) as follows. First, it is easy to see that the result of the subtraction operation is a scalar between $[-1, 1]$, due to the constraints placed on $\mathbf{h}$ in (1). If the image-text pair are similar, we would like the result of $\mathbf{b}_{i\mathcal{X}}^T \mathbf{b}_{j\mathcal{Y}}$ to be very close to L so that the loss goes to 0. For this to occur, the positions of the '1' values in $\mathbf{b}_{i\mathcal{X}}$ and $\mathbf{b}_{j\mathcal{Y}}$ should be the same, indicating an agreement on the indices of the maximum embedded feature dimensions across modalities. Otherwise, if the image-text pair are dissimilar, we would like the result of $\mathbf{b}_{i\mathcal{X}}^T \mathbf{b}_{j\mathcal{Y}}$ to be very close to 0, indicating a difference in the positions of the '1' values in $\mathbf{b}_{i\mathcal{X}}$ and $\mathbf{b}_{j\mathcal{Y}}$. Ultimately, this criterion accomplishes the goal of pushing the hash codes for similar image-text pairs close together, and pulling the hash codes of dissimilar image-text pairs far apart.

The overall similarity loss term $\mathcal{S}$ is the aggregate similarity loss for all $s_{ij} \in \mathrm{S}$ and is given as follows:

$$\mathcal{S}(\mathbf{W}_\mathcal{X}, \mathbf{W}_\mathcal{Y}) = \left\|\frac{1}{L}\mathbf{B}_\mathcal{X}{}^T \mathbf{B}_\mathcal{Y} - \mathrm{S}\right\|_F^2, \tag{3}$$

where $\mathrm{S} \in \{0,1\}^{N \times N}$ is the similarity matrix with s_{ij} defined as in 3.1, and $\mathbf{B}_* \in \{0,1\}^{LK \times N}$ is the matrix of vectorized hash codes for all samples. Note that $\mathcal{S}$ is a function of $\mathbf{W}_\mathcal{X}$ and $\mathbf{W}_\mathcal{Y}$ due to the use of the hash function $h(\mathbf{z}_*; \mathbf{W}_*)$.

3.4.2 Bit Balancer. In addition to the similarity term $\mathcal{S}$, we will introduce a bit balancing term $\mathcal{B}$ to balance the distribution of the K-ary digits in the hash code and thus prevent underutilization of the information capacity of the code. Since most hashing algorithms deal with binary hash codes, they need only to balance the occurrence of 1's and 0's (or 1's and -1's) in the code. Thus one can achieve balance simply by minimizing $|\mathbf{B} \cdot \mathbf{1}|$, where $\mathbf{B} \in \{-1,1\}^{L \times N}$ is the matrix of binary codes and $\mathbf{1}$ is is a vector of 1's of size N.

Binary codes are actually a special case for our algorithm, which must attempt to balance the occurrence of all $\{0, 1, .., K-1\}$ in a K-ary hash code. Then, for each bit position $l \in \{1, 2, ..L\}$ in the hash code, we would like each $d \in \{0, 1, .., K-1\}$ to occur roughly N/K times across the N instances. We can achieve this by minimizing (4):

$$\mathcal{B}(\mathbf{W}_{\mathcal{X}}, \mathbf{W}_{\mathcal{Y}}) = \left\|\mathbf{B}_{\mathcal{X}} \cdot \mathbf{1} - \frac{N}{K} \cdot \mathbf{1}'\right\|_F^2 + \left\|\mathbf{B}_{\mathcal{Y}} \cdot \mathbf{1} - \frac{N}{K} \cdot \mathbf{1}'\right\|_F^2, \quad (4)$$

where $\mathbf{B}_* \in \{0,1\}^{LK \times N}$, $\mathbf{1}$ is a vector of 1's of size N, and $\mathbf{1}'$ is a vector of 1's of size LK. For further explanation, let $\mathbf{C} = \mathbf{B}_* \cdot \mathbf{1} \in \mathbb{R}^{LK \times 1} \geq 0$. Then $\mathbf{C}_i$ counts the number of occurrences of the K-ary digit $d = i \mod K$ in bit position $l = i/L$ across all N instances.

3.4.3 Quantization. For binary hash functions, quantization loss terms aim to achieve a maximum margin between instances classified on either side of the threshold value. Given the classical hash function $h(\mathbf{X}) = \text{sign}(\mathbf{W}_{\mathcal{X}}^T \mathbf{X})$, a good quantizer would encourage $\mathbf{W}_{\mathcal{X}}^T \mathbf{X}$ to be far from 0 to minimize the risk of similar instances being on either side of the threshold value and obtaining different hash codes. Of course, our algorithm does not use a threshold value to quantize the bits; rather, each hash code bit is assigned by using the argmax function over K values. Accordingly, our quantization loss term aims to maximize the gap between the maximum value and the other $K-1$ values. Note that although the implementation of our quantization loss term differs from the classical binary thresholding case, the motivation is the same: we wish to minimize the risk of similar instances obtaining different bit values by a narrow margin, while also minimizing the risk of dissimilar instances obtaining the same bit values by a narrow margin.

Because the formal equation is best explained after the network structure has been introduced, in (5) we simply refer to the quantization loss term as $Q(\mathbf{W}_{\mathcal{X}}, \mathbf{W}_{\mathcal{Y}})$. It is formally defined in (7).

3.4.4 Overall Objective Function. The overall objective is to learn parameters $\mathbf{W}_{\mathcal{X}}$ and $\mathbf{W}_{\mathcal{Y}}$ that minimize

$$\min \ \mathcal{S}(\mathbf{W}_{\mathcal{X}}, \mathbf{W}_{\mathcal{Y}}) + \alpha \mathcal{B}(\mathbf{W}_{\mathcal{X}}, \mathbf{W}_{\mathcal{Y}}) + \lambda Q(\mathbf{W}_{\mathcal{X}}, \mathbf{W}_{\mathcal{Y}}), \quad (5)$$

where $\mathcal{S}$ is the similarity loss term defined in (3), $\mathcal{B}$ is the bit balancing term defined in (4), Q is the quantization loss term to be defined in (7), and α and λ are hyperparameters of the algorithm. The following section describes how to optimize this equation.

3.5 Optimization

Unfortunately, due to the discontinuous and non-convex nature of the argmax term in (1), the objective function in (5) is difficult to optimize. Thus, we will reformulate (1) by using the softmax function to create a continuous probabilistic approximation to the ranking hash function:

$$h(\mathbf{z}; \mathbf{W}) \approx \sigma(\phi(\mathbf{z}; \mathbf{W})), \quad (6)$$

where σ represents the softmax function, and $*$'s are omitted to remove notational clutter. Now h still outputs a vector of size K, but the output values are continuous values between $[0,1]$ that sum to 1. Importantly, the smoothness of the softmax approximation can be tuned such that its output converges to the binary indicator vector $\mathbf{h}$ in (1).

In order to achieve a good set of nonlinear embedding functions $\{\phi_*^{(l)}\}_{l=1}^L$ for each modality, we propose the following hierarchical deep neural network which is the first to use de-correlated nonlinear subspace ranking hashing for cross-modal retrieval. We optimize the embeddings outputted by the neural network by combining the proposed similarity and bit balancing terms with novel adaptations of de-correlation and quantization measures for subspace ranking hashing, described in the following sections.

3.6 Network Architecture

Our deep neural network consists of two independently pre-trained feature learning networks, one for each modality, each followed by a hashing segment and connected by a cross-modal loss segment. A depiction of the full network during the cross-modal training stage is given in Fig. 1. In the figure, image-text pairs are shown being fed into the network along with a similarity label (inputs are given by wide arrows). A detailed explanation of each segment of the network is given in the following sections.

3.7 Feature Learning Segment

The feature learning segment is constructed by pre-training two independent classifier networks, one for each data modality. The structure of the image classifier is an AlexNet [14] convolutional neural network (CNN) with 5 convolutional layers and 3 fully-connected layers. The text classifier is a deep neural network with three hidden layers, each of size 2048. A rectifying linear unit (ReLU) and dropout are employed after each hidden layer.

Each classifier is trained on the appropriate modality of the dataset using binary cross entropy loss. After the classifiers have been trained, the features of the second-to-last fully-connected layer (denoted in Fig. 1 as layer c_{1*}) are useful as input to the hashing segment of the network. Thus, we effectively remove the output layer of the classifiers (the third fully-connected layer), resulting in the feature learning segment shown in Fig. 1. Layer c_{1*} is then connected to the hashing segment, described in the next section.

3.8 Hashing Segment

The hashing segment's purpose is to determine the hash value of the input image or text. It does this by learning L distinct K-dimensional subspaces, where L is the length of the K-ary hash code to be determined. Thus the output of the hashing segment is effectively the projection of the input onto each of the L latent subspaces.

Fig. 1 shows that the layers in the hashing segment can each be divided into L equally-sized groups, where each group corresponds to one subspace being learned and thus one hash bit. (In Fig. 1 we only show two such groups to conserve space). Thus layer h_{1*} is divided into L groups of size $4096/L$, while layers h_{2*} and h_{3*} are each divided into L groups of size K. Note that for each of the L groups of neurons in layer h_{2*}, we use the softmax function to transform the values such that for each group in layer h_{3*}, the sum of the outputs in that group is 1. To obtain the hash value of the input image/text, each group of neurons in layer h_{3*} reports the index of the neuron with the maximum output (shown by the white neurons in Fig. 1.) Assuming that the first neuron in each group is at index 0, the corresponding hash code for both the image and the text in Fig. 1 would be the quaternary code 21 (in practice the code would be longer for a network with more than two groups of neurons.)

3.8.1 De-correlation. It is important for each hash bit to contain information that is de-correlated, or independent from, the other hash bits in order to utilize the full information capacity of the hash code. This requirement motivates an important design characteristic of our deep network. Looking again at Fig. 1, observe that while layers c_{1*} and h_{1*} are fully-connected, only corresponding *groups* of neurons are fully- connected between layers h_{1*} and h_{2*}. Since each group is responsible for one hash bit, the lack of interconnections between the groups should greatly reduce information redundancy and correlation between the hash bits.

3.8.2 Quantization Loss Term. In section 3.4.3, we explained in non-mathematical terms the motivation and reasoning behind our quantization approach. In order to design a quantization loss term to suit our method, notice that each group of K outputs in layer h_{3*} sums to exactly 1. In the ideal case, we would like one output to be exactly 1, and the rest to be 0. To see how this relates to sign-thresholding in the binary quantization case, note that we can essentially reduce our approach to the binary case when we set $K = 2$. Then, the quantized value is determined by thresholding either output at 0.5 rather than 0.

Regardless of the subspace dimension K, we can encourage one output in h_{3*} to be close to 1 and the rest to be close to 0 by minimizing the following equation:

$$Q(\mathbf{W}_{\mathcal{X}}, \mathbf{W}_{\mathcal{Y}}) = -\left\|\mathbf{B}_{\mathcal{X}} - 0.5\right\|_1 - \left\|\mathbf{B}_{\mathcal{Y}} - 0.5\right\|_1 \quad (7)$$

where $\mathbf{B}_* = \sigma(\mathbf{W}_*^T \mathbf{Z}_*) \in [0,1]^{LK \times N}$ is the output of the final hashing layer h_{3*}. Since Q subtracts the distance from 0.5 for all elements of $\mathbf{B}_{\mathcal{X}}$ and $\mathbf{B}_{\mathcal{Y}}$, the quantization term is minimized when all of the outputs of h_{3*} are exactly 0 or 1.

3.9 Training the Network

Training consists of two stages: classifier pre-training, and cross-modal training. For the image classifier, we use a replica of AlexNet that has been pre-trained by The Berkeley Vision and Learning Center [1]on the ImageNet [21] dataset using Caffe [11], and fine-tune the weights for each of the experimental datasets. The text classifier weights are randomly initialized and trained only on each of the experimental datasets.

The proposed DDSRH model is implemented using Torch [7]. In the cross-modal training stage, the weights learned during the classifier pre-training stage are kept relatively constant by setting a low learning rate of 10^{-6} to all of the weights in the feature learning segment. Learning rates for the weights in the hashing segment begin at .05. After 10 epochs, this learning rate for these weights is decreased to .01 and after 50 epochs it is decreased to .005.

The cross-modal training stage is accomplished by feeding image-text pairs into the network, along with a similarity indicator (1 or 0). Note that the same validation and test sets that are used for the classifier pre-training phase are also used for the cross-modal training phase. In this work, we use stochastic gradient descent (SGD) to optimize the weights for our model. All models are trained using a momentum coefficient of 0.9 and without weight decay. We use a batch size of 200 training pairs during training, where 50 pairs are similar pairs and 150 pairs are dissimilar pairs. Using a validation set, we have selected α to be .015 and λ to be .25.

[1]Pretrained model is publicly available for download at https://github.com/BVLC/caffe/tree/master/models/bvlc_alexnet

4 EXPERIMENTS

4.1 Datasets

Brief descriptions of the datasets are given in the following subsections. Please note that the terms *label* (or *class label*) and *concept* are interchangeable. Also, note that the term *image-text couplet* specifically refers to an image from the database and its associated textual tags, while the term *training pair* instead refers to a image and a set of tags that are not necessarily associated.

4.1.1 MIRFLICKR. The MIRFLICKR-25000 dataset [9] consists of 25,000 image-text couplets, each of which is annotated with one or more of 24 semantic labels. Textual tags that occur less than 20 times are removed, and then couplets without tags are removed, resulting in 18,159 image-text couplets. Each set of tags is represented by a 1,075-dimensional bag-of-words vector, representing the 1,075 most common tags across the dataset. Following the experimental setup in CHN and CDQ [3, 4], we randomly select 1,000 image-text couplets for the query set, 1,000 couplets for the validation set, and 4,000 couplets for the training set.

4.1.2 NUS-WIDE. The NUS-WIDE dataset [6] consists of 269,648 image-text couplets, each of which is annotated with one or more of 81 concepts. Following the experimental setup in CHN and CDQ [3, 4], we use the 195,834 image-text couplets that belong to the 21 largest concepts. Tags are represented by a 1,000 bag-of-words vector that corresponds to the 1,000 most frequent tags. Again, following CHN and CDQ, we randomly select 500 couplets per concept for the training set, 100 couplets per concept for the query set, and 50 couplets per concept for the validation set. Couplets are only selected once to avoid duplicates.

4.1.3 Training Pairs. For the single-modality classifier pre-training phase, all images and texts except those that exist in the query set or validation set are used for training. During the cross-modal training phase, a *training pair* consists of any one image and any one text from the training set. *Dissimilar* training pairs are chosen at random by choosing pairs of images and texts that share no class labels. Rather than choosing the *similar* training pairs at random, we employ a similarity threshold function that is based on the following notion: similar training pairs whose image and text component share multiple class labels are more likely to be useful for training the network than similar pairs that share only one or two of many class labels. Thus we choose the *similar* training pairs by using the following similarity threshold function:

$$\tau(\mathbf{x}_i, \mathbf{y}_j) = \frac{C_i^T C_j}{0.5 * (sum(C_i) + sum(C_j))}, \quad (8)$$

where C_i and C_j are the binary class label vectors for image $\mathbf{x}_i$ and text $\mathbf{y}_j$ respectively, and $sum(C_i)$ is the number of classes to which example $\mathbf{x}_i$ belongs. Higher values of τ then indicate that $\mathbf{x}_i$ and $\mathbf{y}_j$ share a large fraction of the classes to which they belong. Since such pairs with high τ values are likely to be more useful for training the network, we only use similar training pairs that satisfy $\tau > 0.5$. We also use all dissimilar pairs where, trivially, $\tau = 0$.

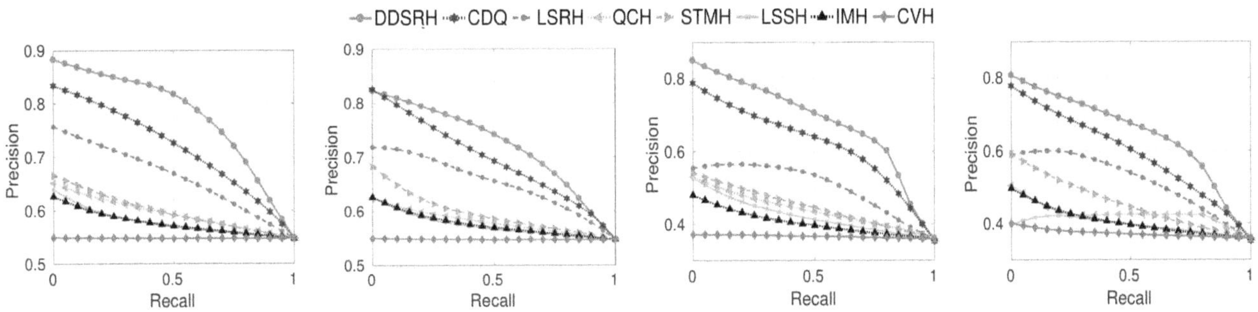

(a) MIRFLICKR, Text to Image (b) MIRFLICKR, Image to Text (c) NUS-WIDE, Text to Image (d) NUS-WIDE, Image to Text

Figure 2: Precision-recall curves using a 32-bit hash code. DDSRH outperforms the other baselines in all cases.

Table 1: Mean average precision at top 50 (mAP@50) results for our method versus baseline methods. The best results are shown in bold. The bit lengths given refer to the number of binary bits in the hash code L_B. All methods were tested using the same data splits and results reported are the average over five runs.

	MIRFLICKR						NUS-WIDE					
	Text query Image			Image query Text			Text query Image			Image query Text		
Method	16 bits	32 bits	64 bits	16 bits	32 bits	64 bits	16 bits	32 bits	64 bits	16 bits	32 bits	64 bits
QCH	0.7055	0.7015	0.6911	0.6651	0.6682	0.6655	0.6407	0.5993	0.5683	0.5383	0.6014	0.6171
STMH	0.6718	0.7055	0.7341	0.6844	0.7158	0.7370	0.5942	0.6081	0.6499	0.6274	0.6689	0.7200
LSSH	0.6934	0.7106	0.7160	0.6455	0.6679	0.6851	0.6034	0.6235	0.6468	0.5651	0.5716	0.5609
IMH	0.6878	0.6875	0.6823	0.6862	0.6883	0.6884	0.5344	0.5647	0.5731	0.5624	0.5990	0.6101
CVH	0.5957	0.6149	0.6395	0.5797	0.5834	0.5834	0.4304	0.4090	0.3972	0.5023	0.4886	0.4794
LSRH	0.7709	0.7825	0.7959	0.7323	0.7393	0.7465	0.5658	0.5799	0.5621	0.6437	0.6381	0.6383
CDQ	0.8429	0.8517	0.8567	**0.8414**	**0.8495**	**0.8542**	0.7900	0.8090	0.8102	0.7921	0.8115	0.8136
DDSRH	**0.8894**	**0.9020**	**0.9037**	0.8297	0.8431	0.8505	**0.8657**	**0.8887**	**0.8991**	**0.8159**	**0.8412**	**0.8463**

4.2 Comparison with Baselines

The retrieval task is divided into two categories: image-query-text and text-query-image. The first uses images as queries to retrieve the top k relevant texts from the database, and the second performs the opposite task. Here, we compare the performance of our model against other works by using mean average precision obtained at the top 50 results (mAP@50), as well as precision-recall curves.

Table 1 shows the mAP@50 results for our method versus CDQ [4], a state-of-the art deep nonlinear hashing method, and several linear hashing methods: QCH [25], STMH [23], LSSH [29], IMH [22], CVH [15], and LSRH [16]. For each experiment, we vary the number of bits from 16 to 64. All methods were trained and tested using our data splits. For the linear hashing methods, the input is the deep features outputted from our feature learning segment. For CDQ, we selected the most optimal parameters by using the same validation set used to tune our own model. It is important to note that every experiment in this paper is run five times so that each reported result is the average across the five runs.

DDSRH outperforms the compared methods by approximately 5% or more on both datasets for the text-query-image task. For the image-query-text task, DDSRH still shows competitive performance. In fact, on the NUS-WIDE dataset, DDSRH exhibits the highest image-query-text performance by a margin of approximately 4%. This shows that DDSRH can perform equally well on both large datasets such as NUS-WIDE and small datasets such as MIRFLICKR.

We believe that the overall lower performance seen on the image-query-text task is due to the semantic gap between images and texts in the datasets. In both datasets, texts belonging to the same category are more similar to each other than images belonging to the same category. As noted in [16, 29], since texts are better able to describe the semantic concept than images, higher mean average precision can be expected for text queries.

Fig. 2 shows the precision-recall curves for DDSRH compared to each baseline. It is evident that DDSRH obtains the best performance. Note that in each case, the precision for DDSRH remains relatively high until the recall reaches approximately 0.75, indicating that DDSRH is capable of returning more relevant results even for larger queries when many items are retrieved.

4.3 Ablation Study

To evaluate the effectiveness of the de-correlation, quantization, and bit balance components of our method, we ran several experiments in which each component was either utilized or not utilized. To eliminate the bit balance or quantization components, we simply set α or λ in (5) to 0 respectively. To eliminate the de-correlation component, we modify the neural network architecture such that

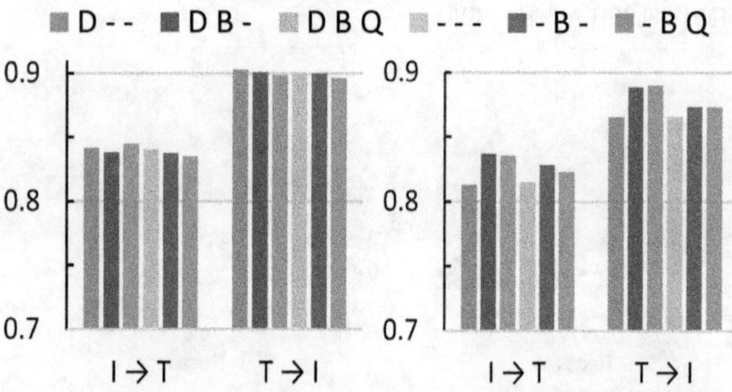

(a) MIRFLICKR (b) NUS-WIDE

Figure 3: mAP @ 50 observed by varying which features are turned "on" among de-correlation (D), bit balancing (B), and quantization (Q). In the legend, a capital letter denotes that the corresponding feature is turned "on". Image-query-text (I → T) and text-query-image (T → I) results are shown for both MIRFLICKR (a) and NUS-WIDE (b).

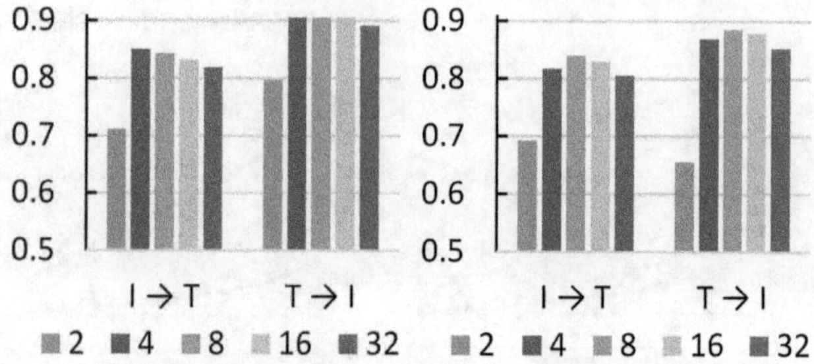

(a) MIRFLICKR (b) NUS-WIDE

Figure 4: mAP @ 50 observed by altering the subspace dimension K, while keeping the bit length of the hash code fixed at $L_B = 60$. Image-query-text (I → T) and text-query-image (T → I) results are shown for both MIRFLICKR (a) and NUS-WIDE (b).

h_{1*} and h_{2*} in Fig. 1 are fully connected. The experiments were run using a hash code length of 32 bits.

The mAP@50 results of this experiment are shown in Fig. 3. The legend indicates which features have been turned "on", where D = de-correlation, B = bit balance, and Q = quantization. Observing the results for NUS-WIDE, we find that the de-correlation component can be very powerful when coupled with bit balancing. While adding de-correlation alone or bit balancing alone only improves the performance by a small amount, adding both together improves the mAP by almost 3% for both retrieval tasks. The results for MIRFLICKR do not indicate the same improvements, which we speculate is due to the fact that it is a much smaller dataset and thus the model can still benefit from a fully-connected architecture with fewer regularization terms.

Finally, we observe that the addition of the quantization term does not consistently improve the mAP results. We believe that this is because the similarity loss term from (3) can only be truly minimized when the outputs of h_{3*} are exactly 0 or 1, such that no quantization loss would occur. Thus, even though the similarity loss term is designed to enforce similarity learning, it appears to be sufficient enough for quantization as well. Note that the results shown in Fig. 2 and Table 1 were gathered using de-correlation, bit balancing, and quantization (see Section 3.9 for the hyperparameter values that determine the weight of the bit balancing and quantization components.) However, as can be seen from Fig. 3, similar results could be achieved by setting λ in (5) to 0 and effectively removing the quantization component from the loss function.

4.4 Effect of Subspace Dimension

This experiment studies the effect of varying the different subspace dimension K. The experiment is designed such that for each value of K, the amount of information contained in the hash code is held constant by using the same number of binary bits, $L_B = 60$. To accomplish this, we test $K = 2^1, 2^2, .., 2^5$ and set the number of K-ary digits L as $L = 60/\log_2 K$. ($L_B = 60$ is chosen since 60 is a common multiple of 1 to 5.) Fig. 4 shows the effect of changing the subspace dimension K. It is evident that K values between 4 and 16 perform well for both MIRFLICKR and NUS-WIDE. This is similar to the findings in LSRH, which found the optimal subspace dimension to be 4 across several datasets. However, it is advisable to use cross-validation to choose the optimal subspace dimension for the given dataset.

5 CONCLUSION

In this paper, we have proposed a novel ranking-based cross-modal hashing method called Deep De-correlated Subspace Ranking Hashing, the first of its kind to exploit de-correlated nonlinear ranking-based hashing for cross-modal retrieval. The nonlinear, de-correlated subspaces learned by the deep neural network were proven to be much more effective at preserving the cross-modal similarity than the linear subspaces proposed in prior works. Additionally, we have proposed adaptations of de-correlation, bit balancing, and quantization for ranking-based hashing; and we have demonstrated that de-correlation and bit balancing in particular can significantly improve the performance of the model. Comparing DDSRH to several modern baselines, we have shown that DDSRH significantly outperforms current state-of-the-art methods on the text-query-image task, while achieving competitive or superior performance on the image-query-text task.

ACKNOWLEDGMENTS

This work is partially supported by Crystal Photonics, Inc. under research ID 1063271. Any opinions, findings, and conclusions expressed in this paper are those of the authors and do not necessarily reflect the views of Crystal Photonics, Inc.

REFERENCES

[1] Andrei Z Broder, Moses Charikar, Alan M Frieze, and Michael Mitzenmacher. 2000. Min-wise independent permutations. *J. Comput. System Sci.* 60, 3 (2000), 630–659.

[2] Michael M Bronstein, Alexander M Bronstein, Fabrice Michel, and Nikos Paragios. 2010. Data fusion through cross-modality metric learning using similarity-sensitive hashing. In *Computer Vision and Pattern Recognition (CVPR), 2010 IEEE Conference on.* IEEE, 3594–3601.

[3] Yue Cao, Mingsheng Long, and Jianmin Wang. 2016. Correlation hashing network for efficient cross-modal retrieval. *arXiv preprint arXiv:1602.06697* (2016).

[4] Yue Cao, Mingsheng Long, Jianmin Wang, and Shichen Liu. 2017. Collective Deep Quantization for Efficient Cross-Modal Retrieval.. In *AAAI*. 3974–3980.
[5] Yue Cao, Mingsheng Long, Jianmin Wang, Qiang Yang, and S Yu Philip. 2016. Deep Visual-Semantic Hashing for Cross-Modal Retrieval.. In *KDD*. 1445–1454.
[6] Tat-Seng Chua, Jinhui Tang, Richang Hong, Haojie Li, Zhiping Luo, and Yantao Zheng. 2009. NUS-WIDE: a real-world web image database from National University of Singapore. In *Proceedings of the ACM international conference on image and video retrieval*. ACM, 48.
[7] Ronan Collobert, Koray Kavukcuoglu, and Clément Farabet. 2011. Torch7: A matlab-like environment for machine learning. In *BigLearn, NIPS Workshop*.
[8] Guiguang Ding, Yuchen Guo, and Jile Zhou. 2014. Collective matrix factorization hashing for multimodal data. In *Proceedings of the IEEE Conference on Computer Vision and Pattern Recognition*. 2075–2082.
[9] Mark J Huiskes and Michael S Lew. 2008. The MIR flickr retrieval evaluation. In *Proceedings of the 1st ACM international conference on Multimedia information retrieval*. ACM, 39–43.
[10] Piotr Indyk and Rajeev Motwani. 1998. Approximate nearest neighbors: towards removing the curse of dimensionality. In *Proceedings of the thirtieth annual ACM symposium on Theory of computing*. ACM, 604–613.
[11] Yangqing Jia, Evan Shelhamer, Jeff Donahue, Sergey Karayev, Jonathan Long, Ross Girshick, Sergio Guadarrama, and Trevor Darrell. 2014. Caffe: Convolutional architecture for fast feature embedding. In *Proceedings of the 22nd ACM international conference on Multimedia*. ACM, 675–678.
[12] Qing-Yuan Jiang and Wu-Jun Li. 2017. Deep Cross-Modal Hashing. In *The IEEE Conference on Computer Vision and Pattern Recognition (CVPR)*.
[13] Lu Jin, Kai Li, Hao Hu, Guo-Jun Qi, and Jinhui Tang. 2018. Semantic Neighbor Graph Hashing for Multimodal Retrieval. *IEEE Transactions on Image Processing* 27, 3 (2018), 1405–1417.
[14] Alex Krizhevsky, Ilya Sutskever, and Geoffrey E Hinton. 2012. Imagenet classification with deep convolutional neural networks. In *Advances in neural information processing systems*. 1097–1105.
[15] Shaishav Kumar and Raghavendra Udupa. 2011. Learning hash functions for cross-view similarity search. In *IJCAI proceedings-international joint conference on artificial intelligence*, Vol. 22. 1360.
[16] Kai Li, Guojun Qi, Jun Ye, and Kien Hua. 2016. Linear subspace ranking hashing for cross-modal retrieval. *IEEE transactions on pattern analysis and machine intelligence* (2016).
[17] Kai Li, Guo-Jun Qi, and Kien A Hua. 2017. Learning label preserving binary codes for multimedia retrieval: A general approach. *ACM Transactions on Multimedia Computing, Communications, and Applications (TOMM)* 14, 1 (2017), 2.
[18] Zijia Lin, Guiguang Ding, Mingqing Hu, and Jianmin Wang. 2015. Semantics-preserving hashing for cross-view retrieval. In *Proceedings of the IEEE Conference on Computer Vision and Pattern Recognition*. 3864–3872.
[19] Mingsheng Long, Yue Cao, Jianmin Wang, and Philip S Yu. 2016. Composite correlation quantization for efficient multimodal retrieval. In *Proceedings of the 39th International ACM SIGIR conference on Research and Development in Information Retrieval*. ACM, 579–588.
[20] Jonathan Masci, Michael M Bronstein, Alexander M Bronstein, and Jürgen Schmidhuber. 2014. Multimodal similarity-preserving hashing. *IEEE transactions on pattern analysis and machine intelligence* 36, 4 (2014), 824–830.
[21] Olga Russakovsky, Jia Deng, Hao Su, Jonathan Krause, Sanjeev Satheesh, Sean Ma, Zhiheng Huang, Andrej Karpathy, Aditya Khosla, Michael Bernstein, et al. 2015. Imagenet large scale visual recognition challenge. *International Journal of Computer Vision* 115, 3 (2015), 211–252.
[22] Jingkuan Song, Yang Yang, Yi Yang, Zi Huang, and Heng Tao Shen. 2013. Inter-media hashing for large-scale retrieval from heterogeneous data sources. In *Proceedings of the 2013 ACM SIGMOD International Conference on Management of Data*. ACM, 785–796.
[23] Di Wang, Xinbo Gao, Xiumei Wang, and Lihuo He. 2015. Semantic Topic Multimodal Hashing for Cross-Media Retrieval.. In *IJCAI*. 3890–3896.
[24] Wei Wang, Beng Chin Ooi, Xiaoyan Yang, Dongxiang Zhang, and Yueting Zhuang. 2014. Effective multi-modal retrieval based on stacked auto-encoders. *Proceedings of the VLDB Endowment* 7, 8 (2014), 649–660.
[25] Botong Wu, Qiang Yang, Wei-Shi Zheng, Yizhou Wang, and Jingdong Wang. 2015. Quantized Correlation Hashing for Fast Cross-Modal Search.. In *IJCAI*. 3946-3952.
[26] Jay Yagnik, Dennis Strelow, David A Ross, and Ruei-sung Lin. 2011. The power of comparative reasoning. In *Computer Vision (ICCV), 2011 IEEE International Conference on*. IEEE, 2431–2438.
[27] Dongqing Zhang and Wu-Jun Li. 2014. Large-Scale Supervised Multimodal Hashing with Semantic Correlation Maximization.. In *AAAI*, Vol. 1. 7.
[28] Yi Zhen and Dit-Yan Yeung. 2012. Co-regularized hashing for multimodal data. In *Advances in neural information processing systems*. 1376–1384.
[29] Jile Zhou, Guiguang Ding, and Yuchen Guo. 2014. Latent semantic sparse hashing for cross-modal similarity search. In *Proceedings of the 37th international ACM SIGIR conference on Research & development in information retrieval*. ACM, 415–424.

Learning Multilevel Semantic Similarity for Large-Scale Multi-Label Image Retrieval

Ge Song
Nanjing University of Aeronautics and Astronautics
Nanjing, China
sunge@nuaa.edu.cn

Xiaoyang Tan
Nanjing University of Aeronautics and Astronautics
Nanjing, China
x.tan@nuaa.edu.cn

ABSTRACT

We present a novel Deep Supervised Hashing with code operation (DSOH) method for large-scale multi-label image retrieval. This approach is in contrast with existing methods in that we respect both the intention gap and the intrinsic multilevel similarity of multi-labels. Particularly, our method allows a user to simultaneously present multiple query images rather than a single one to better express her intention, and correspondingly a separate sub-network in our architecture is specifically designed to fuse the query intention represented by each single query. Furthermore, as in the training stage, each image is annotated with multiple labels to enrich its semantic representation, we propose a new margin-adaptive triplet loss to learn the fine-grained similarity structure of multi-labels, which is known to be hard to capture. The whole system is trained in an end-to-end manner, and our experimental results demonstrate that the proposed method is not only able to learn useful multilevel semantic similarity-preserving binary codes but also achieves state-of-the-art retrieval performance on three popular datasets.

CCS CONCEPTS

• **Information systems → Image search**;

KEYWORDS

Multi-Label Image Retrieval; Hashing; Deep Learning

ACM Reference Format:
Ge Song and Xiaoyang Tan. 2018. Learning Multilevel Semantic Similarity for Large-Scale Multi-Label Image Retrieval. In *Proceedings of 2018 International Conference on Multimedia Retrieval (ICMR '18)*. ACM, New York, NY, USA, 9 pages. https://doi.org/10.1145/3206025.3206027

1 INTRODUCTION

With the popularization of social media and the explosive growth of the web images, content-based image retrieval, which aims to search the images displaying the same objects categories or visual content as the query, has attracted increasing attention. The field has a wide range of application scenarios (e.g., product search, automatic image annotation) but is challenging as well. There are three types of difficulties commonly encountered in practice [32]: the first is known as semantic gap, which is originated from the limited representative of low-level visual features for high-level semantic concepts; the second one concerns about the storage and retrieval efficiency due to the large-scale data to be retrieved; last but not the least, the user's intention is usually hard to be precisely expressed as the expected visual content by a query at hand, which is known as intention gap in literature and is less studied compared to the previous two.

One of the most recent popular techniques to address these issues is the method of deep hashing [2, 13, 16, 18, 21, 28]. It combines the advantages of the feature learning capability of deep convolutional neural networks and the low storage and computational cost of the hashing method to map images into compact binary codes that preserve semantic similarity. In this sense, deep hashing methods address both the semantic gap and the computational efficiency issue of image retrieval but leave the third challenge, i.e., the intention gap, mostly untouched. As a matter of fact, it is almost unrealistic to rely only on a single image to accurately reflect the complex query intention of a user. In literatures, the intention gap is often tackled with multiple alternative query formations, e.g., sketch-based [20, 24, 26, 29] and image-text [7, 12]. Such alternatives serve to be the complement to the original query and allow the user to express her query intention in more flexible ways. Unfortunately, these methods may not always work, for example, under the situations when users are not good at sketching. In addition, they impose an extra burden to learning algorithms to handle different modal data.

To alleviate such problems and inspired by the previous work [12], we propose to leverage data from the same modal to augment query semantic, i.e., allowing a user to freely select multiple query images (e.g., a 'bicycle' image and 'person' image) to express more complex query intention (e.g., 'a person riding a bicycle'). Another way to narrow the intention gap is by exploiting semantic information of each image. Previous work [7] showed that there exists high consistency between users' query intention and human-annotated region-level captions, which means that the labels of query images have a close connection with the user's intention. Fortunately, nowadays many images are associated with more than one

ICMR '18, June 11–14, 2018, Yokohama, Japan

ACM ISBN 978-1-4503-5046-4/18/06...$15.00
https://doi.org/10.1145/3206025.3206027

tags (referred as multi-label) which provide a valuable rich semantic description of the corresponding image.

However, multi-label image retrieval is not straightforward, and query images with multiple labels may actually enlarge the intention gap, as the multiple labels would increase the entropy of user's intention over those labels. Another issue lies in the inherent complexity of the similarity between multi-label images, which involves the measurement of similarity not only at the image-level but the semantic (label) level as well. Many early deep hashing schemes [1, 3, 14, 15, 18–20, 22, 25] are designed for single-label images, which only concern about the preservation of simple binary semantic similarity (i.e., similar or dissimilar), and the Hamming distance between the learned codes cannot accurately reflect the hierarchical relevance in semantics.

Several more recent deep hashing methods [13, 21, 28, 31] have specifically devoted to the topic of multi-label image retrieval. One popular way for this is to explicitly model the similarity between multi-labels, for example, by forcing the codes of 'dog+person' and 'dog+cat' images as close as possible to those of 'dog' images. One side effect of imposing such constraints in the semantic space is that the learned hashing codes are prone to be too ambiguous to express fine-grained concepts, i.e., making the companying individual concepts (e.g., the person' and 'cat' in the previous example) less distinguishable in the representation space. Moreover, due to the imbalance and sparsity problem commonly encountered in multi-label image retrieval, the learned codes tend to be biased to only a few tags. This urges the need to construct more informative codes to respect the complex similarity structure involved in such conditions.

In this work, we introduce a novel deep supervised hashing with code operation (DSOH) for multi-label image retrieval. An overview of the proposed framework is illustrated in Fig. 1. To simultaneously deal with the intention gap problem and learn multilevel similarity of multi-label images, a specific sub-network in our approach is designed to fuse multiple codes at the semantic level, which is named code operation. In training phase, it is able to generate codes that contain rich semantic information to reflect the inherent complex similarity structure. For this, a new margin-adaptive triplet loss is proposed to learn the fine-grained similarity among images with multiple labels. This loss, along with the weighted cross-entropy classification loss, is employed to guide the end-to-end training of the model. While in the testing phase, this sub-network allows a user to present multiple images to express her intention better. Our main contributions are summarised as follows:

- A novel deep hashing method, named DSOH, is proposed to learn multilevel semantic similarity-preserving and operable binary codes for multi-label image retrieval. Unlike the previous hashing methods that ignore the *intention gap* problem in retrieval, a new Code Operation Network is designed to perform the 'union,' 'intersect' and 'substract' operations on semantic concepts of multiple query image codes, which effectively enables users to expand their query intention in a more flexible and friendly manner.
- A new margin-adaptive triplet loss is introduced to capture fine-grained multilevel similarity among images with multiple labels.
- Both standard multi-label retrieval task and complex semantic retrieval tasks are conducted using the proposed DSOH approach on three multi-label image datasets, and state-of-the-art retrieval performance is achieved.

The remainder of this paper is organized as follows. We first discuss related work in section 2. The DSOH model is detailed in section 3, and experimental results are given in section 4. The paper is concluded in section 5.

2 RELATED WORK

Recently several deep hashing schemes [13, 20, 21, 28, 31] have been proposed to learn efficient binary codes for multi-label image retrieval. DSRH (Deep Semantic Ranking based Hashing) [31] tries to learn hashing functions that preserve multilevel semantic similarity via optimizing an adaptively weighted triplet loss which aims to penalize undesired orders with different similarity degrees. IAH (Instance-Aware Hashing) [13] focuses on learning instance-aware hashing for multi-label images with weighted triplet loss functions, in which images are represented by multiple pieces of semantic binary codes corresponds to different categories. MSDH (Multi-label Supervised Deep Hashing) [21] uses multi-layer non-linear transformations as the hashing function and learns similarity via weighted pairwise loss, while DMSSPH (Deep Multilevel Semantic Similarity Preserving Hashing) [28] designs a pairwise loss with adaptive margins that imposes constraints on the distance between the learned codes.

Although most of these supervised hashing methods are successful in performing multi-label semantic retrieval to some extent, seldom of them have attempted to exploit the learn codes to express complex query intention. Closely related works are [7, 12, 23, 30]. Among them, [7] learns a joint embedding of visual and textual cues, allowing one to query the database using a text modifier in addition to editing the query image for semantic retrieval, and [30] introduces a memory-augmented Attribute Manipulation Network to manipulate image representation at the attribute level with a given set of attribute tags for fashion search. Both methods allow users to enrich their query intention by adjusting image representation with directly provided semantic information, the success which, however, heavily depends on the skill of users when using these tools.

3 THE PROPOSED APPROACH

In this section, we first give the notations used in this paper. And then the configurations of the proposed DSOH is detailed, including two sub-networks and the corresponding loss function.

3.1 The problem definition

Assume that we are given a set of N images $\{I_n\}_{n=1}^{N}$. Each image I_n is associated with C classes and its corresponding label l_n is denoted as a binary vector $\{0, 1\}^C$. Each image is

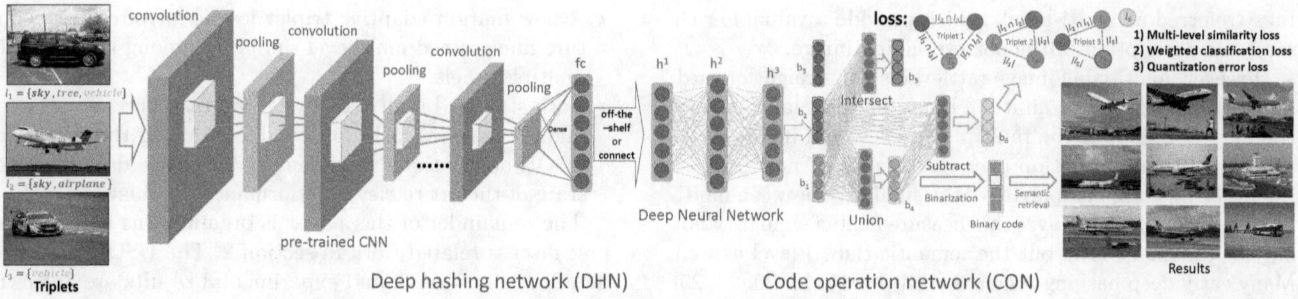

Figure 1: The architecture of the proposed deep supervised hashing network with code operation (DSOH), which includes two sub-networks, one deep hashing network (DHN), and one code operation network (CON). In the training phase, the hashing network takes as input a triplet images I_1,I_2,I_3 and their labels and outputs correspondingly three hashing codes b_1, b_2, b_3, which are then processed by the CON network with three types of code operations, i.e., union, substraction and intersection, respectively. The resulting codes can be used in the testing phase for multi-label image retrieval.

also represented by a D-dimensional visual features $x_i \in R^D$. Our goal is to learn a set of K ($K \ll D$) hashing functions $h_i(x), i = 1...K$, each of which maps a given visual feature x to a binary code $\{-1, 1\}^1$ and jointly they forms a K-dimensional hashing codes $h(x) = [h_1(x), h_2(x), \ldots, h_k(x)]$ which the semantic similarity among images is preserved.

3.2 Deep Hashing Network

Our deep hashing network (DHN) consists of a CNN-based feature learner and a fully-connect deep neural network (DNN). The CNN-based feature learner we adopted is the commonly-used CNN model such as VGG and ResNet pre-trained on the ImageNet. The structure of DNN with M layers is detailed as follows,

$$\begin{aligned} h^1 &= \tanh(w^1 x + bias^1) \\ h^m &= \tanh(w^{m-1} x + bias^1) \\ h^M &= \tanh(w^M h^{M-1} + bias^M) \end{aligned} \tag{1}$$

where x denotes feature vectors from the outputs of the last layer of CNN (i.e., $x = f_{CNN}(I)$, where f_{CNN} is a CNN network.), h^m and w^m respectively being the output and the weights of the m-th layer. The hashing codes can be obtained with a thresholding process on the output of DNN:

$$b = sign(h(x)) = \begin{cases} 1 , h(x) > 0 \\ -1 , h(x) \leq 0 \end{cases} \tag{2}$$

3.3 Code Operation Network

The learned codes of previous semantic hashing methods are independent and cannot be used collaboratively to express more complex queries. Therefore a code operation network (CON) is designed based on the output of the deep hashing network to manipulate them at the semantic level. Three types of code operation are supported in our work, i.e., union, substraction and intersection, all of which are the pairwise operator which takes in a pair of hashing codes and transforms them into a new one. For two codes $h(x_1)$ and $h(x_2)$, a union operator f_u fuses them into one $h_{x_{1\vee 2}} = f_u(h(x_1), h(x_2))$ with label $l_u = l_1 \oplus l_2 = l_1 \cup l_2$; a intersect f_t to fuse them into codes $h_{x_{1\wedge 2}} = f_t(h(x_1), h(x_2))$ with label $l_t = l_1 \otimes l_2$, defined as $l_1 \cap l_2$; and a substractor f_s substracts $h(x_1)$ with $h(x_2)$ to give $h_{x_{1\setminus 2}} = f_s(h(x_1), h(x_2))$ with label $l_s = l_1 \ominus l_2$, which is equal to $l_1 - l_1 \cap l_2$ if $|l_1| > |l_1 \cap l_2|$, and $l_s = l_1$ otherwise.

Union and Intersection Operation. Given two hashing codes $h(x_1)$, $h(x_2)$, both the union and intersection operation are defined as a linear function as follows:

$$h_{x_{1\vee 2}} = f_u(h(x_1), h(x_2)) \equiv W_u[h(x_1), h(x_2)] \tag{3}$$

$$h_{x_{1\wedge 2}} = f_t(h(x_1), h(x_2)) \equiv W_t[h(x_1), h(x_2)] \tag{4}$$

where $[h_1, h_2]$ denotes the concatenation operation, W_u, W_t are two matrices to be learnt for union and intersection respectively, and $h_{x_{1\vee 2}}, h_{x_{1\wedge 2}}$ are the fusion codes with label $l_1 \oplus l_2$ and $l_1 \otimes l_2$ respectively.

Substraction Operation. The situation for the substraction operation can be tricky - it is not a good practice to randomly generating a training pairs for it as in the case of union and intersection, because $l_1 \cap l_2 = \emptyset$ is meaningless for $l_1 - l_1 \cap l_2$. To handle this problem, we cascade the substraction to the union operation and define it as follows:

$$h_{x_{1\vee 2\setminus 2}} = f_s(h_{x_{1\vee 2}}, h(x_2)) \equiv W_s[h_{x_{1\vee 2}}, h(x_2)] \tag{5}$$

where W_s is the parameter matrix for the substraction operator, $h_{x_{1\vee 2\setminus 2}}$ is the subtracted code with multi-label $l_1 \oplus l_2 \ominus l_2$.

The advantages of operating codes are three folds: first, through code operator network, feature sets can be augmented in training, which effectively alleviates the imbalance and sparsity problem of multi-label learning; second, one can easily construct useful triplets using codes operation to capture more complicate similarity structure of data. For example, one can use the union operation to combine any two concepts (even though they rarely appear together, and hence it is difficult to obtain their training samples) and to generate the corresponding hashing codes; and finally, complex similarity level can be simulated with the three basic operations. As we will see, this is useful in handle the multilevel similarity problem in the multi-label context.

3.4 Loss Function

The goal of DSOH is to learn binary codes that preserve multilevel semantic similarity of images. i.e., the codes of *very similar* items should be as close as possible, while the codes of *normally similar* images should be a certain distance away, and those of *dissimilar* images very far away. Besides, to facilitate the code operation at the semantic level, the generated hashing codes should be discriminative. For these purposes, the loss function in this work is designed based on the following criterions: 1) the distance between the learned codes should be adaptive according to their similarity levels; 2) the hashing codes corresponding to different concepts should be distinguishable in the semantic space.

Multi-level similarity loss. One commonly used similarity measurement for hashing codes is the Hamming distance (denoted as d_H), which counts how many bits are different for a given pair of hashing codes b_1 and b_2. Intuitively, the more similar their semantics are (i.e., share more number of labels), the closer their learned codes are. We formalize this as a Lipschitz-like requirement that essentially connects the similarity in the feature space and that in the label space in a meaningful way, as follows,

$$d_L(l_1, l_2) \leq d_H(b_1, b_2) \cdot \frac{1}{m} \tag{6}$$

where m is a scale number whose value is determined by the bits length of underlying hashing codes (see Section 4.2 for details), and d_L is the pairwise distance between the corresponding labels (denoted as l_1 and l_2, respectively) of the two points b_1 and b_2, defined as follows,

$$d_L(l_1, l_2) = \frac{\max\{|l_1|, |l_2|\} - |l_1 \cap l_2|}{\max\{|l_1|, |l_2|\}} \tag{7}$$

where $\|\cdot\|$ denotes the L-1 length of a label vector.

We adopt the scheme of triplets to capture the similarity structure between the hashing codes. Specifically, for a given triplet of images $\{I_1, I_2, I_3\}$ and their labels $\{l_1, l_2, l_3\}$, we first obtain their hashing codes $b_1 = sign(h(f_{CNN}(I_1)))$, $b_2 = sign(h(f_{CNN}(I_2)))$, $b_3 = sign(h(f_{CNN}(I_3)))$, and three derived hashing codes through the CON network [1], i.e., $b_4 = f_u(b_1, b_2)$, $b_5 = f_t(b_1, b_2)$, and $b_6 = f_s(b_4, b_2)$. Hence totally we have six hashing codes and we partition them into three triplets, i.e., $\{b_1, b_2, b_3\}$, $\{b_1, b_2, b_4\}$, and $\{b_1, b_2, b_5\}$, each of which reflects some aspect of the similarity structure and corresponds to a separate triplet loss term in the final loss function.

For the triplet $\{b_1, b_2, b_3\}$, we first select one point from them with most tags as the reference point, based on which we evaluate the similarity between the remaining two points and the reference point using Eq. (7). In this way, we can re-order $\{b_1, b_2, b_3\}$ and denote them as $\{b_{*,1}, b_*, b_{*,2}\}$, where b_* is the reference point, and $b_{*,1}$ is the one that is more similar to b_* than the other ($b_{*,2}$). Finally, we formulate the triplet loss needed as follows,

$$\begin{aligned} L_{tr1}(b_1, b_2, b_3) =& [d_H(b_*, b_{*,1}) - d_H(b_*, b_{*,2}) + \alpha_1]_+ \\ & s.t.\ b \in \{-1, 1\}^k \end{aligned} \tag{8}$$

where $[\cdot]_+ = max\{0, \cdot\}$, and α_1 is the margin and is defined as $\alpha_1 = \frac{|l_* \cap l_{*,1}| - |l_* \cap l_{*,2}|}{|l_*|} \cdot m$. Note that the margin α_1 is adaptive according to their similarity levels.

Similarly, for the group $\{b_1, b_2, b_4\}$ and $\{b_1, b_2, b_5\}$ (where $l_4 = l_1 \cup l_2$ and $l_5 = l_1 \cap l_2$), their relative similarity relationship should respectively satisfy:

$$\begin{aligned} |l_1| > |l_2| &\Rightarrow d_H(b_1, b_4) < d_H(b_1, b_2), d_H(b_2, b_5) < d_H(b_1, b_2) \\ |l_1| < |l_2| &\Rightarrow d_H(b_2, b_4) > d_H(b_1, b_2), d_H(b_1, b_5) < d_H(b_1, b_2) \\ |l_1| = |l_2| &\Rightarrow d_H(b_1, b_4) = d_H(b_2, b_4), d_H(b_1, b_5) = d_H(b_2, b_5) \end{aligned} \tag{9}$$

It can be easily verified that these constraints meet the Lipschitz condition given by Eq. (6). Based on these, the second part of our loss function according to the above two triplets is defined as follows:

$$\begin{aligned} L_{tr2}(b_1, b_2, b_3) =& [y d_H(b_1, b_4) + (1 - y) d_H(b_2, b_4) \\ & - d_H(b_1, b_2) + \alpha_2]_+ + [y d_H(b_2, b_5) \\ & + (1 - y) d_H(b_1, b_5) - d_H(b_1, b_2) + \alpha_3]_+ \\ & s.t.\ b \in \{-1, 1\}^k \end{aligned} \tag{10}$$

where margin $\alpha_2 = \frac{(yn_1 + (1-y)n_2)^2 - n_3 n_4}{n_3(yn_1 + (1-y)n_2)} \cdot m$ and $\alpha_3 = \frac{|n_1 - n_2| n_4}{n_1 n_2} \cdot m$, $n_1 = |l_1|$, $n_2 = |l_2|$, $n_3 = |l_1 \cup l_2|$, $n_4 = |l_1 \cap l_2|$, and if $n_1 > n_2$ then $y = 1$ otherwise $y = 0$.

Combining Eq. 8 and Eq. 10, we obtain the margin-adaptive triplet loss for the three groups of hashing codes as follows:

$$L_{tr}(b_1, b_2, b_3) = L_{tr1}(b_1, b_2, b_3) + L_{tr2}(b_1, b_2, b_3) \tag{11}$$

Weighted classification loss. We also adopt the following weighted cross-entropy loss to ensure that each individual hashing codes consistent with its own semantic concept,

$$L_{cl}(b, l) = -\sum_{j=1}^{C} \left(w_{pos} \cdot l_j \log(\hat{l_j}) + (1 - l_j) \log(1 - \hat{l_j}) \right) \tag{12}$$

where $\hat{l}$ is the predicted value of DSOH, and w_{pos} is the weight of positive samples.

Finally, the overall loss function for N training triplets $\{b_{i1}, b_{i2}, b_{i3}\}_{i=1}^{N}$ is defined as follows:

$$\begin{aligned} \mathcal{L} = \sum_{i=1}^{N} \Big(\sum_{j=1}^{3} L_{cl}(b_{ij}, l_{ij}) + \lambda_1 (L_{cl}(b_{i4}, l_{i4}) + L_{cl}(b_{i5}, l_{i5}) \\ + L_{cl}(b_{i6}, l_{i6})) + \lambda_2 L_{tr}(b_{i1}, b_{i2}, b_{i3}) \Big) \end{aligned} \tag{13}$$

where λ_1 and λ_2 are parameters that balance the classification loss of operating codes and the triplet loss.

3.5 Optimization

Note that the problem of Eq. (13) is a discrete optimization problem, which is NP-hard to solve. To address this issue we

[1] Note that in principle we can generate more hashing codes using the CON network but for simplicity and w.l.o.g., here only a set involving two binary codes are used.

use two types of relaxation over the loss function. First, *tanh* activation function is used to approximate the binary codes. Second, Hamming distance is substituted with Euclidean distance, i.e. $d(h_1, h_2) = ||h_1 - h_2||_2^2$. The final loss function Eq. (13) is hence rewritten as follows:

$$\mathcal{L} = \sum_{i=1}^{N} \{ \sum_{j=1}^{3} L_{cl}(h_{ij}, l_{ij}) + \lambda_1(L_{cl}(h_{i4}, l_{i4}) + L_{cl}(h_{i5}, l_{i5}) + L_{cl}(h_{i6}, l_{i6})) + \lambda_2 L_{tr}(h_{i1}, h_{i2}, h_{i3}, l_{i1}, l_{i2}, l_{i3}) + \lambda_3 \sum_{j=1}^{3}(|||h_{i,j}| - \mathbf{1}||_1) \} \tag{14}$$

where $h_* = h(f_{CNN}(I_*))$ for short, $h_{i4} = f_u(h_{i1}, h_{i2})$, $h_{i5} = f_t(h_{i1}, h_{i2})$, $h_{i6} = f_s(h_{i4}, h_{i2})$. $\mathbf{1}$ is a vector with all element one. $||\cdot||_1$ denotes L1-norm and λ_3 controls the weight of quantization. As this new objective is smooth, the optimization for the whole model is performed using stochastic gradient descent based on Adaptive Moment Estimation (Adam).

4 EXPERIMENTS

4.1 Experimental Settings

We validate the proposed DSOH on three multi-label image datasets, MIRFLICKR25K [9], VOC2012 [4] and Microsoft COCO [17]. MIRFLICKR25K [9] consists of 25,000 multi-label images. Each image is associated 24 classes. In our experiments, samples with no tags are discarded, and 20,006 are remaining. VOC2012 [4] consists of 22,531 images in 20 classes. Since the ground truth labels of the test images are not available, only 11,540 images from its training set are used. For the above two datasets, we randomly sample 2,000 images as the test query set, and the remaining images are used for training. Microsoft COCO [17] contains 82,783 training images and 40,504 testing images. Each image is associated with 90 categories. After pruning images with no category information, we generate 82,081 training samples and 4,956 random test samples.

We perform multi-label retrieval with three kinds of retrieval tasks, which are defined as follows.

- **Task 1** . Retrieve relevant images in the training set using the code of a test image.
- **Task 2** . Retrieve relevant images in the training set using a pair of queries with *Union.*
- **Task 3** . Retrieve relevant images in the training set using a pair of queries with *Substract or Intersect.*

We adopt the commonly-used Average Cumulative Gain (ACG) [10], Normalized Discounted Cumulative Gain (NDCG), and weighted mean Average Precision (weighted mAP) as the performance metric.

4.2 Implementation details

Our DSOH is implemented with Tensorflow[2]. The detailed configurations are illustrated in Table 1. During training, the batch size is set to 64, the learning rate to 0.0001, the λ_1 to 0.01, the λ_2 to 0.1, the λ_3 to 10^{-5}, the w_{pos} is set to 20 for MIRFLICKR25k, VOC2012 and 30 for COCO. The margin parameter m is heuristically set to $2k$ to encourage the codes of dissimilar images to differ in no less than a half of bit length. To make the best use of limited computational resources, all image triplets are generated online from the shuffled training set after each epoch.

[2]https://www.tensorflow.org

Table 1: The configuration of the Deep Semantic Operation Hashing network in experiments.

sub-DHN	
CNN	ResNet-152→2,048 / VGG16→4,096
full1	1,024, tanh
full2	hash code length k, tanh
sub-CON	
Concat.	[k,k]
full3	hash code length k

Table 2: Comparison at Top 100 of End-to-End and Off-the-shelf configuration of DSOH on VOC2012.

Method	NDCG	ACG	mAP_w	Train Time(s)
$DSOH_{off-the-shelf}$	0.7712	1.053	1.073	6.2×10^2
$DSOH_{end2end}$	0.7877	1.080	1.098	2.8×10^4

Because the CNN model in DSOH is optionally connected, we firstly investigate the influence of joint learning of CNN. We perform CNN fine-tuning and DSOH learning in an end-to-end architecture, named $DSOH_{end2end}$. Then it was compared with $DSOH_{off-the-shelf}$ which adopts off-the-shelf CNN feature. CNN models of them are the same VGG16 pre-trained in ImageNet. And two models are trained with 50 epochs. The results on retrieval task 1 are shown in Table 2. We can see that $DSOH_{off-the-shelf}$ achieves competitive performance to $DSOH_{end2end}$. While its computation cost is lower than $DSOH_{end2end}$ by two orders of magnitude. Therefore, considering the time cost, DSOH adopts the off-the-shelf CNN feature in the following experiments.

4.3 Experimental Result

Comparative methods: We compared DSOH with unsupervised hashing LSH [5], SH [27], ITQ [6] and state-of-the-art deep methods MSDH [21], DRSH [31], DMSSPH [28] and our DSOH-NO which removes CON. For a fair comparison, all methods are based on the off-the-shelf 2,048-D ResNet-152 [8] features which are pre-trained on ImageNet with Caffe [11]. LSH, SH, and ITQ were implemented using source codes provided by the authors. To eliminate the effect of the network structures, we implement DMSH, DRSH, DMSSPH and our DSOH with the same network structure as Table 1 shows. All parameters were set optimally based on experimental verification. For retrieval task 2, the fusion code of DSOH-L, DSOH-NO-L and other methods and are empirically obtained by logical OR operation of two query codes, which is consistent with the fusion manner of query label.

Table 3: NDCG@100, ACG@100 and mAP$_w$ of `Task 1` on three datasets with different bits length.

Methods	MIRFLICKR25K				VOC2012				COCO			
	16 bits	32 bits	64 bits	128 bits	16 bits	32 bits	64 bits	128 bits	16 bits	32 bits	64 bits	128 bits
	NDCG@100											
DSOH	**0.5307**	**0.5603**	**0.5872**	**0.5966**	**0.7819**	**0.8047**	**0.8195**	**0.8242**	**0.4663**	**0.5178**	**0.5400**	**0.5439**
DSOH-NO	0.4925	0.5359	0.5658	0.5712	0.7664	0.7908	0.8074	0.8077	0.4234	0.4747	0.5101	0.5221
DMSSPH [28]	0.4835	0.4877	0.5004	0.5241	0.7037	0.7136	0.7310	0.7353	0.4337	0.4817	0.5053	0.5026
DRSH [31]	0.4396	0.4774	0.5113	0.5301	0.6895	0.7290	0.7572	0.7785	0.2994	0.3747	0.4267	0.4553
MSDH [21]	0.3950	0.4265	0.4527	0.4602	0.6479	0.7032	0.7081	0.6922	0.3338	0.4066	0.4464	0.4721
ITQ [6]	0.3577	0.4063	0.4297	0.4482	0.5794	0.6418	0.6694	0.6882	0.2761	0.3799	0.4345	0.4674
SH [27]	0.3238	0.3636	0.3757	0.3849	0.5315	0.5689	0.5662	0.5512	0.2809	0.3686	0.4044	0.4244
LSH [5]	0.2377	0.2635	0.3207	0.3723	0.2586	0.3306	0.4512	0.5450	0.1683	0.2370	0.3231	0.4009
	ACG@100											
DSOH	**2.426**	**2.529**	**2.617**	**2.645**	**1.065**	**1.095**	**1.106**	**1.125**	**1.439**	**1.570**	**1.628**	**1.640**
DSOH-NO	2.306	2.454	2.548	2.569	1.040	1.073	1.097	1.095	1.307	1.440	1.544	1.589
DMSSPH [28]	2.225	2.238	2.292	2.318	0.9525	0.9688	0.9875	0.9943	1.355	1.453	1.509	1.523
DRSH [31]	2.200	2.316	2.434	2.475	0.9448	0.9965	1.033	1.064	1.079	1.248	1.362	1.432
MSDH [21]	1.983	2.086	2.166	2.184	0.8733	0.9494	0.9557	0.9368	1.072	1.258	1.367	1.432
ITQ [6]	1.857	2.016	2.081	2.150	0.7959	0.8738	0.9130	0.9362	0.9962	1.222	1.348	1.428
SH [27]	1.681	1.805	1.831	1.875	0.7303	0.7672	0.7509	0.7239	0.9920	1,164	1.233	1.278
LSH [5]	1.346	1.460	1.681	1.873	0.3885	0.4763	0.6340	0.7536	0.6678	0.8434	1.074	1.266
	mAP$_w$@100											
DSOH	**2.467**	**2.566**	**2.656**	**2.683**	**1.87**	**1.112**	**1.123**	**1.142**	**1.464**	**1.599**	**1.657**	**1.671**
DSOH-NO	2.351	2.496	2.589	2.609	1.059	1.094	1.116	1.114	1.344	1.481	1.584	1.629
DMSSPH [28]	2.267	2.294	2.344	2.371	0.9729	0.9921	1.016	1.023	1.376	1.476	1.533	1.551
DRSH [31]	2.216	2.334	2.453	2.504	0.9682	1.023	1.055	1.087	1.085	1.265	1.384	1.462
MSDH [21]	2.018	2.130	2.222	2.256	0.8936	0.9742	0.9862	0.9701	1.091	1.292	1.402	1.472
ITQ [6]	1.886	2.067	2.142	2.213	0.8249	0.9081	0.9527	0.9792	1.024	1.260	1.385	1.470
SH [27]	1.767	1.902	1.945	2.001	0.7917	0.8432	0.8484	0.8398	1.035	1.216	1.295	1.347
LSH [5]	1.393	1.531	1.767	1.978	0.4442	0.5496	0.7139	0.8357	0.7111	0.9015	1.140	1.328

Similarity r	4	3	2	1	0
mean d_H	1.372	3.409	4.519	6.194	9.113

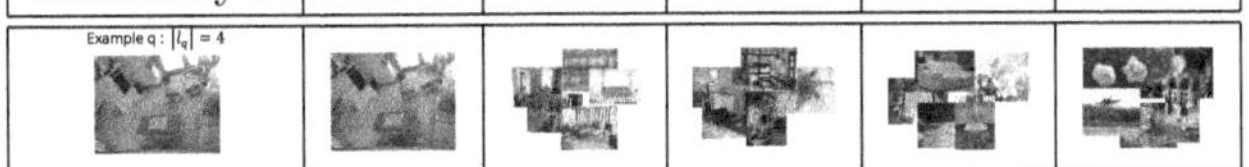

Figure 2: The consistency of Hamming Distance d_H and Semantic Similarity r on VOC2012 with 16 bits.

Results on Task 1: From Table 3, we can observe that 1) the proposed DSOH substantially outperforms other compared methods with three evaluation criteria on all used datasets. E.g., The NDCG@100 results of DSOH indicate a 3.2% $\sim$ 4.1% relative increase over the second best baseline on COCO. 2)DSOH outperforms DSOH-NO 3% NDCG scores in average, which means the effectiveness of the code operation. 3) Compared with multilevel similarity-based DMSSPH, DSOH can exploit more similarity information in triplets and discriminative supervised information to capture the multilevel similarity structure accurately.

Besides, it is worth noting that both DSOH and DRSH learn hashing functions based on triplet ranking loss, the results in Table 3 shows that DSOH gains all-around advantages over DRSH on three datasets. To be more specific, the NDCG@100, ACG@100, and weighted mAP@100 results indicate the relative increase of 8.8%$\sim$16.6%, 20.8%$\sim$36% and 20.9%$\sim$37.9% respectively over DRSH on COCO. This effectively demonstrates the benefit of using our adaptive margin loss.

To verify the consistency of hamming distance of learned codes and multilevel semantic similarity, we select all training samples with four tags as reference images and average the hamming distance between them and others samples according to their semantic similarity. Fig. 2 shows the results. we can see the d_H exactly satisfies the requirement of Eq. (6).

Results on Task 2: From table 4, we can observe that: 1) DSOH leads to superior results with 16.3%,17.9% and 10.9% improvements (NDCG@100) over the best-performing comparison methods on the three datasets with 128 bits. It demonstrates that our hashing code is operable to perform complex retrieval task. 2) Because of the non-considering on the consistency between the logical operation of hashing codes and corresponding semantic label, simple OR operation of hashing code from DSOH-L cannot accomplish complex semantic retrieval task well. Besides, DSOH-NO-L is inferior to DSOH-L because of no CON. 3) With code length increasing, the performance of our DSOH intends to be stable, which implies that a proper length of code can obtain optimal performance while longer is useless.

Furthermore, compared with deep baselines DRSH and DMSSPH, we can find that 1) since DMSSPH considering p-reserving multilevel semantic similarity with certain distance

Table 4: NDCG@100, ACG@100 and mAP$_w$ of Task 2 on three datasets with different bits length.

Methods	MIRFLICKR25K				VOC2012				Microsoft COCO			
	16 bits	32 bits	64 bits	128 bits	16 bits	32 bits	64 bits	128 bits	16 bits	32 bits	64 bits	128 bits
	NDCG@100											
DSOH	**0.3343**	**0.4022**	**0.4354**	**0.4597**	**0.6408**	**0.6969**	**0.7040**	**0.7336**	**0.2406**	**0.3141**	**0.3570**	**0.3783**
DSOH-L	0.1603	0.2093	0.2578	0.2994	0.4194	0.4518	0.6202	0.6130	0.2075	0.2282	0.2743	0.2584
DSOH-NO-L	0.1386	0.1933	0.2045	0.2538	0.4339	0.4962	0.5381	0.5579	0.1563	0.1857	0.1785	0.2521
DMSSPH [28]	0.1986	0.2347	0.2716	0.2184	0.3994	0.4778	0.5061	0.4682	0.1379	0.2332	0.2389	0.2687
DRSH [31]	0.1729	0.1935	0.2382	0.2965	0.3612	0.4430	0.4844	0.5539	0.1274	0.1635	0.1974	0.2306
MSDH [21]	0.1461	0.1519	0.1685	0.2094	0.3695	0.3818	0.3654	0.4149	0.1509	0.1742	0.2098	0.2057
	ACG@100											
DSOH	**3.297**	**3.724**	**3.905**	**3.939**	**1.302**	**1.386**	**1.412**	**1.459**	**1.634**	**1.949**	**2.109**	**2.182**
DSOH-L	2.288	2.651	3.056	3.268	0.8833	0.9708	1.264	1.250	1.452	1.497	1.676	1.655
DSOH-NO-L	2.048	2.628	2.691	3.087	0.9228	1.033	1.102	1.152	1.131	1.285	1.214	1.599
DMSSPH [28]	2.455	2.795	2.976	2.562	0.8666	1.002	1.041	0.9911	1.005	1.531	1.478	1.634
DRSH [31]	2.464	2.659	2.971	3.316	0.7803	0.9658	1.032	1.158	1.020	1.246	1.347	1.499
MSDH [21]	2.151	2.137	2.307	2.646	0.7916	0.8598	0.8128	0.9240	1.091	1.194	1.396	1.334
	mAP$_w$@100											
DSOH	**3.499**	**3.846**	**3.991**	**4.087**	**1.353**	**1.445**	**1.457**	**1.506**	**1.640**	**1.970**	**2.142**	**2.217**
DSOH-L	2.322	2.684	3.071	3.311	0.9151	0.9850	1.301	1.284	1.446	1.509	1.694	1.670
DSOH-NO-L	2.113	2.632	2.711	3.113	0.9606	1.059	1.144	1.186	1.149	1.317	1.223	1.619
DMSSPH [28]	2.501	2.795	3.072	2.633	0.9252	1.071	1.104	1.038	1.012	1.545	1.478	1.649
DRSH [31]	2.424	2.640	2.951	3.318	0.7946	0.9720	1.053	1.185	1.009	1.217	1.348	1.497
MSDH [21]	2.147	2.155	2.327	2.675	0.8091	0.8769	0.8389	0.9389	1.102	1.201	1.401	1.339

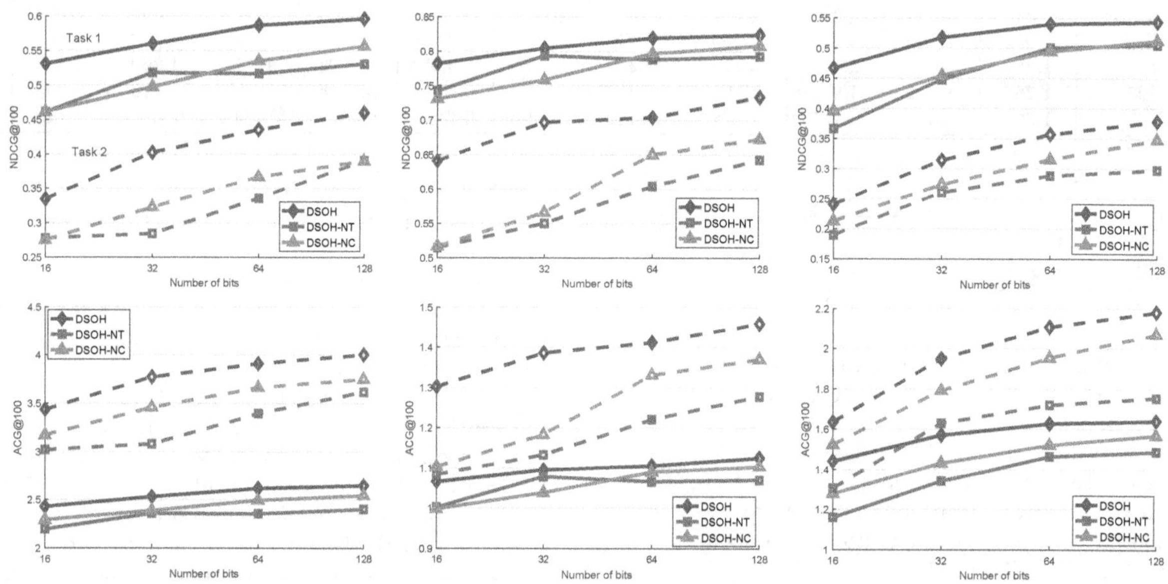

(a) MIRFLICKR25K (b) VOC2012 (c) Microsoft COCO

Figure 3: NDG@100 and ACG@100 of two retrieval tasks with different components and various hashing bits.

constraint in Hamming space, it produces a superior performance to DRSH. 2) Although both DSOH and DMSSPH use adaptive margin in loss function to capture multilevel similarity, DSOH leads to higher accuracies. This performance gap between them may be caused by 1) the exploitation of discriminative supervised information for fused code in DSOH can guide more effective fusion, 2) comprehensive similarity relationship between original codes and fused code in triplet is helpful to improve the generalization of DSOH, 3) the operation of code in DSOH is actually a linear transformation, which can select relevant components from pre-operated codes to integrate and avoid introducing noise in fusion process, while logical OR cannot.

Some retrieval results of Task 2 and Task 3 are presented in Figure 4. From sub-figure (a), we can see the semantic concepts of the query pairs are well fused, and meaningful

(a) Semantic retrieval with hashing codes union operation in DSOH

(b) Semantic retrieval with hashing codes subtract operation in DSOH

(c) Semantic retrieval with hashing codes intersect operation in DSOH

Figure 4: Retrieval examples on VOC2012 with 128 bits. Top 12 results for each query pairs are shown. Results with red border denotes $|l_q \cap l_{res}| = 1$, blue denotes $|l_q \cap l_{res}| = 2$ and green denotes $|l_q \cap l_{res}| > 2$.

results are returned. For instance, 'car + motorbike' returns 'A motorbike parked beside a car.' It is worth noted that DSOH could handle more complex semantic fusion. E.g., 'Person is riding a bicycle + car' returns 'a person rides a bicycle in front of a car.' Besides, from sub-figure (b), it can be seen the semantic concepts of the first query hashing code is partially removed by 'subtracting' the second query code. E.g., 'car, person, dog - car' returns 'A person is playing with a dog.' While in sub-figure (c), the overlap semantic concepts are used for more precise retrieval.

4.4 Effect of Model Configuration

To analyze the effectiveness of different loss term in the proposed DSOH, we separately remove L_{cl} and L_{tr} with other parameters remained to evaluate their influence on the final performance. These two models are called DSOH-NC and DSOH-NT. Here NC denotes no classification loss L_{cl} term and NT denotes no multi-level triplet loss L_{tr} term. Figure 3 shows the result of two tasks.

We can see that jointly using the margin-adaptive triplet loss and classification loss can apparently improve the ranking quality of top-100 relevant items in terms of NDCG, ACG and mAP at the expense of the averaged ranking performance, as it adaptively assigns margins according to the related multilevel similarity and simultaneously encodes rich discriminative information. Besides, for Task 1, with the increasing of the bits number, the performance of DSOH-NC increases firstly and then tends to be flat, which indicates the term L_{cl} cannot take advantage of longer bits to boost performance. For Task 2, DSOH-NT performances worse than DSOH-NC which implies that the term L_{tr} is more important than L_{cl} to capture multilevel similarity.

5 CONCLUSIONS

In this paper, we have presented a novel deep hashing method, named DSOH, to learn multilevel similarity-preserving and operable binary codes for multi-label image retrieval. Unlike many previous works that ignore the *intention gap* issue, we propose a new Code Operation Network to perform the 'union,' 'intersect' and 'subtract' operations on semantic concepts of multiple query image codes, which effectively enables users to expand their query intention in a more flexible and friendly manner. The whole system is learned in an end-to-end way with the help of a newly designed adaptive-margin based triplet loss function. Our experimental results demonstrate that the proposed method is able to learn useful multilevel semantic similarity-preserving binary codes and achieves state-of-the-art retrieval performance on three popular datasets.

ACKNOWLEDGMENTS

This work is partially supported by National Natural Science Foundation of China (61672280,61373060,61732006), the Pre-research fund of Equipments of China, Jiangsu 333 Project (BRA2017377) and Qing Lan Project.

REFERENCES

[1] Jiale Bai, Bingbing Ni, Minsi Wang, Yang Shen, Hanjiang Lai, Chongyang Zhang, Lin Mei, Chuanping Hu, and Chen Yao. 2017. Deep Progressive Hashing for Image Retrieval. In *Proceedings of the 2017 ACM on Multimedia Conference, MM 2017, Mountain View, CA, USA, October 23-27, 2017*. 208–216.

[2] Zhangjie Cao, Mingsheng Long, Jianmin Wang, and Philip S. Yu. 2017. HashNet: Deep Learning to Hash by Continuation. In *IEEE International Conference on Computer Vision, ICCV 2017, Venice, Italy, October 22-29, 2017*. 5609–5618.

[3] Yueqi Duan, Jiwen Lu, Ziwei Wang, Jianjiang Feng, and Jie Zhou. 2017. Learning Deep Binary Descriptor with Multi-quantization. In *2017 IEEE Conference on Computer Vision and Pattern Recognition, CVPR 2017, Honolulu, HI, USA, July 21-26, 2017*. 4857–4866.

[4] Mark Everingham, Luc Gool, Christopher K Williams, John Winn, and Andrew Zisserman. 2010. The Pascal Visual Object Classes (VOC) Challenge. *International Journal of Computer Vision* 88, 2 (2010), 303–338.

[5] Aristides Gionis, Piotr Indyk, and Rajeev Motwani. 1999. Similarity Search in High Dimensions via Hashing. In *International Conference on Very Large Data Bases*. 518–529.

[6] Yunchao Gong, Svetlana Lazebnik, Albert Gordo, and Florent Perronnin. 2013. Iterative Quantization: A Procrustean Approach to Learning Binary Codes for Large-Scale Image Retrieval. *IEEE Transactions on Pattern Analysis and Machine Intelligence* 35, 12 (2013), 2916–2929.

[7] Albert Gordo and Diane Larlus. 2017. Beyond Instance-Level Image Retrieval: Leveraging Captions to Learn a Global Visual Representation for Semantic Retrieval. In *IEEE Conference on Computer Vision and Pattern Recognition*. 5272–5281.

[8] Kaiming He, Xiangyu Zhang, Shaoqing Ren, and Jian Sun. 2016. Deep Residual Learning for Image Recognition. In *2016 IEEE Conference on Computer Vision and Pattern Recognition, CVPR 2016, Las Vegas, NV, USA, June 27-30, 2016*. 770–778.

[9] Mark J. Huiskes and Michael S. Lew. 2008. The MIR flickr retrieval evaluation. In *ACM International Conference on Multimedia Information Retrieval*. 39–43.

[10] Kalervo Järvelin and Jaana Kekäläinen. 2000. IR evaluation methods for retrieving highly relevant documents. In *International ACM SIGIR Conference on Research and Development in Information Retrieval*. 41–48.

[11] Yangqing Jia, Evan Shelhamer, Jeff Donahue, Sergey Karayev, Jonathan Long, Ross B. Girshick, Sergio Guadarrama, and Trevor Darrell. 2014. Caffe: Convolutional Architecture for Fast Feature Embedding. In *Proceedings of the ACM International Conference on Multimedia, MM '14, Orlando, FL, USA, November 03 - 07, 2014*. 675–678.

[12] Gunhee Kim, Seungwhan Moon, and Leonid Sigal. 2015. Ranking and retrieval of image sequences from multiple paragraph queries. In *IEEE Conference on Computer Vision and Pattern Recognition*. 1993–2001.

[13] H. Lai, P. Yan, X. Shu, Y. Wei, and S. Yan. 2016. Instance-Aware Hashing for Multi-Label Image Retrieval. *IEEE Transactions on Image Processing* 25, 6 (2016), 2469–2479.

[14] Qi Li, Zhenan Sun, Ran He, and Tieniu Tan. 2017. Deep Supervised Discrete Hashing. In *International Conference on Neural Information Processing Systems*.

[15] Wu-Jun Li, Sheng Wang, and Wang-Cheng Kang. 2016. Feature Learning Based Deep Supervised Hashing with Pairwise Labels. In *Proceedings of the Twenty-Fifth International Joint Conference on Artificial Intelligence, IJCAI 2016, New York, NY, USA, 9-15 July 2016*. 1711–1717.

[16] Jie Lin, Olivier Morère, Antoine Veillard, Ling-Yu Duan, Hanlin Goh, and Vijay Chandrasekhar. 2017. DeepHash for Image Instance Retrieval: Getting Regularization, Depth and Fine-Tuning Right. In *Proceedings of the 2017 ACM on International Conference on Multimedia Retrieval, ICMR 2017, Bucharest, Romania, June 6-9, 2017*. 133–141.

[17] Tsung Yi Lin, Michael Maire, Serge Belongie, James Hays, Pietro Perona, Deva Ramanan, Piotr Dollr, and C. Lawrence Zitnick. 2014. Microsoft COCO: Common Objects in Context. In *European Conference on Computer Vision*. 740–755.

[18] Haomiao Liu, Ruiping Wang, Shiguang Shan, and Xilin Chen. 2016. Deep Supervised Hashing for Fast Image Retrieval. In *The IEEE Conference on Computer Vision and Pattern Recognition (CVPR)*.

[19] Li Liu, Ling Shao, Fumin Shen, and Mengyang Yu. 2017. Discretely Coding Semantic Rank Orders for Supervised Image Hashing. In *IEEE Conference on Computer Vision and Pattern Recognition*. 5140–5149.

[20] Li Liu, Fumin Shen, Yuming Shen, Xianglong Liu, and Ling Shao. 2017. Deep Sketch Hashing: Fast Free-hand Sketch-Based Image Retrieval. In *Computer Vision and Pattern Recognition*.

[21] Jiwen Lu, Venice Erin Liong, and Jie Zhou. 2017. Deep Hashing for Scalable Image Search. *IEEE Transactions on Image Processing* 26, 5 (2017), 2352–2367.

[22] Yadong Mu and Zhu Liu. 2017. Deep Hashing: A Joint Approach for Image Signature Learning. In *Proceedings of the Thirty-First AAAI Conference on Artificial Intelligence, February 4-9, 2017, San Francisco, California, USA*. 2380–2386.

[23] Amaia Salvador, Nicholas Hynes, Yusuf Aytar, Javier Marín, Ferda Ofli, Ingmar Weber, and Antonio Torralba. 2017. Learning Cross-Modal Embeddings for Cooking Recipes and Food Images. In *2017 IEEE Conference on Computer Vision and Pattern Recognition, CVPR 2017, Honolulu, HI, USA, July 21-26, 2017*. 3068–3076.

[24] Omar Seddati, Stéphane Dupont, and Saïd Mahmoudi. 2017. Quadruplet Networks for Sketch-Based Image Retrieval. In *Proceedings of the 2017 ACM on International Conference on Multimedia Retrieval, ICMR 2017, Bucharest, Romania, June 6-9, 2017*. 184–191.

[25] Ge Song and Xiaoyang Tan. 2017. Hierarchical deep hashing for image retrieval. *Frontiers Comput. Sci.* 11, 2 (2017), 253–265.

[26] Giorgos Tolias and Ondrej Chum. 2017. Asymmetric Feature Maps with Application to Sketch Based Retrieval. In *2017 IEEE Conference on Computer Vision and Pattern Recognition, CVPR 2017, Honolulu, HI, USA, July 21-26, 2017*. 6185–6193.

[27] Yair Weiss, Antonio Torralba, and Rob Fergus. 2008. Spectral hashing. In *International Conference on Neural Information Processing Systems*. 1753–1760.

[28] Dayan Wu, Zheng Lin, Bo Li, Mingzhen Ye, and Weiping Wang. 2017. Deep Supervised Hashing for Multi-Label and Large-Scale Image Retrieval. In *ACM International Conference on Multimedia Retrieval*. 150–158.

[29] Changcheng Xiao, Changhu Wang, Liqing Zhang, and Lei Zhang. 2015. Sketch-based Image Retrieval via Shape Words. In *Proceedings of the 5th ACM on International Conference on Multimedia Retrieval, Shanghai, China, June 23-26, 2015*. 571–574.

[30] Bo Zhao, Jiashi Feng, Xiao Wu, and Shuicheng Yan. 2017. Memory-Augmented Attribute Manipulation Networks for Interactive Fashion Search. In *IEEE Conference on Computer Vision and Pattern Recognition*. 6156–6164.

[31] Fang Zhao, Y. Huang, L. Wang, and Tieniu Tan. 2015. Deep semantic ranking based hashing for multi-label image retrieval. In *IEEE Conference on Computer Vision and Pattern Recognition*. 1556–1564.

[32] Wengang Zhou, Houqiang Li, and Qi Tian. 2017. Recent Advance in Content-based Image Retrieval: A Literature Survey. *arXiv* (2017).

Multi-view Collective Tensor Decomposition for Cross-modal Hashing

Limeng Cui
School of Computer and Control Engineering, University of Chinese Academy of Sciences
Beijing, China
lmcui932@163.com

Zhensong Chen
School of Economics and Management, University of Chinese Academy of Sciences
Beijing, China
wxzmczs@163.com

Jiawei Zhang
IFM Lab, Department of Computer Science, Florida State University
Tallahassee, FL
jzhang@cs.fsu.edu

Lifang He
Weill Cornell Medicine, Cornell University
New York, NY
lifanghescut@gmail.com

Yong Shi
Key Laboratory of Big Data Mining and Knowledge Management, Chinese Academy of Sciences
Beijing, China
yshi@ucas.ac.cn

Philip S. Yu
Department of Computer Science, University of Illinois at Chicago
Chicago, IL

ABSTRACT

Multimedia data available in various disciplines are usually heterogeneous, containing representations in multi-views, where the cross-modal search techniques become necessary and useful. It is a challenging problem due to the heterogeneity of data with multiple modalities, multi-views in each modality and the diverse data categories. In this paper, we propose a novel multi-view cross-modal hashing method named Multi-view Collective Tensor Decomposition (MCTD) to fuse these data effectively, which can exploit the complementary feature extracted from multi-modality multi-view while simultaneously discovering multiple separated subspaces by leveraging the data categories as supervision information. Our contributions are summarized as follows: 1) we exploit tensor modeling to get better representation of the complementary features and redefine a latent representation space; 2) a block-diagonal loss is proposed to explicitly pursue a more discriminative latent tensor space by exploring supervision information; 3) we propose a new feature projection method to characterize the data and to generate the latent representation for incoming new queries. An optimization algorithm is proposed to solve the objective function designed for MCTD, which works under an iterative updating procedure. Experimental results prove the state-of-the-art precision of MCTD compared with competing methods.

CCS CONCEPTS

• **Information systems → Multimedia and multimodal retrieval**;

ICMR '18, June 11–14, 2018, Yokohama, Japan

ACM ISBN 978-1-4503-5046-4/18/06...$15.00
https://doi.org/10.1145/3206025.3206065

KEYWORDS

Cross-modal hashing; tensor factorization; metric learning; multi-view learning

ACM Reference Format:
Limeng Cui, Zhensong Chen, Jiawei Zhang, Lifang He, Yong Shi, and Philip S. Yu. 2018. Multi-view Collective Tensor Decomposition for Cross-modal Hashing. In *ICMR '18: 2018 International Conference on Multimedia Retrieval, June 11–14, 2018, Yokohama, Japan.* ACM, New York, NY, USA, 9 pages. https://doi.org/10.1145/3206025.3206065

1 INTRODUCTION

With the prevalence of multimedia big data in social networks and search engines, data of multi-modality has becoming ubiquitous and abundant. What's more, in some scenarios, each modality can further have representations in multiple views. For instance, as shown in Figure 1, each news article has information in texts and images (i.e., multi-modality), and information in each modality can have different representations in the feature space (depending on the specific feature extraction emphases), which form different views of the article. Since these data presented in different modalities may have strong semantic correlations, cross-modal retrieval has attracted growing attentions, which aims at using one kind of modality to retrieve semantically relevant objects of different modality.

In the past few years, this has become a fundamental problem in several emerging applications including visual search [2], image annotation [6, 25], and object detection/recognition [4]. A promising solution to cross-modal retrieval is the hashing method, which embeds multi-modal data into a common latent representation space and generates similar binary codes for similar objects [28]. However, effective cross-modal hashing still remains a challenge due to the heterogeneous data: features obtained in multi-modality and multi-view, and complementary supervision information, e.g., data categories. In this paper, we focus on how to fuse these data properly to facilitate the cross-modal retrieval task.

Existing cross-modal retrieval methods fail to fully exploit the useful features, which may limit their performance. To be more specific, the features extracted through different views in each modality can provide complementary information. In this paper, we refer to the feature representations extracted with different emphases as "multi-view features". For example, hand-crafted features and deep-learnt features characterize the different aspects of image data [1, 9, 26]. Similarly, explicit and latent features play different roles for text data characterization. Since the relationship among these multi-view features in each modality can be highly nonlinear, simply concatenating the features may result in that dense views dominate the feature space and override the effects of others. An effective fusion strategy is needed to explore feature interactions across different views.

In terms of the supervision information, like news article categories as shown in Figure 1, it also has not been explored effectively in current methods. It represents the class label of the multi-modal data, such as the topic of a news coverage. Most existing methods enforce the same-class samples lie as close as possible in the representation space. However, as separating different subspaces that correspond to different classes is widely ignored, they lose interclass discriminant ability. Motivated by this, we propose to utilize the supervision information to learn a more discriminative representation space.

In this paper, we study the correlations of the multi-view features and construct a novel latent space with the help of supervision information, which is the first attempt to fuse the aforementioned data together for cross-modal retrieval. It is a non-trivial task due to the following problems:

- The features of each modality are available from multiple views and provide complementary information. How do we fuse the features and explore the potential correlations to facilitate the cross-modal retrieval task?
- In order to learn a more discriminative latent space, we should enforce different-class samples to be embedded far apart. How do we incorporate the class information into the learning process?
- For incoming new queries, how do we map their multi-view features into the latent representation space and obtain the hash code?

This paper presents a novel multi-view cross-modality hashing method, termed as Multi-view Collective Tensor Decomposition (MCTD), which addresses the above issues under a collective tensor decomposition framework, shown in Figure. 1. To our best knowledge, the tensor decomposition has not been studied in the problem of cross-modal retrieval so far. Motivated by the issues that early fusion strategies, i.e. concatenating views, would lead to the problem of dominant views, we first propose a fusion approach for modeling the multi-view data of different modalities, and collectively learn a novel latent tensor representation between them by using tensor decomposition technique. Next, we consider enforcing supervision information as maintaining the block-diagonal structure of the latent tensor representation between different modalities, which eventually boils down to a block-diagonal structure loss term in the objective function. Finally, for new queries, we map the original features into the latent representation space by proposing a group

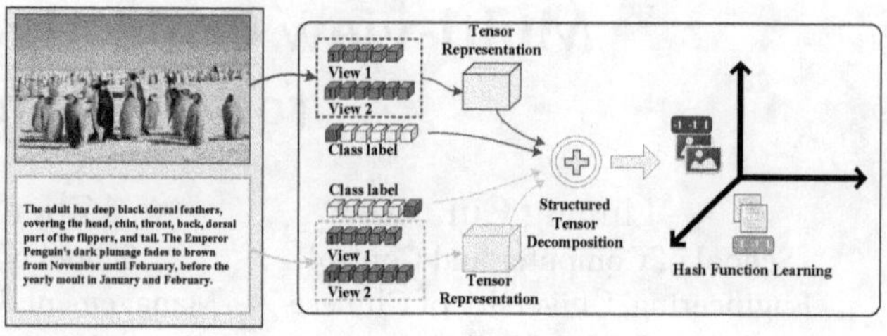

Figure 1: Multi-view Tensor Decomposition Hashing (MCTD) for cross-modal retrieval of images and text sentences.

of linear projections for each modality respectively. Extensive experiments show that MCTD yields state-of-the-art cross-modal retrieval performance.

2 RELATED WORK

Numerous papers have been published on cross-modal retrieval over the past decades [2, 8, 12, 14–16, 25, 27, 32, 35, 36]. Interested readers are referred to [29] for a comprehensive survey of various cross-modal retrieval methods. We now discuss related work in subspace learning and supervised cross-modal hashing.

Subspace Learning: In [37], authors proposed to perform cross-modal similarity search by employing Sparse Coding and Matrix Factorization (SCMF) to bridge the semantic gap and capture high-level latent semantic information. In [15], the Non-negative Matrix Factorization (NMF) was applied across the different modalities to tackle the multi-modal problem. In [31], authors proposed Semantic Consistency Hashing (SCH) method by learning a shared semantic space. A cross-modality hashing method based on matrix factorization (SMFH) [27] was proposed to consider the label consistency across different modalities. In [13], authors proposed a ranking-based method which constructs a common Hamming space where the cross-modal similarity can be measured by using Hamming distance.

Our collective tensor decomposition differs from these methods. On one hand, we explore the correlations of the input multi-view features. Different from traditional multi-view methods [24], MCTD considers multi-view features. On the other hand, inspired by the idea of collective matrix factorization, we propose to use tensor decomposition to learn the latent space which captures a broader view of features.

Supervised Cross-modal Hashing: The prior cross-modal hashing methods can be roughly divided into three categories including unsupervised, semi-supervised [33] and supervised cross-modal hashing. Here we only discuss several techniques that have explored the use of supervision information. In [32], Semantic Correlation Maximization (SCM) was proposed to seamlessly integrate semantic labels into the hashing learning procedure for large-scale data modeling. Semantics-Preserving Hashing (SePH) was proposed in [14], which can transform the given semantic affinities of training data into a probability distribution and approximate it with the hash codes in Hamming space. Semi-paired Discrete Hashing (SPDH) [23] jointly learns the latent features and hash codes with a factorization-based coding scheme. Discrete Cross-modal Hashing

(DCH) was proposed in [30], which directly learns discriminative binary codes while retaining the discrete constraints. As for deep learning methods, [8] presented a deep hashing model to capture the cross-modal correspondences between visual data and natural language. [34] used GAN for unsupervised representation learning to exploit the underlying manifold structure of cross-modal data. [19] proposed a hierarchical network with multi-grained fusion for cross-modal correlation learning. Cross-media multiple deep network (CMDN) was proposed in [18] to exploit the cross-modal correlation by hierarchical learning.

In contrast to previous work, we maintain the intraclass similarity and the interclass dissimilarity at the same time. This allows us to learn more subtle variations in data structure and leads to a more accurate and efficient algorithm.

3 MULTI-VIEW COLLECTIVE TENSOR DECOMPOSITION

Suppose that we have training data with n instances drawn from two modalities $\mathcal{I}$ and $\mathcal{T}$, where the data from each modality are composed with $V \in \mathbb{R}$ views. Specifically, $\mathbf{X}_I = [\mathbf{X}_I^{(1)}; \mathbf{X}_I^{(2)}; \cdots; \mathbf{X}_I^{(V)}] \in \mathbb{R}^{(m_I^1+\cdots+m_I^V)\times n}$ and $\mathbf{X}_T = [\mathbf{X}_T^{(1)}; \mathbf{X}_T^{(2)}; \cdots; \mathbf{X}_T^{(V)}] \in \mathbb{R}^{(m_T^1+\cdots+m_T^V)\times n}$ are the training data matrices drawn from modality $\mathcal{I}$ and modality $\mathcal{T}$ respectively, where $\mathbf{X}_I^{(v)} \in \mathbb{R}^{m_I^v \times n}$ and $\mathbf{X}_T^{(v)} \in \mathbb{R}^{m_T^v \times n}$ are the data matrix for the v-th view, m_I^v and m_T^v are the corresponding dimensions of view $v \in [1:V]$. The goal of MCTD is to learn two groups of hash functions for the data from each modality that are able to generate unified hash codes.

Multi-view Collective Tensor Decomposition (MCTD) is a unified framework with three main components for supervised learning to hash, as shown in Figure 2. The framework accepts input in an image-text pairwise form and processes them through latent representation learning: (1) collective tensor decomposition to generate a common latent representation space between two modalities represented in full-order tensor form; (2) a block-diagonal loss for exploiting supervision information; and (3) two groups of linear projections for mapping the new queries into the latent space.

3.1 Collective Tensor Decomposition

Most cross-modal hashing methods are built upon a reasonable assumption that heterogeneous data with the same semantic label share a common subspace [15, 27, 38], called latent representation space. In the latent space, the semantic representations of relevant data from different modalities are close to each other. We follow this idea and pursue a more general framework. In this part, we explore the correlations on multi-views across different modalities and propose a novel latent representation space learning method by using collective tensor decomposition.

Modeling Correlations on Multi-view: In order to capture interactions among the features across multiple views on two modalities, here we propose a fusion strategy by exploring the concept of Factorization Machines [21] to capture the second-order interactions as well as the concept of Multi-view Machines [3] to capture higher order interactions.

Hence, to fully utilize the complementary information provided by multiple views, we use the full-order interactions among all the V views to represent each data instead of the direct concatenating. Specifically, for each instance $\mathbf{x}_I = [\mathbf{x}_I^{(1)}; \cdots; \mathbf{x}_I^{(V)}]$ from modality $\mathcal{I}$, we can compose the full-order interactions among different views through the outer product of the feature vectors from different views as follows:

$$
\begin{aligned}
&1^{st}\ order: \mathbf{x}_I^{(v)} \quad \forall v \in [1:V] \\
&2^{nd}\ order: \mathbf{x}_I^{(v_1)} \circ \mathbf{x}_I^{(v_2)} \quad \forall v_1, v_2 \in [1:V], v_1 \neq v_2 \\
&\cdots \\
&V^{th}\ order: \mathbf{x}_I^{(1)} \circ \cdots \circ \mathbf{x}_I^{(V)}
\end{aligned} \tag{1}
$$

It is easy to integrate all the interactions into a unified tensor representation by adding a constant value "1" to each feature vector $\mathbf{x}_I^{(v)}$, $v \in [1:V]$. Let $\mathbf{k}_I^{(v)} = [1; \mathbf{x}_I^{(v)}]$, we have the tensor representation for each instance as $\mathcal{K}_I = \mathbf{k}_I^{(1)} \circ \cdots \circ \mathbf{k}_I^{(V)} \in \mathbb{R}^{d_I^1 \times \cdots \times d_I^V}$, where $d_I^v = m_I^v + 1$ for all $v \in [1:V]$. Different from directly modeling the interactions of feature $\mathbf{x}_I^{(v)}$, now we can get feature interactions with different orders which reflects complementary insights.

Then, the data matrix from modality $\mathcal{I}$ can be transformed into the data tensor $\mathcal{X}_I = [\mathcal{K}_{I1}, \mathcal{K}_{I2}, \cdots, \mathcal{K}_{In}] \in \mathbb{R}^{d_I^1 \times \cdots \times d_I^V \times n}$. Similarly, we can get the tensor representation for the data matrix of modality $\mathcal{T}$: $\mathcal{X}_T \in \mathbb{R}^{d_T^1 \times \cdots \times d_T^V \times n}$, where $d_T^v = m_T^v + 1$ for all $v \in [1:V]$.

Learning Latent Representation Space: In cross-modal hashing, heterogenous data are mapped into a unified latent representation space so that the similarity can be directly compared. Learning such latent space is of great importance. In this section, we propose a method called Collective Tensor Decomposition (CTD) to obtain the common representation. We apply Tucker tensor decomposition, which can be considered as a higher-order generalization of Principal Component Analysis (PCA). It decomposes a tensor into a core tensor multiplied by a matrix along each mode [10].

Suppose that we are given two heterogeneous data tensors $\mathcal{X}_I \in \mathbb{R}^{d_I^1 \times \cdots \times d_I^V \times n}$ and $\mathcal{X}_T \in \mathbb{R}^{d_T^1 \times \cdots \times d_T^V \times n}$. According to [17], the results of CTD on $\mathcal{X}_I$ and $\mathcal{X}_T$ can be expressed by

$$
\begin{cases}
\mathcal{X}_I \approx \mathcal{V} \times_1 \mathbf{U}_I^{(1)} \times_2 \mathbf{U}_I^{(2)} \cdots \times_V \mathbf{U}_I^{(V)} \\
\mathcal{X}_T \approx \mathcal{V} \times_1 \mathbf{U}_T^{(1)} \times_2 \mathbf{U}_T^{(2)} \cdots \times_V \mathbf{U}_T^{(V)}
\end{cases} \tag{2}
$$

where $\{\mathbf{U}_I^{(v)} \in \mathbb{R}^{d_I^v \times R}\}_{v=1}^V$, $\{\mathbf{U}_T^{(v)} \in \mathbb{R}^{d_T^v \times R}\}_{v=1}^V$ are the factor matrices (which are usually orthogonal) and can be thought of as the *principal components in each view*, $\mathcal{V} \in \mathbb{R}^{R \times \cdots \times R \times n}$ is the *core tensor* and its entries show the level of interaction between the different components. The $(V+1)$-th order tensor $\mathcal{V}$ is the common latent representation of $\mathcal{X}_I$ and $\mathcal{X}_T$.

The average decomposition loss for CTD is defined as

$$
\begin{aligned}
\mathcal{L}_{ctd} = &\alpha ||\mathcal{X}_I - \mathcal{V} \times_1 \mathbf{U}_I^{(1)} \cdots \times_V \mathbf{U}_I^{(V)}||^2 \\
&+ (1-\alpha) ||\mathcal{X}_T - \mathcal{V} \times_1 \mathbf{U}_T^{(1)} \cdots \times_V \mathbf{U}_T^{(V)}||^2
\end{aligned} \tag{3}
$$

where α is a trade-off parameter.

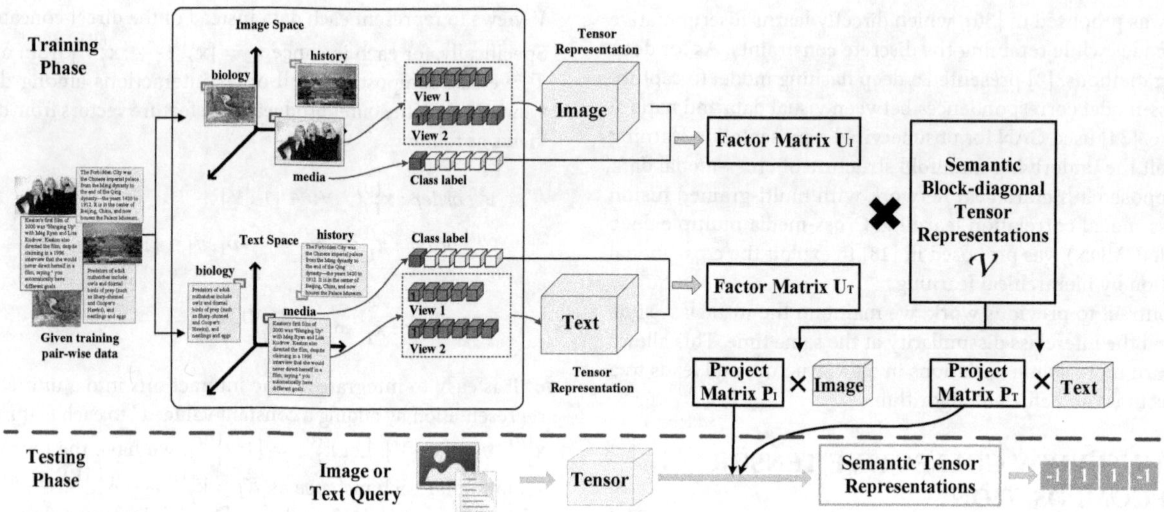

Figure 2: MCTD constitutes: (1) collective tensor decomposition to generate a common latent representation space between two modalities represented in full-order tensor form; (2) a block-diagonal loss for exploiting supervision information; and (3) two groups of linear projections for mapping the new queries into the latent space.

3.2 Block-diagonal Structure Loss

It is natural to assume that the intrinsic representations of data points from the same class are embedded in the same subspace and that these subspaces are separated. Therefore, it is straightforward to explicitly purse the block-diagonal structure of the latent tensor representation by exploring the labeled data. A novel loss named block-diagonal structure loss is proposed in this part.

Assume that these n data points are sampled from C classes and each instance is labeled with one class label. To better illustrate the block-diagonal structure, the labeled data instances are arranged according to their labels. For the tensor instances that belong to c class $\mathcal{X}_{Ic}$ and $\mathcal{X}_{Tc}$, their ideal common representation is denoted by $\mathcal{V}_c^* \in \mathbb{R}^{r\times\cdots\times r\times n_c}$, where r is the dimensionality of each subspace, n_c is the instance number of class c and $c \in [1:C]$. Since then, the ideal block-diagonal structured tensor representation $\mathcal{V}^*$ of data tensors $\mathcal{X}_I$ and $\mathcal{X}_T$ is shown as follows:

$$\mathcal{V}^* = diag(\mathcal{V}_1^*, \mathcal{V}_2^*, \cdots, \mathcal{V}_C^*) \quad (4)$$

However, the dimension of $\mathcal{V}$ is defined by hash code length, not by r. So we introduce a group of auxiliary matrices $\mathbf{Z}^{(v)}$ to change the mode of $\mathcal{V}$ into $\mathcal{V}^*$ with arbitrary dimension:

$$\mathcal{V}^* = \mathcal{V} \times_1 \mathbf{Z}^{(1)} \cdots \times_V \mathbf{Z}^{(V)} \quad (5)$$

where $\mathbf{Z}^{(v)} \in \mathbb{R}^{rC\times R}$ and $v \in [1:V]$. To enforce the block-diagonal structure of $\mathcal{V}$, we propose a loss function. In detail, let $\mathcal{E}_0 \in \mathbb{R}^{rC\times\cdots\times rC\times n}$ and $\mathcal{E}_c^* \in \mathbb{R}^{r\times\cdots\times r\times n_c}$ $(c \in [1:C])$ be the tensors with all elements equal "1". We first define an indicator tensor as

$$\mathcal{E} = \mathcal{E}_0 - diag(\mathcal{E}_1^*, \mathcal{E}_2^*, \cdots, \mathcal{E}_C^*) \quad (6)$$

Then, we have the loss of Block-diagonal Structure (BDS) as follows:

$$\mathcal{L}_{bds} = \frac{1}{2}||\mathcal{E} * (\mathcal{V} \times_1 \mathbf{Z}^{(1)} \cdots \times_V \mathbf{Z}^{(V)})||^2 \quad (7)$$

in which $*$ is the *Hadamard product*, which denotes the element-wise multiplication operator.

In fact, the block-diagonal structure loss can be seen as a global form of structural regularization that can influence the representations of all the classes. In this step, pursuing block-diagonal representations of the latent space guarantees that the representations of data points from the same class will be embedded in the same subspace and that different subspaces can be easily separated.

3.3 New Query Projection

For new queries, we can map the original feature interactions into the latent representation space by two groups of linear projections respectively:

$$\begin{cases} \mathcal{V}_I = \mathcal{X}_I \times_1 \mathbf{P}_I^{(1)} \times_2 \mathbf{P}_I^{(2)} \cdots \times_V \mathbf{P}_I^{(V)} \\ \mathcal{V}_T = \mathcal{X}_T \times_1 \mathbf{P}_T^{(1)} \times_2 \mathbf{P}_T^{(2)} \cdots \times_V \mathbf{P}_T^{(V)} \end{cases} \quad (8)$$

where $\mathbf{P}_I^{(v)} \in \mathbb{R}^{R\times d_I^v}$ and $\mathbf{P}_T^{(v)} \in \mathbb{R}^{R\times d_T^v}$ are the projecting matrix groups for all $v \in [1:V]$.

Since the tensors from different modalities that describing the same objects have the same semantic representations, we can present the loss for linear projections as

$$\begin{aligned} \mathcal{L}_{lp} &= ||\mathcal{V} - \mathcal{V}_I||^2 + ||\mathcal{V} - \mathcal{V}_T||^2 \\ &= ||\mathcal{V} - \mathcal{X}_I \times_1 \mathbf{P}_I^{(1)} \cdots \times_V \mathbf{P}_I^{(V)}||^2 \\ &\quad + ||\mathcal{V} - \mathcal{X}_T \times_1 \mathbf{P}_T^{(1)} \cdots \times_V \mathbf{P}_T^{(V)}||^2 \end{aligned} \quad (9)$$

3.4 Overall Objective Function

The overall objective function, consisting of the collective tensor decomposition term $\mathcal{L}_{ctd}$ in Eq. (3), the block-diagonal structure term $\mathcal{L}_{bds}$ in Eq. (7), the linear projection term $\mathcal{L}_{lp}$ in Eq. (9) and a regularization term, is given as follows:

$$
\begin{aligned}
\min \mathcal{L} &= \mathcal{L}_{ctd} + \mu \mathcal{L}_{bds} + \beta \mathcal{L}_{lp} \\
&\quad + \lambda \Psi(\{\mathbf{U}_I^{(v)}\}, \{\mathbf{U}_T^{(v)}\}, \{\mathbf{P}_I^{(v)}\}, \{\mathbf{P}_T^{(v)}\}, \{\mathbf{Z}^{(v)}\}, \mathcal{V}) \\
&= \alpha ||\mathcal{X}_I - \mathcal{V} \times_1 \mathbf{U}_I^{(1)} \cdots \times_V \mathbf{U}_I^{(V)}||^2 \\
&\quad + (1-\alpha)||\mathcal{X}_T - \mathcal{V} \times_1 \mathbf{U}_T^{(1)} \cdots \times_V \mathbf{U}_T^{(V)}||^2 \\
&\quad + \frac{\mu}{2}||\mathcal{E} * (\mathcal{V} \times_1 \mathbf{Z}^{(1)} \cdots \times_V \mathbf{Z}^{(V)})||^2 \\
&\quad + \beta(||\mathcal{V} - \mathcal{X}_I \times_1 \mathbf{P}_I^{(1)} \cdots \times_V \mathbf{P}_I^{(V)}||^2 \\
&\quad + ||\mathcal{V} - \mathcal{X}_T \times_1 \mathbf{P}_T^{(1)} \cdots \times_V \mathbf{P}_T^{(V)}||^2) \\
&\quad + \lambda \Psi(\{\mathbf{U}_I^{(v)}\}, \{\mathbf{U}_T^{(v)}\}, \{\mathbf{P}_I^{(v)}\}, \{\mathbf{P}_T^{(v)}\}, \{\mathbf{Z}^{(v)}\}, \mathcal{V})
\end{aligned} \tag{10}
$$

where μ, β and λ are the trade-off parameters of the corresponding terms, and the regularization term $\Psi(\cdot)$ is used to prevent overfitting.

The proposed formulation in (10) is hard to be directly solved since it is not convex or smooth with matrices $\{\mathbf{U}_I^{(v)}\}_{v=1}^V$, $\{\mathbf{U}_T^{(v)}\}_{v=1}^V$, $\{\mathbf{P}_I^{(v)}\}_{v=1}^V$, $\{\mathbf{P}_T^{(v)}\}_{v=1}^V$, $\{\mathbf{Z}^{(v)}\}_{v=1}^V$ and tensor $\mathcal{V}$. Therefore, we adopt an iterative multiplicative strategy. Specifically, the optimization procedure can be divided into the following steps:

Step 1: With $\{\mathbf{P}_I^{(v)}\}_{v=1}^V$, $\{\mathbf{P}_T^{(v)}\}_{v=1}^V$, $\{\mathbf{Z}^{(v)}\}_{v=1}^V$ and $\mathcal{V}$ fixed, the minimization over $\{\mathbf{U}_I^{(v)}\}$ and $\{\mathbf{U}_T^{(v)}\}$ are given by

$$
\begin{aligned}
\frac{\partial \mathcal{L}}{\partial \mathbf{U}_I^{(v)}} &= -2\alpha\Big(\mathbf{X}_{I(v)} - \mathbf{U}_I^{(v)}\mathbf{V}_{(v)}\big(\otimes \prod_{\substack{v'=V+1\\ v'\neq v}}^{1} \mathbf{U}_I^{(v')}\big)^T\Big) \\
&\quad \cdot \Big(\big(\otimes \prod_{\substack{v'=V+1\\ v'\neq v}}^{1} \mathbf{U}_I^{(v')}\big)\mathbf{V}_{(v)}^T\Big) + \lambda \frac{\partial \Psi\big(\mathbf{U}_I^{(v)}\big)}{\partial \mathbf{U}_I^{(v)}}
\end{aligned} \tag{11}
$$

and

$$
\begin{aligned}
\frac{\partial \mathcal{L}}{\partial \mathbf{U}_T^{(v)}} &= -2(1-\alpha)\Big(\mathbf{X}_{T(v)} - \mathbf{U}_T^{(v)}\mathbf{V}_{(v)}\big(\otimes \prod_{\substack{v'=V+1\\ v'\neq v}}^{1} \mathbf{U}_T^{(v')}\big)^T\Big) \\
&\quad \cdot \Big(\big(\otimes \prod_{\substack{v'=V+1\\ v'\neq v}}^{1} \mathbf{U}_T^{(v')}\big)\mathbf{V}_{(v)}^T\Big) + \lambda \frac{\partial \Psi\big(\mathbf{U}_T^{(v)}\big)}{\partial \mathbf{U}_T^{(v)}}
\end{aligned} \tag{12}
$$

where $\mathbf{X}_{I(v)}$, $\mathbf{X}_{T(v)}$ and $\mathbf{V}_{(v)}$ are the mode-v matricization of tensor $\mathcal{X}_I$, $\mathcal{X}_T$ and $\mathcal{V}$ respectively, $\otimes$ is the *Kronecker product* of matrices, and $\mathbf{U}_I^{(V+1)} = \mathbf{U}_T^{(V+1)} = \mathbf{E} \in \mathbb{R}^{n\times n}$ is the identity matrix.

Step 2: With $\{\mathbf{U}_I^{(v)}\}_{v=1}^V$, $\{\mathbf{U}_T^{(v)}\}_{v=1}^V$, $\{\mathbf{P}_I^{(v)}\}_{v=1}^V$, $\{\mathbf{P}_T^{(v)}\}_{v=1}^V$ and $\{\mathbf{Z}^{(v)}\}_{v=1}^V$ fixed, we have

$$
\begin{aligned}
\frac{\partial \mathcal{L}}{\partial \mathcal{V}} &= -2\alpha\Big((\mathcal{X}_I \times_1 \mathbf{U}_I^{(1)T} \cdots \times_V \mathbf{U}_I^{(V)T} - \mathcal{V}\Big) \\
&\quad - 2(1-\alpha)\Big((\mathcal{X}_T \times_1 \mathbf{U}_T^{(1)T} \cdots \times_V \mathbf{U}_T^{(V)T} - \mathcal{V}\Big) \\
&\quad + 2\beta\Big((\mathcal{V} - \mathcal{X}_I \times_1 \mathbf{P}_I^{(1)} \cdots \times_V \mathbf{P}_I^{(V)}) \\
&\quad + (\mathcal{V} - \mathcal{X}_T \times_1 \mathbf{P}_T^{(1)} \cdots \times_V \mathbf{P}_T^{(V)})\Big) \\
&\quad + \mu(\mathcal{E} \times_1 \mathbf{Z}^{(1)T} \cdots \times_V \mathbf{Z}^{(V)T}) * \mathcal{V} + \lambda \frac{\partial \Psi(\mathcal{V})}{\partial \mathcal{V}}
\end{aligned} \tag{13}
$$

Step 3: With $\{\mathbf{U}_I^{(v)}\}_{v=1}^V$, $\{\mathbf{U}_T^{(v)}\}_{v=1}^V$, $\{\mathbf{P}_I^{(v)}\}_{v=1}^V$, $\{\mathbf{P}_T^{(v)}\}_{v=1}^V$ and $\mathcal{V}$ fixed, the gradient w.r.t $\{\mathbf{Z}^{(v)}\}$ is shown as

$$
\begin{aligned}
\frac{\partial \mathcal{L}}{\partial \mathbf{Z}^{(v)}} &= \mu(\mathbf{E}_{(v)} * \mathbf{Z}^{(v)}\mathbf{V}_{(v)}\big(\otimes \prod_{\substack{v'=V+1\\ v'\neq v}}^{1} \mathbf{Z}^{(v')}\big)^T)) \\
&\quad \cdot \Big(\big(\otimes \prod_{\substack{v'=V+1\\ v'\neq v}}^{1} \mathbf{Z}^{(v')}\big)\mathbf{V}_{(v)}^T\Big) + \lambda \frac{\partial \Psi\big(\mathbf{Z}^{(v)}\big)}{\partial \mathbf{Z}^{(v)}}
\end{aligned} \tag{14}
$$

in which $\mathbf{E}_{(v)}$ is the mode-v matricization of tensor $\mathcal{E}$ and $\mathbf{Z}^{(V+1)} = \mathbf{E} \in \mathbb{R}^{n\times n}$ is the identity matrix.

Step 4: Similarly, with all the $\{\mathbf{U}_I^{(v)}\}_{v=1}^V$, $\{\mathbf{U}_T^{(v)}\}_{v=1}^V$, $\{\mathbf{Z}^{(v)}\}_{v=1}^V$ and $\mathcal{V}$ fixed, we can obtain

$$
\begin{aligned}
\frac{\partial \mathcal{L}}{\partial \mathbf{P}_I^{(v)}} &= -2\beta\Big(\mathbf{V}_{(v)} - \mathbf{P}_I^{(v)}\mathbf{X}_{I(v)}\big(\otimes \prod_{\substack{v'=V+1\\ v'\neq v}}^{1} \mathbf{P}_I^{(v')}\big)^T\Big) \\
&\quad \cdot \Big(\big(\otimes \prod_{\substack{v'=V+1\\ v'\neq v}}^{1} \mathbf{P}_I^{(v')}\big)\mathbf{X}_{I(v)}^T\Big) + \lambda \frac{\partial \Psi\big(\mathbf{P}_I^{(v)}\big)}{\partial \mathbf{P}_I^{(v)}}
\end{aligned} \tag{15}
$$

and

$$
\begin{aligned}
\frac{\partial \mathcal{L}}{\partial \mathbf{P}_T^{(v)}} &= -2\beta\Big(\mathbf{V}_{(v)} - \mathbf{P}_T^{(v)}\mathbf{X}_{T(v)}\big(\otimes \prod_{\substack{v'=V+1\\ v'\neq v}}^{1} \mathbf{P}_T^{(v')}\big)^T\Big) \\
&\quad \cdot \Big(\big(\otimes \prod_{\substack{v'=V+1\\ v'\neq v}}^{1} \mathbf{P}_T^{(v')}\big)\mathbf{X}_{T(v)}^T\Big) + \lambda \frac{\partial \Psi\big(\mathbf{P}_T^{(v)}\big)}{\partial \mathbf{P}_T^{(v)}}
\end{aligned} \tag{16}
$$

in which $\mathbf{P}_I^{(V+1)} = \mathbf{P}_T^{(V+1)} = \mathbf{E} \in \mathbb{R}^{n\times n}$ is the identity matrix. The optimization procedure of MCTD is summarized in Algorithm 1.

Overall, for any new instance $\mathbf{x}_I = [\mathbf{x}_I^{(1)}; \cdots; \mathbf{x}_I^{(V)}]$ and $\mathbf{x}_T = [\mathbf{x}_T^{(1)}; \cdots; \mathbf{x}_T^{(V)}]$ drawn from each modality, we first transfer them into the full-order interactions presented in the form of tensor representations $\mathcal{K}_I$ and $\mathcal{K}_T$ according to Eq. (1). Then, the MCTD is to learn two groups of hash functions for the data from each modality that are able to generate unified hash codes, i.e., $f(\mathcal{K}_I) = sign(\mathcal{K}_I \times_1 \mathbf{P}_I^{(1)} \cdots \times_V \mathbf{P}_I^{(V)}) : \mathbb{R}^{d_I^1 \times \cdots \times d_I^V} \rightarrow \{-1,+1\}^{R^V}$ and $g(\mathcal{K}_T) = sign(\mathcal{K}_T \times_1 \mathbf{P}_T^{(1)} \cdots \times_V \mathbf{P}_T^{(V)}) : \mathbb{R}^{d_T^1 \times \cdots \times d_T^V} \rightarrow \{-1,+1\}^{R^V}$, where d_I^v and d_T^v are the dimensions of mode-v fiber of tensor $\mathcal{K}_I$ and $\mathcal{K}_T$, and R^V is the length of binary codes.

3.5 Complexity Analysis

In the application, MCTD firstly generates the latent representation for a new query based on the achieved projection matrix groups $\{\mathbf{P}_I^{(v)}\}$ and $\{\mathbf{P}_T^{(v)}\}$, and then the hash codes can be obtained. The main time consumption of the proposed MCTD is the tensor decomposition, its complexity is $O(\Pi_{v=1}^V (d_I^v + d_T^v) R^{V-1} n^2)$. The parameters in Algorithm 1 are updated simultaneously, which indicates that the computation procedure can be paralleled. Therefore, the complexity caused by the interaction across V views is ameliorated. The convergence criterion used in our experiments is that the number of iterations is greater than a threshold (e.g. 200) or the decrease of the objective function value is smaller than a threshold.

Algorithm 1 MCTD

Require: Image feature matrix $\mathbf{X}_I$ and text feature matrix $\mathbf{X}_T$ both in V views, the length of hash codes R, the category C, and the model parameters α, β, μ and λ.
Ensure: Unified hash codes $\mathbf{H}$, and the projection matrix groups $\{\mathbf{P}_I^{(v)}\}_{v=1}^V$ and $\{\mathbf{P}_T^{(v)}\}_{v=1}^V$.
Transforming the data matrix $\mathbf{X}_I$ and $\mathbf{X}_T$ into the tensor representations $\mathcal{X}_I$ and $\mathcal{X}_T$.
Randomly initializing $\{\mathbf{U}_I^{(v)}\}$, $\{\mathbf{U}_T^{(v)}\}$, $\{\mathbf{P}_I^{(v)}\}$, $\{\mathbf{P}_T^{(v)}\}$, $\{\mathbf{Z}^{(v)}\}$ and $\mathcal{V}$ respectively.
while not converged **do**
  for $v := 1$ to V **do**
    Fixing $\{\mathbf{P}_I^{(v)}\}$, $\{\mathbf{P}_T^{(v)}\}$, $\{\mathbf{Z}^{(v)}\}$ and $\mathcal{V}$, update $\mathbf{U}_I^{(v)}$ and $\mathbf{U}_T^{(v)}$.
  end for
  Fixing $\{\mathbf{U}_I^{(v)}\}$, $\{\mathbf{U}_T^{(v)}\}$, $\{\mathbf{P}_I^{(v)}\}$, $\{\mathbf{P}_T^{(v)}\}$ and $\{\mathbf{Z}^{(v)}\}$, update $\mathcal{V}$.
  for $v := 1$ to V **do**
    Fixing $\{\mathbf{U}_I^{(v)}\}$, $\{\mathbf{U}_T^{(v)}\}$, $\{\mathbf{P}_I^{(v)}\}$, $\{\mathbf{P}_T^{(v)}\}$ and $\mathcal{V}$, update $\mathbf{Z}^{(v)}$.
  end for
  for $v := 1$ to V **do**
    Fixing $\{\mathbf{U}_I^{(v)}\}$, $\{\mathbf{U}_T^{(v)}\}$, $\{\mathbf{Z}^{(v)}\}$ and $\mathcal{V}$, update $\mathbf{P}_I^{(v)}$ and $\mathbf{P}_T^{(v)}$.
  end for
end while
Generating the hash codes by $\mathbf{H} = sign(\mathbf{V}_{(V+1)})$.

4 EXPERIMENTS

In this section, we conduct extensive experiments to evaluate the effectiveness of the proposed method MCTD comparing with several state-of-the-art hashing methods on two public cross-modal datasets.

4.1 Datasets

Experiments are conducted to validate the advantages of the proposed cross-modality hashing method on two real-world datasets.

Wiki[1]: Wiki dataset is collected from Wikipedia consisting of 2173/693 (training/testing) multimedia documents. Each document contains a single image and at least 70 words. Totally 10 categories are considered in this dataset and each image-text pair is labeled by one of them. Documents are considered to be similar if they belong to the same category.

Pascal VOC[2]: The data set [7] consists of 5011/4952 (training/testing) image-tag pairs, which can be categorized into 20 different classes. Since some images are multi-labeled, researchers usually select images with only one object as the way in [22], resulting in 1865 training and 1905 testing data. The image features include histograms of bag-of-visual-words, GIST and color. The text features are 399-D tag occurrence features.

4.2 Compared Methods

We compare the performance of our method with several state-of-the-art hashing based cross-modal retrieval methods including **CMFH**[3] [5], **LSSH**[4] [37], **SCM** [32], **SePH**[5] [14], **SMFH**[6] [27] and **DCMH**[7] [8], which can be organized into three categories:

- **Unsupervised hashing: LSSH** is an unsupervised method, which learns a joint abstraction space for image and text by using sparse coding and matrix factorization.
- **Supervised hashing (with shallow architecture): SCM** is a representative supervised method for cross-modal hashing, which is proposed to seamlessly integrate semantic labels into the hashing learning procedure. **CMFH** and **SMFH** are two methods based on matrix factorization, which both lean a common latent space for image and text. **SePH** uses the semantic affinities of training instances into a probability distribution and aims to approximate it in Hamming space. In the experiments, we use RBF kernel and take 500 as sampling size as advised in [14].
- **Supervised hashing (with deep architecture): DCMH** is the most recent work on deep cross-modal hashing, which integrates feature learning and hash-code learning into the same framework.

As existing cross-modal hashing methods can not deal with the multiple views, we concatenate the features to fit the model.

4.3 Evaluation Protocols

For Wiki dataset, each image is represented by a 128-D SIFT histogram and a 128-D CNN feature. We use the output of layer *fc8* in the Alexnet [11], which is pretrained on ImageNet. Each text is represented by a 200-D bag-of-words feature and a 10-D topics' vector generated by Latent Dirichlet Allocation (LDA) model [20]. For Pascal VOC dataset, each image is also represented by both hand-crafted features and deep features. The ground-truth neighbors are defined as those image-text pairs which share category label.

We perform two cross-modal retrieval tasks: using image queries to search relevant text ($I \rightarrow T$) and text query on image databases ($T \rightarrow I$). Following [14, 27, 32], we evaluate the retrieval performance based on two metrics: Mean Average Precision (MAP) and precision-recall curves. In our experiments, we repeat ten times for each group of parameters and report the mean MAP score. The results of numerical experiments are summarized in Table 1.

For our method, based on the rule of thumb, we set the parameters $r = 2$, $\alpha = 0.5$, and $\lambda = 0.05$ throughout the paper. The grid searching is applied to identify optimal values for the parameters from $\mu \in [0.001, 10]$ and $\beta \in [1, 200]$.

4.4 Quantitative Results

We evaluate all methods with different lengths of hash codes, i.e. 16, 32, 64 and 128 bits, and report their MAP results in Table 1, where the best results are presented in bold figures. From the experimental results, we can observe that the proposed MCTD method substantially outperforms all compared methods for cross-modal retrieval tasks which well demonstrates its effectiveness. Specifically,

[1] http://www.svcl.ucsd.edu/projects/crossmodal/
[2] htt p://www.cs.utexas.edu/~grauman/research/datasets.html
[3] http://ise.thss.tsinghua.edu.cn/MIG/code_data_cm.zip
[4] http://ise.thss.tsinghua.edu.cn/MIG/LSSH_code.rar
[5] https://bitbucket.org/linzijia72/
[6] We thank the authors for kindly providing the codes.
[7] https://github.com/jiangqy/DCMH-CVPR2017

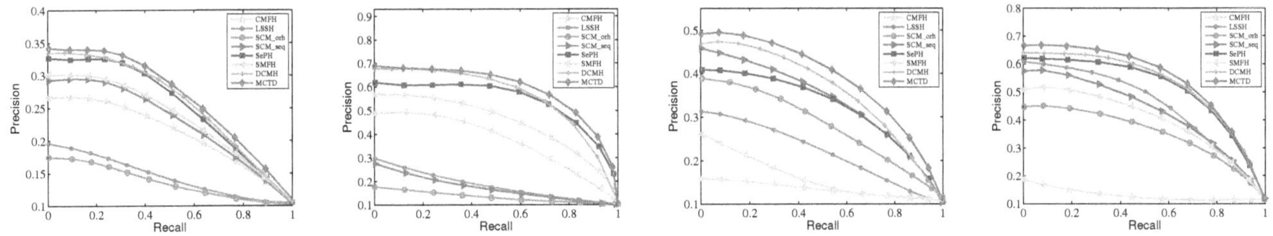

(a) Wiki (I→T) (b) Wiki (T→I) (c) Pascal (I→T) (d) Pascal (T→I)

Figure 3: Precision-recall curves of cross-modal retrieval on Wiki and Pascal.

Table 1: Mean Average Precision (MAP) for cross-modal retrieval tasks on two datasets. Items in bold indicate the best performance.

Task	Method	Wiki				Pascal VOC			
		16bits	32bits	64bits	128bits	16bits	32bits	64bits	128bits
I → T	CMFH	0.2115	0.2230	0.2238	0.2351	0.1575	0.1508	0.1490	0.1429
	LSSH	0.1541	0.1546	0.1544	0.1521	0.2988	0.3083	0.3194	0.3166
	SCM_orth	0.1527	0.1331	0.1216	0.1172	0.4063	0.4040	0.4067	0.4144
	SCM_seq	0.2257	0.2459	0.2461	0.2510	0.3842	0.4868	0.3972	0.4115
	SePH	0.2562	0.2654	0.2793	0.2823	0.4356	0.4424	0.4242	0.4245
	SMFH	0.2507	0.2646	0.2715	0.2787	0.2291	0.2477	0.2586	0.2500
	DCMH	0.2798	0.2809	0.2910	0.2993	0.4564	0.4613	0.4793	0.4801
	MCTD	**0.2919**	**0.3048**	**0.3068**	**0.3138**	**0.4921**	**0.4927**	**0.5194**	**0.5072**
T → I	CMFH	0.5351	0.5445	0.5586	0.5616	0.1576	0.1550	0.1523	0.1463
	LSSH	0.2641	0.2723	0.2795	0.2803	0.6145	0.6177	0.6042	0.5906
	SCM_orth	0.1532	0.1393	0.1297	0.1273	0.4791	0.4526	0.4962	0.4721
	SCM_seq	0.2341	0.2410	0.2445	0.2554	0.4816	0.5455	0.4526	0.4866
	SePH	0.6276	0.6324	0.6513	0.6514	0.6476	0.6524	0.6153	0.6571
	SMFH	0.4481	0.4827	0.4920	0.5038	0.4189	0.4942	0.6035	0.7388
	DCMH	0.6292	0.6524	0.6674	0.6720	0.6513	0.6504	0.6638	0.6708
	MCTD	**0.6482**	**0.6832**	**0.6898**	**0.6972**	**0.6567**	**0.6553**	**0.7074**	**0.7464**

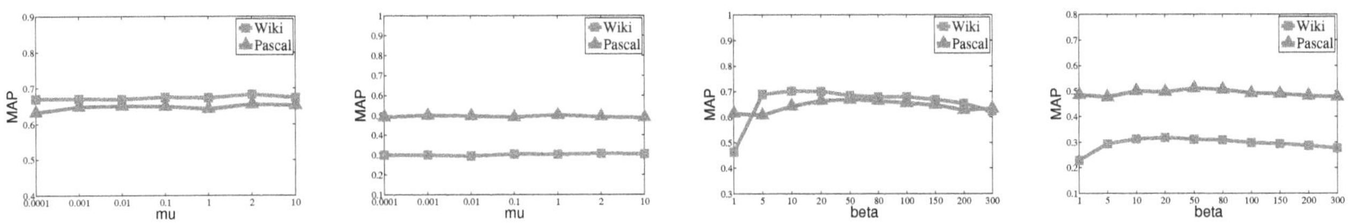

(a) μ (T→I @32 bits) (b) μ (I→T @32 bits) (c) β (T→I @32 bits) (d) β (I→T @32 bits)

Figure 4: Parameter sensitive analysis: the MAP score @32 bits on both the cross-modal retrieval tasks.

compared to the best results of CMFH, LSSH, SCM_orth, SCM_seq, SePH and SMFH, MCTD achieves absolute increases of 1.66%/2.44% and 3.36%/3.24% in average MAP score for two cross-modal tasks $I \rightarrow T$ and $T \rightarrow I$ on Wiki and Pascal VOC datasets. This indicates that MCTD can not only effectively leverage the complementary information provided by the interactions among multi-view features, but also make full use of the category information to purse the block-diagonal representations that can boost the discriminant ability among different classes.

An interesting observation is that our method performs better than deep method DCMH. We assume that our model can use both hand-crafted features and deep-learned features from multiple views and exploit the complex feature correlations effectively. To confirm our assumption, we further test the effect of correlations on multi-views in Section 4.5.

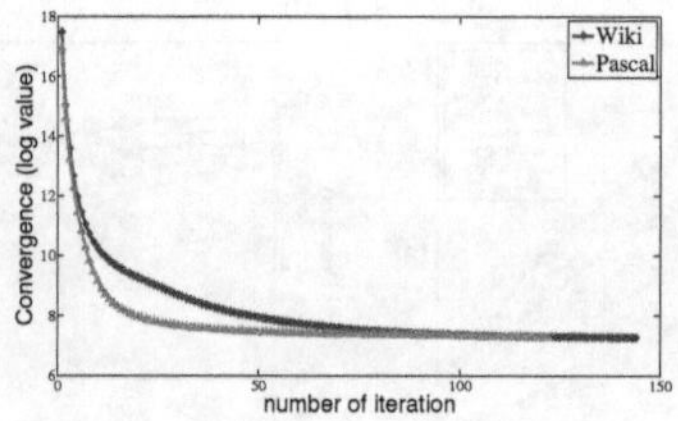

Figure 5: The curves of convergence validation: objective function value @32 bits on both datasets.

Table 2: The training time (seconds) of each method on Wiki.

Method	Dataset	
	Wiki	Pascal VOC
CMFH	14.02	16.38
LSSH	432.22	361.86
SCM_orth	2.90	29.72
SCM_seq	2.11	8.76
SePH	189.85	154.40
SMFH	39.02	60.78
MCTD	45.33	73.24

The precision-recall curves with 32 bits for the two cross-modal tasks $I \rightarrow T$ and $T \rightarrow I$ on these two datasets are presented in Figure 3, respectively. As it is shown, MCTD achieves the highly competitive results. Specifically, it achieves the second best precision at some lower recall values and obtains the best performance at the other recall levels on both datasets.

We then validate the convergence with 32 bits on these two datasets during each iteration. For making a clear show, we adjust the objective value to the log value. As shown in Figure 5, we can see that our method provides a satisfactory convergence rate in the optimization procedure on both datasets.

Finally, we investigate the training time of all these methods. The experiments are conducted on the Wiki dataset and run on a PC with 2.5 GHz Intel Core i7 CPU and 16GB RAM. As for experiments on DCMH, we use a server with NVIDIA GeForce GTX 1080 Ti GPU, so the training time is not included. Here we only evaluate the case that the code length is 32 bits. The results are reported in Table 2. We can observe that the time consumption of MCTD is of the same order of magnitude as that of CMFH and SMFH, both of which involve the computation of matrix inversion. The time cost is acceptable in comparison with that of LSSH and SePH. As MCTD needs to solve the object function in an iterative way, it spends a little more time than others in the training phase.

4.5 Effect of Correlations on Multi-views

To validate the advantage of correlations on multi-views, we present two variants of the proposed algorithm for comparison. The first one only uses the directly concatenated features and the second one only uses the highest-order correlations among all the views, where these two methods are referred as MCTD_c and MCTD_h. We evaluate their performance on the dataset Wiki with different lengths of hash codes and the MAP scores are summarized in Table 3. From this table, we can learn that the correlations on multi-views produce positive results and the full-order correlations can lead to the better performance by providing complementary information, which verifies the effectiveness of the proposed strategy.

Table 3: Effect of Correlations on Multi-views. Items in bold indicate the best performance.

Task	Method	Wiki			
		16bits	32bits	64bits	128bits
I → T	MCTD_c	0.2594	0.2783	0.2817	0.2909
	MCTD_h	0.2708	0.2865	0.2902	0.2944
	MCTD	**0.2919**	**0.3048**	**0.3068**	**0.3138**
T → I	MCTD_c	0.5536	0.6054	0.6231	0.6504
	MCTD_h	0.6024	0.6365	0.6592	0.6467
	MCTD	**0.6482**	**0.6832**	**0.6898**	**0.6972**

4.6 Parameter Sensitivity

We further discuss the performance of MCTD w.r.t the model parameters to analyze the effects of different parameter settings. The experiments are performed by varying the value of one parameter while fixing the others. Due to the space limit, here we only compute the MAP score @ 32 bits on both the cross-modal retrieval tasks, and the results with two important parameters β and μ are shown in Figure 4. From the figures, we can see that these two parameters are not sensitive and MCTD can yield satisfactory results in a wide range of parameter values.

5 CONCLUSION

In this paper, we propose an effective cross-modal hashing method called MCTD. Our framework builds upon complementary features from multi-views and combines this representation with tensor decomposition. More importantly, our method can discover multiple separated subspaces by leveraging the supervision information. Our innovations are shown as follows: Firstly, we propose to use collective tensor decomposition to capture the latent representation space between different modalities. Secondly, introducing a block-diagonal structure loss makes it possible to exploit the supervision information and maintain the global structure of the subspace. Thirdly, a group of linear projections for each modality, is proposed to map the original features of new queries into the latent representation space. In addition, we propose an optimization algorithm to solve the objective function, which can solve the problem effectively and is able to update multiple parameters simultaneously. Experimental results prove the effectiveness of our method in cross-modal retrieval compared to several competing methods.

Source code will be online shortly.

ACKNOWLEDGMENTS

The work is supported by the National Natural Science Foundation of China under Grant No.: 61672313, 61503253, 91546201 and 71331005, the National Science Foundation under Grant No.: IIS-1526499 and CNS-1626432, and Natural Science Foundation of Guangdong Province under Grant No.: 2017A030313339.

REFERENCES

[1] Grigory Antipov, Sid-Ahmed Berrani, Natacha Ruchaud, and Jean-Luc Dugelay. 2015. Learned vs. hand-crafted features for pedestrian gender recognition. In *Proceedings of the 23rd ACM international conference on Multimedia*. ACM, 1263–1266.

[2] Michael M Bronstein, Alexander M Bronstein, Fabrice Michel, and Nikos Paragios. 2010. Data fusion through cross-modality metric learning using similarity-sensitive hashing. In *Computer Vision and Pattern Recognition (CVPR), 2010 IEEE Conference on*. IEEE, 3594–3601.

[3] Bokai Cao, Hucheng Zhou, Guoqiang Li, and Philip S Yu. 2016. Multi-view machines. In *Proceedings of the Ninth ACM International Conference on Web Search and Data Mining*. ACM, 427–436.

[4] Changxing Ding and Dacheng Tao. 2015. Robust face recognition via multimodal deep face representation. *IEEE Transactions on Multimedia* 17, 11 (2015), 2049–2058.

[5] Guiguang Ding, Yuchen Guo, and Jile Zhou. 2014. Collective matrix factorization hashing for multimodal data. In *Proceedings of the IEEE Conference on Computer Vision and Pattern Recognition*. 2075–2082.

[6] Yunchao Gong, Qifa Ke, Michael Isard, and Svetlana Lazebnik. 2014. A multi-view embedding space for modeling internet images, tags, and their semantics. *International journal of computer vision* 106, 2 (2014), 210–233.

[7] Sung Ju Hwang and Kristen Grauman. 2012. Reading between the lines: Object localization using implicit cues from image tags. *IEEE transactions on pattern analysis and machine intelligence* 34, 6 (2012), 1145–1158.

[8] Qing-Yuan Jiang and Wu-Jun Li. 2017. Deep Cross-Modal Hashing. In *Computer Vision and Pattern Recognition (CVPR), 2017 IEEE Conference on*. IEEE, 3270–3278.

[9] Lu Jin, Shenghua Gao, Zechao Li, and Jinhui Tang. 2014. Hand-crafted features or machine learnt features? together they improve RGB-D object recognition. In *Multimedia (ISM), 2014 IEEE International Symposium on*. IEEE, 311–319.

[10] Tamara G Kolda and Brett W Bader. 2009. Tensor decompositions and applications. *SIAM review* 51, 3 (2009), 455–500.

[11] Alex Krizhevsky, Ilya Sutskever, and Geoffrey E Hinton. 2012. Imagenet classification with deep convolutional neural networks. In *Advances in neural information processing systems*. 1097–1105.

[12] Shaishav Kumar and Raghavendra Udupa. 2011. Learning hash functions for cross-view similarity search. In *IJCAI proceedings-international joint conference on artificial intelligence*, Vol. 22. 1360.

[13] Kai Li, Guo-Jun Qi, Jun Ye, and Kien A Hua. 2017. Linear subspace ranking hashing for cross-modal retrieval. *IEEE transactions on pattern analysis and machine intelligence* 39, 9 (2017), 1825–1838.

[14] Zijia Lin, Guiguang Ding, Jungong Han, and Jianmin Wang. 2017. Cross-view retrieval via probability-based semantics-preserving hashing. *IEEE transactions on cybernetics* 47, 12 (2017), 4342–4355.

[15] Hong Liu, Rongrong Ji, Yongjian Wu, and Gang Hua. 2016. Supervised matrix factorization for cross-modality hashing. In *Proceedings of the Twenty-Fifth International Joint Conference on Artificial Intelligence*. AAAI Press, 1767–1773.

[16] Sean Moran and Victor Lavrenko. 2015. Regularised cross-modal hashing. In *Proceedings of the 38th International ACM SIGIR Conference on Research and Development in Information Retrieval*. ACM, 907–910.

[17] Morten Mørup, Lars Kai Hansen, and Sidse M Arnfred. 2008. Algorithms for sparse nonnegative Tucker decompositions. *Neural computation* 20, 8 (2008), 2112–2131.

[18] Yuxin Peng, Xin Huang, and Jinwei Qi. 2016. Cross-Media Shared Representation by Hierarchical Learning with Multiple Deep Networks.. In *IJCAI*. 3846–3853.

[19] Yuxin Peng, Jinwei Qi, Xin Huang, and Yuxin Yuan. 2018. CCL: Cross-modal Correlation Learning With Multigrained Fusion by Hierarchical Network. *IEEE Transactions on Multimedia* 20, 2 (2018), 405–420.

[20] Nikhil Rasiwasia, Jose Costa Pereira, Emanuele Coviello, Gabriel Doyle, Gert RG Lanckriet, Roger Levy, and Nuno Vasconcelos. 2010. A new approach to cross-modal multimedia retrieval. In *Proceedings of the 18th ACM international conference on Multimedia*. ACM, 251–260.

[21] Steffen Rendle. 2010. Factorization machines. In *Data Mining (ICDM), 2010 IEEE 10th International Conference on*. IEEE, 995–1000.

[22] Abhishek Sharma, Abhishek Kumar, Hal Daume, and David W Jacobs. 2012. Generalized multiview analysis: A discriminative latent space. In *Computer Vision and Pattern Recognition (CVPR), 2012 IEEE Conference on*. IEEE, 2160–2167.

[23] Xiaobo Shen, Fumin Shen, Quan-Sen Sun, Yang Yang, Yun-Hao Yuan, and Heng Tao Shen. 2017. Semi-paired discrete hashing: Learning latent hash codes for semi-paired cross-view retrieval. *IEEE transactions on cybernetics* 47, 12 (2017), 4275–4288.

[24] Xiaobo Shen, Fumin Shen, Quan-Sen Sun, and Yun-Hao Yuan. 2015. Multi-view latent hashing for efficient multimedia search. In *Proceedings of the 23rd ACM international conference on Multimedia*. ACM, 831–834.

[25] Jingkuan Song, Yang Yang, Yi Yang, Zi Huang, and Heng Tao Shen. 2013. Inter-media hashing for large-scale retrieval from heterogeneous data sources. In *Proceedings of the 2013 ACM SIGMOD International Conference on Management of Data*. ACM, 785–796.

[26] Jinhui Tang, Lu Jin, Zechao Li, and Shenghua Gao. 2015. RGB-D object recognition via incorporating latent data structure and prior knowledge. *IEEE Transactions on Multimedia* 17, 11 (2015), 1899–1908.

[27] Jun Tang, Ke Wang, and Ling Shao. 2016. Supervised matrix factorization hashing for cross-modal retrieval. *IEEE Transactions on Image Processing* 25, 7 (2016), 3157–3166.

[28] Jingdong Wang, Heng Tao Shen, Jingkuan Song, and Jianqiu Ji. 2014. Hashing for similarity search: A survey. *arXiv preprint arXiv:1408.2927* (2014).

[29] Kaiye Wang, Qiyue Yin, Wei Wang, Shu Wu, and Liang Wang. 2016. A Comprehensive Survey on Cross-modal Retrieval. *arXiv preprint arXiv:1607.06215* (2016).

[30] Xing Xu, Fumin Shen, Yang Yang, Heng Tao Shen, and Xuelong Li. 2017. Learning discriminative binary codes for large-scale cross-modal retrieval. *IEEE Transactions on Image Processing* 26, 5 (2017), 2494–2507.

[31] Tao Yao, Xiangwei Kong, Haiyan Fu, and Qi Tian. 2016. Semantic consistency hashing for cross-modal retrieval. *Neurocomputing* 193 (2016), 250–259.

[32] Dongqing Zhang and Wu-Jun Li. 2014. Large-Scale Supervised Multimodal Hashing with Semantic Correlation Maximization.. In *AAAI*, Vol. 1. 7.

[33] Jian Zhang and Yuxin Peng. 2017. SSDH: semi-supervised deep hashing for large scale image retrieval. *IEEE Transactions on Circuits and Systems for Video Technology* (2017).

[34] Jian Zhang, Yuxin Peng, and Mingkuan Yuan. 2018. Unsupervised Generative Adversarial Cross-modal Hashing. (2018).

[35] Yi Zhen and Dit-Yan Yeung. 2012. Co-regularized hashing for multimodal data. In *Advances in neural information processing systems*. 1376–1384.

[36] Yi Zhen and Dit-Yan Yeung. 2012. A probabilistic model for multimodal hash function learning. In *Proceedings of the 18th ACM SIGKDD international conference on Knowledge discovery and data mining*. ACM, 940–948.

[37] Jile Zhou, Guiguang Ding, and Yuchen Guo. 2014. Latent semantic sparse hashing for cross-modal similarity search. In *Proceedings of the 37th international ACM SIGIR conference on Research & development in information retrieval*. ACM, 415–424.

[38] Xiaofeng Zhu, Zi Huang, Heng Tao Shen, and Xin Zhao. 2013. Linear cross-modal hashing for efficient multimedia search. In *Proceedings of the 21st ACM international conference on Multimedia*. ACM, 143–152.

Binary Coding by Matrix Classifier for Efficient Subspace Retrieval

Lei Zhou
School of Computer Science and Engineering and Beijing Advanced Innovation Center for Big Data and Brain Computing, Beihang University
Beijing, China
leizhou@buaa.edu.cn

Xiao Bai*
School of Computer Science and Engineering and Beijing Advanced Innovation Center for Big Data and Brain Computing, Beihang University
Beijing, China
baixiao@buaa.edu.cn

Xianglong Liu
School of Computer Science and Engineering, Beihang University
Beijing, China
xlliu@nlsde.buaa.edu.cn

Jun Zhou
School of Information and Communication Technology,
Griffith University
Queensland, Australia
jun.zhou@griffith.edu.au

ABSTRACT

Fast retrieval in large-scale database with high-dimensional subspaces is an important task in many applications, such as image retrieval, video retrieval and visual recognition. This can be facilitated by approximate nearest subspace (ANS) retrieval which requires effective subspace representation. Most of the existing methods for this problem represent subspace by point in the Euclidean space or the Grassmannian space before applying the approximate nearest neighbor (ANN) search. However, the efficiency of these methods can not be guaranteed because the subspace representation step can be very time consuming when coping with high dimensional data. Moreover, the transforming process for subspace to point will cause subspace structural information loss which influence the retrieval accuracy. In this paper, we present a new approach for hashing-based ANS retrieval. The proposed method learns the binary codes for given subspace set following a similarity preserving criterion. It simultaneously leverages the learned binary codes to train matrix classifiers as hash functions. This method can directly binarize a subspace without transforming it into a vector. Therefore, it can efficiently solve the large-scale and high-dimensional multimedia data retrieval problem. Experiments on face recognition and video retrieval show that our method outperforms several state-of-the-art methods in both efficiency and accuracy.

*Corresponding author (baixiao@buaa.edu.cn)

ICMR '18, June 11–14, 2018, Yokohama, Japan

ACM ISBN 978-1-4503-5046-4/18/06...$15.00
https://doi.org/10.1145/3206025.3206058

CCS CONCEPTS

• **Information systems → Nearest-neighbor search**; *Image search*; *Video search*;

KEYWORDS

Large-Scale Multimedia Data Retrieval; Subspace Retrieval; Binary Coding; Hashing; Matrix Classifier

ACM Reference Format:
Lei Zhou, Xiao Bai, Xianglong Liu, and Jun Zhou. 2018. Binary Coding by Matrix Classifier for Efficient Subspace Retrieval. In *ICMR '18: 2018 International Conference on Multimedia Retrieval, June 11–14, 2018, Yokohama, Japan.* ACM, New York, NY, USA, 9 pages. https://doi.org/10.1145/3206025.3206058

1 INTRODUCTION

Linear subspace is important for data representation in many multimedia and machine learning tasks. It has demonstrated excellent property in capturing the structural information of some specific data, e.g., face images under different illuminations [3], sequential frames in the video clips [22], classes of similar object [2]. In a high dimensional space, data can be either represented as subspaces or vectors. In practice, it is better to represent these data by subspaces rather than vector features because the intrinsic dimension of high-dimensional data is often much smaller than the ambient dimension [24].

When a query is a vectorized image representation and the dataset is composed of vectors, the problem can be solved by the nearest neighbor search. Thanks to the recent growth of multimedia contents, rapid search in a large dataset is greatly demanded. Many studies aim at efficiently retrieving relevant data from large-scale datasets. Because of the high-computational cost, traditional linear search (or exhaustive search) is not appropriate for searching in a large-scale database. Instead of linear search, many practical strategies are proposed for approximate nearest neighbor (ANN) search [7, 14, 15, 21]. The most general known approach is hashing algorithm which can efficiently solve high-dimensional and large-scale problems [1, 11, 25, 29].

When subspace is used as the representation, how to efficiently find the approximate nearest subspace (ANS) for a given query subspace has to be studied. This problem is related to a wide range of multimedia and pattern recognition applications such as image retrieval [12, 31], video retrieval [30], face recognition [5, 19], and action recognition [23]. A well known work on ANS retrieval was proposed by Basri *et al.* [2]. A mapping was used to transform subspaces to points, then the problem is solved by well-studied ANN search on points. Motivated by this work, some recent approaches [13, 26] utilized the idea of locality sensitive hashing (LSH) [6] to accelerate the searching process. More recently, Xu *et al.* [30] proposed a video retrieval framework, which defined a similarity-preserving distance metric between an image and its orthogonal projection in the subspace of the video. These approaches, however, represent subspaces by points in the Euclidean space or Grassmannian space before applying the traditional ANN methods. A subspace with dimension D will be transformed into a vector whose size is $\Theta(D^2)$. In addition, the transforming process for subspace to point may cause subspace structural information loss and additional calculational cost. Therefore, they can not efficiently solve the ANS retrieval problem, specifically for very high-dimensional data in a large-scale dataset.

In this paper, we present an efficient method for linear subspace retrieval based on hashing algorithm. The superiority of hashing algorithm in information retrieval includes two main aspects. First, binary signature generated by hashing can significantly reduce the storage space for large-scale data. In addition, pairwise data similarity can be fast estimated by calculating the Hamming distance between the corresponding binary signatures. Motivated by these two properties, we develop a method which can efficiently binarize the subspace and simultaneously preserve the similarity between subspaces. First we learn the binary codes for given subspace set following defined similarity preserving criterion. In order to solve the out-of-sample problem (a new query which is not used in training set), our algorithm leverages the learned binary codes to train a set of matrix classifiers to predict the code for query subspace. Here each bit of the binary code for subspace is considered as a class label for that subspace. Then we train r binary classifiers for the r bits binary code. For any given out-of-sample query subspace, the corresponding r bits binary code can be efficiently generated by the r trained binary classifiers. In our method, we use the Support Matrix Machines (SMM) [18] as the binary matrix classifier due to its excellent capability in capturing the structure information within the matrix data.

Compared with the previous works [2, 13, 26, 30], the advantages of our method are that it achieves fast computation without converting a subspace into a vector in the data space, and the classifier set can generate compact hash codes efficiently. In the offline stage, we learn the binary codes for given subspace set with the similarity between subspaces and simultaneously train binary classifiers by the learned codes. All calculations in this stage are done directly on subspace matrices. In the online stage, the query subspace matrix is directly binarized by the trained classifiers. Then we can use the Hamming distance between binary codes to quickly retrieve the ANS. Thus, our method can efficiently solve the ANS retrieval problem even with a high-dimensional and large-scale subspace dataset.

The main contributions of this paper are as follows.

(1) We propose an efficient hashing based solution for the ANS retrieval problem. Our method binarizes a subspace by defined similarity preserving criterion. The compact binary code can significantly reduce the storage and computational cost.

(2) The proposed method directly binarizes the subspace by a matrix classifier without transforming the subspace matrix into the vector form. Therefore, the proposed method can represent a subspace by a shorter binary code with less subspace structural information loss.

(3) Our method can efficiently deal with large-scale and high-dimensional multimedia data retrieval problem due to the compact and discriminative binary codes. Experimental results on face recognition and video retrieval show that our method outperforms the state-of-the-art in both retrieval efficiency and accuracy.

2 RELATED WORK

In this section, we review the related works on ANS retrieval. One of the earliest method in this area was proposed by Basri, Hassner and Zelnik-Manor (BHZ) [2], which represents a subspace $\mathcal{S}$ as its orthogonal bases matrix S [1]. Then a scalable mapping is defined to map S to a vector by taking the entries of the upper triangular portion of SS^T with the diagonal entries scaled by $1/\sqrt{2}$. This allows traditional ANN vector search methods to be applicable on the data. Based on this mapping, this method can solve the ANS problem when both query and database elements may be either points or subspaces of different dimensions. However, when the dimension D of the subspace is very high, the corresponding vector has size $D(D+1)/2$, so the efficiency of this method suffers from high-dimensional data.

Motivated by the above method, Wang *et al.* provided a LSH-based solution to the ANS retrieval problem [26]. This method represents the subspace as a point on Grassmannian, which is named as GLH (Grassmannian-based Locality Hashing). The LSH takes advantage of the geometric position of different subspaces as encoded in their principal angles with random lines, so this method provides good results in high ambient dimension. However, there still exists instability due to the strong randomness of LSH which will make the retrieval accuracy decreased when the training dataset is small [6]. A similar approach proposed by Stephen and Bruce introduces a subspace forest for determining the approximate nearest neighbors of points on Grassmann manifolds [20], which can be used to rapidly classify actions by

[1]Similarly, in our paper, all operations on subspace are done on its orthogonal bases matrix.

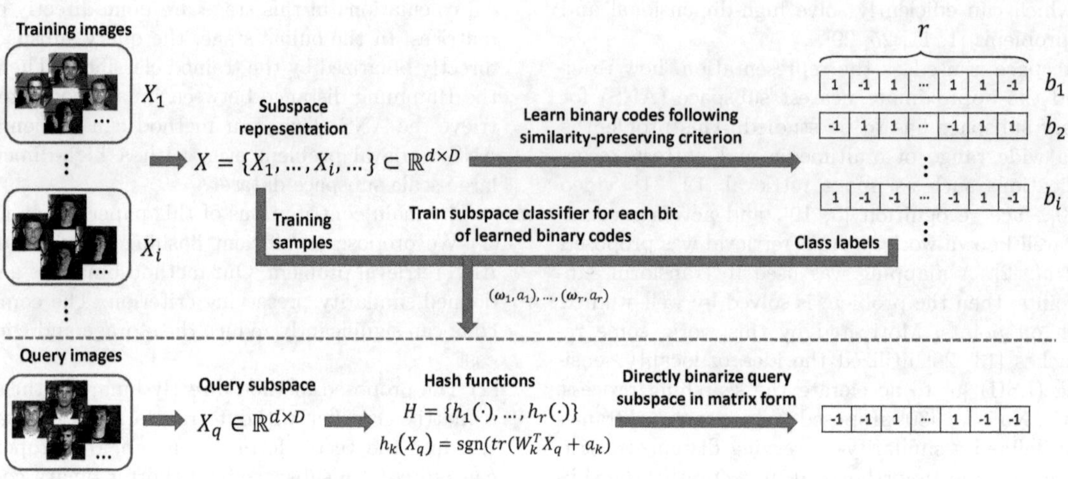

Figure 1: The proposed hashing based method for approximate nearest subspace retrieval. The process above the dashed line is the offline training stage which aims to learn a set of matrix classifiers that map subspaces to corresponding binary codes. The process under the dashed line is the online searching stage which directly binarizes the query subspace by the trained matrix classifiers. Then we can calculate the Hamming distance between binary codes to quickly retrieve the approximate nearest subspace.

a set of labeled samples. The subspace forest works in a manner conceptually similar to randomized forests for ANN computations, but respects the Grassmann manifold geometry.

Another hash-based ANS retrieval was reported by Ji *et al.*[13]. They presented a method to produce similarity preserving Binary Signatures for Subspaces (BSS). In this method, the angular similarity and angular distance between subspaces are first defined. Then a sign-random-projection function is applied to generate binary signatures for subspace. Ji *et al.* proved that the Hamming distance between the binary signatures is an unbiased estimator of the pairwise angular distance. Hence, they applied LSH to the ANN vector search problem. Since this method transforms the subspace matrix into higher dimensional vector, it needs a long binary code to preserve the similarity between subspaces.

More recently, Xu *et al.* [30] proposed a video retrieval framework, which defines a similarity-preserving distance metric between an image and its orthogonal projection in the subspace of the video. They first represented videos as subspaces of frames, and then asymmetrically projected images and videos into a common Hamming space, where they could efficiently retrieve the most relevant videos provided with an image query. Actually, their method also converts the subspace matrix into vector, and then learns similarity-preserving binary codes by the Euclidean distance between images and video subspaces.

The transforming process converting subspace to vector may cause subspace structural information loss and additional calculational cost. The problems of these methods have been solved in our algorithm. We leverage the binary classifier as hash function to encode the subspace into binary code without transforming the subspace matrix into the vector form. On one hand, the compact binary code for subspace can significantly reduce the storage space and computational cost for large-scale data. On the other hand, experiments show that our method can represent a subspace by very short binary code with less information loss.

3 PROPOSED METHOD

In this section, we describe the proposed hashing based method that solves the ANS retrieval problem. We first define the similarity between subspaces and construct an affinity matrix for learning the binary codes. Then the binary codes for given subspace set can be learned by the similarity preserving criterion. In order to solve the out-of-sample problem, our algorithm leverages the learned binary codes to train a set of binary classifiers as hash functions. Here each bit of the binary code for subspace is considered as a class label for that subspace. Then we can train r binary classifiers for the r bits binary code. For any given out-of-sample query subspace, the corresponding r bits binary code can be efficiently generated by the r trained binary classifiers. The process of the proposed method is shown in Figure 1.

3.1 Similarity and Affinity Matrix between Subspaces

First we define the similarity between linear subspaces. In our method, we use the definition of principal angles proposed in [10] which reveal the relative position of two subspaces. Let $\mathcal{F}$ and $\mathcal{G}$ be linear subspaces in $\mathbb{R}^d$, whose dimensions satisfy

$$p = \dim(\mathcal{F}) \geq \dim(\mathcal{G}) = q \geq 1 \tag{1}$$

The principal angles $\{\theta_i\}_{i=1}^q \in [0, \pi/2]$ between these two subspaces are defined recursively by

$$\cos\theta_k = f_k^T g_k = \max_{\substack{f\in\mathcal{F},\|f\|_2=1 \\ f^T[f_1,...,f_{k-1}]=0}} \max_{\substack{g\in\mathcal{G},\|g\|_2=1 \\ g^T[g_1,...,g_{k-1}]=0}} f^T g \quad (2)$$

Let F be an $d \times p$ matrix whose columns are orthonormal bases for subspace $\mathcal{F}$. Let G be an $d \times q$ matrix whose columns are orthonormal bases for subspace $\mathcal{G}$. It is easy to prove that the cosine of each principal angles equals a singular value of $F^T G$. Assume that the SVD of $F^T G$ is

$$F^T G = U diag(\sigma_1, \sigma_2, ..., \sigma_q) V^T \quad (3)$$

Where $1 \geq \sigma_1 \geq \sigma_2 \geq ... \geq \sigma_q \geq 0$. Assume that the principal angles satisfy $0 \leq \theta_1 \leq \theta_2 \leq ... \leq \theta_q \leq \pi/2$, we can get

$$\cos\theta_i = \sigma_i, \quad i = 1, 2, ..., q \quad (4)$$

Then the similarity[2] which reflects the angle similarity between subspaces $\mathcal{F}$ and $\mathcal{G}$ can be defined as

$$S_{\mathcal{F},\mathcal{G}} = \cos\theta_{\mathcal{F},\mathcal{G}} = \frac{\sum_{i=1}^q \cos^2\theta_i}{\sqrt{p}\sqrt{q}} = \frac{\sum_{i=1}^q \sigma_i^2}{\sqrt{p}\sqrt{q}} \quad (5)$$

With the property of singular value that $\sum_{i=1}^q \sigma_i^2 = \|F^T G\|_F^2$, where $\|A\|_F$ is the Frobenius norm of A, we can rewrite the similarity between subspaces as

$$S_{\mathcal{F},\mathcal{G}} = \frac{\|F^T G\|_F^2}{\sqrt{p}\sqrt{q}} \quad (6)$$

Given the defined similarity between subspaces and $S \in [0, 1]$, we can construct an $n \times n$ affinity matrix S for a subspace set $\{\mathcal{X}_1, \mathcal{X}_2, ..., \mathcal{X}_n\}$. Assume that $\{X_1, X_2, ..., X_n\}$ are matrices whose columns are orthonormal bases for $\{\mathcal{X}_1, ..., \mathcal{X}_n\}$, then the affinity matrix S between subspaces can be defined as

$$S_{ij} = \begin{cases} S_{X_i,X_j} & \text{if } S_{X_i,X_j} \geq \epsilon \\ 0 & \text{otherwise} \end{cases} \quad (7)$$

Where $\epsilon \in [0, 1]$. We select ϵ to make S a sparse matrix which shows the local similarity structure of the subspace set. The sparsity of affinity matrix not only leads to much lower storage space, but also brings a significant reduction to the computational cost of subsequent operations.

3.2 Learning Binary Codes for Subspaces

Given a set of linear subspaces $\mathcal{X} = \{\mathcal{X}_1, \mathcal{X}_2, ..., \mathcal{X}_n\} \subset \mathbb{R}^d$, the problem we address is to retrieve the approximate nearest subspace from the subspace dataset for the given query subspace. In order to rapid retrieval, we transform the subspace into binary code. Here we assume that X_i is a matrix whose columns are orthonormal bases of $\mathcal{X}_i$ and b_i is the corresponding r bit binary code for X_i. Our goal is to learn a set of hash functions which can well preserve the similarity between $\mathcal{X}$. Formally, the Hamming distance between two binary codes b_i and b_j is small when $\mathcal{X}_i$ and $\mathcal{X}_j$ is similar (S_{ij} is close to 1), the Hamming distance between b_i and b_j is large when $\mathcal{X}_i$ and $\mathcal{X}_j$ is dissimilar (S_{ij} is close to 0).

Based on the definition of the affinity matrix between subspaces, we first calculate the ground-truth affinity matrix S for $\mathcal{X}$. Where S shows the local similarity structure of $\mathcal{X}$. $H(\cdot)$ is a set of r hash functions we want to learn, $H(\cdot) = \{h_1(\cdot), h_2(\cdot), ..., h_r(\cdot)\}$. We learn the binary codes and hash functions simultaneously. In other words, our method aims to learn a set of binary codes $B = \{b_i\}_{i=1}^n \in \{-1, 1\}^r$ which can well preserve the similarity between $\mathcal{X}$ and simultaneously learn a set of matrix classifiers as hash functions which can map $\mathcal{X}$ to the learned binary codes.

The Hamming distance between b_i and b_j is given by the number of different bits between them. Since $\{b_i\}_{i=1}^n \in \{-1, 1\}^r$, the Hamming distance can be calculated as

$$d_{Ham}(b_i, b_j) = \frac{r - b_i^T b_j}{2} \quad (8)$$

To meet the similarity preserving objective, the optimization objective can be written as

$$\min_{B\in\{-1,1\}^{r\times n}} \sum_{i=1}^n \sum_{j=1}^n S_{ij} \frac{r - b_i^T b_j}{2} \quad (9)$$

Here $\sum_{i=1}^n \sum_{j=1}^n S_{ij} r$ is constant and $b_i^T b_i = r$. Let L be a diagonal matrix given by $L_{ii} = \sum_{j=1}^n S_{ij}$, the objective function Eq. (9) is equal to

$$\min_{B\in\{-1,1\}^{r\times n}} tr(B^T (L - S) B) \quad (10)$$

It is easy to find that except the constraint $B \in \{-1, 1\}^{r\times n}$, the above objective Eq. (10) forms a Laplacian Eigenmap problem. So we relax this constraint but still keep the similarity preserving objective. Then we can get the following Laplacian Eigenmap problem

$$\min_{\bar{B}} \ tr(\bar{B}^T (L - S) \bar{B}) \quad (11)$$

$$\text{subject to } \bar{B}^T L \bar{B} = I, \bar{B}^T L 1 = 0$$

The solution of this Laplacian Eigenmap problem is the r eigenvectors corresponding to the r minimal non-zero eigenvalues of $L - S$. Assume that the solution is given by $\bar{B} = \{\bar{b}_i\}_{i=1}^n \in \{-1, 1\}^r$ whose columns are the r eigenvectors, they are not binary codes but real-valued vectors.

Next we need to transform $\bar{B}$ into binary codes via a r-dimensional thresholding vector. As mentioned in Spectral Hashing [27], a good binary code should satisfy that each bit has 50% chance of being 1 or -1, and different bits are independent of each other. Therefore, we respectively select the median value of the r eigenvectors as a thresholding vector $v = (v_1, v_2, ..., v_r)$. If the l-th element of $\bar{b}_i$ is larger than v_l, $b_i^{(l)} = 1$ ($b_i^{(l)}$ is the l-th bit of b_i). Otherwise, $b_i^{(l)} = -1$. Furthermore, as the solution eigenvectors of Eq. (11) are orthogonal to each other, different bits $\{b_i^{(1)}, b_i^{(2)}, ..., b_i^{(r)}\}$ in the learned binary codes will be independent of each other. Then we get discriminative binary codes B which can well preserve the similarity between subspaces $\mathcal{X}$.

[2]Another definition in [26] is similar to Eq. (5). Here, we normalize the similarity for convenient calculation.

3.3 Training Matrix Classifiers

Although we have learned the binary codes for subspace set $\mathcal{X}$, it does not mean that the ANS retrieval problem has been solved. For a given new query subspace, if we add it into the subspace set $\mathcal{X}$ and update all binary codes according to the method we present above, the high computational cost obviously can not be accepted for practical application. According to the idea of hashing algorithm, we need a set of hash functions which can map the query subspace to corresponding binary code.

Since the subspace is generally represented as matrix composed by its orthonormal bases, we leverage the matrix classifier as hash function. Let each bit of the binary code for subspace can be considered as a class label (class '1' or class '−1') for that subspace. A binary matrix classifier can be trained for each bit of the learned binary codes. Then we use the r binary matrix classifiers to obtain the r-bit binary code for any query subspace.

In this paper, we use the Support Matrix Machine (SMM) [18] as the matrix classifier model due to its excellent ability in capturing the structure information within the matrix data. To capture the correlation among columns or rows within the matrix data, SMM imposes a low-rank constraint on regression matrix W to leverage the structure information. Since the nuclear norm $\|W\|_*$ is the best convex approximation of rank(W) over the unit ball of matrices, and the hinge loss is well fit for large margin principle, the formulation of SMM model is

$$\min_{W,a}\frac{1}{2}\|W\|_F^2+\tau\|W\|_*+C\sum_{i=1}^{n}\{1-y_i[tr(W^TX_i)+a]\}_+ \quad (12)$$

Where $\{1-e\}_+ = \max\{0, 1-e\}$ is the hinge loss function, W is the matrix of regression coefficients, a is an offset term, C is a regularization parameter, and y_i is the class label of X_i. SMM is based on a penalty function which is the combination of the squared Frobenius norm $\|W\|_F^2$ and the nuclear norm $\|W\|_*$.

Because each bit of the binary code is independent of each other, the binary classifiers of each bit can be trained independently. For the bit $b_i^{(k)}$, the corresponding SMM can be trained by following formulation

$$\min_{W_k,a_k}\frac{1}{2}\|W_k\|_F^2+\tau\|W_k\|_*+C\sum_{i=1}^{n}\{1-b_i^{(k)}[tr(W_k^TX_i)+a_k]\}_+ \quad (13)$$

Here we consider $b_i^{(k)}$ as a class label for X_i. After learning the binary classifier, the corresponding hash function can be formulated as $h_k(X) = sgn(tr(W_k^TX)+a_k)$.

Since the objective function Eq. (13) is convex in both W and a, we use the Alternating Direction Method of Multipliers (ADMM) [9] to optimize this convex problem. The objective function Eq. (13) can be equivalently written as

$$\min_{W_k,a_k,V_k} H(W_k,a_k)+G(V_k) \quad (14)$$

$$\text{subject to} \quad V_k - W_k = 0$$

Where

$$H(W_k,a_k)=\frac{1}{2}\|W_k\|_F^2+C\sum_{i=1}^{n}\{1-b_i^{(k)}[tr(W_k^TX_i)+a_k]\}_+$$

and

$$G(V_k)=\tau\|W_k\|_*$$

Then the augmented Lagrangian function of Eq. (14) is

$$\begin{aligned}L(W_k,a_k,V_k,\Lambda) =& H(W_k,a_k)+G(V_k)+tr[\Lambda^T(V_k-W_k)]\\ &+(\rho/2)\|V_k-W_k\|_F^2\end{aligned} \quad (15)$$

Where $\rho > 0$ is augmented Lagrangian parameter, and Λ is penalty parameter. ADMM solves Eq. (15) with the iterative equations

$$(W_k^{(i+1)}, a_k^{(i+1)}) = \min_{W_k,a_k} L(W_k,a_k,V_k^{(i)},\Lambda^{(i)}) \quad (16)$$

$$V_k^{(i+1)} = \min_{V_k} L(W_k^{(i+1)},a_k^{(i+1)},V_k,\Lambda^{(i)}) \quad (17)$$

$$\Lambda^{(i+1)} = \Lambda^{(i)} + \rho(V_k^{(i+1)} - W_k^{(i+1)}) \quad (18)$$

The condition of stopping iteration is that primal residual $r^{(i+1)} = \|V_k^{(i+1)} - W_k^{(i+1)}\|_F^2$ and dual residual $t^{(i+1)} = \rho\|V_k^{(i+1)} - V_k^{(i)}\|_F^2$ converge to 0.

From the solution of Eq. (13), we can successively obtain r hash functions $\{h_1(\cdot), h_2(\cdot), ..., h_r(\cdot)\}$, where

$$h_k(X) = sgn(tr(W_k^TX)+a_k) \quad (19)$$

Then we can efficiently get the corresponding r bits binary code for query subspace by these hash functions.

In our method, the dimension of query subspace must be equal to the training subspace due to the restriction by W_k. However, in practice, the dimension of query subspace may be different from training subspace (for example, when query is an image). Here we expand our method with the query subspace of different dimensions. Assume that the dimension of training subspace is d_t, and d_q for query subspace. In the case that $d_q < d_t$, we can add $d_t - d_q$ bases by randomly choosing from the orthogonal bases of query subspace. In the case that $d_q > d_t$, we can only select the first d_t orthogonal bases of query subspace. Experiments show that our method can be applied in query subspace of different dimensions, with little loss in retrieval accuracy.

3.4 Complexity Analysis

The whole process of proposed method is described in Algorithm 1. Here we analyse the time complexity of our algorithm. In the offline training process, if the given subspace set $X = \{X_i\}_{i=1}^n \subset \mathbb{R}^{d\times D}$, the matrix multiplication for similarity between subspaces in Eq. (6) needs $O(dD^2)$. The affinity matrix can be computed in $O(n^2dD^2)$. In the online searching process, computing the r bit binary code by Eq. (19) for query subspace costs $O(rDd)$. Therefore, the encoding time for query subspace in our algorithm is linearly dependent on the dimension d of training subspaces, regardless the size of training set. Experiments show that our method outperforms the previous works in the query time.

Table 1: The top 1 retrieval accuracy of four methods on two face databases, with different dimensions d_q of query subspaces. Here we show the accuracy of BSS with binary code length $r = 2000$, and the accuracy of our method with binary code length $r = 32$.

Method	Extended YaleB			YouTube Faces		
	$d_q = 4$	$d_q = 9$	$d_q = 13$	$d_q = 4$	$d_q = 9$	$d_q = 13$
BHZ [2]	0.8158	0.7865	0.7749	0.7318	0.7015	0.6803
GLH [26]	0.8772	0.8919	0.9001	0.7693	0.8014	0.8130
BSS [13]	0.9094	0.9653	0.9240	0.8072	0.8251	0.8062
Ours	**0.9415**	**0.9812**	**0.9561**	**0.8414**	**0.8821**	**0.8572**

Table 2: The query time (second) for one retrieval by four methods on two face databases, with different dimensions d_q of query subspaces. Here we show the query time of BSS with binary code length $r = 2000$, and the query time of our method with binary code length $r = 32$.

Method	Extended YaleB			YouTube Faces		
	$d_q = 4$	$d_q = 9$	$d_q = 13$	$d_q = 4$	$d_q = 9$	$d_q = 13$
BHZ [2]	0.3102	0.6980	1.086	0.9517	2.174	3.381
GLH [26]	0.0824	0.0824	0.1282	0.2415	0.2415	0.3757
BSS [13]	5.006e-3	5.006e-3	5.006e-3	0.0221	0.0221	0.0221
Ours	**6.257e-5**	**6.257e-5**	**6.257e-5**	**2.735e-4**	**2.735e-4**	**2.735e-4**

Algorithm 1: The proposed method for ANS retrieval.

Input: Training subspaces $X = \{X_i\}_{i=1}^{n}$ and the hash bits r.
Output: Hash functions $H = \{h_i\}_{i=1}^{r}$ and the binary codes $B = \{b_i\}_{i=1}^{n}$ of X.
Steps:
1. Compute similarity between subspaces by Eq. (6).
2. Construct affinity matrix S for X.
3. Optimize the Laplacian Eigenmap problem Eq. (11), the solution is $\bar{B} = \{\bar{b}_i\}_{i=1}^{n}$
4. Choose the r median values $v_1, v_2, ..., v_r$ of the r eigenvectors obtained in step 3 as thresholding.

```
for i = 1, ..., n do
    for l = 1, ..., r do
        If the l-th element of b̄_i is larger than v_l, b_i^(l) = 1.
        Otherwise, b_i^(l) = −1.
    end
end
5.Optimize Eq. (13) with B fixed.
for k = 1, ..., r do
    Optimize Eq. (13) by ADMM algorithm, achieving W_k and a_k.
    h_k(X) = sgn(tr(W_k^T X) + a_k).
end
```

4 EXPERIMENTS

To evaluate the performance of our ANS retrieval method, we undertook two sets of experiments on three public datasets. The first experiment was face recognition with two datasets: the extended Yale Face Database B [16] (including the Yale Face Database B [8]) and the YouTube Faces Database [28]. Another was video retrieval on the Big Bang Theory (BBT) [17].

4.1 Face Recognition

As subspace is commonly used to capture the appearance of faces under varying illuminations, we test the performance of our method by searching the approximate nearest neighbors on the extended Yale Face Database B and the YouTube Faces Database. We compared our result with several state-of-the-art methods BHZ [2], GLH [26], and BSS [13] in both query time and accuracy.

The extended Yale Face Database B (including 10 human subjects from the Yale Face Database B) contains 38 human subjects each with about 576 face images under 64 different illumination conditions and nine poses. The YouTube Faces Database contains 3425 videos of 1595 different people. For each people, there are 2.15 videos on average. We used the frame-images database which contains sequential frames extracted from the videos, and cropped only the face from each image.

In our experiment, we first resized all the face images to 32×32. For the extended Yale Face Database B, we constructed 9-dimensional training subspaces by randomly choosing 30 images out of the 64 images for each people in one pose, vectorized them to 30 1024-dimensional vectors and computed their first 9 principal components. The rest images were used for constructing query subspaces in the same manner. In practice, the dimension of query subspace may be different from training subspace. Therefore, we constructed query subspaces with different dimensions $d_q = 4, 9, 13$ which include dimensions smaller or equal or larger than the dimension of training subspaces. Thus there

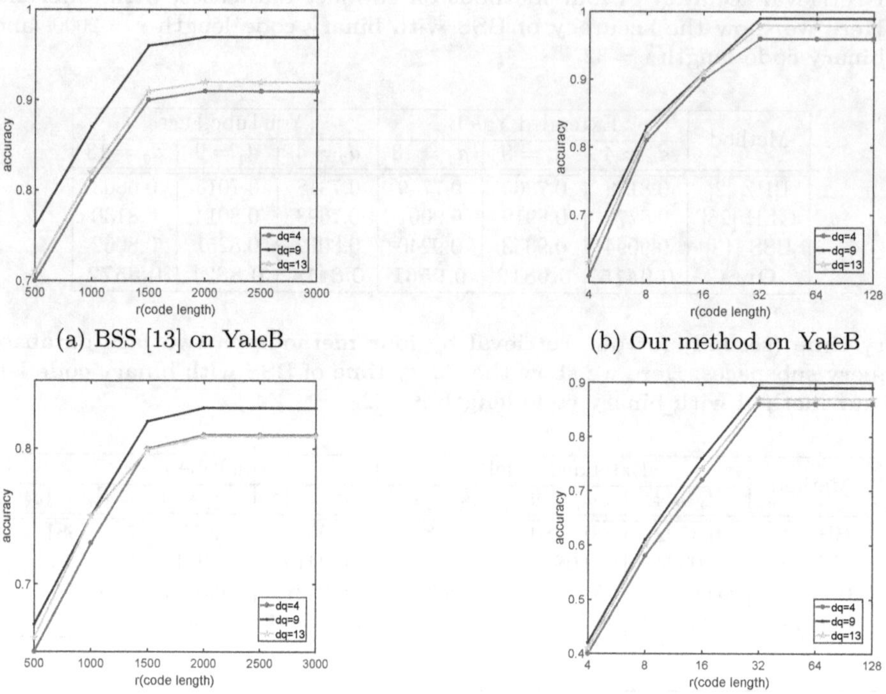

(a) BSS [13] on YaleB

(b) Our method on YaleB

(c) BSS [13] on Youtube Faces

(d) Our method on Youtube Faces

Figure 2: (a) The accuracy of BSS method with different code length on the extended Yale Face Database B. (b) The accuracy of our method with different code length on the extended Yale Face Database B. (c) The accuracy of BSS method with different code length on the YouTube Faces Database. (d) The accuracy of our method with different code length on the YouTube Faces Database.

were $38 \times 9 = 342$ training subspaces and $38 \times 9 \times 3 = 1026$ query subspaces (three different dimensions). In the training process, we set $\epsilon = 0.6$ in Eq. (7). For the YouTube Faces Database, we randomly chose 30 frame-images from each video as the training set, and the rest images were used for the query set. Then we constructed training subspaces and query subspaces by the same manner used in the extended Yale Face Database B. In the training process, we set $\epsilon = 0.6$. For each query subspace, we first encoded it by the learned hash functions Eq. (19). Then we retrieved for the nearest subspace in the training set in terms of Hamming distance between the binary codes. The top 1 retrieval accuracy of our method, compared with BHZ [2], GLH [26] and BSS [13], are shown in Table 1. Here we show the accuracy of BSS with binary code length $r = 2000$, and the accuracy of our method with binary code length $r = 32$. Due to the strong ability of classifiers to express the mapping of subspaces and binary codes, our method achieves better accuracy than previous work with shorter code.

As BSS also produces binary codes for subspaces, we compared our method with BSS by using different code lengths on the extended Yale Face Database B. As shown in Figure 2, when $r = 32$, our method achieves an accuracy of nearly 100%. BSS needs more than 1000 bit binary codes to

Table 3: The storage cost (byte) of two face databases. Here we show the storage cost of BSS with binary code length $r = 2000$, and the storage cost of our method with binary code length $r = 32$.

Method	Extended YaleB	YouTube Face
Original subspace	6.981e7	6.290e9
BSS [13]	3.561e5	3.209e7
Ours	**7.596e3**	**6.846e5**

achieve a good result. In our experiment, BHZ stores subspace with a vector in $1024 \times (1024 + 1)/2 = 524800$ dimensions, GLH stores subspace in 1024 dimensions, BSS stores subspace with 2000 bit binary code, and our method stores subspace with only 32 bit binary code. Thus our method has superiority in both query time and storage cost. Table 2 and Table 3 show the query time and storage cost respectively, where the query time includes both encoding time and retrieval time. We can see from Table 2 that our method is about 80 times faster than the state-of-the-art in query time due to the shorter code length.

4.2 Video Retrieval

Subspace is also a good representation of video clips. In this section, we show the superiority of our method by a video retrieval experiment on the Big Bang Theory (BBT). We compared our method with state-of-the-art methods HER [17], and IBC, BBC [30].

The Big Bang Theory (BBT) is a sitcom (about 20 minutes each episode) which includes many full-view shots of about 5 to 8 characters at a time. BBT1 (The Big Bang Theory Season 1) consists of 3,341 face videos of the first 6 episodes which are represented by block Discrete Cosine Transformation (DCT) feature as used in [4], which forms a 240×240 covariance video representation. For the training process, we set $\epsilon = 0.5$ in Eq. (7).

We constructed two sets of experiments, query by image and query by video. For query by image experiment, the experiment set of HER, IBC, and BBC are as done in [17] and [30]. For our method, we randomly extracted 300 videos for training and 100 images from the rest as query for the retrieval task. We first represent training videos as subspaces and learn the corresponding binary codes. Then we train a set of classifiers as hash functions. The binary codes of query images can be efficiently obtained by the learned classifiers, where an image is considered as one-dimensional subspace. The retrieval mAP with different length of hash code is shown in Table 4. Our proposed method outperforms the state-of-the-art methods. In addition, the query time of our method is also faster than previous methods.

Table 4: Comparison with the state-of-the-art methods on BBT1 database with different length of hash code.

Method	Query-by-image mAP			
	16-bit	32-bit	64-bit	128-bit
HER [17]	0.5049	0.5227	0.5490	0.5539
IBC [30]	0.5152	0.5369	0.5561	0.5645
BBC [30]	0.5080	0.5401	0.5643	0.5718
Ours	**0.5520**	**0.5915**	**0.6014**	**0.6083**

Although HER, IBC, and BBC are designed for query-by-image video retrieval, they can also be applied to query-by-video video retrieval. We use their definition of distance between projected image and video subspace to calculate the distance between video subspaces, and then apply their coding method. For our method, we first represent training and query videos as subspaces and then use our ANS retrieval algorithm. For query by video experiment, we randomly extracted 300 videos for training and 100 videos from the rest as query. Table 5 shows the result that our method significantly performs better than the state-of-the-art methods.

4.3 Parameter Analysis

In our method, we need set suitable parameter ϵ in Eq. (7). Here, we report experimental results on different databases

Table 5: Comparison with the state-of-the-art methods on BBT1 database with different length of hash code.

Method	Query-by-video mAP			
	16-bit	32-bit	64-bit	128-bit
HER [17]	0.5214	0.5431	0.5614	0.5854
IBC [30]	0.5425	0.5542	0.5736	0.5904
BBC [30]	0.5378	0.5537	0.5752	0.5968
Ours	**0.6013**	**0.6415**	**0.6523**	**0.6595**

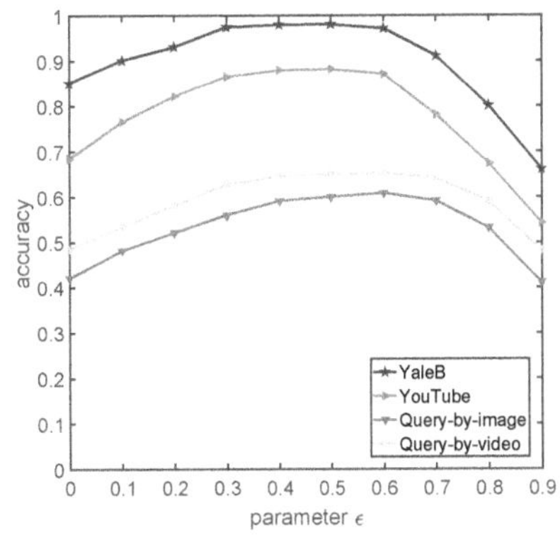

Figure 3: The accuracy of our methods with different parameter ϵ.

to illustrate the sensitivity of our methods to parameter variations. Figure 3 shows the recognition and retrieval accuracy of our method with different $\epsilon \in \{0, 0.1, 0.2, ..., 0.8, 0.9\}$. We can see that when $\epsilon = 0.5$, our method achieves best result for face recognition. When $\epsilon = 0.6$, the video retrieval accuracy reaches the highest.

5 CONCLUSION

We have presented a hashing based method to solve the ANS retrieval problem. This method first learn the binary codes for training subspaces following the similarity preserving criterion. Then the learned binary codes are used to train a set of matrix binary classifiers as hash functions. The compact binary code for query subspace can be efficiently generated by these matrix classifiers. Moreover, our method is further expanded to cope with the case that query subspaces have different dimensions. Several experiments on face datasets and video dataset show that our method can achieve a significant improvement in query time and storage cost with a competitive accuracy, when compared with the state-of-the-art approaches. This suggests that our method is potentially more suitable than previous work on large-scale multimedia retrieval task for real world applications.

ACKNOWLEDGMENTS

This work was supported by the National Natural Science Foundation of China project no. 61772057, in part by Beijing Natural Science Foundation project no. 4162037, and the support funding from State Key Lab. of Software Development Environment.

REFERENCES

[1] Xiao Bai, Haichuan Yang, Jun Zhou, Peng Ren, and Jian Cheng. 2014. Data-Dependent Hashing Based on p-Stable Distribution. *IEEE Transactions on Image Processing* 23, 12 (2014), 5033–5046.

[2] Ronen Basri, Tal Hassner, and Lihi Zelnikmanor. 2011. Approximate Nearest Subspace Search. *IEEE Transactions on Pattern Analysis and Machine Intelligence* 33, 2 (2011), 266–278.

[3] Ronen Basri and David W Jacobs. 2003. Lambertian reflectance and linear subspaces. *IEEE Transactions on Pattern Analysis and Machine Intelligence* 25, 2 (2003), 218–233.

[4] Martin Bauml, Makarand Tapaswi, and Rainer Stiefelhagen. 2013. Semi-supervised Learning with Constraints for Person Identification in Multimedia Data. In *Computer Vision and Pattern Recognition*. 3602–3609.

[5] Xinyuan Cai, Chunheng Wang, Baihua Xiao, Xue Chen, and Ji Zhou. 2012. Deep nonlinear metric learning with independent subspace analysis for face verification. In *Proceedings of the 2012 ACM International Conference on Multimedia*. ACM, 749–752.

[6] Mayur Datar, Nicole Immorlica, Piotr Indyk, and Vahab S Mirrokni. 2004. Locality-sensitive hashing scheme based on p-stable distributions. In *Symposium on Computational Geometry*. 253–262.

[7] Simone Ercoli, Marco Bertini, and Alberto Del Bimbo. 2017. Compact Hash Codes for Efficient Visual Descriptors Retrieval in Large Scale Databases. *IEEE Transactions on Multimedia* 19, 11 (2017), 2521–2532.

[8] Athinodoros S Georghiades, Peter N Belhumeur, and David Kriegman. 2001. From few to many: illumination cone models for face recognition under variable lighting and pose. *IEEE Transactions on Pattern Analysis and Machine Intelligence* 23, 6 (2001), 643–660.

[9] Tom Goldstein, Donoghue, and Simon Setzer. 2014. Fast Alternating Direction Optimization Methods. *Siam Journal on Imaging Sciences* 7, 3 (2014).

[10] Gene H Golub and Charles F Van Loan. 1996. Matrix computations. 1996. *Johns Hopkins University, Press, Baltimore, MD, USA* (1996), 374–426.

[11] Yunchao Gong and Svetlana Lazebnik. 2013. Iterative quantization: A procrustean approach to learning binary codes. In *Computer Vision and Pattern Recognition*. 817–824.

[12] Xiaofei He. 2004. Incremental semi-supervised subspace learning for image retrieval. In *Proceedings of the 2004 ACM International Conference on Multimedia*. ACM, 2–8.

[13] J. Ji, J. Li, Q. Tian, S. Yan, and B. Zhang. 2015. Angular-Similarity-Preserving Binary Signatures for Linear Subspaces. *IEEE Transactions on Image Processing* 24, 11 (2015), 4372–80.

[14] Yu-Gang Jiang, Jun Wang, Xiangyang Xue, and Shih-Fu Chang. 2013. Query-adaptive image search with hash codes. *IEEE Transactions on Multimedia* 15, 2 (2013), 442–453.

[15] Yin-Hsi Kuo, Kuan-Ting Chen, Chien-Hsing Chiang, and Winston H Hsu. 2009. Query expansion for hash-based image object retrieval. In *Proceedings of the 2009 ACM International Conference on Multimedia*. ACM, 65–74.

[16] Kuangchih Lee, Jeffrey Ho, and David Kriegman. 2005. Acquiring linear subspaces for face recognition under variable lighting. *IEEE Transactions on Pattern Analysis and Machine Intelligence* 27, 5 (2005), 684–698.

[17] Yan Li, Ruiping Wang, Zhiwu Huang, Shiguang Shan, and Xilin Chen. 2015. Face video retrieval with image query via hashing across Euclidean space and Riemannian manifold. In *Computer Vision and Pattern Recognition*. 4758–4767.

[18] Luo Luo, Yubo Xie, Zhihua Zhang, and Wujun Li. 2015. Support Matrix Machines. *International Conference on Machine Learning* (2015), 938–947.

[19] Nam Nguyen, Wanquan Liu, and Svetha Venkatesh. 2007. Random subspace two-dimensional PCA for face recognition. In *Pacific-Rim Conference on Multimedia*. Springer, 655–664.

[20] S O'Hara and B. A Draper. 2012. Scalable action recognition with a subspace forest. In *Computer Vision and Pattern Recognition*. 1210–1217.

[21] Fumin Shen, Wei Liu, Shaoting Zhang, Yang Yang, and Heng Tao Shen. 2015. Learning Binary Codes for Maximum Inner Product Search. In *International Conference on Computer Vision*. 4148–4156.

[22] Mei-Ling Shyu, Zongxing Xie, Min Chen, and Shu-Ching Chen. 2008. Video semantic event/concept detection using a subspace-based multimedia data mining framework. *IEEE Transactions on Multimedia* 10, 2 (2008), 252–259.

[23] Litian Sun and Kiyoharu Aizawa. 2013. Action recognition using invariant features under unexampled viewing conditions. In *Proceedings of the 2013 ACM International Conference on Multimedia*. ACM, 389–392.

[24] René Vidal. 2011. Subspace clustering. *IEEE Signal Processing Magazine* 28, 2 (2011), 52–68.

[25] Daixin Wang, Peng Cui, Mingdong Ou, and Wenwu Zhu. 2015. Learning compact hash codes for multimodal representations using orthogonal deep structure. *IEEE Transactions on Multimedia* 17, 9 (2015), 1404–1416.

[26] Xu Wang, Stefan Atev, John Wright, and Gilad Lerman. 2013. Fast Subspace Search via Grassmannian Based Hashing. In *International Conference on Computer Vision*. 2776–2783.

[27] Yair Weiss, Antonio Torralba, and Robert Fergus. 2008. Spectral Hashing. In *Advances in Neural Information Processing Systems*. 1753–1760.

[28] L. Wolf, T. Hassner, and I. Maoz. 2011. Face recognition in unconstrained videos with matched background similarity. In *Computer Vision and Pattern Recognition*. 529–534.

[29] Dayan Wu, Zheng Lin, Bo Li, Mingzhen Ye, and Weiping Wang. 2017. Deep Supervised Hashing for Multi-Label and Large-Scale Image Retrieval. In *Proceedings of the 2017 ACM International Conference on Multimedia Retrieval*. ACM, 150–158.

[30] Ruicong Xu, Yang Yang, Fumin Shen, Ning Xie, and Heng Tao Shen. 2017. Efficient Binary Coding for Subspace-based Query-by-Image Video Retrieval. In *Proceedings of the 2017 ACM International Conference on Multimedia*. ACM, 1354–1362.

[31] Mingmin Zhen, Wenmin Wang, and Ronggang Wang. 2016. Regional Subspace Projection Coding for Image Retrieval. In *Proceedings of the 2016 ACM International Conference on Multimedia Retrieval*. ACM, 205–212.

Instance Image Retrieval by Aggregating Sample-based Discriminative Characteristics

Zhongyan Zhang
School of Computing and Information Technology
University of Wollongong Australia

Lei Wang
School of Computing and Information Technology
University of Wollongong Australia

Yang Wang
Data61,CSIRO

Luping Zhou
School of Electrical and Information Engineering
University of Sydney

Jianjia Zhang
Data61,CSIRO

Fang Chen
Data61,CSIRO

ABSTRACT

Identifying the discriminative characteristic of a query is important for image retrieval. For retrieval without human interaction, such characteristic is usually obtained by average query expansion (AQE) or its discriminative variant (DQE) learned from pseudo-examples online, among others. In this paper, we propose a new query expansion method to further improve the above ones. The key idea is to learn a "unique" discriminative characteristic for each database image, in an offline manner. During retrieval, the characteristic of a query is obtained by aggregating the unique characteristics of the query-relevant images collected from an initial retrieval result. Compared with AQE which works in the original feature space, our method works in the space of the unique characteristics of database images, significantly enhancing the discriminative power of the characteristic identified for a query. Compared with DQE, our method needs neither pseudo-labeled negatives nor the online learning process, leading to more efficient retrieval and even better performance. The experimental study conducted on seven benchmark datasets verifies the considerable improvement achieved by the proposed method, and also demonstrates its application to the state-of-the-art diffusion-based image retrieval.

KEYWORDS

Instance Image Retrieval, Query Expansion, Discriminative Characteristic

ACM Reference Format:

Zhongyan Zhang, Lei Wang, Yang Wang, Luping Zhou, Jianjia Zhang, and Fang Chen. 2018. Instance Image Retrieval by Aggregating Sample-based Discriminative Characteristics. In *ICMR '18: 2018 International Conference on Multimedia Retrieval, June 11–14, 2018, Yokohama, Japan.* ACM, New York, NY, USA, 9 pages. https://doi.org/10.1145/3206025.3206069

ICMR '18, June 11–14, 2018, Yokohama, Japan

ACM ISBN 978-1-4503-5046-4/18/06...$15.00
https://doi.org/10.1145/3206025.3206069

1 INTRODUCTION

Instance image retrieval aims to retrieve images that contain an object similar to the one presented in a query image submitted by users. In the past decade, the performance of instance retrieval has been significantly improved by utilizing various powerful visual representations, especially the recent ones based on convolutional neural networks (CNN) [7, 14, 15, 25, 32]. Nevertheless, even with the state-of-the-art CNN-based feature representation [2, 27, 29], simply applying a Euclidean search for retrieval still cannot obtain satisfying performance, because it does not fully take the characteristic of a query into account. In other words, for a given query, an ideal retrieval scheme should adaptively identify its characteristic and utilize them to search for query-relevant images. To achieve this goal, a set of query-adaptive methods have been developed in the literature, and they can be roughly categorized into the following three groups.

The methods in the first group focus on using multiple visual features, and aim to design an adaptive feature fusion scheme with respect to a query. A rule for adaptively combining multiple features therefore needs to be learned [30, 31]. However, how to adapt a retrieval scheme in the case of a single feature is not in the focus of these methods. Also, they are less relevant to our work when compared with the following two groups. The second group consists of the methods using user relevance feedback. With human in the loop of retrieval, user's feedback provides more precise and straightforward information, for example true positive and true negative images, for learning the characteristic of a query and its class adaptively [23]. During the past two decades, a great deal of methods have been developed for this scenario, and there has been a large body of literature [35]. However, this kind of feedback requires human users to manually label the retrieved images, and such interaction is not always available for a retrieval task. In this paper, we do not assume the availability of such feedback, and our work is more related to the third group introduced as follows.

When there is no explicit user relevance feedback, query expansion (QE) [5, 26] becomes an effective mechanism to adaptively identify the characteristic of a query to enhance retrieval. Query expansion can be regarded as a kind of blind relevance feedback retrieval [6], which automatically "pseudo-labels" part of retrieved images according to an initial ranking result to mimic user relevance feedback. The characteristic of a query or its class is obtained through these pseudo-labeled examples to help construct a query-adaptive retrieval scheme. Generally, a query expansion method contains two crucial components: one is how to make the pseudo-labeling more precise in order to collect the true positive/negative images, and the other is on what characteristic should be learned with these collected images. The earliest query expansion method applied to content-based image retrieval is average query expansion (AQE) [6]. It labels the k-nearest neighbors of a given query as true positive images, and then computes the mean of their feature representations as a new query to refine the retrieval. Another work [1], which is most related to ours, proposes a discriminative query expansion (DQE). It simply regards the top- and bottom-ranked images in an initial ranking list as true positive and negative examples, respectively, and trains an SVM classifier in an online manner. The projection direction of this SVM classifier identifies the discriminative characteristic of a query and its class, and is used to realize a query-adaptive similarity measure.

Although the existing query expansion methods (e.g., AQE and DQE) dramatically improve the retrieval performance, this paper proposes a new query expansion method to further improve them at the following aspects. Specifically, for AQE, it works on the original feature representations, and does not effectively exploit the unique characteristic of each image when compared with the remaining ones in a database. For DQE, the limited pseudo-labeled negative examples usually cannot faithfully represent the class of true negatives, and this degrades the quality of the trained SVM classifier. In addition, training a classifier online prolongs the retrieval process and therefore affects its real-time performance usually required. To address these issues, we actively learn the unique characteristic (e.g., with the well known Exemplar-SVM [16]) of each image in a database with respect to the remaining ones. The characteristic of a query (again as a projection direction) is then obtained by aggregating the unique characteristics of the images collected as "true positive" ones. Such a direction plays a role similar as the weight vector of the SVM classifier in DQE to indicate the discriminative characteristic of a query and its class. Hence, it can produce better retrieval than the averaged relevant feature representations used by AQE. Compared with DQE, our method does not need to pseudo-label any true negatives or perform an online learning of classifier. This advantage is again attributed to our idea on exploiting the unique characteristic of each database image, which can be readily learned in an offline manner. In this way, only the aggregation of some unique characteristics needs to be performed online, which makes the computational cost of our method as light as that of AQE and the the retrieval performance better.

Besides, note that similar as AQE our method also critically depends on collecting true positive images. To achieve this, advanced k-nearest neighbor search methods have been developed, for example, the work in [8, 20]. Both search methods require a good enough initial set of k-reciprocal neighbors with respect to a query. Nevertheless, this requirement may not be met in practice due to the lack of sufficient true positives and the wrong inclusion of true negatives in this set. In this paper, we again exploit our "aggregating unique characteristics" idea proposed above to enhance the quality of this initial set. This not only improves the overall performance of our whole method, but also allows us to maximally utilize the potential of such an idea.

In addition, our method essentially gives rise to a better similarity measure between images. It can therefore be applied to any scenario where image similarity needs to be evaluated. For example, diffusion process has recently produced the state-of-the-art performance for image retrieval by working with deep convolutional feature [11]. One key component of diffusion process in this case is to construct an affinity matrix over an image database. To demonstrate the usefulness of our method, we also apply it to construct this affinity matrix to further improve the retrieval performance of the diffusion-based method.

The contributions of our work are summarized as follows:

1) We propose to identify the characteristic of a query by aggregating the unique characteristics of proper images in a database. This not only helps to find more discriminative characteristic to enhance retrieval, but also switches classifier learning from online to offline to shorten system response time.

2) Considering the importance of collecting true positive images for query expansion methods, we also improve existing k-nearest neighbor search methods by using our "aggregating unique characteristics" idea. This helps to improve the initial set required by these methods with more true positives and less false positives.

3) To show its usefulness, we apply the proposed method to construct the affinity matrix of the state-of-the-art diffusion-based image retrieval and this further improves its performance.

Experimental study is conducted on seven benchmark data sets to verify the effectiveness and advantage of the proposed method. As demonstrated, the proposed method achieves the overall best retrieval performance when compared with existing methods such as AQE, DQE, and other related ones.

The remaining part of this paper is organized as follows. We first introduce the related work in Section 2. Section 3 describes the detail of the proposed method and its application to diffusion process. Experimental study and result analysis are presented in Section 4. Finally, Section 5 draws the conclusion of the paper.

2 RELATED WORK

There are three lines of literature that are related to our work. We first give the overview of query expansion methods that are related to the proposed method. Then, Exemplar-SVM [16] which we utilize as our tool to learn the unique characteristic of each database image is reviewed. At last, as an application to verify the effectiveness of the proposed method, diffusion-based image retrieval is introduced.

After firstly being brought into content-based image retrieval by Chum et al. [6], query expansion (QE) has become a widely used post-processing for instance retrieval tasks to improve the performance. As introduced in Section 1, AQE labels the k-nearest neighbors of a query as the positive images and generates a new feature vector by averaging the features of these positives to refine the retrieval. In this method, the feature representation of each positive is regarded as a portion of the characteristic of the query and its class, and the averaging operation enriches the characteristic to help enhance the representation of the query. However, the enriched representation does not necessarily contain sufficient discriminative information that compares this query to the rest of database images. DQE obtains the discriminative characteristic of a query and its class by training an SVM classifier based on "pseudo-labeled" positives and negatives in an online manner. Even though the retrieval performance benefits from the discriminative characteristic, the effectiveness of classifier could be compromised by the poor precision of "pseudo-labeling" and the limited number of training samples. Besides, the online training delays the retrieval response. On the other hand, the underlying relationship among top-ranked images, such as the reciprocity of samples, has been utilized to build the re-ranking list for database images. Qin et al. [20] re-rank the database images by separating it into a "close set" and a "far set". They enlarge an initial "close set" with searching more the k-reciprocal neighbors of the images in the "close set" to form the final "close set" related to a query. There are also several query expansion methods [8, 13] built upon the analysis of the underlying relationship among database images. However, for either the discriminative characteristic aspect or the query-relevant image collection aspect, there is still room to improve.

Exemplar-SVM is proposed by Malisiewicz et al. [16] to solve object detection tasks. This method is based on a simple but effective idea to learn a separate classifier for each exemplar in a category. By combining and calibrating the classification results of all separate classifiers corresponding to the exemplars belonging to a specific category, a powerful detector is built based on the refined classification score. For each separate classifier's training, the exemplar is regarded as the only positive sample and a large number of images that do not contain any instances of the exemplar's category are collected as negative samples. This training scheme gives the Exemplar-SVM classifier two properties: 1) it gives the ensemble of multiple Exemplar-SVM classifiers the capability of generalization; 2) as shown in [16], the weight vector of the Exemplar-SVM can be used for similarity measure by projecting the feature representations of images along with it when the exemplar is seen as the query. These two properties perfectly match the design of our proposed method, and we will further explain it in Section 3.2.

Diffusion process is an effective mechanism to improve image retrieval accuracy, which propagates the similarities among database images through an affinity matrix [9, 34]. The affinity matrix is built offline with the similarity between each pair of database images, and the retrieval performance largely depends on the quality of this affinity matrix. Even though many successful methods of diffusion process have been proposed to improve retrieval performance, such as [3, 11, 22], the similarity measure that calculates the similarity between each pair of database images has not been paid enough attention. Our work utilizes the proposed similarity measure to build a better affinity matrix to further improve the performance of image retrieval.

3 PROPOSED METHOD

3.1 The basic idea

As introduced above, the discriminative query expansion (DQE) [1] offers a query adaptive projection direction $\mathbf{w}_q$ which is learned online with query-relevant and -irrelevant images obtained via an initial ranking result. The main drawback of this method is that, the labels offered by the initial ranking are not accurate enough and the number of the training samples is small, so that the SVM classifier learned based on these samples may not well identify the discriminative characteristic of the query and its class. In addition, the time cost for training that SVM classifier delays the response of a retrieval system. Our motivation is that, if we can identify a query adaptive projection direction without any online training to contain more discriminative characteristics of the class of query, then the issues of effectiveness and efficiency can be solved simultaneously.

Our idea is based on an assumption that, the discriminative characteristic of a semantic concept (e.g., dog, train, or chair) can be viewed as a combination of the unique characteristic corresponding to each sample belonging to that concept. For instance, in a visual recognition task, a classifier that recognizes the category "dog" should be trained based on many different dogs, that offer various views, illuminations, occlusions, and species to form and enrich the concept "dog". This assumption is enlightened by [4] which tries to construct a classifier for an unseen class by a weighted combination of classifiers trained for related seen classes. Then we argue that the unknown discriminative characteristic of the class of query could also be obtained by properly combining the unique characteristics of the images that are related to the query.

According to the assumption, the proposed query adaptive projection direction is built with the following three components: 1) learn the unique characteristic of each database image offline; 2) search for query-relevant images from a database to find the images that most likely belong to the class of query; 3) collect the unique characteristic of each of the obtained images to form the discriminative characteristic of the class corresponding to the query image.

3.2 Unique characteristic of each image

We utilize the Exemplar-SVM [16] to obtain the unique discriminative characteristic of each database image for the following reasons: 1) the Exemplar-SVM is able to identify the discriminative information of an individual sample with respect to a large number of negatives; 2) according to the first property we introduced for Exemplar-SVM in Section 2, it has strong generalization capability so that ensemble will not compromise the classification efficiency. This satisfies the idea that we want to combine unique characteristics to obtain the characteristic of the query and its class; 3) the authors of [16] has shown that the learned Exemplar-SVM weight vector can be used to define a good distance function. This capability is what we need in our retrieval task.

More specifically, in a database $\mathcal{X} := \{\mathbf{x}_1, \mathbf{x}_2, \ldots, \mathbf{x}_n\}$, for each database image $\mathbf{x}_i$, we train a separate linear SVM classifier that treats $\mathbf{x}_i$ as the only positive training sample and all the other dataset images $\mathcal{N}_i := \{\mathcal{X} \setminus \mathbf{x}_i\}$ as the negative ones:

$$\Omega_i(\mathbf{w}, b) = \|\mathbf{w}\|^2 + h(\mathbf{w}^\top \mathbf{x}_i + b) + C \sum_{\mathbf{x}_j \in \mathcal{N}_i} h(-\mathbf{w}^\top \mathbf{x}_j - b) \quad (1)$$

where $\mathbf{w}$ denotes the classifier weight vector, and the hinge loss function $h(x) = \max(0, 1 - x)$ is used. Each weight vector $\mathbf{w}_i$ is normalized to a unit length to represent the unique discriminative characteristic corresponding to the database image $\mathbf{x}_i$.

There is one difference between the proposed and original Exemplar-SVM. That is we cannot guarantee that the negatives (i.e., the remaining database images) do not contain any instances belonging to the exemplar's class. Theoretically, if they do, the performance of image retrieval could be affected. However, it is found that the proposed method still produces promising result in all the experiments. Theoretical justification to its robustness will be provided in the extended version of this work.

3.3 Search for query-relevant images

Since the unique characteristic of each database image has been obtained, the following part of our method is to find as many true query-relevant images from the database as possible.

Intuitively, the simplest approach is to collect query's k-nearest neighbors as the query-relevant set. This approach is used in AQE [6], and since different query has different number of relevant images, the parameter k can only be given empirically. The concept of k-reciprocal neighbors, which describes the relationship that two samples are the k-nearest neighbors to each other, has been used to better evaluate the relevance of database images to a query as $\mathcal{R}(k, \mathbf{q})$. For example, Qin et al. [20] propose an approach called hello neighbor (HN) to form a query-relevant set, which they call "close set", by searching for more relevant images satisfying two conditions to enlarge an initial set. In addition, Delvinioti et al. [8] define a query-relevant set $\mathcal{R}_s(k, \mathbf{q})$ with a more strict bound with the k-reciprocal neighbors according to a query. Even though the reciprocity relationship keeps more false positive (query-irrelevant) out of the query-relevant set, the precision of the search approach can still be improved.

Since the proposed query-relevant image search approach is modified based on HN, we firstly have a quick review of the "close set" forming part in HN method. In order to form the "close set", an initial "close set" C_{q,t_0} (t_0 denotes the index of search round) is formed with the k-reciprocal nearest neighbors of the query. Then they search for the database images that satisfy one of two conditions to enlarge the set. For each image $\mathbf{x} \in C_{q,t_0}$, add its k-reciprocal nearest neighbors when it satisfies: 1) the set of its k-reciprocal nearest neighbors $\mathcal{R}(k, \mathbf{x})$ contains more than half of the images in the initial set, i.e. $|C_{q,t_0} \bigcap \mathcal{R}(k, \mathbf{x})| > \frac{1}{2}|C_{q,t_0}|$; 2) the neighborhood would add less unknown samples than the known ones, i.e. $|C_{q,t_0} \bigcap \mathcal{R}(k, \mathbf{x})| > |\mathcal{R}(k, \mathbf{x}) \setminus C_{q,t_0}|$. This search strategy repeats from t_0 to t_2 to ensure that the "close set" includes enough true positive images.

Nevertheless, since the number of true positives varies with different query, a fixed parameter k chosen for all queries will lead to an unsatisfied search result. Besides, the reciprocal relationship cannot guarantee the good precision of collecting true positives in the initial set, which further affects the final search accuracy. To improve that situation, we therefore modify the HN search strategy by the following approach.

We first replace the parameter k with a similarity threshold T_s[1] to select the database images that have a higher similarity than this threshold to form the initial set, that is

$$C_{q,t_0} := \{\mathbf{x} | s(\mathbf{q}, \mathbf{x}) > T_s\} \tag{2}$$

where $s(\mathbf{q}, \mathbf{x})$ denotes the similarity between image $\mathbf{x}$ and image $\mathbf{q}$ by an inner product. This process assigns different number of query-relevant images to different query to form an initial set. However, sometimes this process still cannot guarantee to collect enough true positives. Therefore, we decide to utilize Exemplar-SVM to search for true positives in this case. As verified in [16], each Exemplar-SVM weight vector can be used for similarity measure when the corresponding exemplar is regarded as a query. When the number of query-relevant images collected by the approach in Eq. (2) is less than a pre-set threshold N_s, we will utilize Exemplar-SVM to search for true positives. To enhance the capability of Exemplar-SVM, we average the Exemplar-SVM weight vectors of the query's several (for example, two is uniformly used in this work) nearest neighbors to form a projection direction as $\mathbf{w}_e = \frac{1}{2}\sum_i \mathbf{w}_i$, where $\mathbf{w}_i$ corresponds to the image $\mathbf{x}_i \in \mathcal{N}(2, \mathbf{q})$. The projected score $s(\mathbf{q}, \mathbf{x}) = \mathbf{w}_e^\top \mathbf{x}$ is utilized to re-rank the database images. The top-K_s images are then chosen to form the initial query-relevant set when the approach in Eq. (2) fails (i.e., when the number of collected query-relevant images is less than N_s). Figure 1 gives an example for this Exemplar-SVM based re-ranking method to form an initial "close set".

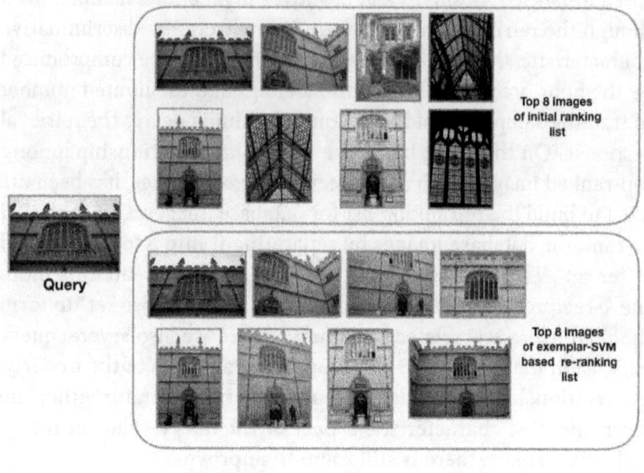

Figure 1: The initial "close set" formed based on an inner product (top) and our proposed Exemplar-SVM based method (bottom).

After constructing the initial set for a query, we add new samples to enlarge the initial set with three rounds. Different from HN [20], we do not keep the parameter k fixed during the three search rounds but make it change with the number of newly added images in each round as $k_{t+1} = |C_{q,t+1} \setminus C_{q,t}|$. This modification reduces the impact brought by the samples in $C_{q,t}$ in the last search round. In addition, if the neighbors of an image have been searched, then this image will be ignored in the next search round to avoid the repetitive search. So, we separate the query-relevant set into "active" C_{act} and "inactive" C_{iac} sets. For the initial set, all the images are labeled as "active". Then for each round, only the images newly added in the last round are assigned into the active set and involved in the search in this round. After three search rounds, all added samples and the initial set form the final query-relevant set together. The detail of our search approach is shown in Algorithm 1.

[1] Since all the feature representations in our method are normalized and the inner product operation is used as the similarity measure, the range of T_s is [-1,1].

Algorithm 1: Proposed Search Strategy

```
C_act ← C_{q,t_0}, C_iac ← ∅;
for t ← 0 to 2 do
    k ← |C_act|
    for x ∈ C_act do
        if |C_act ∩ R(k, x)| > 1/2 |C_act| or
           |C_act ∩ R(k, x)| > |R(k, x) \ C_act| then
            add R(k, x) ∪ C_act to C_{q,t+1}
        C_iac ← x
    C_act ← C_{q,t+1} \ C_iac
```

3.4 Aggregating the unique characteristics

This section describes how we combine the unique characteristic of each image in a database to form the discriminative characteristic of the class corresponding to a query. The unique characteristic of each image that belongs to a class can be regarded as a specific representation of that class. The database images collected by our query-relevant image search approach can be treated as some sampled data from the class of the query. Following the simplest and most intuitive way, we estimate the characteristic of the class by averaging these unique characteristics. In our method, the classifier weight vectors of the images from the query-relevant set are averaged to form the discriminative characteristics of a query's class as follows:

$$\mathbf{w}_q = \frac{1}{k} \sum_{\mathbf{x}_i \in C_q}^{k} \mathbf{w}_i \tag{3}$$

where $\mathbf{w}_i$ means the weight vector learned with an Exemplar-SVM, and C_q denotes the query-relevant set. Certainly, there could be many other ways to better estimate $\mathbf{w}_q$, and we leave this investigation to our further work. With the final aggregated query-adaptive projection direction $\mathbf{w}_q$, the value $\mathbf{w}_q^\top \mathbf{x}$ is used to sort all database images for retrieval.

3.5 Application to diffusion process based image retrieval

In order to demonstrate the effectiveness of the proposed query-adaptive similarity measure, we apply our method to diffusion process, which achieves the state-of-the-art retrieval performance. We first have a quick review of the diffusion method in [11].

Instead of calculating the similarity between each pair of database images, Iscen et al. [11] only use the similarity between each database image $\mathbf{x}_i$ and its k-reciprocal neighbors $\mathbf{x}_j \in \mathcal{R}(k, \mathbf{x}_i)$ to form the affinity matrix. This design makes the matrix sparse to save a lot of computational time and is efficient to be applied to regional feature based diffusion process. In detail, for a dataset $\mathcal{X} := \{\mathbf{x}_1, \ldots, \mathbf{x}_n\} \subset \mathcal{R}^d$, the affinity matrix is defined as $\mathbf{A} = (a_{ij}) \in \mathcal{R}^{n \times n}$ which consists of the elements of pairwise similarities between the points of $\mathcal{X}$:

$$a_{ij} := s(\mathbf{x}_i, \mathbf{x}_j), \forall (i, j) \in [n]^2 \tag{4}$$

where $[n] := 1, \ldots, n$ and $s(.,.)$ is a similarity measure such as $\mathbf{x}_i^\top \mathbf{x}_j$. Usually, this affinity matrix is normalized as:

$$\mathbf{S} := \mathbf{D}^{-1/2}\mathbf{A}\mathbf{D}^{-1/2} \tag{5}$$

where $\mathbf{D} := \mathrm{diag}(\mathbf{A}\mathbf{1}_n)$ is the degree matrix of the graph corresponding to $\mathbf{A}$. Let a vector $\mathbf{y} \in \mathcal{R}^n$ denotes the similarity between a query and all database images. In this vector, only the similarity between the query and its k-nearest neighbors are kept but all the remaining ones are set as zero. This vector is defined as:

$$y_i = s_k(\mathbf{x}_i | \mathbf{q}), \forall i \in [n] \tag{6}$$

With a probability $0 < \alpha < 1$, one jumps to an adjacent vertex of this graph according to the distribution stated in S. Zhou et al. [34][33] proved that, the final ranking score can be obtained as

$$\mathbf{f}^* = (1 - \alpha)(\mathbf{I}_n - \alpha \mathbf{S})^{-1}\mathbf{y}. \tag{7}$$

We focus on building a better affinity matrix $\mathbf{A}$ with the similarity measure proposed by us. For each database image $\mathbf{x}_i$, we first collect its k-reciprocal nearest neighbors $\mathbf{x}_j \in \mathcal{R}(k, \mathbf{x}_i)$. Then we calculate the similarity between $\mathbf{x}_i$ and each $\mathbf{x}_j$ with the learned Exemplar-SVM weight vectors as follows: Firstly the Exemplar-SVM weight vector of image $\mathbf{x}_i$ and those of its k_{dif}-nearest neighbors are averaged to form a projection direction:

$$\mathbf{w}_{dif} = \frac{1}{k_{dif} + 1}(\mathbf{w}_i + \sum_{j=1}^{k_{dif}} \mathbf{w}_j) \tag{8}$$

where $\mathbf{w}_j$ corresponds to the image $\mathbf{x}_j \in \mathcal{N}(k_{dif}, \mathbf{x}_i)$. Then the similarity between the image $\mathbf{x}_i$ and each neighbor image $\mathbf{x}_j$ is computed as:

$$s(\mathbf{x}_i, \mathbf{x}_j) = \exp(-\bar{\mathbf{w}}_{dif}^\top (\mathbf{x}_i - \mathbf{x}_j)) \tag{9}$$

where $\bar{\mathbf{w}}_{dif}$ is the $\mathbf{w}_{dif}$ normalized to the unit length.

4 EXPERIMENTAL RESULT

The experiment aims to verify the effectiveness of the proposed approach at the following aspects:

i) By aggregating the learned unique characteristics of the database images belonging to a query's class, whether it can capture its discriminative characteristic;

ii) Whether the query-relevant set formed by our approach contains enough true positive images and less false positive images.

iii) With the combination of the unique characteristic learning approach and the query-relevant set search approach, will the retrieval performance be improved?

iv) By applying the proposed query-adaptive similarity measure to diffusion-based image retrieval, can we further improve its performance?

4.1 Experimental Settings

4.1.1 Datasets. The experiments are conducted on seven image retrieval benchmarks, which are Oxford5k [18], Paris6k [19], Oxford105k, Paris106k, INSTRE [28], Holidays [12], and Ukbench [17]. Oxford5k consists of 5,063 images corresponding to 11 distinct buildings in Oxford, England. Paris6k contains 6,392 images containing particular landmarks in Paris. For both of them, the bounding boxes of 55 images in the database are cropped as queries. In order to extend the experiments to large-scale datasets, 100k distractor images from Flickr [18] are added to form datasets Oxford105k and Paris106k, respectively. The dataset INSTRE is an instance retrieval dataset which contains various objects with different scales, rotations, and occlusions. It consists of 28,543 images belonging to 250 different object classes. More precisely, 100 classes of them are retrieved from online sources, 100 classes are taken by the dataset creators, and 50 classes contain the objects belonging to two categories. We follow the protocol used in [11] to partition this dataset into 1,250 queries with five per class. And all the remaining 27,293 images form the gallery dataset. Holidays dataset consists of 1,491 holiday photos of 500 categories of scenes or objects. One image of each category is picked as a query. The dataset Ukbench contains 10,200 images of 2,550 indoor objects, and each indoor object has four images. One image of every indoor object is chosen as a query. For the first six datasets, the mean average precision (mAP) is used to measure the retrieval performance. The metric for Ukbench is called N-S score which counts the average recall of top-4 images in a ranking result.

4.1.2 Representation. Since CNN based features have taken over the traditional hand-crafted features, we focus on global feature representations extracted by CNN models. In particular, R-MAC [21] feature representation extracted with a fine-tuned VGG19 architecture is used to describe images for all datasets. In order to verify the robustness of the proposed method, another feature representations extracted with ResNet101 architecture [10] is utilized in our experiments for all datasets as well. For the first five datasets, we directly download these two features extracted by [11][2]. And we extract the features of images in the last two datasets, Holidays and Ukbench, with the architectures offered in [10, 21]. All experiments are conducted with these two features.

4.2 On the discriminative ability of the aggregated characteristic

To demonstrate that the aggregated direction is more capable of capturing the discriminative characteristics of the class of a query, we compare different query expansion methods including AQE [6], DQE [1], and the unique characteristics obtained with Exemplar-SVM (ExE) based on the query-relevant sets. In order to eliminate the impact of the samples that are not true query-relevant images, we temporarily use the ground-truth (i.e., true positive) images to form the query-relevant set to show the upper bound of these methods. Since query images have different numbers of true positive images, we use the percentage to denote how many ground-truth images are involved into aggregating the direction. For AQE, the ground-truth images are utilized to form the new query by averaging them. In the DQE method, the ground-truth images are collected as the positive samples and 30 bottom-ranked images are regarded as the negative samples to train a linear SVM classifier. As shown in Figure 2, our method ExE outperforms the other two methods consistently on all datasets except on Oxford105k and Paris106k when the percentage is less than 40. The performance of DQE fails because the number of negative samples is not enough for training a good classifier when the number of true positive samples increases. This experiment verifies that by aggregating the unique characteristics of each database image belonging to the class of a query, the discriminative characteristics of the query's class can be well obtained and this makes the proposed method produce better retrieval than the AQE and DQE methods.

4.3 On forming a better query-relevant set

To verify the effectiveness of our modified query-relevant image search approach (QRS in short), we compare our approach with k-nearest neighbors (k-NN), hello neighbors (HN) [20], and the approach used in [8] which we call RS. For all these methods, the scale of the query-relevant set depends on a parameter, which is k in k-NN, HN, and RS, and the threshold T_s in our approach which defines the scale of the initial set. We display the precision-recall result with different choice of parameters to compare their search efficiency. Figure 3 shows that, the search approach of RS performs worst on all datasets. The search approach proposed by us gives higher precision and recall than the other three approaches on Oxford5k and Oxford105k regardless of the choice of parameter. On dataset Paris6k and Paris106k, our approach is comparable with HN. On the dataset INSTRE, HN is better than ours and k-NN. The reason is that, the number of the true positive images of the queries in INSTRE is large and equal. This situation is more suitable to use a fixed k to search for the query-relevant images.

4.4 On the impact of parameters

Since the threshold T_s in our method controls the scale of the initial set, we change this parameter to check its impact on the performance of retrieval. Different from the parameter k used in other approaches, conversely, when the threshold T_s increases, the number of chosen query-relevant images will decrease. Besides, we observe that when the threshold T_s is smaller than 0.3, almost all of the database images will be collected by Eq. (2). So, we only show the case when T_s is equal or larger than 0.3.

Figure 4 shows that, with the number of images collected into the initial query-relevant set decreases (i.e., T_s increases), the retrieval performance firstly increases and then decreases to a stable situation. When the threshold T_s is set between 0.4 and 0.7, our method can always be better than the baseline (i.e., the retrieval performance obtained by an inner product). The plots of AQE and DQE are the results obtained with a fine-tuned parameter k.

4.5 Comparison to other query expansion

In this part, we compare the proposed method with existing state-of-the-art query-adaptive methods including Average Query Expansion (AQE) [6], Spatially Constrained Similarity Measure (SCSM) [24], Hello Neighbors (HN) [20], and Discriminative Query Expansion (DQE) [1]. We summarize the result on five datasets in Table 1. The Holidays and Ukbench datasets are not included since the query expansion process is traditionally not applied to these datasets. Except the result of DQE [1] and our method, all the results are quoted from [11]. Except for threshold T_s in Eq. (2), the remaining two parameters N_s and K_s in the query-relevant image search part (Section 3.3) are uniformly set as 5 and 10, respectively, on all datasets. To obtain the result of DQE, the top-10 and bottom-30 ranked images are chosen as the positive and negative samples, respectively, in the online training process. As we can see in Table 1, for the feature representation in [21], our method performs best on Oxford5k, Oxford105k, and Paris106k. However, it is a bit worse

[2] ftp://ftp.irisa.fr/local/texmex/corpus/diffusion/data/

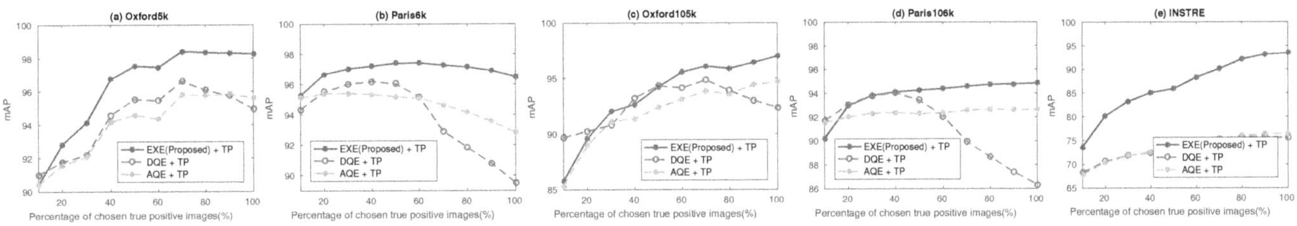

Figure 2: mAP performance based on a query-relevant set formed by different percentage of true positive (TP) samples. R-MAC representations in [21] is used as the feature representation on all the five datasets.

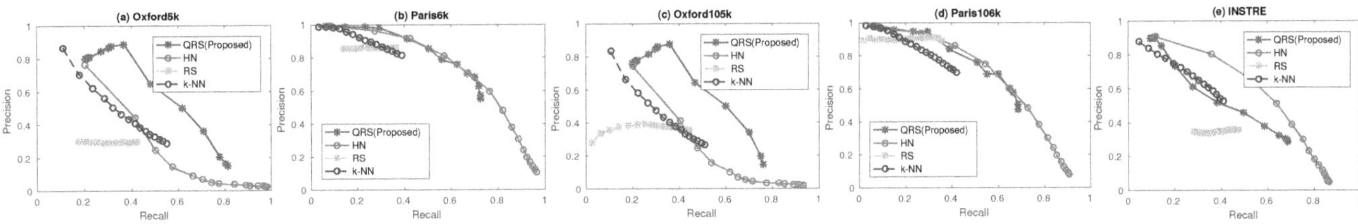

Figure 3: Precision v.s. recall of the query-relevant image search approaches on five datasets. We use the R-MAC representations in [21] for this experiment on all the five datasets.

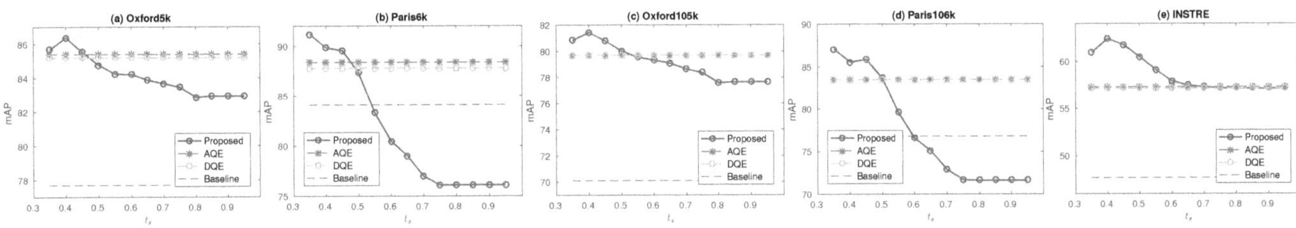

Figure 4: Comparison to the baseline (retrieval by using the inner product as the image similarity): the mAP performance with different choices of parameter T_s in Eq. (2) on five datasets with feature representations in [21].

than HN [20] on datasets Paris6k and INSTRE. This result is in accord with the query-relevant image search result on these two datasets in Figure 3 (b, e). For the feature representation in [10], the proposed method outperforms all of the methods especially on INSTRE (75.1). This result in Table 1 shows that our method can obtain the discriminative characteristics of a query class well and help improve retrieval performance effectively. In addition, our method does not have any spatial verification step which is usually a key element for obtaining more precise retrieval. It further verifies the efficiency of our method since the spatial verification process could cost much time which delays the response of real time retrieval.

4.6 Application to diffusion process based image retrieval

To verify the effectiveness of the proposed query-adaptive similarity measure, we focus on improving the affinity matrix with our method and conduct experiments on the above seven benchmark datasets by following the work of [11].

4.6.1 Impact of parameter. Since there is a parameter k_{dif} in Eq. (8) which controls the number of chosen nearest neighbors for constructing the query-adaptive similarity measure, we experiment with different k_{dif} to investigate its impact. Figure 5 shows that, our proposed method performs better than the baseline [11] on a large range of the k_{dif}'s choice. However, on Holidays and Ukbench, since the number of true positive images for a query is much smaller than that of the other datasets, compared to the rest five datasets, the choice of parameter k_{dif} becomes more critical.

4.6.2 Comparison with baseline. To verify the effectiveness of the affinity matrix we built with the proposed query-adaptive similarity measure, we compare the performance of the proposed with the baseline we use [11]. For diffusion process except the affinity matrix building part, we use the same parameters as in [11]. And since Holidays and Ukbench contain much fewer true positive images per query, we set the parameter k in Eq. (6) as $k = 3$. The parameter $k_{dif} = 4$ on the first five datasets but $k_{dif} = 3$ on Holidays and Ukbench. For the efficiency of computation, the Exemplar-SVM for the feature representation in [10] on Oxford105k and Paris106k is obtained by a simplified version of Eq. (1) as $\mathbf{w}_i \approx \mathbf{x}_i - \mu_0$, where μ_0 is the center of all database images, which means we can approximately obtain the unique characteristic of each database image by

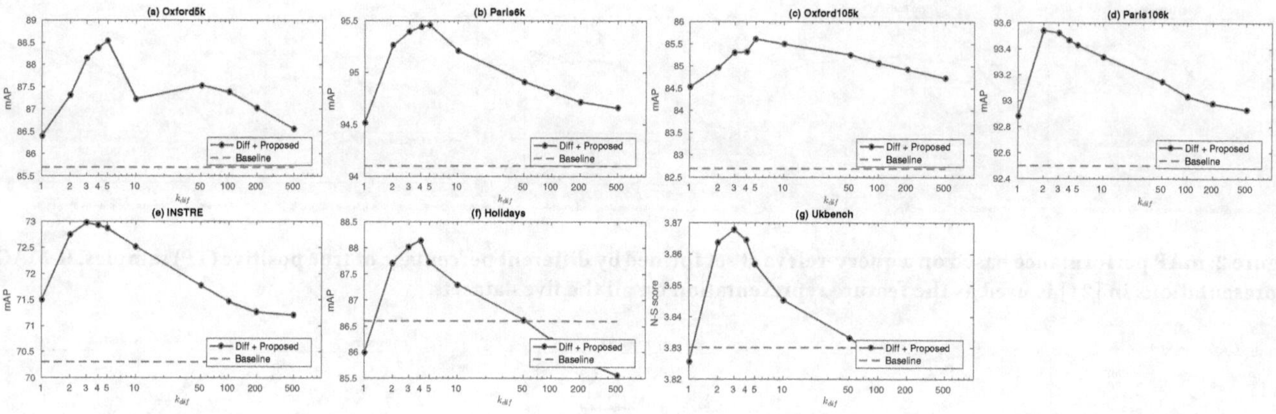

Figure 5: Comparison to the baseline [11] to show the impact of the parameter k_{dif} in Eq. (8) to retrieval performance on seven benchmark datasets.

Table 2: Retrieval performance of the diffusion process with the proposed similarity and the baseline [11] on seven datasets with two feature descriptors [10, 21]. The better results are in bold.

Method	Ox5k	Ox105k	Pa6k	Pa106k	INST	Hol	Uk
R-MAC[21]							
+Diff[11]	85.7	82.7	94.1	92.5	70.3	86.6	3.83
Proposed	**88.4**	**85.7**	**95.4**	**95.3**	**72.9**	**88.0**	**3.87**
R-MAC[10]							
+Diff[11]	87.1	87.4	96.5	**95.4**	80.5	83.8	3.83
Proposed	**89.4**	**88.6**	**97.1**	95.3	**82.1**	**86.1**	**3.88**

Table 1: Comparison of the proposed method with the existing state-of-the-art query adaptive methods based on two feature descriptors [10, 21] on five image retrieval datasets. The two baselines denote the performance with Euclidean search and Dim. presents the dimensions of feature descriptors. The state-of-the-art and the second best results on each dataset are in bold.

Method	Dim.	Ox5k	Ox105k	Pa6k	Pa106k	INST
Baseline: nearest neighbor search with Euclidean distance						
R-MAC[21]	512	77.7	70.1	84.1	76.8	47.7
Query Expansion Methods						
R-MAC[21]+AQE[6]	512	**85.4**	79.7	88.4	83.5	57.3
R-MAC[21]+SCSM[24]	512	85.3	**80.5**	89.4	**84.5**	60.1
R-MAC[21]+HN[20]	512	79.9	-	**92.0**	-	**64.7**
R-MAC[21]+DQE[1]	512	85.2	79.7	87.8	83.5	57.1
Proposed	512	**86.4**	**81.4**	**89.8**	**85.5**	**62.4**
Baseline: nearest neighbor search with Euclidean distance						
R-MAC[10]	2048	83.9	80.8	93.8	89.9	62.6
Query Expansion Methods						
R-MAC[10]+AQE[6]	2048	**89.6**	**88.3**	95.3	92.7	70.5
R-MAC[10]+SCSM[24]	2048	89.1	87.3	**95.4**	92.5	**71.4**
R-MAC[10]+DQE[1]	2048	88.7	87.5	95.3	**93.1**	69.8
Proposed	2048	**89.6**	**88.7**	**95.8**	**93.7**	**75.1**

calculating the direction which points from a database image to the center of all the database images. [3]

As we can see in Table 2, after re-computing the similarity with our method, the performance increases almost on all datasets except when using the feature representation in [10] on Paris106k. This may be due to the simplified version of Exemplar-SVM weight vector we used. However, the overall result still verifies the efficiency of our method. And this demonstrates the importance of similarity measure used in an affinity matrix building process.

[3] Note that the dual solution of SVM's weight vector can be represented as $\mathbf{w} = \sum_{i=1}^{n} \alpha_i y_i \mathbf{x}_i$ with $\sum_{i=1}^{n} \alpha_i y_i = 0$. Since the class label $y_i = 1$ and $y_{j \neq i} = -1$, we can set $\alpha_i = 1$ and $\alpha_j = \frac{1}{n-1}$ for all $j \neq i$, so $\mathbf{w}_i = \mathbf{x}_i - \frac{1}{n-1} \sum_{j \neq i}^{n} \mathbf{x}_j = \frac{n}{n-1}(\mathbf{x}_i - \frac{1}{n} \sum_j \mathbf{x}_j)$. When $n \to +\infty$, $\mathbf{w}_i \to (\mathbf{x}_i - \mu_0)$, where μ_0 is defined as $\frac{1}{n} \sum_j \mathbf{x}_j$.

5 CONCLUSION

In this paper, we propose a framework to construct a query-adaptive similarity measure which captures the discriminative characteristic of the class of a query without online training. Compared with the existing state-of-the-art query expansion methods, our method outperforms them on most of the instance retrieval datasets. The experiment conducted on a diffusion process based image retrieval task also demonstrates the effectiveness and advantage of our proposed method. Future work will focus on training a more effective Exemplar-SVM, better combining the unique characteristics, and applying this query-adaptive similarity measure to other computer vision tasks.

REFERENCES

[1] Relja Arandjelović and Andrew Zisserman. 2012. Three things everyone should know to improve object retrieval. In *Computer Vision and Pattern Recognition (CVPR), 2012 IEEE Conference on*. IEEE, 2911–2918.

[2] Artem Babenko, Anton Slesarev, Alexandr Chigorin, and Victor Lempitsky. 2014. Neural codes for image retrieval. In *European conference on computer vision*. Springer, 584–599.

[3] Sergey Brin and Lawrence Page. 2012. Reprint of: The anatomy of a large-scale hypertextual web search engine. *Computer networks* 56, 18 (2012), 3825–3833.

[4] Soravit Changpinyo, Wei-Lun Chao, Boqing Gong, and Fei Sha. 2016. Synthesized classifiers for zero-shot learning. In *Proceedings of the IEEE Conference on Computer Vision and Pattern Recognition*. 5327–5336.

[5] Ondřej Chum, Andrej Mikulik, Michal Perdoch, and Jiří Matas. 2011. Total recall II: Query expansion revisited. In *Computer Vision and Pattern Recognition (CVPR), 2011 IEEE Conference on*. IEEE, 889–896.

[6] Ondrej Chum, James Philbin, Josef Sivic, Michael Isard, and Andrew Zisserman. 2007. Total recall: Automatic query expansion with a generative feature model for object retrieval. In *Computer Vision, 2007. ICCV 2007. IEEE 11th International Conference on*. IEEE, 1–8.

[7] Ritendra Datta, Jia Li, and James Z Wang. 2005. Content-based image retrieval: approaches and trends of the new age. In *Proceedings of the 7th ACM SIGMM international workshop on Multimedia information retrieval*. ACM, 253–262.

[8] Agni Delvinioti, Hervé Jégou, Laurent Amsaleg, and Michael E Houle. 2014. Image retrieval with reciprocal and shared nearest neighbors. In *Computer Vision Theory and Applications (VISAPP), 2014 International Conference on*, Vol. 2. IEEE, 321–328.

[9] Michael Donoser and Horst Bischof. 2013. Diffusion processes for retrieval revisited. In *Proceedings of the IEEE Conference on Computer Vision and Pattern Recognition*. 1320–1327.

[10] Albert Gordo, Jon Almazan, Jerome Revaud, and Diane Larlus. 2017. End-to-end learning of deep visual representations for image retrieval. *International Journal of Computer Vision* 124, 2 (2017), 237–254.

[11] Ahmet Iscen, Giorgos Tolias, Yannis Avrithis, Teddy Furon, and Ondřej Chum. 2017. Efficient diffusion on region manifolds: Recovering small objects with compact cnn representations. In *2017 IEEE Conference on Computer Vision and Pattern Recognition (CVPR)*. IEEE, 926–935.

[12] Herve Jegou, Matthijs Douze, and Cordelia Schmid. 2008. Hamming embedding and weak geometric consistency for large scale image search. *Computer Vision–ECCV 2008* (2008), 304–317.

[13] Herve Jegou, Hedi Harzallah, and Cordelia Schmid. 2007. A contextual dissimilarity measure for accurate and efficient image search. In *Computer Vision and Pattern Recognition, 2007. CVPR'07. IEEE Conference on*. IEEE, 1–8.

[14] Albert Jiménez, Jose M Alvarez, and Xavier Giró Nieto. 2017. Class-weighted convolutional features for visual instance search. In *Proceedings of the 28th British Machine Vision Conference 2017*. 1–12.

[15] Yannis Kalantidis, Clayton Mellina, and Simon Osindero. 2016. Cross-dimensional weighting for aggregated deep convolutional features. In *European Conference on Computer Vision*. Springer, 685–701.

[16] Tomasz Malisiewicz, Abhinav Gupta, and Alexei A Efros. 2011. Ensemble of exemplar-svms for object detection and beyond. In *Computer Vision (ICCV), 2011 IEEE International Conference on*. IEEE, 89–96.

[17] Panagiotis Papadakis, Ioannis Pratikakis, Theoharis Theoharis, and Stavros Perantonis. 2010. PANORAMA: A 3D shape descriptor based on panoramic views for unsupervised 3D object retrieval. *International Journal of Computer Vision* 89, 2 (2010), 177–192.

[18] James Philbin, Ondrej Chum, Michael Isard, Josef Sivic, and Andrew Zisserman. 2007. Object retrieval with large vocabularies and fast spatial matching. In *Computer Vision and Pattern Recognition, 2007. CVPR'07. IEEE Conference on*. IEEE, 1–8.

[19] James Philbin, Ondrej Chum, Michael Isard, Josef Sivic, and Andrew Zisserman. 2008. Lost in quantization: Improving particular object retrieval in large scale image databases. In *Computer Vision and Pattern Recognition, 2008. CVPR 2008. IEEE Conference on*. IEEE, 1–8.

[20] Danfeng Qin, Stephan Gammeter, Lukas Bossard, Till Quack, and Luc Van Gool. 2011. Hello neighbor: Accurate object retrieval with k-reciprocal nearest neighbors. In *Computer Vision and Pattern Recognition (CVPR), 2011 IEEE Conference on*. IEEE, 777–784.

[21] Filip Radenović, Giorgos Tolias, and Ondřej Chum. 2016. CNN image retrieval learns from BoW: Unsupervised fine-tuning with hard examples. In *European Conference on Computer Vision*. Springer, 3–20.

[22] Matthew Richardson and Pedro Domingos. 2002. The intelligent surfer: Probabilistic combination of link and content information in pagerank. In *Advances in neural information processing systems*. 1441–1448.

[23] Yong Rui, Thomas S Huang, Michael Ortega, and Sharad Mehrotra. 1998. Relevance feedback: a power tool for interactive content-based image retrieval. *IEEE Transactions on circuits and systems for video technology* 8, 5 (1998), 644–655.

[24] Xiaohui Shen, Zhe Lin, Jonathan Brandt, and Ying Wu. 2014. Spatially-constrained similarity measurefor large-scale object retrieval. *IEEE transactions on pattern analysis and machine intelligence* 36, 6 (2014), 1229–1241.

[25] Arnold WM Smeulders, Marcel Worring, Simone Santini, Amarnath Gupta, and Ramesh Jain. 2000. Content-based image retrieval at the end of the early years. *IEEE Transactions on pattern analysis and machine intelligence* 22, 12 (2000), 1349–1380.

[26] Giorgos Tolias and Hervé Jégou. 2014. Visual query expansion with or without geometry: refining local descriptors by feature aggregation. *Pattern recognition* 47, 10 (2014), 3466–3476.

[27] Giorgos Tolias, Ronan Sicre, and Hervé Jégou. 2015. Particular object retrieval with integral max-pooling of CNN activations. *arXiv preprint arXiv:1511.05879* (2015).

[28] Shuang Wang and Shuqiang Jiang. 2015. INSTRE: a new benchmark for instance-level object retrieval and recognition. *ACM Transactions on Multimedia Computing, Communications, and Applications (TOMM)* 11, 3 (2015), 37.

[29] Joe Yue-Hei Ng, Fan Yang, and Larry S Davis. 2015. Exploiting local features from deep networks for image retrieval. In *Proceedings of the IEEE Conference on Computer Vision and Pattern Recognition Workshops*. 53–61.

[30] Shaoting Zhang, Ming Yang, Timothee Cour, Kai Yu, and Dimitris N Metaxas. 2015. Query specific rank fusion for image retrieval. *IEEE Transactions on Pattern Analysis and Machine Intelligence* 37, 4 (2015), 803–815.

[31] Liang Zheng, Shengjin Wang, Lu Tian, Fei He, Ziqiong Liu, and Qi Tian. 2015. Query-adaptive late fusion for image search and person re-identification. In *Proceedings of the IEEE conference on computer vision and pattern recognition*. 1741–1750.

[32] Liang Zheng, Yi Yang, and Qi Tian. 2018. SIFT Meets CNN: A Decade Survey of Instance Retrieval. *IEEE Trans. Pattern Anal. Mach. Intell.* 40, 5 (2018), 1224–1244. https://doi.org/10.1109/TPAMI.2017.2709749

[33] Denny Zhou, Olivier Bousquet, Thomas N Lal, Jason Weston, and Bernhard Schölkopf. 2004. Learning with local and global consistency. In *Advances in neural information processing systems*. 321–328.

[34] Denny Zhou, Jason Weston, Arthur Gretton, Olivier Bousquet, and Bernhard Schölkopf. 2004. Ranking on data manifolds. In *Advances in neural information processing systems*. 169–176.

[35] Xiang Sean Zhou and Thomas S Huang. 2003. Relevance feedback in image retrieval: A comprehensive review. *Multimedia systems* 8, 6 (2003), 536–544.

Deep Extreme Multi-label Learning

Wenjie Zhang
East China Normal University
Shanghai, China
izhangwenjie@gmail.com

Junchi Yan
Shanghai Jiao Tong University
Shanghai, China
yanesta13@163.com

Xiangfeng Wang*
East China Normal University
Shanghai, China
xfwang@sei.ecnu.edu.cn

Hongyuan Zha
East China Normal University
Shanghai, China
zha@sei.ecnu.edu.cn

ABSTRACT

Extreme multi-label learning (XML) or classification has been a practical and important problem since the boom of big data. The main challenge lies in the exponential label space which involves 2^L possible label sets especially when the label dimension L is huge, *e.g.*, in millions for Wikipedia labels. This paper is motivated to better explore the label space by originally establishing an explicit label graph. In the meanwhile, deep learning has been widely studied and used in various classification problems including multi-label classification, however it has not been properly introduced to XML, where the label space can be as large as in millions. In this paper, we propose a practical deep embedding method for extreme multi-label classification, which harvests the ideas of non-linear embedding and graph priors-based label space modeling simultaneously. Extensive experiments on public datasets for XML show that our method performs competitive against state-of-the-art result.

KEYWORDS

Extreme Multi-label Learning; Deep Embedding; Extreme Classification

ACM Reference Format:
Wenjie Zhang, Junchi Yan, Xiangfeng Wang, and Hongyuan Zha. 2018. Deep Extreme Multi-label Learning. In *ICMR '18: 2018 International Conference on Multimedia Retrieval, June 11–14, 2018, Yokohama, Japan.* ACM, New York, NY, USA, 8 pages. https://doi.org/10.1145/3206025.3206030

1 INTRODUCTION

The eXtreme Multi-label Learning (XML) addresses the problem of learning a classifier which can automatically tag a data sample with the most relevant subset of labels from a large label set. For instance, there are more than a million labels (*i.e.*, categories) on Wikipedia and it is expect to build a classifier that can annotate a new article or a web page with a subset of relevant Wikipedia categories. However, XML becomes significantly challenging in order to simultaneously deal with massive labels, dimensions and training samples. Compared with traditional multi-label learning methods [26], the *extreme* multi-label learning methods even more focus on tackling the problem with both extremely high input feature dimension and label dimension. It should also be emphasized that multi-label learning is distinct from multi-class classification [32] which only aims to predict a single mutually *exclusive* label. But in contrast, multi-label learning allows for the co-existence of more than one labels for a single data sample.

One straightforward method is to train an independent one-against-all classifier for each label, which is clearly not optimal for multi-label learning because the dependency between class labels should not be leveraged. Furthermore, for extreme multi-label leaning, this is not practical since it becomes computationally intractable to train a massive number of classifiers, *e.g.*, one million classifiers. Although the issue could possibly be ameliorated if the label hierarchy is established, it is usually impracticable to guarantee this structure in many applications [4]. The issue also lies in the prediction stage, where all the classifiers need to be evaluated in every testing data sample procedure. To address all these challenges, state-of-the-art extreme multi-label learning methods have been proposed recently, which in general can be divided into two categories: tree based methods and embedding based methods.

Tree based methods [1, 21, 30] become popular as they enjoy notable accuracy improvement over traditional embedding based methods. The idea is how to learn the hierarchy from training data. Usually the root is initialized to contain the whole label set. Further the node partition scheme is introduced to determine which labels should be assigned to the left child or the right. Nodes are recursively partitioned till each leaf contains a small number of labels. As follows, in the prediction stage, the testing sample passes down the well-established tree until it arrives at the leaf node whereby its labels are finally determined.

The embedding based method is another fundamental technique to handle the issue [3, 6, 12, 17, 25, 35]. These approaches attempt to make the training and prediction procedures tractable by assuming low-rank training label matrix (of which each column/row corresponds a training sample's label vector) and linearly embedding the high-dimensional label vectors to low-dimensional label vectors to reduce the effective number of labels. As for the prediction stage, labels for a novel sample are determined through a lifting decompression matrix, which maps the embedded label vectors back to

*Contact author is Xiangfeng Wang.

ICMR '18, June 11–14, 2018, Yokohama, Japan

ACM ISBN 978-1-4503-5046-4/18/06…$15.00
https://doi.org/10.1145/3206025.3206030

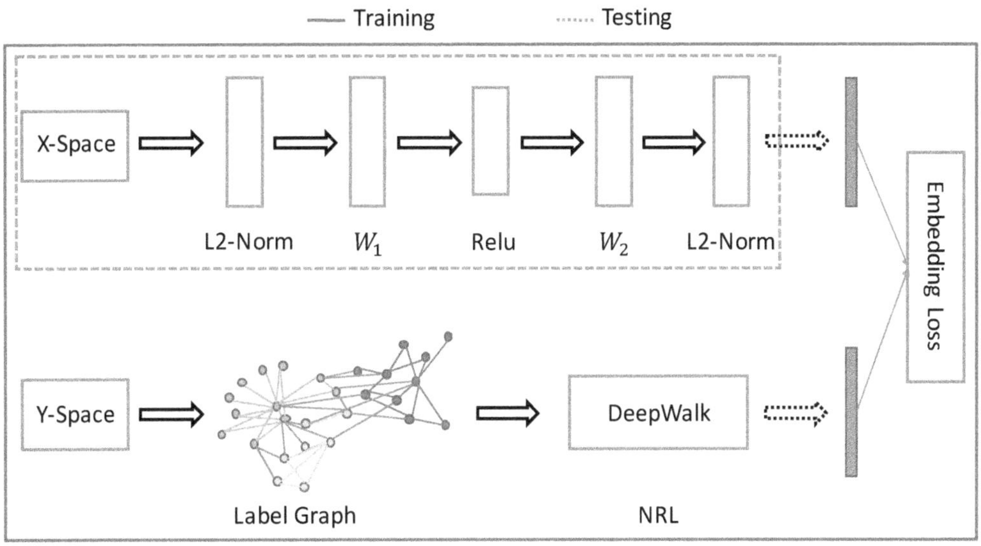

Figure 1: Approach framework: the solid red box represents the training stage, while the dashed blue box represents the mapping function from the high-dimensional feature space to the low-dimensional non-linear embedding space. "L2-Norm" denotes the ℓ_2-normalization layer, "W_1" and "W_2" both denote the fully-connected layers, "Relu" denotes the non-linear activation function, "Label Graph" is built from label space (there exist an edge between labels if the two labels ever co-exist with each other in any sample), "NRL" stands for network representation learning.

the original extremely high-dimensional label space. However, the fundamental problem of the embedding method is the low-rank label space assumption, which is violated in most real world applications [4]. In general, traditional embedding type methods are usually more computationally efficient than tree based methods but with the expense of accuracy.

Notably, the state-of-the-art embedding based method SLEEC (**S**parse **L**ocal **E**mbeddings for **E**xtreme Multi-label **C**lassification) [4] achieves not only significant accuracy but also computationally efficiency, which is a formulation for learning a small ensemble of local distance preserving embeddings. It is intriguing to take a deep neural network approach for non-linearity modeling. To the best of our knowledge, there is very few prior art on deep learning for XML. Furthermore we observe that the label structure is also very important in tree based methods whereby the labels are denoted by nodes. However, they seem to be totally ignored in state-of-the-art embedding based methods. For instance, SLEEC focuses on dimension reduction on the raw *label matrix* (of which each column/row corresponds a training sample's label vector) rather than explore label graph structure.

In this paper, we propose a deep learning based approach for extreme multi-label learning. We extend traditional deep learning framework on multi-label classification problem by establishing non-linear embedding in both feature and label spaces. To our best knowledge, our method is devotes an initial attempt to model the feature space non-linearity and label graph structure simultaneously for the XML problem.

The present work possesses several unique contributions compared with previous work:

- To the best of our knowledge, this is the first work to introduce explicit label graph structure into the *extreme* multi-label learning. It is worth noting that label graph structure is different from the label hierarchy explored by the tree based methods.
- An early work for adapting deep learning to the XML setting, and specifically the first work to our best knowledge for using deep network for embedding in XML – see the approach overview in Figure 1. As a matter of fact, we are unable to identify any prior art for exploring deep learning either for feature space reduction or for label space reduction in the XML setting.
- Extensive experiments on various public benchmark datasets show that without ensemble, our method can perform competitively against or even outperform state-of-the-art ensemble method SLEEC [4].

The paper is organized as follows. Section 2 introduces the related work. The details of the above mentioned concept and idea will be detailed in Section 3. Section 3.5 and Section 4 contain implementation details and numerical experiment results respectively, while the Section 5 concludes this paper.

2 RELATED WORK

2.1 Classification Methods for XML

The XML problem is in general algorithmically intractable for one-against-all classifier[1], as mentioned in Section 1, various tree based and embedding based models are devised.

[1]The recent effort [2] shows that one-vs-rest mechanism is attainable with competitive accuracy against state-of-the-arts *e.g.* FastXML [21] and SLEEC [4], by intensive system level parallel optimization.

Tree based methods for XML: The label partitioning by sub-linear ranking (LPSR) method [30] focuses on reducing the prediction time by establishing a hierarchy structure over a benchmark classifier. However, expensive cost still be an issue since LPSR needs to learn the hierarchy additionally. The multi-label random forest method (MLRF) [1] seeks to learn an ensemble of randomized trees instead of relying on a fundamental classifier. MLRF also suffers the extremely high training cost as LPSR. FastXML [21], which is considered the state-of-the-art tree based method for XML, is proposed to learn the hierarchy not over the label space but the feature space. FastXML defines the set of labels active in a region as the union of the labels of all training points in that region. Predictions are made by returning the ranking list of the leaf nodes according to occurring frequency in the ensemble containing the novel point.

Embedding methods for XML: In order to more practically implement the training and prediction procedures, embedding based approaches aim to reduce the effective number of labels by assuming low-rank structure. Specifically, given n training samples $\{x_i, y_i\}$, $x_i \in \mathbb{R}^d$ denotes the feature vector and $y_i \in \{0,1\}^L$ denotes the related label vector, whereby d and L are both supposed to be huge. Embedding based methods attempt to establish the linear mapping $U \in \mathbb{R}^{\ell \times L}$ which maps the label vectors y_i to a significantly low-dimensional vector $\hat{y}_i \in \mathbb{R}^{\ell}$ ($\ell \ll d, L$), *i.e.*,

$$\hat{y}_i = U y_i.$$

The testing procedure is to predict the labels of a testing sample $\bar{x} \in \mathbb{R}^d$ by lifting the guaranteed low-dimensional vector $\bar{y} \in \mathbb{R}^{\ell}$ to the original label space through another linear or non-linear mapping.

In fact, the main difference of existing embedding based models often lies in the compression and decompression techniques for embedding and lifting respectively, *e.g.*, compressed sensing [17], output codes [35], SVD-type [25], landmark labels [3, 6], Bloom filters [12] and etc. The recent embedding based method SLEEC [4] significantly increases the accuracy of embedding based methods. SLEEC differs from previous embedding based methods from two perspectives: i) in the training procedure, instead of training a global mapping matrix to a linear low-rank subspace, it incorporates the non-linear neighborhood constraints in the low-dimensional embedding space; ii) in the prediction procedure, rather than introducing a decompression matrix for dimension lifting, it employs a simple k-nearest neighbor (k-NN) classifier in the embedding space. Our method falls into the embedding based approach group, but we take one step further by exploring neural networks to model the label space structure as well as for feature space embedding.

2.2 Traditional Multi-label Classification

Multi-label classification (MLC) is a fundamental problem in machine learning area. Traditionally MLC can be tackled with a moderate number of labels [26]. This makes it different from the XML problem where it involves millions of or more labels for each data sample. Previous MLC methods [7] transform the MLC problem either into one or more single-label classification or regression. Recent approaches [5, 10] try to solve the multi-label learning directly. However, when the number of labels grows rapidly, these methods can easily become computationally unaffordable. For instance, if tree based models are employed to traditional MLC [5, 34], the trees will become giant with huge feature dimension and samples number, which leads to the intractability for training. There is also a principled generalization for the naive one-against-all method [15] which cost-effectively explores the label priors, which is similar with one-vs-all method lacking algorithmically scalable ability to XML.

Meanwhile, in cross modal retrieval field, deep neural network [28, 29] has been designed for learning the shared embedding space between images and texts. However, the input feature vectors are usually with small dimension and therefore existing deep embedding frameworks can not be directly applied to the extreme multi-label learning.

3 DEEP LEARNING FOR XML

Our approach involves the training stage and the prediction stage. In the training stage, we map the high-dimensional feature vector and high-dimensional label vector into a common embedding space, and the graphical display of approach framework is proposed in Figure 1. In the prediction stage, a standard k-NN based classifier is used in the embedded feature space to determine the final label predictions. We first briefly introduce three foundation components of our proposed approach framework and further describe the training and prediction stages in details.

3.1 Preliminaries

Let $\mathcal{D} = \{(x_1, y_1), \ldots, (x_n, y_n)\}$ be the given training dataset, $x_i \in \mathbb{R}^d$ be the input feature vector, $y_i \in \{0,1\}^L$ be the corresponding label vector, and $(y_i)_j = 1$ iff the j-th label is turned on for x_i. Let $X = [x_1, \cdots, x_n]$ be the data matrix and $Y = [y_1, \cdots, y_n]$ be the original label matrix. For any unseen instance $x \in \mathbb{R}^d$, the multi-label classifier $h(x) : \mathbb{R}^d \rightarrow \{0,1\}^L$ predicts the proper labels of x. Matrix $V \in \mathbb{R}^{\ell \times L}$ denotes the embedded label matrix, which is learned by the deep label graph embedding detailed as follows.

3.2 Deep Label Graph Embedding

In our work, we aim at simultaneously taking advantage of non-linear embedding and label structure information, while the state-of-the-art embedding based method SLEEC ignores to model the label structure. We focus on using label graph to reflect the label structure. Our approach can efficiently incorporate the label structure cues, which is missing in many popular embedding based methods as it is nontrivial to incorporate even the classical label hierarchy information.

We first establish a label graph. *There exists an edge if the two labels ever co-exist with each other in any sample.* If the prior label hierarchy information is guaranteed, we will directly incorporate it instead of establishing the label graph. Further we intend to learn a representation, where we assume that two nearby labels in the graph have similar representation. Inspired by word2vec, which learns word representation based on the sentence context information, we exploit the local context information of the labels by exploiting the label node context information in the graph. There are many advanced methods for network representation leaning (NRL) or network embedding, which studies the problem of embedding information networks into low-dimensional spaces, *i.e.*, each vertex is represented by a low-dimensional vector. The precedent work DeepWalk [20] uses random walk to collect sequences as contexts and establish the word2vec representation for all nodes in the graph. In this paper, we adopt DeepWalk in our framework, because of its significant computational efficiency and scalability.

3.3 Deep Non-linear Embedding

In this paper, we aim to learn a non-linear mapping from X to the embedding space, while previous embedding based methods usually transfer the high-dimensional feature vectors to a low-dimensional space under a linear mapping. The feature representation of $\boldsymbol{x} \in \mathbb{R}^d$ in the embedding space is denoted as $f_{\boldsymbol{x}} := F(\boldsymbol{x}; \boldsymbol{W}) \in \mathbb{R}^\ell$ where $\boldsymbol{W}$ denotes the embedding parameter, and the feature representation of $\boldsymbol{y} \in \mathbb{R}^L$ in the latent space is denoted as $f_{\boldsymbol{y}} \in \mathbb{R}^\ell$. Therefore, the distance between $\boldsymbol{x}$ (*e.g.* document features) and the corresponding $\boldsymbol{y}$ (*e.g.* label features) can be represented by the distance between $f_{\boldsymbol{x}}$ and $f_{\boldsymbol{y}}$, *i.e.*,

$$d(\boldsymbol{x}, \boldsymbol{y}) := d(f_{\boldsymbol{x}}, f_{\boldsymbol{y}}) = \sum_j^{\ell} h\left((f_{\boldsymbol{x}})_j, (f_{\boldsymbol{y}})_j\right), \tag{1}$$

where

$$h(a, b) = \begin{cases} 0.5(a-b)^2 & \text{if } |a-b| \le 1, \\ |a-b| - 0.5 & \text{otherwise,} \end{cases} \tag{2}$$

which denotes the robust smooth-ℓ_1 loss [13] which is less sensitive to outliers than the classical ℓ_2 loss. The objective function that we will minimize can be formulated as

$$\mathcal{L}(\boldsymbol{W}) := \sum_{i=1}^{n} d(\boldsymbol{x}_i, \boldsymbol{y}_i) = \sum_{i=1}^{n} d(f_{\boldsymbol{x}_i}, f_{\boldsymbol{y}_i}), \tag{3}$$

where $\boldsymbol{W}$ represents the model parameters for X branch network. In Figure 1, the embedding loss refers to a class of deep metric learning loss such as contrastive loss [11] or triplet loss [16, 22], as well as their variants which are widely used in image retrieval, face recognition and person re-identification. Although they are able to achieve good performance, but the training stage is still difficult and its overhead is slightly larger, because we need to sample lots of appropriate tuples or triplets. In this paper, with the purpose to propose a much simpler and more effective method, we use the smooth-ℓ_1 loss instead in our proposed framework.

3.4 Cluster Embedding Space

State-of-the-art embedding based method SLEEC introduces a clustering step of all training points in high-dimensional feature space as pre-processing. Further they apply their approach in each of the clusters separately for large-scale datasets. As we know owing to the curse-of-dimensionality, clustering usually turns out to be unstable for large dimensional feature datasets and frequently leads to some drop in the prediction accuracy. To safeguard against such instability, they use an ensemble of models which are generated with different sets of clusters, although this technique will increase the model size and training cost. In our paper, instead of clustering all the training points in high-dimensional feature space, we only cluster all the training points in low-dimensional embedding space after our single learner established. The clustering step becomes significantly more computational efficient and stable.

Algorithm 1 DXML: Training Algorithm

Input $\mathcal{D} = \{(\boldsymbol{x}_1, \boldsymbol{y}_1), \ldots, (\boldsymbol{x}_n, \boldsymbol{y}_n)\}$, Embedding dimensionality: ℓ, No. of clusters: m, No. of iteration: T

1: Build the label graph, in which there exist an edge between labels if the two labels ever co-exist with each other in any sample;

2: Use DeepWalk [20] transfer label graph to embedded label matrix $\boldsymbol{V}$;

3: Project original label matrix Y to

$$f_Y = \left\{ f_{\boldsymbol{y}} \mid f_{\boldsymbol{y}} = \frac{1}{nnz(\boldsymbol{y})} \boldsymbol{V}\boldsymbol{y},\ \boldsymbol{y} \in Y \right\};$$

4: Train the deep neural network shown in Figure 1 to obtain the mapping from original feature vector set X to embedded feature vector set $f_X = \{f_{\boldsymbol{x}}\}$. Update $\boldsymbol{W}$ for T epochs to

$$\min \mathcal{L}(\boldsymbol{W}) = \sum_{i=1}^{n} d(f_{\boldsymbol{x}_i}, f_{\boldsymbol{y}_i});$$

5: Partition f_X into $Z^1, \ldots, Z^m$.

Output $\{Z^1, \ldots, Z^m\}$

Algorithm 2 DXML: Test Algorithm

Input Test point $\boldsymbol{x}$, No. of k-NN: k, No. of desired labels: p

1: $\bar{\boldsymbol{x}} \leftarrow f(\boldsymbol{x})$

2: $Z^{i^\star}$: partition closest to $\bar{\boldsymbol{x}}$;

3: $K_{\bar{\boldsymbol{x}}} \leftarrow k$ nearest neighbors of $\bar{\boldsymbol{x}}$ in $Z^{i^\star}$;

4: $P_{\boldsymbol{x}} \leftarrow$ empirical label dist, for points $\in K_{\bar{\boldsymbol{x}}}$;

5: $\boldsymbol{y}_{pred} \leftarrow Top_p(P_{\boldsymbol{x}})$

Output $\boldsymbol{y}_{pred}$

3.5 Algorithm Framework

The training algorithm is shown in Algorithm 1, termed by DXML (Deep embedding for **XML** classification). The test algorithm is shown in Algorithm 2. In the following, we will discuss more details of these two stages.

Training stage

- Label space embedding: We first build the label graph, in which each node denotes a label and there is an edge if the two connecting labels co-appear on at least one sample in Figure 1. Then, we use DeepWalk to learn low-dimensional continuous feature representations, which is the embedded label matrix $\boldsymbol{V} \in \mathbb{R}^{\ell \times L}$ for all nodes in the label graph.
- Feature embedding: Given the low-dimensional representation of $\boldsymbol{y} \in \{0, 1\}^L$ by $f_{\boldsymbol{y}} = \frac{1}{nnz(\boldsymbol{y})} \boldsymbol{V}\boldsymbol{y}$, where $nnz(\boldsymbol{y})$ denotes the number of non-zero elements of the original binary vector $\boldsymbol{y}$. The X branch deep neural network is trained to find the mapping that the sample's feature vector is embedded into the same space with the low-dimensional representation of $\boldsymbol{y}$. Moreover $f_{\boldsymbol{x}}$ and $f_{\boldsymbol{y}}$ are close to each other as measured by the embedding loss.

- Cluster embedding space: After getting the feature embedding set $\{f_{x_i}\}$, we partition the set into several clusters with k-means.

Prediction stage The prediction is relatively standard: given a test sample $\boldsymbol{x}$, we first get its low-dimensional feature representation $f_{\boldsymbol{x}}$, then assign the index for it by

$$i^\star = \arg \min_{i \in \{1,\cdots,m\}} \|f_{\boldsymbol{x}} - z_c^i\|_2, \tag{4}$$

where z_c^i denotes the center of the i-th cluster Z^i. In the following, we perform k-NN search in its low-dimensional feature representation to find its similar samples from the training dataset in the corresponding cluster $Z^{i^\star}$. Finally, the average (or simply sum) of the k-nearest neighbors' labels is set as the final label prediction.

4 EXPERIMENTS

Experiments are carried out on publicly available XML benchmark datasets from the Extreme Classification Repository[2], which contains both small-scale datasets [21] and large-scale datasets [4]. We compare with some state-of-the-art peer methods, which includes both embedding based and tree based methods.

4.1 Protocol

Platform The experiments are implemented under CentOS-6.5 64-bit system, with Intel(R) Xeon(R) CPU E5-2680 v2 @ 2.80GHz ×6 CPU, GeForce GTX 1080 Ti and 128G RAM. The code is implemented parlty in Python and partly in MATLAB and the network is built by MXNet[3] [8], which is a flexible and efficient library for deep learning and has been chosen by Amazon as the official deep learning framework for its web service.

Datasets The extreme multi-label classification datasets include Amazon-670K [19], Delicious-200K [31] and Wiki10-31K [36]. All the datasets are publicly available. It should be noted that some other methods are not scalable enough on such large datasets. Furthermore, we also present comparisons on public relatively small datasets such as BibTex [18], Delicious [27], MediaMill [23]. The statistics of the benchmarks are listed in Table 1.

Baseline algorithms for comparison Our primary focus is to compare with those state-of-the-art extreme multi-label classification methods, such as embedding based methods like SLEEC [4] and LEML [33], tree based methods like FastXML [21] and LPSR [30]. SLEEC was shown to beat all other embedding based methods on the benchmark datasets and LEML uses trace norm regularization to identify a low-dimensional representation of the original high-dimensional label space. Our method can be considered as a natural combination of label graph and deep embedding. Techniques such as compressed sensing (CS) [17], CPLST [9], ML-CSSP [6], one-vs-all [14] can only be trained on small datasets using commodity computational hardware.

Evaluation metrics The evaluation metric in [4] is *Precision@k* (*P@k*) has been widely adopted as the metric of choice for evaluating multi-label algorithms. The *P@k* is the fraction of correct positive labels, which is the number of correct predictions over k. It decrease with the number of k increases. Such metric encourages the correct label to be ranked higher. *Precision@k* and *nDCG@k* defined for a predicted score vector $\hat{\boldsymbol{y}} \in \mathbb{R}^L$ and ground truth label vector $\boldsymbol{y} \in \{0,1\}^L$ as

$$P@k = \frac{1}{k} \sum_{j \in rank_k(\hat{\boldsymbol{y}})} \boldsymbol{y}_j,$$

$$DCG@k = \sum_{j \in rank_k(\hat{\boldsymbol{y}})} \frac{\boldsymbol{y}_j}{\log(j+1)},$$

$$nDCG@k = \frac{DCG@k}{\sum_{j=1}^{\min(k, \|\boldsymbol{y}\|_0)} 1/\log(j+1)},$$

where $rank_k(\boldsymbol{y})$ returns the k largest indices of $\boldsymbol{y}$ ranked in descending order.

Network Structure We propose to learn a non-linear embedding in a deep neural network framework. As shown in the top half of Figure 1, it composes of a fully connected layer with weight W_1, a successive Rectified Linear Unit (**ReLU**) layers and another fully connected layer with weight W_2. Set $W_1 \in \mathbb{R}^{d\times 256}$ and $W_2 \in \mathbb{R}^{256\times \ell}$ for small-scale datasets, while $W_1 \in \mathbb{R}^{d\times 512}$ and $W_2 \in \mathbb{R}^{512\times \ell}$ for large-scale datasets. We apply dropout technique [24] right after the last linear layer. At the end of the network, we add a ℓ_2 normalization layer.

Hyper-parameter Setting For our method, we set the embedding dimension ℓ to be 100 for small-scale and 300 for large-scale datasets respectively. We train our networks using vanilla SGD (stochastic gradient descent) with momentum 0.9, weight decay 0.0005 and the fixed learning rate 0.015. The remaining key hyper-parameter k in k-NN is set by cross-validation on a validation set.

4.2 Results and Ablation Analysis

The performance of all methods in *P@k* and *nDCG@k* on all six datasets are summarized in Tables 2, 3, 4 and 5. In general, **DXML** performs competitively even without ensemble.

Results on small datasets The results in Tables 2 and 4 are averaged over 10 train-test split for each dataset. From two tables, one can see that our method DXML can mostly be ranked as top 2 on all the three datasets. DXML almost outperforms all the other baseline algorithms. On Bibtex and MediaMill datasets, DXML outperforms LEML and FastXML by nearly 4% for $\{P, nDCG\}$ @ $\{3, 5\}$ and outperforms state-of-the-art embedding based method SLEEC by nearly 1%. On Delicious dataset, DXML also outperforms SLEEC by nearly 1% for $\{P, nDCG\}$ @ $\{1, 3, 5\}$, while slightly underperforms the tree based method FastXML.

Results on large datasets As observed from Table 3 and 5, DXML's predictions could be significantly more accurate than all the other baseline methods (except on Delicious-200K where DXML was ranked second). On the Amazon-670K dataset, our method outperforms LFML and LPSR-NB by around 28% and 9% respectively for $\{P, nDCG\}$ @ $\{1, 3, 5\}$.

Training and test time The training and test time in seconds for our deep learning based method DXML and state-of-the-art embedding method SLEEC on the six benchmark datasets are summarized in Table 6. Notice that DXML and SLEEC are implemented for running on CPU at test stage, while DXML are implemented for running on GPU and SLEEC are implemented for running on

[2] http://research.microsoft.com/en-us/um/people/manik/downloads/XC/XMLRepository.html
[3] https://github.com/apache/incubator-mxnet

Table 1: Statistics of the datasets used in experiments. Point denotes the data sample.

Scale	Dataset	Train	Test	Features	Labels	Avg. points per label	Avg. labels per point
Small	Bibtex	4,880	2,515	1,836	159	111.71	2.40
	Delicious	12,920	3,185	500	983	311.61	19.03
	MediaMill	30,993	12,914	120	101	1902.15	4.38
Large	Wiki10-31K	14,146	6,616	101,938	30,938	8.52	18.64
	Delicious-200K	196,606	100,095	782,585	205,443	72.29	75.54
	Amazon-670K	490,449	153,025	135,909	670,091	3.99	5.45

Table 2: P@k on small scale datasets.

Dataset	P@k	Embedding based							Tree based		Other	
		DXML	SLEEC	LEML	WSABIE	CPLST	CS	ML-CSSP	FastXML	LPSR	1-vs-All	KNN
Bibtex	P@1	**66.03**	65.08	62.54	54.78	62.38	58.87	44.98	63.42	62.11	62.62	57.04
	P@3	**40.21**	39.64	38.41	32.39	37.84	33.53	30.43	39.23	36.65	39.09	34.38
	P@5	27.51	**28.87**	28.21	23.98	27.62	23.72	23.53	28.86	26.53	28.79	25.44
Delicious	P@1	68.17	67.59	65.67	64.13	65.31	61.36	63.04	**69.61**	65.01	65.02	64.95
	P@3	62.02	61.38	60.55	58.13	59.95	56.46	56.26	**64.12**	58.96	58.88	58.89
	P@5	57.45	56.56	56.08	53.64	55.31	52.07	50.16	**59.27**	53.49	53.28	54.11
MediaMill	P@1	**88.73**	87.82	84.01	81.29	83.35	83.82	78.95	84.22	83.57	83.57	82.97
	P@3	**74.05**	73.45	67.20	64.74	66.18	67.32	60.93	67.33	65.78	65.50	67.91
	P@5	58.83	**59.17**	52.80	49.83	51.46	52.80	44.27	53.04	49.97	48.57	54.23

Table 3: P@k on large scale datasets.

Dataset	P@k	Embedding based			Tree based	
		DXML	SLEEC	LEML	FastXML	LPSR-NB
Wiki10-31K	P@1	**86.45**	85.88	73.47	83.03	72.72
	P@3	70.88	**72.98**	62.43	67.47	58.51
	P@5	61.31	**62.70**	54.35	57.76	49.50
Delicious-200K	P@1	**48.13**	47.85	40.73	43.07	18.59
	P@3	**43.85**	42.21	37.71	38.66	15.43
	P@5	**39.83**	39.43	35.84	36.19	14.07
Amazon-670K	P@1	**37.67**	35.05	8.13	36.99	28.65
	P@3	**33.72**	31.25	6.83	33.28	24.88
	P@5	29.86	28.56	6.03	**30.53**	22.37

CPU at training stage separately. From the table, one can see that our method DXML has comparable time complexities as SLEEC in testing.

Results for ablation test We also perform ablation test to study the efficacy of non-linear embedding in our framework (see Figure 1) compared with the linear embedding, which do not use non-linear activation function (e.g. **ReLU**) in our framework. As shown in Figure 2 DXML with nonlinearities outperforms the DXML without nonlinearities.

In summary, extensive experiments were carried out on six extreme multi-label classification benchmark datasets demonstrating that our deep learning based model DXML can often achieve higher prediction accuracies as compared to the-state-of-the-art embedding method SLEEC. In particular, DXML also shows competitiveness not only on large datasets but also on smaller ones. our method exhibits certain nice properties over SLEEC: i) DXML can be trained with off-the-shelf stochastic optimization solvers and its memory cost can be flexibly adjusted by the mini-batch size. ii) For new arrival data, SLEEC has to be trained from scratch, while in contrast, DXML allows for incremental learning too.

5 CONCLUSION

For the extreme multi-label learning (XML) problem, this paper starts with modeling the large-scale label space via the label graph.

Table 4: nDCG@k on small scale datasets.

Dataset	nDCG@k	Embedding based							Tree based		Other	
		DXML	SLEEC	LEML	WSABIE	CPLST	CS	ML-CSSP	FastXML	LPSR	1-vs-All	KNN
Bibtex	nDCG@1	**66.03**	65.08	62.54	54.78	62.38	58.87	44.98	63.42	62.11	62.62	57.04
	nDCG@3	**60.71**	60.47	58.22	50.11	57.63	52.19	44.67	59.51	56.50	59.13	52.29
	nDCG@5	62.03	**62.64**	60.53	52.39	59.71	53.25	47.97	61.70	58.23	61.58	54.64
Delicious	nDCG@1	68.17	67.59	65.67	64.13	65.31	61.36	63.04	**69.61**	65.01	65.02	64.95
	nDCG@3	63.45	62.87	61.77	59.59	61.16	57.66	57.91	**65.47**	60.45	60.43	60.32
	nDCG@5	59.89	59.28	58.47	56.25	57.80	54.44	63.36	**61.90**	56.38	56.28	56.77
MediaMill	nDCG@1	**88.73**	87.82	84.01	81.29	83.35	83.82	78.95	84.22	83.57	83.57	82.97
	nDCG@3	**81.87**	81.50	75.23	72.92	74.21	75.29	68.97	75.41	74.06	73.84	75.44
	nDCG@5	**80.03**	79.22	71.96	69.37	70.55	71.92	62.88	72.37	69.34	68.18	72.83

Table 5: nDCG@k on large scale datasets.

		Embedding based			Tree based	
Dataset	nDCG@k	**DXML**	SLEEC	LEML	FastXML	LPSR-NB
Wiki10-31K	nDCG@1	**86.45**	85.88	73.47	83.03	72.72
	nDCG@3	**76.32**	76.02	64.92	71.01	61.71
	nDCG@5	67.11	**68.13**	58.69	63.36	54.63
Delicious-200K	nDCG@1	**48.13**	47.85	40.73	43.07	18.59
	nDCG@3	**43.95**	43.52	38.44	39.70	16.17
	nDCG@5	**41.73**	41.37	37.01	37.83	15.13
Amazon-670K	nDCG@1	**37.67**	35.05	8.13	36.99	28.65
	nDCG@3	33.93	32.74	7.30	**35.11**	26.40
	nDCG@5	32.47	31.53	6.85	**33.86**	25.03

Table 6: Comparing training and test times (in seconds) of different methods.

		DXML		SLEEC	
Scale	Dataset	train (GPU)	test (CPU)	train(CPU)	test(CPU)
Small	Bibtex	353	2.1	307	1.5
	Delicious	1630	7.8	1763	6.1
	MediaMill	9403	40.2	9906	35.3
Large	Wiki10-31K	3047	16.3	3241	11.4
	Delicious-200K	14537	1471	16302	1347
	Amazon-670K	67038	3573	71835	3140

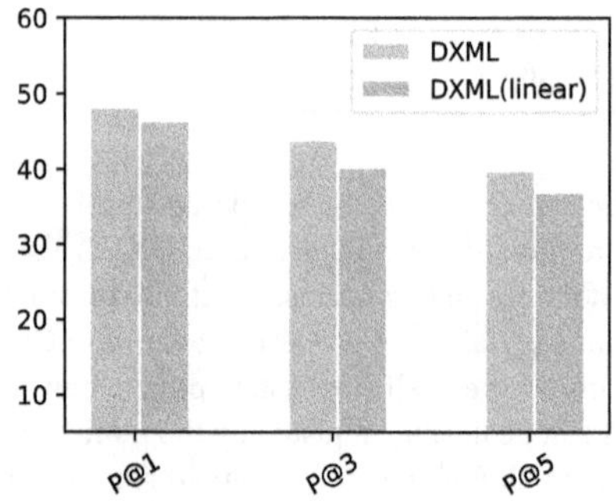

Figure 2: Ablation test for precision@k comparison of deep non-linear embedding (see Figure 1) and deep linear embedding on Delicious-200K.

In contrast, existing XML methods either explore the label hierarchy as done by many tree based method or perform dimension reduction on the original label/sample matrix. Moreover, a deep neural network is devised to explore the label space effectively. We also explore deep neural network for learning the embedding function for the feature space as induced by the embedding label space. Extensive experimental results corroborate the efficacy of our method. We leave for future work for more advanced training mechanism for end-to-end deep learning paradigm for XML classification.

6 ACKNOWLEDGMENTS

This work is supported by the NSFC (Grant No.11501210, 61602176, 61672231 and 61628203), the NSFC-Zhejiang Joint Fund for the Integration of Industrialization and Information (Grant No. U1609220) and the Key Program of Shanghai Science and Technology Commission (Grant No. 15JC1401700). We also would like to thank Liwei Wang for discussions on label graph modeling.

REFERENCES

[1] Rahul Agrawal, Archit Gupta, Yashoteja Prabhu, and Manik Varma. 2013. Multi-label learning with millions of labels: Recommending advertiser bid phrases for web pages. In *WWW*.

[2] Rohit Babbar and Bernhard Schölkopf. 2017. DiSMEC: Distributed Sparse Machines for Extreme Multi-label Classification. In *WSDM*.

[3] Krishnakumar Balasubramanian and Guy Lebanon. 2012. The landmark selection method for multiple output prediction. In *ICML*.

[4] Kush Bhatia, Himanshu Jain, Purushottam Kar, Prateek Jain, and Manik Varma. 2015. Sparse Local Embeddings for Extreme Multi-label Classification. In *NIPS*.

[5] Wei Bi and James T Kwok. 2011. Multi-label classification on tree-and dag-structured hierarchies. In *ICML*.
[6] Wei Bi and James Tin-Yau Kwok. 2013. Efficient Multi-label Classification with Many Labels.. In *ICML*.
[7] Matthew R Boutell, Jiebo Luo, Xipeng Shen, and Christopher M Brown. 2004. Learning multi-label scene classification. *Pattern recognition* 37, 9 (2004).
[8] Tianqi Chen, Mu Li, Yutian Li, Min Lin, Naiyan Wang, Minjie Wang, Tianjun Xiao, Bing Xu, Chiyuan Zhang, and Zheng Zhang. 2015. Mxnet: A flexible and efficient machine learning library for heterogeneous distributed systems. *arXiv preprint arXiv:1512.01274* (2015).
[9] Yao-Nan Chen and Hsuan-Tien Lin. 2012. Feature-aware label space dimension reduction for multi-label classification. In *NIPS*.
[10] Weiwei Cheng, Eyke Hüllermeier, and Krzysztof J Dembczynski. 2010. Bayes optimal multilabel classification via probabilistic classifier chains. In *ICML*.
[11] Sumit Chopra, Raia Hadsell, and Yann LeCun. 2005. Learning a similarity metric discriminatively, with application to face verification. In *CVPR*.
[12] Moustapha M Cisse, Nicolas Usunier, Thierry Artieres, and Patrick Gallinari. 2013. Robust bloom filters for large multilabel classification tasks. In *NIPS*.
[13] Ross Girshick. 2015. Fast r-cnn. In *ICCV*.
[14] Bharath Hariharan, SVN Vishwanathan, and Manik Varma. 2012. Efficient max-margin multi-label classification with applications to zero-shot learning. *Machine learning* 88, 1-2 (2012).
[15] Bharath Hariharan, Lihi Zelnik-Manor, Manik Varma, and Svn Vishwanathan. 2010. Large scale max-margin multi-label classification with priors. In *ICML*.
[16] Elad Hoffer and Nir Ailon. 2015. Deep metric learning using triplet network. In *International Workshop on Similarity-Based Pattern Recognition*. Springer.
[17] D. Hsu, S. Kakade, J. Langford, and T. Zhang. 2009. Multi-label prediction via compressed sensing. In *NIPS*.
[18] Ioannis Katakis, Grigorios Tsoumakas, and Ioannis Vlahavas. 2008. Multilabel text classification for automated tag suggestion. *ECML PKDD discovery challenge* (2008).
[19] Julian McAuley and Jure Leskovec. 2013. Hidden factors and hidden topics: understanding rating dimensions with review text. In *Proceedings of the 7th ACM conference on Recommender systems*. ACM, 165–172.
[20] Bryan Perozzi, Rami Al-Rfou, and Steven Skiena. 2014. Deepwalk: Online learning of social representations. In *KDD*.
[21] Yashoteja Prabhu and Manik Varma. 2014. FastXML: a fast, accurate and stable tree-classifier for extreme multi-label learning. In *KDD*.
[22] Florian Schroff, Dmitry Kalenichenko, and James Philbin. 2015. Facenet: A unified embedding for face recognition and clustering. In *CVPR*.
[23] Cees GM Snoek, Marcel Worring, Jan C Van Gemert, Jan-Mark Geusebroek, and Arnold WM Smeulders. 2006. The challenge problem for automated detection of 101 semantic concepts in multimedia. In *ACM-MM*.
[24] Nitish Srivastava, Geoffrey E Hinton, Alex Krizhevsky, Ilya Sutskever, and Ruslan Salakhutdinov. 2014. Dropout: a simple way to prevent neural networks from overfitting. *Journal of machine learning research* 15, 1 (2014), 1929–1958.
[25] Farbound Tai and Hsuan-Tien Lin. 2012. Multilabel classification with principal label space transformation. *Neural Computation* 24, 9 (2012).
[26] Grigorios Tsoumakas and Ioannis Katakis. 2006. Multi-label classification: An overview. *International Journal of Data Warehousing and Mining* 3, 3 (2006).
[27] G. Tsoumakas, I. Katakis, and I. Vlahavas. 2008. Effective and effcient multilabel classification in domains with large number of labels. In *ECML/PKDD*.
[28] Liwei Wang, Yin Li, Jing Huang, and Svetlana Lazebnik. 2018. Learning two-branch neural networks for image-text matching tasks. *IEEE Transactions on Pattern Analysis and Machine Intelligence* (2018).
[29] Liwei Wang, Yin Li, and Svetlana Lazebnik. 2016. Learning Deep Structure-Preserving Image-Text Embeddings. In *CVPR*.
[30] Jason Weston, Ameesh Makadia, and Hector Yee. 2013. Label partitioning for sublinear ranking. In *ICML*.
[31] Robert Wetzker, Carsten Zimmermann, and Christian Bauckhage. 2008. Analyzing social bookmarking systems: A del. icio. us cookbook. In *ECAI Mining Social Data Workshop*.
[32] Ting-Fan Wu, Chih-Jen Lin, and Ruby C Weng. 2004. Probability estimates for multi-class classification by pairwise coupling. *JMLR* 5, Aug (2004).
[33] Hsiang-Fu Yu, Prateek Jain, Purushottam Kar, and Inderjit S Dhillon. 2014. Large-scale Multi-label Learning with Missing Labels.. In *ICML*.
[34] Min-Ling Zhang and Kun Zhang. 2010. Multi-label learning by exploiting label dependency. In *KDD*.
[35] Yi Zhang and Jeff G Schneider. 2011. Multi-Label Output Codes using Canonical Correlation Analysis.. In *AISTATS*.
[36] Arkaitz Zubiaga. 2012. Enhancing navigation on wikipedia with social tags. *arXiv preprint arXiv:1202.5469* (2012).

Multimodal Network Embedding via Attention based Multi-view Variational Autoencoder

Feiran Huang
State Key Laboratory of Software Development Environment, Beihang University
Beijing, China
huangfr@buaa.edu.cn

Xiaoming Zhang*
State Key Laboratory of Software Development Environment, Beihang University
Beijing, China
yolixs@buaa.edu.cn

Chaozhuo Li
State Key Laboratory of Software Development Environment, Beihang University
Beijing, China
lichaozhuo@buaa.edu.cn
yolixs@buaa.edu.cn

Zhoujun Li
State Key Laboratory of Software Development Environment, Beihang University
Beijing, China
lizj@buaa.edu.cn

Yueying He
National Computer Network Emergency Response Technical Team/Coordination Center of China
Beijing, China
hyy@cert.org.cn

Zhonghua Zhao
National Computer Network Emergency Response Technical Team/Coordination Center of China
Beijing, China
zhaozh@cert.org.cn

ABSTRACT

Learning the embedding for social media data has attracted extensive research interests as well as boomed a lot of applications, such as classification and link prediction. In this paper, we examine the scenario of a multimodal network with nodes containing multimodal contents and connected by heterogeneous relationships, such as social images containing multimodal contents (e.g., visual content and text description), and linked with various forms (e.g., in the same album or with the same tag). However, given the multimodal network, simply learning the embedding from the network structure or a subset of content results in sub-optimal representation. In this paper, we propose a novel deep embedding method, i.e., Attention-based Multi-view Variational Auto-Encoder (AMVAE), to incorporate both the link information and the multimodal contents for more effective and efficient embedding. Specifically, we adopt LSTM with attention model to learn the correlation between different data modalities, such as the correlation between visual regions and the specific words, to obtain the semantic embedding of the multimodal contents. Then, the link information and the semantic embedding are considered as two correlated views. A multi-view correlation learning based Variational Auto-Encoder (VAE) is proposed to learn the representation of each node, in which the embedding of link information and multimodal contents are integrated and mutually reinforced. Experiments on three real-world datasets demonstrate the superiority of the proposed model in two applications, i.e., multi-label classification and link prediction.

*Correspongding author.

ICMR '18, June 11–14, 2018, Yokohama, Japan

ACM ISBN 978-1-4503-5046-4/18/06...$15.00
https://doi.org/10.1145/3206025.3206035

CCS CONCEPTS

• **Information systems → Social networks**; **Multimedia and multimodal retrieval**;

KEYWORDS

multimodal, multi-view, network embedding, VAE, attention

ACM Reference Format:

Feiran Huang, Xiaoming Zhang, Chaozhuo Li, Zhoujun Li, Yueying He, and Zhonghua Zhao. 2018. Multimodal Network Embedding via Attention based Multi-view Variational Autoencoder. In *ICMR '18: 2018 International Conference on Multimedia Retrieval, June 11–14, 2018, Yokohama, Japan.* ACM, New York, NY, USA, 9 pages. https://doi.org/10.1145/3206025.3206035

1 INTRODUCTION

Data with both network structure and multimodal contents have become increasingly popular on social media platforms such as Flickr and Twitter. Learning an effective representation for social media data has gained great success in network-oriented and content-centric applications, such as node classification [2], link prediction [21], community detection [18], and network visualization [31]. Therefore, how to represent the networked data to a vectorized space, also called network embedding, has been increasingly attracting attention in both academia and industry, which subsequently posits a significant challenge to the multimodal network embedding: can both the multimodal contents and various links information be combined for effective network embedding learning?

Though network embedding has attracted a lot of attention in both academia and industry, it is a challenging task to deal with the social media data for network embedding. First, the data such as social images contain diverse patterns of manifestation such as visual content and text description. These data modalities are heterogeneous in the feature spaces. Second, there also exists link relations between different data objects besides the content, which suggests that an effective embedding method should be able to leverage both the nonlinear network information and data content to learn a unified representation. Third, the amount of data on

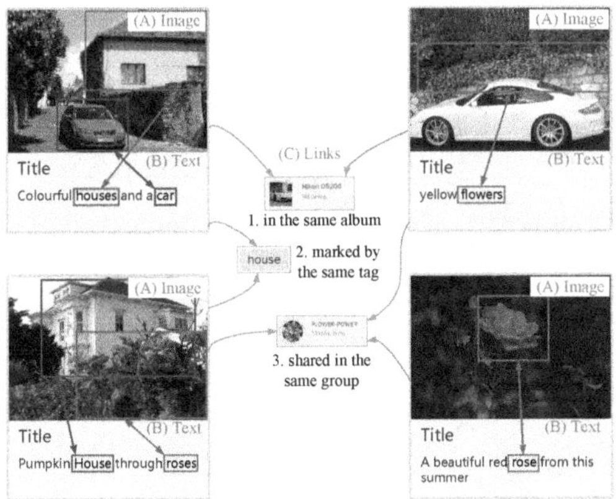

Figure 1: An example of social image: (A) a shared image; (B) the title provided by the owner; (C) Links between similar images. (A) and (B) constitute the multi-modal content of social image and (C) forms the network between images.

social websites has been increasing exponentially and the network is dynamic with new nodes joining in continuously. Therefore, an efficient method is needed to learn the embedding of a large number of data and handle new nodes in the meantime.

Recently, there has been a large number of network embedding methods proposed to learn node representation [1, 27, 32, 34]. For example, Deepwalk [27] uses the skip-gram to learn the latent representations of social network nodes, by transforming the truncated random walks into node sequences. With the development of deep learning, there are also some works based on the deep models. For example, SDNE [34] uses a deep model to exploit the first-order and second-order proximity jointly. In [3], a deep graph embedding model is proposed to encode each node as a low dimensional vector representation. However, these models only take the network structure into consideration. Recently, several methods [4, 19, 25, 36] have been proposed to combine both the content and network structure for a joint representation. However, they only consider one modality in each node. In reality, each node usually contains multiple data modalities and different modalities have a close correlation among them, such as some textual words usually correlate with the corresponding visual regions in social images. Moreover, it is time-consuming for most of these methods to embed new coming nodes since they need to retrain the whole model.

Meanwhile, the multimodal and interconnected characteristics of social media data provide opportunities for network embedding. Figure 1 shows an example of linked social images. First, though different modalities of content are heterogeneous, there exists a close correlation between them. For example, some visual regions visualize the semantic meaning of the corresponding words in the sentence. If the correlation is parsed accurately, these words and visual regions can be modeled jointly in an intimate fashion and thus provide a more efficient representation of the multimodal contents. Second, social media data does not exist in isolation but are linked explicitly or implicitly. Though the interconnection violates the assumption of independently and identically distributed data, the two views of the data contents and interconnection information can be exploited to complement each other. For example, two linked social images are more likely to have similar visual content and textual description than two randomly selected social images, and vice versa.

To tackle the challenges make use of the opportunities, we propose to take advantage of the link information and the correlation in multimodal contents for deep network embedding. In particular, we investigate: (1) how to learn an effective representation to capture the correlation between different data modalities; (2) how to combine both link information and multimodal contents for deep network embedding. Our solutions to these questions result in a new approach for social media network embedding. In particular, we propose an Attention based Multi-view Variational Auto-Encoder (AMVAE) embedding method to jointly integrate multimodal contents and network structure for embedding learning. LSTM with attention model is used to learn a visual-textual representation and prevent the model from being dominated by single modality, in which the alignment between image regions and textual words is well exploited. Then, the link information and the visual-textual representation are considered as two correlated views. A multi-view Variational Auto-Encoder (VAE) is proposed to comprehensively model network structure and multimodal contents and embed them into a unified vector space. The main contributions are summarized as follows:

- Different from traditional network embedding methods, we investigate the problem of linkage-embedded multimodal data embedding. The learned embedding can effectively incorporate the network structure and multimodal contents. Our approach is unsupervised and task independent, which is suitable for different types of data and applications.
- We proposed a joint deep model (AMVAE) to address the challenges of incorporating the link information and multimodal contents for embedding learning. The embedding is integrated and mutually reinforced by the attention based multi-view variational autoencoder.
- We conduct extensive experiments to compare AMVAE with several baselines on 3 real-world datasets. The experimental results demonstrate the superiority of AMVAE.

The rest of this paper is organized as follows. Section 2 summarizes the related works. Then we formally define the studied problem. Section 4 introduces AMVAE in details, and section 5 presents the experimental results. Finally, we conclude in section 6.

2 RELATED WORKS

Most of existing network embedding methods can be categorized into methods based on network structure only and methods combining node content and network information.

Earlier methods focus on generating node embedding using the shallow model, e.g., MDS [6], LLE [29], and IsoMap [33]. These methods typically first construct an affinity graph based on the link information and then extract the leading eigenvectors as the representations of nodes. DeepWalk [27] uses the skip-gram to learn the latent representations of network nodes, by transforming the truncated random walks into node sequences. node2vec [13] exploits biased random walks to generate context nodes, and then applies DeepWalk [27] to learn node representations. Despite

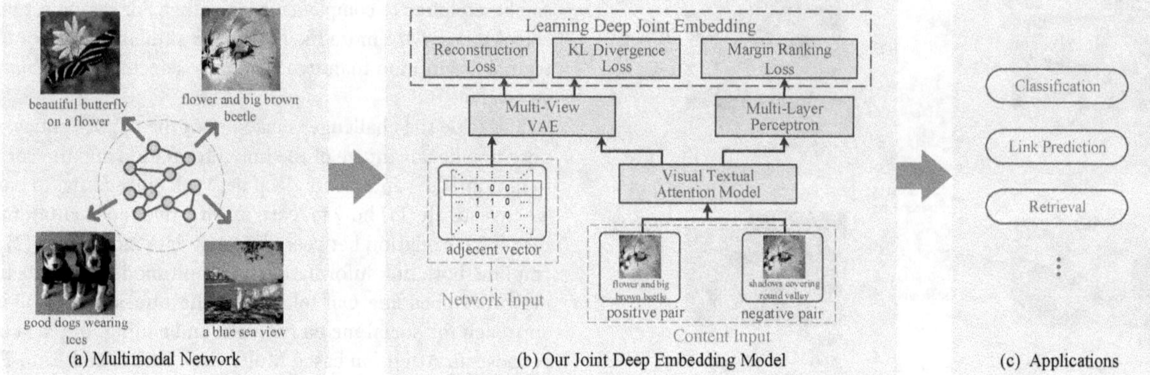

Figure 2: The framework of the proposed AMVAE.

these approaches have achieved certain performance on network embedding, the shallow model is difficult to effectively capture the non-linear structure of the underlying network. Recently, many deep model-based methods [3, 34] have been proposed for network embedding. SDNE [34] is a semi-supervised deep model that exploits the first-order proximity and second-order proximity to characterize the local and global network structure. However, these models exploit only the link information and cannot be directly applied to the scene where nodes have abundant content.

On the other side, some works [4, 19, 25, 36, 38] have been proposed to combine both the content and link information to learn a joint representation for the nodes. In [19], an effective network embedding model is built by introducing variational autoencoder. It concatenates the text and adjacency vector and then encodes the joint vector for classification. However, this model tends to reconstruct the view with a longer vector, which results in the learned embedding lose information of the view with a shorter vector. Text-associated DeepWalk (TADW) [36] is the first attempt to import textual features for network embedding. By proving DeepWalk is equivalent to matrix factorization, TADW incorporates textual features into network embedding through matrix factorization. However, TADW cannot handle large social network because it is very time and memory consuming to perform matrix factorization. HNE [4] proposes a heterogeneous network embedding method using deep architecture, in which each node is an image or a text. However, the social media data usually contains multi-modal contents, and the internal relation between different data modalities makes it not suitable to embed them independently.

3 PROBLEM STATEMENT

A multimodal network is defined as a graph with each node contains multiple modalities of contents. Suppose there is a multimodal network $G = (V, E, C)$, where V is the set of nodes, E denotes the edges between nodes, and C denotes the multimodal contents on the nodes. $e_{u,v}$ represents the edge between the two nodes u and v if there exist links between them. Each node may contain two types of content, i.e., the visual content (i) and the text description (t). Then, for each node $v \in V$, our goal is to learn a distributed representation $z_v \in \mathbb{R}^d$, where $d \ll |V|$ is the dimension of embedding space, from the three input vectors of the visual content (i_v), textual content (t_v), and link information (y_v).

Figure 2 illustrates the framework of our approach. First, the visual-textual attention model is proposed to learn the semantic embedding for the multimodal contents, where the correlation between textual words and visual regions is exploited to learn a better representation. Then the semantic embedding and the network information are considered as two views, and a multi-view correlation learning based Variational Auto-Encoder (VAE) is proposed to learn the representation of each node. To integrate the two modules, a novel joint embedding model termed Attention based Multi-view Variational Autoencoder (AMVAE) is proposed, which simultaneously conducts the semantic embedding and multi-view embedding by exploring their intrinsic correlations.

4 MULTIMODAL NETWORK EMBEDDING

4.1 Visual-Textual Attention Model

Attention is a mechanism which allows for an alignment of the input and output sequence, by which the salient features are allowed to dynamically come to the forefront as needed. Recently, it has been proven to be beneficial for visual semantic tasks such as image captioning [20, 35], image question answering [22, 37] and image embedding [14]. Different from these works, our model is formulated in multimodal network architecture to capture the correlation between visual regions and sequential words. Particularly, we utilize LSTM with attention model to capture the underlying mapping between the spatial structures of the image and the linguistic structures, so as to facilitate a robust semantic embedding of the multimodal contents to support network embedding. Based on this semantic embedding, the multimodal contents can be incorporated with the link information to learn an embedding for the multimodal network.

Given a node $v \in V$, let $t_v = \{w_1, w_2, ..., w_m\}$ denotes a sentence with m words and $i_v = \{r_1, r_2, ..., r_n\}$ denotes the n image regions. Our goal is to automatically find the correlation between the words and the visual regions. In the attention model, for each word w_i, a score $\alpha_{ij} (1 \le j \le n)$ between 0 and 1 is assigned to each image region r_j based on its relevance to the word w_i. We empirically use a softmax function to calculate α_{ij}:

$$\alpha_{ij} = \frac{\exp(e_{ij})}{\sum_{j=1}^{n} \exp(e_{ij})} \quad (1)$$

where

$$e_{ij} = \varphi(w_i^T U r_j + b) \quad (2)$$

is the unnormalized attention score which measures how well the image region r_j and the word w_i match. The weight matrix U and the bias term b are the parameters to be learned. $\varphi(\cdot)$ is a nonlinear activation function to make the model nonlinearity, of which usually a tanh function is adopted. $\alpha_{i.}$s are used to normalize attentions for word w_i over all the regions $\{r_j\}$.

The normalized attention scores are then used to modulate the strength of attention on different regions. Attended visual features can be reweighted as sum of the whole regions for word w_i:

$$r^i = \sum_{j=1}^{n} \alpha_{ij}(Ur_j) \quad (3)$$

Compared with the original independent visual features shared by all words, the weighted visual feature mapping r^i is more effective to reflect the image regions related to the current word w_i. Let $c_i = [r^i; w_i]$ be the concatenation of r^i and w_i, which is the output of the attention process and input to the LSTM memory cell at time step i. In this way, we are able to integrate the visual and textual contents as a joint sequence $\{c_1, c_2, ..., c_m\}$ to the LSTM network. The output of the last LSTM cell acts as the final representation of the multimodal contents, as shown in Figure 3.

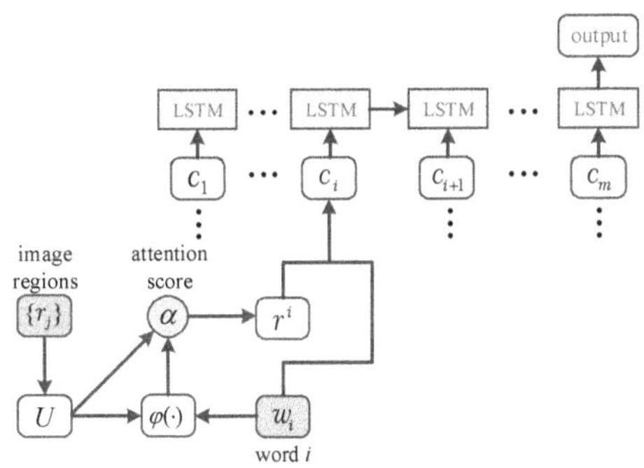

Figure 3: The architecture of LSTM with attention model.

We expect the visual-textual attention model can assign the correct attention weights between the input words and the visual regions for an image and sentence pair. However, there is no explicit information to learn the alignments. Inspired by the recent works of semantic embedding [11, 17], we apply siamese similarity to pilot the learning of attention model. Given an image and sentence pair (i_v, t_v), a negative sentence t_v^- is first sampled. Then both (i_v, t_v) and (i_v, t_v^-) are input to LSTM, and the pairwise margin ranking loss function is optimized to learn the semantic embedding:

$$L_1(i_v, t_v, t_v^-) = max(0, M - f(g(i_v, t_v)) + f(g(i_v, t_v^-))) \quad (4)$$

where $f(\cdot)$ learns the match score given the output vectors $g(i_v, t_v)$ and $g(i_v, t_v^-)$ of the sequential LSTM. This loss function aims to make sure that the match score defined by $f(\cdot)$ is at least greater than margin M for the correct pair (i_v, t_v) compared to the negative pair (i_v, t_v^-). We use a multi-layer perceptron (MLP) with activations tanh to learn the match score, as shown in Figure 4.

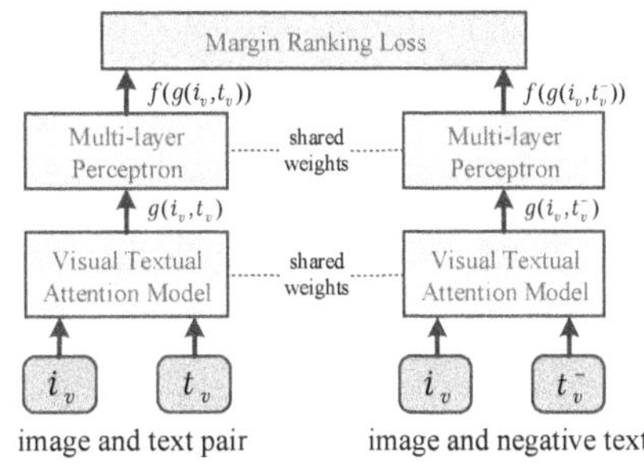

Figure 4: Siamese learning for the attention model.

4.2 Multi-View VAE for Embedding

Variational auto-encoder (VAE) is an effective generative model [16, 28]. VAE based models have yielded state-of-the-art results in image generation [8, 12] and reinforcement learning [10, 24]. Compared to traditional auto-encoder, VAE has a KL divergence term beside the reconstruction cost that tries to converge the current state of AE to an expected probability distribution.

Given the input data of one view x, the object of VAE is to find the underlying variables z to represent x. During the encoding phase, the MLP with nonlinear activation functions is used to map the input data x to a nonlinear latent features h. Different from autoencoder, VAE obtains two vectors μ and σ from h. They can be treated as the mean and variance of the distribution of h respectively. Furthermore, a random variable ε is sampled from a previous distribution (e.g., Gaussian distribution). The reparameterized z is considered as the final representation of x:

$$z = \phi(\mu, \sigma, \varepsilon) \quad (5)$$

where $\phi(\cdot)$ is a linear function used to reparameterize h. Then the encoding process is reversed to obtain the reconstructed data $\hat{x}$ of x. The loss function of VAE is composed of the reconstruction term and the KL regularizer:

$$L_{vae}(x) = KL(q(z|x)||p(z)) + H(x, \hat{x}) \quad (6)$$

where $KL(\cdot)$ is the KL divergence function used as a measure of the difference between two distributions. $H(x, \hat{x})$ is a cross-entropy function used to measure the difference between x and $\hat{x}$.

In the scenario of multimodal network, the link information and the semantic embedding are considered as two correlated views, where the content view x_v ($v \in V$) is obtained from visual-textual attention model as $x_v = g(i_v, t_v)$, and the network view y_v is the adjacent vector of v.

Separate mode. To learn the network embedding, a straightforward approach is to train two VAE models for the two views separately as shown in Figure 5a. Then, the two encoded hidden variables $z_v^{(1)}$ and $z_v^{(2)}$ corresponding to x_v and y_v are concatenated as a new representation of the data. It is possible for this model to learn a representation such that $z_v^{(1)}$ is tuned for the content view

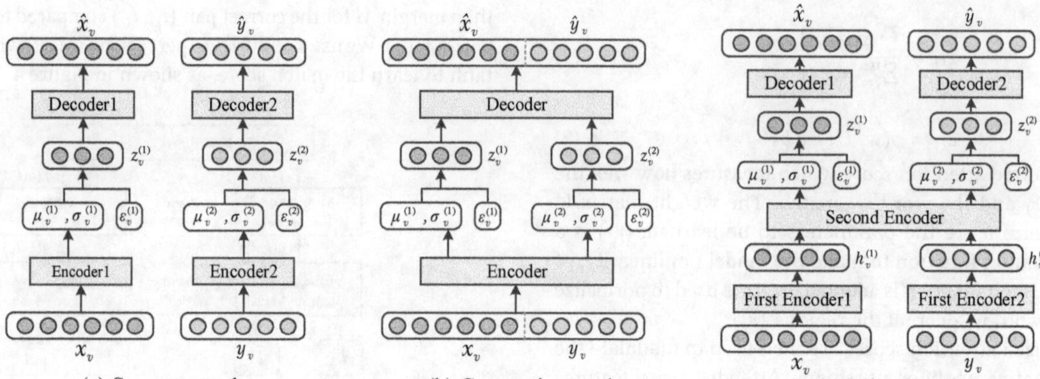

(a) Separate mode (b) Connective mode (c) Mixed mode

Figure 5: Three types of Variational Auto-encoder for multi-view data

while $z_v^{(2)}$ is tuned for the network view. However, this method neglects the correlation between two views.

Connective mode. The second method is to train a VAE on the concatenation of vectors x_v and y_v (Figure 5b). In the last layer of encoder, we obtain two sets of output: $(\mu_v^{(1)}, \sigma_v^{(1)})$ and $(\mu_v^{(2)}, \sigma_v^{(2)})$ for the two views. They can be treated as the mean and variance of the distribution of the content and network information respectively. The multi-view embedding is the concatenation of $z_v^{(1)}$ and $z_v^{(2)}$, which can be learned by training this connective VAE network. This method is used in [19] to embed network with both text content and network structure. However, this method is not effective especially when there is a great divergence on the vector length of two views x_v and y_v. The view with the longer vector is likely to dominate the objective function of both KL divergence and data reconstruction.

Mixed mode. To address the problems of the previous two methods, we propose a mixed mode (Figure 5c), which first encodes the two views to two vectors $h_v^{(1)}$ and $h_v^{(2)}$ with the same length. Then $h_v^{(1)}$ and $h_v^{(2)}$ are concatenated together and input to the second encoder to jointly models the distribution of the two views. Since $h_v^{(1)}$ and $h_v^{(2)}$ have the same length, the objective function of KL divergence can make less bias between the two views. Then, the view reconstruction objective is applied to reconstruct the two views separately, which will be balanced between the two views. The final multi-view representation z_v is the concatenation of the hidden vector $z_v^{(1)}$ and $z_v^{(2)}$. Based on Eq. (6), The loss function of this mode is formulated as follows:

$$L_2(i_v, t_v, y_v) = KL(q(z_v^{(1)}|x_v, y_v)||p(z_v^{(1)})) + H(x_v, \hat{x}_v) + KL(q(z_v^{(2)}|x_v, y_v)||p(z_v^{(2)})) + H(y_v, \hat{y}_v) \tag{7}$$

4.3 Attention based Multi-view Variational Autoencoder

As discussed above, we have proposed two independent models to learn the semantic embedding of the multimodal contents and the embedding of two views. In order to perform multimodal network embedding, a straightforward two-step approach can be used, i.e., first learn the semantic embedding and then feed it together with the link information into the multi-view VAE. One limitation of this approach is that the intrinsic correlation between the multimodal contents and link information is not well explored to reinforce the performance of each other.

Therefore, we propose a novel joint embedding model AMVAE, which simultaneously conducts the semantic embedding and multi-view embedding by exploring their intrinsic correlations. The fundamental design principle of AMVAE lies in that the semantic embedding model and the multi-view embedding model should form a mutually-reinforcing learning loop. Based on the analysis, we formulate the loss function of AMVAE as the summation of the margin ranking loss (4) and the multi-view VAE cost (7):

$$L(i_v, t_v, t_v^-, y_v) = L_1(i_v, t_v, t_v^-) + \alpha L_2(i_v, t_v, y_v) \tag{8}$$

where the hyperparameter α controls the importance of the two losses. Then, the final loss function of the proposed model for training can be formulated as:

$$\begin{aligned}\mathcal{L} &= \sum_{v \in V} L(i_v, t_v, t_v^-, y_v) + \beta L_{reg} \\ &= \sum_{v \in V} L_1(i_v, t_v, t_v^-) + \sum_{v \in V} \alpha L_2(i_v, t_v, y_v) + \beta L_{reg}\end{aligned} \tag{9}$$

where L_{reg} is an L2-norm regularizer term for parameters to prevent overfitting and β is a trade-off hyperparameter.

The joint model is automatically learned by minimizing the joint loss function over the training set. We use stochastic gradient descent over the shuffled mini-batches with an adaptive learning rate to optimize the loss function.

5 EXPERIMENTS

In this section, we evaluate the performance of AMVAE on three multimodal network datasets through two tasks.

5.1 Experimental Preparation

The experiments are conducted on three datasets, i.e., PASCAL, MIR, and NUS-WIDE, which are collected from Flickr and have been manually labeled. Based on these collections, [23] gathered the meta-information of images. The details are described below:

- PASCAL [9] is widely used as a benchmark for multi-label classification. PASCAL 2007 contains 9963 images. Among them, 9,474 of the annotated images are available in Flickr.
- MIR contains one million images, but only 25,000 of them are annotated [15]. Among them, 13,368 of the annotated images are available in Flickr.
- NUS-WIDE [5] is intended for several visual tasks. It contains 269,648 images, of which 226,912 are available in Flickr.

Table 1: Statistics of the datasets

	PASCAL	MIR	NUS-WIDE
#node	6,267	5,330	126,574
#edge	84,794	127,770	23,716,443

We remove the images that do not belong to any of their corresponding groundtruth labels. The title of each image is extracted as the text content, and the images with no title are removed. Since many titles are meaningless, we remove these images. As for the network structure, we make use of five types of links, i.e., marked by the same tag, taken in the same location, submitted to the same group, posted by the same user, and commented by the same user. For simplification, we build a weighted network where an edge between two nodes is established once they have at least one type of link, and the weight is set as the number of links. The statistics of these datasets are shown in Table 1.

We take the images with size 224×224 and channel RGB as the visual input, and the multi-layer CNN is used to extract visual features. The CNN layers employ the VGG19 network [30] pre-trained on ImageNet 2012 classification dataset [7] with tensorflow framework. Similar to [35], we use the output of the convolutional layer "conv5_4" as the region features, of which the feature dimension is 196×512. As for the textual content, we employ the pre-trained word features built on GloVe [26], and each word is represented by a 300-dimensional GloVe vector. The dimension of the LSTM in visual textual attention model are set to be 512, which is also the dimension of the representation of the multimodal contents. The margin for siamese learning in Eq.(4) is set to be 0.4 in the experiments. And the MLP for siamese learning is set to be 3 fully connected layers with structure 256-128-1 with *tanh* activation function. The structure of encoders and decoders in multi-view VAE for different datasets is set as in Table 2 with *tanh* activation function. We choose the embedding dimension $d = 256$, thus the hidden variables $z_v^{(1)}$ and $z_v^{(2)}$ are set to have 128 neurons respectively. The hyper-parameters α and β are set to be 1.5 and 0.02 for a relatively good experimental performance.

5.2 Baselines

We evaluate the performance of our models by comparing it with the state-of-the-art approaches introduced below:

Methods based on network structure

- **node2vec** [13] proposes a biased random walk algorithm based on DeepWalk [27] for graph embedding.
- **SDNE** [34] is a deep network embedding model with both the local and global network structure preserved.

Table 2: Neural network structure for multi-view VAE.

Dataset	PASCAL	MIR	NUS-WIDE
First Encoder1	512-256	512-256	512-256
First Encoder2	1024-256	1024-256	2048-256
Second Encoder	256	256	256
Decoder1	256-512	256-512	256-512
Decoder2	1024-6267	1024-5330	2048-126574

Methods combining content and network structure

- **SDNE+cont** concatenate the network embedding learned from SDNE [34] and multimodal content.
- **HNE** [4] is a heterogeneous network embedding method via deep structure, in which each node has only one modality.
- **TADW** [36] incorporates rich text information into the network embedding process under matrix factorization.
- **VAEBNR** [19] builds an effective network representation model by introducing variational autoencoder.

Our methods for multimodal network embedding

- **AMVAE**$_{mixed}$ is a variation of our method using the multi-view VAE of the mixed mode without the attention model.
- **AMVAE**$_{att+separate}$ combines the visual-textual attention model and the multi-view VAE of the separate mode.
- **AMVAE**$_{att+connective}$ combines the visual-textual attention model and the multi-view VAE of the connective mode.
- **AMVAE**$_{att+mixed}$ combines the visual-textual attention model and the multi-view VAE of the mixed mode.

The content input for SDNE+cont, TADW, VAEBNR, and AMVAE$_{mixed}$ is the concatenation of visual features from VGG19 and text features from GloVe. For the methods of node2vec, SDNE, and TADW, parameters are set to be the default values on the papers.

5.3 Multi-Label Classification

The node representations generated by various network embedding methods are used as the input for classification. To ensure a fair comparison, we build the same MLP classifier for all the methods. Since the datasets are multi-labeled with unbalanced distribution over classes, we use the mean average precision (mAP) to evaluate the performance. We randomly sample $p\%$ of the labeled nodes as training data and use the rest for testing. Similar to [27], we repeat this process 10 times and report the average value of mAP.

Experimental results on the 3 datasets are illustrated in table 3. Here, "-" indicates TADW cannot handle the large network of NUS-WIDE due to its time and memory consuming for matrix factorization. From Table 3, it is evident AMVAE consistently outperforms compared methods on all the datasets. node2vec and SDNE show relatively low mAP because the two models only take the network structure for embedding. SDNE+cont obtains better performance compared to SDNE by simply concatenation of node embedding learned from SDNE and multimodal content. It indicates the importance of content information for embedding learning. HNE, TADW, and VAEBNR outperform SDNE+cont on each metric which confirms the necessity of capturing the relation between node content and network structure. Compared to HNE, TADW

Table 3: Multi-label classification performance (mAP %) for 3 datasets

Dataset	PASCAL			MIR			NUS-WIDE		
p%	10%	20%	30%	10%	20%	30%	10%	20%	30%
node2vec	33.5	39.6	45.5	52.6	57.1	59.8	39.9	42.5	43.9
SDNE	34.7	40.2	45.2	53.7	57.2	61.0	40.6	43.4	41.7
SDNE+cont	41.2	42.1	46.4	59.7	64.8	65.6	42.3	47.4	48.9
HNE	44.1	48.2	52.2	65.9	70.1	72.0	50.5	51.6	53.3
TADW	45.1	49.3	52.1	64.3	68.2	70.8	-	-	-
VAEBNR	46.8	51.9	53.3	66.2	68.1	71.3	48.7	50.1	53.2
$AMVAE_{mixed}$	49.0	53.0	55.2	68.1	71.4	74.2	51.7	53.6	55.3
$AMVAE_{att+separate}$	50.8	54.7	56.1	69.1	72.3	74.1	53.3	56.8	58.0
$AMVAE_{att+connective}$	53.3	55.5	59.2	70.5	74.0	76.4	52.0	55.5	57.1
$AMVAE_{att+mixed}$	**54.3**	**57.6**	**59.9**	**72.1**	**75.3**	**77.1**	**56.9**	**59.1**	**60.4**

and VAEBNR, our model $AMVAE_{mixed}$ obtains a solid improvement, which validates the effectiveness of our mixed multi-view VAE model for multimodal network embedding. With the attention model, $AMVAE_{att+mixed}$ boosts mAP about 3%-5% compared to $AMVAE_{mixed}$ and makes larger improvement comparing to HNE and TADW. This is because the attention model makes alignments between the multimodal contents for a more efficient representation. From the comparison of the three types of multi-view VAE, i.e., separate mode, connective mode, and mixed mode, we can find that $AMVAE_{att+mixed}$ presents the best performance.

5.4 Link Prediction

Link prediction can show the predictability of different network embedding methods. It is very useful when one user wants to recommend similar social images to the current image.

We conduct the experiments for the link prediction as follows. First, we randomly removed 50% edges from the original network and consider them as the links for prediction. The node representations are learned from the residual network by different embedding methods. We take the node pairs with removed links as the positive samples and randomly sample the same number of unlinked node pairs to form a balanced dataset for this task. Given a node pair in the sample sets, the cosine similarity score is calculated according to their representation vectors. Area Under Curve (AUC) is used to evaluate the consistency between the similarity scores and the real link state. Table 4 shows the experimental results of link prediction. From this table, one can observe that our proposed models perform consistently better than the baseline methods. Compared to HNE and TADW, $AMVAE_{att+mixed}$ improves the AUC score by about 10%, which demonstrates the effectiveness of our model in learning the node representation for link prediction.

For fine-grained analysis for link prediction on the sparse network, we tune the proportion of removed links from 50% to 100% in the original network and then follow the aforementioned procedure to report the results of different network embedding methods over dataset NUS-WIDE. The result is as shown in Figure 6. One can see that $AMVAE_{att+mixed}$ performs significantly and consistently better than the baselines. And the margin between $AMVAE_{att+mixed}$ and other methods becomes larger when the network is sparser. It confirms that our method can learn more robust representations when the network is very sparse.

Table 4: Link prediction results (AUC) on three datasets

Datasets	PASCAL	MIR	NUS-WIDE
node2vec	0.584	0.689	0.651
SDNE	0.597	0.697	0.686
SDNE+cont	0.671	0.719	0.723
HNE	0.734	0.751	0.757
TADW	0.728	0.716	-
VAEBNR	0.762	0.787	0.751
$AMVAE_{mixed}$	0.764	0.817	0.785
$AMVAE_{att+separate}$	0.789	0.852	0.828
$AMVAE_{att+connective}$	0.797	0.870	0.834
$AMVAE_{att+mixed}$	**0.811**	**0.873**	**0.864**

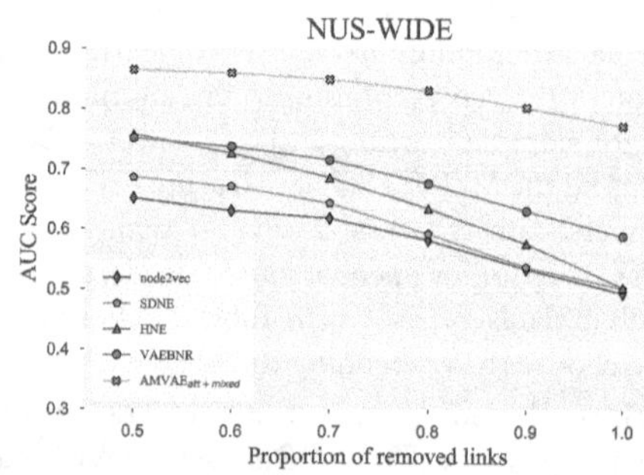

Figure 6: Link prediction results on sparse network.

5.5 Case Study

One advantage of including the attention mechanism is the ability to visualize what the model "sees". To better understand the interpretability of meaningful attention drawn from each word to the visual regions, we present two examples in Figure 7. Similar to [35], in order to visualize the attention scores for the model, we simply upsample the scores by a factor of $2^4 = 16$ and apply a Gaussian filter. The final attended images are the original images masked with upsampled attention scores. Thus, if the attention scores of the regions are bigger, attended regions are colored whiter.

From the figure, it can be seen that our model draws the right attention on the words. For the sentence "flowers by the road", "flowers" and "road" are attended on the right positions on the corresponding image. "by" and "the" are not attended obviously on the image, because these two words have no specific semantics meaning to be manifested visually. The proposed attention mechanism makes the relations between multimodal content explicit and interpretable. The visual-textual attention model finds the fine-granularity correlation between the multimodal contents, which is useful to obtain a more robust and precise semantic embedding.

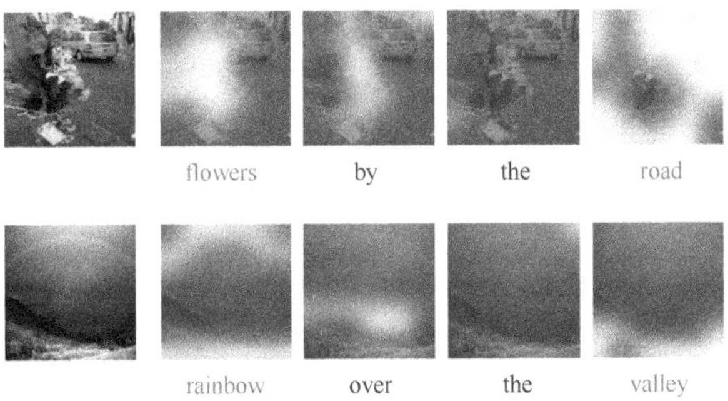

Figure 7: Examples of learned attentions.

5.6 Parameter Sensitivity

In order to evaluate how changes to the parametrization of AMVAE affect its performance, we present the results of mAP for multi-label classification with $p\% = 30\%$. Specifically, we evaluate how different sizes of the embedding dimensions and different values of the balance parameters α and β can affect the result.

Embedding dimensions: We first fix $\alpha = 1.5$ and $\beta = 0.02$ and show how the dimensionality of the embedding vector affects the performance in Figure 8a. We can see that the performance raises initially when the size of dimension increases. This is intuitive as more bits can encode more useful information in the increasing bits. However, when the size of dimension continuously increases, the performance starts to drop slowly. The reason is that too large size of the dimension may introduce noises which will deteriorate the performance. Overall, it is always important to determine the size of dimension, but our method is not very sensitive to it.

Balance parameters: We have two balance parameters in the model, i.e., α which is used to balance the importance of the visual-textual attention model and the multi-view VAE, and β which is a trade-off parameter for L2-norm regularizer. We fix the dimensionality $d = 256$ and vary α and β to evaluate the performance of multi-label classification on NUS-WIDE. Based on the curves in Figure 8b, we can observe that it is important to set a trade-off term to prevent overfitting because the model shows relatively bad performance when $\beta = 0$. However, when β is set to be a large value, the performance decreases too. The reason is that the too large trade-off term influences the optimization of embedding learning.

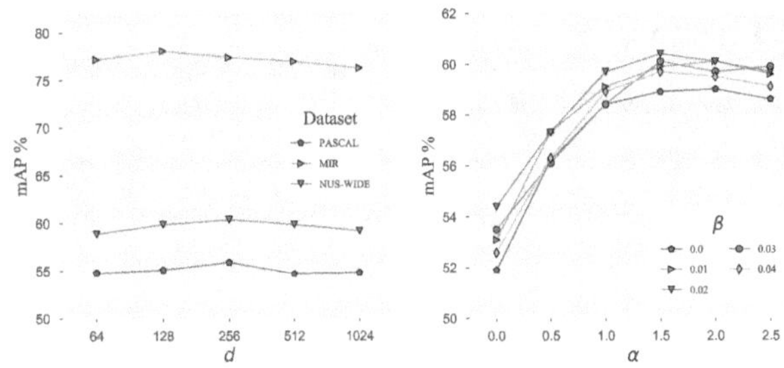

(a) Embedding dimenstion **(b) Balance parameters**

Figure 8: Parameter sensitivity study for d and α.

On the other side, the value of parameter α has more impact on the performance of the model. When $\alpha = 0$, the performance is totally determined by the visual-textual attention model, which results in that the model is unable to learn from network information. And the larger the α, the more the model concentrates on the optimization of multi-view VAE. From Figure 8b, we can see that the model obtains the best performance when $\alpha = 1.5$ and $\beta = 0.02$. Note that we didn't present the curves for datasets MIR and PASCAL because they are similar to Figure 8b.

6 CONCLUSION AND FUTURE WORK

In this paper, we explore learning a deep multimodal network embedding model to capture both multimodal contents and link information for social media data applications. A novel multimodal network embedding method called AMVAE is proposed to incorporate both the link information and multimodal contents for more effectively and efficiently embedding. Our work is different from current network embedding researches that mainly explore the link information and can not effectively exploit the multimodal content in each node. It is also different from the current data embedding methods that ignore the link information and are mainly task dependent, such as image caption and classification. Meanwhile, our model is more efficient to train and handle new nodes compared to most of the existing approaches. The experiment results on multi-label classification and link prediction indicate that capturing the correlation between different data modalities and the network structure are helpful for a better embedding.

Our method can be used to embed other multimodal network data, e.g., social music, social videos, microblogging, etc. In the future, we will explore to introduce more information, such as the first-order proximity beside the adjacency vectors used in this paper, to better model the network structure. Furthermore, we can incorporate other heterogeneous information, such as user profiles and user network, for better embedding.

7 ACKNOWLEDGEMENT

This work was supported by the National Natural Science Foundation of China (Grand Nos. U1636211, 61672081, 61602237, 61370126), Beijing Natural Science Foundation of China (No. 4182037), National High Technology Research and Development Program of China (No.2015AA016004) and Fund of the State Key Laboratory of Software Development Environment (No. SKLSDE-2017ZX-19).

REFERENCES

[1] Amr Ahmed, Nino Shervashidze, Shravan M. Narayanamurthy, Vanja Josifovski, and Alexander J. Smola. 2013. Distributed large-scale natural graph factorization. In *WWW*, Daniel Schwabe, Virgílio A. F. Almeida, Hartmut Glaser, Ricardo A. Baeza-Yates, and Sue B. Moon (Eds.). International World Wide Web Conferences Steering Committee / ACM, 37–48. http://dl.acm.org/citation.cfm?id=2488393

[2] Smriti Bhagat, Graham Cormode, and S. Muthukrishnan. 2011. Node Classification in Social Networks. In *Social Network Data Analytics*. Springer, 115–148. https://doi.org/10.1007/978-1-4419-8462-3_5

[3] Shaosheng Cao, Wei Lu, and Qiongkai Xu. 2016. Deep Neural Networks for Learning Graph Representations. In *AAAI*. AAAI Press, 1145–1152. http://www.aaai.org/ocs/index.php/AAAI/AAAI16/paper/view/12423

[4] Shiyu Chang, Wei Han, Jiliang Tang, Guo-Jun Qi, Charu C Aggarwal, and Thomas S Huang. 2015. Heterogeneous network embedding via deep architectures. In *SIGKDD*. ACM, 119–128.

[5] Tat-Seng Chua, Jinhui Tang, Richang Hong, Haojie Li, Zhiping Luo, and Yantao Zheng. 2009. NUS-WIDE: a real-world web image database from National University of Singapore. In *CIVR*. ACM. https://doi.org/10.1145/1646396.1646452

[6] Trevor F Cox and Michael AA Cox. 2000. *Multidimensional scaling*. CRC press.

[7] Jia Deng, Wei Dong, Richard Socher, Li-Jia Li, Kai Li, and Fei-Fei Li. 2009. ImageNet: A large-scale hierarchical image database. In *CVPR*. IEEE Computer Society, 248–255. https://doi.org/10.1109/CVPRW.2009.5206848

[8] Alexey Dosovitskiy and Thomas Brox. 2016. Generating Images with Perceptual Similarity Metrics based on Deep Networks. In *NIPS*, Daniel D. Lee, Masashi Sugiyama, Ulrike von Luxburg, Isabelle Guyon, and Roman Garnett (Eds.). 658–666. http://papers.nips.cc/paper/6158-generating-images-with-perceptual-similarity-metrics-based-on-deep-networks

[9] Mark Everingham, Luc J. Van Gool, Christopher K. I. Williams, John M. Winn, and Andrew Zisserman. 2010. The Pascal Visual Object Classes (VOC) Challenge. *IJCV* 88, 2 (2010), 303–338. https://doi.org/10.1007/s11263-009-0275-4

[10] Kai Fan, Chunyuan Li, and Katherine A. Heller. 2016. A Unifying Variational Inference Framework for Hierarchical Graph-Coupled HMM with an Application to Influenza Infection. In *AAAI*, Dale Schuurmans and Michael P. Wellman (Eds.). AAAI Press, 3828–3834. http://www.aaai.org/ocs/index.php/AAAI/AAAI16/paper/view/11865

[11] Andrea Frome, Gregory S. Corrado, Jonathon Shlens, Samy Bengio, Jeffrey Dean, Marc'Aurelio Ranzato, and Tomas Mikolov. 2013. DeViSE: A Deep Visual-Semantic Embedding Model. In *NIPS*. 2121–2129. http://papers.nips.cc/paper/5204-devise-a-deep-visual-semantic-embedding-model

[12] Karol Gregor, Ivo Danihelka, Alex Graves, Danilo Jimenez Rezende, and Daan Wierstra. 2015. DRAW: A Recurrent Neural Network For Image Generation. In *ICML (JMLR Workshop and Conference Proceedings)*, Vol. 37. JMLR.org, 1462–1471. http://jmlr.org/proceedings/papers/v37/gregor15.html

[13] Aditya Grover and Jure Leskovec. 2016. node2vec: Scalable Feature Learning for Networks. In *SIGKDD*. ACM, 855–864. https://doi.org/10.1145/2939672.2939754

[14] Feiran Huang, Xiaoming Zhang, Zhoujun Li, Tao Mei, Yueying He, and Zhonghua Zhao. 2017. Learning Social Image Embedding with Deep Multimodal Attention Networks. In *Proceedings of the on Thematic Workshops of ACM Multimedia 2017, Mountain View, CA, USA, October 23 - 27, 2017*. ACM, 460–468. https://doi.org/10.1145/3126686.3126720

[15] Mark J. Huiskes and Michael S. Lew. 2008. The MIR flickr retrieval evaluation. In *SIGMM*. ACM, 39–43. https://doi.org/10.1145/1460096.1460104

[16] Diederik P. Kingma and Max Welling. 2013. Auto-Encoding Variational Bayes. *CoRR* abs/1312.6114 (2013). http://arxiv.org/abs/1312.6114

[17] Ryan Kiros, Ruslan Salakhutdinov, and Richard S. Zemel. 2014. Unifying Visual-Semantic Embeddings with Multimodal Neural Language Models. *CoRR* abs/1411.2539 (2014). http://arxiv.org/abs/1411.2539

[18] Jure Leskovec, Kevin J. Lang, and Michael W. Mahoney. 2010. Empirical comparison of algorithms for network community detection. In *WWW*, Michael Rappa, Paul Jones, Juliana Freire, and Soumen Chakrabarti (Eds.). ACM, 631–640. https://doi.org/10.1145/1772690.1772755

[19] Hang Li, Haozheng Wang, Zhenglu Yang, and Masato Odagaki. 2017. Variation Autoencoder Based Network Representation Learning for Classification. In *ACL*. Association for Computational Linguistics, 56–61. https://doi.org/10.18653/v1/P17-3010

[20] Linghui Li, Sheng Tang, Lixi Deng, Yongdong Zhang, and Qi Tian. 2017. Image Caption with Global-Local Attention. In *AAAI*, Satinder P. Singh and Shaul Markovitch (Eds.). AAAI Press, 4133–4139. http://aaai.org/ocs/index.php/AAAI/AAAI17/paper/view/14880

[21] David Liben-Nowell and Jon M. Kleinberg. 2007. The link-prediction problem for social networks. *JASIST* 58, 7 (2007), 1019–1031. https://doi.org/10.1002/asi.20591

[22] Jiasen Lu, Jianwei Yang, Dhruv Batra, and Devi Parikh. 2016. Hierarchical Question-Image Co-Attention for Visual Question Answering. In *NIPS*, Daniel D. Lee, Masashi Sugiyama, Ulrike von Luxburg, Isabelle Guyon, and Roman Garnett (Eds.). 289–297. http://papers.nips.cc/paper/6202-hierarchical-question-image-co-attention-for-visual-question-answering

[23] Julian J. McAuley and Jure Leskovec. 2012. Image Labeling on a Network: Using Social-Network Metadata for Image Classification. In *ECCV (Lecture Notes in Computer Science)*, Vol. 7575. Springer, 828–841. https://doi.org/10.1007/978-3-642-33765-9_59

[24] Shakir Mohamed and Danilo Jimenez Rezende. 2015. Variational Information Maximisation for Intrinsically Motivated Reinforce-ment Learning. In *NIPS*. 2125–2133. http://papers.nips.cc/paper/5668-variational-information-maximisation-for-intrinsically-motivated-reinforcement-learning

[25] Shirui Pan, Jia Wu, Xingquan Zhu, Chengqi Zhang, and Yang Wang. 2016. Tri-Party Deep Network Representation. In *IJCAI*. IJCAI/AAAI Press, 1895–1901. http://www.ijcai.org/Abstract/16/271

[26] Jeffrey Pennington, Richard Socher, and Christopher D. Manning. 2014. Glove: Global Vectors for Word Representation. In *ACL*. ACL, 1532–1543. http://aclweb.org/anthology/D/D14/D14-1162.pdf

[27] Bryan Perozzi, Rami Al-Rfou, and Steven Skiena. 2014. Deepwalk: Online learning of social representations. In *SIGKDD*. ACM, 701–710.

[28] Danilo Jimenez Rezende, Shakir Mohamed, and Daan Wierstra. 2014. Stochastic Backpropagation and Approximate Inference in Deep Generative Models. In *ICML (JMLR Workshop and Conference Proceedings)*, Vol. 32. JMLR.org, 1278–1286. http://jmlr.org/proceedings/papers/v32/rezende14.html

[29] Sam T Roweis and Lawrence K Saul. 2000. Nonlinear dimensionality reduction by locally linear embedding. *science* 290, 5500 (2000), 2323–2326.

[30] Karen Simonyan and Andrew Zisserman. 2014. Very Deep Convolutional Networks for Large-Scale Image Recognition. *CoRR* abs/1409.1556 (2014). http://arxiv.org/abs/1409.1556

[31] Jian Tang, Jingzhou Liu, Ming Zhang, and Qiaozhu Mei. 2016. Visualizing Large-scale and High-dimensional Data. In *WWW*, Jacqueline Bourdeau, Jim Hendler, Roger Nkambou, Ian Horrocks, and Ben Y. Zhao (Eds.). ACM, 287–297. https://doi.org/10.1145/2872427.2883041

[32] Jian Tang, Meng Qu, Mingzhe Wang, Ming Zhang, Jun Yan, and Qiaozhu Mei. 2015. LINE: Large-scale Information Network Embedding. In *WWW*. ACM, 1067–1077. https://doi.org/10.1145/2736277.2741093

[33] Joshua B Tenenbaum, Vin De Silva, and John C Langford. 2000. A global geometric framework for nonlinear dimensionality reduction. *science* 290, 5500 (2000), 2319–2323.

[34] Daixin Wang, Peng Cui, and Wenwu Zhu. 2016. Structural deep network embedding. In *SIGKDD*. ACM, 1225–1234.

[35] Kelvin Xu, Jimmy Ba, Ryan Kiros, Kyunghyun Cho, Aaron C. Courville, Ruslan Salakhutdinov, Richard S. Zemel, and Yoshua Bengio. 2015. Show, Attend and Tell: Neural Image Caption Generation with Visual Attention. In *ICML (JMLR Workshop and Conference Proceedings)*, Vol. 37. JMLR.org, 2048–2057. http://jmlr.org/proceedings/papers/v37/xuc15.html

[36] Cheng Yang, Zhiyuan Liu, Deli Zhao, Maosong Sun, and Edward Y. Chang. 2015. Network Representation Learning with Rich Text Information. In *IJCAI*. AAAI Press, 2111–2117. http://ijcai.org/Abstract/15/299

[37] Zichao Yang, Xiaodong He, Jianfeng Gao, Li Deng, and Alexander J. Smola. 2016. Stacked Attention Networks for Image Question Answering. In *CVPR*. IEEE Computer Society, 21–29. https://doi.org/10.1109/CVPR.2016.10

[38] Daokun Zhang, Jie Yin, Xingquan Zhu, and Chengqi Zhang. 2017. User Profile Preserving Social Network Embedding. In *IJCAI*, Carles Sierra (Ed.). ijcai.org, 3378–3384. https://doi.org/10.24963/ijcai.2017/472

Exploiting Relational Information in Social Networks using Geometric Deep Learning on Hypergraphs

Devanshu Arya
Informatics Institute
University of Amsterdam
d.arya@uva.nl

Marcel Worring
Informatics Institute
University of Amsterdam
m.worring@uva.nl

ABSTRACT

Online social networks are constituted by a diverse set of entities including users, images and posts which makes the task of predicting interdependencies between entities challenging. We need a model that transfers information from a given type of relations between entities to predict other types of relations, irrespective of the type of entity. In order to devise a generic framework, one needs to capture the relational information between entities without any entity dependent information. However, there are two challenges: (a) a social network has an intrinsic community structure. In these communities, some relations are much more complicated than pairwise relations, thus cannot be simply modeled by a graph; (b) there are different types of entities and relations in a social network, taking into account all of them makes it difficult to formulate a model. In this paper, we claim that representing social networks using hypergraphs improves the task of predicting missing information about an entity by capturing higher-order relations. We study the behavior of our method by performing experiments on CLEF dataset consisting of images from Flickr, an online photo sharing social network.

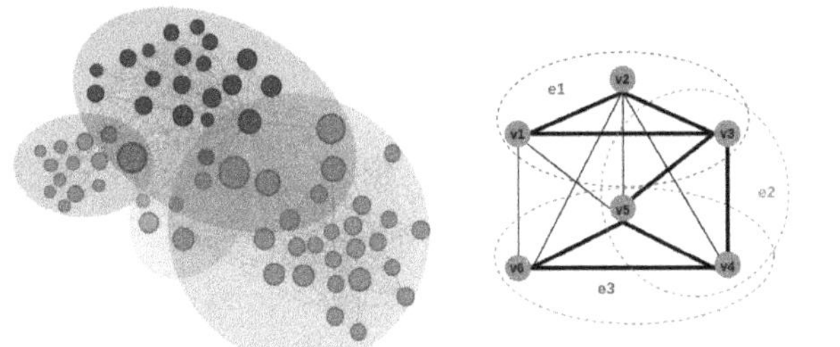

(a) Overlapping Community Structure in Social Network (b) Hypergraph vs Traditional Graph Representation of Relations

Figure 1: Figure (a) represents the overlapping community structure within a social network with the size of node proportional to its degree. As can be seen, the higher degree nodes forms a sub-unit to which other low degree nodes are densely connected. Figure (b) shows a comparison between the hypergraph and traditional graph representation. The higher-order relation between vertices cannot be captured using the pairwise edges. However, it can be easily captured using the hyperedges e1,e2 and e3.

CCS CONCEPTS

• **Computing methodologies** → *Multi-task learning*; *Neural networks*;

KEYWORDS

Social Network; Hypergraph; Geometric Deep Learning

ACM Reference Format:

Devanshu Arya and Marcel Worring. 2018. Exploiting Relational Information in Social Networks using Geometric Deep Learning on Hypergraphs. In *ICMR '18: 2018 International Conference on Multimedia Retrieval, June 11–14, 2018, Yokohama, Japan.* ACM, New York, NY, USA, 9 pages. https://doi.org/10.1145/3206025.3206062

1 INTRODUCTION

The structure of an online social network contains an enormous amount of information within the intrinsic relationships among entities. Capturing implicit relations within these structure allows to perform tasks such as clustering, classification and link prediction. In order to extract these relational information sources, data representation plays a key role. In multimedia, the problem of learning one type of relations between entities to predict other types of relations has been a topic of significant interest. In particular, exploiting relations in online social networks, brings up the problem of generalization across different types of entities. The entities can be users in social communication networks (Facebook, Twitter), images/videos in media sharing networks (Flickr, Instagram), posts in discussion forums (Reddit, Quora) or resources in 'sharing economy' networks (Airbnb, Uber). There exists a multitude of relations within these social networks, even for a small dataset which reveals another hindrance to extract meaningful information. One of the key solutions for these problems is to design a model that can efficiently capture large amounts of relational information between entities, so one can perform tasks irrespective of any entity specific knowledge. Hence, there is a need for a representation which is scalable and a formulation which is neutral to all kinds of social networks.

Traditional graph-based representations of a social network leads to a loss in information, as it implicitly takes into account only pairwise connections between the entities. These pairwise relations fail to represent higher-order relations among the entities. Moreover, a simple binary representation of relations does not depict a collective flow of information. For instance, consider Twitter which

ICMR '18, June 11–14, 2018, Yokohama, Japan

ACM ISBN 978-1-4503-5046-4/18/06...$15.00
https://doi.org/10.1145/3206025.3206062

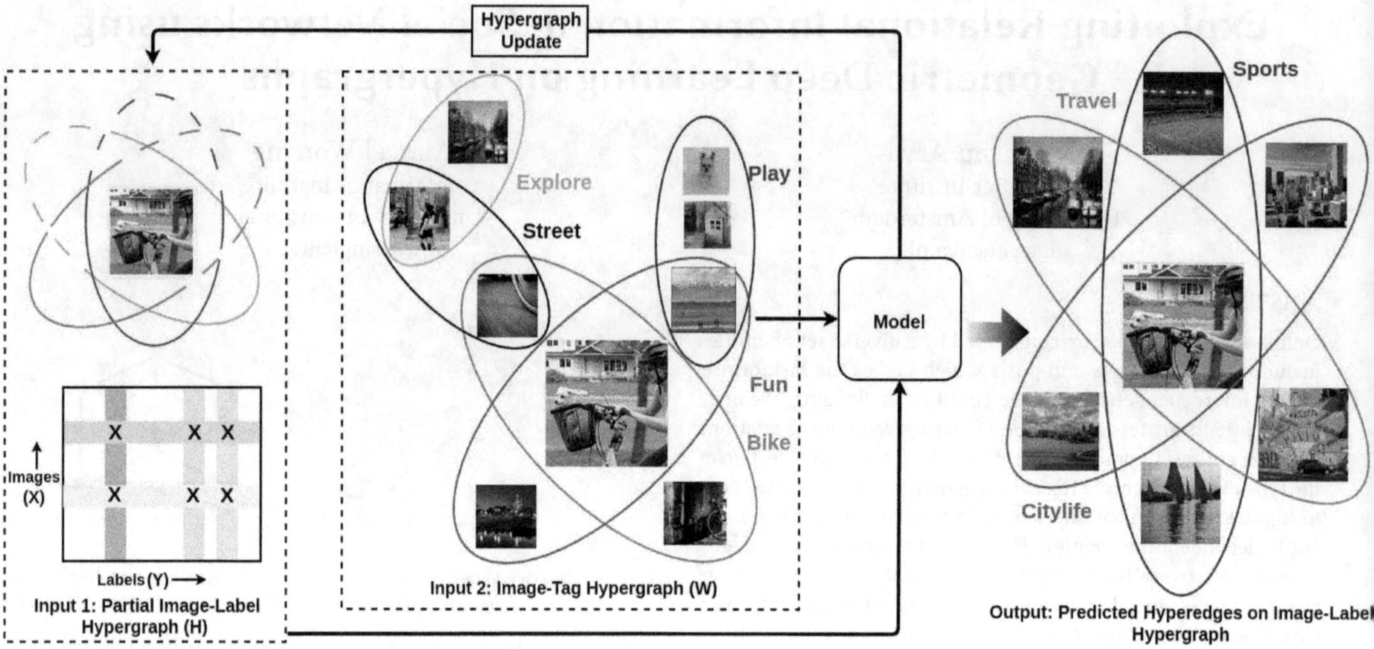

Figure 2: An example of the proposed method on the CLEF dataset of Flickr. The goal is to predict any type of metadata for images given two sets of input. Input 1 is the partial information about the images in one of the metadata spaces represented by an incomplete hypergraph (implying an incomplete incidence matrix). Input 2 is the complete information for the images in the other metadata space. Finally, the output is the set of predicted hyperedges between the images in the partial metadata space.

has users, tweets, hashtags, lists etc.. Representing even a ternary relation of a user releasing a tweet containing multiple hashtags is infeasible using traditional graphs [24]. Or even in the simple case of a co-authorship network, one cannot know whether three or more authors that link together in the network were co-authors of the same paper or not [50] as seen in Fig.1(b). Thus to capture higher-order relations in social networks, traditional graph-based representation of the network proves to be insufficient.

Another characteristic of social networks is the presence of overlapping communities [28]. Most importantly a social network possesses the special property of being a scale-free network [32] [35]. Scale-free networks are a class of power-law networks where the nodes that have many connections (high-degree nodes) tend to be connected to other nodes with many connections, while they are surrounded by many small clusters of low-degree nodes. In other words, social networks contain a structure of communities, where smaller communities in the network are joined to larger communities by highly connected nodes that play the role of local hubs [39]. Graphically, these communities form subunits within the network which show relatively high levels of connection within them and a lower connectivity among them as seen in Fig.1(a). This implies that high-degree nodes in the core of a subunit are crucial for an efficient flow of information and to maintain strong connectivity in these networks. To efficiently capture the relational information within a social network one needs to exploit this dense overlapping community structure.

Various approaches have been proposed in the past to exploit relational information in social networks [31] [10] [36] [19] [29]. However, they do not fully capture the structural features shared within the overlapping community structure of the entities. In order to utilize this property, in this paper we represent social networks as hypergraphs where each entity is represented as a set of vertices and the edges represent the overlapping relations between them. A hypergraph [3] is a generalization of the simple graph in which the edges, called hyperedges, are arbitrary non-empty subsets of the vertex set and may therefore connect any number of vertices. The hyperedges form the key difference between a hypergraph and a traditional graph. The nodes are kept the same as in a simple graph but a hyperedge can connect even all the nodes at once as compared to a traditional graph where an edge is always a connection between 2 nodes. Especially, a set of multimodal entities in a social network can be viewed as a hypergraph whose vertices are the individuals and whose hyperedges are the communities. Finally, a hypergraph representation can be computationally advantageous as compared to the simple graph model since the incidence matrix of a hypergraph requires less storage space in depicting the same volume of information [47]. In this way, a hypergraph is a natural framework to capture the community structure as well as higher-order relations between nodes in the network.

In order to infer relations between entities using only its relational information requires not only a good representation of data, but also a robust powerful model to integrate them. In this work, we propose a methodology which can perform multiple tasks and can be generalized to all social networks. We develop a model to predict missing information (metadata) about an entity by learning relations between entities, without requiring any content-specific features of the entity. To build a multi-functional model for predicting missing metadata, we introduce a multi-graph convolutional neural network model for hypergraphs based on the recent works in deep learning on graphs, specifically graph convolutional networks.

Deep convolutional neural networks [22] have been proven to offer an efficient framework to extract deep meaningful statistical patterns in signals like image, speech or video, in which there is a latent Euclidean structure. However, most of the definitions of convolution, utilize the properties of stationarity and locality which holds for Euclidean data spaces. Recent works [13] [21] on *geometric deep learning* aims to extend the framework of convolutional neural networks to data represented on graphs. The key idea in geometric deep learning is to devise a method for representation learning that can capture structural information within non-Euclidean domains, especially graphs. The applications of graph convolutional network ranges from describing shapes in different human poses [42], semi-supervised classification of authors in citation networks [21] and learning molecular fingerprints [11]. However, regular graph CNNs provide only a partial solution for learning dense information within a group of nodes. The two basic drawbacks of such models in a social network scenario have been due to the compact structure of data which makes the model unscalabale and the inability to share relational information across entities. Hence, we focus on developing a framework that can represent the scale-free properties of a social network and is generalizable to all social networks.

The points below highlight the contributions of this paper:

- We propose a generic framework which can transfer relational information from one type of relation to predict other types of relations between entities. Our approach is entity independent and captures higher-order relations by using hypergraph-based representation of a social network.
- We formulate a model for geometric deep learning on hypergraphs to perform tasks such as multi-label classification, link prediction and recommendation. Our results shows significant improvement as compared to previous graph-based methods.
- We further establish that a hypergraph-based representation of a social network is the most efficient way to build a model for learning the same volume of information in a network as compared to traditional pairwise simple or weighted graphs.

2 BACKGROUND

In this section, we introduce some background on the three concepts on which we base our methodology i.e. hypergraphs, matrix completion and geometric deep learning.

2.1 Notation and Formulation of a Hypergraph

A hypergraph G is formally represented as $H = (V, E)$, where V is a set of vertices and E is a set of hyperedges where each $e \in E$ is a subset of V. The *degree* of a hyperedge e, denoted as $\delta(e)$, is the number of vertices in e. In case of a simple graph, $\delta(e) = 2$ and hence they are known as "2-graph". The diagonal matrices containing the degrees of all vertices (v) and hyperedges (e) are denoted by D_v and D_e respectively. We say that there is a *hyperpath* between vertices v_1 and v_k when there is a sequence of distinct vertices and hyperedges $v_1, e_1, v_2, e_2, ..., e_{k-1}, v_k$ such that $\{v_i, v_{i+1}\} \subseteq e_i$ for $1 \leq i \leq k-1$. One of the key differences of hypergraphs as compared to pairwise simple graphs is its representation using an incidence matrix. It is represented by a $|V| \times |E|$ matrix H with entries $h(v, e) = 1$ if $v \in e$ and 0 otherwise. A simple graph is commonly represented by a square $|V| \times |V|$ matrix A which is known as the adjacency matrix, such that its element a_{ij} is 1 when there is an edge from vertex i to vertex j and 0 when there is no edge. There are many advantages of the incidence matrix (H) over the adjacency matrix (A) to model relational data [47]. The three key advantages are: (i) the incidence matrix of the hypergraph requires less storage space in comparison with the graph adjacency matrix to represent the same volume of information; (ii) hypergraph incidence matrices require fewer operations for matrix-vector multiplication; and (iii) most importantly, the benefits of using the Laplacian of a hypergraph incidence matrix which will be discussed in detail in section 4.2.

2.2 Matrix Completion

Matrix completion is the task of finding the missing values of a partially observed $p \times q$ matrix M. That is, we only observe a sparse set E of observations $M_{i,j} : \forall(i,j) \in E$, with $|E| << pq$. The goal is to estimate the rest of the values $M_{i,j} \notin E$. A particularly popular model is to assume that the values lie in a smaller subspace, resulting in M being a low-rank matrix, which leads to solving a rank minimization problem. Let $\Xi(\bullet)$ be the projection operator selecting only those entries that lie in the set E and let R be the target matrix to be reconstructed using $M_{i,j} : \forall(i,j) \in E$. Then the rank minimization problem is given by:

$$\widetilde{R} = \min_{R \in \mathbb{R}^{p \times q}} rank(R) \text{ s.t. } \Xi(R) = \Xi(M), \tag{1}$$

However, in reality the observed entries always contain a small amount of noise. For example, in movie recommmender systems the rating given by user contains noisy input and in wireless communications the signals received are contaminated with noise. To make the low-rank matrix completion problem more robust to noise, Candes et.al. [8] relaxed eq.1 by nuclear norm minimization given by eq.2.

$$\widetilde{R} = \min_{R} \frac{1}{2}||R||_* + \lambda_R||\Xi(M - R)||_F^2 \tag{2}$$

The number of unknown variables in this formulation are in the order of $p \times q$ which makes it practically unscalable for large matrices. One of the solutions is to use a factorized representation of matrix R i.e. $R = XY^T$, where X, Y are $p \times r$ and $q \times r$, matrices respectively with $r << min(p, q)$, which formulates as eq.3 [43].

$$\widetilde{X}, \widetilde{Y} = \min_{X,Y} \frac{1}{2}||X||_F^2 + \frac{1}{2}||Y||_F^2 + \lambda_{X,Y}||\Xi(M - XY^T)||_F^2 \tag{3}$$

Low-rank further implies linear dependence of rows/columns of M which can be utilized to constraint the space of solutions to be smooth. In many scenarios, the rows/columns form communities which can further optimize computation by incorporating proximity information among rows/columns. Recent work on geometric matrix completion has shown the importance of these relations by using them as side information to the matrix completion problem [20] [34] [2] [38]. It assumes that there exists a graph $G_r = (V^X, E^X)$ whose adjacency matrix encodes the relationships between the p rows of X and a graph $G_c = (V^Y, E^Y)$ for q rows of Y. The geometric matrix completion can then be written as

$$\min_{X,Y} \frac{1}{2}||X||^2_{G_r} + \frac{1}{2}||Y||^2_{G_c} + \lambda_{X,Y}||\Xi(M - XY^T)||^2_F \quad (4)$$

where, $||X||^2_{G_r} = trace(X\Delta_r X^T)$ and $||Y||^2_{G_c} = trace(Y\Delta_c Y^T)$ are the graph Dirichlet semi-norm for rows and columns respectively. Δ_r and Δ_c are the row and column laplacian matrices.

2.3 Geometric Deep Learning

As defined by Bronstein et.al. [5]; "Geometric deep learning is an umbrella term for emerging techniques attempting to generalize (structured) deep neural models to non-Euclidean domains such as graphs and manifolds". One of the early attempts on generalizing neural network to graphs are due to Scarselli et.al. in 2005 [15], who proposed a combination of recurrent neural networks and random walk models called Graph Neural Networks (GNN). The first formulation of convolution neural networks on graphs used the definition of convolutions from graph signal processing in the spectral domain [6].

In this work, we focus on applying convolution network on graphs in order to learn the intrinsic relations in social networks. A convolutional layer in the spectral domain is defined as

$$f_l^{out} = \xi(\sum_{l'=1}^{p} \Phi_k \hat{G}_{l,l'} \Phi_K^T f_{l'}^{in}) \quad (5)$$

where, $F_{in}^{n \times p} = (f_1^{in} ... f_p^{in})$ and $F_{out}^{n \times q} = (f_1^{out} ... f_p^{out})$ represent the p and q−dimensional input and output signals on the vertices of the graph. Φ_k is the $n \times k$ matrix of the eigenvectors from the spectral decomposition of the graph. $\hat{G}_{l,l'}$ are the learnable spectral filters and ξ is the ReLU non-linearity. Further advancement to this definition have been proposed in order to make a *Graph Convolution Network* (GCN) generic and scalable [16] [11] [21].

3 RELATED WORK

We review two categories of related work: studies on context/network based learning of relational information in social networks and applications of deep learning approaches on graphs.

3.1 Learning Relational Information in Social Networks

Several approaches have been introduced for learning relations within a social network. They can be grouped in five main categories based on their representation of social network data.

In the first one, [26] proposed one of the earliest approaches where they use network topology in which, they model a social network as a simple homogeneous graph where each node represents an entity and each link denotes social relationships. [45] proposed Link Prediction using Social Features (*LPSF*), based on features extracted from patterns of prominent interactions across the network for each entity pair. These features are very useful in identifying similar node pairs, even when they are far away. They propose a simple yet powerful model to capture relations between entities. However, these approaches are not made generic across all networks and lack scalability due to their dependence on pre-defined methods for feature extraction.

In the second type of approach [48] proposed to model social networks as pairwise heterogeneous graphs as opposed to homogeneous ones and apply a random walk algorithm to calculate link proximity. Online photo sharing networks have been of particular interest in learning relations due to the generation of large amounts of metadata. [31] proposed a graphical model that treats image classification as a problem of simultaneously predicting binary labels for a network of photos. They represent each image by a node while the edges are formed between images that have some common property. The first two approaches model social relations between entities as pairs and then apply a structural learning algorithm. These approaches can be scalable to large networks but they still fail to capture any higher-order relations. Therefore, they cannot make use of the community structure in social networks leading to loss in information. Moreover, their applicability to real-world networks is confined as they use parametric methods for modeling relations [19].

The third category of approaches represents data on an ego network, which consist of a focal node ("ego") and the nodes to whom ego is directly connected to ("alters"). Egos and alters are tied to each other by social relations, in [12] and [23], the authors propose to learn social circles by representing the data in ego networks. Li et. al. [25] further study the problem of profiling user attributes in social networks by capturing the correlation between attributes and social connections in an ego network. These approaches however does not generalize for all types of social networks and to learn all kinds of relations between entities and metadata.

Another kind of approaches are based on hypergraph theory. Hypergraph-based models have been widely used in the multimedia domain for solving the problems of community detection [49] [27], multi-label classification [9] [44], tag-based social image searching [14], music recommendation [7] and link prediction in social networks [24]. In this work, we use hypergraph-based approach to represent data, for precisely capturing the high-order relations, in order to build a generic framework for classification, recommendation and link prediction.

Several "non-graph" based approaches to exploit relational information across domains have also been a field of particular interest. Earlier works on multi-domain collaborative filtering includes interaction-associated information of users and items as side information for recommendation. Cross-domain collaborative filtering (CDCF) [18] has recently started to draw significant research attention. The basic concept of CDCF is to borrow rating knowledge for each user from some related auxiliary domains, whose rating matrices are relatively dense, to alleviate the rating sparsity problem in the sparse target domain. These approaches rely mostly on implicit domain correlations that are mined solely from user preference data, and and no explicit links are exploited. There are two major questions surrounding this approach [41]. First, what could be the common knowledge that can be transferred/shared between different domains, and, second, what could be the optimal way to transfer/share knowledge between different domains [37].

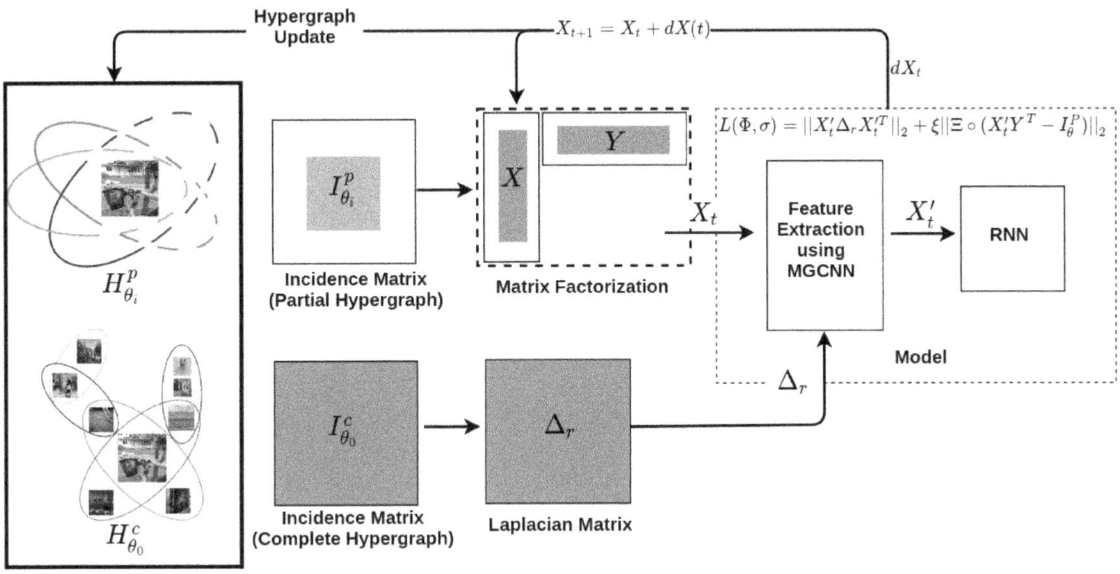

Figure 3: A block-diagram of the proposed model. The input to the model are the partial $H\theta_i^p$ and complete $H\theta_0^c$ hypergraphs corresponding to the two types of metadata θ_i and θ_0 respectively. $I\theta_0^c$ and $I\theta_i^p$ are the incidence matrices (the grey color depicts data used for training whereas white represents missing data). The model updates the hypergraph incrementally by updating the incidence matrix using geometric deep learning based model.

3.2 Application of Deep Learning based Approaches on Graphs

There has been a recent surge of interest to formulate deep learning methods on non-euclidean domain especially in graphs. The effectiveness of deep learning graph-based approaches ranges from computer graphics [4] to chemistry [13]. The spectral graph convolutional neural networks (*GCN*), originally proposed in [6] and extended in [11] have proven effective in classification of handwritten digits and news texts. [21] proposed a simplified *GCN* for semi-supervised classification of authors in a citation network. In the computer vision community, *GCN* has been extended by [30] to describe shapes in different human poses, [42] to demonstrate classification of point clouds and [33] for image and 3D shape analysis. In multimedia, [40] proposed an approach to categorize user posts for political extremism content based on their discussion topics. Deep learning on graphs for social networks is yet to be explored for their ability to uncover hidden relations between multimedia items. In this paper, we take a step further to devise a generic model for learning relations in social networks using geometric deep learning methods.

4 PROPOSED MODEL

In this work, we define a trainable graphical model that treats predicting metadata for an entity, as the unified problem of generating sets of hyperedges across entities. The basic hypothesis of the model is that entities related through one set of metadata carry imperative information which can be learnt to predict other relational properties between them. In this paper, we will use $H_\Theta^{p/c}$ (with $I_\Theta^{p/c}$ as its incidence matrix) to denote a partial(p) or a complete (c) hypergraph. The subscript Θ is the type of metadata used to construct the hyperedges i.e. $\Theta = t/l/g/u$ for tags (t), labels (l), groups (g) and users (u) respectively. The inputs to the model are: (a) a complete hypergraph of entities constructed using one type of metadata denoted by H_Θ^c and (b) a partial hypergraph on the same sets of entities constructed from the required metadata denoted by H_Θ^p. The training of the model has three phases: constructing the model by formulating it as a factorized matrix completion problem, relational feature extraction using geometric deep learning and finally updating the partial hypergraph by predicting hyperedges across entities. Fig.3 shows these three phases as a block diagram.

4.1 Formulating Hyperedge Prediction as Matrix Completion

The computational advantage of using a hypergraph for the above mentioned problems instead of a simple graph is the representation of its vertices and edges by an incidence matrix. As compared to traditional graphs where the incidence matrix has an additional constraint of only two non-zero values in each column ("2-graph" property), the incidence matrix of a hypergraph can have as many as all non-zero values in each column. Therefore, generating hyperedges in a hypergraph can be termed equivalent to the problem of filling missing entries in its corresponding incidence matrix. In this work, we represent the relation between entities using their metadata by hypergraphs. Each entity corresponds to a vertex and the edges depict all unique values of the corresponding metadata. The respective incidence matrix ($I_\Theta^{p/c}$) is of dimension $n \times \theta$, where n is the total number of entities and θ are the unique values corresponding to the metadata Θ. Hence, the problem of predicting hyperedges between entities in H_Θ^p reduces to completing the incidence matrix I_Θ^p with multiple missing entries corresponding to each column and at least one known entry in each row, where each row is an entity and the columns are values of the metadata.

In order to incorporate relational information from H^c_Θ to fill I^p_Θ, we further take motivation from geometric matrix completion. This is achieved by factorizing I^p_Θ into its row (X_p) and column (Y_p) matrices such that $I^p_\Theta = X_p Y_p^T$. The matrix X with dimension $n \times q$ represents the entities (vertices) and Y with dimension $\theta \times q$ represents values of metadata (edges), with $q << min(n, \theta)$. The implicit relation between the individual entities in X_p (row matrix) is captured using H^c_Θ. We consider identity relations between values in the column-matrix Y_p i.e. each value of the metadata is related to itself only. This is because the unique values of metadata (Θ) do not contain any relational information among them. That is, we treat all the values of a metadata to be independent and uniformly distributed in space. Thus eq.4 can be re-formulated with $H^c_\Theta \equiv G_r$, I^p_Θ as the partially filled matrix M and $||Y||_{Gc}$ as a constant, which leads to the following minimization problem

$$\min_X ||X||^2_{H^c_\Theta} + \lambda_X ||\Xi \circ (I^p_\Theta - XY^T)||^2_F \quad (6)$$

4.2 Feature Extraction using Multi-Graph CNNs on Hypergraph

The second phase of our model aims at jointly extracting features from H^c_Θ and H^p_Θ. In this way, we can transfer the relational information from the complete hypergraph H^c_Θ to predict the missing hyperedges in H^p_Θ. In this paper, we devise our solution based on recent work on multi-graph convolution (*MGCNN*) [34]. It uses the formulation for GCN using recurrent Chebyshev polynomials which simplifies eq.5 [11]. The motivation behind multi-graph convolution is that, a Fourier transform of a 2-dimensional signal can be simplified by formulating it as applying a one-dimensional Fourier transform to its rows and columns. In particular, multi-graph convolution proposes a method of matrix completion, given the rows and columns of a matrix possess relational information within themselves. In our framework, we extract features combining I^p_Θ and I^c_Θ by stacking multi-graph CNN layers given by

$$X'_t = \sum_{j=0}^{q} \Phi_j T_j(\Delta_r) X_t \quad (7)$$

where Φ_j are the learnable filter coefficients, $\Delta_r^{n \times n}$ is the row-hypergraph Laplacian and T_j is the representation of filters using Chebyshev polynomials. In this way a multi-graph CNN on $X_t^{n \times q}$ with a single channel produces a k dimensional output $X_t'^{n \times q \times k}$.

The other advantage of the above formulation is the use of the Laplacian to encode information from data defined on hypergraph H^c_Θ. The Laplacian matrix of a hypergraph has been shown to be useful for learning higher-order relations [1] [44], spectral clustering of edges [50] and to measure the relatedness between two entities [7]. In this paper, we use the normalized hypergraph Laplacian matrix (Δ_r) [50] given by

$$\Delta_r = \mathbb{I} - D_v^{-\frac{1}{2}} I^c_\Theta D_e^{-1} I^{cT}_\Theta D_v^{-\frac{1}{2}} \quad (8)$$

where D_v and D_e are the vertex and edge degree matrices of hypergraph H^c_Θ respectively, $\mathbb{I}$ is the identity matrix and I^{cT}_Θ is the transpose of incidence matrix I^c_Θ. The Laplacian will be used for incorporating the structure of the hypergraph H^c_Θ in eq.7. In this way, we extract relational features using combined information from the complete and the partial hypergraph.

	Task1	**Task2**	**Task3**	**Task4**
θ_0	Tags (t)	Tags(t)	Tags (t)	Labels (l)
θ_i	Labels (l)	User (u)	Groups (g)	Tags (t)
$\|\|rel_{\theta_i}\|\|$	613,014	51,804	70,226,414	91,485,864
$\|\|rel(H^c_{\theta_0})\|\|$	45,766	45,766	45,766	55,396
$\|\|rel(G^c_{\theta_0})\|\|$	85,802	85,802	85,802	95,766

Table 1: Table showing the details about the 4 tasks. The goal is to predict relations given a partial set of rel_{θ_i} and complete set of relations represented on hypergraph ($rel(H^c_{\theta_0})$) or on simple and weighted-graph ($rel(G^c_{\theta_0})$).

4.3 Incremental Updates of the Hypergraph

The next step is to diffuse the features extracted by coupling the structures of the two hypergraphs (H^c_Θ and H^p_Θ). The partial hypergraph is updated incrementally as a consequence of the completion of its incidence matrix. We use a Recurrent Neural Network (RNN) [17] to predict small incremental changes (dX) to the matrix X [34]. One of the main advantages of using an RNN for predicting accurate small changes is its ability to store information for longer temporal steps. The model is finally trained by feeding the features extracted from multi-graph CNN (X'_t) to an RNN and perform training by using the minimization eq.6 in geometric matrix completion as the loss function.

$$L(\Phi, \sigma) = ||X'_{t,\sigma} \Delta_r X'_{t,\sigma}{}^T||_2 + \lambda_X ||\Xi \circ (X'_{t,\sigma} Y^T - I^P_\theta)||_2 \quad (9)$$

where $X't$ is the feature extracted by multi-graph convolution with Φ as the learning coefficient, σ denotes the parameter for RNN and the subscript t denotes the number of diffusion iterations.

5 EXPERIMENTS

In this section, we perform extensive experiments to show the advantages of learning higher-order relations in a social network using geometric deep learning on hypergraphs as compared to other approaches. We design our experiments to investigate the following:

- Performance of the proposed generic framework to predict multiple types of relations between entities
- Advantages of using geometric deep learning over existing simple graph as well as hypergraph-based learning
- Efficiency in representing relational information of a network using hypergraphs as compared to pairwise simple graph representation

To evaluate our model, we explore the online photo sharing social network Flickr, which generates a huge amount of metadata and hence relations for each image. Flickr has been particularly very popular in using social network metadata for image classification among other implications [19] [31]. The metadata, such as user-generated tags and community-curated groups in Flickr are used by people as a means to communicate with other people, and

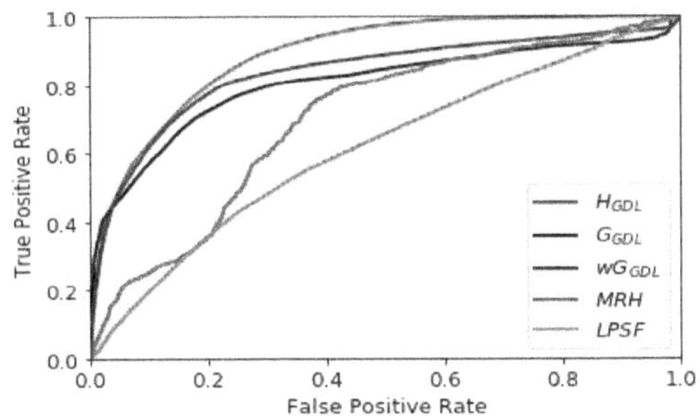

(a) Task1: Multi-Label Image Classification

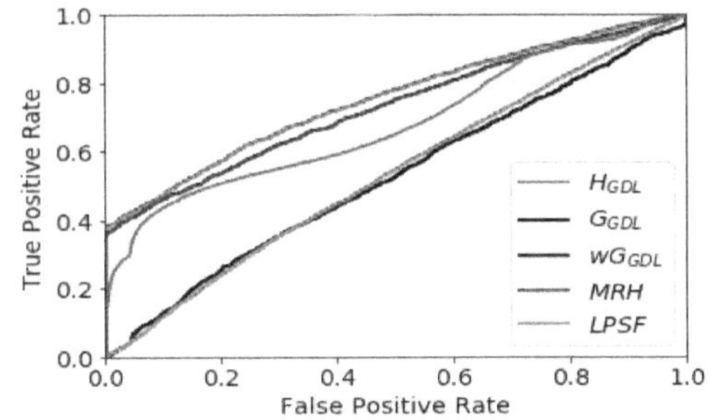

(b) Task2: Image-User Link Prediction

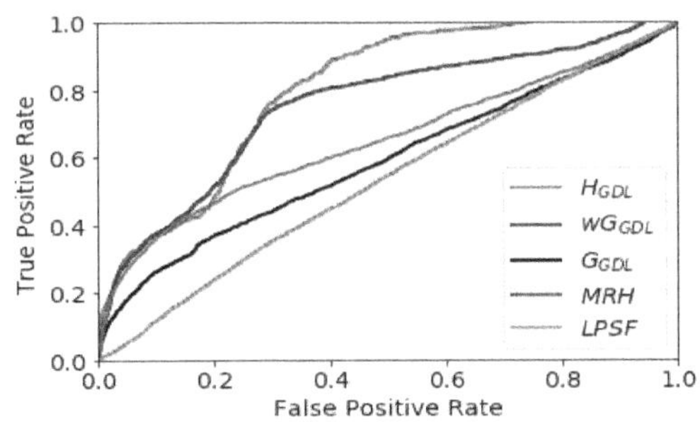

(c) Task3: Group Recommendation

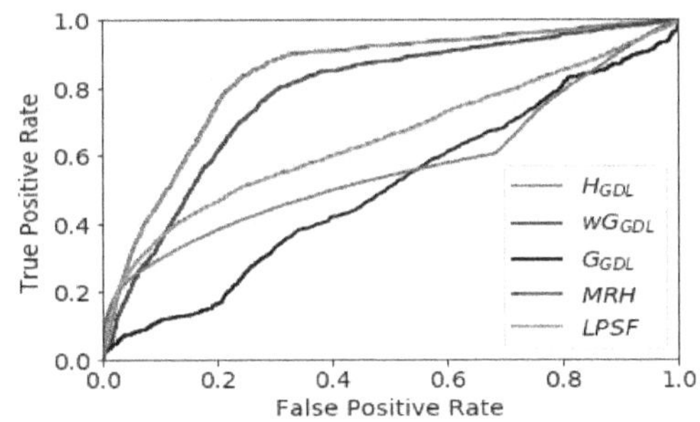

(d) Task4: Tag Recommendation

Figure 4: Experiment 1 - Receiver Operating Characteristics (ROC) curve showing the performance of the models on each of the 4 tasks. The hypergraph-based geometric deep learning model (H_{GDL}) has significant advantage as compared to other methods.

as a means to describe the image and its location. But not every image is annotated with all the information, hence using relational information can be highly informative in unveiling the missing information of every image.

Data Setup For our experiments, we study the CLEF dataset [31] comprising of images from Flickr which has social network metadata and has labels provided by human annotators for each image. The dataset consists of 4,546 images with 99 labels (l), 21,192 tags (t), 10,575 groups (g) and 2,663 users (u). We show that our framework can be used as a generic multi-functional setup for generating information for an image by performing 4 types of tasks using our model: $Task1$: Multi-Label Image Classification, $Task2$: Image-User Link Prediction, $Task3$: Group Recommendation and $Task4$: Tag Recommendation. Given a set of known-metadata (θ_0) for each image, we first construct the complete hypergraph $H^c_{\theta_0}$. Our goal is to predict other sets of partially known metadata (θ_i) associated with the images.

Training The total number of relations, $||rel_{\theta_i}||$ between the images and the target metadata (θ_i) is tabulated in Table1. As seen from the table, each image has multiple values of metadata in common with other images, resulting in a multitude of relations. We randomly sample 40% of these relations and keep them aside to use them as test set. The remaining relations are used to construct the partial hypergraph $H^p_{\theta_i}$ for training the model along with the complete hypergraph $H^c_{\theta_0}$.

Evaluation To show the efficiency in representing social network information with a hypergraph, we compare our result with the data represented by hypergraph (H), simple graph (G) and weighted graph (wG) using the same model. Simple graph (G) indicates a binary relation between entities with a value 1 if the two entities share at least one common value of the metadata. The weighted graph (wG) is constructed by assigning weights equal to the count of values of the metadata common between two entities. The hypergraph-based representation reduces the total number of relations between entities and the known metadata significantly by representing higher-order relations as community. This can be seen from Table1 where $||rel(H^c_{\theta_0})||$ and $||rel(G^c_{\theta_0})||$ denote the total number of relations in a hypergraph and graph based representation respectively.

We evaluate the performance of our geometric deep learning based model as compared to the previous hypergraph based algorithm (MRH) [7] [24] and a graph-based model trained on social network features ($LPSF$) [45] [46] for the same tasks. $LPSF$ as mentioned under the first approach in section 3.1, trains a neural network on popular features like Page Rank, Number of Common Neighbors, Preferential Attachment etc. extracted from a social network. We use the notation H_{GDL}, wG_{GDL} and G_{GDL} for our geometric deep learning (GDL) model on hypergraph, weighted graph and regular graph respectively.

5.1 Experiment 1: Learning Relational Information in a Social Network

We start our experimental evaluation by showing the performance of our model, MRH and $LPSF$ on the 4 tasks. To evaluate the performance of our model and show its advantages over other methods, we show the Receiver Operating Characteristic (ROC) curves for each tasks. The ROC curve depicts how well a model is able to

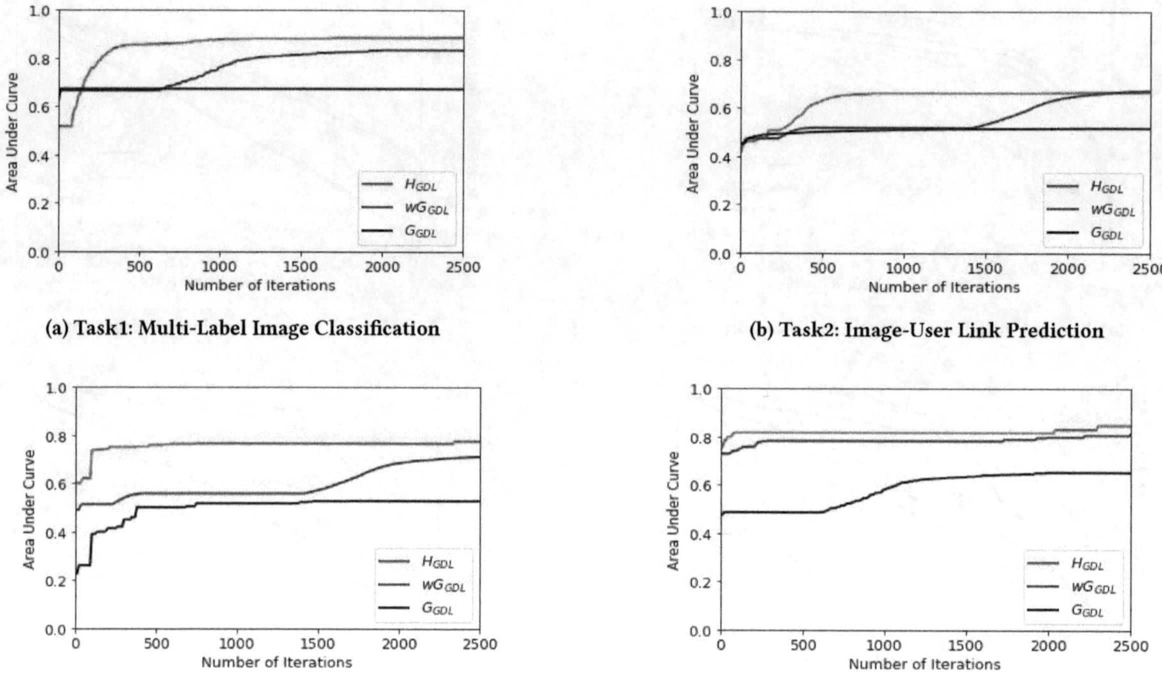

(a) Task1: Multi-Label Image Classification

(b) Task2: Image-User Link Prediction

(c) Task3: Group Recommendation

(d) Task4: Tag Recommendation

Figure 5: Experiment 2 - Figure showing the rate of learning with each iteration of the proposed model using hypergraph (H_{GDL}), weighted graph (wG) and simple graph (G). As can be seen, the hypergraph-based model converges faster for all the 4 tasks implying a better representation to learn relational information.

predict the presence/absence of a relation among images with the corresponding metadata. Fig.4 shows the performance of the models on the 4 tasks. The Geometric Deep Learning based approach outperforms existing hypergraph-based *MRH* and graph-based *LPSH* methods in all the 4 tasks. This confirms, the significant advantage of using a hypergraph representation of the network as compared to simple and weighted graphs using the same model. Most importantly, this proves the advantage of learning relations using geometric deep learning techniques as compared to existing hypergraph-based model.

5.2 Experiment 2: Measuring the efficiency of representing data from social network

To explore the advantage of representing a social network using hypergraphs as compared to traditional graphs, we evaluate their efficiency in learning relational information. We compare the rate of convergence of our algorithm on the three graph frameworks mentioned above i.e. hypergraph (H), weighted graph (wG) and simple graph (G) on the 4 tasks. The faster the algorithm converges, the better the framework is in capturing the same volume of relational information. We plot the area under the ROC curve against the number of iterations used to update the matrix incrementally. As can be seen from Fig.5, the hypergraph-based representation converges faster than simple and weighted graphs for all the 4 tasks. This concludes the efficiency of a hypergraph in capturing information which makes it the best choice to represent data on a social network.

6 CONCLUSIONS

In this paper, a generic method to exploit relational information between entities in a social network for predicting missing information about an entity has been presented. In contrast with traditional graph representation, we model a social network using hypergraphs. We show the importance of using hypergraphs in order to capture all types of entities and either the pair wise or high-order relations among them to avoid loss of any information. Moreover, our approach is content independent i.e. it does not depend on any entity-specific information and hence can be generalized to all types of social networks. We formulate the learning problem as matrix completion on graphs and extend the methods on geometric deep learning to hypergraphs. We evaluate our model on 4 tasks: multi-label image classification, image-user link prediction, group and tag recommendation in a Flickr dataset. Experimental results show a significant advantage in representing social networks by hypergraphs and using deep learning based method for exploiting relational information within the network. We also prove the computational effectiveness of representing the same volume of information from a social network on a hypergraph as compared to the traditional pairwise graphs.

ACKNOWLEDGMENTS

This research has received funding from the European Union's Horizon 2020 research and innovation programme under grant agreement 700381.

REFERENCES

[1] Sameer Agarwal, Kristin Branson, and Serge Belongie. 2006. Higher order learning with graphs. In *Proceedings of the 23rd international conference on Machine learning*. ACM, 17–24.

[2] Kirell Benzi, Vassiiis Kalofolias, Xavier Bresson, and Pierre Vandergheynst. 2016. Song recommendation with non-negative matrix factorization and graph total variation. In *Acoustics, Speech and Signal Processing (ICASSP), 2016 IEEE International Conference on*. Ieee, 2439–2443.

[3] Claude Berge. 1973. *Graphs and Hypergraphs (North-Holland mathematical library; v. 6)*. Elsevier.

[4] Davide Boscaini, Jonathan Masci, Emanuele Rodolà, and Michael Bronstein. 2016. Learning shape correspondence with anisotropic convolutional neural networks. In *Advances in Neural Information Processing Systems*. 3189–3197.

[5] Michael M Bronstein, Joan Bruna, Yann LeCun, Arthur Szlam, and Pierre Vandergheynst. 2017. Geometric deep learning: going beyond euclidean data. *IEEE Signal Processing Magazine* 34, 4 (2017), 18–42.

[6] Joan Bruna, Wojciech Zaremba, Arthur Szlam, and Yann Lecun. 2014. Spectral networks and locally connected networks on graphs. In *International Conference on Learning Representations (ICLR2014), CBLS, April 2014*.

[7] Jiajun Bu, Shulong Tan, Chun Chen, Can Wang, Hao Wu, Lijun Zhang, and Xiaofei He. 2010. Music recommendation by unified hypergraph: combining social media information and music content. In *Proceedings of the 18th ACM international conference on Multimedia*. ACM, 391–400.

[8] Emmanuel J Candes and Yaniv Plan. 2010. Matrix completion with noise. *Proc. IEEE* 98, 6 (2010), 925–936.

[9] Gang Chen, Jianwen Zhang, Fei Wang, Changshui Zhang, and Yuli Gao. 2009. Efficient multi-label classification with hypergraph regularization. In *Proceedings of Computer Vision and Pattern Recognition, 2009. CVPR*. IEEE, 1658–1665.

[10] Jinpeng Chen, Hongbo Gao, Zhenyu Wu, and Deyi Li. 2013. Tag co-occurrence relationship prediction in heterogeneous information networks. In *Parallel and Distributed Systems (ICPADS), 2013 International Conference on*. IEEE, 528–533.

[11] Michaël Defferrard, Xavier Bresson, and Pierre Vandergheynst. 2016. Convolutional neural networks on graphs with fast localized spectral filtering. In *Advances in Neural Information Processing Systems*. 3844–3852.

[12] Christopher P Diehl, Galileo Namata, and Lise Getoor. 2007. Relationship identification for social network discovery. In *AAAI*, Vol. 22. 546–552.

[13] David K Duvenaud, Dougal Maclaurin, Jorge Iparraguirre, Rafael Bombarell, Timothy Hirzel, Alán Aspuru-Guzik, and Ryan P Adams. 2015. Convolutional networks on graphs for learning molecular fingerprints. In *Advances in neural information processing systems*. 2224–2232.

[14] Yue Gao, Meng Wang, Huanbo Luan, Jialie Shen, Shuicheng Yan, and Dacheng Tao. 2011. Tag-based social image search with visual-text joint hypergraph learning. In *Proceedings of the 19th ACM international conference on Multimedia*. ACM, 1517–1520.

[15] Marco Gori, Gabriele Monfardini, and Franco Scarselli. 2005. A new model for learning in graph domains. In *Neural Networks, 2005. IJCNN'05. Proceedings. 2005 IEEE International Joint Conference on*, Vol. 2. IEEE, 729–734.

[16] Mikael Henaff, Joan Bruna, and Yann LeCun. 2015. Deep convolutional networks on graph-structured data. *arXiv preprint arXiv:1506.05163* (2015).

[17] Sepp Hochreiter and Jürgen Schmidhuber. 1997. Long short-term memory. *Neural computation* 9, 8 (1997), 1735–1780.

[18] Liang Hu, Jian Cao, Guandong Xu, Jie Wang, Zhiping Gu, and Longbing Cao. 2013. Cross-domain collaborative filtering via bilinear multilevel analysis. In *International Joint Conference on Artificial Intelligence*. IJCAI/AAAI.

[19] Justin Johnson, Lamberto Ballan, and Li Fei-Fei. 2015. Love thy neighbors: Image annotation by exploiting image metadata. In *Proceedings of the IEEE international conference on computer vision*. 4624–4632.

[20] Vassilis Kalofolias, Xavier Bresson, Michael Bronstein, and Pierre Vandergheynst. 2014. Matrix completion on graphs. *arXiv preprint arXiv:1408.1717* (2014).

[21] Thomas N Kipf and Max Welling. 2016. Semi-supervised classification with graph convolutional networks. *arXiv preprint arXiv:1609.02907* (2016).

[22] Alex Krizhevsky, Ilya Sutskever, and Geoffrey E Hinton. 2012. Imagenet classification with deep convolutional neural networks. In *Advances in neural information processing systems*. 1097–1105.

[23] Jure Leskovec and Julian J Mcauley. 2012. Learning to discover social circles in ego networks. In *Advances in neural information processing systems*. 539–547.

[24] Dong Li, Zhiming Xu, Sheng Li, and Xin Sun. 2013. Link prediction in social networks based on hypergraph. In *Proceedings of the 22nd International Conference on World Wide Web*. ACM, 41–42.

[25] Rui Li, Chi Wang, and Kevin Chen-Chuan Chang. 2014. User profiling in an ego network: co-profiling attributes and relationships. In *Proceedings of the 23rd international conference on World wide web*. ACM, 819–830.

[26] David Liben-Nowell and Jon Kleinberg. 2007. The link-prediction problem for social networks. *journal of the Association for Information Science and Technology* 58, 7 (2007), 1019–1031.

[27] Yu-Ru Lin, Jimeng Sun, Paul Castro, Ravi Konuru, Hari Sundaram, and Aisling Kelliher. 2009. Metafac: community discovery via relational hypergraph factorization. In *Proceedings of the 15th ACM SIGKDD international conference on Knowledge discovery and data mining*. ACM, 527–536.

[28] Dajie Liu, Norbert Blenn, and Piet Van Mieghem. 2012. A social network model exhibiting tunable overlapping community structure. *Procedia Computer Science* 9 (2012), 1400–1409.

[29] Yun-Fu Liu, Jing-Ming Guo, and Lingling An. 2017. Multimedia Classification Using Bipolar Relation Graphs. *IEEE Transactions on Multimedia* 19, 8 (2017), 1860–1869.

[30] Jonathan Masci, Davide Boscaini, Michael Bronstein, and Pierre Vandergheynst. 2015. Geodesic convolutional neural networks on riemannian manifolds. In *Proceedings of the IEEE international conference on computer vision workshops*. 37–45.

[31] Julian McAuley and Jure Leskovec. 2012. Image labeling on a network: using social-network metadata for image classification. *Computer Vision–ECCV 2012* (2012), 828–841.

[32] Alan Mislove, Massimiliano Marcon, Krishna P Gummadi, Peter Druschel, and Bobby Bhattacharjee. 2007. Measurement and analysis of online social networks. In *Proceedings of the 7th ACM SIGCOMM conference on Internet measurement*. ACM, 29–42.

[33] Federico Monti, Davide Boscaini, and Jonathan Masci. 2017. Geometric deep learning on graphs and manifolds using mixture model CNNs. In *Proceedings of Computer Vision and Pattern Recognition, CVPR*.

[34] Federico Monti, Michael Bronstein, and Xavier Bresson. 2017. Geometric matrix completion with recurrent multi-graph neural networks. In *Advances in Neural Information Processing Systems*. 3700–3710.

[35] André A Moreira, Demétrius R Paula, Raimundo N Costa Filho, and José S Andrade Jr. 2006. Competitive cluster growth in complex networks. *Physical Review E* 73, 6 (2006), 065101.

[36] Zhenxing Niu, Gang Hua, Xinbo Gao, and Qi Tian. 2014. Semi-supervised relational topic model for weakly annotated image recognition in social media. In *Proceedings of the IEEE Conference on Computer Vision and Pattern Recognition*. 4233–4240.

[37] Weike Pan, Nathan N Liu, Evan W Xiang, and Qiang Yang. 2011. Transfer learning to predict missing ratings via heterogeneous user feedbacks. In *IJCAI Proceedings-International Joint Conference on Artificial Intelligence*, Vol. 22. 2318.

[38] Nikhil Rao, Hsiang-Fu Yu, Pradeep K Ravikumar, and Inderjit S Dhillon. 2015. Collaborative filtering with graph information: Consistency and scalable methods. In *Advances in neural information processing systems*. 2107–2115.

[39] Erzsébet Ravasz and Albert-László Barabási. 2003. Hierarchical organization in complex networks. *Physical Review E* 67, 2 (2003), 026112.

[40] Stevan Rudinac, Iva Gornishka, and Marcel Worring. 2017. Multimodal Classification of Violent Online Political Extremism Content with Graph Convolutional Networks. In *Proceedings of the on Thematic Workshops of ACM Multimedia 2017*. ACM, 245–252.

[41] Yue Shi, Martha Larson, and Alan Hanjalic. 2014. Collaborative filtering beyond the user-item matrix: A survey of the state of the art and future challenges. *ACM Computing Surveys (CSUR)* 47, 1 (2014), 3.

[42] Martin Simonovsky and Nikos Komodakis. 2017. Dynamic Edge-Conditioned Filters in Convolutional Neural Networks on Graphs. In *Proceedings of Computer Vision and Pattern Recognition, 2017. CVPR*.

[43] Nathan Srebro, Jason Rennie, and Tommi S Jaakkola. 2005. Maximum-margin matrix factorization. In *Advances in neural information processing systems*. 1329–1336.

[44] Liang Sun, Shuiwang Ji, and Jieping Ye. 2008. Hypergraph spectral learning for multi-label classification. In *Proceedings of the 14th ACM SIGKDD international conference on Knowledge discovery and data mining*. ACM, 668–676.

[45] Xi Wang and Gita Sukthankar. 2013. Link prediction in multi-relational collaboration networks. In *Proceedings of the 2013 IEEE/ACM international conference on advances in social networks analysis and mining*. ACM, 1445–1447.

[46] Xi Wang and Gita Sukthankar. 2014. Link prediction in heterogeneous collaboration networks. In *Social network analysis-community detection and evolution*. Springer, 165–192.

[47] Michael M Wolf, Alicia M Klinvex, and Daniel M Dunlavy. 2016. Advantages to modeling relational data using hypergraphs versus graphs. In *High Performance Extreme Computing Conference (HPEC), 2016 IEEE*. IEEE, 1–7.

[48] Zhijun Yin, Manish Gupta, Tim Weninger, and Jiawei Han. 2010. Linkrec: a unified framework for link recommendation with user attributes and graph structure. In *Proceedings of the 19th international conference on World wide web*. ACM, 1211–1212.

[49] Yi-Liang Zhao, Qiang Chen, Shuicheng Yan, Tat-Seng Chua, and Daqing Zhang. 2013. Detecting profilable and overlapping communities with user-generated multimedia contents in LBSNs. *ACM Transactions on Multimedia Computing, Communications, and Applications (TOMM)* 10, 1 (2013), 3.

[50] Denny Zhou, Jiayuan Huang, and Bernhard Schölkopf. 2007. Learning with hypergraphs: Clustering, classification, and embedding. In *Advances in neural information processing systems*. 1601–1608.

Automatic Prediction of Building Age from Photographs

Matthias Zeppelzauer
St. Pölten University of Applied Sciences
matthias.zeppelzauer@fhstp.ac.at

Miroslav Despotovic
Kufstein University of Applied Sciences
miroslav.despotovic@fh-kufstein.ac.at

Muntaha Sakeena
St. Pölten University of Applied Sciences
muntaha.sakeena@fhstp.ac.at

David Koch
Kufstein University of Applied Sciences
david.koch@fh-kufstein.ac.at

Mario Döller
Kufstein University of Applied Sciences
mario.doeller@fh-kufstein.ac.at

ABSTRACT

We present a first method for the automated age estimation of buildings from unconstrained photographs. To this end, we propose a two-stage approach that firstly learns characteristic visual patterns for different building epochs at patch-level and then globally aggregates patch-level age estimates over the building. We compile evaluation datasets from different sources and perform an detailed evaluation of our approach, its sensitivity to parameters, and the capabilities of the employed deep networks to learn characteristic visual age-related patterns. Results show that our approach is able to estimate building age at a surprisingly high level that even outperforms human evaluators and thereby sets a new performance baseline. This work represents a first step towards the automated assessment of building parameters for automated price prediction.

CCS CONCEPTS

• **Information systems → Information retrieval;** • **Computing methodologies → Visual content-based indexing and retrieval**; *Supervised learning*; *Neural networks*;

KEYWORDS

Content-based image retrieval, visual pattern extraction, image classification, building analysis, building age estimation, deep learning.

ACM Reference Format:

Matthias Zeppelzauer, Miroslav Despotovic, Muntaha Sakeena, David Koch, and Mario Döller. 2018. Automatic Prediction of Building Age from Photographs. In *ICMR '18: 2018 International Conference on Multimedia Retrieval, June 11–14, 2018, Yokohama, Japan.* ACM, New York, NY, USA, 9 pages. https://doi.org/10.1145/3206025.3206060

1 INTRODUCTION

The vision behind this research is the automated valuation of real estate objects. The valuation of building prices is a difficult task

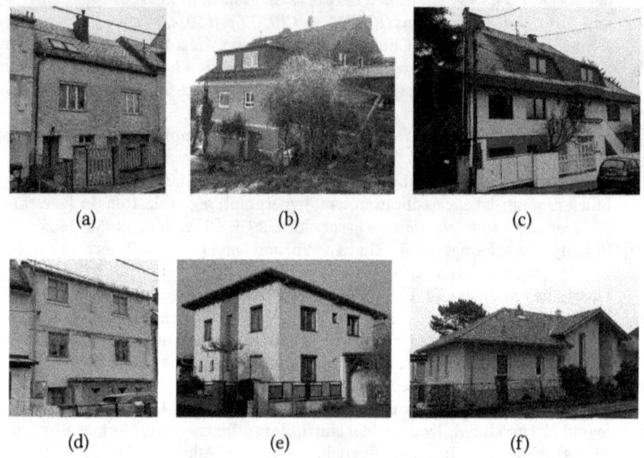

Figure 1: Buildings from different building epochs starting with 1960 until today. Which building does stem from which epoch? The answer is in the footnote[1].

that takes into account many aspects (e.g. location, infrastructure, building size and condition etc.) and till date is mostly performed manually by domain experts. The most common approach for manual real estate price estimation are hedonic price models, which are regression models that take building-specific parameters into account [16]. Research on hedonic price models has shown that building age has a strong influence on real estate and rent prices [2, 31]. Age information of buildings is, however, often not available.

The goal of this research is to improve real estate price estimation by automatically extracting the age of buildings and thereby mitigating the need for additional meta-data. We suggest that building age can be extracted by analyzing images showing the external view of houses. Figure 1 shows an example of six different buildings from different building epochs. For a human observer, it is relatively easy to distinguish a rather old building from a newer one. The assignment of a distinct building epoch for each building is, however, a complex task. We invite the reader to guess the approximate building epoch of each building in Figure 1. The answer is here[1].

Although the task is challenging, there are certain visual clues that provide indications about coarse age or building epoch such as the fiber cement plates frequently used in the 1960s in Figure

[1]Answer: (a) 1960s, (b) 1970s, (c) 1980s, (d) 1990s, (e) 2000s, (f) 2010s

ICMR '18, June 11-14, 2018, Yokohama, Japan

ACM ISBN 978-1-4503-5046-4/18/06...$15.00
https://doi.org/10.1145/3206025.3206060

1(a), the rounded dorner typical for the 1980s in Figure 1(c), and the typical monopitch roof of a low-energy building from the 2000s in Figure 1(e). The major research question behind this work is if we can automatically capture such characteristical patterns by automated image analysis and leverage them for the automatic prediction of building age.

We present an automated method for the estimation of building age. This task has to the best of our knowledge not been investigated before. The classification of buildings from unconstrained external views, as employed in this work, is a complex task since buildings can appear in different locations of the image, from different distances and perspectives as well as under different weather and lighting conditions. Additionally, foreground objects like cars and trees often cover significant areas of the facade. We break down the problem by first trying to learn characteristic visual primitives for each building epoch. Based on age estimations of these primitives we derive enhanced age assessments for an entire building.

Aside from our novel approach, the contribution of this paper is fourfold: *First*, we assemble several image datasets of buildings from different data sources which contain images from six different building epochs starting with 1960s until today. *Second*, we perform a comprehensive analysis of the capabilities of our method and in particular investigate its generalization ability to new data and the influence of dataset bias. *Third*, we establish a first *human baseline* for building age assessment and show that our approach clearly outperforms human evaluators. *Fourth*, we analyze the employed neural networks and show that building-related visual patterns are learned at several abstraction levels.

2 RELATED WORK

In recent years a lot of research has been performed on the analysis of buildings, especially from satellite imagery [3]. While this works well for the detection and segmentation of land covers [20] and building footprints [5], satellite images cannot provide more specific visual information like the architectural style and the current state of the building which is necessary to estimate its age. More suitable for the detection of age (and potentially other parameters in future) are photos of the external view of buildings which are provided for example by real estate companies, real estate search engines, street view services, and social media platforms. Such images are, however, in most cases user-generated and unconstrained which impedes automated analysis.

Related methods on the analysis of building images focus rather on the retrieval of building-related photographs than on the analysis of the buildings themselves. A popular application is to find images showing the same building from different perspectives and distances. Related approaches have been introduced in [13, 15, 22, 29]. In [29], the authors use an edge-based approach based on the Hough transform to parameterize buildings which is effective in detecting buildings with strong linear edges. In [22], the authors propose a building retrieval method based on the combination of color and line features. An approach for the retrieval of buildings by local oriented features (using steerable filters and maximum pooling) is proposed in [13]. A content-based image retrieval system based on consistent line clusters that further detect the approximate region of a building has been proposed in [15].

Li et al.[14] propose a method to predict the type of building (e.g. residential vs. non-residential building) from Google Street View images based on Histograms of Oriented Gradients (HOG), Scale Invariant Feature Transform (SIFT) and Fisher Vectors. A first approach to extract higher-level building parameters has been introduced in [6], where the authors try to visually derive the approximate heating energy demand of a building from building photographs. Other approaches try to segment the facade out of the image as a basis for a more detailed analysis [17]. The authors use a split and merge strategy to find the facade region. Based on vertical and horizontal line scans, patches with repetitive structures are extracted and merged to find the coarse facade region. Beyond this, methods for the analysis and mining of different architectural styles have been introduced. A first approach to classify old buildings into different styles (Gothic, Baroque, and Romanesque) has been introduced by [24]. The authors extract SIFT features and Bag of Visual Words (BoVW) histograms to predict different architectural styles. A more recent paper applies deformable parts models (DPMs) to classify building facades into 25 different architectural styles [28]. The authors extract HOG pyramids and train DPMs for each style. A similar approach is presented in [30] where the authors first decompose facade images into basic building blocks by object localization techniques and then model the spatial relationships between detected blocks (so called blocklets). Style recognition is then formulated as matching blocklets of different buildings. Note that compared to classical architectural styles the intra-class heterogeneity of the building epochs addressed in this work is larger because our classes do not represent individual styles but temporal epochs which may exhibit different styles. Furthermore, similar styles may appear in different epochs making the task even more challenging.

Finding typical patterns for a given class of objects (buildings) can also be considered as a pattern mining problem. Related work includes [4] where the authors represent buildings by recurring spatial configurations of neighboring local features. From these configurations they build graphs and perform graph mining to discover typical configurations. A similar approach is presented in [8]. The authors first detect local features and cluster them into visual words. Next they group frequently co-occurring visual words into pairs and mine those pairs that are most discriminatory for a given class. Based on this representation the authors mine representative image patches for different architectural styles. A problem of these approaches is that they do not scale well to large training sets of thousands of images and that their level of abstraction is limited.

An alternative approach has been introduced in [7] where the authors try to discover meaningful image patches for different cities. They search for patches in street view images which are discriminative and frequently occur for certain cities. Lee et al. [12] extend this method for the clustering of buildings into coarse age groups. For this purpose, they align a cadastre map with construction dates to street view images and generate a training data set. They apply pattern discovery similarly to [7] to extract characteristic patches for different building epochs.

A limitation of the works in [7] and [12] is that the patch matching is based on HOG descriptors. Initial experiments with our data has shown that HOG-based patch matching yields unintuitive similarity estimates and is computationally expensive. Inspired by [12],

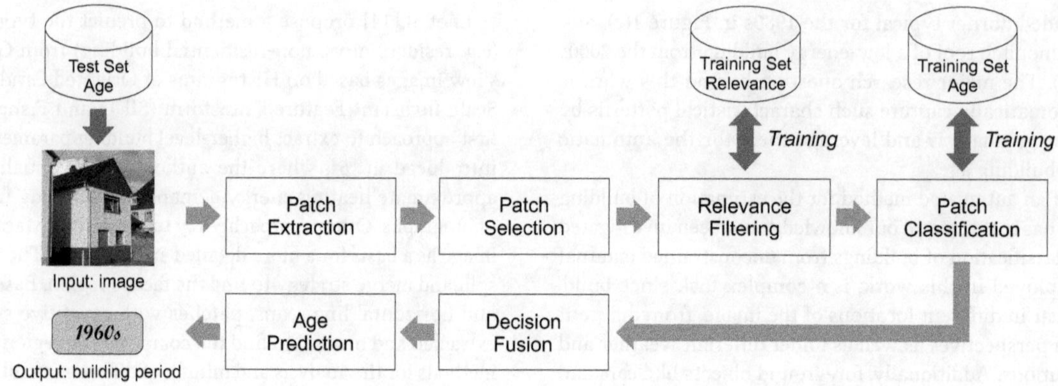

Figure 2: Overview of our approach for building age estimation.

our approach introduces a number of extensions: (i) patch selection is not random but steered by the underlying structure in the images, (ii) it circumvents the limitations introduced by pair-wise HOG matching by training a classifier directly from the patches and (iii) we employ a more powerful representation of the patches based on Convolutional Neural Networks (CNNs).

3 APPROACH

The basic assumption behind our approach is that certain visual building-specific elements provide useful indicators for different building epochs and the approximate construction year. We expect the entire input image of a building to be too unspecific to extract age-related patterns from buildings (or rather it would need a tremendous amount of input images and training time to learn important structures completely autonomously). To accelerate learning and to decrease the amount of necessary training data we base the analysis on image patches. Image patches contain less complex content and may better match individual characteristic building-specific elements. Two major questions in this context are: (i) where in the image patches should best be extracted and (ii) which patches are discriminative and characteristical for a given building epoch? To answer the first question we investigate different patch sampling strategies (see Sections 3.1 and 3.2). To account for the second question, we leverage Convolutional Neural Networks (CNNs) and learn patterns from the patches in a supervised manner. An overview of our method is depicted in Figure 2. The input is an unconstrained image of a building from which we extract patches and heuristically select the most representative ones. Additionally, we apply a specifically trained relevance filter to remove patches not related to buildings. From the remaining patches we train a classifier for different building epochs. Finally, decision fusion and age prediction infer the most likely building epoch for entire buildings.

3.1 Patch Extraction

In contrast to previous work on patch-based pattern mining [7, 12] we do not sample patches randomly from the input image because this may lead to a bad spatial coverage. First experiments trying to leverage SIFT feature detection to identify suitable patch locations led to strongly imbalanced sampling across the image and were thus discarded [18]. To obtain a better coverage and to save computation time, we apply sampling at regular intervals (as in dense SIFT) and extract overlapping patches of different scales at each sampling location, see Figure 3. This leads to a large number of candidate patches which cover the entire image at different scales. After extraction all patches are rescaled to the same size.

Figure 3: Patches of different scales extracted at a given location (left, yellow squares), resulting rescaled patches (right).

3.2 Patch Selection

Patch selection aims at removing patches which do not represent building-related information, for example sky in the background or occluding objects like cars in the foreground of the building. This reduction of data is necessary to speed up the training of the subsequent CNNs. Furthermore, it helps to direct the further analysis to building-related content, which facilitates CNN training and enables to use smaller training sets. We propose two heuristics for the extraction of meaningful building-related patches.

High-contrast patches: patches with low contrast are likely to represent unimportant information (e.g. homogeneous sky in the background or homogeneous areas of a smooth facade). To obtain a measure for the amount of contrast inside a patch we compute the norm of its (unnormalized) SIFT descriptor, i.e. the norm of the gradient histogram. The norm provides an estimate of the amount of gradient variation inside the patch in different directions. From all input patches we select only the $t\%$ patches with the maximum norm to obtain a smaller set of high-contrast patches, see Figure 4.

High-contrast patch clusters: The first strategy may be biased towards similar and frequently occurring structures (e.g. corners

Figure 4: The top 3% patches with highest contrast according to the norm of their SIFT descriptors. The patches cover well the area of the building (facade).

of windows) resulting in visually similar image patches. To obtain more visual heterogeneity we first cluster the extracted image patches. Therefore, each patch is represented by its (normalized) SIFT descriptor. K-Means is applied to obtain K clusters of patches for each input image. From each cluster we select the patch which is closest to its cluster center. These patches are more likely to represent visually different content. From the resulting K patches, we select the t% patches with highest contrast as in the first selection strategy. Figure 5 shows the difference between both strategies.

Figure 5: Different patch selection strategies: patches selected through clustering (red) represent more heterogeneous structures while high-contrast patches (yellow) exhibit higher redundancy (more repetative visual structures).

3.3 Relevance Filtering

A problem that remains after patch selection is that many patches represent information from the image which indeed have a lot of structure but are not related to the depicted building, e.g. parts of cars, trees, fences, etc. To better distinguish building-related from non-related patches, we train a classifier at patch-level that categorizes patches into different object types. We manually compile a training set of image patches from our training set (see Section 4.1) for 12 different object categories which often appear in outdoor photographs of buildings: cars, people, trees, grass, asphalt, poles, sunblind, furniture, fence, firewood, sign, a class containing miscellaneous patches of other type, and one positive class (building). The total training set for relevance filtering contains 8.000 patches. As a classifier we employ a pre-trained CNN (AlexNet trained on ImageNet [11]) and adapt its output layer to 13 classes. We chose a multi-class setup instead of a binary setup (building vs. non-building) to enable the network to better model the structure of the data and to learn a more powerful representation. We fine-tune all layers of the network. The trained net is then applied as filter to remove all patches from further processing that are not classified as building.

3.4 Patch Classification & Decision Fusion

Each patch that remains after relevance filtering is input to patch classification. To increase heterogeneity during training we apply data augmentation. Each patch is flipped, cropped, and scaled with a random probability. Additionally, brightness, contrast, and saturation are shifted randomly to account for illumination variations.

For patch classification we employ two different CNN architectures: Alexnet [11] with 8 layers and ResNet [9] with 50 layers. Alexnet is a widely used CNN consisting of five convolutional layers (with max pooling, local response normalization, and rectified linear units (ReLu) as activation function), three fully connected layers and a softmax layer on top. ResNet50 consists of larger stacks of convolutional layers with batch normalization [10]. ResNet employs direct connections that skip individual layers (skip connections). These connections accelerate training and enable the construction of deeper networks. Although the ResNet architecture has many more layers, it has less parameters than Alexnet and is thus faster to train. For both employed architectures we rescale the last layer to the number of building epochs that should be distinguished.

The patches are fed into the networks with all RGB color channels and are rescaled to the input size of the networks (224x224). The networks are applied either individually (for comparison) or in combination as an ensemble. In case of ensemble classification, we fuse the outputs of the networks by averaging their respective class likelihoods from the softmax layers. The result is again a probability distribution from which we retrieve the class with the maximum likelihood as the final prediction.

3.5 Age Prediction

All analyses and predictions so far have been made at patch-level. To get a prediction for an entire building, the patch-level predictions need to be aggregated into a global estimate. We investigate two different strategies:

- *Majority voting:* To get a robust estimate we take all patch-level predictions for an entire image and return the building epoch which is predicted most often.
- *Overall likelihood:* To get a more sensitive decision, we average the class likelihoods and return the building epoch with the highest overall likelihood for all patches.

A source of confusion may be patches with *ambiguous age predictions*, i.e. patches where the most likely class c_{max} is not remarkably more likely than the other classes. Such patches may represent age-invariant visual patterns that impede age prediction. We define a patch as ambiguous if the difference between the likelihood c_{max} and the likelihood for the second most likely class is below a threshold t_u. We remove such ambiguous patches during age prediction.

4 EXPERIMENTAL SETUP

4.1 Datasets

The employed data comes from two different sources: a database of real estate evaluation reports and from web platforms[2]. We restrict the analysis to those building epochs for which a sufficient number of houses could be retrieved (see below).

Building epochs. Epochs employed in real estate industry usually capture entire decades (e.g. 1960s, 1970s...) as defined by [21]. In contrast to the official counting where each epoch begins with the first odd year of the decade (e.g. 1961) we set the begin of each epoch to the beginning of the decade, i.e. 1960. This is due to the fact that for houses where only the decade but not the exact year of construction (YoC) is known, real estate agents and valuers often denote the YoC simply with the belonging decade. Thus, the official counting in such cases would lead to artificial class confusions.

We have compiled three datasets which all contain images of houses from all six building epochs. Due to the different availability of buildings for the different epochs, the datasets are not completely balanced, see Table 1.

dataset \ epoch	1960s	1970s	1980s	1990s	2000s	2010s	sum
training T_{tr}	649	1.075	1.378	1.424	1.315	579	6.450
validation T_v	84	153	205	207	201	80	930
test T_t	194	299	420	431	372	178	1.894
web images W_t	209	269	198	229	227	253	1.385
human baseline H_t	47	53	61	118	139	52	470

Table 1: Datasets used for our experiments with the number of images per building epoch.

Real estate valuation reports: From a real estate valuation company we obtained a dataset of 17.241 valuation reports of single family houses generated by real estate experts. We first remove all reports that do not contain a photo of the building. The remaining reports contain at least one or more pictures, postal code, YoC, and the so called fictitious year of construction (FYoC). The FYoC is a number determined by the real estate valuers and is computed as $FYoC = YoC + N$, where N represents the number of years the total lifespan of a building has been extended by renovations and modernizations. Modernizations (e.g. of the facade) often change the appearance of a building significantly, making its real age difficult to discover visually. Since our method operates purely on visual information, we exclude such renovated houses from this dataset to avoid a bias during training. The final dataset contains 9.250 RGB images of the single family houses. For the training of our classifiers we split the dataset into three subsets: training T_{tr} with 6.450 images (≈70%), validation T_v with 930 images (≈10%) and test T_t with 1.894 images (≈20%). Since the original dataset may contain several images for each house, we have taken special caution that no house appears in more than one partition.

Web images: In order to evaluate the influence of the dataset bias [25] to our approach, we have compiled a separate dataset by crawling images together with meta-data from real estate offers on respective websites. Only offers where an exact YoC was available were crawled. Redundant offers (from the same or several platforms) were removed. Overall, a set of 1.385 images has been compiled, which we refer to as W_t. This dataset serves as an additional independent test set. Note that in this dataset we cannot guarantee that YoC equals $FYoC$. Thus, renovated buildings with a changed (and thus unauthentic) visual appearance may be included. This strongly increases the complexity of the dataset.

Human Baseline Data: To get a better feeling for the complexity of the task of building age estimation, we establish a human baseline for building age prediction. To this end, we assemble a third dataset which is again disjoint to all other sets. The dataset stems from additional (previously not used) real estate reports and comprises of images from 470 distinct houses from all six epochs and is referred to as H_t in the following. To establish a fair and objective comparison with our approach we take our pre-trained method and apply it directly on this dataset.

4.2 Method Setup & Training

The proposed method has a number of parameters that are defined as follows. For patch extraction, we employ square patches of side length 16, 24, 32, and 40 pixels (see Figure 3) and sample them for each scale continuously over the image with 50% horizontal and vertical overlap. SIFT descriptors are extracted with standard parameters [26]. For the first patch selection strategy (high-contrast patches) we employ $t = 0.5\%$, $t = 1\%$, and $t = 1.5\%$ of high-contrast patches to evaluate the sensitivity of parameter t. For the second selection strategy (high-contrast patch clusters) we employ $K = 50$ clusters for each image and percentages of 7%, 14% and 21% for t.

For *relevance filtering* we employ Alexnet [11] pre-trained on ImageNet adapted to 13 selected object classes (see Section 3.3). We train the network for 20 epochs with a learning rate of 0.0001, decay of 0.0005, momentum of 0.9 and a batch size of 256.

For *patch classification* we employ extensive data augmentation (see Section 3.4) during training for both employed networks Alexnet and ResNet (both pre-trained on ImageNet). For both nets the output is reduced to 6 neurons representing the six building epochs. Common training parameters for both nets are 20 epochs with a learning rate of 0.0001, decay of 0.0005, momentum of 0.9 and a batch size of 256. All nets were trained with cross-entropy loss and stochastic gradient descent [1].

For the detection of ambiguous patches, we set parameter $t_u = 0.25$ (empirically estimated on validation set). All experiments were performed in MATLAB on a workstation with Ubuntu 14 OS, 64 GB RAM and an NVIDIA T1080. The MatConvNet framework was used for training the networks [27].

4.3 Evaluation & Research Questions

The primary goal of the evaluation is to investigate how well the age of a building can be estimated from a photo. To assess the performance we train our method on training set T_{tr} and employ the validation set T_v to monitor training progress and overfitting behavior. Finally, we evaluate the method with the independent test set T_t. We employ the classification accuracy as well as top-1 error (=1-accuracy) as performance measures for all experiments at patch-level as well as on image-level. Accuracy represents the portion of correctly classified images in the entire test set. Note

[2]The images used in this work are not under creative commons license and thus cannot be shared, we will, however, publicly share extracted features and trained networks under https://phaidra.fhstp.ac.at/detail_object/o:2960.

that, classification accuracy is a reasonable choice since the dataset is mostly balanced.

Beyond pure classification performance, we aim at answering the following research questions (RQ):

- **RQ1**: How large is the generalization ability and is there a notable dataset bias, i.e., do results generalize to data from different sources?
- **RQ2**: How well does the method perform compared to human evaluators?
- **RQ3**: Can we automatically discover characteristic age-related visual primitives from unconstrained building photographs

To account for **RQ1** we evaluate the approach on the independent partition T_t (test set) and on the data from the second platform W_t to investigate dataset bias (see Section 5.3). **RQ2** is investigated by letting expert users guess building epochs on the human baseline H_t, see Section 5.4. To answer **RQ3**, we visually inspect those patches from the test set T_t which obtain the highest likelihoods for a building epoch. Additionally, we investigate neural network activations and visualize the learned filters (see Section 5.5).

5 RESULTS

5.1 Parameter Sensitivity

In a preliminary evaluation, we assess the sensitivity of our method to its parameters. Especially the parameters for patch selection and extraction are essential, as they strongly influence the selection of training patches for the subsequently trained networks and thereby the overall performance. Table 2 summarizes the results of the experiments and shows that larger percentages, i.e. larger numbers of patches lead to slightly better (lower) top-1 error for the validation set. Furthermore, the selection strategy with patch clustering provides better results than just selecting the highest contrast patches globally. This is most likely due to the better visual heterogeneity obtained by clustering. Finally, relevance filtering "RF" improves results consistently by a small margin.

Experiments presented in Table 2 were obtained after 10 epochs of fine-tuning ResNet. We take the best result obtained so far (last row in Table 2 and continue the training for additional 30 epochs to see if performance further improves. Retraining mainly reduces the training error (down to 14%). The validation error decreases only slightly and starts to oscilate around 58%. This shows that the network starts to overfit on the training data after 10 epochs.

From Table 2 we observe that the validation errors are relatively high compared to the training errors (around 60%, corresponding to a classification accuracy of 40%). Note that both measures are computed at patch-level and are thus not directly representative for the overall task of predicting the age of an entire building.

5.2 Age Prediction

Age prediction aggregates the individual patch-wise age estimates over an entire building. Results for our approach from Section 3.5 with majority voting as aggregation function for the validation set T_v are shown in Figure 6. Similarly to the results in Table 2 more patches (higher percentages) lead to better performance and relevance filtering (solid lines) in most cases improves performance. The clustering-based patch selection clearly outperforms the purely

Patch selection	Perc.	RF.	#patches	err_{trn}	err_{val}
Hi-C.	0.5%	N	86.596	0.49	0.65
Hi-C.	1%	N	181.676	0.38	0.61
Hi-C.	1.5%	N	267.552	0.31	0.62
Hi-C. Cluster	7%	N	102.328	0.53	0.63
Hi-C. Cluster	14%	N	179.208	0.48	0.61
Hi-C. Cluster	21%	N	274.585	0.43	0.60
Hi-C.	0.5%	Y	34.842	0.52	0.61
Hi-C.	1%	Y	73.779	0.44	0.60
Hi-C.	1.5%	Y	109.714	0.39	0.60
Hi-C. Cluster	7%	Y	48.735	0.54	0.63
Hi-C. Cluster	14%	Y	86.208	0.50	0.59
Hi-C. Cluster	21%	Y	137.808	0.44	0.58

Table 2: Training results for different patch selection strategies (high-contrast patches, "Hi-C." and high-contrast patch clusters "Hi-C. Cluster" with K=50), different percentages "Perc.", as well as with and without relevance filtering "RF". ResNet with 10 epochs is used as network model. We provide the number of resulting patches, the top-1 error err_{trn} for the training set T_{tr} and the top-1 error err_{val} for the validation set T_v.

contrast-based selection (orange line with square markers). The obtained accuracy on the validation set of 52% clearly outperforms the random baseline of approx. 18% (according to zero rule) as well as the patch-level accuracy of approx. 40% from Section 5.1. These results show that fusion of the patch-wise predictions for the entire image strongly contributes to the classification performance.

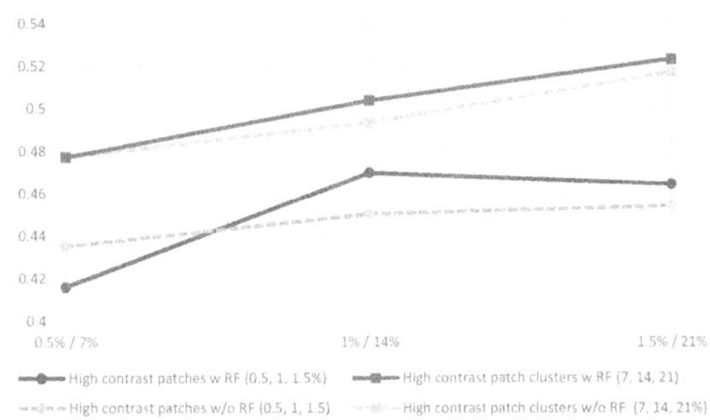

Figure 6: Classification accuracy on the validation set at building-level for the different configurations of Table 2.

We further evaluate the two different aggregation functions as well as the filtering of ambiguous patches from Section 3.5. Majority voting slightly outperforms averaging the likelihoods by a small margin of 1-2% accuracy which indicates that this strategy is more robust. The removal of ambiguous patches improves results slightly (around 1%) but not consistently in all experiments. Peak performance is, however, obtained by filtering ambiguous patches.

In a next step, we compare different network architectures and the effect of their combination in an ensemble. Additionally to the ResNet architecture, we train Alexnet with the same inputs. The peak performance of Alexnet on the validation set is an accuracy of 47.5%. Alexnet does not reach the performance level of ResNet

(51.5%). When both nets are combined in an ensemble, however, the overall performance on the validation set increases to 54.0%. This represents the best result obtained during training. Thus, this configuration is used in all further experiments on the test sets.

5.3 Generalization Ability and Dataset Bias

After having evaluated the different components of our approach we evaluate it on the independent test set T_t to estimate its generalization ability. We achieve an overall accuracy for building age prediction of 61.35%. This clearly outperforms the best result obtained for the validation set (54%, see Section 5.2). This proves a good generalization ability of our approach. A confusion matrix for the experiment is shown in Figure 7(a). The highest values are obtained along the diagonal (correct predictions). Most confusions occur between neighboring classes, which is due to the fuzziness at the epoch boundaries (decades).

Additionally, we test our approach on the second test set W_t, which comes from another data source (web images, see Section 4.1) to estimate the influence of dataset bias and obtain an accuracy of 34.94%. This performance is notable smaller and shows that there is an influence from the data source [25]. We assume the main reason for the drop in performance is that the test set W_t contains also renovated and modernized buildings (see Section 4.1). Renovations change the visual appearance of a building and usually make it look newer. This is reflected by the confusion matrix in Figure 7(b), which is skewed towards age predictions which underestimate the age (confusions in the upper triangular part of the matrix). This is particularly noticeable for older buildings (1960s-1990s).

true \ prediction	1960s	1970s	1980s	1990s	2000s	2010s
1960s	**89**	33	35	14	23	0
1970s	23	**158**	84	16	15	3
1980s	11	45	**264**	72	24	4
1990s	2	11	55	**286**	74	3
2000s	2	10	12	61	**274**	13
2010s	5	2	6	11	63	**91**

(a) Test set T_t

true \ prediction	1960s	1970s	1980s	1990s	2000s	2010s
1960s	**55**	56	42	14	42	0
1970s	33	**86**	90	25	32	3
1980s	16	40	**82**	22	32	6
1990s	13	18	79	**49**	68	2
2000s	17	8	21	38	**137**	6
2010s	8	14	13	6	137	**75**

(b) Test set W_t

Figure 7: Confusion matrix for age prediction on the two employed test sets: (a) the approach generalizes well to test set T_t with an overall accuracy of 61.35%; (b) the additional complexity of dataset W_t (inclusion of renovated buildings) represents an notable challenge and results in frequent underestimations of building age.

5.4 Human Baseline Comparison

To better understand the complexity of the task of visual building age estimation we set up an experiment utilizing LabelMe [23] to generate a human baseline, see also Section 4.1. The experiment has been performed within the scope of a case study at the Real Estate Industry Department of the University of Applied Sciences in Kufstein, Austria during winter term 2017 with a group of seven bachelor students from the Facility & Real Estate Management curriculum. The dataset H_t was split into seven partitions. Each partition was assigned to one evaluator who assessed the building epoch for each house by looking at the respective photo and selecting an epoch from a list.

For a fair and objective comparison, the same data was then provided to our pre-trained method. The human evaluators achieved an overall accuracy of 36% (170 correct assignments from 470). This result shows that building age assessment is far from being trivial and poses a considerable challenge to humans. Our approach achieves an accuracy of 55.1% on the same data (without any adaption or retraining) and thus strongly outperforms human performance. This demonstrates strong capabilities of our approach for automated age estimation. It further confirms a good generalization ability on H_t which is an independent test set similarly to T_t.

5.5 Network Analysis

To get a deeper understanding on the inner workings of the trained networks and to verify the learning process, we perform a series of qualitative analyses. In a first step, we investigate the capabilities of the network to learn discriminative patches for certain building epochs (**RQ3** from Section 4.3). To this end, we extract the top 100 patches from our test set T_t that were assigned to the correct class with highest probability, i.e. those patches the network is most confident about. Figure 8(a) shows example patches from three selected building epochs (1960s, 1980s, and 2000s) which achieve high likelihoods for their respective class (≥ 0.99). We observe, that a majority of the extracted patches represent typical building characteristics which confirms that the network is able to learn meaningful visual primitives. The experiment further shows that the most characteristic patches capture a rather large scale and thus larger parts of the buildings. This indicates that a larger spatial context facilitates capturing discriminative patterns.

Figure 8(b) shows those patches the network is most uncertain about. From visual inspection we conclude that there are two major reasons for the uncertainty. First, the network seems to be unable to clearly decide for a class when there is a lack of structure as e.g. in the case of the patch which contains mostly the roof in the bottom-left corner of Figure 8(b) and second when the scale is to small and the spatial context is insufficient. Larger scales seem to facilitate finding typical age-related patterns. Finally, Figure 8(c) shows patches which unintendedly pass the relevance filtering. A common pattern observed for such false positives patches is a strong contrast across the patch and a rich structure in the image (e.g. the patch in the bottom left corner of Figure 8(c).

We further investigate to which degree the learned filters in our networks reflect patterns that can be assigned to particular elements of buildings. To this end, we input patches to the network, perform a forward pass and extract the activations for all convolutional layers. For visualization we scale them up to the input image size. Results of selected filters for an example patch are shown in Figure 9. We observe that building-related patterns are captured already in the second convolutional layer. In higher layers more specific structures are represented such as the spike of the roof and the gable (the triangular part of the wall underneath the roof) in the 4th convolutional layer, see Figure 9, first two images in last row.

To verify which structures are actually learned by the individual filters, we apply the DeepDream approach [19] to the individual

(a) most likely (b) most unsure (c) noise patches

Figure 8: Test patches from our experiment: (a) patches classified correctly by our network (ResNet) with highest likelihood for the correct class; (b) patches with lowest confidence for a certain class; (c) non-building patches that pass the relevance filtering.

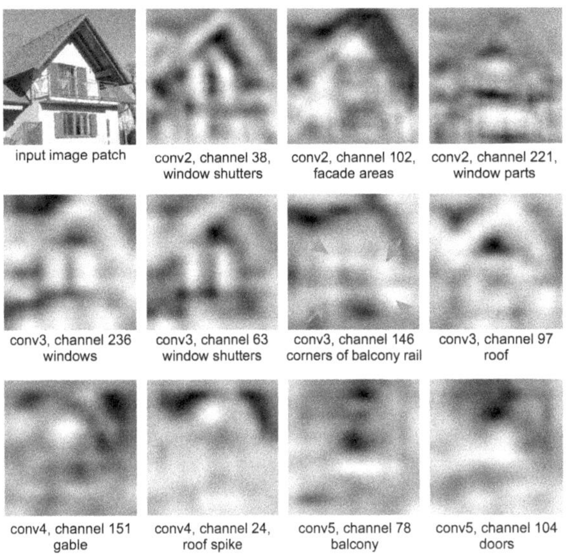

Figure 9: Activations for an input patch of different convolutional layers of our trained network (2nd to 5th convolutional layer) capturing different architectural elements of buildings.

convolutional filters. We apply DeepDream with three pyramid levels with a spacing of 1.05 and run the back propagation for 20 iterations. Results for representative filters learned are shown in Figure 10 (best viewed in color). We frequently observe triangular roof-like structures, as in the top-left image in Figure 10. Other filters represent textures, such as areas covered by roof tiles (top-right image in Figure 10). In higher-layer filters, we observe larger structures, such as windows (bottom-left image) but even house-like structures (see white circle in bottom-left image in Figure 10).

6 CONCLUSION

Real estate image analysis (REIA) is a research field that attracts increasing attention. In this context, we have presented a first method for the estimation of building age from unconstrained photographs.

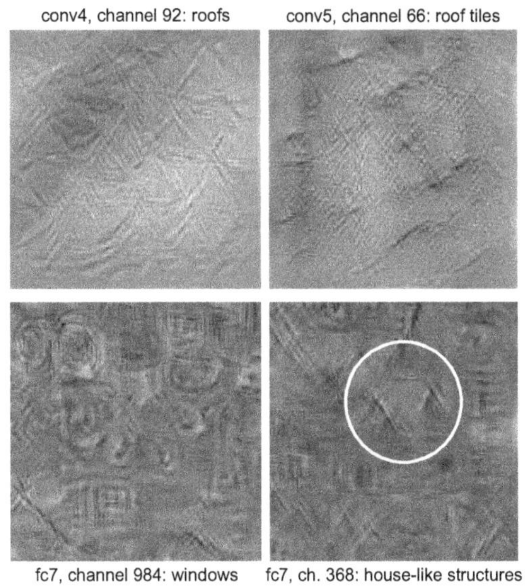

Figure 10: Filters reconstructed with DeepDream capturing building-related patterns, such as windows, roofs and typical building contours (best viewed in color).

We mine promising image patches from building images at different scales and learn representations for different building epochs using CNNs. Our results show that different epochs can be discriminated with a probability of approx. 61% which is far beyond random probability (18% according to zero rule). Our approach is able to capture meaningful building characteristics for different building epochs. Furthermore, we clearly beat the human baseline and set a first automatic analysis baseline for this task. A major insight from the in-depth analysis of the trained networks is that the discovered structures represent more abstract patterns than those reported by e.g. object recognition networks [19]. The reason for this is that the classes employed in this work (building epochs) have a much higher intra-class variation than typical object classes (e.g. cats, cars, and dogs). The presented task is thus more difficult because it requires not only to learn a particular type of object (e.g. house) but also its typical characteristics that differentiate it from other objects of the *same* class (e.g. house from the 1960s vs. house from the 1970s). To further improve results we will investigate deeper network architectures to obtain more powerful hierarchies, the effect of a more fine-grained ground truth for training (i.e. annotations of individual building elements instead of coarse image-level categories), and building segmentation techniques to better filter out non-building patches. Furthermore, we will investigate age prediction for renovated houses in detail to see whether the date of renovation can be predicted visually and to which degree indications for the original YoC can be inferred for such buildings.

7 ACKNOWLEDGMENTS

We thank Sprengnetter Austria GmbH for providing real estate images and meta-data for our experiments. This work was supported by the Austrian Research Promotion Agency (FFG), Project No. 855784 and Project No. 856333.

REFERENCES

[1] Léon Bottou. 2010. Large-scale machine learning with stochastic gradient descent. In *Proceedings of COMPSTAT'2010*. Springer, 177–186.

[2] Wolfgang A Brunauer, Stefan Lang, Peter Wechselberger, and Sven Bienert. 2010. Additive hedonic regression models with spatial scaling factors: An application for rents in Vienna. *The Journal of Real Estate Finance and Economics* 41, 4 (2010), 390–411.

[3] Gong Cheng and Junwei Han. 2016. A Survey on Object Detection in Optical Remote Sensing Images. *ISPRS Journal of Photogrammetry and Remote Sensing* 117 (2016), 11–28.

[4] Wei-Ta Chu and Ming-Hung Tsai. 2012. Visual pattern discovery for architecture image classification and product image search. In *Proceedings of the 2nd ACM International Conference on Multimedia Retrieval*. ACM, 27.

[5] Joseph Paul Cohen, Wei Ding, Caitlin Kuhlman, Aijun Chen, and Liping Di. 2016. Rapid building detection using machine learning. *Applied Intelligence* 45, 2 (2016), 443–457.

[6] M. Despotovic, M. Sakeena, D. Koch, M Döller, and M. Zeppelzauer. 2017. Predicting Heating Energy Demand by Computer Vision. *Journal on Computer Science - Research and Development* 33, 1 (2017), 231–232.

[7] C. Doersch, S. Singh, A. Gupta, J. Sivic, A. Efros, and W. Makes. 2012. What Makes Paris Look like Paris? *ACM Transactions on Graphics* 31, 4 (2012), 1–9.

[8] Abhinav Goel, Mayank Juneja, and CV Jawahar. 2012. Are buildings only instances?: exploration in architectural style categories. In *Proceedings of the Eighth Indian Conference on Computer Vision, Graphics and Image Processing*. ACM, 1.

[9] Kaiming He, Xiangyu Zhang, Shaoqing Ren, and Jian Sun. 2016. Deep Residual Learning for Image Recognition. In *The IEEE Conference on Computer Vision and Pattern Recognition (CVPR)*.

[10] Sergey Ioffe and Christian Szegedy. 2015. Batch normalization: Accelerating deep network training by reducing internal covariate shift. In *International Conference on Machine Learning*. 448–456.

[11] Alex Krizhevsky, Ilya Sutskever, and Geoffrey E Hinton. 2012. Imagenet classification with deep convolutional neural networks. In *Advances in neural information processing systems*. 1097–1105.

[12] S. Lee, N. Maisonneuve, D. Crandall, A. A. Efros, and J. Sivic. 2015. Linking Past to Present: Discovering Style in Two Centuries of Architecture. *IEEE International Conference on Computational Photography (ICCP)* (2015).

[13] J. Li, N. Allinson, and Senior member IEEE. 2013. BUILDING RECOGNITION USING LOCAL ORIENTED FEATURES. *IEEE Transactions of industrial informatics* 9 (2013).

[14] Xiaojiang Li, Chuanrong Zhang, and Weidong Li. 2017. Building block level urban land-use information retrieval based on Google Street View images. *GIScience and Remote Sensing* 54, 6 (2017).

[15] Y. L. Y. Li and L. G. Shapiro. 2002. Consistent line clusters for building recognition in CBIR. *IEEE International Conference on Pattern Recognition* 6 (2002), 0–4.

[16] Wen-Chi Liao and Xizhu Wang. 2012. Hedonic house prices and spatial quantile regression. *Journal of Housing Economics* 21, 1 (2012), 16–27.

[17] Fei Liu and Stefan Seipel. 2014. Detection of Façade Regions in Street View Images from Split-and-Merge of Perspective Patches. *Journal of Image and Graphics* 2, 1 (2014).

[18] David G Lowe. 1999. Object recognition from local scale-invariant features. In *Computer vision, 1999. The proceedings of the seventh IEEE international conference on*, Vol. 2. Ieee, 1150–1157.

[19] Christopher Mordvintsev, Alexanderand Olah and Mike Tyka. 2015. Inceptionism: Going Deeper into Neural Networks, Google Research. (2015). https://research.googleblog.com/2015/06/inceptionism-going-deeper-into-neural.html

[20] V. Muhr, M. Despotovic, D. Koch, M. Döller, and M. Zeppelzauer. 2017. Towards Automated Real Estate Assessment from Satellite Images with CNNs. In *Proceedings of the 10th Forum Media Technology (FMT)*, Vol. 2009. CEUR Workshop Proceedings, 14–23.

[21] Andreas Oberhuber and Daniel Denk. 2014. Zahlen, Daten, Fakten zu Wohnungspolitik und Wohnungswirtschaft in Österreich. (2014).

[22] Y.-I. Pyo, J. W. Lee, and R.-H. Park. 2009. Building image retrieval using color and line features. *9th International Symposium on Communications and Information Technology* 9 (2009), 1381—1386.

[23] Bryan C Russell, Antonio Torralba, Kevin P Murphy, and William T Freeman. 2008. LabelMe: a database and web-based tool for image annotation. *International journal of computer vision* 77, 1-3 (2008), 157–173.

[24] G. Shalunts, Y. Haxhimusa, and R. Sablatnig. 2011. Architectural style classification of building facade windows. *Advances in Visual Computing* 6939 (2011), 280—-289.

[25] Antonio Torralba and Alexei A Efros. 2011. Unbiased look at dataset bias. In *Computer Vision and Pattern Recognition (CVPR), 2011 IEEE Conference on*. IEEE, 1521–1528.

[26] A. Vedaldi and B. Fulkerson. 2008. VLFeat: An Open and Portable Library of Computer Vision Algorithms. http://www.vlfeat.org/. (2008).

[27] Andrea Vedaldi and Karel Lenc. 2015. Matconvnet: Convolutional neural networks for matlab. In *Proceedings of the 23rd ACM international conference on Multimedia*. ACM, 689–692.

[28] Z. Xu, D. Tao, Y. Zhang, J. Wu, and A. C. Tsoi. 2014. Architectural style classification using multinomial latent logistic regression. *European Conference on Computer Vision* 8689 (2014), 600–615.

[29] X. Yuan and C.-T. Li. 2008. CBIR APPROACH TO BUILDING IMAGE RETRIEVAL BASED ON INVARIANT CHARACTERISTICS IN HOUGH DOMAIN. *Proc. Int. Conf. Acoust. Speach Signal Process.* 2, 2 (2008), 1209–1212.

[30] L. Zhang, M. Song, X. Liu, L. Sun, C. Chen, and J. Bu. 2002. Recognizing architecture styles by hierarchical sparse coding of blocklets. *Information Sciences: an International Journal* 254 (2002), 141–154.

[31] Joachim Zietz, Emily Norman Zietz, and G Stacy Sirmans. 2008. Determinants of house prices: a quantile regression approach. *The Journal of Real Estate Finance and Economics* 37, 4 (2008), 317–333.

The PMEmo Dataset for Music Emotion Recognition

Kejun Zhang
State Key Lab of CAD&CG, Zhejiang University
38, Zheda Road
Hangzhou, China 310027
zhangkejun@zju.edu.cn

Hui Zhang
State Key Lab of CAD&CG, Zhejiang University
38, Zheda Road
Hangzhou, China 310027
huiz@zju.edu.cn

Simeng Li
State Key Lab of CAD&CG, Zhejiang University
38, Zheda Road
Hangzhou, China 310027
li.simeng@zju.edu.cn

Changyuan Yang
International User Experience Business Unit, Alibaba Group
Hangzhou, China 310000
changyuan.yangcy@alibaba-inc.com

Lingyun Sun
State Key Lab of CAD&CG, Zhejiang University
Hangzhou, China 310027
sunly@zju.edu.cn

ABSTRACT

Music Emotion Recognition (MER) has recently received considerable attention. To support the MER research which requires large music content libraries, we present the PMEmo[1] dataset containing emotion annotations of 794 songs as well as the simultaneous electrodermal activity (EDA) signals. A Music Emotion Experiment was well-designed for collecting the affective-annotated music corpus of high quality, which recruited 457 subjects.

The dataset is publically available to the research community, which is foremost intended for benchmarking in music emotion retrieval and recognition. To straightforwardly evaluate the methodologies for music affective analysis, it also involves pre-computed audio feature sets. In addition to that, manually selected chorus excerpts (compressed in MP3) of songs are provided to facilitate the development of chorus-related research.

In this article, We describe in detail the resource acquisition, subject selection, experiment design and annotation collection procedures, as well as the dataset content and data reliability analysis. We also illustrate its usage in some simple music emotion recognition tasks which testified the PMEmo dataset's competence for the MER work. Compared to other homogeneous datasets, PMEmo is novel in the organization and management of the recruited annotators, and it is also characterized by its large amount of music with simultaneous physiological signals.

CCS CONCEPTS

• **Applied computing → Sound and music computing**;

KEYWORDS

Dataset; Music Emotion Recognition; Experiment; EDA

ACM Reference format:
Kejun Zhang, Hui Zhang, Simeng Li, Changyuan Yang, and Lingyun Sun. 2018. The PMEmo Dataset for Music Emotion Recognition. In *Proceedings of 2018 International Conference on Multimedia Retrieval, Yokohama, Japan, June 11–14, 2018 (ICMR'18)*, 8 pages.
https://doi.org/10.1145/3206025.3206037

1 INTRODUCTION

Emotion plays an important role in music, which means considerable requirements for organizing music by emotional association. Music emotion recognition (MER) is concerned with automatically extracting affective information from music and predicting the perceived emotion of it. MER has became a hot topic in music information retrieval (MIR) and received increased attention in wide-range fields, e.g., Computer Science, Psychology, Human-Computer Interaction.

Most researchers working on MER adopt methods in supervised machine learning to implement music emotion prediction [23], which usually need a large number of songs with emotion labels provided by listeners to train the models. However, it is obviously time-consuming and also labour-consuming to acquire sufficient emotion feedback especially in controlled experimental setting. As a result, there is a scarcity of music datasets containing emotion annotations though a number of widely used datasets do exist for music information research.

To support the development of MER, we present a new dataset and refer it as PMEmo. The dataset contains 794 music clips annotated by 457 subjects, which is created to develop and evaluate MER models. Specially, to eliminate the effects of cultural and educational background [8], we invite subjects from various countries and majors.

Moreover, it is worth concerning that all the music clips in PMEmo are chorus parts of their full songs, manually selected by students majoring in music. This makes the dataset a useful corpus for research on chorus-section detection. Meanwhile, the electrodermal activity (EDA) of subjects when listening to these music are also recorded, making it possible to analyse emotion states in multiple modes.

[1] PMEmo means popular music with emotional annotations

ICMR'18, June 11–14, 2018, Yokohama, Japan

ACM ISBN 978-1-4503-5046-4/18/06...$15.00
https://doi.org/10.1145/3206025.3206037

Table 1: Some Existing Music Datasets with Emotion Annotations

Name	Stimulus	Data	with Audio
Emotify[2]	400 excerpts	induced emotion	yes
MoodSwings[3]	240 excerpts (30s)	arousal and valence	no
Amg1608[4]	1608 excerpts (30s)	valence and arousal	no
emoMusic[5]	744 excerpts (45s)	arousal and valence	yes
DEAM[6]	1802 excerpts	valence and arousal	yes
SoundTracks[7]	360 +110 excerpts	valence, energy, tension and mood	yes
GMD[8]	1400 songs	genre, valence and arousal	downloadable
DEAPDataset[9]	120 music video excerpts	valence, arousal, dominance and physiological data	no
PMEmo	794 music chorus	valence, arousal and physiological data	yes

To briefly summarize, the PMEmo dataset provides:

- song metadata (song title, artists, beginning and ending timestamps of chorus section),
- manually selected music chorus clips (MP3),
- pre-computed audio features for use in MER tasks,
- manually annotated emotion labels: static labels for the whole clips (i.e., overall labels), and dynamic labels for each 0.5-second segment (i.e., continuous labels over time),
- Corresponding EDA physiological signals.

In what follows, we first review related datasets for music emotion recognition (Section 2). Subsequently, we describe the details of the dataset in Section 3, including the song selection, experiment design, the dataset's structure and content, basic data statistics and annotation reliability. In Section 4, we further implement baseline MER method to assess the quality of the dataset empirically and then discuss the results and findings. Finally, we conclude the paper and present some possible extensions (Section 5).

2 RELATED WORK

Since the early years of the MER, there have been numerous efforts to build datasets with emotional annotations facilitating the development and evaluation of music emotion recognition. Table 1 shows some well-known work on that.

Furthermore, the relationship between music and emotion has been studied by psychologists for a long period, who often divide emotion into three categories: expressed emotion, perceived emotion, and felt (or evoked) emotion [22]. As shown in Table 1, a large proportion of datasets in MER focuses on the second one: perceived emotion (i.e., emotions that are perceived by listeners). There are various approaches used to describe perceived emotion and report listeners' responses, most of which belong to one of the following methods: the categorical method and the dimensional method.

For categorical method, emotions are considered as categories that are distinct from each other. Emotify [1], which consists of 400 song excerpts (1 minute long) in 4 genres (rock, classical, pop, electronic), applied the GEMS scale (Geneva Emotional Music Scales) [24] for collecting annotations and accepted the concept of nine basic factors for music-induced emotions (i.e., wonder, transcendence, tenderness, nostalgia, peacefulness, power, joyful activation, tension and sadness).

Although the categorical method is an understandable approach to emotion conceptualization, there exits a major drawback on it. The key to a categorical model is its basic emotion classes, the number of which is usually too small compared to the richness of emotion perceived by humans [22]. Considering this, dimensional models of emotion have gained support among MER researchers.

The two-dimensional, valence-arousal model (VA model) proposed by Russell [12] is one of the most popular dimensional emotion approaches, which is adopted by the major of datasets mentioned in Table 1. The MoodSwings dataset [18] contains per-second VA ratings for 240 clips of US pop songs and the AMG1608 dataset [4] comprises the VA annotations for 1,608 Western music of different genres. Yi-Hsuan et al. developed the emoMusic dataset [17] in 2013, which consists entirely of CC (Creative Commons) music from the Free Music Archive (744 songs). Then in 2016, he aggregated these data into the DEAM dataset [2], which was provided as a baseline dataset in the "Emotion in Music" task at MediaEval Multimedia Evaluation Campaign. Considering the demand for large amount of human labour, these datasets have turned to crowdsourcing through Amazon Mechanical Turk with their own verification steps to remove unreliable data.

Different from the datasets mentioned before, SoundTracks [5] and GMD [11] did not utilize Western music as emotion stimuli. the SoundTracks dataset selected film soundtracks (approx. 15 second) as stimulus sets while the GMD datasets collected 1400 Greek tracks to induce emotion.

In addition to the subjective label annotated by listeners, recent advances in emotion recognition (e.g., Chen [3] and Gao [7]'s recent work of emotion recognition from electroencephalogram (EEG) signals) have motivated the creation of novel datasets containing emotional expressions in different modalities, including physiological responses which could represent the felt emotion of listeners. the DEAPDataset [10] recorded the emotion rating and corresponding EEG signals from 32 volunteers, among whom 22

[2]http://www.projects.science.uu.nl/memotion/emotifydata/
[3]http://music.ece.drexel.edu/research/emotion/moodswingsturk
[4]https://amg1608.blogspot.ca/
[5]http://cvml.unige.ch/databases/emoMusic/
[6]http://cvml.unige.ch/databases/DEAM/
[7]https://www.jyu.fi/hytk/fi/laitokset/mutku/en/research/projects2/past-projects/coe/materials/emotion/soundtracks/Index
[8]https://hilab.di.ionio.gr/en/music-information-research/
[9]http://www.eecs.qmul.ac.uk/mmv/datasets/deap/readme.html

participants' frontal face videos were also recorded. The PMEmo dataset provides VA annotations for 794 music choruses, each of which was labelled by at least 10 people, and all the EDA records of 457 subjects are also included.

3 THE PMEMO DATASET

The whole PMEmo dataset of approximately 1.3 GB can be downloaded from www.happiness.zju.edu.cn. Considering copyright restrictions, full songs are not included in this dataset but the chorus excerpts are available in PMEmo. To make the data accessible and compatible for a wide range of platforms, the metadata of songs, the acoustic features and the annotations are all stored in CSV files (delimited by comma).

In this section, we outline the song acquisition and chorus selection procedure, describe the information of subjects who participant in this work, introduce the experiment designed to collect annotation, list in detail the dataset's components and analyze basic statistical properties of the dataset, which could be used to evaluate annotation reliability.

3.1 Song Acquisition and Chorus Selection

Our target music is pop song, therefore, we search some well-known music charts for gathering songs popular all around the world: the Billboard Hot 100[10], the iTunes Top 100 Songs (USA)[11] and the UK Top 40 Singles Chart[12]. In order to fetch sufficient music resources, we downloaded the songs available on these three charts from 2016 to 2017 and collected 1000 songs all together. However, we later discovered a set of duplicates (though they do have slightly different song titles or artists from the original ones). After filtering out the reduplicative music, we obtain a full song set of 794 pop songs. Table 2 illustrates some basic statistical data of the music sources.

Table 2: The Sources of Music

Charts	Start Time	End Time	Songs
Billboard Hot 100	19th week, 2016	23rd week, 2017	487
iTunes Top 100	15th week, 2016	21st week, 2017	616
UK Top 40 Singles	37th week, 2016	21st week, 2017	226

To reduce the heavy cognitive load and improve the stability of emotion annotation, almost every dataset in MER utilize music segments as emotion-inducing materials and the PMEmo does this as well. Specifically, each clip in this dataset is manually selected as one of the chorus parts of each song, which is implemented by university students in music major. But what distinguishes the PMEmo from most of the other MER datasets is that the clips are of various length which are exact the duration of the chorus parts. This enables the PMEmo dataset useful in chorus detection research.

3.2 Subject Selection

A total of 457 subjects (236 females and 221 males) are recruited to participant in this work. Among them, 366 are Chinese university students who are in non-music major while 44 are majoring in music recruited to ensure high quality labelling. Meanwhile, to weaken the impact of cultural background (almost all the songs are in English), 47 English speakers are invited to annotate the datasets. Each song receives a total of at least 10 emotion annotations including one by music-majoring student and one by English speaker. Since the limitation of EDA signal acquisition device, we are unable to utilize crowdsourcing method, which means subjects can not annotate the dataset directly via the Internet. Considering this, we design an experiment to acquire the data we want and describe that in the following.

3.3 Experiment Design and Annotation Collection

We use MP150 Biopac system (Biopac Systems, Inc., Goleta, CA) to monitor the the electrodermal activity continuously at a sampling rate of 50 Hz and export the signals from AcqKnowledge software. A desktop application was developed for annotating the songs (shown in Figure 1). The annotation was done with the sliding area collecting dynamic annotations, on a scale from 1 to 9, at a sampling rate of 2 Hz and annotators should make a static annotation for the whole music excerpt on nine-point scale after finishing dynamic labelling. Furthermore, the annotators were asked to listen to the same music twice to annotate on valence and arousal separately.

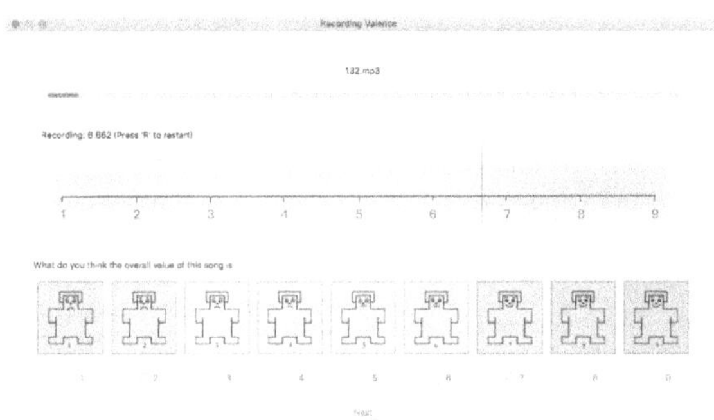

Figure 1: The Annotation Interface

Firgure 2 is a flow diagram of this experiment, for which each subject spent 50 minutes on average. At the very beginning, subjects were shown a document used to inform consent of the experiment, by which it was ensured that all the participants were aware of the purpose, potential risk and other necessary information about the experiment. After signing that paper, we displayed a video to the subjects and introduce the procedure and details in the annotation task to them. We also had a training session conducted to ensure their precise understanding of this task, during which process 4 clips representing extreme emotion (extremely large and small value in valence and arousal respectively) were played and subjects were enabled to get familiar with operating the annotation interface. Only after completely trained can subjects start the formal experiment.

It is a known issue that multiple cognitive processes will interact on each other, in other words, subjects need some buffer time to relax and remove the interference from the previous stimulus. Therefore, we set a relaxing procedure before starting annotating

[10] https://y.qq.com/n/yqq/toplist/108.html
[11] https://y.qq.com/n/yqq/toplist/123.html
[12] https://y.qq.com/n/yqq/toplist/107.html

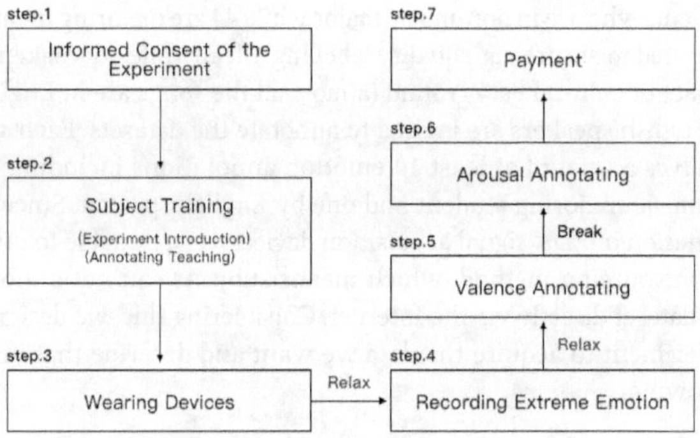

Figure 2: Experimental Procedures

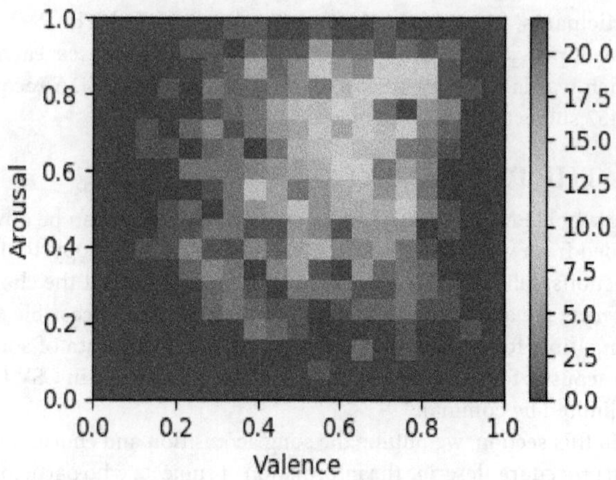

Figure 3: The Distribution of Static Annotations

and a short break (10 seconds) between each song-listening. At the relaxing procedure, subjects were required to calm down with the help of *In My Life*, a song by Kevin Kern, whose light music were proved to be in favour of relieving people's emotion [9]. EDA finger transducer (BSL-SS3LA) were equipped to subjects' fingers of the non-dominant hand before this step so that we can check the subjects' response with assistance of the skin conductance recorded by the device. Particularly, subjects' EDA responses to 4 clips with extreme emotion were also stored in order to study individual difference in the subsequent research work.

After finishing all these preparation procedures, subjects were asked to conduct annotation work. Specifically, each subject listened to 20 excerpts and one of those was duplicated to guarantee the high quality data as what was done in [4] (the annotations from this subject were accepted only if the bias between duplicated clips were within 0.25 in the Valence-Arousal space), but we did not inform the subject of the existence of identical songs. Completing the experiment, subjects were paid 50 yuan per person.

In total, 457 subjects have participated in this experiment and we finally received 401 person-time valid annotations (87.7 percent). Each music clip was annotated by at least 10 annotators including English speakers and semi-experts from music academy. As we can see from Figure 3 that a large proportion of music chorus clips have overall annotations falling in the first quadrant. Moreover, Figure 4 enumerates several emotion changing curves of various music excerpts (5 randomly chosen clips from the PMEmo dataset), which illustrates the significant difference of emotion between songs and comparatively stable tendency for the same song.

3.4 Data Reliability

Initial orientation time (IOT) is a known concept in MER that annotators need some preliminary time before they can give meaningful and reliable annotations. Schubert [14] found that the median IOT for valence was 8 seconds and for arousal that was 12 seconds. Yi-Hsuan's work in 2013 [16] showed that the annotations began converging around the 10th second and after that, he obtained a similar result in 2017 [2]. Taking into account the previous work, we discard the first 15-second dynamic annotations from the data.

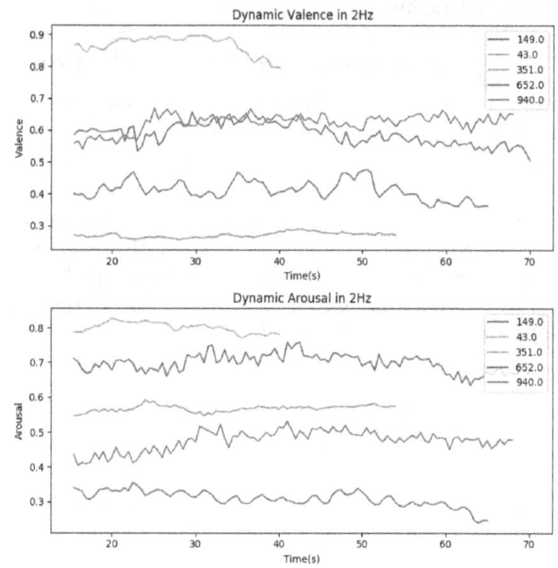

Figure 4: Emotion curves of song NO. 43, 149, 351, 652 and 940 (the first 15-second labels are removed).

We use the Cronbach's α [13] to evaluate annotation consistency. Cronbach's α is often used in psychometric test to estimate the reliability that represents the degree to which a set of items measures a single unidimensional latent construct. In this article, we compute the Cronbach's α on the sequences of annotations for each song.

Annotations are sampled in 2Hz and as what is usually done to normalize the continuous annotations [2], we process the annotations by

$$a_{j,i} = a_{j,i} + (\overline{A_j} - \overline{A}) \tag{1}$$

where $a_{j,i}$ is the label annotated by subject j at time i, and $\overline{A}$ is the mean of all the labels for this song by all subjects while $\overline{A_j}$ is the mean of dynamic labels by subject j.

Table 3 shows the mean (averaged across songs) and the standard deviation of Cronbach's α for the annotations in the PMEmo dataset. The quite high results for both valence and arousal indirectly indicate excellent internal consistency of the collected annotations.

Table 3: Cronbach's α

Dimension	The Mean Value	The Standard Deviation
Valence	0.998	0.005
Arousal	0.998	0.008

4 MUSIC EMOTION RECOGNITION EXPERIMENTS USING PMEMO

It is necessary to have a large-scale dataset for music emotion recognition, which has become an important task recently. While the PMEmo dataset is not restricted to this task, we illustrate its use for implementing and evaluating a music emotion recognition system that aims to predict the static and dynamic emotion of a song automately. In the following, we firstly introduce the features and methodologies used in the assessment. Then we present the setting and performance in each experiment.

4.1 MER Feature Set

Feature extraction is a critical step for MER model, which could affect the recognition performance to a large extent. However, for generic MER there has been no attempt made at defining a "standard" feature set. This is probably resulted from the rather young and multi-faceted characteristic of music emotion computing field. What is fortunate to researchers in MER is that the INTERSPEECH 2013 Computational Paralinguistics Evaluation (ComParE) Campaign [15] has proposed a well-evolved feature set for detecting paralinguistic phenomena automately. In this set, the key factors are frame-wise acoustic low-level descriptors (LLDs, briefly shown in Table 4) including MFCCs, energy, etc. These descriptors are very relevant for both Music Information Retrieval and other general sound analysis. The ComParE 2013 has also applied quite a number of statistical functions, such as mean and moments, to LLD contours and the calculated results constitute a large set of suprasegmental features. All of these obtained features form the ComParE 2013 baseline feature set with a 6373-dimension scale, which has been exhaustively listed at Weninger's work [20] and proved to work effectively for the task of music mood regression.

In particular, PMEmo dataset provides all the 6373-dimension features in song level for the sake of static emotion task. In comparison to the considerable size for overall mood recognition, we only extract the core 260-dimension features in segment level (the average and the standard deviation of the 65 LLDs as well as their first-order derivatives, calculated in 1s window with 0.5s overlap) for dynamic recognition task to properly reduce the computing load. Extraction of these features is done with the open-source toolkit openSMILE [6]. Furthermore, no feature selection procedure is implemented in order to fully demonstrate PMEmo's capability to MER task.

Table 4: A Simple Profile for Low-Level Descriptors Provided in ComParE Acoustic Feature Set

Category	Dimension	Content
Energy related	4	Auditory weighted frequency bands and their sum
Spectral	55	Centroid, roll-of point, skewness, sharpness, and spectral flux
Voicing related	6	fundamental frequency and harmonics-to-noise ratio

4.2 MER Methodology

In this article, we adopt two well-accepted methods, Multivariate Linear Regression (MLR) and Support Vector Regression (SVR), as the base classifiers to model emotions in valence and arousal.

For the whole song, we train and test the classifiers using the 6373-dimension features $x_1, x_2, ..., x_{6373}$ and separate static labels of valence and arousal $y_{valence}, y_{arousal}$ respectively.

$$\{X_1, X_2, ..., X_m\} \overset{static\ model}{\longrightarrow} \{e_1, e_2, ..., e_m\} \tag{2}$$

where m is the number of songs, $X_i = \{x_1, x_2, ..., x_6 373\}$ is the feature set of the ith song and e_i is the value of valence or arousal for this song.

With respect to continuous mood of a song, it is natural to consider the multi-scale structure in music. Xianyu et al. proposed a double-scale SVR [21], which decoupled dynamic emotion into two scales and then recognized them separately. We are inspired by the outstanding idea and organize the dynamic MER model in a similar way: building a global classifier with 6373 song-level global features to fit the mean value of dynamic emotion, meanwhile utilizing the 260 segment-level local features to reveal the fluctuation over time.

$$\begin{aligned} &\{X_1, X_2, ..., X_m\} \overset{global\ model}{\longrightarrow} \{\overline{L_1}, \overline{L_2}, ..., \overline{L_m}\} \\ &\{Y_1^{t_1}, Y_2^{t_2}, ..., Y_m^{t_3}\} \overset{local\ model}{\longrightarrow} \{D_1^{t_1}, D_2^{t_2}, ..., D_m^{t_m}\} \\ &\text{Dynamic emotion}: L_i = \overline{L_i} + D_i^{t_i} \end{aligned} \tag{3}$$

where m is the number of songs and for the ith song, X_i is the global feature set of it while $Y_i^{t_i}$ is a matrix of 260 columns and t_i rows (t_i is the number of timestamps in the ith song), which represents the local features of this song. $\overline{L_i}$ is the mean of dynamic emotion and $D_i^{t_i}$ is the fluctuation at each timestamp.

Before building the regression models, we resized all the annotations (both of static annotations and dynamic ones) into $[0, 1]$ for a more intuitive understanding of the performance in the following experiments.

4.3 Performance of Static MER

Static task is to predict the overall emotion of a whole song, which is represented by single valence value and arousal value. To train and test the static MER regression models, the data in PMEmo was divided into 11 folds. 10 folds of that constituted the training set while the remaining one was used to test the trained models. A

10-fold cross-validation procedure was carried out on the training set for parameter optimization. In this article, Root Mean Square Error (*RMSE*) and Pearson Correlation Coefficient (r) were calculated individually for valence and arousal as the evaluation metrics. Table 5 presents 2 running results on static emotion.

- Run 1: Based on MLR, trained on the 10 training folds;
- Run 2: Based on SVR with Radial Basis kernel function, $C = 1.0$, trained on the 10 training folds.

Table 5: Evaluation Results on Static Emotion

Dimension	Run	*RMSE*	r
Valence	Run 1	0.136	0.546
	Run 2	0.124	0.638
Arousal	Run 1	0.111	0.719
	Run 2	0.102	0.764

In this evaluation procedure, Run 1 (MLR) and Run 2 (SVR) had similar results, both of which achieved good performance and revealed the bright prospect of the PMEmo dataset in the field of static MER.

4.4 Performance of Dynamic MER

As mentioned before, a hierarchical regression model aiming to recognize the global trend as well as local variation was built. It is worth notice that the lengths of music clips are not fixed in the PMEmo dataset, and resulted from that, for global scale and local scale we did the following operation respectively:

- **Global-scale operation** For each song, extracting only one global feature and mapping it into one global emotion value.
- **Local-scale operation** For each song, dividing it into 1-second segments with 50% overlap (leading to 2 Hz fluctuation frequency), then extracting the local features from these fragments and project them onto mood space.

The strategy of splitting pre-existing data into training and testing set here is the same as the previous experiment. However, there is slight distinction existing in the evaluation calculation due to the difference of predicted music units. In global scale, *RMSE* and r were calculated in the whole testing set (in song unit). While in local scale, these metrics were computed for each song and then averaged across songs. Table 6 reports the evaluation metrics for dynamic MER.

The *RMSE* results of dynamic MER also performed well. Furthermore, it can be seen from Table 6 that the major error arose in global scale (much larger than the local-scale error), presenting consistency with the result of [21]. However, the r results was not desirable in local scale, which obviously limited the dynamic emotion recognition performance. This may result from the difficulty of instantaneous perception. In other words, annotators could not perceive and report emotion changes well in very short time, affecting the description of emotion fluctuation in real time. Altogether, these two experiments indicated the advantage of PMEmo in terms of establishing MER system.

Table 6: Evaluation Results on Dynamic Emotion

Dimension	Run	Scale	*RMSE*	r
Valence	Run 1	global	0.103	0.673
		local	0.016	0.047
		fusion	0.089	0.047
	Run 2	global	0.106	0.675
		local	0.016	0.095
		fusion	0.088	0.095
Arousal	Run 1	global	0.113	0.816
		local	0.020	0.103
		fusion	0.093	0.103
	Run 2	global	0.101	0.844
		local	0.019	0.115
		fusion	0.085	0.115

4.5 Predict Music Emotion using EDA

Considering the requirements of multi-modal information research on MER, the PMEmo dataset has recorded the electrodermal activity of subjects simultaneously when listening to music. In this part, we demonstrate one of the potential approaches to taking advantage of these EDA signals and detecting corresponding music mood. Specifically, we only performed dynamic MER arbitrarily as both dynamic annotations and EDA vary over time.

Firstly, a low-pass filter of 0.6 Hz was employed to diminish the noise from motion and artifacts [19]. Then the filtered skin electric conductance data was scaled in z-scores (z-score $= \frac{X-\mu}{\sigma}$, where μ is the mean of vector X and σ is the standard variation of it) due to the great individual distinctions, by which we could obtain the variation of EDA as the music emotion varying. Because of the different acquisition rates of EDA and continuous emotion (50 Hz and 2 Hz, respectively), we resampled the EDA signals into 2 Hz. Finally, we trained and tested MLR and SVR models with pre-processed EDA data as well as the dynamic affective value.

Table 7: Evaluation Results using EDA Data

Dimension	Run	Scale	*RMSE*	r
Valence	Run 1	global	0.139	0.063
		local	0.016	0.060
		fusion	0.118	0.059
	Run 2	global	0.141	0.017
		local	0.016	0.059
		fusion	0.119	0.048
Arousal	Run 1	global	0.186	0.011
		local	0.019	0.097
		fusion	0.157	0.106
	Run 2	global	0.194	0.040
		local	0.019	0.099
		fusion	0.160	0.110

Table 7 shows the prediction performance using EDA data, which represented the feasibility of indicating music emotion from listeners' physiological data. The comparatively low value of *RMSE* revealed the correlation between perceived emotion and evoked emotion. The PMEmo dataset enables researchers to study MER in other respects besides acoustic feature space.

5 CONCLUSION AND FUTURE WORK

We have created a brand new dataset, PMEmo, that enables music retrieval and emotion recognition research in multiple modalities. It has been released to public and are available for free download. The PMEmo dataset contains information on the level of songs, manually selected chorus excerpts and their features in common MER use. In addition to the standard valence-arousal annotations appearing in other homogeneous datasets as well, PMEmo is characterized by its large amount of music with simultaneous physiological signals, and it is also novel in the components of annotators recruited. We set several procedures to ensure the quality of labelling and all the annotations as well as physiological data were acquired under the strictly controlled laboratory conditions.

Despite the good performance of the PMEmo dataset at music retrieval and emotion recognition tasks in multiple modalities, we would like to consider further extensions in the future. In particular, we are thinking about enriching the cultural background of songs since it does affect the perception of valence to large extent. Beyond that, we intend to add text-based features that allow analysis of lyrics, which is also an important composition of music content but ignored in our current work. Next to the music descriptors, abundant categories of physiological information are required to distinguish listeners' emotion state more accurately. Finally, other popular emotion dimensions such as dominance may be included to increase the comprehensive ability of the dataset in various applications.

To support these further research work in the future, we have developed a crowdsourcing platform customized for annotating multimedia content, especially for music emotion labelling. Researchers are allowed to use multimedia resources on this platform and release their experiments easily. It is a practical network application which can help experimenters quickly gather and assess multimedia affective data. We will publish this platform soon and believe it can actually bring convenience to Affective Computing research community.

ACKNOWLEDGMENTS

This project is supported by the National Key Research and Development Program of China (2016YFC0200700), National Natural Science Foundation of China (No. 61672451 and No. 61402141), National Basic Research Program of China (973 Program, No. 2015CB352503), and Alibaba-Zhejiang University Joint Institute of Frontier Technologies. It would not have been possible without the help of numerous students, in particular, Lumin Huang, Mengqi Jin, Ke Duan, Yingping Cao, Jun Zheng, Xiaoyi Huang, and Kaili Zhu from Happy Lab, Zhejiang University. Finally, we would like to thank Prof. Li for providing an experimental research facility, which ensured the smooth progress of the experiment.

REFERENCES

[1] Anna Aljanaki, Frans Wiering, and Remco C Veltkamp. 2016. Studying emotion induced by music through a crowdsourcing game. *Information Processing & Management* 52, 1 (2016), 115–128.

[2] Anna Aljanaki, Yi-Hsuan Yang, and Mohammad Soleymani. 2017. Developing a benchmark for emotional analysis of music. *PloS one* 12, 3 (2017), e0173392.

[3] Tanfang Chen, Shangfei Wang, Zhen Gao, and Chongliang Wu. 2016. Emotion Recognition from EEG Signals Enhanced by User's Profile. In *Proceedings of the 2016 ACM on International Conference on Multimedia Retrieval.* ACM, 277–280.

[4] Yu-An Chen, Yi-Hsuan Yang, Ju-Chiang Wang, and Homer Chen. 2015. The AMG1608 dataset for music emotion recognition. In *Acoustics, Speech and Signal Processing (ICASSP), 2015 IEEE International Conference on.* IEEE, 693–697.

[5] Tuomas Eerola and Jonna K Vuoskoski. 2011. A comparison of the discrete and dimensional models of emotion in music. *Psychology of Music* 39, 1 (2011), 18–49.

[6] Florian Eyben, Felix Weninger, Florian Gross, and Björn Schuller. 2013. Recent developments in opensmile, the munich open-source multimedia feature extractor. In *Proceedings of the 21st ACM international conference on Multimedia.* ACM, 835–838.

[7] Zhen Gao and Shangfei Wang. 2015. Emotion recognition from eeg signals using hierarchical bayesian network with privileged information. In *Proceedings of the 5th ACM on International Conference on Multimedia Retrieval.* ACM, 579–582.

[8] Xiao Hu and Yi-Hsuan Yang. 2017. Cross-dataset and cross-cultural music mood prediction: A case on Western and Chinese Pop songs. *IEEE Transactions on Affective Computing* 8, 2 (2017), 228–240.

[9] Chia-Hui Ko, Yi-Yu Chen, Kuan-Ta Wu, Shu-Chi Wang, Jeng-Fu Yang, Yu-Yin Lin, Chia-I Lin, Hsiang-Ju Kuo, Chia-Yen Dai, and Meng-Hsuan Hsieh. 2017. Effect of music on level of anxiety in patients undergoing colonoscopy without sedation. *Journal of the Chinese Medical Association* 80, 3 (2017), 154–160.

[10] Sander Koelstra, C Muhl, M Soleymani, JS Lee, A Yazdani, T Ebrahimi, T Pun, A Nijholt, and I Patras. [n. d.]. DEAP dataset (2012). *URL http://www. eecs. qmul. ac. uk/mmv/datasets/deap/index. html. BibliographyA* 6 ([n. d.]).

[11] Dimos Makris, Ioannis Karydis, and Spyros Sioutas. 2015. The greek music dataset. In *Proceedings of the 16th International Conference on Engineering Applications of Neural Networks (INNS).* ACM, 22.

[12] Jonathan Posner, James A Russell, and Bradley S Peterson. 2005. The circumplex model of affect: An integrative approach to affective neuroscience, cognitive development, and psychopathology. *Development and psychopathology* 17, 3 (2005), 715–734.

[13] J Reynaldo A Santos. 1999. Cronbach's alpha: A tool for assessing the reliability of scales. *Journal of extension* 37, 2 (1999), 1–5.

[14] Emery Schubert. 2013. Reliability issues regarding the beginning, middle and end of continuous emotion ratings to music. *Psychology of music* 41, 3 (2013), 350–371.

[15] Björn Schuller, Stefan Steidl, Anton Batliner, Alessandro Vinciarelli, Klaus Scherer, Fabien Ringeval, Mohamed Chetouani, Felix Weninger, Florian Eyben, Erik Marchi, et al. 2013. The INTERSPEECH 2013 computational paralinguistics challenge: social signals, conflict, emotion, autism. In *Proceedings INTERSPEECH 2013, 14th Annual Conference of the International Speech Communication Association, Lyon, France.*

[16] Mohammad Soleymani, Anna Aljanaki, Yi-Hsuan Yang, Michael N Caro, Florian Eyben, Konstantin Markov, Björn W Schuller, Remco Veltkamp, Felix Weninger, and Frans Wiering. 2014. Emotional analysis of music: A comparison of methods. In *Proceedings of the 22nd ACM international conference on Multimedia.* ACM, 1161–1164.

[17] Mohammad Soleymani, Micheal N Caro, Erik M Schmidt, Cheng-Ya Sha, and Yi-Hsuan Yang. 2013. 1000 songs for emotional analysis of music. In *Proceedings of the 2nd ACM international workshop on Crowdsourcing for multimedia.* ACM, 1–6.

[18] Jacquelin A Speck, Erik M Schmidt, Brandon G Morton, and Youngmoo E Kim. 2011. A Comparative Study of Collaborative vs. Traditional Musical Mood Annotation.. In *ISMIR.* 549–554.

[19] Iris Van Den Bosch, Valorie N Salimpoor, and Robert J Zatorre. 2013. Familiarity mediates the relationship between emotional arousal and pleasure during music listening. *Frontiers in human neuroscience* 7 (2013).

[20] Felix Weninger, Florian Eyben, Björn W Schuller, Marcello Mortillaro, and Klaus R Scherer. 2013. On the acoustics of emotion in audio: what speech, music, and sound have in common. *Frontiers in psychology* 4 (2013).

[21] Haishu Xianyu, Xinxing Li, Wenxiao Chen, Fanhang Meng, Jiashen Tian, Mingxing Xu, and Lianhong Cai. 2016. SVR based double-scale regression for dynamic emotion prediction in music. In *Acoustics, Speech and Signal Processing (ICASSP), 2016 IEEE International Conference on.* IEEE, 549–553.

[22] Yi-Hsuan Yang and Homer H. Chen. 2011. *Music Emotion Recognition* (1st ed.). CRC Press, Inc., Boca Raton, FL, USA.

[23] Yi-Hsuan Yang and Homer H Chen. 2012. Machine recognition of music emotion: A review. *ACM Transactions on Intelligent Systems and Technology (TIST)* 3, 3 (2012), 40.

[24] Marcel Zentner, Didier Grandjean, and Klaus R Scherer. 2008. Emotions evoked by the sound of music: characterization, classification, and measurement. *Emotion* 8, 4 (2008), 494.

Interpretable Partitioned Embedding for Customized Multi-item Fashion Outfit Composition

Zunlei Feng
Zhejiang University
Hangzhou, Zhejiang
zunleifeng@zju.edu.cn

Zhenyun Yu
Zhejiang University
Hangzhou, Zhejiang
zhenyunyu@zju.edu.cn

Yezhou Yang
Arizona State University
Phoenix, Arizona
yz.yang@asu.edu.cn

Yongcheng Jing
Zhejiang University
Hangzhou, Zhejiang
ycjing@zju.edu.cn

Junxiao Jiang
Alibaba Group
Hangzhou, Zhejiang
junxiao.jjx@alibaba-inc.com

Mingli Song*
Zhejiang University
Hangzhou, Zhejiang
brooksong@zju.edu.cn

ABSTRACT

Intelligent fashion outfit composition becomes more and more popular in these years. Some deep learning based approaches reveal competitive composition recently. However, the uninterpretable characteristic makes such deep learning based approach cannot meet the designers, businesses and consumers' urge to comprehend the importance of different attributes in an outfit composition. To realize interpretable and customized multi-item fashion outfit compositions, we propose a partitioned embedding network to learn interpretable embeddings from clothing items. The network consists of two vital components: attribute partition module and partition adversarial module. In the attribute partition module, multiple attribute labels are adopted to ensure that different parts of the overall embedding correspond to different attributes. In the partition adversarial module, adversarial operations are adopted to achieve the independence of different parts. With the interpretable and partitioned embedding, we then construct an outfit composition graph and an attribute matching map. Extensive experiments demonstrate that 1) the partitioned embedding have unmingled parts which corresponding to different attributes and 2) outfits recommended by our model are more desirable in comparison with the existing methods.

CCS CONCEPTS

• **Computing methodologies** → *Image representations*; *Neural networks*; *Learning latent representations*;

*Corresponding author.

ICMR '18, June 11–14, 2018, Yokohama, Japan

ACM ISBN 978-1-4503-5046-4/18/06...$15.00
https://doi.org/10.1145/3206025.3206048

KEYWORDS

Outfit composition, interpretable, adversarial, embedding

ACM Reference Format:
Zunlei Feng, Zhenyun Yu, Yezhou Yang, Yongcheng Jing, Junxiao Jiang, and Mingli Song. 2018. Interpretable Partitioned Embedding for Customized Multi-item Fashion Outfit Composition. In *ICMR '18: 2018 International Conference on Multimedia Retrieval, June 11–14, 2018, Yokohama, Japan.* ACM, New York, NY, USA, 9 pages. https://doi.org/10.1145/3206025.3206048

1 INTRODUCTION

"Costly thy habit as thy purse can buy, But not expressed in fancy; rich, not gaudy, For the apparel oft proclaims the man."

William Shakespeare

Fashion style tells a lot about one's personality. With the fashion industries going online, clothing fashions are becoming a much more popular topic among the general public. There have been a number of research studies on clothes retrieval and recommendation [8, 9, 12, 19, 37, 40], clothing category classification [4, 20, 30, 38], attribute prediction [1, 2, 5, 15, 39] and clothing fashion analysis [10, 19, 22]. However, due to the fact that the fashion concept is often subtle and subjective, the composition of fashion outfit keeps being an open problem to reach consensus for the general public.

Until now, there are few works [18] studying multi-item fashion outfit composition. Most existing works [4, 13, 14, 23, 25, 29, 33] are proposed to recommend tops (bottoms) to given bottoms (tops). Some early works [4, 13, 14] adopt hand-crafted features to represent items. Those hand-crafted attribute features are usually mixed with other attribute features. Other deep network based works [23, 25, 29, 33] adopt the mixed embedding to represent item of outfit, which is uninterpretable. Very recently, Li *et al.* [18] present a deep neural network based multi-modal method by adopting mixed multi-modal embedding to represent an outfit item as a whole. However, the obtained embedding is uninterpretable and does not bring attribute information. Unfortunately, in many practical applications, it is necessary to understand the importance of different attributes in an outfit composition for designers, businesses and consumers. That is to

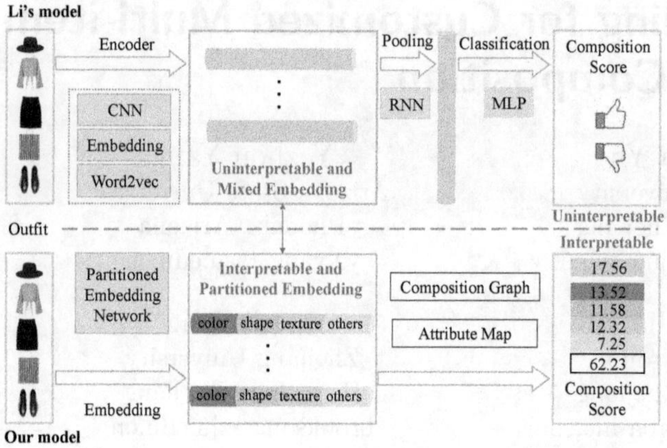

Figure 1: Comparative framework between our model and Li's [18] model. Features used by Li's method are usually mixed and uninterpretable, which lead to uninterpretable outfit composition. Different parts of embedding extracted by our model correspond to different attributes. With the partitioned embedding, our model can recommend outfit composition with interpretable matching scores.

say, an interpretable and partitioned embedding is vital for a practical fashion outfit composition system.

To address the aforementioned problems, we propose a partitioned embedding network in this paper. The network consists of two vital components: attribute partition module and partition adversarial module. In the attribute partition module, multiple attribute labels are adopted to ensure that different parts of the overall embedding correspond to different attributes. In the partition adversarial module, adversarial operations are adopted to achieve independence of different parts. Meanwhile, some indefinable attributes (such as style and occasion) can be extracted by the partition adversarial module. Then, considering that matching items may appear multiple times in different outfits, we propose a fashion composition graph to model matching relationships in outfit with the extracted partitioned embeddings. Meanwhile, an attribute matching map which learns the importance of different attributes in the composition is also built. Comparative framework between our model and the multimodal embeddings based method [18] is shown in Figure 1.

To summarize, our work has three primary contributions: 1) We present a partitioned embedding network, which can extract interpretable partitioned embeddings from fashion outfit items. 2) We put forward a weakly-supervised multi-item fashion outfit composition model, which depends solely on a large number of outfits without quality scores of outfits as others. Besides, our model can be extended to a dataset with annotated quality scores. 3) An iterative and customized fashion outfit composition scheme is given. Since fashion trends alter directions quickly and dramatically, our model can keep up with the fashion trends by easily incorporating new fashion outfit dataset.

2 RELATED WORK

Clothing embedding. In recent years, there are several models [22, 30, 34] can be used to get embeddings of clothes. Vittayakorn *et al.* [34] extract five basic feature (color, texture, shape, parse and style) of outfit appearance and concatenated them to form a vector for representing outfit. They use the vector to learning the outfit similarity and analyze visual trends in fashion. Matzen *et al.* [22] adopt deep learning method to train several attribute classifiers and used high-level features of the trained classifiers to create a visual embedding of clothing style. Then, using the embedding, millions of Instagram photos of people sampled worldwide are analyze to study spatio-temporal trends in clothing around the globe. Simo-Serra *et al.* [30] train a classifier network with ranking as the constraint to extract discriminative feature representation and also used high level feature of the classifier network as embeddings of fashion style. Kingma *et al.* [16] introduce a novel estimator of the variational lower bound for approximate inference with continuous latent variables. The continuous latent embedding usually contains mixed and uninterpretable features of original images.

Disentangled embedding. In the supervised setting, supervised methods [17, 26, 35] take the advantage of labeled data and try to disentangle the factors as expected. However, those methods require massive accurate labeled data and the learned disentangle units miss some complicated attribute feature of clothing. In the unsupervised setting, methods [6, 11, 27, 36] can learn interpretable embeddings but fail to anchor a specific meaning into the disentanglement. In the semi-supervised setting, Bouchacourt *et al.* [3] propose the ML-VAE that can learn disentangled representations from a set of grouped observations. Due to complicated of clothing's attribute feature, it hard to build grouped observations. Siddharth *et al.* [28] learn disentangled representations with an auxiliary variable, which also can't contain all complicated attribute feature of clothing. Most closely with our method, Veit *et al.* [32] propose Conditional Similarity Networks (C-SN) that learn embeddings differentiated into semantically distinct subspaces that capture the different attributes of similarities. However, Veit's method will need larger number of triplet data when dealing with more attributes.

Fashion outfit composition. As described above, due to the difficulty in modeling outfit composition, there are several works [4, 13, 14, 18, 23, 25, 29, 33] studying fashion outfit composition. Iwata *et al.* [13] present an approach by concatenating hand-crafted features into a vector as an embedding for each clothing item. Liu *et al.* [4] developed an occasion oriented clothing recommendation and pairing system, which explores the matching rules of upper and lower-body clothing with specified occasions. Jagadeesh *et al.* [14] propose four models to discover key fashion insights from large quantities of online fashion images. These works [4, 13, 14] adopt hand-crafted feature to represent attribute features, where the extracted specified hand-crafted attribute features are usually mixed with other attribute features. Oramas *et al.* [25] present a hierarchical method to discover patterns of co-occurring activations of base-level elements that define visual compatibility between pairs of object classes. McAuley *et al.* [23] adopt features extracted by Convolutional Neural Network (CNN) to model human preference for the appearance of one item given that of another in terms of more than just the visual similarity between the two. Veit *et al.* [33] use a Siamese Convolutional Neural Network architecture to learn clothing matching from the Amazon co-purchase dataset, focusing on the representative problem of learning compatible clothing style. Simo-Serral *et al.* [29] introduce a Conditional Random Field to learn the different outfits, types of people and settings. The model is used to predict how fashionable a person looks on a particular photograph. Very recently, Li *et al.* [18] use the quality scores as the label and multi-modal embeddings as features to train a grading model. The framework of Li's approach is shown in Figure 1(a). However, the embeddings extracted by above deep learning based methods [23, 25, 29, 33] and the mixed multi-modal embedding used by Li's model is uninterpretable, which leads to uninterpretable outfit composition.

3 THE PROPOSED METHOD

To overcome the limitations of existing fashion outfit composition approaches, we propose an interpretable partitioned embedding based method to achieve customized multi-item fashion outfit composition. In this section, the partitioned embedding network is firstly presented to partition an embedding into independent parts which correspond to different attributes. Then, we introduce how to build composition relationship in our proposed composition graph and the attribute map with the interpretable and partitioned embedding.

3.1 Interpretable Partitioned Embedding

Let I denote an outfit item, $\mathcal{R}(I)$ denote the extracted embedding of I. To make the extracted embedding interpretable and partitionable, there are two constraints to be satisfied: on one hand, the fixed parts of the whole embedding should correspond to specific attributes; on the other hand, different parts of the whole embedding should be mutually independent. Thus, the embedded attribute embedding $\mathcal{R}(I)$ of item I can be described as below:

$$\begin{aligned} \mathcal{R}(I) &= [r_1; r_2; ...; r_N], \\ s.t.\ \mathcal{P}(r_i|\{r_j, j \neq i\}) &= \mathcal{P}(r_i) \end{aligned} \tag{1}$$

where r_i corresponds to different parts of embedding and N is the total number of parts. $\mathcal{P}(r_i|\{r_j, j \neq i\}) = \mathcal{P}(r_i)$ implies that r_i does not depend on $\{r_j, j \neq i\}$. To get interpretable and partitioned embedding, we propose the partitioned embedding network, which is shown in Figure 2. The partitioned embedding network consists of two vital components: attribute partition module and partition adversarial module, which can fulfill above two constraints. Thus, the loss of the partitioned embedding network is defined as follows:

$$\mathcal{L} = \mathcal{L}_a(I, \mathcal{R}(I)) + \alpha\mathcal{L}_t(I, Label), \tag{2}$$

where α is a balancing parameter, $\mathcal{L}_a(I, \mathcal{R}(I))$ is the partition adversarial loss, $\mathcal{L}_t(I, Label) = \frac{1}{N}\sum_{k=1}^{N} loss(I, Label\ k)$ is the summed loss of each attribute loss $loss(I, Label\ k)$.

3.1.1 Attribute Partition Module. As aforementioned, there are several attributes [20, 22, 34] for describing fashion, such as color, shape, texture, style and so on. To get the importance of attributes in the fashion cloth, we administer a questionnaire among 30 professional stylists. Statistically, attributes are split into 4 classes in the order of color, shape, texture and remaining attributes (style, occasion and others). In Figure 2, *Bnet* is used to extract an initial embedding of a clothing item, which is uninterpretable. To get interpretable embedding, the attribute partition module is introduced. The attribute partition module is composed of attribute networks *Anet* 1, *Anet* 2, *Anet* 3, which are used to ensure that *Part 1'*, *Part 2'*and *Part 3'* of the overall embedding correspond to color, shape and texture attribute, respectively.

Color is a primary element in the fashion outfit composition. To get the color label, we adopt the latest proposed color theme extraction method [7] to extract color themes. This method can extract large span and any number of ranked color themes. We modify it to just extract color in the foreground area of an item. To get an explicit mapping relationship between **shape** and embedded codes, we adopt the Variational Auto-Encoder model [16] to encode and decode shape information. **Texture** attribute used in our paper are classified into 6 category: pure, strip, letter, repeating pattern, single pattern and stitching. In total, 100 thousand data are labeled for each category in our paper.

3.1.2 Partition Adversarial Module. With the attribute partition module, *Part 1'*, *Part 2'* and *Part 3'* of the initial embedding contain color, shape and texture information, respectively. However, the extracted initial embedding has two drawbacks: different parts of the initial embedding may still mix other attribute information and remaining attribute (style and others) does not have explicitly corresponding part in the whole embedding.

To address the above problems, our partition adversarial module is introduced. The partition adversarial module includes adversarial prediction networks and decoder network. Decoder network *Dnet* guarantees that embedding contains all useful information of the original clothing item. Adversarial prediction networks *Pnet* 1, *Pnet* 2, ..., *Pnet* N ensure that different parts of whole embedding are independent. Under the influence of decoder network and adversarial prediction networks, the last part of the embedding solely contains the remaining attribute corresponding information. Thus, the partition adversarial loss $\mathcal{L}_a(I, \mathcal{R}(I))$ can be defined as follows:

$$\mathcal{L}_a(I, \mathcal{R}(I)) = \mathcal{L}_c(I, I') + \beta\mathcal{L}_d(r_1, r_2, ..., r_N), \tag{3}$$

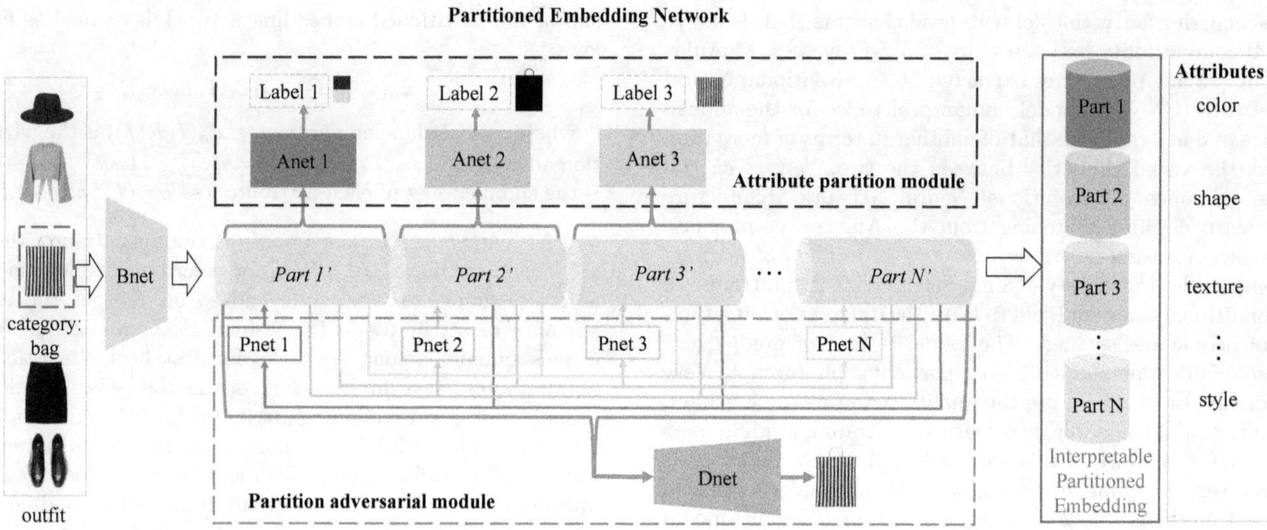

Figure 2: The framework of partitioned embedding network. The network consists of two vital components: attribute partition module and partition adversarial module. The attribute partition module is composed of attribute networks *Anet* 1, *Anet* 2, *Anet* 3, which are used to ensure that *Part 1'*, *Part 2'* and *Part 3'* of the overall embedding correspond to color, shape and texture attribute, respectively. The partition adversarial module includes adversarial prediction networks *Pnet* 1, *Pnet* 2, ..., *Pnet* *N* and decoder network *Dnet*. The adversarial prediction networks can ensure that different parts of the whole embedding are independent. The decoder network guarantees that embedding contains all useful information of original clothing item.

where β is a balancing parameter, I' is the decoded image of I, $\mathcal{L}_c(I, I')$ is the decoded loss and $\mathcal{L}_d(r_1, r_2, ..., r_N)$ is mutually independent loss, respectively.

Inspired by the adversarial approach in [27], we adopt adversarial operation to meet the mutually independent constraint. Thus, the mutually independent loss $\mathcal{L}_d(r_1, r_2, ..., r_N)$ includes predicting loss $\mathcal{L}_p$ and encoding loss $\mathcal{L}_e$. In the prediction stage, each prediction net *Pnet i* tries to predict the corresponding embedding part r_i as much as possible to maximize the predictability. The predicted loss $\mathcal{L}_p$ can be defined as:

$$\mathcal{L}_p = \sum_{i=1}^{N} \mathbb{E}[r_i - \mathcal{F}_{\theta(i)}(r_1, ..., r_{i-1}, r_{i+1}, ..., r_N)]^2, \quad (4)$$

where $\mathcal{F}$ is the prediction net *Pnet* and $\theta(i)$ is the parameters of prediction net *Pnet i* . In the encoding stage, all encoder nets *Bnet i* are trying to make all the prediction net $\mathcal{F}_{\theta(i)}$ fail to predict corresponding embedding, which means to minimize predictability. The encoded loss $\mathcal{L}_e$ thus could be defined as:

$$\mathcal{L}_e = -\sum_{i=1}^{N} \mathbb{E}[r_i - \mathcal{F}_{\theta(i)}(r_1, ..., r_{i-1}, r_{i+1}, ..., r_N)]^2. \quad (5)$$

In summary, attribute partition module makes sure that different parts of the whole embedding contain corresponding attribute information. Parts adversarial module ensures that different parts of embedding are only related to corresponding attributes and the last part of embedding contains all remaining attribute information.

3.2 Fashion Outfit Composition

3.2.1 Outfit Composition Graph. Considering that some matching items may appear many times in different outfits, we propose a fashion composition graph to model matching relationship in outfit. According to category, items in outfits are classified into five categories: tops, bottoms, hats, bags and shoes. For each category, we first cluster all items into N_p cluster centers $P_k, k \in \{1, 2, 3, ..., N_p\}$ according to color embedding. Then, for each cluster P_k, items that belongs to it is clustered into N_q cluster centers $Q_k, k \in \{1, 2, 3, ..., N_q\}$ according to shape embedding. For each cluster Q_k, items that belongs to it is clustered into N_t cluster centers $T_k, k \in \{1, 2, 3, ..., N_t\}$ according to texture embedding. Lastly, items belonging to texture cluster center are clustered into N_r cluster centers $R_k, k \in \{1, 2, 3, ..., N_r\}$ according to the remaining embedding. Then, we can get $\mathcal{N} = N_p N_q N_t N_r$ cluster centers $\mathcal{C}_k, k \in \{1, 2, 3, ..., \mathcal{N}\}$. After getting all clustering centers, fashion composition graph $\mathcal{G}$ is defined as follow:

$$\mathcal{G} = (\mathcal{V}, \mathcal{E}, \mathcal{W}), \quad (6)$$

where $\mathcal{V}$ is the vertex set of all cluster center $\mathcal{C}_k$, $\mathcal{E}$ is the edge set and $\mathcal{W}$ is the weight set.

At the initial stage, all vertexes $v \in \mathcal{V}$ have no connections and all weights $w \in \mathcal{W}$ are set to zeros. If item $I \in v_i$ and item $I' \in v_j$ appear in the same outfit and there is no connection between v_i and v_j, a connection is created and weight $w_{i,j}$ is set as one. If corresponding vertices v_i and v_j already have connection, the weight between them will be

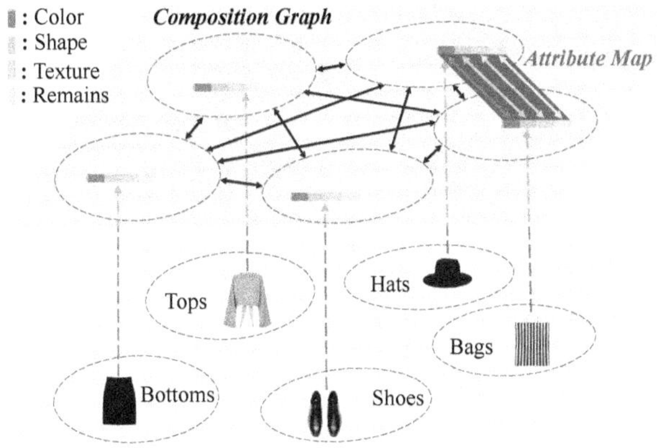

Figure 3: Fashion outfit composition graph. In the graph, all items are classified into five classes according to the category. For each category, items are clustered into different cluster centers according to attributes' importance. With these cluster centers as vertexes, edges and weights of fashion composition graph are learned from outfit dataset. Meanwhile, an attribute map are built, which model significance of different attributes.

updated as follow:

$$w_{i,j} = w'_{i,j} + \rho, \quad (7)$$

where $w'_{i,j}$ is the weight in the last stage. Figure 3 shows an example of the connection process.

3.2.2 Attribute Matching Map. In the process of building fashion outfit graph $\mathcal{G}$, an attribute matching map $\mathcal{M}$ of different attributes is also built. which is defined as:

$$\begin{aligned} \mathcal{M} = \{\{\mathcal{U}_x^k, \mathcal{A}\}, \{\mathcal{H}_y^k, \mathcal{B}\}, \{\mathcal{J}_z^k, \mathcal{D}\}, \{\mathcal{O}_q^k, \mathcal{T}\}\}, \quad (8) \\ k \in \{1, 2, .., \mathcal{K}\}, x \in \{1, 2, .., \mathcal{X}\}, y \in \{1, 2, .., \mathcal{Y}\}, \\ z \in \{1, 2, .., \mathcal{Z}\}, q \in \{1, 2, .., \mathcal{Q}\} \end{aligned}$$

where $\mathcal{K}$ is the number of categories, $\mathcal{X}, \mathcal{Y}, \mathcal{Z}, \mathcal{Q}$ are clusters' number of color, shape, texture and the remaining features respectively, $\mathcal{U}_x^k$ is the x-th color attribute cluster of category k, $\mathcal{H}_y^k$ is the y-th shape attribute cluster of category k, $\mathcal{J}_z^k$ is the z-th texture attribute cluster of category k, $\mathcal{O}_q^k$ is the q-th remaining attributes cluster of category k, $\mathcal{A}, \mathcal{B}, \mathcal{D}, \mathcal{T}$ are score values set and all initial score value in set are set to zero.

When an item I of category k and an item I' of category k' appear together in the same outfit, score value $a(i,j)$ between color cluster $\mathcal{U}_i^k$ ($r_1 \in \mathcal{U}_i^k$, $\mathcal{R}(I) = [r_1; r_2; r_3]$) and color cluster $\mathcal{U}_j^{k'}$ ($r'_1 \in \mathcal{U}_j^{k'}$, $\mathcal{R}(I') = [r'_1; r'_2; r'_3]$) will be updated using the following equation:

$$a(i,j) = a'(i,j) + 1, a(i,j) \in \mathcal{A}, \quad (9)$$

where, $a'(i,j)$ is last stage score value. $b(i,j) \in \mathcal{B}$, $d(i,j) \in \mathcal{D}$ and $t(i,j) \in \mathcal{T}$ are updated in the same way.

After getting the outfit composition graph $\mathcal{G}$ and the attribute map $\mathcal{M}$, composition score $\mathcal{S}$ of an outfit o is defined as follows:

$$\begin{aligned} \mathcal{S}(o) = \mathcal{S}_1 + \eta \mathcal{S}_2, \quad (10) \\ \mathcal{S}_1 = \frac{\sum_{k=1}^{K} w_k}{K\sigma(w_1, w_2, ..., w_K)}, \\ \mathcal{S}_2 = \sum_{t=1}^{3} \frac{\sum_{k=1}^{K} s_k^t}{K\sigma(s_1^t, s_2^t, ..., s_K^t)} \end{aligned}$$

where, η is a balancing parameter, $\mathcal{S}_1$ is the weight matching score in composition graph, $\mathcal{S}_2$ is attribute matching scores. K is the number of matching weights in outfit o, $\sigma(w_1, w_2, ..., w_K)$ is variance among matching weights $w_k, k \in \{1, 2, ..., K\}$. To get an matching outfit for an item I, an exhaustion algorithm is adopted to search the most matching outfit. In order to reduce time complexity, only top N_c connected items of each category are taken into account.

4 EXPERIMENTS

4.1 Implementation Details

DataSet. Until now, there are many clothing related datasets (such as HipsterWars [15], DeepFashion [20], FCDB [1] and so on) as been summarized in [1]. However, the number of validation image in these datasets is insufficient for multi-item outfit composition. As a consequence, we collect a dataset from Polyvore.com, which is the most popular fashion oriented website in the US with tens of thousands of fashion outfits creating every day. In the dataset, fashion outfits are associated with the number of *likes* and some fashion items. Each fashion item has a corresponding image, category and *like*. In practical application, an outfit may contain many items, such as tops (blouse, cardigan, sweater, sweatshirt, hoodie, tank, tunic), bottoms (pant, skirt, short), hats, bags, shoes, glasses, watches, jewelry and so on. In this article, we choose five prerequisite categories (tops, bottoms, hats, bags and shoes). Through discarding items that mix human body, we finally get a set of 1.56 million outfits and 7.53 million items.

Network architectures. The number of parts N equals to 4. The basic network *Bnet* includes four branching networks *Bnet* 1, *Bnet* 2, *Bnet* 3 and *Bnet* 4, which encode color, shape, texture and remaining attribute feature, respectively. In attribute partition module, *Anet* 1, *Anet* 2 and *Anet* 3 are color, shape and texture attribute extracting network, respectively. *Anet* 1 is a Generative Adversarial Network architecture, which includes a generative model G_c and a discriminative model D_c. In partition adversarial module, all prediction networks *Pnet* 1, *Pnet* 2, *Pnet* 3, *Pnet* 4 share the same architecture. Let Ci denote a Convolution-BatchNorm-ReLU layer with i filters. CDj denotes a Convolution-BatchNorm-Dropout-ReLU layer with a dropout rate of 30% and j filters. DCk denotes a deconvolution-ReLU layer with k filters, and FCt denotes a Full Connection with t neuron.

Table 1: Architecture of all networks

Network		Architecture
Bnet	Bnet 1	CD16-CD32-CD64-FC100
	Bnet 2	CD16-CD32-CD64-C64-FC100
	Bnet 3	CD16-CD32-CD64-CD64-FC100
	Bnet 4	CD32-CD64-CD128-C128-C128-FC100
Dnet		DC128-DC128-DC64-DC32-DC1
Anet 1	G_c	FC64-FC32-FC15
	D_c	FC256-FC128-FC64-FC1
Anet 2		C64-DC64-DC32-DC1
Anet 3		FC64-FC6
Pnet		FC256-FC128-FC100

All convolutions are 4×4 spatial filters with stride 2. Convolutions in both encoder and the discriminator are downsampled by a factor of 2, where as in the decoder they upsample by a factor of 2. Input size of clothing item is $128 \times 128 \times 3$. The size of whole embedding is 400×1 and the size of each part is 100×1. All the network architectures are summarized in Table 1. In our experiment, we adopt the Adam optimizer during training. Unless otherwise specified, the learning rate is fixed to be 0.001 and the minibatch size is 64. Weights are initialized from a Gaussian distribution with mean as 0 and standard deviation as 0.02. Before training the whole network, *Bnet* 1, *Bnet* 2 and *Bnet* 3 have been pre-trained on a small subset of dataset with 50,000 clothing items. The learning rate of *Bnet* 1, *Bnet* 2, *Bnet* 3 and *Pnet* are 0.0005, 0.001, 0.007 and 0.0003, respectively.

Parameters setting. In our experiment, α is 1, β is 0.7 and η is 1. The color themes number of each clothing item is 5. Connected items of each category N_c is 10. The number of cluster center for color, shape, texture and remaining attribute are 1000, $\sqrt{N_{color\ i}}$, $\sqrt{N_{shape\ j}}$ and $\sqrt{N_{texture\ k}}$, respectively. $N_{color\ i}$, $N_{shape\ j}$ and $N_{texture\ j}$ are the total number of items in cluster i, cluster j and cluster k, respectively.

4.2 Outfits' Psycho-Visual Tests

To verify the effectiveness of our proposed method, we make a pairwise comparison study. In this experiment, a total of one hundred items are used, along with 20 items for each category. For each item, each method will give an outfit. 30 professional stylists take part in the psychophysical experiment, 13 males and 17 females. In the paired comparison, a stylist is presented with a pair of the recommended outfit. The stylists are asked to choose the most matching composition. All pairs are presented twice to avoid mistakes in individual preferences. The number of pairs is $n(n-1)N_o/2$, where n is the number of composition methods and N_o is the total number of test outfits. For each pair, the outfit chosen by an observer is given a score of 1, the other outfit is given a score of 0 and both of them got a score of 0.5 when equally matching. After obtaining the raw data, we converted it to

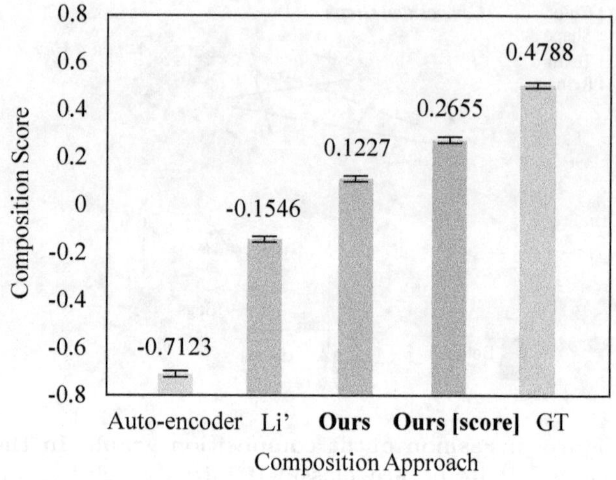

Figure 4: Score of composition for the ranking experiment with all professional stylists.

frequency matrix $F = (f_{ij})_{1 \leqslant i,j \leqslant n}$, where the entry f_{ij} denotes the score given to composition method j as compared with composition method i. From matrix F, percentage matrix $M = (m_{ij})_{1 \leqslant i,j \leqslant n}$ is calculated through $M = F/N_b$, where N_b denotes total number of observations.

To get preference scales from the matrix M, we apply the case V of Thurstone's law of comparative judgment [31] following Morovic's thesis [24]. Firstly, a logistic matrix $G = (g_{ij})_{1 \leqslant i,j \leqslant n}$ is calculated through Equation (11) as

$$g_{ij} = ln\left(\frac{N_b m_{ij} + \tau}{N_b(1 - m_{ij}) + \tau}\right), \tag{11}$$

where τ is an arbitrary additive constant (0.5 is also been used in our experiment). Logistic matrix G are then transformed to z-scores matrix $Z = (z_{ij})_{1 \leqslant i,j \leqslant n}$ by using a simple scaling in the form of $Z = \lambda * G$ where coefficient λ is determined by linear regression between z-scores and corresponding logistic values. We calculate this value of λ to be 0.5441 with $N_b = 3000$ observations for each pair of algorithms. From the matrix Z, an accuracy score of composition method i is calculated by averaging the scores of the ith column of the matrix Z. The final matching scores are contained in an interval around 0. The interval can be estimated as $\pm 1.96/\sqrt{2N_b}$ at the 95% confidence level. The resulting z-scores and confidence intervals for all outfits are shown in Figure 4, where 'Ours [score]' means our method with normalized user favorite scores and 'GT' means the original outfit composition. It is evident that our model performs superiorly to other methods and auto-encoder is the least suitable. The matching scores of five composition methods are -0.7123, -0.1546, 0.1227, 0.2655 and 0.4788 separately with ± 0.0253 confidence interval. Figure 6 depicts directly visual comparative results of representative composition outfits. From the figure, we can see that our method get more satisfactory composition results. The method with score label gives a more reasonable composition. It is obvious that

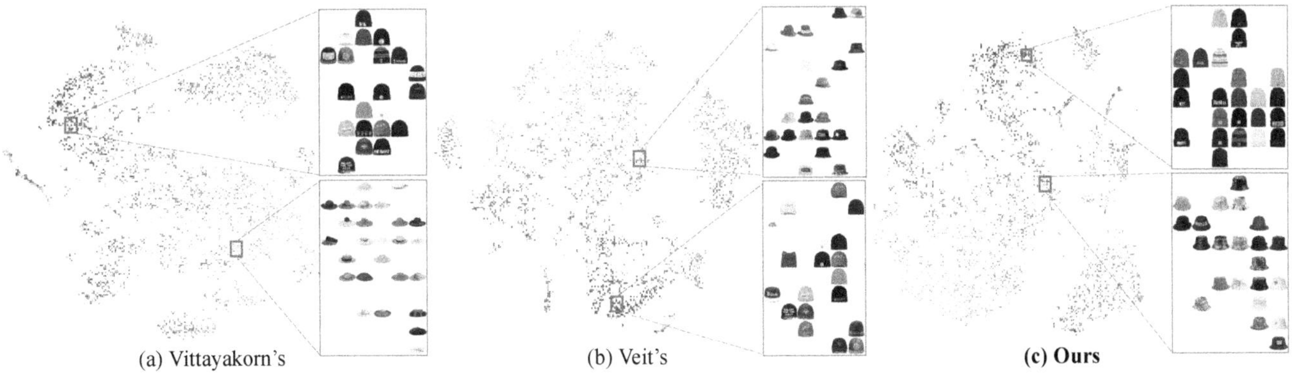

Figure 5: Visualization of the shape space of hand-crafted shape features used in Vittayakorn's method [34], shape embedding extracted by Veit's CSN [32] and our partitioned shape embedding using t-SNE [21].

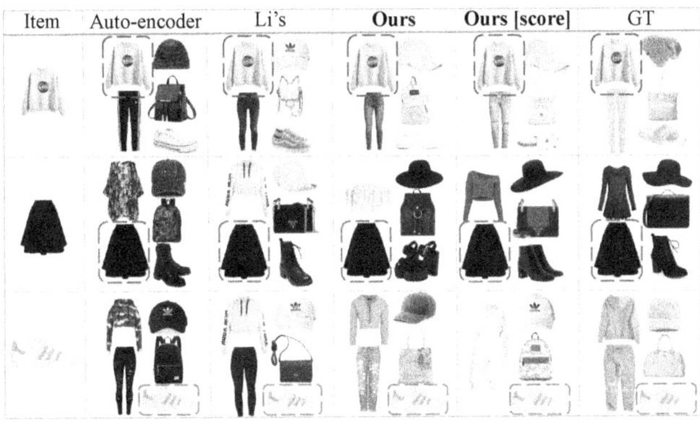

Figure 6: Composition visual comparison among different methods.

our method produces better composition outfit than the other methods.

4.3 Tests on E-commerce Platform

To further validate the effectiveness of our proposed method. We test our outfit composition result on word famous e-commerce platform. In this part, we compare outfits generated by our method with original outfits and outfits generated by other two methods. For each category of item, five thousands outfits are generated with each method. Then, total 125 thousand outfits are exhibited on the e-commerce platform with 500 thousand pageview (PV). The average click-through rate (CTR) and the average second click-through rate (SCTR) are shown in Table 2, where we can see that original outfit composition (GT) has the highest CTR and SCTR. What's more, CTR and SCTR of our method are higher than the other two methods, which proves that our method can generate more desirable outfit than other two methods.

Table 2: CTR & SCTR for the test outfits

	Auto-encoder	Li's	**Ours**	**Ours [score]**	GT
CTR	3.57%	4.21%	4.56%	4.63%	5.20%
SCTR	53.78%	61.43%	60.96%	62.75%	68.47%

4.4 Validity of Partitioned Embedding

To validate the discriminative ability of embedding partitioned by our method, we compare with other two embeddings: hand-crafted features used in Vittayakorn's method [34] and embedding extracted by Veit's CSN [32]. In this part, we visualize the shape space of three shape embeddings using t-SNE [21], which is shown in Figure 5. For each visualized map, a dense region and a common region are magnified with red bounding boxes. From Figure 5(c), we can see that hats in the red bounding box share same shape and vary color and texture. However, hats in the red bounding box of Vittayakorn's and Veit's visualized map are usually mixed with different shape, which indicates that shape embedding extracted by our method is more unmingled that other two methods.

4.5 Personalized Attributes Composition

In the stage of building composition graph, we cluster the attributes corresponding parts of embeddings into different level cluster centers as vertexes in the graph. In the testing stage, users can specify their preferred attribute, such as "color=red", "shape=circle" or "texture=strip", our model can give a series of specified attribute items with interpretable matching scores for users to choose. Figure 7 shows some ordered recommended matching items with six composition scores. For example, sum composition score of the recommended hat in the green box is 65.46. Weight composition score in the blue box is 16.45. Attributes matching scores corresponding to color, shape, texture and remaining attribute are 14.36, 11.74, 13.59 and 9.32, respectively. From attribute matching scores in the red bounding box, we can see that color and texture attributes give more contribution to the final composition than other attributes. Meanwhile, for the user

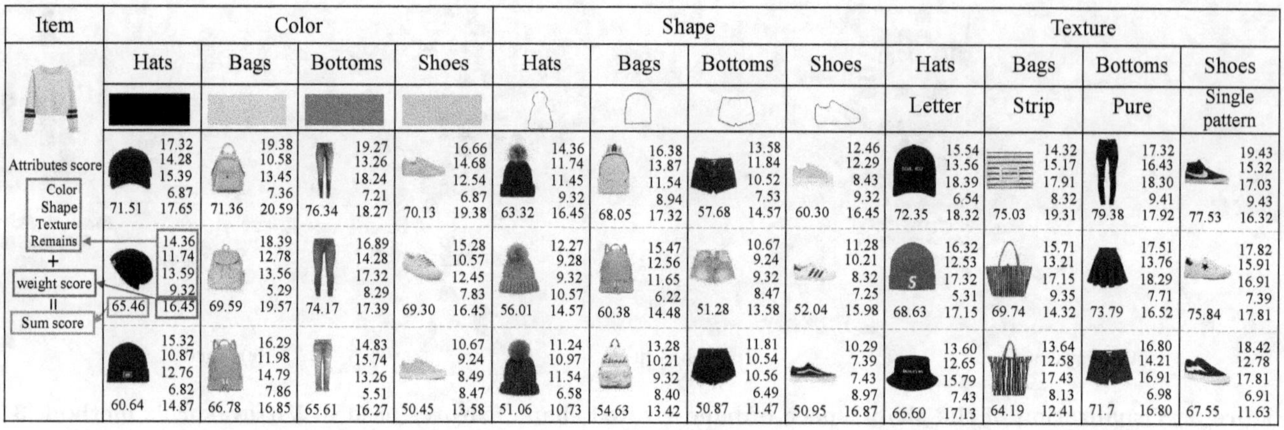

Figure 7: Outfit composition with user specify attribute (color, shape or texture).

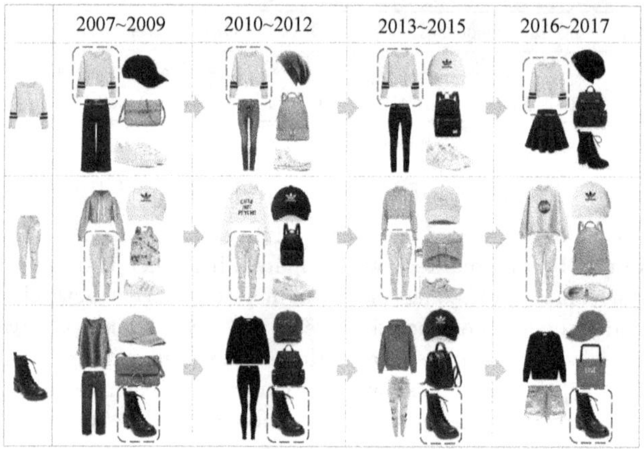

Figure 8: Fashion trends with different years.

specified attribute, the recommended items are satisfactory with user preference.

4.6 Outfit Composition's Extension

As described above, our fashion composition graph is weakly supervised. Our model can also be extended to a dataset with matching score labels. After normalizing the user favorite scores, the fashion composition graph with the score is built using Eq.(7) by setting ρ to the normalized score. Outfit composition result with normalized scores are given in Table 2, Figure 6 and Figure 4.

The fashion trends are known for its quick and dogmatical variation [1]. The proposed technique enables us to keep up with the fashion trend along time. When new trend outfit dataset joints, old $\mathcal{W}$ of composition graph is divided by $\sqrt{N_m}$, where N_m is the max weight of the graph. Then, the fashion composition graph is updated following Eq.(7) with $\rho > 1$. In the experiments, we classify our whole outfit dataset into four groups according to years: dataset1 (2007–2009), dataset2 (2010–2012), dataset3 (2013–2015), dataset4 (2016 – 2017). We use our proposed iterated model with dataset1 (2007 – 2009) as the basic dataset to get initial outfit composition graph. Then, by constantly adding new dataset into the basic dataset, we can get new outfit composition graph, by which fashion trend is kept up with. Figure 8 gives the visual most popular outfit along years. We can see that our iterated model can keep up with fashion trends tightly.

5 CONCLUSION

Fashion style tells a lot about one's personality. Interpretable embeddings of items are fatal in design, market and clothing retrieval. In this paper, we propose a partitioned embedding network, which can extract interpretable partitioned embedding from clothing items. The network consists of two vital components: attribute partition module and partition adversarial module. In the attribute partition module, multiple attribute labels are adopted to ensure that different parts of the overall embedding correspond to different attributes. In the partition adversarial module, adversarial predicted networks and encoded network are adopted to achieve the independence of different parts. Then, using the extracted partitioned embeddings, a composition graph and an attribute matching map are built. When users specify their preference attributes, such as color and shape, our model can recommend desirable outfit with interpretable attribute matching scores. In practice, people's skin color and stature have great influence on the outfit composition. Thus, personalization would be taken into consideration in our future work.

ACKNOWLEDGMENTS

This work is supported by National Key Research and Development Program (2016YFB1200203), National Natural Science Foundation of China (61572428,U1509206), Fundamental Research Funds for the Central Universities (2017FZA5014) and Key Research and Development Program of Zhejiang Province (2018C01004).

REFERENCES

[1] Kaori Abe, Teppei Suzuki, Shunya Ueta, Akio Nakamura, Yutaka Satoh, and Hirokatsu Kataoka. 2017. Changing Fashion Cultures. *arXiv preprint arXiv:1703.07920* (2017).

[2] Lukas Bossard, Matthias Dantone, Christian Leistner, Christian Wengert, Till Quack, and Luc Van Gool. 2012. Apparel classification with style. In *Asian conference on computer vision*. Springer, 321–335.

[3] Diane Bouchacourt, Ryota Tomioka, and Sebastian Nowozin. 2017. Multi-level variational autoencoder: Learning disentangled representations from grouped observations. *arXiv preprint arXiv:1705.08841* (2017).

[4] Huizhong Chen, Andrew Gallagher, and Bernd Girod. 2012. Describing clothing by semantic attributes. *Computer Vision–ECCV 2012* (2012), 609–623.

[5] Qiang Chen, Junshi Huang, Rogerio Feris, Lisa M Brown, Jian Dong, and Shuicheng Yan. 2015. Deep domain adaptation for describing people based on fine-grained clothing attributes. In *Proceedings of the IEEE conference on computer vision and pattern recognition*. 5315–5324.

[6] Xi Chen, Yan Duan, Rein Houthooft, John Schulman, Ilya Sutskever, and Pieter Abbeel. 2016. Infogan: Interpretable representation learning by information maximizing generative adversarial nets. In *Advances in Neural Information Processing Systems*. 2172–2180.

[7] Zunlei Feng, Wolong Yuan, Chunli Fu, Jie Lei, and Mingli Song. 2017. Finding intrinsic color themes in images with human visual perception. *Neurocomputing* (2017).

[8] Jianlong Fu, Jinqiao Wang, Zechao Li, Min Xu, and Hanqing Lu. 2012. Efficient clothing retrieval with semantic-preserving visual phrases. In *Asian Conference on Computer Vision*. Springer, 420–431.

[9] M Hadi Kiapour, Xufeng Han, Svetlana Lazebnik, Alexander C Berg, and Tamara L Berg. 2015. Where to buy it: Matching street clothing photos in online shops. In *Proceedings of the IEEE International Conference on Computer Vision*. 3343–3351.

[10] Ruining He and Julian McAuley. 2016. Ups and downs: Modeling the visual evolution of fashion trends with one-class collaborative filtering. In *proceedings of the 25th international conference on world wide web*. International World Wide Web Conferences Steering Committee, 507–517.

[11] Irina Higgins, Loic Matthey, Arka Pal, Christopher Burgess, Xavier Glorot, Matthew Botvinick, Shakir Mohamed, and Alexander Lerchner. 2016. beta-vae: Learning basic visual concepts with a constrained variational framework. (2016).

[12] Junshi Huang, Rogerio S Feris, Qiang Chen, and Shuicheng Yan. 2015. Cross-domain image retrieval with a dual attribute-aware ranking network. In *Proceedings of the IEEE International Conference on Computer Vision*. 1062–1070.

[13] Tomoharu Iwata, Shinji Wanatabe, and Hiroshi Sawada. 2011. Fashion coordinates recommender system using photographs from fashion magazines. In *IJCAI*, Vol. 22. 2262.

[14] Vignesh Jagadeesh, Robinson Piramuthu, Anurag Bhardwaj, Wei Di, and Neel Sundaresan. 2014. Large scale visual recommendations from street fashion images. In *Proceedings of the 20th ACM SIGKDD international conference on Knowledge discovery and data mining*. ACM, 1925–1934.

[15] M Hadi Kiapour, Kota Yamaguchi, Alexander C Berg, and Tamara L Berg. 2014. Hipster wars: Discovering elements of fashion styles. In *European conference on computer vision*. Springer, 472–488.

[16] Diederik P Kingma and Max Welling. 2014. Auto-Encoding Variational Bayes. *stat* 1050 (2014), 1.

[17] Tejas D Kulkarni, William F Whitney, Pushmeet Kohli, and Josh Tenenbaum. 2015. Deep convolutional inverse graphics network. In *Advances in Neural Information Processing Systems*. 2539–2547.

[18] Yuncheng Li, Liangliang Cao, Jiang Zhu, and Jiebo Luo. 2017. Mining Fashion Outfit Composition Using An End-to-End Deep Learning Approach on Set Data. *IEEE Transactions on Multimedia* (2017).

[19] Qiang Liu, Shu Wu, and Liang Wang. 2017. DeepStyle: Learning User Preferences for Visual Recommendation. In *Proceedings of the 40th International ACM SIGIR Conference on Research and Development in Information Retrieval*. ACM, 841–844.

[20] Ziwei Liu, Ping Luo, Shi Qiu, Xiaogang Wang, and Xiaoou Tang. 2016. Deepfashion: Powering robust clothes recognition and retrieval with rich annotations. In *Proceedings of the IEEE Conference on Computer Vision and Pattern Recognition*. 1096–1104.

[21] Laurens van der Maaten and Geoffrey Hinton. 2008. Visualizing data using t-SNE. *Journal of machine learning research* 9, Nov (2008), 2579–2605.

[22] Kevin Matzen, Kavita Bala, and Noah Snavely. 2017. StreetStyle: Exploring world-wide clothing styles from millions of photos. *arXiv preprint arXiv:1706.01869* (2017).

[23] Julian McAuley, Christopher Targett, Qinfeng Shi, and Anton Van Den Hengel. 2015. Image-based recommendations on styles and substitutes. In *Proceedings of the 38th International ACM SIGIR Conference on Research and Development in Information Retrieval*. ACM, 43–52.

[24] Jan Morovic. 1998. To develop a universal gamut mapping algorithm. (1998).

[25] Jose Oramas and Tinne Tuytelaars. 2016. Modeling visual compatibility through hierarchical mid-level elements. *arXiv preprint arXiv:1604.00036* (2016).

[26] Guim Perarnau, Joost van de Weijer, Bogdan Raducanu, and Jose M Álvarez. 2016. Invertible conditional gans for image editing. *arXiv preprint arXiv:1611.06355* (2016).

[27] Jürgen Schmidhuber. 2008. Learning factorial codes by predictability minimization. *Learning* 4, 6 (2008).

[28] N Siddharth, Brooks Paige, Alban Desmaison, Jan-Willem van de Meent, Frank Wood, Noah D Goodman, Pushmeet Kohli, and Philip HS Torr. 2016. Learning Disentangled Representations in Deep Generative Models. (2016).

[29] Edgar Simo-Serra, Sanja Fidler, Francesc Moreno-Noguer, and Raquel Urtasun. 2015. Neuroaesthetics in fashion: Modeling the perception of fashionability. In *Proceedings of the IEEE Conference on Computer Vision and Pattern Recognition*. 869–877.

[30] Edgar Simo-Serra and Hiroshi Ishikawa. 2016. Fashion style in 128 floats: Joint ranking and classification using weak data for feature extraction. In *Proceedings of the IEEE Conference on Computer Vision and Pattern Recognition*. 298–307.

[31] Louis L Thurstone. 1927. A law of comparative judgment. *Psychological review* 34, 4 (1927), 273.

[32] Andreas Veit, Serge Belongie, and Theofanis Karaletsos. 2017. Conditional similarity networks. *Computer Vision and Pattern Recognition (CVPR 2017)* (2017).

[33] Andreas Veit, Balazs Kovacs, Sean Bell, Julian McAuley, Kavita Bala, and Serge Belongie. 2015. Learning visual clothing style with heterogeneous dyadic co-occurrences. In *Proceedings of the IEEE International Conference on Computer Vision*. 4642–4650.

[34] Sirion Vittayakorn, Kota Yamaguchi, Alexander C Berg, and Tamara L Berg. 2015. Runway to realway: Visual analysis of fashion. In *Applications of Computer Vision (WACV), 2015 IEEE Winter Conference on*. IEEE, 951–958.

[35] Chaoyue Wang, Chaohui Wang, Chang Xu, and Dacheng Tao. 2017. Tag disentangled generative adversarial network for object image re-rendering. In *Proceedings of the Twenty-Sixth International Joint Conference on Artificial Intelligence, IJCAI*. 2901–2907.

[36] Xiaolong Wang and Abhinav Gupta. 2016. Generative image modeling using style and structure adversarial networks. In *European Conference on Computer Vision*. Springer, 318–335.

[37] Xianwang Wang and Tong Zhang. 2011. Clothes search in consumer photos via color matching and attribute learning. In *Proceedings of the 19th ACM international conference on Multimedia*. ACM, 1353–1356.

[38] Kota Yamaguchi, M Hadi Kiapour, Luis E Ortiz, and Tamara L Berg. 2012. Parsing clothing in fashion photographs. In *Computer Vision and Pattern Recognition (CVPR), 2012 IEEE Conference on*. IEEE, 3570–3577.

[39] Kota Yamaguchi, Takayuki Okatani, Kyoko Sudo, Kazuhiko Murasaki, and Yukinobu Taniguchi. 2015. Mix and Match: Joint Model for Clothing and Attribute Recognition.. In *BMVC*. 51–1.

[40] Zhengzhong Zhou, Yifei Xu, Jingjin Zhou, and Liqing Zhang. 2016. Interactive Image Search for Clothing Recommendation. In *Proceedings of the 2016 ACM on Multimedia Conference*. ACM, 754–756.

A Multi-Oriented Scene Text Detector with Position-Sensitive Segmentation

Peirui Cheng
University of Chinese Academy of Sciences
Beijing, China
chengpeirui16@mails.ucas.edu.cn

Weiqiang Wang
University of Chinese Academy of Sciences
Beijing, China
wqwang@ucas.ac.cn

ABSTRACT

Scene text detection has been studied for a long time and lots of approaches have achieved promising performances. Most approaches regard text as a specific object and utilize the popular frameworks of object detection to detect scene text. However, scene text is different from general objects in terms of orientations, sizes and aspect ratios. In this paper, we present an end-to-end multi-oriented scene text detection approach, which combines the object detection framework with the position-sensitive segmentation. For a given image, features are extracted through a fully convolutional network. Then they are input into text detection branch and position-sensitive segmentation branch simultaneously, where text detection branch is used for generating candidates and position-sensitive segmentation branch is used for generating segmentation maps. Finally the candidates generated by text detection branch are projected onto the position-sensitive segmentation maps for filtering. The proposed approach utilizes the merits of position-sensitive segmentation to improve the expressiveness of the proposed network. Additionally, the approach uses position-sensitive segmentation maps to further filter the candidates so as to highly improve the precision rate. Experiments on datasets ICDAR2015 and COCO-Text demonstrate that the proposed method outperforms previous state-of-the-art methods. For ICDAR2015 dataset, the proposed method achieves an F-score of 0.83 and a precision rate of 0.87.

CCS CONCEPTS

• **Computing methodologies** → **Image segmentation**; **Object detection**; **Neural networks**;

KEYWORDS

scene text detection, fully convolutional network, text detection branch, position-sensitive segmentation branch

ICMR '18, June 11–14, 2018, Bunkyo, Japan
© 2018 Association for Computing Machinery.
ACM ISBN 978-1-4503-5046-4/18/06...$15.00
https://doi.org/10.1145/3206025.3206043

ACM Reference Format:
Peirui Cheng and Weiqiang Wang. 2018. A Multi-Oriented Scene Text Detector with Position-Sensitive Segmentation. In *ICMR '18: 2018 International Conference on Multimedia Retrieval, June 11–14, 2018, Bunkyo, Japan.* ACM, New York, NY, USA, 8 pages. https://doi.org/10.1145/3206025.3206043

1 INTRODUCTION

Natural scene text detection is becoming more and more popular with the development of computer vision and fast increase of image data. It plays an important role in various applications, such as image retrieval [11], automatic driving, blind navigation [33]. It is also a very challenging task due to multiple orientations, perspective distortions, motion blur and variation of text sizes, colors and aspect ratios.

In recent years, various methods [4, 11, 17, 30, 35] have demonstrated their success on diverse benchmarks for scene text detection. Early text detection [3, 10, 34] methods mainly depend on artificial features to detect characters.They normally need some post-processing steps such as character proposals clustering, text lines filtering and text lines segmentation to refine the precision rate and reduce the efficiency of text detection.

Currently, several deep Convolutional Neural Network (CNN) based approaches [4, 8, 12, 17, 21, 30, 32, 36, 39] have shown expressive accuracy and efficiency. They can be classified into three categories: proposals based methods [4, 17, 21, 30, 38], segmentation based methods [32, 36] and direct regression methods [4, 39]. The proposals based methods utilize the object detection framework, such as Faster R-CNN [27], SSD [20], to generate proposals and then filter these proposals. The segmentation based methods, inspired by semantic segmentation [22, 37], exploit the Fully Convolutional Network (FCN) to generate text segmentation maps, then cluster the salient pixels into characters and go through several steps to obtain the final detection results. The direct regression methods, inspired by YOLO [26] and Densebox [9], also exploit the FCN to generate text score map and regress the size or coordinates of text boxes directly so that they can detect scene text efficiently.

Generally, proposals based methods need a vast number of proposals and post-processing steps due to multiple orientations and variation of text sizes [17, 21], which lowers the efficiency of detection. Direct regression methods, by contrast, are suitable for non-horizontal and multi-scale text detection with a high efficiency. But, their accuracies are always inferior to those of proposals based methods due to the lack of post-processing for candidates.

In this paper, we present a novel multi-oriented scene text detection pipeline that fully utilizes the advantages of position-sensitive segmentation [16] and direct regression methods. The pipeline simultaneously generates multi-oriented rectangles as candidates and generates position-sensitive segmentation maps. We aim to predict candidates through direct regression methods and then filter these candidates using the corresponding pixels in the segmentation maps to improve the detection accuracy. However, scene texts are always so compact or connected closely that we cannot confirm that the salient pixels of a certain candidate in segmentation map belong to one ground-truth box. So we adopt position-sensitive segmentation maps to handle the problem, inspired by instance-aware segmentation methods [1, 16]. After predicting text candidates and generating position-sensitive segmentation maps, we propose Position-Sensitive Non-Maximum Suppression(PS-NMS) to filter redundant candidates and obtain the final results.

We summarize the contributions of this paper as follows:

- We propose a multi-oriented scene text detection approach by combining direct regression detection with position-sensitive segmentation, which significantly improves the performance of scene text detection.
- The expressiveness of shared features are improved due to the position-sensitive segmentation, which improves the performance of the detection module.
- We propose PS-NMS to utilize position-sensitive segmentation maps to filter redundant candidates, which significantly improves the precision rate.
- Without many bells and whistles, the proposed algorithm outperforms state-of-the-art methods on ICDAR2015 [14] and COCO-Text [31] text detection benchmarks.

2 RELATED WORK

Conventional detection methods use hand-crafted features, such as stroke width [3], extremal region [23, 24], symmetry [35], to detect text. Among them, Stroke Width Transform (SWT) [3] based methods and Maximally Stable Extremal Regions (MSER) [24] based methods are the mainstream. They mainly obtain character candidates by extracting connected components, followed by false positive filtering, character pairing, text line grouping and word partition. The performance of these approaches heavily degrades on some challenging benchmarks (ICDAR2015 [14], COCO-Text [31]) due to the use of low-level features. Additionally they suffer from low efficiency due to multiple complex steps in them.

Recently, the progress of deep neural network has tremendously promoted the performance of semantic segmentation [22, 37] and it also offers a new framework for scene text detection. Zhang *et al.* [36] use the FCN to generate text saliency map and use component based information and context of the text block to locate text lines. Yao *et al.* [32] utilize a single network for predicting text regions, character candidates and linking orientation map so that it can detect multi-oriented and curved text from multiple channels. Although the semantic segmentation based methods are able to carry out multi-oriented text detection, they often need multiple steps and their robustness suffers from character-level segmentation.

At present, the majority of scene text detection methods [17, 21, 30, 38] are based on object detection methods, such as Faster R-CNN [27], SSD [20], and the state-of-the-art performance is achieved on public benchmarks, e.g., ICDAR2013 [15], ICDAR2015 [14] and COCO-Text [31]. Zhong *et al.* [38] modify the Faster R-CNN framework with Inception-RPN and Ambiguous Text Category to detect scene text. Textboxes [17] is an improved version of SSD for scene text detection, which changes the size and ratio of convolutional kernels to fit the property of scene text. Liu and Jin [21] utilize quadrangle rather than rectangle in the SSD based framework for exactly detecting multi-oriented text. These proposal based methods obtain leading performance on text detection benchmarks. Since these methods need a large number of proposals to deal with multi-oriented text, it makes the cost of calculation become expensive.

Inspired by YOLO [26] and Densebox [9], the researchers develop the idea that candidates can be directly regressed without proposals or default boxes. Zhou *et al.* [39] propose a approach which uses the FCN to generate a pixel-wise text score map and geometry maps to represent the rotated candidates. It gained the high recall rate using feature pyramid network [18] and direct regression without proposals. Also, many methods [7, 25] aim to combine object detection with semantic segmentation to improve the precision of text detection. He *et al.* [7] propose a single shot detector combining semantic segmentation with proposal based text detection. It embeds a saliency network into the SSD framework to improve the performance. Qin *et al.* [25] cascade a YOLO-like direct regression network to a pixel-wise segmentation network. These methods mainly intend to reduce the number of false positive candidates and focus on the candidates containing target objects. However, the semantic segmentation they use only focuses on whether each pixel belongs to text, and does not concern whether each pixel belongs to a certain text instance, which is more important for improving the precision of text detection.

In the proposed method, the position-sensitive segmentation [16] is used to represent whether each pixel belongs to a certain part of text instances. Compared with the semantic segmentation, it can improve the performance of scene text detection better. Additionally, we propose PS-NMS to further use position-sensitive segmentation maps for filtering redundant and false positive candidates to improve the precision of scene text detection.

3 PROPOSED METHODOLOGY

The proposed algorithm is an end-to-end method for detecting multi-oriented text in natural scenes. It consists of four modules: feature extraction, text detection branch, position-sensitive segmentation branch and PS-NMS.

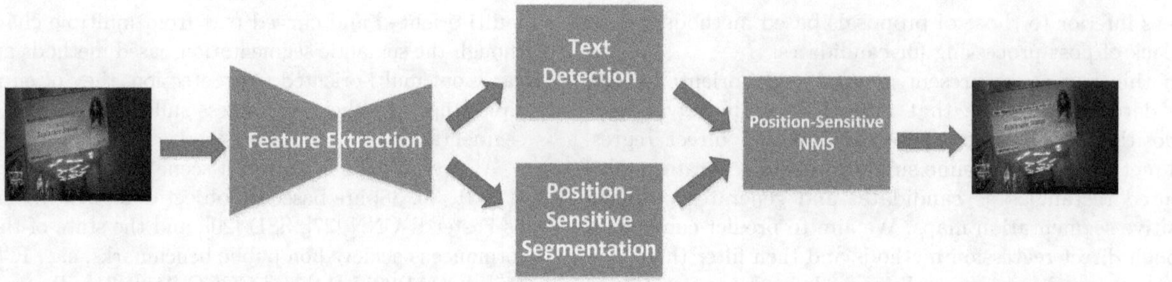

Figure 1: Overall architecture of the proposed method. Feature Extraction is an FCN and features are then input into Text Detection Branch and Position-Sensitive Segmentation Branch respectively. Position-Sensitive NMS is a post-processing for filtering candidates.

The overall architecture of proposed method is shown in Figure 1. First, the features are extracted through a CNN inspired by feature pyramid network [18]. Then, text detection branch and position-sensitive segmentation branch simultaneously process convolutional features. Finally, PS-NMS filters the candidates obtained by text detection branch utilizing the information from position-sensitive segmentation branch. The remaining bounding boxes are the final output.

3.1 Feature extraction

The architecture of feature extraction network is shown in Figure 2. We use ResNet-50 [6] as the backbone of this network. The feature maps output by each stage's last residual block of ResNet-50 are extracted for concatenation, and a 1×1 bottleneck convolution is used to reduce the number of feature maps. The size of final feature maps is defined as quarter size of an input image in view of the efficiency and accuracy of proposed method.

3.2 Text detection branch

In the text detection branch, a score map F_s and multi-channel geometry maps F_g are obtained [39]. The positive area of one text box on the score map is a shrunk version of the original quadrangle. The geometry maps are made up of five channels. Among them, four channels respectively represent the distances from a pixel location to the top, right, bottom, left edges of the relevant minimum enclosing rectangles of scene text, and the fifth channel represents the angle of inclination of the relevant rectangle. Candidates are obtained by the text detection branch. If the score of a pixel on the score map is higher than a threshold, the corresponding candidate is a positive one. The size and orientation of the candidate is defined by the corresponding pixels on the geometry maps.

3.3 Position-sensitive segmentation branch

Since some of the candidates obtained by text detection branch may not enclose text regions perfectly and some of them may locate on background, we utilize position-sensitive segmentation [16] to improve the precision of proposed method.

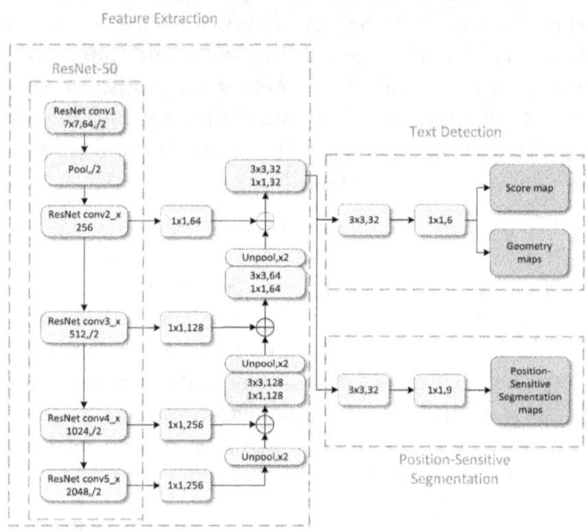

Figure 2: Architecture of feature extraction network. ResNet-50 consists of $conv1 - conv5$**. The unpooling operation is the upsampling operation implemented by linear interpolation. The feature maps of the same size are concatenated. The output of text detection branch consists of a score map and five geometry maps. The output of position-sensitive segmentation branch consists of nine segmentation maps.**

As shown in Figure 3(c), the blue candidate and the red candidate are all the candidates obtained by text detection branch. It is obvious that the average value of pixels in segmentation map involved by the blue candidate is larger since the candidate exactly overlaps with a word. False positive candidates, e.g., the red candidate in Figure 3(c), can be filtered easily by utilizing the segmentation map, as shown in Figure 3(b). It should be noticed that scene texts are often very close to each other so that their masks generated by conventional semantic segmentation are connected, as shown in Figure 3(b). If a candidate locates between two words, and it does not obviously overlap with a certain word exactly, as the red candidate in Figure 3(d), it is hard to filter the candidate according to the segmentation map in Figure 3(b), since the pixels in the segmentation map involved by the candidate are all salient although they belong to different text instances. Inspired by instance-aware segmentation [1, 5, 16], if the segmentation maps can distinguish different text instances based on different colors or channels, we can eliminate the red candidate easily, as shown in Figure 3(e). So, the proposed method utilizes the position-sensitive segmentation to generate segmentation maps which are sensitive to text instances.

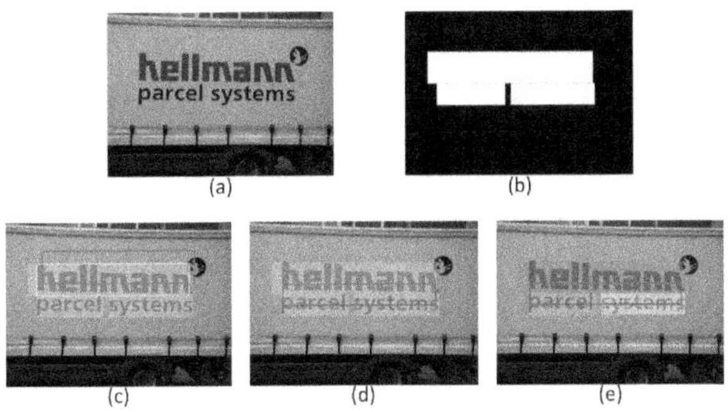

Figure 3: Instance-aware segmentation. (a) The input image. (b) The ground truth of segmentation. (c) The blue box is a truly positive bounding box and the red one is a false positive one. (d) A candidate generated wrongly can not be filtered by a conventional segmentation map. (e) Instance-aware segmentation.

In the position-sensitive segmentation branch, nine position-sensitive segmentation maps are generated through nine 1×1 convolution on the feature maps extracted by feature extraction module. The value of each pixel in segmentation maps represents the probability that the pixel belongs to a particular part of text instances. As shown in Figure 4(b), the nine segmentation maps encode the cases of {*top-left, top-center, top-right, center-left, center, center-right, bottom-left, bottom-center, bottom-right*} of text instances. In the training step, for a quadrangle given by the annotation, we first project it as a positive area onto a binary map which is quarter size of the input image. Then we draw the minimum enclosing rectangle of the positive area and set a 3×3 regular grid on it. Finally we project positive area in each grid onto the corresponding mask as the ground truth of the corresponding segmentation map.

By generating the nine position-sensitive segmentation maps, a fine-grained classification is carried out on the basis of text or non-text classification and bounding box regression. In this case, pixels are not only classified as text or non-text but also classified as whether they belong to a particular part of text instances or not, which makes the network be able to distinguish relative positions and improves the performance.

3.4 Loss Function

In the proposed method, the loss L is formulated as

$$L = L_{cof} + \lambda_{loc} L_{loc} + \lambda_p L_p, \quad (1)$$

where L_{cof}, L_{loc}, L_p denote the loss for score map F_s, geometry maps F_g and position-sensitive segmentation maps, respectively. λ_{loc} and λ_p are the weights of relevant losses. In our system, we set λ_{loc} as 10 and set λ_p as 1.

Many object detection methods use the cross-entropy loss function as the loss for a score map. The class-balanced cross-entropy loss function, which tackles the imbalanced distribution of target objects, is used in many scene text detection methods [32, 39]. In our method, We use the Generalized Dice Loss [29] function as the loss for score map, which is more suitable for segmentation and more robust when facing the severe imbalance situation [29]. It is defined as

$$L_{cof} = 1 - 2\frac{(1-\beta)P^*P + \beta(1-P^*)(1-P)}{(1-\beta)(P^*+P) + \beta[(1-P^*)+(1-P)]}, \quad (2)$$

where P^* denotes the binary ground truth of the score map and $P = F_s$ denotes the predicted score map. β is the weight for adjusting the balance between positive and negative samples. P^*P represents the sum of the products of corresponding pixels in two maps. We set β as the ratio of the number of text pixels to the size of feature map.

We adopt the loss for geometry maps L_{loc} in [39] and it is given by

$$L_{loc} = \text{IOU}(R, R^*) + \lambda_\theta(1 - \cos(\theta - \theta^*)), \quad (3)$$

where $\text{IOU}(R, R^*)$ denotes the IOU loss [13] between the predicted bounding box R and the ground truth R^*. λ_θ is the weight parameter and it is set to 10 in our system. θ denotes the predicted rotation angle and θ^* denotes the ground truth orientation.

The loss for position-sensitive segmentation maps L_p is similar to L_{cof}:

$$L_{pss} = \frac{1}{N}\sum_{i=1}^{N}(1 - 2\frac{M_i P_p^* P_i'}{M_i P_p^* + P_i'}), \quad (4)$$

where N denotes the number of segmentation maps and M_i is the i-th mask. The pixels in mask M_i are set to 1 if they belong to the i-th grid of any text's minimum enclosing rectangle and 0 otherwise. P_p^* is the ground truth for segmentation, where pixels belonging to original quadrangles are set to 1 and 0 otherwise, as shown in Figure 4(b). P_i' denotes the i-th predicted position-sensitive segmentation map.

3.5 Position-Sensitive NMS

To eliminate the redundant candidates and the false positive candidates, the PS-NMS is proposed. The PS-NMS is used to mainly handle two problems. One is that there are many candidates corresponding to the same text instance and these candidates always severely overlap with each other. These candidates contain much useful location information for text

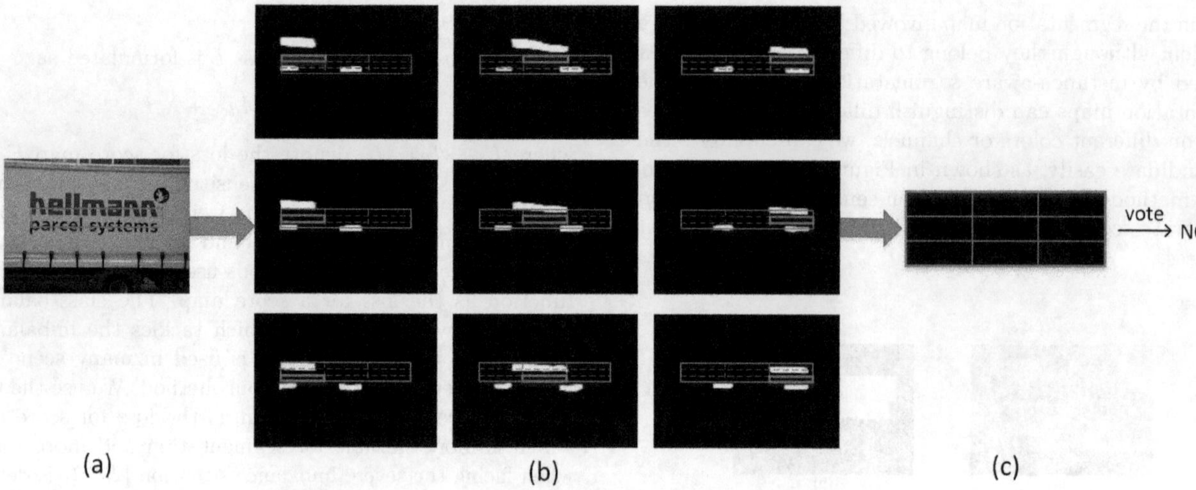

Figure 4: Position-Sensitive NMS. (a) The input image. (b) 9 position-sensitive segmentation maps. (c) The result of the red candidate through the Position-Sensitive NMS.

boxes regression and suppressing them directly seems unsuitable. The other problem is that there are many false positive candidates located on the space between words.

The proposed PS-NMS has two steps. First,we sort candidates according to the scores, compare the candidate with other remaining candidates in turn and merge them if they have a high overlap. The merged candidate's coordinates are calculated by the weighted sum of the corresponding candidates' coordinates with corresponding score values as the weights. This step has the same complexity of $O(n^2)$ as the conventional NMS. After this step, only dozens of number of candidates are left. Then we project the candidates onto position-sensitive segmentation maps and set a 3×3 regular grid on them, as shown in Figure 4(b). We can extract the value of pixels in each grid from the corresponding maps and decide whether a certain candidate encloses a text instance well by average pooling of each grid and vote. The candidates will be eliminated if their scores are lower than a threshold. As shown in Figure 4(c), a false positive candidate can be eliminated easily, while the conventional semantic segmentation fails to eliminate the candidate(Figure 3(d)). If a candidate encloses a certain text instance well, each grid of this candidate also overlaps with the positive area of the corresponding segmentation maps. Therefore, these candidates will not be eliminated wrongly. The proposed PS-NMS can effectively improve performance for multi-oriented scene text detection.

4 EXPERIMENTS

To verify the effectiveness of the proposed algorithm, we conducted quantitative experiments on two public benchmark datasets: ICDAR2015 [14] and COCO-Text [31].

4.1 Datasets

ICDAR2015 is used in the Challenge 4 of ICDAR2015 Robust Reading Competition [14]. It contains 1000 training images and 500 testing images. The scene text regions are annotated by 4 vertices of word-level irregular quadrangles. The images in this dataset are taken by Google Glasses from various scenarios in an incidental way. Therefore, it is a very challenging dataset due to motion blur, large variation in text scales, multiple orientations and complex background. In the training step, we add 229 training images from ICDAR2013 to the training set.

COCO-Text is the largest scene text detection dataset and it is from MS-COCO [19] dataset. The whole dataset consists of a total of 63686 images annotated with 43686 images as training set and the other 20000 images as test set. In this dataset, since word-level regions are annotated by horizontal rectangles, we set angle to 0.

4.2 Implementation Details

We pretrained the ResNet-50 [6] on the ImageNet [2] and fine-tuned the network on ICDAR2015 and COCO-Text respectively. We crop regions with random scales from the training images and resize them to 512×512 pixels with an invariant aspect ratio. In the training stage, we do not apply any other data augmentation. The whole experiments are conducted on Tensorflow and run on a workstation with 2.8GHz CPU, 16G RAM and GTX 1080Ti. The network is optimized by Adam and the number iteration is 10^5. The learning rate starts from 10^{-4} and decays with a factor of 0.94 every 10000 steps.

4.3 Results

Figure 5 shows some detection examples used in quanlitative study. The upper row shows the results on ICDAR2015 and

Figure 5: Results on ICDAR2015 and COCO-Text. Top: results on ICDAR2015. Bottom: results on COCO-Text.

Table 1: Results on ICDAR2015 Challenge 4 Incidental Scene Text Localization task.

Algorithm	Recall	Precision	F-score
HUST-MCLAB [14]	0.38	0.44	0.41
Zhang [36]	0.43	0.71	0.54
Yao [32]	0.59	0.72	0.65
DMPNet [21]	0.68	0.73	0.71
Seglink [28]	0.77	0.73	0.75
He [8]	0.73	0.80	0.77
EAST [39]	0.78	0.83	0.81
He [7]	0.80	0.82	0.81
Proposed	0.79	0.87	0.83

Table 2: Results on COCO-Text.

Algorithm	Recall	Precision	F-score
Baseline model C [31]	0.05	0.19	0.07
Baseline model B [31]	0.11	0.90	0.19
Baseline model A [31]	0.23	0.84	0.36
Yao [32]	0.27	0.43	0.33
He [7]	0.31	0.46	0.37
EAST [39]	0.32	0.50	0.39
Proposed	0.38	0.48	0.42

the lower row shows the results on COCO-Text. The results show that the proposed method performs well for scene text detection with large variation in scales and orientations.

Table 1 summarizes the result of the proposed method on ICDAR2015 [14] compared with previous state-of-the-art methods. In Table 1, the proposed method achieves an F-score of 0.83 and performs better than the state-of-the-art methods [7, 39]. It should be noticed that we directly input the original test images into the network without any modification. The proposed method not only uses the position-sensitive segmentation as a multiple task to improve the performance but also uses it to eliminate the candidates which are not located accurately. So the proposed method achieves a precision of 0.87 which is nearly 4% higher than the best method [39]. Besides, our method does not lower the speed of testing compared with EAST [39] since it does not increase the number of parameters of network almost, and only a dozen of candidates need to be filtered through position-sensitive segmentation maps after the merging step.

For the COCO-Text [31], the results of the proposed method and some previous state-of-the-art methods [7, 32, 39] are shown in Table 2. In our implementation, we use the identical framework and training manner as the one for ICDAR2015 while testing images are resized to 720 × 600. The proposed method achieves a precision of 0.48 and an F-score of 0.42, which is significantly higher than the above state-of-the-art methods [7, 32, 39]. The experimental result shows that the proposed method can still maintain high precision while it achieves a high recall.

Table 3 shows the effectiveness of different components of our method on ICDAR2015 [14] and COCO-Text [31]. The Proposed(without segmentation) represents the framework which does not involve position-sensitive segmentation

Table 3: The effectiveness of different components of our method on ICDAR2015 and COCO-Text text detection datasets.

Algorithm	ICDAR2015			COCO-Text		
	Recall	**Precision**	**F-score**	**Recall**	**Precision**	**F-score**
Proposed(without segmentation)	0.77	0.84	0.80	0.38	0.36	0.37
Proposed(without PS-NMS)	0.79	0.85	0.82	0.41	0.40	0.40
Proposed	0.79	0.87	0.83	0.38	0.48	0.42

branch. In this framework, the candidates obtained by text detection branch are directly filtered by NMS. The Proposed(without PS-NMS) represents the framework containing both text detection branch and position-sensitive segmentation branch, while it does not use position-sensitive segmentation maps to filter the candidates. The architecture of the Proposed(without segmentation) is similar to EAST [39] and in our implementation it achieves an F-score of 0.80 on ICDAR2015 and 0.37 on COCO-Text. When we add position-sensitive segmentation branch into the framework, the proposed(without PS-NMS) achieves an F-score of 0.82 on ICDAR2015 and 0.40 on COCO-Text. The improvement results from the position-sensitive segmentation as a multiple task and a fine-grained classification. When we add the PS-NMS operation, the proposed method achieves an F-score of 0.83 on ICDAR2015 and 0.42 on COCO-Text. For the ICDAR2015, it improves the precision rate by 2% with recall rate constant, compared with the proposed(without PS-NMS). For the COCO-Text, the recall rate decreases by 3% while the precision rate increases by 8%. It demonstrates that utilizing position-sensitive segmentation maps to filter candidates can effectively eliminate false positive candidates.

Based on the experimental results on the two datasets, it can be concluded that the proposed method performs well for scene text detection and combining position-sensitive segmentation with text detection can effectively improve the performance of scene text detection.

5 CONCLUSIONS

In the work, we present an end-to-end method for multi-oriented scene text detection. By combining position-sensitive segmentation with text detection framework, the proposed method can effectively improve the performance of scene text detection. The results on two challenging datasets, ICDAR2015 and COCO-Text, demonstrate that the proposed method outperforms the state-of-the-art methods.

Acknowledgments

This work is supported by National Key R&D Program of China under contract No.2017YFB1002203, and also supported by National Nature Science Foundation of China (NSFC) under Grant No.61772495.

REFERENCES

[1] Jifeng Dai, Kaiming He, Yi Li, Shaoqing Ren, and Jian Sun. 2016. Instance-sensitive fully convolutional networks. In *European Conference on Computer Vision*. Springer, 534–549.

[2] Jia Deng, Wei Dong, Richard Socher, Li Jia Li, Kai Li, and Fei Fei Li. 2009. ImageNet: A large-scale hierarchical image database. In *Computer Vision and Pattern Recognition, 2009. CVPR 2009. IEEE Conference on*. 248–255.

[3] Boris Epshtein, Eyal Ofek, and Yonatan Wexler. 2010. Detecting text in natural scenes with stroke width transform. In *Computer Vision and Pattern Recognition*. 2963–2970.

[4] Ankush Gupta, Andrea Vedaldi, and Andrew Zisserman. 2016. Synthetic Data for Text Localisation in Natural Images. In *Computer Vision and Pattern Recognition*. 2315–2324.

[5] Kaiming He, Georgia Gkioxari, Piotr Dollár, and Ross Girshick. 2017. Mask r-cnn. In *Computer Vision (ICCV), 2017 IEEE International Conference on*. IEEE, 2980–2988.

[6] Kaiming He, Xiangyu Zhang, Shaoqing Ren, and Jian Sun. 2016. Deep residual learning for image recognition. In *Proceedings of the IEEE conference on computer vision and pattern recognition*. 770–778.

[7] Pan He, Weilin Huang, Tong He, Qile Zhu, Yu Qiao, and Xiaolin Li. 2017. Single shot text detector with regional attention. In *The IEEE International Conference on Computer Vision (ICCV)*.

[8] Wenhao He, Xu-Yao Zhang, Fei Yin, and Cheng-Lin Liu. 2017. Deep direct regression for multi-oriented scene text detection. *arXiv preprint arXiv:1703.08289* (2017).

[9] Lichao Huang, Yi Yang, Yafeng Deng, and Yinan Yu. 2015. DenseBox: Unifying Landmark Localization with End to End Object Detection. *Computer Science* (2015).

[10] Weilin Huang, Yu Qiao, and Xiaoou Tang. 2014. Robust scene text detection with convolution neural network induced mser trees. In *European Conference on Computer Vision*. Springer, 497–511.

[11] Max Jaderberg, Karen Simonyan, Andrea Vedaldi, and Andrew Zisserman. 2014. Reading Text in the Wild with Convolutional Neural Networks. *International Journal of Computer Vision* 116, 1 (2014), 1–20.

[12] Max Jaderberg, Andrea Vedaldi, and Andrew Zisserman. 2014. Deep Features for Text Spotting. In *European Conference on Computer Vision*. 512–528.

[13] Yuning Jiang, Yuning Jiang, Zhimin Cao, Zhimin Cao, and Thomas Huang. 2016. UnitBox: An Advanced Object Detection Network. In *ACM on Multimedia Conference*. 516–520.

[14] Dimosthenis Karatzas, Lluis Gomez-Bigorda, Anguelos Nicolaou, Suman Ghosh, Andrew Bagdanov, Masakazu Iwamura, Jiri Matas, Lukas Neumann, Vijay Ramaseshan Chandrasekhar, and Faisal Shafait. 2015. ICDAR 2015 competition on Robust Reading. In *International Conference on Document Analysis and Recognition*. 1156–1160.

[15] Dimosthenis Karatzas, Faisal Shafait, Seiichi Uchida, Masakazu Iwamura, Lluis Gomez I Bigorda, Sergi Robles Mestre, Joan Mas, David Fernandez Mota, Jon Almazn Almazn, and Llus Pere De Las Heras. 2013. ICDAR 2013 Robust Reading Competition. In *International Conference on Document Analysis and Recognition*. 1484–1493.

[16] Yi Li, Haozhi Qi, Jifeng Dai, Xiangyang Ji, and Yichen Wei. 2017. Fully convolutional instance-aware semantic segmentation. In *IEEE Conf. on Computer Vision and Pattern Recognition (CVPR)*. 2359–2367.

[17] Minghui Liao, Baoguang Shi, Xiang Bai, Xinggang Wang, and Wenyu Liu. 2017. TextBoxes: A Fast Text Detector with a Single Deep Neural Network.. In *AAAI*. 4161–4167.

[18] Tsung Yi Lin, Piotr Dollar, Ross Girshick, Kaiming He, Bharath Hariharan, and Serge Belongie. 2017. Feature Pyramid Networks for Object Detection. In *IEEE Conference on Computer Vision and Pattern Recognition*. 936–944.

[19] Tsung-Yi Lin, Michael Maire, Serge Belongie, James Hays, Pietro Perona, Deva Ramanan, Piotr Dollár, and C Lawrence Zitnick.

2014. Microsoft coco: Common objects in context. In *European conference on computer vision*. Springer, 740–755.

[20] Wei Liu, Dragomir Anguelov, Dumitru Erhan, Christian Szegedy, Scott Reed, Cheng-Yang Fu, and Alexander C Berg. 2016. Ssd: Single shot multibox detector. In *European conference on computer vision*. Springer, 21–37.

[21] Yuliang Liu and Lianwen Jin. 2017. Deep matching prior network: Toward tighter multi-oriented text detection. In *Proceedings of the IEEE Conference on Computer Vision and Pattern Recognition*, Vol. 2. 8.

[22] Jonathan Long, Evan Shelhamer, and Trevor Darrell. 2015. Fully convolutional networks for semantic segmentation. In *IEEE Conference on Computer Vision and Pattern Recognition*. 3431–3440.

[23] Lukas Neumann and Jiri Matas. 2010. A Method for Text Localization and Recognition in Real-World Images. In *Computer Vision - ACCV 2010 - Asian Conference on Computer Vision, Queenstown, New Zealand, November 8-12, 2010, Revised Selected Papers*. 770–783.

[24] L. Neumann and J. Matas. 2012. Real-time scene text localization and recognition. In *Computer Vision and Pattern Recognition*. 3538–3545.

[25] Siyang Qin and Roberto Manduchi. 2017. Cascaded Segmentation-Detection Networks for Word-Level Text Spotting. *arXiv preprint arXiv:1704.00834* (2017).

[26] Joseph Redmon, Santosh Divvala, Ross Girshick, and Ali Farhadi. 2016. You Only Look Once: Unified, Real-Time Object Detection. In *Computer Vision and Pattern Recognition*. 779–788.

[27] Shaoqing Ren, Ross Girshick, Ross Girshick, and Jian Sun. 2017. Faster R-CNN: Towards Real-Time Object Detection with Region Proposal Networks. *IEEE Transactions on Pattern Analysis and Machine Intelligence* 39, 6 (2017), 1137.

[28] Baoguang Shi, Xiang Bai, and Serge Belongie. 2017. Detecting oriented text in natural images by linking segments. In *Proc. CVPR*, Vol. 3.

[29] Carole H Sudre, Wenqi Li, Tom Vercauteren, Sebastien Ourselin, and M Jorge Cardoso. 2017. Generalised Dice overlap as a deep learning loss function for highly unbalanced segmentations. In *Deep Learning in Medical Image Analysis and Multimodal Learning for Clinical Decision Support*. Springer, 240–248.

[30] Zhi Tian, Weilin Huang, Tong He, Pan He, and Yu Qiao. 2016. Detecting Text in Natural Image with Connectionist Text Proposal Network. In *European Conference on Computer Vision*. 56–72.

[31] Andreas Veit, Tomas Matera, Lukas Neumann, Jiri Matas, and Serge Belongie. 2016. Coco-text: Dataset and benchmark for text detection and recognition in natural images. *arXiv preprint arXiv:1601.07140* (2016).

[32] Cong Yao, Xiang Bai, Nong Sang, Xinyu Zhou, Shuchang Zhou, and Zhimin Cao. 2016. Scene text detection via holistic, multi-channel prediction. *arXiv preprint arXiv:1606.09002* (2016).

[33] Chucai Yi and Yingli Tian. 2011. Assistive text reading from complex background for blind persons. In *International Workshop on Camera-Based Document Analysis and Recognition*. 15–28.

[34] X. C. Yin, X. Yin, K. Huang, and H. W. Hao. 2014. Robust Text Detection in Natural Scene Images. *IEEE Transactions on Pattern Analysis and Machine Intelligence* 36, 5 (2014), 970–83.

[35] Zheng Zhang, Wei Shen, Cong Yao, and Xiang Bai. 2015. Symmetry-based text line detection in natural scenes. In *IEEE Conference on Computer Vision and Pattern Recognition*. 2558–2567.

[36] Zheng Zhang, Chengquan Zhang, Wei Shen, Cong Yao, Wenyu Liu, and Xiang Bai. 2016. Multi-oriented text detection with fully convolutional networks. *arXiv preprint arXiv:1604.04018* (2016).

[37] Shuai Zheng, Sadeep Jayasumana, Bernardino Romera-Paredes, Vibhav Vineet, Zhizhong Su, Dalong Du, Chang Huang, and Philip HS Torr. 2015. Conditional random fields as recurrent neural networks. In *Proceedings of the IEEE International Conference on Computer Vision*. 1529–1537.

[38] Zhuoyao Zhong, Lianwen Jin, Shuye Zhang, and Ziyong Feng. 2016. DeepText: A Unified Framework for Text Proposal Generation and Text Detection in Natural Images. *Architecture Science* 12 (2016), 1–18.

[39] Xinyu Zhou, Cong Yao, He Wen, Yuzhi Wang, Shuchang Zhou, Weiran He, and Jiajun Liang. 2017. EAST: an efficient and accurate scene text detector. *arXiv preprint arXiv:1704.03155* (2017).

Scene Text Detection and Tracking in Video with Background Cues

Lan Wang
State Key Laboratory for Novel Software Technology
Nanjing University
Nanjing, China
mg1633077@smail.nju.edu.cn

Yang Wang
State Key Laboratory for Novel Software Technology
Nanjing University
Nanjing, China
mf1733064@smail.nju.edu.cn

Susu Shan
State Key Laboratory for Novel Software Technology
Nanjing University
Nanjing, China
mf1433008@smail.nju.edu.cn

Feng Su*
State Key Laboratory for Novel Software Technology
Nanjing University
Nanjing, China
suf@nju.edu.cn

ABSTRACT

To detect scene text in the video is valuable to many content-based video applications. In this paper, we present a novel scene text detection and tracking method for videos, which effectively exploits the cues of the background regions of the text. Specifically, we first extract text candidates and potential background regions of text from the video frame. Then, we exploit the spatial, shape and motional correlations between the text and its background region with a bipartite graph model and the random walk algorithm to refine the text candidates for improved accuracy. We also present an effective tracking framework for text in the video, making use of the temporal correlation of text cues across successive frames, which contributes to enhancing both the precision and the recall of the final text detection result. Experiments on public scene text video datasets demonstrate the state-of-the-art performance of the proposed method.

CCS CONCEPTS

• **Information systems → Information retrieval**; • **Computing methodologies → Computer vision**;

KEYWORDS

Text detection; tracking; scene text; background; video

ACM Reference Format:

Lan Wang, Yang Wang, Susu Shan, and Feng Su. 2018. Scene Text Detection and Tracking in Video with Background Cues. In *ICMR'18: 2018 International Conference on Multimedia Retrieval, June 11–14, 2018, Yokohama, Japan.* ACM, New York, NY, USA, 9 pages. https://doi.org/10.1145/3206025.3206051

*Corresponding author

ICMR'18, June 11–14, 2018, Yokohama, Japan

ACM ISBN 978-1-4503-5046-4/18/06...$15.00
https://doi.org/10.1145/3206025.3206051

1 INTRODUCTION

The rapid development of image/video capturing, storage and processing technologies has brought significant growth of video data. Among various types of objects appearing in video, scene text usually carries rich and direct semantic meaning and is often a key and reliable category of information source in the video, and thus plays an important role in semantic-based video analysis, indexing, summarization, retrieval and many other related applications.

A wide variety of methods for detecting scene text in videos have been proposed in recent years [36], which can be divided into two main categories: individual frame based and multiple frames based. The former usually exploits the large numbers of text detection techniques designed for static images, which focus on the exploitation of visual characteristics of scene text and can be further categorized into connected component based [3, 7, 8, 19, 35] and region based [2, 13, 14, 20, 27, 30]. On the basis of text detection techniques for individual frame or image, the multiple frames based video text detection methods further exploit the temporal cues of the text across video frames to improve detection performance. Variant techniques have been proposed for this purpose such as spatial-temporal analysis [22, 32, 38], multi-frame integration [29, 31] and tracking [26, 34, 39]. Despite the promising results that have been achieved, to reliably detect scene text in videos remains a challenging task, due to the wide diversity of scene text appearance on size, style, color, layout as well as the varied contextual factors such as complicated background and lighting condition, low contrast, interfering objects, and so on.

In this paper, we propose a novel scene text detection method for videos. The main difference of our method from most existing ones is, instead of treating the background as a subsidiary or negligible information to the text, we extract both text and their background from image and exploit the correlations between the text and the background to enhance text detection performance. Moreover, we propose an effective tracking framework for text in the video, exploiting the correlation and redundancy of text cues across video frames to further enhance the accuracy and completeness of the text detection result. Fig. 1 shows the flowchart of the proposed method, which consists of three main components: 1) initial extraction of text candidates and background regions, 2) refinement

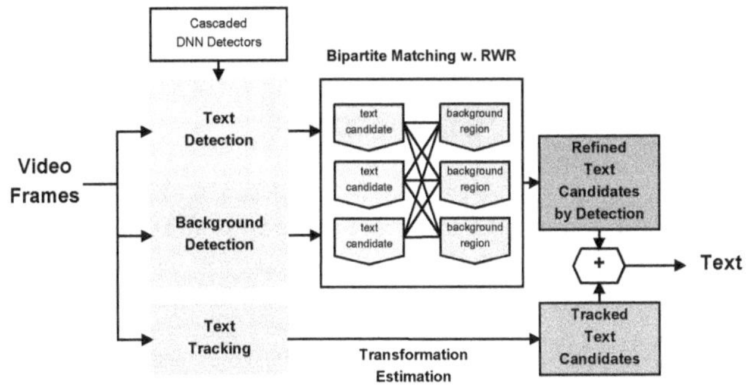

Figure 1: The flowchart of the proposed method.

of text candidates with a bipartite graph model on the basis of background regions, and 3) tracking of text across video frames.

The key contributions of the proposed method are summarized as follows:

- To the best of our knowledge, it is the first work to exploit background cues for scene text detection in videos.
- We present effective detection algorithms for scene text and their potential background regions in the video frames.
- We propose a robust matching scheme for text and corresponding background regions based on a bipartite graph model integrating variant text-background correlations and random walk algorithm, which effectively improves text detection performance.
- We propose an effective tracking framework for scene text in the video based on transformation estimation as well as a robust combination mechanism of tracking and detection, which significantly enhance both precision and recall of the detected text on the basis of the intraframe detection.

The remainder of the paper is organized as follows. Section 2 introduces the related work on text detection in videos. Section 3 describes the detection of text candidates in individual frame by a cascaded detection model based on deep neural networks. Section 4 describes the extraction of potential background regions of text and the refinement of text candidates exploiting text-background correlations. Section 5 describes the tracking framework for text in the video and the combination mechanism of tracking and detection results. Section 6 presents the results of the experiment.

2 RELATED WORK

Existing work on text detection in videos can be generally divided into two main schemes: individual frame based and multiple frames based, depending on whether the correlated text cues from different frames are exploited for the detection of text.

2.1 Text Detection in Individual Frame

Individual frame based text detection methods localize text in the video frame by frame using text detection techniques basically designed for static images, while exploit no integration measures for corresponding text cues in multiple frames. There are a variety of text localization techniques of this scheme in the literature, which can be further divided into two main categories: (1) connected component based and (2) sliding window based.

Recent works on connected component based scene text detection [3, 7, 8, 19, 35] utilize connected component analysis to extract character candidates from the image, whose pixels share similar text characteristics such as stroke width and extremal regions, and then classify the character candidates to either true text or no-text objects. For example, Stroke Width Transform (SWT) [3] and Maximally Stable Extremal Region (MSER) [16] are two widely exploited techniques for localizing potential text regions based on characteristics of text components [7, 35]. In [24], Shivakumara *et al.* presented a Bayesian classifier based text detection method that combines Laplacian and Sobel operations, followed by boundary growing to localize multi-oriented text. Yin *et al.* [35] employed an effective MSERs tree pruning algorithm based on minimizing regularized variations to extract MSERs as character candidates, and uses a single-link clustering algorithm with distance metric learning to extract text lines.

The sliding window based methods [20, 27, 30] detect text in an image by shifting a multi-scale window onto all possible locations in the image to extract relevant features and then employing certain classifiers (e.g. SVM and AdaBoost) to determine a window being text candidate or not. For example, Kim *et al.* [13] classified a window on a pyramid of images of variant resolutions into text or nontext by analyzing its textural properties using a SVM, and then applied a continuously adaptive mean shift algorithm to identify text regions. Wang *et al.* [30] used a random ferns classifier on the HOG feature of a sliding window to localize characters in an image, which are further grouped into words using a pictorial structures framework for a small fixed lexicon. Tian *et al.* [27] combined the sliding window scheme with a fast cascade boosting algorithm for detecting character candidates, which are aggregated into text lines using a min-cost flow network model.

Over the past few years, there has emerged a new development trend of adopting deep neural networks such as convolutional neural network (CNN) and recurrent neural network (RNN) for scene text detection [5, 21, 27, 28, 37]. For example, Zhang *et al.* [37] extracted text lines in the image based on the symmetry property of character groups and exploits CNN to exclude false text candidates. Tian *et al.* [28] proposed a novel Connectionist Text Proposal Network (CTPN) for localizing text lines in the image, which detects a text line as a sequence of correlated fixed-width text proposals in the convolutional feature maps using a RNN. Shi *et al.* [21] proposed an effective text detection method that uses a sophisticated CNN model to detect both the segments of text and the links between them simultaneously.

2.2 Text Detection in Multiple Frames

The individual frame based text detection methods aforementioned exploit text cues in single video frame solely. For some of the video frames that certain unfavorable detection conditions (e.g. blurring, highlight, low contrast, skew distortion) happen to present, these methods may fail to obtain reliable detection results. On the other hand, by exploiting the temporal redundancy and correlation of text cues across frames, multiple frames based text detection methods can transfer text cues detected in relatively well-conditioned frames (e.g. less motion blurring) to adjacent worse-conditioned frames to assist detection or rectify the results, thereby improving the holistic detection performance. A variety of video text detection methods following this strategy [22, 26, 29, 31, 32, 34, 38, 39] have been proposed, exploiting techniques such as tracking, multi-frame integration and spatial-temporal analysis. For instance, Khare *et al.* [12] introduced a Histogram Oriented Moments (HOM) descriptor for filtering of text candidates from sliding windows, and then identified the text based on its motion pattern computed from optical flow properties. In [11], Khare *et al.* further proposed a method combining temporal information, gradient direction analysis and boundary growing for identifying text candidates in the video. Wu *et al.* [32] exploited the spatial cues of text based on Delaunay triangulation for detecting text in video frames and a tracking algorithm of video text by matching the subgraphs of triangulation of text candidates. Yang *et al.* [34] proposed a tracking based video text detection framework, which fuses multi-information in each frame to localize text candidates, and then exploits a dynamic programming algorithm to acquire the optimal tracking trajectory and refine the detection results.

3 DETECTION OF TEXT CANDIDATES

In this work, we adopt a two-level cascaded detection scheme for extracting text candidates from individual video frames, which complementarily combines the SegLink detector model [21] and a component-level CNN classifier.

3.1 Text Candidate Localization

To extract the initial text candidates from a video frame, we employ the SegLink text detection model proposed in [21], which exploits a sophisticated CNN model to detect both the segments of text and the cross-layer and within-layer links between text segments in a fully-convolutional manner. The model uses a pretrained VGG-16 network [25] as its backbone with the fully-connected layers of VGG-16 being converted into convolutional layers and a few extra feature layers being added, for detecting text segments and links at different scales. Then, SegLink finds the connected segments of a text object using a depth-first search algorithm, and combines them into appropriate words.

3.2 Component-Level Filtering of Text Candidates

As SegLink operates on the linked windows in the image and enforces no component-level constraints of text, the bounding box of the text candidate extracted may not enclose precisely the characters, and sometimes may correspond to non-text regions that falsely exhibit certain holistic text-alike characteristics, as shown in Fig. 2. Therefore, we propose to apply a CNN-based component-level filtering on the text candidate regions to further exclude non-text ones, so as to increase the detection accuracy in a video frame.

Specifically, we first learn a CNN classifier similar to the one used in [33] based on the training character samples from the synthetic scene text dataset [4]. Then, for each text candidate region extracted by SegLink, we extract the MSERs within the region and feed them to the CNN to compute their text-alike confidence scores, which are then filtered by Non-Maximum Suppression (NMS) and averaged

Figure 2: Examples of incorrect text candidates (marked by yellow boxes) extracted by SegLink.

to acquire the holistic *text confidence* of the text candidate. By further thresholding on this confidence score, a number of false text candidates extracted by SegLink such as those shown in Fig. 2 can be effectively excluded.

4 REFINEMENT OF TEXT CANDIDATES WITH BACKGROUND CUES

Different from most existing scene text detection schemes that focus on the characterization and extraction of the text objects solely, in this work, we propose to simultaneously extract the background regions in the video frame that potentially contain text objects, such as various signs in the scene. We further exploit the correlation and conformity between the text and its background region on spatial, shape and motion cues to enhance the detection accuracy of text.

4.1 Detection of Background Regions

We adapt the method proposed in [1] to efficiently localize potential background regions of text, which are considered to be local homogeneous regions in the image that contain foreground objects of a contrasting color.

The detection process consists of three main steps. First, we divide the image into a grid of non-overlapping patches of $L \times L$ size. We then measure the homogeneity of one patch on luminance by applying three binary templates (or weight matrices) $\mathbf{W}^{(m=1,2,3)} \in \{+1,-1\}^{L\times L}$ with $\sum_{i=1}^{L}\sum_{j=1}^{L}\mathbf{W}_{i,j}^{(m)} = 0$ (as used in [1]) on the patch, which compute the luminance contrast between the two horizontally, vertically, and diagonally divided interior parts of the patch respectively. The variation $\delta^{(m)}$ of the luminance inside the patch quantified by the m-th template is then computed as $\delta^{(m)} = |\frac{2}{L^2}\sum_{i=1}^{L}\sum_{j=1}^{L}\mathbf{I}_{i,j}\mathbf{W}_{i,j}^{(m)}|$, where $\mathbf{I}_{i,j}$ is the luminance value of the pixel at position (i, j) in the patch. One patch is considered homogeneous if the L_∞ norm of the vector $[\delta^{(1)}, \delta^{(2)}, \delta^{(3)}]$ is less than a threshold $\mathcal{T}_h = 1.0$ and at least one of its four neighbouring patches also meets the same condition. We adopt a bottom-up scheme for looking for homogeneous patches in a video frame, which begins with an initial patch size $L = 2$ and iteratively doubles the patch size as long as the patch remains homogeneous.

Next, for a homogeneous patch detected in the video frame, we add all its pixels to a seed pixel set S. We then grow from every pixel $p_i \in$ S to its four-connectivity neighbouring pixels p_j, and add p_j to S if the luminance difference between p_i and p_j is less than a threshold $\mathcal{T}_g = 4.0$, which is looser than the relatively strict threshold $\mathcal{T}_h$ used for localizing homogeneous patches to accommodate local smooth variation of luminance in background regions. Such growing is repeated until no pixel can be grouped into S. The resulting connected set of homogeneous pixels is then taken as a candidate background region.

We further determine the candidate background region to be a potentially text-containing one based on localizing *valid* holes in the region, which have sufficient area and luminance contrast to the background, as a text instance typically appears. Specifically, there should exist at least one valid hole, which corresponds to the potential text, in the candidate region. Moreover, we propose two constraints on the background region and the contained holes:

(1) The number of *invalid* holes is below a threshold proportional to the area of the background region.
(2) The variance of luminance among pixels located in the inner ring (with width of $\frac{1}{8}$ region size) along the background region boundary is smaller enough, and the average luminance is similar to that of the other parts of the region.

If both constraints are satisfied, the region is considered a background region potentially enclosing certain text.

4.2 Bipartite Matching of Text and Background

The text in a video frame and its background region are correlated in variant aspects. For example, they should have the similar spatial positions and particularly, the conformable motion patterns, based on the fact that text always moves together with the object it's attached to. To exploit such correlations to refine the text detection results (i.e. to exclude false text candidates as well as reinforce the confidence of true text candidates weakened by contextual interference and degradation) on the basis of the potentially text-containing background regions detected, we propose to measure and make use of three types of correlations between a text t and its background region b:

(1) **spatial overlapping** $o(t, b)$: the proportion of the overlapping area between t and b to the area of t, which depicts the positional correspondence between text and background.
(2) **shape matching** $s(t, b)$: the ratio of the overlapping area between the holes in b and t to the area of t, which measures the matching degree between the shapes of the text and the background holes.
(3) **motional conformity** $m(t, b)$: the cosine similarity between the average optical flow vectors of t and b, which measures the consistency between the motion patterns of the text and the background region.

We further depict the matching between the text and the background regions with a bipartite graph model, in which the two disjoint sets of vertices, **T** and **B**, each constituting one part of the graph, represent the text candidates and background regions, respectively. An edge connecting one text $t \in \mathbf{T}$ to one background region $b \in \mathbf{B}$ represents the relation between t and b, which is quantified by the weight $\mathbf{w}_{t,b}$ associated with the edge. We compute $\mathbf{w}_{t,b}$ by integrating spatial overlapping $o(t, b)$, shape matching $s(t, b)$ and motional conformity $m(t, b)$ between t and b:

$$\mathbf{w}_{t,b} = o(t,b) \times s(t,b) \times \exp(m(t,b)) \quad (1)$$

It's easy to see that, the larger overlapping or the better matching of the shapes or the more conformable motion patterns between the text and the background region, the higher weight is assigned to their connection edge.

We then employ a random walk with restart (RWR) algorithm on the bipartite graph to revise the confidence of each text candidate, using the normalized weights of graph edges as the transition probabilities. Specifically, we define a background-to-text state transition matrix $\mathbf{B2T}_{M\times N}$, where M and N denote the number of text candidates and background regions respectively, and $\mathbf{B2T}_{i,j}$ is the transition probability of the random walker moving from the j-th background region b_j to the i-th text candidate t_i:

$$\mathbf{B2T}_{i,j} = \frac{w_{t_i,b_j}}{\sum_{k=1}^{M} w_{t_k,b_j}} \quad (2)$$

Similarly, we define a text-to-background state transition matrix $\mathbf{T2B}_{N\times M}$, where $\mathbf{T2B}_{j,i}$ denotes the transition probability of the walker moving from text candidate t_i to background region b_j:

$$\mathbf{T2B}_{j,i} = \frac{w_{t_i,b_j}}{\sum_{k=1}^{N} w_{t_i,b_k}} \quad (3)$$

Given the state transition probability matrices and the state distribution vector $\pi^{(l)} = [\pi_1^{(l)}, \pi_2^{(l)}, \ldots, \pi_M^{(l)}]^T$ representing the probabilities of the walker staying at the text candidate t_i at moment l, the new state distribution vector $\pi^{(l+1)}$ at the next moment $l+1$ can then be obtained as:

$$\pi^{(l+1)} = (1-\rho)\mathbf{B2T}\cdot\mathbf{T2B}\cdot\pi^{(l)} + \rho\mathbf{r} \quad (4)$$

where, the composite state transition matrix $[\mathbf{B2T}\cdot\mathbf{T2B}]_{i,j}$ depicts the probability of the walker moving from text candidate t_j (passing through any intermediate background regions) to text candidate t_i. $\mathbf{r} = [\mathbf{r}_1, \mathbf{r}_2, \ldots, \mathbf{r}_M]^T$ denotes a restarting distribution representing the probability of the walker restarting at each text candidate. ρ denotes the restarting probability, by which the random walker jumps according to the restarting distribution $\mathbf{r}$ instead of the distribution $\mathbf{B2T}\cdot\mathbf{T2B}\cdot\pi^{(l)}$.

We employ an uniform initial state distribution $\pi^{(0)}$ and use the normalized confidence scores of the text candidates computed by the CNN classifier described in Section 3.2 as the restarting distribution. Then, after iteratively updating $\pi^{(l)}$ according to Eq. (4), the converged stationary distribution $\pi_{i=1..M}$ gives the revised confidence of each text candidate in the graph, with their correlations with the background regions taken into account.

By the definition of the state transition probability (2)(3), the higher probability of the existence of background region that matches with a text candidate t will generally lead to the higher stationary probability of t, in which the background region acts as an effective filtering cue for false text candidates and thereby can be exploited to improve the accuracy of text detection. Specifically, a confidence threshold $\mathcal{T}_{conf} = 0.5$ is applied on the text candidates in the graph, and those having a revised confidence score lower than $\mathcal{T}_{conf}$ will be excluded from subsequent processing. Note that, as the elements of $\pi_{i=1..M}$ are probabilities reflecting the relative strength of confidence among text candidates in the graph, which will change with the number of candidates (i.e. M), we accordingly scale $\pi_{i=1..M}$ by M before comparing them with $\mathcal{T}_{conf}$.

5 TEXT TRACKING IN VIDEO

Text in videos are vulnerable to complex scene context, poor lighting condition as well as the degraded quality of the text, resulting in usually a number of missed detections and false alarms in extracted text candidates, which are difficult to recover based on information in individual video frame solely. Accordingly, we devise a robust tracking algorithm for text in the video to make use of temporal redundancy and correlation of text cues across successive frames, which has two aspects of contributions to the final text detection performance. First, it helps to improve the detection accuracy by identifying and discarding transient false text candidates detected in few frames, which usually have a sparse trajectory across frames. Second (and more important), it helps to significantly increase the recall of those text objects with temporarily unfavorable detection conditions (e.g. local highlight or occlusion) in some frames of the trajectory, by propagating hypotheses on the locations of the text across frames, which are estimated based on the detection or tracking results in previous frames.

Moreover, different from the existing methods for tracking text in videos that adopt a tracking-by-detection scheme based on matching text candidates detected in different frames, we propose to explicitly estimate the motion transformation of a text to generate the tracked candidate of the text apart from the detected one, which effectively complements the insufficiency of the intraframe detector faced with accidentally unfavoured detection conditions.

5.1 Tracking By Transformation Estimation

For a text candidate in the video, we model its geometric transformation across two successive video frames with a matrix $T \in \mathbb{R}^{2\times2}$, whose elements depict the potential translation, rotation and scaling transformations of the text.

Similar to [6], we estimate the transformation matrix T using a generalized Hough voting algorithm on the basis of the set of matched pixels in the text candidate region between two successive video frames. Specifically, we first densely sample in the bounding box of the text to create a set of pixel points p_i^t in frame t, then we compute the optical flow vector $\vec{\mathbf{o}}_i^t$ at p_i^t and add it to p_i^t to obtain its corresponding point $p_i^{t+1} = p_i^t + \vec{\mathbf{o}}_i^t$. Then, given every two pairs (p_i^t, p_i^{t+1}) and (p_j^t, p_j^{t+1}) of matched points between frame t and $t+1$, we estimate the values of the four transformation parameters of T by solving the linear equation system constructed on these points, which casts a vote to the corresponding bin in the 4-D Hough parameter space. We then find the K highest peaks in the Hough matrix, which correspond to the K most likely geometric transformation matrices $T_{k\in[1,K]}$ of the text. By applying each resulting transformation matrix to the position of the text in frame t, we finally obtain K candidate locations of the text in frame $t+1$.

On the other hand, some of the pixels in a video frame may lack significant enough motion cues for robust estimation of the transformation parameters. We accordingly learn a SVM classifier on-line for each text candidate being tracked, based on the HOG features of its instances in all previous frames. Then, for a text candidate p^t located at the position (x_o^t, y_o^t) in frame t whose average optical flow magnitude over pixels in its region is lower than a threshold (0.5 in this work), we scan in a local neighboring rectangle region in frame $t+1$ centered at $(x_o^{t+1} = x_o^t, y_o^{t+1} = y_o^t)$ with the height and width being 4 times of those of p^t, to find K best matched candidate locations $\{(x_k^{t+1}, y_k^{t+1})\}_{k\in[1,K]}$ where the SVM classifier yields the highest K confidence scores on the local patches p_k^{t+1} $(k \in [1,K])$ centered at (x_k^{t+1}, y_k^{t+1}) and samely sized as p^t. Note that, the patches at candidate locations generated by transformation estimation in frame $t+1$ are also evaluated by the SVM to acquire their confidence scores.

Finally, among all candidate locations (either from transformation estimation or from SVM-based scanning), the patch at the location with the highest confidence score is taken as the final text candidate generated by tracking. If this candidate's confidence score is lower than 0.5, however, it's considered an invalid text instance, so that the tracking is terminated.

5.2 Combination of Tracking and Detection

As tracked text candidates provide a reliable and important supplement to the intraframe detection results, especially for frames with significantly unfavorable detection conditions, we devise an effective combination algorithm for text candidates from both sources.

Given the two lists D and T of text candidates acquired by the text detector and the tracker respectively in one frame, the combination algorithm merges D and T into the final set of text candidates as accurate and complete as possible, by looking for an optimal matching relationship between D and T as described by Alg. 1.

Algorithm 1 Combine tracked and detected text candidates

```
INPUT: the detected (D) and tracked (T) text candidates
OUTPUT: the combined text candidates M
Compute the matching cost matrix P ∈ R^{|T|×|D|}
α ← HungarianAlgorithm(P)
M ← ∅
for each pair(t, d) ∈ α do
  if overlap(t, d) > T_ro then
    m ← merge(t, d), M ← M ∪ {m}
  else
    M ← M ∪ {t, d}
  end if
end for
```

To compute the matching cost matrix $\mathbf{P}_{t,d}$ for each pair of a tracked text candidate t and a detected text candidate d, we evaluate and integrate their similarities on position, color histogram and optical flow, which depict spatial, appearance and motion characteristics of the text candidates. Specifically, we compute the differences between the positions and color histograms of the tracked and detected text candidates by:

$$\mathbf{p}_{pos}(t,d) = \exp(\frac{\mathbf{dist}(\mathbf{t_p}, \mathbf{d_p})}{\sigma_p}) \quad \mathbf{p}_{col}(t,d) = \exp(\frac{\mathbf{dist}(\mathbf{t_c}, \mathbf{d_c})}{\sigma_c}) \tag{5}$$

where, $\mathbf{dist}(\cdot,\cdot)$ is the Euclidean distance. $\mathbf{t_p}$ and $\mathbf{d_p}$ are the centroid coordinates of the tracked text candidate t and the detected text candidate d, $\mathbf{t_c}$ and $\mathbf{d_c}$ are their color histograms, respectively. σ_p and σ_c are the normalization scale factors for the spatial and color histogram distances respectively.

To measure the dissimilarity on motion patterns between the tracked text candidate t and the detected text candidate d, given their average optical flow vectors $\mathbf{t_o}$ and $\mathbf{d_o}$, we compute the difference between $\mathbf{t_o}$ and $\mathbf{d_o}$ as:

$$\mathbf{p}_{opf}(t,d) = \exp(-\frac{\mathbf{t_o} \cdot \mathbf{d_o}}{\|\mathbf{t_o}\|\|\mathbf{d_o}\|}) \tag{6}$$

The final matching cost of the pair of the tracked and detected text candidates is then defined as:

$$P_{t,d} = p_{pos}(t,d) \times p_{col}(t,d) \times p_{opf}(t,d) \quad (7)$$

Given the list of optimally matched pairs of tracked and detected text candidates obtained by the Hungarian algorithm, the function **overlap**(t,d) in Alg. 1 further computes the overlapping area between a pair of text candidates t and d divided by the area of the smaller one, which is then verified whether to be larger than a threshold $\mathcal{T}_{ro}$ (0.3 in this work) denoting the minimum overlapping ratio of two text candidates that should be merged into one candidate. If satisfied, the function **merge**(t,d) merges two text candidates t and d into one candidate m, in which the width of m will be equal to the larger width of the two candidates, and the height of m takes the height of the detected candidate, which is usually more accurate than that of the tracked candidate.

5.2.1 Trajectory-based Filtering of Text Candidates. We maintain a trajectory for each tracked text instance during its tracking process, which is exploited to filter out falsely detected and tracked text candidates before carrying out Alg. 1, so as to increase the precision of the final result. A trajectory of a tracked text instance is created from the earliest frame that the text is initially detected, and further tracked through the corresponding text candidates found by the tracker in adjacent frames.

Specifically, as the transformation estimation may be inaccurate in certain confusing circumstances such as violent vibrations of the camera, the resulting tracked text candidate may deviate significantly from its true location or even correspond to non-text regions. To eliminate these false tracked text candidates, we record the number of frames in the trajectory of a tracked text candidate t in which t can find at least one matched peer from detection whose Intersection over Union (IoU) with t is larger than 0.4. Such frames are then identified as the *matched frames*, and we compute the proportion of the matched frames to all frames in the trajectory. If this ratio is lower than 0.5, we will regard the trajectory as invalid and discard all tracked candidates in it. Furthermore, as the text candidates by intraframe detection may also include false ones such as those corresponding to transient noises, if the proportion of the matched frames in a trajectory further falls below 0.25, the detected text candidates involved in the trajectory (i.e. those matching the tracked candidates) will be discarded as well.

Moreover, to timely stop tracking of no longer existing text candidates such as those moving out of the frame, if a tracked text candidate cannot find matched candidates from detection in more than 3 – 5 successive frames, the tracked candidates in these frames are discarded and the tracking of current trajectory is terminated.

6 EXPERIMENTS

6.1 Dataset

To evaluate the performance of the proposed video text detection and tracking method, we adopt two public scene text video datasets in the experiment - the dataset [18] and the dataset of ICDAR 2013 Robust Reading Competition Challenge 3: Text in Videos [10].

The dataset [18] consists of 5 video sequences of varied outdoor scenes, which last from around 6 seconds to 41 seconds with a typical frame rate of 30 fps and have an uniform image size of 640 × 480 pixels. The ICDAR 2013 dataset consists of 28 video sequences lasting from 10 seconds to 1 minute and including text in different languages, with the frame rate ranging from 24 to 30 fps and the image size ranging from 307 × 93 to 3888 × 2592 pixels. The text regions in the video samples may have arbitrary motion patterns and are usually affected by nature noises, low contrast, distortion, blurring, hard illumination change and occlusion.

Table 1: Comparison of Intraframe Detection Performance by SegLink and the Proposed Cascaded Model on Dataset [18] and ICDAR 2013 Dataset.

Dataset [18]

Method	Precision	Recall	F-measure
SegLink	71.1	**78.2**	74.32
SegLink + CNN (**Proposed**)	**79.9**	77.0	**78.12**

ICDAR 2013 Dataset

Method	Precision	Recall	F-measure
SegLink	54.32	**47.02**	49.38
SegLink + CNN (**Proposed**)	**56.56**	46.71	**51.05**

6.2 Evaluation Protocol

We adopt the standard evaluation protocol for text detection as used in the work [3, 35], in which, the precision rate p, the recall rate r, and the f measure (the harmonic mean value $\frac{2*p*r}{p+r}$) are used to evaluate and compare different methods.

6.3 Evaluation of Intraframe Text Detection

To verify the complementarity of the proposed CNN-based component level filter for text candidates to the Seglink [21] detector, in Table 1, we compare the performances of the intraframe text detection described in Section 3 with and without exploiting the CNN-based filter on both dataset [18] and ICDAR 2013 dataset.

As shown by Table 1, compared to exploiting the Seglink detector solely, the proposed cascaded model achieves an average increase of 3.8% on the f-measure on dataset [18] and 1.67% on ICDAR 2013 dataset. It shows that the CNN-based component-level filtering of text candidates is effective for further enhancing the detection precision on the basis of SegLink by excluding false text candidates extracted by the latter, at the cost of a slight decrease of the recall rate. This usually results from some locally interfered or degraded text (e.g. those affected by illumination change or blurring), on which the CNN filter fails due to the weakened text characteristics, while SegLink acquires the correct detection result by exploiting correlations (i.e. linkings) between segments of the text.

6.4 Evaluation of Exploiting Background Cues in Text Detection

Exploiting background cues to assist the detection of text in the video is a key component of the proposed method. To investigate its effectiveness, we compare the detection performances with and without exploiting the background cues in detection. Table 2 shows the comparison results on dataset [18] and ICDAR 2013 dataset. It can be seen that, compared to the scheme that no background cue

Table 2: Comparison of Detection Performance with (as Proposed) or without Exploitation of Background Cues on Dataset [18] and ICDAR 2013 Dataset.

Dataset [18]

Method	Precision	Recall	F-measure
Without Background Cues	80	82.55	80.96
Proposed	**88.80**	**87.53**	**88.14**

ICDAR 2013 Dataset

Method	Precision	Recall	F-measure
Without Background Cues	55.37	49.81	51.76
Proposed	**58.34**	**51.74**	**54.45**

(a) (b)

Figure 3: Illustration of the effect of background-based refinement of text candidates. (a) Text detection results without exploiting background cues. (b) Text detection results with the proposed background-based refinement. Note the false text candidates detected (marked by yellow boxes) in (a) are finally discarded in (b).

is exploited, the introduction of background-based refinement of the detection result enhances both the precision and the recall, as the non-text candidates extracted by the detector without corresponding background regions will be assigned a low confidence score by the bipartite matching algorithm and get filtered out eventually. Accordingly, the proposed method achieves a significant increase of the f-measure by 7.18% on dataset [18] and 2.69% on ICDAR 2013 dataset, compared to the scheme without exploitation of background cues.

Fig. 3 illustrates the effect of the background-based refinement on improving the text detection result. In both examples, the marked false text candidates extracted by the detector lack matched valid background regions. Consequently, their confidence scores are reduced during the random walking on the text-background bipartite graph, resulting in the exclusion of these false candidates from the refined detection result.

Table 3: Comparison of Detection Performance with (as Proposed) or without Text Tracking on Dataset [18] and ICDAR 2013 Dataset.

Dataset [18]

Method	Precision	Recall	F-measure
Without Tracking	76.12	81.22	78.34
Track w/o Trajec. Filtering	80.16	**87.69**	83.57
Proposed	**88.80**	87.53	**88.14**

ICDAR 2013 Dataset

Method	Precision	Recall	F-measure
Without Tracking	56.17	49.13	51.42
Track w/o Trajec. Filtering	57.61	**51.79**	52.73
Proposed	**58.34**	51.74	**54.45**

6.5 Evaluation of Text Tracking Framework

To evaluate the effectiveness of the proposed tracking framework for scene text in the video, we compare the text detection performances with and without combination of the tracking results in Table 3. Specifically, the latter scheme is based on the text candidates detected in every individual frame only, while the former further combines the tracked text candidates with the detected ones to yield the final result as described in Section 5. We also compare the proposed method with one variant of it (the line 'Track w/o Trajec. Filtering' in Table 3), which omits the trajectory-based filtering of text candidates.

The result shows that introducing the text tracking measures is an effective supplement to the detection capability on the basis of the intraframe detection. Compared to the intraframe detection only scheme, the proposed scheme combining tracking and detection achieves a significant increase of the f-measure by 9.8% on dataset [18] and 3.03% on ICDAR 2013 dataset, revealing the very encouraging effect of the proposed transformation estimation based tracking framework on enhancing the text detection performance on videos. Moreover, as shown by the result, the trajectory-based filtering of false text candidates is effective for improving the detection performance, which, for example, contributes to the significant increases of the precision by 8.64% and the f-measure by 4.57% with a slight decrease of the recall rate by 0.16% on dataset [18], on the basis of combining tracking and detection results.

Fig. 4 further illustrates how the proposed text tracking framework helps to tackle certain detection insufficiency. In example (a), the temporary highlight appearing on the local part of the text keeps the intraframe detection algorithm from acquiring the correct bounding box of the whole text in the affected frames, while the proposed method successfully rectifies the detection result by incorporating the tracked text candidate that is propagated from previous well-conditioned frames. Similarly, in example (b), the text missed by the intraframe detection in the current frame can be effectively recovered by the tracking algorithm based on previous successful detection and transformation estimation.

Figure 4: Illustration of the effect of the proposed text tracking framework on the detection of text in videos.

Table 4: Comparison of Video Text Detection Performance on Dataset [18] (%).

Method	Precision	Recall	F-measure
Proposed	**88.80**	**87.53**	**88.14**
Yang *et al.* [34]	85	77	81
Zuo *et al.* [39]	84	68	75
Baseline	71.1	78.2	74.32
Minetto *et al.* [18]	61	69	63

Table 5: Comparison of Video Text Detection Performance on ICDAR 2013 Dataset (%).

Method	Precision	Recall	F-measure
Proposed	**58.34**	51.74	**54.45**
Khare *et al.* [11]	57.91	**55.9**	51.7
Yin *et al.* [35]	48.62	54.73	51.56
Shivakumara *et al.* [24]	51.15	53.71	50.67
Shivakumara *et al.* [23]	51.10	50.10	50.59
Baseline	54.32	47.02	49.38
Zhao *et al.* [38]	47.02	46.30	46.65
Khare *et al.* [12]	41.4	47.6	44.3
Liu *et al.* [15]	44.60	38.91	41.62
Epshtein *et al.* [3]	39.80	32.53	35.94
Mi *et al.* [17]	26.92	40.30	32.76
Huang *et al.* [9]	32.50	32.35	32.42

6.6 Comparison with State-of-the-Art Methods

We compare the performance of the proposed method with some state-of-the-art video text detection methods on dataset [18] and ICDAR 2013 dataset in Table 4 and Table 5, respectively. We also include a 'Baseline' method in the comparison, which exploits the SegLink method [21] to perform intraframe text detection only.

On dataset [18], our method achieves the highest scores on all three evaluation metrics among the compared methods. Specifically, the f-measure of our method precedes the second best method [34] by 7.14%, which mainly owes to the enhancement of the recall score by introducing effective tracking measures for video text and combination of tracking and detection results.

Figure 5: Examples of text detection results by the proposed method.

On the more complex ICDAR 2013 dataset, in which text usually have largely varied qualities resulting from degradation, complicated illumination and contextual interference, the proposed method again achieves the highest precision and f-measure among the compared methods, with a precedence of 2.75% on the f-measure over the second best method [11]. The comparison results on both datasets demonstrate the effectiveness of the proposed mechanism of exploiting background cues and tracking measures on scene text detection in the video.

Fig. 5 shows some scene text detection results in video samples of the datasets by the proposed method, which exhibits sufficient robustness to the largely varied qualities of text in the videos.

7 CONCLUSION

We presented a novel scene text detection method for videos, which exploits the correlations between the text and its background region in video images to enhance text detection performance. We further presented an effective tracking framework for scene text in the video, which makes use of temporal correlation of text cues across successive frames and enhances both the precision and the recall of the final text detection result.

ACKNOWLEDGMENTS

Research supported by the Natural Science Foundation of Jiangsu Province of China under Grant No. BK20171345 and the National Natural Science Foundation of China under Grant Nos. 61003113, 61321491, 61672273.

REFERENCES

[1] Katherine L. Bouman, Golnaz Abdollahian, Mireille Boutin, and Edward J. Delp. 2011. A Low Complexity Sign Detection and Text Localization Method for Mobile Applications. *IEEE Transactions on Multimedia* 13, 5 (Oct. 2011), 922–934. https://doi.org/10.1109/TMM.2011.2154317

[2] Xiangrong Chen and Alan L. Yuille. 2004. Detecting and reading text in natural scenes. In *2004 IEEE Computer Society Conference on Computer Vision and Pattern Recognition (CVPR)*, Vol. 2. II–366–II–373 Vol.2. https://doi.org/10.1109/CVPR.2004.1315187

[3] Boris Epshtein, Eyal Ofek, and Yonatan Wexler. 2010. Detecting Text in Natural Scenes with Stroke Width Transform. In *2010 IEEE Computer Society Conference on Computer Vision and Pattern Recognition*. 2963–2970. https://doi.org/10.1109/CVPR.2010.5540041

[4] Ankush Gupta, Andrea Vedaldi, and Andrew Zisserman. 2016. Synthetic Data for Text Localisation in Natural Images. In *2016 IEEE Conference on Computer Vision and Pattern Recognition (CVPR)*. 2315–2324. https://doi.org/10.1109/CVPR.2016.254

[5] Tong He, Weilin Huang, Yu Qiao, and Jian Yao. 2016. Text-Attentional Convolutional Neural Network for Scene Text Detection. *IEEE Transactions on Image Processing* 25, 6 (June 2016), 2529–2541. https://doi.org/10.1109/TIP.2016.2547588

[6] Yang Hua, Karteek Alahari, and Cordelia Schmid. 2015. Online Object Tracking with Proposal Selection. In *2015 IEEE International Conference on Computer Vision (ICCV)*. 3092–3100. https://doi.org/10.1109/ICCV.2015.354

[7] Weilin Huang, Zhe Lin, Jianchao Yang, and Jue Wang. 2013. Text Localization in Natural Images Using Stroke Feature Transform and Text Covariance Descriptors. In *2013 IEEE International Conference on Computer Vision*. 1241–1248. https://doi.org/10.1109/ICCV.2013.157

[8] Weilin Huang, Yu Qiao, and Xiaoou Tang. 2014. Robust Scene Text Detection with Convolution Neural Network Induced MSER Trees. In *Computer Vision – ECCV 2014*. 497–511.

[9] Xiaodong Huang. 2011. A novel approach to detecting scene text in video. In *2011 4th International Congress on Image and Signal Processing*, Vol. 1. 469–473. https://doi.org/10.1109/CISP.2011.6099945

[10] Dimosthenis Karatzas, Faisal Shafait, Seiichi Uchida, Masakazu Iwamura, Lluis Gomez i Bigorda, Sergi Robles Mestre, Joan Mas, David Fernandez Mota, Jon Almazan Almazan, and Lluis Pere de las Heras. 2013. ICDAR 2013 Robust Reading Competition. In *2013 12th International Conference on Document Analysis and Recognition*. 1484–1493. https://doi.org/10.1109/ICDAR.2013.221

[11] Vijeta Khare, Palaiahnakote Shivakumara, Raveendran Paramesran, and Michael Blumenstein. 2017. Arbitrarily-oriented multi-lingual text detection in video. *Multimedia Tools and Applications* 76, 15 (Aug 2017), 16625–16655. https://doi.org/10.1007/s11042-016-3941-x

[12] Vijeta Khare, Palaiahnakote Shivakumara, and Paramesran Raveendran. 2015. A New Histogram Oriented Moments Descriptor for Multi-oriented Moving Text Detection in Video. *Expert Systems with Applications* 42, 21 (Nov 2015), 7627–7640. https://doi.org/10.1016/j.eswa.2015.06.002

[13] Kwang In Kim, Keechul Jung, and Jin Hyung Kim. 2003. Texture-based approach for text detection in images using support vector machines and continuously adaptive mean shift algorithm. *IEEE Transactions on Pattern Analysis and Machine Intelligence* 25, 12 (Dec 2003), 1631–1639. https://doi.org/10.1109/TPAMI.2003.1251157

[14] Jung-Jin Lee, Pyoung-Hean Lee, Seong-Whan Lee, Alan Yuille, and Christof Koch. 2011. AdaBoost for Text Detection in Natural Scene. In *2011 International Conference on Document Analysis and Recognition*. 429–434. https://doi.org/10.1109/ICDAR.2011.93

[15] Chunmei Liu, Chunheng Wang, and Ruwei Dai. 2005. Text detection in images based on unsupervised classification of edge-based features. In *Eighth International Conference on Document Analysis and Recognition (ICDAR'05)*. 610–614 Vol. 2. https://doi.org/10.1109/ICDAR.2005.228

[16] Jiri Matas, Ondrej Chum, Martin Urban, and Tomas Pajdla. 2004. Robust Wide-Baseline Stereo From Maximally Stable Extremal Regions. *Image and Vision Computing* 22, 10 (Sep. 2004), 761–767. https://doi.org/10.1016/j.imavis.2004.02.006

[17] Congjie Mi, Yuan Xu, Hong Lu, and Xiangyang Xue. 2005. A Novel Video Text Extraction Approach Based on Multiple Frames. In *2005 5th International Conference on Information Communications Signal Processing*. 678–682. https://doi.org/10.1109/ICICS.2005.1689133

[18] Rodrigo Minetto, Nicolas Thome, Matthieu Cord, Neucimar J. Leite, and Jorge Stolfi. 2011. Snoopertrack: Text detection and tracking for outdoor videos. In *2011 18th IEEE International Conference on Image Processing*. 505–508. https://doi.org/10.1109/ICIP.2011.6116563

[19] Lukas Neumann and Jiri Matas. 2012. Real-time Scene Text Localization and Recognition. In *2012 IEEE Conference on Computer Vision and Pattern Recognition*. 3538–3545. https://doi.org/10.1109/CVPR.2012.6248097

[20] Lukas Neumann and Jiri Matas. 2013. Scene Text Localization and Recognition with Oriented Stroke Detection. In *2013 IEEE International Conference on Computer Vision*. 97–104. https://doi.org/10.1109/ICCV.2013.19

[21] Baoguang Shi, Xiang Bai, and Serge Belongie. 2017. Detecting Oriented Text in Natural Images by Linking Segments. In *2017 IEEE Conference on Computer Vision and Pattern Recognition (CVPR)*. 3482–3490. https://doi.org/10.1109/CVPR.2017.371

[22] Palaiahnakote Shivakuamra, Mohamed Lubani, KokSheik Wong, and Tong Lu. 2014. Optical flow based dynamic curved video text detection. In *2014 IEEE International Conference on Image Processing (ICIP)*. 1668–1672. https://doi.org/10.1109/ICIP.2014.7025334

[23] Palaiahnakote Shivakumara, Trung Quy Phan, and Chew Lim Tan. 2010. New Fourier-Statistical Features in RGB Space for Video Text Detection. *IEEE Transactions on Circuits and Systems for Video Technology* 20, 11 (Nov 2010), 1520–1532. https://doi.org/10.1109/TCSVT.2010.2077772

[24] Palaiahnakote Shivakumara, Rushi Padhuman Sreedhar, Trung Quy Phan, Shijian Lu, and Chew Lim Tan. 2012. Multioriented Video Scene Text Detection Through Bayesian Classification and Boundary Growing. *IEEE Transactions on Circuits and Systems for Video Technology* 22, 8 (Aug 2012), 1227–1235. https://doi.org/10.1109/TCSVT.2012.2198129

[25] Karen Simonyan and Andrew Zisserman. 2014. Very Deep Convolutional Networks for Large-Scale Image Recognition. *CoRR* abs/1409.1556 (2014). arXiv:1409.1556 http://arxiv.org/abs/1409.1556

[26] Makoto Tanaka and Hideaki Goto. 2007. Autonomous Text Capturing Robot Using Improved DCT Feature and Text Tracking. In *Ninth International Conference on Document Analysis and Recognition (ICDAR 2007)*, Vol. 2. 1178–1182. https://doi.org/10.1109/ICDAR.2007.4377101

[27] Shangxuan Tian, Yifeng Pan, Chang Huang, Shijian Lu, Kai Yu, and Chew Lim Tan. 2015. Text Flow: A Unified Text Detection System in Natural Scene Images. In *2015 IEEE International Conference on Computer Vision (ICCV)*. 4651–4659. https://doi.org/10.1109/ICCV.2015.528

[28] Zhi Tian, Weilin Huang, Tong He, Pan He, and Yu Qiao. 2016. Detecting Text in Natural Image with Connectionist Text Proposal Network. In *Computer Vision – ECCV 2016*. 56–72.

[29] Baokang Wang, Changsong Liu, and Xiaoqing Ding. 2013. A research on Video text tracking and recognition. *Proceedings of SPIE* 8664 (2013), 8664–8664–10. https://doi.org/10.1117/12.2009441

[30] Kai Wang, Boris Babenko, and Serge Belongie. 2011. End-to-End Scene Text Recognition. In *2011 International Conference on Computer Vision*. 1457–1464. https://doi.org/10.1109/ICCV.2011.6126402

[31] Christian Wolf, Jean-Michel Jolion, and Francoise Chassaing. 2002. Text Localization, Enhancement and Binarization in Multimedia Documents. In *16th International Conference on Pattern Recognition*, Vol. 2. 1037–1040 vol.2. https://doi.org/10.1109/ICPR.2002.1048482

[32] Liang Wu, Palaiahnakote Shivakumara, Tong Lu, and Chew Lim Tan. 2015. A New Technique for Multi-Oriented Scene Text Line Detection and Tracking in Video. *IEEE Transactions on Multimedia* 17, 8 (Aug 2015), 1137–1152. https://doi.org/10.1109/TMM.2015.2443556

[33] Hailiang Xu and Feng Su. 2015. Robust Seed Localization and Growing with Deep Convolutional Features for Scene Text Detection. In *2015 5th ACM International Conference on Multimedia Retrieval (ICMR 2015)*. 387–394. https://doi.org/10.1145/2671188.2749370

[34] Chun Yang, Xu-Cheng Yin, Wei-Yi Pei, Shu Tian, Ze-Yu Zuo, Chao Zhu, and Junchi Yan. 2017. Tracking Based Multi-Orientation Scene Text Detection: A Unified Framework With Dynamic Programming. *IEEE Transactions on Image Processing* 26, 7 (July 2017), 3235–3248. https://doi.org/10.1109/TIP.2017.2695104

[35] Xu-Cheng Yin, Xuwang Yin, Kaizhu Huang, and Hong-Wei Hao. 2014. Robust Text Detection in Natural Scene Images. *IEEE Transactions on Pattern Analysis and Machine Intelligence* 36, 5 (May 2014), 970–983. https://doi.org/10.1109/TPAMI.2013.182

[36] Xu-Cheng Yin, Ze-Yu Zuo, Shu Tian, and Cheng-Lin Liu. 2016. Text Detection, Tracking and Recognition in Video: A Comprehensive Survey. *IEEE Transactions on Image Processing* 25, 6 (June 2016), 2752–2773. https://doi.org/10.1109/TIP.2016.2554321

[37] Zheng Zhang, Wei Shen, Cong Yao, and Xiang Bai. 2015. Symmetry-based text line detection in natural scenes. In *2015 IEEE Conference on Computer Vision and Pattern Recognition (CVPR)*. 2558–2567. https://doi.org/10.1109/CVPR.2015.7298871

[38] Xu Zhao, Kai-Hsiang Lin, Yun Fu, Yuxiao Hu, Yuncai Liu, and Thomas S. Huang. 2011. Text From Corners: A Novel Approach to Detect Text and Caption in Videos. *IEEE Transactions on Image Processing* 20, 3 (March 2011), 790–799. https://doi.org/10.1109/TIP.2010.2068553

[39] Ze-Yu Zuo, Shu Tian, Wei yi Pei, and Xu-Cheng Yin. 2015. Multi-strategy tracking based text detection in scene videos. In *2015 13th International Conference on Document Analysis and Recognition (ICDAR)*. 66–70. https://doi.org/10.1109/ICDAR.2015.7333727

Recognizing Actions in Wearable-Camera Videos by Training Classifiers on Fixed-Camera Videos

Yang Mi
University of South Carolina
miy@email.sc.edu

Kang Zheng
University of South Carolina
zheng37@email.sc.edu

Song Wang*
Tianjin University
University of South Carolina
songwang@cec.sc.edu

ABSTRACT

Recognizing human actions in wearable camera videos, such as videos taken by GoPro or Google Glass, can benefit many multimedia applications. By mixing the complex and non-stop motion of the camera, motion features extracted from videos of the same action may show very large variation and inconsistency. It is very difficult to collect sufficient videos to cover all such variations and use them to train action classifiers with good generalization ability. In this paper, we develop a new approach to train action classifiers on a relatively smaller set of fixed-camera videos with different views, and then apply them to recognize actions in wearable-camera videos. In this approach, we temporally divide the input video into many shorter video segments and transform the motion features to **stable** ones in each video segment, in terms of a fixed view defined by an anchor frame in the segment. Finally, we use sparse coding to estimate the action likelihood in each segment, followed by combining the likelihoods from all the video segments for action recognition. We conduct experiments by training on a set of fixed-camera videos and testing on a set of wearable-camera videos, with very promising results.

KEYWORDS

Action recognition; Wearable camera; Stable motion features; Sparse coding

ACM Reference Format:
Yang Mi, Kang Zheng, and Song Wang. 2018. Recognizing Actions in Wearable-Camera Videos by Training Classifiers on Fixed-Camera Videos. In *ICMR '18: 2018 International Conference on Multimedia Retrieval, June 11–14, 2018, Yokohama, Japan.* ACM, New York, NY, USA, 9 pages. https://doi.org/10.1145/3206025.3206041

1 INTRODUCTION

In this paper, we study the problem of recognizing the human actions present in a video that is taken by wearable camera, such as GoPro and Google Glass. Compared to static cameras, wearable camera can cover wider areas and better capture the actions of interest, with the subjective motion of the camera wearer. This research can benefit many important applications. In law enforcement, from the videos taken by police-officer-worn cameras, we can identify abnormal people and behavior to enhance security in public areas. In kindergarten, from the videos taken by teacher-worn cameras, we can identify kids with insufficient or atypical activities, which may imply possible social difficulties.

So far, the most effective approach for video-based action recognition is to first extract spatial-temporal motion features, and then use these motion features to train classifiers for recognizing different human actions. The performance of this approach highly relies on the consistency of the extracted motion features, which may not be well preserved when the input video is taken by a wearable camera. On one hand, the extracted motion features may not accurately reflect the desired human action by mixing undesired camera motion. On the other hand, continuous camera motion leads to varying camera view in the duration of the action, as illustrated in the bottom row of Fig. 1, and it is well known that many motion features are very sensitive to the view change. Clearly, it is very difficult to collect sufficient videos to cover all such variations, i.e., cover all possible camera motions and view changes in the duration of an action, which, however, is necessary for training classifiers with good generalization ability.

Figure 1: Sample videos from a fixed camera (top) and a wearable camera (bottom).

Identifying and compensating camera motions to construct stable motion features can effectively address this problem. If we can transform all the frames in a video and the motion features extracted from these frames to a fixed camera view, then for each action we only need to collect a relatively small set of fixed-camera videos from different view angles for training, since the space of possible fixed-camera view is of much lower dimension than the space of possible wearable-camera motion in the duration of an action. However, given the accumulated errors in estimating and compensating the camera motion between two temporally distant frames, it is difficult to transform all the frames and their motion features in a video of an action to one single fixed camera view.

*corresponding author

ICMR '18, June 11–14, 2018, Yokohama, Japan

ACM ISBN 978-1-4503-5046-4/18/06...$15.00
https://doi.org/10.1145/3206025.3206041

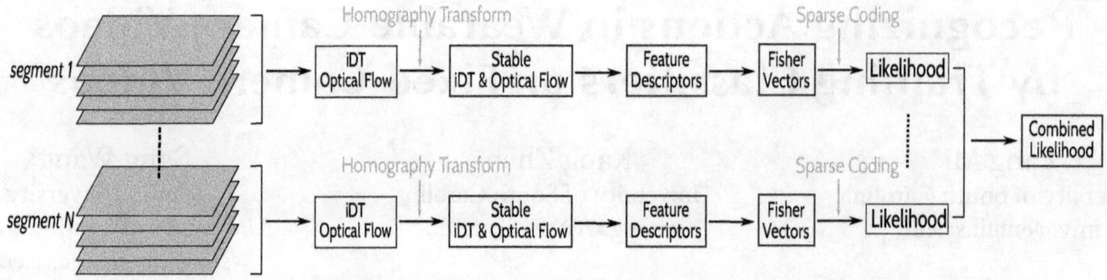

Figure 2: Workflow of the proposed method for action recognition in wearable camera videos.

In this paper, we propose a new approach to address this problem by dividing the video of an action into a sequence of shorter video segments. In each video segment, we extract *stable* motion features corresponding to a fixed camera view, defined by an anchor frame in the segment. This is achieved by computing and applying homography transforms between the anchor frame and other frames assigned to this video segment. By controlling the length of video segment, the desired homography transforms can be estimated by composing the adjacent-frame homography transforms without high accumulation errors. However, stable features extracted for different video segments correspond to different views because each video segment has its own anchor frame. Combining the stable features from all the video segments for action classification still leads to feature inconsistency.

To address this issue, we further propose to use a sparse-coding model to estimate the action likelihood in each video segment independently, followed by combining the likelihoods from all the video segments for final action recognition. In estimating the action likelihood of each video segment, its stable motion features are consistent to those extracted from the corresponding segment of the training videos, since the training videos are taken by fixed cameras in many different views. The combination of the video subdivision and motion-feature stabilization enables the action classifiers trained on fixed-camera videos to be applicable to recognize actions in wearable-camera videos. In the experiments, we apply the proposed method to recognize eight human actions: *jump, handwave, pickup, punch, standup, sitdown, kick, throw* from wearable-camera videos, with very promising results.

The remainder of this paper is organized as follows. Section 2 briefly overviews the related work. Section 3 introduces the proposed method in detail. Section 4 reports the experimental results, followed by a brief conclusion in Section 5.

2 RELATED WORK

Most video-based human action recognition approaches extract **spatial-temporal features**, such as hand-crafted features based on trajectories extracted from videos [9, 30–33, 38]. For example, the improved dense trajectory (iDT) [33] based descriptors of HOG (histograms of oriented gradients) [5], HOF (histograms of optical flow) [3], and MBH (motion boundary histogram) [31] have been shown to be effective in action recognition on many challenging datasets, e.g. HMDB51 [15] and UCF101 [28]. Recently, convolutional neural networks (CNNs) have been used to extract deeply-learned features from videos [6, 10, 13, 16, 27, 29, 35]. Many action-recognition approaches [6, 16, 29, 35] combine deeply-learned features and hand-crafted features to achieve better performance. However, most of these methods do not explicitly consider the feature inconsistency caused by camera motion.

Most recent works [1, 18, 19, 22] on **action recognition based on wearable camera videos** are focused on ego-centric action recognition, i.e., recognizing the actions of the camera wearers, which are completely different from the work proposed in this paper – our goal is to recognize the action of a performer present in the video. [19] developed an approach to recognize actions and interactions present in a wearable camera video by using iDT in foreground. This work, however, does not consider the feature stability – the foreground iDT contains both the motion of the action performer and the camera. [41] detect actions of interest from long streaming wearable-camera videos by directly extracting iDT, without computing stable features. Different from these works, in this paper we not only extract iDT, but also make them stable for action recognition.

Many recent action recognition works [9, 11, 32, 33, 38] include a step of **camera motion compensation** in extracting motion features, e.g., trajectory-based features, from videos taken by moving cameras. In [9], 2D affine motion models are used to approximate the camera motion between adjacent frames. In [38], a low rank optimization algorithm is developed to estimate camera-induced and object-induced motions: only the latter is used for action recognition. In [11], the motion patterns of dense trajectories [30] are clustered to characterize foreground-foreground or foreground-background relationships. In iDT [32, 33], dense trajectory locations [30] between two adjacent frames are transformed to a fixed view for camera motion compensation. In this paper, we extend iDT by making it stable over a video segment instead of only two adjacent frames.

Another group of related works are **cross-view action recognition** [4, 12, 14, 21, 34, 36, 39, 40], which extract view-invariant features from videos recorded in different views. In particular, [36] also used sparse coding for cross-view action recognition as in the proposed work. However, most of these works assume that videos are taken by fixed cameras. This is different from the proposed work where videos are taken by wearable cameras that may move and change view frame by frame. In the experiments, we will also show the performance of the proposed method on fixed-camera videos by comparing with several existing cross-view action recognition methods.

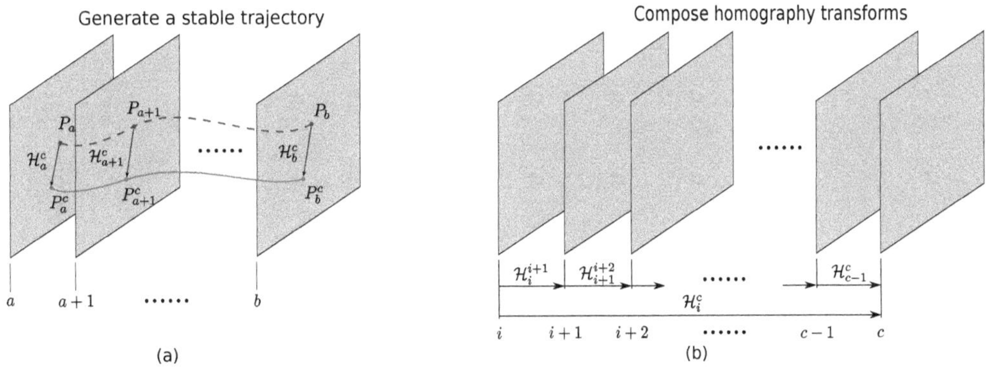

Figure 3: An illustration of (a) transforming a trajectory to a fixed camera view underlying an anchor frame c by (b) composing a sequence of adjacent-frame homography transforms.

3 PROPOSED METHOD

This paper is focused on video-based action recognition [17, 25, 29, 33], where each input video just contains one action of interest and tightly covers its duration. Our goal is to develop classifiers to recognize the action in this video. We will not tackle the more general problem of action detection from a long streaming video [20, 41]. As illustrated in Fig. 2, we uniformly divide an input video into a sequence of video segments and extract stable features for each video segment in terms of the view underlying an anchor frame. Finally we use a sparse-coding based algorithm to estimate the action likelihood for each video segment, followed by combining the likelihoods of all the video segments for action classification.

Many effective spatial-temporal motion features [9, 30–33] are defined on dense trajectories detected over multiple frames and/or optical flow calculated between adjacent frames. In the following, we first calculate stable dense trajectories and optical flow in terms of an anchor frame, and then introduce the anchor frame selection, stable feature definition and the proposed action classifiers.

3.1 Stable Dense Trajectories

Dense trajectories are points of interests and their tracking over a number of consecutive frames. In this paper, we use the iDT (improved dense trajectories) algorithm [33] to extract dense trajectories from the input video, where the trajectory length L, i.e., the number of frames traversed by the trajectory, can be priorly set. Let's consider one trajectory $(P_a, P_{a+1}, \dots, P_b)$, $b = a + L - 1$, where P_i is the location of this trajectory on frame i, $a \leq i \leq b$. These L trajectory locations (and their corresponding frames) are generated under different camera views, as in iDT. Different from iDT, to make dense trajectories stable over a video segment, we transform these locations into a fixed camera view underlying an anchor frame c in this segment. We denote the resulting stable trajectory as $(P_a^c, P_{a+1}^c, \dots, P_b^c)$. Obviously, if c is a frame traversed by the trajectory, i.e., $a \leq c \leq b$, we have $P_c^c = P_c$. We will elaborate on the selection of anchor frame later.

As illustrated in Fig. 3(a), for each trajectory point P_i, $i \neq c$, we estimate the homography transform $\mathcal{H}_i^c$ from frame i to frame c and calculate the stable location $P_i^c = \mathcal{H}_i^c(P_i)$. The estimation of the homography transform requires a set of matched feature points between the two frames and these matched feature points can be very difficult to detect when two frames are not adjacent or close to each other. To address this issue, we propose to estimate the homography transform between adjacent frames and then compose them to estimate a homography transform between non-adjacent frames. Without loss of generality, let's consider the case of $i < c$. We estimate the adjacent-frame homography transforms $\mathcal{H}_j^{j+1}$ from frame j to frame $j+1$, $j = i, i+1, \cdots, c-1$, by applying RANSAC [8] to the matched background feature points in terms of SURF descriptors and dense optical flow, as in [33]. Each estimated homography transform is represented by a homography matrix, e.g., $[h_{ij}]_{3\times 3}$ and transforms a 2D location (x, y) to (x', y') as

$$\begin{cases} x' = \frac{h_{11}x + h_{12}y + h_{13}}{h_{31}x + h_{32}y + h_{33}} \\ y' = \frac{h_{21}x + h_{22}y + h_{23}}{h_{31}x + h_{32}y + h_{33}}. \end{cases} \quad (1)$$

By composing the adjacent-frame homography transforms, as illustrated in Fig. 3(b), we can construct the transform from frame i to anchor frame c by

$$\mathcal{H}_i^c = \mathcal{H}_{c-1}^c \circ \mathcal{H}_{c-2}^{c-1} \circ \cdots \circ \mathcal{H}_i^{i+1}. \quad (2)$$

Similarly, if $i > c$, we can construct the homography transform from frame i to anchor frame c by

$$\mathcal{H}_i^c = \mathcal{H}_{c+1}^c \circ \mathcal{H}_{c+2}^{c+1} \circ \cdots \circ \mathcal{H}_i^{i-1}. \quad (3)$$

3.2 Stable Optical Flow

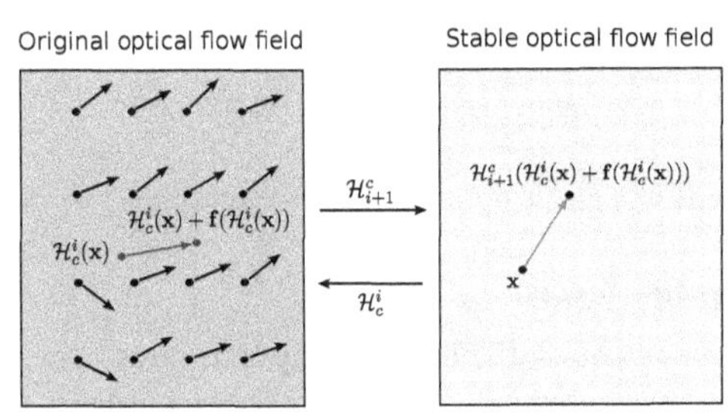

Figure 4: An illustration of calculating stable optical flow with view angle defined by anchor frame c. An original optical flow vector (blue) is transformed to a stable optical flow vector (red).

In this paper, we first use iDT to calculate optical flow on each frame of the video, and then transform this optical flow to a stable one, i.e., corresponding to a fixed view underlying anchor frame c. Note that the optical flow computed in iDT has compensated the camera motion between adjacent frames. In this paper, we

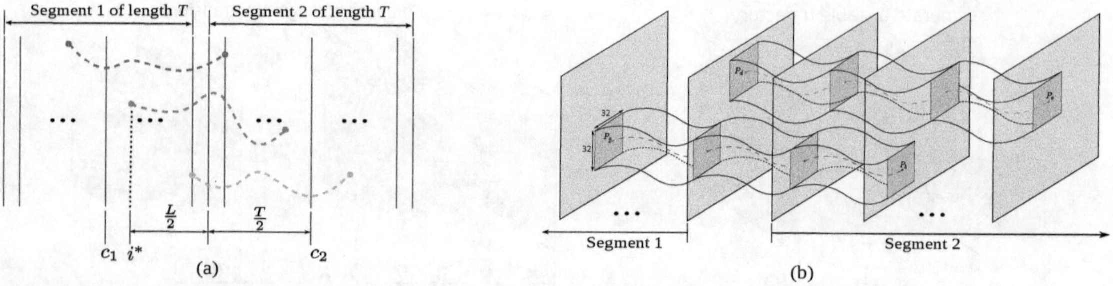

Figure 5: An illustration of (a) the temporal distance $|i^* - c|$ for composing homography transforms and (b) the bundling of the optical flow and trajectories.

further stabilize the optical flow by compensating camera motions between non-adjacent frames, i.e., between the anchor frame and one of its non-adjacent frames. Without loss of generality, let's consider the optical flow calculated on frame i which we denote as $\mathbf{f}(\mathbf{x})$. At each pixel $\mathbf{x} = (x, y)$, the optical flow vector actually points from the location $\mathbf{x}$ in frame i to its corresponding location $\mathbf{x} + \mathbf{f}(\mathbf{x})$ in frame $i + 1$. One straight-forward approach to make it view consistent is to apply the one-way homography transform to transform both endpoints of the flow vector to the view-consistent ones in terms of frame c. However, the transformed location $\mathcal{H}_i^c(\mathbf{x})$ may not show integer $x-$ and $y-$coordinates and the transformed optical-flow vector field may not uniformly cover the image. We need to perform 2D interpolation on the transformed non-uniform 2D vector field to estimate the view-consistent optical flow at each pixel, which can introduce high inaccuracies.

We propose a two-way homography transform to address this problem. As illustrated in Fig. 4, starting from each pixel $\mathbf{x}$ on frame i after transforming to the fixed view, we first estimate its corresponding location on the original frame i as $\mathcal{H}_c^i(\mathbf{x})$. On the original frame i, we have uniform optical flow field $\mathbf{f}(\cdot)$ available for each integer-coordinate pixel. Therefore, even if $\mathcal{H}_c^i(\mathbf{x})$ has non-integer coordinates, we can perform 2D interpolation to get an accurate estimation of the optical flow at this location, which we denote as $\mathbf{f}(\mathcal{H}_c^i(\mathbf{x}))$. This way, we estimate the flow location on the original frame $i + 1$ as $\mathcal{H}_c^i(\mathbf{x}) + \mathbf{f}(\mathcal{H}_c^i(\mathbf{x}))$ and its stable location in the fixed view underlying frame c is $\mathcal{H}_{i+1}^c(\mathcal{H}_c^i(\mathbf{x}) + \mathbf{f}(\mathcal{H}_c^i(\mathbf{x})))$. Based on this, after transforming to the fixed view, at each pixel $\mathbf{x}$ on frame i, we can calculate a stable flow vector as

$$\mathcal{H}_{i+1}^c(\mathcal{H}_c^i(\mathbf{x}) + \mathbf{f}(\mathcal{H}_c^i(\mathbf{x}))) - \mathbf{x},$$

which leads to a stable optical flow field on frame i.

3.3 Stable Features

As mentioned above, the homography transform between non-adjacent frames is computed by composing a sequence of adjacent-frame homography transforms. In practice, each adjacent-frame homography transform may contain an error and such errors may accumulate in composition. The larger the value of $|i - c|$, i.e., the temporal distance between frame i and the anchor frame c, the higher the accumulated errors in constructing $\mathcal{H}_c^i$ and $\mathcal{H}_i^c$. In this paper, we relieve such accumulation errors by uniformly dividing the input video into N shorter video segments, as well as selecting an appropriate anchor frame for each video segment.

More specifically, we first apply iDT algorithm to detect length-L dense trajectories on the input video and assign each detected trajectory to the video segment with the largest temporal overlap. Let T be the length of video segment for the considered input video. Typically, we have $L < T$ and by picking the *middle frame as the anchor frame* c for a video segment, we will have smallest possible $|i^* - c| \approx \frac{T+L}{2}$, where i^* indicates the furthest frame (from frame c) that may contain a trajectory location to be transformed to the view underlying frame c, as shown by the red trajectory in Fig. 5(a). For optical flow, it is calculated on each frame using the algorithm in [7]. As in [33], optical flow is bundled with trajectories in defining motion features: optical flow near/around a trajectory, e.g., a 32×32-pixel region around the trajectory on each frame, is included to the video segment to which the trajectory is assigned. As a result, the frames traversed by the trajectory will be assigned to the same video segment and their optical flow will be transformed to the corresponding fixed view. Some frames may be traversed by multiple trajectories that are assigned to different video segments. The optical flow in these frames, e.g., the three middle frames in Fig. 5(b), need to be transformed to different fixed views when bundled to different trajectories. Given the bundling of optical flow and trajectories, we have the same $|i^* - c| \approx \frac{T+L}{2}$ in computing stable optical flows.

To improve the robustness and efficiency of feature extraction, we only extract features associated to the detected person, in the form of a rectangular bounding box on each frame. As in [33], we calculate the motion features of HOF (histograms of optical flow) [3] and MBH (motion boundary histogram) [31] for each video segment, but using the proposed stable trajectories and optical flow. Stable trajectories that are partly located outside any involved frame will be discarded in calculating these motion features. Also following [33], we calculate the appearance feature of HOG (histograms of oriented gradients) [5] without any further transforms. For each video segment, we finally construct a feature vector by concatenating Fisher vectors [23] of stable trajectories, HOG, HOF and MBH, with normalizations. Camera motion over a video segment has been compensated in computing the motion features and therefore, the motion features are consistent to the ones extracted from a fixed camera over the video segment. Together with the video-segment based action classifiers to be discussed in the following, we can achieve the goal of training the action classifiers on fixed-camera videos and then applying them to process wearable-camera videos. The original iDT can only provide feature stabilization between

Figure 6: Exemplar frames of the collected videos for the eight different actions of interest, where each column shows one action separately, The first and second rows show the videos collected in two different scenarios respectively.

two adjacent frames, and this local stabilization could not provide sufficient information for action classification.

3.4 Action Classifiers

Based on the stable features extracted in each video segment, we use a sparse-coding model for supervised action recognition [2]. More specifically, we estimate the likelihood of action k on a video V as $\mathcal{P}(k|V) = \frac{1}{N}\sum_{j=1}^{N}\mathcal{P}(k|V^j)$, where V^j is the j-th video segment and

$$\mathcal{P}(k|V^j) = \frac{1}{\sqrt{2\pi\sigma^2}}\exp\left(\frac{-\|\mathbf{p}^j - \mathbf{A}_k^j\mathbf{z}^*\|^2}{2\sigma^2}\right) \quad (4)$$

with $\mathbf{p}^j$ being the stable feature extracted from video segment V^j, $\mathbf{A}_k^j$ being the basis matrix for the j-th segment of the action k. The sparse-coding coefficient $\mathbf{z}^*$ can be calculated by

$$\mathbf{z}^* = \min_{\mathbf{z}}\{\|\mathbf{p}^j - \mathbf{A}_k^j\mathbf{z}\|^2 + \lambda\|\mathbf{z}\|_0\}. \quad (5)$$

The basis matrix $\mathbf{A}_k^j$ is constructed from a set of training video samples of action k – Each row of $\mathbf{A}_k^j$ is the feature vector extracted from the j-th segment of a training video. We use the $\mathbf{L}^1$ norm approximation via Orthogonal Matching Pursuit (OMP) implementation [26] to solve this minimization problem.

As mentioned in Section 1, given that the features extracted in each video segment is stable, i.e., corresponding to a fixed view, we only need collect training video samples such that 1) the camera view stay unchanged in each video segment, 2) training videos well cover all possible camera views in each video segment. This can be achieved by using fixed-camera videos – *for each action, we simply use fixed cameras to collect multiple videos of this action from different views as the training set.* In practice, due to the use of the sparse-coding model, we only need to collect videos from a sparsely sampled set of views for training. The constructed basis matrix $\mathbf{A}_k^j$ can help represent features from other views not covered in the training videos. This not only reduces the load and difficulty in collecting the training videos, but also improves the algorithm efficiency.

4 EXPERIMENTS

4.1 Dataset and Experimental Setup

The proposed method takes fixed-camera videos from different views for training (as the basis of the sparse-coding matrix) and then test on videos taken by wearable cameras with complex motions. We did not find existing video datasets that are appropriate for our experiments. Therefore, we collect our own video dataset, which will be released to public. We choose eight human actions that are very common in daily life: *jump, handwave, pickup, punch, standup, sitdown, kick, throw.* Each of the collected video reflects one of these actions, as illustrated in Fig. 6. In each video, only one person (the performer of action) is present and the video temporally well cover the duration of the underlying action. The average length of the collected videos is approximately 3.5 seconds. All the videos are recorded by GoPro cameras with 30fps frame rate. Each frame is downsampled to the spatial resolution of 720 × 405 pixels.

Training data are collected in an outdoor setting by fixed cameras that faces the performer from eight uniformly distributed horizontal views. For each action, we take ten videos from each view, resulting in 640 training videos in total. For the testing data, each video also contains one action performed by one person. But it is taken by a GoPro camera worn by a camera wearer over his head. The wearer freely moves in recording the action of the performer – the wearer's motion includes both body motion, such as walking, and head motion, such as head rotation. Four different performers and five different camera wearers are used to collect the testing videos. The testing videos are recorded in two different outdoor scenarios. One of them is in an area surrounded by buildings which is the same scenario where we collect the training videos. The other scenario is an open playground. We collected 237 and 171 testing videos in the first and second scenarios respectively, which leads to 408 videos in total, with 51 testing videos for each action. We annotate these videos for the performer (in the form of a bounding box on each frame) and each instance of the actions, by using the open-source video annotation tool of VATIC [24].

For feature descriptors, we choose trajectory length $L = 9$. Other than using the proposed stable iDT and stable optical flow to replace the original iDT and optical flow, all the other settings and parameters in defining HOG and MBH follow [33]. Different from [33], we use 8 bins without an additional zero bin, for HOF. In particular, optical flow is bundled to nearby trajectories for defining these feature descriptors and their bundling relation is defined by a distance no more than 32 pixels in both x- and y-directions on each frame. The dimensions of these descriptors are: 18 for stable trajectories, 96 for HOG, 96 for HOF and 192 for MBH.

We use the fisher vector [23] for feature encoding., For each type of feature descriptor, we construct a 256-component Gaussian Mixture Model (GMM) using 256,000 randomly sampled features from our training data. We follow the setting in [23] to encode features into fisher vectors and normalize them, within each segment of each video. Finally, we concatenate the normalized fisher vectors of different feature descriptors as the feature vector of this video segment.

One sparse-coding (SC) classifier is trained for each action. We divide each video (either training and testing one) into $N = 10$ equal-length video segments. We set parameters $\sigma = 6$ in Eq. (4) and $\lambda = 10^{-2}$ in Eq. (5). The action $k^* = \arg\max_k \mathcal{P}(k|V)$ with the highest likelihood will be taken as the recognized action for video V.

4.2 Results

Figure 7 shows the action recognition accuracies of the proposed method on the testing data, when dividing each video into different number of video segments. We can see that, when dividing a video into $N = 10$ segments, we achieve the highest accuracy of 70.1%. An overly large N may lead to very short video segments with low-discriminative motion features. An overly small N, e.g., $N = 1$ (no video subdivision), may lead to very long video segments with high accumulation errors in composing homography transforms for computing stable features. We use $N = 10$ for the remaining experiments.

Figure 8 shows the recognition accuracy for each action class in each recording scenario. Figure 9 shows the confusion matrix of the proposed method on the testing data. We can see that the performance on the testing data collected in the second scenario is not good as that in the first scenario. This is partly due to the use of the first scenario for collecting the training data. Actions *jump* and *kick* show high accuracy, because their features are more discriminative than other action classes. Recognition accuracy of *handwave* are low since they only involve relatively small-scale hand movements.

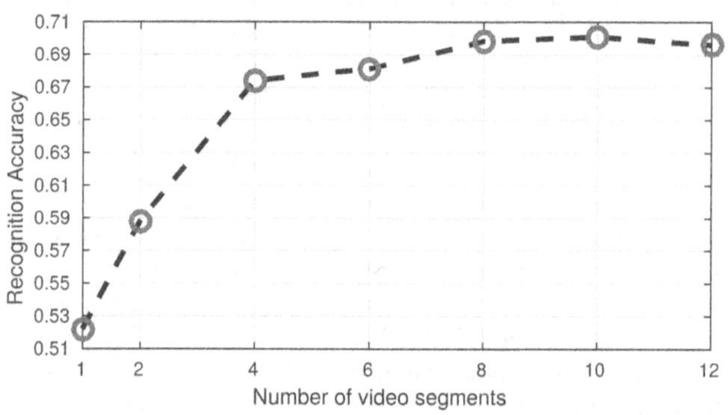

Figure 7: The testing performance of the proposed method, when dividing each video into different number of video segments.

Figure 10 shows the accumulation error in composing homography transforms over a temporal distance $|i - c|$. We can see that, with the increase of $|i - c|$, the composed homography transform gets more inaccurate – the (red) edge points in the background of anchor frame c are dislocated from the edge after applying the composed homography transform over a sequence of 11 frames, i.e., $i = c - 11$. In this paper, we divide each video into shorter video segments to avoid such accumulation errors.

We choose three existing methods for comparison. The first one is Zheng et al [41], where videos from two different fixed views are taken for training. It uses traditional iDT, HOG, HOF and MBH features, encoded by bag-of-features (BOF). Sparse coding is used as the classifiers. The second one is Wang et al [32], which detects iDT for action recognition, with camera motion compensated between adjacent frames. It uses iDT, HOG, HOF and MBH features encoded by the fisher vector [23]. A linear SVM (support vector machine) is used as the classifiers. The third one is Tran et al [29], where deep 3D convolutional networks are used to learn deep features. All the deep features are extracted from fixed-length video clips without any further feature encoding, followed by using linear SVM as the classifiers. Wang et al [32] and Tran et al [29] have reported state-of-the-art performances on several challenging action recognition datasets, including UCF101 [28], which contains videos recorded by moving cameras. For all the three comparison methods, we use their default settings and parameters.

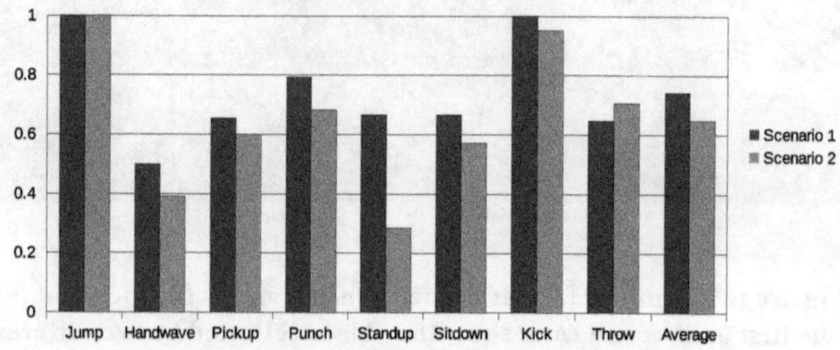

Figure 8: The recognition accuracy of the proposed method for each action class and each recording scenario.

	Jump	Handwave	Pickup	Punch	Standup	Sitdown	Kick	Throw
Jump	1.00	0.00	0.00	0.00	0.00	0.00	0.00	0.00
Handwave	0.02	0.45	0.00	0.12	0.00	0.08	0.18	0.16
Pickup	0.00	0.00	0.63	0.00	0.20	0.14	0.04	0.00
Punch	0.00	0.00	0.00	0.75	0.02	0.16	0.04	0.04
Standup	0.00	0.00	0.02	0.00	0.51	0.45	0.02	0.00
Sitdown	0.02	0.00	0.00	0.02	0.31	0.63	0.02	0.00
Kick	0.00	0.00	0.00	0.00	0.00	0.00	0.98	0.02
Throw	0.00	0.00	0.00	0.00	0.06	0.08	0.20	0.67

Figure 9: Confusion matrix of the proposed method on the testing data.

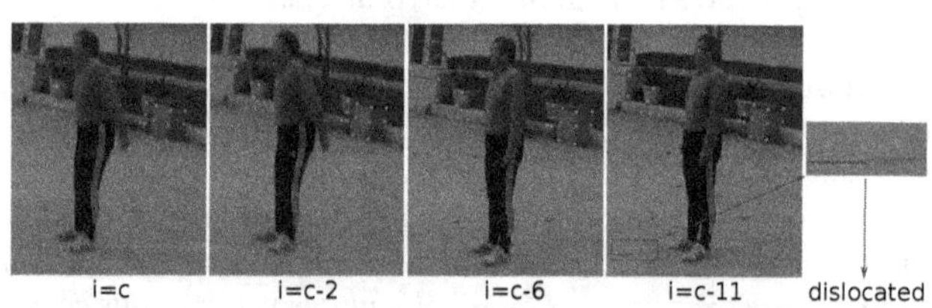

Figure 10: An illustration of accumulation error in composing homography transforms.

Method	Training Set	Testing Set	Classifier	Accuracy
Zheng et al [41]	Fixed-camera videos from eight views	All wearable-camera videos	Sparse coding	25%
Tran et al [29]	Fixed-camera videos from eight views	All wearable-camera videos	linear SVM	20.1%
	One subset of wearable-camera videos	The other subset of wearable-camera videos	linear SVM	34.1%
Wang et al [32]	Fixed-camera videos from eight views	All wearable-camera videos	linear SVM	54.4%
	One subset of wearable-camera videos	The other subset of wearable-camera videos	linear SVM	45.8%
Baseline	Fixed-camera videos from eight views	All wearable-camera videos	Sparse coding	55.6%
Proposed + linear SVM	Fixed-camera videos from eight views	All wearable-camera videos	linear SVM	62.3%
Proposed	Fixed-camera videos from eight views	All wearable-camera videos	Sparse coding	**70.1%**

Table 1: Comparison results against several existing action recognition methods on the testing dataset.

From Table 1, we can see that, when trained on fix-camera videos and testing on wearable-camera videos, all three comparison methods obtain much lower action recognition accuracy, than the proposed method, due to serious feature inconsistency between training data and testing data. Another approach to address this feature inconsistency problem is to use wearable camera videos for training. We conduct additional experiments for Wang et al [32] and Tran et al [29] by randomly separating all the collected wearable camera videos into two subsets of similar size: one subset used for training and the other subset used for testing. This way, we can perform two-fold cross-validation for performance evaluation. From Table 1, we can see that, by using wearable camera videos for training, Wang et al [32] even does not show any performance improvement over the use of fixed camera videos for training. The main reason is the complexity of the wearable camera motion in practice: it is difficult to use a limited number of training videos to cover all the possible motions of wearable cameras in the duration of an action.

The effectiveness of sparse-coding (SC) classifier is also verified: if we replace them by linear SVMs in the proposed method, the action recognition accuracy substantially decreases, as shown in the row of "Proposed + Linear SVM" in Table 1. The main reason is that sparse coding can linearly combine the features from seen views to approximate the features from unseen views. In Table 1, we also include the performance of a "Baseline" method, which follows the general setting of the proposed method, but does not divide each video into segments, i.e., $N = 1$, and does not transform the trajectories and optical flow to stable ones. We can see that "Baseline" performs much worse than the proposed method with $N = 10$. This further verifies the effectiveness of the proposed video subdivision and feature stabilization methods.

Figure 11 shows the recognition accuracy in terms of each action class, using the proposed method and the three comparison methods, respectively. Note that, for Tran et al [29] and Wang et al [32], their performances are dependent on the adopted training set. As shown in Table 1, Tran et al [29] performs better when using wearable camera videos for training, while Wang et al [32] performs better when using 640 fixed camera videos for training. In Fig. 11, we report the best performance for each of these comparison methods. We can see that, the proposed method outperforms the comparison methods on six out of eight action classes, and achieves the second highest performance in the other two action classes. We notice that the comparison methods also show low accuracy on the action of *handwave*, where Wang et al [32] obtains an accuracy of indeed 0%, due to only small-scale motion of hand.

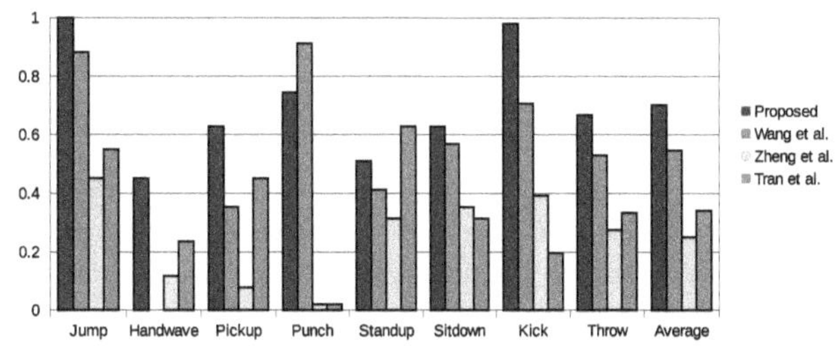

Figure 11: Per-class action recognition accuracy of the proposed method and comparison methods on the testing dataset.

4.3 Results on Fixed-Camera Videos

We also conduct experiments on a multi-view action recognition dataset IXMAS [37], to further test the performance of the proposed method on fixed-camera videos, and show the effectiveness of the proposed video-subdivision approach and the sparse-coding classifier. The IXMAS dataset contains twelve human actions, each of which is performed three times by eleven actors, and recorded by four side view cameras and one top view camera. The proposed method is trained on the data from four views and tested on the data from the remaining view. We still divide each video into 10 video segments as in Section 4.2.

Method	Cam1	Cam2	Cam3	Cam4	Cam5	Average
Junejo et al [12]	66.6%	65.5%	65.0%	62.4%	49.6%	61.9%
Yan et al [39]-1	75.5%	74.6%	77.1%	69.7%	63.3%	72.1%
Yan et al [39]-2	77.3%	74.1%	79.3%	71.3%	65.1%	73.4%
Wang et al [36]	81.9%	82.1%	80.5%	78.5%	73.0%	79.2%
Ciptadi et al [4]	83.9%	81.8%	87.6%	83.0%	73.6%	82.0%
Proposed	**97.5%**	**98.2%**	**95.5%**	**91.2%**	**79.0%**	**92.3%**

Table 2: Action recognition performance of the proposed method and several comparison methods on the IXMAS dataset.

Figure 12 shows the confusion matrix of the proposed method on the IXMAS dataset. Table 2 shows the recognition accuracies of the proposed method and several comparison cross-view action recognition methods, on this dataset. Cam *i* indicates the case of

	Checkwatch	Crossarms	Scratchhead	Sitdown	Getup	Turnaround	Walk	Wave	Punch	Kick	Pickup	Point
Checkwatch	0.91	0.00	0.02	0.02	0.01	0.00	0.01	0.00	0.00	0.00	0.00	0.03
Crossarms	0.01	0.70	0.08	0.03	0.05	0.00	0.01	0.02	0.01	0.04	0.01	0.04
Scratchhead	0.00	0.01	0.90	0.01	0.01	0.00	0.00	0.05	0.01	0.00	0.00	0.02
Sitdown	0.00	0.00	0.00	0.99	0.00	0.00	0.00	0.00	0.00	0.00	0.01	0.00
Getup	0.00	0.00	0.00	0.00	0.99	0.00	0.00	0.00	0.00	0.00	0.01	0.00
Turnaround	0.00	0.00	0.00	0.04	0.02	0.92	0.01	0.00	0.00	0.00	0.01	0.00
Walk	0.00	0.00	0.00	0.00	0.00	0.01	0.99	0.00	0.00	0.00	0.00	0.00
Wave	0.01	0.00	0.01	0.00	0.00	0.00	0.00	0.96	0.00	0.01	0.00	0.00
Punch	0.00	0.00	0.02	0.00	0.02	0.00	0.00	0.01	0.90	0.03	0.02	0.00
Kick	0.01	0.00	0.00	0.01	0.01	0.00	0.00	0.00	0.00	0.96	0.01	0.01
Pickup	0.00	0.00	0.00	0.01	0.00	0.00	0.00	0.00	0.00	0.00	0.99	0.00
Point	0.04	0.00	0.04	0.01	0.01	0.00	0.00	0.02	0.01	0.01	0.02	0.84

Figure 12: Confusion matrix of the proposed method on the IXMAS dataset.

testing on data from view-i, and training on data from other four views. We can see that, in general, the action recognition accuracies on fixed-camera videos are much higher than those on wearable-camera videos. On this dataset, the proposed method outperforms all the comparison methods. We believe this owes to the capability of sparse coding in using motion features taken from very few sparse views to represent the ones taken from many other views. The result proves the effectiveness of the proposed video subdivision approach and the sparse-coding classifier. It also shows that the proposed method can deal with the fixed-camera videos. The recognition accuracies of *crossarms* and *point* are low due to their small-scale motions involving only a small part of the body. Performance on "Cam5" is worse, because the classifiers are trained on the data from four side views and tested on the data from the top view.

5 CONCLUSION

This paper introduced an approach to recognizing human actions in wearable-camera videos by training classifiers on fixed-camera videos. In this method, we first divided a video of an action into a sequence of shorter video segments, and then extracted stable motion features in each video segment, by transforming them to a fixed view defined by an anchor frame in this segment. We then used a sparse-coding model to compute the action likelihood for each video segment independently, and finally averaged the likelihoods over all the video segments for action recognition. The combination of video subdivision and feature stabilization enables the motion feature consistency between training (fixed-camera) videos and testing (wearable-camera) videos. We tested the proposed method on both wearable/fixed-camera videos, with competitive results. We believe the proposed method can also handle action recognition in videos taken by other moving cameras, besides wearable cameras. We plan to study this in the future.

Acknowledgment This work was supported in part by NSFC-61672376 and NSF-1658987.

REFERENCES

[1] Alejandro Betancourt, Pietro Morerio, Carlo S Regazzoni, and Matthias Rauterberg. 2015. The evolution of first person vision methods: A survey. *IEEE Transactions on Circuits and Systems for Video Technology* 25, 5 (2015), 744–760.

[2] Yu Cao, Daniel Barrett, Andrei Barbu, Siddharth Narayanaswamy, Haonan Yu, Aaron Michaux, Yuewei Lin, Sven Dickinson, Jeffrey Mark Siskind, and Song Wang. 2013. Recognize human activities from partially observed videos. In *Proceedings of the IEEE Conference on Computer Vision and Pattern Recognition.* 2658–2665.

[3] Rizwan Chaudhry, Avinash Ravichandran, Gregory Hager, and René Vidal. 2009. Histograms of oriented optical flow and binet-cauchy kernels on nonlinear dynamical systems for the recognition of human actions. In *Proceedings of the IEEE Conference on Computer Vision and Pattern Recognition.* 1932–1939.

[4] Arridhana Ciptadi, Matthew S Goodwin, and James M Rehg. 2014. Movement pattern histogram for action recognition and retrieval. In *Proceedings of the European Conference on Computer Vision.* 695–710.

[5] Navneet Dalal and Bill Triggs. 2005. Histograms of oriented gradients for human detection. In *Proceedings of the IEEE Conference on Computer Vision and Pattern Recognition*, Vol. 1. 886–893.

[6] César Roberto de Souza, Adrien Gaidon, Eleonora Vig, and Antonio Manuel López. 2016. Sympathy for the details: Dense trajectories and hybrid classification architectures for action recognition. In *Proceedings of the European Conference on Computer Vision.* 697–716.

[7] Gunnar Farnebäck. 2003. Two-frame motion estimation based on polynomial expansion. *Image analysis* (2003), 363–370.

[8] Martin A Fischler and Robert C Bolles. 1981. Random sample consensus: a paradigm for model fitting with applications to image analysis and automated cartography. *Commun. ACM* 24, 6 (1981), 381–395.

[9] Mihir Jain, Herve Jegou, and Patrick Bouthemy. 2013. Better exploiting motion for better action recognition. In *Proceedings of the IEEE Conference on Computer Vision and Pattern Recognition.* 2555–2562.

[10] Shuiwang Ji, Wei Xu, Ming Yang, and Kai Yu. 2013. 3D convolutional neural networks for human action recognition. *IEEE Transactions on Pattern Analysis and Machine Intelligence* 35, 1 (2013), 221–231.

[11] Yu-Gang Jiang, Qi Dai, Xiangyang Xue, Wei Liu, and Chong-Wah Ngo. 2012. Trajectory-based modeling of human actions with motion reference points. In *Proceedings of the European Conference on Computer Vision.* 425–438.

[12] Imran N Junejo, Emilie Dexter, Ivan Laptev, and Patrick Perez. 2011. View-independent action recognition from temporal self-similarities. *IEEE Transactions on Pattern Analysis and Machine Intelligence* 33, 1 (2011), 172–185.

[13] Andrej Karpathy, George Toderici, Sanketh Shetty, Thomas Leung, Rahul Sukthankar, and Li Fei-Fei. 2014. Large-scale video classification with convolutional neural networks. In *Proceedings of the IEEE Conference on Computer Vision and Pattern Recognition.* 1725–1732.

[14] Yu Kong, Zhengming Ding, Jun Li, and Yun Fu. 2017. Deeply Learned View-Invariant Features for Cross-View Action Recognition. *IEEE Transactions on Image Processing* 26, 6 (2017), 3028–3037.

[15] Hildegard Kuehne, Hueihan Jhuang, Estíbaliz Garrote, Tomaso Poggio, and Thomas Serre. 2011. HMDB: A large video database for human motion recognition. In *Proceedings of the IEEE International Conference on Pattern Recognition.* 2556–2563.

[16] Yingwei Li, Weixin Li, Vijay Mahadevan, and Nuno Vasconcelos. 2016. Vlad3: Encoding dynamics of deep features for action recognition. In *Proceedings of the IEEE Conference on Computer Vision and Pattern Recognition.* 1951–1960.

[17] Xiaodan Liang, Liang Lin, and Liangliang Cao. 2013. Learning latent spatio-temporal compositional model for human action recognition. In *Proceedings of the ACM Multimedia Conference.* 263–272.

[18] Minghuang Ma, Haoqi Fan, and Kris M Kitani. 2016. Going deeper into first-person activity recognition. In *Proceedings of the IEEE Conference on Computer Vision and Pattern Recognition.* 1894–1903.

[19] Sanath Narayan, Mohan S Kankanhalli, and Kalpathi R Ramakrishnan. 2014. Action and interaction recognition in first-person videos. In *Proceedings of the IEEE Conference on Computer Vision and Pattern Recognition Workshops.* 512–518.

[20] Xiaojiang Peng and Cordelia Schmid. 2016. Multi-region two-stream R-CNN for action detection. In *Proceedings of the European Conference on Computer Vision.* 744–759.

[21] Hossein Rahmani and Ajmal Mian. 2015. Learning a non-linear knowledge transfer model for cross-view action recognition. In *Proceedings of the IEEE Conference on Computer Vision and Pattern Recognition.* 2458–2466.

[22] Michael S Ryoo and Larry Matthies. 2013. First-person activity recognition: What are they doing to me?. In *Proceedings of the IEEE Conference on Computer Vision and Pattern Recognition.* 2730–2737.

[23] Jorge Sánchez, Florent Perronnin, Thomas Mensink, and Jakob Verbeek. 2013. Image classification with the fisher vector: Theory and practice. *International Journal of Computer Vision* 105, 3 (2013), 222–245.

[24] Christian Schuldt, Ivan Laptev, and Barbara Caputo. 2004. Recognizing human actions: A local SVM approach. In *Proceedings of the IEEE International Conference on Pattern Recognition*, Vol. 3. 32–36.

[25] Paul Scovanner, Saad Ali, and Mubarak Shah. 2007. A 3-dimensional sift descriptor and its application to action recognition. In *Proceedings of the ACM Multimedia Conference.* 357–360.

[26] Victor Shia, Allen Y Yang, S Shankar Sastry, Andrew Wagner, and Yi Ma. 2011. Fast l1-minimization and parallelization for face recognition. In *ASILOMAR on Signals, Systems, and Computers*. 1199–1203.

[27] Karen Simonyan and Andrew Zisserman. 2014. Two-stream convolutional networks for action recognition in videos. In *Proceedings of the Neural Information Processing Systems Conference*. 568–576.

[28] Khurram Soomro, Amir Roshan Zamir, and Mubarak Shah. 2012. UCF101: A dataset of 101 human actions classes from videos in the wild. *arXiv preprint arXiv:1212.0402* (2012).

[29] Du Tran, Lubomir Bourdev, Rob Fergus, Lorenzo Torresani, and Manohar Paluri. 2015. Learning spatiotemporal features with 3d convolutional networks. In *Proceedings of the IEEE International Conference on Computer Vision*. 4489–4497.

[30] Heng Wang, Alexander Kläser, Cordelia Schmid, and Cheng-Lin Liu. 2011. Action recognition by dense trajectories. In *Proceedings of the IEEE Conference on Computer Vision and Pattern Recognition*. 3169–3176.

[31] Heng Wang, Alexander Kläser, Cordelia Schmid, and Cheng-Lin Liu. 2013. Dense trajectories and motion boundary descriptors for action recognition. *International Journal of Computer Vision* 103, 1 (2013), 60–79.

[32] Heng Wang, Dan Oneata, Jakob Verbeek, and Cordelia Schmid. 2016. A robust and efficient video representation for action recognition. *International Journal of Computer Vision* 119, 3 (2016), 219–238.

[33] Heng Wang and Cordelia Schmid. 2013. Action recognition with improved trajectories. In *Proceedings of the IEEE International Conference on Computer Vision*. 3551–3558.

[34] Jiang Wang, Xiaohan Nie, Yin Xia, Ying Wu, and Song-Chun Zhu. 2014. Cross-view action modeling, learning and recognition. In *Proceedings of the IEEE Conference on Computer Vision and Pattern Recognition*. 2649–2656.

[35] Limin Wang, Yu Qiao, and Xiaoou Tang. 2015. Action Recognition With Trajectory-Pooled Deep-Convolutional Descriptors. In *Proceedings of the IEEE Conference on Computer Vision and Pattern Recognition*. 4305–4314.

[36] Wei Wang, Yan Yan, Luming Zhang, Richang Hong, and Nicu Sebe. 2016. Collaborative sparse coding for multiview action recognition. *IEEE Transactions on Multimedia* 23, 4 (2016), 80–87.

[37] Daniel Weinland, Remi Ronfard, and Edmond Boyer. 2006. Free viewpoint action recognition using motion history volumes. *Computer Vision and Image Understanding* 104, 2 (2006), 249–257.

[38] Shandong Wu, Omar Oreifej, and Mubarak Shah. 2011. Action recognition in videos acquired by a moving camera using motion decomposition of lagrangian particle trajectories. In *Proceedings of the IEEE International Conference on Computer Vision*. 1419–1426.

[39] Yan Yan, Elisa Ricci, Ramanathan Subramanian, Gaowen Liu, and Nicu Sebe. 2014. Multitask linear discriminant analysis for view invariant action recognition. *IEEE Transactions on Image Processing* 23, 12 (2014), 5599–5611.

[40] Jingjing Zheng and Zhuolin Jiang. 2013. Learning view-invariant sparse representations for cross-view action recognition. In *Proceedings of the IEEE International Conference on Computer Vision*. 3176–3183.

[41] Kang Zheng, Yuewei Lin, Youjie Zhou, Dhaval Salvi, Xiaochuan Fan, Dazhou Guo, Zibo Meng, and Song Wang. 2014. Video-based action detection using multiple wearable cameras. In *Proceedings of the European Conference on Computer Vision Workshops*. 727–741.

Annotating, Understanding, and Predicting Long-term Video Memorability

Romain Cohendet*
Technicolor
Rennes, France
Romain.Cohendet@technicolor.com

Karthik Yadati*
Delft University of Technology
Delft
N.K.Yadati@tudelft.nl

Ngoc Q. K. Duong
Technicolor
Rennes, France
Quang-Khanh-Ngoc.Duong@technicolor.com

Claire-Hélène Demarty
Technicolor
Rennes, France
Claire-Helene.Demarty@technicolor.com

ABSTRACT

Memorability can be regarded as a useful metric of video importance to help make a choice between competing videos. Research on computational understanding of video memorability is however in its early stages. There is no available dataset for modelling purposes, and the few previous attempts provided protocols to collect video memorability data that would be difficult to generalize. Furthermore, the computational features needed to build a robust memorability predictor remain largely undiscovered. In this article, we propose a new protocol to collect long-term video memorability annotations. We measure the memory performances of 104 participants from weeks to years after memorization to build a dataset of 660 videos for video memorability prediction. This dataset is made available for the research community. We then analyze the collected data in order to better understand video memorability, in particular the effects of response time, duration of memory retention and repetition of visualization on video memorability. We finally investigate the use of various types of audio and visual features and build a computational model for video memorability prediction. We conclude that high level visual semantics help better predict the memorability of videos.

KEYWORDS

Video memorability, Long-term memory, Scene understanding, Measurement protocol, Global video features, Attributes

ACM Reference Format:
Romain Cohendet*, Karthik Yadati*, Ngoc Q. K. Duong, and Claire-Hélène Demarty. 2018. Annotating, Understanding, and Predicting Long-term Video Memorability. In *ICMR '18: 2018 International Conference on Multimedia Retrieval, June 11–14, 2018, Yokohama, Japan.* ACM, New York, NY, USA, 9 pages. https://doi.org/10.1145/3206025.3206056

*Both authors contributed equally to this work.

ACM ISBN 978-1-4503-5046-4/18/06...$15.00
https://doi.org/10.1145/3206025.3206056

1 INTRODUCTION

Enhancing the relevance of multimedia occurrences in our everyday life requires new ways to organize – in particular, to retrieve – digital content. Like other metrics of video "importance", such as aesthetics [13] or interestingness [12], memorability can be regarded as useful to help make a choice between competing videos. In addition, memorability has the advantage of being clearly definable and objectively measurable (i.e., using a measure that is not influenced by the observer's personal judgment). Image memorability has initially been defined as the probability for an image to be recognized **a few minutes** after a single view, when presented amidst a stream of images [21]. This definition has been widely accepted within subsequent work (e.g., [9, 24, 25, 27, 29]).

The computational understanding of video memorability (VM) follows on from the study of image memorability (IM) prediction which has attracted increasing attention since the seminal work of Isola *et al.* [21]. With the recent introduction of deep learning to address the challenge of IM prediction, models also achieved very good results [2, 24, 37]. As a result of this success, researchers have recently extended this challenge to videos. However, to the best of our knowledge, only two available studies focus on VM prediction [17, 36].

Several problems could explain this scarcity of studies on VM. Firstly, there is no publicly available dataset to train and test models. This is probably the most serious obstacle to the rapid expansion of research in VM prediction. Following the foot steps of researchers in IM [21, 24], providing data and ground truth for VM should be one of our first objectives. The second point, closely related to the previous one, is the lack of a common definition for VM. The previous attempts to predict VM [17, 36] were based on different measures of memorability. Furthermore, in comparison to images, videos have supplementary dimensions – sound and visual movement – that critically contribute to the semantic and emotional information conveyed and this makes it difficult to come up with a common definition of VM. But the videos used and the way memorability is measured have a critical impact on what we understand by VM. Similarly, the definition of IM [21] inevitably limited researchers. In particular, previous research on IM focused on the measurement of memory performances only a few minutes after memorization. But these short-term memory performances might be poor predictors of longer term memory performances. For example, the memorability of emotional images would decrease in a non-harmonious way between two measures of memory performance (a few minutes and one day after memorization), inducing in a dataset a change in the ranking of memorability values over time [10]. To this end, VM data would be expected to benefit from a protocol that would measure lasting long-term memory performance.

Regarding modelling, the previous attempts at predicting VM [17, 36] highlighted several features which contribute to the prediction of VM, such as semantic, saliency and color features. But the work is far from complete and our capacity to propose efficient computational models will participate to answer the challenge of VM prediction.

While participating in the expansion of research on VM, the contributions of this paper are threefold:

- We propose a new protocol that measures very long-term memory performances (from weeks to years after memorization) to collect ground truth data of good quality and make the corresponding dataset available for the research community (section 3).
- We assess and analyze the collected data and provide useful insights on the understanding of VM (section 4).
- We build a computational model based on machine learning techniques which allows to predict a VM score for a given video. For this purpose, we investigate the use of various types of audio and visual features, ranging from low-level characteristics to emotional and (highly) semantic features (section 5).

2 PREVIOUS WORK

In this section, we review previous work on IM and VM prediction, focusing on annotation protocols and modelling aspects.

2.1 Measurement of memorability

Long-term memory has been studied for over a century in psychology, from multiple perspectives, since the seminal experimental studies of Ebbinghaus [14] until the more recent neuro-imaging studies [3]. This work provided researchers, interested in computational understanding of IM and VM, with several memory tests (see [34] for an extensive overview), such as the recognition test [17, 21, 24] or the textual questions-based recall survey [36]. It also demonstrated that humans have an extensive long-term visual memory, which enables them to recall a great amount of images [38] and image details [6], as well as of videos [15]. This is one of the observations at the origin of the work on memorability in computer science [21]. Several factors have also been highlighted for their critical influence on long-term memory, such as emotion [23], semantics [33], several demographic factors [11], memory re-evocation [32], or passage of time [30]. These different factors are all important to better understand memorability, and are found valuable computational features for IM and VM prediction.

Focusing on the work in computer vision, most studies on IM prediction made use of one of the two available large datasets designed specifically to meet this challenge [21, 24]. To address more specific problems, several other datasets have also been publicly released concerning memorability of face photographs [1], visualization pictures [4], emotional images [11] and scene categories [7]. To build the most used datasets presented in [21, 24], the authors, possibly constrained by the difficulty in conducting long crowdsourcing studies, measured memory performance a few minutes after memorization to obtain their memorability annotations. This could be a problem if we conceive that memorability reflects a lasting memory performance [10]. Indeed, it has been shown that long-term memories continue to change long after their memorization through an ongoing process called consolidation, which lasts weeks to years [30]. Because several factors influence the consolidation process (e.g., emotions, sleep, re-evocation), which does not equally affect all memories, the order of memorability ratings measured for content, and especially videos, is susceptible to change over time [10]. A protocol to collect memorability annotations would benefit from the capacity to capture long-lasting memory performances, averaged to obtain what we will later refer to as "long-term memorability".

To our knowledge, the first attempt at measuring VM [17] partially adapted the protocol proposed to measure IM [21] to videos. The resulting protocol is however much heavier than the memory game protocol [21]. They followed a classical recognition process, which consists of two steps: a free viewing task, followed two days later by a recall task. The task duration, for each of the 20 participants, was about 24 hours, spread over 10 sessions (five free viewing tasks and five recall tasks) of about two hours each. The authors used the same proportion of fillers (i.e., non repeated videos) in the free viewing and recall tasks (i.e., 4/5 of fillers and 1/5 of repeated videos named targets) to guarantee that viewers were unaware of targets. If it was mandatory in [21] for which encoding and recall tasks were interlaced, there is a way here to alleviate the task without impacting its quality; indeed, reducing the number of fillers in the free viewing task would have very little impact on the memorability scores (often authors even use only material interrogated later in the learning/free viewing task). Furthermore, the long time span of the experiment makes the generalization of this protocol difficult, in particular if one targets the construction of an extensive dataset. Moreover, authors measured memory after two days, but, as aforementioned, it is known that the consolidation process lasts weeks to years: it would be interesting to collect even longer term memory performances.

In another earlier approach for VM measurement, the participants performed a crowdsourcing experiment that consisted of a free viewing task during which they saw a series of videos, followed by a recall task in which they had to answer textual questions (such as: "Did you see a man juggling?", "Did you see a car on road?") [36]. The major drawback of the study comes from the use of questions instead of a classic visual recognition task. Indeed, the memorability scores computed for the videos may reflect not only the differences in memory performances but also the differences between the questions in terms of difficulty. The authors tested the complexity of the chosen textual questions using the Flesch-Kincaid Grade Level readability metric, which is designed to quantify how difficult to understand an English text is [26]. However, this measure might not be sufficient to represent the questions in all their complexities, such as the ease for a person to draw images from the words, to connect the words to the associated concepts in memory, to associate the words to the corresponding scene, etc. Moreover, there is an unequal distribution of the reading comprehension of English among Amazon Mechanical Turk workers, who are not necessary native English speakers. This problem of a potential unequal complexity of the question becomes even more important in view of the use by authors of the response time to calculate memorability scores, which might also critically depend on the complexity of the questions. One will note that this potential bias could have also affected the measure of inter-human consistency. Furthermore, the questions were handcrafted, and the choices for types of questions and videos were very limited (e.g., the question "Did you see a car on road?" implies that in a whole experimental session only one car on a road should appear to connect the memory performance to one particular video). The authors also manually ensured that no textual questions nor videos in a session were similar in content. This makes it difficult to generalize this protocol to the construction of an extensive dataset.

2.2 Memorability modelling

Previous attempts at predicting image and video memorability highlighted quite a few features that correlate with memorability.

The pioneering work of Isola *et al.* focused primarily on building computational models to predict IM from low-level visual features [21]. From their work, it appeared that the degree of an image's memorability can be predicted to a certain extent. Several characteristics have also been found to be relevant for predicting memorability in subsequent work, for example saliency [29], interestingness and aesthetics [19], or emotions [24]. The best results were finally obtained by using fine-tuned deep features, which outperformed all other features in [24], reaching a rank correlation of .64 which is near human consistency (.68) when measured for the ground truth collected in the study. This result was later confirmed by other researchers [2, 37].

Regarding VM prediction, Han *et al.* proposed a method which combines the power of audio-visual and fMRI-derived features [17]. They preliminary built a computational model learned with fMRI features, which supposedly conveys the brain activity of memorizing videos. This enabled them to finally predict VM without the use of fMRI scans in a second step. However, the method would be difficult to generalize. Shekhar *et al.* conducted a performance analysis of several computationally extracted features before building their memorability predictor [36]. The analysis encompassed C3D deep learning features, semantic features obtained from some video captioning process, saliency features, dense trajectories, and color features. They found that the most predictive feature combination used captioning features, dense trajectories, saliency and color features. The features that performed the best when used alone were image captioning features, i.e., those conveying more semantics. Due to the particularity of the dataset of Shekhar *et al.* – that is, their aforementioned use of questions to measure memorability –, it would be interesting to confirm if this combination works equally well on another dataset, and in particular if image captioning features also perform the best.

3 MEMORABILITY DATASET CONSTRUCTION

3.1 Video collection

We want our protocol to measure memory performance after a significant retention period. This can be achieved either with a longitudinal study, or by measuring a memory created prior to the experiment. We chose the latter because it enabled us to immediately measure very long-term memory. Thus, the main characteristic of the proposed protocol, in contrast with previous work, is the absence of learning (often, free viewing) task. It is replaced with a questionnaire designed to collect information about the participants' prior memory. In order to repeat measures of memory performances for different persons on the same material, to obtain average performance, we worked with movies famous enough to have been seen by several of our participants.

We first established a list of 100 occidental movies, taking care of mixing popularity and genres. We then manually selected seven videos of 10 seconds from each movie. To maintain a high intra-video semantic cohesion, we did not make cuts that would impair the understanding of the scene, nor did we aggregate shots that belong to different scenes. Indeed, since the semantics is linked to the memorability of images [19], we can expect it is linked to the memorability of videos too.

We also gave preference to the videos we called "neutral", by contrast to the "typical" ones. According to our definition, a neutral video is a part of a movie which contains no element that would enable someone to easily guess this video belongs to a particular movie. The list of undesirable elements includes but is not limited to: recognizable famous actors, typical music, style, etc. Typical videos are simply defined as non-neutral videos. In most movies, just a few or no 10-second neutral videos exist. That explains why we obtained only 127 neutral videos for 573 typical ones (while we expected two neutral and five typical videos per movie, i.e., 200 neutral and 500 typical videos in total).

3.2 Annotation protocol

The protocol is composed of two tasks. Firstly, participants had to fill in a questionnaire intended to collect data about whether they have seen the 100 selected movies. Secondly, participants performed a recognition task on videos selected based on their responses to the questionnaire.

104 participants (22 – 58 years of age; age average = 37.1; stdev = 10.4; 26% females; mostly educated persons – engineers or researchers mainly), participated in the experiment on a voluntary basis. The experiment was taking place in a well-controlled environment: a room insulated from noise and equipped with subdued lights. The videos, of HD or DVD quality, were displayed on a 60 inch monitor. The participants were seated at a distance of about 220 centimeters from the screen (three times the screen height). Having provided basic demographics, participants answered the questionnaire. For each of the 100 movies, they were asked whether they remembered watching fully the movie. In case of a positive answer, three additional questions followed: 1/ their confidence of watching the movie (*not confident / slightly confident / 50% confident / considerably confident / 100% confident*), 2/ the last time they saw

the movie (*less than month / 1 year / 5 years / 10 years / more than 10 years*), and 3/ the number of times they saw the movie (*once / 2-4 times / 5-9 times / 10-19 times / more than 20 times*). In case of a negative answer, only one question was asked, related to their confidence of not having seen the movie. The questionnaire required about 20 minutes to complete.

Based on the answers to the questionnaire, an algorithm automatically selected 80 targets (i.e., videos from seen movies) and 40 fillers (i.e., videos from never seen movies) among the movies associated with the highest degree of certitude, with a maximum of two videos from the same movie. The fillers enable to quantify how much lucky confusions account for the correct recognitions. During the video selection, the current number of annotations was also taken into account to equally balance the annotations among all the videos. Given such 120 videos selected, participants performed a recognition task where they saw the videos separated by an inter-stimuli interval of 2 seconds. They had to press the space bar when they recognized a video in particular, and not when they were guessing that a particular video came from a movie they had seen (which was possible only for the typical videos).

3.3 Memorability score calculation

After collecting the data, we kept only the 660 videos that had been seen at least 4 times as targets (from the initial set of 700 videos). On average, each video of our dataset had been viewed as a target by 10.7 participants; which corresponds to the mean number of observations that enter into the calculation of a memorability score. We then assigned a memorability score to each video, defined as the correct recognition rate of the video when viewed as target. The average percentage of correct detections for all participants was 46.71% (stdev = 14.65%), and the average false alarm rate (i.e., the percentage of answers on fillers) was 4.16% (stdev = 5.27%). Figure 2(a) provides a distribution of the videos according to their degree of memorability. The dataset is publicly released here[1]. In addition to the videos and corresponding ground truth, we also provide the features used in section 5.

4 STUDY OF THE MEMORABILITY ANNOTATIONS

In this section, we conduct an analysis of the ground truth data collected through the protocol described above. We firstly perform a human consistency analysis. Then we compare neutral videos with typical videos. We finally study which factors affect the memorability among response time, duration of memory retention and repetition of visualization. In what follows, error bars in the graphs correspond to standard error of the mean, μ to the mean, Mdn to the median and N to the number of observations in the statistics.

4.1 Consistency analysis

We follow the method proposed in [19] to measure human consistency when assessing memorability of videos. We randomly split our 104 participants into two independent groups of equal size, and calculate how well VM scores from the first group of participants match with VM scores from the second group. Averaging over 25 random half-split trials, an average Spearman's rank correlation (i.e., a global human consistency) of 0.57 is observed between these pairs of scores.

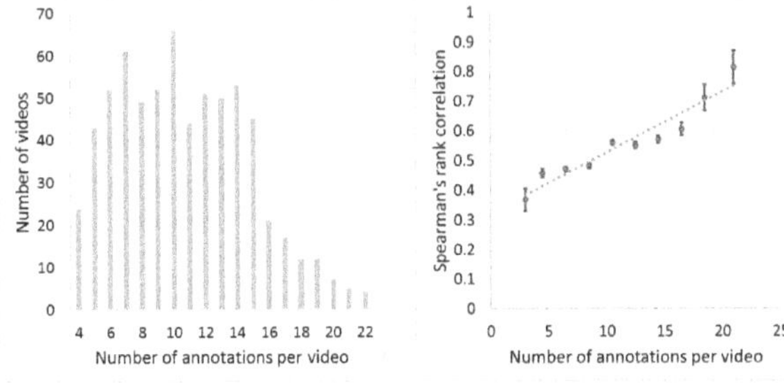

Figure 1: (a) Distribution of the number of videos according to the number of annotations per video. (b) Human consistency (with linear trendline).

We reproduced this calculation to obtain human consistency as a function of the number of annotations per video, presented in Figure 1(b). This graph is to be compared with the histogram presented in Figure 1(a), which shows that the number of videos for each number of annotations was unequal. According to the graph, we achieved a consistency of .70 from about 18 annotations, which is consistent with the previous finding [17]. This number also corresponds to the maximal consistency obtained when collecting IM scores [21, 24], but for a much bigger number of annotations (80) per image. It must be noted that the protocols are different between the IM experiments conducted in [21, 24] and ours or the work in [17]. We conducted a measure of long-term memory performance after at least two days of memorization, whereas in [21, 24] it is measured after a dozen of seconds to a few minutes. In addition, VM annotations were collected through in-lab experiments, and IM annotations through crowdsourcing experiments. However, it would be interesting in the future to confirm if an important difference exists between images and videos regarding the number of annotations necessary to achieve a high human consistency. Apart from the conclusions we could draw about the universality of the intrinsic memorability of videos compared to images, this would mean that the magnitude of the work to carry out to build an extensive database for VM prediction is substantially smaller than one could expect from work on IM prediction.

4.2 Neutral and typical videos

In our experiment, participants were given clear instructions that they had to really recognize any video they were presented as already seen, and not only guess that a video was coming from a movie whose title was proposed in the questionnaire. However, a number of participants reported difficulty in making the distinction between guessing and recognizing: sometimes, because they knew that a video belonged to a movie they had seen, they had the false feeling of recognizing it. In this section, we perform an analysis to compare neutral videos, which contain no element that would enable participants to easily guess that a video belongs to a particular

[1] https://www.technicolor.com/dream/research-innovation/movie-memorability-dataset

movie, and typical videos, that could be more or less easily related to the movie they belong to.

A Wilcoxon rank-sum test indicated that the memorability was lower for neutral ($Mdn = .20, \mu = .24$) than for typical ($Mdn = .53, \mu = .53$) videos, with $Z = 10.22, p < .00001$. This result does not necessarily mean that participants tended to guess when it was possible to do so – rather than simply recognize – videos selected from movies they have seen. Indeed, neutral videos contain far less contextual elements useful for recognition than typical ones, making the latter - if more easily "guessable" - at least more easily recognizable. However, it should draw our attention to the possibility that our measure is not purely objective, but – to some extent – context dependent. This would constitute the main weakness of our protocol, that one should counteract by adapted measures of control.

We can also note that the average false alarm rate (that is, the percentage of wrongly recognized filler videos) was low for neutral videos (.05%) as well as for typical videos (.03%). Specifically, we expect lucky confusions to account for little of correct detections on average for the two sorts of videos.

4.3 Response time

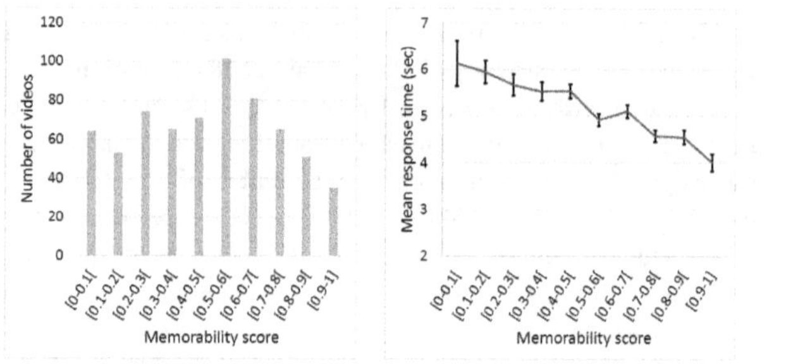

(a) (b)

Figure 2: (a) Distribution of the number of videos depending on memorability score ranges. (b) Mean response time for correct recognitions against memorability scores.

Figure 2 (b) shows that the response time to do a correct detection decreases when the memorability of the video increases. We also observed a Pearson's correlation of −0.36 ($p < .0001$) between the response time on the targets and their memorability scores. These two results indicate that participants tended to answer quicker when the videos were more memorable, even though the participants did not receive any instruction to do so. This suggests that people tend to naturally answer rapidly after having recognized the video. This also suggests either that the most memorable videos are also the most accessible in memory, and/or that the most memorable videos contain more early recognizable elements than the less memorable ones. In [36], the response time of the participants was taken to be the measure of VM. The authors chose this measure to avoid a long gap between viewing and recall stage. Our results validate – to some extent – their modus operandi: the fact that the response time decreases linearly when the memorability increases suggest that the response time is a good indicator of the memorability of the videos (at least, in a recognition task).

4.4 User context and memorability

To provide us with insights on which context-related factors collected through our questionnaire were linked to memorability, we processed to a logistic regression, using demographics and answers to the questionnaire as regressors, and the detection of a target video (with two possible discrete outcomes, detected or not) as observations to fit. Regarding the participants' nationality, we grouped them into occidental (69 pers) and non-occidental (35 pers) categories, motivated by our use of occidental movies, which could have more meaning for occidental than for non-occidental people. We also tested age and gender to reveal a potential bias in our movies' choice, that may be more memorable for people of a certain age and gender. The model, in case of a single observation n, can be written as:

$$y_n = \begin{cases} 1 & if \beta_0 + \sum_{k=1}^{K} x_{n,k}\beta_k + \epsilon_n > 0 \\ 0 & else \end{cases} \quad (1)$$

where y_n denotes the dependent variable which can take two values, 1 for recognition or 0 for omission of the n-th target observation, $x_{n,k}$ our k-th feature value (last view, number of views, nationality, age, gender), β_k are the coefficients to be estimated, and ϵ_n indicates the error term.

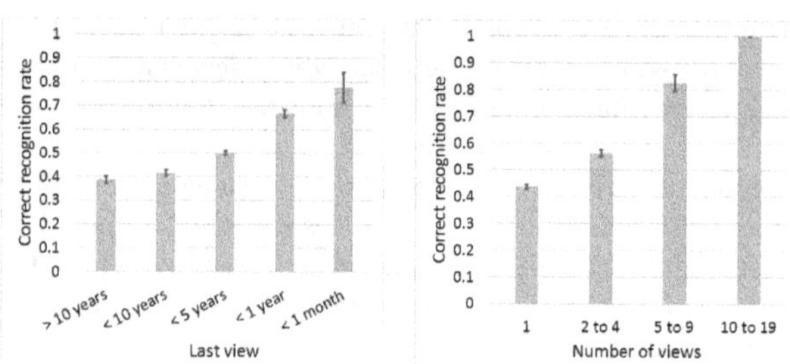

(a) (b)

Figure 3: Correct recognition rate depending on (a) when occurred the last viewing, and (b) the number of views.

According to the results of the logistic regression, the retention duration (last view) is highly negatively correlated with the probability to recognize a video ($\beta = -.37, p < .0001$). Figure 3 (a) shows that this decrease in memory for videos over time is continuous. This result indicates that long-term memory of videos continues to be altered over time for years. In the context or experiment, it implies that, to provide an accurate representation of an average long-term memory performance, a memorability score should correspond to a memory measure carried out as late as possible after the memorization.

The results of the logistic regression also show that the number of views is highly correlated with the probability to recognize a video ($\beta = .44, p < .0001$). As expected, the more a movie was seen, the better the videos were memorized. Figure 3 (b) shows that this continues to be true even with more than 9 viewings (however, the number of observations – 12 – was very low for videos which belong to movies with 10 or more views). One should note that the repetition of a viewing could not be the (only) factor involved in the above phenomenon; in particular, viewing again a movie may be the sign of a special interest which would explained a better memorization (e.g., via a greater attentional and emotional investment). The fact remains that repetition is an important factor to ask people when measuring their prior memory. Furthermore, a protocol used to build an extensive database for VM prediction should, in case of multiple measures of memory (e.g., after the memorization and then after a longer delay), avoid measuring twice the same items, because this repetition could artificially increase the performance measured for the last items.

We observed no significant effects of the demographic factors (nationality, age and gender). This suggests that the videos were equally susceptible to be recognized by the different participants (or, that the relations between these factors and the observations are too complex to have been captured by the model).

5 MEMORABILITY PREDICTION

Until now, we have presented the video collection and the annotation protocol together with some insights on human VM. In this section, we move towards building a machine learning model that can learn and then predict the VM score of a video from its audio-visual features. The main goal of modelling is to understand if VM is predictable, and if yes identify which features: generic, perceptual, or semantic, are suitable for such prediction. We pose the problem as a standard regression problem and Figure 4 illustrates different steps in our method. In the following sub-sections, we explain our choice of features and models to address the problem in hand.

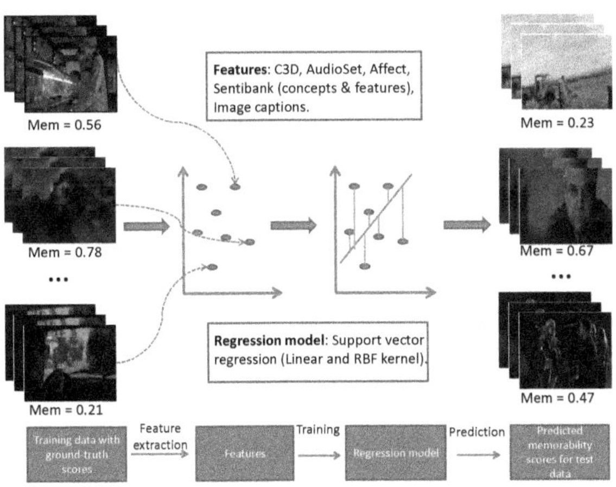

Figure 4: Proposed approach for memorability score prediction.

To build our predictive model, we split the dataset, at the level of movies, into training (70%), validation (15%) and test (15%) data, which translates into 70 movies in the training set and 15 movies each in the validation and test sets. We chose to split our dataset at the level of movies, instead of the videos, in order to avoid videos from the same movie being present in the training as well as the evaluation (validation+test) set. To ensure that such random split did not lead to any mismatch, we computed the average number of annotations per video in each of them. We observe that the numbers of annotations are balanced: each video in the test set has around 10 annotations while there are 9 annotations for each one in the train set on an average.

5.1 Feature extraction

The task of remembering a specific video has a high cognitive complexity in general, suggesting that it requires a semantic understanding of the content and/or some other perceptual factors such as the emotion conveyed by the video. Many users who participated in our experiments indicated that it is a difficult task. While trying to build a machine learning model for such a task, we explore different kinds of features that can be extracted from the audio-visual signal. We investigate a variety of generic state-of-the-art features ([39], [16]) and compare them with other semantic ([22]) and perceptual (emotion) features ([5]).

5.1.1 Spatio-temporal visual features (C3D). These features are extracted from the C3D model, a 3-dimensional convolutional network proposed for generic video analysis [39]. The main motivation to use C3D is that it encodes both the spatial and temporal information in the video. The model has been proposed for video analysis and is not an extension of a model for image analysis, unlike other state-of-the-art models like VGG16 [28]. We use the publicly available model trained on the Sports-1M dataset [39] and extract the output of the fully connected layer – fc6 of the network with a dimensionality of 4096. We additionally explore the use of principal component analysis (PCA) (named C3D (PCA) in Table 1) for the dimension reduction, as the original dimensionality is very high when compared to other features.

5.1.2 Audio features (AudioSet). Using a recently released AudioSet [16] model, which was trained on a large dataset for event detection, we extract 128-dimensional embeddings for each audio track associated with a video in our dataset. We use these embeddings for training the regression models. The motivation to use these features is that they are state-of-the-art in the audio event detection research and events could play a major role in how people remember sequences in movies. Additionally, we wanted to investigate how the audio channel contributes to building a model for VM prediction.

5.1.3 Emotion related features (SentiBank and Affect). As research in psychology showed that emotion and memory are correlated [8], we investigate the use of emotion-related feature in our prediction system. For modelling emotion from the visual content, we resort to a visual sentiment concept detector: SentiBank [5]. SentiBank is a set of 1200 trained visual concept detectors providing a mid-level representation of sentiment from visual content. We use the binary code for concept detection, from images, provided by the authors. The SentiBank concept detector provides two pieces of information: concepts with probabilities and features. Concepts are adjective–noun pairs and the probability represents how likely each concept is depicted visually in an image. Examples of some concepts in the SentiBank ontology are: *young driver, scary face, terrible pain*, etc.

We sample one frame for every second of the video in our dataset, resulting in 10 frames per video. We run the SentiBank concept detector on each of these 10 frames and rank the concepts based on the probability of their occurrence in the frame and take the top-50 concepts. We extract 300-dimensional word embeddings (Word2Vec [31]), for each of the 50 concepts and take an average to obtain a single vector per frame. We repeat this process for all the 10 frames and take the average of all the vectors to obtain a single feature vector for each video. Sentibank detectors also provide a 4096-dimensional feature for each frame and we take the average across all the frames to obtain one 4096-dimensional feature vector for each video. In the end, we use a 300-dimensional concept vector and a 4096-dimensional feature vector.

In addition to SentiBank concepts, we investigate other ways to capture emotional content in a video. Following a circumplex model of affect (the experience of emotion) [35], we define arousal as the dimension of affect that measures the excitement in the video, while valence measures whether the video invokes positive or negative emotion. We resort to an audio-visual analysis of the video to obtain its arousal and valence scores using the method described in [18]. For each frame in the video, we compute the arousal and valence scores using the method proposed in [18]. In order to keep a fixed dimensionality of the feature vector, we take the first 200 frames in the video because of the varying frame rates across the videos. We concatenate the arousal and valence scores for the first 200 frames in each video resulting in a 400-dimensional feature vector (200 for arousal and 200 for valence) for a video.

5.1.4 Visual semantic features (Image captions). Visual semantics are known to play an important role in image memorability ([20], [37]). We utilize the state-of-the-art research in image captioning to capture such high-level semantics of the video [22]. We sample one frame for every second of the video in our dataset, resulting in 10 frames per video. For each of these 10 frames, we run the caption detector (code provided by the authors) and obtain a caption for the frame. For each non-functional word in the caption, we extract 300-dimensional word embeddings (Word2Vec [31]) and take an average across all the words to obtain a single vector per frame. We repeat this process for all the 10 frames and take the average of all the vectors to obtain a single 300-dimensional feature vector for each video.

5.2 Modelling and evaluation metric

We use the features discussed in Section 5.1 to train a Support Vector Regression (SVR) model for the VM score prediction. The choice of SVR is guided by the nature of the problem as well as by the small size of the dataset. We have chosen to go with the same regressor for all the features because our focus is mainly on identifying which features are more important for VM prediction. This way we ensure that the difference in performances is because of the features themselves. Note that, in addition to the variety of features explained in Section 5.1, we also explore a combination of all the features by concatenating them into a single feature vector. While performing such a concatenation, we use the low-dimension version of the features for C3D and SentiBank features, obtained after applying a dimension reduction method (PCA) to the original set. In the experiments where we use PCA for C3D and SentiBank features, we retain 95% of variance in the data while reducing the feature dimensions. Note that we investigated other models like LSTM, to model the sequential nature of videos. The results were not very encouraging and this could be because of the relatively smaller size of our dataset.

We use the grid search strategy to obtain the best hyper-parameters for SVR in term of the Mean Squared Error (*MSE*) between the predicted scores and the ground-truth on the validation set. The choice of hyper-parameters in the grid search are: kernel = {linear, RBF}, $C = \{0.1, 1, 10, 100, 1000\}$ and $\gamma = \{0.01, 0.1, 1, 10, 100\}$.

The prediction performance is evaluated by the Spearman correlation (*SpCorr*), which measures the rank correlation between the predicted memorability scores and the ground-truth scores. This metric is chosen as (1) we focus more on the relative memorability between videos rather than on their absolute memorability scores, and (2) it gives an indication of how close the predicted memorability scores are to the human consistency when annotating memorability scores.

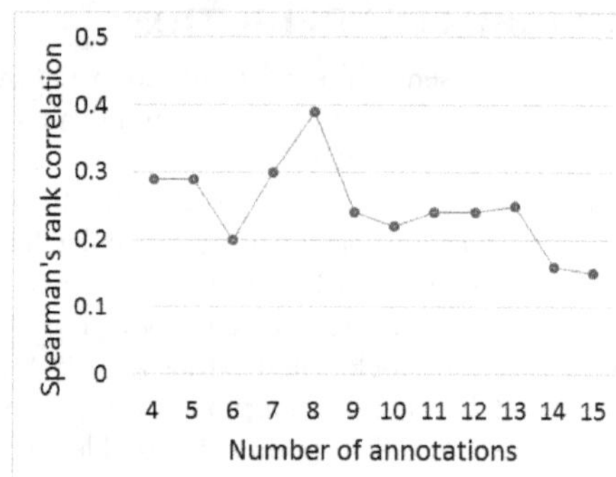

Figure 5: Spearman correlation on the validation set with models using image captioning features trained on videos with varying number of annotations.

5.3 Memorability prediction results

In this section, we will discuss how the models trained on different features perform while predicting memorability scores of new videos. Table 1 reports the prediction results obtained by the SVR model when trained on different features, for the validation and test sets. Two sets of results are reported: *SpCorr* ($\geq$ 4 annotations) and *SpCorr* ($\geq$ 8 annotations). The former corresponds to the prediction capability of the model when trained on videos with at least 4 annotations, and the latter corresponds to the results when trained on videos with at least 8 annotations where the ground-truth is better annotated.

As it can be seen, visual semantic features derived from image captioning clearly offer better prediction results compared to all other considered features. This is not surprising as they capture visual attributes along the scene, which are known to play an important role in human memory. This is also inline with a previous study in IM [37] where image captioning-based features helped better predict IM than the conventional CNN features. When predicting VM on the test set, C3D features showed to be quite effective to the task as they encode the visual spatio-temporal information of the

Feature	Feature type	Dimension	*SpCorr*(≥ 4 annotations)		*SpCorr* (≥ 8 annotations)	
			validation set	*test set*	*validation set*	*test set*
C3D	visual spatio-temporal	4096	0.20	0.26	0.31	0.34
C3D (PCA)	visual spatio-temporal	225	0.24	0.21	0.18	0.17
AudioSet	audio related	128	0.23	0.22	0.21	0.24
Affect	affect related	400	0.19	0.17	0.26	0.23
SentiBank concepts	emotion related	300	0.16	0.13	0.15	0.17
SentiBank features	emotion related	4096	0.25	0.21	0.27	0.26
SentiBank features (PCA)	emotion related	225	0.22	0.21	0.22	0.23
Captions	visual semantics	300	**0.29**	**0.31**	**0.39**	**0.38**
Combination (PCA)	combine all features	1578	0.24	0.23	0.29	0.27

Table 1: Prediction results in terms of Spearman correlation scores on validation and test data for different features with models trained on videos that have at least 4 (columns 4-5) or 8 (columns 6-7) annotations.

video. On the contrary, audio information captured by AudioSet features does not seem to be enough for VM prediction. One of our initial hypotheses was that emotion would play an important role in VM, supported by literature from psychology [8]. However, when observing the results in Table 1, both Affect [18] and SentiBank [5] performed quite poorly compared to the image captioning features. Another observation from Table 1 is that the combination of all the features (last row in the table) does not appear in the top-3 best performing features. One of the reasons for this could be that there is a lot of redundance when combining all the features into a single feature vector, or it could be that the size of the combined feature vector is too big when compared to the size of the dataset. Thus, in future work we could look at selectively combining the features to investigate if that improves the performance.

As our dataset contains videos with different numbers of annotations, we further investigate the effect of the number of annotations on the prediction performance. For this purpose, we train a first SVR model, using image captioning features, on videos with at least 4 annotations and use this model to predict the memorability score for videos in the validation set. We repeat this process for different numbers of annotations per video (from 4 to 15) in the training set. Please note that the validation set in each of the repetitions is fixed and only the training set changes. We provide a demonstration of how *SpCorr* varies with an increasing number of annotations in the training set in Figure 5. As can be seen, *SpCorr* first increases up to 5 annotations and then remains more or less constant before decreasing (beyond 10 annotations). In the wake of this observation, we also investigated the performance of all the features when we train the regression model with videos that have at least 8 annotations as reported in the second part of Table 1: *SpCorr* (≥ 8 annotations).

Comparing the two sets of results in Table 1, we observe that globally the models trained on videos with at least 8 annotations perform better than the models trained on videos with at least 4 annotations. These results are comparable to the human consistency analysis shown in Section 4.1. We finally performed an additional 10-fold cross-validation on videos with at least 8 annotations (train+validation set) using the image captioning features. From this study, we re-confirmed that there is no overfitting issue in our model and we observed the average value of *SpCorr* across the 10 folds to be 0.33, which is close to the performance on the test set.

6 CONCLUSIONS

In this paper, we have presented a novel protocol to collect long-term memorability annotations for videos, which enabled us to build a dataset to support research in this subject. We then performed a range of statistical studies on this dataset to understand important factors in the annotation process as well as how they can affect video memorability. The main strength of our protocol is that it enables to measure memory performance weeks to years after memorization without requiring a longitudinal study. It appears from the analysis that memory of videos continues to decrease for years, which justifies such a distant measurement, in contrast to previous work. The counterpart is that we cannot control the memorizing process. In particular, the correctness of the answers to the questionnaire designed to collect information about the participants' prior memory is not absolute. Even with additional information about the movies (e.g. showing an excerpt/trailer), the possibility would remain that a participant falsely answers he/she has already seen/never seen a movie. Our current work focuses on collecting VM annotations at a large scale using crowdsourcing, measuring VM in a more objective manner, by controlling the memorizing step. We proceed of the measurement after different periods of retention (from a few minutes to a few days), which enables us also to study long-term memory, although not as long as in the present experiment. Another limitation of the presented protocol is the limited choice of content. To design our experiment, we needed contents broadly disseminated among the population surveyed. In our current work, we are not limited anymore by this problem, and decided to work on neutral videos.

We finally proposed computational models for VM prediction where we investigated the use of various audio and visual features for the task. For this, we observed that the visual semantic features offer the best prediction result, which re-confirms the correlation between the visual attributes and memorability. Although very promising, these results seem to be limited by the relative small size of the dataset. Again, our current work might enable us to reconfirm these results on a larger dataset and for more general videos.

REFERENCES

[1] Wilma A Bainbridge, Phillip Isola, and Aude Oliva. 2013. The intrinsic memorability of face photographs. *Journal of Experimental Psychology: General* 142, 4 (2013), 1323.

[2] Yoann Baveye, Romain Cohendet, Matthieu Perreira Da Silva, and Patrick Le Callet. 2016. Deep Learning for Image Memorability Prediction: the Emotional Bias. In *Proc. ACM Int. Conf. on Multimedia (ACMM)*. 491–495.

[3] Robert S Blumenfeld and Charan Ranganath. 2007. Prefrontal cortex and long-term memory encoding: an integrative review of findings from neuropsychology and neuroimaging. *The Neuroscientist* 13, 3 (2007), 280–291.

[4] Michelle A Borkin, Azalea A Vo, Zoya Bylinskii, Phillip Isola, Shashank Sunkavalli, Aude Oliva, and Hanspeter Pfister. 2013. What makes a visualization memorable? *IEEE Transactions on Visualization and Computer Graphics* 19, 12 (2013), 2306–2315.

[5] Damian Borth, Tao Chen, Rongrong Ji, and Shih-Fu Chang. 2013. SentiBank: Large-scale Ontology and Classifiers for Detecting Sentiment and Emotions in Visual Content. In *Proc. ACM International Conference on Multimedia (ACMM)*. 459–460.

[6] Timothy F Brady, Talia Konkle, George A Alvarez, and Aude Oliva. 2008. Visual long-term memory has a massive storage capacity for object details. *Proceedings of the National Academy of Sciences* 105, 38 (2008), 14325–14329.

[7] Zoya Bylinskii, Phillip Isola, Constance Bainbridge, Antonio Torralba, and Aude Oliva. 2015. Intrinsic and extrinsic effects on image memorability. *Vision research* 116 (2015), 165–178.

[8] Larry Cahill and James Mcgaugh. 1996. A Novel Demonstration of Enhanced Memory Associated with Emotional Arousal. 4 (01 1996), 410–21.

[9] Bora Celikkale, Aykut Erdem, and Erkut Erdem. 2013. Visual attention-driven spatial pooling for image memorability. In *Proc. IEEE Int. Conf. on Computer Vision and Pattern Recognition Workshops*. 976–983.

[10] Romain Cohendet. 2016. *Prédiction computationnelle de la mémorabilité des images: vers une intégration des informations extrinsèques et émotionnelles*. Ph.D. Dissertation. Nantes.

[11] Romain Cohendet, Anne-Laure Gilet, Matthieu Perreira Da Silva, and Patrick Le Callet. 2016. Using individual data to characterize emotional user experience and its memorability: Focus on gender factor. In *Proc. Int. Conf. on Quality of Multimedia Experience (QoMEX)*. IEEE, 1–6.

[12] Claire-Hélène Demarty, Mats Viktor Sjöberg, Bogdan Ionescu, Thanh-Toan Do, Hanli Wang, Ngoc Q. K. Duong, and Frédéric Lefebvre. 2016. Mediaeval 2016 predicting media interestingness task. In *Proc. MediaEval Workshop*.

[13] Sagnik Dhar, Vicente Ordonez, and Tamara L Berg. 2011. High level describable attributes for predicting aesthetics and interestingness. In *Proc. IEEE Int. Conf. on Computer Vision and Pattern Recognition (CVPR)*. IEEE, 1657–1664.

[14] Hermann Ebbinghaus. 1913. *Memory: A contribution to experimental psychology*. Number 3. University Microfilms.

[15] Orit Furman, Nimrod Dorfman, Uri Hasson, Lila Davachi, and Yadin Dudai. 2007. They saw a movie: long-term memory for an extended audiovisual narrative. *Learning & memory* 14, 6 (2007), 457–467.

[16] Jort F. Gemmeke, Daniel P. W. Ellis, Dylan Freedman, Aren Jansen, Wade Lawrence, R. Channing Moore, Manoj Plakal, and Marvin Ritter. 2017. Audio Set: An ontology and human-labeled dataset for audio events. In *Proc. IEEE Int. Conf. on Audio, Speech and Language Processing (ICASSP)*.

[17] Junwei Han, Changyuan Chen, Ling Shao, Xintao Hu, Jungong Han, and Tianming Liu. 2015. Learning computational models of video memorability from fMRI brain imaging. *IEEE transactions on cybernetics* 45, 8 (2015), 1692–1703.

[18] A. Hanjalic and Li-Qun Xu. 2005. Affective video content representation and modeling. *IEEE Transactions on Multimedia* 7, 1 (Feb 2005), 143–154.

[19] Phillip Isola, Jianxiong Xiao, Devi Parikh, Antonio Torralba, and Aude Oliva. 2014. What makes a photograph memorable? *IEEE Transactions on Pattern Analysis and Machine Intelligence* 36, 7 (2014), 1469–1482.

[20] Phillip Isola, Jianxiong Xiao, Devi Parikh, Antonio Torralba, and Aude Oliva. 2014. What Makes a Photograph Memorable? *IEEE Trans. Pattern Anal. Mach. Intell.* 36, 7 (July 2014), 1469–1482.

[21] Phillip Isola, Jianxiong Xiao, Antonio Torralba, and Aude Oliva. 2011. What makes an image memorable?. In *Proc. IEEE Int. Conf. on Computer Vision and Pattern Recognition (CVPR)*. IEEE, 145–152.

[22] Andrej Karpathy and Li Fei-Fei. 2017. Deep Visual-Semantic Alignments for Generating Image Descriptions. *IEEE Trans. Pattern Anal. Mach. Intell.* 39, 4 (April 2017), 664–676.

[23] Elizabeth A Kensinger and Daniel L Schacter. 2008. Memory and emotion. *Handbook of emotions* 3 (2008), 601–617.

[24] Aditya Khosla, Akhil S Raju, Antonio Torralba, and Aude Oliva. 2015. Understanding and predicting image memorability at a large scale. In *Proc. IEEE Int. Conf. on Computer Vision (ICCV)*. 2390–2398.

[25] Jongpil Kim, Sejong Yoon, and Vladimir Pavlovic. 2013. Relative spatial features for image memorability. In *Proceedings of the 21st ACM international conference on Multimedia*. ACM, 761–764.

[26] J Peter Kincaid, Robert P Fishburne Jr, Richard L Rogers, and Brad S Chissom. 1975. *Derivation of new readability formulas (automated readability index, fog count and flesch reading ease formula) for navy enlisted personnel*. Technical Report. Naval Technical Training Command Millington TN Research Branch.

[27] Souad Lahrache, Rajae El Ouazzani, and Abderrahim El Qadi. 2016. Bag-of-features for image memorability evaluation. *IET Computer Vision* 10, 6 (2016), 577–584.

[28] S. Liu and W. Deng. 2015. Very deep convolutional neural network based image classification using small training sample size. In *Proc. Asian Conference on Pattern Recognition (ACPR)*. 730–734.

[29] Matei Mancas and Olivier Le Meur. 2013. Memorability of natural scenes: The role of attention. In *Proc. IEEE Int. Conf. on Image Processing (ICIP)*. 196–200.

[30] James L McGaugh. 2000. Memory–a century of consolidation. *Science* 287, 5451 (2000), 248–251.

[31] Tomas Mikolov, Kai Chen, G.s Corrado, and Jeffrey Dean. 2013. Efficient Estimation of Word Representations in Vector Space. 2013 (01 2013).

[32] Lynn Nadel and Morris Moscovitch. 1997. Memory consolidation, retrograde amnesia and the hippocampal complex. *Current opinion in neurobiology* 7, 2 (1997), 217–227.

[33] M Ross Quillan. 1966. *Semantic memory*. Technical Report. Bolt Beranek and Newman Inc Cambridge MA.

[34] Alan Richardson-Klavehn and Robert A Bjork. 1988. Measures of memory. *Annual review of psychology* 39, 1 (1988), 475–543.

[35] James Russell. 1980. A Circumplex Model of Affect. 39 (12 1980), 1161–1178.

[36] Sumit Shekhar, Dhruv Singal, Harvineet Singh, Manav Kedia, and Akhil Shetty. 2017. Show and Recall: Learning What Makes Videos Memorable. In *Proceedings of the IEEE Conference on Computer Vision and Pattern Recognition*. 2730–2739.

[37] Hammad Squalli-Houssaini, Ngoc Q. K. Duong, Marquant Gwenaëlle, and Claire-Hélène Demarty. 2018. Deep learning for predicting image memorability. In *Proc. IEEE Int. Conf. on Audio, Speech and Language Processing (ICASSP)*.

[38] Lionel Standing. 1973. Learning 10000 pictures. *Quarterly Journal of Experimental Psychology* 25, 2 (1973), 207–222.

[39] Du Tran, Lubomir Bourdev, Rob Fergus, Lorenzo Torresani, and Manohar Paluri. 2015. Learning Spatiotemporal Features with 3D Convolutional Networks. In *Proc. IEEE Int. Conf. on Computer Vision (ICCV)*. 4489–4497.

Optimally Grouped Deep Features Using Normalized Cost for Video Scene Detection

Daniel Rotman, Dror Porat, Gal Ashour, Udi Barzelay
IBM Research
Haifa, Israel
[danieln,drorp,ashour,udib]@il.ibm.com

ABSTRACT

Video scene detection is the task of temporally dividing a video into its semantic sections. This is an important preliminary step for effective analysis of heterogeneous video content. We present a unique formulation of this task as a generic optimization problem with a novel normalized cost function, aimed at optimal grouping of consecutive shots into scenes. The mathematical properties of the proposed normalized cost function enable robust scene detection, also in challenging real-world scenarios. We present a novel dynamic programming formulation for efficiently optimizing the proposed cost function despite an inherent dependency between subproblems. We use deep neural network models for visual and audio analysis to encode the semantic elements in the video scene, enabling effective and more accurate video scene detection. The proposed method has two key advantages compared to other approaches: it inherently provides a temporally consistent division of the video into scenes, and is also parameter-free, eliminating the need for fine-tuning for different types of content. While our method can adaptively estimate the number of scenes from the video content, we also present a new non-greedy procedure for creating a hierarchical consensus-based division tree spanning multiple levels of granularity. We provide comprehensive experimental results showing the benefits of the normalized cost function, and demonstrating that the proposed method outperforms the current state of the art in video scene detection.

CCS CONCEPTS

• **Computing methodologies** → **Computer vision**; **Computer vision tasks**; **Visual content-based indexing and retrieval**; Hierarchical representations; • **Theory of computation** → *Discrete optimization*; *Dynamic programming*;

KEYWORDS

video scene detection; temporal segmentation; optimization; normalized cost; dynamic programming; hierarchy creation

ACM Reference Format:
Daniel Rotman, Dror Porat, Gal Ashour, Udi Barzelay. 2018. Optimally Grouped Deep Features Using Normalized Cost for Video Scene Detection. In *ICMR '18: 2018 International Conference on Multimedia Retrieval, June 11–14, 2018, Yokohama, Japan.* ACM, New York, NY, USA, 9 pages. https://doi.org/10.1145/3206025.3206055

ICMR '18, June 11–14, 2018, Yokohama, Japan

ACM ISBN 978-1-4503-5046-4/18/06...$15.00
https://doi.org/10.1145/3206025.3206055

1 INTRODUCTION

Video scene detection is the task of temporally dividing a heterogenous video into its semantic sections, called *scenes*. Scenes typically relay a specific concept or theme which acts as a component of the story delivered by the video. Formally, scenes are defined as a sequence of semantically related and temporally adjacent shots depicting a high-level concept or story [23]. The *shots* that compose the scenes are a series of frames taken from the same camera at the same time; different shots are separated by a shot boundary, usually in the form of an abrupt cut or gradual fade transition. Due to the relative uniformity of the frames in a shot, detecting the boundaries of shots is relatively simple and usually considered to be a solved problem [27]. There are a number of available methods for this task that can be used off-the-shelf with impressive performance [1, 4]. However, dividing videos into scenes, which is the goal of this work, is considered to be a much more challenging task on account of the semantic nature of scenes.

The rise in video content volume in recent years [17] has increased the importance of developing technologies that can help manage, recommend, and consume video content. For long heterogeneous videos, it can be difficult for consumers, and in particular for data analysts (in a professional context), to understand the contents of the video and the location of the information they seek. For this, video scene detection is a powerful tool. We can use the ability to partition the video into scenes to help build a table-of-contents, enable fast browsing and skipping between scenes, and identify the contextual boundaries of the content in the video. In addition, the tasks of summarizing, retrieving, understanding, and classifying video content can benefit greatly when dealing with multi-chaptered videos. For video navigation in particular, creating a hierarchy of division over multiple levels of granularity can be especially beneficial for providing insight as to the structure of the video (see Section 6).

A common approach for video scene detection is to equate the problem to a standard clustering task. Such an approach neglects an important element, which is the *temporal consistency* of video scenes: Since video scenes have an obvious ingrained temporal structure and sequence, clustering shots independently of their location and order in the video can lead to situations of marking a scene as a non-contiguous segment. Not only does this not make sense, but it also contradicts the definition of a scene. One obvious problematic example is classic ping-pong shot sequences, in which the camera alternates between two entities/views. Another involves

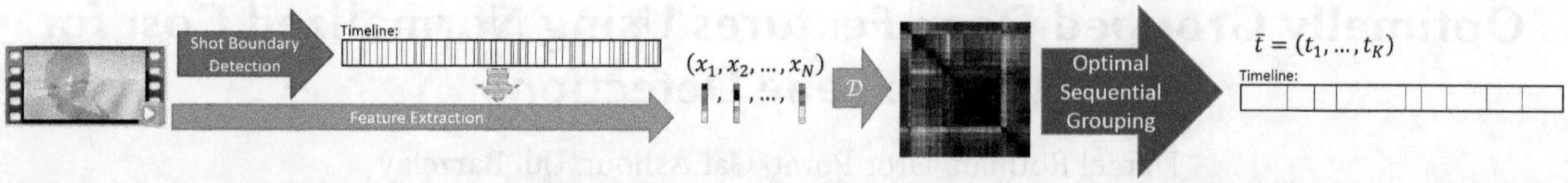

Figure 1: An overview of the proposed video scene detection method. Given a video shot boundary detection is performed (blue arrow) and from each shot a representative feature is extracted (green arrow). A distance matrix D is created from the features (orange arrow) on which the optimal sequential grouping algorithm can be performed (purple arrow) to result in the optimal division into scenes. (Best viewed in color.)[1]

outlier shots, where a single shot in a sequence looks completely different because of a close-up or angle shift. Even when a method considers the temporal distance of shots and enforces temporal consistency using some heuristics, the result remains suboptimal since the video structure is treated as an enforcement instead of as an integral property.

In contrast, in this paper we extend our work in [20], which formalizes video scene detection as an optimization process of sequential grouping. Utilizing the structure of the video, we choose optimal locations for division based on features that represent the shots in the video, and a distance metric to measure the (dis-)similarity between them. As opposed to our previous approach [20], we incorporate a normalized cost function which has important mathematical properties that make it appropriate for difficult situations such as widely varying scene lengths and weak scene indications (as detailed in Section 3.3). In addition, we incorporate the use of deep neural networks to better capture the semantic elements in a video scene. Using deep features helps to more accurately identify the underlying and correlative elements in a scene, enabling scene partitioning which requires high-level understanding.

A general overview of the proposed method is shown in Figure 1. Given a video, we perform shot boundary detection [4] and extract a representative feature vector from each shot, which allows a distance between each pair of shots to be calculated. We formulate an optimization problem with a normalized cost function over the computed distance values. We minimize the cost function to obtain the optimal division into scenes.

The proposed method for video scene detection has substantial advantages. It is parameter-free, and thus avoids the need for fine-tuning to make the method applicable to different types of content. It is also efficient due to a novel dynamic programming scheme which allows fast scene partitioning. Furthermore, we formulate the method as a general optimization process for sequential data, thus making it applicable to various other tasks, such as audio partitioning or data analysis for change point detection. For video scene detection, our comprehensive evaluation shows that the proposed method outperforms the state of the art on real-world videos of a variety of genres.

The major contributions in this work are as follows: 1. Development of a novel normalized cost function, which we show to be superior for performing the sequential grouping task, both analytically and in practice. 2. A novel dynamic programming formulation for efficiently optimizing the proposed cost function despite an inherent dependency between subproblems (see Section 4.1). 3. Incorporation of deep neural networks for visual and audio analysis to identify semantic elements that compose a scene. 4. A novel non-greedy algorithm for constructing a hierarchical division tree using a set of optimal divisions.

This paper is organized as follows: In Section 2, we review the relevant literature on the problem of video scene detection. In Section 3, we detail the problem definition and our formulation, and introduce the normalized cost function. Section 4 details the optimization process. In Section 5 we describe the incorporation of deep neural networks for multimodal feature extraction. Section 6 details our non-greedy algorithm for constructing a hierarchical division tree. Section 7 presents our evaluation, and in Section 8 we draw conclusions.

2 PREVIOUS WORK

In this section, we review some of the previous work in video scene detection. We limit ourselves to methods that aim to perform an entire partitioning of a video as opposed to scene extraction. For a more general review, see [8].

One methodology for video scene detection makes assumptions about video editing and uses *editing rules* to isolate video scenes [7, 10]. These methods use heuristics derived from the film industry to attempt to identify scene changes by recognizing the types of shots (wide shot, close-up, etc.) and learning the predictable behavior. Many of these rules are highly prevalent in the mainstream film industry (e.g., Hollywood movies). However, relying on them drastically limits the capabilities to a very particular genre and production type. For example, the rules learned for documentary films will most likely be completely different than the rules for news broadcasts or sports videos. This limitation makes these methods suitable only for application-specific tasks.

Clustering methods [2, 3, 5, 18] use a variety of advanced schemes to depict shots and the relationship between them. These methods then typically group the shots together using standard clustering techniques. As mentioned above, this results in the need to introduce heuristics that enforce temporal consistency, since the shot clusters may not all be temporally aligned. Specifically, situations such as outlier shots and ping-pong shot sequences are likely to cause complete mislabeling of the scene (see Figure 2).

Graph methods for video scene detection are also quite prevalent [19, 24, 25, 28]. These model the video as a connected graph and employ known algorithms such as graph cuts or dominant sets to detect the video scene boundaries. One state-of-the-art method [25] uses high-level and low-level audio-visual representations over

[1] Image taken from Sintel ©copyright Blender Foundation | durian.blender.org

Figure 2: Examples of shot sequences which can lead to a temporally inconsistent division to scenes. (Top) Ping-pong sequences where there is an interaction between two entities in a scene. (Bottom) Outlier shots, where a single shot (fourth from the left) in the middle of a scene looks very different. (Best viewed in color.)[2]

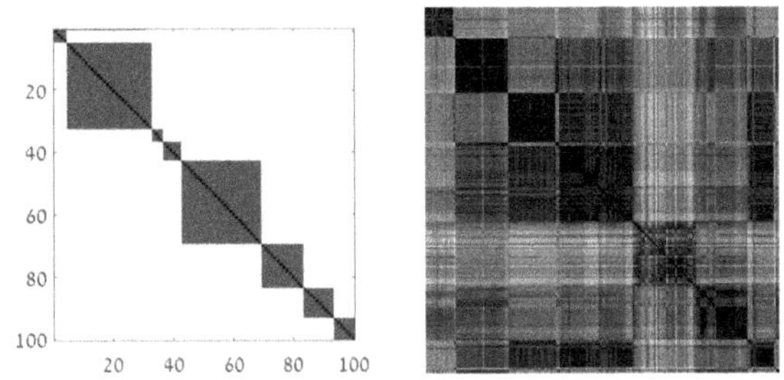

Figure 3: D matrices: illustration (left) and real data (right). Brighter pixels represent larger distance values.

multiple scene transition graphs to calculate the probabilistic confidence of a scene transition. It is interesting to note that these methods lack a unified agreement on how to represent the video. For example, some represent shots as nodes while others represent shot clusters as nodes. Since there is a lack of a joint formulation, the motivation, rationalities, and conclusions from experiments cannot be shared or migrated between methods.

More advanced methods use probabilistic models and stochastic processes [6, 15, 32] to describe a video. Developing or learning a probabilistic model enables a mathematical representation of the video and calculating the probabilities for the existence of scene boundaries. These methods typically cannot guarantee an optimal solution, and often rely on multiple initializations in order to explore and test multiple probabilistic configurations.

3 PROBLEM DEFINITION AND NOTATION

We now present our method for video scene detection with normalized cost. Since the formulation and the optimization process can be applied to multiple types of features and even to different problems, we represent our method in a general formulation as a sequential grouping problem. For the problem of video scene detection, the features can be, for example, color histograms representing each shot, high-level visual concepts, audio features, a multimodal combination, and so forth [21]. In Section 5 we discuss the deep features we use in this work to achieve accurate and robust video scene detection.

3.1 Notation and Definitions

Let us define a series of N feature vectors of length m with a defined order $X_1^N = \{x_1, \ldots, x_N\}$, where $\forall i, x_i \in \mathbb{R}^m$. To measure the distance between feature vectors, we define: $\mathcal{D} : \mathbb{R}^m \times \mathbb{R}^m \rightarrow \mathbb{R}$ such that $\mathcal{D}$ fulfills the mathematical conditions of a distance metric. $\mathcal{D}$ is chosen to return a low value for feature vectors that are similar.

The goal is to find a vector of indexes: $\bar{t} = (t_1, \ldots, t_K)$ that denotes the partitioning into segments. K represents the number of segments (scenes, in the problem of video scene detection). We discuss estimating this parameter in Section 4.2. The vector $\bar{t}$ is limited to $\forall i, t_i \in \mathbb{N}$, and must be monotonically increasing ($t_i > t_j$ for $i > j$), with t_i indicating the last feature vector index in segment i. Thus $t_K = N$, and we can define $t_0 = 0$ to simplify mathematical notation. The monotonicity is enforced to ensure that every segment has at least one feature. We use $\Omega^K \subsetneq \mathbb{N}^K$ to denote the set of all possible $\bar{t}$'s that fulfill these restrictions.

[2]Images taken from (top) Big Buck Bunny ©copyright Blender Foundation | peach.blender.org and (bottom) Tears of Steel ©copyright Blender Foundation | mango.blender.org

3.2 Intuition

Before entering the technical mathematical formulation, we provide a visualization of the problem to explain our intuition regarding the effectiveness of the method. Taking the values of $\mathcal{D}$ and placing them in a two-dimensional array, we arrive at a matrix D in which the value at the i-th row and j-th column is the value obtained by $\mathcal{D}(x_i, x_j)$. This matrix is symmetrical due to the symmetry property of the distance metric, and the elements on the main diagonal are zeros because $\mathcal{D}(x_i, x_i) = 0$.

Our goal in dealing with the problem of video scene detection is to choose the features and distance metric to return a small distance between feature vectors belonging to the same scene, and large distances for features from different scenes. In an ideal case, we would expect the matrix D to look similar to the illustration in Figure 3. In this visualization, larger values are portrayed by brighter pixels. In the ideal matrix D there is an obvious *block-diagonal* structure, in which groups of features extracted from adjacent shots return low distance values between them, resulting in low valued blocks on the diagonal. It is necessary to create a cost function in which placing the elements of $\bar{t}$ on the edges of the blocks on the diagonal would return the global minimum when minimizing this cost.

3.3 Cost Function

Given the motivation described above, we define a cost function $\mathcal{H} : \Omega^K \rightarrow \mathbb{R}$ that maps a possible $\bar{t}$ to a value indicating the quality of the division.

There are various possibilities for the cost function $\mathcal{H}$. The most obvious form is an *additive cost function*

$$\mathcal{H}_{add}(\bar{t}) = \sum_{i=1}^{K} \sum_{j_1=t_{i-1}+1}^{t_i} \sum_{j_2=t_{i-1}+1}^{t_i} \mathcal{D}(x_{j_1}, x_{j_2}). \quad (1)$$

This cost function, used in our previous work [20], sums up all the values in the blocks on the diagonal. The assumption is that these values bordered by $\bar{t}$ should be substantially lower than the values outside the blocks on the diagonal. Another possible cost

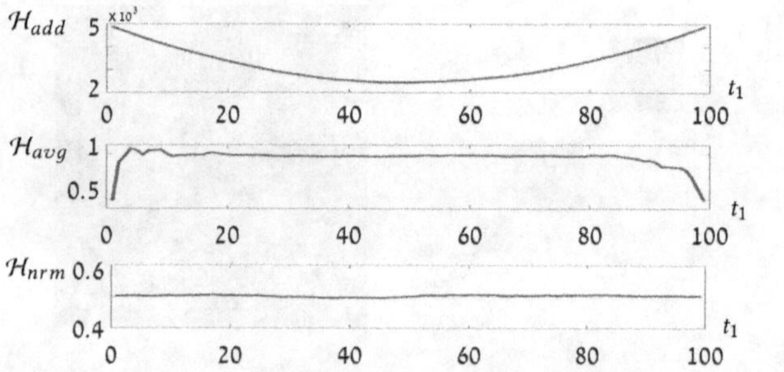

Figure 4: From top to bottom: $\mathcal{H}_{add}$, $\mathcal{H}_{avg}$, and $\mathcal{H}_{nrm}$ for uniformly distributed values of D. Presented here is the cost function value for $N = 100$ and $K = 2$ as a function of the point of division t_1.

function is the *average cost function*

$$\mathcal{H}_{avg}(\bar{t}) = \sum_{i=1}^{K} \frac{\sum_{j_1=t_{i-1}+1}^{t_i} \sum_{j_2=t_{i-1}+1}^{t_i} \mathcal{D}(x_{j_1}, x_{j_2})}{(t_i - t_{i-1})^2}, \tag{2}$$

which sums up the average value of each block on the diagonal.

In this paper we propose the *normalized cost function*

$$\mathcal{H}_{nrm}(\bar{t}) = \frac{\sum_{i=1}^{K} \sum_{j_1=t_{i-1}+1}^{t_i} \sum_{j_2=t_{i-1}+1}^{t_i} \mathcal{D}(x_{j_1}, x_{j_2})}{\sum_{i=1}^{K} (t_i - t_{i-1})^2 - N}, \tag{3}$$

which measures the average value of the entire block diagonal as partitioned by $\bar{t}$. Note that the N subtracted in the denominator is optional and is intended to exclude the values on the main diagonal itself (which are zero) from being taken into account.

To better understand the properties of the different cost functions, we conduct the following experiment: We create a synthetic simulation under a null hypothesis of the data showing no inclination toward a specific division. This is achieved by creating values of D that are uniformly distributed, and thus all points of division should be equally acceptable. Figure 4 shows the three cost functions as a function of t_1 for a division into $K = 2$. We expect the cost function to have a constant response over the point of division due to the null hypothesis stated above. However, we can see that only $\mathcal{H}_{nrm}$ results in the expected behavior, while $\mathcal{H}_{add}$ and $\mathcal{H}_{avg}$ introduce certain biases for the division location.

These biases are mathematical properties of the $\mathcal{H}_{add}$ and $\mathcal{H}_{avg}$ cost functions. For the additive cost function, there is a strong inclination to divide the sequence roughly in the middle since the number of values being summed is the smallest ($N^2/2$ compared to roughly N^2 at the borders). There are two typical scenarios in which the additive cost function will fail to locate a correct partitioning: 1. when the blocks vary greatly in size (see Figure 8), and 2. when the block structure is not very pronounced (see Figure 5). Portraying the opposite behavior, the average cost function prefers partitioning near the borders. This is because a small block has a much higher probability of giving an extremely low average value compared to bigger blocks (since there are less values being accumulated). This results in the algorithm always partitioning as many sequences into single-feature blocks as possible. Due to this limitation it is unusable in practice and therefore not considered further in this paper.

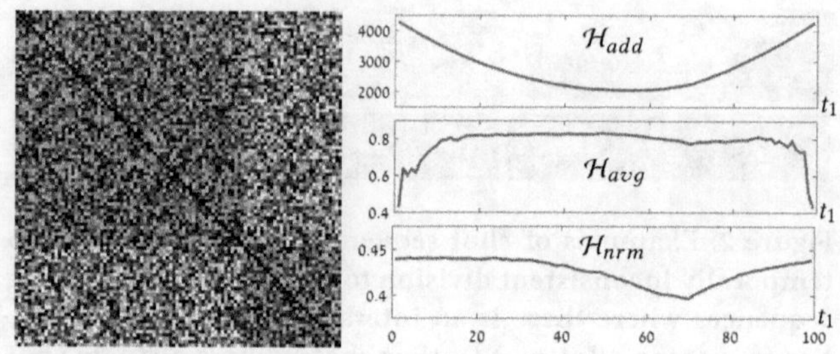

Figure 5: (Left) A synthetic D matrix with a slight inclination for division. (Right) From top to bottom, $\mathcal{H}_{add}$, $\mathcal{H}_{avg}$, and $\mathcal{H}_{nrm}$ in a similar representation as in Figure 4. Only $\mathcal{H}_{nrm}$ allows the identification of the subtle inclination for a division in D.

The normalized cost function gives the desired mathematical formulation to allow unbiased and correct partitioning overcoming the difficulties mentioned above. We evaluate the normalized cost function versus the additive cost function over large permutations of synthetic data in Section 7.1.

4 OPTIMAL SEQUENTIAL GROUPING WITH NORMALIZED COST

Given the normalized cost function, we perform an optimization to find the $\bar{t}$ that globally minimizes $\mathcal{H}_{nrm}$ using dynamic programming.

Dynamic programming is a method to solve complex problems by breaking them down into subproblems and conserving their solutions. Minimizing $\mathcal{H}_{nrm}$, as opposed to $\mathcal{H}_{add}$ and $\mathcal{H}_{avg}$, is especially difficult since the solution to any given subproblem depends on the solution of the complete problem. For example, given $X_n^N = \{x_n, \ldots, x_N\}$, we want to find the solutions to the subproblems of dividing a subset of the features $X_{i>n}^N$. This is possible with $\mathcal{H}_{add}$ and $\mathcal{H}_{avg}$ due to the linearity of their outer sum. However, in $\mathcal{H}_{nrm}$, finding the optimal t_i depends on $(t_1, \ldots, t_n, \ldots, t_{i-1})$ since they affect the denominator.

In the next subsection (4.1), we develop a novel and unique dynamic programming scheme to solve the optimization problem, while overcoming this difficulty.

4.1 Optimization

In our dynamic programming scheme, the only external element that affects the sub-sequence optimizations is a single value—the denominator in (3). The denominator can be treated as an unknown parameter $p \in \mathbb{N}$, and the optimization process can be applied to every possible value of this parameter. We call this parameter *area*, since in effect this is the area of the blocks on the diagonal. We show in Section 4.3 that although the evaluation over all possible values of the parameter might seem costly, in practice the number of possibilities can be greatly limited. In Section 7.1 we present actual running times showing that the method is very practical even in real-world scenarios.

We now detail the optimization procedure using our novel dynamic programming scheme. We define superscripts $\mathcal{H}^{n,k}$ to indicate a subproblem in which a sub-sequence of the feature vectors

$X_n^N = \{x_n, \ldots, x_N\}$ is divided into k segments. When we omit the superscripts, the assumption is that $n = 1$ and $k = K$. Three tables $\mathcal{C}$, $\mathcal{I}$, and $\mathcal{P}$ are defined as follows: $\mathcal{C}(n,k,p)$ is the optimal value of $\mathcal{H}_{nrm}^{n,k}$ where the unknown parameter equals p. p is assumed to be the area added to the denominator from dividing the rest of the sequence X_1^{n-1}. $\mathcal{I}(n,k,p)$ preserves the optimal t_1 of the solution to $\mathcal{H}_{nrm}^{n,k}$ in order to enable recreation of the partitioning, and $\mathcal{P}(n,k,p)$ is the area used in this optimal solution contributed by X_n^N.

We initialize the tables for $k = 1$. This leaves only one possibility, grouping all the features together, which results in:

$$\mathcal{C}(n,1,p) = \frac{\sum_{j_1=n}^{N}\sum_{j_2=n}^{N}\mathcal{D}(x_{j_1},x_{j_2})}{p + (N-n+1)^2 - N}, \tag{4}$$

$$\mathcal{I}(n,1,p) = N, \tag{5}$$

and

$$\mathcal{P}(n,1,p) = (N-n+1)^2, \tag{6}$$

for every n and p. We then fill the rest of the table for k in ascending order.

The logic is as follows. Given a sequence of features X_n^N, allocate the group of features X_n^i into a single group, and the rest X_{i+1}^N into $k-1$ groups. By choosing the i that minimizes the cost, we ensure that as k grows, the optimal solution is chosen. For mathematical neatness, we define:

$$G(n,k,p)(i) = \frac{\sum_{j_1=n}^{i}\sum_{j_2=n}^{i}\mathcal{D}(x_{j_1},x_{j_2})}{p + (i-n+1)^2 + \mathcal{P}\left(i+1,k-1,p+(i-n+1)^2\right) - N} \tag{7}$$

as the contribution of X_n^i to the cost function. The denominator includes the entire area of the blocks on the diagonal, composed of three elements: p, which is the area of solving for X_1^{n-1}; $(i-n+1)^2$, which is the area for X_n^i; and $\mathcal{P}\left(i+1,k-1,p+(i-n+1)^2\right)$, which is the area for X_{i+1}^N.

Therefore, the tables are filled with the following formulas:

$$\mathcal{C}(n,k,p) = \min_i \left\{G_{n,k,p}(i) + \mathcal{C}\left(i+1,k-1,p+(i-n+1)^2\right)\right\}, \tag{8}$$

$$\mathcal{I}(n,k,p) = \operatorname*{argmin}_i \left\{G_{n,k,p}(i) + \mathcal{C}\left(i+1,k-1,p+(i-n+1)^2\right)\right\}, \tag{9}$$

and

$$\mathcal{P}(n,k,p) = (\mathcal{I}(n,k,p)-n+1)^2 + \mathcal{P}\left(\mathcal{I}(n,k,p)+1,k-1,p+(\mathcal{I}(n,k,p)-n+1)^2\right). \tag{10}$$

See Figure 6 for an illustration of this dynamic programming scheme. The value of $\mathcal{P}(n,k,p)$ is composed of contributions to the denominator from X_n^i and X_{i+1}^N, where the optimal point for division i is chosen as $\mathcal{I}(n,k,p)$.

Once the tables have been filled, the optimal cost function value is then $\tilde{\mathcal{H}}_{nrm}^K = \mathcal{C}(1,K,0)$. To recreate the optimal division locations $\tilde{t}$, we use the following recursive formula: initialize $\mathcal{P}_{tot} = 0$ and $\tilde{t}_0$, and then for i running from 1 to K:

$$\tilde{t}_i \leftarrow \mathcal{I}\left(\tilde{t}_{i-1}+1, K-i+1, \mathcal{P}_{tot}\right), \tag{11}$$

$$\mathcal{P}_{tot} \leftarrow \mathcal{P}_{tot} + \left(\tilde{t}_i - \tilde{t}_{i-1}\right)^2. \tag{12}$$

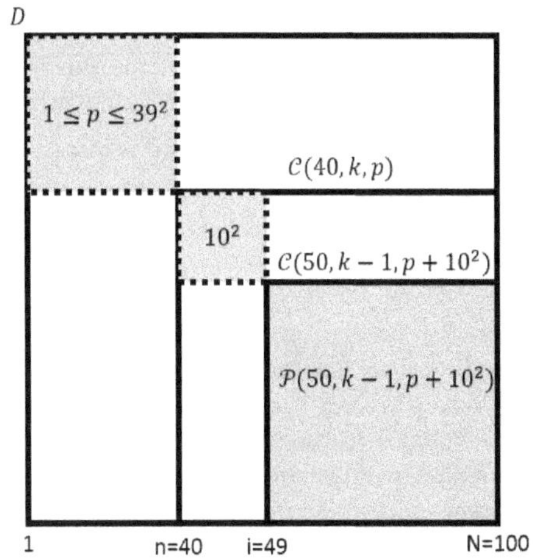

Figure 6: An illustration depicting the operation of the dynamic programming scheme. The entire block represents D, and presented is solving the subproblem beginning at $n = 40$. One of the possibilities $i = 49$ is calculated over possible values of p—the area contributed from the preceding feature vectors (orange). The calculated value $\mathcal{C}(40,k,p)$ uses a subsolution $\mathcal{C}(50,k-1,p+10^2)$ (blue) which begins at index 50, divides into $k-1$ blocks, and the area outside of the subsolution is p plus the area for the segmented block of features 40-49 (green). (Best viewed in color.)

As a sanity check, the process should end meeting the following equality:

$$\mathcal{P}_{tot} = \mathcal{P}(1,K,0). \tag{13}$$

4.2 Estimating the Number of Scenes K

In the process above, we performed the sequential grouping given a particular number of groups K. In many applications, K can be left as an adjustable parameter used to customize the partitioning to a particular level of granularity. Furthermore, a series of results over multiple values of K could be returned denoting a hierarchy of group partitioning. In Section 6 we detail our novel non-greedy algorithm for creating a hierarchical division tree.

When a hard decision has to be made, such as for the analytical evaluation of performance, K can be estimated similar to the estimation of the number of clusters in a classic clustering problem. The gap statistic [30] is an especially noteworthy candidate; it calculates the number of scenes according to the improvement in clustering distance compared with data under a null hypothesis. In practice, we use our method in [20] which automatically detects the *elbow_index*—the elbow in the graph of the log singular values of the matrix D. This index has been shown to reliably estimate the number of blocks on the diagonal of the matrix D due to the equivalence between the problem and low-rank matrix approximation.

4.3 Limiting p

The tables detailed in the optimization process above have to be calculated for all possible values of the parameter p. However, it can be useful to remove values of p that are not plausible. Given n for a specific subproblem, one way to limit p is by keeping it within the range $[n, n^2]$. If k is also known, the range can be further limited to $\left[\left\lceil\frac{n^2}{k}\right\rceil, (n-k+1)^2+k-1\right]$. This is due to the fact that the maximum area is obtained for one large group of size $n-k+1$, and $k-1$ single-featured groups. The minimum area is obtained by dividing the n features into k groups as equally as possible, resulting in an area of $\lceil k \cdot (\frac{n}{k})^2 \rceil$.

The process can be improved further by calculating exactly which values of p are possible, and which are not: We can define a static binary lookup table $\mathcal{B}(n, k, p)$ that denotes when p is a possible area of dividing n features into k groups. This table can be calculated completely offline and is independent of the choice of feature or distance metric. We initialize:

$$\mathcal{B}(n, 1, p) = true \quad \text{iff} \quad n = p^2. \tag{14}$$

The rest of the table can be filled as k increases with the recursive formula (utilizing the logical OR operation):

$$\mathcal{B}(n, k, p) = \bigvee_i \mathcal{B}\left(n-i, k-1, p-i^2\right). \tag{15}$$

This essentially attempts to divide n features into one group of i features and the rest of the features into $k-1$ groups, for any possible i.

5 FEATURE EXTRACTION USING DEEP NEURAL NETWORKS

In recent years, deep Convolutional Neural Networks (CNNs) have enjoyed great success in large-scale image and video recognition, yielding substantial gains in various benchmarks. Deep CNN architectures such as AlexNet [13], VGG [26], Inception [29], and ResNet [11] can be trained on large datasets like ImageNet [9] and then used as powerful feature extractors, with the extracted features incorporating useful semantic information. Similarly, it has been shown that CNN architectures can also offer very promising results on audio classification (e.g., [12]).

For enabling effective video scene detection, the features extracted from the different shots must encode high-level, semantic information about the video content. Given that the low-level information in the video can vary greatly even with small camera shifts, it can be highly useful to identify a shot with the high-level concepts, which will make comparison to adjacent shots more meaningful. Therefore, our hypothesis in this work is that deep features (encoding both the visual and audio information in the video) can prove useful also for the task of video scene detection.

More specifically, for encoding the visual information, we use the Inception-v3 architecture [29] (pre-trained on ImageNet) and apply it to frames in the video (middle frame of each shot) to extract semantic information representing each shot. This is done by removing the final classification layer of the network and extracting the next-to-last layer of the CNN to obtain a high-level representation. The resulting 2048-dimensional vector per shot allows distances between shots to be measured in a semantic and more meaningful way.

In addition, we evaluated the performance when incorporating also audio features to obtain a multimodal representation of the video. For this, we use the VGGish model [12] which represents each 0.96 seconds of audio with a 128-dimensional deep feature vector. When using both visual and audio together, we create separate D matrices for each modality, which are then normalized and averaged together. We note that this merging is not equivalent to averaging the normalized feature vectors together, since the D matrices already incorporate the similarities and dissimilarities between vectors. The merging essentially averages the relative similarity between each pair of shots, allowing both modalities to contribute to the preference of partitioning.

6 HIERARCHY CREATION

In this section we detail our novel non-greedy hierarchy creation method, an optional component when a hierarchical division tree is desired.

In the field of video browsing it can often be beneficial to compute more than a single partitioning for a video, where a hierarchy of the divisions across multiple granularity levels (from coarse to fine temporal partitioning) allows the consumer to better understand the high-level structure of the content in the video. For this, it is particularly important that the multitude of divisions over various granularity levels adhere to a hierarchical structure.

In general, there are two main approaches for hierarchy creation: Divisive methods (e.g., [14]) begin with the coarsest level (no division) and sequentially choose the best location for a division at each finer granularity level. Agglomerative methods (e.g., [16]) begin at the finest granularity level (a partition at each possible location) and choose the best location to remove a partition at each coarser granularity level. The problem with these methods is that they are inherently greedy and typically lead to suboptimal solutions, since at each stage the best location for division or grouping is chosen and cannot be retracted.

To overcome this limitation, we propose a non-greedy hierarchy creation procedure: Using multiple sets of optimal divisions at different granularity levels, we measure the consensus for division at particular indexes and determine the hierarchy of divisions according to this consensus score. If in a classical hierarchy creation method an index of division/grouping indicates that it was the best choice at that granularity level, in our method it indicates that there was a strong correlation over the set of optimal divisions to divide/group at that particular index. This method leads to a much more consistent and reliable hierarchy, where points of division are more accurate due to the larger consensus between multiple sets of optimal divisions.

6.1 Notation

We now define the notation used for our hierarchy tree creation method (see Figure 7 for a visualization of the process). We assume that we have consolidated a collection of optimal divisions $\{\overline{t}^{(K)}\}_{K \in \mathcal{K}}$, with K (as defined in Section 3.1) running over a set of different values $\mathcal{K}$. We wish to determine the hierarchy boundary locations $\overline{T}$, with T_i indicating the i-th chosen boundary. This boundary, per the definition of a hierarchy, exists in the hierarchical tree beginning from level i and onward. Thus, the resulting division in the i-th level of the hierarchy includes the boundaries: $(T_1, \ldots, T_i)$.

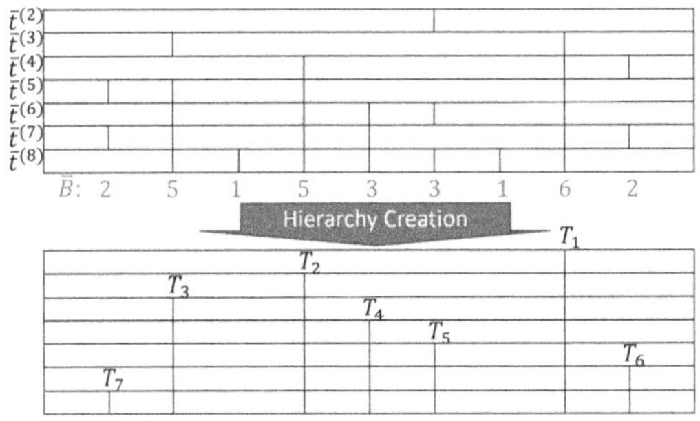

Figure 7: Visualization of our hierarchy creation method. The optimal divisions $\{\bar{t}^{(K)}\}_{K\in\mathcal{K}}$ are used to calculate the hierarchical division tree $\overline{T}$.

To avoid confusion, we note that unlike $\bar{t}$ above, $\overline{T}$ is not monotonically increasing, and that $\overline{T}$'s last value is not necessarily N, rather $0 < T_i < N$ indicates a boundary *after* element i.

6.2 Non-Greedy Hierarchical Division Tree Creation

We define the indicator function $\mathbf{1}_A = 1$ if A is true, and 0 otherwise. This enables counting the number of instances that a boundary was chosen over the entire set of optimal divisions:

$$B_l = \sum_{K\in\mathcal{K}} \sum_{i=1}^{K} \mathbf{1}_{\bar{t}_i^{(K)}=l}. \qquad (16)$$

The values $0 \le B_l \le |\mathcal{K}|$ indicate how many of the optimal divisions in the collection chose to place a boundary at index $l \in [1, \ldots, N-1]$. Dividing by $|\mathcal{K}|$ (this is not mathematically necessary and is not performed in practice) would indicate the probability that a division should be placed at a particular location. With $\hat{B}$ containing the elements in B sorted in descending order, we can determine the indexes that have the most consensus for placing a division. The hierarchy division locations $\overline{T}$ are therefore calculated by assigning partition locations to higher consensus values:

$$T_i = l, \text{ such that } b_l = \hat{b}_i. \qquad (17)$$

This results in a hierarchical division tree $\overline{T}$ where the existence of a particular division is determined by the consensus across the set of optimal divisions.

7 EVALUATION

7.1 Cost Function Evaluation

As explained in Section 4.1, $\mathcal{H}_{nrm}$ is computationally more difficult to minimize compared to $\mathcal{H}_{add}$. However, the latter adds an undesired bias for the point of division. We perform an evaluation between these two cost functions to assess the benefit of the normalized cost function in practice. By creating synthetic simulations of the fundamental optimization problem, we can run a large-scale evaluation using randomized permutations of a typical matrix D, and test the quality of division.

We randomly generated instances of the matrix D with a block-diagonal structure by creating a random matrix D_s with $N = 100$ and uniformly distributed values in the range $[0, 1]$. We chose a random K between 1 and 10, and generated a random permutation of K numbers that sum to N to denote scene blocks. We squared the values inside the blocks on the diagonal, and square-rooted the values outside to keep the values within the $[0, 1]$ range. Finally, we zeroed the values on the diagonal itself $D(i, i) = 0$. Figure 3 shows an example of a synthetic matrix D, and a matrix D created from real video data.

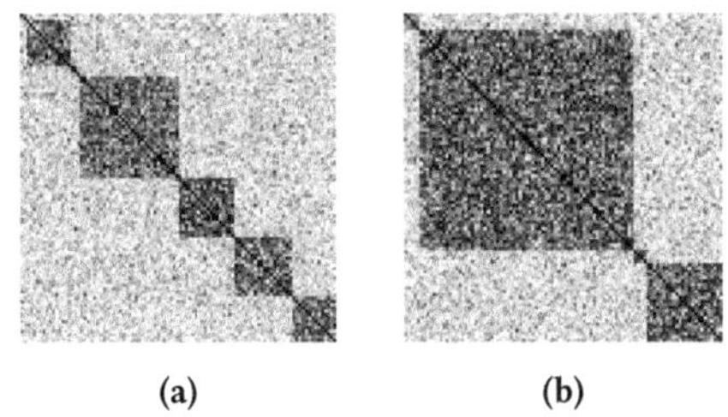

Figure 8: Two examples of synthetic D matrices. $\mathcal{H}_{nrm}$ returned an F-score of 0.92 and 1 for D in 8a and 8b respectively, while $\mathcal{H}_{add}$ returned 0.77 and 0.4. Specifically, the low performance of $\mathcal{H}_{add}$ for 8b is a result of the inherent undesired mathematical bias which tends toward same-sized blocks (as described in Section 3.3).

For evaluation, we used the widely accepted Coverage C and Overflow O metrics [31], with a single F-score as an overall quality measure for scene detection computed as the harmonic mean of C and $1 - O$. Performing 1000 random iterations of the process and assuming a known K, we performed the optimal sequential grouping with the normalized cost function $\mathcal{H}_{nrm}$ and the additive cost function $\mathcal{H}_{add}$.

The results show an average F-score of 0.9 for $\mathcal{H}_{nrm}$ and 0.73 for $\mathcal{H}_{add}$. This shows an obvious advantage for the normalized cost function over the additive cost function. Figure 8 shows two examples of the experiments which stress in particular that the normalized cost function is particularly favorable for varying block sizes. For video scene detection, one real-world example where this is important is when attempting to correctly partition between a video and embedded advertisements, where typically the advertisements are substantially shorter than the video content.

Runtimes averaged at 0.92 seconds for $\mathcal{H}_{nrm}$ with C++ code on a 2.8 GHz Intel ®Core™i7 processor, while $\mathcal{H}_{add}$ resulted in an approximate 5x acceleration. With these numbers, it is possible to decide on the tradeoff between quality and runtime for a specific application. For offline video scene detection, a runtime of under a second for a video with $N = 100$ shots (which in practice relates to a video roughly 10 minutes long) is extremely fast even for large corpuses of videos, which one might find in industry.

7.2 Scene Detection Evaluation

The availability of common datasets to evaluate video scene detection algorithms is limited [8]. Many methods rely on performing evaluation on feature films that are not publicly available. Even some published video scene detection datasets feature videos with no clear licenses or permissions; this can present legal difficulties especially for researchers outside academia.

Consequently, we use the Open Video Scene Detection dataset (OVSD) [22], which comprises 21 full-length freely available videos

Figure 9: The first six scenes of the video ToS from the OVSD dataset as partitioned by our method. In this visualization each cluster consists of a single frame from each shot in the scene. (Best viewed in color.)[3]

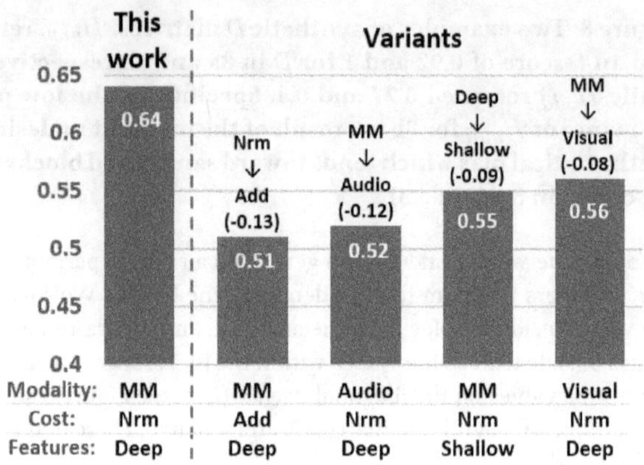

Figure 10: An evaluation of the contribution of each of the elements in our improved method. When using the additive ('Add') cost instead of the normalized ('Nrm') cost function we see the largest drop in F-score value, and so forth replacing the multimodal approach with only audio features, replacing deep features with shallow features, and replacing the multimodal approach with only visual features.

from a variety of genres. We performed shot boundary detection and extracted deep features (see Section 5), and as a distance metric we used L_2-norm. We distinguish between a method that uses only visual results versus methods that incorporate multiple modalities.

Table 1 presents our results over the OVSD dataset against two state-of-the-art methods, and Figure 9 shows some visual results. We compare our normalized cost method using deep visual features to the visual-features-based method in [2] and to our previous method [20], and we compare our multimodal method incorporating the additional use of deep audio features (see Section 5) to the multimodal method in [25]. The results show a significant performance boost for our methods compared to the state of the art.

Additionally, we evaluate the relative gain obtained from various potential design choices of our method. In Figure 10 changing a single element of the algorithm (normalized cost function, multimodal features, and deep features) is tested. We see the largest drop in F-score performance (-0.13) when replacing the normalized cost with the additive cost. This demonstrates again the superiority of the normalized cost function. Next is using only deep audio features (-0.12), using shallow features (RGB histograms and Mel Frequency Cepstrum Coefficients) instead of deep features (-0.09), and using only deep visual features (-0.08). This gives an indication of the relative contribution of each element to the final performance of the complete method.

[3]Images taken from Tears of Steel ©copyright Blender Foundation | mango.blender.org

Table 1: Results on OVSD dataset. Best *F*-score in bold.

Video Name	Multimodal		Visual		
	Ours MM	[25]	Ours V	[20]	[2]
1000	**0.60**	0.50	**0.64**	0.57	0.39
BBB	**0.63**	0.49	0.38	**0.69**	0.46
BWNS	**0.70**	0.61	**0.55**	0.20	0.43
CH7	**0.60**	0.52	**0.58**	0.49	0.26
CL	**0.51**	0.45	0.37	**0.53**	0.07
ED	**0.61**	0.56	0.33	**0.69**	0.55
FBW	0.59	**0.61**	**0.67**	0.14	0.52
Honey	**0.63**	0.38	**0.64**	0.38	0.36
JW	**0.63**	0.28	**0.69**	0.64	0.22
LCDP	**0.72**	0.18	**0.49**	0.42	0.22
LM	0.64	**0.71**	**0.57**	0.25	0.28
Meridian	**0.79**	0.63	0.66	0.71	**0.82**
Oceania	**0.61**	0.51	**0.61**	0.45	0.26
Pentagon	**0.65**	0.48	**0.63**	0.18	0.16
Route 66	**0.60**	0.36	**0.50**	0.31	0.05
SDM	0.70	**0.81**	**0.67**	0.18	0.55
Sintel	0.58	**0.59**	0.36	**0.66**	0.51
SStB	**0.62**	0.43	**0.57**	0.48	0.22
SW	**0.61**	0.40	**0.61**	0.36	0.13
ToS	0.73	**0.75**	0.46	**0.62**	0.23
Valkaama	0.70	**0.73**	0.70	**0.73**	0.16
Average	**0.64**	0.52	**0.56**	0.46	0.33

8 CONCLUSION

In this paper, we presented a unique formulation of the task of video scene detection as a generic optimization problem with a novel normalized cost function to optimally group consecutive shots into scenes. The proposed normalized cost function enables robust scene detection, and is efficiently optimized using a novel dynamic programming scheme despite an inherent dependency between subproblems. In addition, we incorporated the use of deep neural network models for visual and audio analysis to obtain a semantic representation of the elements in the video scene, enabling effective and more accurate video scene detection. We offered two ways to determine the granularity of division: an adaptive estimation of the number of scenes, and a novel non-greedy procedure for creating a hierarchical consensus-based division tree spanning multiple levels of granularity. Our comprehensive experimental analysis showed the clear advantages of the normalized cost function, and demonstrated that the proposed method outperforms the current state of the art in video scene detection.

REFERENCES

[1] Evlampios Apostolidis and Vasileios Mezaris. 2014. Fast shot segmentation combining global and local visual descriptors. In *2014 IEEE International Conference on Acoustics, Speech and Signal Processing (ICASSP)*. IEEE, 6583–6587.

[2] Lorenzo Baraldi, Costantino Grana, and Rita Cucchiara. 2015. Analysis and Re-Use of Videos in Educational Digital Libraries with Automatic Scene Detection. In *11th Italian Research Conference on Digital Libraries*. Springer, 155–164.

[3] Lorenzo Baraldi, Costantino Grana, and Rita Cucchiara. 2015. A deep siamese network for scene detection in broadcast videos. In *Proceedings of the 23rd ACM international conference on Multimedia*. ACM, 1199–1202.

[4] Lorenzo Baraldi, Costantino Grana, and Rita Cucchiara. 2015. Shot and scene detection via hierarchical clustering for re-using broadcast video. In *International Conference on Computer Analysis of Images and Patterns*. Springer, 801–811.

[5] Lorenzo Baraldi, Costantino Grana, and Rita Cucchiara. 2017. Recognizing and presenting the storytelling video structure with deep multimodal networks. *IEEE Transactions on Multimedia* 19, 5 (2017), 955–968.

[6] Vasileios T Chasanis, Aristidis C Likas, and Nikolaos P Galatsanos. 2009. Scene detection in videos using shot clustering and sequence alignment. *IEEE transactions on multimedia* 11, 1 (2009), 89–100.

[7] Lei Chen and M Tamer Ozsu. 2002. Rule-based scene extraction from video. In *Image Processing. 2002. Proceedings. 2002 International Conference on*, Vol. 2. IEEE, II–II.

[8] Manfred Del Fabro and Laszlo Böszörmenyi. 2013. State-of-the-art and future challenges in video scene detection: a survey. *Multimedia systems* 19, 5 (2013), 427–454.

[9] Jia Deng, Wei Dong, Richard Socher, Li-Jia Li, Kai Li, and Li Fei-Fei. 2009. Imagenet: A large-scale hierarchical image database. In *Computer Vision and Pattern Recognition, 2009. CVPR 2009. IEEE Conference on*. IEEE, 248–255.

[10] Mehdi Ellouze, Nozha Boujemaa, and Adel M Alimi. 2010. Scene pathfinder: unsupervised clustering techniques for movie scenes extraction. *Multimedia Tools and Applications* 47, 2 (2010), 325–346.

[11] Kaiming He, Xiangyu Zhang, Shaoqing Ren, and Jian Sun. 2016. Deep residual learning for image recognition. In *Proceedings of the IEEE conference on computer vision and pattern recognition*. 770–778.

[12] Shawn Hershey, Sourish Chaudhuri, Daniel PW Ellis, Jort F Gemmeke, Aren Jansen, R Channing Moore, Manoj Plakal, Devin Platt, Rif A Saurous, Bryan Seybold, et al. 2017. CNN architectures for large-scale audio classification. In *Acoustics, Speech and Signal Processing (ICASSP), 2017 IEEE International Conference on*. IEEE, 131–135.

[13] Alex Krizhevsky, Ilya Sutskever, and Geoffrey E Hinton. 2012. Imagenet classification with deep convolutional neural networks. In *Advances in neural information processing systems*. 1097–1105.

[14] Kaiyang Liao, Fan Zhao, Yuanlin Zheng, Congjun Cao, and Mingzhu Zhang. 2017. Parallel N-Path Quantification Hierarchical K-means Clustering Algorithm for Video Retrieval. *International Journal of Pattern Recognition and Artificial Intelligence* (2017), 1750029.

[15] Tong Lin, HongJiang Zhang, and Qing-Yun Shi. 2001. Video Scene Extraction by Force Competition.. In *IEEE International Conference on Multimedia and Expo, 2001. ICME 2001*. 753–756.

[16] Jakub Lokoč, Klaus Schoeffmann, and Manfred del Fabro. 2015. Dynamic hierarchical visualization of keyframes in endoscopic video. In *International Conference on Multimedia Modeling*. Springer, 291–294.

[17] Mary Meeker. 2015. Internet trends 2015-code conference. *Glokalde* 1, 3 (2015).

[18] Rameswar Panda, Sanjay K Kuanar, and Ananda S Chowdhury. 2017. Nyström Approximated Temporally Constrained Multisimilarity Spectral Clustering Approach for Movie Scene Detection. *IEEE Transactions on Cybernetics* (2017).

[19] Zeeshan Rasheed and Mubarak Shah. 2005. Detection and representation of scenes in videos. *IEEE transactions on Multimedia* 7, 6 (2005), 1097–1105.

[20] Daniel Rotman, Dror Porat, and Gal Ashour. 2016. Robust and Efficient Video Scene Detection Using Optimal Sequential Grouping. In *Multimedia (ISM), 2016 IEEE International Symposium on*. IEEE, 275–280.

[21] Daniel Rotman, Dror Porat, and Gal Ashour. 2017. Optimal Sequential Grouping for Robust Video Scene Detection Using Multiple Modalities. *International Journal of Semantic Computing* 11, 02 (2017), 193–208.

[22] Daniel Rotman, Dror Porat, and Gal Ashour. 2017. Robust video scene detection using multimodal fusion of optimally grouped features. In *Multimedia Signal Processing (MMSP), 2017 IEEE 19th International Workshop on*. IEEE, 1–6.

[23] Yong Rui, Thomas S Huang, and Sharad Mehrotra. 1999. Constructing table-of-content for videos. *Multimedia systems* 7, 5 (1999), 359–368.

[24] Ufuk Sakarya and Ziya Telatar. 2008. Video scene detection using dominant sets. In *2008 15th IEEE International Conference on Image Processing*. IEEE, 73–76.

[25] Panagiotis Sidiropoulos, Vasileios Mezaris, Ioannis Kompatsiaris, Hugo Meinedo, Miguel Bugalho, and Isabel Trancoso. 2011. Temporal video segmentation to scenes using high-level audiovisual features. *IEEE Transactions on Circuits and Systems for Video Technology* 21, 8 (2011), 1163–1177.

[26] Karen Simonyan and Andrew Zisserman. 2014. Very deep convolutional networks for large-scale image recognition. *arXiv preprint arXiv:1409.1556* (2014).

[27] Alan F Smeaton, Paul Over, and Aiden R Doherty. 2010. Video shot boundary detection: Seven years of TRECVid activity. *Computer Vision and Image Understanding* 114, 4 (2010), 411–418.

[28] Jeong-Woo Son, Wonjoo Park, Minho Han, and Sun-Joong Kim. 2017. Scene boundary detection with graph embedding. In *Advanced Communication Technology (ICACT), 2017 19th International Conference on*. IEEE, 451–453.

[29] Christian Szegedy, Vincent Vanhoucke, Sergey Ioffe, Jon Shlens, and Zbigniew Wojna. 2016. Rethinking the inception architecture for computer vision. In *Proceedings of the IEEE Conference on Computer Vision and Pattern Recognition*. 2818–2826.

[30] Robert Tibshirani, Guenther Walther, and Trevor Hastie. 2001. Estimating the number of clusters in a data set via the gap statistic. *Journal of the Royal Statistical Society: Series B (Statistical Methodology)* 63, 2 (2001), 411–423.

[31] Jeroen Vendrig and Marcel Worring. 2002. Systematic evaluation of logical story unit segmentation. *IEEE Transactions on Multimedia* 4, 4 (2002), 492–499.

[32] Yun Zhai and Mubarak Shah. 2006. Video scene segmentation using Markov chain Monte Carlo. *IEEE Transactions on Multimedia* 8, 4 (2006), 686–697.

Transductive Zero-Shot Hashing via Coarse-to-Fine Similarity Mining

Hanjiang Lai
School of Data and Computer Science, Sun Yat-sen University
Guangdong Key Laboratory of Big Data Analysis and Processing
Guangzhou, China
laihanj3@mail.sysu.edu.cn

ABSTRACT

Zero-shot Hashing (ZSH) is to learn hashing models for novel/target classes without training data, which is an important and challenging problem. Most existing ZSH approaches exploit transfer learning via an intermediate shared semantic representations between the seen/source classes and novel/target classes. However, the hash functions learned from the source dataset may show poor performance when directly applied to the target classes due to the dataset bias. In this paper, we study the transductive ZSH, i.e., we have unlabeled data for novel classes. We put forward a simple yet efficient joint learning approach via coarse-to-fine similarity mining which transfers knowledges from source data to target data. It mainly consists of two building blocks in the proposed deep architecture: 1) a shared two-streams network to learn the effective common image representations. The first stream operates on the source data and the second stream operates on the unlabeled data. And 2) a coarse-to-fine module to transfer the similarities of the source data to the target data in a greedy fashion. It begins with a coarse search over the unlabeled data to find the images that most dissimilar to the source data, and then detects the similarities among the found images via the fine module. Extensive evaluation results on several benchmark datasets demonstrate that the proposed hashing method achieves significant improvement over the state-of-the-art methods.

CCS CONCEPTS

• **Information systems** → **Image search**;

KEYWORDS

Image Retrieval; Zero-Shot Hashing; Deep-Learning; Domain Adaptation

ICMR '18, June 11–14, 2018, Yokohama, Japan

ACM ISBN 978-1-4503-5046-4/18/06...$15.00
https://doi.org/10.1145/3206025.3206026

ACM Reference Format:
Hanjiang Lai. 2018. Transductive Zero-Shot Hashing via Coarse-to-Fine Similarity Mining. In *ICMR '18: 2018 International Conference on Multimedia Retrieval, June 11–14, 2018, Yokohama, Japan.* ACM, New York, NY, USA, Article 4, 8 pages. https://doi.org/10.1145/3206025.3206026

1 INTRODUCTION

Due to the ever-growing large-scale image data on the web, image retrieval has attracted increasing interest. Hashing [2] is a popular nearest neighbor search method that learns similarity-preserving hash functions to encode the images into binary codes.

Many algorithms have been proposed for learning the similarity-preserving hash functions [3, 19, 33]. One of the leading approaches is the deep-networks-based hashing [13, 18, 39], which learn the powerful image representations as well as the binary hash codes. Lin et al. [16] proposed to learn the hash codes and image representations in a point-wised manner. Li et al. [13] and Liu et al. [17] presented deep pairwise-supervised hashing. Further, Zhao et al. [40] presented a deep ranking based method for multi-label images, and Zhuang et al. [41] proposed a triplet-based deep hash network.

However, as the image data continue to grow, many new semantic concepts emerge rapidly. And those brand novel classes may emerge with zero or litter labeled images. Zero-shot learning (ZSL) [14, 36] is to build recognition models that capable of recognising novel classes without labeled training samples. The main idea behind ZSL is to exploit knowledge transfer via embedding both classes into a common semantic representation, e.g., the word-vectors [22] of the class names. Inspired by that, Yang et al. [37] firstly proposed zero-shot hashing (ZSH), which sets up a tunnel to transfer supervised knowledge between the source and target classes via an intermediate-level semantic representation. However, due to source data and target data have different data distributions, using the hash functions learned from the source dataset without any adaptation to the target dataset may causes an unknown bias, which is called *projection domain shift problem* [1, 25]. Pachori et al. [24] introduced an unsupervised domain-adaptation model for ZSH, which updated the learned hash model by the query data from the target dataset.

In this paper, we focus on ZSH with transductive setting [1, 5], i.e., the unlabeled images from the target dataset are

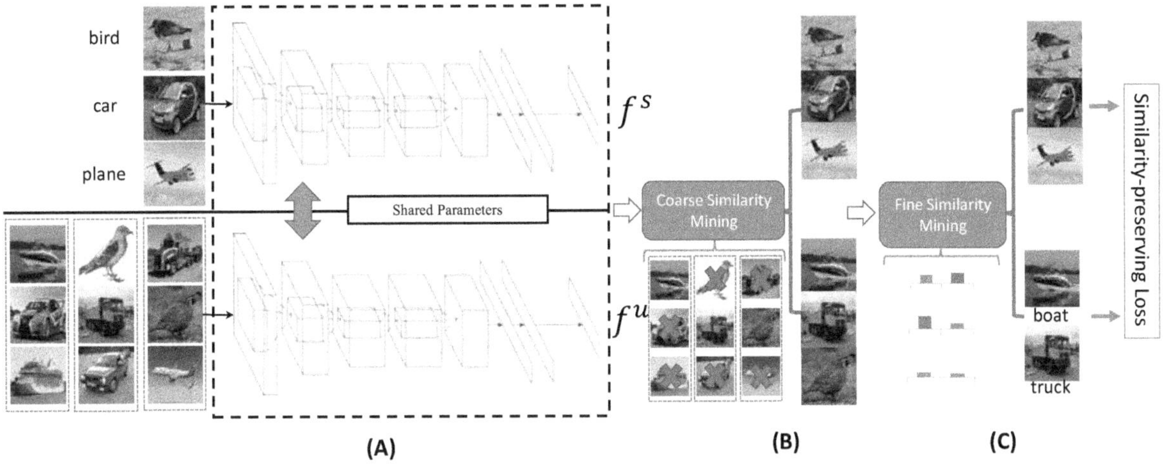

Figure 1: Overview of the proposed deep architecture for the transductive zero-shot hashing. Our architecture is a two-streams network, in which the first stream operates on the labelled images of the seen classes while the second stream operates on the unlabelled images. The architecture firstly (A) encodes the images into the image representations via stacked convolutional and fully-connected layers. With this, it can obtain the common feature representations for both the source and target data. And then it (B) detects the most informative images from the large set of unlabeled images. We propose a greedy binary classification network with the proposed cross-images selection layer to achieve the goal. (C) is a fine similarity mining module to further finding the similarities among the informative images. It greedily selects the image which has the highest probability score come from a novel class, and then assigns the label of the image as its class. After that, a similarity-preserving loss function is conducted to learn the hash functions for both the source and target classes.

available. In the real world, the images of the source classes are usually more common than the novel ones. It is unrealistic to assume that the source data are never existing in the unlabelled dataset. Thus, we do not require the unlabelled data are all from the target classes. Specially, two datasets are considered in TZSH: 1) a labelled source dataset where all samples are from source classes and 2) an unlabelled dataset that includes the images from both of the source and novel classes.

The main problem becomes how to utilize the unlabeled images. Suppose that we have the knowledges from the source images (since labels are available) and there are some unknown and novel knowledges in the unlabeled set. Since the known knowledges and the unknown knowledges are totally different, the unlabeled images that look most dissimilar to the source images are most informative and important to find the novel knowledges. Based on this, we firstly propose a coarse stage to find the images from the unlabeled dataset that look most dissimilar to the labeled images. Further, there are several novel classes and each novel class has its own unknown knowledge. Based on this, we secondly propose a fine stage to detect the similarities among the found images. We consider a simple method in which the found images are assigned to the novel classes one at a time in a greedy fashion based on similarities learned from the semantic representations of the class names.

Specially, we propose a deep architecture to transfer similarities of the seen images to that of the novel classes via coarse-to-fine similarities mining. As shown in Fig. 1, our architecture is a two-streams neural network. The first stream is for labeled images and the second stream for unlabeled images, which are designed to relate the target data to the source ones. Then, we propose coarse-to-fine similarity mining module to transfer the similarities of the labeled source data to the target data. We begin with the coarse stage which is to find the most dissimilar samples. We formulate it as a binary classification problem: the source images are regarded as negative samples and the images from the target dataset are positive samples. Then we greedily select the unlabeled images that have the highest possibility scores belong to positive samples as the found images. Note that these found unlabeled images are most dissimilar to the source images, With the images found in the coarse stage, we also formulate it as a multi-class problem in the fine stage, each output for one novel class. Similar with the binary classification problem, we greedily select the images that have the highest probability scores for each novel class. Finally, a loss function is proposed to capture the similarities among the images, and a hash model is learned to encode all the images into binary codes.

The main contributions of this work are three-folds.

- We propose a deep transductive zero-shot hashing framework to solve the projection domain shift problem, which learns the hash functions for both the source and target data.
- We propose a simple yet efficient coarse-to-fine similarity mining method for transferring the knowledge from the source classes to the novel classes.
- We conduct extensive evaluations on several benchmark datasets. The empirical results demonstrate that the proposed method achieves superior performance to the baselines.

2 RELATED WORK

Due to the rapidly increasing data, hashing has become a popular method for nearest neighbor search. Many methods have been proposed for hashing, including data independent hashing [2] and data dependent hashing [3, 10, 11, 19, 20, 23, 26, 32, 33].

Among the supervised methods, learning the hash codes with deep frameworks, e.g., CNN based methods [4], has been emerged as one of the leading approaches. Lin et al. [16] proposed to learn the hash codes and image representations in a point-wised manner, which is suitable for large-scale training datasets. Zhang et al. [38] presented a novel regularization term to learn the deep hash functions. Wang et al. [31] proposed deep multimodal hashing with orthogonal regularization (DMHOR) method for multi-modal data. Zhao et al. [40] proposed a deep semantic ranking based method for learning hash functions that preserve multi-level semantic similarity between multi-label images. Zhuang [41] proposed a fast deep network for triplet supervised hashing. Liu et al. [17] proposed deep supervised hashing (DSH) to learn compact similarity-preserving binary code for a huge body of image data. Zhang et al. [39] proposed an efficient training algorithm for very deep neural network by alternating direction method of multipliers. Liu et al. [18] proposed deep sketch hashing (DSH) for free-hand sketch-based image retrieval. Mandal et al. [21] and Jiang et al. [7] present deep hashing framework for cross-modal retrieval.

Although the success of the supervised deep hashing methods, they need a lot of label information. Recently, Lin et al. [15] proposed an unsupervised deep learning approach to learn compact binary codes. Three criterions on binary codes are learned in their network: 1) minimal loss quantization, 2) evenly distributed codes, and 3) uncorrelated bits. Wu et al. [34] present an end-to-end unsupervised deep video hashing (UDVH) which integrates the feature clustering and feature binarization to preserve the neighborhood structure of the binary space, and a smart rotation to balance the binary codes. Xia et al. [35] proposed a novel unsupervised heterogeneous deep hashing framework, in which the auto-encoder and Restricted Boltzmann Machine (RBM) are utilized to learn the binary codes. Venkateswara et al. [30] introduced a new dataset called office-home to evaluate domain adaptation algorithms.

While, existing unsupervised hashing methods do not consider to leverage useful knowledge from the related datasets. Yang et al. [37] proposed zero-shot hashing for encoding the images of the unseen classes to the binary codes. In their work, they firstly use NLP model to transform data labels into semantic embedding space, in which the relationships among the seen and unseen classes can be well characterized. Then, the embedding space is rotated for better aligning the visual feature space. Finally, hash functions are learned to transform visual feature space into the embedding space.

Since the underlying data distributions of the seen classes and the novel classes are different, the projection functions learned by the seen classes without any adaptation to the novel classes may cause data bias problem. Fu et al. [1] proposed transductive multi-view embedding to solve the projection domain shift problem. Guo et al. [29] proposed transductive zero-shot recognition via jointly learning the shared model space for transferring the knowledge between the classes. The most similar work is [24], which formulated it as the domain adaptation problem for zero-shot hashing. Given the features of a mini-batch of images belong to the unseen classes, it updates the transformation matrix learned from the seen classes in each iteration.

Although success, most existing zero-shot hashing methods firstly represent each input image by a fixed visual descriptors (e.g., extracted from the pre-train deep models [37]), then followed by separate projection and quantization steps to encode the representation into a binary code. Such fixed visual features may not be optimal and it is expected to learn the visual features that can sufficiently preserve the images similarities. In this paper, we propose a deep framework for learning better common representation.

3 TRANSDUCTIVE ZERO-SHOT HASHING

In this section, we describe an architecture of deep convolution network designed for transductive zero-shot hashing (TZSH).

We firstly introduce notations to formalise the TZSH setting. There is a labeled source dataset $S = \{I_i^s, Y_i^s\}_{i=1,\cdots,n}$, where I_i^s is an image and Y_i^s is the class name/label of the i-th image. We also have a large set of unlabeled data $U = \{I_i^u\}_{i=1,\cdots,n_u}$, which includes the images from both the source classes Y^s and the novel classes Y^u but no annotations. The novel classes Y^u are disjoint from the source ones, that is $Y^u \cap Y^s = \varnothing$. The goal of TZSH is to learn a deep model from the labeled source dataset S and the unlabeled dataset U, while the similarities among the novel images and source images should also be preserved.

As shown in Fig. 1, the proposed architecture mainly contains two parts: 1) a shared deep network for learning the common semantic image representations for both the source and target datasets, and 2) a coarse-to-fine similarity mining module for finding the similarities of the target images with the help of the semantic word spaces. By the word representations of class names, we transfer the similarities from the source classes to the novel ones by the proposed cross-images selection layer in a greedy manner. Finally, we can easily construct the loss function by using the above found similarities.

3.1 Common Semantic Representation via Shared Two-streams Network

To encode both the source and target images into the same semantic space, we introduce a two-streams architecture, which includes two inputs. The first stream operates on the labelled source data $\{I_i^s, Y_i^s\}_{i=1,\cdots,r^s}$, and the second stream operates on the unlabelled data $\{I_i^u\}_{i=1,\cdots,r^u}$, where r^s and r^u are the sizes of mini-batch, respectively. These images go through the deep network with the stacked convolutional and full-connected layers, and are encoded to a common representation space. Note that the weights of the corresponding layers are shared between the two streams, and are trained jointly. The output common semantic representations are denoted as $\mathbf{f}_i^s = \psi(I_i^s)$ and $\mathbf{f}_i^u = \psi(I_i^u)$, where ψ is the proposed deep network.

3.2 Coarse-to-Fine Similarity Mining

We use the following two stages to find the similarities among the target data: 1) we first greedily select the most informative images in the coarse stage, and then 2) we further greedily select an image from the coarse set for each target class, respectively.

3.2.1 Coarse Similarity Mining. The main idea behind our method is that there is commonly a difference between the distributions of the images from the novel classes and the images from source classes. Thus, we can formulate it as a binary classification problem: the images from the source classes are the negative samples and that of the novel classes are the positive samples. To train the model, we can use the labeled images (all from the source classes) as the negative samples. Due to no annotations, the greedy method is applied and the cross-image selection layer is proposed to find the positive samples.

More specifically, we add a fully-connected layer with 2-dimensional after the semantic representations $\mathbf{f}^u$ and $\mathbf{f}^s$, respectively. We have the deep features $\mathbf{c}^u \in \mathbb{R}^{r^u \times 2}$ and $\mathbf{c}^s \in \mathbb{R}^{r^s \times 2}$, in which the i-th row of $\mathbf{c}^u$ represents the probability of the image coming from the source classes is $\mathbf{c}_{i1}^u$ or from the novel classes is $\mathbf{c}_{i2}^u$. We divide the $\mathbf{c}^u$ into m groups with equal length $r' = r^u/m$, and each group selects one image which has the highest score come from target classes. We propose a cross-images selection layer in our network for solving the problem that the target data are unlabeled. Fig. 2 illustrates the proposed greedily selection procedure. Formally, we greedily select m images that has the highest scores coming from the novel classes, which can be formulated as

$$\begin{aligned} j_1 &= arg\max\{\mathbf{c}_{j2}^u, j = 1, \cdots, r'\}, \\ &\cdots, \\ j_m &= arg\max\{\mathbf{c}_{j2}^u, j = (m-1)r' + 1, \cdots, r^u\}. \end{aligned} \tag{1}$$

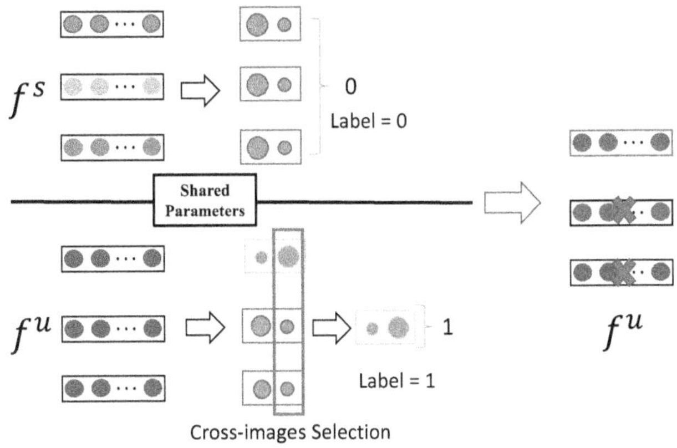

Figure 2: Coarse similarity mining module. To detect the most informative target images, we formulate it as a binary classification problem, in which images of the source classes are regarded as the negative samples and images of the novel classes are positive samples. Without annotations of images, we propose a cross-images selection layer to find the positive samples. For all r' images, the network generates a 2-dimensional probability vector for each image, in which the first value represents the probability score coming from the source classes and the second one represents the probability score from the novel classes. The cross-images selection layer greedily selects one image that has the highest possibility score, i.e., the maximum in the second values of all the r' images.

If the j-th image has a relatively higher/lower score, the j-th image likely/unlikely belongs to the novel classes. The highest score means most likely belong to the novel classes. Thus, these selected m images are most informative images from the mini-batch images, we can use them as positive samples.

To learn the parameters, the problem is a traditional binary classification problem. We can use the softmax loss [9] to optimize this problem, which is widely used loss function for classification problem in neural networks. The loss objective in coarse stage can be formulated as

$$\min -\frac{1}{m}\sum_{i=1}^{m}\log(\mathbf{c}_{j_1 2}^u) - \frac{1}{r^s}\sum_{i=1}^{r^s}\log(\mathbf{c}_{i1}^s). \tag{2}$$

Discussions. First, we show that our proposed deep architecture is able to detect the novel images. Suppose that j-th image is not from the novel classes, it is of a source class. In this case, the first stream will assign the low probability score to this image due to the images of the source classes are regarded as negative samples and the network's parameters are shared. Thus, the probability score can be suppressed in the next iteration and make this image not to be chosen again.

Second, the cross-images selection layer is attractive because it also allows end-to-end training. Specially, the gradient of the objective (2) is $\mathbf{g}$. Then, we can just put the gradient to the place where the image came from and let the gradients of other images to be zero, that is the gradients of informative images are $\mathbf{g}$ and other images are $\mathbf{0}$ in the cross-images selection layer when back propagation.

3.2.2 Fine Similarity Mining. With the found m images from the unlabelled data, we need a fine stage to find the similarities among these images. Although without the annotations, fortunately, the similarities among the class names are available, e.g., we can obtain them via the existing word2vec [22] model. Specially, suppose the i-th class name is Y_i, we denote $Z_i = g(Y_i)$ as the word-vector for the i-th class name. The similarity between the i-th class and the j-th class is defined as

$$Sim(Y_i, Y_j) = \frac{Z_i Z_j}{||Z_i|| \cdot ||Z_j||}, \tag{3}$$

where $Sim(Y_i, Y_j)$ is the cosine similarity between the two vectors.

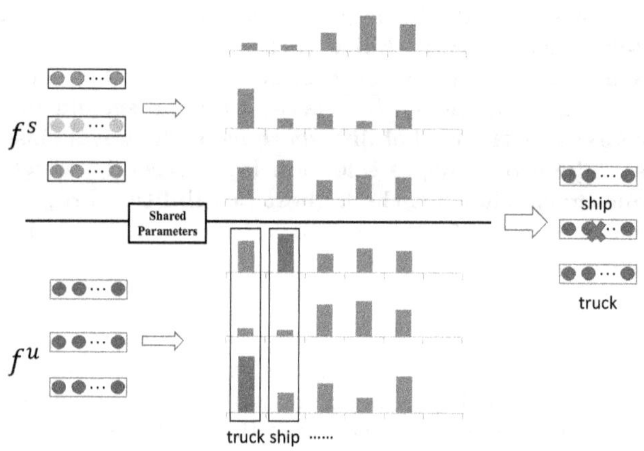

Figure 3: Illustration of the proposed fine similarity mining module. For the m images (in n_y novel classes), our network generates a probability vector for each images, e.g., $\mathbf{p}_i^u \in \mathbb{R}^{n_y}$ $(i = 1, \cdots, m)$. After that, the cross-images selection layer is used to select the n_y images. Each image corresponds to one target class.

Inspired by that, we also use a multi-label classification approach to detect the similarities among the target images. Fig. 3 shows the framework of our method. We project the source classes into the target classes. More specially, we add another fully-connected layer with n_y dimensional features for $\{\mathbf{f}_i^s\}_{i=1,\cdots,r}$ and $\{\mathbf{f}_i^u\}_{i=j_1,\cdots,j_m}$, where n_y is denoted as the number of target classes. These images go through the deep neural network and output the probability scores: $\mathbf{p}^u \in \mathbb{R}^{m \times n_y}$ and $\mathbf{p}^s \in \mathbb{R}^{r^s \times n_y}$. We also use the cross-images selection layer to greedy select the images which have the largest probability come from the novel classes:

$$j_1 = arg\max\{\mathbf{p}_{j1}^u, j = 1, \cdots, m\},$$
$$j_2 = arg\max\{\mathbf{p}_{j2}^u, j = 1, \cdots, m\},$$
$$\cdots,$$
$$j_{n_y} = arg\max\{\mathbf{p}_{jn_y}^u, j = 1, \cdots, m\}.$$

For training the parameters, we also use the softmax loss to optimize the problem. For the source data, we firstly calculate the similarities between the labels Y_i^s and all target classes according to (3):

$$\hat{Sim}_i = [Sim(Y_i^s, Y_1^u), \cdots, Sim(Y_i^s, Y_{n_y}^u)]. \tag{4}$$

Then, a normalization process is calculated as to make sure that $\sum_k \hat{Sim}_{ik} = 1$. $\hat{Sim}_i$ is the probability scores that the image looks like the novel classes, which is used as the label for the i-th image. For the target data, the selected images are assigned to the corresponding classes, respectively. The softmax loss can be defined as

$$\min -\frac{1}{r^s}\sum_{i=1}^{r^s}\sum_{j=1}^{n_y} \hat{Sim}_{ij}\log(\mathbf{p}_{ij}^s) - \frac{1}{n_y}\sum_{i=1}^{n_y}\log(\mathbf{p}_{j_i i}^u) \tag{5}$$

In the proposed fine similarity mining module, the performance depends on the similarities between the source and novel classes. If the novel class has high similarity with one source class, our method can work well. If the novel class is not related to any source classes, our method may fail.

3.3 Similarity-Preserving Loss

As we aim to learn the l-dimensional binary codes, we use a fully-connected layer to compact each $\mathbf{f}$ into a l-dimensional vector $\mathbf{h}$. Through the coarse-to-fine module, we have the deep binary features $\{\mathbf{h}_i^s\}_{i=1,\cdots,r^s}$ and $\{\mathbf{h}_i^u\}_{i=j_1,\cdots,j_{n_y}}$ for the source data and the most representative target data.

The hamming distance between the similar images should be small and the hamming distance between the dissimilar images should be large. For the source data, the similarities can be obtained via the classes Y^s, i.e, $\hat{s}_{ik} = 1$ if $Y_i^s = Y_k^s$, otherwise $\hat{s}_{ik} = 0$. For the i-th image comes from the source classes and the k-th image from the target classes, the similarity is $\hat{s}_{ik} = 0$. For the similarities among the target images, we use both the hamming distance and detected similarities as the supervised information to make sure not introduce too much wrong annotations. Specially, if the indices of the largest value in $\mathbf{p}_{j_i}^u$ and $\mathbf{p}_{j_k}^u$ are the same and the hamming distance between $\mathbf{h}_{j_i}^u$ and $\mathbf{h}_{j_k}^u$ is small, the two images are similar, i.e., $\hat{s}_{ik} = 1$. When the indices are not the same and the hamming distance is large, they are dissimilar, i.e., $\hat{s}_{ik} = 0$. The overall loss function can be defined as

$$\begin{aligned} \min \sum_{i=1}^{r^s+n_y}\sum_{k=1}^{r^s+n_y} & \hat{s}_{ik}||\mathbf{h}_i - \mathbf{h}_k||^2 \\ & + (1-\hat{s}_{ik})\max(0, \epsilon - ||\mathbf{h}_i - \mathbf{h}_k||^2). \end{aligned} \tag{6}$$

4 EXPERIMENTS

In this section, we evaluate and compare the performance of the proposed method with several state-of-the-art algorithms.

4.1 Datasets and Experimental Settings

We conduct extensive evaluations of the proposed Transductive Zero-Shot Hashing (TZSH) on three benchmark datasets.

- **ImageNet** [1] is a subset of the large hand-labeled dataset. It consists of about 1.2 million images and 1,000 categories.
- **Animals with Attributes (AwA)** [2] consists of 30,475 images of 50 animals classes, which 85 numeric attribute values are provided for each class.
- **CIFAR-10** [3] consists of 60,000 images in 10 classes, which each class has 6,000 images. It is labeled subset of the 80 million tiny images dataset.

In each dataset, we resize images of all these databases into 256×256. We randomly select 2,500 images from the target classes as the test set, and the rest images are used as the retrieval database. In the retrieval database, 10,000 images from the seen classes are randomly chosen as the labeled set S and the other images are used as unlabeled set U.

We evaluate the performance by the popular metric: Mean Average Precision (MAP)and the precision scores within Hamming distance 2 as the evaluation metric.

We implement the proposed method using the open-source *Caffe* [6] framework. The mini-batch sizes are setted to $r^s = 128$, $r^u = 256$, and m is setted to 32 for all experiments. In this paper, we use AlexNet [9] as our basic network. For all deep learning-based methods, the weights of layers are initialized by the pre-trained AlexNet model [4] unless noted otherwise. IMH [28], COSDISH [8], SDH [27], ZSH [37], One-Stage Hashing [12] and Domain Adaptation Zero-shot Hashing (DA-ZSH) [24] are selected as the baselines.

4.2 Results on ImageNet

ImageNet is a large dataset and consists of 1.2 million color images from 1,000 categories. For fair comparison, we following the setting of [37]. Precisely, 100 classes that have corresponding semantic word vectors learned from Wikipedia text corpus are selected. We randomly select 10 categories as the target classes and the rest 90 categories as the seen classes.

The pre-trained AlexNet model uses all 1,000 classes in training. It is not suitable for the setting of zero-shot hashing. Thus, we train a new AlexNet model only using the rest 900 classes. The weights of our network are initialized by the new model. And the new model is also used to extract features for the images.

We compare the proposed method with several state-of-the art methods as shown in Fig 4. Note that the results of other methods are directly cited from the work [37]. As can be seen, the proposed TZSH performs better than the baselines in ImageNet dataset. Note that ZSH is the recent proposed method, which achieves an excellent performance on this

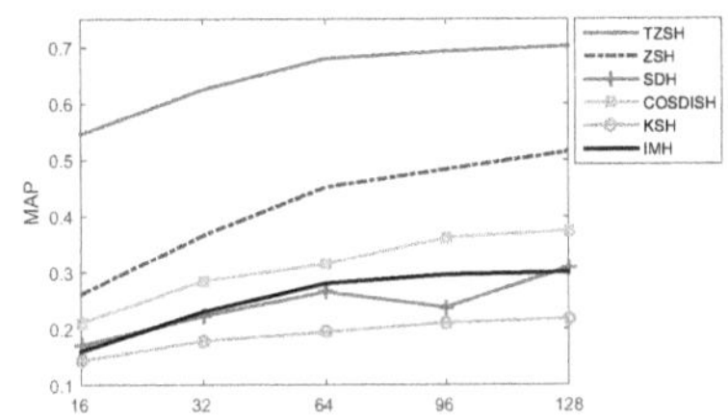

(a) MAP

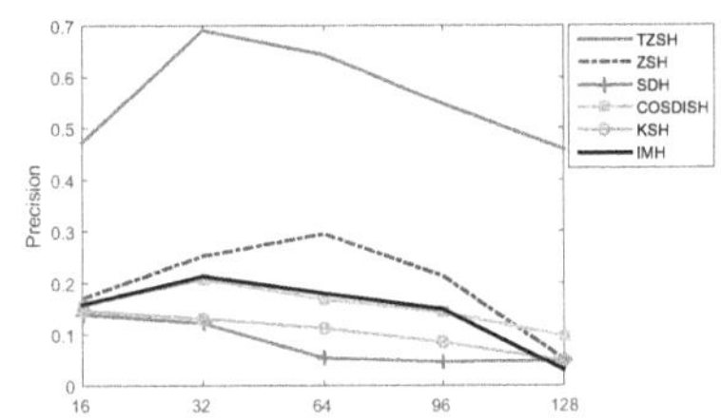

(b) Precision scores within Hamming distance 2

Figure 4: MAP and precision scores within Hamming distance 2 w.r.t. different numbers of bits on ImageNet dataset.

dataset. Even so, our method also performances better than ZSH.

4.3 Results on AwA Dataset

AwA dataset contains 50 animals species. For fair comparison, we following the setting of the most similar work domain adaptation zero-shot hashing (DA-ZSH) [24], which also uses the unlabeled data of the novel classes. Specially, 10 classes are selected as the target classes and the rest 40 classes as the seen classes. The 85 numeric attribute values for each class are used as semantic vectors.

Table 1: MAP of Hamming ranking w.r.t different numbers of bits on AwA dataset.

Method	AwA (MAP)				
	16 bits	32 bits	64 bits	96 bits	128 bits
IMH	0.1082	0.1092	0.1102	0.1102	0.1103
SDH	0.0948	0.0743	0.1127	0.1266	0.1135
COSDISH	0.0779	0.1045	0.1184	0.1115	0.1035
ZSH	0.1087	0.1051	0.1219	0.1171	0.1208
NDA-ZSH	0.0834	0.1067	0.1148	0.1278	0.1281
DA-ZSH	0.1030	0.1261	0.1375	0.1432	0.1432
TZSH	**0.4010**	**0.4803**	**0.5327**	**0.5428**	**0.5442**

The comparison results are shown in Table 1. Note that the results of other methods are directly cited from the paper [24],

[1] http://image-net.org/challenges/LSVRC/2012/
[2] http://attributes.kyb.tuebingen.mpg.de/
[3] http://www.cs.toronto.edu/ kriz/cifar.html
[4] http://dl.caffe.berkeleyvision.org/bvlc_alexnet.caffemodel

which also uses the features extracted from the deep network. Again, our method yields the highest accuracy and beats all the baselines. Note that we only train our model by the labelled images of the seen classes and the unlabelled data, which indicate that our model can performance well on the novel classes even without the annotations.

4.4 Results on CIFAR-10

This dataset consists of color images from 10 classes, i.e., airplane, automobile, bird, cat, deer, dog, frog, horse, ship and truck. For fair comparison, we follow the setting of the most similar work domain adaptation zero-shot hashing (DA-ZSH) [24]. We enrich each class with 300-dimensional semantic word vectors with real number by the pre-trained word2vec model [22]. Two classes are randomly selected as target classes and the rest eight classes as seen classes.

Table 2 shows the performances of all comparing approaches. We take ship-truck, automobile-deer, dog-truck and cat-dog as target classes for zero-shot hashing, respectively. We can see that our method can achieve very high accuracy compared to the baselines. For instant, DA-ZSH achieves an excellent performance on this dataset. Even so, the MAP of TZSH is 0.5502 on average when the number of bits is 16, while the second best algorithm DA-ZSH is 0.4126.

The main reason for the good performance of our method is that TZSH can find the similarities of the target images via the proposed similarity mining module. Thus, similarities of target classes can be incorporated and help to obtain a good performance. However, for cat and dog, these two classes are dissimilar to the other eight classes, leading to hard to transfer the similarities of the seen classes to the novel ones. Thus it is not supervising that the results are poor.

Table 2: MAP w.r.t different numbers of bits on CIFAR-10 dataset.

Method	CIFAR-10 (MAP)				
	16 bits	32 bits	64 bits	96 bits	128 bits
IMH	0.1975	0.2035	0.2087	0.2172	0.2233
SDH	0.1715	0.2022	0.2136	0.2214	0.2396
COSDISH	0.1721	0.2036	0.2164	0.2270	0.2424
ZSH	0.1921	0.2168	0.2223	0.2430	0.2663
One-Stage	0.2128	0.2462	0.2526	0.2632	0.2512
NDA-ZSH	0.2290	0.2018	0.1954	0.1927	0.1875
DA-ZSH	0.4126	0.4313	0.4580	0.5325	0.5529
ship-truck	0.6644	0.6768	0.6848	0.6908	0.6828
dog-truck	0.6263	0.6370	0.6345	0.6395	0.6400
auto-deer	0.6212	0.6266	0.6359	0.6347	0.6405
cat-dog	0.3093	0.3221	0.3118	0.3102	0.3140

To better understand our proposed method, we do further analysis in the following subsections.

4.4.1 Effect of Seen Category Ratio. In this set of experiments, we compare the performance of our method w.r.t different number of seen classes, in which the number of seen classes vary from 2 to 8 [5].

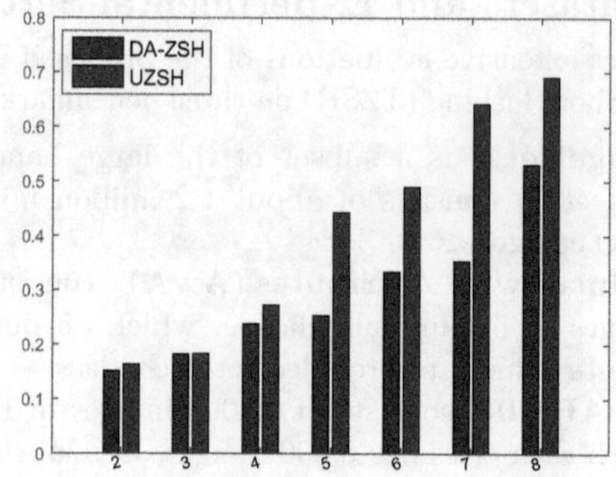

Figure 5: MAP on different number of the seen classes.

Since the DA-ZSH [24] is the most similar work and it performs very well, we choose it as the baseline. Fig 5 shows the comparison results, from which it can be seen that: our method performs best in all different numbers of the seen classes. For example, the MAP of our method is 0.6908 compared to 0.5325 of the DA-ZSH when the number of the novel classes is two. We can also observe that our method achieves significant improvement over the baseline when the number of the seen classes is larger than the number of the novel ones. This is because it is hard to transfer the similarities of the seen classes to the novel ones when the number of the seen classes is small.

4.4.2 Effect of the Unlabeled Size. In training, we have an unlabeled set U. In this set of experiments, we explore the effects on MAP with respect to different numbers of the unlabeled size. We take ship-truck as target classes and the rest 8 classes as seen classes.

For exploring the effect of unlabeled size, the numbers of the unlabeled set are varying from 10,000 to 40,000. Table 3 shows the results. We can observe that our method can perform well on different numbers of the unlabeled set. This is because our method can detect the similarities among the ship-truck images.

Table 3: MAP of Hamming ranking w.r.t different numbers of unlabeled images on CIFAR-10 dataset.

Method	MAP				
	10,000	20,000	30,000	40,000	47,500
TZSH	0.6767	0.6727	0.6786	0.6833	0.6768

[5] Note that we do not give the results when the number of seen classes is one and nine. The reason is that we cannot construct hashing functions with only one seen class and we know all the annotations in transductive setting when the number of seen class is nine.

5 CONCLUSION

In this paper, we proposed a deep-network-based transductive zero-shot hashing method for image retrieval. In the proposed deep architecture, we designed coarse-to-fine similarity mining for finding the similarities of the novel classes. A deep binary classification network was proposed to find the most informative images from the target classes in the unlabelled data. Then, we transferred the similarities of the seen classes to the found images by the help of word representations. Based on the found similarities, we finally proposed a ranking loss function for preserving the similarities. Empirical evaluations on three datasets showed that the proposed method significantly outperforms the state-of-the-art methods.

In future work,we plan to study zero-shot hashing for multi-label image retrieval, in which the image may contain objects of multiple categories.

ACKNOWLEDGMENT

This work is supported by the National Natural Science Foundation of China under Grants (U1611264, 61602530, U1711262, 61472453, U1401256 and U1501252). This work is also supported by the Research Foundation of Science and Technology Plan Project in Guangdong Province (2017B030308007).

REFERENCES

[1] Yanwei Fu, Timothy M Hospedales, Tao Xiang, and Shaogang Gong. 2015. Transductive multi-view zero-shot learning. *TPAMI* 37, 11 (2015), 2332–2345.

[2] Aristides Gionis, Piotr Indyk, and Rajeev Motwani. 1999. Similarity search in high dimensions via hashing. In *VLDB*. 518–529.

[3] Yunchao Gong and Svetlana Lazebnik. 2011. Iterative quantization: A procrustean approach to learning binary codes. In *CVPR*. 817–824.

[4] Jinma Guo and Jianmin Li. 2015. CNN Based Hashing for Image Retrieval. *arXiv preprint arXiv:1509.01354* (2015).

[5] Yuchen Guo, Guiguang Ding, Xiaoming Jin, and Jianmin Wang. 2016. Transductive Zero-Shot Recognition via Shared Model Space Learning.. In *AAAI*, Vol. 3. 8.

[6] Yangqing Jia. 2013. Caffe: An open source convolutional architecture for fast feature embedding. *http://caffe. berkeleyvision. org* (2013).

[7] Qing-Yuan Jiang and Wu-Jun Li. 2017. Deep cross-modal hashing. *CVPR* (2017).

[8] Wang-Cheng Kang, Wu-Jun Li, and Zhi-Hua Zhou. 2016. Column Sampling Based Discrete Supervised Hashing.. In *AAAI*. 1230–1236.

[9] Alex Krizhevsky, Ilya Sutskever, and Geoff Hinton. 2012. Imagenet classification with deep convolutional neural networks. In *NIPS*. 1106–1114.

[10] Brian Kulis and Trevor Darrell. 2009. Learning to hash with binary reconstructive embeddings. In *NIPS*. 1042–1050.

[11] Brian Kulis and Kristen Grauman. 2009. Kernelized locality-sensitive hashing for scalable image search. In *ICCV*. 2130–2137.

[12] Hanjiang Lai, Yan Pan, Ye Liu, and Shuicheng Yan. 2015. Simultaneous Feature Learning and Hash Coding with Deep Neural Networks. In *CVPR*. 3270–3278.

[13] WuJun Li. 2016. Feature Learning based Deep Supervised Hashing with Pairwise Labels. In *IJCAI*. 3485–3492.

[14] Yanan Li, Donghui Wang, Huanhang Hu, Yuetan Lin, and Yueting Zhuang. [n. d.]. Zero-shot recognition using dual visual-semantic mapping paths.

[15] Kevin Lin, Jiwen Lu, Chu-Song Chen, and Jie Zhou. 2016. Learning Compact Binary Descriptors with Unsupervised Deep Neural Networks. In *CVPR*.

[16] Kevin Lin, Huei-Fang Yang, Jen-Hao Hsiao, and Chu-Song Chen. 2015. Deep Learning of Binary Hash Codes for Fast Image Retrieval. In *CVPR*. 27–35.

[17] Haomiao Liu, Ruiping Wang, Shiguang Shan, and Xilin Chen. 2016. Deep supervised hashing for fast image retrieval. In *CVPR*. 2064–2072.

[18] Li Liu, Fumin Shen, Yuming Shen, Xianglong Liu, and Ling Shao. 2017. Deep sketch hashing: Fast free-hand sketch-based image retrieval. *CVPR* (2017).

[19] Wei Liu, Jun Wang, Rongrong Ji, Yu-Gang Jiang, and Shih-Fu Chang. 2012. Supervised hashing with kernels. In *CVPR*. 2074–2081.

[20] Wei Liu, Jun Wang, Sanjiv Kumar, and Shih-Fu Chang. 2011. Hashing with graphs. In *ICML*. 1–8.

[21] Devraj Mandal, Kunal Chaudhury, and Soma Biswas. 2017. Generalized Semantic Preserving Hashing for n-Label Cross-Modal Retrieval. *CVPR* (2017).

[22] Tomas Mikolov, Ilya Sutskever, Kai Chen, Greg S Corrado, and Jeff Dean. 2013. Distributed representations of words and phrases and their compositionality. In *NIPS*. 3111–3119.

[23] Mohammad Norouzi and David M Blei. 2011. Minimal loss hashing for compact binary codes. In *ICML*. 353–360.

[24] Shubham Pachori, Ameya Deshpande, and Shanmuganathan Raman. 2018. Hashing in the zero shot framework with domain adaptation. *Neurocomputing* 275 (2018), 2137–2149.

[25] Sinno Jialin Pan and Qiang Yang. 2010. A survey on transfer learning. *TKDE* 22, 10 (2010), 1345–1359.

[26] Ruslan Salakhutdinov and Geoffrey Hinton. 2007. Learning a Nonlinear Embedding by Preserving Class Neighbourhood Structure. In *AISTATS*. 412–419.

[27] Fumin Shen, Chunhua Shen, Wei Liu, and Heng Tao Shen. 2015. Supervised discrete hashing. In *CVPR*. 37–45.

[28] Fumin Shen, Chunhua Shen, Qinfeng Shi, Anton Van Den Hengel, and Zhenmin Tang. 2013. Inductive hashing on manifolds. In *CVPR*. 1562–1569.

[29] Richard Socher, Milind Ganjoo, Christopher D Manning, and Andrew Ng. 2013. Zero-shot learning through cross-modal transfer. In *NIPS*. 935–943.

[30] Hemanth Venkateswara, Jose Eusebio, Shayok Chakraborty, and Sethuraman Panchanathan. 2017. Deep hashing network for unsupervised domain adaptation. *CVPR* (2017).

[31] Daixin Wang, Peng Cui, Mingdong Ou, and Wenwu Zhu. 2015. Deep Multimodal Hashing with Orthogonal Regularization. In *IJCAI*. 2291–2297.

[32] Jun Wang, Sanjiv Kumar, and Shih-Fu Chang. 2010. Semi-supervised hashing for scalable image retrieval. In *CVPR*. 3424–3431.

[33] Yair Weiss, Antonio Torralba, and Rob Fergus. 2008. Spectral hashing. In *NIPS*. 1753–1760.

[34] Gengshen Wu, Li Liu, Yuchen Guo, Guiguang D-ing, Jungong Han, Jialie Shen, and Ling Shao. 2017. Unsupervised deep video hashing with balanced rotation. IJCAI.

[35] Zhaoqiang Xia, Xiaoyi Feng, Jinye Peng, and Abdenour Hadid. 2016. Unsupervised deep hashing for large-scale visual search. In *IPTA*. IEEE, 1–5.

[36] Yongqin Xian, Bernt Schiele, and Zeynep Akata. 2017. Zero-shot learning-the good, the bad and the ugly. In *CVPR*. 4582–4591.

[37] Yang Yang, Yadan Luo, Weilun Chen, Fumin Shen, Jie Shao, and Heng Tao Shen. 2016. Zero-Shot Hashing via Transferring Supervised Knowledge. In *MM*. 1286–1295.

[38] Ruimao Zhang, Liang Lin, Rui Zhang, Wangmeng Zuo, and Lei Zhang. 2015. Bit-scalable deep hashing with regularized similarity learning for image retrieval and person re-identification. *TIP* 24, 12 (2015), 4766–4779.

[39] Ziming Zhang, Yuting Chen, and Venkatesh Saligrama. 2016. Efficient training of very deep neural networks for supervised hashing. In *CVPR*. 1487–1495.

[40] Fang Zhao, Yongzhen Huang, Liang Wang, and Tieniu Tan. 2015. Deep Semantic Ranking Based Hashing for Multi-Label Image Retrieval. *arXiv preprint arXiv:1501.06272* (2015).

[41] Bohan Zhuang, Guosheng Lin, Chunhua Shen, and Ian Reid. 2016. Fast training of triplet-based deep binary embedding networks. In *CVPR*. 5955–5964.

Asymmetric Discrete Cross-Modal Hashing

Xin Luo
Shandong University
luoxin.lxin@gmail.com

Peng-Fei Zhang
Shandong University
mima.zpf@gmail.com

Ye Wu
Shandong University
kimiwadewu@gmail.com

Zhen-Duo Chen
Shandong University
chenzd.sdu@gmail.com

Hua-Junjie Huang
Shandong University
185031297@qq.com

Xin-Shun Xu*
Shandong University
xuxinshun@sdu.edu.com

ABSTRACT

Recently, cross-modal hashing (CMH) methods have attracted much attention. Many methods have been explored; however, there are still some issues that need to be further considered. 1) How to efficiently construct the correlations among heterogeneous modalities. 2) How to solve the NP-hard optimization problem and avoid the large quantization errors generated by relaxation. 3) How to handle the complex and difficult problem in most CMH methods that simultaneously learning the hash codes and hash functions. To address these challenges, we present a novel cross-modal hashing algorithm, named Asymmetric Discrete Cross-Modal Hashing (ADCH). Specifically, it leverages the collective matrix factorization technique to learn the common latent representations while preserving not only the cross-correlation from different modalities but also the semantic similarity. Instead of relaxing the binary constraints, it generates the hash codes directly using an iterative optimization algorithm proposed in this work. Based the learnt hash codes, ADCH further learns a series of binary classifiers as hash functions, which is flexible and effective. Extensive experiments are conducted on three real-world datasets. The results demonstrate that ADCH outperforms several state-of-the-art cross-modal hashing baselines.

CCS CONCEPTS

• **Computing methodologies → Learning paradigms; Visual content-based indexing and retrieval;** • **Information systems → Multimedia and multimodal retrieval;**

KEYWORDS

Multimedia Retrieval; Cross-Modal Retrieval; Hashing; Learning to Hash; Discrete Optimization.

ACM Reference Format:

Xin Luo, Peng-Fei Zhang, Ye Wu, Zhen-Duo Chen, Hua-Junjie Huang, and Xin-Shun Xu. 2018. Asymmetric Discrete Cross-Modal Hashing. In *ICMR '18: 2018 International Conference on Multimedia Retrieval, June 11–14, 2018, Yokohama, Japan.* ACM, New York, NY, USA, 9 pages. https://doi.org/10.1145/3206025.3206034

*Corresponding author.

ICMR '18, June 11–14, 2018, Yokohama, Japan

ACM ISBN 978-1-4503-5046-4/18/06...$15.00
https://doi.org/10.1145/3206025.3206034

1 INTRODUCTION

Last decade has witnessed the tremendous explosion of multimedia data on the Internet [7, 8, 12, 24, 26, 27, 32–34, 42, 48]. Besides, the dimensionality of data has become higher and higher. Therefore, exact nearest neighbor search, which requires an expensive cost in time or space, becomes unpractical in some real multimedia retrieval applications. To tackle this, a lot of efforts have been devoted to approximate nearest neighbors (ANN) search. It returns approximate nearest neighbors of a given query; however, it is fast and scalable to large-scale problems. Especially, hashing based ANN search has attracted a lot of attention. It first transforms examples into binary codes, minimizing the Hamming distance of similar examples and maximizing that of dissimilar ones; then, pairwise comparisons can be carried out extremely efficiently in the Hamming space, using XOR operations. Moreover, the storage cost can be dramatically reduced. Therefore, hashing methods have become more and more popular for ANN search. Thus, many hashing methods have been explored [15, 21, 37, 39, 40].

Existing hashing methods can be divided into two categories, i.e., data-independent and data-dependent. The former usually uses random projections to generate binary codes of data without considering the specific data. For example, Locality Sensitive Hashing (LSH) [9] is one of the most popular data-independent methods. On the contrary, the latter category generates more compact binary codes by considering specific data, which can be further categorized into unsupervised [17, 37, 41] and supervised methods [11, 44, 46].

In addition, from the point of view of how to construct hash functions, pioneer hashing methods can be classified into symmetric and asymmetric ones. The former methods learn the same hash functions for both the database and the query data; however, the latter ones use different hash functions to generate the hash codes of the database and the query data. For example, two-step hashing [4, 20, 30, 44] is a typical kind of asymmetric hashing methods, decomposing the hashing learning problem into two steps: a binary code inference step and a hash function learning step based on the learnt codes. It has been theoretically proven to obtain superior accuracy with shorter codes [1, 10].

More recently, cross-modal retrieval [31, 49] has become more and more appealing. Accordingly, many cross-modal hashing (CMH) approaches have been proposed. In terms of utilizing of label information or not, existing CMH methods can be divided into two categories, i.e., unsupervised and supervised. Unsupervised CMH learns the projections which can transform the multi-modal features into binary codes by modelling the intra-modal and inter-modal similarity of the training data. For example, Inter-Media Hashing (IMH) [38] learns the linear hash functions for mapping the features in different views into a common Hamming space by preserving the intra-view and inter-view consistency. Collective Matrix Factorization Hashing (CMFH) [6] learns the unified hash codes by collective matrix factorization with latent factor model from different modalities. Latent Semantic Sparse Hashing (LSSH) [51] employs sparse coding to capture the salient structures of the images and matrix factorization to learn the latent concepts from texts; thereafter, the learnt latent semantic features are mapped to a joint abstraction space. Composite Correlation Quantization (CCQ) [28] jointly finds correlation-maximal mappings that transform different modalities into the isomorphic latent space, and learns the composite quantizers that convert the isomorphic latent features into the compact binary codes. Fusion Similarity Hashing (FSH) [23] constructs an undirected asymmetric graph to model the fusion similarity among different modalities, upon which a graph hashing scheme with alternating optimization is introduced to learn the binary codes that embeds such fusion similarity. In contrast, supervised CMH methods further leverage the available supervised information, e.g., semantic labels, to learn the binary codes and hash functions. For example, Cross View Hashing (CVH) [18], which extends the Spectral Hashing [43] to multi-view field, formulates the problem of hash functions learning as a NP-hard minimization problem and then tackles the problem by solving a relaxed tractable eigenvalue problem. Semantic Correlation Maximization (SCM) [49] seamlessly integrates the semantic labels into the hashing learning procedure for large-scale data modeling. Semantics Preserving Hashing (SePH) [21] transforms the semantic affinities of training data into a probability distribution and approximates it with the to-be-learnt hash codes via minimizing the Kullback-Leibler divergence. Semi-Relaxation Supervised Hashing (SRSH) [50] tackles the binary constraint optimization problem by relaxing a part of the binary constraints and replacing one binary matrix with an intermediate representation matrix. Besides, some deep CMH models have been proposed, such as Deep Cross-Modal Hashing (DCMH) [14], Pairwise Relation Guided Deep Hashing (PRDH) [47], and Dual deep neural networks cross-modal hashing (DDCMH) [2]. These deep CMH methods have obtained competitive performance. However, our work is not a deep CMH one, the reason is that we want to concentrate on the design of loss function, which is an important criterion of generating the compact hash codes.

Although many promising cross-modal hashing methods have been proposed, there are still some issues that need to be further considered. 1) How to construct the correlation among heterogeneous multiple modalities is still an open problem for CMH. To solve this problem, CMFH [6] and SMFH [22] leverage collective matrix factorization (CMF) to learn the cross-correlation. However, CMFH is a unsupervised hashing which cannot make use of the label information; SMFH cannot fully explore the information of semantic labels because of the adopted sampling technique. 2) The discrete optimization problem is hard to solve. Most pioneer CMH methods relax the discrete constraints and quantize the real-valued solution, leading to large quantization errors. 3) Most pioneer cross-modal hashing methods learn the hash codes and hash functions simultaneously, making the learning problem complex and difficult. Some two-step hashing methods have been proposed to tackle this; however, most of them can only work on the unimodal data or cannot considering the cross-correlation of different modalities.

To address the aforementioned challenges, we propose a novel cross-modal hashing method, namely, Asymmetric Discrete Cross-Modal Hashing (ADCH), which is a supervised CMF-based two-step hashing method. Specifically, it first leverages collective matrix factorization to find a shared latent semantic space of different modalities and obtain the representations of all instances in the latent space. Then, the learnt representations and the hash codes are formulated to approximate the semantic similarity. In light of this, instead of relaxing the binary constraints, ADCH can learn the hash codes directly by using a four-step alternative optimization scheme. Therefore, it can avoid the large quantization error problem. In addition, ADCH adopts the two-step hashing strategy to learn hash functions for new samples not in the training set, making it flexible. To summarize, the main contributions of this work are as follows:

- We present a novel discrete cross-modal hashing method, i.e., ADCH. It can fully exploit the cross-correlations among different modalities and the semantic similarity to learn precise hash codes. Moreover, instead of relaxing the discrete constraints, it learns the hash codes discretely, avoiding the large quantization error problem.
- A four-step alternative optimization algorithm is proposed. In each step, the variable has a closed-form solution, making the optimization efficient.
- Extensive experiments are conducted on three benchmark datasets. The results demonstrate that ADCH outperforms several state-of-the-art cross-modal hashing methods.

The rest of this paper is organized as follows. Section 2 details the proposed cross-modal hashing method. Section 3 presents the experimental settings and results on three benchmark datasets, followed by conclusion and future work in Section 4.

2 OUR METHODOLOGY

2.1 Notations

Suppose there are n training instances and m different modalities. $\mathbf{X}^{(t)} = [\mathbf{x}_1^{(t)}, \mathbf{x}_2^{(t)}, \ldots, \mathbf{x}_n^{(t)}] \in \mathbb{R}^{d_t \times n}$ is the feature matrix of the t-th modality, where $\mathbf{x}_i^{(t)}$ is the feature vector of i-th instance, d_t denotes the dimensionality of the corresponding feature space and $t = 1, \cdots, m$. Without loss of generality, we further assume that the instances in each modality are zero-centered, i.e., $\sum_{i=1}^{n} \mathbf{x}_i^{(t)} = 0$. In addition, $\mathbf{S} \in \{-1, 1\}^{n \times n}$ is the semantic similarity matrix, where $\mathbf{S}_{ij} = 1$ denotes points i and j are semantically similar and $\mathbf{S}_{ij} = -1$ otherwise. $\mathbf{B} \in \{-1, 1\}^{r \times n}$ is the to-be-learnt hash code matrix of the training set, where r is the length of hash codes. $||\cdot||_F$ and $Tr(\cdot)$ denote the Frobenius norm and the trace of a matrix, respectively. $sgn(\cdot)$ is an element-wise sign function defined as $sgn(x) = 1$ if $x \geq 0$, and -1 otherwise.

2.2 Common Latent Representation Learning

To ensure that ADCH is able to perform cross-modal retrieval and capture the correlations among different modalities simultaneously, we first adopt the Collective Matrix Factorization (CMF) [5] technique to find a common latent space and learn the representations of all instances in the latent space. Specifically, we define the following problem,

$$\min_{\mathbf{U}^{(t)},\mathbf{V}} \theta_t \parallel \mathbf{X}^{(t)} - \mathbf{U}^{(t)}\mathbf{V} \parallel_F^2, \quad s.t. \quad t = 1, ..., m, \tag{1}$$

where $\mathbf{U}^{(t)} \in \mathbb{R}^{d_t \times r}$ is the mapping matrix, $\mathbf{V} \in \mathbb{R}^{r \times n}$ is the common latent representations of all training samples and θ_t is the balance parameter. Theoretically, $\mathbf{V}$ can capture the intrinsic and latent structure of data; therefore, it is able to preserve the cross-correlation of the multiple modalities.

2.3 Semantic Similarity Embedding

Many supervised hashing methods preserve the semantic similarity with the learnt binary codes. For example, a commonly used formula is as follows,

$$\min_{\mathbf{B}} \parallel r\mathbf{S} - \mathbf{B}^\top \mathbf{B} \parallel_F^2, \quad s.t. \quad \mathbf{B} \in \{-1, 1\}^{r \times n}. \tag{2}$$

In Eq. (2), the inner product is leveraged to approximate the semantic similarity with the square loss. And [25] has revealed that the inner product of the hash codes can reflect the opposite of the Hamming distance. Thus, the precise hash codes can be learnt by minimizing the Hamming distances of similar pairs and maximizing those of dissimilar pairs.

As mentioned previously, we leverage the Collective Matrix Factorization (CMF) to map all instances into a common latent space. In order to further build a connection between the hash codes and the representations in the learnt latent space, we reformulate Eq. (2) into the following one,

$$\min_{\mathbf{B}} \parallel r\mathbf{S} - \mathbf{B}^\top \mathbf{R}\mathbf{V} \parallel_F^2, \quad s.t. \quad \mathbf{B} \in \{-1, 1\}^{r \times n}, \tag{3}$$

where $\mathbf{R} \in \mathbb{R}^{r \times r}$ is a mapping matrix. Compared with Eq. (2), one $\mathbf{B}$ is replaced by the real-valued matrix $\mathbf{RV}$, which can approximate the similarity more accurately [4, 10]. In another word, we assume that the representations in the common latent space can be mapped with the matrix $\mathbf{R}$ to approximate the hash codes. Moreover, by replacing one $\mathbf{B}$ with the real-valued matrix $\mathbf{RV}$, the optimization problem becomes easy to solve, shown in subsection 2.6

2.4 Kernelization

In hashing literature [11, 25], kernelization is a popular and powerful technique for better capturing the non-linear structure of data. In this work, we also adopt it to map each instance into a k-dimensional kernel feature representation. Specifically, we adopt the RBF kernel, i.e., $\phi(\mathbf{x}^{(t)}) = [exp(\parallel \mathbf{x}^{(t)} - \mathbf{o}_1 \parallel^2/\sigma), \cdots, exp(\parallel \mathbf{x}^{(t)} - \mathbf{o}_k \parallel^2/\sigma)]$, where $\mathbf{o}_1, \mathbf{o}_2, \cdots, \mathbf{o}_k$ are k randomly sampled anchor points and σ is the kernel width. In this work, we set $k = 500$ and $\sigma = \frac{1}{kn}\sum_{i=1}^{n}\sum_{j=1}^{k} \parallel \mathbf{x}_i - \mathbf{o}_j \parallel_2$.

2.5 Overall Objective Function

Combining Eq. (1) and Eq. (3) together, and replacing the original features $X^{(t)}$ with the kernel features $\phi(\mathbf{X}^{(t)})$, we have the following overall objective function,

$$\min_{\mathbf{U}^{(t)},\mathbf{V},\mathbf{R},\mathbf{B}} \sum_{t=1}^{m} \theta_t \parallel \phi(\mathbf{X}^{(t)}) - \mathbf{U}^{(t)}\mathbf{V} \parallel_F^2 + \lambda \parallel r\mathbf{S} - \mathbf{B}^\top \mathbf{R}\mathbf{V} \parallel_F^2, \quad s.t. \quad \mathbf{B} \in \{-1, 1\}^{r \times n}, \tag{4}$$

where λ is the tradeoff parameter.

2.6 Optimization

By optimizing Eq. (4), we can generate the binary codes $\mathbf{B}$ of all training samples. However, it is not convex and hard to solve. Therefore, we proposed a four-step iterative scheme to alternatively update $\mathbf{U}^{(t)}, \mathbf{V}, \mathbf{R}$, and $\mathbf{B}$. The details of the optimization algorithm are elaborated as follows.

Step 1: Update $\mathbf{U}^{(t)}$ by fixing $\mathbf{V}, \mathbf{R}$, and $\mathbf{B}$.
The problem is then simplified into the following one,

$$\min_{\mathbf{U}^{(t)}} \parallel \phi(\mathbf{X}^{(t)}) - \mathbf{U}^{(t)}\mathbf{V} \parallel_F^2, \tag{5}$$

It becomes a least square problem and easy to solve. For example, we can obtain a closed-form solution to it by setting the derivative of Eq. (5) with respect to $\mathbf{U}^{(t)}$ equal to zero,

$$\mathbf{U}^{(t)} = (\phi(\mathbf{X}^{(t)})\mathbf{V}^\top)(\mathbf{V}\mathbf{V}^\top)^{-1}. \tag{6}$$

Step 2: **Update V by fixing $\mathbf{U}^{(t)}$, R, and B.**
The problem in Eq. (4) becomes as follows,

$$\min_{\mathbf{V}} \sum_{t=1}^{m} \theta_t \parallel \phi(\mathbf{X}^{(t)}) - \mathbf{U}^{(t)}\mathbf{V} \parallel_F^2 + \lambda \parallel r\mathbf{S} - \mathbf{B}^\top \mathbf{R}\mathbf{V} \parallel_F^2, \quad s.t. \quad \mathbf{B} \in \{-1, 1\}^{r \times n}, \tag{7}$$

Setting the derivative of Eq. (7) with respect to $\mathbf{V}$ equal to zero, we can also obtain the closed-form solution shown below,

$$\mathbf{V} = (\lambda \mathbf{R}^\top \mathbf{B}\mathbf{B}^\top \mathbf{R} + \sum_{t=1}^{m} \theta_t (\mathbf{U}^{(t)})^\top \mathbf{U}^{(t)})^{-1} \cdot (\lambda r \mathbf{R}^\top \mathbf{B}\mathbf{S} + \sum_{t=1}^{m} \theta_t (\mathbf{U}^{(t)})^\top \phi(\mathbf{X}^{(t)})). \tag{8}$$

Step 3: Update R by fixing $\mathbf{U}^{(t)}$, V, and B.
The problem in (4) is then rewritten as,

$$\min_{\mathbf{R}} \lambda \parallel r\mathbf{S} - \mathbf{B}^\top \mathbf{R}\mathbf{V} \parallel_F^2, \quad s.t. \quad \mathbf{B} \in \{-1, 1\}^{r \times n}, \tag{9}$$

Setting the derivative of (9) with respect to $\mathbf{R}$ equal to zero, we can obtain the closed-form solution of $\mathbf{R}$,

$$\mathbf{R} = (\mathbf{B}\mathbf{B}^\top)^{-1}\mathbf{B}\mathbf{S}\mathbf{V}^\top(\mathbf{V}\mathbf{V}^\top)^{-1}. \tag{10}$$

Step 4: Update B by fixing $\mathbf{U}^{(t)}$, V, and R.
The problem in Eq. (4) becomes the following one,

$$\min_{\mathbf{B}} \lambda \parallel r\mathbf{S} - \mathbf{B}^\top \mathbf{R}\mathbf{V} \parallel_F^2, \quad s.t. \quad \mathbf{B} \in \{-1, 1\}^{r \times n}. \tag{11}$$

It is a NP-hard optimization problem due to the binary constraint. To tackle the binary constraint, most existing hashing methods first relax it and solve a continuous learning problem; then, generate the approximate binary solution via quantization. As mentioned previously, the relaxation scheme may generate large quantization errors and the approximate solution becomes suboptimal.

To address this issue, we discretely learn it bit-by-bit, inspired by the method in [36], i.e., discrete cyclic coordinate descent (DCC). We first rewrite Eq. (11) as follows,

$$\begin{aligned} &\min_{\mathbf{B}} \| r\mathbf{S} \|_F^2 - 2rTr(\mathbf{S}^\top \mathbf{B}^\top \mathbf{R}\mathbf{V}) + \| \mathbf{B}^\top \mathbf{R}\mathbf{V} \|_F^2, \\ &s.t. \quad \mathbf{B} \in \{-1, 1\}^{r \times n}. \end{aligned} \tag{12}$$

Discarding the constant term, i.e., $\| r\mathbf{S} \|_F^2$, we obtain the following problem,

$$\begin{aligned} &\min_{\mathbf{B}} \| \mathbf{B}^\top \mathbf{P} \|_F^2 - 2rTr(\mathbf{B}^\top \mathbf{Q}), \\ &s.t. \quad \mathbf{B} \in \{-1, 1\}^{r \times n}, \end{aligned} \tag{13}$$

where $\mathbf{P} = \mathbf{R}\mathbf{V}$, $\mathbf{Q} = \mathbf{R}\mathbf{V}\mathbf{S}^\top$. Then, we learn $\mathbf{B}$ bit by bit. Specifically, we use $\mathbf{b}^\top$ to denote the k-th row of $\mathbf{B}$ ($k = 1, \cdots r$) and $\mathbf{B}'$ to denote the matrix of $\mathbf{B}$ excluding $\mathbf{b}$. Similarly, let $\mathbf{p}^\top$ be the k-th row of $\mathbf{P}$, $\mathbf{P}'$ the matrix of $\mathbf{P}$ excluding $\mathbf{p}$ and let $\mathbf{q}^\top$ be the k-th row of $\mathbf{Q}$, $\mathbf{Q}'$ the matrix of $\mathbf{Q}$ excluding $\mathbf{q}$. Thereafter, we have,

$$\begin{aligned} \| \mathbf{B}^\top \mathbf{P} \|_F^2 &= Tr(\mathbf{B}^\top \mathbf{P}\mathbf{P}^\top \mathbf{B}), \\ &= \| \mathbf{b}\mathbf{p}^\top \|_F^2 + 2\mathbf{p}^\top \mathbf{P}'^\top \mathbf{B}'\mathbf{b} + const. \end{aligned} \tag{14}$$

Here $\| \mathbf{b}^\top \mathbf{p} \|_F^2 = Tr(\mathbf{p}^\top \mathbf{b}\mathbf{b}^\top \mathbf{p}) = n\mathbf{p}^\top \mathbf{p} = const$. Similarly, we have $Tr(\mathbf{B}^\top \mathbf{Q}) = \mathbf{q}^\top \mathbf{b}$. Then, we obtain the following optimization problem,

$$\begin{aligned} &\min_{\mathbf{b}} (\mathbf{p}^\top \mathbf{P}'^\top \mathbf{B}' - \mathbf{q}^\top)\mathbf{b}, \\ &s.t. \quad \mathbf{b} \in \{-1, 1\}^n. \end{aligned} \tag{15}$$

Apparently, the optimal solution of problem (15) is as follows,

$$\mathbf{b} = sgn(\mathbf{q} - \mathbf{B}'^\top \mathbf{P}'\mathbf{p}). \tag{16}$$

From Eq. (16), we can see that current bit of $\mathbf{b}$ is based on the pre-learnt bits. We can iteratively update each bit until the procedure converges to a set of better codes. In our experiments, the whole r-bit hash codes for the training data can be iteratively learnt in tr times by 16, where $t = 3$.

By repeating the above 4 steps until it is convergent, we can obtain the final hash codes of all instances in the training set. It is worth noting that all variables in Eq. (4) have closed-form solutions; therefore, the precise hash codes can be learnt. The whole alternative optimization scheme is summarized in Algorithm 1.

2.7 Hash Functions Learning

As mentioned previously, ADCH is an asymmetric hashing method, adopting different encoding strategies for instances in the retrieval set and query set. And the hash codes of the retrieval set are generated by optimizing the overall objective function, i.e, Eq. (4). Thereafter, we learn the hash functions to generate hash codes of new instances not in the training set, e.g., those in the query set. For this purpose, we can train r binary classifiers based on the feature matrix and the learnt code matrix, acting as hash functions, which has been demonstrated to be an effective scheme [16, 20, 40, 49]. Any

Algorithm 1 The optimization algorithm in ADCH.

Input: The similarity matrix $\mathbf{S}$, the kernel features of training data $\phi(\mathbf{X}^{(t)}), t = 1, \cdots, m$, the parameters $\theta_t, t = 1, \cdots, m$ and λ, the iteration number C and hash code length r.

```
Randomly initialize U^(t), V, R, and B.
for iter = 1 → C do
    Update U^(t) using Eq. (6).
    Update V using Eq. (8).
    Update R using Eq. (10).
    Update B using Eq. (16).
end for
```

Output: $\mathbf{U}^{(t)}$, $\mathbf{V}$, $\mathbf{R}$, and $\mathbf{B}$.

effective predictive model can be leveraged in such a scheme, e.g., linear classifiers [16, 40, 49], SVM with RBF kernel [20], boosted decision trees [16, 19], and deep convolutional network [44]. Generally, more powerful classifiers can ensure better accuracy; however, more training time is consumed. Considering the efficiency, in this work, we adopt linear classifier as the hash functions. Specifically, the projection matrix $\mathbf{W}^{(t)}$ for the t-th modality, transforming the kernel features of the k-th modality $\phi(\mathbf{X}^{(t)})$ to $\mathbf{B}$, can be learnt by optimizing the following problem,

$$\| \mathbf{B} - \mathbf{W}^{(t)}\phi(\mathbf{X}^{(t)}) \|_F^2 + \beta \| \mathbf{W}^{(t)} \|_F^2, \tag{17}$$

where β is a balance parameter, and $\| \mathbf{W}^{(t)} \|_F^2$ is a regularization term. And the optimal $\mathbf{W}^{(t)}$ can be computed as,

$$\mathbf{W}^{(t)} = B\phi(\mathbf{X}^{(t)})^\top (\phi(\mathbf{X}^{(t)})\phi(\mathbf{X}^{(t)})^\top + \beta\mathbf{I})^{-1}. \tag{18}$$

Thereafter, we can easily generate the hash code of a new query sample $\mathbf{x}_{query}$. For example, given the t-th modality, we can obtain its hash code with the following equation,

$$\mathbf{B}_{query} = sgn(\mathbf{W}^{(t)}\phi(\mathbf{x}_{query}^{(t)})), \tag{19}$$

where $\phi(\cdot)$ is the nonlinear embedding with the RBF kernel as mentioned in Section 2.4.

3 EXPERIMENTS

To evaluate the performance of ADCH, we carried out extensive experiments on three widely-used benchmark datasets and compared it with nine state-of-the-art cross-modal hashing methods.

3.1 Experimental Settings

3.1.1 Datasets. Experiments are conducted on three benchmark datasets, i.e., Wiki [35], MIRFlickr [13], and NUS-WIDE [3]. All of the datasets are with two modalities, i.e., image and text.

Wiki: It consists of 2,866 image-text pairs and was collected from Wikipedia. Each instance is annotated with one of 10 semantic classes. In addition, the image of each instance is represented by a 128-dimension *SIFT* [29] feature vector, and the text is represented by a 10-dimension topic vector. Wiki was initially split into a training set with 2,173 instances and a test set of 693 instances.

MIRFlickr: It consists of 25,000 instances collected from Flickr website, each being manually annotated with at least one of 24 labels. The image modality is described by a 150-dimension edge histogram [29] and the text modality is described by a 500-dimension feature vector generated from PCA on its index tagging vector. We randomly selected 25% instances of the dataset as the query set, and the remaining 75% ones as the training set.

NUS-WIDE: It is a large-scale real-world dataset crawled from Flickr, containing 269, 648 instances. Each instance has an image with its associated textual tags and is manually annotated with at least one of 81 provided labels. However, some instances' labels are scarce; so we followed the same settings of previous works [21, 45, 51] and selected 10 most common concepts and the corresponding 186, 577 instances. For each instance, the visual view is represented by a 500-dimension bag-of-visual SIFT feature vector and the textual view is represented by a binary tagging vector w.r.t. the top 1, 000 most frequent tags. We selected 2% of the data as the query set and the rest as the training set.

On Wiki, if two instances have the same class label, they are considered to be semantically similar and dissimilar otherwise. For the multi-label datasets MIRFlickr and NUS-WIDE, two instances are considered to be semantically similar only if they share at least one semantic tag. Following previous works [21, 45, 50], we randomly selected 5,000 instances on MIRFlickr and 10,000 instances on NUS-WIDE from the original training set to train our method and all baselines.

3.1.2 Baselines and Implementation Details. Considering that ADCH is a shallow model, we compared ADCH with nine sate-of-the-art shallow cross-modal hashing methods, i.e., CVH [18], IMH[38], SCM-seq [49], LSSH [51], CMFH [6], SePH-km [21], CCQ [28] FSH [23], and SRSH [50]. They can be divided into two categories: IMH, LSSH, CMFH, CCQ, and FSH are unsupervised ones, while CVH, SCM-seq, SePH-km, and SRSH are supervised ones.

The source codes of most baselines are kindly provided by the authors. We carefully tuned their parameters according to the scheme suggested by the authors. All experiments are repeated 10 times with random data partitions, and the averaged results are reported. For ADCH, its parameters are selected by a validation procedure, i.e., $\theta_1 = 0.1, \theta_2 = 0.9, \lambda = 0.001$, and $\beta = 1$. In addition, the total iterative number C of Algorithm 1 is set to 3.

3.1.3 Evaluation Metrics. We conducted two cross-modal retrieval tasks: 1) Image-to-Text using image as query to search similar texts; 2) Text-to-Image using text as query to search similar images. In the testing phase, the Hamming distance is adopted to measure the similarity between the binary codes of the query instances and the ones in image/text database. In addition, we adopt three widely-used performance measures for multi-modal hashing to evaluate all methods, namely mean average precision (MAP), top-N precision and precision-recall curves. For all metrics, a larger value indicates a better retrieval performance.

3.2 Retrieval performance

3.2.1 Results on Wiki. The MAP results of ADCH and all baselines on Wiki are listed in Table 1. And the top-N precision and precision-recall curves in the cases of 8-bit and 32-bit are plotted in Figure 1. From these results, we can observe that:

- ADCH significantly outperforms all baselines in all cases, well demonstrating its effectiveness.

Table 1: The MAP results of various models on WIKI. The best results are in boldface.

Task	Method	8 bits	16 bits	24 bits	32 bits	64 bits
Image to Text	CVH	0.1881	0.1777	0.1706	0.1643	0.1532
	IMH	0.1628	0.1678	0.1662	0.1651	0.1670
	SCM-seq	0.1845	0.1898	0.2102	0.2284	0.2127
	LSSH	0.1885	0.2180	0.2104	0.2071	0.2068
	CMFH	0.2065	0.1965	0.2179	0.2281	0.2371
	SePH-km	0.2542	0.2548	0.2931	0.3002	0.3040
	CCQ	0.1660	0.1667	0.1622	0.1685	0.1686
	FSH	0.2062	0.2476	0.2521	0.2526	0.2454
	SRSH	0.2867	0.3250	0.3524	0.3611	0.3690
	ADCH	**0.3218**	**0.3626**	**0.3774**	**0.3968**	**0.3864**
Text to Image	CVH	0.1834	0.1612	0.1506	0.1372	0.1227
	IMH	0.1312	0.1376	0.1391	0.1402	0.1329
	SCM-seq	0.1545	0.1812	0.1916	0.1993	0.1944
	LSSH	0.4231	0.4977	0.5083	0.5227	0.5266
	CMFH	0.4655	0.4726	0.4967	0.5139	0.5331
	SePH-km	0.6215	0.5991	0.6479	0.6506	0.6678
	CCQ	0.2188	0.2322	0.2469	0.2493	0.2544
	FSH	0.4235	0.5077	0.5326	0.5152	0.5118
	SRSH	0.5960	0.6882	0.7190	0.7313	0.7466
	ADCH	**0.7332**	**0.7462**	**0.7581**	**0.7585**	**0.7563**

- In general, the results of most methods at Text-to-Image task are much better than those at Image-to-Text task. The reason for this phenomenon may be that text modality can better describe the content of an image-text pair than the image modality.
- The performance of unsupervised LSSH and CMFH are always better than supervised IMH and CVH since the qualitative latent semantic features are well exploited.
- ADCH obtains better results when the hash code length becomes longer. The main reason is that, in ADCH, the binary codes are learnt bit by bit and the useful information in the pre-learnt bits can be incorporated incrementally when updating the current bit.

From Table 1 and Figure 1, we can conclude that ADCH is effective on Wiki.

3.2.2 Results on MIRFlickr. Table 2 contains the MAP results of all methods on MIRFlickr and Figure 2 illustrates the top-N precision and precision-recall curves with 8 and 32 bits. From these results, we have the following observations:

- ADCH obtains the best results in all cases, which further shows its effectiveness.
- Similar to the results on Wiki, most methods perform better at Text-to-Image task than Image-to-Text task and ADCH obtains better accuracy with longer codes.
- The MAP results of most methods on MIRFlickr are much better than those on Wiki. The reason is that MIRFlickr is a multi-label dataset and one instance has more semantically similar neighbours on MIRFlickr, while Wiki is a multi-class one.

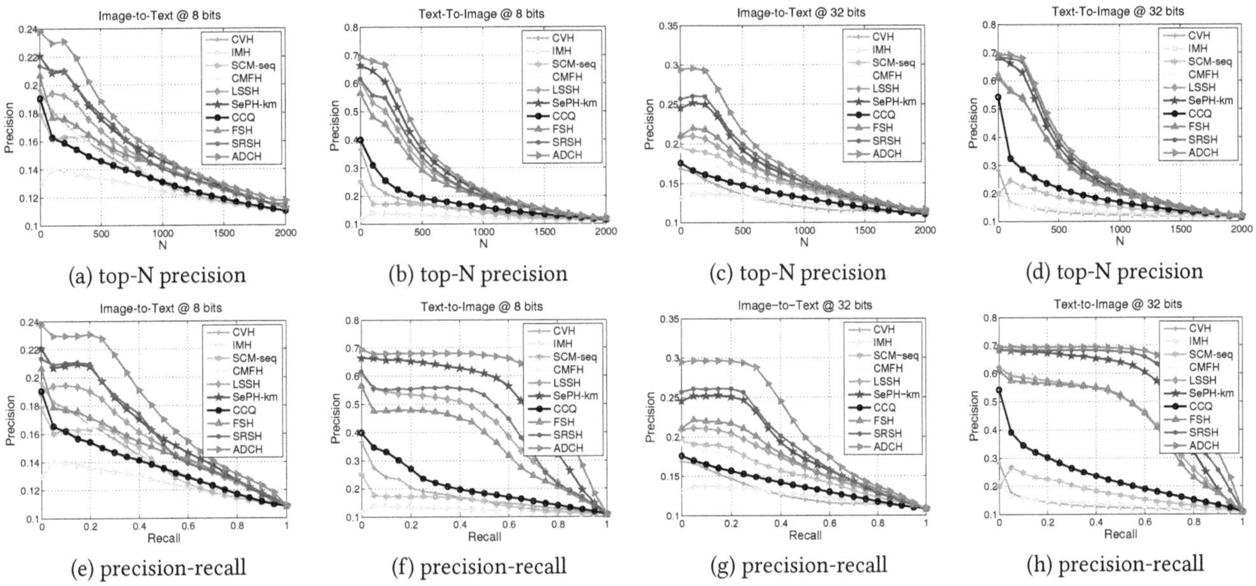

(a) top-N precision (b) top-N precision (c) top-N precision (d) top-N precision

(e) precision-recall (f) precision-recall (g) precision-recall (h) precision-recall

Figure 1: The top-N precision and precision-recall curves in the cases of 8-bit and 32-bit code length on Wiki.

Table 2: The MAP results of various models on MIRFlickr. The best results are in boldface.

Task	Method	8 bits	16 bits	24 bits	32 bits	64 bits
Image to Text	CVH	0.5785	0.5739	0.5714	0.5699	0.5673
	IMH	0.5656	0.5680	0.5678	0.5686	0.5677
	SCM-seq	0.6121	0.6280	0.6316	0.6357	0.6473
	LSSH	0.5705	0.5733	0.5725	0.5704	0.5745
	CMFH	0.5808	0.5807	0.5823	0.5716	0.5716
	SePH-km	0.6676	0.6843	0.6860	0.6873	0.6882
	CCQ	0.5710	0.5738	0.5741	0.5741	0.5748
	FSH	0.5845	0.5905	0.5939	0.5944	0.6005
	SRSH	0.6884	0.7062	0.7124	0.7035	0.7091
	ADCH	**0.7123**	**0.7130**	**0.7169**	**0.7197**	**0.7238**
Text to Image	CVH	0.5786	0.5736	0.5713	0.5699	0.5674
	IMH	0.5647	0.5669	0.5671	0.5687	0.5672
	SCM-seq	0.6034	0.6149	0.6176	0.6214	0.6285
	LSSH	0.5871	0.5832	0.5896	0.5895	0.5921
	CMFH	0.5915	0.5888	0.5913	0.5656	0.5658
	SePH-km	0.7232	0.7389	0.7409	0.7456	0.7476
	CCQ	0.5898	0.5955	0.5969	0.5995	0.5993
	FSH	0.5877	0.5932	0.5979	0.5949	0.6061
	SRSH	0.7374	0.7718	0.7774	0.7829	0.7936
	ADCH	**0.7776**	**0.7980**	**0.7956**	**0.8046**	**0.8134**

Table 3: The MAP results of various models on NUS-WIDE. The best results are in boldface.

Task	Method	8 bits	16 bits	24 bits	32 bits	64 bits
Image to Text	CVH	0.3781	0.3644	0.3591	0.3559	0.3504
	IMH	0.3480	0.3486	0.3463	0.3480	0.3487
	SCM-seq	0.4852	0.4965	0.5272	0.5097	0.5213
	LSSH	0.3843	0.3850	0.3884	0.3865	0.3925
	CMFH	0.3577	0.3542	0.3547	0.3558	0.3558
	SePH-km	0.5512	0.5613	0.5688	0.5652	0.5764
	CCQ	0.3723	0.3748	0.3671	0.3792	0.3796
	FSH	0.3892	0.4214	0.4320	0.4292	0.4533
	SRSH	0.5648	0.6065	0.6176	0.6283	**0.6404**
	ADCH	**0.6108**	**0.6136**	**0.6276**	**0.6287**	0.6343
Text to Image	CVH	0.3751	0.3629	0.3582	0.3551	0.3507
	IMH	0.3490	0.3489	0.3461	0.3435	0.3473
	SCM-seq	0.4745	0.4951	0.5185	0.5071	0.5184
	LSSH	0.4126	0.4178	0.4201	0.4210	0.4224
	CMFH	0.3610	0.3570	0.3579	0.3594	0.3586
	SePH-km	0.6401	0.6582	0.6619	0.6619	0.6732
	CCQ	0.3606	0.3636	0.3658	0.3670	0.3661
	FSH	0.3906	0.4258	0.4379	0.4427	0.4715
	SRSH	0.5853	0.6676	0.6810	0.6955	0.7088
	ADCH	**0.6777**	**0.7103**	**0.7287**	**0.7084**	**0.7399**

To summarize, from the above results , we can find that ADCH performs well on this dataset.

3.2.3 Results on NUS-WIDE. The MAP results and two kinds of curves on NUS-WIDE are displayed in Table 3 and Figure 3, respectively. From these results, we have the following observations, similar to those on Wiki and MIRFlickr:

- ADCH outperforms the baselines in nine cases.
- All methods performs better at Text-to-Image task than Image-to-Text task, consistent with that on Wiki and MIR-Flickr.
- ADCH also obtains better results on this dataset when the code length becomes longer.
- ADCH, SRSH and SePH-km perform much better than other methods.

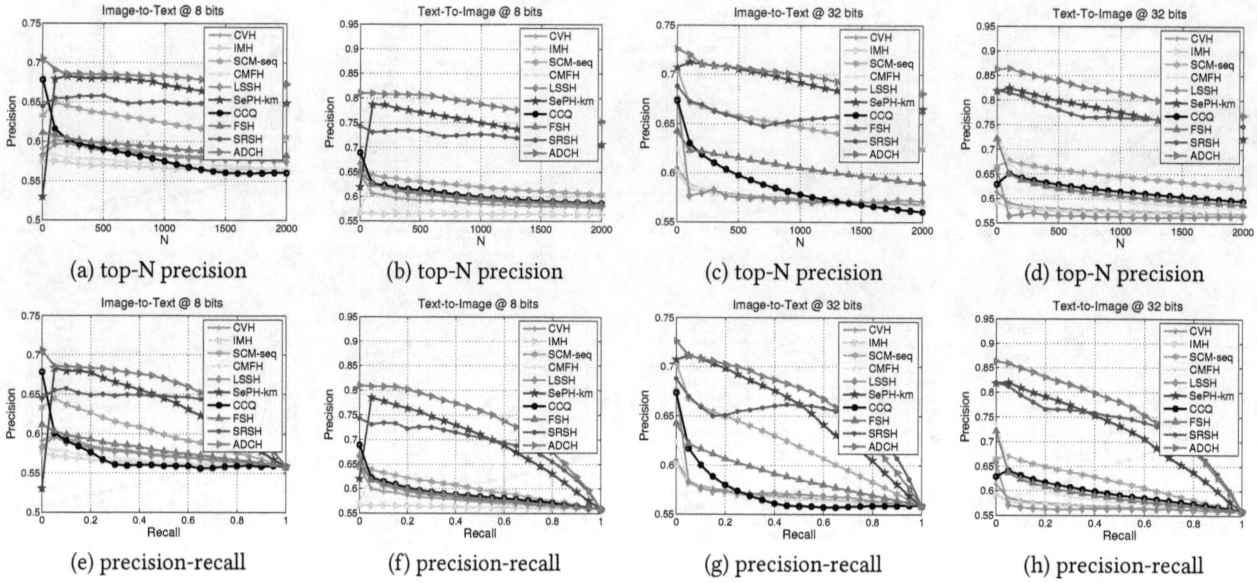

(a) top-N precision (b) top-N precision (c) top-N precision (d) top-N precision

(e) precision-recall (f) precision-recall (g) precision-recall (h) precision-recall

Figure 2: The top-N precision and precision-recall curves in the cases of 8-bit and 32-bit code length on MIRFlickr.

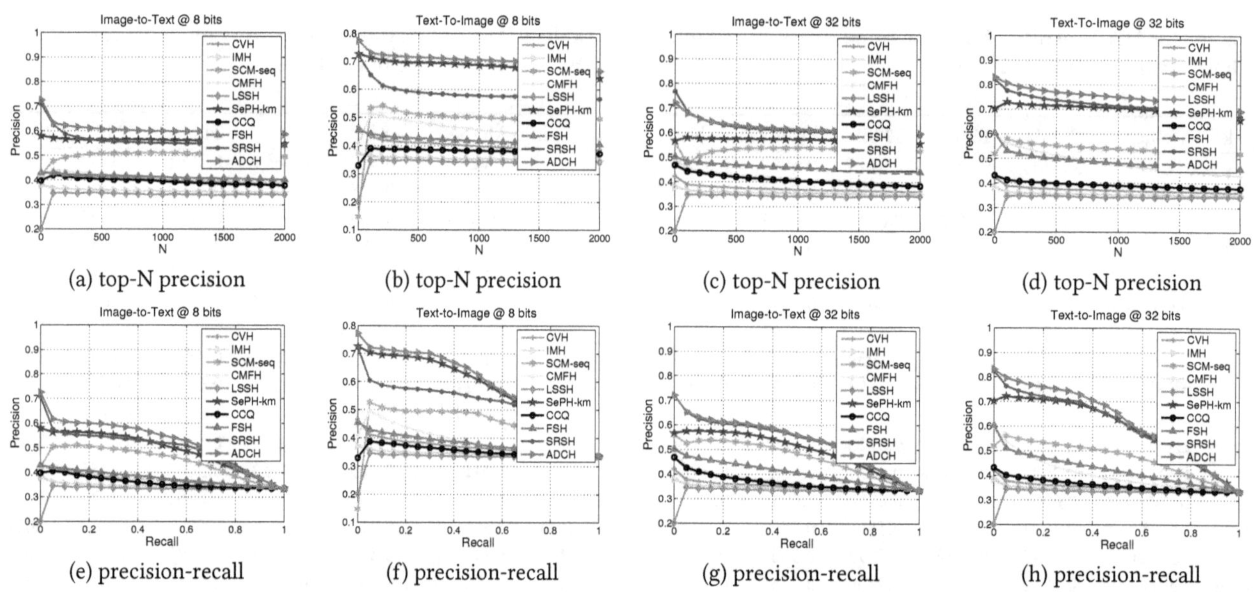

(a) top-N precision (b) top-N precision (c) top-N precision (d) top-N precision

(e) precision-recall (f) precision-recall (g) precision-recall (h) precision-recall

Figure 3: The top-N precision and precision-recall curves in the cases of 8-bit and 32-bit code length on NUS-WIDE.

In a nutshell, from the results on NUS-WIDE, we can conclude that ADCH works well on this dataset.

3.3 Comprehensive Analysis

3.3.1 Time Cost Analysis. Furthermore, to demonstrate the efficiency of ADCH, we investigated the training time of the proposed method in comparison with all of the baselines on three datasets. The length of hash codes varies from 8 to 64. The training time results of all of the methods are summarized in Table 4. We can observe that:

- The training time of ADCH is acceptable. Especially, its training time is much shorter than that of SRSH and SePH-km.
- The training time of ADCH gets longer with the hash code length becoming longer. The reason is that ADCH learns the hash codes bit by bit and more time will be consumed with longer codes.

Table 4: The training time of all methods on Wiki, MIRFlickr, and NUS-WIDE.

Method	Wiki					MIRFlickr					NUS-WIDE				
	8bits	16bits	24bits	32bits	64bits	8bits	16bits	24bits	32bits	64bits	8bits	16bits	24bits	32bits	64bits
CVH	0.02	0.02	0.03	0.03	0.03	0.06	0.06	0.06	0.07	0.08	1.19	1.21	1.19	1.22	1.23
IMH	2.00	1.99	2.02	1.98	2.03	15.58	17.36	15.22	14.05	14.22	110.88	111.84	110.91	110.22	110.62
SCM-seq	0.11	0.17	0.28	0.33	0.53	0.23	0.39	0.41	0.47	1.11	5.02	8.70	12.14	13.67	30.48
CMFH	0.16	0.13	0.15	0.17	0.19	0.15	0.16	0.17	0.18	0.20	0.67	0.70	0.74	0.75	0.77
LSSH	6.73	6.63	7.22	7.41	7.42	11.05	11.09	11.63	11.63	12.89	20.38	20.72	20.89	21.52	23.53
SePH-km	147.51	161.36	176.82	211.90	261.68	682.79	715.46	753.29	784.61	836.78	1482.61	2724.39	2967.88	3120.40	3531.11
CCQ	0.27	1.19	3.45	4.38	6.26	1.66	2.84	4.30	5.52	15.65	4.25	5.99	7.84	9.52	23.48
FSH	2.80	3.00	2.89	3.08	3.75	9.31	9.09	9.29	9.54	9.94	39.54	39.46	39.31	39.77	40.84
SRSH	5.03	5.21	5.77	6.40	8.67	30.70	31.23	31.75	32.29	32.88	267.08	270.63	272.46	273.42	285.65
ADCH	0.22	0.35	0.50	0.65	1.49	0.77	1.26	1.83	2.64	6.12	2.82	4.73	7.02	9.76	20.10

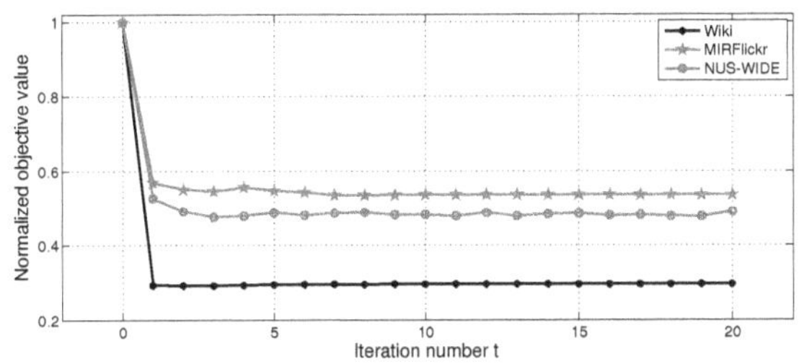

Figure 4: Convergence curves in the case of 32-bit code length on Wiki, MIRFlickr, and NUS-WIDE.

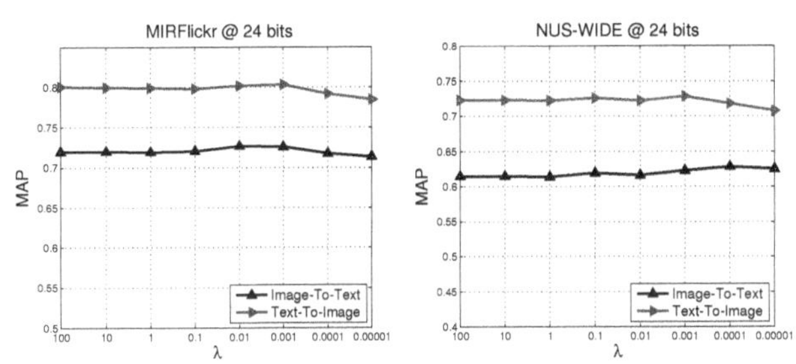

Figure 5: Parameter sensitivity analysis of parameter λ in the cases of 24-bit code length on MIRFlickr and NUS-WIDE.

- Some baselines, such as CVH, SCM-seq and CMFH, can be trained fast. However, as shown in Section 3.2, their retrieval performance are much worse than ADCH. Thus, ADCH is more practical than them.

To conclude, our proposed ADCH is more practical than all of the baselines for cross-modal retrieval.

3.3.2 Convergence Analysis. To show that the proposed alternative optimization method can converge efficiently, we validated the convergence by experiments. Specifically, the convergence curves on three datasets with 32-bit codes are illustrated in Figure 4. For convenience, the objective values are normalized by dividing the maximum on each dataset. Clearly, the proposed algorithm converges in less than 5 iterations, which demonstrates the high convergence rate.

3.3.3 Parameter Sensitivity Analysis. We conducted experiments to further analyse the influence of parameter λ on the performance. The MAP curves of ADCH in the cases of 24-bits on MIRFlickr and NUS-WIDE are plotted in Figure 5. From this figure, we can observe that ADCH is not sensitive to the parameter λ over a wide range, it obtains the best result when λ is about 0.001.

4 CONCLUSION AND FUTURE WORK

In this paper, we present a novel supervised cross-modal hashing method, i.e., Asymmetric Discrete Cross-Modal Hashing (ADCH). We address three issues in most CMH: (1) how to efficiently construct the correlations among heterogeneous data from different modalities; (2) how to solve the discrete NP-hard optimization problem; (3) how to handle the complex and difficult problem in most CMH methods that simultaneously learning the hash codes and hash functions. To address these issues, ADCH leverages CMF technique to learn common latent representations preserving not only the cross-correlation from different modalities but also the semantic similarity. Instead of relaxing the binary constraints, it learns the hash codes directly using an iterative optimization algorithm proposed in this work. Based on the learnt hash codes, ADCH further learns a series of binary classifiers as hash functions. Extensive experimental results demonstrate that ADCH outperforms nine state-of-the-art baselines for cross-modal retrieval task.

In this work, we present ADCH as a shallow model because we want to concentrate on the design of loss function, which is an important criterion of generating compact hash codes. However, we believe that it can be easily transformed into a deep model when combined with a deep neural network. We leave this for our future work.

5 ACKNOWLEDGEMENTS

This work was partially supported by the Key Research and Development Program of Shandong Province (2016GGX101044) and National Natural Science Foundation of China (61573212).

REFERENCES

[1] Neyshabur Behnam, Srebro Nati, Salakhutdinov Ruslan, Makarychev Yury, and Yadollahpour Payman. 2013. The power of asymmetry in binary hashing. In *Proceedings of the Advances in Neural Information Processing Systems*. 2823–2831.

[2] Zhen-Duo Chen, Wan-Jin Yu, Chuan-Xiang Li, Liqiang Nie, and Xin-Shun Xu. 2018. Dual deep neural networks cross-modal hashing. In *Proceedings of the AAAI Conference on Artificial Intelligence*.

[3] Tat-Seng Chua, Jinhui Tang, Richang Hong, Haojie Li, Zhiping Luo, and Yantao Zheng. 2009. NUS-WIDE: A real-world web image database from National University of Singapore. In *Proceedings of the ACM International Conference on Image and Video Retrieval*. 48.

[4] Cheng Da, Shibiao Xu, Kun Ding, Gaofeng Meng, Shiming Xiang, and Chunhong Pan. 2017. AMVH: Asymmetric multi-valued hashing. In *Proceedings of the IEEE Conference on Computer Vision and Pattern Recognition*. 736–744.

[5] Scott Deerwester, Susan T Dumais, George W Furnas, Thomas K Landauer, and Richard Harshman. 1990. Indexing by latent semantic analysis. *J. Am. Soc. Inf. Sci.* 41, 6 (1990), 391.

[6] Guiguang Ding, Yuchen Guo, and Jile Zhou. 2014. Collective matrix factorization hashing for multimodal data. In *Proceedings of the IEEE Conference on Computer Vision and Pattern Recognition*. 2075–2082.

[7] Fuli Feng, Xiangnan He, Yiqun Liu, Liqiang Nie, and Tat-Seng Chua. 2018. Learning on partial-order hypergraphs. In *Proceedings of the International World Wide Web Conferences*. 1523–1532.

[8] Fuli Feng, Liqiang Nie, Xiang Wang, Richang Hong, and Tat-Seng Chua. 2017. Computational social indicators: A case study of chinese university ranking. In *Proceedings of the International ACM SIGIR Conference on Research and Development in Information Retrieval*. 455–464.

[9] Aristides Gionis, Piotr Indyk, Rajeev Motwani, et al. 1999. Similarity search in high dimensions via hashing. In *Proceedings of the International Conference on Very Large Data Bases*. 518–529.

[10] Albert Gordo, Florent Perronnin, Yunchao Gong, and Svetlana Lazebnik. 2014. Asymmetric distances for binary embeddings. *IEEE Trans. Pattern Anal. Mach. Intell.* 36, 1 (2014), 33–47.

[11] Jie Gui, Tongliang Liu, Zhenan Sun, Dacheng Tao, and Tieniu Tan. 2018. Fast supervised discrete hashing. *IEEE Trans. Pattern Anal. Mach. Intell.* 40, 2 (2018), 490–496.

[12] Xiangnan He and Tat-Seng Chua. 2017. Neural factorization machines for sparse predictive analytics. In *Proceedings of the AAAI Conference on Artificial Intelligence*. 355–364.

[13] Mark J Huiskes and Michael S Lew. 2008. The MIR flickr retrieval evaluation. In *Proceedings of the ACM International Conference on Multimedia Information Retrieval*. 39–43.

[14] Qing-Yuan Jiang and Wu-Jun Li. 2017. Deep cross-modal hashing. In *Proceedings of the IEEE Conference on Computer Vision and Pattern Recognition*. 3270–3278.

[15] Yu-Gang Jiang, Jun Wang, Xiangyang Xue, and Shih-Fu Chang. 2013. Query-adaptive image search with hash codes. *IEEE Trans. Multimedia* 15, 2 (2013), 442–453.

[16] Wang-Cheng Kang, Wu-Jun Li, and Zhi-Hua Zhou. 2016. Column sampling based discrete supervised hashing. In *Proceedings of the AAAI Conference on Artificial Intelligence*. 1230–1236.

[17] Weihao Kong and Wu-Jun Li. 2012. Isotropic hashing. In *Proceedings of the Advances in Neural Information Processing Systems*. 1646–1654.

[18] Shaishav Kumar and Raghavendra Udupa. 2011. Learning hash functions for cross-view similarity search. In *Proceedings of the International Joint Conference on Artificial Intelligence*. 1360–1365.

[19] Guosheng Lin, Chunhua Shen, Qinfeng Shi, Anton Van den Hengel, and David Suter. 2014. Fast supervised hashing with decision trees for high-dimensional data. In *Proceedings of the IEEE Conference on Computer Vision and Pattern Recognition*. 1963–1970.

[20] Guosheng Lin, Chunhua Shen, David Suter, and Anton van den Hengel. 2013. A general two-step approach to learning-based hashing. In *Proceedings of the International Conference on Computer Vision*. 2552–2559.

[21] Zijia Lin, Guiguang Ding, Mingqing Hu, and Jianmin Wang. 2015. Semantics-preserving hashing for cross-view retrieval. In *Proceedings of the IEEE Conference on Computer Vision and Pattern Recognition*. 3864–3872.

[22] Hong Liu, Rongrong Ji, Yongjian Wu, and Gang Hua. 2016. Supervised matrix factorization for cross-modality hashing. In *Proceedings of the International Joint Conference on Artificial Intelligence*. 1767–1773.

[23] Hong Liu, Rongrong Ji, Yongjian Wu, Feiyue Huang, and Baochang Zhang. 2017. Cross-modality binary code learning via fusion similarity hashing. In *Proceedings of the IEEE Conference on Computer Vision and Pattern Recognition*. 7380–7388.

[24] Meng Liu, Liqiang Nie, Meng Wang, and Baoquan Chen. 2017. Towards micro-video understanding by joint sequential-sparse modeling. In *Proceedings of the ACM International Conference on Multimedia*. 970–978.

[25] Wei Liu, Jun Wang, Rongrong Ji, Yu-Gang Jiang, and Shih-Fu Chang. 2012. Supervised hashing with kernels. In *Proceedings of the IEEE Conference on Computer Vision and Pattern Recognition*. 2074–2081.

[26] Xianglong Liu, Cheng Deng, Bo Lang, Dacheng Tao, and Xuelong Li. 2016. Query-adaptive reciprocal hash tables for nearest neighbor search. *IEEE Trans. Image Process.* 25, 2 (2016), 907–919.

[27] Xianglong Liu, Lei Huang, Cheng Deng, Bo Lang, and Dacheng Tao. 2016. Query-adaptive hash code ranking for large-scale multi-view visual search. *IEEE Trans. Image Process.* 25, 10 (2016), 4514–4524.

[28] Mingsheng Long, Yue Cao, Jianmin Wang, and Philip S Yu. 2016. Composite correlation quantization for efficient multimodal retrieval. In *Proceedings of the AAAI Conference on Artificial Intelligence*. 579–588.

[29] David G Lowe. 2004. Distinctive image features from scale-invariant keypoints. *Int. J. Comput. Vis.* 60, 2 (2004), 91–110.

[30] Xin Luo, Ye Wu, and Xin-Shun Xu. 2018. Scalable supervised discrete hashing for large-scale search. In *Proceedings of the International World Wide Web Conferences*. 1603–1612.

[31] Jonathan Masci, Michael M Bronstein, Alexander M Bronstein, and Jürgen Schmidhuber. 2014. Multimodal similarity-preserving hashing. *IEEE Trans. Pattern Anal. Mach. Intell.* 36, 4 (2014), 824–830.

[32] Liqiang Nie, Xuemeng Song, and Tat-Seng Chua. 2016. *Learning from multiple social networks*. Morgan & Claypool Publishers.

[33] Liqiang Nie, Meng Wang, Zheng-Jun Zha, and Tat-Seng Chua. 2012. Oracle in image search: A content-based approach to performance prediction. *ACM Trans. Inf. Syst.* 30, 2 (2012), 13.

[34] Liqiang Nie, Shuicheng Yan, Meng Wang, Richang Hong, and Tat-Seng Chua. 2012. Harvesting visual concepts for image search with complex queries. In *Proceedings of the ACM International Conference on Multimedia*. 59–68.

[35] Nikhil Rasiwasia, Jose Costa Pereira, Emanuele Coviello, Gabriel Doyle, Gert RG Lanckriet, Roger Levy, and Nuno Vasconcelos. 2010. A new approach to cross-modal multimedia retrieval. In *Proceedings of the ACM International Conference on Multimedia*. 251–260.

[36] Fumin Shen, Chunhua Shen, Wei Liu, and Heng Tao Shen. 2015. Supervised discrete hashing. In *Proceedings of the IEEE Conference on Computer Vision and Pattern Recognition*. 37–45.

[37] Fumin Shen, Chunhua Shen, Qinfeng Shi, Anton Hengel, and Zhenmin Tang. 2013. Inductive hashing on manifolds. In *Proceedings of the IEEE Conference on Computer Vision and Pattern Recognition*. 1562–1569.

[38] Jingkuan Song, Yang Yang, Yi Yang, Zi Huang, and Heng Tao Shen. 2013. Inter-media hashing for large-scale retrieval from heterogeneous data sources. In *Proceedings of the ACM SIGMOD Conference on Management of Data*. 785–796.

[39] Jinhui Tang, Zechao Li, Meng Wang, and Ruizhen Zhao. 2015. Neighborhood discriminant hashing for large-scale image retrieval. *IEEE Trans. Image Process.* 24, 9 (2015), 2827–2840.

[40] Jun Wang, Sanjiv Kumar, and Shih-Fu Chang. 2010. Semi-supervised hashing for scalable image retrieval. In *Proceedings of the IEEE Conference on Computer Vision and Pattern Recognition*. 3424–3431.

[41] Jian Wang, Xin-Shun Xu, Shanqing Guo, Lizhen Cui, and Xiao-Lin Wang. 2016. Linear unsupervised hashing for ANN search in Euclidean space. *Neurocomputing* 171 (2016), 283–292.

[42] Meng Wang, Weisheng Li, Dong Liu, Jialie Shen, and Shuicheng Yan. 2015. Facilitating image search with a scalable and compact semantic mapping. *IEEE Trans. Cybern.* 45, 8 (2015), 1561–1574.

[43] Yair Weiss, Antonio Torralba, and Rob Fergus. 2009. Spectral hashing. In *Proceedings of the Advances in Neural Information Processing Systems*. 1753–1760.

[44] Rongkai Xia, Yan Pan, Hanjiang Lai, Cong Liu, and Shuicheng Yan. 2014. Supervised hashing for image retrieval via image representation learning. In *Proceedings of the AAAI Conference on Artificial Intelligence*. 2156–2162.

[45] Xing Xu, Fumin Shen, Yang Yang, Heng Tao Shen, and Xuelong Li. 2017. Learning discriminative binary codes for large-scale cross-modal retrieval. *IEEE Trans. Image Process.* 26, 5 (2017), 2494–2507.

[46] Ting-Kun Yan, Xin-Shun Xu, Shanqing Guo, Zi Huang, and Xiaolin Wang. 2016. Supervised robust discrete multimodal hashing for cross-media retrieval. In *Proceedings of the ACM International Conference on Information and Knowledge Management*. 1271–1280.

[47] Erkun Yang, Cheng Deng, Wei Liu, Xianglong Liu, Dacheng Tao, and Xinbo Gao. 2017. Pairwise relationship guided deep hashing for cross-modal retrieval. In *Proceedings of the AAAI Conference on Artificial Intelligence*. 1618–1625.

[48] Yang Yang, Zheng-Jun Zha, Yue Gao, Xiaofeng Zhu, and Tat-Seng Chua. 2014. Exploiting web images for semantic video indexing via robust sample-specific loss. *IEEE Trans. Multimedia* 16, 6 (2014), 1677–1689.

[49] Dongqing Zhang and Wu-Jun Li. 2014. Large-scale supervised multimodal hashing with semantic correlation maximization. In *Proceedings of the AAAI Conference on Artificial Intelligence*. 2177–2183.

[50] Peng-Fei Zhang, Chuan-Xiang Li, Meng-Yuan Liu, Liqiang Nie, and Xin-Shun Xu. 2017. Semi-relaxation supervised hashing for cross-modal retrieval. In *Proceedings of the ACM International Conference on Multimedia*. 1762–1770.

[51] Jile Zhou, Guiguang Ding, and Yuchen Guo. 2014. Latent semantic sparse hashing for cross-modal similarity search. In *Proceedings of the AAAI Conference on Artificial Intelligence*. 415–424.

Collaborative Subspace Graph Hashing for Cross-modal Retrieval

Xiang Zhang
State Key Laboratory of High Performance Computing, National University of Defense Technology & College of Computer, National University of Defense Technology
Changsha, Hunan, P.R. China
zhangxiang08@nudt.edu.cn

Guohua Dong*
Science and Technology on Parallel and Distributed Laboratory, National University of Defense Technology & College of Computer, National University of Defense Technology
Changsha, Hunan, P.R. China
dghzz1991@163.com

Yimo Du*
Unit 31008
Beijing, P.R. China
duyimo86@163.com

Chengkun Wu
State Key Laboratory of High Performance Computing, National University of Defense Technology & College of Computer, National University of Defense Technology
Changsha, Hunan, P.R. China
chengkun_wu@nudt.edu.cn

Zhigang Luo*
Science and Technology on Parallel and Distributed Laboratory, National University of Defense Technology & College of Computer, National University of Defense Technology
Changsha, Hunan, P.R. China
zgluo@nudt.edu.cn

Canqun Yang
Science and Technology on Parallel and Distributed Laboratory, National University of Defense Technology & College of Computer, National University of Defense Technology
Changsha, Hunan, P.R. China
canqun@nudt.edu.cn

ABSTRACT

Current hashing methods for cross-modal retrieval generally attempt to learn the separate modality-specific transformation matrices to embed multi-modality data into a latent common subspace, and usually ignore the fact that respecting the diversity of multi-modality features in the latent subspace could be beneficial for retrieval improvements. To this, we propose a collaborative subspace graph hashing method (CSGH) to perform a two-stage collaborative learning framework for cross-modal retrieval. Particularly, CSGH first embeds multi-modality data into separate latent subspaces through individual modality-specific transformation matrices, and then connects these latent subspaces to a common Hamming space through a shared transformation matrix. In this framework, CSGH considers the modality-specific neighborhood structure and the cross-modal correlation within multi-modality data through the Laplacian regularization and the graph based correlation constraint, respectively. To solve CSGH, we develop an alternative procedure to optimize it, and fortunately, each sub-problem of CSGH has the elegant analytical solution. Experiments of cross-modal retrieval on Wiki, NUS-WIDE, Flickr25K and Flickr1M datasets show the effectiveness of CSGH compared with the state-of-the-art cross-modal hashing methods.

*Corresponding author.

ICMR'18, June 11–14, 2018, Bunkyo, Japan

ACM ISBN 978-1-4503-5046-4/18/06...$15.00
https://doi.org/10.1145/3206025.3206042

CCS CONCEPTS

• **Information systems → Multimedia and multimodal retrieval**;

KEYWORDS

cross-modal hashing, cross-modal retrieval, subspace learning, graph hashing, cross-modal correlation

ACM Reference Format:
Xiang Zhang, Guohua Dong, Yimo Du, Chengkun Wu, Zhigang Luo, and Canqun Yang. 2018. Collaborative Subspace Graph Hashing for Cross-modal Retrieval. In *Proceedings of 2018 International Conference on Multimedia Retrieval (ICMR'18).* ACM, New York, NY, USA, 9 pages. https://doi.org/10.1145/3206025.3206042

1 INTRODUCTION

Hashing has witnessed great advances in computer vision tasks such as classification [5, 13], person re-identification [51, 63, 68] and information retrieval [11, 20, 21, 24, 28, 39, 52, 54, 64], for its low storage cost and fast search speed. It seeks to map the data points from original feature space to a Hamming Space with binary hashing codes as well as to preserve the neighborhood structure. Many hashing methods such as Locally Sensitive Hashing (LSH) [9], Iterative Quantization (ITQ) [14] and Spectral Hashing (SH) [47] are developed to focus on this issue. However, most of them consider solving single-modal learning problem, where the query is conducted over one modality.

With the rapid growth of multimedia data including text, image, etc, cross-modal retrieval [3, 15, 34, 45, 46, 62] has become a challenging yet interesting issue. Recently, a lot of studies of cross-modal hashing have been done in this field [4, 23, 49, 53, 55, 56, 65]. According to whether supervised information such as similarity data or class labels is used, these efforts can be divided into either unsupervised methods or supervised ones. Generally speaking, supervised cross-modal hashing methods such as Cross-Modal-Sensitive Hashing (CMSSH) [1], Semantic Correlation Maximization (SCM) [60] and Quantized Correlation Hashing (QCH) [48], achieve great gains in retrieval performance but might rely heavily on manual annotations, compared with the unsupervised counterparts. In practice, these methods could fail, especially when supervised information is neither available nor easy to collect. In such situations, unsupervised cross-modal hashing methods are the proper candidate and still work well without any supervised information. This is because they encode cross-modal data points into hashing codes by looking into the data itself. Thus, unsupervised cross-modal hashing methods have attracted wide attention from the machine learning community.

Among unsupervised cross-modal hashing methods, many attempts focus on maximizing the correlation between the hashing codes across domains, which include Cross-View Hashing (CVH) [17], Inter-Media Hashing (IMH) [40], Composite Correlation Quantization (CCQ) [26], etc. To be specific, CVH proposed a principled method to learn the hash functions to map similar instances into identical codes across modalities. IMH developed a hash function by employing linear projection coupled with the mean thresholds. CCQ jointly learned a correlation-maximal latent space and a similarity-preserving composite quantization in a unified optimization framework. Although these methods learn the separate modality-specific transformation matrices to embed multi-modality data into a latent common subspace, most of them ignore the promising potential of the diversity of multi-modal features in the latent subspace.

To address the issue as mentioned above, we develop an unsupervised cross-modal hashing model dubbed the collaborative subspace graph hashing method (CSGH), and the corresponding flowchart is shown in Fig. 1. As Fig. 1 shows, CSGH performs the two-stage collaborative learning framework: it first projects multi-modality data into separate latent subspaces via individual modality-specific transformation matrices, and then connects the latent subspace to a Hamming space by the shared transformation matrix. In light of the insights above, we formulate the collaborative learning process above as multi-view low-rank regression (MVLR) problem [66]. To some degree, we assign the MVLR with the novel physical interpretation, i.e., the proposed two-stage collaborative learning framework. As we know, few studies involved this point. Since we relax the consistence of the features in the latent subspace, our collaborative learning can capture the diversity of the latent features across modalities whilst reducing the quantization loss from continuous latent subspace to discrete Hamming space. For convenience, we refer to the continuous subspace as the collaborative subspace. In such collaborative subspace, CSGH endeavors to capture the modality-specific neighborhood structure and the cross-modal correlation through the Laplacian regularization and the correlation constraint. These regularization terms assist in ensuring the collaborative and latent features of two modalities to be semantically correlated within and between modalities, respectively. To solve CSGH, we develop an alternative iteration optimization algorithm to optimize it, and fortunately, each sub-problem of CSGH has the elegant analytical solution. Experiments of cross-modal retrieval on Wiki [38], NUS-WIDE [6], Flickr25K [16] and Flickr1M [30] datasets show the effectiveness of CSGH compared with the state-of-the-art cross-modal hashing methods.

2 RELATED WORK

Cross-modal retrieval plays an indispensable role in large-scale multimedia data analysis. Past efforts mainly focus on single-modal retrieval and challenges stemming from the "media-gap", that is, representations from different modalities are inconsistent [35], thus it is difficult to measure similarities among them. Many works are explored to address this issue by capturing correlations across modalities, such as common space learning based methods and graph regularization based methods. In fact, both types of cross-modal retrieval methods are categorized in terms of different aspects, thus they may have a certain overlaps. They are closely related with our model.

2.1 Common space learning based methods

Recently, common space learning is one of the research hot spots in cross-modal retrieval. The main assumption of such methods is that cross-modal data share relevant semantic information, thus making it possible to transform data to a common space and to perform similarity measurement across modalities. Here we only introduce three types of common space learning based cross-modal retrieval methods: 1) **traditional statistical correlation analysis based methods** such as Canonical correlation analysis (CCA) based methods [7, 37], mainly learn respective linear transformation matrices and project data points of different modalities into a common space through the learned transform matrices, and are the most popular baselines for cross-modal retrieval. These methods are easy to implement and efficient for training, but they may fail to describe complex correlations of real-world cross-modal data through linear projections. 2) **Deep neural network (DNN) based methods** gain a lot of attention of cross-modal retrieval researchers recently, and have been used to learning the common space across cross-modal data [12, 32, 41]. Most of such existing DNN based methods use shared or private deep structure as the framework and usually learning to transform data to a common space by a shared layer. They can learn nonlinear relationships and might achieve the state-of-the-art performance for cross-modal retrieval, but most of them have too many parameters and take a lot of time for training. Besides, they have a lot of dependency on training data, and need large storage source. For the low storage cost and fast search speed, 3) **hashing based methods** [2, 10, 17, 22, 26, 29, 31, 33, 40, 42, 48, 61, 67, 70] are proposed to perform cross-modal retrieval. Most of them follow the two-step learning procedure: first, transform multi-modal data to a common space to bridge the modality discrepancy; second, learn hashing codes by connecting the common space with the Hamming space. However, most of these existing methods mainly focus on projecting the data points of different modalities into a common space by individual modality-specific transformation matrices, and usually ignore the promising potential of the diversity of the latent features.

2.2 Graph regularization based methods

Among cross-modal retrieval methods, graph regularization based methods [19, 36, 43, 48, 50, 58], either supervised or unsupervised, can capture correlations of cross-modal data, such as semantic relevance, intra-modality neighborhood structure and inter-modality relationships, through graph regularization. Supervised methods

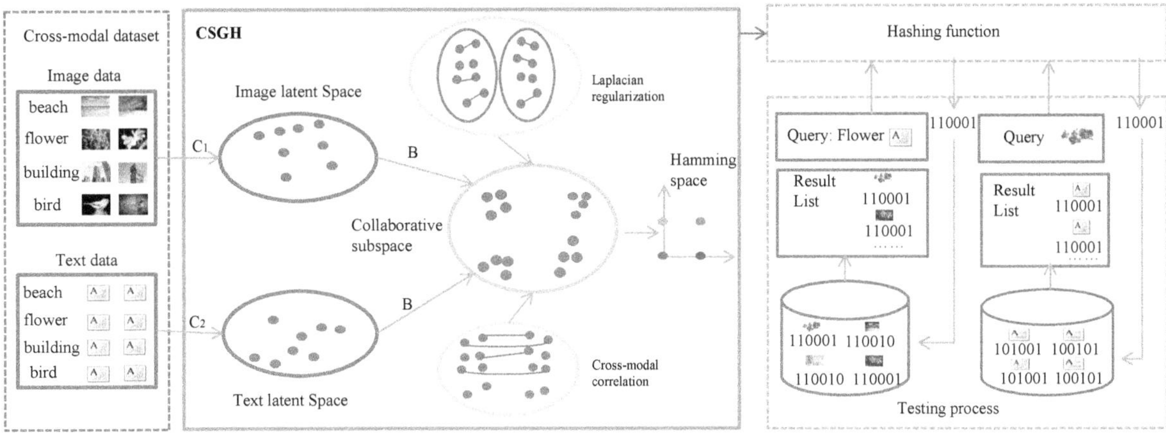

Figure 1: The flowchart of the proposed CSGH.

usually construct a graph through supervised information like class labels or similarity data, while unsupervised methods use the information within data itself, such as clustering information. To be specific, joint graph regularized heterogeneous metric learning (JGRHML) [58] used data in the learned metric space to construct the joint graph regularization term. Quantized correlation hashing (QCH) [48] calculated the similarity matrix across two modalities through similarity information to capture the cross-modal relationship. Moreover, the graph based methods can easily extend to retrieve multi-media data up to two modalities. For instance, joint representation learning (JRL) [59] considered the modality correlations and semantic information in a unified framework for up to five modalities. Peng et al. [36] proposed a semi-supervised cross-media feature learning algorithm with the unified graph regularization, and utilized one joint graph to simultaneously model all the media types exceeding five modalities in empirical experiments. Although graph regularization has been proven effective in cross-modal retrieval, however, constructing a graph may cost too much time and space, especially for large-scale real-word datasets. To speed up the graph construction, Liu et al. [25] proposed an efficient way to construct single-modality graph in the hashing framework. Based on the efficiency and efficacy of graph regularization as above, we also integrate it into our model for cross-modal retrieval tasks. Different from the mentioned methods above, we regularize the features in both collaborative and latent subspaces.

3 THE PROPOSED MODEL

3.1 Collaborative Subspace Graph Hashing

As analyzed in section 2, most of existing cross-modal hashing methods [17, 26, 40] aim at learning the separate modality-specific transformation matrices to embed multi-modality data into a latent common subspace. However, most of them ignore the promising power of the diversity of the features in the latent subspace. This implies that the semantic subspace might be not optimal. In this regard, we adopt a two-stage collaborative learning framework to address this issue, as shown in Fig. 1. In the collaborative learning framework, the modality-specific transformation matrices and the shared transformation matrix are learned jointly. We use the learned modality-specific transformation matrices to project each modality data to their respective latent subspaces in which the features are transformed to a common collaborative subspace again through the shared transformation matrix. As a result, the collaborative features are connected to Hamming space. In light of the insights above, we formulate the two-stage collaborative learning as the multi-view low-rank regression (MVLR) problem [66]. Without loss of generality, we treat the images and the texts as two modalities to demonstrate our model. Given that $X_1 \in R^{d_1 \times n}$ and $X_2 \in R^{d_2 \times n}$ represent the features of image and text, respectively, where n is the number of training samples, and both d_1 and d_2 are the dimensionality of image and text features, respectively. We can obtain the following formulation:

$$J_1 = \left\| \begin{bmatrix} I_n \\ I_n \end{bmatrix} Y - \begin{bmatrix} X_1^T C_1 \\ X_2^T C_2 \end{bmatrix} B \right\|_F^2 + \left\| \begin{bmatrix} \sqrt{\lambda_1} C_1 \\ \sqrt{\lambda_2} C_2 \end{bmatrix} B \right\|_F^2, \quad (1)$$

where $Y \in R^{n \times r}$ indicates the hashing codes shared by two modalities. $C_1 \in R^{d_1 \times s}$ and $C_2 \in R^{d_2 \times s}$ indicate the modality-specific transformation matrices of image and text data, respectively. $B \in R^{s \times r}$ is the shared transformation matrix and maps the latent features to a shared collaborative subspace whilst reducing the quantization loss for hashing codes. $\left\| \begin{bmatrix} \sqrt{\lambda_1} C_1 \\ \sqrt{\lambda_2} C_2 \end{bmatrix} B \right\|_F^2$ is the regularization term to avoid the trivial solutions over $C_1 B$ and $C_2 B$, where $\lambda_1 \geq 0$ and $\lambda_2 \geq 0$ are two regularized parameters.

We note that the first term of Eq. (1) considers our two-stage collaborative learning framework. To some degree, we make the first attempt to assign the MVLR with a novel physical interpretation. To our knowledge, few studies involve this issue. During the collaborative learning, the latent features across two modalities are not necessarily identical through the modality-specific transformations. This can capture the diversity of the features in the latent subspace. In terms of our empirical results, we note that the diversity does not hurt the efficacy of our model because our major aim is to keep the consistency of the resultant collaborative features. To this, we explicitly impose the Laplacian regularization and cross-modal correlation constraint to capture the neighborhood structure and the cross-modal correlation within the dataset as described below. In this way, the collaborative subspace can adaptively accommodate themselves to guarantee the consistence of hashing codes in a Hamming space. It is beneficial for automatically assigning semantic information to both the shared transformation matrix and the modality-specific transformation matrices. As a byproduct, it is also helpful for the optimization.

In both single-modal and cross-modal retrieval, the neighborhood structure within the dataset is always the focus of the hashing methods. Thus, we directly utilize the Laplacian regularization over the collaborative subspace in the context of graph hashing framework [25, 47] and then obtain the following formulation:

$$J_2 = tr(B^T \begin{bmatrix} C_1^T X_1 & C_2^T X_2 \end{bmatrix} \begin{bmatrix} \alpha_1 L_1 & 0 \\ 0 & \alpha_2 L_2 \end{bmatrix} \begin{bmatrix} X_1^T C_1 \\ X_2^T C_2 \end{bmatrix} B), \quad (2)$$

where $L_1 \in R^{n \times n}$ and $L_2 \in R^{n \times n}$ denote the Laplacian matrices of image and text, respectively. Both Laplacian matrices can be easily calculated by anchor graph construction method [25].

As mentioned above, Eq. (2) merely employs the intra-modality Laplacian regularization. Motivated by QCH [48], we attempt to treat the graph matrix as the weights to capture the cross-modal correlation in a completely unsupervised manner. The reweight formulation can be written as below:

$$J_3 = tr(B^T \begin{bmatrix} C_1^T X_1 & C_2^T X_2 \end{bmatrix} \begin{bmatrix} \beta_2 S_1 & -\beta_1 S \\ -\beta_1 S & \beta_2 S_2 \end{bmatrix} \begin{bmatrix} X_1^T C_1 \\ X_2^T C_2 \end{bmatrix} B), \quad (3)$$

where S is the cross-modal graph weight matrix. Given $M = Z_1 \Lambda_1^{-1} Z_1^T + Z_2 \Lambda_2{}^{-1} Z_2{}^T$, where Z_1 and Z_2 are the similarity matrix of image and text data calculated according to [25], and $\Lambda_1 = diag(Z_1{}^T \mathbf{1})$ and $\Lambda_2 = diag(Z_2{}^T \mathbf{1})$. Then, we obtain $S = (M + M^T)/2$. Both S_1 and S_2 are the diagonal matrix of the row sum and the column sum of S, respectively. Obviously, different from [48], we capture the cross-modal correlation in an unsupervised manner. The developed regularization term not only explicitly ensures the collaborative features to be correlated but also implicitly guarantees the latent features of two modalities to be semantically correlated. This claim holds because maximizing Eq. (8) approximates to minimizing its denominator which implicitly indicates maximizing the correlation of the latent features.

Finally, we formulate the above thoughts as our final unsupervised model dubbed the Collaborative Subspace Graph Hashing method (CSGH), i.e.,

$$\min_{Y,B,C} J = J_1 + J_2 + J_3 = \left\|EY - X_c^T CB\right\|_F^2 + \|I_\lambda CB\|_F^2 + tr(B^T C^T X_c L X_c^T CB) + tr(B^T C^T X_c \tilde{S} X_c^T CB), \quad (4)$$

where $X_c = \begin{bmatrix} X_1 & 0 \\ 0 & X_2 \end{bmatrix}$, $C = \begin{bmatrix} C_1 \\ C_2 \end{bmatrix}$, $E = \begin{bmatrix} I_n \\ I_n \end{bmatrix}$, $I_\lambda = \begin{bmatrix} \sqrt{\lambda_1} I_{d_1} & 0 \\ 0 & \sqrt{\lambda_2} I_{d_2} \end{bmatrix}$, $L = \begin{bmatrix} \alpha_1 L_1 & 0 \\ 0 & \alpha_2 L_2 \end{bmatrix}$, and $\tilde{S} = \begin{bmatrix} \beta_2 S_1 & -\beta_1 S \\ -\beta_1 S & \beta_2 S_2 \end{bmatrix}$.

3.2 Optimization

Although Eq. (4) is jointly non-convex with respect to all the variables, we can solve it through the use of an iterative optimization method, where Y, B and C are solved alternatively. Fortunately, each subproblem has the elegant closed-form solution. The details of the optimization procedure are listed as below:

***B*-subproblem:** When Y and C are fixed, setting the gradient of Eq. (4) over B to zero, we can obtain:

$$C^T X_c EY = (C^T X_c X_c^T C + C^T I_\lambda^T I_\lambda C + C^T X_c L X_c^T C + C^T X_c \tilde{S} X_c^T C)B. \quad (5)$$

Let $H = C^T X_c EY$ and $G = C^T X_c X_c^T C + C^T I_\lambda^T I_\lambda C + C^T X_c L X_c^T C + C^T X_c \tilde{S} X_c^T C$. The solution of B is:

$$B = G^{-1} H. \quad (6)$$

***C*-subproblem:** When Y and B are fixed, substituting Eq. (6) into Eq. (4), after that the objective function become:

$$\min_C J = -2tr(H^T B) + tr(GBB^T) = -tr(G^{-1} H H^T), \quad (7)$$

which is equal to:

$$\max_C tr\left[(C^T S_t C)^{-1} C^T S_b C\right], \quad (8)$$

where $S_b = X_c EYY^T E^T X_c^T$, and $S_t = X_c X_c^T + I_\lambda^T I_\lambda + X_c L X_c^T + X_c \tilde{S} X_c^T$. Thus, the solution of C is the eigenvector of $S_t{}^{-1} S_b$ corresponding to the s largest eigenvalues [66].

***Y*-subproblem:** When C and B are fixed, Eq. (4) can be written as:

$$\max_Y tr(Y^T E^T X_c^T CB). \quad (9)$$

According to [18], we solve Eq. (9) by

$$Y(\mathbf{rank}(i,j),j) = \begin{cases} 1, & i \le \frac{n}{2} \\ -1, & otherwise, \end{cases} \quad (10)$$

where **rank** is the sorted index of $E^T X_c^T CB$ in descending order, and both i and j are the indices of the matrix **rank**.

Initialization: During the optimization procedure, B and C are related to Y. Thus, we decide to firstly initialize Y. To initialize Y, we respectively calculate the r eigenvectors of the two-modality normalized similarity matrix A_1 and A_2 corresponding to the r largest eigenvalues, and then collect them as two eigenvector matrices. Further, we calculate the sum of such two eigenvector matrices and then sort the resultant matrix in the row-wise descending order to induce the sorted index. After that, we utilize the sorted index to initialize Y, according to Eq. (10). When Y is initialized, C is calculated according to C-subproblem and B is initialized by Eq. (6).

The overall optimization procedure for our model is summarized in **Algorithm 1**. Since the objective function is minimized at each step, the optimization problem in Eq. (4) is non-increasing under the iterative update rules. Thus, the convergence analysis of our optimization algorithm is:

$$J(B^t, C^t, Y^t) \le J(B^{t+1}, C^t, Y^t) \le J(B^{t+1}, C^{t+1}, Y^t) \le J(B^{t+1}, C^{t+1}, Y^{t+1}), \quad (11)$$

Algorithm 1: Optimization for CSGH

Input: The hashing code length r; two similarity matrices Z_1 and Z_2; six parameters $\lambda_1, \lambda_2, \alpha_1, \alpha_2, \beta_1$ and β_2; the maximum number of iterations N; the training data X_c.
Output: C and B

```
Initialize Y, compute L and S̃;
repeat
    Solve C-subproblem;
    Solve B-subproblem via (6);
    Solve Y-subproblem via (10);
until Convergence;
```

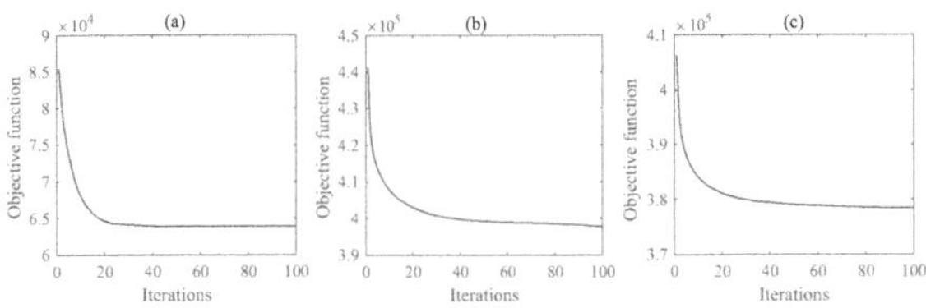

Figure 2: The objective value of CSGH for 32-bit cross-modal retrieval versus different iterations on (a) Wiki, (b) NUS-WIDE and (c) Flickr1M datasets, respectively.

where B^t, C^t and Y^t signify the shared transformation matrix, the modality-specific transformation matrices and the hashing codes at the tth round iteration, respectively. To accelerate its convergence, we have treated Eq. (12) as the termination condition of **Algorithm 1**.

$$\left|(J(B^t, C^t, Y^t) - J(B^{t+1}, C^{t+1}, Y^{t+1}))/J(B^t, C^t, Y^t)\right| \leq \delta, \quad (12)$$

where the tolerance $\delta = 10^{-4}$ is used in all the experiments.

As shown in Fig. 2, the objective function curve takes on the tendency of a monotone decrease, and converges around 40 iterations on all the compared datasets for 32-bit cross-modal retrieval task.

When a new sample $x \in R^{d_1}$ comes, if it belongs to the image data, we minimize

$$\min_{y} \left\|y - x^T C_1 B\right\|_F^2, \quad (13)$$

and the hashing codes y is:

$$y = \Pi_0(x^T C_1 B), \quad (14)$$

where $\Pi_0(s)$ denotes the element-wise operation over the vector s, of which $s_i = 1$ if the i-th entry value s_i is larger than zero; otherwise, $s_i = 0$. Likewise, if the new sample belongs to the text data, the hashing code is $y = \Pi_0(x^T C_2 B)$.

4 EXPERIMENT

In this section, we verify the effectiveness of CSGH by conducting experiments of cross-modal retrieval on four popular cross-modal datasets including Wiki [38], NUS-WIDE [6], Flickr25K [16] and Flickr1M [30].

Table 1: The values of six regularized parameter on Wiki, NUS-WIDE, Flickr25K and Flickr1M datasets, respectively.

Parameter	Dataset		
	Wiki	NUS-WIDE	Flickr25K/1M
α_1	10^{-5}	0.2	0.1
α_2	10^{-3}	0.2	0.1
β_1	0.1	0.1	0.1
β_2	0.2	0.2	0.2
λ_1	10^{-5}	10^4	10^4
λ_2	10^{-3}	10^4	10^4

4.1 Datasets

- The **Wiki** dataset [38] consists of 2,866 image-text pairs collected from Wikipedia's featured articles. All the image-text pairs are annotated with semantic labels of 10 categories. Each image is represented by a 128-dimensional bag-of-words feature vector based on SIFT descriptors while each text is represented by a 10-dimensional feature vector. Following the original partition [8, 26, 38], we use the released 693 pairs as testing set and the 2,173 pairs as training set. We employ the training set as the gallery database.
- The **NUS-WIDE** dataset [6] comprises 269,648 images and the associated tags from Flickr, with the 81 ground-truth concepts used for evaluation. Following [26, 44, 69], we select the most 21 frequently-used concepts to construct a new dataset of 195,834 image-text pairs. Each image is represented by a 500-dimensional bag of words feature vector based on SIFT descriptors, and meanwhile each text is encoded as a 1000-dimensional tag occurrence feature vector. From the new dataset, we randomly sample 2,000 image-text pairs as the testing set, and the rest image-text pairs are used as the gallery database. From the gallery database, we randomly select 10,000 image-text pairs as the training set.
- The **Flickr1M** dataset [30] consists of one million Flickr images, with 25,000 labelled and 975,000 unlabelled image-text pairs. As in [16], the dataset with 25,000 labelled pairs is dubbed **Flickr25K**. The ground-truth of the labelled pairs contain 38 concepts. Each image is represented by a 3,857-dimensional vector, and each text is represented by a 2000-dimensional vector generated by tag occurrences [41]. The testing set includes 1,000 image-text pairs randomly sampled from the 25,000 labelled pairs, while the remaining 24,000 pairs form the gallery database. In this paper, we not only utilize the gallery database as the training set for evaluating both unsupervised and supervised methods (Results on Flickr25K) but also select 10,000 unlabelled pairs as the training set for evaluating unsupervised methods (Results on Flickr1M).

4.2 Comparison models and protocols

We compare CSGH with six state-of-the-art cross-modal hashing methods including supervised models such as CMSSH [1], SCM [60] and QCH [48], and unsupervised models like CVH [17], IMH [40] and CCQ [26].

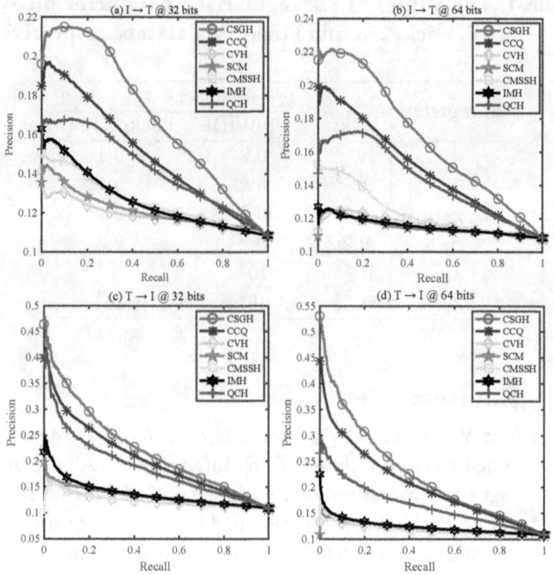

Figure 3: The precision-recall curves on Wiki dataset.

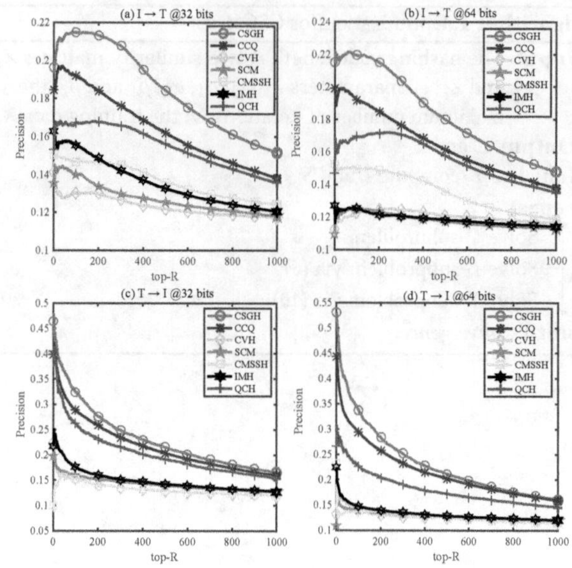

Figure 4: The precision@top-R curves on Wiki dataset.

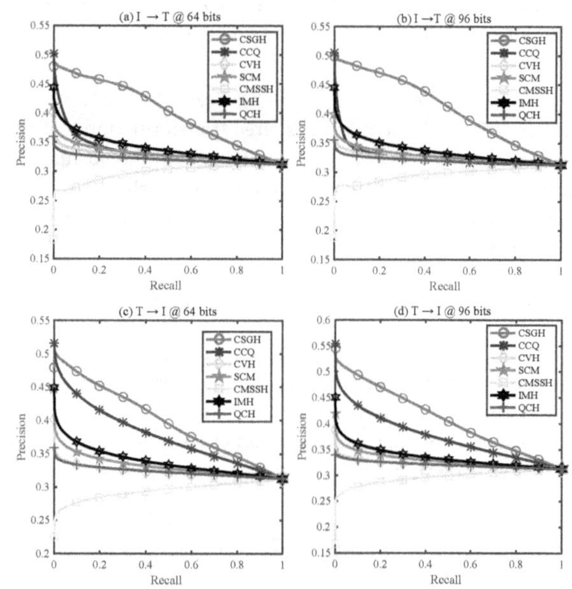

Figure 5: The precision-recall curves on NUS-WIDE dataset.

Two types of cross-modal retrieval tasks are performed: 1) I→T: image data as the query, and text data as the gallery database; 2) T→I: text data as the query, and image data as the gallery database.

We employ the mean average precision (MAP) to evaluate the effectiveness of our model. Following [27, 44, 57], we report MAP@R = 50, where R is the number of retrieved samples. We also display the precision-recall curves and precision@top-R curves of all the retrieval tasks in figures.

CSGH has seven parameters: the dimension s of the modality-specific transformation matrices and the shared transformation matrix, and six regularized parameters λ_1, λ_2, β_1, β_2, α_1 and α_2. For all the mentioned datasets, s can be adaptively decided by the number of the non-zero eigenvalues of ${S_t}^{-1}S_b$, in which the kept non-zero eigenvalues are over or equal to 10^{-5}. The settings of six regularized parameters on four datasets are shown in Table 1.

4.3 Experimental results

Results on Wiki. We evaluate CSGH against six state-of-the-art cross-modal hashing models with different hashing bits (32, 64, 96 and 128), and report the MAP results in Table 2. For all the evaluated cross-modal tasks, CSGH is superior to all of the compared supervised and unsupervised methods for all the bits on Wiki dataset. The precision-recall curves and the precision@top-R curves evaluated on Wiki dataset are illustrated in Figs. 3 and 4, respectively. From Figs. 3 and 4, we can also draw the conclusion that CSGH performs better than the other compared methods for these cross-modal retrieval tasks.

Results on NUS-WIDE. Table 2 also reports the MAP results on NUS-WIDE dataset. As we can see from Table 2, CSGH performs better when the bits grow, while several methods such as SCM, CVH and IMH have the downtrend. For the 32-bit retrieval task, CSGH is slightly inferior to CCQ but show the competitive results, especially for the long bits. The precision-recall curves and the precision@top-R curves shown in Fig. 5 and Fig. 6, respectively, show that CSGH is also superior to almost all the other compared methods and has competitive performance to CCQ.

Results on Flickr25K and Flickr1M. Since supervised models need labels, for fair comparison, we evaluate all the methods on the labelled Flickr25K dataset. To further assess the effectiveness of CSGH against the other unsupervised models, we do experiments on Flickr1M. The MAP results on Flickr25K and Flickr1M are shown in Table 3 and Table 4, respectively. The MAP results on Flickr25K is similar to that on NUS-WIDE dataset. On Flickr1M dataset, CSGH

Table 2: The MAP on Wiki and NUS-WIDE, respectively

Tasks	Methods	Dataset							
		Wiki				NUS-WIDE			
		32 bits	64 bits	96 bits	128 bits	32 bits	64 bits	96 bits	128 bits
I→T	CMSSH	0.1759	0.1560	0.1581	0.1764	0.2641	0.2799	0.2981	0.3075
	SCM	0.1839	0.1648	0.1786	0.1657	0.4633	0.4430	0.4305	0.4255
	QCH	0.2153	0.2170	0.2019	0.1842	0.3783	0.4025	0.4033	0.4044
	CVH	0.1806	0.1582	0.1590	0.1687	0.4417	0.4302	0.4221	0.4195
	IMH	0.2007	0.1658	0.1577	0.1493	0.4781	0.4726	0.4695	0.4666
	CCQ	0.2366	0.2366	0.2366	0.2290	**0.5212**	0.5275	0.5304	0.5222
	CSGH	**0.2658**	**0.2682**	**0.2716**	**0.2655**	0.5108	**0.5331**	**0.5405**	**0.5426**
T→I	CMSSH	0.1762	0.2011	0.2386	0.2454	0.2827	0.2830	0.2840	0.2746
	SCM	0.2376	0.2053	0.2027	0.2011	0.4754	0.4477	0.4442	0.4353
	QCH	0.3970	0.3198	0.3034	0.2442	0.4198	0.4073	0.4041	0.3994
	CVH	0.2517	0.2231	0.2237	0.2178	0.4333	0.4222	0.4193	0.4179
	IMH	0.2784	0.2384	0.2344	0.2062	0.4832	0.4758	0.4685	0.4661
	CCQ	0.4077	0.4130	0.4171	0.3545	**0.5428**	**0.5524**	0.5532	0.5502
	CSGH	**0.4436**	**0.4809**	**0.4880**	**0.4891**	0.5209	0.5496	**0.5637**	**0.5692**

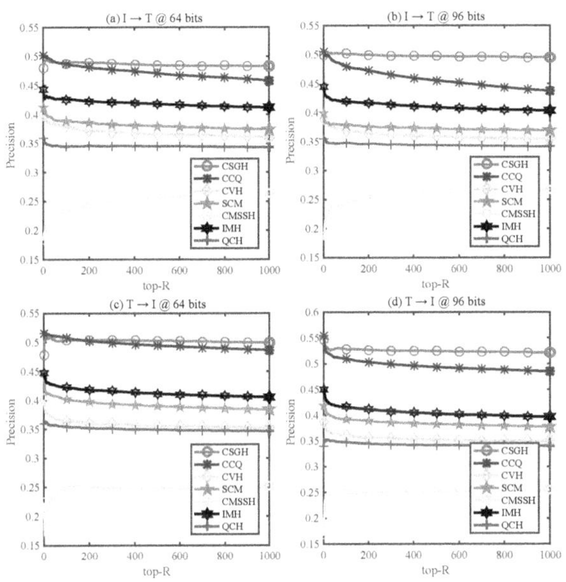

Figure 6: The precision@top-R curves on NUS-WIDE dataset.

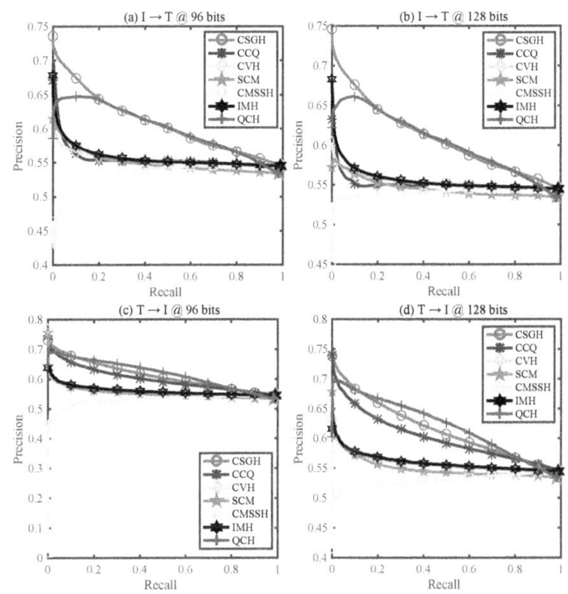

Figure 7: The precision-recall curves on Flickr25K dataset.

is superior to all the compared methods in terms of MAP, and thus this verifies the advantage of CSGH on unlabelled scenarios. The precision-recall curves on Flick25K dataset shown in Fig. 7 indicate that our model is superior to most of the compared unsupervised methods and two supervised methods including CMSSH and SCM, and is competitive to QCH for I→T task. For T→I task, CSGH is slightly inferior to QCH. The precision-recall results are reasonable because QCH is a supervised model and can benefits from the labels. The precison@top-R curves on Flickr25K is shown in Fig. 8. From Fig. 8, CSGH outweighs the other compared methods, especially QCH, in light of the precison@top-R curves.

5 CONCLUSION

This paper proposes a new cross-modal hashing method dubbed the Collaborative Subspace Graph Hashing (CSGH). CSGH is able to produce the hashing codes of different modalities by the so-called collaborative subspace learning based on the modality-specific transformation matrices and the shared transformation matrix. Meanwhile, it can capture the neighborhood structure and cross-modal correlation via the intra-modality Laplacian regularization and cross-modal correlation constraint, respectively. During optimizing CSGH, each sub-problem of CSGH can yield the elegant analytical solution. Experiments of cross-modal retrieval on four popular datasets verify the effectiveness of CSGH compared with six

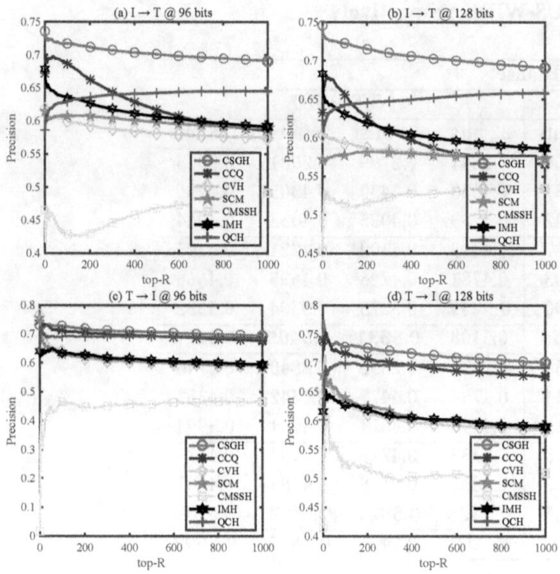

Figure 8: The precision@top-R curves on Flickr25K dataset.

Table 3: The MAP on Flickr25K dataset

Tasks	Methods	Flickr25K			
		32 bits	64 bits	96 bits	128 bits
I→T	CMSSH	0.5039	0.5509	0.4946	0.5521
	SCM	0.6229	0.6288	0.6089	0.6118
	QCH	0.6285	0.6431	0.6398	0.6610
	CVH	0.6514	0.6459	0.6372	0.6334
	IMH	0.6941	0.6822	0.6744	0.6714
	CCQ	**0.7320**	0.7154	0.7181	0.6989
	CSGH	0.7214	**0.7338**	**0.7434**	**0.7493**
T→I	CMSSH	0.4758	0.5148	0.4193	0.6044
	SCM	0.6635	0.6695	0.6579	0.6560
	QCH	0.6971	0.7100	0.7081	0.7177
	CVH	0.6984	0.6954	0.7039	0.6925
	IMH	0.6928	0.6837	0.6628	0.6667
	CCQ	0.7288	0.7378	0.7479	0.7565
	CSGH	**0.7309**	**0.7415**	**0.7490**	**0.7575**

Table 4: The MAP on Flickr1M dataset

Tasks	Methods	Flickr1M			
		32 bits	64 bits	96 bits	128 bits
I→T	CVH	0.5567	0.5680	0.5612	0.5580
	IMH	0.6610	0.6597	0.6439	0.6380
	CCQ	0.6346	0.6254	0.6390	0.6355
	CSGH	**0.7055**	**0.7365**	**0.7402**	**0.7397**
T→I	CVH	0.5673	0.5596	0.5815	0.5803
	IMH	0.6304	0.6387	0.6311	0.6374
	CCQ	0.6818	0.6963	0.7117	0.7047
	CSGH	**0.7171**	**0.7508**	**0.7426**	**0.7486**

state-of-the-art supervised and unsupervised cross-modal hashing methods.

ACKNOWLEDGMENTS

The authors would like to thank Dr. Long Lan and the anonymous referees for their valuable comments and helpful suggestions.

This work was supported by the National Key Research and Development Program of China under Grant No.: 2016YFB0200401, and the National Natural Science Foundation of China under Grant No.: U1435222.

REFERENCES

[1] M. M. Bronstein, A. M. Bronstein, F. Michel, and N. Paragios. 2010. Data fusion through cross-modality metric learning using similarity-sensitive hashing. In *CVPR*. 3594–3601.

[2] M. M. Bronstein, A. M. Bronstein, F. Michel, and N. Paragios. 2013. Data fusion through cross-modality metric learning using similarity-sensitive hashing. In *CVPR*. 3594–3601.

[3] Y. Cao, M Long, J. Wang, and S. Liu. 2017. Collective deep quantization for efficient cross-modal retrieval. In *AAAI*. 3974–3980.

[4] Z. Cao, M. Long, J. Wang, and Q. Yang. 2017. Transitive hashing network for heterogeneous multimedia retrieval. In *AAAI*. 81–87.

[5] L. Chi, B. Li, X. Zhu, S. Pan, and L. Chen. 2017. Hashing for adaptive real-time graph stream classification with concept drifts. *IEEE TCB* (2017).

[6] T. S. Chua, J. Tang, R. Hong, H. Li, Z. Luo, and Y. T. Zheng. 2009. NUS-WIDE: a real-world web image database from national university of singapore. In *CIVR*. ACM, 48.

[7] P. J. Costa, E. Coviello, G. Doyle, N. Rasiwasia, G. R. Lanckriet, R. Levy, and N. Vasconcelos. 2014. On the role of correlation and abstraction in cross-modal multimedia retrieval. *IEEE TPAMI* 36, 3 (2014), 521–35.

[8] J. Costa Pereira, E. Coviello, G. Doyle, N. Rasiwasia, G. Lanckriet, R. Levy, and N. Vasconcelos. 2014. On the role of correlation and abstraction in cross-modal multimedia retrieval. *IEEE TPAMI* 36, 3 (March 2014), 521–535.

[9] M. Datar, N. Immorlica, P. Indyk, and V. S. Mirrokni. 2004. Locality-sensitive hashing scheme based on P-stable distributions. In *SCG*. ACM, 253–262.

[10] G. Ding, Y. Guo, and J. Zhou. 2014. Collective matrix factorization hashing for multimodal data. In *CVPR*. 2083–2090.

[11] G. Dong, X. Zhang, L. Lan, X. Huang, and Z. Luo. 2018. Discrete graph hashing via affine transformation. In *ICME*.

[12] F. Feng, X. Wang, and R. Li. 2014. Cross-modal retrieval with correspondence autoencoder. In *MM*. ACM, 7–16.

[13] L. Feng, X. S. Xu, S. Guo, and X. L. Wang. 2017. Supervised class graph preserving hashing for image retrieval and classification. In *MMM*. Springer, 391–403.

[14] Y. Gong, S. Lazebnik, A. Gordo, and F. Perronnin. 2013. Iterative quantization: a procrustean approach to learning binary codes for large-scale image retrieval. *IEEE TPAMI* 35, 12 (2013), 2916–2929.

[15] L. He, X. Xu, H. Lu, Y. Yang, F. Shen, and H. T. Shen. 2017. Unsupervised cross-modal retrieval through adversarial learning. In *ICME*. 1153–1158.

[16] M. J. Huiskes and M. S. Lew. 2008. The MIR Flickr retrieval evaluation. In *MIR*. ACM, 39–43.

[17] S. Kumar and R. Udupa. 2011. Learning hash functions for cross-view similarity search. In *IJCAI*. 1360–1365.

[18] X. Li, D. Hu, and F. Nie. 2017. Large graph hashing with spectral rotation.. In *AAAI*. 2203–2209.

[19] J. Liang, Z. Li, D. Cao, R. He, and J. Wang. 2016. Self-paced cross-modal subspace matching. In *SIGIR*. ACM, 569–578.

[20] J. Lin, Z. Li, and J. Tang. 2017. Discriminative deep hashing for scalable face image retrieval. In *IJCAI*.

[21] J. Lin, A. Veillard, L. Y. Duan, V. Chandrasekhar, and T. Poggio. 2017. Nested invariance pooling and RBM hashing for image instance retrieval. In *ICMR*. ACM, 260–268.

[22] Z. Lin, G. Ding, M. Hu, and J. Wang. 2015. Semantics-preserving hashing for cross-view retrieval. In *CVPR*. 3864–3872.

[23] L. Liu, Z. Lin, L. Shao, F. Shen, G. Ding, and J. Han. 2017. Sequential discrete hashing for scalable cross-modality similarity retrieval. *IEEE TIP* 26, 1 (2017), 107–118.

[24] L. Liu, F. Shen, Y. Shen, X. Liu, and L. Shao. 2017. Deep sketch hashing: fast free-hand sketch-based image retrieval. In *arXiv*.

[25] W. Liu, J. Wang, S. Kumar, and S. F. Chang. 2011. Hashing with graphs. In *ICML*. 1–8.

[26] M. Long, Y. Cao, J. Wang, and P. S. Yu. 2016. Composite correlation quantization for efficient multimodal retrieval. In *SIGIR*. ACM, 579–588.

[27] X. Lu, F. Wu, S. Tang, Z. Zhang, X. He, and Y. Zhuang. 2013. A low rank structural large margin method for cross-modal ranking. In *SIGIR*. ACM, 433–442.
[28] X. Lu, X. Zheng, and X. Li. 2017. Latent semantic minimal hashing for image retrieval. *TIP* 26, 1 (2017), 355–368.
[29] Jonathan M., Michael M. B., Alexander M. B., and JÍzrgen S. 2014. Multimodal Similarity-Preserving Hashing. *IEEE TPAMI* 36, 4 (2014), 824–30.
[30] B. Thomee M. J. Huiskes and M. S. Lew. 2010. New trends and ideas in visual concept detection: the MIR Flickr retrieval evaluation initiative. In *MIR*. ACM, 527–536.
[31] S. Moran and V. Lavrenko. 2015. Regularised cross-modal hashing. (2015), 907–910.
[32] J. Ngiam, A. Khosla, M. Kim, J. Nam, H. Lee, and A. Y. Ng. 2011. Multimodal deep learning. In *ICML*. 689–696.
[33] M. Ou, P. Cui, F. Wang, J. Wang, W. Zhu, and S. Yang. 2013. Comparing apples to oranges:a scalable solution with heterogeneous hashing. In *SIGKDD*. ACM, 230–238.
[34] Yuxin Peng, Xin Huang, and Yunzhen Zhao. 2017. An overview of cross-media retrieval: concepts, methodologies, benchmarks and challenges. *TCSVT* (2017).
[35] Y. Peng, J. Qi, X. Huang, and Y. Yuan. 2018. CCL: Cross-modal Correlation Learning with Multi-grained Fusion by Hierarchical Network. *IEEE Transactions on Multimedia* 20, 2 (2018), 405–420.
[36] Y. Peng, X. Zhai, Y. Zhao, and X. Huang. 2016. Semi-supervised cross-media feature learning with unified patch graph regularization. *IEEE TCSVT* 26, 3 (2016), 583–596.
[37] V. Ranjan, N. Rasiwasia, and C. V. Jawahar. 2015. Multi-label cross-modal retrieval. In *ICCV*. 4094–4102.
[38] N. Rasiwasia, J. Costa Pereira, E. Coviello, G. Doyle, G.R.G. Lanckriet, R. Levy, and N. Vasconcelos. 2010. A new approach to cross-modal multimedia retrieval. In *MM*. ACM, 251–260.
[39] R. Salakhutdinov and G. Hinton. 2009. Semantic hashing. *International Journal of Approximate Reasoning* 50, 7 (2009), 969–978.
[40] J. Song, Y. Yang, Y. Yang, Z. Huang, and H. T. Shen. 2013. Inter-media hashing for large-scale retrieval from heterogeneous data sources. In *SIGMOD*. ACM, 785–796.
[41] N. Srivastava and R. R. Salakhutdinov. 2012. Multimodal learning with deep boltzmann machines. In *NIPS*, F. Pereira, C. J. C. Burges, L. Bottou, and K. Q. Weinberger (Eds.). Curran Associates, Inc., 2222–2230. http://papers.nips.cc/paper/4683-multimodal-learning-with-deep-boltzmann-machines.pdf
[42] D. Wang, X. Gao, X. Wang, and L. He. 2015. Semantic topic multimodal hashing for cross-media retrieval. In *IJCAI*. 3890–3896.
[43] K. Wang, R. He, L. Wang, W. Wang, and T. Tan. 2016. Joint feature selection and subspace learning for cross-modal retrieval. *IEEE TPAMI* 38, 10 (2016), 2010–2023.
[44] W. Wang, B. C. Ooi, X. Yang, D. Zhang, and Y. Zhuang. 2014. Effective multi-modal retrieval based on stacked auto-encoders. *Proceedings of the VLDB Endowment* 7, 8 (2014), 649–660.
[45] Y. Wei, Y. Zhao, C. Lu, Sh. Wei, L. Liu, Zh. Zhu, and S. Yan. 2017. Cross-modal retrieval with CNN visual features: a new baseline. *IEEE TCB* 47, 2 (2017), 449–460.
[46] Y. Wei, Y. Zhao, Z. Zhu, S. Wei, Y. Xiao, J. Feng, and S. Yan. 2016. Modality-Dependent Cross-Media Retrieval. *Acm Transactions on Intelligent Systems and Technology* 7, 4 (2016), 57.
[47] Y. Weiss, A. Torralba, and R. Fergus. 2009. Spectral hashing. In *NIPS*. 1753–1760.
[48] B. Wu, Q. Yang, W. S. Zheng, Y. Wang, and J. Wang. 2015. Quantized correlation hashing for fast cross-modal search. In *IJCAI*. 3946–3952.
[49] D. Wu, Z. Lin, B. Li, M. Ye, and W. Wang. 2017. Deep supervised hashing for multi-label and large-scale image retrieval. In *ICMR*. ACM, 150–158.
[50] F. Wu, Y. Zhou, Y. Yang, S. Tang, Y. Zhang, and Y. Zhuang. 2014. Sparse multi-modal hashing. *IEEE TMM* 16, 2 (2014), 427–439.
[51] L. Wu and Y. Wang. 2017. Structured deep hashing with convolutional neural networks for fast person re-identification. In *arXiv*.
[52] L. Xie, J. Shen, J. Han, L. Zhu, and L. Shao. 2017. Dynamic multi-view hashing for online image retrieval. In *IJCAI*. 3133–3139.
[53] X. Xu, F. Shen, H. T. Shen, and X. Li. 2017. Learning discriminative binary codes for large-scale cross-modal retrieval. *IEEE TIP* 26, 5 (2017), 2494–2507.
[54] Y. Xu, Y. Yang, F. Shen, X. Xu, Y. Zhou, and H. T. Shen. 2017. Attribute hashing for zero-shot image retrieval. In *ICME*. IEEE, 133–138.
[55] E. Yang, C. Deng, W. Liu, Liu .X, D. Tao, and X. Gao. 2017. Pairwise relationship guided deep hashing for cross-modal retrieval. In *AAAI*. 1618–1625.
[56] T. Yao, X. Kong, H. Fu, and Q. Tian. 2017. Supervised coarse-to-fine semantic hashing for cross-media retrieval. *Digital Signal Processing* 63 (2017), 135–144.
[57] Z. Yu, F. Wu, Y. Yang, Q. Tian, J. Luo, and Y. Zhuang. 2014. Discriminative coupled dictionary hashing for fast cross-media retrieval. In *SIGIR*. ACM, 395–404.
[58] X. Zhai, Y. Peng, and J. Xiao. 2013. Heterogeneous metric learning with joint graph regularization for cross-media retrieval. In *AAAI*. 1198–1204.
[59] X. Zhai, Y. Peng, and J. Xiao. 2014. Learning cross-media joint representation with sparse and semisupervised regularization. *IEEE TCSVT* 24, 6 (2014), 965–978.
[60] D. Zhang and W.J. Li. 2014. Large-scale supervised multimodal hashing with semantic correlation maximization. In *AAAI*. 2177–2183.
[61] D. Zhang, F. Wang, and L. Si. 2011. Composite hashing with multiple information sources. In *SIGIR*. ACM, 225–234.
[62] L. Zhang, B. Ma, G. Li, Q. Huang, and Q. Tian. 2017. Cross-modal retrieval using multi-ordered discriminative structured subspace learning. *TMM* 19, 6 (2017), 1220–1233.
[63] R. Zhang, L. Lin, R. Zhang, W. Zuo, and L. Zhang. 2015. Bit-scalable deep hashing with regularized similarity learning for image retrieval and person re-Identification. *IEEE TIP* 24, 12 (2015), 4766–4779.
[64] W. Zhao, Z. Guan, H. Luo, J. Peng, and J. Fan. 2017. Deep multiple instance hashing for object-based image retrieval. In *IJCAI*. 3504–3510.
[65] X. Zhao, G. Ding, Y. Guo, J. Han, and Y. Gao. 2017. TUCH: turning cross-view hashing into single-view hashing via generative adversarial nets. In *IJCAI*. 3511–3517.
[66] S. Zheng, X. Cai, C. Ding, F. Nie, and H. Huang. 2015. A closed form solution to multi-view low-rank regression. In *AAAI*. 1973–1979.
[67] J. Zhou, G. Ding, and Y. Guo. 2014. Latent semantic sparse hashing for cross-modal similarity search. In *SIGIR*. ACM, 415–424.
[68] F. Zhu, X. Kong, L. Zheng, H. Fu, and Q. Tian. 2017. Part-based deep hashing for large-scale person re-identification. *IEEE TIP* 26, 10 (2017), 4806–4817.
[69] X. Zhu, Z. Huang, H. T. Shen, and X. Zhao. 2013. Linear cross-modal hashing for efficient multimedia search. In *MM*. ACM, 143–152.
[70] Y. Zhuang, Z. Yu, W. Wang, F. Wu, S. Tang, and J. Shao. 2014. Cross-media hashing with neural networks. (2014), 901–904.

Dictionary Learning based Supervised Discrete Hashing for Cross-Media Retrieval

Ye Wu
Shandong University
kimiwadewu@gmail.com

Xin Luo
Shandong University
luoxin.lxin@gmail.com

Xin-Shun Xu*
Shandong University
xuxinshun@sdu.edu.com

Shanqing Guo*
Shandong University
guoshanqing@sdu.edu.com

Yuliang Shi
Shandong University
shiyuliang@sdu.edu.com

ABSTRACT

Hashing technique has attracted considerable attention for large-scale multimedia retrieval due to its low storage cost and fast query speed. Moreover, many hashing models have been proposed for cross-modal retrieval task. However, there are still some problems that need to be further considered. For example, a majority of them directly use linear projection matrix to project heterogeneous data into a common space, which may lead to large error as there are some heterogeneous data with semantic similarity hard to be close in latent space when linear projection is used. Besides, most existing cross-modal hashing methods use a simple pairwise similarity matrix for preserving the label information when learning. This kind of pairwise similarity cannot fully utilize the discriminative property of label information. Furthermore, most existing supervised ones try to solve a relaxed continuous optimization problem by dropping the discrete constraints, which may lead to large quantization error. To overcome these limitations, in this paper, we propose a novel cross-modal hashing method, called Dictionary Learning based Supervised Discrete Hashing (DLSDH). Specifically, it learns dictionaries and generates sparse representation for every instance, which is more suitable to be projected to a latent space. To make full use of label information, it uses cosine similarity to construct a new pairwise similarity matrix which can contain more information. Moreover, it directly learns the discrete hash codes instead of relaxing the discrete constraints. Extensive experiments are conducted on three benchmark datasets and the results demonstrate that it outperforms several state-of-the-art methods for cross-modal retrieval task.

CCS CONCEPTS

• **Computing methodologies → Learning paradigms; Visual content-based indexing and retrieval;** • **Information systems → Multimedia and multimodal retrieval;**

KEYWORDS

Approximate Nearest Neighbor; Hashing; Cross-Modal Retrieval; Dictionary Learning; Multiple Modalities

ACM Reference Format:
Ye Wu, Xin Luo, Xin-Shun Xu*, Shanqing Guo*, and Yuliang Shi. 2018. Dictionary Learning based Supervised Discrete Hashing for Cross-Media Retrieval. In *ICMR '18: 2018 International Conference on Multimedia Retrieval, June 11–14, 2018, Yokohama, Japan.* ACM, New York, NY, USA, 9 pages. https://doi.org/10.1145/3206025.3206045

1 INTRODUCTION

In recent years, more and more multimedia data are generated; correspondingly, the demand for efficient large-scale multimedia retrieval technologies is significantly growing [6, 7, 10, 26, 28, 34]. The multimedia data usually come from different data sources, and exist in different media types, e.g., texts, images and videos. Usually, given a query, a multimedia retrieval model is expected to return a candidate list containing similar samples. Most similarity search methods can only handle the unimodal setting [9, 21, 24, 31, 33, 42], in which the query and the returned candidates are in the same modality. However, in many applications, we hope that a model can deal with different modalities, i.e. cross-modal retrieval. As an example, we can use a query of one modality (e.g., images) to retrieve relevant items of other modalities (e.g., texts and videos). Recently, quite a few studies have tried to tackle the cross-modal retrieval problem [12, 14, 27, 35, 37]. However, one major limitation of these methods is that they are not able to deal with large-scale multi-modal data since the scalability issue is not fully considered.

In order to tackle the efficiency challenge, some promising works which leverage hashing techniques have been proposed to do the cross-modal retrieval tasks [3, 5, 32, 38, 49]. To consider the scalability issue, they find linear projections to embed the heterogeneous data into a common Hamming space, in which the multi-modal features can be represented by low dimensional binary hash codes. In this way, the underlying correlations between different modalities can be captured. Besides, once the multi-modal features are transformed into short binary codes, pairwise comparisons can then be carried out extremely efficiently in the Hamming space, using bit-wise XOR operation. Moreover, by storing short hash codes instead of high dimensional multi-modal features, the storage cost can be dramatically reduced. Generally, multi-modal hashing can be divided into two categories: modality-specific and integrated hashing methods. Modality-specific ones learn independent hash codes for each modality. Typical examples are Cross-Modal Similarity

*Corresponding author.

ICMR '18, June 11–14, 2018, Yokohama, Japan

ACM ISBN 978-1-4503-5046-4/18/06...$15.00
https://doi.org/10.1145/3206025.3206045

Sensitive Hashing (CMSSH) [1], Cross-View Hashing (CVH) [17], and Inter-Media Hashing (IMH) [30]. Integrated ones learn unified hashing codes for different modalities. Representative methods are Composite Hashing with Multiple Information Sources (CHMIS) [44], Latent Semantic Sparse Hashing (LSSH) [49], and Collective Matrix Factorization Hashing (CMFH) [5].

In addition, from the perspective of the utilization of label information, existing cross-modal hashing methods can be grouped into unsupervised [5, 30, 49] and supervised ones [1, 19, 43, 48]. Unsupervised ones, including Collective Matrix Factorization Hashing (CMFH) [5] and Composite Correlation Quantization (CCQ) [22], exploit the intra- and inter-modal relations of training data and generate hash codes without utilizing the label information. Different from unsupervised cross-modal hashing methods, supervised ones can further exploit the available label information to improve performance which can better preserve the semantic similarity of cross-modal data. Generally, label information is helpful for the supervised models to achieve better retrieval performance than unsupervised ones. Many supervised methods have been proposed, such as Semantic Correlation Maximization (SCM) Hashing [43] and Semantics-Preserving Hashing (SePH) [19].

More recently, several deep cross-modal hashing methods have been proposed. For example, Deep Cross-Modal Hashing (DCMH) [13] integrates both feature learning and hash codes learning into a same deep learning framework with one deep neural network for all modalities. Pairwise Relation Guided Deep Hashing (PRDH) [40] further exploits different pairwise constraints to enforce the hash codes from not only intra-modality but also inter-modality. Deep Visual-Semantic Hashing (DVSH) [2] uses CNN and Long Short Term Memory (LSTM) to separately learn hash codes for each modality, but it is constrained to sentences or other sequential texts.

As shown above, many cross-modal hashing methods have been proposed and achieved promising results; however, there are still some problems that should be further considered. (1) Most existing cross-modal hashing methods directly use linear projection matrices to project heterogeneous data into a common space. This kind of approaches could lead to large error as there are some heterogeneous data with semantic similarity hard to be close in latent space when linear projection is used. (2) Most supervised cross-modal hashing methods use pairwise similarities which are defined by the given labels. For example, two instances are usually defined to be similar if they share at least one common label; however, this kind definition of pairwise similarity is particularly simple and ignores a lot of useful information. For example, suppose that there are three instances x_1, x_2, and x_3 with labels $l_1 = [1, 1, 1, 0], l_2 = [1, 1, 0, 0]$, and $l_3 = [0, 0, 1, 0]$; most cross-modal hashing methods treat the similarity between x_1 and x_2 and that between x_1 and x_3 equally; but apparently, x_1 and x_2 are more similar than x_1 and x_3 as they share more labels. (3) Most existing supervised cross-modal hashing methods try to solve a relaxed continuous optimization problem by dropping the discrete constraints which may lead to large errors. Some methods have been proposed to solve the discrete optimization problem directly, such as Supervised Discrete Hashing(SDH) [29], Fast Supervised Discrete Hashing(FSDH) [8], Discrete Weakly-Supervised Hashing [45], and Column Sampling based Discrete Supervised Hashing (COSDISH) [15]. However, they are proposed for unimodal case. Inspired by [29], Discrete Cross-Modal Hashing(DCMH) [25] uses the discrete cyclic coordinate descent method to optimize the formulation.

Considering these problems, we propose a novel cross-modal hashing method, i.e., Dictionary Learning based Supervised Discrete Hashing (DLSDH). Specifically, instead of projecting data directly, it learns dictionaries and generates sparse representations for instances, which are more suitable to be projected to a latent space. In order to further make full use of the label information, it utilizes cosine similarity to construct a new pairwise similarity matrix which can contain more information than that the commonly used one. Moreover, it directly solves the discrete optimization problem without relaxing the binary constraints. DLSDH is extensively evaluated on three benchmark datasets including Wiki, MIRFlickr, and NUS-WIDE. The results demonstrate that DLSDH outperforms several state-of-the-art cross-modal hashing methods.

The rest of this paper is organized as follows. Section 2 introduces the proposed DLSDH model. Section 3 presents the optimization schemes for the problems in DLSDH. In Section 4, we give some further discussions, e.g., out-of-sample query extension and extension to more modalities. Experimental results and corresponding analysis on three benchmark datasets are presented in Section 5, followed by conclusion in Section 6.

2 OUR METHODOLOGY

In this section, we describe the details of the proposed cross-modal retrieval method, i.e., Dictionary Learning based Supervised Discrete Hashing (DLSDH). For simplicity of presentation, we give a description on bimodal case consisting of images and texts which are the most common modalities in real world. But, as described in Section 4.2, it is very easy to extend the proposed method to general cases with more than two modalities.

2.1 Notation and Problem Definition

Suppose we have n training points $O = \{\mathbf{o}_i\}_{i=1}^n$ where $\mathbf{o}_i = (\mathbf{x}_i^{(1)}, \mathbf{x}_i^{(2)})$ denotes the i-th instance; $\mathbf{x}_i^{(1)} \in \mathbb{R}^{d_1}$ is the d_1-dimensional image feature and $\mathbf{x}_i^{(2)} \in \mathbb{R}^{d_2}$ is the d_2-dimensional text feature (usually, $d_1 \neq d_2$). $\mathbf{L} = \{\mathbf{l}_i\}_{i=1}^n \in \{0, 1\}^{n \times c}$ is the overall label matrix where $\mathbf{l}_i = [l_{i1}, l_{i2}, \cdots, l_{ic}]$ is the label vector of the i-th instance, c is the total number of labels, and $l_{ij} = 1$ if $\mathbf{o}_i$ belongs to class j and 0 otherwise.

Following the scheme of integrated models, DLSDH learns a unified hash code for two different modalities of one instance. Given the binary code length r, DLSDH aims to learn hash codes $\mathbf{Y} = \{\mathbf{y}_i\}_{i=1}^n \in \mathbb{R}^{r \times n}$ for training instances and modality-specific hash functions $H_I(\mathbf{x}^{(1)})$ and $H_T(\mathbf{x}^{(2)})$ for image and text modalities, respectively, where $\mathbf{y}_i = \{-1, 1\}^r$ is the r-bit binary hash code. Note that the binary hash code can also be $\mathbf{y}_i = \{0, 1\}^r$. In this paper, we use $\mathbf{y}_i = \{-1, 1\}^r$. The more semantically similar between $\mathbf{o}_i$ and $\mathbf{o}_j$, the smaller their Hamming distance between their corresponding hash codes $\mathbf{y}_i$ and $\mathbf{y}_j$ should be, and vice versa.

2.2 Pairwise Similarity Construction

As mentioned previously, in most existing supervised cross-modal hashing methods, the semantic similarity is represented as a semantic pairwise similarity matrix $\mathbf{S} \in \{-1, 0, 1\}^{n\times n}$ defined by the label information where $\mathbf{S}_{ij}$ is set to 1 when instance $\mathbf{o}_i$ and $\mathbf{o}_j$ share at least one common label, which also means that these two instances are semantically similar; $\mathbf{S}_{ij}$ is set to -1 when instance $\mathbf{o}_i$ and $\mathbf{o}_j$ do not have similar labels; and $\mathbf{S}_{ij} = 0$ means that whether instance $\mathbf{o}_i$ and instance $\mathbf{o}_j$ are semantically similar or not is unknown. In this paper, following previous works [15] we assume that all instances' label information is fully observed without missing entries, i.e., $\mathbf{S} \in \{-1, 1\}^{n\times n}$.

However, this kind of semantic similarity matrix may discard some useful information contained in original data, especially for multi-label data, which are commonly seen in real world [46]. For example, if we have $\mathbf{l}_1 = [1, 1, 1, 0]$, $\mathbf{l}_2 = [1, 1, 0, 0]$ and $\mathbf{l}_3 = [0, 0, 1, 0]$, according to the above definitions, we have $\mathbf{S}_{12} = \mathbf{S}_{13} = 1$. Apparently, instances $\mathbf{o}_1$ and $\mathbf{o}_2$ are more similar than instances $\mathbf{o}_1$ and $\mathbf{o}_3$ as they share more labels. Therefore, the same value of $\mathbf{S}_{12}$ and $\mathbf{S}_{13}$ may discard some useful information contained in original label information.

To consider this problem, we redefine the pairwise similarity matrix $\mathbf{S}$ to make binary hash codes preserve label information as same as that in original data so that it can leverage more label information to supervise the binary codes learning. More specially, we use cosine similarity to construct the similarity matrix $\mathbf{S}$,

$$\mathbf{S}_{ij} = \frac{\sum_{k=1}^{c} \mathbf{l}_{ik}\mathbf{l}_{jk}}{\sqrt{\sum_{k=1}^{c} \mathbf{l}_{ik}^2}\sqrt{\sum_{k=1}^{c} \mathbf{l}_{jk}^2}}. \tag{1}$$

Obviously, if instances $\mathbf{o}_i$ and $\mathbf{o}_j$ are semantically dissimilar, $\mathbf{S}_{ij} = 0$, and we set these $\mathbf{S}_{ij} = -1$ instead; if instances $\mathbf{o}_i$ and $\mathbf{o}_j$ are semantically similar, $0 < \mathbf{S}_{ij} \leq 1$; $\mathbf{S}_{ij} = 1$ means the label information of instance $\mathbf{o}_i$ is exactly same as that of instance $\mathbf{o}_j$. By doing this, the similarity matrix can contain more information about the similarity of original data points, which means that DLSDH can make full use of it to learn better hash codes preserving the similarities in original space.

2.3 Hash Codes Learning

The proposed DLSDH is a two-step method. It first learns the binary hash codes; thereafter, learns hash functions based on the derived hash codes. Inspired by KSH [20], to learn the binary hash codes, we do not directly work on Hamming distance and try to manipulate codes inner product instead.

The correlation between hash code inner product and Hamming distance is as follows,

$$\mathbf{y}_i \circ \mathbf{y}_j = r - 2\mathcal{D}_h(\mathbf{o}_i, \mathbf{o}_j), \tag{2}$$

where operation $\circ$ is the inner product; $\mathcal{D}_h(\mathbf{o}_i, \mathbf{o}_j)$ is the Hamming distance between $\mathbf{o}_i$ and $\mathbf{o}_j$.

Thereafter, the hash codes learning problem can be formulated as,

$$\begin{aligned} &\min_{\mathbf{Y}} \| \mathbf{Y}^\top\mathbf{Y} - r \cdot \mathbf{S} \|_2^2, \\ &s.t.\ \ \mathbf{Y} \in \{-1, 1\}^{r\times n}. \end{aligned} \tag{3}$$

2.4 Hash Functions Learning

After deriving the optimal hash codes, the learning of hash functions is open for any effective predictive models, like linear regression, SVM, and logistic regression, etc. Actually, as revealed in [1], for any bit of the hash code, learning the corresponding hash function to project features into it can be modeled as a binary classification problem.

Most existing cross-modal hashing methods directly use a linear projection matrix to project heterogeneous data into a common space. This kind of approaches may lead to large error as there are some heterogeneous data with semantic similarity hard to be close in latent space when linear projection is used. To avoid this, in this paper, we use dictionary learning to learn dictionaries and generate sparse representations for instances, and then learn projections which map data from the dictionary space to a low-dimensional Hamming space. Data from the same category are reconstructed by the similar dictionary atoms, and the sparse representation of each instance is more suitable to be projected to the latent space.

Then, for image modality, the hash function learning problem can be formulated as,

$$\min_{\mathbf{D}^1,\mathbf{S}^1,\mathbf{R}^1} \| \mathbf{X}^1 - \mathbf{D}^1\mathbf{S}^1 \|_2^2 + \rho_1 \sum_{i=1}^{n} | \mathbf{S}_i^1 | + \lambda_1 \| \mathbf{Y} - \mathbf{R}^1\mathbf{S}^1 \|_2^2, \tag{4}$$

where $\mathbf{D}^1 \in \mathbb{R}^{d_1\times k_1}$ is the dictionary of image modality and k_1 is the size of dictionary. $\mathbf{S}^1 \in \mathbb{R}^{k_1\times n}$ is the sparse representation matrix of all instances, and $\mathbf{S}_i^1$ is the sparse representation of the i-th instance. $\mathbf{R}^1 \in \mathbb{R}^{r\times k_1}$ is a projection matrix. ρ_1, λ_1 are weight parameters.

Similarly, for text modality, the hash function learning problem can be defined as,

$$\min_{\mathbf{D}^2,\mathbf{S}^2,\mathbf{R}^2} \| \mathbf{X}^2 - \mathbf{D}^2\mathbf{S}^2 \|_2^2 + \rho_2 \sum_{i=1}^{n} | \mathbf{S}_i^2 | + \lambda_2 \| \mathbf{Y} - \mathbf{R}^2\mathbf{S}^2 \|_2^2, \tag{5}$$

where $\mathbf{D}^2 \in \mathbb{R}^{d_2\times k_2}$ is the dictionary of text modality and k_2 is the size of dictionary. $\mathbf{S}^2 \in \mathbb{R}^{k_2\times n}$ is the sparse representation matrix of all instances, and $\mathbf{S}_i^2$ is the sparse representation of the i-th instance. $\mathbf{R}^2 \in \mathbb{R}^{r\times k_2}$ is the projection matrix for text modality. ρ_2, λ_2 are weight parameters.

3 OPTIMIZATION ALGORITHM

As shown above, there are two optimization problems, i.e., hash codes learning and hash functions learning, which are shown in Eq. (3), (4), and (5), respectively. In this section, we present the optimization schemes for them.

Hash codes learning

Obviously, Eq. (3) is a discrete optimization problem which is hard to solve. As mentioned previously, most supervised hashing methods relax the discrete constraints, and transform the discrete optimization problem into a continuous one; finally, derive the approximate binary solution via quantization. Such scheme may deteriorate the accuracy of the learned binary codes due to the accumulated quantization error. Some supervised hashing methods try to directly solve the discrete optimization [18], but the time-complexity is $O(n^2)$ which is rather expensive when the number of training instances is large.

To tackle these problems, we propose an alternating optimization scheme to solve Eq. (3) directly. At the same time, we utilize the column sampling strategy [15, 47] to effectively make use of all training instances, and avoid the $O(n^2)$ time complexity problem in hash codes learning. More specifically, in each iteration a set of instances $\mathcal{I}$ with size $|\mathcal{I}|$ is randomly sampled from $O = \{\mathbf{o}_i\}_{i=1}^n$, and we use $\mathcal{N}$ to denote the unsampled instances in O, i.e., $\mathcal{N} = O - \mathcal{I}$. Then, in each iteration, the optimization problem in Eq. (3) can be rewritten as follows,

$$\min_{\mathbf{Y}^{\mathcal{I}},\mathbf{Y}^{\mathcal{N}}} \| \mathbf{Y}^{\mathcal{N}}[\mathbf{Y}^{\mathcal{I}}]^\top - r\mathbf{S}_{\mathcal{N}\mathcal{I}} \|_2^2 + \| \mathbf{Y}^{\mathcal{I}}[\mathbf{Y}^{\mathcal{I}}]^\top - r\mathbf{S}_{\mathcal{I}} \|_2^2, \quad s.t.\ \ \mathbf{Y}^{\mathcal{I}} \in \{-1,1\}^{|\mathcal{I}|\times r}, \mathbf{Y}^{\mathcal{N}} \in \{-1,1\}^{|\mathcal{N}|\times r}, \tag{6}$$

where $\mathbf{Y}^{\mathcal{I}}$ is the hash codes of sampled instances in $\mathcal{I}$, $\mathbf{Y}^{\mathcal{N}}$ is those of unsampled instances in $\mathcal{N}$; $\mathbf{S}_{\mathcal{N}\mathcal{I}} \in \mathbb{R}^{|\mathcal{N}|\times|\mathcal{I}|}$ represents the pairwise similarity among $\mathcal{N}$ and $\mathcal{I}$, $\mathbf{S}_{\mathcal{I}} \in \mathbb{R}^{|\mathcal{I}|\times|\mathcal{I}|}$ is the pairwise similarity of instances in $\mathcal{I}$. To learn both $\mathbf{Y}^{\mathcal{I}}, \mathbf{Y}^{\mathcal{N}}$, we propose an alternate optimization scheme which contains several iterations with each iteration divided into two alternating steps, i.e., solving $\mathbf{Y}^{\mathcal{I}}, \mathbf{Y}^{\mathcal{N}}$.

Step 1: Update $\mathbf{Y}^{\mathcal{N}}$ by fixing $\mathbf{Y}^{\mathcal{I}}$
When $\mathbf{Y}^{\mathcal{I}}$ is fixed, then we can rewrite Eq.(6) as,

$$\min_{\mathbf{Y}^{\mathcal{N}} \in \{-1,1\}^{|\mathcal{N}|\times r}} \| \mathbf{Y}^{\mathcal{N}}[\mathbf{Y}^{\mathcal{I}}]^\top - r\mathbf{S}_{\mathcal{N}\mathcal{I}} \|_2^2 . \tag{7}$$

The above optimization problem is a discrete least square problem which can be solved by relaxing the $Y^{\mathcal{N}}$ into continuous values. But, as mentioned previously, that will generate large quantization errors. To avoid this, we solve this problem by solving an approximate problem and get a constant-approximation solution. Specifically, we rewrite Eq. (7) as follows,

$$\min_{\mathbf{Y}^{\mathcal{N}} \in \{-1,1\}^{|\mathcal{N}|\times r}} \| \mathbf{Y}^{\mathcal{N}}[\mathbf{Y}^{\mathcal{I}}]^\top - r\mathbf{S}_{\mathcal{N}\mathcal{I}} \|_1 . \tag{8}$$

Then, we have the following theorem.

THEOREM 3.1. *Suppose $\mathbf{Y}^{\mathcal{N}} = \mathbf{A}^*$ makes Eq.(8) reach its minimum, then $\mathbf{A}^*$ is a $2r$-approximation solution of Eq.(7).*

Inspired by [15], we give the proof of Theorem 3.1 as follows.

PROOF. Suppose that $\mathbf{B}^*$ makes Eq. (7) reach its minimum. For simplicity of representation, we use $f_1(\cdot)$ and $f_2(\cdot)$ to denote Eq. (7) and Eq. (8), respectively. Then, we have

$$\begin{aligned} f_1(\mathbf{A}^*) &= \| \mathbf{A}^*[\mathbf{Y}^{\mathcal{I}}]^\top - r\mathbf{S}_{\mathcal{N}\mathcal{I}} \|_2^2 \\ &= r^2 \| \frac{1}{r}\mathbf{A}^*[\mathbf{Y}^{\mathcal{I}}]^\top - \mathbf{S}_{\mathcal{N}\mathcal{I}} \|_2^2 . \end{aligned}$$

As all elements of $\mathbf{A}^*, \mathbf{Y}^{\mathcal{I}}$ and $\mathbf{S}_{\mathcal{N}\mathcal{I}}$ have values in $[-1,1]$, we thus have $\frac{1}{r}\mathbf{A}^*[\mathbf{Y}^{\mathcal{I}}]^\top - S_{\mathcal{N}\mathcal{I}} \in [-2,2]^{|\mathcal{N}|\times|\mathcal{I}|}$. Then,

$$\| \frac{1}{r}\mathbf{A}^*[\mathbf{Y}^{\mathcal{I}}]^\top - \mathbf{S}_{\mathcal{N}\mathcal{I}} \|_2^2 \le 2 \| \frac{1}{r}\mathbf{A}^*[\mathbf{Y}^{\mathcal{I}}]^\top - \mathbf{S}_{\mathcal{N}\mathcal{I}} \|_1$$

$$f_1(\mathbf{A}^*) \le 2r^2 \| \frac{1}{r}\mathbf{A}^*[\mathbf{Y}^{\mathcal{I}}]^\top - \mathbf{S}_{\mathcal{N}\mathcal{I}} \|_1 = 2rf_2(\mathbf{A}^*).$$

It's easy to find that $f_2(\mathbf{B}^*) \le f_1(\mathbf{B}^*)$. Finally, we have $f_1(\mathbf{A}^*) \le 2rf_2(\mathbf{A}^*) \le 2rf_2(\mathbf{B}^*) \le 2rf_1(\mathbf{B}^*)$ □

Therefore, based on Theorem 3.1, we can solve the problem in Eq. (7) in a discrete way with an error bound, and get $\mathbf{Y}^{\mathcal{N}} = sgn(\mathbf{S}_{\mathcal{N}\mathcal{I}}\mathbf{Y}^{\mathcal{I}})$ which makes Eq. (8) reach its minimum.

Step 2: Update $\mathbf{Y}^{\mathcal{I}}$ by fixing $\mathbf{Y}^{\mathcal{N}}$
When $\mathbf{Y}^{\mathcal{N}}$ is fixed, the optimization problem becomes,

$$\min_{\mathbf{Y}^{\mathcal{I}} \in \{-1,1\}^{|\mathcal{I}|\times r}} \| \mathbf{Y}^{\mathcal{N}}[\mathbf{Y}^{\mathcal{I}}]^\top - r\mathbf{S}_{\mathcal{N}\mathcal{I}} \|_2^2 + \| \mathbf{Y}^{\mathcal{I}}[\mathbf{Y}^{\mathcal{I}}]^\top - r\mathbf{S}_{\mathcal{I}} \|_2^2 . \tag{9}$$

To solve this problem, we transform it into binary quadratic(BQP) problem. We first let $\mathbf{Q}_{i,j}^{(k)} = -2(r\mathbf{S}_{\mathcal{I}_{i,j}} - \sum_{m=1}^{k-1} \mathbf{y}_i^m \mathbf{y}_j^m)$, when $i \neq j$; $\mathbf{Q}_{i,j}^{(k)} = 0$, when $i = j$; and $\mathbf{p}_i^{(k)} = -2\sum_{l=1}^{|\mathcal{N}|} \mathbf{Y}_{l,k}^{\mathcal{N}}(r\mathbf{S}_{\mathcal{N}\mathcal{I}_{l,i}} - \sum_{m=1}^{k-1} \mathbf{Y}_{l,m}^{\mathcal{N}} \mathbf{Y}_{i,m}^{\mathcal{I}})$. Thereafter, we can easily get the optimization problem for the k-th bit of $\mathbf{Y}^{\mathcal{I}}$ by solving the following optimization problem.

$$\min_{\mathbf{y}^k \in \{-1,1\}^{|\mathcal{I}|}} [\mathbf{y}^k]^\top \mathbf{Q}^{(k)} \mathbf{y}^k + [\mathbf{y}^k]^\top \mathbf{p}^{(k)}. \tag{10}$$

Eq. (10) is still an intractable problem to optimize. In [41], the following BQP problem is studied.

$$\min [\bar{\mathbf{y}}^k]^\top \bar{\mathbf{Q}}^{(k)} \bar{\mathbf{y}}^k, \quad s.t.\ \ \bar{\mathbf{y}}^k \in \{0,1\}^n, \bar{\mathbf{b}}_n^k = 1 \tag{11}$$

where the diagonal elements of $\bar{\mathbf{Q}}^{(k)}$ are zero and n is number of training data which is $|\mathcal{I}|$ in this paper.

To complete the transformation from Eq. (10) to Eq. (11), we firstly transform the value of $\mathbf{y}^k$ from $\{-1,1\}^{|\mathcal{I}|}$ to $\{0,1\}^{|\mathcal{I}|}$, which can be easily realized by denoting $\bar{\mathbf{y}}^k$ as $\frac{1}{2}(\mathbf{y}^k + 1)$. In addition, we need to make sure the problem has no linear term. Then, we have the following equation which is equivalent to Eq. (10),

$$\min [\widetilde{\mathbf{y}}^k]^\top \widetilde{\mathbf{Q}}^{(k)} \widetilde{\mathbf{y}}^k, \quad s.t.\ \ \widetilde{\mathbf{y}}^k \in \{0,1\}^{|\mathcal{I}|+1}, \widetilde{\mathbf{b}}_{|\mathcal{I}|+1}^k = 1 \tag{12}$$

where $\mathbf{y}^k = [\bar{\mathbf{y}}^k, 1]^\top$, $\widetilde{\mathbf{Q}}^{(k)} = \begin{pmatrix} 4\mathbf{Q}^{(k)} & \frac{1}{2}\mathbf{p}_0^{(k)} \\ \frac{1}{2}[\mathbf{p}_0^{(k)}]^\top & 0 \end{pmatrix}$ and $\mathbf{p}_0^{(k)} = 2[\mathbf{p}_i^{(k)} - \sum_{l=1}^{|\mathcal{I}|}(\mathbf{Q}_{i,l}^{(k)} + \mathbf{Q}_{l,i}^{(k)})]$.

To get a balanced partition of the dataset, we further add a constraint which requires the number of values 0 and 1 to be same in each bit. Thereafter, Eq. (12) becomes

$$\min [\widetilde{\mathbf{y}}^k]^\top \widetilde{\mathbf{Q}}^{(k)} \widetilde{\mathbf{y}}^k, \quad s.t.\ \ \widetilde{\mathbf{y}}^k \in \{0,1\}^{|\mathcal{I}|+1}, \widetilde{\mathbf{b}}_{|\mathcal{I}|+1}^k = 1, \sum_{i=1}^{|\mathcal{I}|+1} \widetilde{\mathbf{y}}_i^k = \frac{|\mathcal{I}|+1}{2}. \tag{13}$$

The above problem can be well solved by using the method in [41]. As shown in [41], there exists a 2-approximation algorithm for Eq. (13). To save space, we do not give the details.

To further have an overall look of the optimization scheme of hash codes learning, we summarize it in Algorithm 1.

Hash functions learning
Once we obtain the hash codes $\mathbf{Y}$, we need to further learn the hash functions, i.e., the mapping matrices, which can map out-of-sample query instances to hash codes. As shown in Eq. (4) and (5),

Algorithm 1 Optimization Scheme for Hash codes Learning.

Input: The label matrix L, a sub set $\mathcal{I}$ of $\mathcal{O}$ for column sampling, the number of column sampling times T, the number of times t alternating optimization for $\mathbf{Y}^{\mathcal{I}}$ and $\mathbf{Y}^{\mathcal{N}}$ runs in each sampling, the bit length r.
Initialize binary hash codes $\mathbf{Y}_0$ by randomization.
for $iter = 1 \to T$ **do**
  Generate $\mathcal{I}$, $\mathcal{N}$, and the corresponding pairwise similarity matrices.
  for $i = 1 \to t$ **do**
    for $k = 1 \to r$ **do**
      Construct problem (10).
      Construct problem (12) from (10).
      Construct problem (13) from (12).
      Solving problem (13) by using the 2-approximation algorithm in [41] and get the k-th column of $\mathbf{Y}^{\mathcal{I}}_{(i)}$.
    end for
    $\mathbf{Y}^{\mathcal{N}}_{(i)} = sgn(\mathbf{S}_{\mathcal{N}\mathcal{I}}\mathbf{Y}^{\mathcal{I}}_{(i-1)})$.
  end for
end for
Output: Integrated hash codes $\mathbf{Y}$.

we need to learn the sparse representations $\mathbf{S}^1$ and $\mathbf{S}^2$, and dictionaries $\mathbf{D}^1$ and $\mathbf{D}^2$, mapping matrices $\mathbf{R}^1$ and $\mathbf{R}^2$ for different modalities. To save space, we just show the scheme to learn the corresponding matrices for image modality, which is also an alternate method.

Step 1: Update $\mathbf{S}^1$ by fixing $\mathbf{D}^1$ and $\mathbf{R}^1$
Once $\mathbf{D}^1$ and $\mathbf{R}^1$ are fixed, Eq. (4) can be rewritten as,

$$\min_{\mathbf{S}^1} \| \mathbf{X}^1 - \mathbf{D}^1\mathbf{S}^1 \|_2^2 + \rho \sum_{i=1}^{n} | \mathbf{S}^1_i | + \lambda \| \mathbf{Y} - \mathbf{R}^1\mathbf{S}^1 \|_2^2, \tag{14}$$

which is equivalent to,

$$\min_{\mathbf{S}^1} \| \begin{bmatrix} \mathbf{X}^1 \\ \sqrt{\lambda}\mathbf{Y} \end{bmatrix} - \begin{bmatrix} \mathbf{D}^1 \\ \sqrt{\lambda}\mathbf{R}^1 \end{bmatrix} \mathbf{S}^1 \|_2^2 + \rho \sum_{i=1}^{n} | \mathbf{S}^1_i | . \tag{15}$$

The problem in Eq.(15) can be efficiently solved by using standard toolboxes, e.g., SLEP (Sparse Learning with Efficient Projections) package[1].

Step 2: Update $\mathbf{D}^1$ by fixing $\mathbf{S}^1$ and $\mathbf{R}^1$
When $\mathbf{S}^1$ and $\mathbf{R}1$ are fixed, Eq.(4) can be rewritten as,

$$\min_{\mathbf{D}^1} \| \mathbf{X}^1 - \mathbf{D}^1\mathbf{S}^1 \|_2^2, \quad s.t. \quad \| \mathbf{D}^1_{\cdot i} \|_2 \leq 1. \tag{16}$$

To solve this problem, we can introduce a diagonal matrix Θ with diagonal elements being the Larangian multipliers $\Theta_{ii} = \theta_i$. Thereafter, we have the following optimization problem,

$$g(\mathbf{D}^1, \Theta) = \| \mathbf{X}^1 - \mathbf{D}^1\mathbf{S}^1 \|_2^2 + \sum_{i=1}^{n} \theta_i(\| \mathbf{B}_{\cdot i} \| - 1). \tag{17}$$

Apparently, we can get the closed form solution by setting the derivation with respect to $\mathbf{D}^1$ equal to zero, i.e.,

$$\mathbf{D}^1 = \mathbf{X}^1(\mathbf{S}^1)^\top(\mathbf{S}^1(\mathbf{S}^1)^\top + \Theta)^{-1}. \tag{18}$$

[1] http://parnec.nuaa.edu.cn/jliu/largeScaleSparseLearning.htm

Substituting $\mathbf{D}^1$ Eq. (17) with Eq. (18), we obtain the Lagrangian dual problem,

$$\min_{\Theta} Tr\{\mathbf{X}^1(\mathbf{S}^1)^\top(\mathbf{S}^1(\mathbf{S}^1)^\top + \Theta)^{-1}\mathbf{S}^1(\mathbf{X}^1)^\top\} + Tr\{\Theta\}, \quad s.t. \quad \Theta_{ii} \geq 0,\ i = 1, ..., k, \tag{19}$$

where $Tr\{\cdot\}$ denotes the trace of a matrix. Eq.(19) can be solved by using Newton's method or conjugate gradient. Thereafter, we can obtain $\mathbf{D}^1$ by substituting Θ into Eq. (18).

Step 3: Update $\mathbf{R}^1$ by fixing $\mathbf{S}^1$, $\mathbf{D}^1$
Eq. (4) is rewritten as follows,

$$\min_{\mathbf{R}^1} \lambda_1 \| \mathbf{Y} - \mathbf{R}^1\mathbf{S}^1 \|_2^2, \quad s.t. \quad \| \mathbf{R}^1_{\cdot i} \|_2 \leq 1. \tag{20}$$

We can see the learning problem of $\mathbf{R}^1$ is same as that in Step 2.

4 DISCUSSIONS

4.1 Out-of-Sample Extension

We can easily obtain the hash code of an out-of-sample query instance q. For example, when the image modality of query q is given, denoted as $\mathbf{x}^{(1)}_q$, we first generate a sparse vector $\mathbf{s}^1_q$ to represent $\mathbf{x}^{(1)}_q$ by solving the following problem,

$$\min_{\mathbf{s}} \| \mathbf{x}^{(1)}_q - \mathbf{D}^1\mathbf{s}^1_q \|_2^2 + \rho_1 | \mathbf{s}^1_q | . \tag{21}$$

As demonstrated previously, the problem can be efficiently solved; thereafter, the hash code of query q can be obtained by $\mathbf{y} = sgn(\mathbf{R}^1\mathbf{s}^1_q)$.

When the text modality of query q is given, denoted as $\mathbf{x}^{(2)}_q$, we first solve the following problem, and obtain a sparse vector $\mathbf{s}^2_q$ to represent $\mathbf{x}^{(2)}_q$,

$$\min_{\mathbf{s}} \| \mathbf{x}^{(2)}_q - \mathbf{D}^2\mathbf{s}^2_q \|_2^2 + \rho^2 | \mathbf{s}^2_q | . \tag{22}$$

Then, we can generate the hash code of query q by $\mathbf{y} = sgn(\mathbf{R}^2\mathbf{s}^2_q)$.

4.2 Extension to More Modalities

DLSDH can be easily extended to cases with three or more modalities. Actually, the training processes of hash codes learning in those cases are nearly same as that mentioned previously, except that hash functions for more modalities need to be learnt independently. Specifically, Eq. (4) can be generalized to the following problem for the i-th modality.

$$\min_{\mathbf{D}^i, \mathbf{S}^i, \mathbf{R}^i} \| \mathbf{X}^i - \mathbf{D}^i\mathbf{S}^i \|_2^2 + \rho_i \sum_{i=1}^{n} | \mathbf{S}^i_i | + \lambda_i \| \mathbf{Y} - \mathbf{R}^i\mathbf{S}^i \|_2^2, \tag{23}$$

where $\mathbf{D}^i \in \mathbb{R}^{d_i \times k_i}$ is the dictionary for the i-th modality, and k_i is the size of dictionary; $\mathbf{R}^i \in \mathbb{R}^{r \times k_i}$ is a projection matrix for the i-th modality; ρ_i, λ_i are weight parameters.

5 EXPERIMENTS

In this section, extensive experiments on three real-world multi-modal datasets are conducted to verify the effectiveness of our proposed DLSDH. Its performance is compared with several state-of-the-art cross-modal hashing methods.

5.1 Experimental Settings

5.1.1 Datasets. Experiments are conducted on three benchmark datasets, i.e., Wiki [27], MIRFlickr [11], and NUS-WIDE [4], which are described below.

Wiki consists of 2, 866 image-text pairs and was collected from Wikipedia. For each instance, the image is represented by 128-dimension *SIFT* [23] feature vector and the text is represented by a 10-dimension topic vector generated by Latent Dirichlet Allocation (LDA). Each instance belongs to ones of 10 semantic classes. It was initially split into a training set with 2, 173 instances and a test set of 693 instances.

MIRFlickr consists of 25, 000 instances collected from Flickr website. Each instance is manually annotated with at least one of 24 labels. The image is described by a 150-dimension edge histogram [23] and the text is described by a 500-dimension feature vector generated from PCA on its index tagging vector. We used 25% instances of the dataset as the query set, and the remaining 75% ones as the training set.

NUS-WIDE is a large-scale real-world web image dataset, containing 269, 648 instances. Each instance has an image with its associated textual tags and is manually annotated with at least one of 81 provided labels. However, some instances' labels are rare; so we followed the same settings of previous works [19, 36, 49] and select 10 most common concepts and the corresponding 186, 577 images. For each instance, its image is represented by a 500-dimension SIFT feature vector and its text is represented by a binary tagging vector w.r.t. the top 1,000 most frequent tags. We select 2% of the data as the query set and the rest as the training set.

Considering computation consumption, we ramdomly selected 5,000 and 10,000 samples from original training data on MIRFlickr and NUS-WIDE, respectively.

5.1.2 Baseline Methods. Considering that DLSDH is a shallow model, we compared DLSDH with nine sate-of-the-art shallow cross-modal hashing methods including four unsupervised ones, i.e., IMH[30], LSSH [49], CMFH [5], and CCQ [22], and five supervised ones, i.e., CVH [17], SCM-orth [43], SCM-seq [43], SePH-km [19], and SRDMH [39]. Source codes of most baselines are kindly provided by the authors. We carefully tuned their parameters according to the scheme suggested by the authors.

5.1.3 Evaluation Metrics. To fully evaluate the proposed method and baselines, we adopted three widely used performance measures for multi-modal hashing, i.e., mean average precision (MAP), top-N precision and precision-recall curves. For all metrics, a larger value indicates better retrieval performance.

5.1.4 Implementation Details. In the experiment, we set the parameters of DLSDH according to empirical analysis on parameter sensitivity. Finally, we set the size of dictionaries D^1, D^2 to the same, i.e., $k^1 = k^2 = 512$; however, different size is acceptable. We set $\rho_1 = \rho_2 = 0.2$ and $\lambda_1 = \lambda_2 = 0.02$. In order to remove any randomness caused by random initialization and random selection of training set, all of the results are averaged over 10 runs. In Algorithm 1, we set $T = 10$, $t = 3$ and $|\mathcal{I}| = r$.

In addition, we also adopted nonlinear kernel functions (RBF) to generate kernel features which is widely used in previous hashing applications [16, 19, 20, 29]. Specifically, we randomly sampled $m(m < n)$ anchor points $a_1, a_2, \cdots, a_m$ from training data.

Table 1: MAP comparison on Wiki. The best results are in boldface.

Task	Method	8 bits	16 bits	32 bits	64 bits
Image to Text	CVH	0.1701	0.1569	0.1483	0.1502
	IMH	0.1656	0.1648	0.1637	0.1655
	SCM-orth	0.1543	0.1465	0.1387	0.1286
	SCM-seq	0.2341	0.2366	0.2410	0.2437
	LSSH	0.2142	0.2088	0.2098	0.2089
	CMFH	0.2069	0.2206	0.2261	0.2349
	SePH-km	0.2796	0.2796	0.2820	0.3076
	CCQ	0.1679	0.1689	0.1683	0.1684
	SRDMH	**0.3272**	**0.3161**	0.3217	0.3045
	DLSDH	0.3083	0.3105	**0.3231**	**0.3298**
Text to Image	CVH	0.1586	0.1448	0.1398	0.1293
	IMH	0.1377	0.1393	0.1400	0.1324
	SCM-orth	0.1539	0.1438	0.1338	0.1277
	SCM-seq	0.2257	0.2426	0.2459	0.2480
	LSSH	0.4972	0.5099	0.5221	0.5272
	CMFH	0.4688	0.5129	0.5055	0.5347
	SePH-km	0.6379	0.6379	0.6451	0.6662
	CCQ	0.2426	0.2457	0.2509	0.2546
	SRDMH	0.6419	0.6653	0.6800	0.6799
	DLSDH	**0.7265**	**0.7365**	**0.7436**	**0.7519**

Then, with the RBF kernel, kernel features can be represented as $\phi(x) = exp(\frac{-\|x-a_t\|_2^2}{2\sigma^2})$, where σ is the kernel width. In this paper, we calculate it with $\sigma = \frac{1}{mn}\sum_{i=1}^{n}\sum_{t=1}^{m} \| x_i - a_t \|_2$, $m = 500$. However, as shown in [36], kernelization may not ensure better results for all time. It can boost the performance when training instances are represented with low dimension features. Thus, we only used nonlinear embedding on Wiki dataset as image features and text features on this dataset are only 128- and 10-dimension, respectively.

5.2 Results

5.2.1 Results on Wiki. The MAP results of all methods on Wiki are listed in Table 1. From Table 1, we can find that our proposed method DLSDH obtains the best results on most cases. To gain deep insights into DLSDH and all baselines, we further plotted the top-N precision and precision-recall curves with 32 bits in Figure 1. From this figure, we can observe that

- DLSDH outperforms or is comparable to those baseline methods on this dataset.
- Note that in Figure 1, some baselines gets better results than DLSDH when N is large; however, DLSDH is better than all baseline methods when N is small. This means that DLSDH can get more similar samples when N is small. This is very important for search tasks because users can get more related instances at beginning.

5.2.2 Results on MIRFlickr. The MAP results on MIRFlickr of our proposed DLSDH and all baseline methods are summarized in Table 2. The top-N precision curves and precision-recall curves are plotted in Figure 2. From Table 2, we can find that our proposed DLSDH obtains the best results on all cases. From Table 2 and Figure 2, we have the following observations:

- DLSDH outperforms all baseline methods on this dataset.

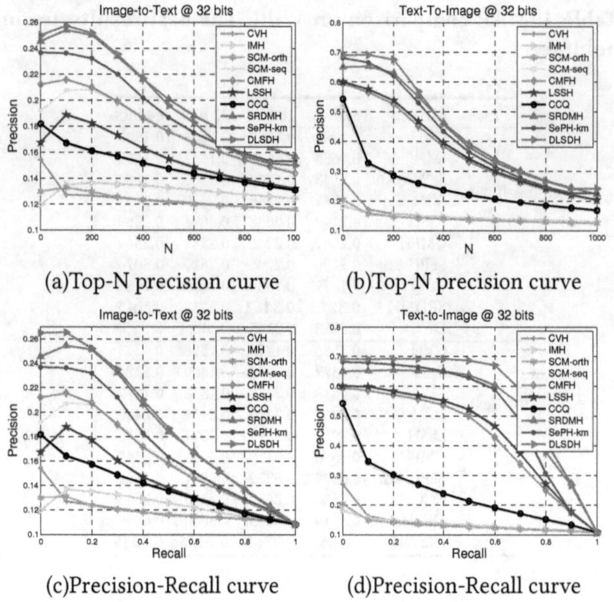

(a)Top-N precision curve (b)Top-N precision curve

(c)Precision-Recall curve (d)Precision-Recall curve

Figure 1: Top-N precision and Precision-Recall curves on Wiki with 32 bits.

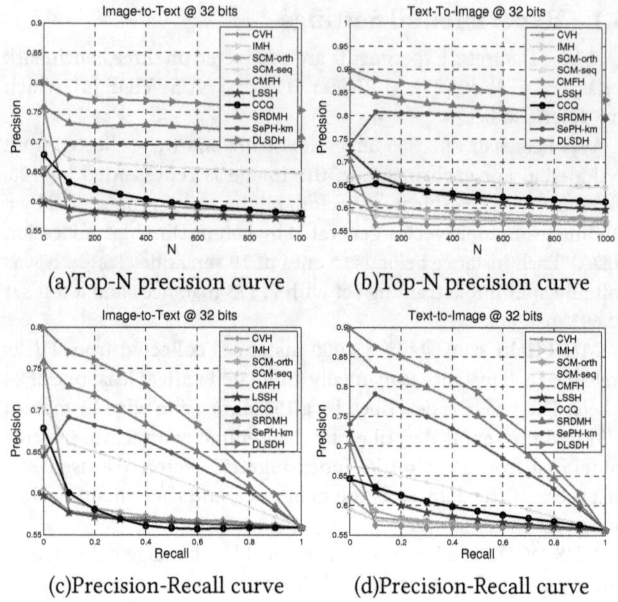

(a)Top-N precision curve (b)Top-N precision curve

(c)Precision-Recall curve (d)Precision-Recall curve

Figure 2: Top-N precision and Precision-Recall curves on MIRFlickr with 32 bits.

Table 2: MAP comparison on MIRFlickr. The best results are in boldface.

Task	Method	8 bits	16 bits	32 bits	64 bits
Image to Text	CVH	0.5739	0.5714	0.5699	0.5673
	IMH	0.5680	0.5678	0.5686	0.5677
	SCM-orth	0.5876	0.5809	0.5765	0.5723
	SCM-seq	0.6280	0.6316	0.6357	0.6473
	LSSH	0.5733	0.5731	0.5705	0.5762
	CMFH	0.5810	0.5802	0.5722	0.5725
	SePH-km	0.6726	0.6881	0.6716	0.6811
	CCQ	0.5732	0.5734	0.5744	0.5741
	SRDMH	0.6893	0.6899	0.7066	0.6889
	DLSDH	**0.7164**	**0.7470**	**0.7460**	**0.7306**
Text to Image	CVH	0.5736	0.5713	0.5699	0.5674
	IMH	0.5669	0.5671	0.5687	0.5672
	SCM-orth	0.5862	0.5808	0.5736	0.5670
	SCM-seq	0.6149	0.6176	0.6214	0.6285
	LSSH	0.5835	0.5887	0.5897	0.5917
	CMFH	0.5939	0.5910	0.5664	0.5664
	SePH-km	0.7183	0.7502	0.7233	0.7310
	CCQ	0.5944	0.5974	0.5992	0.5991
	SRDMH	0.7361	0.7483	0.7770	0.7529
	DLSDH	**0.7743**	**0.8084**	**0.8095**	**0.8048**

- The results of Text-to-Image are generally better than those of Image-to-Text. The main reason is that text can better describe the content of an image-text pair than image.
- Most supervised methods obtain better results than unsupervised ones.

5.2.3 Results on NUS-WIDE. The MAP results on NUS-WIDE with various code lengths are summarized in Table 3. The curves of top-N retrieved samples and precision-recall curves are plotted in Figure 3. From Table 3, we can find that DLSDH obtains the best results on all cases. From Figure 3, we can find that DLSDH

Table 3: MAP comparison on NUS-WIDE. The best results are in boldface.

Task	Method	8 bits	16 bits	32 bits	64 bits
Image to Text	CVH	0.3368	0.3372	0.3365	0.3378
	IMH	0.3422	0.3422	0.3414	0.3405
	SCM-orth	0.3818	0.3705	0.3656	0.3547
	SCM-seq	0.5252	0.5248	0.5261	0.5328
	LSSH	0.3633	0.3612	0.3642	0.3680
	CMFH	0.3419	0.3369	0.3483	0.3393
	SePH$_{km}$	0.5724	0.5724	0.5648	0.5743
	CCQ	0.3684	0.3686	0.3678	0.3699
	SRDMH	0.5589	0.5760	0.5843	0.5815
	DLSDH	**0.5770**	**0.5828**	**0.6052**	**0.6025**
Text to Image	CVH	0.3370	0.3369	0.3368	0.3394
	IMH	0.3426	0.3426	0.3435	0.3410
	SCM-orth	0.3770	0.3665	0.3627	0.3531
	SCM-seq	0.4993	0.5013	0.5071	0.5134
	LSSH	0.4001	0.4011	0.4032	0.4056
	CMFH	0.3413	0.3375	0.3457	0.3384
	SePH$_{km}$	0.6242	0.6782	0.6825	0.6816
	CCQ	0.3636	0.3656	0.3644	0.3659
	SRDMH	0.6216	0.6443	0.6583	0.6512
	DLSDH	**0.6934**	**0.7014**	**0.7085**	**0.7172**

outperforms or is comparable to those baseline methods. Note that, in Figure 3, we can find that the precision of SRDMH is better than that of DLSDH; however, we can also observe that the precision of our proposed method is much better than that of SRDMH in the beginning, which is very important for retrieval task.

5.2.4 Parameter Sensitivity Analysis. To evaluate the influence of parameters, we conducted experiments on NUS-WIDE by changing one parameter while fixing others with prefixing the code length as 32 bits.

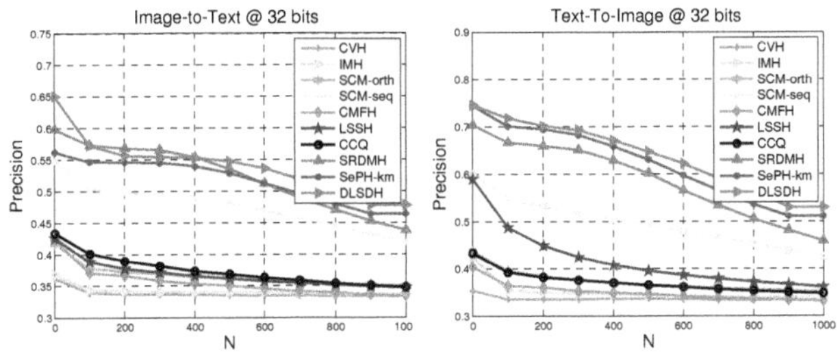

(a)Top-N precision curve (b)Top-N precision curve

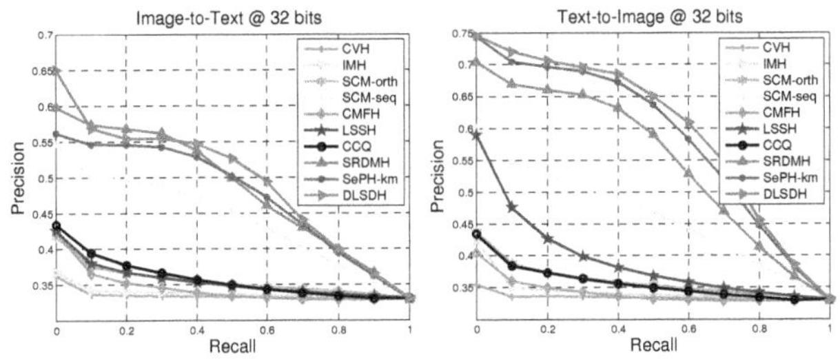

(c)Precision-Recall curve (d)Precision-Recall curve

Figure 3: Top-N precision and Precision-Recall curves on NUS-WIDE with 32 bits.

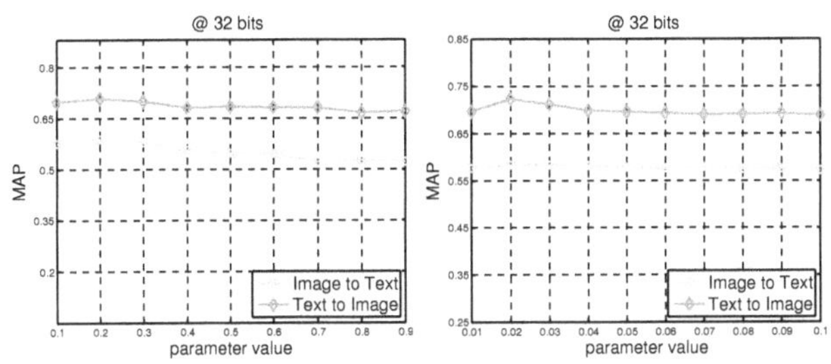

(a)ρ_1 and ρ_2 (b)λ_1 and λ_2

Figure 4: Sensitivity analysis of parameters.

Parameters ρ_1 and ρ_2 control the balance between the reconstruction error and sparsity for modality image and text. The results are plotted in Figure 4(a), where we can see that the MAP value is influenced by ρ_1 and ρ_2. For example, when ρ_1 and ρ_2 increase, the performance degrades.

Parameters λ_1 and λ_2 control the linear connection of latent semantic spaces for modality image and text. The MAP results with different parameter values are plotted in Figure 4(b). We can see that with λ_1 and λ_2 getting larger, the performance becomes poorer.

According to the above results, in this paper, we set $\rho_1 = \rho_2 = 0.2$ and $\lambda_1 = \lambda_2 = 0.02$.

5.3 Similarity Matrix Construction Comparison

As mentioned previously, we use Cosine Similarity to construct the similarity matrix S rather than the scheme used in most existing methods. Besides, we also tried other two similarity measurements,

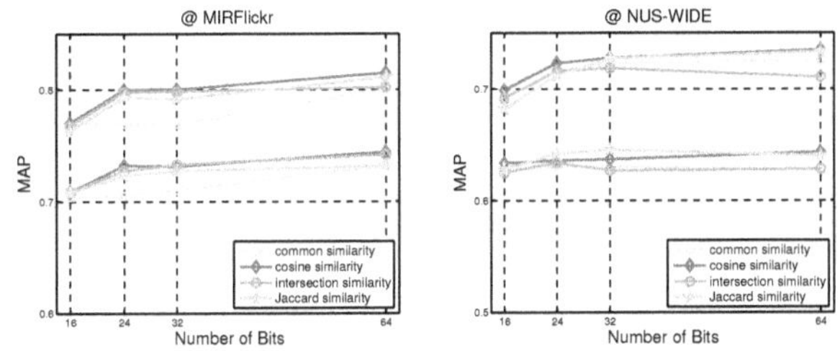

Figure 5: MAP of DLSDH with different similarity matrix construction schemes. Common similarity is the scheme adopted by most existing cross-modal hashing approaches

i.e., Jaccard Similarity and Intersection Similarity. The pairwise similarity matrix based on Jaccard Similarity can be defined by,

$$S_{ij} = \frac{|L_i \cap L_j|}{|L_i \cup L_j|}, \tag{24}$$

where $|\cdot|$ is the number of elements in a set, L_k is the set of categories that instance o_k belongs to.

The pairwise similarity matrix based Intersection Similarity is defined by,

$$S_{ij} = \sum_{k=1}^{c} \min(l_{ik}, l_{jk}). \tag{25}$$

In order to demonstrate that Cosine Similarity is a proper choice for constructing S, we conducted experiments on MIRFlickr and NUS-WIDE with code length varying from 16 to 64. The curves of DLSDH with different similarity matrices are plotted in Figure 5. Note that there are two groups of curves in each figure. The upper one is the results of Text-to-Image; the lower one is the those of Image-to-Text. From this figure, we can observe DLSDH with Cosine Similarity obtains the best results on most cases, which confirms that Cosine Similarity is a proper choice for constructing the similarity matrix S.

6 CONCLUSIONS

In this paper, a novel supervised hashing method for cross-modal retrieval is presented, named Dictionary Learning based Supervised Discrete Hashing (DLSDH). To better supervise the hash codes learning, we use cosine similarity to construct the pairwise similarity matrix which can make full use of label information. In order to avoid the large error caused by relaxing the discrete constraints, DLSDH directly optimizes the binary codes and uses column sampling methods to tackle the $O(n^2)$ complexity cost problem for pairwise similarity. Besides, to overcome the limitation of linear projection, dictionary learning is leveraged to generate sparse representation for every instance which is suitable to be projected into latent space. Extensive experiments are conducted on three benchmark datasets. The results demonstrate that DLSDH outperforms or is comparable to several state-of-the-art methods for cross-modal retrieval task.

7 ACKNOWLEDGEMENTS

This work was partially supported by the Key Research and Development Program of Shandong Province (2016GGX101044) and National Natural Science Foundation of China (61573212).

REFERENCES

[1] Michael M Bronstein, Alexander M Bronstein, Fabrice Michel, and Nikos Paragios. 2010. Data fusion through cross-modality metric learning using similarity-sensitive hashing. In *Proceedings of the IEEE Conference on Computer Vision and Pattern Recognition*. 3594–3601.

[2] Yue Cao, Mingsheng Long, Jianmin Wang, Qiang Yang, and Philip S Yu. 2016. Deep visual-semantic hashing for cross-modal retrieval. In *Proceedings of the ACM International Conference on Knowledge Discovery and Data Mining*. 1445–1454.

[3] Zhen-Duo Chen, Wan-Jin Yu, Chuan-Xiang Li, Liqiang Nie, and Xin-Shun Xu. 2018. Dual deep neural networks cross-modal hashing. In *Proceedings of the AAAI Conference on Artificial Intelligence*.

[4] Tat-Seng Chua, Jinhui Tang, Richang Hong, Haojie Li, Zhiping Luo, and Yantao Zheng. 2009. NUS-WIDE: A real-world web image database from National University of Singapore. In *Proceedings of the ACM International Conference on Image and Video Retrieval*. 48.

[5] Guiguang Ding, Yuchen Guo, and Jile Zhou. 2014. Collective matrix factorization hashing for multimodal data. In *Proceedings of the IEEE Conference on Computer Vision and Pattern Recognition*. 2075–2082.

[6] Fuli Feng, Xiangnan He, Yiqun Liu, Liqiang Nie, and Tat-Seng Chua. 2018. Learning on partial-order hypergraphs. In *Proceedings of the International World Wide Web Conferences*. 1523–1532.

[7] Fuli Feng, Liqiang Nie, Xiang Wang, Richang Hong, and Tat-Seng Chua. 2017. Computational social indicators: A case study of chinese university ranking. In *Proceedings of the International ACM SIGIR Conference on Research and Development in Information Retrieval*. 455–464.

[8] Jie Gui, Tongliang Liu, Zhenan Sun, Dacheng Tao, and Tieniu Tan. 2017. Fast supervised discrete hashing. *IEEE Transactions on Pattern Analysis and Machine Intelligence* 40, 2 (2017), 490 – 496.

[9] Yanbin Hao, Tingting Mu, John Y. Goulermas, Jianguo Jiang, Richang Hong, and Meng Wang. 2017. Unsupervised t-distributed video hashing and its deep hashing extension. *IEEE Transactions on Image Processing* 26, 11 (2017), 5531–5544.

[10] Xiangnan He and Tat-Seng Chua. 2017. Neural Factorization Machines for Sparse Predictive Analytics. In *Proceedings of the International ACM SIGIR Conference on Research and Development in Information Retrieval*. 355–364.

[11] Mark J Huiskes and Michael S Lew. 2008. The MIR flickr retrieval evaluation. In *Proceedings of the ACM International Conference on Multimedia Information Retrieval*. 39–43.

[12] Sung Ju Hwang and Kristen Grauman. 2012. Learning the relative importance of objects from tagged images for retrieval and cross-modal search. *International Journal of Computer Vision* 100, 2 (2012), 134–153.

[13] Qing-Yuan Jiang and Wu-Jun Li. 2017. Deep cross-modal hashing. In *Proceedings of the IEEE Conference on Computer Vision and Pattern Recognition*. 3270–3278.

[14] Cuicui Kang, Shiming Xiang, Shengcai Liao, Changsheng Xu, and Chunhong Pan. 2015. Learning consistent feature representation for cross-modal multimedia retrieval. *IEEE Transactions on Multimedia* 17, 3 (2015), 370–381.

[15] Wang-Cheng Kang, Wu-Jun Li, and Zhi-Hua Zhou. 2016. Column sampling based discrete supervised hashing. In *Proceedings of the AAAI Conference on Artificial Intelligence*. 1230–1236.

[16] Brian Kulis and Trevor Darrell. 2009. Learning to hash with binary reconstructive embeddings. In *Proceedings of the Advances in Neural Information Processing Systems*. 1042–1050.

[17] Shaishav Kumar and Raghavendra Udupa. 2011. Learning hash functions for cross-view similarity search. In *Proceedings of the International Joint Conference on Artificial Intelligence*. 1360–1365.

[18] Guosheng Lin, Chunhua Shen, Qinfeng Shi, Anton van den Hengel, and David Suter. 2014. Fast supervised hashing with decision trees for high-dimensional data. In *Proceedings of the IEEE Conference on Computer Vision and Pattern Recognition*. 1963–1970.

[19] Zijia Lin, Guiguang Ding, Mingqing Hu, and Jianmin Wang. 2015. Semantics-preserving hashing for cross-view retrieval. In *Proceedings of the IEEE Conference on Computer Vision and Pattern Recognition*. 3864–3872.

[20] Wei Liu, Jun Wang, Rongrong Ji, Yu-Gang Jiang, and Shih-Fu Chang. 2012. Supervised hashing with kernels. In *Proceedings of the IEEE Conference on Computer Vision and Pattern Recognition*. 2074–2081.

[21] Xianglong Liu, Cheng Deng, Bo Lang, Dacheng Tao, and Xuelong Li. 2016. Query-adaptive reciprocal hash tables for nearest neighbor search. *IEEE Transactions on Image Processing* 25, 2 (2016), 907–919.

[22] Mingsheng Long, Yue Cao, Jianmin Wang, and Philip S Yu. 2016. Composite correlation quantization for efficient multimodal retrieval. In *Proceedings of the International ACM SIGIR Conference on Research and Development in Information Retrieval*. 579–588.

[23] David G Lowe. 2004. Distinctive image features from scale-invariant keypoints. *International Journal of Computer Vision* 60, 2 (2004), 91–110.

[24] Xin Luo, Ye Wu, and Xin-Shun Xu. 2018. Scalable supervised discrete hashing for large-scale search. In *Proceedings of the International World Wide Web Conferences*. 1603–1612.

[25] Dekui Ma, Jian Liang, Xiangwei Kong, Ran He, and Ying Li. 2017. Discrete cross-modal hashing for efficient multimedia retrieval. In *Proceedings of the IEEE International Symposium on Multimedia*. 38–43.

[26] Liqiang Nie, Shuicheng Yan, Meng Wang, Richang Hong, and Tat-Seng Chua. 2012. Harvesting visual concepts for image search with complex queries. In *Proceedings of the ACM International Conference on Multimedia*. 59–68.

[27] Nikhil Rasiwasia, Jose Costa Pereira, Emanuele Coviello, Gabriel Doyle, Gert RG Lanckriet, Roger Levy, and Nuno Vasconcelos. 2010. A new approach to cross-modal multimedia retrieval. In *Proceedings of the ACM International Conference on Multimedia*. 251–260.

[28] Zhaochun Ren, Shangsong Liang, Edgar Meij, and Maarten de Rijke. 2013. Personalized time-aware tweets summarization. In *Proceedings of the International ACM SIGIR Conference on Research and Development in Information Retrieval*. 513–522.

[29] Fumin Shen, Chunhua Shen, Wei Liu, and Heng Tao Shen. 2015. Supervised discrete hashing. In *Proceedings of the IEEE Conference on Computer Vision and Pattern Recognition*. 37–45.

[30] Jingkuan Song, Yang Yang, Yi Yang, Zi Huang, and Heng Tao Shen. 2013. Inter-media hashing for large-scale retrieval from heterogeneous data sources. In *Proceedings of the ACM SIGMOD International Conference on Management of Data*. 785–796.

[31] Jinhui Tang, Zechao Li, Meng Wang, and Ruizhen Zhao. 2015. Neighborhood discriminant hashing for large-scale image retrieval. *IEEE Transactions on Image Processing* 24, 9 (2015), 2827–2840.

[32] Daixin Wang, Peng Cui, Mingdong Ou, and Wenwu Zhu. 2015. Deep multimodal hashing with orthogonal regularization. In *Proceedings of the International Joint Conference on Artificial Intelligence*. 2291–2297.

[33] Jian Wang, Xin-Shun Xu, Shanqing Guo, Lizhen Cui, and Xiaolin Wang. 2016. Linear unsupervised hashing for ANN search in Euclidean space. *Neurocomputing* 171 (2016), 283–292.

[34] Meng Wang, Weisheng Li, Dong Liu, Bingbing Ni, Jialie Shen, and Shuicheng Yan. 2015. Facilitating image search with a scalable and compact semantic mapping. *IEEE Transactions on Cybernetics* 45, 8 (2015), 1561–1574.

[35] Fei Wu, Xinyang Jiang, Xi Li, Siliang Tang, Weiming Lu, Zhongfei Zhang, and Yueting Zhuang. 2015. Cross-modal learning to rank via latent joint representation. *IEEE Transactions on Image Processing* 24, 5 (2015), 1497–1509.

[36] Xing Xu, Fumin Shen, Yang Yang, Heng Tao Shen, and Xuelong Li. 2017. Learning discriminative binary codes for large-scale cross-modal retrieval. *IEEE Transactions on Image Processing* 26, 5 (2017), 2494–2507.

[37] Xing Xu, Yang Yang, Atsushi Shimada, Rin-ichiro Taniguchi, and Li He. 2015. Semi-supervised coupled dictionary learning for cross-modal retrieval in internet images and texts. In *Proceedings of the ACM International Conference on Multimedia*. 847–850.

[38] Xin-Shun Xu. 2016. Dictionary learning based hashing for cross-modal retrieval. In *Proceedings of the ACM International Conference on Multimedia*. 177–181.

[39] Ting-Kun Yan, Xin-Shun Xu, Shanqing Guo, Zi Huang, and Xiao-Lin Wang. 2016. Supervised robust discrete multimodal hashing for cross-media retrieval. In *Proceedings of the ACM International Conference on Information and Knowledge Management*. 1271–1280.

[40] Erkun Yang, Cheng Deng, Wei Liu, Xianglong Liu, Dacheng Tao, and Xinbo Gao. 2017. Pairwise relationship guided deep hashing for cross-modal retrieval. In *Proceedings of the AAAI Conference on Artificial Intelligence*. 1618–1625.

[41] Rui Yang. 2013. *New results on some quadratic programming problems*. Ph.D. Dissertation. University of Illinois at Urbana-Champaign.

[42] Yang Yang, Yadan Luo, Weilun Chen, Fumin Shen, Jie Shao, and Heng Tao Shen. 2016. Zero-shot hashing via transferring supervised knowledge. In *Proceedings of the ACM International Conference on Multimedia*. 1286–1295.

[43] Dongqing Zhang and Wu-Jun Li. 2014. Large-Scale supervised multimodal hashing with semantic correlation maximization. In *Proceedings of the AAAI Conference on Artificial Intelligence*. 2177–2183.

[44] Dan Zhang, Fei Wang, and Luo Si. 2011. Composite hashing with multiple information sources. In *Proceedings of the International ACM SIGIR Conference on Research and Development in Information Retrieval*. 225–234.

[45] Hanwang Zhang, Na Zhao, Xindi Shang, Huanbo Luan, and Tat-seng Chua. 2016. Discrete image hashing using large weakly annotated photo collections. In *Proceedings of the AAAI Conference on Artificial Intelligence*. 3669–3675.

[46] Min-Ling Zhang and Zhi-Hua Zhou. 2014. A review on multi-label learning algorithms. *IEEE Transactions on Knowledge and Data Engineering* 26, 8 (2014), 1819–1837.

[47] Peichao Zhang, Wei Zhang, Wu-Jun Li, and Minyi Guo. 2014. Supervised hashing with latent factor models. In *Proceedings of the International ACM SIGIR Conference on Research and Development in Information Retrieval*. 173–182.

[48] Peng-Fei Zhang, Chuan-Xiang Li, Meng-Yuan Liu, Liqiang Nie, and Xin-Shun Xu. 2017. Semi-relaxation supervised hashing for cross-modal retrieval. In *Proceedings of the ACM International Conference on Multimedia*. 1762–1770.

[49] Jile Zhou, Guiguang Ding, and Yuchen Guo. 2014. Latent semantic sparse hashing for cross-modal similarity search. In *Proceedings of the International ACM SIGIR Conference on Research and Development in Information Retrieval*. 415–424.

Feature Reconstruction by Laplacian Eigenmaps for Efficient Instance Search

Bingqing Ke
Center for Future Media
School of Computer Science & Engineering
University of Electronic Science and Technology of China
kebingqing@std.uestc.edu.cn

Jie Shao*
Center for Future Media
School of Computer Science & Engineering
University of Electronic Science and Technology of China
shaojie@uestc.edu.cn

Zi Huang
School of Information Technology & Electrical Engineering
The University of Queensland
huang@itee.uq.edu.au

Heng Tao Shen
Center for Future Media
School of Computer Science & Engineering
University of Electronic Science and Technology of China
shenhengtao@uestc.edu.cn

ABSTRACT

Instance search aims at retrieving images containing a particular query instance. Recently, image features derived from pre-trained convolutional neural networks (CNNs) have been shown to provide promising performance for image retrieval. However, the robustness of these features is still limited by hard positives and hard negatives. To address this issue, this work focuses on reconstructing a new representation based on conventional CNN features to capture the intrinsic image manifold in the original feature space. After the feature reconstruction, the Euclidean distance can be applied in the new space to measure the pairwise distance among feature points. The proposed method is highly efficient, which benefits from the linear search complexity and a further optimization for speedup. Experiments demonstrate that our method achieves promising efficiency with highly competitive accuracy. This work succeeds in capturing implicit embedding information in images as well as reducing the computational complexity significantly.

CCS CONCEPTS

• **Information systems** → **Image search**;

KEYWORDS

Laplacian eigenmaps; instance search; feature reconstruction

ACM Reference Format:

Bingqing Ke, Jie Shao, Zi Huang, and Heng Tao Shen. 2018. Feature Reconstruction by Laplacian Eigenmaps for Efficient Instance Search. In *ICMR'18: 2018 International Conference on Multimedia Retrieval, June 11–14, 2018, Yokohama, Japan.* ACM, New York, NY, USA, 9 pages. https://doi.org/10.1145/3206025.3206032

*Corresponding author.

ICMR'18, June 11–14, 2018, Yokohama, Japan

ACM ISBN 978-1-4503-5046-4/18/06...$15.00
https://doi.org/10.1145/3206025.3206032

1 INTRODUCTION

Given a query instance, which is presented in the form of a bounding box, the task of instance search aims to retrieve database images that contain the query instance. It has attracted wide attention over the last decade [25]. Recent studies have shown that the visual descriptors derived from the convolutional layer activations can achieve state-of-the-art performance for many computer vision tasks, such as object detection [7, 20], segmentation [8, 14, 22] and question answering [4]. After the last convolutional layer is produced, a certain pooling strategy [1, 2, 24] is used to generate features of the input. The most common pooling strategies include sum-pooling [2] and max-pooling [1]. Recently, Tolias et al. [24] proposed maximum activations of convolutions (MAC) and regional maximum activation of convolutions (R-MAC) to achieve excellent performance.

Manifold learning aims to find meaningful low-dimensional structures of data points hidden in their high-dimensional observations [3, 21, 23, 26]. Assume that we have a collection of images plotted in the feature spaces as illustrated in Figure 1. The points in the same color indicate similar distance to the query Q. When conducting a similarity ranking on a set of images (e.g., x_1 to x_7) in the Euclidean space based on their distances to the query Q, x_6 and x_7 are top-ranked and they are supposed to be *positive* images. However they are actually *negative* images for the task of instance search (known as *false positives*) because the object described in Q does not appear in x_6 or x_7. Images x_4 and x_5 are regarded as *negative* images for the query because of their large distance to Q. However, they should be considered as *junk* images[1]. The data points such as x_4 and x_5 are called as *false negatives.* Figure 1(b) demonstrates that searching using Euclidean distance after manifold learning is more semantically accurate than the same search in the original feature space.

Yu et al. [27] propose the fuzzy objects matching (FOM) scheme in order to achieve effective instance search. In their work, the fuzzy objects are generated from 300 object proposals by clustering and the default number of fuzzy objects is 20 per image. They factorize

[1] In the task of instance search, positive images mean that more than 25% of the query object is clearly visible, negative images do not contain the target object, and junk images contains the query object but less than 25% of the object appears [15].

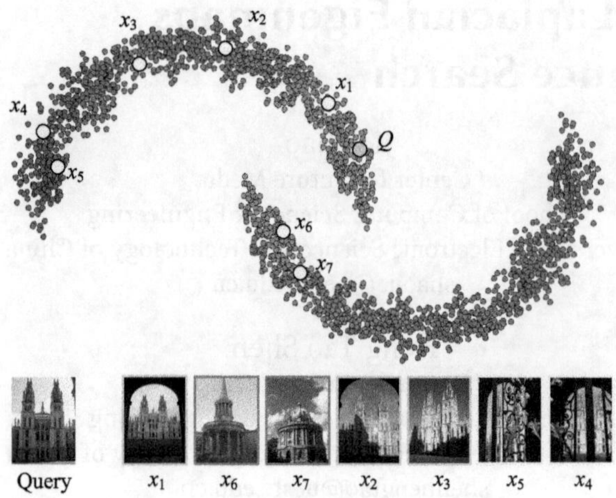

(a) Euclidean space.

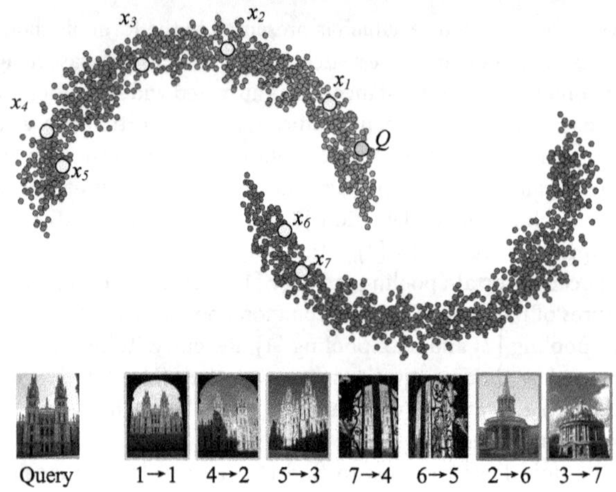

(b) Manifold space.

Figure 1: A similarity ranking on example images for instance search. The query data and the data to be ranked are shown in green and yellow respectively. The points in the same color have similar distance to the query, where the points in orange are most similar to the query and the purple points are dissimilar to the query. Compared with the image ranking in the Euclidean space (a), the rank change of each image in the manifold space (b) is explicitly denoted underneath. Positive/negative/junk images are depicted with green/red/yellow border.

the feature matrix of all the object proposals from one reference image into the product of a set of fuzzy objects. Although the method achieves satisfactory performance, the dimensionality of the visual descriptors is too high (13k), which is impractical for handling large-scale datasets. Razavian et al. [19] extract local features by exploiting multi-scale schemes, which take geometric invariance into explicit consideration. Gao et al. [6] propose an unsupervised deep hashing method to generate compact binary codes for instance search. The main contribution of this method is the search efficiency can be improved by using hashing. The methods by Iscen et al. [9, 10] achieve the state-of-the-art results. They perform a diffusion process on a graph of image regions linked based on the region similarities, which is time-consuming. Mohedano et al. [13] demonstrate the suitability of the bag of words (BoW) aggregation scheme based on local CNN features. They apply sliding window principle which leads to the large number of possible windows. Exhaustive search is extremely costly.

In this work, we focus on unfolding the underlying manifold in original feature space for the task of instance search. This method first reconstructs new features based on MAC and R-MAC, which are the most effective CNN features. To explore the intrinsic manifold structure of data points, we use Laplacian eigenmaps [3]. Our work is able to achieve competitive performance while the search process is much faster. It turns out that our method not only achieves excellent performance on high-dimensional features, but also provides competitive performance with very short codes.

In summary, we make the following contributions:

- We take advantages of MAC and R-MAC features to construct a better image representation for instance search.
- As the features derived from CNNs are limited by hard positives and hard negatives, we reconstruct a low-dimensional representation that captures the manifold structure of images by Laplacian eigenmaps.
- An approach to improve the efficiency of instance search is proposed. The major process is executed off-line and the query stage is essentially a linear search with a low computational cost.
- Extensive experiments are conducted to verify the effectiveness and the efficiency of the proposed new representation. Our method outperforms the state-of-the-art on several instance retrieval benchmarks, and the performance on extremely short codes (the dimensionality is as low as 16) is still better than most of the existing approaches.

2 RELATED WORK

This section discusses existing methods for instance search by using CNN features. We also review some manifold learning techniques, which are used to exploit nonlinear information hidden in original data and meanwhile improve the search efficiency.

CNN based representation. CNN based visual descriptors are proven to show satisfactory performance on image retrieval [11, 13, 27]. Mohedano et al. [13] use a BoW framework to encode the local convolutional features of an image into a single vector. However, the dimensionality of the feature vector is too high (25k). Tolias et al. [24] propose maximum activations of convolutions (MAC) and regional maximum activation of convolutions (R-MAC) features. Given an input image I, the output of CNN is in the form of a 3D tensor of $W_c \times H_c \times K_c$ dimensions, where W_c and H_c are the width and height of feature map respectively, and K_c denotes the number of feature channels. The MAC feature is produced by performing a max-pooling on each feature channel over all locations. Then, they propose a region sampling method to sample regions at different scales. R-MAC is produced by extracting MAC feature on each region and then combining them into a single vector. In this paper, we adopt the same strategy to extract the candidate regions.

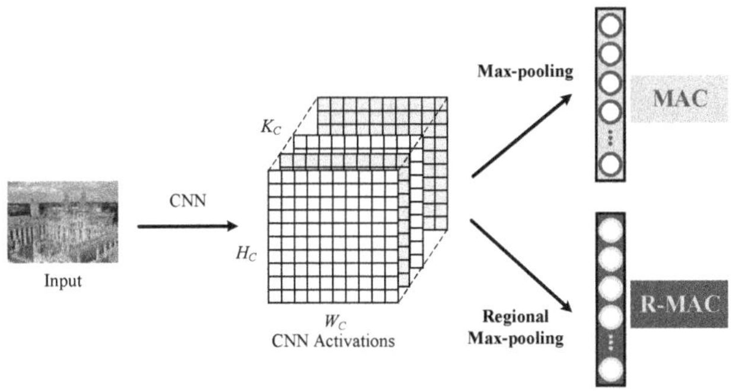

(a) Two types of features extracted from CNN.

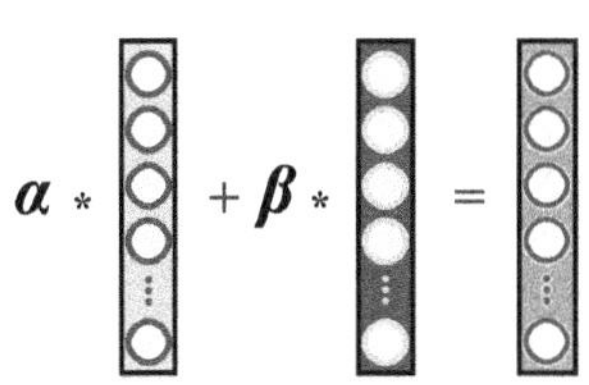

(b) Weighted average.

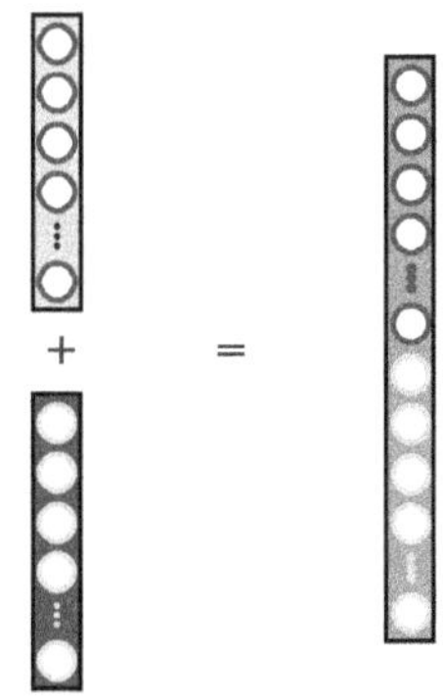

(c) Concatenate.

Figure 2: Illustration of proposed feature fusion methods. Two types of excellent features MAC and R-MAC are first derived from a CNN through conducting different pooling strategies. 2(b) and 2(c) are two approaches to combine the two features.

Manifold learning. Manifold learning techniques extract low-dimensional feature from high-dimensional data in an unsupervised manner. These techniques aim to unfold the underlying manifold so that the Euclidean distance in the new space is a meaningful measure of distance between any pair of points. Several powerful manifold learning techniques have been proposed, such as Isomap [23], local linear embedding (LLE) [21], Laplacian eigenmaps [3] and semi-definite embedding (SED) [26]. The power of these methods lies in capturing the underlying low-dimensional manifold structure within data. In this paper, we utilize Laplacian eigenmaps which relies on the spectral decomposition criterion to learn a low-dimensional embedding of data. Laplacian eigenmaps is a classic method of manifold learning. Compared with other methods of manifold learning, Lapacian eigenmaps has good theoretical properties and it is simple. It provides an effective technique for exploiting nonlinear information hidden in manifold structure of data and dimensionality reduction. These properties make Laplacian eigenmaps a good choice for manifold learning.

Table 1: Performance comparison of MAC, R-MAC and two features we propose on the Oxford5K and Paris6k datasets. Dim denotes the corresponding feature dimensionality.

Method	Dim	Oxford5k	Paris6k
MAC	512	82.6	85.8
R-MAC	512	79.3	86.9
Weighted Average	512	82.8	85.4
Joint	1024	**83.7**	**87.2**

3 FEATURE FUSION STRATEGIES

Both of MAC and R-MAC [24] achieve competitive performance in the task of instance search. We consider that different visual descriptors may capture different aspects of information of an image. To adequately take advantages of MAC and R-MAC features, we propose two strategies to combine these two features. In the following, we use $X_{mac}(X_{rmac}) \in \mathbb{R}^{512}$ to represent MAC (RMAC) feature of an image, and $X_{mac}(i)$ ($X_{rmac}(i)$) denotes the ith element of X_{mac} (X_{rmac}).

Weighted average. First, we adopt a common pooling strategy to obtain a new feature by simply summing up R-MAC and MAC as shown in Figure 2(b). The obtained new feature denoted by $X_{wa} \in \mathbb{R}^{512}$ is computed as follows:

$$X_{wa}(i) = \alpha X_{mac}(i) + \beta X_{rmac}(i), \quad 1 \le i \le 512, \tag{1}$$

where $X_{wa}(i)$ represents the ith element of vector X_{wa}. Note that, when we set $\alpha = \beta$, it is mean-pooling.

Concatenate. In this strategy, we directly concatenate two features to generate a new descriptor as shown in Figure 2(c). Suppose the new feature is $X_{joint} \in \mathbb{R}^{1024}$, the ith elements of vector X_{joint} can be defined as follows:

$$X_{joint}(i) = \begin{cases} X_{mac}(i), & \text{if } 1 \le i \le 512, \\ X_{rmac}(i-512), & \text{otherwise.} \end{cases} \tag{2}$$

To compare the performances on these four types of regional visual descriptors, we adopt a simple search strategy without query expansion (which uses neighbors of query feature vector for new search). Given an instance in the form of a bounding box, the cosine similarity between the query and the candidate regions are computed first. The score of an image I is defined as $score_i = max\{s(q,r_1), s(q,r_2), \cdots, s(q,r_m)\}$, where $s(q,r_j)$ denotes the cosine similarity between the query q and the jth region of I, and m is the number of regions extracted from image I. In this work, we adopt the same strategy used in [24] and extract $m = 21$ regions per image. The results are shown in Table 1. We can find that, the MAC feature achieves a better performance on Oxford5k dataset compared with Paris6k, and the R-MAC feature is the opposite. Note that since it is observed that the performance of the weighted average pooling with $\alpha = \beta$ is better than the setting of $\alpha \neq \beta$, we only report the result of the mean-pooling (i.e., $\alpha = \beta$). Our new joint feature achieves the best performance on both datasets.

In this work, we extract the joint feature as the original descriptor of a region.

4 LAPLACIAN EIGENMAPS FOR DATA REPRESENTATION AND DIMENSIONALITY REDUCTION

Although our joint feature provides a good performance on instance search, its dimensionality is 1,024, and it cannot capture the image manifold structure. In this section, we reconstruct a new feature based on the joint feature through Laplacian eigenmaps.

First, we briefly review Laplacian eigenmaps. Suppose

$$X = [x_1, \ldots, x_N] \in \mathbb{R}^{D_s \times N}$$

is a set of N data points in original feature space, and D_s is the dimensionality of data. The purpose of Laplacian eigenmaps is to find a low-dimensional data representation that best preserves neighborhood relations. To this end, the algorithm works as follows [3, 12]:

- Construct an affinity matrix $W = (w_{ij}) \in \mathbb{R}^{N \times N}$ of pairwise similarities among N data points, where w_{ij} denotes the similarity between x_i and x_j. In this work, we adopt the strategy proposed by [17] to define w_{ij} as follows:

$$top(q,k) \subset DB, DB \in \mathbb{R}^{D \times N}, \quad (3)$$

$$|top(q,k)| = k, \quad (4)$$

$$sim(q,x_i) > sim(q,x_j), \quad \forall \quad x_i \in top(q,k), \; x_j \notin top(q,k), \quad (5)$$

where DB represents the database and $sim(q,x)$ denotes the cosine similarity between q and x. The similarity measure is symmetric which means $sim(q,x) = sim(x,q)$. Then, we define the element w_{ij} of the affinity matrix W as

$$w_{ij} = \begin{cases} sim(x_i,x_j), \text{ if } j \in top(x_i,k) \text{ and } i \in top(x_j,k), \\ 0, \text{ otherwise.} \end{cases} \quad (6)$$

- Compute the normalized Laplacian matrix

$$L = I - D^{-\frac{1}{2}} W D^{-\frac{1}{2}},$$

where D is the diagonal matrix and I denotes an identity matrix of size N. The ith element d_{ii} of D corresponds to the summation of all the similarities related to x_i, which is $d_{ii} = \sum_{j=1}^{N} w_{ij}$.

- Compute $U \in \mathbb{R}^{N \times d}$ by solving the following constrained optimization:

$$\min_{U \in \mathbb{R}^{N \times d}} < UU^T, L > \; s.t. \; U^T U = I, \quad (7)$$

where $d \leq D_s$.

- Normalize each row of $U \in \mathbb{R}^{N \times d}$ to obtain a new matrix $\hat{U}$.

In the third stage of Laplacian eigenmaps, the columns of U indeed come from the first d eigenvectors corresponding to the smallest d eigenvalues of L by its eigendecomposition.

Note that, the rows of U is exactly the new d-dimensional representation of the original D_s-dimensional features X. The elements of UU^T represent the cosine similarity between pairs of new representations (the rows of U), and thus Laplacian eigenmaps can find a low-dimensional data representation that best preserves neighborhood relations.

Form new queries. When we conduct an instance search by a given query in the form of a bounding box, we can just get its joint feature X_{joint} from a CNN. Therefore, as shown in Figure 4(a), to obtain the corresponding d-dimensional query feature, a common practice is to add the query to database, construct a new affinity matrix W and conduct Laplacian eigenmaps, which is extremely time-consuming.

We introduce a simple strategy to form a d-dimensional feature of query, as shown in Figure 4(b). First, we define a mapping function f as follows:

$$f : X \to Y, \quad (8)$$

where X is an original joint feature and Y denotes the corresponding d-dimensional vector in new feature space.

Suppose the joint feature of query extracted from a CNN is X_q, and Y_q denotes the d-dimensional feature of query we expect. The function g is defined as

$$g : X_q \to Y_q. \quad (9)$$

Our strategy uses the joint feature X_q of query to find the nearest neighbor X'_q in database. Then, $f(X'_q) = Y_q$ is obtained by the mapping function. Y_i is the expected query in the new feature space. In this way, we have $g(X_q) = f(N(X_q))$, where $N(X)$ denotes the nearest neighbor of X. As the search space is not changed, most computations can be conducted off-line and hence our search is in linear complexity. Note that, if the nearest neighbor $N(X)$ of the query is dissimilar to X, we can get that there is no image which contains the instance of the given query in database.

5 FURTHER OPTIMIZATION FOR SPEEDUP

Given a new query, we first obtain its joint feature with 1,024 dimensions, and then we compute the similarity between the query and all regions to perform 1-nearest neighbor search, which is time-consuming. In this section, we propose a simple and reliable enhancement method to improve the search efficiency by using a tree structure.

Spectral clustering [5] is proven to provide excellent performance on clustering task. It can be divided into two steps: 1) Laplacian eigenmaps, and 2) clustering. Thus, a clustering algorithm is performed in the new feature space generated by Laplacian eigenmaps instead of the original joint features in this work. We employ the k-means algorithm on the rows of $\hat{U}$ (normalized U which is extracted from Eq. 7) to partition N data points into K groups. Since the dimensionality of the new feature is lower than the joint feature, 1-nearest neighbor search is faster. The clustering information is then mapped back to the joint features as Figure 3 shows.

Considering that there are K clusters and N/K region descriptors in each cluster on average, as Figure 5 shows, we perform a two-stage search to find the nearest neighbor by following steps:

- First, we compute the similarities between the joint feature of query and all cluster centroids to obtain the cluster C_s that is most similar to the original query.
- We then traverse all region descriptors in cluster C_s to find the most similar region to the query. X'_q is the nearest neighbor of X_q.

It is obvious that the above two-stage search can significantly reduce the original search time. Note that, since we only need to find the 1-nearest neighbor of the original query, the result is reliable.

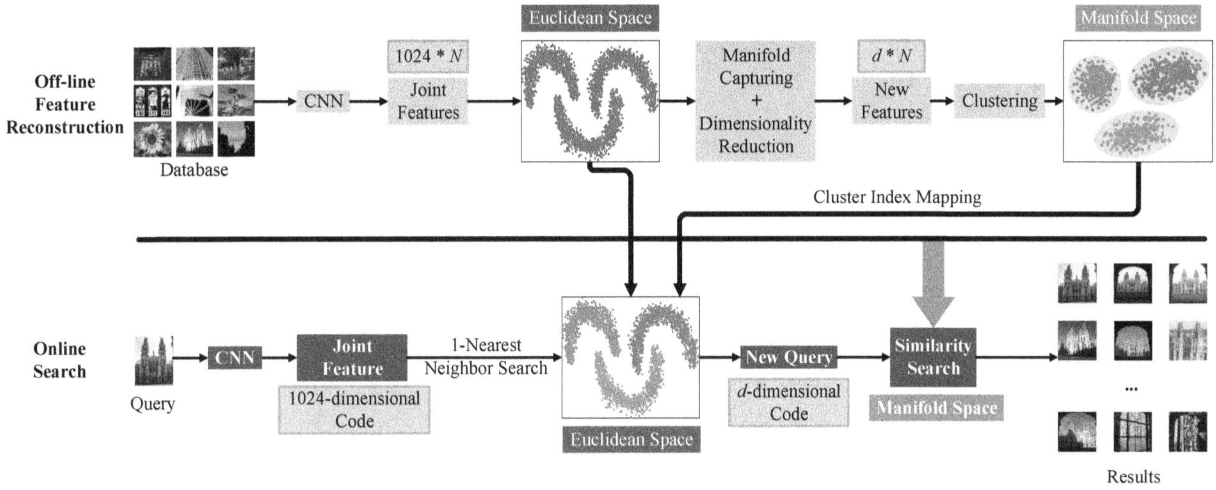

Figure 3: Overview of our method for instance search. The top row shows the off-line feature reconstruction. We obtain d-dimensional features which capture image manifold. Then, a clustering algorithm is conducted on the new features for accelerating the online retrieval. The bottom row shows the online search process. We first conduct 1-nearest neighbor search by using the clustering information generated off-line to obtain a d-dimensional query, and then the new query is used to perform a similarity search in the new feature space.

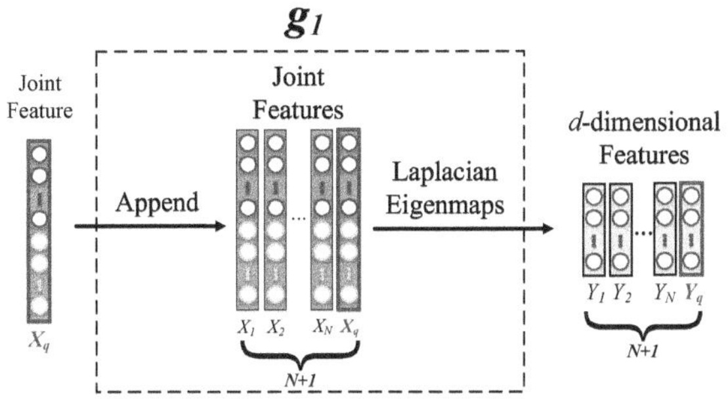

(a) Common practice to form new query.

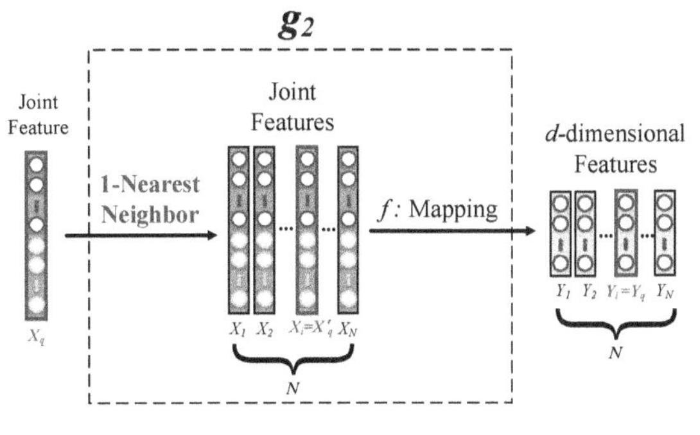

(b) Our method to generate new query.

Figure 4: Form new query.

Time complexity analysis. Suppose we have obtained K clusters. Our searching process can be summarized as two steps: 1) generate corresponding d-dimensional feature for the query Y_q; and 2) use Y_q to conduct instance search. The performance improvement is reflected in the following two aspects.

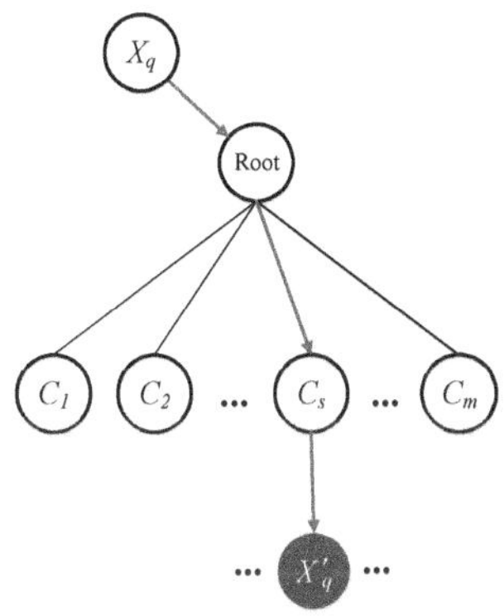

Figure 5: A tree structure for 1-nearest neighbor search.

For the first aspect, suppose we partition N data points into K clusters and there are N/K points on average per cluster. According to the discussion above, we compute the similarity between the original query and all K cluster centroids to find a cluster C_s to conduct the exact search. Then, we traverse all data points in C_s. Thus, it costs $O(DK + \frac{DN}{K})$ time complexity where D denotes the dimensionality of original features. We set $K = \sqrt{N}$ and it leads to $O(2D\sqrt{N})$ time complexity in general. If $N = 100,000$, the efficiency is improved by around 150 times.

On the other hand, Laplacian eigenmaps can reduce the feature dimensionality greatly, resulting in a significant acceleration of the search process especially when extremely short codes are used for retrieval. Suppose the length of the codes we obtain is d (we set

$16 \leq d \leq 512$ in this work), and the common dimensionality of existing features is 512, the search efficiency is enhanced by $512/d$ times. The complexity of our method is $O(dN + 2D\sqrt{N})$.

6 EXPERIMENTAL RESULTS

6.1 Experimental Setup

Our experiments are conduced on Oxford buildings dataset [15] and Paris dataset [16], which are referred to as Oxford5k and Paris6k respectively. In addition, 100k Flickr images [15] are added to form the so called Oxford105k and Paris106k. We use mean average precision (MAP) as the performance measure in all datasets. The experiments are conducted on a machine with a 12-core Intel Xeon 2.20GHz CPU.

Visual descriptors. As most of the existing CNNs are trained for the task of image classification, the descriptors produced from them are suboptimal for other tasks. In [18], a fine-tuned CNN for image retrieval is introduced. In this work, we employ this CNN to extract visual descriptors. The binary codes (DRH) [6] are extracted from the same CNN for the instance search task. A method called diffusion [10] applies R-match, a multi-scale scheme proposed by [19], on the fine-tuned CNN can be selected as a baseline. In addition, fast spectral ranking (FSR) proposed by [9] further improves the efficiency of [10]. In our experiments, we compare these methods with our proposal.

Regions reduction. Tolias et al. [24] propose a region sampling method to sample regions for each image at different scales. In this work, we adopt the same strategy to extract regions at 3 different scales and there are 21 regions per image on average. Iscen et al. [10] learn a Gaussian mixture model (GMM) on the features of each image to reduce the number of regions per image from 21 to 5. The size of affinity matrix on Oxford105k is reduced from 2.2M×2.2M to 0.5M×0.5M. We employ the same strategy on all datasets to reduce the computation cost. We do not experiment on large-scale datasets without GMM, because there is not much improvement any more [9, 10] and it is time-consuming.

Number of nearest neighbors. We vary the number of nearest neighbors for constructing the affinity matrix for different scale datasets, and the results are reported in Figure 6. In the rest of the paper, we set $k = 220$ for Oxford5k and Paris6k. When GMM is conducted, we set $k = 70, 170$ for small datasets (Oxford5k and Paris6k) and large-scale datasets (Oxford105k and Paris106k) respectively. Note that, since the features contain less information when the dimensionality of feature d or the number of regions per image (corresponding to the size of affinity matrix for Laplacian eigenmaps) becomes smaller, we set $k = 100, 350$ for Oxford5k (Paris6k) and Oxford105k (Paris106k) with GMM respectively, and the results are shown in Table 4.

Effect of feature reconstruction. Figure 7 shows the examples of the top retrieved images before (top) and after (bottom) feature reconstruction, both using joint feature combining MAC and R-MAC. The bottom bounding box with blue border (X'_q) is the nearest neighbor of the given query instance (X_q) in the original feature space. From the search results, we can observe the superiority of using reconstructed new features with Laplacian eigenmaps.

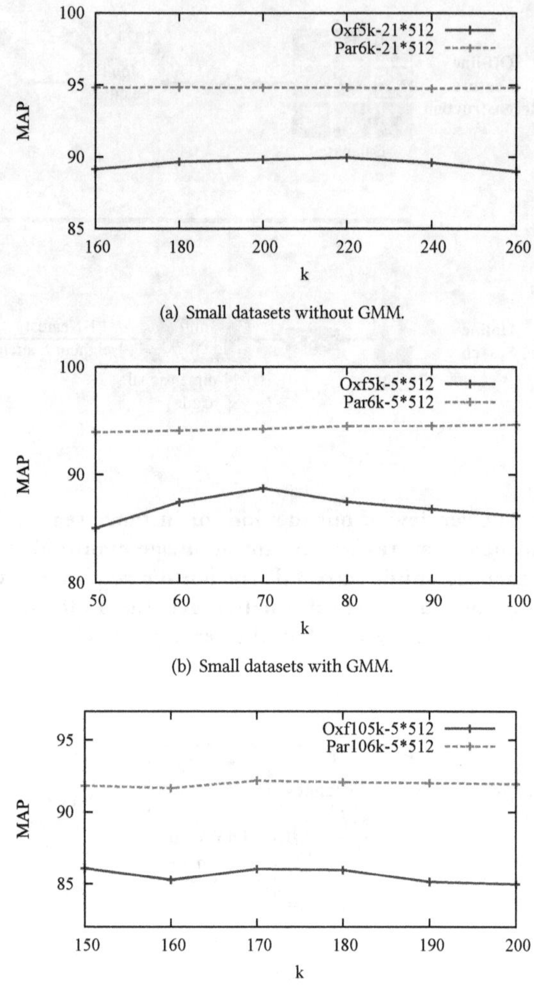

(a) Small datasets without GMM.

(b) Small datasets with GMM.

(c) Large-scale datasets with GMM.

Figure 6: Effect of the number of nearest neighbors k used for the affinity matrix.

6.2 Comparison with the State-of-the-art Methods

Retrieval performance. We compare with two state-of-the-art methods, diffusion [10] and FSR [9]. Tables 2, 3 and 4 present the results. Compared with diffusion [10], we achieve the same MAP on Oxford5k and outperform it on Paris6k and Oxford105k with GMM, while we run much faster. Compared with FSR [9], we achieve the same performance on Paris106k and outperform it on Oxford5k and Paris6k with GMM.

Note that when d is set to be 430 (we do not report this result in the table because 430 is not a common dimensionality used as a feature), the MAP is 90.7 on Oxford5k without GMM. Eventually, we achieve 93.9 MAP when query expansion is conducted, which outperforms the state-of-the-art. For Paris6k with GMM, we achieve 96.0 MAP on 16-dimensional features which is nearly perfect. In

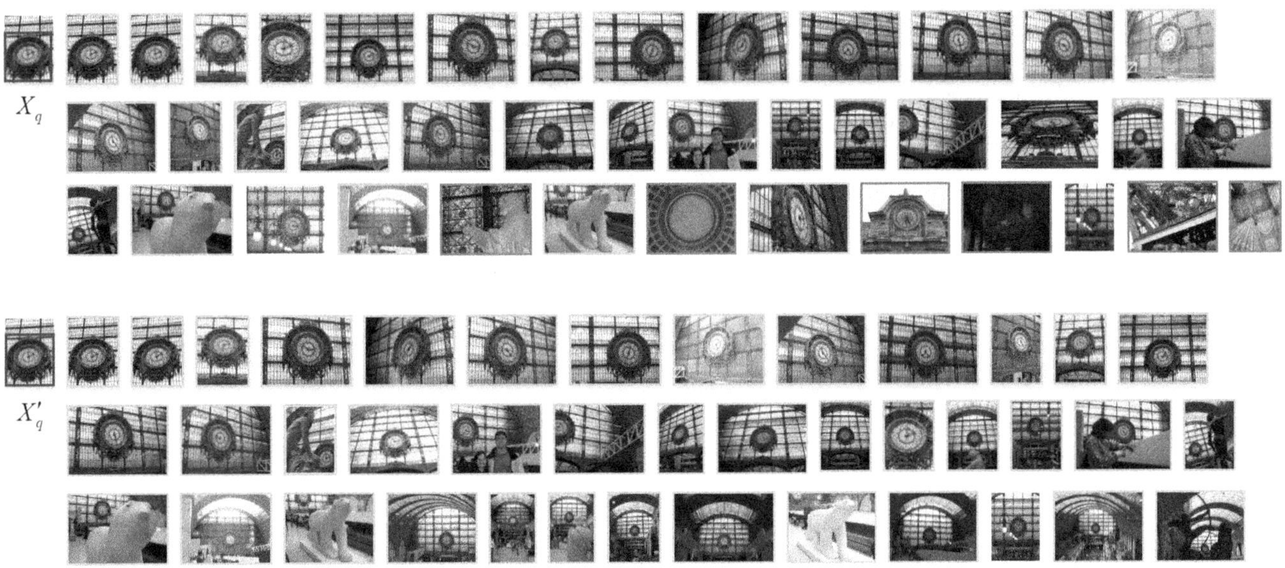

Figure 7: Examples of top retrieved images before (top) and after (bottom) feature reconstruction by Laplacian eigenmaps. X_q represents the joint feature of query, and X_q' denotes the corresponding new feature after Laplacian eigenmaps. We depict the query instance with blue border. Positive/negative/junk images are depicted with green/red/yellow borders.

addition, since query expansion also tries to exploit the manifold of images, it is quite difficult to perform even better.

Dimensionality reduction. We set the dimensionality of features d as 16, 32, 128, 256 and 512 for all datasets. We can find that on Oxford dataset, the performance becomes worse with the decrease of dimensionality. That is because the information that image contains is lost when the feature dimensionality is reduced. Note that, when we set $d = 16$, our method can still achieve competitive performance. For Paris6k dataset, when d becomes lower, the MAP value increases. That is because the features on Paris6k can be considered extremely low-dimensional features (e.g., 16-dimensional) embedded in a high-dimensional space.

Extreme short codes. In Laplacian eigenmaps, we use the first d eigenvectors of L corresponding to the smallest d eigenvalues to compose the new searching space. As we mentioned above, d is the length of the new features. To measure the performance on extremely low-dimensional features we obtained, the value of d can be set as 32 and 16. The results of a simple instance search without query expansion are shown in Table 4, and we can achieve competitive performance on 32- and 16-dimensional features. Note that we achieve 96.0 MAP on Patis6k with GMM which outperforms the art-of-the-state, although the dimensionality is just 16. The power of our method lies in its ability to capture the intrinsic manifold structure of the data.

Query time. In this work, running time refers to the searching time excluding the construction of query vector, which is the basic procedure in all baseline and our methods. We compare the query time with the two state-of-the-art methods [10] and [9]. The running time for instance search on different datasets is reported in Table 5. The search time is just 0.1s per query in large-scale datasets (Oxford105k and Paris106k), which outperforms the other

Table 2: Performance comparison with the state-of-the-art.

Regional Search			
Method	Dim	Oxf5k	Par6k
Ours	21×512	90.0	94.8
	21×256	87.9	95.4
	21×128	88.4	95.1
	21×32	86.1	95.6
	21×16	81.5	96.0
R-match	21×512	81.5	86.1
DRH	40×1024	78.3	80.1
Query Expansion			
Method	Dim	Oxf5k	Par6k
Ours	21×512	93.2	95.5
	21×16	81.6	96.2
R-match	21×512	83.6	87.0
DRH	40×1024	85.1	84.9
Diffusion	21×512	93.2	96.5
FSR	21×512	93.0	96.5

two methods. We use 16-dimensional features to conduct the search in Paris106k, and our method requires just 98ms per query. Note that, the performance on 16-dimensional features is excellent.

The online complexity of [10] is high. Although they improve the search efficiency recently [9], the online complexity is still $O(rN)$ where N denotes the number of regions and r is pre-defined and set to be large enough, such as 5k.

As we demonstrated in the above complexity analysis, the improvement comes from two aspects: searching the new query and dimensionality reduction. Diffusion [10] requires the most time

Table 3: Regional representation with 5 descriptors per image using GMM.

Regional Search					
Method	Dim	Oxf5k	Par6k	Oxf105k	Par106k
	5×512	88.7	94.2	86.0	92.2
Ours	5×256	86.4	94.4	81.8	92.1
	5×128	86.7	94.7	81.6	91.4
Query Expansion					
Method	Dim	Oxf5k	Par6k	Oxf105k	Par106k
Ours	5×512	91.0	94.3	86.1	92.4
Diffusion	5×512	91.5	95.6	84.7	93.0
FSR	5×512	91.6	95.6	86.5	92.4

Table 4: Performance on extremely short codes.

Regional Search					
Method	Dim	Oxf5k	Par6k	Oxf105k	Par106k
Ours	5 × 32	85.4	96.0	77.6	90.2
	5 × 16	81.3	96.0	72.8	89.4

Table 5: Time cost (ms) for different methods. Our method with optimization for acceleration is marked with *.

Method	Dim	Oxf5k	Par6k	Oxf105k	Par106k
Diffusion	512	636.4	745.5	1078.2	1259.8
FSR	512	21.0	21.0	140.0	-
Ours	512	14.5	17.5	101.4	103.7
	16	13.9	16.3	97.0	98.4
Ours*	512	13.2	15.3	95.2	96.1
	16	12.7	14.7	90.9	91.9

to search as it conducts random walk online. Our approach is the fastest as Table 5 shows. When the dimensionality of features becomes lower, the query process becomes faster.

7 CONCLUSION

We conduct Laplacian eigenmaps on the joint MAC/R-MAC feature to capture the intrinsic manifold structure of images hidden in their high-dimensional data representations. The feature dimensionality reduction achieved by the feature reconstruction significantly reduces the computational cost of the search process. A comprehensive performance study has demonstrated the strengths of the proposed method in both accuracy and efficiency for instance search. The new feature generated by our method with extremely low dimensionality can still achieve outstanding accuracy in some cases (e.g., Table 4, Dim = 5× 16 for Par6k).

ACKNOWLEDGMENTS

This work is supported by the National Natural Science Foundation of China (grants No. 61672133 and No. 61632007), and the Fundamental Research Funds for the Central Universities (grants No. ZYGX2015J058 and No. ZYGX2014Z007).

REFERENCES

[1] Hossein Azizpour, Ali Sharif Razavian, Josephine Sullivan, Atsuto Maki, and Stefan Carlsson. 2015. From generic to specific deep representations for visual recognition. In *2015 IEEE Conference on Computer Vision and Pattern Recognition Workshops, CVPR Workshops, Boston, MA, USA, June 7-12, 2015.* 36–45.

[2] Artem Babenko and Victor S. Lempitsky. 2015. Aggregating Deep Convolutional Features for Image Retrieval. *CoRR* abs/1510.07493 (2015). http://arxiv.org/abs/1510.07493

[3] Mikhail Belkin and Partha Niyogi. 2001. Laplacian Eigenmaps and Spectral Techniques for Embedding and Clustering. In *Advances in Neural Information Processing Systems 14 [Neural Information Processing Systems: Natural and Synthetic, NIPS 2001, December 3-8, 2001, Vancouver, British Columbia, Canada].* 585–591.

[4] Jie Chen, Jie Shao, Fumin Shen, Chengkun He, Lianli Gao, and Heng Tao Shen. 2017. Movie Fill in the Blank with Adaptive Temporal Attention and Description Update. In *Proceedings of the 2017 ACM on Conference on Information and Knowledge Management, CIKM 2017, Singapore, November 06 - 10, 2017.* 1039–1048.

[5] Nello Cristianini, John Shawe-Taylor, and Jaz S. Kandola. 2001. Spectral Kernel Methods for Clustering. In *Advances in Neural Information Processing Systems 14 [Neural Information Processing Systems: Natural and Synthetic, NIPS 2001, December 3-8, 2001, Vancouver, British Columbia, Canada].* 649–655.

[6] Lianli Gao, Tao He, Jingkuan Song, Xing Xu, and Heng Tao Shen. 2018. Deep Region Hashing for Efficient Large-scale Instance Search from Images. In *Proceedings of the Thirty-Second AAAI Conference on Artificial Intelligence, February 2-7, 2018, New Orleans, Louisiana, USA.*

[7] Spyros Gidaris and Nikos Komodakis. 2016. LocNet: Improving Localization Accuracy for Object Detection. In *2016 IEEE Conference on Computer Vision and Pattern Recognition, CVPR 2016, Las Vegas, NV, USA, June 27-30, 2016.* 789–798.

[8] Bharath Hariharan, Pablo Andrés Arbeláez, Ross B. Girshick, and Jitendra Malik. 2015. Hypercolumns for object segmentation and fine-grained localization. In *IEEE Conference on Computer Vision and Pattern Recognition, CVPR 2015, Boston, MA, USA, June 7-12, 2015.* 447–456.

[9] Ahmet Iscen, Yannis S. Avrithis, Giorgos Tolias, Teddy Furon, and Ondrej Chum. 2017. Fast Spectral Ranking for Similarity Search. *CoRR* abs/1703.06935 (2017). http://arxiv.org/abs/1703.06935

[10] Ahmet Iscen, Giorgos Tolias, Yannis S. Avrithis, Teddy Furon, and Ondrej Chum. 2017. Efficient Diffusion on Region Manifolds: Recovering Small Objects with Compact CNN Representations. In *2017 IEEE Conference on Computer Vision and Pattern Recognition, CVPR 2017, Honolulu, Hawaii, USA, July 22-25, 2017.* 2077–2086.

[11] Jie Lin, Olivier Morère, Antoine Veillard, Ling-Yu Duan, Hanlin Goh, and Vijay Chandrasekhar. 2017. DeepHash for Image Instance Retrieval: Getting Regularization, Depth and Fine-Tuning Right. In *Proceedings of the 2017 ACM on International Conference on Multimedia Retrieval, ICMR 2017, Bucharest, Romania, June 6-9, 2017.* 133–141.

[12] Canyi Lu, Shuicheng Yan, and Zhouchen Lin. 2016. Convex Sparse Spectral Clustering: Single-View to Multi-View. *IEEE Trans. Image Processing* 25, 6 (2016), 2833–2843.

[13] Eva Mohedano, Kevin McGuinness, Noel E. O'Connor, Amaia Salvador, Ferran Marqués, and Xavier Giró i Nieto. 2016. Bags of Local Convolutional Features for Scalable Instance Search. In *Proceedings of the 2016 ACM on International Conference on Multimedia Retrieval, ICMR 2016, New York, New York, USA, June 6-9, 2016.* 327–331.

[14] Hyeonwoo Noh, Seunghoon Hong, and Bohyung Han. 2015. Learning Deconvolution Network for Semantic Segmentation. In *2015 IEEE International Conference on Computer Vision, ICCV 2015, Santiago, Chile, December 7-13, 2015.* 1520–1528.

[15] James Philbin, Ondrej Chum, Michael Isard, Josef Sivic, and Andrew Zisserman. 2007. Object retrieval with large vocabularies and fast spatial matching. In *2007 IEEE Computer Society Conference on Computer Vision and Pattern Recognition (CVPR 2007), 18-23 June 2007, Minneapolis, Minnesota, USA.*

[16] James Philbin, Ondrej Chum, Michael Isard, Josef Sivic, and Andrew Zisserman. 2008. Lost in quantization: Improving particular object retrieval in large scale image databases. In *2008 IEEE Computer Society Conference on Computer Vision and Pattern Recognition (CVPR 2008), 24-26 June 2008, Anchorage, Alaska, USA.*

[17] Danfeng Qin, Stephan Gammeter, Lukas Bossard, Till Quack, and Luc J. Van Gool. 2011. Hello neighbor: Accurate object retrieval with k-reciprocal nearest neighbors. In *The 24th IEEE Conference on Computer Vision and Pattern Recognition, CVPR 2011, Colorado Springs, CO, USA, 20-25 June 2011.* 777–784.

[18] Filip Radenovic, Giorgos Tolias, and Ondrej Chum. 2016. CNN Image Retrieval Learns from BoW: Unsupervised Fine-Tuning with Hard Examples. In *Computer Vision - ECCV 2016 - 14th European Conference, Amsterdam, The Netherlands, October 11-14, 2016, Proceedings, Part I.* 3–20.

[19] Ali Sharif Razavian, Josephine Sullivan, Stefan Carlsson, and Atsuto Maki. 2016. Visual Instance Retrieval with Deep Convolutional Networks. *ITE Transactions on Media Technology and Applications* 4, 3 (2016), 251–258.

[20] Shaoqing Ren, Kaiming He, Ross B. Girshick, and Jian Sun. 2017. Faster R-CNN: Towards Real-Time Object Detection with Region Proposal Networks. *IEEE Trans. Pattern Anal. Mach. Intell.* 39, 6 (2017), 1137–1149.

[21] Sam T. Roweis, , and Lawrence K. Saul. 2000. Nonlinear Dimensionality Reduction by Locally Linear Embedding. *Science* 290, 5500 (2000), 2323–2326.

[22] Evan Shelhamer, Jonathan Long, and Trevor Darrell. 2017. Fully Convolutional Networks for Semantic Segmentation. *IEEE Trans. Pattern Anal. Mach. Intell.* 39, 4 (2017), 640–651.

[23] Joshua B. Tenenbaum, Vin de Silva, and John C. Langford. 2000. A Global Geometric Framework for Nonlinear Dimensionality Reduction. *Science* 290, 5500 (2000), 2319–2323.

[24] Giorgos Tolias, Ronan Sicre, and Hervé Jégou. 2015. Particular object retrieval with integral max-pooling of CNN activations. *CoRR* abs/1511.05879 (2015). http://arxiv.org/abs/1511.05879

[25] Bo Wang, Jie Shao, Chengkun He, Gang Hu, and Xing Xu. 2017. Spatial Verification via Compact Words for Mobile Instance Search. In *MultiMedia Modeling - 23rd International Conference, MMM 2017, Reykjavik, Iceland, January 4-6, 2017, Proceedings, Part II.* 356–367.

[26] Kilian Q. Weinberger and Lawrence K. Saul. 2006. An Introduction to Nonlinear Dimensionality Reduction by Maximum Variance Unfolding. In *Proceedings, The Twenty-First National Conference on Artificial Intelligence and the Eighteenth Innovative Applications of Artificial Intelligence Conference, July 16-20, 2006, Boston, Massachusetts, USA.* 1683–1686.

[27] Tan Yu, Yuwei Wu, Sreyasee Das Bhattacharjee, and Junsong Yuan. 2017. Efficient Object Instance Search Using Fuzzy Objects Matching. In *Proceedings of the Thirty-First AAAI Conference on Artificial Intelligence, February 4-9, 2017, San Francisco, California, USA.* 4320–4326.

Image Annotation Retrieval with Text-Domain Label Denoising

Zachary Seymour
SUNY Binghamton
Binghamton, New York
zseymou1@binghamton.edu

Zhongfei (Mark) Zhang
SUNY Binghamton
Binghamton, New York
zhongfei@cs.binghamton.edu

ABSTRACT

This work explores the problem of making user-generated text data, in the form of noisy tags, usable for tasks such as automatic image annotation and image retrieval by denoising the data. Earlier work in this area has focused on filtering out noisy, sparse, or incorrect tags by representing an image by the accumulation of the tags of its nearest neighbors in the visual space. However, this imposes an expensive preprocessing step that must be performed for each new set of images and tags and relies on assumptions about the way the images have been labelled that we find do not always hold. We instead propose a technique for calculating a set of probabilities for the relevance of each tag for a given image relying soley on information in the text domain, namely through widely-available pretrained continous word embeddings. By first clustering the word embeddings for the tags, we calculate a set of weights representing the probability that each tag is meaningful to the image content. Given the set of tags denoised in this way, we use kernel canonical correlation analysis (KCCA) to learn a semantic space which we can project into to retrieve relevant tags for unseen images or to retrieve images for unseen tags. This work also explores the deficiencies of the use of continuous word embeddings for automatic image annotation in the existing KCCA literature and introduces a new method for constructing textual kernel matrices using these word vectors that improves tag retrieval results for both user-generated tags as well as expert labels.

CCS CONCEPTS

• **Computing methodologies** → **Canonical correlation analysis**; *Kernel methods*; Object recognition; • **Information systems** → Data cleaning;

KEYWORDS

Kernel canonical correlation analysis, automatic image annotation, label denoising

ICMR '18, June 11–14, 2018, Yokohama, Japan

ACM ISBN 978-1-4503-5046-4/18/06...$15.00
https://doi.org/10.1145/3206025.3206063

ACM Reference Format:
Zachary Seymour and Zhongfei (Mark) Zhang. 2018. Image Annotation Retrieval with Text-Domain Label Denoising. In *ICMR '18: 2018 International Conference on Multimedia Retrieval, June 11–14, 2018, Yokohama, Japan.* ACM, New York, NY, USA, 9 pages. https://doi.org/10.1145/3206025.3206063

1 INTRODUCTION

Many of the recent advances in image recognition have come from the broad availability of high-quality, large-scale image datasets. However, such datasets represent a significant commitment in terms of time and human labor to insure the labels are accurate and dense. On the other hand, across many forms of social media, images with user-provided labels have either become the primary means of interaction with other users or one of the few types of media that easily translates between networks. For instance, between Facebook and Twitter, the amount of text a user can write in a post differs greatly, but an image appears the same and can share the same (hash)tags across each. As such, there is great opportunity in understanding how users interact with images, particularly in assigning them textual metadata in the form of captions, tags, and labels.

One path to this end is the development of automated image annotation systems, capable of learning from and, at least in part, recreating human annotation. Commonly, the assumption is made that a human will assign an image visually meaningful labels, corresponding to the content of that image. This corresponds to several machine learning tasks that are themselves subsets of image annotation, namely object recognition, object detection, and scene recognition, among others. However, given the social nature of such image annotation, user-generated labels are frequently noisy and generally selfish. Users often annotate images for their own ends. Such tags can be used to interact with large communities (*#vegansofig*, *#petstagram*) or other cultural phenomena (*#tbt*,*#ootd*) or to act as livestreams of personal events (*#foreveryounge*, *#wedlongandprosper*). For the purposes of learning to assign tags to an image given just its visual information, many of these types of tags can register as noise; *i.e.*, they do not directly correspond to something actually depicted in the image. However, more and more of this type of real-world data is being produced, so it would be beneficial to make use of it. To meaningfully draw knowledge from this data, the noise needs to be modeled and partially removed.

One such proposed method is to use the image-label correspondence to learn an underlying "semantic space" of textually-informed image embeddings and then to assign more weight to the tags that occur more frequently among an image's nearest neighbors in this space [27]. However, for many datasets, finding the several nearest neighbors for every training image in order to denoise the tags adequately is a computationally expensive task. Furthermore, denoising in this way relies on the assumption that users will agree on a uniform lexicon for describing classes of objects. For instance, one user may favor the tag *bird* while another may favor *birds*, regardless of whether the image content is truly singular or plural. As a result, the model could fail to recall the correct tag for the first instance by transfering the label from the other, even though both labels are correct and similar meaning. We instead consider giving more weight to tags in the case where many similar words are used together, such as *bird*, *feather*, and *sky* versus just *birds* alone.

Building off of the rich literature regarding continuous word embeddings and the wide availability of pretrained language models in numerous languages [19, 2], we propose a model to instead denoise sets of tags using only text domain information. Rather than group labels by their frequency of use by other users, we instead estimate the probability that a particular label is relevant, given the other labels or tags provided for that single example. Our chief contribution is three-fold:

(1) We introduce a technique for reducing the noise of a list of user-generated tags given only pretrained word embeddings (which can be learned and used independent of a particular image set).
(2) We use this technique to re-introduce the semantically-powerful vector representations of the tag words into kernel-based automatic image annotation methods, such as kernel CCA with label transfer.
(3) Given our derived probabilities for the relevance of a set of tags, we also demonstrate how this technique can improve the semantic embedding of clean, expert labels.

2 RELATED WORK

Many of the capabilities of this model to extract semantically meaningful representations of images come from the development of convolutional neural networks (CNN) [16] and the availability of large-scale image datasets, such as ImageNet [5]. Our model also benefits significantly from the extensive work towards extracting semantically meaningful text representations in an unsupervised setting, which allows for powerful vector representations of words to be learned easily from large-scale text data [19, 20, 2].

Our work is synergistic with other recent work on automatic image annotation using deep CNNs [30] and the learning of joint embeddings of images and their labels. WSABIE [31] and DeViSE [6] learn to rank the top k labels using neural architectures and the weight approximate-rank pairwise (WARP) loss. Our work compares more closely with works deriving the jointly-learned semantic space via canonical correlation analysis, particularly KCCA. KCCA was first applied to paired image-text data by Hardoon et al. [12]. There are a large number of works in the literature employing CCA or variants of CCA for cross-modal retrieval of images or tags [27, 21, 32, 8, 11, 23]. Particularly, we highlight the work of Murthy et al. [21] that makes use of both CNN image features and word embeddings, but their experiments are limited to small datasets with only expert labels. Furthermore, Uricchio et al. [27] both demonstrate the need for kernel CCA, to allow for non-linear relationships between the visual and textual data, and the necessity of denoising user-generated labels.

We also acknowledge work being done in this area in the deep learning community, particularly in combining convolutional and recurrent neural networks [30]. Recent work in this area has sought to deal with the issues presented by user-generated tags. The "skip-image" technique [22] modifies the skip-gram method [19] to model the label co-occurrences and more effectively deal with rare tags. The Recurrent Image Annotator model [15] also takes the approach of combining a CNN and RNN to generate tags; however it attempts to directly model and predict the number of objects present in an image to generate an appropriate number of tags. As such, that model fails to appropriately account for non-object descriptive tags. We instead first deprioritize irrelevant tags and use our new representation to directly model the underlying semantic space.

3 METHODOLOGY

Before introducing our denoising technique, which is the primary contribution of this paper, we first establish the necessary background for KCCA with images and labels.

3.1 Image Features

Given an image, we represent its features using the activations from the last fully connected layer of a VGG-Net [24] convolutional neural network pre-trained on ImageNet [5]. Such a representation has proven useful in many visual recognition and classification tasks [7].

Maintaining the same notation used in [27], let $\phi^V(I_i)$ be the extracted feature of I_i. For image features given by neural network activations, we employ the ArcCosine kernel:

$$K_n^V(\phi^V(I_i), \phi^V(I_j)) = \frac{1}{\pi}||\phi^V(I_i)||^n||\phi^V(I_j)||^n J_n(\theta) \quad (1)$$

where J_n is defined according to the order of the kernel. Following [3], we set $n = 2$ which gives us:

$$J_2(\theta) = 3\sin\theta\cos\theta + (\pi - \theta)(1 + 2\cos^2\theta) \quad (2)$$

where θ is the angle between the inputs $\phi^V(I_i)$, $\phi^V(I_j)$. Uricchio et al. [27] demonstrate that other kernels, such as linear and radial basis function, obtain a similar but slightly inferior performance (~1%).

3.2 Text Features

3.2.1 Expert Labels. For expert labels, we can use simple binary indicator vectors as textual features. Letting D be the vocabulary size (*i.e.*, the number of labels used for annotation), we map the labels of an image I_i to a D-dimensional vector $\phi^T(I_i) = [w_1^i, \cdots, w_D^i]$, where w_k is 1 if that image has been annotated with label l_k, and 0 otherwise. Given this highly sparse representation, we can use a linear kernel, effectively counting the number of labels in common between two images:

$$K^T(\phi^T(I_i), \phi^T(I_j)) = \sum_{k=1}^{D} w_k^i w_k^j. \quad (3)$$

Here, we measure the similarity of two images by the co-occurrence of their labels. However, this representation lacks expressibility of label relationships, for it models each label independently. Previous works have shown that exploiting semantic relations by weighting each label differently can improve performance [13]. Uricchio et al. [27] explore two textual kernels that consider semantic relations between labels: an ontology-based textual kernel using bag-of-words and a two-stage kernel that takes the mean of the continuous vector representations of the label words. Concretely, given the learned representation of a label w_k as $\zeta(w_k) \in \mathbb{R}^P$, a set of labels of an image I_i can be represented by using average pooling

$$\phi^T(I_i) = \frac{1}{N} \sum_{k}^{D} w_k^i \cdot \zeta(l_k^i), \quad (4)$$

followed by a linear kernel

$$K^T(\phi^T(I_i), \phi^T(I_j)) = \phi^T(I_i)\phi^T(I_j)^\intercal. \quad (5)$$

We will refer to the vector $\phi^T(I_i)$ resulting from the pooling of an image's labels as a *document vector*, in that it is intended to be representative of the list of tags as a whole. However, works exploring the semantic properties of embeddings such as those produced by word2vec have shown that simply averaging the features for each word in a document does not guarantee that the resulting document vector will be actually representative. Rather, all that is guaranteed is that this document vector lies somewhere in the convex hull of its constituent word vectors [17]. Consequently, better results are achieved by using a weighted average to pool the word vectors. For example, Lev et al. [17] suggest using Fisher Vectors derived from Gaussian Mixture Models to provide the weighted document vectors. In Figure 1, we demonstrate several examples of the nearest neighbors (by cosine distance) of such document vectors in the original word embedding space using two methods: average pooling of the vectors for each user tag and taking a weighted average using weights derived from our scheme described in Section 3.2.2. First, Figure 1a demonstrates the case where both document vectors are seemingly relevant: *plexiglass* and *paris*. However, *paris* provided in the weighted case not only directly recalls one of the user's tags but also captures something of the uniqueness of this particular image that distinguishes it from other images of glass and steel structures; *i.e.*, it is a picture of the Louvre in Paris, France. Figure 1b demonstrates what we have found to be the most common case, particularly when the tags are numerous and varied: the averaged document vector bares little resemblance to what the user's set of tags attempts to convey, while the weighted case again recalls one of the provided tags.[1] Finally, in the best case (Figure 1c), both document vectors agree. Nonetheless, in terms of cosine distance, the weighted document vector is *more* similiar to the most similar word than in the simple averaged case.

3.2.2 Denoising User-generated Tags. While weighting the tags by relevance can aid the textual representation of clean, expert labels, estimating the probability that a tag is relevant is unquestionably necessary in the presence of noisy, user-generated tags. In this setting, user tags are both sparse and noisy. Furthermore, each user can be assumed to use tags in different ways and for their own ends. Once extremely infrequent tags are discarded, some sets of user tags are on a level with the preprocessed expert tags, clean and representative of the image content. Other types of users employ tags to keep track of their own life events or to participate in the social apsect of the sites on which they are posted. For example, many of the NUS-WIDE images with the highest tag counts are labelled with (nearly) every geographical tag in the dataset, presumably to attract other users interested in, say, travel, certainly not to assert that each of these diverse locations is pertinent to the image content. As such, an essential preprocessing step is to downplay the significance of some tags and boost others. Uricchio et al. [27] propose cleaning the tag vector by taking the available visual information as ground truth, transforming the tag vector for a given image into one composed by aggregating the tags from its nearest neighbors in the visual space, defined by the visual kernel K^V (computed in (1)). However, finding the nearest neighbors of each of tens of thousands of images incurs a large computational cost that must be repeated for each dataset in turn. Instead, we propose to utilize the many readily-available precomputed word vectors to infer which labels in a given tag set are more or less relevant.

Our goal is to obtain a denoised tag feature-vector $\hat{\phi}^T(I_i) = [\hat{w}_{i,1}, \cdots, \hat{w}_{i,D}]$ with which we can compute the textual kernel K^T. Our intuition is that many tags describe similar things (animals, colors, places, materials, etc.). Consequently, if we perform clustering of the tags in the word embedding space, we can use the cluster information and the relative distance of each tag from its cluster centroid to infer its relevance.

To this end, we use agglomerative hierarchical clustering [25] to induce clusters of the tag embeddings. Beginning with the binary indicator representation of each tag vector $\phi^T(I_i) = [w_1^i, \cdots, w_D^i]$, where w_k is 0 or 1 if the image I_i has been annotated with the corresponding tag t_k, we use the linear kernel defined above to construct a $D \times D$ connectivity matrix; *i.e.*, two tags are considered neighbors proportional to the frequency they co-occur. We then employ the average linkage algorithm using cosine distance as the metric to learn a set of clusters $[C_1, \cdots, C_C]$ with corresponding centroids $[c_1, \cdots, c_C]$.[2] Then, we construct binary cluster indicator

[1] Frequently, when the English language word vectors were trained on Unicode data, we also note that the document vectors for samples with large numbers of tags seem to settle on a select few Chinese characters, typically in our experience either 凹 or 鍾

[2] We found setting C equal to 5% the number of tags to give good results (*i.e.*, few singleton clusters).

(a) User tags: light, paris, sun, louvre, evening, silhouettes, glass, steel, france, geometry, pyramid
Most similar (average): plexiglass (0.63)
Most similar (weighted): paris (0.65)

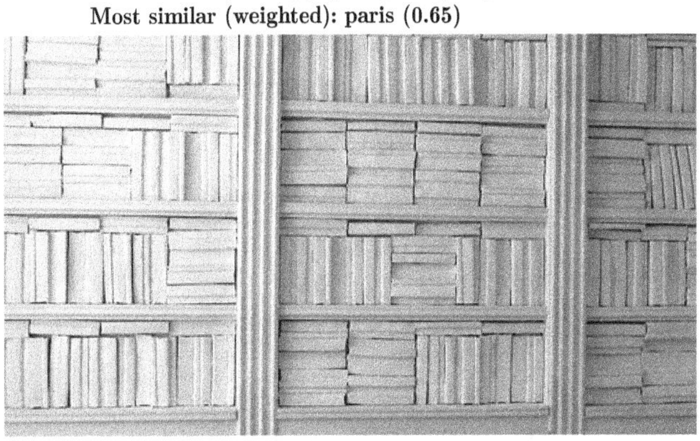

(b) User tags: shelf, book, pattern, white, ukraine
Most similar (average): 凹 (0.63)
Most similar (weighted): shelf (0.82)

(c) User tags: harbour, ocean, sea, oceans, atlantic, boat, boats, canada, newfoundland, north, history, fishing, rural, orca
Most similar (average): ocean (0.73)
Most similar (weighted): ocean (0.84)

Figure 1: Examples of images from the NUS-WIDE training set and their user tags. We show the most similar word to the simple average and weighted average of the tag word vectors, along with their respective cosine distances.

vectors $\phi^T_{C_i} = [w_1, \cdots, w_D]$, where w_k is given by

$$w_k = \begin{cases} \exp\left(\frac{-d(\zeta(t_k), c_i)}{\sigma}\right) & \text{if } t_k \in C_i \\ 0 & \text{if } t_k \notin C_i \end{cases} \tag{6}$$

where $d(x, y)$ is the Euclidean distance and σ is the mean distance to the centroid across all clusters. Finally, the cleaned tag vector $\hat{\phi}^T(I_i)$ is given by

$$\hat{\phi}^T(I_i) = \sum_{k=1}^{C} \left[(\phi^T(I_i) \otimes \phi^T_{C_k}) \frac{|\phi^T(I_i)|_{C_k}}{|C_k|} \right], \tag{7}$$

where $\otimes$ denotes element-wise product and $|\phi^T(I_i)|_{C_k}$ denotes the number of tags from cluster k with which image I_i was annotated. By normalizing each $\hat{\phi}^T$ to sum to 1, we can treat this new tag vector as a vector of probablities that a particular tag is relevant to the image content, based on the surrounding tags, repetition of similar words, etc. To compare two such vectors, we can use the exp-χ^2 kernel:

$$K^T(\hat{\phi}^T(I_i), \hat{\phi}^T(I_j)) = \exp\left(-\frac{1}{2C} \sum_{k=1}^{D} \frac{(\hat{w}_{i,k} - \hat{w}_{j,k})^2}{(\hat{w}_{i,k} + \hat{w}_{j,k})} \right) \tag{8}$$

where C is the mean of the χ^2 distances.

Importantly, these new weights also allow us to introduce the new word2vec-based kernel discussed above, where now we weight the average of the word vectors by the probablities we have derived above:

$$\phi^T(I_i) = \sum_{k=1}^{D} \hat{w}^i_k \cdot \zeta(t_k), \tag{9}$$

again, followed by a linear kernel

$$K^T(\phi^T(I_i), \phi^T(I_j)) = \phi^T(I_i)\phi^T(I_j)^\intercal. \tag{10}$$

3.3 KCCA

Given two data views, such as the ones provided by visual and textual features, our next task is to learn a multimodal space with which we can exploit the combined semantic properties of each set of features. First, we briefly describe CCA and then use our kernels defined above to implement the KCCA algorithm. CCA seeks to use the paired data views to find projections from each feature space into a shared semantic space by maximizing the correlation between the projected representations.

Formally, given N training pairs of visual and textual features $\{(\phi^V(I_1), \phi^T(I_1)), \ldots, (\phi^V(I_N), \phi^T(I_N))\}$, the CCA algorithm finds directions z^*_V and z^*_T that maximize the correlation of the projections of ϕ^V and ϕ^T onto z^*_V and z^*_T, respectively. This is expressed as:

$$\begin{aligned} z^*_V, z^*_T &= \underset{z_V, z_T}{\arg\max} \frac{\mathrm{E}[\langle \phi^V, z_V \rangle \langle \phi^T, z_T \rangle]}{\sqrt{\mathrm{E}[\langle \phi^V, z_V \rangle^2] \mathrm{E}[\langle \phi^T, z_T \rangle^2]}} \\ &= \underset{z_V, z_T}{\arg\max} \frac{z_V^\intercal C_{vt} z_T}{\sqrt{z_V^\intercal C_{vv} z_V z_T^\intercal C_{tt} z_T}} \end{aligned} \tag{11}$$

with the empircal expectation denoted by E[·] and where C_{vv} and C_{tt} respectively denote the covariance matrices for ϕ^V and ϕ^T, and C_{vt} denotes the between-sets covariance matrix.

By default, however, the CCA algorithm can only model linear relationships. As a result, KCCA was introduced to exploit the kernel trick to allow projecting the data into a higher-dimensional feature space [12]. Thus, the problem becomes finding values of z^*_V and z^*_T that lie in the span of the N training instances $\phi^V(I_i)$ and $\phi^T(I_i)$:

$$z^*_V = \sum_{i=1}^{N} \alpha_i \phi^V(I_i), \qquad z^*_T = \sum_{i=1}^{N} \beta_i \phi^T(I_i). \tag{12}$$

The objective of KCCA is to identify the weights $\alpha, \beta \in \mathbb{R}^N$ that maximize:

$$\alpha^*, \beta^* = \arg\max_{\alpha,\beta} \frac{\alpha^\intercal K^V K^T \beta}{\sqrt{\alpha^\intercal (K^V)^2 \alpha \beta^\intercal (K^T)^2 \beta}} \tag{13}$$

where K^V and K^T are the $N \times N$ kernel matrices over a sample of N visual-textual pairs. As shown by Hardoon et al. [12], regularization should be used during learning to avoid trivial solutions. Hence, the norms of the projection vectors are penalized by the term $\kappa \in [0, 1]$, and we obtain the generalized eigenvalue problem:

$$(K^V + \kappa I)^{-1} K^T (K^T + \kappa I)^{-1} K^V \alpha = \lambda^2 \alpha. \tag{14}$$

The top M eigenvectors of this problem yield bases $A = [\alpha_1 \ldots \alpha_M]$ and $B = [\beta_1 \ldots \beta_M]$ that we can use to project the training and test kernels into the semantic space. The corresponding eigenvalue r_j of each pair (α_j, β_j) measures the correlation between projected input pairs, with higher r_j meaning higher correlation. Consequently, it helps to give more weight to the dimensions with higher energy. As a result, the final features can be obtained by

$$\psi(I) = (K^V A) R \tag{15}$$

where $R = \text{diag}([r_1, \ldots, r_M])$. Because ψ only depends on the visual kernel K^V, projecting new test images requires only visual features, which makes this approach suitable for automatic image annotation.

3.4 Transfer in the Semantic Space

Because the canonical correlations are learned jointy from the spaces of the visual and textual kernels described above, the space into which the images are projected by (15) forces similar images to have similar features. As a result, the neighborhood around each image contains similar images whose embeddings have been informed by both their visual and textual data. Thus, given an unlabeled test image, we are able to automatically annotate it by projecting it into the shared semantic space and transfering known labels from the other images in its neighborhood.

Following the introduction of four nearest-neighbor voting algorithms by Uricchio et al. [27], we choose the most straightforward, dubbed "NNvot," to use in the semantic space to automatically annotate images. While those authors exhaustively cover a variety of voting algorithms and their respective relevance functions [18], simple nearest-neighbor voting was found to work well in most scenarios, so we focus our experiments there.

Given an image and a vocabulary of labels, we perform automatic image annotation by projecting the test image onto the semantic space and then identifying its K nearest-neighbors. Here we rank the vocabulary labels according to the their frequency in the set of retrieved neighbors. The relevance function f for an image-tag pair (I, t) is defined as:

$$f(I, t) := k_t \tag{16}$$

where k_t is the number of images labeled as t in the K neighborhood of I.

Dataset	Images	Labels	Tags
IAPR-TC12	19,627	291	–
ESP-GAME	20,770	268	–
MIRFlickr-25k	25,000	18	1,386
NUS-WIDE	269,648	81	5,018

Table 1: Summary of statistics for our datasets. For clarity, "labels" refers to annotations generated by experts and "tags" refers to user-generated annotations.

4 EXPERIMENTS

4.1 Datasets

IAPR-TC12. The IAPR-TC12 dataset [9] was first introduced for the task of multilingual information retrieval. The dataset contains 19,627 images made up of natural scenes, including depictions of people, sporting events, animals, cities, etc. We use the same setting as previous work [10], with 17,664 training images and 1,962 test images. Out of 291 possible labels, each image is annotated with 5.7 labels on average.

ESP-GAME. Unlike the other datasets here, which derived in part from user labels on online images, the ESP-GAME dataset [1] was collected using a computer game in which two players would jointly describe images and earn points when they agreed on the annotation. This encouraged the players to provide visually-meaningful descriptions. Again using the same splits as described in previous works [10], we use 18,689 training images and 2,081 test images. Each image has 4.68 annotations on average, drawn from 268 possible labels.

NUS-WIDE. The NUS-WIDE dataset [4] contains 269,648 images released with tags at three levels of granularity and six different types of low-level image features. The dataset contains 5,018 unique tags provided by the original users. The images are also manually annotated with an additional 81 ground-truth "concepts" (of which there is some overlap with the set of user-generated tags). URLs are also provided to retrieve the raw image data from Flickr. Since the dataset was released, many images have been taken down by the user or are no longer available; therefore, our dataset (in keeping with contemporary literature) contains 127,302 images in the training set and 85,137 in the test set. On average, each image has 1.76 concept labels and 5.97 user labels.

MIRFlickr-25k. The MIRFLICKR-25k open evaluation project [14] comprises 25,000 images retrieved from Flickr through its public API paired with manual annotations of 18 different labels. The original user tags are also available, of which 1,386 occur in at least 20 images. These are the same labels utilized elsewhere in the literature [29]. Because they are drawn from the same source, the tags annotate similar concepts as NUS-WIDE, though the images and labels have been selected by the dataset's creators to promote "interestingness." Each image contains approximately 2.78 expert labels and 8.94 user tags.

4.2 Implementation Details

To increase the computational efficiency of the model, particularly in the presence of larger datasets like NUS-WIDE, we approximate the Gram matrices for the KCCA algorithm using the Partial Gram-Schmidt Orthogonalization (PGSO) algorithm provided by Hardoon et al. [12]. Across all of our experiments, we fix the KCCA regularization parameter (see (14)) $\kappa = 0.5$. Rather than stopping PGSO at a certain value of the norm, we instead fix the dimensionality of the semantic space (*i.e.*, the dimensionality of $\psi(I)$ in (15)) to 4,096.

Because we wished to make use of publicly-available word vectors, the dimensionality of all word embeddings (*e.g.*, $\hat{\phi}^T(I_i)$ in (7)) is fixed to 300. The embeddings were trained on the English Wikipedia using fastText [2].[3] We found no noticable difference between these vectors and those trained on similar data with word2vec [19], although the subword-level vectors avoided any instances where the tags were outside of the original vocabulary.

Information about the various baselines can be found in their respective references.

4.3 Experiment 1: Performance on Denoised User Tags

Our results for denoising user-generated tags are shown in Table 2. On the MIRFlickr dataset, with only 1400 tags, our model outperforms the state-of-the-art in all measures; however, we see that using our weights as a probability over the tags with the exp-χ^2 kernel gave better recall than taking the weighted average of continuous word vectors. In terms of precision, our weighted averaging outperforms all other methods. In Figure 2, we provide some examples drawn from MIRFlickr-25k. The first two columns give an original image from the test set and its corresponding ground truth user tags. We then project the image into the semantic space learned via KCCA using (15) and retrieve its nearest two image neighbors and nearest five tag neighbors learned using the two different word vector pooling methods as described above: average pooling and our weighted average technique.

[3]Pre-trained vectors are available from https://github.com/facebookresearch/fastText/blob/master/pretrained-vectors.md

Method	MAP	P@5	R@5
TagProp [29]	38.4	-	-
FisherBoxes [28]	54.8	-	-
Nearest Neighbors Voting [27]	59.3	34.2	37.1
Uricchio et al.(exp(χ^2)) [27]	60.6	35.4	68.8
Ours (exp(χ^2))	61.2	34.9	**70.1**
Ours (Weighted Average)	**62.3**	**35.8**	69.5

(a) MIRFlickr-25k

Method	MAP	P@5	R@5
FisherBoxes [28]	39.7	-	-
Nearest Neighbors Voting [27]	43.1	30.1	46.3
Uricchio et al. (exp(χ^2)) [27]	43.7	**36.3**	48.0
Ours (exp(χ^2))	44.0	33.8	**48.4**
Ours (Weighted Average)	**44.3**	34.3	47.4

(b) NUS-WIDE

Table 2: Results on user-generated tags from MIRFlickr-25k and NUS-WIDE. When relevant, kernels used for KCCA are given in parentheses.

In the first three rows, we can see that the ability of the model to retrieve similar images given an input image is very strong. In particular, in the first and third examples, the model retrieved images with the exact same subject matter, and, while the breeds of dog in the second examples may differ between the original image and its neighbors, they are still similar in appearance. Between the fourth and fifth columns, we can especially see the power of weighting the average of the continous word vectors. When the tags are specific or all centered around a single topic, such as graffiti, art, and urban areas in the first example, both methods return roughly the same tags, in similar orders. For instance, we see both models learn that *graffiti* is more relevant than the more general *art* for the first image. The other examples, though, demonstrate the polluting effect color word embeddings seem to have on the pooled representations. In the second example, where the image depicts a red standard poodle, our model chooses *dog* and *dogs* as the most relevant tags; however, it also manages to retrieve both *poodle* and the highly-specific *standardpoodle.* However, when the tag vectors are just averaged, the color word quickly overwhelms the model: the *dog* is returned due to visual similarity, but the model is also semantically close to images labelled with many other colors (*green* and *blue*). The third example is similar but more subtle: both models retrieve not only the art form but also the technique (*crochet* and *amigurimi*, respectively). Nevertheless, in the pooling example, *explored* appears, which is simply a frequently-occurring but irrelevant tag. Though not included in the ground truth, our model also manages to recall *etsy*, indicative of many such images being posted on the popular online storefront.[4]

[4]www.etsy.com

Image	User Tags	Nearest Images		Weighted Average	Pooling
	art graffiti losangeles msk awr			**graffiti** **art** sanfrancisco **msk** **losangeles**	**graffiti** **art** sanfrancisco **losangeles** **msk**
	red dog poodle standard standardpoodle			**dog** dogs **poodle** **standard** **standardpoodle**	**dog** explore **red** green blue
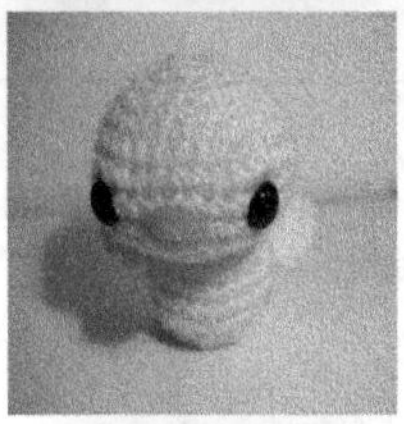	yellow bird handmade crochet amigurimi			**amigurimi** **crochet** toy **handmade** etsy	**amigurimi** **crochet** macro explored toy
	green pink home studio owl			cup vintage retro coffee **home**	sky sunset explore silhouette clouds

Figure 2: Examples from the MIRFlickr-25k test set with tags transferred in the semantic space using two different pooling methods before a linear text kernel: simple average of word vectors followed by a linear kernel and weighted average of word vectors. Correctly recalled tags are shown in bold.

The last row of Figure 2 represents an error case. The original tags themselves are rather non-descript and vague as to the particular content of the image. For denoising, our model weights *pink* and *green* the same, followed by *home*. From the visual neighbors, it appears that the hat boxes in the picture with some forms of glassware sitting on tables, thus *cup* and *coffee*, while the particular tones of green and pink in the image are reminiscent of other images tagged *vintage* or *retro*. Despite the poor performance of our model, in the average pooling case, the tag retrieval is even worse, again exhibiting the combined effect of vastly differing tags polluting the pooled representation and label transfer misrepresenting the original image.

4.4 Experiment 2: "Denoising" Expert Tags

We also performed experiments to use our technique to weight the average of document vectors of tag sets with no assumption of noisiness. These labels were provided manually by experts; therefore, every label should be relevant to the image. However, as we have shown, there are many instances where simply pooling the label word embeddings distorts the overall representation, particularly when an image depicts more than one distinct object.

	MIRFlickr-25k			NUS-Wide		
	MAP	**P@5**	**R@5**	**MAP**	**P@5**	**R@5**
Baselines [27]						
Nearest Neighbors	69.9	44.7	69.2	49.3	39.6	44.0
TagProp	70.8	45.5	70.1	50.9	41.3	44.6
SVM	72.7	38.8	72.4	50.2	34.6	**60.6**
Uricchio et al. [27]						
Linear Kernel	72.9	46.1	73.1	51.7	40.2	50.5
Average Pooling	72.3	46.9	**73.4**	50.6	**40.8**	50.1
Ours						
Weighted Average	**73.0**	**47.1**	72.8	**52.2**	40.4	51.9

Table 3: Results on *expert* tags for MIRFlickr-25k and NUS-WIDE.

	IAPR-TC12			ESP-GAME		
Method	**MAP**	**P@5**	**R@5**	**MAP**	**P@5**	**R@5**
Baselines [27]						
Nearest Neighbors	36	39	29	28	31	28
TagProp	38	40	32	32	34	32
2PKNN	41	41	39	36	43	36
Uricchio et al. [27]						
Linear Kernel	**43**	49	**38**	**39**	45	**39**
Ours						
Weighted Average	42	**50**	**38**	37	**47**	38

Table 4: Results on ESP-GAME and IAPR

We first give results for expert tags on same images tested with user-generated tags in Section 4.3, shown in Table 3. The trend of these results on MIRFlickr-25k is consistent with our early experiment: our model outperforms the state-of-the-art in terms of precision but falls slightly behind in recall. On NUS-WIDE, our model performs favorably against the state-of-the-art in terms of precision; however, it also fails to outperform the performance of the SVM baseline introduced in Uricchio et al. [27].

Next, we also demonstrate the performance of our model on IAPR-TC12 and ESP-GAME. These datasets contain many more possible labels than either MIRFlickr-25k or NUS-WIDE; however, both sets of images were manually annotated with the intention of describing the image, so despite their sparsity, there is still an expectation that the labels are of a high quality. We show our results in Table 4. As is to be expected, the scores are relatively lower than those provided for the less sparse datasets above. On IAPR-TC12, we outperform the currently state-of-the-art in terms of both Precision@5 and Recall@5 (Uricchio et al. [27] did not apply their method with a simple average pooling over the label words, so we compare our model against their best results). On ESP-GAME, however, our model fails to outperform the state-of-the-art in anything but Precision@5. We speculate that this is because the labellers of ESP-GAME were discouraged from providing more common or obvious labels which our model may have been able to make better use of to determine the appropriate weights for the word embeddings.

5 CONCLUSION AND FUTURE WORK

In this work, we have introduced a new technique for denoising user-generated tags in image datasets and shown its effectiveness not only in learning semantic spaces for label transfer from such noisy labels but also in enhancing representations of already-clean expert labels. For future work, we are particularly interested in incorporating additional data views to contribute to the learning of the semantic space. Previous works have addressed the limited expressiveness of CCA by utilizing more than two views of the data, such as including categories alongside the image and tag data [8]. We feel that such approaches could be extended to the kernel-based scenario as used here to further increase the expressivity of the model. Furthermore, many large, professionally-released image datasets now include both user tags and expert labels, just as with NUS-WIDE and MIRFlickr-25k. Potential future work could seek to exploit this predefined correspondence between expert labels and user tags to assist in the denoising process, with the expert labels acting similarly to the clustering used here. However, text in the form of labels, tags, or captions is not the only other possible view of the data to use alongside the visual. Many images such as those drawn from Flickr or Instagram contain several other modalities of data such as GPS and Exif data that could also be exploited either to denoise the tag metadata or to enhance the learned semantic represention of the images and text. Given proper encodings of this type of metadata, future work in this area could utilize newer canonical correlation methods such as generalized CCA or KGCCA [26] to accumulate an arbitrary number of views on the data as part of constructing the underlying semantic space.

REFERENCES

[1] Luis von Ahn and Laura Dabbish. 2004. Labeling images with a computer game. In *Proceedings of the 2004 Conference on Human Factors in Computing Systems, CHI 2004, Vienna, Austria, April 24 - 29, 2004*, 319–326. DOI: 10.1145/985692.985733. http://doi.acm.org/10.1145/985692.985733.

[2] Piotr Bojanowski, Edouard Grave, Armand Joulin, and Tomas Mikolov. 2017. Enriching word vectors with subword information. *TACL*, 5, 135–146. https://transacl.org/ojs/index.php/tacl/article/view/999.

[3] Youngmin Cho and Lawrence K. Saul. 2009. Kernel methods for deep learning. In *Advances in Neural Information Processing Systems 22: 23rd Annual Conference on Neural Information Processing Systems 2009. Proceedings of a meeting held 7-10 December 2009, Vancouver, British Columbia, Canada*. 342–350. http://papers.nips.cc/paper/3628-kernel-methods-for-deep-learning.

[4] Tat-Seng Chua, Jinhui Tang, Richang Hong, Haojie Li, Zhiping Luo, and Yantao Zheng. 2009. NUS-WIDE: a real-world web image database from national university of singapore. In *Proceedings of the 8th ACM International Conference on Image and Video Retrieval, CIVR 2009, Santorini Island, Greece, July 8-10, 2009*. DOI: 10.1145/1646396.1646452. http://doi.acm.org/10.1145/1646396.1646452.

[5] Jia Deng, Wei Dong, Richard Socher, Li-Jia Li, Kai Li, and Fei-Fei Li. 2009. Imagenet: A large-scale hierarchical image database. In *2009 IEEE Computer Society Conference on Computer Vision and Pattern Recognition (CVPR 2009), 20-25 June 2009, Miami, Florida, USA*, 248–255. DOI: 10.1109/CVPRW.2009.5206848. https://doi.org/10.1109/CVPRW.2009.5206848.

[6] Andrea Frome, Gregory S. Corrado, Jonathon Shlens, Samy Bengio, Jeffrey Dean, Marc'Aurelio Ranzato, and Tomas Mikolov. 2013. Devise: A deep visual-semantic embedding model. In *Advances in Neural Information Processing Systems 26: 27th Annual Conference on Neural Information Processing Systems 2013. Proceedings of a meeting held December 5-8, 2013, Lake Tahoe, Nevada, United States*. 2121–2129. http://papers.nips.cc/paper/5204-devise-a-deep-visual-semantic-embedding-model.

[7] Ross B. Girshick, Jeff Donahue, Trevor Darrell, and Jitendra Malik. 2014. Rich feature hierarchies for accurate object detection and semantic segmentation. In *2014 IEEE Conference on Computer Vision and Pattern Recognition, CVPR 2014, Columbus, OH, USA, June 23-28, 2014*, 580–587. DOI: 10.1109/CVPR.2014.81. https://doi.org/10.1109/CVPR.2014.81.

[8] Yunchao Gong, Qifa Ke, Michael Isard, and Svetlana Lazebnik. 2014. A multi-view embedding space for modeling internet images, tags, and their semantics. *International Journal of*

Computer Vision, 106, 2, 210–233. DOI: 10.1007/s11263-013-0658-4. https://doi.org/10.1007/s11263-013-0658-4.

[9] Michael Grubinger, Paul Clough, Henning Müller, and Thomas Deselaers. 2006. The iapr tc-12 benchmark: a new evaluation resource for visual information systems. In *International workshop ontoImage*. Vol. 5, 10.

[10] Matthieu Guillaumin, Thomas Mensink, Jakob J. Verbeek, and Cordelia Schmid. 2009. Tagprop: discriminative metric learning in nearest neighbor models for image auto-annotation. In *IEEE 12th International Conference on Computer Vision, ICCV 2009, Kyoto, Japan, September 27 - October 4, 2009*, 309–316. DOI: 10.1109/ICCV.2009.5459266. https://doi.org/10.1109/ICCV.2009.5459266.

[11] AmirHossein Habibian, Thomas Mensink, and Cees G. M. Snoek. 2015. Discovering semantic vocabularies for cross-media retrieval. In *Proceedings of the 5th ACM on International Conference on Multimedia Retrieval, Shanghai, China, June 23-26, 2015*, 131–138. DOI: 10.1145/2671188.2749403. http://doi.acm.org/10.1145/2671188.2749403.

[12] David R. Hardoon, Sándor Szedmák, and John Shawe-Taylor. 2004. Canonical correlation analysis: an overview with application to learning methods. *Neural Computation*, 16, 12, 2639–2664. DOI: 10.1162/0899766042321814. https://doi.org/10.1162/0899766042321814.

[13] Hexiang Hu, Guang-Tong Zhou, Zhiwei Deng, Zicheng Liao, and Greg Mori. 2016. Learning structured inference neural networks with label relations. In *2016 IEEE Conference on Computer Vision and Pattern Recognition, CVPR 2016, Las Vegas, NV, USA, June 27-30, 2016*, 2960–2968. DOI: 10.1109/CVPR.2016.323. https://doi.org/10.1109/CVPR.2016.323.

[14] Mark J. Huiskes and Michael S. Lew. 2008. The MIR flickr retrieval evaluation. In *Proceedings of the 1st ACM SIGMM International Conference on Multimedia Information Retrieval, MIR 2008, Vancouver, British Columbia, Canada, October 30-31, 2008*, 39–43. DOI: 10.1145/1460096.1460104. http://doi.acm.org/10.1145/1460096.1460104.

[15] Jiren Jin and Hideki Nakayama. 2016. Annotation order matters: recurrent image annotator for arbitrary length image tagging. In *23rd International Conference on Pattern Recognition, ICPR 2016, Cancún, Mexico, December 4-8, 2016*, 2452–2457. DOI: 10.1109/ICPR.2016.7900004. https://doi.org/10.1109/ICPR.2016.7900004.

[16] Alex Krizhevsky, Ilya Sutskever, and Geoffrey E. Hinton. 2012. Imagenet classification with deep convolutional neural networks. In *Advances in Neural Information Processing Systems 25: 26th Annual Conference on Neural Information Processing Systems 2012. Proceedings of a meeting held December 3-6, 2012, Lake Tahoe, Nevada, United States.* 1106–1114. http://papers.nips.cc/paper/4824-imagenet-classification-with-deep-convolutional-neural-networks.

[17] Guy Lev, Benjamin Klein, and Lior Wolf. 2015. In defense of word embedding for generic text representation. In *Natural Language Processing and Information Systems - 20th International Conference on Applications of Natural Language to Information Systems, NLDB 2015 Passau, Germany, June 17-19, 2015 Proceedings*, 35–50. DOI: 10.1007/978-3-319-19581-0_3. https://doi.org/10.1007/978-3-319-19581-0_3.

[18] Xirong Li, Tiberio Uricchio, Lamberto Ballan, Marco Bertini, Cees G. M. Snoek, and Alberto Del Bimbo. 2016. Socializing the semantic gap: A comparative survey on image tag assignment, refinement, and retrieval. *ACM Comput. Surv.*, 49, 1, 14:1–14:39. DOI: 10.1145/2906152. http://doi.acm.org/10.1145/2906152.

[19] Tomas Mikolov, Ilya Sutskever, Kai Chen, Gregory S. Corrado, and Jeffrey Dean. 2013. Distributed representations of words and phrases and their compositionality. In *Advances in Neural Information Processing Systems 26: 27th Annual Conference on Neural Information Processing Systems 2013. Proceedings of a meeting held December 5-8, 2013, Lake Tahoe, Nevada, United States.* 3111–3119. http://papers.nips.cc/paper/5021-distributed-representations-of-words-and-phrases-and-their-compositionality.

[20] Tomas Mikolov, Wen-tau Yih, and Geoffrey Zweig. 2013. Linguistic regularities in continuous space word representations. In *Human Language Technologies: Conference of the North American Chapter of the Association of Computational Linguistics, Proceedings, June 9-14, 2013, Westin Peachtree Plaza Hotel, Atlanta, Georgia, USA*, 746–751. http://aclweb.org/anthology/N/N13/N13-1090.pdf.

[21] Venkatesh N. Murthy, Subhransu Maji, and R. Manmatha. 2015. Automatic image annotation using deep learning representations. In *Proceedings of the 5th ACM on International Conference on Multimedia Retrieval, Shanghai, China, June 23-26, 2015*, 603–606. DOI: 10.1145/2671188.2749391. http://doi.acm.org/10.1145/2671188.2749391.

[22] Karl Ni, Kyle Zaragoza, Charles Foster, Carmen Carrano, Barry Chen, Yonas Tesfaye, and Alex Gude. 2016. Sampled Image Tagging and Retrieval Methods on User Generated Content. arXiv: 1611.06962v3 [cs.CV].

[23] Nikhil Rasiwasia, Jose Costa Pereira, Emanuele Coviello, Gabriel Doyle, Gert R. G. Lanckriet, Roger Levy, and Nuno Vasconcelos. 2010. A new approach to cross-modal multimedia retrieval. In *Proceedings of the 18th International Conference on Multimedia 2010, Firenze, Italy, October 25-29, 2010*, 251–260. DOI: 10.1145/1873951.1873987. http://doi.acm.org/10.1145/1873951.1873987.

[24] Karen Simonyan and Andrew Zisserman. 2014. Very Deep Convolutional Networks for Large-Scale Image Recognition. arXiv: 1409.1556v6 [cs.CV].

[25] Robert R Sokal and Charles D Michener. 1958. A statistical method for evaluating systematic relationship. *University of Kansas science bulletin*, 28, 1409–1438.

[26] Arthur Tenenhaus, Cathy Philippe, and Vincent Frouin. 2015. Kernel generalized canonical correlation analysis. *Computational Statistics & Data Analysis*, 90, 114–131. DOI: 10.1016/j.csda.2015.04.004. https://doi.org/10.1016/j.csda.2015.04.004.

[27] Tiberio Uricchio, Lamberto Ballan, Lorenzo Seidenari, and Alberto Del Bimbo. 2017. Automatic image annotation via label transfer in the semantic space. *Pattern Recognition*, 71, 144–157. DOI: 10.1016/j.patcog.2017.05.019. https://doi.org/10.1016/j.patcog.2017.05.019.

[28] Tiberio Uricchio, Marco Bertini, Lorenzo Seidenari, and Alberto Del Bimbo. 2015. Fisher encoded convolutional bag-of-windows for efficient image retrieval and social image tagging. In *2015 IEEE International Conference on Computer Vision Workshop, ICCV Workshops 2015, Santiago, Chile, December 7-13, 2015*, 1020–1026. DOI: 10.1109/ICCVW.2015.134. https://doi.org/10.1109/ICCVW.2015.134.

[29] Jakob J. Verbeek, Matthieu Guillaumin, Thomas Mensink, and Cordelia Schmid. 2010. Image annotation with tagprop on the MIRFLICKR set. In *Proceedings of the 11th ACM SIGMM International Conference on Multimedia Information Retrieval, MIR 2010, Philadelphia, Pennsylvania, USA, March 29-31, 2010*, 537–546. DOI: 10.1145/1743384.1743476. http://doi.acm.org/10.1145/1743384.1743476.

[30] Jiang Wang, Yi Yang, Junhua Mao, Zhiheng Huang, Chang Huang, and Wei Xu. 2016. CNN-RNN: A unified framework for multi-label image classification. In *2016 IEEE Conference on Computer Vision and Pattern Recognition, CVPR 2016, Las Vegas, NV, USA, June 27-30, 2016*, 2285–2294. DOI: 10.1109/CVPR.2016.251. https://doi.org/10.1109/CVPR.2016.251.

[31] Jason Weston, Samy Bengio, and Nicolas Usunier. 2011. WSABIE: scaling up to large vocabulary image annotation. In *IJCAI 2011, Proceedings of the 22nd International Joint Conference on Artificial Intelligence, Barcelona, Catalonia, Spain, July 16-22, 2011*, 2764–2770. DOI: 10.5591/978-1-57735-516-8/IJCAI11-460. https://doi.org/10.5591/978-1-57735-516-8/IJCAI11-460.

[32] Jun Yu, Xiaokang Yang, Fei Gao, and Dacheng Tao. 2017. Deep multimodal distance metric learning using click constraints for image ranking. *IEEE Trans. Cybernetics*, 47, 12, 4014–4024. DOI: 10.1109/TCYB.2016.2591583. https://doi.org/10.1109/TCYB.2016.2591583.

Multi-label Triplet Embeddings for Image Annotation from User-Generated Tags

Zachary Seymour
SUNY Binghamton
Binghamton, New York
zseymou1@binghamton.edu

Zhongfei (Mark) Zhang
SUNY Binghamton
Binghamton, New York
zhongfei@cs.binghamton.edu

ABSTRACT

This work studies the representational embedding of images and their corresponding annotations–in the form of tag metadata–such that, given a piece of the raw data in one modality, the corresponding semantic description can be retrieved in terms of the raw data in another. While convolutional neural networks (CNNs) have been widely and successfully applied in this domain with regards to detecting semantically simple scenes or categories (even though many such objects may be simultaneously present in an image), this work approaches the task of dealing with image annotations in the context of noisy, user-generated, and semantically complex multi-labels, widely available from social media sites. In this case, the labels for an image are diverse, noisy, and often not specifically related to an object, but rather descriptive or user-specific. Furthermore, the existing deep image annotation literature using this type of data typically utilizes the so-called CNN-RNN framework, combining convolutional and recurrent neural networks. We offer a discussion of why RNNs may not be the best choice in this case, though they have been shown to perform well on the similar captioning tasks. Our model exploits the latent image-text space through the use of a triplet loss framework to learn a joint embedding space for the images and their tags, in the presence of multiple, potentially positive exemplar classes. We present state-of-the-art results of the representational properties of these embeddings on several image annotation datasets to show the promise of this approach.

CCS CONCEPTS

• **Computing methodologies** → **Neural networks**; *Object recognition*; Ranking; • **Information systems** → *Multimedia and multimodal retrieval*;

KEYWORDS

Triplet embeddings, image annotation, convolutional neural networks

ACM Reference Format:

Zachary Seymour and Zhongfei (Mark) Zhang. 2018. Multi-label Triplet Embeddings for Image Annotation from User-Generated Tags. In *ICMR '18: 2018 International Conference on Multimedia Retrieval, June 11–14, 2018, Yokohama, Japan.* ACM, New York, NY, USA, 8 pages. https://doi.org/10.1145/3206025.3206061

ICMR '18, June 11–14, 2018, Yokohama, Japan

ACM ISBN 978-1-4503-5046-4/18/06...$15.00
https://doi.org/10.1145/3206025.3206061

1 INTRODUCTION

In recent years, architectures based on deep convolutional neural networks (CNNs) have shown remarkable and consistently improving performance on image classification and single object detection. Models variously combining CNNs with a recurrent neural network have also been shown to be highly performant in terms of generating sentence-level captions and describing the relationships between detected objects in an image. In all of these cases, the labels or captions that supervise the training of such models are relatively clean and chosen to be particularly descriptive of the content in the images. However, outside of such manually-annotated data, the popularity of social media, particularly on picture-oriented social networks such as Flickr, Instagram, and Pinterest, has produced an abundance of user-generated image labels. These annotations differ from those typically used in a labeling scenario, in that they are typically multiple and noisy for semantically complex scenes (see Figure 1). Here we refer to semantically simple scenes as those that are clearly present and can be directly named in an image such as flowers, vehicles, and buildings, and refer to semantically complex scenes as those that are not clearly present or that must be inferred from an image, such as the nature of the depicted event (football game, baseball game, or concert), its location, or the weather. Since these labels are directly provided by users of the platform, the labels can be assumed to be representative of how a human thinks that the image should be categorized. Certainly, these labels often represent the types of objects or scenes that might be detected by traditional single- or multi-label setups (e.g., *deer, shoes, wood*); however, we also find labels that are descriptive of attributes of the scene but not any specific content, such as a location (*colorado*) or the nature of an event (*vacation*). On a platform like Instagram, where in large part the tags–rather than the images–mitigate the social interactions of the network, the labels have assumed a life of their own, providing a structure to the network external to any particular content of the images associated with them (consider, for example, the popularity of *#tbt*).

We take as a motivating example the image depicted in Figure 2. Combining the visual information with that included in the tags, one can infer that the image depicts a crowd at a relief concert in Wales, on the field of an indoor sports stadium; *concert* is the defining activity occurring in the image, whereas all of the other tags provide additional details or context. However, there is very little visual information to distinguish between a concert and other events that might occur in a *stadium*, namely the stage occupies a very small portion of the image (and appears at an odd

china, politics, world, sport, shoes, running, track — *bravo, wow, baby, deer, colorado, fawn* — *travel, colors, asia, vacation, wood, vietnam*

Figure 1: We present three randomly selected images from the NUS-Wide training dataset along with their tags (drawn, in this case, from the provided set of 1,000 tags).

crowd, concert, wales, relief, stadium

Figure 2: A challenging example from the NUS-WIDE training set.

angle) and the alternate color of the pitch and crowd of people are not easily distinguishable at the resolutions typically handled by CNNs. Furthermore, the tags *concert*, *wales*, and *relief* are ranked (in the ground truth) more highly than *stadium*, arguably the largest visually-distinguishable object in the image, while *relief* can only be understood in context with *concert*. Also, the tag *wales* has no correlation with either the rest of the tags or the image (or, in fact, with most of the other Welsh images). Recently, work from within Flickr [1] discusses models for dealing with this type of data as well, as they view it in-house. The authors note that before approaching these models, they manually review the top 10,000 tags from the site; of particular interest here is the fact that they remove the location-based tags, offloading prediction of these tags to a module that instead makes use of embedded GPS information. However, in the current state-of-the-art datasets, GPS or other such metadata is generally either unavailable or not available at a scale to be able to capture all such tags. As a result, our model must still attempt to handle this information via a combination of visual data and tag co-occurrence.

This scenario renders simply estimating the probability of one or more labels corresponding to an image difficult. We instead frame the problem as seeking to retrieve a set of relevant tags for a given image. Consequently, we reformulate the training scenario to directly optimize this problem by learning a structured, joint embedding space of images and tags rather than predicting the probability of the tags for a given image at each step. This allows each image to be clustered with its relevant tags on a low-dimensional manifold and allows for the bidirectional annotation of images with matching tags or of words with matching images.

The contribution of this work is two-fold:

(1) We present an end-to-end framework for modeling the semantic space of the image-tag pairs using a structured triplet loss, beginning with raw pixel data and text features.
(2) We introduce into the literature of triplet-loss-based models a technique for sampling triplets in the presence of multiple labels and thus handling ambiguity in selecting positive and negative exemplars.

2 RELATED WORK

Many of the capabilities of this model to extract semantically meaningful representations of images come from the development of deep CNN models [11] and the availability of large-scale image datasets, such as ImageNet [4]. Our work is synergistic with other recent work on multi-label classification using deep CNNs [7, 26]. It also lies within a family of work surrounding learning a joint embedding of images and labels. Both WSABIE [28, 5] and DeViSE [6] learn to rank the top k labels using the weight approximate-rank pairwise (WARP) loss. Also similar to this work, metric learning [12] learns a metric to discriminate the similarity between images and their labels. However, all of these methods fail to appropriately model label co-occurrences. More recent work in this area has sought to deal with the issues presented by user-generated tags. The "skip-image" model [17] modifies the skip-gram method [16] to model the label co-occurrences and more effectively deal with rare tags. Fast0Tag [29] approaches the problem from a zero shot scenario, aligning images along the principal directions in the tag space to predict unseen labels from those seen. However, the majority of contemporary models for image annotation combine convolutional and recurrent neural networks to iteratively predict appropriate tags given an image, following the CNN-RNN framework [26]. The RIA model [9] also takes the approach of combining a CNN and RNN to generate tags; however it attempts to directly model and predict the number of objects present in an image to generate an appropriate number of tags. As such, that model fails to appropriately account for non-object descriptive tags. The current state-of-the-art S-CNN-RNN model [14] introduces semantic regularization to the CNN-RNN training procedure by introducing side information in the form of more diverse tags. Our approach differs in that we seek to model the structure of that space directly, while preserving the ability of the model to recall more of the complex, non-visual tags.

Triplet loss has recently gained a greater popularity as it was successfully applied to facial recognition and clustering [20]. Our model builds upon the triplet sampling technique described there. While in Schroff et al. [20] each element of the triplet is generated from the output of a deep CNN, other work has treated the positive and negative exemplars as sequences and produced the embedding using an RNN [2]. As an example of using heterogeneous, visual-textual triplets, this model also draws inspiration from earlier such models [27]; however, we distinguish this work from the earlier

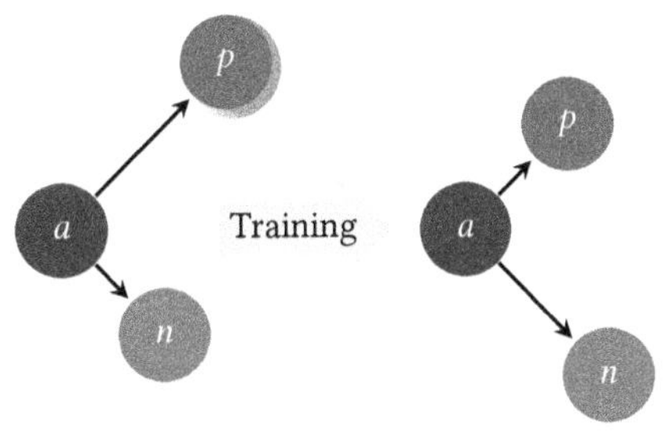

Figure 3: Training under the triplet loss minimizes the distance between the *anchor* and a *positive* example, while maximizing the distance between *anchor* and a *negative* example.

work in that our model shows the success of utilizing the triplet loss in an end-to-end framework, beginning with raw pixel and text data.

3 MODEL

Our model is composed of two branches: one CNN embeds images into a low-dimensional space to extract semantically useful representations and another CNN embeds sequences of labels into this space and models their dependencies.

The goal of the model is, given an image x and a sequence of tags $(y_1, y_2, \ldots, y_n)$, to produce embeddings $f_I(x)$ and $f_T(y_1, y_2, \ldots, y_n)$ in some latent feature space $\mathbb{R}^d$, such that the squared distance between an image and its relevant tags is small and, conversely, that the squared distance between an image and invalid tags is large.

3.1 Triplet Loss

More precisely, an embedding of x is represented by $f(x) \in \mathbb{R}^d$. Furthermore, this embedding is constrained to lie on the d-dimensional hypersphere, i.e., $\|f(x)\|_2 = 1$. Then, we intend to insure that the three embeddings, x_i^a, y_i^p, y_i^n (the *anchor*, *positive*, and *negative*, respectively), satisfy

$$\left\|f_I(x_i^a) - f_T(y_i^p)\right\|_2^2 + \alpha < \|f_I(x_i^a) - f_T(y_i^n)\|_2^2, \quad \forall (f_I(x_i^a), f_T(y_i^p), f_T(y_i^n)) \in \mathcal{T} \tag{1}$$

where f_I and f_T represent the respective embedding functions for the images and text, α is the enforced margin between the positive and negative label sequences, and $\mathcal{T}$ is the set of all possible triplets with $|\mathcal{T}| = N$. This process is illustrated in Figure 3.

Letting $d(x, y) = \|f_I(x) - f_T(y)\|_2^2$, the loss that is minimized, then, is

$$\mathcal{L}_{I \to T} = \sum_{i=1}^{N} \left[d(x_i^a, y_i^p) - d(x_i^a, y_i^n) + \alpha\right]_+ \tag{2}$$

3.2 Triplet Selection and the Importance of Annotation Order

Generating all such triplets not only contributes orders of magnitude more training data but also signficantly slows convergence during training, as the majority of the possibile triplets trivially fulfill the constraints of (1), so, for many iterations, the gradient updates performed are minimal. Proper selection of these triplets is discussed by Schroff et al. [20]; however, we note that for our model, because our data are drawn from two different modalities, the anchor-positive pairs do not need to be sampled and are inferred from the training data; that is, an image and its ground truth annotations form the initial anchor-positive pair. What remains is the online sampling of the negative exemplars from each mini-batch. We follow the protocol of Parkhi et al. [18], where rather than finding the maximally-offending example from each mini-batch (which is computationally expensive), we randomly sample one triplet that satisfies

$$\|f_I(x_i^a) - f_T(y_i^n)\|_2^2 - \left\|f_I(x_i^a) - f_T(y_i^p)\right\|_2^2 < \alpha, \tag{3}$$

i.e., the negative exemplar lies within the margin α. In this way, we only select "semi-hard" examples, those which violate the triplet criterion (but not necessarily those which maximally violate it). This speeds up both the training of the network and its convergence.

The idea of learning embeddings from triplet sampling is not new, even in the deep learning literature. It has been successfully applied in fields as diverse as facial recognition [20] and speaker identification [2]. However, in all of these fields, the problem of discerning which training samples constitute a positive or negative exemplar for the purposes of (3) is trivial; i.e., a sample is either in a class or it is not. However, in the case of image annotation, this problem is less clear; when an image can have a whole range of labels, it is not satisfactory to simply treat each label individually or to treat a given set of labels, used together, as a unique class. In the former case, this limits our ability to consider the effect of label co-occurrence; in the latter, there may be too few examples for a given set of labels.

Thus, for our purposes, we consider a set of tags to positively annotate an image if it either matches the ground truth or is some proper subset of the ground truth. For example, in the case of the image shown in Figure 2, while (*crowd, concert, wales, relief, stadium*) is the best annotation in terms of the ground truth, (*crowd, stadium*) also constitutes a valid labeling. Even in cases where the entire dataset was labeled by experts, one person's idea of the subject(s) of an image may differ from another's; as such, any subset of the correct tags must also be considered valid and the embeddings updated accordingly. Conversely, because the negative exemplars are sampled from the current mini-batch, we also do not want to tell the model that some subset of the ground truth annotation is "invalid." Consequently, when selecting the negative exemplar for a given training sample, we insure not only that the triplet satisfies (3) but also that $y_i^p \cap y_i^n = \emptyset$.

Futhermore, recent literature in image annotation has placed a lot of focus on the order of the annotations during training [9]. Notably, the tags in NUS-WIDE are, by default, in order of descending frequency so training to recurrently predict these tags can obscure rare labels in favor of less descriptive but more popular ones. Randomly shuffling the tags or reversing the frequency ordering has been shown to help in this regard.[1] We note however that image annotations in the real-world are not strictly–or at least not linearly–ordered.

[1] In [9], the authors show a 5–10% improvement on recall from either shuffling the labels or ordering them rarest first.

Original Tags: africa, egypt, middleeast, motorvehicle, passenger, road, streets, taxi, transportation, urbanscenes, vehicle
NUS-WIDE Tags: road, africa, streets, egypt, vehicle, transportation

Figure 4: An example from NUS-WIDE, showing the tags provided by the original Flickr user and those from the dataset.

Consider the example in Figure 4. Here, along with the most-frequent-first tag ordering from NUS-WIDE, we also provide the tags in the order given by the original Flickr user. We can see that the tags are ordered locally and occur in three distinct groups: annotations about the location of the photograph, annotations about the objects in the image, and more general annotations about those objects. It seems, often, that a user has an object or topic in mind, provides tags corresponding to that object, then moves on to the next object and so forth. Annotations in this case can be seen as hierarchical, with several known objects and child tags related to them, annotated in depth-first order. For this reason, we feel the Inception-style CNN architecture [22], with several filter sizes capturing multi-scale sliding windows of the list of tags, more faithfully represents the nature of the raw data than generating tags recurrently. Because, in cases like the NUS-WIDE dataset, the original ordering of the tags cannot be recovered or, is no longer meaningful (due to relabeling), we randomly shuffle tags when constructing the embedding matrix.

3.3 Joint Image-Tag Embeddings

We propose a triplet-based dual-CNN framework for multi-label image annotation (Figure 5). Rather than recurrently predicting one or more labels for an image, we encode a sequence of labels using several convolutional filters at different scales to jointly learn embeddings for both the images and annotations to later retrieve labels from the structured embedding space. Once the embedding functions for the two branches of the model are learned, the set of tags for an input image (or, conversely, a known image for an input set of tags) can be retrieved from the embedding space by finding those objects at the smallest Euclidean distance from the input embedding.

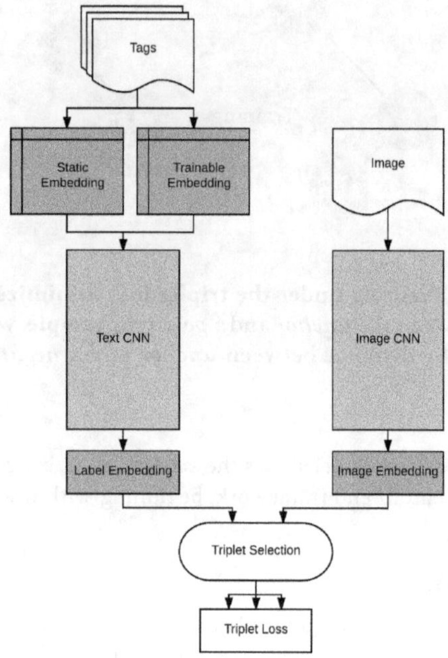

Figure 5: An overview of the architecture for our proposed model. The dual outputs of the convolutional neural networks are embedded into a shared space in which the distance between corresponding images and tag sequences is minimized.

Concretely, the input consists of an image $\mathcal{I}_p$ and a sequence of labels $L_p = (\ell_1, \ell_2, \ldots, \ell_m)$ annotating $\mathcal{I}_p$. Each ℓ_k is encoded as a one-hot vector $e_k = [0, \ldots, 0, 1, 0, \ldots, 0]$, where $e_k[k] = 1$ and 0 otherwise. The embedding w_k for each label is given by multiplying this one-hot vector with two separate embedding matrices, W_{static} and $W_{\text{nonstatic}}$, where the k-th row of each is the embedding of label k. Following the practice introduced in convolutional text classification [10], we randomly initialize $W_{\text{nonstatic}}$ and train it along with the rest of the model while W_{static} is initialized with pre-trained word vectors (such as from word2vec [16]) which are fixed during training. In this case, using the parlance common in computer vision, the fixed and trainable word embeddings each act as a "channel" of the input data, both inducing distributed representations of the tags at training time and supplementing them with external knowledge about the word co-occurrence. These embeddings are passed through our textual CNN [10], whereby the features of the tags are extracted using several different filter widths (in our case, we use filters of width 3, 4, and 5) to model the interactions between the tags at various scales. The CNN then outputs a d-dimensional embedding of the tag sequence, x_p.

Letting $I_p = \text{CNN}(\mathcal{I}_p)$, where CNN represents some convolutional neural network, be the extracted semantic features of image $\mathcal{I}_p$, we select some other x_n in the same mini-batch as (I_p, x_p) that satisfies (3) and calculate the triplet loss, given by (2).

Finally, we found through our experiments that the model was either slow to converge or that the loss [(2)] continued to decrease

Dataset	Images	Labels	Tags
NUS-WIDE	269,648	81	1000
MS-COCO	123,287	80	-
MIRFlickr-25k	25,000	18	1,386

Table 1: Summary of statistics for our datasets. For clarity, "labels" refers to annotations generated by experts and "tags" refers to user-generated annotations.

while the number of triplets satisfying (3) remained constant, indicating that the embeddings of both the positive and negative exemplars were settling around the imposed margin, rather than the model forcing the negatives away. We thus employed some structure-preserving techniques [27] to regularize the model. To this end, we also require images that have some subset of their tags in common to be embedded near each other (along with embedding each near their corresponding images). Following a similar process to that described above, we take each image as the anchor and randomly sample a different positive and a negative exemplar matching the criteria from each mini-batch, one sharing some or all tags with the anchor and the other sharing none. Letting $d(x, y) = \| f_I(x) - f_I(y) \|_2^2$, we have

$$\mathcal{L}_{I \to I} = \sum_{i=1}^{N} \left[d(x_i^a, x_i^p) - d(x_i^a, x_i^n) + \alpha \right]_+ , \tag{4}$$

with tags y_a matching each image x^p and not image x^n. Thus, our complete loss to be minimized is given as:

$$\mathcal{L} = \mathcal{L}_{I \to T} + \lambda \mathcal{L}_{I \to I} \tag{5}$$

3.4 Training

Our model largely relies on a deep CNN for quality high-level image features. For fair comparison with the existing literature, we use features from VGGNet [21], pretrained on the ImageNet 2012 classification dataset [19]. We train the model using rmsprop [24] to mitigate the effects of vanishing gradients. The dimension of all embeddings is 256. All training was conducted on a K40 GPU using Tensorflow [15].

4 EVALUATION

4.1 Datasets

NUS-WIDE. The NUS-WIDE dataset [3] contains 269,648 images released with tags at three levels of granularity and six different types of low-level image features. The data contain 5,018 unique tags and a set of 1,000 cleaner tags, both provided by the original users. The images are also manually annotated with an additional 81 ground-truth "concepts" (of which there is some overlap with the set of 1,000 tags). URLs are also provided to retrieve the raw image data from Flickr. Since the dataset was released, many images have been taken down by the user or are no longer available, our dataset (in keeping with contemporary literature) contains 127,302 images in the training set and 85,137 in the test set.

The tags included in this dataset, even after being narrowed down to 1,000 from the original set of 5,018, represent a very diverse set of labels. The most common are descriptive of the content or at least visual characteristics of the image: *nature, sky, blue, water, clouds.* However, there are also annotations for compositional aspects–*portrait, macro*–, user reactions–*bravo, wow, interestingness*–, many geographical locations–*finland, philadelphia, barcelona*–, and even bookkeeping information leftover from the user profile–e.g., *delete.* On average, each image contains 1.76 concept labels and 5.97 user labels.

Method	P@3	R@3	F1@3
Softmax	60.2	62.1	61.1
WARP	59.8	61.4	60.7
CNN-RNN	61.7	49.9	55.2
RIA	66.8	69.0	67.9
S-CNN-RNN	**71.4**	70.6	71.0
Ours	70.0	**72.5**	**71.2**

Table 2: Comparisons of our proposed model on 81 concepts from NUS-WIDE.

Microsoft COCO. The Microsoft COCO (MS-COCO) dataset [13] is an image dataset targeted toward object detection, image segmentation, and captioning tasks. The dataset is comparable in scope with NUS-WIDE, with 82,783 training images and 40,504 test images, annotated with 80 object instances as labels. The images from this dataset were also collected from Flickr; however, the original user tags are not present, and all images have been separately and manually annotated. Interestingly, most of the images in the dataset contain more than one category of object (the images, on average, contain between 4 and 5 distinct object types), and there is a strong co-occurrence dependency between types. However, unlike NUS-WIDE, the labels are less noisy and all of the labels in this setting correspond directly to some object *visually* contained in the image. The difficulty then lies in detecting smaller objects, which global image features may not be able to discern. Each image contains, on average, 7.34 labeled objects. While the user tags in NUS-WIDE follow a more common long-tail distribution, the object instances in MS-COCO are more evenly distributed, with the exception of the label *person*, which occurs five times more frequently than the second-most frequent label (*chair*).

MIRFlickr-25k. The MIRFLICKR-25k open evaluation project [8] comprises 25,000 images retrieved from Flickr through its public API paired with manual annotations of 18 different labels. The original user tags are also available, of which 1,386 occur in at least 20 images. These are the same labels used in [25]. Because they are drawn from the same source, the tags annotate similar concepts as NUS-WIDE, though the images have been selected by the dataset's creators to promote "interestingness." Each image contains approximately 2.78 expert labels and 8.94 user tags; for our purposes, we focus solely on retrieving the user tags.

4.2 Results

We evaluate our proposed model on both the NUS-WIDE 81- and 1000-label datasets and the 80-object dataset from MS-COCO, as examples of both clean and relatively clean annotation datasets. We also compare the performance of our model and the current

Method	P@10	R@10	F1@10
Softmax	17.7	28.8	21.5
WARP	18.3	30.8	22.9
CNN-RNN	18.5	31.2	23.3
S-CNN-RNN	19.0	30.2	23.3
Ours	**19.8**	**32.7**	**24.7**

Table 3: Comparisons of our proposed model on 1,000 tags from NUS-WIDE.

Method	P@3	R@3	F1@3	P@1
Softmax	60.2	62.1	61.1	–
WARP	59.8	61.4	60.7	–
CNN-RNN	69.2	66.4	67.8	–
RIA	74.2	64.6	69.1	–
S-CNN-RNN	**76.6**	68.7	72.5	**77.1**
Ours	70.1	**75.5**	**72.7**	76.9

Table 4: Comparisons of our proposed model on 80 object instances from MS-COCO.

Method	P@3	R@3	F1@3
S-CNN-RNN	14.2	28.3	18.9
Ours	**17.1**	**30.5**	**21.9**

Table 5: Comparisons of our proposed model on 1,386 user tags from MIRFlickr-25k.

NUS-WIDE state-of-the-art on the 1,386 tags from MIRFlickr-25k as an example of performance of each on sparse, noisy, personal user-generated content. We follow the existing experimental procedure from the literature [14], reporting precision, recall, and F1 score (harmonic mean of precision and recall) at $k = 3$, with the exception of the NUS-WIDE user tags, for which we follow the example of [26] by reporting precision and recall at $k = 10$.

Across all datasets, as shown in Tables 2 to 4, our model outperforms the existing state-of-the-art on this in terms of recall and F1 score. On the cleaner, expert-labeled datasets (that is, NUS-WIDE-81 and MS-COCO), our model is outperformed in terms of precision by the RNN-based tag models. This is because, for a given k, our model will always retrieve k labels, while the ground truth number of labels may be less than k. On the other hand, the RNN may be able to generate fewer than k in these instances, so the precision will be higher, but the potential recall lower. Due to the noisiness of the data, as previously discussed, it may be advantageous to weigh recall more importantly than precision, as tags ranking more highly than the ground truth can, in some cases, be treated as instances of missing annotations (see, for example, Figure 6). As a means of normalizing this advantage of the RNN, we compare the Precision@1 of our model against S-CNN-RNN in Table 4. Looking at the precision of only the top result, our model compares much more favorably with the state-of-the-art.

Finally, in Table 5, we present results of our model evaluted on MIRFlickr-25k. This dataset is seldom used in the literature, so for brevity, we compare our model against only the best performing model on the other datasets, as a baseline. Here, as well, even in the presence of sparse and noisy user-generated content, our triplet-loss-based model outperforms the exisiting recurrent state-of-the-art.

4.3 Annotation Case Studies

Figures 6 and 7 show some example images from MS-COCO and NUS-WIDE, respectively. On the left of each figure, we give an example of an image with good recall of the ground truth tags. Figure 6 in particular demonstrates the much higher performance of the model on the MS-COCO dataset. All of the correct objects in the image (*mouse, keyboard,* and *laptop*) are correctly annotated, and we also show the next closest tags, which denote a recognition of some notion of furniture and the tag *tv.* We notice that the visual features from our CNN (which is pretrained on ImageNet) are often insufficient in distinguishing between a television and a computer monitor (and, furthermore, there are several instances in MS-COCO where a monitor is labeled as both). While many of the most frequent tags are missing from our annotation of the first image in Figure 7, we note that many of the other retrieved tags, while incorrect, are seemingly more relevant: *bright* and *street* versus *bravo* and *interestingness.*

The second image in each figure provides an error case for each dataset. For the MS-COCO image in Figure 6, again because of the quality of the object annotations, our model still manages to retrieve the single correct tag (*toilet*), while also picking up the visual similarities of the bathtub with a *sink* (MS-COCO does not contain an annotation for either bathtub or shower). However, the top-5 set of tags (after the three used to evaluate the model) contains two irrelevant but visually defensible tags; for instance, we can identify the model conflating the marble in the background with snow.

In the case of the NUS-WIDE example on the right of Figure 7, none of the correct labels occur in the nearest five tags to the image; however, we note that many of the retrieved tags are still relevant. The tags *nature, africa,* and *safari* all seem to accurately capture the content of the image, though without an acknowledgement of the actual objects present. We necessarily note that *nature* occurs twenty times more often than *elephant* and more than twice as often as *people,* so nearness to that tag (often indicated by a large presence of green color in the image) likely overwhelms the object detection, instead favoring more qualitative labels. Finally, the elephant image provides one example of our model's handling of geographical tags, as discussed in Section 1. Although the elephant is not specifically recalled by the model, it has learned that such scenes (also mitigated by the nearness of tags *nature* and *safari*) often take place in Africa, demonstrating the ability of our model to capture such non-visual dependencies between the images and other tags.

Finally, the image and tags presented in Figure 8 exemplify several of the characteristics of the ground truth tags discussed above, as well as the capabilities of our model. To begin, the most frequently-occurring tag with which the image is labeled is *china,*

Tags: laptop, mouse, keyboard	Tags: toilet
Predictions: mouse, keyboard, laptop, bed, couch, tv	Predictions: toilet, sink, toothbrush, snowboard, zebra

Figure 6: Two example predictions from our model on images from MS-COCO.

Tags: bravo, explore, light, people, night, city, interestingness, urban, colors	Tags: people, elephant
Predictions: night, city, street, lights, lines, bright	Predictions: nature, africa, army, safari, shadow

Figure 7: Two example predictions from our model on images from NUS-WIDE.

and it is unlikely anyone–other than a seasoned architectural historian–would be able to recall this from the image alone. The second tag of the image, *museum*, is an interesting case study in itself. The majority of the images labeled with *museum* in the dataset are either interior shots–depicting works of art, various exhibits, or rooms, staircases, and the like–or exterior shots of buildings as diverse in form as the world's museums. Thus, we see that the annotation for museum comes to represent either some general notion of "art" or the general concept of architectural spaces, depending on which tags it co-occurs with in that instance. For the predictions of our model, then, we first see the grouping of *sky, blue,* and *clouds.* The image is clearly taken outdoors, so due to its frequency in the dataset (and the lack of greenery discounting, say, *nature*), the concept of outside is denoted with *sky,* which nearly always brings *clouds* along with it. Although the specificity of museum is not captured here, the model still exhibits an ability to recognize such outdoor spaces, retrieving both *building* and *architecture.* Also, quite nicely, not just the blueness of the image but also the quality of the glass is denoted by the nearness of the embedding for *reflection.* In a similar manner, the image also embeds closely to *ice* as a further example of something that may also be blue, out-of-doors, and reflective.

Tags: china, museum
Predictions: sky, blue, clouds, architecture, reflection, building, ice, military

Figure 8: An example from the NUS-WIDE test data with ground truth and our predicted tags

5 CONCLUSION AND FUTURE WORK

We have demonstrated the effectiveness of learning multi-label triplet embeddings for performing image annotation, in the presence of noisy labels. While conceptually simple, our model achieves state-of-the-art performance on publicly-available datasets. In future work, we would like to continue this idea forward to utilize more of the metadata available alongside public image data. Works such as [5] have shown the increased effectiveness of models that incorporate user information on the instance level. Furthermore, several recent datasets also crawled from Flickr data, such as the Yahoo Flickr Creative Commons 100M (YFCC100M) Dataset [23], provide much larger sets of tags and much more training data than that used here. YFCC100M even provides "expansion" packs including GPS and Exif data for many of the images. However, for the data that is publicly available in these datasets, either specific users occur too infrequently as to limit the learning capacity of a model or the metadata is too sparse to be used effectively. Thus, a way forward for this work may involve the collection of additional datasets, perhaps utilized in a semi-supervised fashion as supplement to the larger, well-annotated datasets above, to leverage the way different users or different social networks reason about image content by gaining an understanding of such side information.

REFERENCES

[1] Kofi Boakye, Sachin Farfade, Hamid Izadinia, Yannis Kalantidis, and Pierre Garrigues. 2017. Tag prediction at Flickr: A view from the darkroom. In *Proceedings of the on Thematic Workshops of ACM Multimedia 2017, Mountain View, CA, USA, October 23 - 27, 2017*, 376–384. DOI: 10.1145/3126686.3126745. http://doi.acm.org/10.1145/3126686.3126745.

[2] Hervé Bredin. 2017. Tristounet: triplet loss for speaker turn embedding. In *2017 IEEE International Conference on Acoustics, Speech and Signal Processing, ICASSP 2017, New Orleans, LA, USA, March 5-9, 2017*, 5430–5434. DOI: 10.1109/ICASSP.2017.7953194. https://doi.org/10.1109/ICASSP.2017.7953194.

[3] Tat-Seng Chua, Jinhui Tang, Richang Hong, Haojie Li, Zhiping Luo, and Yantao Zheng. 2009. NUS-WIDE: a real-world web image database from national university of singapore. In *Proceedings of the 8th ACM International Conference on Image and Video Retrieval, CIVR 2009, Santorini Island, Greece, July 8-10, 2009.* DOI: 10.1145/1646396.1646452. http://doi.acm.org/10.1145/1646396.1646452.

[4] Jia Deng, Wei Dong, Richard Socher, Li-Jia Li, Kai Li, and Fei-Fei Li. 2009. Imagenet: A large-scale hierarchical image database. In *2009 IEEE Computer Society Conference on Computer Vision and Pattern Recognition (CVPR 2009), 20-25 June 2009, Miami, Florida, USA*, 248–255. DOI: 10.1109/CVPRW.2009.5206848. https://doi.org/10.1109/CVPRW.2009.5206848.

[5] Emily Denton, Jason Weston, Manohar Paluri, Lubomir D. Bourdev, and Rob Fergus. 2015. User conditional hashtag prediction for images. In *Proceedings of the 21th ACM SIGKDD International Conference on Knowledge Discovery and Data Mining, Sydney, NSW, Australia, August 10-13, 2015*, 1731–1740. DOI: 10.1145/2783258.2788576. http://doi.acm.org/10.1145/2783258.2788576.

[6] Andrea Frome, Gregory S. Corrado, Jonathon Shlens, Samy Bengio, Jeffrey Dean, Marc'Aurelio Ranzato, and Tomas Mikolov. 2013. Devise: A deep visual-semantic embedding model. In *Advances in Neural Information Processing Systems 26: 27th Annual Conference on Neural Information Processing Systems 2013. Proceedings of a meeting held December 5-8, 2013, Lake Tahoe, Nevada, United States.* 2121–2129. http://papers.nips.cc/paper/5204-devise-a-deep-visual-semantic-embedding-model.

[7] Yunchao Gong, Yangqing Jia, Thomas Leung, Alexander Toshev, and Sergey Ioffe. 2013. Deep Convolutional Ranking for Multilabel Image Annotation. arXiv: 1312.4894v2 [cs.CV].

[8] Mark J. Huiskes and Michael S. Lew. 2008. The MIR flickr retrieval evaluation. In *Proceedings of the 1st ACM SIGMM International Conference on Multimedia Information Retrieval, MIR 2008, Vancouver, British Columbia, Canada, October 30-31, 2008*, 39–43. DOI: 10.1145/1460096.1460104. http://doi.acm.org/10.1145/1460096.1460104.

[9] Jiren Jin and Hideki Nakayama. 2016. Annotation order matters: recurrent image annotator for arbitrary length image tagging. In *23rd International Conference on Pattern Recognition, ICPR 2016, Cancún, Mexico, December 4-8, 2016*, 2452–2457. DOI: 10.1109/ICPR.2016.7900004. https://doi.org/10.1109/ICPR.2016.7900004.

[10] Yoon Kim. 2014. Convolutional neural networks for sentence classification. In *Proceedings of the 2014 Conference on Empirical Methods in Natural Language Processing, EMNLP 2014, October 25-29, 2014, Doha, Qatar, A meeting of SIGDAT, a Special Interest Group of the ACL*, 1746–1751. http://aclweb.org/anthology/D/D14/D14-1181.pdf.

[11] Alex Krizhevsky, Ilya Sutskever, and Geoffrey E. Hinton. 2012. Imagenet classification with deep convolutional neural networks. In *Advances in Neural Information Processing Systems 25: 26th Annual Conference on Neural Information Processing Systems 2012. Proceedings of a meeting held December 3-6, 2012, Lake Tahoe, Nevada, United States.* 1106–1114. http://papers.nips.cc/paper/4824-imagenet-classification-with-deep-convolutional-neural-networks.

[12] Jun Li, Xun Lin, Xiaoguang Rui, Yong Rui, and Dacheng Tao. 2015. A distributed approach toward discriminative distance metric learning. *IEEE transactions on neural networks and learning systems*, 26, 9, 2111–2122.

[13] Tsung-Yi Lin, Michael Maire, Serge J. Belongie, James Hays, Pietro Perona, Deva Ramanan, Piotr Dollár, and C. Lawrence Zitnick. 2014. Microsoft COCO: common objects in context. In *Computer Vision - ECCV 2014 - 13th European Conference, Zurich, Switzerland, September 6-12, 2014, Proceedings, Part V*, 740–755. DOI: 10.1007/978-3-319-10602-1_48. https://doi.org/10.1007/978-3-319-10602-1_48.

[14] Feng Liu, Tao Xiang, Timothy M. Hospedales, Wankou Yang, and Changyin Sun. 2017. Semantic regularisation for recurrent image annotation. In *2017 IEEE Conference on Computer Vision and Pattern Recognition, CVPR 2017, Honolulu, HI, USA, July 21-26, 2017*, 4160–4168. DOI: 10.1109/CVPR.2017.443. http://doi.ieeecomputersociety.org/10.1109/CVPR.2017.443.

[15] Martn Abadi et al. 2015. TensorFlow: large-scale machine learning on heterogeneous systems. Software available from tensorflow.org. (2015). http://tensorflow.org/.

[16] Tomas Mikolov, Ilya Sutskever, Kai Chen, Gregory S. Corrado, and Jeffrey Dean. 2013. Distributed representations of words and phrases and their compositionality. In *Advances in Neural Information Processing Systems 26: 27th Annual Conference on Neural Information Processing Systems 2013. Proceedings of a meeting held December 5-8, 2013, Lake Tahoe, Nevada, United States.* 3111–3119. http://papers.nips.cc/paper/5021-distributed-representations-of-words-and-phrases-and-their-compositionality.

[17] Karl Ni, Kyle Zaragoza, Charles Foster, Carmen Carrano, Barry Chen, Yonas Tesfaye, and Alex Gude. 2016. Sampled Image Tagging and Retrieval Methods on User Generated Content. arXiv: 1611.06962v3 [cs.CV].

[18] Omkar M. Parkhi, Andrea Vedaldi, and Andrew Zisserman. 2015. Deep face recognition. In *Proceedings of the British Machine Vision Conference 2015, BMVC 2015, Swansea, UK, September 7-10, 2015*, 41.1–41.12. DOI: 10.5244/C.29.41. https://doi.org/10.5244/C.29.41.

[19] Olga Russakovsky et al. 2015. Imagenet large scale visual recognition challenge. *International Journal of Computer Vision*, 115, 3, 211–252. DOI: 10.1007/s11263-015-0816-y. https://doi.org/10.1007/s11263-015-0816-y.

[20] Florian Schroff, Dmitry Kalenichenko, and James Philbin. 2015. Facenet: A unified embedding for face recognition and clustering. In *IEEE Conference on Computer Vision and Pattern Recognition, CVPR 2015, Boston, MA, USA, June 7-12, 2015*, 815–823. DOI: 10.1109/CVPR.2015.7298682. https://doi.org/10.1109/CVPR.2015.7298682.

[21] Karen Simonyan and Andrew Zisserman. 2014. Very Deep Convolutional Networks for Large-Scale Image Recognition. arXiv: 1409.1556v6 [cs.CV].

[22] Christian Szegedy, Wei Liu, Yangqing Jia, Pierre Sermanet, Scott E. Reed, Dragomir Anguelov, Dumitru Erhan, Vincent Vanhoucke, and Andrew Rabinovich. 2015. Going deeper with convolutions. In *IEEE Conference on Computer Vision and Pattern Recognition, CVPR 2015, Boston, MA, USA, June 7-12, 2015*, 1–9. DOI: 10.1109/CVPR.2015.7298594. https://doi.org/10.1109/CVPR.2015.7298594.

[23] Bart Thomee, David A. Shamma, Gerald Friedland, Benjamin Elizalde, Karl Ni, Douglas Poland, Damian Borth, and Li-Jia Li. 2016. YFCC100M: the new data in multimedia research. *Commun. ACM*, 59, 2, 64–73. DOI: 10.1145/2812802. http://doi.acm.org/10.1145/2812802.

[24] T. Tieleman and G. Hinton. 2012. Lecture 6.5—RmsProp: Divide the gradient by a running average of its recent magnitude. COURSERA: Neural Networks for Machine Learning. (2012).

[25] Jakob J. Verbeek, Matthieu Guillaumin, Thomas Mensink, and Cordelia Schmid. 2010. Image annotation with tagprop on the MIRFLICKR set. In *Proceedings of the 11th ACM SIGMM International Conference on Multimedia Information Retrieval, MIR 2010, Philadelphia, Pennsylvania, USA, March 29-31, 2010*, 537–546. DOI: 10.1145/1743384.1743476. http://doi.acm.org/10.1145/1743384.1743476.

[26] Jiang Wang, Yi Yang, Junhua Mao, Zhiheng Huang, Chang Huang, and Wei Xu. 2016. CNN-RNN: A unified framework for multi-label image classification. In *2016 IEEE Conference on Computer Vision and Pattern Recognition, CVPR 2016, Las Vegas, NV, USA, June 27-30, 2016*, 2285–2294. DOI: 10.1109/CVPR.2016.251. https://doi.org/10.1109/CVPR.2016.251.

[27] Liwei Wang, Yin Li, and Svetlana Lazebnik. 2016. Learning deep structure-preserving image-text embeddings. In *2016 IEEE Conference on Computer Vision and Pattern Recognition, CVPR 2016, Las Vegas, NV, USA, June 27-30, 2016*, 5005–5013. DOI: 10.1109/CVPR.2016.541. https://doi.org/10.1109/CVPR.2016.541.

[28] Jason Weston, Samy Bengio, and Nicolas Usunier. 2011. WSABIE: scaling up to large vocabulary image annotation. In *IJCAI 2011, Proceedings of the 22nd International Joint Conference on Artificial Intelligence, Barcelona, Catalonia, Spain, July 16-22, 2011*, 2764–2770. DOI: 10.5591/978-1-57735-516-8/IJCAI11-460. https://doi.org/10.5591/978-1-57735-516-8/IJCAI11-460.

[29] Yang Zhang, Boqing Gong, and Mubarak Shah. 2016. Fast zero-shot image tagging. In *2016 IEEE Conference on Computer Vision and Pattern Recognition, CVPR 2016, Las Vegas, NV, USA, June 27-30, 2016*, 5985–5994. DOI: 10.1109/CVPR.2016.644. https://doi.org/10.1109/CVPR.2016.644.

Linguistic Patterns and Cross Modality-based Image Retrieval for Complex Queries

Chandramani Chaudhary
BITS Pilani
Pilani India
chandramani.chaudhary@pilani.bits-pilani.ac.in

Poonam Goyal
BITS Pilani
Pilani India
poonam@pilani.bits-pilani.ac.in

Joel Ruben Antony Moniz
BITS Pilani
Pilani India
f2012106@pilani.bits-pilani.ac.in

Navneet Goyal
BITS Pilani
Pilani India
goyal@pilani.bits-pilani.ac.in

Yi-Ping Phoebe Chen
La Trobe University
Melbourne, Australia
phoebe.chen@latrobe.edu.au

ABSTRACT

With the rising prevalence of social media, coupled with the ease of sharing images, people with specific needs and applications such as known item search, multimedia question answering, etc., have started searching for visual content, which is expressed in terms of complex queries. A complex query consists of multiple concepts and their attributes are arranged to convey semantics. It is less effective to answer such queries by simply appending the search results gathered from individual or subsets of concepts present in the query. In this paper, we propose to exploit the query constituents and relationships among them. The proposed approach finds image-query relevance by integrating three models – the linguistic pattern-based textual model, the visual model, and the cross modality model. We extract linguistic patterns from complex queries, gather their related crawled images, and assign relevance scores to images in the corpus. The relevance scores are then used to rank the images. We experiment on more than 140k images and compare the NDCG@n scores with the state-of-the-art image ranking methods for complex queries. Also, ranking of images obtained by our approach outperforms than that of obtained by a popular search engine.

CCS CONCEPTS

• **Information systems → Information systems applications; Information retrieval**

ICMR'18, June 11-14, 2018, Yokohama, Japan.

ACM ISBN 978-1-4503-5046-4/18/06...$15.00.
DOI: https://doi.org/10.1145/3206025.3206050

KEYWORDS

Linguistic pattern, cross-modality; nearest neighbor; complex query; image retrieval

ACM Reference format:

Chandramani Chaudhary, Poonam Goyal, Joel Ruben Antony Moniz, Navneet Goyal, and Yi-Ping Phoebe Chen. 2018. Linguistic patterns and cross modality-based image retrieval for complex queries. In Proceedings of ICMR '18, Yokohama, Japan, June 11-14, 2018 (ICMR'18), 9 pages.
DOI: https://doi.org/10.1145/3206025.3206050

1 INTRODUCTION

The exponential growth in social image hosting sites and multimedia technologies in the last few years has rendered the web an opulent source of multimedia data. The availability of the Internet and communication facilities has given users access to a rich source of multimedia data. This data is used by many image retrieval applications in entertainment, medicine, advertising, etc. Images not only contain visual information but also textual information which can be used for concept abstraction or to give a special name to the objects. As a result of the availability of visual and textual information, there have been major advances in retrieving images based on simple queries viz. single label [1], multi-label [2-4], and structured [5] which is evident by reasonably good results of the commercial search engines.

The average query length is getting longer as mentioned by Nie et al. [12]. Moreover, according to Clickture [39] dataset, more than 50% of the queries have two or more key terms. Nowadays, users surf for specific need/visual concepts such as objects or scenes with particular attributes, hence their queries are becoming complex, more specific and longer [39]. These complex queries are popular in many media search applications, such as multimedia question answering, text illustration, known item search and some domain specific search systems.

Complex queries usually comprise of multiple interrelated visual concepts and their attributes, adjectives and actions for example – *a boy walking with an old man and a dog in a park* [39], where there are four visual concepts *boy, old man, dog* and *park.* The concepts are associated with other concepts, for example, *boy* with man and *dog, old* with *man,* and *walking* with *boy.* However, current image retrieval systems are unable to perform well on complex queries with such rich semantics. Fig.1 shows top four retrieved images by the Google image search for the two queries. It can be seen that a few of the retrieved images contain all the concepts, but the relations (such as spatial and action) between them are not understood. Also, some of the retrieved images do not have all the constituents of the complex query. The same kind of results are obtained for many other complex queries and it is observed that relations between concepts are not properly captured. Moreover, some retrieved images do not have all the concepts incorporated in complex query.

Search engines [6, 8, 9] which largely use the image title and the surrounding text on web pages, do not provide satisfactory results. Recently, concept-based image searches [10, 11], where images containing the detected visual concepts are returned, become more popular than simple text-based image searches [6]. However, these methods cannot effectively deal with complex queries. This is because, only the presence of multiple concepts is considered. The concepts in a text do not appear in isolation rather, they interact with each other providing semantics to the text. These interactions can help bridge the semantic gap in the image search process

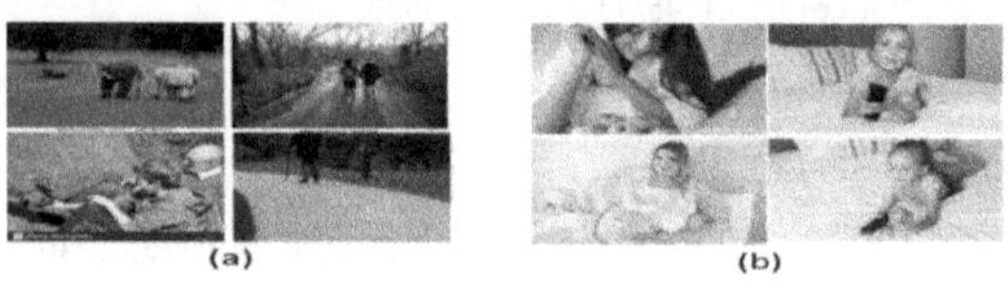

Figure 1: Top four retrieved images from a popular search engine for queries (a) a boy walking with an old man and a dog in a park (b) a baby with an apple lying in the bed

A few attempts [12-17, 31] have been made to tackle the problem of complex queries. Nie et al. [12] proposed an approach which exploits web sources, apart from visual and textual information for query-image relevance estimation. It gives more importance to the most co-occurring concepts. Its performance degrades when rare visual concepts (or their rare combination) are present in the query. It also fails to handle spatial and action relationship among concepts. Guo et al. [13] extended Nie's approach to establish concept-image relevance. Both of these methods are image reranking frameworks, where Guo et al. [13] uses Flickr search result and Nie et al. [12] uses Google search results for reranking. Cui et al. [15] introduced a learning based rank technique for visual concept-based image search. Learning based methods often require large training dataset. Noise-free training labels with sufficient positive examples are very expensive and difficult to get for complex queries. All these methods concentrate only on the presence of visual concepts, leaving out the interaction/relationship between the concepts. A method which deals with complex queries for videos uses concept bundle which integrates multiple concepts in a bundle [16]. This approach is again a learning based approach that selects concept bundles and primitive concepts based on their web video search frequencies. However, images are not always surrounded by sentences and are sometimes labeled only with a few tags. Siddiquie et al. [17] proposed a unified framework which mainly exploits the objects' spatial relationships for more descriptive queries. Recently, Chen et al. [31] used K-parser to parse the query and text associated with the images. However, they only used text to estimate query-image relevance.

To overcome the limitations of general *n*-gram based query matching, we propose to use concepts, attributes, and their relationships (used interchangeably with linguistic patterns) as important components for retrieval. For a sports query, *Elise of Belgium hits a shot against Elina,* our approach considers the relationships such as (1) there is *Elise,* (2) there is *Elina,* (3) *Elise hits* a *shot,* etc. and we evaluate images based on their support for these relationships, thus reducing the semantic gap between the images and the complex queries. All the relationships from text associated with images are extracted using natural language processing techniques and they are linked to the image content and textual cues to give query relevance scores to images. In particular, we use the Stanford Dependency Tree (SDT) parser [18] and our proposed rule-based semantic parser to extract linguistic patterns. The SDT parser (currently defines 55 binary relationships) is used to extract the grammatical relationships in a sentence. Our rule-based parser generates binary and ternary linguistic patterns using these grammatical relationships. These linguistic patterns are then used to estimate query-image relevance using textual and visual modality-based models. The linguistic patterns for the query in Fig. 1 (a) are (boy, walking, man), (old, man), (dog, in, park), etc. The textual and visual modality-based models focus on the existence of the linguistic patterns in the image content and its textual cues, which allows us to estimate query-image relevance with respect to different constituents of the query and the image. It is possible that the image in consideration has incomplete or missing information (Void of Information (VoI)). To overcome this, we exploit k-nearest neighbors (*k*-NN) in our proposed *cross modality* model for query-image relevance. The model gives score to an image using both primitive concepts (e.g. boy, dog, etc.) and the linguistic patterns on the basis of the image neighbors.

In the proposed method, we combine three models linearly to assign a final score of relevance to images for a given query. Experiments are conducted on two datasets, one, with nearly 150k images for 100 queries and the other with nearly 9k images for 25 queries. However, no existing work [12, 13, 16, 31] has used more than fifty queries to the best of our knowledge. Also, there is no publically available dataset for complex queries. The results show that the proposed approach outperforms the existing image retrieval approaches for complex queries. We analyzed our reranked results from Google image search engine and found that our approach provides better reranking of the images as compared to the existing methods. Following are the main contributions of the paper.

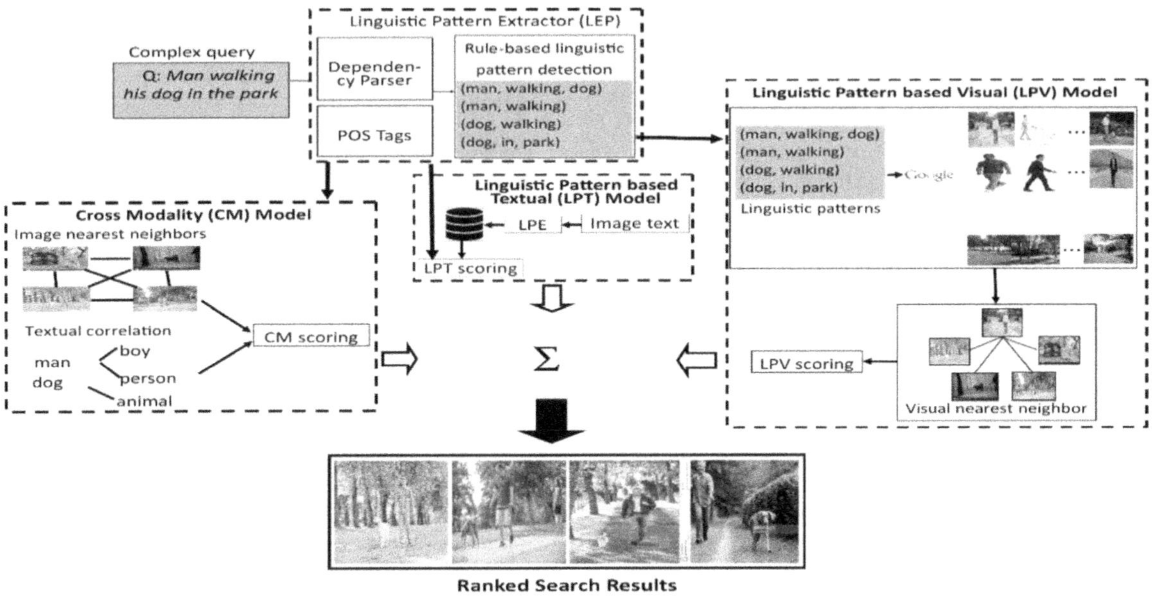

Figure 2: The proposed query-image relevance approach for complex

- A rule-based semantic parser is developed to extract linguistic patterns from a given text.
- Two models are developed based on linguistic patterns, one using visual modality and the other using textual modality, to exploit the constituents of the query and the image.
- A cross modality (textual and visual modality) model is also developed to exploit the contribution of primitive concepts and linguistic patterns, and to tackle VoI for query-image relevance. The proposed approach integrates all three models for image ranking and reranking

2 RELATED WORK

Many researchers have dealt with complex queries in text-based information systems. Two Major approaches, query term re-weighting [7, 19, 20] and query reduction [8, 21] are the most explored. In spite of their success, they cannot be used directly for image retrieval due to the sematic gap between queries and images. The sematic gap occurs due to different modalities of the query and search domain.

In an earlier work on image retrieval for complex queries, concepts are extracted and their individual search results are aggregated and presented as the results [22]. However, these results were far from what was expected. Natsev et al. [23] proposed a combination of two learning models – first, the nearest neighbor model on positive examples and second, the support vector machine model which considers both positive and negative examples. Chang et al. [24] weighted the individual concept detectors according to their training performance. However, such approaches do not guarantee the coexistence of these concept in a retrieved image. To present this coexistence Li et al. [25] learned bi-concept detectors from social tagged images, and applied them in a search engine to retrieve images relevant to bi-concept queries. Yuan et al. [16] proposed a concept-based video retrieval search for complex queries, leveraging the plentiful but partially related samples and users' feedback. They proposed a higher-level semantic descriptor named *concept bundle* which is a set of multiple primitive concepts, which exploited only the existence of concept bundles.

Nie et. al [12] proposed a scheme where visual concepts are considered and a heterogeneous probabilistic network is constructed to establish the relationships between the query and retrieved images. The network consist of three components, namely sematic, visual, and cross-modality. Based on these components, a final ranked list of images is retrieved. Guo et al. [13] extended this idea by establishing concept-query and the concept-image probabilistic model. Each model estimates relevance based on visual content, web and image text. Cui et al. [15] proposed a learning method based on concepts. Concept detectors are built by leveraging visual features and then the weights of each concept in a query are learnt. Siddiquie et al. [17] proposed a framework which handles queries consisting of objects, attributes and spatial relationships. They proposed a unique multi-modal hashing algorithm capable of mapping queries of different modalities to the same binary sematic representation. Chen et al. [31] considered only textual information for retrieval. Both query and image text are represented in the form of RDF (Resource Description Framework) data and a query is taken as a SPARQL query. Matching RDFs are retrieved for a given query. However, the RDF data is constructed only for nouns and verbs.

Most of the aforementioned methods are concept based and mostly consider the co-occurrences of two or more concepts but do not exploit the interaction between these concepts and/or their attributes. In this paper, we tackle this issue by utilizing the dependency among the concepts and their attributes, thus producing a ranking of images that matches to user expectations.

3 PROPOSED APPROACH

Our approach consists of three main models: (1) the linguistic pattern-based textual (LPT) model (2) the linguistic pattern-based visual (LPV) model, and (3) the cross-modality (CM) model. The architecture of our framework is illustrated in Fig. 2. A linguistic pattern extractor (LPE) generates patterns from text associated with images and queries and feeds them to all models. The cross-modality model exploits both the textual and visual information related to images for both primitive concepts and linguistic patterns. The final query-image relevance score is computed as a weighted sum of the normalized scores given by the models. The final relevance score $Rel(Q, i_q)$ is as follows

$$Rel(Q, i_q) = \alpha_1 LPT(Q, i_q) + \alpha_2 LPV(Q, i_q) + \alpha_3 CM(Q, i_q) \quad (1)$$

where Q denotes a query and i_q denotes an image. $\alpha_1, \alpha_2, and\ \alpha_3$ are the respective fusing weights of the models with their sum being 1. We take these weights according to the average performance of the each model. Table 1 lists the key notations and definitions used throughout the paper.

Table 1: Summary of key notations and definitions

Notation	Definition
$I = \{i_1, i_2, \dots i_M\}$	*I is* an image dataset containing M images and i_r is *r-th* image of *I*
Q	A specific complex query
S	*S* is a piece of text/sentence containing *n tokens*
a,b,c,d and h	Tokens of sentence *S*
L_Q={$l_1, l_2, \dots l_z$}	L_Q is set of linguistic pattern for query *Q*, and l_j is the *j*-th pattern
L_{i_q}	A linguistic pattern set of surrounding text of image i_q
$T = \{t_1, t_2, \dots t_m\}$	*T* is concept set (for whole dataset), and t_r is *r-th* concept
$r(t_u, i_r)$	Indicates the existence of concept t_u with i_r.
k	Number of visual nearest neighbors
$NN_v(i_q)$	Set of *k* visual NNs of image i_q and *v* is the cosine visual similarity function for two images
$I'(t_k)$	Set of images labeled with concept t_k
$TT(t_k, t_r)$	Concept-to-concept relevance between two concept t_k and t_r based on concept co-occurrence in the whole dataset.
$I'_{NN(i_q)}(t_p)$	Set of neighborhood images of i_q labeled with concept t_p
$TT_{NN}(t_k, t_r)$	Concept-to-concept relevance between t_k and t_r based on their co-occurrence in the visual neighbors of the test image
$T'(i_r)$	Set of concepts which are labeled to image i_r
$T'_{NN}(i_q)$	Set of concepts which are labeled to image set $NN_v(i_q)$
$I_{web}(l_g)$	Set of images downloaded for linguistic pattern l_g
ω	Weight used for ternary and binary patterns in the LPT model
$\delta(l_j, l_r)$	$\delta(l_j, l_r) = 1$ if linguistic pattern l_j and l_r are same else zero

3.1 Linguistic Pattern Extractor (LPE)

The query text or text associated with the images is parsed and converted into semantic patterns. Our pattern extractor consists of two components, the first being the Stanford dependency tree (SDT) parser which generates a dependency tree from a given text. A dependency tree is a set of grammatical relationships in a sentence which are close to shallow semantic representations and a good starting point for generating semantic patterns. Currently, it defines 55 binary relations. These grammatical relationships are used to generate binary and ternary semantic relationships (linguistic patterns). Fig. 3 presents the dependency trees generated for four sample queries. Second is a rule-based parser which is designed to extract relationships that give more semantics as compared to visual concepts. The dependency tree is an input to the rule-based parser. To generate these rules we have considered various type of sentence e.g. declarative, interrogative, compound, etc. The rules in the rule-based parser cover almost all the important relationships between objects and their attributes. The following rules are developed to enumerate linguistic patterns by traversing the dependency tree paths either top to bottom or bottom to top. We refer to the parent node as the head and the child node as dependent. In Fig. 3 (b) *playing* is head of *boy*, or *boy* is a dependent of *playing* and *boy* is a sibling of *with.* Let *S* be a sentence/text with *n* tokens and let *w* be the current token for which we are generating pattern(s)

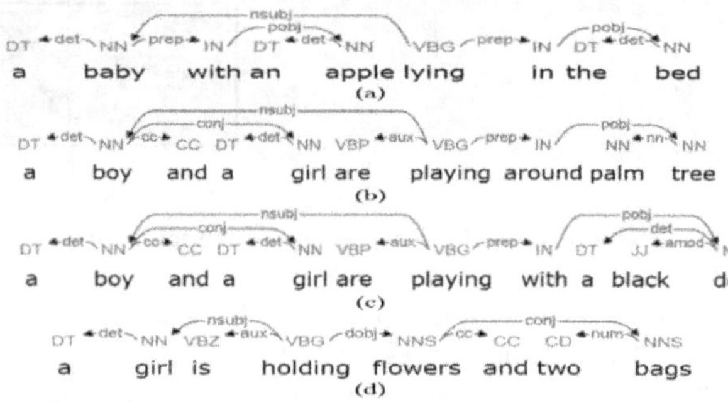

Figure 3: Dependency trees for queries (a) q1: a baby with an apple lying in the bed (b) q2: a boy and a girl are playing around palm tree (c) q3: a boy and a girl are playing with a black dog (d) q4: a girl is holding flowers and two bags.

The following rules extract binary and ternary patterns:

R1: If *w* is the subject of its first encountered head verb *a* in the tree $\xRightarrow{extract}$ (*w*, *a*) as (entity, action) pattern.

Eg: In query q1, *baby* is the subject and its first encountered head verb is *lying*, resulting in the pattern (*baby, lying*)

R2: If *w* is the head verb of a first encountered object *a* in the tree $\xRightarrow{extract}$(*w*, a) as (action, entity) pattern.

Eg: In q1, *lying* is the head verb and *bed* is the first encountered object, resulting in the pattern (*lying, bed*)

R3: If (entity, action) pattern is extracted through R1, extract the first encountered object *b* of a $\xRightarrow{extract}$ (*w*, *a*, *b*) as (entity, action, entity) pattern.

Eg: In q1, according to R1 we have (*baby, lying*), and *bed* is the first encountered object, resulting in the pattern (*baby, lying, bed*)

R4: If *w*is the noun of its head noun *a* $\xRightarrow{extract}$(*w*, *a*) as (attribute, Entity) pattern.

Eg: In q2, *tree* is the head noun of noun *palm*, resulting in the pattern (*palm, tree*)

R5: If *w* is a preposition then extract dependent noun *b* and the first encountered head noun *a* $\xRightarrow{extract}$(*a*, *w*, *b*) as (entity, preposition, entity) pattern

Eg: In q3, *with* is the preposition, *boy* is the head noun and *dog* is the dependent noun, resulting in the pattern (*boy, with, dog*)

R6: If w is preposition of its dependent a and b is head of the preposition phrase $\xrightarrow{extract}$ (b, w, a) as (action, preposition, entity) pattern.
Eg: In q3, *with* is the preposition, *dog* is the dependent and *playing* is the head of the preposition phrase, resulting in the pattern (*playing, with, dog*)
R7: If w is the conjunction of its head h and sibling a, where h and a have a conjunct relationship, extract the first encountered node c with a subject relationship with h or a $\xrightarrow{extract}$ (c, h) and (c, a) both as (entity, action) or (modifier, entity) or (attribute, entity).
Eg: In q3, *and* is the conjunction, *boy* is its head and *girl* is the sibling with the conjunction relationship with *boy. playing* is the node with the subject relationship with *boy* resulting in the pattern (*playing, boy*) and (*playing, girl*)
R7.1: If there is no first encountered subject node c and there is a head node b (verb or noun) of h, and there exist a subject relationship between b and d. $\xrightarrow{extract}$ (b, h), (b, a), (d, b, h) and (d, b, a) patterns.
Eg: In q4, *and* is the conjunction, *flowers* is its head and *bags* is the sibling with the conjunction relationship with *flowers. holding* is the node with the subject relation with *girl* resulting in the pattern (*holding, flowers*), (*holding, bags*), (*girl, holding, flowers*), (*girl, holding, bags*)
R8: Some of the patterns are directly present in the dependency tree. These patterns are binary and they are (Entity, modifier), (Entity, attribute), (Number modifier, entity), (Number compound, entity), (Negation modifier, entity) and Compound pattern.
Eg: In q3, *black* is the modifier and *dog* is the entity resulting in the pattern (*black, dog*)
These rules help in matching partial or complete query with the image text.

3.1.1 SDT Parser Modifications. We use a few additional tools and rules to improve the SDT parser output as follows:
Variation1: Sometimes wrong POS (Parts-Of-Speech) tags are given by the SDT parser to the words in a sentence. To minimize this inaccuracy, we parsed the sentence using two more parsers viz. TurboParser [35] and NLTK POS tagger [36] and majority voting by these three parser is used to decide the final POS of the word. If majority of the voting results in a tie, we use the original SDT output. The ensemble of parsers reduces the error rate of individual parser from 12% to 4%.
Variation2: In some cases subject and object relationships are not given by SDT. In such cases, we take the verb a and its first encountered head noun b and dependent noun c and extracted three patterns (b, a), (a, c), and (b, a, c).

3.2 Linguistic Pattern-based Textual model (LPT model)

In this model, we establish relationships between linguistic patterns $L_Q = \{l_1, l_2, ..., l_z\}$ of a query Q found by LPE with that of image (i_q). To do this, we count the number of patterns of L_Q which are present in the set of linguistic patterns of i_q, L_{i_q}. Patterns extracted by LPE are binary and ternary patterns. We give more weightage to the ternary patterns than to the binary patterns, because the former has more semantic information. We give weight value, ω=1, to the binary patterns and, ω=2, for the ternary patterns. $LPT(Q, i_q)$ is then calculated as the weighted sum of the binary and ternary patterns. Existing methods [12, 13] use co-occurrence information of the visual concepts in complex queries. But, they are unable to exploit the dependency among them. The LPT score for query Q and image i_q is given as follows:

$$LPT(Q, i_q) = \sum_{l_j \in L_Q} \sum_{l_r \in L_{i_q}} \omega * \delta(l_j, l_r) \tag{2}$$

where $\delta(l_j, l_r) = 1$ if linguistic pattern l_j and l_r are same else it is zero.

3.3 Linguistic Pattern-based Visual model (LPV model)

To find the linguistic patterns-based visual relevance $LPV(Q, i_q)$ between a query Q and an image $i_q \epsilon I$, each pattern $l_g \in L_Q$ is considered as a simple query and is fired on a commercial search engine to get the top N retrieved images, $I_{web}(l_g)$. For each image i_r from $I_{web}(l_g)$, k-nearest neighbors are identified from our dataset. If i_q is present in k-NN of i_r then the similarity between i_q and i_r is considered for the visual relevance score. The nearest neighbor approach eliminates unrelated images from being considered and thus prevents retrieval of unrelated images. The linguistic pattern based approach when considered with k-NN images, reduces the sematic gap for visual models. Most of the existing approaches [12, 13, 15] use only visual concepts instead of linguistic patterns to estimate visual relatedness and do not give satisfactory results. N is taken to be 20 and k taken to be 50. We empirically found these optimal values by looking at MAP values with increasing value of N and k as shown in Fig. 4(a) and 4(b). The LPV score used is as follows:

$$LPV(Q, i_q) = \sum_{l_g \in L_Q} \sum_{i_r \in I_{web}(l_g)} sim\,(i_q, i_r) \tag{3}$$

The visual similarity between two images, i_q and i_r, is computed using Gaussian similarity as:

$$\mathrm{sim}(i_q, i_r) = \begin{cases} \exp(-\left\|i_q - i_r\right\|^2 / \sigma^2) & if\ i_q \epsilon NN_v(i_r) \\ 0 & otherwise \end{cases} \tag{4}$$

where σ is the median of the Euclidean distances of all the related image pairs [32, 33].

3.4 Cross Modality model (CM model)

This model considers both text and visual modalities along with linguistic patterns to find the relevance between a query and an image. This model also incorporates visual concepts, which are not considered in LPT and LPV models. We use concept to refer both visual concepts and linguistic patterns. Relevance is computed based on the following factors: 1) how frequently a concept is occurring in the image's visual neighbors; 2) how a concept and an image text concepts co-occur in the visual neighbors. These intuitions work well if a large amount of supporting data is available. However, many social images do not have a sufficient number of concepts and thus, these factors may not contribute fully towards the relevance score. We handle this VoI by utilizing the concepts of the visual neighbors of the image, in the context of the above two factors, to improve concept relevance. These factors together contribute towards the development of an image-concept relevance score.

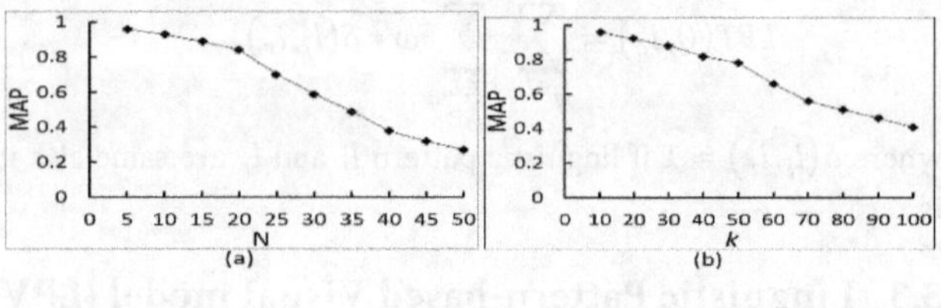

Figure 4: (a) Effect of different N values on MAP for fifty queries (b) Effect of different k values on MAP for hundred images.

3.4.1 Factor 1: Concept existence in visual neighbors [26]: cm_1 Given an Image set $I = \{i_1, i_2, \dots i_l\}$ labeled with concepts from concept set, $T = \{t_1, t_2, \dots t_m\}$. Let r be an indicator variable defined as:

$$r(t_u, i_r) = \begin{cases} 1 & \text{if image } i_r \text{ is labeled with concept } t_u \\ 0 & \text{otherwise} \end{cases} \quad (5)$$

For each image, $i_q \in I$, k-nearest neighbors $NN_v(i_q)$, are given based on visual similarity v:

$$v(i_q, i_r) = cosine\_similarity(i_q, i_r) \quad (6)$$

The nearest neighbor vote for test image i_q and concept t_p is:

$$cm_1(t_p, i_q) = |\{i_r \in NN_v(i_q) | \, r(t_p, i_r) = 1\}| \quad (7)$$

3.4.2 Factor 2: Concept boosting: cm_2. To formulate concept boosting, we first describe concept co-occurrence: To leverage text information and to exploit the dependency between concepts, we utilize concept co-occurrence (how two concepts together are assigned to images). We exploit concept co-occurrence between pair-wise concepts, t_k and t_r, in the whole dataset. We normalize concept co-occurrence by the union of t_k and t_r to find the relatedness between the concepts. Different normalization factors, such as the frequency of one of the concepts is used in [34,28], and the co-occurrences of a concept is summed with all the other concepts to reduce the bias in [29]. We normalize concept co-occurrence by the union of t_k and t_r to find the relatedness between the concepts.

$I'(t_k) = \{i_r \,|\, r(t_k, i_r) = 1, i_r \in I\}$ denotes the set of images labeled with t_k and $T'(i_r)$ denotes the set of concepts which are labeled to image i_r. Concept-to-concept relevance, $TT(t_k, t_r)$, between t_k and t_r ($t_k \neq t_r$) is given by the Jaccard coefficient.

$$TT(t_k, t_r) = \frac{|I'(t_k) \cap I'(t_r)|}{|I'(t_k) \cup I'(t_r)|} \quad (8)$$

Two concepts that are related to an image/topic can be more informative and reliable if they occur together in many of the visual neighbors of the image. Based on this observation, we consider co-occurrences of t_p and the concept of image i_q in the visual neighbors. This is to reduce the effect of noisy concepts cm_2 is calculated using a similar measure as given in eq (8), but with respect to $NN_v(i_q)$. Let $I'_{NN(i_q)}(t_p) = \{i_r \,|\, r(t_p, i_r) = 1, i_r \in NN_v(i_q)\}$ be the set of neighborhood images of i_q labeled with concept t_p. The concept-to-concept relevance, $TT_{NN}(t_p, t_r)$, between t_p and $t_r \in T'(i_q)$, ($t_p \neq t_r$), and cm_2 are defined as follows

$$TT_{NN}(t_p, t_r) = \frac{|I'_{NN(i_q)}(t_p) \cap I'_{NN(i_q)}(t_r)|}{|I'_{NN(i_q)}(t_p) \cup I'_{NN(i_q)}(t_r)|} \quad (9)$$

$$cm_2(t_p, i_q) = \sum_{t_r \in T'(i_q)} TT_{NN}(t_p, t_r) \quad (10)$$

The cross modality model calculates the relevance between concept t_p and image i_q as $CM(t_p, i_q) = cm_1 * cm_2$. Concept co-occurrence works reliably under the assumption that enough supporting data is available. If concepts are missing or no information can be extracted from concepts [27, 28], cm_2 becomes zero, thus wiping out the effect of factor cm_1 (as factors are multiplied in the relevance score [28, 29]). We handle this by estimating cm_2 using the additional information of the visual neighborhood of the image i_q.

3.4.3 Factor 3: Handling void of information: cm_3. If image i_q does not have any concepts or if the co-occurrence information of the concepts of i_q with other concepts is not available, we consider the concepts of the images belonging to set $NN_v(i_q)$ and T' is replaced with T'_{NN} in cm_2 equation to obtain concept boosting measures:

$$cm_3(t_p, i_q) = \sum_{t_r \in T'_{NN}(i_q)} TT_{NN}(t_p, t_r) \,/\, k \quad (11)$$

The cross modality model is now defined as follows:

$$CM(t_p, i_q) = \begin{cases} cm_1 * cm_2 & \text{if } cm_2 \neq 0 \\ cm_1 * cm_3 & \text{otherwise} \end{cases} \quad (12)$$

The proposed measure not only gives importance to concept t_p and image i_q, but also to its visual neighbors. The *CM* score given by eq (12), is estimated for each concept of query Q and then aggregated for final cross modality relevance score, $CM(Q, i_q)$. The component, $cm_1 * cm_2$, gives importance to the test concept and test image, while $cm_1 * cm_3$, gives importance to image, its visual neighbors and concepts. We take product of cm_1 and cm_2 because it boosts the importance of the informative terms [42]. If cm_2 becomes zero, we will consider cm_3. Many times, text associated with images may not be in sentence form therefore no linguistic patterns can be obtained. This case is also handled by the proposed CM model

4 EXPERIMENTAL ANALYSIS

4.1 Dataset

There are two types of data, viz., tag-based [40, 41] and sentence-based [37, 38] available for evaluating image retrieval. MIRFlickr [40] and NUS-WIDE [41] are two leading benchmark datasets for tag-based image retrieval. They provide 14 and 81 test tags respectively, with their ground truth. The ground truth is developed only for single tag queries. In contrast to this, Flickr8k and MSCOCO have sentences which briefly describe main objects and scenes in an image. Therefore, complex queries can be applied on them and we use them to evaluating our approach. However, no ground truth is available for such queries. Also, these datasets have only a few relevant images with respect to a query. Therefore, we include google search result images to our dataset to have sufficient number of relevant images. To obtain the ground truth for each image we used crowdsourcing. Following Gua et al. [13] procedure to give score to images, we give three values viz. relevant (score=2), partially relevant (score=1), and irrelevant (score=0) with respect to the query.

We create two datasets WCQ9K and WCQ148K. WCQ9K is created using 25 complex queries fired on the Google image search engine. The top 400 (limited by Google at the time of scraping) images are crawled with their surrounding text of a 300-word window. Text from the "alt" and "title" tags of image-tag is also considered, whereas, WCQ148K is created by combining three sources, viz. MSCOCO [37] consisting of 81K images, flickr8k consisting of 8K images [38], and Google search results consisting of 59K images. The top 600 Google search result images are crawled in the same manner for 100 complex queries as previously described. These queries are extracted from Clickture using top frequent concepts from both MSCOCO and Filckr8k datasets to ensure related images from all three datasets. The dataset also consist of images which are visually similar.

Linguistic patterns are extracted using LPE for image with associated text and query text. The linguistic patterns extracted for each query are fired as simple queries to the Google search engine and the top 10 images are retrieved for each pattern. We use CNN features. A trained CNN model called VGGNet [30] consisting of 16 layers with (3x3) convolution filters is used to obtain the visual features of each image. The CNN features of dimension 4096 are generated from the last fully connected layers of ReLU activation.

4.2 Evaluation Measure: NDCG@*n*

NDCG is commonly used to evaluate top ranked results in information retrieval systems, because top images search results are visited by most of the users. A higher value of NDCG indicates that images with higher relevance scores are ahead of less relevant images for a given query. It is defined as follows:

$$NDCG@n(Q) = \frac{DCG_n(Q)}{IDCG_n(Q)} \tag{13}$$

where $DCG_n(Q) = \sum_{j=1}^{n} \frac{2^{rel_j - 1}}{log_2(j+1)}$, rel_j is the graded relevance of the image at rank j and $IDCG_n(Q)$ is a normalization constant equal to the maximum possible DCG value till rank n. NDCG equals 1 for a perfect ranking and is achieved when DCG and IDCG values are the same.

4.3 Parameter settings

The proposed approach is unsupervised and considers three models. Each model has a fair share in the final results. The weights in eq (1) are to be associated with each model. The method used for estimating weights α_1, α_2, and α_3 is based on the individual performance of each model and is as follows

$$\begin{cases} \alpha_1 : \alpha_2 : \alpha_3 = A_{LPT} : A_{LPV} : A_{CM} \\ \alpha_1 + \alpha_2 + \alpha_3 = 1 \end{cases} \tag{14}$$

where A_{LPT}, A_{LPV}, and A_{CM} are the normalized average retrieval precision when using the LPT model, the LPV model, and the CM model, respectively [13].

4.4 Results

To demonstrate the effectiveness of our approach, we compare our approach with Guo et al. [13], Cui et al. [15], and Gao et al. [14]. Guo et al. compared their approach with the other existing approaches and demonstrated the superiority of their result over the other complex query-based approaches [12]. For each of the methods, the parameters with the best performance are considered. Fig. 5 presents the mean NDCG@*n* over all queries of WCQ148K for different values of *n*. Fig. 5 shows that our approach is better than the existing approaches at all values of *n*. The difference in the NDCG score of our method with Gao et al. is almost constant at all values of *n*, whereas for Cui et al. the difference increases for higher values of *n*. Fig. 5 shows that Cui et al. approach gives very irrelevant values after *n*=50, whereas Gao et al. and our approach tends to give relevant images even at n=100. Our approach is better than the other methods as evident from Fig. 5 because it considers concepts, attributes, and relationships such as spatial and action. None of the existing methods exploit these rich semantics.

An experiment is conducted to evaluate the performance of our approach in relation to image reranking with the Google search results and Guo et al. work. We use the WCQ9K dataset as it contains only Google search results. It can be observed from Fig. 6 that the difference between the mean NDCG of the Google search results and ours widen for higher values of *n* from 0.63 to 0.91. This is because, the top google search results for some queries are relevant and the later results are mix of partially relevant and irrelevant images. All methods give best performance at a lower value of *n* and degrade as *n* increases. In Fig. 5, LPCM is slightly going up with the increase in NDCG depth whereas in Fig. 6 it is going down. This is due to the fact that the average number of relevant images per query is low in the WCQ9K, i.e. approximately 30 images per query. Therefore, no method can achieve a good score for higher values of *n* which is obvious from Fig. 6. In Fig. 5 NDCG curve rises with an increase in *n* as WCQ148K has significant number of relevant images. For example, the query "*group of people walking on the beach at sunset*", from WCQ148K has almost 150 relevant images and nearly 500 partially relevant images, whereas query "*lorry full of mangoes*" in WCQ9K has almost 6 relevant images and 26 partially relevant images.

Fig. 7 shows the effect of each model individually using our approach through mean NDCG@*n*. The LPT model performs the best among the three models. This is because the LPT model is able to exploit a good textual description available for images. The LPV model is found to perform better than the CM model, on an

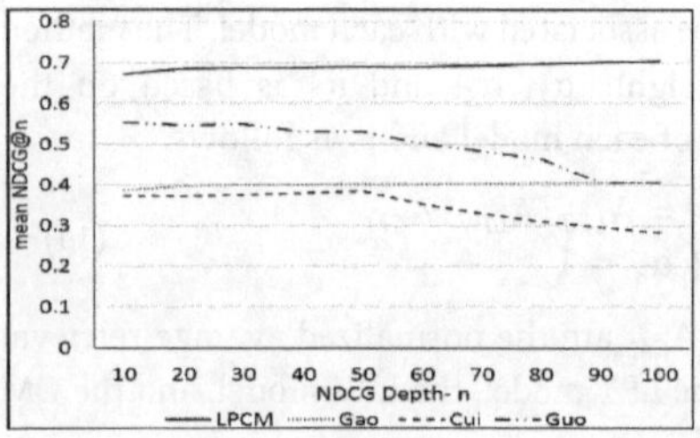

Figure 5: Average performance comparison of different approaches over WCQ148K

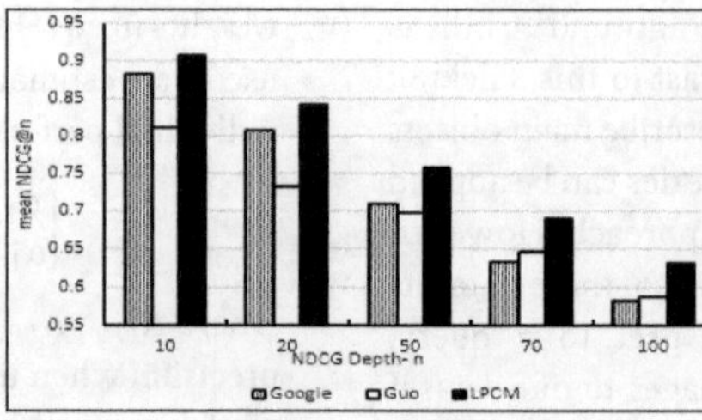

Figure 6: Comparison of the search result reranking of different approaches over WCQ9K

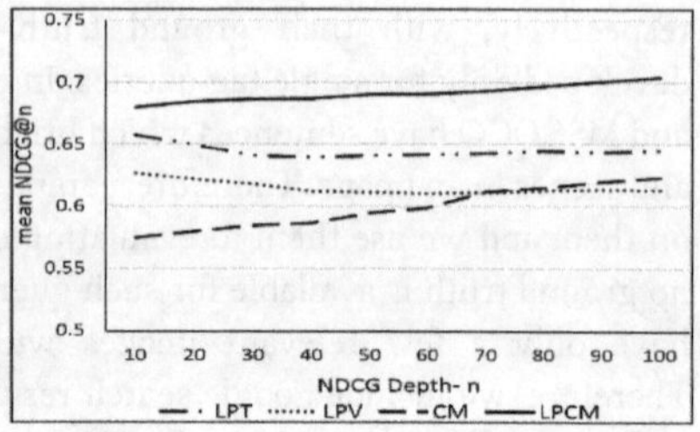

Figure 7: Comparison of individual model in the proposed approach over WCQ148K

average, but in some cases, at a lower value of *n*, the LPV model gives a null value as there are no nearest neighbours present in the data. In Fig. 7, the NDCG for both LPT and LPV decreases for higher value of *n*, whereas, the NDCG of CM increases for a higher value of *n*. Both CM and our approach curve follow the same pattern, which proves that CM helps to lift the curve of our method at higher values of *n*. The LPT model for a lower value of *n* performs better than our approach for a couple of queries, because it exactly matches the associated text of images.

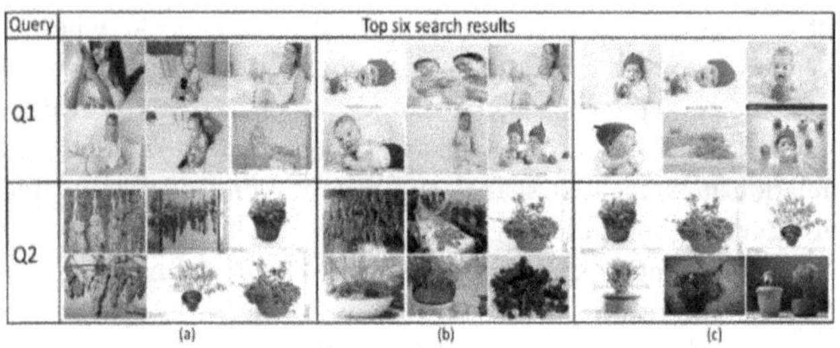

Figure 8: Search results for queries Q1: a baby with an apple lying in the bed and Q2: dried plant in a pot using (a) Google search (b) Guo's approach, and (c) LPCM over WCQ9K

Fig. 8 shows the results of image reranking for Google, Guo et al., and our approaches on WCQ9K. The top six ranked images for the two queries are presented in Fig. 8. It can be seen from the figure that the performance of the proposed approach is significantly better than that of the other two approaches. In Fig. 8(a), we see that the Google retrieved images are mix of relevant and partially relevant images. For query Q1, the top results contain a woman and a girl rather than a baby. None of the result is a perfect match to the query. For Q2, pot is considered as marijuana which returns many images of dried marijuana. Fig. 8(b) shows that the resultant images of Guo's approach have two partially relevant and four relevant images for query Q1. However, only one relevant image is retrieved for Q2. This is due to the fact that the concept of pot exists in many of Marijuana images. Also, a dried plant and marijuana share many visual cues. Fig. 8(c) shows the results of our approach. For query Q1, our approach retrieves all six relevant images. This is because of the availability of rich text with the relevant images where the concepts and patterns exist. For Q2 our method retrieves one marijuana image which is because of the similarity between dried marijuana and a dried plant.

We analyzed the performance of each model individually for ten queries from WCQ9K. The performance of the LPT and CM models is better than the LPV model, because of the presence of good textual information compared to visual. The LPV model works better when the query contains visual concepts which have some unique visual features. The LPT model performs better for almost all queries except in the case of simple queries where CM model performs better. The performance of the CM model is moderate for all queries compared to LPT and LPV. Unlike other existing methods which demonstrate their performance on filtered data, our method considers dataset where we have a significant amount of partial overlap among images w.r.t. visual appearance.

5 CONCLUSIONS AND FUTURE WORK

In this paper, we proposed a novel approach for estimating the query-image relevance for complex queries, which exploits the linguistic patterns of a query. We built a rule-based semantic parser which is applied on the results of the Stanford dependency tree parser to identify them. Our approach consists of three models. LPT and LPV give the relevance score on the biases of linguistic patterns to an image based on textual and visual modalities, respectively. We also built a cross modality model on both primitive concepts and the linguistic patterns for query-image relevance. The model exploits concepts in an image neighborhood to utilize its additional information. It also handles the unavailability of supporting text for images. Experiments were conducted to evaluate and compare our approach with the state-of-the-art methods on real world data of size more than 148K images. The results demonstrated the effectiveness of our approach while having significant amount of partial overlap among images.

The limitation of our approach is that it does not consider constraints like the spatial relationship among the objects and it does not deal with abstract queries. Our future work will handle these issues in image retrieval for complex queries.

REFERENCES

[1] R. Fergus, L. Fei-Fei, P. Perona, and A. Zisserman. 2005. Learning Object Categories from Google's Image Search. In Proc. ICCV, vol. 2, pp. 1816 - 1823

[2] D. Grangier and S. Bengio. A Discriminative Kernel-based Model to Rank Images from Text Queries. IEEE Trans. Pattern Analysis and Machine Intelligence, vol. 30, no. 8, pp. 1371 - 1384

[3] M. Guillaumin, T. Mensink, J. Verbeek, C. Schmid, and C. Schmid. 2009. TagProp: Discriminative metric learning in nearest neighbor models for image auto-annotation. In Proc. Computer Vision, pp. 309–316

[4] N. Kumar, P. Belhumeur, and S. Nayar. 2008. FaceTracer: A Search Engine for Large Collections of Images with Faces. In Proc. European conference on Computer Vision, Lecture Notes in Computer Science, vol.s 5305. Springer, Berlin

[5] T. Lan, W. Yang, Y. Wang, and G. Mori. 2012. Image Retrieval with Structured Object Queries Using Latent Ranking SVM. In Proc. European conference on Computer Vision, vol. 4, pp. 129-142

[6] C. Frankel, M. J. Swain, and V. Athitsos. 1996. WebSeer: An Image Search Engine for the World Wide Web How to Find Images on the Web. Technical report, University of Chicago

[7] P. Li, M. Sanderson, and M. Carman. 2016. On the Effectiveness of Query Weighting for Adapting Rank Learners to New Unlabelled Collections. In Proc. CIKM, pp. 1413-1422

[8] N. Balasubramanian and G. Drive. 2010. Exploring Reductions for Long Web Queries Categories and Subject Descriptors. In Proc. SIGIR pp. 571–578.

[9] M. Bendersky, M. Rey, and W. B. Croft. 2011 . Parameterized Concept Weighting in Verbose Queries. In Proc. SIGIR, pp. 605–614.

[10] S. Tang et al.. 2008. TRECVID 2008 High-Level Feature Extraction By MCG-ICT-CAS. In Proc. The TRECVID Workshop, 566

[11] Y. Han et al. 2015. Semi-Supervised Feature Selection via Spline. IEEE Trans. Neural Networks and Learning Systems, vol. 26, no. 2, pp. 252-264

[12] L. Nie, S. Yan, M. Wang, R. Hong, and T. Chua. 2012 . Harvesting Visual Concepts for Image Search with Complex Queries. ACM Multimedia, pp. 59–68

[13] D. Guo and P. Gao. 2016. Complex-query web image search with concept-based relevance estimation. WWW, vol. 19, no. 2pp. 247–264

[14] Y. Gao, M. Wang, Z. J. Zha, J. Shen, X. Li, and X. Wu. 2013. Visual-textual joint relevance learning for tag-based social image search. IEEE Trans. Image Process., vol. 22, no. 1, pp. 363–376

[15] C. Cui, J. Shen, Z. Chen, S. Wang, and J. Ma. 2017. Learning to rank images for complex queries in concept-based search. Neurocomputing, DOI: https://doi.org/10.1016/j.neucom.2016.05.118

[16] J. Yuan, Z. Zha, Y. Zheng, X. Zhou, and M. Wang. 2011. Learning Concept Bundles for Video Search with Complex Queries. In Proc. MM, pp. 453–462

[17] B. Siddiquie, B. White, A. Sharma, and L. S. Davis. 2014. Multi-Modal Image Retrieval for Complex Queries using Small Codes. In Proc. ICMR.

[18] M.-C. de Marneffe and C. D. 2008. Manning, The Stanford typed dependencies representation. In workshop on Cross-Framework and Cross-Domain Parser Evaluation, pp. 1-8.

[19] M. Bendersky and W. B. Croft. 2008. Discovering Key Concepts in Verbose Queries. In Proc. SIGIR, pp. 491–498,.

[20] M. Lease, J. Allan, and B. Croft. 2009. Regression Rank: Learning to Meet the Opportunity of Descriptive Queries. Advances in Information Retrieval, ECIR, Lecture Notes in Computer Science, vol 5478

[21] G. Kumaran and J Allan. 2008. Effective and efficient user interaction for long queries. In Proc SIGIR, pp. 11-18

[22] R. Aly, D. Hiemstra, and R. Ordelman. 2007.Building detectors to support searches on combined semantic concepts. In MIR Workshop

[23] A. P. Natsev and M. R. Naphade. 2005. Learning the Semantics of Multimedia Queries and Concepts from a Small Number of Examples. In Proc. MULTIMEDIA, pp. 598–607.

[24] S. Chang, W. Hsu, L. Kennedy, and L. Xie. 2006 Video Search and High-Level Feature Extraction. In Proc. TREC Video Retrieval Evaluation

[25] X. Li, C. G. M. Snoek, S. Member, M. Worring, and A. W. M. Smeulders. 2012. Harvesting Social Images for Bi-Concept Search. IEEE Trans. Multimedia, vol. 14, no. 4, pp. 1091–1104

[26] X. Li, C. G.M.Snoek, and M. Worring. 2009. Learning Social Tag Relavevance by Neighbor Voting. IEEE trans. Multimedia, vol. 11, no. 7, pp. 1310–1322

[27] X. Qian, X. S. Hua, Y. Y. Tang, and T. Mei. 2014. Social image tagging with diverse semantics. IEEE Trans. Cybern., vol. 44, no. 12, pp. 2493–2508

[28] S. Lee, W. De Neve, and Y. M. Ro. 2010. Tag refinement in an image folksonomy using visual similarity and tag co-occurrence statistics. Signal Process. Image Commun., vol. 25, no. 10, pp. 761–773

[29] X. Zhang, Z. Huang, H. T. Shen, Y. Yang, and Z. Li. 2012. Automatic tagging by exploring tag information capability and correlation. In Proc. Int. Conf. WWW, vol. 15, no. 3, pp. 233–256

[30] K. Simonyan and A. Zisserman. 2015. Very Deep Convolutional Networks for Large-Scale Image Recognition. In Proc. ICLR, arXiv:1409.1556v6

[31] H. Chen, A. Trouve, K. J. Murakami and A. Fukuda. Semantic image retrieval for complex queries using a knowledge parser. Multimedia Tools and Applications, 2017

[32] G. Song, S. Wang, Q. Huang and Q. Tian. Multimodal Similarity Gaussian Process Latent Variable Model, IEEE Trans. Image Processing, 2017

[33] J. Liang, Y. Han and Q. Hu. Semi-Supervised image clustering with multi-modal information. ACM Multimedia System, vol. 22, no. 2, pp. 149-160, Mar. 2016.

[34] B. Sigurbjörnsson and R. Van Zwol. 2008. Flickr tag recommendation based on collective knowledge. In Proc. Int. Conf. WWW, vol. 6, pp. 327–336

[35] A. Martins, M. Almeida, and N. A. Smith. 2013. Turning on the turbo: Fast third-order nonprojective turbo parsers. In Proc. of the 51st Annual Meeting of the Association for Computational Linguistics, vol. 2, pp. 617–622.

[36] E. Loper, S. Bird. 2002. NLTK: the natural language toolkit. In Proc. of the ACL Workshop on Effective Tools and Methodologies for Teaching Natural Language Processing and Computational Linguistics, pp. 69–72.

[37] Lin, T.-Y., Maire, M., Belongie, S., Hays, J., Perona, P., Ramanan, D., Dollr, P., & Zitnick, C. L. 2014. Microsoft COCO: Common objects in context. In ECCV

[38] C. Rashtchian, P. Young, M. Hodosh, and J. Hockenmaier. 2010. Collecting image annotations using amazon's mechanical turk. In NAACL HLT Workshop on Creating Speech and Language Data with Amazon's Mechanical Turk, pp. 139– 147.

[39] X. S. Hua, L. Yang, J. Wang, J. Wang, M. Ye, K. Wang, Y. Rui, and J. Li. 2013. Clickage: Towards bridging semantic and intent gaps via mining click logs of search engines. ACM Multimedia.

[40] T.-S. Chua, J. Tang, R. Hong, H. Li, Z. Luo, and Y. Zheng, "NUS-WIDE: A real- world web image database from national university of Singapore," Proc. ACM Int. Conf. Image Video Retr. (CIVR), 2009,Article No. 48

[41] K. Simonyan and A. Zisserman, "Very deep convolutional networks for large-scale image recognition," Proc. ICLR, 2015, arXiv:1409.1556v6

[42] C. Tofallis, "Add or Multiply? A Tutorial on Ranking and Choosing with Multiple Criteria.," INFORMS Trans. Edu., 2014, pp. 109–119.

A Context-Aware Late-Fusion Approach for Disaster Image Retrieval from Social Media

Minh-Son Dao
Universiti Teknologi Brunei, Brunei Darussalam
Big Data Analytics Laboratory, NICT, Japan
minh.son@utb.edu.bn

Pham Quang Nhat Minh
Alt Vietnam Co., Ltd, Vietnam
pham.minh@alt.ai

Asem Kasem
Universiti Teknologi Brunei, Brunei Darussalam
asem.kasem@utb.edu.bn

Mohamed Saleem Haja Nazmudeen
Universiti Teknologi Brunei, Brunei Darussalam
mohamed.saleem@utb.edu.bn

ABSTRACT

Natural disasters, especially those related to flooding, are global issues that attract a lot of attention in many parts of the world. A series of research ideas focusing on combining heterogeneous data sources to monitor natural disasters have been proposed, including multi-modal image retrieval. Among these data sources, social media streams are considered of high importance due to the fast and localized updates on disaster situations. Unfortunately, the social media itself contains several factors that limit the accuracy of this process such as noisy data, unsynchronized content between image and collateral text, and untrusted information, to name a few.

In this research work, we introduce a context-aware late-fusion approach for disaster image retrieval from social media. Several known techniques based on context-aware criteria are integrated, namely late fusion, tuning, ensemble learning, object detection and scene classification using deep learning. We have developed a method for image-text content synchronization and spatial-temporal-context event confirmation, and evaluated the role of using different types of features extracted from internal and external data sources. We evaluated our approach using the dataset and evaluation tool offered by MediaEval2017: Emergency Response for Flooding Events Task. We have also compared our approach with other methods introduced by MediaEval2017's participants. The experimental results show that our approach is the best one when taking the image-text content synchronization and spatial-temporal-context event confirmation into account.

CCS CONCEPTS

• **Information systems → Combination, fusion and federated search**; **Image search**; • **Computing methodologies → Machine learning approaches**;

ICMR '18, June 11–14, 2018, Yokohama, Japan

ACM ISBN 978-1-4503-5046-4/18/06...$15.00
https://doi.org/10.1145/3206025.3206047

KEYWORDS

Natural Disaster Image Retrieval; Social Media; Late Fusion; Domain Specific; Content and Context; Discriminative Improvement

ACM Reference Format:

Minh-Son Dao, Pham Quang Nhat Minh, Asem Kasem, and Mohamed Saleem Haja Nazmudeen. 2018. A Context-Aware Late-Fusion Approach for Disaster Image Retrieval from Social Media. In *ICMR '18: 2018 International Conference on Multimedia Retrieval, June 11–14, 2018, Yokohama, Japan.* ACM, New York, NY, USA, 8 pages. https://doi.org/10.1145/3206025.3206047

1 INTRODUCTION

Natural disasters affecting living beings and the environment cause many types of losses and hardships. As reported by the United Nations Office for the Coordination of Humanitarian Affairs[1], flooding events recently form the majority type of observed natural disasters. Along with civilization development, we have learned worth experiences and invented several methods to cope with the permanent threats of natural disasters [18]. The significance of flooding hazards has led many researchers and government agencies to work on the use of technology-based solutions for accurate and timely designation of flooded areas to enable understanding of these areas, estimating hazards impact, and responding quickly to most critical events. This has been typically done by leveraging remote-sensed data [19], and mainly satellite images, and using several techniques to efficiently monitor and assess the damages after natural hazards and disasters [17]. Although remote sensing is known as a rich data source that can cover wide areas with high resolution, it is however expensive, slowly updated, and cannot precisely report activities of people inside affected areas. On the contrary, other data sources such as social media streams are considered to be cheap and fast in reflecting what is happening on the field. This is mainly due to the fast response and locality of such information sources, where even news reporters and concerned officials cannot be timely available.

Social media platforms such as Twitter and Flickr have been heavily exploited for inferring information about different types of events, such as social, sports, and disaster events [15, 26]. Liu et. al. [20] provided a comprehensive survey on event based analysis over social multimedia data, including event enrichment, detection, and categorization. This has led research works to focus on combining remote-sensing with other sources of data, most notably

[1] UNISDR, Sendai Framework for Disaster Risk Reduction 2015-2030. http://www.unisdr.org/files/43291_sendaiframeworkfordrren.pdf

real-time information extracted from social media, in order to provide accurate and comprehensive view of disaster events. In [14], Herfort et. al. presented an approach that relies on the geographical relations between twitter data and flood phenomena to improve situational awareness. The approach used specific geographical features such as hydrological data and digital elevation models to prioritize crisis-relevant twitter messages.

Bischke et. al. [7] demonstrated a system for contextual enrichment of remote-sensed events in satellite imagery by leveraging contemporary content from social media. Similarly, K. Ahmad et. al. [2] introduced a system, JORD, which crawled and linked social media data about environmental disasters to satellite imagery. Bischke et. al. [8] has also set up a challenge to encourage researchers around the world to share their solutions on best ways to integrate remote sensing and social media data to increase the accuracy of information extracted from data relating to a natural disaster.

In this paper, we present a method designed to extract information about flooding events based on images and other metadata retrieved from social media streams. This is in accordance to the first subtask of Mediaeval 2017 [8], which is about Disaster Image Retrieval from Social Media. In particular, we have designed an algorithm that takes a collection of multimedia images and their metadata and is able to identify those images related to a flooding event and properly discriminate the water levels in different areas (e.g., images showing a lake vs. images showing a flooded street).

To achieve that, we have designed a context-aware and late-fusion algorithm that leverages several known techniques, namely late fusion, tuning, ensemble learning, object detection, and used deep learning and temporal-spatial-based event confirmation.

The paper is organized as follows: Section 2 describes our proposed method to retrieve disaster images, in this case "flood" images, from social media data with different restrictions of features that can be used. Section 3 reports the results of the proposed method as well as the comparison with other participants who joined the MediaEval 2017 challenge. Section 4 summarizes the proposed method with its contribution and future works to overcome its current limitations.

2 A CONTEXT-AWARE LATE-FUSION IMAGE RETRIEVAL

A recent survey on content-based image retrieval [30] emphasized various ways to utilize features extracted from images including spatial context embedding information and retrieval fusion scheme to overcome conceptual and contextual semantic gaps. In [20], the authors point out the importance of integrating both visual and text features to link the event's data (i.e. image and its related metadata) to the context where such an event happens. The research introduced in [16] discussed how to bridge the semantic gap between multimedia data and users by taking both content and context components. In [10], the approach used external data with visual and text features extracted from social media to detect event's presence. These external data enhance the consistency between events reported by users and those that really happen under the same context (i.e. spatio-temporal-semantic).

We introduce in this section a context-aware late-fusion image retrieval framework designed with four different categories: (1) using visual features alone, (2) using metadata data alone, (3) fusing visual and text features, and (4) fusing image content, metadata, and external data with context awareness. The proposed framework is designed according to the aforementioned discussions to have a comprehensive comparison between the different ways to utilize social media data to carry out context-aware late-fusion image retrieval.

Following subsections discuss each category of the proposed framework.

2.1 Visual-based Image Retrieval

Visual features play a very important role in a content-based image retrieval. Various visual features have been defined and leveraged for increasing the precision/recall of image retrieving process. These features can be used solely or fused with others by a proper fusion scheme. In [11], an experimental comparison of different visual features for image retrieval was conducted. In [22], an interesting survey of fusion schemes used to utilize a set of features for image retrieval is introduced. These researchers point out that selecting a set of features and a fusing scheme to gain a good result are not trivial issues.

In this section, we describe how to utilize a fixed number of visual features with a proper fusion scheme to retrieve images. Figure 2 illustrates our method that is designed with four stages in order to cope with the similarity of texture, color, and spatial relation of different regions between non-flood and flood images. Figure 1 introduces an example of low-discriminative distance between flood and non-flood images in term of using traditional visual features such as Auto Color Correlogram (ACC), Edge Histogram (EH), Color and Edge Directivity Descriptor (CEDD), Color Layout (CLD), Fuzzy Color and Texture Histogram (FCTH), Joint Composite Descriptor (JCD), GABOR, Scalable Color (SC), and TAMURA.

We formalize the problem as an ensemble learning and tuning task, in which we use visual features associated with each image provided by the organizers of the 2017 Multimedia Satellite Task:Emergency Response for Flooding Events [8] (e.g. ACC, EH, CEDD, CLD, FCTH, JCD, GABOR, SC, and TAMURA). These visual features are used with supervised learners to create classifiers. Our visual-based method includes three components: late fusion, tuning, and ensemble learning, designed as follows:

- **Stage 1**: a set of classifiers associated with each type of features (F_i) is created by using supervised learners (SL_i) with outputs reported in a regression form (i.e. the output variable takes continuous values). The late fusion technique is applied to these outputs to form the multimodal features combination (MFC), as follows: $MFC = \sum_{i=1}^{n}(w_i * SL_i)$ where n is the number of supervised learners, w_i is the weight of the ith supervised learner, and $\sum(w_i) = 1$.
- **Stage 2**: bagging is utilized on these features and learners to increase the accuracy of the system. A multiple data set (MDS) is created by dividing randomly the training data set into m non-intersecting folders (MDS_m). At the end of this stage, the combined classifier is created, namely the combined learner (CL).
- **Stage 3**: after running a testing phase on these data sets, a new training data set for tuning is created and learned by

Figure 1: The similarity of texture, color, and spatial relation of different regions between non-flood and flood images

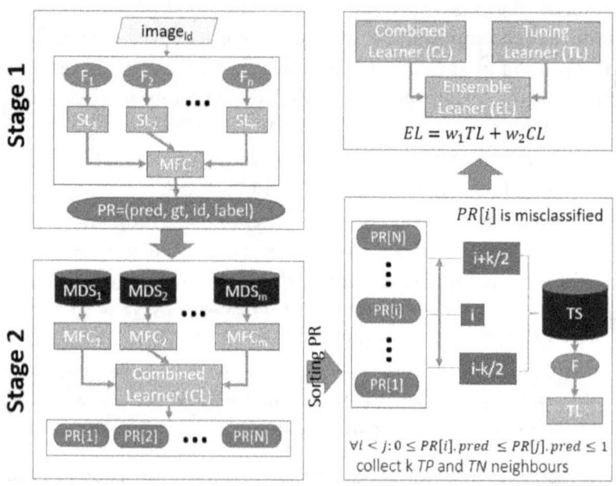

Figure 2: The Visual-based Image Retrieval Diagram

using a specific supervised learner and a certain subset of feature types F. The output of this stage is called the tuning learner (TL). Subsection 2.1.1 describes how to establish this tuning data set.

- **Stage 4**: the ensemble learner (EL) is created as $EL = w1 * TL + w2 * CL$ where $w1 + w2 = 1$.

2.1.1 Creating a tuning data set.

(1) Let $PR = \{pred, gt, id, label\}_{i=1:N}$ be an output array when using CL from stage 2, where N is the number of images, $PR[i] = (pred, gt, id, label)$ denotes the predicted value, the ground-truth label, the *id* and the predicted label of the ith image. Here, the predicted label $PR[i].label$ is calculated by $f(PR[i].pred, threshold)$ where the function f and the *threshold* value are given beforehand. Next, the ascending sort algorithm is applied to PR on the *pred* value to get PR^{sorted} array so that $\forall i < j, 0 \leq PR^{sorted}[i].pred \leq PR^{sorted}[j].pred \leq 1$.

(2) For each $PR^{sorted}[i]$, if $PR^{sorted}[i].gt \neq PR^{sorted}[i].label$, collecting its k nearest neighbour images whose ground-truth and label are equal (i.e. collect k *true positive* and *true negative* neighbours) by getting $k/2$ samples from position $(i-1)$ towards 1 and from position $(i+1)$ towards N, respectively.

Algorithm 1 describes how to generate a tuning data set TS from input data set PR.

ALGORITHM 1: Generating a tuning data set

Input: $PR = \{pred, gt, id, label = 0\}_{i=1:N}$, threshold, k
Output: TS
Function ***generateTS***
  //update "label" with f = "smaller"
  foreach *(pr in PR)* **do**
    if *(pr.pred < threshold)* **then**
      pr.label = 0; //irrelevant
    else
      pr.label = 1 //relevant
    end
  end
  $PR^{sorted} = AscendingSort_{pred}(PR)$;
  $TS = \emptyset$;
  foreach *(pr in* PR^{sorted}*)* **do**
    if *(pr.gt ≠ pr.label)* **then**
      $LB = max(i - k/2, 1)$;
      $UB = min(i + k/2, N)$;
      $TS = TS \cup \{y_m\}_{m=i..LB}$;
      $TS = TS \cup \{y_n\}_{n=i..UB}$;
    end
  end
end

Stages 3 and 4 are the major contribution of our proposed method to improve the accuracy of image retrieval. The idea behind these stages is to apply boosting and bagging techniques to create a tuning classifier (e.g. Random Forest (RF)) for samples which fall into a wrong side of a hyperplane zone of a previous classifier (e.g. Support Vector Machine (SVM)).

2.2 Meta-data-based Image Retrieval

In this section, we present our method for classifying images, which only uses images' metadata. We focus on metadata that may contain useful information for classifying images into one of two classes: **flood-related** or **flood-unrelated**. From our observation, we chose three attributes for the task: title, description, and user's tags, while each image in the data set additionally include other fields such as *image_id*, *image_url*, *date_taken*, *date_uploaded*, *user_nsid*, *user_nickname*, *capture_device*, *license_url*, *latitude*, *longitude*, and *license_name*.

We formalize the image retrieval as a text categorization task, in which we extract textual features from the metadata. Textual features are used as basic features for training a feed forward neural network (FFNN) with just one hidden layer. We chose neural network as the machine learning algorithm because we obtained better results on the development set than other methods that we tried in preliminary experiments. Another reason is that our proposed neural network architecture is very simple, and yet effective, when applied to the development data set.

Our meta-based classification method includes three components: preprocessing, feature extraction, and training neural network, as illustrated in Figure 3. They are described as follows:

(1) **Pre-processing**: we clean text data by removing hyperlinks, image path, and image names. We also remove all URLs in the text. We perform these steps by using some regular expressions. After that, we do word tokenization and remove all punctuations in a text. For a user tag containing multiple words, we join words in the tag to form a phrase and treat that phrase as a single word. We use *nltk toolkit* [5] to perform word tokenization.
(2) **Textual Feature Extraction**: for text categorization task, bag-of-words are basic and straightforward features. We just use bag-of-words features and represent an image as an n-dimension sparse vector in which n is the limit of the number of words in the vocabulary extracted from the training data set. A feature is activated if the metadata of the image contains the corresponding word in the vocabulary. In our experiments, we used $n = 10,000$. We extracted features from the three attributes: title, description, and tags of an image.
(3) **Neural Network Architecture**: we used a feed-forward neural network with one hidden layer containing 128 units. For training the network, we used batch size of 20, and applied drop-out technique with drop-out coefficient 0.5. In the output layer, we used softmax layer so that the final network can output probability values that an image is related to flood or not. We adopted *keras* framework[2] for building the neural network.

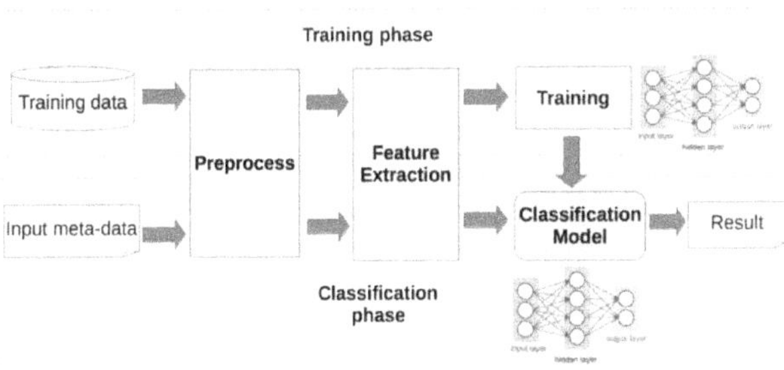

Figure 3: The meta-based classification diagram

[2]https://github.com/fchollet/keras

2.3 Visual-metadata-based Image Retrieval

The research presented in [27] could be considered as the first method that combines text (i.e. context) and image features (i.e. content) into the same semantic space using Latent Semantic Indexing (LSI) to retrieve images. In [26, 30] the authors emphasized the importance of using both visual and text features to retrieve images or detect events, especially with social media data.

Here we introduce a visual-metadata-based image retrieval using both visual and text features. The method used for visual-based image retrieval, described in subsection 2.1 is utilized for this task with some modifications. All features and supervised learners of visual-based and metadata-based methods are reused.

At stage 1, MFC is modified as $MFC = \sum_{i=1}^{N}(w_i^v * SL_i^v) + \sum_{j=1}^{M}(w_j^m * SL_j^m)$ where $\sum(w_i^v) + \sum(w_j^m) = 1$. v and m denote visual and metadata, respectively. N and M denote the number of visual and metadata features, respectively.

In this case, feature sets include visual features provided by the organizer and text features extracted using the method introduced in subsection 2.2. The CL is integrated from both visual-based and metadata-based methods. The TL and EL are performed as usual.

2.4 Visual-metadata-external-resource-based Image Retrieval

Figure 1 and 4 are examples of factors that strongly influence the image retrieval productivity. The former shows that only visual features (i.e. content) cannot work well when lacking the context support. The latter confirms that non-synchronization between image and metadata content also leads to wrong result. Obviously, Figure 4 can tell us that the image content expressed *non-flood* event (i.e. no visual cue can link you to a flood event) whilst metadata content confirmed *related-flood* event.

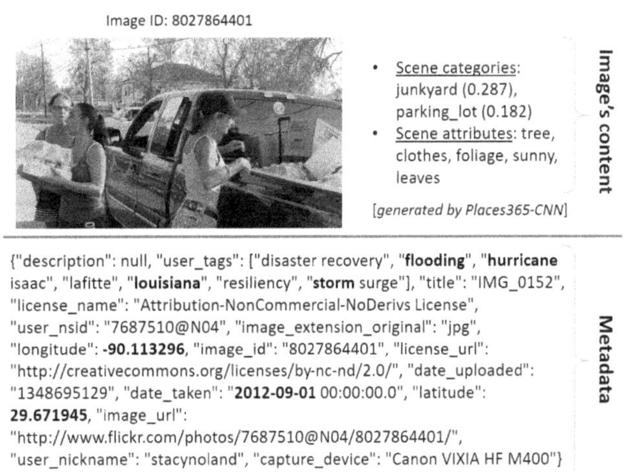

Figure 4: Non synchronization between the content of an image and metadata from the same post

We observed that a water texture and colour and a spatial relation between the water area and its surrounding area can lead to misclassification when using the proposed method with limited visual features provided by the organizer. Besides, a metadata content and its associated image do not always synchronize with an event meaning. Hence, we propose the context-aware method to overcome these obstacles by taking into account both image and metadata content as well as spatio-temporal-context information implied from external resources. The diagram in Figure 5 illustrates the proposed method.

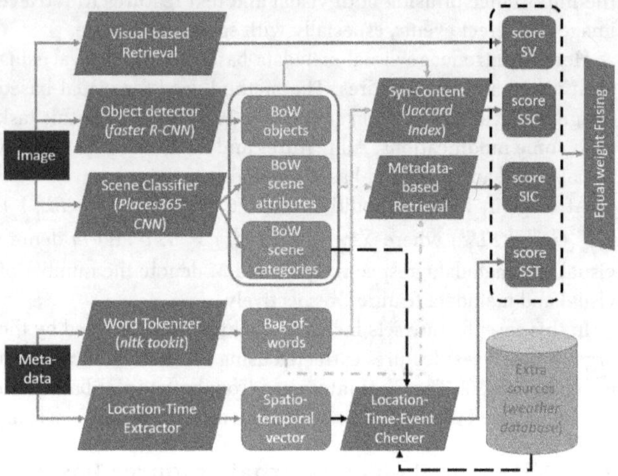

Figure 5: Visual-metadata-external-resource-based Image Retrieval Diagram

Enriching Image's Content: we utilize the faster R-CNN [24] with pre-computed object detection model running on the Tensorflow platform [9] to generate a Bag of Words (BoW) containing objects detected from images (i.e. BoW-object). Then, we use the Places365-CNN [29] pre-computed scene classification to build a bag-of-words of scene categories (i.e. BoW-scene-categories) and scene attributes (i.e. BoW-scene-attributes). These three BoWs are merged to generate image's content (i.e. BoW-image-content).

Enriched Image Content and Metadata Score (SIC): the merged BoW-image-content and the BoW-metadata are integrated and then fed to the metadata-based image retrieval described in 2.2 to generate the **SIC** score.

Syn-Content Score (SSC): the bag-of-words extracted from the text of a given image using the pre-processing stage of the algorithm introduced in subsection 2.2 and the merged BoW-image-content created at the previous stage are utilized to calculate the syn-content score between image and metadata content.

Spatio-Temporal-Context Score (SST): the BoW-scene-categories, a spatio-temporal vector extracted from metadata by leveraging GPS, time, and place-name entity, and extra information implied from various weather databases that can be freely accessed on the Internet (e.g. Europe area[3], America area[4], and Australia area[5]) are integrated to confirm whether a flood report by <image,metadata> really happened. The method introduced in [10] is applied to calculate **SST**.

Visual Features Score (SV): this score is the output of the method described in subsection 2.1 (i.e. using only visual features to retrieve images).

[3] https://www.eswd.eu/
[4] http://www.weather.gov/, https://water.usgs.gov/floods/reports/
[5] http://www.bom.gov.au/climate/data/

These four scores are then fused with equal weights to get the final ranking score. Algorithm 2 formalizes the aforementioned description.

ALGORITHM 2: Calculating a ranking score of a given pair <image, metadata>

Input: <image, metadata>, extraDB, $w = (w_1, w_2, w_3, w_4)$
Output: ranking score SF
Function *calculateRS*
SV = SSC = SIC = SST = 0;
BoW-object = Bow-scene-attributes = Bow-scene-categories = BoW = $\emptyset$;
BoW-object = **ObjectDetector**(image) ;
BoW-scene-attributes = **SceneClassifier**(image, option=scene-attributes) ;
BoW-scene-categories = **SceneClassifier**(image, option=scene-categories) ;
BoW-image-content = <BoW-object, BoW-scene-attributes,BoW-scene-categories> ;
BoW-metadata = **WordTokenizer**(metadata) ;
Spatio-Temporal-Vector = **LocationTimeExtractor**(metadata);
SV = **EL**(image) ;
SSC = **JaccardIndex**(BoW-metadata,BoW-image-content) ;
SIC = **FFNN**(BoW-metadata);
SST = **LocationTimeEventChecker**(Spatio-Temporal-Vector, BoW-scene-categories, extraDB) ;

$SF = w_1SV + w_2SSC + w_3SIC + w_4SST$;
end

3 EXPERIMENTAL RESULTS

We have used the data set and evaluation metrics provided by the organizers of the 2017 Multimedia Satellite Task:Emergency Response for Flooding Events [8]. The data set includes *Development-Set* (5,280 images, along with features and class labels (1=evidence of a flooding event and 0=no evidence) and the *Test-Set* (1,320 images and features). The evaluation metric is the *Average Precision at k* (AP@k) at various cutoffs, k=50, 100, 200, 300, 400, or 500.

The requirements of runs 1, 2, 3, and 4 match the visual-based, metadata-based, visual-metadata-based and visual-metadata-external-resource-based image retrieval methods described in this paper. All parameters used by our approach are set as follows:

- **RUN 1**: (1) *Stage 1*: we use features set $\{CEDD, EH, JCD\}$ and SVM (*SVM-Type: eps-regression, SVM-Kernel: radial, cost: 1, gamma: 0.006944444, epsilon: 0.1*) to create SLs, the weighted w_i's are set to 1/3, (2) *Stage 2*: we divide the development set into $m = 10$ non-intersecting data sets, (3) *Stage 3*: k is set to 10, and random forest (RF) is used to create TL (*type of random forest: regression, number of trees: 500, No. of variables tried at each split: 48*) with the JC feature as the input, and (4) *Stage 4*: we set $w_1 = 0.4, w_2 = 0.6$

- **RUN 2**: we perform 5-fold cross validation on the development set and report the average score of 5 folds. In testing, we train the model using development set and use the trained model for the prediction on test images.
- **RUN 3 and RUN 4**: we used the pre-computed object detection model without changing any parameter [9, 24, 29]. We also reused the methods in RUN 1 and RUN 2 with the same setup.

Table 1 shows the evaluation results on the development and test sets.

Table 1: Evaluation Results on Development and Test Data (MAP: Mean Average Precision, AP@N: Average Precision at N)

	Dev. Set		Test Set	
Run	AP@480	MAP	AP@480	MAP
RUN 1	82.17	88.84	77.62	87.87
RUN 2	83.4	87.8	57.07	57.12
RUN 3	85.78	92.86	85.41	90.39
RUN 4	92.53	98.38	90.69	97.36

For RUN 1 and 2, there is a big gap between results on the development set and on the test set. Possible explanations are that (1) the data distribution of the development set is different than of the test set, and/or (2) there is too much non-synchronization between text and image contents. In the current work, we did not deal with inflections such as "flood" and "flooded", so the feature space is quite sparse.

For RUN 3, the fusion of visual-based and metadata-based outputs improves the accuracy of flood images retrieval (around 3% higher). It proves that these two different approaches can compensate their weaknesses.

For RUN 4, there is a significant improvement in accuracy when using enriched image content, syn-content, and spatio-temporal-context scores, whilst the visual-metadata-based method (e.g. RUN 3) reaches it's limitation. Figure 6 illustrates one example of comparing the productivity between run 3 and run 4. Obviously, run 4 gained a significant improvement when re-ranking the mis-classified image from 48th to 680th position. It should be noted that there are 480 flood images in the test set.

In order to have an objective evaluation of the proposed method, different methods created by participants who joined MediaEval 2017 challenge are briefly introduced and compared. Since these methods and ours use the same dataset and evaluation scores given by the organizer, we hope this will demonstrate the benefit of our method.

Table 4 reports the different type of features, fusion scheme, and classifiers that are investigated by participants. The enriched image content gained by using deep-learning can obviously beat the traditional visual features, as described in Tables 2 and 3. Nevertheless, none of these methods pay attention to checking spatio-temporal-context by using external resources (i.e. do not check whether the event reported by social media really happened). Moreover, the syn-content is totally ignored by these methods. Thus, for *RUN 4*

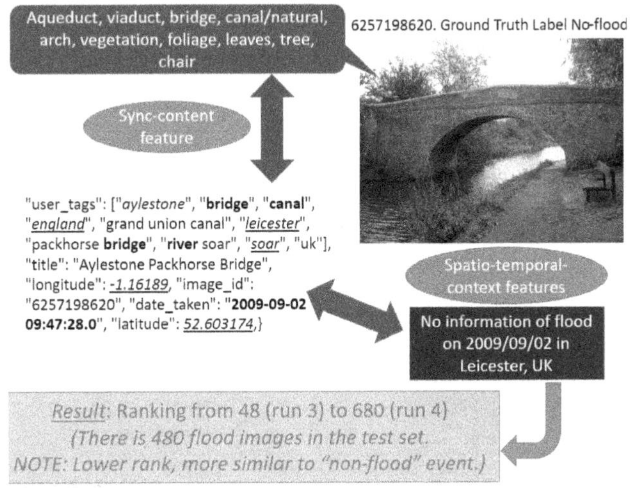

Figure 6: An example of leveraging syn-content, enriched image content, and spatiotemporal-context event confirmation to successfully re-ranking the mis-classified image.

Table 2: AP@480 Ranking Comparison (AP@N: Average Precision at N)

		AP@480			
ID	Methods	Run 1	Run 2	Run 3	Run 4
1.	S. Ahmad et al. [3]	**86.81**	22.83	83.73	na
2.	Tkachenko et al. [25]	50.95	66.78	72.26	71.97
3.	Lopez-Fuentes et al. [21]	61.58	67.54	81.60	68.40
4.	K. Ahmad et al. [1]	84.94	25.88	54.74	73.83
5.	Avgerinakis et al. [4]	78.82	36.15	68.57	na
6.	Nogueira et al. [23]	74.60	**76.71**	**95.84**	82.06
7.	Zhao et al. [28]	51.46	63.70	73.16	na
8.	Hanif et al. [13]	na	na	na	na
9.	Fu et al. [12]	na	na	na	na
10.	Bischke et al. [6]	86.64	63.41	90.45	74.08
	Proposed Method	77.62	57.07	85.41	**90.69**

(i.e. using as much information as possible), our proposed method achieved the best results.

Although the condition of *RUN 1* required to use only visual features given by the organizer (i.e. traditional visual features), most of the participants added extra features collected by using pre-trained neural network models. Nevertheless, among methods that obey the rule (i.e. method 2, 7, and 8), our proposed method still achieved the best result. Tables 2 and 3 show the comparison between the proposed method and others.

4 CONCLUSIONS AND FUTURE WORKS

We have introduced a context-aware late-fusion method to retrieve flood images from social media data. An experimental comparison is investigated with the outcome of ten different methods participating in MediaEval 2017 challenge, Multimedia Satellite Task: Emergency Response to Flooding Events, and evaluation is performed using the same dataset and evaluation tool provided by

Table 3: Mean Average Precision (MAP) Ranking Comparison

		Mean $AP@\{50, 100, 250, 480\}$			
ID	Methods	Run 1	Run 2	Run 3	Run 4
1.	S. Ahmad et al. [3]	**95.73**	18.23	92.55	na
2.	Tkachenko et al. [25]	62.75	74.37	80.87	81.61
3.	Lopez-Fuentes et al. [21]	66.38	70.16	83.96	75.96
4.	K. Ahmad et al. [1]	95.11	31.45	68.12	82.68
5.	Avgerinakis et al. [4]	92.27	39.90	83.37	na
6.	Nogueira et al. [23]	87.88	62.53	85.63	91.59
7.	Zhao et al. [28]	64.70	75.74	85.43	na
8.	Hanif et al. [13]	80.98	71.79	80.84	na
9.	Fu et al. [12]	19.21	12.84	18.30	17.24
10.	Bischke et al. [6]	95.71	**77.64**	**97.40**	64.50
	Proposed Method	87.87	57.12	90.39	**97.36**

the organizers. We introduced a new algorithm to re-rank the retrieval scores so that the ranking score of a misclassified image can be decreased significantly (i.e. increase AP scores). Our proposed method achieved the best results among participating methods when taking the image-text content synchronization and spatial-temporal-context event confirmation into account. We have also confirmed that the synchronization between image content and metadata of the same post as well as the spatio-temporal-context information (i.e. checking whether an event reported in social media really happened) plays an important role in increasing the AP score.

In future, instead of using SVM and RF classifiers with a simple fusion scheme, other classifiers with better fusion scheme could be investigated, aiming for better results. Deep-learning should also be utilized in our future work. Other external data sources can be considered to enhance the accuracy of checking the context of an event. Moreover, the context of pre-disaster and post-disaster events will be considered carefully. This will help to retrieve more images whose content do not relate directly to a disaster event but pre- or post-disaster event.

REFERENCES

[1] Kashif Ahmad, Konstantin Pogorelov, Michael Riegler, Nicola Conci, and Pal Halvorsen. 2017. CNN and GAN Based Satellite and Social Media Data Fusion for Disaster Detection. In *Proc. of the MediaEval 2017 Workshop* (Sept. 13-15, 2017). Dublin, Ireland.

[2] Kashif Ahmad, Michael Riegler, Ans Riaz, Nicola Conci, and Duc-Tien Dang-Nguyen andand Pal Halvorsen. 2017. The JORD System: Linking Sky and Social Multimedia Data to Natural Disasters. In *Proceedings of the 2017 ACM on International Conference on Multimedia Retrieval.* ACM, 461–465.

[3] Sheharyar Ahmad, Kashif Ahmad, Nasir Ahmad, and Nicola Conci. 2017. Convolutional Neural Networks for Disaster Images Retrieval. In *Proc. of the MediaEval 2017 Workshop* (Sept. 13-15, 2017). Dublin, Ireland.

[4] Konstantinos Avgerinakis, Anastasia Moumtzidou, Stelios Andreadis, Emmanouil Michail, Ilias Gialampoukidis, Stefanos Vrochidis, and Ioannis Kompatsiaris. 2017. Visual and Textual Analysis of Social Media and Satellite Images for Flood Detection @ Multimedia Satellite Task MediaEval 2017. In *Proc. of the MediaEval 2017 Workshop* (Sept. 13-15, 2017). Dublin, Ireland.

[5] Steven Bird, Ewan Klein, and Edward Loper. 2009. Natural Language Processing with Python.

[6] Benjamin Bischke, Prakriti Bhardwaj, Aman Gautam, Patrick Helber, Damian Borth, and Andreas Dengel. 2017. Detection of Flooding Events in Social Multimedia and Satellite Imagery using Deep Neural Networks. In *Proc. of the MediaEval 2017 Workshop* (Sept. 13-15, 2017). Dublin, Ireland.

[7] Benjamin Bischke, Damian Borth, Christian Schulze, and Andreas Dengel. 2016. Contextual enrichment of remote-sensed events with social media streams. In *Proceedings of the 2016 ACM on Multimedia Conference.* ACM, 1077–1081.

[8] Benjamin Bischke, Patrick Helber, Christian Schulze, Srinivasan Venkat, Andreas Dengel, and Damian Borth. 2017. The Multimedia Satellite Task at MediaEval 2017: Emergence Response for Flooding Events. In *Proc. of the MediaEval 2017 Workshop* (Sept. 13-15, 2017). Dublin, Ireland.

[9] Xinlei Chen and Abhinav Gupta. 2017. An Implementation of Faster RCNN with Study for Region Sampling. *arXiv preprint arXiv:1702.02138* (2017).

[10] Minh-Son Dao, Giulia Boato, Francesco G.B. De Natale, and Truc-Vien Nguyen. 2013. Jointly Exploiting Visual and Non-visual Information for Event-related Social Media Retrieval. In *Proceedings of the 3rd ACM Conference on International Conference on Multimedia Retrieval (ICMR '13).* ACM, New York, NY, USA, 159–166. https://doi.org/10.1145/2461466.2461494

[11] Thomas Deselaers, Daniel Keysers, and Hermann Ney. 2008. Features for Image Retrieval: An Experimental Comparison. *Inf. Retr.* 11, 2 (April 2008), 77–107. https://doi.org/10.1007/s10791-007-9039-3

[12] Xiyao Fu, Yi Bin, Liang Peng, Jie Zhou, Yang Yang, and Heng Tao Shen. 2017. BMC@MediaEval 2017 Multimedia Satellite Task via Regression Random Forest. In *Proc. of the MediaEval 2017 Workshop* (Sept. 13-15, 2017). Dublin, Ireland.

[13] Muhammad Hanif, Muhammad Atif Tahir, Mahrukh Khan, and Muhammad Rafi. 2017. Flood detection using Social Media Data and Spectral Regression based Kernel Discriminant Analysis. In *Proc. of the MediaEval 2017 Workshop* (Sept. 13-15, 2017). Dublin, Ireland.

[14] Benjamin Herfort, Joao Porto de Albuquerque, Svend-Jonas Schelhorn, and Alexander Zipf. 2014. Exploring the geographical relations between social media and flood phenomena to improve situational awareness. *Connecting a digital Europe through location and place* (2014), 55–71.

[15] Amanda Lee Hughes and Leysia Palen. 2009. Twitter adoption and use in mass convergence and emergency events. *IJEM* (2009), 248–260. Issue 3-4.

[16] Ramesh Jain and Pinaki Sinha. 2010. Content Without Context is Meaningless. In *Proceedings of the 18th ACM International Conference on Multimedia (MM '10).* ACM, New York, NY, USA, 1259–1268. https://doi.org/10.1145/1873951.1874199

[17] Karen E Joyce, Stella E Belliss, Sergey V Samsonov, Stephen J McNeill, and Phil J Glassey. 2009. A review of the status of satellite remote sensing and image processing techniques for mapping natural hazards and disasters. *Progress in Physical Geography* (2009).

[18] I. Kelman, J. C. Gaillard, James Lewis, and Jessica Mercer. 2016. Learning from the history of disaster vulnerability and resilience research and practice for climate change. *Natural Hazards* 82, 1 (01 May 2016), 129–143. https://doi.org/10.1007/s11069-016-2294-0

[19] Victor Klemas. 2017. Remote sensing of floods and flood-prone areas: an overview. *Journal of Coastal Research* 31, 4 (July 2017), 1005–1013. https://doi.org/10.2112/JCOASTRES-D-14-00160.1

[20] Xueliang Liu, Meng Wang, and Benoit Huet. 2015. Event analysis in social multimedia: a survey. *Frontiers of Computer Science* 10 (2015), 433–446.

[21] Laura Lopez-Fuentes, Joost van de Weijer, Marc Bolanos, and Harald Skinnemoen. 2017. Multi-modal Deep Learning Approach for Flood Detection. In *Proc. of the MediaEval 2017 Workshop* (Sept. 13-15, 2017). Dublin, Ireland.

[22] Giorgio Giacinto Luca Piras. 2017. Information fusion in content based image retrieval: A comprehensive overview. *Information Fusion* 37 (2017), 50–60.

[23] Keiller Nogueira, Samuel Fadel, Icaro Dourado, Rafael Werneck, Javier Munoz, Otavio Penatti, Rodrigo Calumby, Lin Li, Jefersson Dos Santos, and Ricardo Torres. 2017. Data-Driven Flood Detection using Neural Networks. In *Proc. of the MediaEval 2017 Workshop* (Sept. 13-15, 2017). Dublin, Ireland.

[24] Shaoqing Ren, Kaiming He, Ross Girshick, and Jian Sun. 2015. Faster R-CNN: Towards Real-Time Object Detection with Region Proposal Networks. In *Advances in Neural Information Processing Systems (NIPS).*

[25] Nataliya Tkachenko, Arkaitz Zubiaga, and Rob Procter. 2017. WISC at MediaEval 2017: Multimedia Satellite Task. In *Proc. of the MediaEval 2017 Workshop* (Sept. 13-15, 2017). Dublin, Ireland.

[26] Christos Tzelepis, Zhigang Ma, Vasileios Mezaris, Bogdan Ionescu, Ioannis Kompatsiaris, Giulia Boato, Nicu Sebe, and Shuicheng Yan. 2016. Event-based media processing and analysis: A survey of the literature. *Image and Vision Computing* (2016), 3–19.

[27] Thijs Westerveld. 2000. Image Retrieval: Content Versus Context. In *Content-Based Multimedia Information Access - Volume 1 (RIAO '00).* LE CENTRE DE HAUTES ETUDES INTERNATIONALES D'INFORMATIQUE DOCUMENTAIRE, Paris, France, France, 276–284. http://dl.acm.org/citation.cfm?id=2835865.2835894

[28] Zhengyu Zhao and Martha Larson. 2017. Retrieving Social Flooding Images Based on Multimodal Information. In *Proc. of the MediaEval 2017 Workshop* (Sept. 13-15, 2017). Dublin, Ireland.

[29] Bolei Zhou, Agata Lapedriza, Aditya Khosla, Aude Oliva, and Antonio Torralba. 2018. Places: A 10 million Image Database for Scene Recognition. *IEEE Transaction on Pattern Analysis and Machine Intelligence* (2018), 1–14. https://doi.org/10.1109/TPAMI.2017.2723009

[30] Wengang Zhou, Houqiang Li, and Qi Tian. 2017. Recent Advance in Content-based Image Retrieval: A Literature Survey. *CoRR* abs/1706.06064 (2017).

Table 4: Features and Classifiers Comparison

ID	Authors	Run 1	Run 2	Run 3	Run 4
1.	S. Ahmad et al. [3]	AlexNet pretrained on ImageNet and Places dataset and SVM	Meta-data with user's tags, date taken along with GPS information and Random Forest	Fusing scores outputs of run 1 and 2 with equal weights	na
2.	Tkachenko et al. [25]	CEDD, CLD and GABOR and Logistic Regression (LGC)	A bag-of-words and word vectors and LGC	Concatenating the image and text vectors and LGC	Concatenating five vectors for visual features, metadata, word vectors of titles, user tags and descriptions and LGC
3.	Lopez-Fuentes et al. [21]	Pre-trained weights on ImageNet and fine-tune the last inception model of the network with convolutional InceptionV3 network	Word embedding initialized by Glove vectors and bidirectional LSTM	Concatenating the image and text features followed by a fully connected layer and a softmax classifier	Same as run 3 with extra images obtained from Google Similar Images
4.	K. Ahmad et al. [1]	Eight feature vectors through four different network architectures from the same image (AlexNet, GoogleNet, VGGNet16, and ResNet) with SVM	Meta-data with user's tags, date taken along with GPS information and Random Tree classifier	Fusing scores of run 1 and run 2 using Induced Ordered Weighting Averaging Operators (IOWA)	Fusing scores of run 1 and run 2 using Particle Swarm Optimization (PSO)
5.	Avgerinakis et al. [4]	Deep Convolutional Neural Network (DCNN) features produced from the Places205 - GoogleNet network with SVM	Meta-data with title, description, and user tags and DBpedia Spotlight	Fusing scores of run 1 and run 2 using non-linear graph based techniques (e.g. random walk, diffusion-based) in a weighted non-linear way	na
6.	Nogueira et al. [23]	Fine-tuned the GoogleNet (pre-trained on ImageNet dataset) using the whole training set, replacing the original last layer by a new one containing two neurons, which correspond to the two classes: "flooding" and "non-flooding".	A set of words extracted from each metadata and Relation Networks (RN) with two outputs	Concatenating output of run 1 and run 2 into a single vector with a fully-connected layer of 512 units and a single sigmoid unit for classification	An alternative version of run 1 with 5 disjoint subsets of a training image dataset.
7.	Zhao et al. [28]	CEDD feature with SVM	Flood-related keywords (e.g. flood(s), flooding, and flooded) in user tags, title and description fields of metadata	Pre-filtering and re-ranking using both visual and metadata information	na
8.	Hanif et al. [13]	ACC, CEDD, CLD, EH, FCTH, GABOR, JCD, SC, and TAMURA features and Kernel Discriminant Analysis using Spectral Regression (SRKDA)	user tags with TF-IDF from metadata and SRKDA	Fusing features of run 1 and run 2 and SRKDA	na
9.	Fu et al. [12]	CNN feature with ResNet-152 and Regression Random Forest (RRF)	GloVe vector generated from words of metadata and RRF	Using both text and images to train the random forest	Same as run 3 with extra 5320 images generated by randomly cropping and flipping horizontally the original images in the development set
10.	Bischke et al. [6]	Pre-trained network DeepSentiBank with the X-ResNet and SVM with RBF kernel	Word2Vec model on the user tags with TF-IDF and SVM with RBF kernel	Fusing two modalities in run 1 and run 2 to create a 1200-dimensional vector and SVM with RBF kernel	Only visual features from an ImageNet pre-trained ResNet152 model and SVM with RBF kernel

Face Retrieval Framework Relying on User's Visual Memory

Yugo Sato
Waseda University
y.sato9372@fuji.waseda.jp

Tsukasa Fukusato
The University of Tokyo
tsukasafukusato@is.s.u-tokyo.ac.jp

Shigeo Morishima
Waseda Research Institute for Science and Engineering
shigeo@waseda.jp

ABSTRACT

This paper presents an interactive face retrieval framework for clarifying an image representation envisioned by a user. Our system is designed for a situation in which the user wishes to find a person but has only visual memory of the person. We address a critical challenge of image retrieval across the user's inputs. Instead of target-specific information, the user can select several images (or a single image) that are similar to an impression of the target person the user wishes to search for. Based on the user's selection, our proposed system automatically updates a deep convolutional neural network. By interactively repeating these process (human-in-the-loop optimization), the system can reduce the gap between human-based similarities and computer-based similarities and estimate the target image representation. We ran user studies with 10 subjects on a public database and confirmed that the proposed framework is effective for clarifying the image representation envisioned by the user easily and quickly.

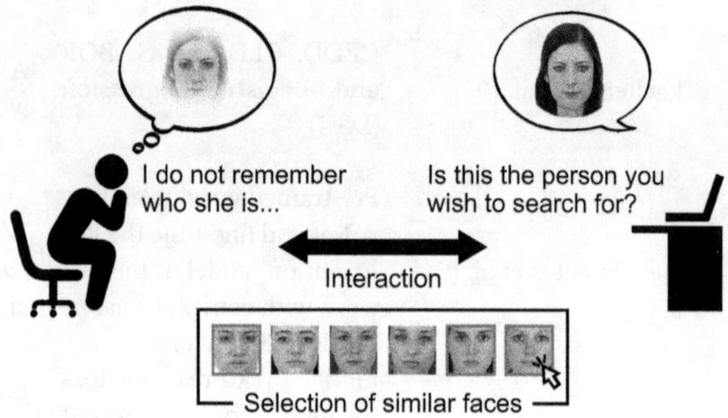

Figure 1: Face retrieval relying on the user's visual memory. The user selects several faces that are similar to their impression of the target face. Based on the selection, the search system can estimate the image representation of the target envisioned by the user and retrieve it from a database.

CCS CONCEPTS

• **Information systems** → *Users and interactive retrieval;*

KEYWORDS

User interaction; Deep convolutional neural network; Relevance feedback; Active learning

ACM Reference Format:
Yugo Sato, Tsukasa Fukusato, and Shigeo Morishima. 2018. Face Retrieval Framework Relying on User's Visual Memory. In *Proceedings of 2018 International Conference on Multimedia Retrieval (ICMR'18).* June 11–14, 2018, Yokohama, Japan, 9 pages. https://doi.org/10.1145/3206025.3206038

1 INTRODUCTION

In recent years, a large number of photos that include a variety of unconstrained subjects, such as generic objects and human faces, have been uploaded to social networks or photo-sharing services. Hence, efficient systems to retrieve images from such a large volume of data are in demand. Web image search systems such as Google, Yahoo!, and Bing utilize several items with embedded information, such as filenames, image captions, and text on web pages [22, 24, 31]. While text-based search techniques have achieved success in document retrieval tasks, these embedded tags are often unreliable for describing image contents, and the quality of manually defined tags can affect the performance of the image retrieval process [5, 20, 45]. In addition, if a user seeks an image with visual characteristics that cannot be easily expressed by keywords, the user would generally have to scroll through large numbers of image results retrieved by using keywords, in search of the desired image.

Computer-vision-based studies generally analyze contents of images; for example, they compute the similarity between a query and each image of a database with image descriptors such as color histograms [9] or Gabor texture features [47]. Using these similarities, the system enables a user to retrieve a set of images easily without text queries, which is a process called content-based image retrieval. However, there is a well-known challenging problem called "semantic gap" between low-level visual features and the high-level intention of the user, which makes it difficult to search for user-desired images [2, 39, 48].

Recently, highly accurate image recognition methods with deep learning have been reported (e.g., image classification tasks). Dense data of raw images are abstracted into high-dimensional sparse representations via convolution and pooling layers. By learning from a large-scale database, deep convolutional neural networks can generate generic representations and classifiers adapted to a given task. By extending its features, Donahue et al. introduced the deep convolutional activation feature (DeCAF), which utilizes the representation layers as image descriptors and can compute image representations with more semantic information compared to low-level visual features [4]. The image representations obtained

ACM ISBN 978-1-4503-5046-4/18/06...$15.00
https://doi.org/10.1145/3206025.3206038

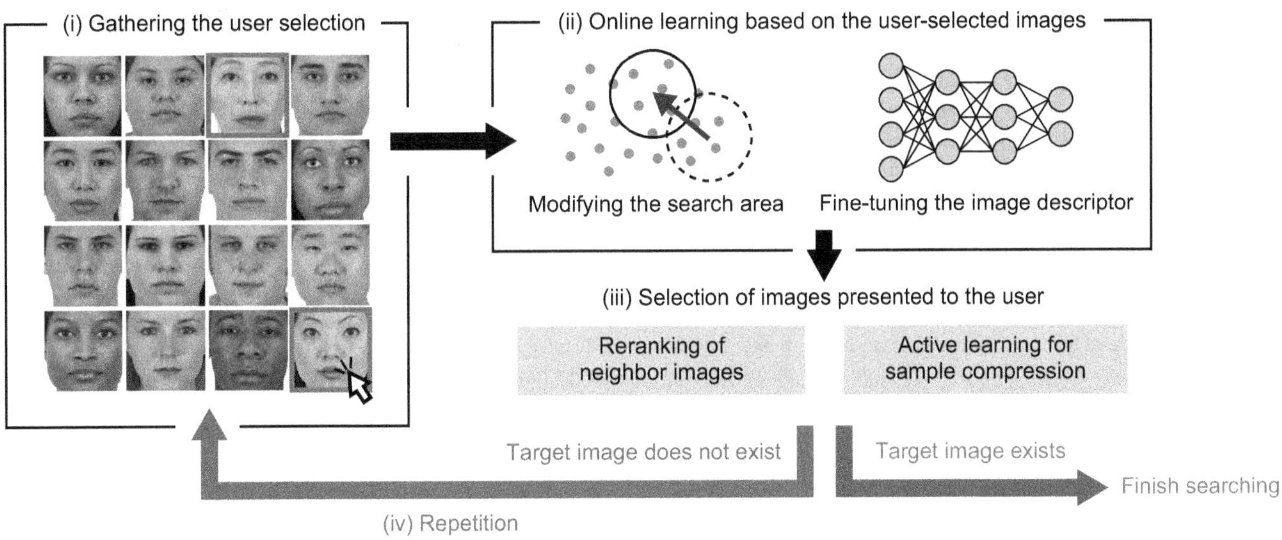

Figure 2: Flowchart of the proposed retrieval framework. By interactively repeating the user's input and the system's search process, the framework can estimate the target image representation envisioned by the user.

through deep learning consistently outperform conventional hand-crafted features and boost the image retrieval performance [1, 38, 51]. However, the image representations are calculated fully automatically, and it is difficult to reflect the intention of a user in the retrieval process.

To ensure that a user's intention is reflected in the retrieval process, many studies have typically utilized the "relevance feedback" approach, which allows the user to interactively refine retrieval results [3, 14, 49]. The main process includes three steps: the system (i) provides initial results of queries provided by the user; (ii) gathers user feedback according to his/her subjective judgment; and (iii) updates the retrieval results based on the user's feedback on whether those results are relevant [3]. However, these systems require an additional user-task of finding text or image queries related to the target in advance because they assume that the user has some specific queries.

In this study, we propose a framework that belongs to a general category of content-based image retrieval but is different from existing techniques in that it clarifies an obscure target image that a user envisions by relying on his/her visual memory. A usage case is provided in Figure 1. The system enables the user to find a person whose name or affiliation is unknown by selecting similar people on a search window. To achieve such a system, we extend the concept of DeCAF and propose an interactive image descriptor based on online learning with multiple feedback instances. Figure 2 shows a flowchart of the proposed retrieval framework. Our search process includes the following steps: (i) gathering a user selection based on relevance feedback (including images that are similar to the target envisioned by the user); (ii) online learning based on the user-selected images (modifying the search area according to the relevant images and fine-tuning an image descriptor); (iii) selection of images presented to the user (re-ranking initial retrieval results based on the fine-tuned image representation and sample compression with active learning). By interactively repeating the user's input and the system's search process, we can estimate the target image representation envisioned by the user.

2 RELATED WORK

2.1 Face Image Retrieval

In general, because face images are taken under different photographic conditions, such as pose, expression, illumination, and occlusion, many stable and highly accurate image retrieval systems for changing environmental conditions have been studied [10, 15, 27, 43]. Among them, facial contour points are mainly used to compute geometric facial attributes [35, 53]. In this system, a user can manipulate facial landmark positions to retrieve various expressions. However, because these systems focus only on the sparse facial shape, it is difficult to determine or quantify facial characteristics such as gender or impression. Kemelmacher-Shilzerman et al. proposed a real-time system that finds a photograph with a similar facial expression to a given query for application to puppetry [16]. In this system, the query is the user's own facial expression, such as a smile or frown, and the system automatically retrieves photographs of different persons who have a similar facial expression. After it aligned faces by using 3D template models, it extracted LBP histograms [25] from face regions for face representations. On the other hand, Kumar et al. employed simple text queries such as "a smiling man with blonde hair and mustache" [19]. This system learned correspondences between image features and manually defined tags, such as "smiling man" or "blonde hair," by using a support vector machine (SVM). However, because the system can only retrieve face images that have some specific attributes defined in the pre-training process, it is necessary to reconstruct face image descriptors to quantify various facial attributes.

2.2 Deep Image Representation for Content-based Image Retrieval

Deep learning for image analysis has been mainly studied in the field of computer vision. Many researchers studied face representations generated by deep convolutional neural networks (CNNs) [32, 37, 42], and they achieved highly accurate verification methods for cropped, incomplete, or occluded face images with the generated face representations. Donahue et al. proposed DeCAF [4], which is a more robust and generic image descriptor compared to conventional descriptors such as GIST [26] and LLC [41]. They also found that activation features closer to the output layer of the network can describe the semantics of an input image. Lin et al. extended the concept of DeCAF to the retrieval of images of clothes [21]. They utilized a pre-trained network model that had learned rich mid-level visual representations and fine-tuned it using their dataset. It has been reported that applying deep feature representations in a new domain, similarity learning, can significantly boost the retrieval performance. This performance boost is much better than the improvements achieved by "shallow" similarity learning with conventional hand-crafted features [8, 38, 40]. Therefore, inspired by these methods, we employ DeCAF as a face image descriptor for accurately computing semantic facial similarity.

Zhu et al. proposed the generative visual manipulation model (GVM) [52] to edit images on a natural image manifold and generate a new query image using generative adversarial nets (GAN) [7] for searching. In this search process, a user can manipulate the appearance of retrieval results through hand sketching, including coloring and warping. However, the retrieval performance significantly depends on the quality of the user's sketch as a search query.

2.3 Interactive User Feedback for Concept Learning

In content-based image retrieval, one challenging task is to reflect a user's search intention in retrieval results. To solve this problem, many researchers have attempted to utilize relevance feedback [29, 30]. In the field of face retrieval, Wu et al. proposed identity-based quantization using a dictionary constructed using the identities of 270 peoples for large-scale face image retrieval [44]. They improved the precision of local ranking by updating the distance metrics of the top k face representations with user-annotated references.

Our framework is similar to that of CueFlik [6], WhittleSearch [18] and AMNet [50], which manipulate the attributes of retrieval results based a user's input. In the search process, the systems can interactively estimate a search concept by the user's editing of various attributes of the retrieval results based on a comparison with a target image envisioned by the user. However, this process requires a large number of annotated parameters to be provided by the user because of the massive number of items for evaluation. Additionally, these systems are based on the assumption that the user can input queries for initial searching. In contrast, in the present study, we assume a situation in which the user cannot input proper image or text queries, and our system can estimate the representation of a face that the user wishes to find by relying on his/her visual memory.

3 INTERACTIVE FACE RETRIEVAL WITH SELECTION OF SIMILAR FACES

In this section, we describe a method to interactively retrieve a face image envisioned by a user by relying on the user's visual memory. In our retrieval process, instead of image or text queries, our system requires the user's decisions on whether each facial candidate is similar to the individual the user is searching for; the user's decisions are recorded when they click on images. After pre-processing (see Section 3.1, 3.2), based on this user interaction, the search area in a database is modified in the direction of interest and an image descriptor is fine-tuned automatically (see Section 3.3), and the initial retrieval results are re-ranked based on the estimation of the target image representation (see Section 3.4).

3.1 Deep Face Representation

For facial image representations, we use a pre-trained CNN model of the VGG-Face CNN descriptor, which has been trained with a dataset containing 2.6 million face images [28]. This network architecture is based on the VGG-Very-Deep-16 CNN [34], which consists of 16 neural network layers (the first 13 are convolutional layers, and the remaining 3 are fully connected layers). Each convolutional layer includes convolution, rectified linear (ReLU) transform ($f(x) = max(x, 0)$), and max-pooling transform. An input image is abstracted into high-dimensional representations via the convolution layers and pooling layers alternately, and it is connected to the fully connected layers. The fully connected layers focus on the activation maps of the previous layer and determine the features with the strongest correlation to a particular class. To construct a face image database, we first detect the face area in images stored in the database [17] and normalize them to 224×224 pixels. Then, we use activations of the second fully connected layer to extract high-dimensional facial representation vectors (i.e., DeCAF; 4096-dimensional representation vectors) from all database images passed through the VGG-Face network.

3.2 Indexing for Searching on Large-scale Database

Generally, as the amount of data increases, a retrieval system requires a greater amount of time for computing all similarities between images stored in the database. Therefore, we create search indexes of the facial representation vectors (see Section 3.1) with the approximate k-nearest neighbor graph (ANNG) [13]. ANNG, which is incrementally constructed with approximate k-nearest-neighbors calculated on a partially constructed graph, is a method for indexing a large-scale database. In addition, the neighborhood graph and tree implementation used for indexing originate from a common library and can perform a similarity search using ANNG, and they have already been applied in several commercial services [12, 36]. Given a centroid vector of a search area, ANNG can retrieve k-nearest neighbors based on the cosine similarity between their facial representation vectors.

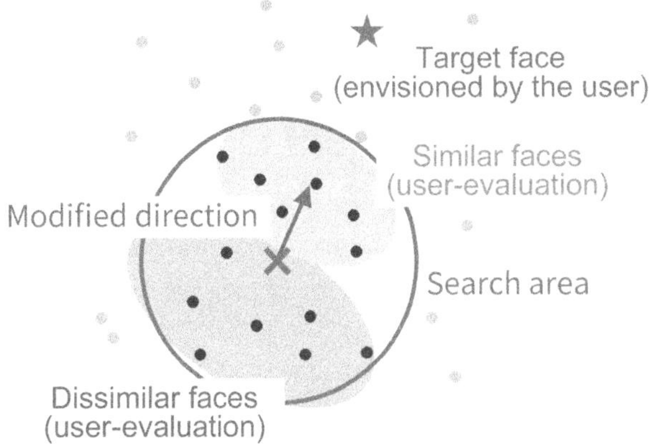

Figure 3: Modifying a search area with user-evaluated faces and the Rocchio algorithm. The centroid of the search area is moved toward the centroid of faces selected as similar by the user.

3.3 Online Learning based on User-selected Images

Modifying Search Area.
In a search process, we first estimate a query vector (i.e., the centroid of a search area in Section 3.2) based on the images selected by the user. In this process, based on the relevance feedback approach, we estimate the query vector that can retrieve more candidates that are similar to the target image in the feature space of the database constructed in Section 3.1. For estimating the query vector, we utilize the Rocchio algorithm [29], which is generally used in the exploratory information searching. The algorithm is based on the assumption that most users have a general conception of which information is relevant or irrelevant. This algorithm modifies the vector to separate the relevant and irrelevant vectors maximally by calculating each of their centroids as follows:

$$\vec{q}_m = \alpha \vec{q}_0 + \beta \frac{1}{|D_r|} \sum_{\vec{d}_j \in D_r} \vec{d}_j - \gamma \frac{1}{|D_{nr}|} \sum_{\vec{d}_k \in D_{nr}} \vec{d}_k, \tag{1}$$

where $\vec{q}_m$ is the modified vector, $\vec{q}_0$ is the original vector, D_r is the set of relevant vectors, D_{nr} is the set of irrelevant vectors, and α, β, and γ are weight values (in this paper, we set $\alpha = 1.0$, $\beta = 0.8$, and $\gamma = 0.1$). The centroid of the search area is moved toward the relevant vectors, i.e., those including similar faces, and away from irrelevant vectors, i.e., those including dissimilar faces (see Figure 3). During a search process, by interactively repeating the user's input and the system's search process, we modify the search area and refer to the database images in an exploratory manner.

Fine-tuning Image Descriptor.
In general, the retrieval results depend on the feature representations obtained via the pre-training of the network and are uniquely determined. Thus, there may be a semantic gap between human-based image representations and computer-based image representations. To solve this problem, we dynamically fine-tune the representation parameters by using user feedback for every search iteration. The fine-tuning process is performed with the pre-trained VGG-Face model initialized in the facial representation extraction (see Section 3.1). The network architecture remains unchanged except for the last layer, which is replaced with a new classification layer (i.e., the 2 classes of similar and dissimilar). The activations of the last layer are given to a softmax function, which is expressed as

$$p_k = \frac{\exp(h_k)}{\sum_{j=1}^{K} \exp(h_j)}, \tag{2}$$

where h_k is the k-th activation of the last layer and K is the number of classes; p_k denotes the probability of the k-th class. In the training process, while all the convolutional layers' parameters are fixed, we fine-tune the fully connected layers by using back-propagation. We minimize the cross-entropy error of every training image set. The cross-entropy error is expressed as

$$E = -\sum_{n=1}^{N} \sum_{k=1}^{K} l_{nk} \log p_k, \tag{3}$$

$$l_{nk} = \begin{cases} 1 & \text{(if } n\text{-th image is similar to the target)} \\ 0 & \text{(otherwise)} \end{cases}, \tag{4}$$

where N is the number of the training image set and l_{nk} is the label vector of the n-th training image provided by the user. The error E is minimized by calculating its gradient and optimizing the network parameters by using AdaDelta [46].

3.4 Active Selection

For gathering detailed user feedback, relevance feedback systems generally present more neighbor samples of a search point in a ranking style to the user. However, as the number of proposed samples increases, the process becomes time-consuming and burdensome because the user is required to evaluate all of them. For example, in WhittleSearch [18], it is necessary for the user to observe approximately 50 images while evaluating 18 attributes. In this section, we propose a novel method to decrease the number of samples presented to the user by estimating the image representation of the target envisioned by the user. We call this method "active selection." Concretely, after performing two-class classification learning with the deep convolutional neural network (see Section 3.3), by re-extracting DeCAF, we re-rank the neighbor samples of the search point. Then, instead of presenting all the re-ranked results to the user, we apply an active learning method to low-ranked images for decreasing the number of images presented.

Re-ranking of Neighbor Images.
In the search process, the user can smoothly find a set of images that includes the target face and similar faces if they are placed at the top of the proposed results. Therefore, we re-rank the neighbors to place particular images having representations envisioned by the user at the top position of the retrieval results. After fine-tuning the image descriptor, in this section, we describe the re-ranking of the neighbor images retrieved by ANNG searching. We

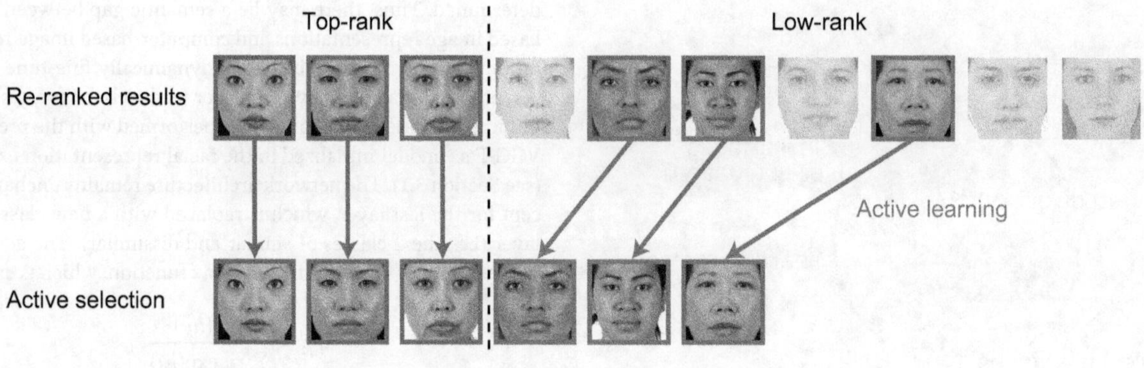

Figure 4: Active selection for decreasing the number of images presented to users. The selection includes a mixture of the top-ranked images, and low-ranked images chosen by active learning.

first re-extract the DeCAF features from k neighbor images with the fine-tuned VGG-Face model, which is the same procedure as in Section 3.1. Then, based on the fine-tuned image representations, we calculate the cosine distance between a query vector, i.e., the centroid of a search area, and each vector of the neighbors. Finally, we define the images that are close to the search point as the top-ranked images.

Active Learning for Sample Compression.
We decrease the number of images presented to the user to reduce the burden on the user for evaluating the proposed images. However, in general, as the number of labeled samples provided by the user decreases, the accuracy of estimation with primitive compression methods (e.g., simply cut the low-ranked images) decreases. Therefore, we propose a novel compression method considering this trade-off relationship. In this paper, we apply the key idea of active learning. The idea of active learning is that a machine learning algorithm can achieve a greater accuracy with fewer training labels if it is allowed to choose the data from which it learns [33]. Namely, active learning can choose images requiring labeling from non-labeled samples for high-accuracy estimation. In this paper, we define the top 30% of the re-ranked results as the top-ranked images and the rest of the images as the low-ranked images. We adopt active learning for low-ranked images, which can choose the images having their class estimated uncertainly by the current trained network model. The images satisfying the requirement defined as follows are chosen from the low-ranked images:

$$\arg\min_{x}(P(y_1|x) - P(y_2|x)), \tag{5}$$

where y_1 and y_2 are the most-probable and second-most-probable class labels (i.e., the similar class or dissimilar class), respectively, and P is the probability of x belonging to the class (so-called the margin sampling method). We pick as many low-ranked images as the number of top-ranked images with the procedure mentioned above. Therefore, we propose active selection, which proposes to the user a mixture of the top-ranked images and the uncertain low-ranked images chosen by active learning (see Figure 4).

4 EXPERIMENTAL RESULTS

4.1 Interface Design

Here, we describe the interface used in the user studies mentioned in the subsequent sections (see Figure 5). To support intuitive browsing, a user can select images on our interface through a drag-and-drop operation. The user can select images that are similar or dissimilar to their impression of the target by dragging and dropping them from the search window (Figure 5: upper-right) to the labeling boxes (Figure 5: left). Note that it is not necessary for the user to select dissimilar images because images that are not selected as similar images are automatically treated as dissimilar. In addition, the interface enables the user to modify the labels of images evaluated in the past searching iterations by moving the images to another box in the search process. The bottom-left image is the nearest-neighbor face in the current search iteration (i.e., a top-ranked image among re-ranked neighbor images) used for supplemental information. Based on the top-ranked image, the user can intuitively understand the process of creating face representations via user-labeling. In these experiments, our retrieval system ran on an Intel Xeon CPU E5-2687W 3.10 GHz with 32 GB RAM and an NVIDIA TITAN X GPU.

4.2 User Study Settings

Database.
For our experiment, we used the Chicago Face Database [23], which consists of 597 face images (290 male and 307 female), as the target database. It provides high-resolution photographs of the subjects' frontal pose with neutral expressions. The subjects have various nationalities and ethnicities and are between the ages of 17 and 65 years. Since previous works used small-scale databases for experiments (for example, WhittleSearch [18] used 772 images including only 8 persons), we assume that the number of images in the Chicago Face Database is sufficient for confirming the usefulness of our retrieval system.

Methodology.
To assess the utility of our face retrieval system, we performed user studies. In the user studies, we invited 10 computer science

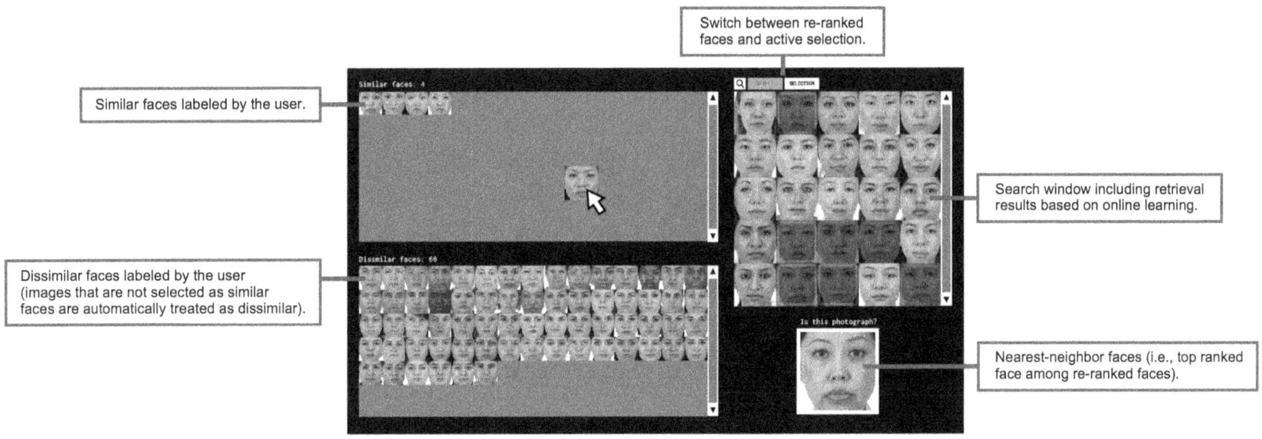

Figure 5: Proposed user interface. A user can select images to retrieve the target image by interactively repeating the drag-and-drop operation.

students (20 to 27 years old; 7 male and 3 female). First, each subject was given a brief overview of our interface and a step-by-step tutorial for familiarization with our retrieval framework. Then, we asked them to perform search tasks using our face retrieval interface.

We evaluated the search task for a specific person as well as its features. In this experiment, the subjects were shown a single face image that was randomly selected from the database. Then, they searched for the person from visual memory without observing further examples (i.e., the subjects repeatedly selected several face candidates that were similar to the target face until it was found). The experiment facilitator did not provide a time constraint or intervene unless the subject had difficulty in completing the task.

Baseline.
Our goal was to observe whether the subjects could independently search for the target face using our system. In addition, since face retrieval relying on a user's visual memory is a new problem; to our knowledge, there has been no existing work on this problem. Thus, in this paper, we assess our framework by changing the contents of images proposed to the user in a search process as follows:

50 neighbors
50 neighbor images of a current search point, i.e., the top 50 images of the original retrieval results of ANNG searching.

25 neighbors
25 neighbor images of a current search point, i.e., the top 25 images of the original retrieval results of ANNG searching.

Active selection
25 images compressed by applying active selection to 50 neighbor images.

The first two are simply cut low-ranked images presented in conventional relevance feedback studies. In this paper, we defined the number of images in active selection as 25 based on the number of images visible on a page of the search window. The images initially proposed to the user were randomly selected.

4.3 Search Cost to Find Target Face

In this section, we report the search cost for a subject to find a specified face using our retrieval interface. We recorded the total search time, total number of search iterations, and frequency of the subjects' dragging and dropping until they found the specified face in a search window. Figure 6 shows the obtained scores. In these experiments, even though the proposed framework used only unstable inputs relying on the subjects' visual memory, it achieved rapid searching for the target image within 1 min on average (50 neighbors: 118.6 s; 25 neighbors: 80.3 s; active selection: 58.5 s). Furthermore, the specified image was found with a small number of search iterations on average (50 neighbors: 5.9; 25 neighbors: 7.2; active selection: 4.5). Because the number of dragging and dropping operations by the subject was reduced as well (50 neighbors: 11.2; 25 neighbors: 7.5; active selection: 7.0), we also confirmed that active selection could reduce the burden on the user for searching. In summary, each chart provides credible evidence that the proposed active selection method outperforms the baseline method and is effective in searching for a specified face image intuitively and efficiently. This is because there is a critical trade-off relationship between the reduction of user burden by simply removing original retrieval results and the probability of presence of the target or similar faces. Active selection can reduce the strength of this trade-off relationship by re-ranking based on the subject's visual similarities and active learning for sample compression. In addition, active selection also contributes to decreasing the size of the scroll panel used in the search window because of the smaller number of images presented to a user.

4.4 Efficiency of Exploratory Searching

Here, we report the efficiency of exploratory searching. In this paper, the distance between a search point and the target image point is used for evaluation. At every search iteration, we observed the cosine distance between the centroid vector of a search point and the representation vector of the specified image. Figure 7 shows

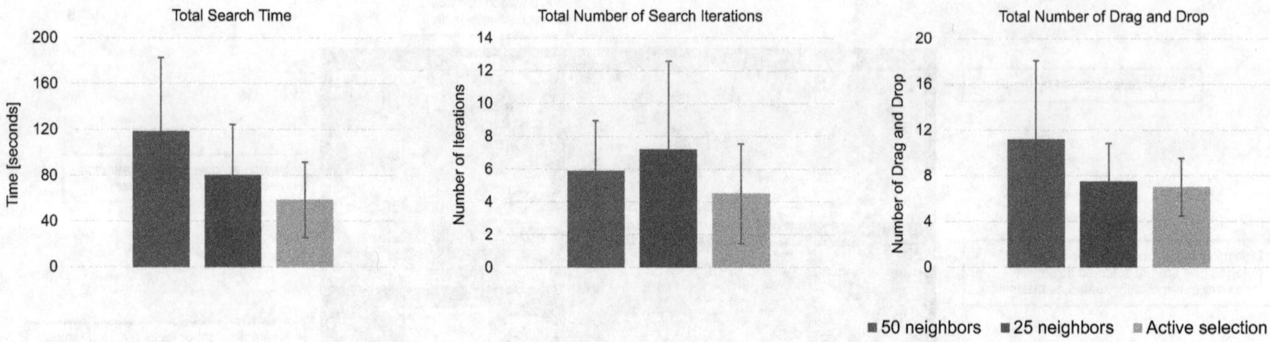

Figure 6: Average search cost for a subject to find a specified face (left: total search time; middle: total number of search iterations; right: frequency of drag and drop). Retrieval of the specified face by using active selection resulted in easy and quick searching.

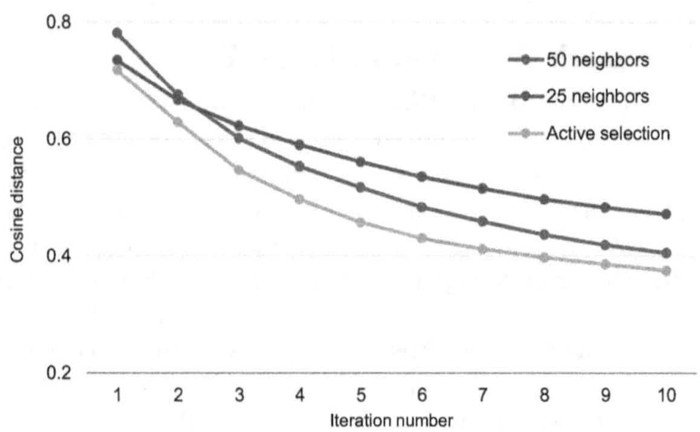

Figure 7: Cosine distance between the centroid of a search point and a target face image at every search iteration. With active selection, the distance converges more rapidly.

that the cosine distance converges as the search progresses. We observed the convergence of the distance in both the baseline methods and active selection. The convergence speed of the distance was higher for active selection than for the baseline methods. The reason for such results was that the subjects could effectively evaluate similarities between proposed faces because of the small number of images visible on a search window, and the system correctly modified the search area. In these experiments, some subjects were confused in the evaluation of similarities when many images were presented simultaneously (for example, when 50 neighbor face images were presented). Therefore, decreasing the number of images proposed to a user with active selection could result in intuitive searching. Note that the performance of convergence when 25 neighbor images were presented was inferior to that of the other methods because the subjects could not find similar images in the small number of proposed images, and the system inefficiently modified the search area.

5 CONCLUSION AND FUTURE WORK

In this paper, we proposed a novel framework for clarifying an image representation envisioned by a user. Our retrieval system enables the user to find a target image by relying on his/her visual memory easily and quickly. In addition, we proposed active selection for decreasing the number of presented images. We confirmed that active selection contributed to reducing the burden on the user for efficient exploratory searching. However, some future works are required for improving the proposed framework further.

Initial Presentation.

First, the total number of search iterations and search time may depend on the images presented initially to the user. In this paper, because the images initially presented to the user were randomly selected, the system might provide images that are not similar to the target. Our framework can flexibly handle such a case by repeating the search process, but further modification of the search area may be required. We plan to solve this problem by initially providing a simple database map showing images in a search space constructed by DeCAF features and ANNG so that the user can easily browse the database overview.

Number of Presented Images.

In our experiment, following previous works, we used a small-scale database and confirmed our retrieval system's usefulness. However, it is necessary to assess the proposed system on a large-scale database such as the LFW Face Database [11] for practical use in many applications. In addition, our framework requires the fine-tuning of the relationship between the scale of the database and the number of presented images.

Since the proposed retrieval framework has demonstrated the potential to flexibly meet the demand of various users interactively, it may be useful for some applications such as criminal investigation. In addition, because our current system mainly focuses on facial images, the extension of the proposed human-in-the-loop framework (e.g., object recognition or an interface that can augment a user's individual memories) may present interesting research opportunities, which we plan to explore in the future. We believe that our perception-based framework is a step toward the acceleration of research in the field of human computation.

ACKNOWLEDGMENTS

This work was supported in part by JST ACCEL Grant Number JPMJAC1602, Japan.

REFERENCES

[1] Artem Babenko, Anton Slesarev, Alexandr Chigorin, and Victor Lempitsky. 2014. Neural codes for image retrieval. In *Proc. of the European Conference on Computer Vision*. Springer, 584–599.

[2] Bor-Chun Chen, Yan-Ying Chen, Yin-Hsi Kuo, and Winston H Hsu. 2013. Scalable face image retrieval using attribute-enhanced sparse codewords. *IEEE Trans. on Multimedia* 15, 5 (2013), 1163–1173.

[3] En Cheng, Feng Jing, and Lei Zhang. 2009. A unified relevance feedback framework for web image retrieval. *IEEE Trans. on Image Processing* 18, 6 (2009), 1350–1357.

[4] Jeff Donahue, Yangqing Jia, Oriol Vinyals, Judy Hoffman, Ning Zhang, Eric Tzeng, and Trevor Darrell. 2014. DeCAF: A Deep Convolutional Activation Feature for Generic Visual Recognition.. In *Proc. of the 31st International Conference on Machine Learning*, Vol. 32. 647–655.

[5] Faezeh Ensan and Ebrahim Bagheri. 2017. Document Retrieval Model Through Semantic Linking. In *Proc. of the Tenth ACM International Conference on Web Search and Data Mining*. ACM, 181–190.

[6] James Fogarty, Desney Tan, Ashish Kapoor, and Simon Winder. 2008. CueFlik: interactive concept learning in image search. In *Proc. of the SIGCHI Conference on Human Factors in Computing Systems*. ACM, 29–38.

[7] Ian Goodfellow, Jean Pouget-Abadie, Mehdi Mirza, Bing Xu, David Warde-Farley, Sherjil Ozair, Aaron Courville, and Yoshua Bengio. 2014. Generative adversarial nets. In *Proc. of the Advances in neural information processing systems*. 2672–2680.

[8] Albert Gordo, Jon Almazán, Jerome Revaud, and Diane Larlus. 2016. Deep image retrieval: Learning global representations for image search. In *Proc. of the European Conference on Computer Vision*. Springer, 241–257.

[9] Ju Han and Kai-Kuang Ma. 2002. Fuzzy color histogram and its use in color image retrieval. *IEEE Trans. on Image Processing* 11, 8 (2002), 944–952.

[10] Christian Herrmann and Jürgen Beyerer. 2015. Face Retrieval on Large-Scale Video Data. In *Proc. of the 12th Conference on Computer and Robot Vision (CRV)*. IEEE, 192–199.

[11] Gary B Huang, Manu Ramesh, Tamara Berg, and Erik Learned-Miller. 2007. Labeled faces in the wild: A database for studying face recognition in unconstrained environments. *Technical Report 07-49, University of Massachusetts, Amherst* (2007).

[12] Masajiro Iwasaki. 2015. NGT: Neighborhood Graph and Tree for Indexing. http://research-lab.yahoo.co.jp/software/ngt/. (2015).

[13] Masajiro Iwasaki. 2016. Pruned Bi-directed K-nearest Neighbor Graph for Proximity Search. In *Proc. of the International Conference on Similarity Search and Applications*. Springer, 20–33.

[14] Zhong Ji, Yanwei Pang, and Xuelong Li. 2015. Relevance preserving projection and ranking for Web image search reranking. *IEEE Trans. on Image Processing* 24, 11 (2015), 4137–4147.

[15] Subhradeep Kayal. 2014. Improved Hierarchical Clustering for Face Images in Videos: Integrating positional and temporal information with HAC. In *Proc. of the International Conference on Multimedia Retrieval*. ACM, 455.

[16] Ira Kemelmacher-Shlizerman, Eli Shechtman, Rahul Garg, and Steven M Seitz. 2011. Exploring photobios. In *ACM Trans. on Graphics (TOG)*, Vol. 30. ACM, 61.

[17] Davis E King. 2009. Dlib-ml: A machine learning toolkit. *Journal of Machine Learning Research* 10, Jul (2009), 1755–1758.

[18] Adriana Kovashka, Devi Parikh, and Kristen Grauman. 2012. Whittlesearch: Image search with relative attribute feedback. In *Proc. of the IEEE Conference on Computer Vision and Pattern Recognition*. IEEE, 2973–2980.

[19] Neeraj Kumar, Alexander Berg, Peter N Belhumeur, and Shree Nayar. 2011. Describable visual attributes for face verification and image search. *IEEE Trans. on Pattern Analysis and Machine Intelligence* 33, 10 (2011), 1962–1977.

[20] Xirong Li, Tiberio Uricchio, Lamberto Ballan, Marco Bertini, Cees GM Snoek, and Alberto Del Bimbo. 2016. Socializing the semantic gap: A comparative survey on image tag assignment, refinement, and retrieval. *ACM Computing Surveys (CSUR)* 49, 1 (2016), 14.

[21] Kevin Lin, Huei-Fang Yang, Kuan-Hsien Liu, Jen-Hao Hsiao, and Chu-Song Chen. 2015. Rapid clothing retrieval via deep learning of binary codes and hierarchical search. In *Proc. of the 5th Conference on Multimedia Retrieval*. ACM, 499–502.

[22] Ying Liu, Dengsheng Zhang, Guojun Lu, and Wei-Ying Ma. 2007. A survey of content-based image retrieval with high-level semantics. *Pattern Recognition* 40, 1 (2007), 262–282.

[23] Debbie S Ma, Joshua Correll, and Bernd Wittenbrink. 2015. The Chicago face database: A free stimulus set of faces and norming data. *Behavior Research Methods* 47, 4 (2015), 1122–1135.

[24] Lyndon Nixon and Raphaël Troncy. 2014. Survey of semantic media annotation tools for the web: towards new media applications with linked media. In *Proc. of the European Semantic Web Conference*. Springer, 100–114.

[25] Timo Ojala, Matti Pietikainen, and David Harwood. 1994. Performance evaluation of texture measures with classification based on Kullback discrimination of distributions. *Pattern Recognition* 1 (1994), 582–585.

[26] Aude Oliva and Antonio Torralba. 2001. Modeling the shape of the scene: A holistic representation of the spatial envelope. *International Journal of Computer Vision* 42, 3 (2001), 145–175.

[27] Enrique G Ortiz, Alan Wright, and Mubarak Shah. 2013. Face recognition in movie trailers via mean sequence sparse representation-based classification. In *Proc. of the IEEE Conference on Computer Vision and Pattern Recognition*. 3531–3538.

[28] Omkar M Parkhi, Andrea Vedaldi, and Andrew Zisserman. 2015. Deep face recognition. In *Proc. of the British Machine Vision Conference*, Vol. 1. 6.

[29] Joseph Rocchio. 1971. Relevance feedback in information retrieval. *The Smart Retrieval System-Experiments in Automatic Document Processing* (1971), 313–323.

[30] Yong Rui, Thomas S Huang, Michael Ortega, and Sharad Mehrotra. 1998. Relevance feedback: a power tool for interactive content-based image retrieval. *IEEE Trans. on Circuits and Systems for Video Technology* 8, 5 (1998), 644–655.

[31] S Sasikala and R Soniya Gandhi. 2015. Efficient content based image retrieval system with metadata processing. *International Journal of Innovative Research in Science and Technology* 1, 10 (2015), 72–77.

[32] Florian Schroff, Dmitry Kalenichenko, and James Philbin. 2015. Facenet: A unified embedding for face recognition and clustering. In *Proc. of the IEEE Conference on Computer Vision and Pattern Recognition*. 815–823.

[33] Burr Settles. 2010. Active learning literature survey. *University of Wisconsin, Madison* 52, 55-66 (2010), 11.

[34] Karen Simonyan and Andrew Zisserman. 2014. Very deep convolutional networks for large-scale image recognition. *ArXiv Preprint ArXiv:1409.1556* (2014).

[35] Brandon M Smith, Shengqi Zhu, and Li Zhang. 2011. Face image retrieval by shape manipulation. In *Proc. of the IEEE Conference on Computer Vision and Pattern Recognition*. IEEE, 769–776.

[36] Kohei Sugawara, Hayato Kobayashi, and Masajiro Iwasaki. 2016. On approximately searching for similar word embeddings. In *Proc. of the 54th Annual Meeting of the Association for Computational Linguistics*, Vol. 1. 2265–2275.

[37] Yi Sun, Xiaogang Wang, and Xiaoou Tang. 2015. Deeply learned face representations are sparse, selective, and robust. In *Proc. of the IEEE Conference on Computer Vision and Pattern Recognition*. 2892–2900.

[38] Ji Wan, Dayong Wang, Steven Chu Hong Hoi, Pengcheng Wu, Jianke Zhu, Yongdong Zhang, and Jintao Li. 2014. Deep learning for content-based image retrieval: A comprehensive study. In *Proc. of the 22nd ACM international conference on Multimedia*. ACM, 157–166.

[39] Changhu Wang, Lei Zhang, and Hong-Jiang Zhang. 2008. Learning to reduce the semantic gap in web image retrieval and annotation. In *Proc. of the 31st annual international ACM SIGIR conference on Research and development in information retrieval*. ACM, 355–362.

[40] Fang Wang, Le Kang, and Yi Li. 2015. Sketch-based 3d shape retrieval using convolutional neural networks. In *Proc. of the IEEE Conference on Computer Vision and Pattern Recognition*. 1875–1883.

[41] Jinjun Wang, Jianchao Yang, Kai Yu, Fengjun Lv, Thomas Huang, and Yihong Gong. 2010. Locality-constrained linear coding for image classification. In *Proc. of the IEEE Conference on Computer Vision and Pattern Recognition*. IEEE, 3360–3367.

[42] Yandong Wen, Kaipeng Zhang, Zhifeng Li, and Yu Qiao. 2016. A discriminative feature learning approach for deep face recognition. In *Proc. of the European Conference on Computer Vision*. Springer, 499–515.

[43] Baoyuan Wu, Yifan Zhang, Bao-Gang Hu, and Qiang Ji. 2013. Constrained clustering and its application to face clustering in videos. In *Proc. of the IEEE Conference on Computer Vision and Pattern Recognition*. 3507–3514.

[44] Zhong Wu, Qifa Ke, Jian Sun, and Heung-Yeung Shum. 2011. Scalable face image retrieval with identity-based quantization and multireference reranking. *IEEE Trans. on Pattern Analysis and Machine Intelligence* 33, 10 (2011), 1991–2001.

[45] Jun Yu, Xiaokang Yang, Fei Gao, and Dacheng Tao. 2016. Deep multimodal distance metric learning using click constraints for image ranking. *IEEE Trans. on Cybernetics* (2016).

[46] Matthew D Zeiler. 2012. ADADELTA: an adaptive learning rate method. *ArXiv Preprint ArXiv:1212.5701* (2012).

[47] Dengsheng Zhang, Aylwin Wong, Maria Indrawan, and Guojun Lu. 2000. Content-based image retrieval using Gabor texture features. *IEEE Trans. on Pattern Analysis and Machine Intelligence* (2000), 13–15.

[48] Hanwang Zhang, Zheng-Jun Zha, Yang Yang, Shuicheng Yan, Yue Gao, and Tat-Seng Chua. 2013. Attribute-augmented semantic hierarchy: towards bridging semantic gap and intention gap in image retrieval. In *Proc. of the 21st ACM international conference on Multimedia*. ACM, 33–42.
[49] Yongdong Zhang, Xiaopeng Yang, and Tao Mei. 2014. Image search reranking with query-dependent click-based relevance feedback. *IEEE Trans. on Image Processing* 23, 10 (2014), 4448–4459.
[50] Bo Zhao, Jiashi Feng, Xiao Wu, and Shuicheng Yan. 2017. Memory-augmented attribute manipulation networks for interactive fashion search. In *Proc. of the IEEE Conference on Computer Vision and Pattern Recognition*. 1520–1528.
[51] Fang Zhao, Yongzhen Huang, Liang Wang, and Tieniu Tan. 2015. Deep semantic ranking based hashing for multi-label image retrieval. In *Proc. of the IEEE Conference on Computer Vision and Pattern Recognition*. 1556–1564.
[52] Jun-Yan Zhu, Philipp Krähenbühl, Eli Shechtman, and Alexei A Efros. 2016. Generative visual manipulation on the natural image manifold. In *Proc. of the European Conference on Computer Vision*. Springer, 597–613.
[53] Shengqi Zhu, Brandon M Smith, and Li Zhang. 2011. FaceSimile: A mobile application for face image search based on interactive shape manipulation. In *Proc. of the IEEE International Conference on Computer Vision Workshops (ICCV Workshops)*. IEEE, 82–83.

Facial Expression Synthesis by U-Net Conditional Generative Adversarial Networks

Xueping Wang
Beijing Advanced Innovation Center for Big Data and Brain Computing, Beihang University
Beijing, China
xpwang@buaa.edu.cn

Weixin Li*
Beijing Advanced Innovation Center for Big Data and Brain Computing, Beihang University
Beijing, China
weixinli@buaa.edu.cn

Guodong Mu
Beijing Advanced Innovation Center for Big Data and Brain Computing, Beihang University
Beijing, China
muyouhang@buaa.edu.cn

Di Huang
Beijing Advanced Innovation Center for Big Data and Brain Computing, Beihang University
Beijing, China
dhuang@buaa.edu.cn

Yunhong Wang
Beijing Advanced Innovation Center for Big Data and Brain Computing, Beihang University
Beijing, China
yhwang@buaa.edu.cn

ABSTRACT

High-level manipulation of facial expressions in images such as expression synthesis is challenging because facial expression changes are highly non-linear, and vary depending on the facial appearance. Identity of the person should also be well preserved in the synthesized face. In this paper, we propose a novel U-Net Conditioned Generative Adversarial Network (UC-GAN) for facial expression generation. U-Net helps retain the property of the input face, including the identity information and facial details. We also propose an identity preserving loss, which further improves the performance of our model. Both qualitative and quantitative experiments are conducted on the Oulu-CASIA and KDEF datasets, and the results show that our method can generate faces with natural and realistic expressions while preserve the identity information. Comparison with the state-of-the-art approaches also demonstrates the competency of our method.

KEYWORDS

Facial expression synthesis; generative adversarial network (GAN); identity preserving

ACM Reference Format:

Xueping Wang, Weixin Li, Guodong Mu, Di Huang, and Yunhong Wang. 2018. Facial Expression Synthesis by U-Net Conditional Generative Adversarial Networks. In *ICMR '18: 2018 International Conference on Multimedia Retrieval, June 11–14, 2018, Yokohama, Japan.* , 8 pages. https://doi.org/10.1145/3206025.3206068

*indicates the corresponding author.

ICMR '18, June 11–14, 2018, Yokohama, Japan

ACM ISBN 978-1-4503-5046-4/18/06...$15.00
https://doi.org/10.1145/3206025.3206068

1 INTRODUCTION

Facial expression synthesis (FES) generally aims to render a face image of a neutral expression with different universal ones, i.e., happiness, sadness, fear, anger, disgust, and surprise. FES has received increasing attention in recent years from both the academia and industry, not only due to its scientific challenges, but also for its wide-range of applications, e.g., human-computer interactions, animation and facial reenactment [30].

The key issue in FES is to transfer expressions by reconstructing texture and deforming shape of the given face, and this is a rather difficult task as the expressions produced are expected to be natural and with typical texture and shape patterns, in particular in the presence of variations of ambient illumination, head pose, image resolution, etc. For example, surprise usually makes the mouth open and the eyes become bigger, while disgust only slightly varies facial geometry but tends to present more detailed wrinkles on the areas around the nose and between the eyebrows. Furthermore, corresponding input and output faces are required to share the same identity, i.e. preserving identity cues after expression editing. In literature, there exist a number of investigations which focus on this topic, and the last two decades have witnessed its development from hand-crafted methods to deep learning based ones.

Specifically, the most majority of the early studies are hand-crafted, and they manipulate faces by warping facial components according to the difference calculated from training samples [17, 18, 38]. Although they sometimes demonstrate promising results, even of high-resolution, modeling differences between expressions needs paired data where one subject has the samples of different expressions. Meanwhile, the face warping phase depends heavily on locations of fiducial landmarks, whose detection accuracies are limited by the discriminative power of traditional features. More importantly, the identity clue in the given face cannot be well protected due to global or local texture warping. Later, deep learning techniques have also been explored in this topic. High-order Boltzmann machine [26] and Flow Variational Auto-Encoder (FVAE) [35] are attempted; however, their faces synthesized are not visually satisfying, mainly because identity cues are lost more or less, making the input and output faces do not look like each other. Expression Generative Adversarial Network (ExprGAN) is proposed for photo-realistic facial expression [5]. It explicitly emphasizes the necessity of identity in FES and adds an identity constraint term in the loss function, aiming to balance expression generation and identity preservation. The results achieved are largely superior to those in the previous work, but the basic encoder-decoder generator framework leaves much space for further improvement.

In this paper, we propose a novel GAN based FES apporach that takes a neutral face as input and synthesizes the ones of the same person, but with different universal expressions. Instead of the encoder-decoder network used in generator [5], we make use of the U-Net model. As U-Net shares low level information between input and output images by skip connections, it helps retain the property of the input, thus better preserving identity information in the faces of synthesized expressions. At meantime, we present a new identity preserving loss, which not only minimizes the similarity between the same person, but maximizes that between different ones as well, to further enhance the proposed model. Finally, we embed the Auxiliary Classifier GAN (AC-GAN) to the framework so that one-to-many (neutral to various expressions) synthesis can be reached simultaneously. Extensive experiments are carried out on the Oulu-CASIA and KDEF databases, and the results are state-of-the-art in terms of both expression editing as well as identity protection, which clearly indicates the effectiveness of the proposed method.

The remainder of this paper is organized as follows. We describe the related work in the next section. The proposed method is introduced in Section 3. Experimental results are shown and analyzed in Section 4. Finally, we conclude the paper in Section 5.

2 RELATED WORK

2.1 Facial Expression Synthesis

In recent years, facial expression synthesis has been widely studied in the field of computer vision. The traditional methods mainly include geometry-controlled image warping based approaches [18, 38] and morphing-based approaches [2, 24, 28]. The methods based on geometry controlled image warping use the feature difference vector of the source and target expression images to generate feature positions for a new face. They can only capture the feature motions of the face but ignore the facial detail changes brought by the changes of facial expressions. Morphing-based approaches [2, 24, 28], can only generate expressions in-between the given expression through interpolation and cannot be used to generate expressions for a new face. The deep learning-based methods can be divided into three subclasses from the perspective of generative modeling, namely Deep Belief Network (DBN) [26, 29], variational autoencoders (VAE) [3, 6, 13, 33, 35, 40], and generative adversarial networks (GAN) [4–7, 11, 14, 16, 23].

In the first subclass, Susskind et al. [29] used a deep belief net to generate expressions for a given identity with elementary facial expressions such as "raised eyebrows". Reed et al. [26] proposed a higher-order Boltzmann machine which incorporates multiplicative interactions to effectively disentangle the variation of facial expression and identity. However, the generated images of these methods are low-resolution with size of 48 x 48, which are not visually satisfying.

In the second subclass, Cheung et al. [3] used augmented autoencoders with a supervised cost and an unsupervised cross-covariance penalty to reatain subject identity in faces. Ghodrati et al. [32] adopted a convolutional encoder-decoder architecture to generate a similar and plausible facial image, based on some desired attributes. Then the images are refined by the refinement network using convolutional filters. Though this model can alter a face without human intervention and with noticeable accuracy, the synthesized facial images has low resolution (32×32) and tend to be blurry. Larsen et al. [14] combined variational autoencoder and generative adversarial networks together to encode, and generate face images with feature-wise error measures. And the latent image representation could disentangle factors of variation, such as simple arithmetic applied in the learned latent space producing images which refect changes in some attributes. Yan et al. [33] interpreted a facial image as a composite of the foreground and background, and adopted a layered generative model to generate object images from high-level description based on images and texts, by using a conditioned variational auto-encoder. Yeh et al. [35] proposed Flow Variational Autoencoder (FVAE) model to edit the facial expression using latent vector arithmetic. Although the generated face image has high resolution, paired data of one subject with different expressions are needed to obtain the face expression interpolation. Zhou et al. [40] proposed the conditional difference adversarial autoencoder (CDAAE) to generate a face image with a target emotion or facial action unit (AU) label. In order to preserve the person identity, a feedforward path was added to an autoencoder model connecting low level features in the encoder to features at the corresponding level in the decoder. Though the method preserved the person identity information, the generated facial images are of low resolution (64×64) and some expression details and hair information are lost.

In the third subclass, Li et al. [16] presented a deep convolutional network model to generate a facial image conditioned on the source input image and the reference attribute, which can preserve the referenced attribute and the same or similar identity of the input image. Choi et al. [4] utilized a mask vector method that enables a novel generative adversarial network named StarGAN to control all available domain labels and translate the input image and domain information into corresponding domain. Olszewski et al. [23] proposed a method to transfer the face of a single RGB target image to a source video sequence with the same expression. Kaneko et al. [11] proposed a conditional filtered generative adversarial network (CF-GAN) to generate or edit an image while intuitively controlling large variations of an attribute. Ding et al. [5] proposed an Expression Generative Adversarial Network (ExprGAN) for photo-realistic facial expression editing to control both the type of the expression and its intensity simultaneously. However, the images this method generates tend to be a little blurry, do not have much expression details and miss the original person identity.

2.2 Generative Adversarial Networks (GANs)

Generative Adversarial Networks (GANs) [7] are a type of parametric method that has been widely applied and studied for image

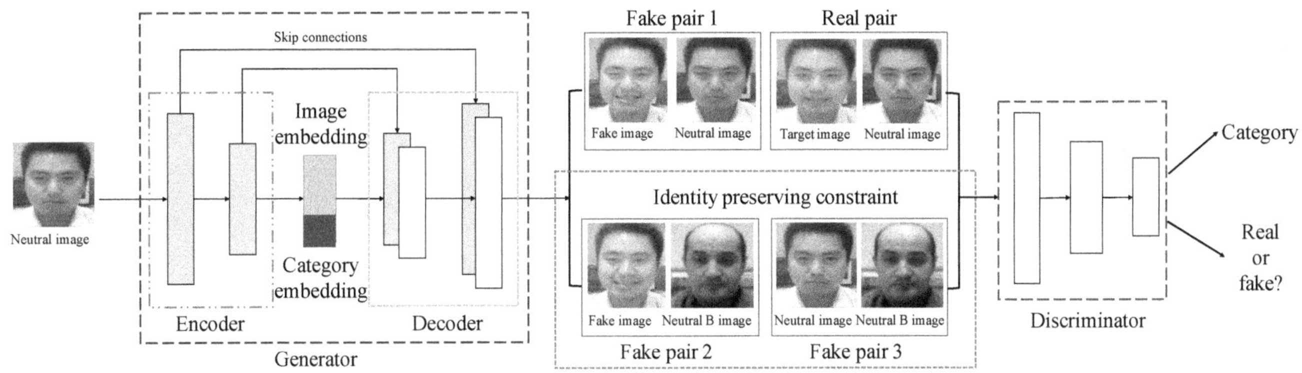

Figure 1: Illustration of the proposed UC-GAN model. Our model contains two parts: the generator G and the discriminator D.

synthesis. The main idea is to train paired generator and discriminator networks at the same time, where the goal of the discriminator is to classify between "real" images and generated "fake" images, and the generator aims to fool the discriminator so that the generated images are indistinguishable from real images. Once trained, the generator can be used to synthesize images driven by a compact vector of noise. Compared to the blurry and low-resolution outcome from other methods, GANs can produce sharp and plausible images. Conditional GAN (cGAN) is an extension of GAN with some conditioned information settings [21, 25]. Ledig et al. [15] presented SRGAN, a generative adversarial network (GAN) for image super-resolution (SR) with a perceptual loss function, which is capable of generating photo-realistic natural images for $4\times$ upscaling factors. Isola et al. [10] explored GANs in the image conditional setting for image-to-image translation in many tasks. This paper uses U-Net model as the generator which shares the low-level information between an input image and a corresponding output image. Odena et al. [22] proposed an auxiliary classifier GAN (AC-GAN) to generate globally coherent high resolution ImageNet samples, where every generated sample has a corresponding class label. Yang et al. [34] presented a novel face age progression method based on GAN. In order to achieve and enhance the aging details, a pyramidal adversarial discriminator was used to convey the high-level age-specific features. Our method is partly inspired by these works.

3 APPROACH

In this section, we describe the proposed UC-GAN for facial expression generation. We first introduce the cGAN, which our UC-GAN is built on. Then we explain the framework and formulation of UC-GAN in detail.

3.1 Conditional Generative Adversarial Networks

The conditional GAN (cGAN) [21] is an extension of the GAN model allowing the generation of images with some extra information y, such as class labels or data from other modalities. The structure of cGAN is just like GAN, including two "adversarial" models: a generative model G and a discriminative model D. G is optimized to capture the real data distribution based on random noise z which is hard for D to discriminate from real data x. D estimates the probability that a sample comes from the training data rather than G. D and G play the two-player minimax game with value function $V(D,G)$. The objective function is defined as

$$\begin{aligned}\min_G \max_D V(D,G) = \mathbb{E}_{x\sim p_{data}(x)}[\log D(x|y)] + \\ \mathbb{E}_{z\sim p_z(z)}[\log(1 - D(G(z|y)))].\end{aligned} \tag{1}$$

3.2 U-Net Conditioned Generative Adversarial Networks (UC-GAN)

The proposed UC-GAN model is illustrated in Fig. 1. As shown in the figure, the generator G is a U-Net conditioned model, including an encoder and a decoder. Different from the traditional U-Net model, the U-Net conditioned model transmits the encoded features, along with the conditional information, to the decoder. The UC-GAN takes neutral images I_N and target category embedding (labels) c as input and outputs a high confidence target facial image of the same person. Here we directly encode RGB facial images instead of latent random noises for two reasons. Firstly, if the GAN model generates images from random noises, the output images may not be controlled. This is undesirable in facial expression synthesis, where we have to ensure that the output face preserves the identity of the input face. Secondly, the conditioned images as a meaningful latent space, can maintain the sharp textures and person identity of the input facial images.

As shown in Fig. 1, the neutral image I_N is first encoded by an encoder E, yielding a facial identity embeddings $E(I_N)$. After combining it with the category embedding c, we now can have the GAN model that can handle multiple expressions at the same time. However, a new problem emerges: the model starts to confuse and mix the expression categories, generating faical images that don't look like any of the target emotions. Inspired by the AC-GAN model [22], we add the multi-class category loss to supervise the discriminator to penalize such scenarios, by predicting the facial expression categories of the generated facial images. The encoder maps the same facial expression into the same vector. The decoder, on the other hand, will take both the facial identity embedding and category embedding to generate the target facial expression.

The discriminator D aims to distinguish between target image and the generated image, and classify expression.

Identity Preserving Loss. Whether a GAN model works well mainly depends on the cooperation between the generator and discriminator. If the discriminator is too weak, it also results in low performance. Whereas, a comparatively strong discriminator can achieve more reasonable and nautral-looking facial expression details and clear facial profile [34]. For facial expression generation method, the person identity should not be changed while generating different facial images. So in terms of identity, it is desired to have the distance between the generated image and input image smaller than that between the generated image and another different person's image. As shown in Fig. 1, the generated fake images should have the same identity as the input, and far away from the "neutral B image". To solve this problem, we add two more fake pairs to enhance the ability of discriminator to preserve the person identity: the first pair consists of the generated facial image $G(I_N, c)$ and another person's neutral face image I_{BN}; the second one consists of the input neutral image I_N and another person's neutral face image I_{BN}. The discriminator D also performs multi-class classification to classify the facial expression category. The identity preserving loss is defined as

$$L_{ip} = 2 * L_{sce}(D(I_N, I_T), 1) + L_{sce}(D(I_{BN}, G(I_N, c)), 0) + L_{sce}(D(I_{BN}, I_T), 0) \quad (2)$$

where L_{sce} denotes the sigmoid cross-entropy loss function. I_T is the real target facial expression image. The value 1 means the pair discriminated is a positive sample for D, and the value 0 means the pair discriminated is a negative sample for D. We multiply 2 to the loss of real pair to balance the number of positive and negative samples.

Category Loss. We use six basic expression categories in this paper. The network D also measures whether an image belongs to a specific fine-grained expression category. Here we use a standard method for classification. The network D takes I_N as input and outputs a six-dimensional vector, which is then turned into class probabilities through a softmax function. The category loss function is defined as

$$L_c = L_{sce}(D(I_N, I_T), c) + L_{sce}(D(I_N, G(I_N, c)), c). \quad (3)$$

Adversarial Loss. In order to generate realistic facial expression images indistinguishable from real facial images, we utilize the adversarial loss

$$L^D_{adv} = L_{sce}(D(I_N, I_T), 1) + L_{sce}(D(I_N, G(I_N, c)), 0) \quad (4)$$

$$L^G_{adv} = L_{sce}(D(I_N, G(I_N, c)), 1) \quad (5)$$

where L^D_{adv} and L^G_{adv} denote the loss function for the discriminator D and the generator G, respectively. D tries to distinguish generated images $G(I_N, c)$ from real image while G produces the facial image $G(I_N, c)$ conditioned on both input image I_N and target label c.

Reconstruction Loss. Though G is trained to generate realistic images with correct target label through minimizing the adversarial and category losses, the generated images cannot be guaranteed to have fine texture details compared to target images. To alleviate this problem, we apply a reconstruction loss to the generator, which is defined as

$$L_{L1} = \|G(I_N, c) - I_T\|_1 \quad (6)$$

where $G(I_N, c)$ is the generated images based on input I_N and corresponding target expression label c. We adopt the $L1$ distance rather than $L2$ in our reconstruction loss for less blurring effects [10].

Full Objective Function. The final objective loss function is defined as

$$G^* = L^D_{adv} + L^G_{adv} + \lambda_1 L_{L1} + \lambda_2 L_c + \lambda_3 L_{ip} \quad (7)$$

where λ_1, λ_2, and λ_3 are hyper-parameters that balance the importance of reconstruction, category, and identity preserving losses, respectively.

Network architecture. For the model architecture, we mainly use the U-Net based architecture [27], which can help ensure the low-level information to be shared between the input and output. The only difference from traditional U-Net is that we combine the category embedding after encoding. The conditioned U-Net model connects each layer i and layer n-i, where n is the total number of layers. Each skip connection simply concatenates all channels at layer i with those at layer n-i. The classifier function and check function of D share parameters except the output layer. This parameter sharing scheme enables the networks to leverage their common information such as features at low-level layers that are close to the data layer, hence helping train model effectively. In addition, it also minimizes the number of parameters and adds minimal complexity to the standard GAN.

4 EXPERIMENTS

4.1 Dataset

Two datasets are mainly used in our experiment, i.e. Oulu-CASIA and KDEF.

Oulu-CASIA. The Oulu-CASIA NIR&VIS facial expression database (Oulu-CASIA) [39] contains 80 subjects with six expressions, i.e., angry, disgust, fear, happy, sad and surprise. The whole image sequences are obtained under three different illumination conditions: dark, strong and weak. In the experiment, we only use the videos with strong illumination captured by a VIS camera, in which the first frame is always neutral and the last frame has the peak expression. For each expression squence of each subject, only the first and the last three frames are used, and we combine the first neutral images with the last three frames respectively to generate three image pairs. The total number of image pairs is 1440. Training and test sets are divided based on identity, with 1296 for training and 144 for testing. We align the faces by Multi-task CNN algorithm [37], and crop them.

KDEF. The Karolinska Directed Emotional Faces (KDEF) [19] dataset includes totally 4900 pictures of human facial expressions. It contains 70 individuals, each displaying 7 different emotional expressions including the neutral expression. Each expression is photographed (twice) from 5 different angles. Each subject appears in two series. In the experiment, we only choose the frontal facial images. So for one subject in each series, we only have seven facial images. Then we combine the neutral expression with the universal expressions. The total number of image pairs is 840. Training and test sets are divided based on identity, with 756 for training and 84 for testing.

4.2 Implementation Details

The UC-GAN mainly contains two parts: a generator G with an encoder and a decoder, and a discriminator D. The encoder contains a traditional convolution layer and seven encoder layers where the numbers of channels are 64, 128, 256, 512, 512, 512, 512, 512, respectively. The traditional convolution layer is 5×5 stride 2 convolution. The encoder layer in a block is composed of Leaky ReLU [20], 5×5 stride 2 convolution and batch normalization [9]. The decoder includes eight decoder layers. The decoder layer in a block is composed of 5×5 deconvolutional operation with stride 2, batch normalization, skip connection and dropout. For the first three decoder layers, the dropout probability is 0.5. For each decoder layers except the last one, the decoder layers have skip connections with the corresponding encoder layers. With skip connections, the decoder's numbers of channels are 1024, 1024, 1024, 1024, 512, 256, 128, and 3. D has two functions: one is for checking if the images are true or false, and the other is for expression classification. Both functions share the first four encoder layers blocks with 64, 128, 256, and 512 channels. Then it is branched to two heads, one for checking and one for classification.

We conduct a ten-fold person-independent cross validation for each dataset, so the number of training set and test set is 9:1. During training, the generator takes a neutral face image and a corresponding label information as input, and the output is a generated expression face image conditioned on the expression label. The input and output face images are 256×256 RGB images $I \in \mathbb{R}^{256\times256\times3}$. The discriminator takes image pairs $(I_N : I_T)$ as positive sample pairs, and $(I_N : G(I_N, c))$, $(I_{BN} : G(I_N, c))$, $(I_{BN} : I_T)$ as negative sample pairs.

On both datasets, we use the Adaptive Moment Estimation (ADAM) [12] optimizer with $\beta_1 = 0.5$. The initial learning rate is set to 0.0002 for both generator and discriminator. The images are scaled to 256×256 and the pixel values are normalized into the range $[-1, 1]$. We empirically set the batch size to 1, and the weights are set as $\lambda_1 = 100$, $\lambda_2 = 1$, $\lambda_3 = 1$, respectively. During testing, we randomly sample a neutral image and set an expression label. The model is implemented using Tensorflow [1].

4.3 Facial Expression Synthesis

We train our model on two datasets mentioned before for facial expression synthesis, respectively. The expression of the input face is fixed as neutral, and the target expression can be any from the six expressions (i.e. happy, surprise, fear, disgust, angry, and sad).

4.3.1 *Qualitative Evaluation.*

To show that our facial expression synthesis method can generate natural facial expressions while preserving the identity, we conduct the qualitative experiment.

Facial expression generation results. The first column shows the input faces, and the rest columns show our results for different expressions. From Fig. 3, we can see that our method can produce natural and reasonable facial expressions, even with variations in race, gender, etc. Our results also preserve the identity information of the input face sufficiently.

Comparison with other methods. We also compare our method with one state-of-the-art method for face expression synthesis, i.e. ExprGAN [5]. The Oulu-CASIA dataset is used for the comparison experiment. The comparison results are shown in Fig. 2. The first column shows input neutral faces for different methods. The other six columns show the generated results for the six expressions. The ground-truth images are also included in the Fig. 2 (in the last row). As shown in Fig. 2, compared with ExprGAN, the proposed UC-GAN has better realistic expression generation results, while the personal identities of the input faces are also well maintained. ExprGAN fails to preserve the personal identity effectively in the synthesis results, and the output faces are not clear.

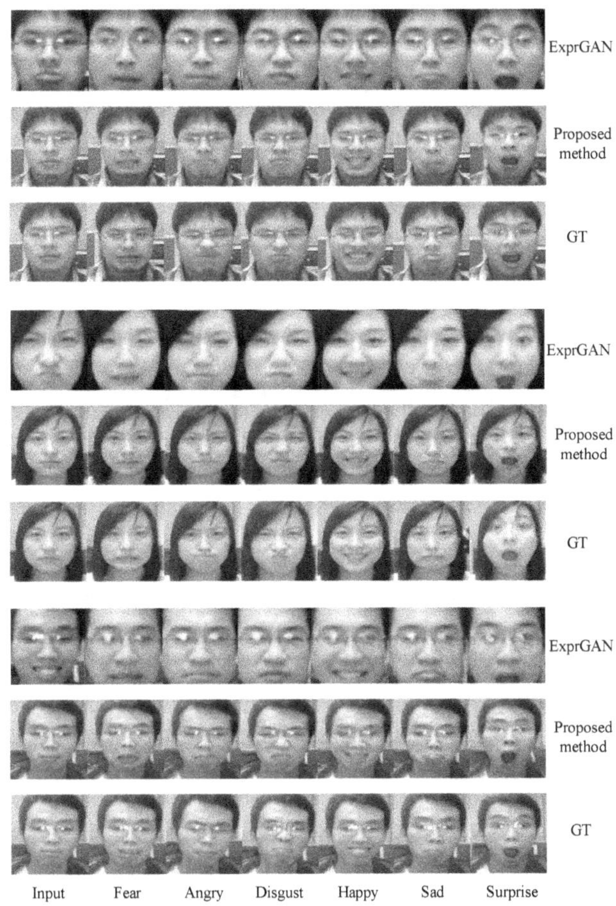

Figure 2: Comparison results of different facial expression synthesis methods on Oulu-CASIA. The ground-truth images (GT) are shown along with the synthesis results.

4.3.2 *User Study.*

We also evaluate our method by user study. Facial expression synthesis aims at generating natural and reasonable expressions while remaining his/her identity intact. So in the user study, we ask the volunteers to check whether the generated images have realistic and reasonable expressions, and whether they can still be recognized as the same person. There are 20 participants in this experiment. Each is shown with several pairs of images and is asked to give a score ranging from 1 to 10 to evaluate whether the generated

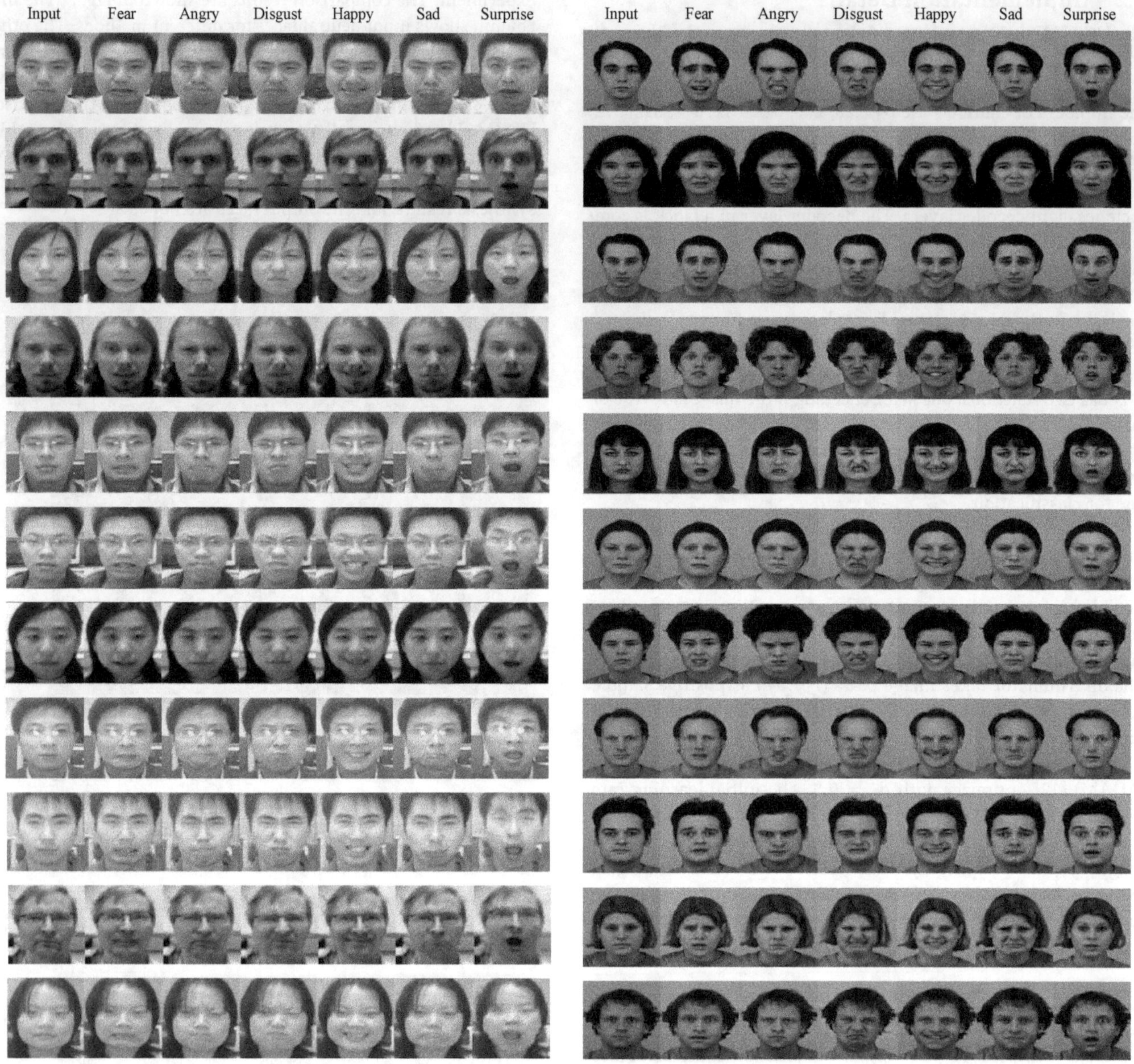

(a) Oulu-CASIA

(b) KDEF

Figure 3: Facial expression synthesis results of our method on the Oulu-CASIA and KDEF datasets.

images are reasonable or not and decide whether they are images from the same person. The average scores of user study are 76.82% and 82.75% for the Oulu-CASIA and KDEF datasets, respectively, which demonstrate that the proposed UC-GAN generates natural and reasonable expressions, even though the number of subjects in the training datasets is small. And 79.64% of the generated faces are judged to be the same person in the input image, which shows that our method can preserve the person identity effectively.

One thing we want to discuss is that even though our method can synthesize natural faces with reasonable expressions, the synthesized expressions may not be personalized. For instance, the synthesized faces in Fig. 4 do not look exactly the same as the ground-truth images (the expression intensities and patterns are different), even though they are perceived to be natural and reasonable. This is also a general problem for most learning based approaches, which tend to learn the most-common expression patterns from the training data and apply them to the test faces. But personalized results are highly demanded in practice. So personalized facial expression synthesis, which has more practical applications, can be one of our future research directions.

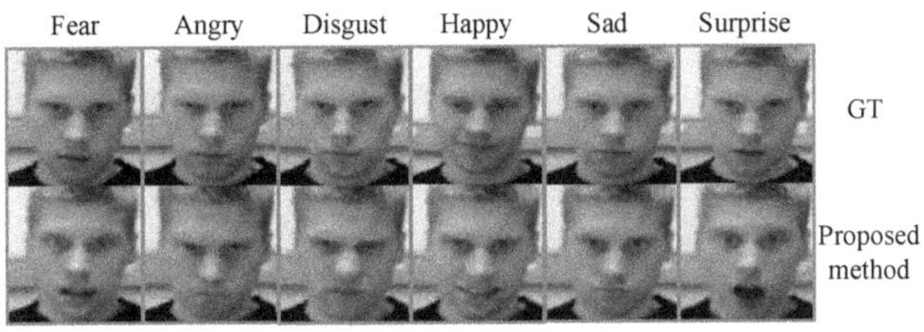

Figure 4: Example facial expression synthesis results on Oulu-CASIA and their corresponding ground-truth images (GT).

4.4 Contribution of Identity Preserving Loss

In this subsection, we demonstrate the discriminator's ability to make generated faces identity-preserving and natural via an ablation study. In detail, we compare the performance of our method with and without the identity preserving loss. Fig. 5 shows the qualitative evaluation results, in which the faces generated using our method with the identity preserving loss are more natural and identity-preserving, compared to those generated using the method without the loss.

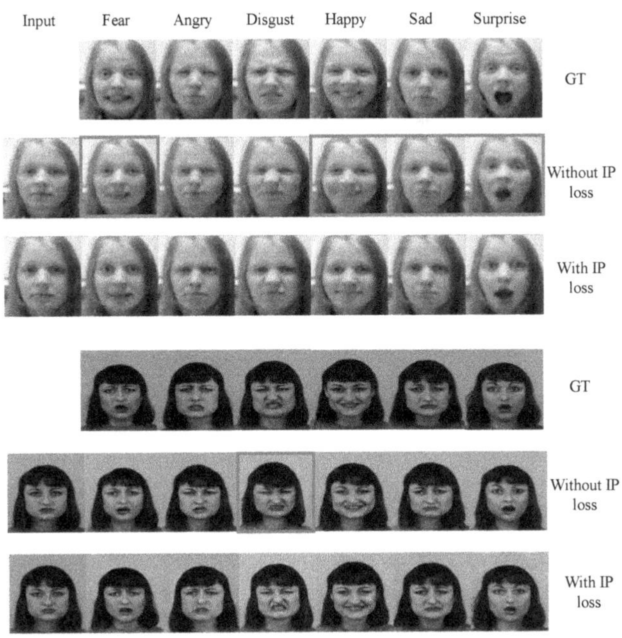

Figure 5: Comparison results of our method with or without identity preserving loss on the Oulu-CASIA and KDEF datasets. The top three rows are the comparison results from Oulu-CASIA, and the rest are from KDEF. The red boxes mark some synthesis results which are blurred or lose the identity information.

Table 1: Face verification results on Oulu-CASIA and KDEF

Dataset name	Dataset accuracy	Without IP loss[1]	With IP loss[1]
Oulu-CASIA	96.18%	92.26%	95.38%
KDEF	96.07%	93.88%	95.98%

[1] IP is the abbreviation of identity preserving.

In order to evaluate the performance of the proposed identity preserving loss quantitatively, we adopt the automatic face verification method by Wen [31] to check if the identity information of the input face is well preserved during expression synthesis. We use their model, which is trained on the CASIA-webface dataset [36], to extract facial features for face verification. A traditional shallow neural network is further used for verification, which includes two convolution layers and the dimension of feature maps for each layer is 128 and 2, respectively. Using this face verification algorithm and feature extracting method, the face verification accuracy on LFW dataset [8] is 98.50%. Inspired by [34], we perform comparisons between the input and the generated facial images for the six expressions, and the statistical analysis among the generated facial images is conducted. So in Oulu-CASIA, we have 144×21 pairs in total. As shown in Table 1, the verification rate of our method with identity preserving loss on Oulu-CASIA rises about 3.12% compared with the method without the loss. The dataset accuracy on the Oulu-CASIA dataset, which measures the accuracy of the verification method using the ground-truth faces with expressions, is 96.18% . For KDEF, there are 98×21 pairs of verifications, and the verification rate rises from 93.88% to 95.98% after adding the identity preserving loss. The dataset accuracy tested on this algorithm is 96.07%. These results quantitatively demonstrate the ability of identity preservation of the proposed method.

5 CONCLUSION

In this paper we propose a U-Net Conditioned Generative Adversarial Networks (UC-GAN) for facial expression synthesis. U-Net is adopted for its ability in keeping the low-level information of the input in the output face image. We also propose a person identity preserving loss to minimize the distance between the same person and maximize that between different ones. This loss constraint further enhances the distinction ability of the discriminator, which is good for producing identity-preserving faces with vivid expression details. Extensive experiments are conducted on the Oulu-CASIA and KDEF datasets. The proposed method outperforms the state-of-the-art method in qualitative evaluations. We also analyze the proposed method comprehensively by ablation studies using qualitative and quantitative evaluations. Both qualitative and quantitative experimental results demonstrate that our method, especially with the identity preserving loss added, can generate satisfactory face images that are natural-looking, and identity-preserving.

ACKNOWLEDGMENTS

This work is funded by the National Natural Science Foundation of China (No. 61673033 and No. 61421003).

REFERENCES

[1] Martín Abadi, Ashish Agarwal, Paul Barham, Eugene Brevdo, Zhifeng Chen, Craig Citro, Greg S Corrado, Andy Davis, Jeffrey Dean, Matthieu Devin, et al. 2016. Tensorflow: Large-scale machine learning on heterogeneous distributed systems. *arXiv preprint arXiv:1603.04467* (Mar 2016).

[2] Thaddeus Beier and Shawn Neely. 1992. Feature-based Image Metamorphosis. *SIGGRAPH Comput. Graph.* 26, 2 (Jul 1992), 35–42.

[3] Brian Cheung, Jesse A Livezey, Arjun K Bansal, and Bruno A Olshausen. 2015. Discovering hidden factors of variation in deep networks. *arXiv preprint arXiv:1412.6583v4* (Jun 2015).

[4] Yunjey Choi, Minje Choi, Munyoung Kim, Jung-Woo Ha, Sunghun Kim, and Jaegul Choo. 2017. StarGAN: Unified Generative Adversarial Networks for Multi-Domain Image-to-Image Translation. *arXiv preprint arXiv:1711.09020* (Nov 2017).

[5] Hui Ding, Kumar Sricharan, and Rama Chellappa. 2018. ExprGAN: Facial Expression Editing with Controllable Expression Intensity. In *2018 Thirty-Second AAAI Conference on Artificial Intelligence (AAAI).*

[6] Jon Gauthier. 2014. Conditional generative adversarial nets for convolutional face generation. *Class Project for Stanford CS231N: Convolutional Neural Networks for Visual Recognition, Winter semester* 2014, 5 (2014), 2.

[7] Ian Goodfellow, Jean Pouget-Abadie, Mehdi Mirza, Bing Xu, David Warde-Farley, Sherjil Ozair, Aaron Courville, and Yoshua Bengio. 2014. Generative Adversarial Nets. In *Advances in Neural Information Processing Systems 27.* 2672–2680.

[8] Gary B. Huang, Manu Ramesh, Tamara Berg, and Erik Learned-Miller. 2007. *Labeled Faces in the Wild: A Database for Studying Face Recognition in Unconstrained Environments.* Technical Report 07-49. University of Massachusetts, Amherst.

[9] Sergey Ioffe and Christian Szegedy. 2015. Batch Normalization: Accelerating Deep Network Training by Reducing Internal Covariate Shift. In *Proceedings of the 32nd International Conference on Machine Learning*, Vol. 37. 448–456.

[10] Phillip Isola, Jun-Yan Zhu, Tinghui Zhou, and Alexei A Efros. 2017. Image-To-Image Translation With Conditional Adversarial Networks. In *2017 IEEE Conference on Computer Vision and Pattern Recognition (CVPR).* 5967–5976.

[11] Takuhiro Kaneko, Kaoru Hiramatsu, and Kunio Kashino. 2017. Generative attribute controller with conditional filtered generative adversarial networks. In *2017 IEEE Conference on Computer Vision and Pattern Recognition (CVPR).* 7006–7015.

[12] Diederik Kingma and Jimmy Ba. 2014. Adam: A method for stochastic optimization. *arXiv preprint arXiv:1412.6980* (Dec 2014).

[13] Diederik P Kingma and Max Welling. 2013. Auto-encoding variational bayes. *arXiv preprint arXiv:1312.6114* (Dec 2013).

[14] Anders Boesen Lindbo Larsen, SÃÿren Kaae SÃÿnderby, Hugo Larochelle, and Ole Winther. 2016. Autoencoding beyond pixels using a learned similarity metric. In *Proceedings of The 33rd International Conference on Machine Learning*, Vol. 48. 1558–1566.

[15] Christian Ledig, Lucas Theis, Ferenc Huszar, Jose Caballero, Andrew Cunningham, Alejandro Acosta, Andrew Aitken, Alykhan Tejani, Johannes Totz, Zehan Wang, et al. 2017. Photo-Realistic Single Image Super-Resolution Using a Generative Adversarial Network. In *2017 IEEE Conference on Computer Vision and Pattern Recognition (CVPR).* 105–114.

[16] Mu Li, Wangmeng Zuo, and David Zhang. 2016. Deep Identity-aware Transfer of Facial Attributes. *arXiv preprint arXiv:1610.05586* (Oct 2016).

[17] James Jenn-Jier Lien, Takeo Kanade, Jeffrey F Cohn, and Ching-Chung Li. 2000. Detection, tracking, and classification of action units in facial expression. *Robotics and Autonomous Systems* 31, 3 (May 2000), 131–146.

[18] Zicheng Liu, Ying Shan, and Zhengyou Zhang. 2001. Expressive Expression Mapping with Ratio Images. In *Proceedings of the 28th Annual Conference on Computer Graphics and Interactive Techniques.* 271–276.

[19] Daniel Lundqvist, Anders Flykt, and Arne Öhman. 1998. The Karolinska directed emotional faces (KDEF). *CD ROM from Department of Clinical Neuroscience, Psychology section, Karolinska Institutet* (1998).

[20] Andrew L Maas, Awni Y Hannun, and Andrew Y Ng. 2013. Rectifier nonlinearities improve neural network acoustic models. In *in ICML Workshop on Deep Learning for Audio, Speech and Language Processing*, Vol. 1. 3.

[21] Mehdi Mirza and Simon Osindero. 2014. Conditional generative adversarial nets. *arXiv preprint arXiv:1411.1784* (Nov 2014).

[22] Augustus Odena, Christopher Olah, and Jonathon Shlens. 2017. Conditional Image Synthesis with Auxiliary Classifier GANs. In *2017 Thirty fourth International Conference on Machine Learning (ICML)*, Doina Precup and Yee Whye Teh (Eds.), Vol. 70. 2642–2651.

[23] Kyle Olszewski, Zimo Li, Chao Yang, Yi Zhou, Ronald Yu, Zeng Huang, Sitao Xiang, Shunsuke Saito, Pushmeet Kohli, and Hao Li. 2017. Realistic Dynamic Facial Textures from a Single Image using GANs. In *2017 IEEE International Conference on Computer Vision (ICCV).* 5439–5448.

[24] Frédéric Pighin, Jamie Hecker, Dani Lischinski, Richard Szeliski, and David H. Salesin. 2005. Synthesizing Realistic Facial Expressions from Photographs. In *ACM SIGGRAPH 2005 Courses.* Article 9.

[25] Alec Radford, Luke Metz, and Soumith Chintala. 2015. Unsupervised representation learning with deep convolutional generative adversarial networks. *arXiv preprint arXiv:1511.06434* (Nov 2015).

[26] Scott Reed, Kihyuk Sohn, Yuting Zhang, and Honglak Lee. 2014. Learning to Disentangle Factors of Variation with Manifold Interaction. In *Proceedings of the 31st International Conference on Machine Learning*, Vol. 32. 1431–1439.

[27] Olaf Ronneberger, Philipp Fischer, and Thomas Brox. 2015. U-net: Convolutional networks for biomedical image segmentation. In *2015 eighteenth International Conference on Medical Image Computing and Computer-Assisted Intervention (MICCAI).* 234–241.

[28] Steven M. Seitz and Charles R. Dyer. 1996. View Morphing. In *Proceedings of the 23rd Annual Conference on Computer Graphics and Interactive Techniques.* 21–30.

[29] Joshua M Susskind, Geoffrey E Hinton, Javier R Movellan, and Adam K Anderson. 2008. Generating facial expressions with deep belief nets. In *Affective Computing.*

[30] Justus Thies, Michael Zollhofer, Marc Stamminger, Christian Theobalt, and Matthias Nießner. 2016. Face2face: Real-time face capture and reenactment of rgb videos. In *2016 IEEE Conference on Computer Vision and Pattern Recognition (CVPR).* 2387–2395.

[31] Yandong Wen, Kaipeng Zhang, Zhifeng Li, and Yu Qiao. 2016. A Discriminative Feature Learning Approach for Deep Face Recognition. In *Computer Vision – ECCV 2016*, Bastian Leibe, Jiri Matas, Nicu Sebe, and Max Welling (Eds.). 499–515.

[32] Marco Pedersoli Xu Jia, Amir Ghodrati and Tinne Tuytelaars. 2016. Towards Automatic Image Editing: Learning to See another You. In *Proceedings of the British Machine Vision Conference (BMVC).* Article 101, 11 pages.

[33] Xinchen Yan, Jimei Yang, Kihyuk Sohn, and Honglak Lee. 2016. Attribute2image: Conditional image generation from visual attributes. In *Computer Vision – ECCV 2016.* Amsterdam, The Netherlands, 776–791.

[34] Hongyu Yang, Di Huang, Yunhong Wang, and Anil K Jain. 2017. Learning Face Age Progression: A Pyramid Architecture of GANs. *arXiv preprint arXiv:1711.10352* (Nov 2017).

[35] Raymond Yeh, Ziwei Liu, Dan B Goldman, and Aseem Agarwala. 2016. Semantic Facial Expression Editing using Autoencoded Flow. *arXiv preprint arXiv:1611.09961* (Nov 2016).

[36] Dong Yi, Zhen Lei, Shengcai Liao, and Stan Z Li. 2014. Learning face representation from scratch. *arXiv preprint arXiv:1411.7923* (Nov 2014).

[37] Kaipeng Zhang, Zhanpeng Zhang, Zhifeng Li, and Yu Qiao. 2016. Joint face detection and alignment using multitask cascaded convolutional networks. *IEEE Signal Processing Letters* 23, 10 (Oct 2016), 1499–1503.

[38] Qingshan Zhang, Zicheng Liu, Gaining Quo, Demetri Terzopoulos, and Heung-Yeung Shum. 2006. Geometry-driven photorealistic facial expression synthesis. *IEEE Transactions on Visualization and Computer Graphics* 12, 1 (Jan-Feb 2006), 48–60.

[39] Guoying Zhao, Xiaohua Huang, Matti Taini, Stan Z. Li, and Matti Pietikäinen. 2011. Facial expression recognition from near-infrared videos. *Image and Vision Computing* 29, 9 (Aug 2011), 607–619.

[40] Yuqian Zhou and Bertram Emil Shi. 2017. Photorealistic Facial Expression Synthesis by the Conditional Difference Adversarial Autoencoder. In *2017 Seventh International Conference on Affective Computing and Intelligent Interaction (ACII).* 370–376.

PatternNet: Visual Pattern Mining with Deep Neural Network

Hongzhi Li [*], Joseph G. Ellis [†], Lei Zhang [*] and Shih-Fu Chang [†]
[*] Microsoft Research, Redmond, WA 98052, USA
[†] Columbia University, New York, NY 10027, USA
hongzhi.li@microsoft.com,jge2105@columbia.edu,leizhang@microsoft.com,sfchang@ee.columbia.edu

ABSTRACT

Visual patterns represent the discernible regularity in the visual world. They capture the essential nature of visual objects or scenes. Understanding and modeling visual patterns is a fundamental problem in visual recognition that has wide ranging applications. In this paper, we study the problem of visual pattern mining and propose a novel deep neural network architecture called PatternNet for discovering these patterns that are both discriminative and representative. The proposed PatternNet leverages the filters in the last convolution layer of a convolutional neural network to find locally consistent visual patches, and by combining these filters we can effectively discover unique visual patterns. In addition, PatternNet can discover visual patterns efficiently without performing expensive image patch sampling, and this advantage provides an order of magnitude speedup compared to most other approaches. We evaluate the proposed PatternNet subjectively by showing randomly selected visual patterns which are discovered by our method and quantitatively by performing image classification with the identified visual patterns and comparing our performance with the current state-of-the-art. We also directly evaluate the quality of the discovered visual patterns by leveraging the identified patterns as proposed objects in an image and compare with other relevant methods. Our proposed network and procedure, PatterNet, is able to outperform competing methods for the tasks described.

KEYWORDS

visual pattern mining; convolutional neural network; image classification; object proposal

ACM Reference Format:

Hongzhi Li [1], Joseph G. Ellis [2], Lei Zhang [1] and Shih-Fu Chang [2]. 2018. PatternNet: Visual Pattern Mining with Deep Neural Network. In *ICMR '18: 2018 International Conference on Multimedia Retrieval, June 11–14, 2018, Yokohama, Japan.* ACM, New York, NY, USA, 9 pages. https://doi.org/10.1145/3206025.3206039

1 INTRODUCTION

Visual patterns are basic visual elements that commonly appear in images but tend to convey higher level semantics than raw pixels. Visual patterns are a reflection of our physical world, in which plants and animals reproduce themselves by repeated replication and we as human being improve our world by constant innovation and duplicative production. As a result, we see in images many similar and repeated patterns at different semantic levels, for example, lines, dots, squares, wheels, doors, cars, horses, chairs, trees, etc.

Understanding and modeling visual patterns is a fundamental problem in visual recognition, and much work has been done in the computer vision community to address this problem, with varied approaches and success. For example, SIFT features can be used to detect robust local points that are scale-invariant and can tolerate limited distortions [20]. The detected SIFT patches are often regarded as low level image patterns.

The convolutional layers in a Convolutional Neural Network can be seen as a form of feature extractor or visual pattern mining. CNNs have recently been shown to exhibit extraordinary power for visual recognition. The breakthrough performance on large-scale image classification challenges [16, 25] is just one example. Many researchers recently have been interested in understanding why CNNs exhibit such strong performance in classification tasks and have been analyzing the changes in the structure and underlying theory of CNNs. One of the the most popular interpretations [31] is that the trained convolution layers are able to capture local texture patterns of the image set. [31] designed a deconvolutional neural network to visually demonstrate the information captured by each convolutional filter in a convolutional neural network [16]. Given any filter, the deconvolution process traces back via the network and finds which *pixels* in the original image contribute to the response of this filter. Using the deconvolution neural network, one can show that each filter is normally sensitive to certain visual appearances or patterns and can demonstrate what type of patterns each filter is sensitive to. For example, the first one or two convolution layers are able to capture simple textures like lines or corners, whereas the upper layers are capable of capturing semantically meaningful patterns with large variances in appearance. A typical CNN, like AlexNet, has 256 filters in its last convolutional layer (conv5), which is a very small number compared with all the possible patterns existing in the real world. This implies that a filter may be triggered by several different patterns that share the same latent structure that is consistent with the filter. We also find that an image patch can trigger several different filters simultaneously when it exhibits multiple latent patterns that conform with multiple filters.

Base on above analysis of CNN filters, we study the problem of visual pattern mining and propose a framework for leveraging the activations of filters in a convolutional neural network to automatically discover patterns. However, filters and activations from CNN architectures as currently constructed can not be used directly to

ICMR '18, June 11–14, 2018, Yokohama, Japan

ACM ISBN 978-1-4503-5046-4/18/06...$15.00
https://doi.org/10.1145/3206025.3206039

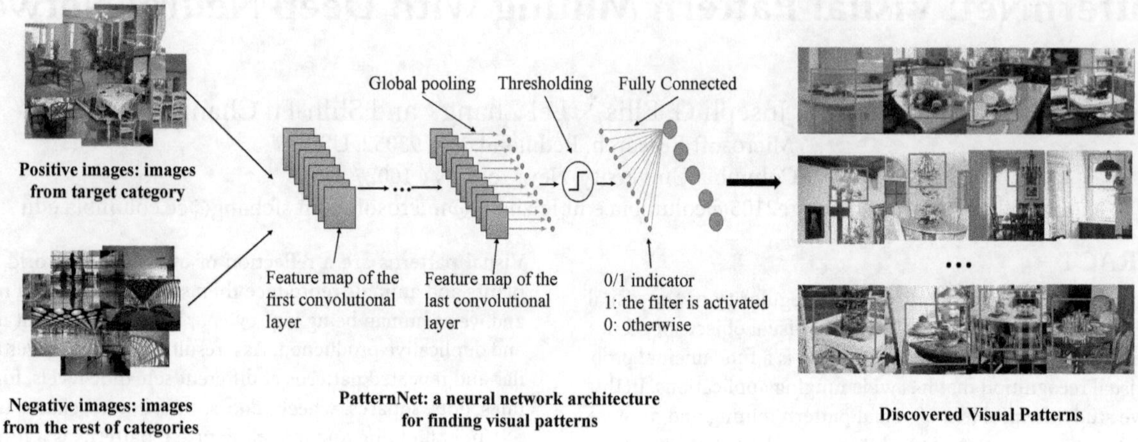

Figure 1: Visual Pattern Mining with Deep Neural Network

find visual patterns. Therefore, we propose a new network structure designed specifically to discover meaningful visual patterns.

Filters can be triggered by image patches from the same visual pattern, but for our definition of a visual pattern a set of similar image patches must be 1) popular and 2) unique. Formally, each of our discovered patterns should be **representative** and **discriminative**. Discriminative means the patterns found from within one image category should be significantly different from those that are found in other categories, and therefore only appear sparingly in those other categories. This means that patterns should represent unique visual elements that appear across images in the same category. Representative requires that the patterns should appear frequently among images in the same category. That is, a visual pattern should not be an odd patch only appearing in one or two images. Patterns that do not appear frequently may be discriminative but will not appear in enough images to be of use.

We formulate the problem of visual pattern mining as follows: given a set of images from a category (images from the target category are referred to as "positive images" throughout this manuscript), and a set of images from other categories as reference (these are referred to as "negative images" in the rest of this paper), find representative and unique visual patterns that can distinguish positive images from negative images. Our discriminative property insures that the patterns we find are useful for this task. If a pattern only appears in positive images but not in negative images, we call it discriminative. If a pattern appears many times in positive images, we call it representative.

In this paper, We follow our two defined criteria for discovering visual patterns (representative and discriminative) and design a neural network inspired by the standard convolutional neural network used for image classification tasks. We name the proposed neural network **PatternNet**. PatternNet leverages the capability of the convolution layers in CNN, where each filter has a consistent response to certain high level visual patterns. This property is used to discover the discriminative and representative visual patterns using a specially designed fully connected layer and loss function to find a combination of filters which have strong response to the patterns in the images from the target category and weak response to the images from other categories.After we introduce the architecture of PatternNet, we will analyze and demonstrate how PatternNet is capable of finding the representative and discriminative visual patterns from images.

The contributions of this paper are highlighted as follows:

- We propose a novel end-to-end neural network architecture called PatternNet for finding high quality visual patterns that are both discriminative and representative.
- By introducing a global pooling layer between the last convolutional layer and the fully connected layer, PatternNet achieves the shift-invariant property on finding visual patterns. This allows us to find visual patterns on image patch level without pre-sampling images into patches.

2 RELATED WORK

Visual pattern mining and instance mining are fundamental problems in computer vision. Many useful and important image understanding research and applications rely on high-quality visual pattern or visual instance mining results, such as the widely used mid-level feature representations for image classification and visual summarization. Most previous works [14, 18, 26, 27] follow the same general procedure. First, image patches are sampled either randomly from images or by using object proposals, such as selective search, saliency detection, or visual attention. Then visual similarity and geometry restrictions are employed for finding and clustering visually similar image patches, which are often referred to as *visual patterns*. Subsequently, the discovered visual patterns are used to build a mid-level feature representation that can improve the performance of image classification.

As well as using visual patterns as middle-level feature representations, visual pattern mining itself can be used in broader research areas. Zhang et al. [33] propose a method to use "thread-of-feature" and "min-Hash" technology to mine visual instances from large-scale image datasets and apply the proposed method on

Figure 2: Visualization of the local response region of filters in the last convolutional layer of CNN on different images. The second row images show the local response region of filter α. Filter α is activated by all the images. The third row images show the local response region of filter β. Filter β is only activated by the "flight" images

the applications of multimedia summarization and visual instance search.

Some works, such as [21] and [15] use the term "parts" to describe a similar concept to "visual patterns" in this paper. They define "part" as a partial object or scene that makes up a larger whole. In part-based approaches, the objects or scenes are broken into parts and a binary classifier is trained for each part. The parts are used as an image representation for image classification. Parts-based image classification works focus on different aspects than our work. First, those works are supervised approaches. The part detectors are learned from labeled data, while PatternNet uses unsupervised learning techniques to find the visual patterns from a set of images. Second, the goal of using parts-based models is to obtain better classification results, while we focus on finding discriminative and representative visual patterns.

More recently, [19] has utilized a Convolution Neural Network for feature representation and has used association rule mining [1], a widely used technique in data mining, to discover visual patterns. The key idea of this approach is to form a transaction for each image based on its neuron responses in a fully connected layer and find all significant association rules between items in the database.

In contrast to most existing approaches that normally have a separate stage to extract patches or construct transactions, followed with a clustering algorithm or an association rule mining algorithm for finding useful visual patterns, we develop a deep neural network framework to discover visual patterns in an end-to-end manner, which enables us to optimize the neural network parameters more effectively for finding the most representative and discriminative patterns.

3 VISUAL PATTERN MINING

In this section, we introduce the architecture and analyze the properties of our novel CNN, PatternNet.

3.1 PatternNet Architecture

The convolutional layers in CNNs can be seen as feature extractors. An excellent visual example demonstrating the capabilities of each CNN as a feature extractor exists in [31]. They demonstrate that the first few convolutional layers tend to capture lower-level image features, such as edges and corners, while the last convolutional layer captures higher-level object information, such as people's faces, wheels, or other complicated structural patterns. Recently, the properties of convolutional layers have been leveraged to address the problem of object segmentation and have shown very promising results in [12]. The activations of convolutional layers can be applied in object segmentation problems because: 1) a filter is normally selective to certain patterns, and 2) a filter is spatially local and its response map can be utilized to localize the image patch that has the object-of-interest in the original input image. We will leverage both of these tendencies, especially the ability for a convolutional filter to provide local information within the image in our construction of PatternNet.

As shown in Figure 2, we visualize the local response region of the same filter in the last convolutional layer of a CNN on different images. We can clearly see that the filter can be activated by different visual patterns. Due to the fact that a filter may be activated by multiple different visual patterns, we cannot directly use the single filter output to discover these visual patterns. On the other hand, a visual pattern may activate multiple filters, as well.

Thusly, we can think of the filters in the last convolutional layer as more like selectors for finding mid-level *latent* visual patterns rather than high-level *semantic* visual patterns.

This observation motivates us to develop a neural network architecture to find visual patterns as a combination of multiple filters from the final convolutional layer. For example, in Figure 2, the visual pattern "flight" can be detected by the filters $\{\alpha, \beta\}$. A typical convolutional neural network has N_c filters in its last convolutional layer, and each filter produces an $M_c \times M_c$ dimensional feature response map. The value of each pixel in a feature map is the response of a filter with respect to a sub-region of an input image. A high value for a pixel means that the filter is activated by the content of the sub-region of the input image. If a filter is activated, the $M_c \times M_c$ dimensional feature map records the magnitude of the response and the location information of where in the input image the filter is activated. We use a tunable threshold T_r to decide

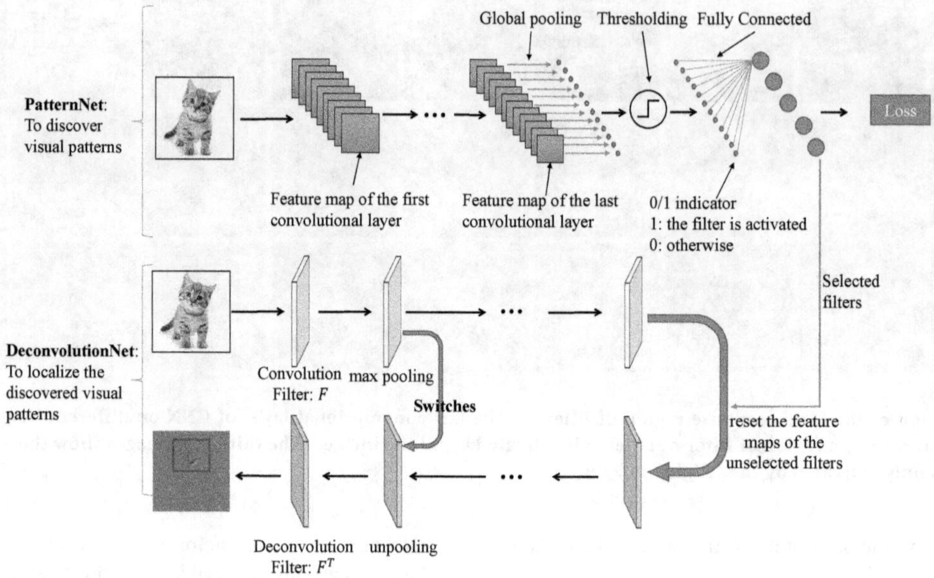

Figure 3: PatternNet Architecture. The proposed system use PatternNet to discover visual patterns. The visual patterns are represented by a set of filters. Once the visual patterns are discovered, a deconvolutional neural network is used to localize the location of the visual pattern in the input image.

whether the response magnitude is sufficiently high such that the filter should be considered activated. We set the response as 1 if the response magnitude is stronger than T_r, or 0 otherwise. To achieve translation-invariance and more effectively utilize image sub-regions, we intentionally ignore the location information. That is, as long as there is at least one response value from the $M_c \times M_c$ feature map larger than T_r, we consider that the filter is activated by the input image.

In PatternNet, we use a global max pooling layer after the last convolutional layer to discard the location information, which leads to a faster and more robust pattern mining algorithm as the feature after global max pooling is more compact and can effectively summarize input patches from any location. We utilize the deconvolutional neural network to obtain the location information later in the process when we need to localize the visual patterns. Each feature map produces one max value after the global pooling layer. This value is then sent to a threshold layer to detect whether the corresponding filter is activated by the input image. After thresholding, we get N_c of 0/1 indicators for N_c filters in the last convolution layer. Each indicator represents if a filter is activated by the input image. We use a fully connected (FC) layer to represent the selection of filters for the visual patterns. Each neuron in the fully connected layer is a linear combination of the outputs from the global pooling layer after thresholding:

$$h_i = \sum_{k=1}^{N_c} W_{i,k} \cdot x_k \qquad (1)$$

where h_i is the response of the i-th ($i = 1, \ldots, N_f$) neuron in the FC layer, and $x_k \in \{0, 1\}$ is the activation status of the k-th filter in the last convolutional layer. The selection of filters is reflected by the values of parameter W in the FC layer. After the fully connected layer, we add a sigmoid layer to map each response $h_i \in \mathbb{R}$ to $p_i \in [0, 1]$, indicating the probability that the pattern appears in the input image:

$$p_i = \frac{1}{1 + e^{-h_i}} \qquad (2)$$

The cost function is defined in Equation 3:

$$Loss = -\frac{1}{N_f} \sum_{i=1}^{N_f} \left(\frac{1}{|\mathcal{B}|} \sum_{j=1}^{|\mathcal{B}|} (1 - y_j)\log(1 - p_{i,j}) + y_j \log(p_{i,j}) \right) \qquad (3)$$

where $y_j \in \{0, 1\}$, $|\mathcal{B}|$ is the size of a mini-batch $\mathcal{B}$, and $p_{i,j}$ is the response of the i-th neuron in the fully connected layer w.r.t. the j-th image in the mini batch. Suppose there are N_f neurons in the fully connected layer. Then we can get N_f linear combinations of filters from PatternNet by checking the weights of the FC layer. Each linear combination of filters represents a visual pattern from the given image set.

The intuition of this loss function is to learn multiple visual patterns and use the visual patterns to distinguish positive and negative classes. Each neuron in the FC layer selects a few filters to represent a pattern. If a filter is activated by an image and its corresponding weights in W are nonzero, it will contribute to the output of the FC layer. The nonzero weights of the parameters of the FC layer control which filters can contribute to the loss function. The loss function encourages the network to discover filters that are triggered by positive images but not by negative images. A collection of filters combined together can effectively represent a unique pattern from positive images. The discovered pattern is representative because most of the positive images are required to trigger the selected filters in the training process. Furthermore, the discovered pattern is also discriminative because most of the negative images cannot trigger those filters.

After we learn the PatternNet, we can discover the visual patterns from the trained network parameters. For example, the fully connected layer has $N_f * N_c$ dimensional weights, where N_c is the number of filters in the last convolution layer, and N_f is a tunable parameter, which represents the expected number of discovered patterns. We can get N_f combinations of filters by checking the weights of the FC layer in PatternNet. Each combination of filters is able to find a visual pattern from the given image set. To be more specific, we use the following example to explain how to find the visual patterns by PatternNet. We use the similar structure of the convolutional layers from AlexNet to design PatternNet. The last convolutional layer has 256 filters. Each filter produces a 13×13 feature map. The global max pooling layer has a 13×13 kernel and produces a single value for each feature map. Therefore, it produces a 256-dimensional vector as the input to the fully connected layer. The fully connected layer has $N_f * N_c$ parameters, in this particular example, we set it to 20×256, where 256 is determined by the number of filters in the last convolutional layer, and 20 is the expected number of visual patterns that can be discovered from the dataset. For each of the 20 neurons in the FC layer, we check the N_c (which is 256 in AlexNet) parameters, and each parameter correspond to a filter in the last convolutional layer. Since these parameters are sparse, we select the top three parameters, which correspond to three convolutional filters. The select three convolutional filters can be used to detect visual patterns from the image set. We can simply feed an image into the convolutional layers, and check the response map of these selected filters. If all of the filters are activated by the image, it means the image contains a visual pattern defined by these three filters.

We use the deconvolutional neural network architecture (see Fig. 3) to localize where a visual pattern appears in the input image. The output of the deconvolutional neural network H_i^{deconv} is the derivative of the response value of the i-th filter H_i^{conv} w.r.t the pixels in the input images.

$$H_i^{deconv}(x, y) = \frac{\partial H_i^{conv}}{\partial P} \tag{4}$$

where H_i^{deconv} is the output of a deconvolutional neural network for the ith filter. It has the same size as the input image I. And P is a pixel (x, y) in the input image I. $H_i^{deconv}(x, y)$ is the deconvolutional results at pixel (x, y). It is the partial derivative of ith feature map $w.r.t.$ the pixel (x, y) of the input image I. The value of $H_i^{deconv}(x, y)$ evaluates the impact of input image pixel (x, y) on the ith feature map. The larger value means that this pixel has greater impact. Thus, the deconvolutional results can be used to find which region of the input image contributes to the response map of the given filter.

A deconvolutional neural network has two passes: a convolution pass and a deconvolution pass. The deconvolution pass shares a similar architecture with the convolution pass, but it performs inverse-like operations, such as pooling vs. unpooling and convolution vs. deconvolution. Unpooling is fairly simple; this operation uses "switches" from the pooling layer to recover the feature map prior to the pooling layer. The "switches" recover the max value at the original location within each pooling kernel and set all the other locations in the feature map to zero. The non-linear operations ("ReLU") in the convolution pass are ignored in the deconvolution pass, because the positive values are passed to the next layer without any change and the negative values are set to zero in ReLU. The deconvolution operation we use is equivalent to the standard weight update equations during the backpropagation. Using the chain-rule, the calculation of partial derivative in Eq. 4 is relatively easy. In the convolutional neural network, we calculate the output of the kth convolutional layer with kernel F by

$$H_k = H_{k-1} * F \tag{5}$$

For each deconvolutional layer, given the feature map H^k from the k-th layer, we use the transpose of the same convolution kernel F^T to compute the output of the deconvolutional layer H^{k-1}:

$$H^{k-1} = \frac{\partial H^k}{\partial F} = H^k * F^T \tag{6}$$

The detailed derivation of Equation 6 can be found in [31]. Based on Equation 6, the calculation of Equation 4 is equivalent to the backpropagation of a single filter activation.

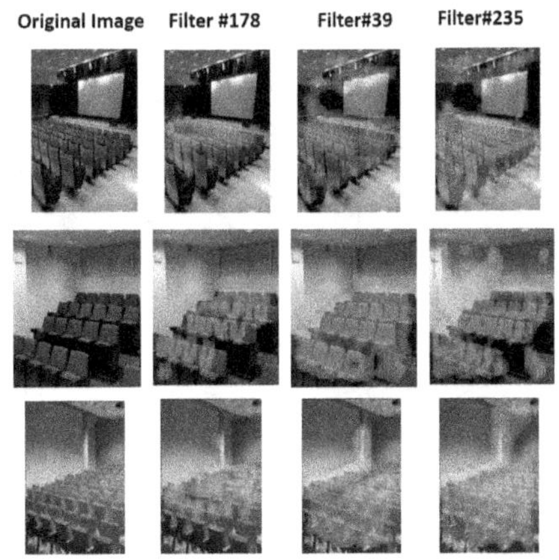

Figure 4: Visualization of the local response magnitude of CNN filters in image patches. The heatmap shows different filters are selective to different *latent* patterns.

H_i^{deconv} reflects the impact of each pixel in the input image to the response value of the ith filter. Let R_i be the region of non-zero pixels in H_i^{deconv}. Only the pixels in this region contribute to the response value of the filter. The region (patch) of a visual pattern in the input image is:

$$R_{\mathcal{P}} = \bigcap_{i \in \mathcal{P}} R_i \tag{7}$$

where $\mathcal{P}$ is a set of filters that define a visual pattern.

To illustrate how a set of filters finds a visual pattern, we generate heat maps to visualize the local response region of CNN filters in Fig. 4. Fig. 4 shows a "seat" pattern is found in the image collection with filter #178, #39 and #235. For each image, all the filters are activated at the same location. The figure clearly shows which region activates the filters and it is obvious that "seat" is the target of this pattern.

3.2 Finding Discriminative Patterns from a Category w.r.t Different Reference Images

In contrast to *Representative*, *Discriminative* is a relative concept. For example, the visual pattern "book shelf" is a *discriminative* pattern in the "library" images w.r.t. to the random background images[1]. But it is not a *discriminative* pattern if we use images from the "bookstore" category as reference images since there are also many "bookshelf" visual instances in the "bookstore" images.

As shown in Fig. 5 (A) and (B), we use random background images as reference images and find visual patterns from "library" images and "bookstore" images. We find that both "books" and "book shelf" visual patterns are *discriminative* patterns for the two categories w.r.t. random background images. But if we want to find the *discriminative* patterns from "library" images w.r.t. "bookstore" images, as shown in Figure 5 (C), the unique patterns like "chairs", "the hall", and "reading desks" are discovered, instead of patterns like "bookshelf", which are shared between the two categories.

This characteristic demonstrates that PatternNet has the capability to find the "true" discriminative patterns from a set of images w.r.t different reference images. This is quite a useful feature. For example, given a set of images taken in London and another set of images taken in New York, we can use this algorithm to find out what are the unique visual characteristics in London.

[1] e.g. random images downloaded from Flickr, or random images selected from all the other categories

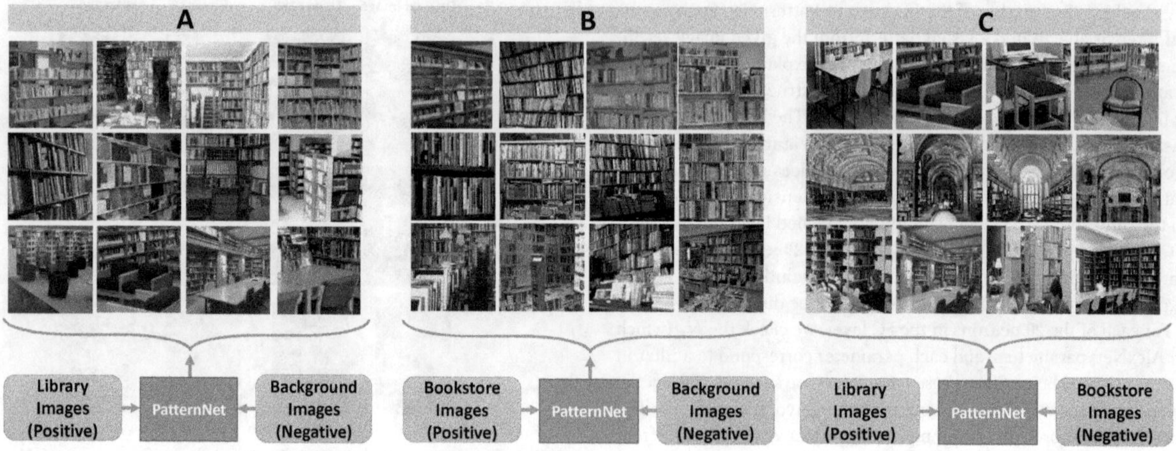

Figure 5: Find discriminative patterns by using different negative images.

4 EXPERIMENT

4.1 Subjective Evaluation

To demonstrate the performance of PatternNet, we first present in Fig. 6 some randomly selected visual patterns discovered from a variety of datasets, including VOC2007, MSCOCO and CUB-Bird-200. The mask images are generated from a deconvolutional neural network [31], which demonstrates the ability of PatternNet to discover and visualize visual patterns in images. We can clearly see that PatternNet is able to find and localize the intricate visual patterns from different datasets.

4.2 Objective Evaluation

It is not easy to directly evaluate visual pattern mining works due to the lack of well-annotated datasets for this task. Some previous works use the image classification task as a proxy to evaluate visual pattern mining results [19]. In this paper, we also conduct experiments for image classification as a proxy to evaluate our work. We compare the PatternNet model with several baseline approaches across a wide variety of datasets. We also compare with several state-of-the-art visual pattern mining or visual instance mining works for scene classification and fine-grained image classification. It is important to note that we use the classification tasks as a proxy to evaluate the quality of visual pattern mining methods. We are not aiming to outperform all the state-of-the-art image classification methods. Instead, we believe that our visual pattern mining approach could be used to improve current image classification methods. Thus, in the following experiments, we only compare our proposed PatternNet with other state-of-the-art visual pattern mining methods on image classification tasks.

We believe that it is not sufficient to evaluate the quality of visual patterns by solely using image classification. Ideally, we should use a dataset with all possible patterns labeled by human beings to measure the precision, recall, and F-score of the discovered visual patterns. However, it is almost impossible to label a large-scale dataset due to the difficulty and amount of human labor required. Instead, we notice that the currently available datasets for object detection can be used to evaluate pattern mining works. This is because the labeled objects for the detection task in those datasets are indeed "discriminative" and "representative" visual patterns. If the pattern mining algorithm is robust, those objects should be detected and found by our approach. In this paper, we follow the evaluation metric proposed in [29] to directly evaluate the quality of visual patterns discovered by our work. [29] developed a technique to propose a bounding box for candidate objects from images. In their paper, they use Mean Average Best Overlap (MABO) as the evaluation metric. *ABO* for a specific class *c* is defined as follows:

$$ABO = \frac{1}{|G^c|} \sum_{g_i^c \in G^c} \max_{l_j \in L} Overlap(g_i^c, l_j) \tag{8}$$

$$Overlap(g_i^c, l_j) = \frac{area(g_i^c) \cap area(l_j)}{area(g_i^c) \cup area(l_j)} \tag{9}$$

where $g_i^c \in G^c$ is the ground truth annotation and L is the bounding box of the detected visual patterns.

4.3 Using Image Classification as a Proxy to Evaluate PatternNet

We follow similar settings to those used by most existing pattern mining or instance mining works to evaluate our approach to image classification. That is, after we discover the visual patterns from the training images, we use the visual patterns to extract a middle-level feature representation for both training and test images. Then, the middle-level feature representations are used in the classification task. As our visual patterns are discovered and represented by a set of filters in the last convolution layer, it is easy and natural for us to integrate the pattern detection, training, and testing phrases together in one neural network. To do this, we add a static fully connected layer on top of the last convolution layer. The parameters of this FC layer are manually initialized using the visual patterns learned in PatternNet. During the training phase, we freeze this static FC layer by setting the learning rate to zero. Assume that we have N_f unique visual patterns for a dataset. Then the FC layer has N_f dimensional outputs. Each dimension collects the response from the filters associated with one visual pattern. After scaling and normalization, the value of each dimension represents the detection score of a visual pattern from an input image. On top of this FC layer, a standard FC layer and softmax layer are used to obtain classification results.

4.3.1 Baseline Comparison. We compare PatternNet with several baseline approaches, including: 1) use the response of fc7 layer of a CNN [25] as image feature representation and train a multi-class SVM model for image classification, 2) use the response of the pool5 layer from a CNN [25] as image feature representation and train a multi-class SVM model for image classification. We simply use a fully connected layer and a softmax layer on top of the PatternNet architecture to classify images. The results can be found in Table 1. PatternNet outperforms the baseline approaches that directly use the response from the pool5 and fc7 layers as image features.

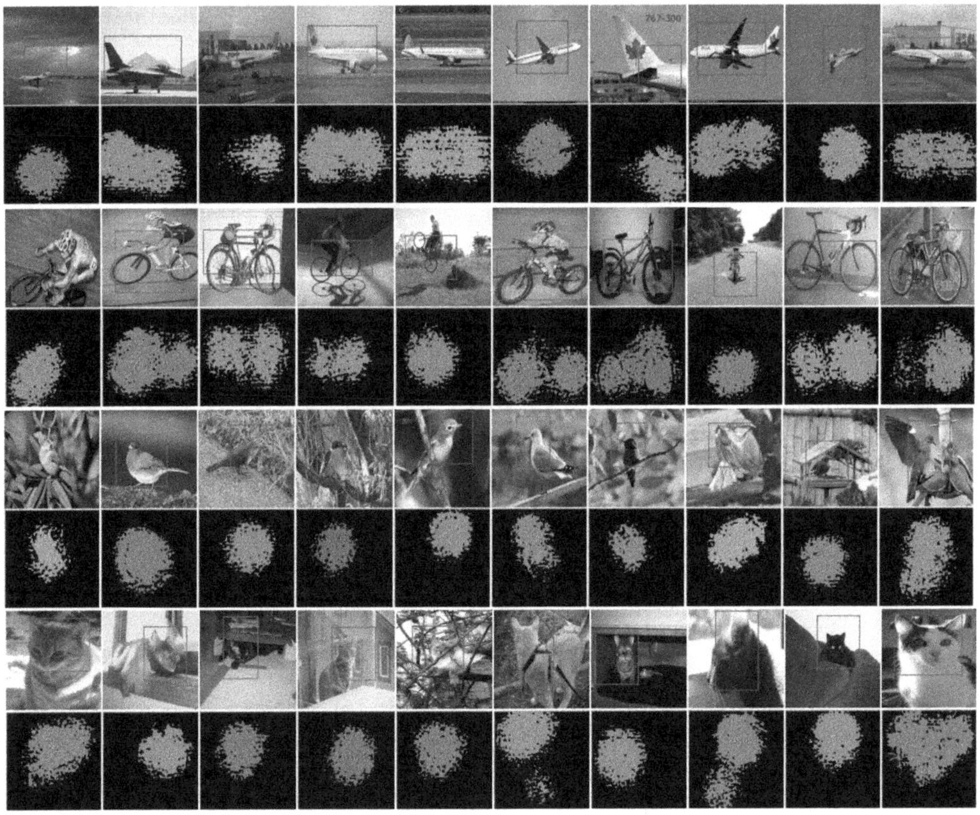

Figure 6: Randomly selected visual patterns discovered by PatternNet from a variety of datasets. The mask images show the localization results of each visual pattern.

Table 1: Comparison with the baseline approaches on some popular benchmark datasets. PatternNet uses the same structure of convolutional layers as in VGG19, and uses their pre-trained model to initialize the convolutional layers

Method	MITIndoor	CUB-BIRD-200	StanfordDogs
VGG19 fc7 + SVM	67.6	54.6	78.1
VGG19 pool5 + SVM	61.6	40.7	67.1
PatternNet	75.3	70.0	83.1

The response of each neuron in the last fully connected layer in PatternNet indicates whether the input image has a certain visual pattern. The results in Table 1 prove that the selected visual patterns are discriminative and can be used as effective image features for classification.

4.3.2 Scene Classification. We use the MITIndoor dataset for scene classification, which has 67 classes of indoor images. We follow the split of training and test images as in [23]: approximately 80 training images and 20 test images per category. About 20 visual patterns are discovered by PatternNet on training images for each category. For each indoor scene category, we use its 80 images as positive samples and the images from other categories as negative samples to train the PatternNet model to discover visual patterns. The convolutional layers are initialized by a pre-trained CNN model [16], and frozen during the training phase. PatternNet converges within approximately 100 iterations, which takes about 1-2 mins on a workstation with GTX Titan X GPU. After this procedure, we find approximately 20-30 unique patterns per scene category. Note that the number of discovered patterns is controllable by using different dimensions of parameters in the fully connected layer of PatternNet. From Table 2, we can see that PatternNet outperforms the state-of-the-art works. Compared with MDPM, we directly modify the current CNN architecture to perform the scene classification task, while their approach has to sample image patches from test images and produce the middle-level feature representation for classification. In addition to enhanced performance, this allows our approach to provide an order of magnitude speedup compared with MDPM.

Table 2: Scene classification results for MITIndoor dataset. PatternNet uses the pre-trained AlexNet to initialize the convolutional layers to achieve a fair comparison.

Method	Accuracy (%)
ObjectBank [17]	37.60
Discriminative Patch [26]	38.10
BoP [14]	46.10
HMVC [18]	52.30
Discriminative Part [27]	51.40
MVED [7]	66.87
MDPM [19]	69.69
PatternNet	71.30

Table 3: Fine-grained object classification results on Stanford dogs dataset

Method	Accuracy (%)
Alignments [10]	36.8
GMTL [22]	39.3
Symb [5]	45.6
Unsupervised Alignments [9]	50.1
SPV [6]	52.0
Google LeNet ft [28]	75.0
Attention [24]	76.8
PatternNet	**83.1**

4.3.3 Fine-grained Object Classification. Recently, fine-grained image classification has attracted much attention in visual recognition. Compared with traditional image classification problems (dogs vs. cars, buildings vs. people), the fine-grained image classification (Labrador vs. Golden Retriever, Husky vs. Samoyed) is a much more challenging problem, since it requires attention to detailed visual features in order to distinguish the fine-grained categories. Similar to the scene classification task, our insight is that discriminative patterns are able to capture the information from local parts of the image/object. With PatternNet, the discriminative patterns of each fine-grained class can be effectively discovered. As is the property of discriminative patterns, the patterns from one category rarely appear in other categories. Hence, such patterns have a great potential to improve the fine-grained object classification task.

We evaluate our approach on two popular datasets for the fine-grained image classification task: CUB-bird 200 and Stanford Dogs. The CUB-200 dataset has 200 classes of different birds, and the Stanford Dogs dataset has 120 categories of different dogs. We follow the suggested training-test split from the original dataset and compare our results with some state-of-the-art works as listed in Tables 3 and 4. The parameters of the convolution layers are imported from a pre-trained CNN model [25] without any fine-tuning. During any of our training phases, we do not fine-tune any parameters from convolution layers in order to prevent over-fitting. The only parameters we learned for PatternNet are the fully connected layer as the indicator of linear combination of convolution filters. The training phase for discovering patterns is stopped after a few hundreds of iterations when the training loss is stable. We notice that some recent works reported significantly high performance by leveraging the manually labeled bounding box information, such as 82.0% reported by PD [15] on the CUB-200 dataset. In our approach, we use neither manually labeled bounding boxes nor parts information. The purpose of this experiment is to evaluate the quality of the discovered visual patterns. It is important to evaluate our approach on the whole image instead of clean objects given by the manually labeled bounding box. Thus, we only compare with the approaches that do not use the manually labeled bounding box information. We also do not compare with works that use additional images to fine-tune a CNN model, since those works involve additional training data and thus are not a fair comparison. From tables 3 and 4, we can see the clear advantage of our approach compared with the state-of-the-art works on the same experiment setup.

4.4 Evaluate PatternNet on Object Proposal Task

As we have discussed before, visual pattern mining technology can be used for the object proposal task. The main difference between pattern mining and traditional object proposal methods ([29] [2]) is that we do not need manually labeled object bounding boxes to train the model. Our algorithm directly mines the regularity from the given image set and finds important ("discriminative" and "representative") objects in images. Also, instead of proposing thousands of object bounding box proposals in [29], we only generate tens of object bounding boxes with a much higher accuracy. As [29] is widely used in many research works for pre-processing images, we compare our approach with the state-of-the-art object proposal works and show the results in Table 5. Our advantage is that we propose far fewer bounding boxes than the traditional object proposal works. We compare the recall rate and MABO reported in the literature when approximately 100 bounding boxes are proposed by those works. The results show that the PatternNet outperforms the other works with a substantially lower number of proposed bounding boxes.

Table 4: Fine-grained classification results on CUB-200 dataset

Method	Accuracy (%)
GMTL [22]	44.2
SPV [6]	48.9
Alignments [10]	53.6
POOF [3]	56.8
R-CNN [11]	58.8
Symb [5]	59.4
PB-R-CNN [32]	65.9
PatternNet	**70.0**

Table 5: Comparison of recall rate and MABO for a variety of methods on the Pascal VOC 2007 test set. For PatternNet, we propose about 5 bounding boxes per image. For the other methods, we compare their reported number when about 100 bounding boxes are proposed.

Method	Recall	MABO	# proposed BB
Sliding window search [13]	0.75	-	100
Jumping windows [30]	0.60	-	100
Objectness [2]	0.77	0.66	100
The boxes around the regions [4]	0.70	0.63	100
The boxes around the regions [8]	0.74	0.65	100
Selective Search [29]	0.74	0.63	100
PatternNet	**0.86**	**0.77**	5

5 CONCLUSION

In this paper, we have presented a novel neural network architecture called PatternNet for discovering visual patterns from image collections. PatternNet leverages the capability of the convolutional layers in a CNN, where each filter normally has consistent response to certain high-level visual patterns. This property is used to discover discriminative and representative visual patterns by using a specially designed fully connected layer and a lost function to find a sparse combinations of filters, which have strong responses to the patterns in images from the target category and weak responses to images from the rest of the categories. We conducted experimental evaluation on both the scene classification task and the fine-grained object classification task. The evaluation result shows that the discovered visual patterns by PatternNet are both representative and discriminative. We believe that PatternNet has shown promising performance in automatically discovering the useful portions of an image and enables advanced computer vision applications without expensive bounding box based labeling of datasets.

REFERENCES

[1] R. Agrawal, T. Imieliński, and A. Swami. Mining association rules between sets of items in large databases. In *ACM SIGMOD Record*, volume 22, pages 207–216. ACM, 1993.

[2] B. Alexe, T. Deselaers, and V. Ferrari. Measuring the objectness of image windows. *Pattern Analysis and Machine Intelligence, IEEE Transactions on*, 34(11):2189–2202, 2012.

[3] T. Berg and P. N. Belhumeur. Poof: Part-based one-vs.-one features for fine-grained categorization, face verification, and attribute estimation. In *Computer Vision and Pattern Recognition (CVPR), 2013 IEEE Conference on*, pages 955–962. IEEE, 2013.

[4] J. Carreira and C. Sminchisescu. Constrained parametric min-cuts for automatic object segmentation. In *Computer Vision and Pattern Recognition (CVPR), 2010 IEEE Conference on*, pages 3241–3248. IEEE, 2010.

[5] Y. Chai, V. Lempitsky, and A. Zisserman. Symbiotic segmentation and part localization for fine-grained categorization. In *Computer Vision (ICCV), 2013 IEEE International Conference on*, pages 321–328. IEEE, 2013.

[6] G. Chen, J. Yang, H. Jin, E. Shechtman, J. Brandt, and T. X. Han. Selective pooling vector for fine-grained recognition. In *Applications of Computer Vision (WACV), 2015 IEEE Winter Conference on*, pages 860–867. IEEE, 2015.

[7] C. Doersch, A. Gupta, and A. A. Efros. Mid-level visual element discovery as discriminative mode seeking. In *Advances in Neural Information Processing Systems*, pages 494–502, 2013.

[8] I. Endres and D. Hoiem. Category independent object proposals. In *Computer Vision–ECCV 2010*, pages 575–588. Springer, 2010.

[9] E. Gavves, B. Fernando, C. G. Snoek, A. W. Smeulders, and T. Tuytelaars. Fine-grained categorization by alignments. In *Proceedings of the IEEE International Conference on Computer Vision*, pages 1713–1720, 2013.

[10] E. Gavves, B. Fernando, C. G. Snoek, A. W. Smeulders, and T. Tuytelaars. Local alignments for fine-grained categorization. *International Journal of Computer Vision*, 111(2):191–212, 2014.

[11] R. Girshick, J. Donahue, T. Darrell, and J. Malik. Rich feature hierarchies for accurate object detection and semantic segmentation. In *Computer Vision and Pattern Recognition (CVPR), 2014 IEEE Conference on*, pages 580–587. IEEE, 2014.

[12] B. Hariharan, P. Arbeláez, R. Girshick, and J. Malik. Hypercolumns for object segmentation and fine-grained localization. In *Proceedings of the IEEE Conference on Computer Vision and Pattern Recognition*, pages 447–456, 2015.

[13] H. Harzallah, F. Jurie, and C. Schmid. Combining efficient object localization and image classification. In *Computer Vision, 2009 IEEE 12th International Conference on*, pages 237–244. IEEE, 2009.

[14] M. Juneja, A. Vedaldi, C. Jawahar, and A. Zisserman. Blocks that shout: Distinctive parts for scene classification. In *Computer Vision and Pattern Recognition (CVPR), 2013 IEEE Conference on*, pages 923–930. IEEE, 2013.

[15] J. Krause, H. Jin, J. Yang, and L. Fei-Fei. Fine-grained recognition without part annotations. In *Proceedings of the IEEE Conference on Computer Vision and Pattern Recognition*, pages 5546–5555, 2015.

[16] A. Krizhevsky, I. Sutskever, and G. E. Hinton. Imagenet classification with deep convolutional neural networks. In *Advances in neural information processing systems*, pages 1097–1105, 2012.

[17] L.-J. Li, H. Su, L. Fei-Fei, and E. P. Xing. Object bank: A high-level image representation for scene classification & semantic feature sparsification. In *Advances in neural information processing systems*, pages 1378–1386, 2010.

[18] Q. Li, J. Wu, and Z. Tu. Harvesting mid-level visual concepts from large-scale internet images. In *Computer Vision and Pattern Recognition (CVPR), 2013 IEEE Conference on*, pages 851–858. IEEE, 2013.

[19] Y. Li, L. Liu, C. Shen, and A. van den Hengel. Mid-level deep pattern mining. In *CVPR*, 2015.

[20] D. G. Lowe. Object recognition from local scale-invariant features. In *Computer vision, 1999. The proceedings of the seventh IEEE international conference on*, volume 2, pages 1150–1157. Ieee, 1999.

[21] S. N. Parizi, A. Vedaldi, A. Zisserman, and P. Felzenszwalb. Automatic discovery and optimization of parts for image classification. *arXiv preprint arXiv:1412.6598*, 2014.

[22] J. Pu, Y.-G. Jiang, J. Wang, and X. Xue. Which looks like which: Exploring inter-class relationships in fine-grained visual categorization. In *Computer Vision–ECCV 2014*, pages 425–440. Springer, 2014.

[23] A. Quattoni and A. Torralba. Recognizing indoor scenes. In *Computer Vision and Pattern Recognition, 2009. CVPR 2009. IEEE Conference on*, pages 413–420. IEEE, 2009.

[24] P. Sermanet, A. Frome, and E. Real. Attention for fine-grained categorization. *arXiv preprint arXiv:1412.7054*, 2014.

[25] K. Simonyan and A. Zisserman. Very deep convolutional networks for large-scale image recognition. *arXiv preprint arXiv:1409.1556*, 2014.

[26] S. Singh, A. Gupta, and A. Efros. Unsupervised discovery of mid-level discriminative patches. *Computer Vision–ECCV 2012*, pages 73–86, 2012.

[27] J. Sun and J. Ponce. Learning discriminative part detectors for image classification and cosegmentation. In *Computer Vision (ICCV), 2013 IEEE International Conference on*, pages 3400–3407. IEEE, 2013.

[28] C. Szegedy, W. Liu, Y. Jia, P. Sermanet, S. Reed, D. Anguelov, D. Erhan, V. Vanhoucke, and A. Rabinovich. Going deeper with convolutions. In *Proceedings of the IEEE Conference on Computer Vision and Pattern Recognition*, pages 1–9, 2015.

[29] J. R. Uijlings, K. E. van de Sande, T. Gevers, and A. W. Smeulders. Selective search for object recognition. *International journal of computer vision*, 104(2):154–171, 2013.

[30] A. Vedaldi, V. Gulshan, M. Varma, and A. Zisserman. Multiple kernels for object detection. In *Computer Vision, 2009 IEEE 12th International Conference on*, pages 606–613. IEEE, 2009.

[31] M. D. Zeiler and R. Fergus. Visualizing and understanding convolutional networks. In *Computer Vision–ECCV 2014*, pages 818–833. Springer, 2014.

[32] N. Zhang, J. Donahue, R. Girshick, and T. Darrell. Part-based r-cnns for fine-grained category detection. In *Computer Vision–ECCV 2014*, pages 834–849. Springer, 2014.

[33] W. Zhang, H. Li, C.-W. Ngo, and S.-F. Chang. Scalable visual instance mining with threads of features. In *Proceedings of the ACM International Conference on Multimedia*, pages 297–306. ACM, 2014.

Steganographer Detection based on Multiclass Dilated Residual Networks

Mingjie Zheng
College of Compute Science and Software Engineering
Shenzhen University
Shenzhen, China
zhengmingjie@email.szu.edu.cn

Sheng-hua Zhong*
College of Compute Science and Software Engineering
Shenzhen University
Shenzhen, China
csshzhong@szu.edu.cn

Songtao Wu
College of Compute Science and Software Engineering
Shenzhen University
Shenzhen, China
csstwu@szu.edu.cn

Jianmin Jiang*
College of Compute Science and Software Engineering
Shenzhen University
Shenzhen, China
jianmin.jiang@szu.edu.cn

ABSTRACT

Steganographer detection task is to identify criminal users, who attempt to conceal confidential information by steganography methods, among a large number of innocent users. The significant challenge of the task is how to collect the evidences to identify the guilty user with suspicious images, which are embedded with secret messages generating by unknown steganography and payload. Unfortunately, existing methods for steganalysis were served for the binary classification. It makes them harder to classify the images with different kinds of payloads, especially when the payloads of images in test dataset have not been provided in advance. In this paper, we propose a novel steganographer detection method based on multiclass deep neural networks. In the training stage, the networks are trained to classify the images with six types of payloads. The networks can preserve even strengthen the weak stego signals from secret messages in much larger receptive filed by virtue of residual and dilated residual learning. In the inference stage, the learnt model is used to extract the discriminative features, which can capture the difference between guilty users and innocent users. A series of empirical experimental results demonstrate that the proposed method achieves good performance in spatial and frequency domains even though the embedding payload is low. The proposed method achieves a higher level of robustness of inter-steganographic algorithms and can provide a possible solution to address the payload mismatch problem.

---

*Sheng-hua Zhong and Jianmin Jiang are the corresponding authors of this paper.

ICMR '18, June 11–14, 2018, Yokohama, Japan

ACM ISBN 978-1-4503-5046-4/18/06...$15.00
https://doi.org/10.1145/3206025.3206031

CCS CONCEPTS

• **Computing methodologies → Neural networks** • **Security and privacy → Software and application security**

KEYWORDS

Steganographer detection; multiclass classification; deep neural networks; multimedia security

ACM Reference format:

M. Zheng, S. Zhong, S. Wu, J. Jiang. 2018. Steganographer Detection based on Multiclass Dilated Residual Networks. In *Proceedings of ACM International Conference on Multimedia Retrieval 2018, Yokohama, Japan, June11–14, 2018 (ICMR'18)*, 9 pages.
DOI: https://doi.org/10.1145/3206025.3206031

1 INTRODUCTION

Image steganography is the technique of concealing secret messages within images, so that the existence of the hidden data is not obvious in covert communication [1]. In general, the image in which the secret messages are intended to be embedded is termed as the *cover* image, and the image which includes messages is referred to the *stego* image [2]. Image steganalysis, from an opponent's perspective, is an art of revealing the presence of secret messages in the images, which are hidden by the steganographer [3]. Steganography and steganalysis are in a hide-and-seek game [3]. They try not only to beat each other, but also to create strategic coalitions to develop.

Currently, most of image steganalytic techniques are devoted to separate a suspicious image as cover image or stego image. This problem is termed as *stego detection* problem. However, in the real-world situation, there exist multiple users, and each user will transmit vast numbers of images. Moreover, only some of users are guilty of using unknown and diverse steganography with unknown embedding parameters such as embedding payload. It's more practical than the "laboratory environment" in most of image steganalytic tasks. Image steganalytic techniques are desired to solve more challenges beyond the laboratory conditions. Therefore, in this paper, we devote to investigate a completely different problem: identifying which users try to hide secret messages into the images with steganography among many innocent users [4]. This kind of user is called as the guilty actor (or guilty user). This problem is known as *steganographer detection* problem. It poses significant challenge in comparisons of stego detection problem, which is how to collect the evidences from multiple images of suspicion, and then to identify the guilty user. We believe that steganographer detection will play an imperative role in many significant multimedia security applications.

Most of existing steganographer detection methods mainly depend on the handcrafted features based on the traditional steganalytic algorithms. As the first attempt, in [5], Ker *et al.* extracted PEV-274 features [6] from each image and calculate the distance of each pair of users by maximum mean discrepancy (MMD) [7]. Finally, they formulated the steganographer detection task as a clustering problem to separate the guilty user from majority innocent users. In 2012 and 2014, Ker *et al.* considered the steganographer as the outlier among innocent users and proposed to replace hierarchical clustering by the local outlier factor (LOF) method [8] to rank user's possibility of being guilty according to the degree of anomaly [9, 10]. In 2016, Li *et al.* proposed a method that used high-order joint features and clustering ensembles [4]. The high-order joint features were procured from high-order joint density matrices of Discrete Cosine Transformation (DCT) coefficients from JPEG images. In 2017, Li *et al.* extended the work in the way of proposing a sampling construction strategy [11]. They designed an embedding probability calculation model and selected DCT blocks with higher embedding probability to reconstruct a sample image. Then, they extracted a 155-D reduced PEV feature set from each sample image. Finally, the agglomerative hierarchical clustering was used to identify the guilty user according to their corresponding MMD distances.

In these years, deep learning based methods have achieved great success in many multimedia tasks, such as image retrieval [12], face recognition [13], emotion recognition [14] and so on. One of the most important contributions of deep learning techniques is extracting more efficient features through features auto-learning rather than handcrafted. Currently, there is limited existing work based on deep learning to solve the steganographer detection task. However, many works [15–24] based on deep learning techniques have been proposed for steganalysis, which is close to steganographer detection task. These methods directly learn the discriminative features to separate stegos from covers, which are benefit from the process in deep learning techniques. For instance, in 2016, Xu *et al.* reported a well-designed convolutional neural network (CNN) architecture which took into account of the knowledge of steganalysis [18]. The results demonstrated that the proposed model was competitive compared with that achieved by the spatial rich model. In 2017, Xu presented an empirical study on applying CNNs to detect JPEG version of the UNIversal WAvelet Relative Distortion [23]. Wu *et al.* proposed the deep residual network for image steganalysis [20]. By virtue of the deep residual learning, the network could capture the weak signals from the secret messages which brought that the proposed model achieved better performance than the classical method spatial rich model and several other CNN-based models.

Inspired by these steganalytic methods based on deep learning, in 2017, we were first to propose the steganographer detection method based on deep residual network [25]. The effective features extracted by residual learning were used to calculate the distance between each pair of users by MMD. Finally, the guilty user was identified by the agglomerative hierarchical clustering algorithm. Although the proposed framework could achieve good detection accuracies in spatial domain when the payload was low, all of stego images must be paired with their corresponding cover images when extracting the features both in training and the inference stage.

Currently, existing methods for the steganographer detection task mainly depend on the features extracted from the steganalytic methods. In other words, the features are utilized to separate stego image from cover image. However, these existing works based on deep learning for steganalysis were served for the binary classification. Thus, these methods ignore the important information from stego images, such as the embedding payload. Let us think about the distortions caused by different payloads. We believe the distance between cover image and stego image with low payload, e.g. 0.1 payload, is smaller than the distance between stego images with 0.1 and 0.4 payloads. But in the binary classification for image steganalysis, this kind of differences has been ignored. This ignorance makes it harder to classify the images with different kinds of payloads, especially when the payloads of images in test dataset have not been provided in advance. This phenomenon belongs to the cover-source mismatch problem [26], which makes the detection accuracy much lower, especially when the payload is low. To solve this challenge, one kind of solution is to train each model for each payload, and then utilizes the ensemble strategy to obtain the final result based on all models. But it inevitably requires high computational complexity.

In our paper, we propose a novel steganographer detection method based on multiclass deep neural networks. In machine learning, multiclass is the problem of classifying instances into one of three or more classes. In our model, the dilated residual networks are trained for multiclass classification of images with six kinds of embedding payloads. In the inference stage, we employ the learnt model as the feature extractor to extract the discriminate features from each image of each user. Then, the agglomerative hierarchical clustering algorithm is used to identify the steganographer according to the corresponding distance metrics. To our best knowledge, we are the first to propose a steganographer detection framework based on multiclass neural networks. This multiclass neural networks are an attempt to solve the payload mismatch problem. In our experiments, we also find that the multiclass neural networks can learn effective features from the information of relatively high payloads and promote to separate the low payload embedded stegos from the covers.

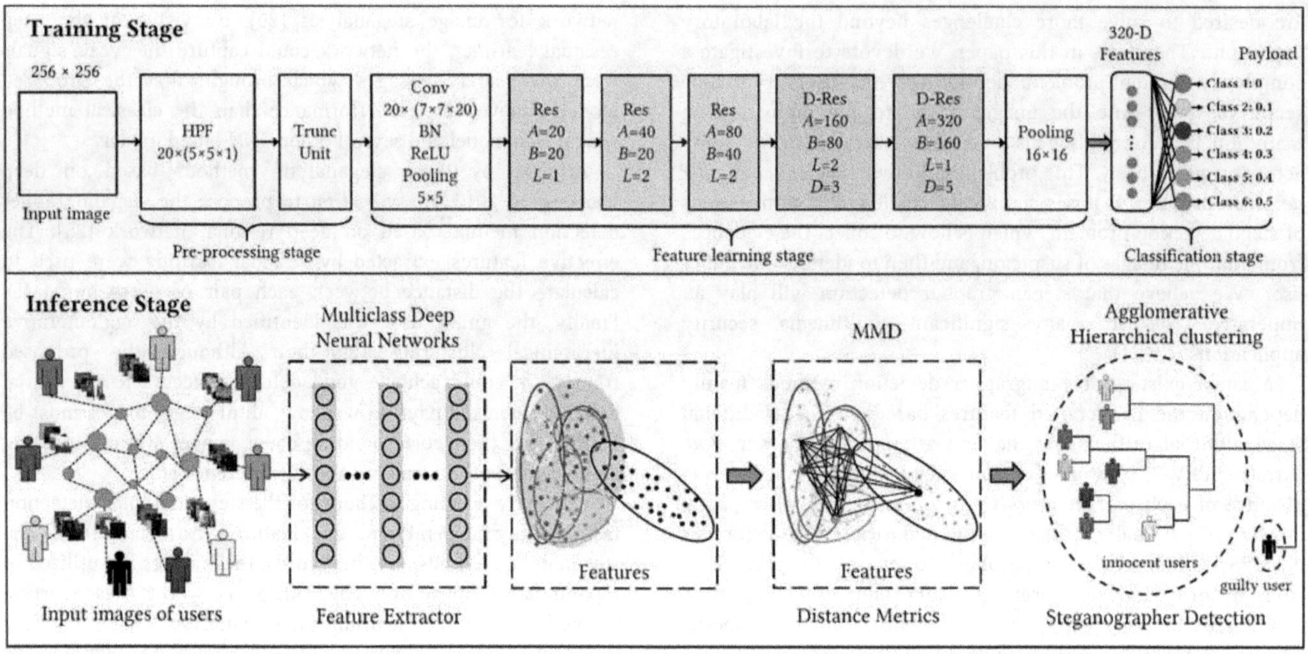

Figure 1: Multiclass deep neural networks based steganographer detection.

2 PROPOSED METHOD

In this paper, we propose a novel steganographer detection method based on multiclass deep neural networks. Fig. 1 illustrates the framework of Multiclass Deep Neural Networks based Steganographer Detection (MDNNSD). In the training stage, the multiclass dilated residual networks are trained for the classification of images with six types of embedding payloads. In the testing stage, the learnt model is utilized to extract features of each image from each user. Then, the distance between each pair of user is calculated based on MMD algorithm. Finally, the agglomerative hierarchical clustering algorithm is performed to identify the guilty user.

2.1 Feature Extraction via Multiclass Neural Networks

As illustrated in Fig. 1, in the learning part, the multiclass neural networks are learnt to classify images with six types of embedding payloads. In the inference part, the learnt model is utilized to extract the features of each image from each user. The proposed networks consist of three parts: the pre-processing stage, the feature learning stage and the classification stage.

The pre-processing stage aims to extract the message (noise) component, which includes two layers: the High-Pass-Filtering (HPF) layer and the truncation layer. As we known, the steganographic algorithm can be considered as adding low-amplitude additive noise to cover images. Hence, it means the weak stego signals have much lower amplitude in comparison of that of the image content. To suppress image content and extract effective information from low signal-to-noise ratio (SNR) stego signals, in the HPF layer, 20 high-pass filters are used to extract the high frequency components from the input. To guarantee the pre-processing stage has the ability to extract the high frequency component, each filter of HPF layer is initialized by a high-pass kernel. In the truncation layer, we try to use the truncation unit to constrain the dynamic range of input feature maps. This setting is also used to improve the convergence speed. The truncation unit is defined by Eq. 1 as follows:

$$Trunc(x) = \begin{cases} -T, & x < -T \\ x, & -T \le x \le T \\ T, & x > T \end{cases} \tag{1}$$

where T denotes the truncation threshold.

The feature learning stage is to extract the discriminative features. This sub-network mainly consists of two kinds of units: the Res and the D-Res units. The structure of the Res and the D-Res units are shown in Fig. 2. In the feature learning stage, the networks first use 20 convolutional kernels with the size of 7×7 to preserve the noise components generated in the pre-processing stage. Then, a series of units are utilized to extract the discriminative features, which include the residual learning units and dilated residual learning units. For the residual learning block in residual learning units, it fits the residual function $F(\mathbf{s}) := H(\mathbf{s}) - \mathbf{s}$ rather than approximating an underlying function $H(\mathbf{s})$ directly, which can be implemented by feedforward networks with the shortcut connections [27]. He *et al.* has proved that the networks could be easier to optimize by the short connections [27]. Some prior works have also proved that deep residual learning is benefit for extracting effective patterns from weak stego signals [20, 25]. Hence, in the feature learning stage, we take advantage of the residual learning to capture the weak stego signals from the steganographer.

Specifically, for the Res unit, it first uses the projection shortcut connection to increase the dimension of feature map, and then directly utilizes the identity shortcut connections in the following repeated building blocks.

The structure of D-Res unit is similar with that of the Res unit in addition to replacing all convolutional layers with the dilated convolutional layers. In our networks, we take advantage of the dilated residual unit with a larger receptive field. It is utilized to preserve the effective information from the weak signals generated by the guilty user. After a series of units processing, an average pooling layer with the size of 16×16 to transform the feature maps into feature vectors.

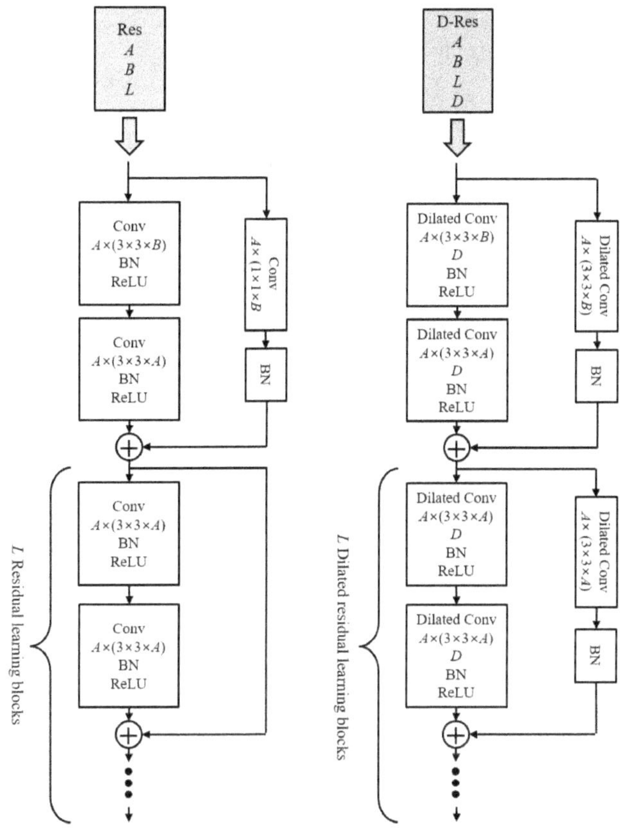

Figure 2: The structure of the Res and the D-Res units. Conv represents convolutional layers, with kernel sizes following (number of kernels) × (height × width × number of channels). *L* denotes the number of residual or dilated residual learning blocks. *D* denotes the dilation value in the dilated convolutional layers.

For the classification stage, in the training phase, the networks map extracted feature vectors into six labels. Six output nodes correspond to the embedding payload of the image, *i.e.*, 0, 0.1, 0.2, 0.3, 0.4 and 0.5, respectively. To train the networks, the feature vectors, which are generated by the last pooling layer in the feature learning stage, are fully connected to the six output nodes for multiclass classification. In the inference stage, we consider the learnt model as the feature extractor. Therefore, 320-D feature vector of each image from each user is generated from the last average pooling layer in the feature learning stage.

2.2 Distance Metrics based on MMD

By virtue of multiclass deep neural networks, the discriminative features of each image from each user are extracted via the learnt model. Then, the distance between each pair of users is calculated by maximum mean discrepancy (MMD) based on the extracted features. Mathematically, MMD is employed to measure the similarity between two probability distributions. In our work, we use MMD as the distance metrics to calculate the similarity between feature sets from any pair of users.

We denote a set of m users as U_1, U_2, ..., U_m, which include one guilty user and m-1 innocent users, and each of them transfers n images. The feature sets $\mathbf{F}_X = (\mathbf{x}_1, \mathbf{x}_2, \ldots \mathbf{x}_n)$ and $\mathbf{F}_Y = (\mathbf{y}_1, \mathbf{y}_2, \ldots, \mathbf{y}_n)$ are extracted from the images transferred by U_X and U_Y, where $\mathbf{x}_i$ and $\mathbf{y}_i$ ($1 \le i \le n$) denote a 320-D feature vector of an image from U_X and U_Y, respectively. The sample estimate for the MMD distance of U_X and U_Y is defined by Eq. 2 as follows:

$$d(U_X, U_Y) = \sqrt{\frac{1}{n^2}\sum_{i,j=1}^{n} k(\mathbf{x}_i, \mathbf{x}_j) - \frac{2}{n^2}\sum_{i,j=1}^{n} k(\mathbf{x}_i, \mathbf{y}_j) + \frac{1}{n^2}\sum_{i,j=1}^{n} k(\mathbf{y}_i, \mathbf{y}_j)} \quad (2)$$

where $k(\mathbf{x}, \mathbf{y})$ represents a positive definite kernel function, including the linear kernel and the Gaussian kernel. In this paper, we employ the Gaussian kernel to calculate the MMD distance.

2.3 Steganographer Detection by Hierarchical Clustering

After the MMD distance between each pair of users is calculated, we identify the steganographer (guilty user) based on the MMD distance by using the agglomerative hierarchical clustering algorithm.

The agglomerative hierarchical clustering algorithm is a representative method of cluster analysis. Initially, each user is considered as a singleton cluster. Then, the nearest two clusters are combined by using the linkage function and form a new larger cluster. It is repeated until the last cluster is linked and a complete binary hierarchical tree is formed. Ideally, for the steganographer detection task, all the innocent users should be clustered as a cluster and the other cluster only consists of the guilty user.

In this paper, we use four kinds of linkage functions to calculate the distance between two clusters based on the MMD distance, including the average linkage, the single linkage, the complete linkage, and the weighted average linkage.

3 EXPERIMENTS

A series of empirical experiments are conducted on two standard datasets. In Section 3.1, we test the proposed method on a standard spatial domain dataset BOSSbase ver 1.01 [28]. Then, in Section 3.2, we further evaluate the proposed method in frequency domain. The images from BOSSbase ver 1.01 are compressed with JPEG quality factor 80, and they are used to test the effectiveness of the proposed method. In the following sections, we call it as JPEG version of BOSSbase ver 1.01.

For the training stage of our proposed networks, parameters are updated by stochastic gradient descent. Each element $\mathbf{W}_{ij}$ in the weight matrix **W** is initialized by the improved "Xavier" method [29], *i.e.*, Gaussian distribution with zero mean and the standard deviation inversely proportional to the number of network's connections. The bias vectors are initialized to zeros. The threshold T in the truncation layer is set to 5. The momentum and weight decay in our networks are set to 0.9 and 0.0001, respectively. A mini-batch with 40 images (20 cover-stego pairs) is used as the input for training. We adaptively adjust the learning rate in the training phase. Specifically, the learning rate is initialized to 0.001 and scheduled to decrease 10% for every 50 training epochs. All of the experiments are conducted on a Tesla K80 GPU.

3.1 Steganographer Detection in Spatial Domain

In this section, we evaluate the proposed method for the steganographer detection task in spatial domain from easy to difficult cases.

3.1.1 Experimental Setting. The standard dataset BOSSbase ver 1.01 is utilized to validate our proposed method. The original BOSSbase ver 1.01 consists of 10,000 grayscale images with the size of 512×512. Following the setting in [16, 20, 25], each image of the original dataset is cropped into four non-overlapping sub-images with the size of 256×256. In the training stage, 20,000 cover images are selected randomly from all cropped images, and their five kinds of stego images are generated by Spatial version of the UNIversal WAvelet Relative Distortion (S-UNIWARD) steganography [30] at five kinds of payloads. The payloads are set from 0.1 to 0.5 bit-per-pixel (bpp) with step 0.1. Thus, these images are constructed 100,000 cover-stego pairs, and they are used for training the multiclass deep neural networks. The remaining 20,000 covers and their corresponding stegos are utilized to evaluate the performance of our model in detecting the guilty user. In our experiments, we randomly selected m users, which include one guilty user and m-1 innocent users, and each of them transfers n images. All the statistical experiments are repeated 100 times, and each time, m is set to 100 and n is set to 200. The average results are reported.

In spatial domain, we use five content-adaptive steganography to embed the messages into the images, *i.e.* S-UNIWARD [30], HIgh-pass Low-pass Low-pass (HILL) [31], Wavelet Obtained Weights (WOW) [32], Highly Undetectable steGO implemented using the Gibbs construction with Bounding Distortion (HUGO-BD) [33], and Minimizing the power of the most POwerful Detector (MiPOD) [34].

We compare our method with the conventional method SRMQ1_SD, and two CNN-based methods, including: ANSD and XuNet_SD. SRMQ1_SD is the steganographer detection method via SRMQ1 [35], which is a well-known spatial rich model with a single quantization step. ANSD is the steganographer detection method via a well-known deep CNN architecture AlexNet [36]. We modify the network slightly. First, the input size of the network is modified as 256×256×3. Second, the number of neurons in the first two fully-connected layers is modified as 1,000. The last fully-connected layer has 2 neurons to classify the covers and stegos. Each image is first filtered by the *KV* filter proposed by Qian *et al.* [16] and the input image of the network is the filtered image. In the training stage, the model is only trained on S-UNIWARD at 0.4bpp. Considering AlexNet is served for the classification of ImageNet Dataset and the number of images of ImageNet is far more than that of BOSSbase. Thus, the size of min-batch is reduced from 256 to 64 (32 cover-stego pairs). To other parameters, we just follow the general setting. XuNet_SD is the abbreviation of the steganographer detection method based on the network proposed by Xu *et al.* [18]. As a matter of convenience, we refer this network as XuNet. It is noticed that the input size of XuNet is modified as 256×256, which is in accord with the input size of our networks. The size of mini-batch is set to 40 (20 cover-stego pairs). In the training phase, the model is only trained on S-UNIWARD at 0.4bpp. In addition, we train the model once and use the learnt model for testing the steganographer detection task instead of training it five times for ensemble learning as described in [18].

3.1.2 A Single Steganographic Algorithm with A single payload. In this subsection, we aim to evaluate our proposed method under a simple condition. In detail, the stego images of the guilty user are generated by one steganographic algorithm (S-UNIWARD) at one payload. The payload is set to 0.05, 0.1, 0.2, 0.3 and 0.4. Here, we employ the single linkage as the clustering linkage function. We compare our proposed method with classical method SRMQ1_SD and two CNN-based methods including ANSD and XuNet_SD. The comparison results are shown in Table 1.

Table 1: The Detection Accuracy Comparisons of Different Methods on S-UNIWARD with a Single Payload.

Payload (bpp)	Method	Feature Dimension	Average Distance AD1	Average Distance AD2	Acc. (%)	STD
0.05	MDNNSD	320	0.0763	0.0836	6	0.24
	ANSD	1,000	0.0771	0.0807	5	0.22
	XuNet_SD	128	0.0757	0.0762	2	0.14
	SRMQ1_SD	12,753	0.0757	0.0753	0	0
0.1	MDNNSD	320	0.0763	0.1148	84	0.37
	ANSD	1,000	0.0773	0.0988	73	0.45
	XuNet_SD	128	0.0761	0.0801	2	0.14
	SRMQ1_SD	12,753	0.0753	0.0757	0	0
0.2	MDNNSD	320	0.0762	0.2028	100	0
	ANSD	1,000	0.0772	0.1610	100	0
	XuNet_SD	128	0.0753	0.0990	71	0.46
	SRMQ1_SD	12,753	0.0751	0.0748	0	0
0.3	MDNNSD	320	0.0763	0.2743	100	0
	ANSD	1,000	0.0771	0.2285	100	0
	XuNet_SD	128	0.0756	0.1324	100	0
	SRMQ1_SD	12,753	0.0747	0.0734	1	0.1
0.4	MDNNSD	320	0.0764	0.3476	100	0
	ANSD	1,000	0.0773	0.2756	100	0
	XuNet_SD	128	0.0754	0.1718	100	0
	SRMQ1_SD	12,753	0.0748	0.0772	2	0.14

From Table 1, we can find that three CNN-based methods can detect the steganographer accurately when the payload is greater than 0.2. However, the classical method, SRMQ1_SD cannot detect the guilty user in most of cases. For the average distance, AD1 and AD2 is the average distance between the features of innocent users, and the average distance between the features of the guilty user and innocent users, respectively. Obviously, the value of AD1/AD2 is high means that the guilty user is more deviated from innocent users. We can find that the value of AD1/AD2 of SRMQ1_SD is smaller than other CNN-based methods. Besides, we can observe that the feature dimension of SRMQ1_SD is 12,573, which is much larger than other CNN-based methods. Although the high-dimensional rich models with ensemble classifiers are benefit for the steganalysis task, the performance of SRMQ1_SD is not good for steganographer detection task due to the high dimension of the extracted features. Based on these results, we can make the conclusion that CNN-based methods can effectively capture features to distinguish the guilty user from innocent users. In addition, the detection accuracies of all methods decrease with the decrease of the payload. However, our proposed method outperforms other CNN-based methods when the payload is lower than or equal to 0.2. It means our proposed method can detect the guilty user more effectively when the payload is low.

3.1.3 Multiple Steganographic Algorithms with A Single Payload. In this subsection, we try to test the performance of the proposed method when the stego images of the guilty user are generated through data embedded by multiple steganographic algorithms (S-UNWARD, HILL, WOW, HUGO-BD, and MiPOD) with a single payload. That is, for the guilty user, the images are equally divided into five groups. The images of each group include messages embedded by each steganographic algorithm. The payload is set to 0.05, 0.1, 0.2 and 0.3, respectively. Here, we also use the single linkage function. The detection accuracies are displayed in Fig. 3.

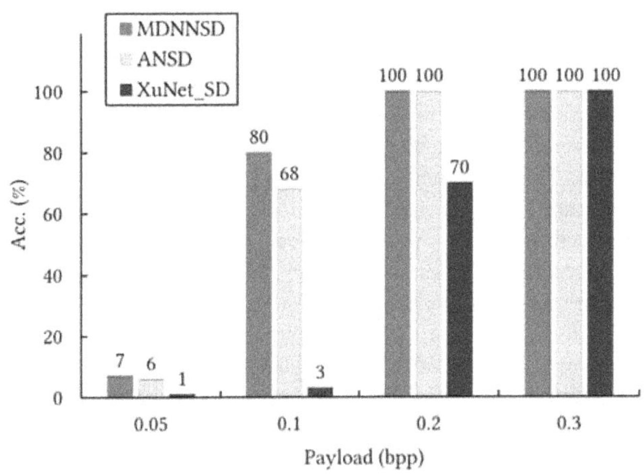

Figure 3: The detection accuracies of MDNNSD, ANSD and XuNet_SD. The models are tested on multiple steganographic algorithms with a single payload.

As Fig. 3 shows, although the condition is more difficult, all of the CNN-based methods can detect the guilty user successfully in most of cases. When the payload is 0.1, the accuracies of our proposed method and ANSD are higher than XuNet_SD. For AlexNet, which is a well-known CNN model for image classification, we can find the features extracted from it can effectively distinguish the stego images and cover images. In spite of this, our proposed method shows a higher level of robustness of inter-steganographic algorithms. However, when the payload is 0.05, all methods cannot detect the guilty user well. As we know, when the embedding payload is low, the stego image is similar to the cover image, making models harder to distinguish the guilty user from innocent users.

3.1.4 The Comparisons of Different Training Strategies. In this subsection, we test the performance of the proposed networks under different training strategies. In detail, the first training strategy is the networks are trained on S-UNIWARD at 0.1bpp, which is named as DNNSD_01. The second is that the networks are trained on S-UNIWARD at 0.4bpp, which is termed as DNNSD_04. Specifically, for these two strategies, the models are trained for binary classification (cover/stego), and the training networks map the input images into two labels. On the contrary, the networks in our proposed method are trained for multiclass classification. All of three models are tested on S-UNIWARD at 0.1 and 0.4bpp, respectively. We compare our proposed method, MDNNSD with these two other training strategies. The performance of the networks under different training strategies is shown in Fig. 4.

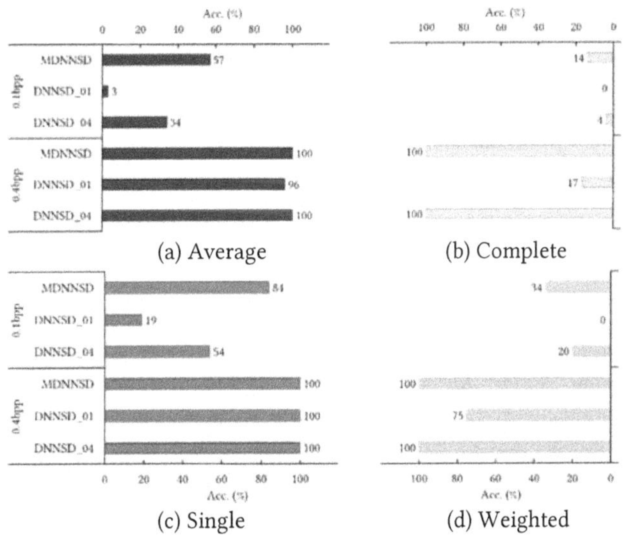

Figure 4: The comparison results of different models on S-UNIWARD at 0.1 and 0.4bpp, respectively. Different colors represent different linkage functions.

Fig. 4 shows that the performance of our proposed method outperforms other strategies. In other words, the model trained for multiclass classification is better than those trained for binary classification even though the payload used in training stage is the same as the testing payload. Moreover, compared with DNNSD_04 testing on 0.1bpp, the performance of DNNSD_01 tested on 0.1bpp is worse. As we all know, when the payload is low, the stego image is much similar to the cover image. Thus, when DNNSD_01 is trained on the images with low payload, the learnt model cannot capture more useful information from the weak stego signal. For a fair comparison, we also test the performance of the similar model but training for binary classification on the images embedded by S-UNIWARD with six kinds of payloads. We can find the performance of that case is worse than the performance of our proposed method. For instance, under the single linkage function, the detection accuracy of this similar model tested on 0.1bpp is 29%, while the detection accuracy of our proposed model is 84%. Thus, we can make the conclusion that the outstanding performance of our method is mainly dependent on the proposed multiclass networks rather than more samples from different payloads.

3.2 Steganographer Detection in Frequency Domain

In Section 3.1, we have evaluated the effectiveness of our proposed method for the steganographer detection task in spatial domain. In this section, we extend the task to frequency domain, and devote to evaluate whether our proposed method can identify the guilty user in frequency domain or not.

3.2.1 Experimental Setting. Consistent with the setting in Section 3.1.1, each image from the original BOSSbase ver 1.01 is cropped into four non-overlapping sub-images. Then, each sub-image is compressed with JPEG quality factor 80 using Matlab's imwrite function. All of these cropped JPEG images compose the JPEG version of BOSSbase ver 1.01 dataset, which is utilized to validate the performance of our method in frequency domain. We also randomly select 20,000 images from the cropped JPEG images and their corresponding stego images generated by JPEG version of the UNIversal WAvelet Relative Distortion (J-UNIWARD) [30] at five kinds of payloads to train the model. The payloads are set from 0.1 to 0.5 bits per non-zeros Alternating Current DCT coefficient (bpnzAC) with step 0.1. The rest 20,000 covers and their corresponding stegos are used to validate our proposed method in steganographer detection task. Keeping the same setting in spatial-domain experiments, m users are randomly selected and each of them transfers n images. All the statistical experiments are repeated for 100 times, and each time, m is set to 100 and n is set to 200. The average accuracy is used as basis for evaluation.

In frequency domain, we use two JPEG-domain steganographic algorithms to embed messages, including: J-UNIWARD [30], and no-shrinkage F5 (nsF5) [37]. J-UNIWARD is a kind of content-adaptive steganographic algorithm, which is more difficult than nsF5. We compare our proposed method with the classical method PEV_SD, and the CNN-based method ANSD. PEV_SD is the steganographer detection framework based on the PEV-274 features. The parameters setting of ANSD is identical to that of ANSD in spatial domain. Similar to what has been done in JPEG-domain steganalytic methods [23, 38], each image in JPEG format is first decompressed into the spatial domain. Then, the decompressed JPEG images are used as the input of all models.

3.2.2 A Single Steganographic Algorithm with A single payload. In the first experiment in frequency domain, we try to compare our proposed method with two other methods under a simple condition. For the guilty user, two hundred stego images include message embedded by a single steganographic algorithm with a single payload. We test the performance of all models in four cases, including: J-UNIWARD at 0.1bpnzAC, J-UNIWARD at 0.4bpnzAC, nsF5 at 0.1bpnzAC, and nsF5 at 0.4bpnzAC, respectively. Here, we use the single linkage as the linkage function in the clustering algorithm. The experiment results are provided in Table 2.

Table 2: The Detection Accuracy Comparisons of Different Methods Tested on a Single Steganographic Algorithm with a Single Payload.

Case	Method	Feature Dimension	Acc. (%)	STD
J-UNIWARD at 0.1bpnzAC	MDNNSD	320	58	0.5
	ANSD	1,000	1	0.1
	PEV_SD	274	0	0
J-UNIWARD at 0.4bpnzAC	MDNNSD	320	100	0
	ANSD	1,000	100	0
	PEV_SD	274	4	0.2
nsF5 at 0.1bpnzAC	MDNNSD	320	65	0.48
	ANSD	1,000	8	0.27
	PEV_SD	274	2	0.14
nsF5 at 0.4bpnzAC	MDNNSD	320	100	0
	ANSD	1,000	100	0
	PEV_SD	274	90	0.3

From Table 2, we can observe that the classical method PEV_SD achieves good performance in the case of nsF5 at 0.4bpnzAC due to the lower dimension of features. However, in the case of J-UNIWARD at 0.4bpnzAC, the accuracy of PEV_SD is low. It is owing to J-UNIWARD is a content-adaptive steganography, which is more difficult than nsF5. For the CNN-based methods, both of them can achieve good performance when the payload is high. This illustrates the CNN-based method is effective for steganographer detection task in frequency domain. However, when the payload is low, *i.e.* 0.1bpnzAC, ANSD and PEV_SD are inferior to our proposed method. In other words, our proposed method can effectively solve the steganographer detection problem in spatial and frequency domain under low payload condition. In addition, compared with the performance of our proposed method in spatial domain, the detection accuracies of that in frequency domain are lower. It is due to these images loss detail information in the compression and decompression procedure, and this detail information are used to hide the weak stego signal.

4 CONCLUSIONS

In this paper, we propose a novel steganographer detection method based on multiclass deep neural networks. To our best knowledge, we are the first to propose a steganographer detection framework based on multiclass neural networks. In the training stage, the proposed multiclass neural networks are trained to classify the images with six types of embedding payloads. In the inference stage, the learnt model is served as the feature extractor, which utilizes to extract the features of each image from each user. Finally, the agglomerative hierarchical clustering algorithm is utilized to identify the steganographer based on the MMD distance metric.

In the experiments, we evaluate the effectiveness of the proposed method on two standard datasets in different image domain. In spatial domain, the proposed method can accurately identify the guilty user from easy to difficult conditions, especially the low embedding payloads. Moreover, the proposed method demonstrates its robustness under inter-steganographic algorithms situations. In frequency domain, the performance of the proposed method outperforms other methods when the payload is low. In future work, we seek to apply our proposed method under the real-world large-scale social media networks.

ACKNOWLEDGMENTS

This work was supported by the National Natural Science Foundation of China (No. 61502311, No. 61620106008), the Natural Science Foundation of Guangdong Province (No. 2016A030310053, 2016A030310039, 2017A030310521), the Science and Technology Innovation Commission of Shenzhen under Grant (No.JCYJ20160422151736824), Shenzhen Emerging Industries of the Strategic Basic Research Project under Grant (No. JCYJ20160226191842793), the Shenzhen high-level overseas talents program, and the Tencent "Rhinoceros Birds" - Scientific Research Foundation for Young Teachers of Shenzhen University (2016).

REFERENCES

[1] R. J. Anderson and F. A. P. Petitcolas. 1998. On the limits of steganography. *IEEE Journal on Selected Areas in Communications.* 16, 4 (May 1998), 474–481. DOI: 10.1109/49.668971

[2] T. Lin, C. Wang, W. Chen, F. Lin and W. Lin. 2017. A novel data hiding algorithm for high dynamic range images. *IEEE Transactions on Multimedia.* 19, 1 (Jan. 2017), 196-211. DOI: 10.1109/TMM.2016.2605499

[3] B. Li, J. He, J. Huang, and Y. Q. Shi. 2011. A survey on image steganography and steganalysis. *Journal of Information Hiding and Multimedia Signal Processing.* 2, 2 (Apr. 2011), 142-172.

[4] F. Li, K. Wu, J. Lei, M. Wen, Z. Bi, and C. Gu. 2016. Steganalysis over large-scale social networks with high-order joint features and clustering ensembles. *IEEE Transactions on Information Forensics and Security.* 11, 2 (Feb. 2016), 344-357. DOI: 10.1109/TIFS.2015.2496910

[5] A. D. Ker and T. Pevný. 2011. A new paradigm for steganalysis via clustering. In *Proceeding of SPIE, Media Watermarking., Security, and Forensics III.* San Francisco Airport, California, U.S. 78800U1–U13.

[6] T. Pevný and J. Fridrich. 2007. Merging Markov and DCT features for multi-class JPEG steganalysis. In *Proceeding of SPIE, Security, Steganography, and Watermarking of Multimedia Contents IX.* San Jose, CA, U.S. 650503–14.

[7] A. Gretton, K. M. Borgwardt, M. Rasch, B. Schöölkopf, and A. J. Smola. 2007. A kernel method for the two-sample-problem. In *Proceeding of Advances in Neural Information Processing Systems (NIPS).* Cambridge, MA, USA, 513–520.

[8] M. M. Breunig, H.-P. Kriegel, R. T. Ng, and J. Sander. 2000. LOF: Identifying density-based local outliers. In *Proceeding of ACM SIGMOD International Conference on Management of Data (ACM SIGMOD'00).* ACM New York, NY, USA. 93–104.

[9] A. D. Ker and T. Pevný. 2012. Identifying a steganographer in realistic and heterogeneous data sets. In *Proceeding of SPIE, Media Watermarking., Security, and Forensics 2012.* Burlingame, California. U.S. 83030N1–N13.

[10] A. D. Ker and T. Pevný. 2014. The steganographer is the outlier: Realistic large-scale steganalysis. *IEEE Transactions on Information Forensics and Security.* 9, 9 (Sep. 2014), 1424–1435.

[11] F. Li, M. Wen, J. Lei, and Y. Ren. 2017. Efficient steganographer detection over social networks with sampling reconstruction. *Peer-to-Peer Networking and Applications.* (Sep. 2017), 1-16. DOI: https://doi.org/10.1007/s12083-017-0603-3

[12] O. Seddati, S. Dupont, and S. Mahmoudi. 2017. Quadruplet Networks for Sketch-Based Image Retrieval. In *Proceedings of the 2017 ACM on International Conference on Multimedia Retrieval (ICMR '17).* ACM, New York, NY, USA, 184-191.

[13] Z. Wang, K. He, Y. Fu, R. Feng, Y. Jiang, and X. Xue. 2017. Multi-task Deep Neural Network for Joint Face Recognition and Facial Attribute Prediction. In *Proceedings of the 2017 ACM on International Conference on Multimedia Retrieval (ICMR '17).* ACM, New York, NY, USA, 365-374.

[14] J. Gao, Y. Fu, Y. Jiang, and X. Xue. 2017. Frame-Transformer Emotion Classification Network. In *Proceedings of the 2017 ACM on International Conference on Multimedia Retrieval (ICMR '17).* ACM, New York, NY, USA, 78-83.

[15] S. Tan and B. Li. 2014. Stacked convolutional auto-encoders for steganalysis of digital images. In *Proceeding of Asia-Pacific Signal and Information Processing Association Annual Summit and Conference (APSIPA).* Siem Reap. 1-4.

[16] Y. Qian, J. Dong, W. Wang, and T. Tan. 2015. Deep learning for steganalysis via convolutional neural networks. In *Proceeding of SPIE, Media Watermarking. Security, and Forensics,* San Francisco, California, U.S. 9409J1–J10.

[17] Y. Qian, J. Dong, W. Wang, and T. Tan. 2016. Learning and transferring representations for image steganalysis using convolutional neural network. In *Proceeding of IEEE International Conference on Image Processing (ICIP),* Phoenix, AZ. 2752-2756.

[18] G. Xu, H. Z. Wu, and Y. Q. Shi. 2016. Structural design of convolutional neural networks for steganalysis. *IEEE Signal Processing Letters.* 23, 5 (May 2016), 708-712. DOI: 10.1109/LSP.2016.2548421

[19] G. Xu, H. Z. Wu, and Y. Q. Shi. 2016. Ensemble of CNNs for steganalysis: An empirical study. In *Proceeding of ACM Workshop on Information Hiding and Multimedia Security (IH&MMSec'16).* ACM New York, NY, USA, 103-107.

[20] S. Wu, S. Zhong, and Y. Liu. 2017. Deep residual learning for image steganalysis. *Multimedia Tools and Applications.* (2017), 1-17. DOI: https://doi.org/10.1007/s11042-017-4440-4

[21] J. Ye, J. Ni, and Y. Yi. 2017. Deep learning hierarchical representations for image steganalysis. *IEEE Transactions on Information Forensics and Security.* 12, 11 (Nov. 2017), 2545-2557. DOI: 10.1109/TIFS.2017.2710946

[22] J. Zeng, S. Tan, B. Li, and J. Huang. 2016. Large-scale JPEG image steganalysis using hybrid deep-learning framework. arXiv: 1611.03233. Retrieved from https://arxiv.org/abs/1611.03233

[23] G. Xu. 2017. Deep convolutional neural network to detect J-UNIWARD. In *Proceeding of ACM Workshop on Information Hiding and Multimedia Security (IH&MMSec'17).* ACM New York, NY, USA, 103-107.

[24] J. Yang, Y. Shi, E. K. Wong, and X. Kang. 2017. JPEG steganalysis based on denseNet. arXiv: 1711.09335. Retrieved from https://arxiv.org/abs/1711.09335

[25] M. Zheng, S. Zhong, S. Wu, and J. Jiang. 2017. Steganographer detection via deep residual network. In *Proceeding of IEEE International Conference on Multimedia and Expo (ICME'17).* Hong Kong, 235-240.

[26] J. Kodovský, V. Sedighi, and J. Fridrich. 2014. Study of cover source mismatch in steganalysis and ways to mitigate its impact. In *Proceeding of SPIE, Media Watermarking. Security, and Forensics.* San Francisco, California, U. S .90280J1–J12.

[27] K. He, X. Zhang, S. Ren, J. Sun. 2016. Deep residual learning for image recognition. In *Proceeding of IEEE Conference on Computer Vision and Pattern Recognition (CVPR).* Las Vegas, NV, USA. 770-778.

[28] P. Bas, T. Filler, and T. Pevný. 2011. "Break our steganographic system": The ins and outs of organizing BOSS. In *Proceeding of the 13th International Workshop on Information Hiding (IH).* Springer, Berlin, Heidelberg, 59–70.

[29] K. He, X. Zhang, S. Ren, and J. Sun. 2015. Delving deep into Rectifiers: Surpassing Human-Level Performance on ImageNet Classification. In *Proceeding of IEEE International Conference on Computer Vision (ICCV).* Santiago, Chile. 1026-1034.

[30] V. Holub and J. Fridrich. 2014. Universal distortion function for steganography in an arbitrary domain. *EURASIP Journal on Information Security.* 2014, 1 (Dec. 2014), 1–13. DOI: https://doi.org/10.1186/1687-417X-2014-1

[31] B. Li, M. Wang, J. Huang, and X. Li. 2014. A new cost function for spatial image steganography. In *Proceeding of IEEE International Conference on Image Processing (ICIP).* Paris, France, 4206-4210.

[32] V. Holub and J. Fridrich. 2012. Designing steganographic distortion using directional filters. In *Proceeding of IEEE International Workshop on Information Forensics and Security (WIFS).* Tenerife, 234-239.

[33] T. Filler and J. Fridrich. 2010. Gibbs construction in steganography. *IEEE Transactions on Information Forensics and Security.* 5, 4 (Dec. 2010), 705-720. DOI: 10.1109/TIFS.2010.2077629

[34] V. Sedighi, R. Cogranne, and J. Fridrich. 2016. Content-Adaptive steganography by minimizing statistical detectability. *IEEE Transactions on Information Forensics and Security.* 11, 2 (Feb. 2016), 221-234. DOI: 10.1109/TIFS.2015.2486744

[35] J. Fridrich and J. Kodovsky. 2012. Rich models for steganalysis of digital images. *IEEE Transactions on Information Forensics and Security.* 7, 3 (Jun. 2012), 868-882. DOI: 10.1109/TIFS.2012.2190402M.
[36] A. Krizhevsky, I. Sutskever, and G. Hinton. 2012. ImageNet classification with deep convolutional neural networks. In *Proceeding of Advances in Neural Information Processing Systems (NIPS).* 1097-1105.
[37] J. Fridrich, T. Pevný, and J. Kodovský. 2007. Statistically undetectable JPEG steganography: Dead ends challenges, and opportunities. In *Proceeding of ACM Workshop on Multimedia & security (MM&Sec'07).* ACM New York, NY, USA. 20-21.
[38] V. Holub and J. Fridrich. 2015. Low-complexity features for JPEG steganalysis using undecimated DCT. *IEEE Transactions on Information Forensics and Security.* 10, 2 (Feb. 2015), 219-228. DOI: 10.1109/TIFS.2014.2364918

An Entropy Model for Loiterer Retrieval across Multiple Surveillance Cameras *

Maguell L.T.L. Sandifort[†,‡], Jianquan Liu[‡], Shoji Nishimura[‡], Wolfgang Hürst[†]
[†]Utrecht University, the Netherlands
[‡]Biometrics Research Laboratories, NEC Corporation, Japan

ABSTRACT

Loitering is a suspicious behavior that often leads to criminal actions, such as pickpocketing and illegal entry. Tracking methods can determine suspicious behavior based on trajectory, but require continuous appearance and are difficult to scale up to multi-camera systems. Using the duration of appearance of features works on multiple cameras, but does not consider major aspects of loitering behavior, such as repeated appearance and trajectory of candidates. We introduce an entropy model that maps the location of a person's features on a heatmap. It can be used as an abstraction of trajectory tracking across multiple surveillance cameras. We evaluate our method over several datasets and compare it to other loitering detection methods. The results show that our approach has similar results to state of the art, but can provide additional interesting candidates.

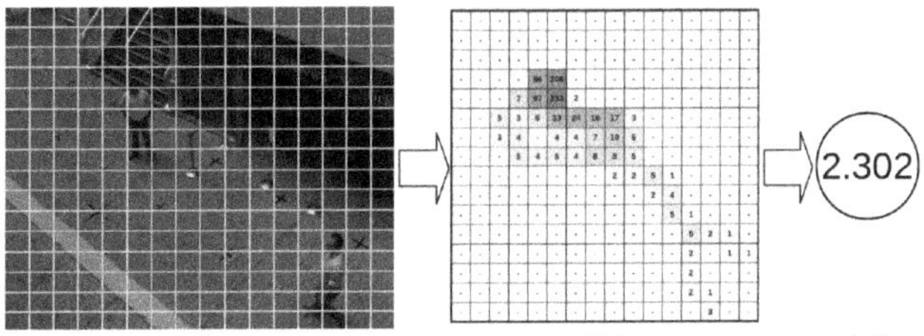

(a) (b) (c)

Figure 1: Overview of the entropy model. a) Split the camera view up into bins. b) Add each feature to the correct bin based on location in camera view. c) Calculate the entropy score

CCS CONCEPTS

• **Information systems → Multimedia information systems**; • **Social and professional topics → Surveillance**;

KEYWORDS

Loitering Discovery; Video Surveillance; Entropy Model; Heatmaps; Repeated Appearance; Ranking System; Loitering Candidate

ACM Reference Format:

Maguell L.T.L. Sandifort[†,‡], Jianquan Liu[‡], Shoji Nishimura[‡], Wolfgang Hürst[†]. 2018. An Entropy Model for Loiterer Retrieval across Multiple Surveillance Cameras . In *ICMR '18: 2018 International Conference on Multimedia Retrieval, June 11–14, 2018, Yokohama, Japan.* ACM, New York, NY, USA, 9 pages. https://doi.org/10.1145/3206025.3206049

1 INTRODUCTION

Loitering is a problem in the public safety domain, where an individual stays in an area for an extended period of time without a clear goal [15]. It is seen as a precursor to illegal behavior such as pickpocketing or illegal entry.

A number of approaches exist for detecting loitering behavior [6]. Detecting loitering is usually done by looking at a single camera view. Loitering behavior is then decided by looking at the duration of appearance, or the trajectory of a person. For duration, if the person is visible on the camera view for a certain amount of time, he or she is considered loitering. For trajectory-based methods, the length or the curvature of the trajectory is used to determine loitering behavior. Some methods also consider people leaving and re-entering the camera's field of view [5, 12].

These works provide a yes/no answer to whether or not a certain candidate is a loiterer. For this, some threshold for time or a score is involved. Choosing this threshold is challenging, as pedestrians showing suspicious behavior that stay in the area below this time threshold will not be detected. Finally, tracking based methods require people to be tracked continuously and therefore struggles in crowded scenes due to occlusions. In contrast to this single view, many areas exist where multiple cameras are installed, covering a larger region of a space or providing different viewing directions. We could apply single-camera methods to all these cameras in parallel. However, this would treat each camera as their own confined space. As a result we will lose insight into the big picture of the entire surveilled scene.

Liu et al. [9] address the problem of loitering across multiple cameras. They forgo tracking approaches and instead propose a scalable approach based on the frequency of the appearance of facial features. This approach works regardless of the amount of cameras used and it does not need to keep the positional relationship between cameras into account. It groups similar facial features together in their proposed similarity tree. It then provides a list of loitering candidates based

*This work is mainly completed during the period of internship.

ICMR '18, June 11–14, 2018, Yokohama, Japan

ACM ISBN 978-1-4503-5046-4/18/06...$15.00
https://doi.org/10.1145/3206025.3206049

on the amounts of facial features captured of one individual. Having a lot of features signifies that a person has been in the area for a long time.

While their method can provide a good list of initial candidates they only use duration to determine loitering behavior. Duration is a good initial indication of loitering, but there are other indicators as well, such as frequently reappearing in the same area. As they do not rely on tracking methods, they do not consider the trajectory of a person either.

To utilize the more in-depth information that tracking approaches provide, without relying too much on detailed tracking, we introduce an entropy model. We use this model to determine the amount that someone moves across a camera view. Using this model, we assign a higher likeliness of loitering to people that move more as opposed to standing still. We combine this entropy model with appearance duration and frequent reappearance to provide a loitering candidate list.

An overview of our entropy model can be seen in Fig. 1. First we input the features of people in the camera view into our system. For each camera view we create a heatmap, by splitting the camera view into bins. Next, we transform the position of features to the heatmap. The heatmap serves as an abstraction for tracking methods. It shows the rough trajectory of a person across the camera view, as well as how long they stood still in a certain location. Then by calculating the entropy of the heatmap, we get a measure for the amount a person moved inside the camera view.

Based on this hybrid approach we can provide a potential list of loiterers in the same level of accuracy and recall as other loitering detection methods. Both single- and multi-camera feature extraction can be used to provide input to our system. Our method scores people that show more aspects of loitering as higher candidates than people that only appear for a long duration. In addition our method provides additional interesting candidates.

In this paper we contribute the following:

- We propose an entropy model applied to a multi-camera surveillance system that models the movement of people. In addition we propose a measure for repeated leaving and entering of an area.
- We combine our measure into a loitering score that can be used to provide a list of potential loitering candidates.
- We conduct experiments over several datasets to evaluate our method and compare it to other loitering retrieval methods. The results show that our method provides similar levels of accuracy and recall as with other state-of-the-art methods, but will rank moving and frequently reappearing candidates higher. Finally, our method provides additional interesting candidates.

2 RELATED WORK

Trajectory. One way to detect loitering behavior is by looking at the trajectory of a pedestrian. Ko et al. [7] transform their camera image to account for the camera's angle and then track the center of an object moving in the camera view. Loitering behavior is then determined if a trajectory has irregular and large direction variations compared to a pre-defined threshold. Li et al. [8] track the trajectory of people moving in their static scene and determine loitering based on the angle of their path and the time duration of the path. Park et al. [13] propose a loitering detection algorithm using a regional histogram and object velocity. While a pedestrian is tracked, their location is stored in a histogram. If they exit and re-enter the same area multiple times, they are considered a loiterer. In addition to that, if the pedestrian's velocity is lower than a pre-defined threshold and the displacement is higher than a pre-defined threshold, the pedestrian is classified as a loiterer.

Looking at the trajectory can be an effective way to detect loitering behavior. However, these approaches require continuous and reliable tracking to obtain the trajectories. In crowded or occupied scenes the tracking could fail, making these methods difficult to use in real scenarios. We will propose the entropy model measure based on tracking that does not require a consistent view of people, but will still provide information on where the tracked person has been.

Entropy. Some methods utilize entropy theory to detect abnormalities. Ren et al. [14] propose a behavior entropy model to detect abnormal behaviors in a crowd. Xiong et al. [17] use a kinetic energy model to determine irregularities in crowd behavior. They create a histogram for each axis of the foreground pixels. Then they calculate the entropy to determine the crowd dispersion, which is used to get the kinetic energy of the crowd. If the crowd dispersion or kinetic energy exceeds a set threshold, an alarm signal is sent.

These works show that entropy theory can be applied to detect irregularities in crowds. Inspired by this, we will apply entropy theory to individuals as a measure to determine how much they are moving.

Classification. Bird et al. [2] use a single camera method to detect loiterers around a bus stop. Their method takes snapshots of people that are clearly visible and then uses the clothing color of people for similarity matching. Loitering is determined based on the duration of appearance. Tomás et al. [16] identify sequential micro-patterns (such as walk, stop, walk, stop) to determine loitering behavior of the elderly. Elhamod et al. [3] provide a semantics-based approach using both features of objects and the relationship between them to define and detect behavior of interest, such as loitering or abandoned luggage.

Nam [12] tracks pedestrians as blobs using a color feature model. Difference in shape, color and distance traveled is then used to track these blobs over multiple frames. It raises a loitering alarm if a person remains in a pre-defined region of interest longer than a loitering time-threshold. The method also accounts for pedestrians briefly moving out of view and re-entering again, without resetting the alarm timer. The loitering time-threshold is adapted automatically during a learning phase.

Table 1: Quick reference to the meanings of notations used through the paper.

Symbol	Meaning of notation
C_i	Camera with id i
CC	Camera count, the amount of cameras the candidates is visible on
CA_j	Camera Appearance with id j
T_{ca}	Camera Appearance Threshold
$RA(C_i)$	Camera i's Reappearance
RAS	ReAppearance Score
$FC(x)$	Feature Count of x
b_i^j	Bin with id i in the heatmap of CA_j
$p_{b_i^j}$	Probability of bin with id i in the heatmap of CA_j ($p_{b_i^j}$ for empty bins)
he_j	Heatmap entropy of the heatmap of CA_j (excludes empty bins)
$Dur(x)$	Duration of x
$P(CA_j)$	Presence of CA_j
WES	Weighted Entropy Score
DS	Duration Score
LS	Loitering Score

Huang et al. [5] extract their features through a color structure approach. They can then track people in a single camera. They define local loitering; someone loitering in the scene for an extended period of time, and global loitering; which keeps in mind that the candidate can temporarily leave the camera view and then return to it if they are loitering around the area. Arsic et al. [1] use multiple cameras surveilling the same scene at different angles to track and detect loiterers and abandoned luggage.

Lu et al. [11] present a summarization method consisting of three steps. First, pre-processing finds and tracks objects. Next, the holistic-level summarization decides on representative images using an energy minimization method. Finally, the object-level summarization provides relevant meta data for each object. Loitering is detected by mapping the trajectory of objects on histograms for each axis. If the ratio between windows of these two histograms exceeds a threshold value the object is considered a loiterer.

Most of the related work on loitering detection only provides a classification of a loiterer. For this, some threshold for time or a score is involved. Choosing this threshold is not easy in practice. For example, pedestrians showing suspicious behavior that stay in the area below this time threshold will not be detected. Additionally, they make no distinction between people who move and people who are waiting. When analyzing a large amount of footage, there could be many potential loiterers. It will be difficult to fine tune an alarm based on a time threshold. We reconsider trying to classify loiterers, by providing a list of candidates instead, with the most likely loiterer at the top. This allows the operator to make the final judgment. Our method can retrieve loiterers and provide other suspicious candidates in an ordered list sorted by suspicion level.

3 OUR APPROACH

Most methods deal with classification of loitering. They classify a person as loitering or not loitering. Such a yes/no answer requires a score or a time threshold. Thresholds will bring misclassification for border cases.

In reality however, there will still be an operator that is using surveillance systems. We do not have to completely replace the operator and instead should focus on assisting them. With this in mind, we rethink the loitering analysis as a *loiterer retrieval* problem in this paper. We propose a ranking measure to retrieve a list of loitering candidates ordered by level of interest. The operator or expert in the surveillance domain can then use this list to determine the actual loiterers. In our model, we take into account three important properties to determine loitering behavior: (1) entropy, (2) reappearance and (3) duration. Finally, we combine these properties into a (4) loitering score. Their details can be found in next subsection.

3.1 Model description

Before we describe our measure, we introduce necessary definitions that will be used in our approach.

Definition 1 (**CA**: Camera Appearance). *A sequence of chronologically ordered features of the same person on the same camera, starting when they enter the camera view and ending when they leave the camera view (after a time threshold T_{ca})*

We then use the camera appearance CA to introduce our entropy model that will be adopted in the ranking measure.

(1) Entropy Model. Two people that appear on a camera for the same amount of time (i.e., duration) can show vastly different behaviors. For example, one person could be entering the scene and then waiting in one spot, before moving again and leaving the scene. The other person could be moving around the camera view before leaving the scene. Using only duration does not distinguish between these two behavior. Likewise, trajectory of a person is not considered either when only using the duration.

To distinguish between these movements we propose an entropy model. For each CA, we construct a heatmap. We map the location of a person on the camera view on this heatmap. This way we get a rough indication of the trajectory of a person in the camera view. In addition, we can identify if the person has been standing still or moving around. The advantage of using this heatmap approach over a direct tracking approach is that we do not need continuous views of a person. It serves as an abstraction of tracking where someone has been on a single or multiple cameras.

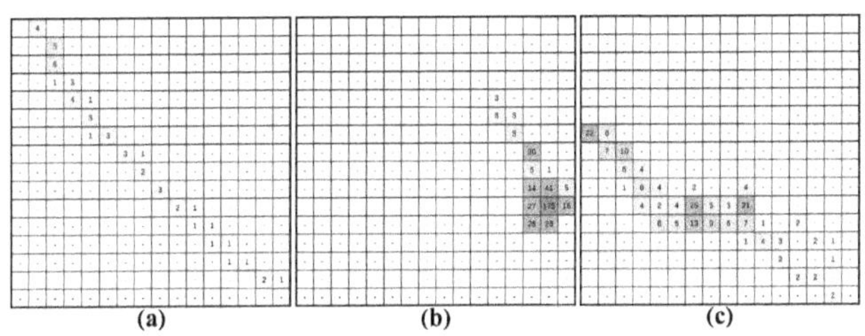

Figure 2: Heatmap examples showing the abstractions of three different movements of a person: a) walk through the area; b) keep waiting in the area; c) walk around, likely loitering in the area.

Fig. 2 shows some heatmap examples. (a) is the heatmap of a person that is walking through the camera view. We can see the person is walking in a straight line and does not stop midway, as the distribution of the moving path is spread out equally. (b) is an example of someone who is waiting. There is a peak in the location the person is waiting, resulting in a skewed distribution. (c) is an example of someone who is loitering, by walking, stopping, changing direction, and repeat. The person moves, stops, changes direction and repeats, causing an uneven distribution with multiple small peaks.

To obtain the latent movement information from these heatmaps, we are inspired by the information entropy theory [4]. We model movement by calculating the entropy over the heatmap. First we determine the probability distribution of the features on the heatmap. In Eq. 1, the probability p_{b_i} of each bin b_i on the heatmap is computed by dividing the count of features ($FC(b_i)$) located in b_i by the total count of features ($FC(CA_j)$) located in the heatmap:

$$p_{b_i} = \frac{FC(b_i)}{FC(CA_j)} \tag{1}$$

Then, we can compute the heatmap entropy (he_j) as follows.

$$he_j = -\sum_{i=1}(p_{b_i}\log(p_{b_i})) \tag{2}$$

Empty bins do not contribute to the entropy, so they are excluded from the computation.

If someone is moving, the features are distributed over the bins, causing the entropy to rise. In addition, if someone has a non-straight trajectory, their path will go through multiple bins, further increasing the entropy. However, if someone is standing still, it skews the distribution over the heatmap, causing the entropy to decrease.

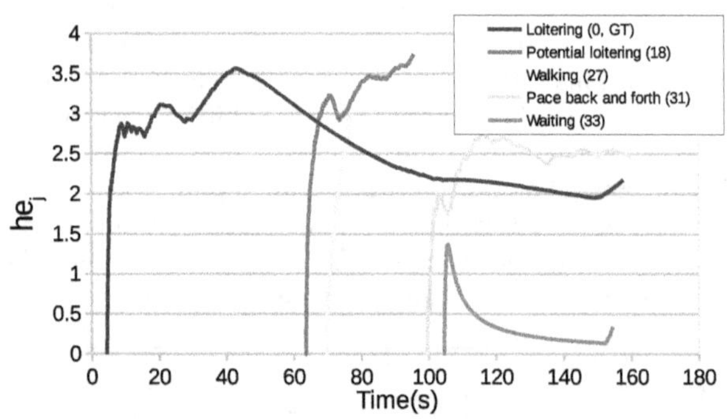

Figure 3: he_j of five persons over time. If someone is moving, the he_j will increase, while standing still causes the he_j to decrease. The he_j going up and down shows move, stop, move, stop behavior. GT indicates the groundtruth loiterer. The legend is associated with the id of a person extracted from the dataset.

Fig. 3 shows the heatmap entropy he_j over time for five persons. Once someone enters the area, their entropy will increase substantially, as only a few bins in the heatmap will be filled. After a few seconds, the entropy will show clear trends depending on the behavior. The ground truth loiterer (blue, 0) starts by pacing through the area causing their entropy to steadily increase. After 40 seconds the person stands still. We see this in the figure as their entropy decreases after that point. The potential loitering candidate (red, 18) enters the area and then stops, changes direction and moves again multiple times causing this person's entropy to increase over time. Note that their entropy is higher than those of people that have been standing still. Someone who is walking through the area (yellow, 27) will have a high entropy as they are only moving, but they score lower than someone who changes direction multiple times. If someone is pacing back and forth (green, 31) in a small area, their entropy will stay roughly the same over time. Finally, if a person is waiting (magenta, 33), their entropy will steadily decrease.

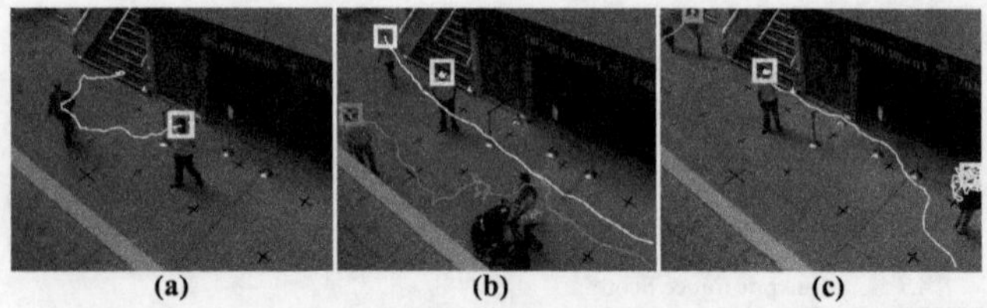

Figure 4: An example selected from the dataset (PETS S1) corresponding to Fig. 3. It shows frames at the times: 40s (a), 70s (b) and 110s (c). In addition, the path is drawn that they will make until the next image. For the last image, the path is drawn until they leave the scene.

If someone is moving through the surveilled scene, they will pass through multiple cameras. For each camera they pass through, we construct a heatmap and calculate its entropy. Next we need to combine the entropy scores into one. Simply adding them up is not a good idea, as this will cause the entropy score of a person to be higher if they pass through more cameras, which is not what we want to measure with the entropy score. Therefore we assign weights to each heatmap, based on their duration. We mainly aim to distinguish between moving and waiting people with this measure. As both of those are associated with a high duration, we weight the heatmaps of cameras the person appeared longer on higher.

We calculate the weight of each heatmap, which we call the presence $P(CA_j)$, based on the duration of the CA_j it belongs to.

$$P(CA_j) = \frac{Dur(CA_j)}{\sum_{j=1}(Dur(CA_j))} \tag{3}$$

Finally, we combine all heatmap entropies of a person together into the weighted entropy score WES.

$$WES = \sum_{j=1}(he_j P(CA_j)) \tag{4}$$

Definition 2 (**WES**: WEIGHTED ENTROPY SCORE). *Given a sequence of CAs, each with their respective heatmap h_j, WES is the weighted combination of the entropy of each h_j. This is a measure for the amount of movement a person shows across multiple cameras.*

In this way, longer CAs are weighted more substantially. Short CAs with high entropy, which will be someone walking through a camera view, will not contribute as much as longer CAs. Someone waiting for a longer time will have low entropy, so while the duration is high, the entropy remains low and therefore will not contribute much to the WES either. Moving in one view for a long time however will have high duration and high entropy, so this will create a high contribution to the WES.

(2) Reappearance. The WES serves as a measure to model the movement of a person. Next we want to model the movement between camera views. Consider two different people moving through the same surveilled area. Person 1 appears on five different cameras once, while person 2 appears on one of the cameras three separate times, and appears once on 2 other cameras. If their duration is the same. They both appear for the same duration and after they leave the area they have 5 CAs each. Using the duration or the entropy is not enough to distinguish between these two behaviors. To be able to model the difference we propose the following definition.

Definition 3 (REAPPEARANCE). *Given a camera C_i, we define reappearance as the same person leaving a camera view and entering it again.*

To use the reappearance into a measure we consider the skewness of reappearance across the cameras as well. For example, someone who goes to do grocery shopping at a nearby store will likely show up on a sequence of cameras twice, once for going to the store and once for returning home. If they appear 2 times on 3 different cameras, they reappear the same amount of times as someone who appears 4 separate times on a single camera. To distinguish between these scenarios, we count each reappearance on a camera as more substantial than the previous one.

With that in mind, we can then calculate a camera reappearance score for a person as follows:

$$RA(C_i) = 2^{a-1} \tag{5}$$

where a is the amount of CAs for that person on camera i. In this way, the more a person reappears on the same camera, the more rapidly the $RA(C_i)$ score increases in exponential scale.

Finally, we need to normalize the $RA(C_i)$ for the amount of cameras. To do this, we add the $RA(C_i)$s together and then divide by the amount of unique the person appeared at least once on. Doing that we get our final ReAppearance Score RAS:

$$RAS = \sum_{i=1}^{n} RA(C_i)/CC \tag{6}$$

Definition 4 (**RAS**: REAPPEARANCE SCORE). *Given all cameras C_i a person has appeared at least once on and their respective $RA(C_i)$, RAS is the weighted combination of reappearances.*

It is a measure of skewed appearance, showing that the person is hanging around a certain area instead of merely walking through it. Therefore, despite the same duration of appearance, someone repeatedly entering and exiting the view of the same camera can be distinguished from someone who only appears once on each camera.

For example, a pickpocket may loiter around a popular meeting spot. To not attract too much attention from bystanders he moves around the area, but keeps returning to look for victims, causing him to repeatedly leave and enter the camera view. This behavior results in a high RAS.

(3) Duration. A person who is in an area for a longer period of time is more likely to be loitering. Therefore, we need to consider the duration as well. First we define the duration of a CA as follows:

Definition 5 ($Dur(CA)$: DURATION OF A CA). *Given the features f_i in CA, we define $Dur(CA)$ as the difference in timestamp between the last and the first f_i in the CA in seconds.*

Then, to calculate the duration measure, we add the duration of all CAs of a person together. In the case that CA durations overlap, we do not count the overlapping durations multiple times. Finally, duration of people can vary substantially, especially in larger surveillance systems. To reduce the impact of these large difference, we scale the duration score as follows by taking the logarithm over the final duration:

$$DS = \log(\sum_{j=1}(Dur(CA_j)) + 1) \tag{7}$$

Note that we add 1 to the duration before calculating the logarithm to prevent negative values for durations less than 1.

(4) Loitering Score. Each of the measures above account for an aspect of loitering behavior. To provide a list of candidates, we combine the measures above into one loitering score. Depending on the situation, an operator might consider one aspect of loitering more important than others. Therefore we provide weights to each of the measures, so the total score can be fine tuned based on the needs of the operator.

$$LS = \alpha RAS + \beta WES + \gamma DS \tag{8}$$

Definition 6 (**LS**: LOITERING SCORE). *Given the RAS, WES and DS, as well as the weights α, β and γ, we define LS as the weighted combination of the three measures. A higher score indicates that the person is more likely to be loitering.*

Each factor can be scaled by its associated weight α, β and γ. As the score is a comparative value, these do not have to add up to 1, only the ratio between the three should be considered.

The LS is used to give a ranking of loitering candidates. The score on its own is meaningless and serves mainly as a comparison value between candidates. Likewise, the score is bound to the system it was obtained in and should not be used to compare to the score of another system.

3.2 Implementation

Next we will go over how we create our candidate list. For this we use Algorithm 2. After some pre-processing, it calculates the measures for entropy, reappearance and duration for each person. The measures are then combined into the loitering score. Finally, it outputs a list of candidates ordered by loitering score. Below we will go over each part of the algorithm.

Algorithm 1: GroupFeatures()

```
Input: Features list FL^j containing features f_i^j of
       person j.
Output: List CAL^j containing CA_i^j
1  begin
2    Sort FL^j on timestamp ;
3    foreach Feature f_i^j do
4      Find CA_i for f_i^j.cameraID ;
5      if f_i^j.timestamp - CA_i.last.timestamp > T_ca
       then
6        CAL^j.push(CA) ;
7        Create new CA for f_i^j.cameraID
8      Add f_i^j to CA ;
9    foreach Open CA_i do
10     CAL^j.push(CA) ;
11   return CAL^j ;
```

Pre-processing. Before we can calculate our measures, we first need to do some pre-processing on our data. Each of the features comes attached with the following metadata: a person identifier, a camera identifier, a timestamp and the position in the camera view. We need to group these features into CAs. See Algorithm 1.

First the features are sorted by timestamp so they are in chronological order (line 2). As people can appear simultaneously on multiple cameras, we keep track of open cameras. For each feature we add to a CA, we compare the timestamp of the last feature added to that CA (line 5). If the time difference exceeds the T_{ca}, we close the old CA and push it to the list. The feature is then added to a new CA for the same camera (line 6 and 7). Otherwise, we just add the feature to the existing CA (line 8).

Finally, after we have added all features to a CA we push the remaining CAs (line 9 and 10) and return the list (line 11). We then use this list of CAs for that person to calculate the measures.

Measures. The construction of the candidate list can be seen in Algorithm 2. For each person, we group the features into CAs (line 3). Then we construct a heatmap for each of the CAs. We split the heatmap into bins according to the hD (line 5). For an hD of 16, we split the heatmap into 16x16 bins, for a total of 256 bins. Next we iterate over the features in the CA. We map the center coordinates of the position

Algorithm 2: BuildCandidateList()

```
Input: Data set ds with features f_i^j grouped by person
       j, RAS scalar α, WES scalar β, Duration scalar
       γ, heatmap Dimension hD
Output: List of candidates CL ordered by score.
1  begin
2    foreach Candidate j ∈ ds do
3      CAL^j ← GroupFeatures() ;
4      foreach CA in CAL do
5        Construct heatmap of CA with hD dims. ;
6        Compute he_j by using Eq. (2) ;
7      Compute WES using Eq. (4) ;
8      Compute RAS using Eq. (6) ;
9      Compute DS using Eq. (7) ;
10     Compute LS using Eq. (8) ;
11     CL.push(j) ;
12   Sort CL by LS ;
13   return CL ;
```

metadata of the feature to the heatmap to the appropriate bin in the heatmap. Next we calculate the entropy over each heatmap (line 6).

After that, we have the information we need to calculate the measures WES, RAS and DS (line 7, 8 and 9). We then calculate the LS by scaling each measure with their appropriate scalar (line 10), after which the processing for that candidate is done. Finally, we push the candidate j to the candidate list CL (line 11) and continue to next person.

After all people have scores assigned to them, we order the candidate list on the LS (line 12).

4 EXPERIMENTS

The experiments were conducted on the Ubuntu 16.04 OS, with an Intel® Core™ i7-6700 CPU @ 3.40GHz and 11 GB of memory. We evaluate our approach using two datasets.

- AntiLoiter Dataset[1] [9, 10], and
- PETS 2007[2] Scenario 1 (PETS S1) and Scenario 3 (PETS S3).

AntiLoiter Dataset. A multi-scene multi-camera dataset containing groups of people walking in public areas. Videos are high resolution (1920x1080). Faces are clearly visible and timestamp information is provided. One designated person acting as a real loiterer shows up repeatedly on multiple cameras.

PETS2007 Dataset. Single-scene multi-camera footage of an airport. The cameras have a resolution of 768x576, which consist of multiple scenes for the detection of loitering and abandoned luggage. To compare our approach to one of the state of the art [12] and to show that we can use our approach on single camera scenes we only use the third

[1] https://github.com/ryukenzen/antiloiter/
[2] http://www.cvg.reading.ac.uk/PETS2007/data.html

camera of each scenario to extract the trajectories of persons. To show that input can be provided by means of a tracking method, we annotate the features semi-manually, by iterating over a subset of the frames (every 4th frame) and selecting the face of each candidate while they are visible on the footage. We receive the features in a similar way as an accurate tracking method that can deal with occlusions. We use the datasets PETS S1 and PETS S3 for our comparison. PETS S1 is a scene that shows one person loitering in the scene. PETS S3 has 2 people waiting and 2 people entering the scene, exchanging bags and leaving the scene. Loitering in this dataset is explicitly defined as someone appearing longer than 60 seconds (see Fig. 4).

4.1 Parameter Evaluation

Heatmap dimensions. One of the parameters in our system is the heatmap bin dimensions. Changing the dimensions will affect the calculation of the WES in a few ways. Using a small amount of bins will make it difficult to distinguish between those standing still and walking around a small area. It also runs the risk of putting someone in a single bin for their entire appearance duration, causing their entropy value to be zero. On the other extreme end, having a bin for each pixel makes it almost impossible to distinguish between waiting and moving. Even the smallest of movements will cause a waiting person to be split across a large amount of bins. Additionally, a large amount of bins will require a lot of processing time. Therefore, our bin count should be as low as possible, without losing too much information about the movement. We have conducted experiments on PETS S1 and S3 by varying the bin dimensions in different sizes.

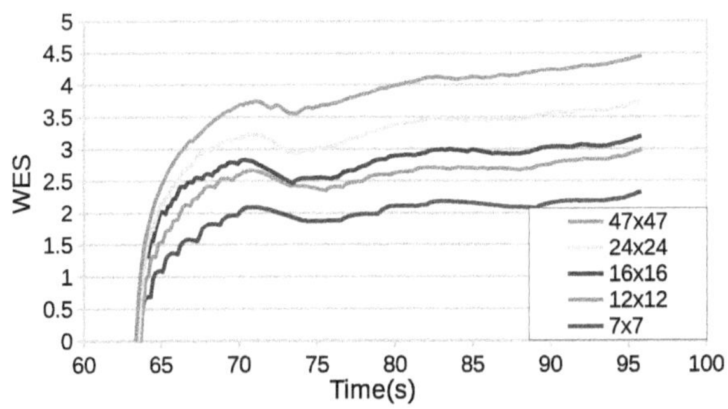

Figure 5: Effect of the heatmap dimensions on the WES over time of a loitering candidate in PETS S1. The WES increases with heatmap dimension size from 7x7 to 47x47.

Fig. 5 shows the WES over time of a loitering candidate in PETS S1 for different heatmap dimensions. As shown in the figure, the WES increases steadily with the dimension size, such as from 7x7 to 47x47.

Fig. 6 shows the results of changing the heatmap dimensions for a waiting person. As this person is mostly standing still, using low heatmap dimensions such as 12x12 and below will cause only one bin to be filled with features, which results in an entropy of 0. Therefore we want to take heatmap

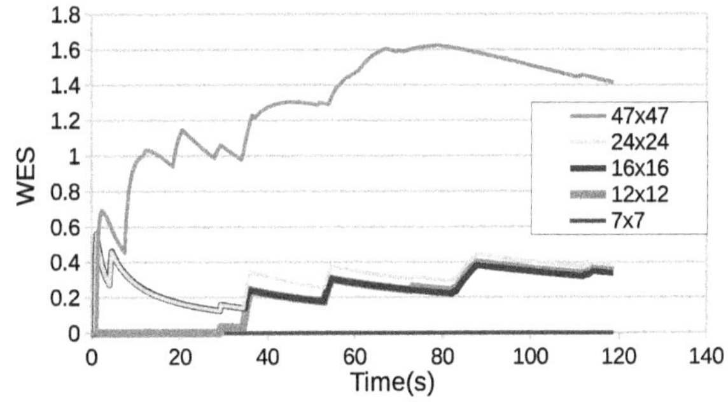

Figure 6: Effect of the heatmap dimensions on the WES over time of a waiting person in PETS S3. Low heatmap dimensions will cause the WES to be 0.

dimensions above 12x12, to make sure that people that are waiting still have a non-zero entropy value.

Scaling Parameters. We cover three different measures that together provide a loitering score. However, depending on the scene, each measure does not contribute equally to the final score. For this we introduced the scaling parameters: α for the RAS, β for the WES and γ for the DS. We have tested several parameter configurations. For each of the datasets, we took several candidates of interests, and plotted their rank for each of the parameter settings. They can be seen in Fig. 7, 8 and 9.

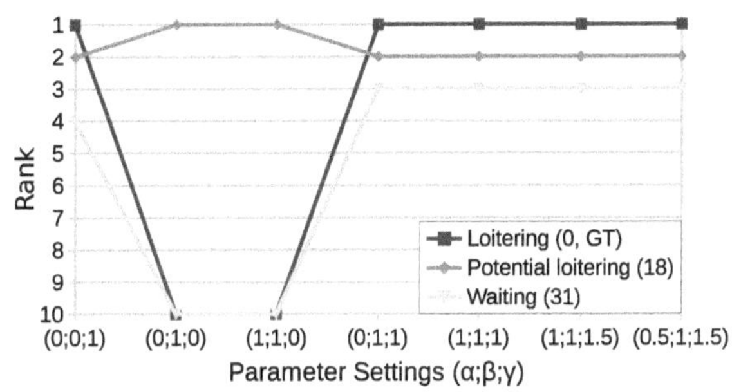

Figure 7: Effect of the scaling parameters on the ranking of several candidates from PETS S1

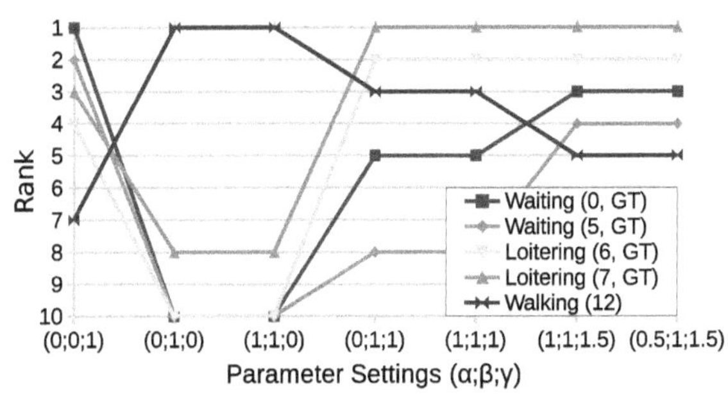

Figure 8: Effect of the scaling parameters on the ranking of several candidates from PETS S3

Using only the duration (0;0;1) like other methods do, we already get reasonable results for PETS2007 and AntiLoiter.

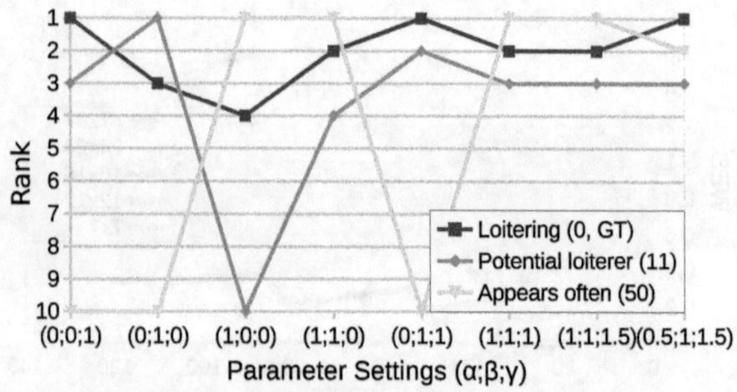

Figure 9: Effect of the scaling parameters on the ranking of several candidates from the AntiLoiter dataset

If we only use the WES (0;1;0) the candidates are ordered by the amount of their movement. Using this measure alone decreases the ranking of the ground truths, as they also stand still occasionally. While the measure does not appear to be sensitive when used alone, it does score the people that move a lot as more likely loitering candidates.

Only using the RAS (1;0;0) will score everyone in the PETS2007 datasets equally, as there are no reappearing candidates in that dataset. Therefore we removed this setting from Fig. 7 and 8. For the AntiLoiter dataset we now focus solely on people that reappear on cameras the most.

When all measures equally contribute (1;1;1) to the loitering score, we see that candidates that move around more are scored higher than those that do not. However, as seen in Fig. 7, people that are just briefly walking through the area are now scoring higher than those waiting for a very long time. Therefore we increase the weight of the duration (1;1;1.5). Finally, we decrease the weight of the RAS (0.5;1;1.5) to decrease the effect of repeated appearance.

4.2 Comparison with Related Work

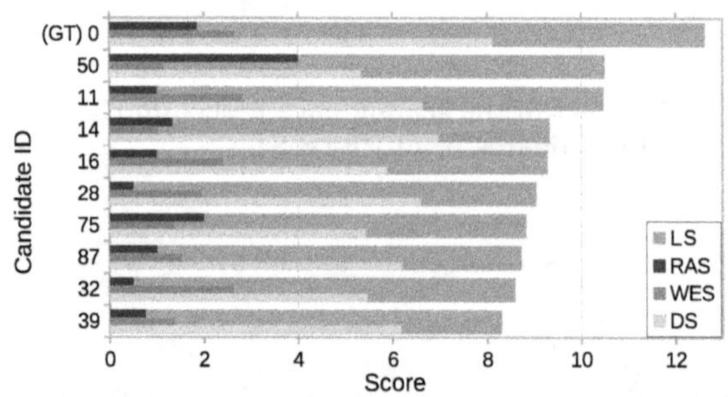

Figure 10: Top 10 candidates on the AntiLoiter Dataset

We compared our method to two states of the art [10, 12]. The following parameters were used: $\alpha = 0.5$, $\beta = 1.0$, $\gamma = 1.5$, heatmap dimensions: 16x16. Fig. 10, 11 and 12 show the top loitering candidates for each dataset. We provide all ground-truth loiterers as candidates ranked at 1st place, without requiring a loitering time threshold to select candidates.

We summarize our comparison with the related work in Table 2 where P denotes the precision and R denotes the recall. Our method accurately provides the list of ground truth loiterers. In addition to this, it provides additional interesting candidates.

Comparison with AntiLoiter is shown in Fig. 10. The ground truth loiterer is given as the first loitering candidate. Candidate with ID 50 reappears in the same scene at different times. This causes the high RAS. It is worth noting that the WES is relatively low, due to the people being grouped as one candidate because they were in a similar area. However, due to our chosen α we account for this, by making the RAS contribute less to the total score. If Candidate 50 would be one person however, (s)he would have very suspicious behavior, repeatedly entering and exiting the same area in a short amount of time. Our method shows other candidates based on reappearance, such as candidate 11, who walks through the area for a moderate duration, but also passes one of the cameras twice.

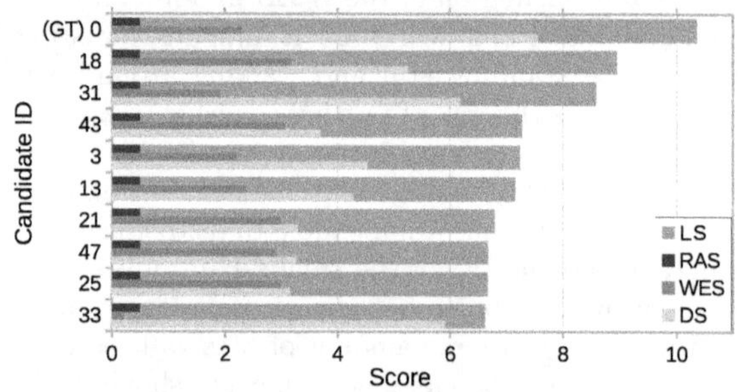

Figure 11: Top 10 candidates on PETS S1

In the comparison on PETS S1 there is one person entering the scene and moving around before leaving. This person with ID 0 is the only ground truth in this scene. As shown in Fig. 11, we provide the person as the top candidate. We provide some other candidates as well. We examined the video to confirm that candidate 18 enters the scene and has very loiter-like behavior: Move, stop, look-around, repeat. Candidate 31 enters the scene and paces around a small area. While staying longer in the scene than candidate 18, this person was staying in one area and therefore is scored lower.

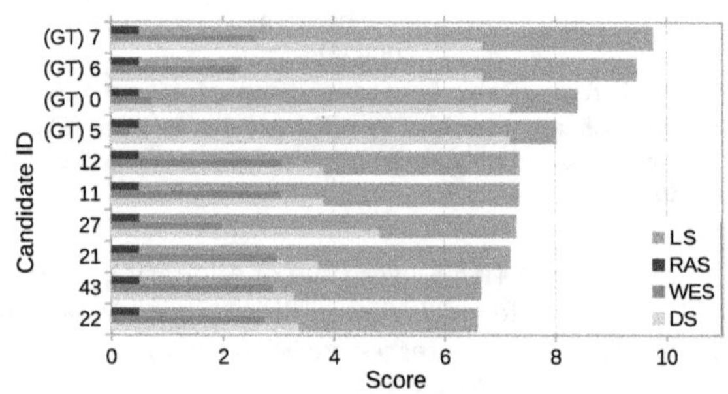

Figure 12: Top 10 candidates on PETS S3

In the comparison on PETS S3 there are two people in view, candidates 0 and 5, that remain in place for the full duration of the footage, only moving slightly every now and

Table 2: Comparison of the results

	Datasets		AntiLoiter	PETS	
Method				S1	S3
MM16 [9],[10]		P	100%	-	-
		R	100%	-	-
MTA15 [12]		P	-	99.8%	100%
		R	-	96.22%	58.85%
Our method	Top 1	P	**100%**	**100%**	-
		R	**100%**	**100%**	-
	Top 4	P	-	-	**100%**
		R	-	-	**100%**

then. Candidates 6 and 7 enter the scene a bit later, move around and exchange bags, before leaving again. These 4 candidates are the ground truth of loiterers for this scene. Despite candidate 6 and 7 having a lower appearance, they score as higher loiterers because they move around a lot in the scene. As shown in Fig. 12, we provide them as the top candidates. We provide another candidate as well: Candidate 27 enters the scene, stops, walks, stops and then leaves the scene, who would be in a high opportunity to be considered as a potential loiterer.

5 DISCUSSION AND FUTURE WORK

We did not have an optimal dataset to test our approach fully. For future work, we should create a dataset that shows loitering, waiting and normal behavior (as well as providing the ground truth for these behaviors) of pedestrians in a multi-camera scene, across a large time period.

A formal definition of loitering should be considered as well. The WES has been made with the assumption that someone who moves around should be considered more suspicious than someone that is standing still. This definition will differ depending on the situation.

The system could be improved by allowing different parameter settings per camera. This could be useful if the system operator has knowledge of the area. For example, a popular meeting area could have a lower WES contribution, as there are many people waiting in this area, but a higher RAS contribution to detect pickpockets who reappear multiple times in the same or multiple cameras

6 CONCLUSION

We proposed an entropy model and ranking measure that can retrieve a list of loitering candidates. The features used for input can either be obtained through tracking, or appearance methods. The results are comparable to state of the art and give additional candidates as potential loiterers. Our approach scores moving people higher than waiting people, despite their appearance being shorter.

REFERENCES

[1] Dejan Arsic, Martin Hofmann, Björn Schuller, and Gerhard Rigoll. 2007. Multi-camera person tracking and left luggage detection applying homographic transformation. In *Proceedings of Tenth IEEE International Workshop on Performance Evaluation of Tracking and Surveillance, PETS.*

[2] Nathaniel D Bird, Osama Masoud, Nikolaos P Papanikolopoulos, and Aaron Isaacs. 2005. Detection of loitering individuals in public transportation areas. *IEEE Transactions on intelligent transportation systems* 6, 2 (2005), 167–177.

[3] Mohannad Elhamod and Martin D Levine. 2013. Automated real-time detection of potentially suspicious behavior in public transport areas. *IEEE Transactions on Intelligent Transportation Systems* 14, 2 (2013), 688–699.

[4] R.M. Gray. 2011. *Entropy and Information Theory.* Springer US. https://books.google.co.jp/books?id=wdSOqgVbdRcC

[5] Chung-Hsien Huang, Yi-Ta Wu, and Ming-Yu Shih. 2009. Unsupervised pedestrian re-identification for loitering detection. In *Pacific-Rim Symposium on Image and Video Technology.* Springer, 771–783.

[6] Shian-Ru Ke, Hoang Le Uyen Thuc, Yong-Jin Lee, Jenq-Neng Hwang, Jang-Hee Yoo, and Kyoung-Ho Choi. 2013. A review on video-based human activity recognition. *Computers* 2, 2 (2013), 88–131.

[7] Jong-Gook Ko and Jang-Hee Yoo. 2013. Rectified trajectory analysis based abnormal loitering detection for video surveillance. In *Artificial Intelligence, Modelling and Simulation (AIMS), 2013 1st International Conference on.* IEEE, 289–293.

[8] Wenting Li, Dongping Zhang, Min Sun, Yibo Yin, and Ye Shen. 2015. Loitering Detection Based on Trajectory Analysis. In *Intelligent Computation Technology and Automation (ICICTA), 2015 8th International Conference on.* IEEE, 530–533.

[9] Jianquan Liu, Shoji Nishimura, and Takuya Araki. 2016. AntiLoiter: A Loitering Discovery System for Longtime Videos across Multiple Surveillance Cameras. In *Proceedings of the 2016 ACM Conference on Multimedia Conference, MM 2016, Amsterdam, The Netherlands, October 15-19, 2016.* 675–679. https://doi.org/10.1145/2964284.2970927

[10] Jianquan Liu, Shoji Nishimura, Takuya Araki, and Yuichi Nakamura. 2017. A Loitering Discovery System Using Efficient Similarity Search Based on Similarity Hierarchy. *IEICE Transactions* 100-A, 2 (2017), 367–375. http://search.ieice.org/bin/summary.php?id=e100-a_2_367

[11] Ruipeng Lu, Hua Yang, Ji Zhu, Shuang Wu, Jia Wang, and David Bull. 2015. Hierarchical video summarization with loitering indication. In *Visual Communications and Image Processing (VCIP), 2015.* IEEE, 1–4.

[12] Yunyoung Nam. 2015. Loitering detection using an associating pedestrian tracker in crowded scenes. *Multimedia Tools and Applications* 74, 9 (2015), 2939–2961.

[13] Keon-woo Park, Doo-sik Kang, Jun-sik Kim, and Myeong-jin Lee. 2016. Loitering Detection based on Regional Histogram and Object Velocity. (2016), 1304–1305.

[14] Wei-Ya Ren, Guo-Hui Li, Jun Chen, and Hao-Zhe Liang. 2012. Abnormal crowd behavior detection using behavior entropy model. In *Wavelet Analysis and Pattern Recognition (ICWAPR), 2012 International Conference on.* IEEE, 212–221.

[15] Scott A. Richmond and Patric R. Spence. 2013. Loitering. In *Encyclopedia of Street Crime in America,* Jeffrey Ian Ross (Ed.). SAGE Publications, Inc, 240–241. https://doi.org/10.4135/9781452274461

[16] Rafael Martínez Tomás, Susana Arias Tapia, Antonio Fernández Caballero, Sylvie Ratté, Alexandra González Eras, Patricia Ludeña González, et al. 2015. Identification of loitering human behaviour in video surveillance environments. In *International Work-Conference on the Interplay Between Natural and Artificial Computation.* Springer, 516–525.

[17] Guogang Xiong, Xinyu Wu, Yen-lun Chen, and Yongsheng Ou. 2011. Abnormal crowd behavior detection based on the energy model. In *Information and Automation (ICIA), 2011 IEEE International Conference on.* IEEE, 495–500.

Visual Question Answering With a Hybrid Convolution Recurrent Model

Philipp Harzig
University of Augsburg
Augsburg, Germany
philipp.harzig@informatik.uni-augsburg.de

Christian Eggert
University of Augsburg
Augsburg, Germany
christian.eggert@informatik.uni-augsburg.de

Rainer Lienhart
University of Augsburg
Augsburg, Germany
rainer.lienhart@informatik.uni-augsburg.de

ABSTRACT

Visual Question Answering (VQA) is a relatively new task, which tries to infer answer sentences for an input image coupled with a corresponding question. Instead of dynamically generating answers, they are usually inferred by finding the most probable answer from a fixed set of possible answers. Previous work did not address the problem of finding all possible answers, but only modeled the answering part of VQA as a classification task. To tackle this problem, we infer answer sentences by using a Long Short-Term Memory (LSTM) network that allows us to dynamically generate answers for (image, question) pairs. In a series of experiments, we discover an end-to-end Deep Neural Network structure, which allows us to dynamically answer questions referring to a given input image by using an LSTM decoder network. With this approach, we are able to generate both less common answers, which are not considered by classification models, and more complex answers with the appearance of datasets containing answers that consist of more than three words.

CCS CONCEPTS

• **Information systems → Multimedia and multimodal retrieval**; • **Computing methodologies → Natural language generation**; **Speech recognition**; **Scene understanding**; **Neural networks**; *Image representations*;

KEYWORDS

VQA, Visual Question Answering, multimodal retrieval, natural language generation, LSTM, multimodal fusion

ACM Reference Format:
Philipp Harzig, Christian Eggert, and Rainer Lienhart. 2018. Visual Question Answering With a Hybrid Convolution Recurrent Model. In *ICMR '18: 2018 International Conference on Multimedia Retrieval, June 11–14, 2018, Yokohama, Japan.* ACM, New York, NY, USA, 8 pages. https://doi.org/10.1145/3206025.3206054

ICMR '18, June 11–14, 2018, Yokohama, Japan

ACM ISBN 978-1-4503-5046-4/18/06...$15.00
https://doi.org/10.1145/3206025.3206054

1 INTRODUCTION

In recent years, the machine learning community rapidly adapted neural networks. Especially, Deep Convolutional Neural Networks (DCNNs) developed into the main method for extracting representations from images. Over time, the models got deeper, more complex [10, 22, 23] and achieved higher accuracies in the ImageNet Challenge [21]. Because these models are trained on a very large dataset of images, they learn to extract a good feature representation of images and, thus, are also used for other problems than image classification. Additionally, methods for interpreting language in form of sentences were also not unaffected by the advances in neural networks. Recurrent Neural Networks (RNNs) have become the standard in extracting information from text or creating sentences. Particularly, a special form of RNNs called Long Short-Term Memory (LSTM) [12] networks are nowadays used widely in natural language processing.

A new task called Visual Question Answering (VQA) emerged lately. In VQA, an image and a question regarding that image are the inputs, and a sentence answering the question is the desired output. In other words, the VQA task is a model that answers questions asked for an input image. This task is challenging, because a good understanding both of images and natural language is essential to be able to predict the answer of a question asked regarding the contents of the image. Its difficulty lies in fusing feature representations of the image and question into a joint representation, which then makes it possible to generate an answer for that very image-question pair. Unlike most other approaches, we use an LSTM network to generate the answers for the VQA task. The general practice is to extract the most common answers from the training set and predict the answers by choosing the most likely answer out of a fixed predefined set. Teney et al. [24] treat VQA as a multi-label classification task, i.e., for a given image and question the answer is predicted from a fixed set of answers. This strategy delivers good scores as the official evaluation metric is the accuracy. Hence, a fixed set of the most common answers has a greater influence on the score than less common answers. We tackle the serious drawback of leaving out the less common answers altogether. We deal with this problem by constructing the answer with an LSTM network, which can produce answers out of the entire vocabulary corpus.

Our main contributions are as follows: (1) We use a CNN network to extract features from the input question, which has been shown to work better than an LSTM encoding in our case. (2) We compare different approaches, which embed the question and image features into a joint semantic space. (3) We do not see the VQA task as a classification problem but rather we see it as a more complex problem that can not be approximated by some 3000 possible answers.

Natural language is more complex than a set of predefined answers, thus, we replace the fully-connected classification layer with an LSTM network, that can produce arbitrary sentences. Finally, (4) we find out that our architecture is able to produce new answers not contained in the training set at all, some of which we show in a qualitative analysis.

2 RELATED WORK

When it comes to VQA, we face the challenge to process image data properly, process natural language and correctly fuse them in order to answer the questions regarding the image accurately. In this section, we give an overview of related work in all of those research areas.

Natural language processing. Natural language processing is a long-studied topic in computer vision. Barnard et al. [3] present a statistical model that learns relationships between visual information from images and text information coming with the images. Farhadi et al. [6] infer triplets consisting of object, action and scene from handcrafted image features and transfer them to text afterwards. Similarly, Li et al. [17] use image features to compose sentences from scratch by using a text corpus comprised of n-grams gathered from the web. Lately, Recurrent Neural Networks (RNNs) in form of Long Short-Term Memory (LSTM) [12] networks became very popular in both understanding text and generating text.
The encoder/decoder structure used by current image captioning approaches as well as our VQA model is heavily influenced by machine translation networks that transform a sentence from one language into another. For example, Google [27] uses LSTM-driven neural networks for their translation system. Facebook [8] goes into another direction and eliminates the LSTM layers by replacing them through ordinary convolutional layers resulting in better performance both in speed and accuracy.

Image Captioning. The image captioning task is closely related to the VQA task. The goal of image captioning is to create a natural language sentence that describes a given input image. VQA can be seen as a special case of image captioning, where the input question modality is added to the model and answers instead of descriptions should be generated. Different approaches appeared over time which try to convert the content of images into text fragments. State-of-the-art approaches still use the idea of extracting features from an image and converting them into a natural language sentence. They use modern image classification DCNNs like [23] as a feature extractor. One such architecture is the Show and Tell model by Vinyals et al. [25, 26], which makes use of recurrent neural networks for sequence modeling to convert image features into human-like sentences. Also Karpathy et al. [15] utilize neural networks for sequence modeling in form of a Bidirectional Recurrent Neural Network to generate captions for images. They refine their model to additionally describe parts of the image instead of captioning the image as a whole and call this method dense captioning [13, 14]. Different approaches and their performances are reported on the website for the MSCOCO [4, 18] captioning challenge.

Joint multimodal embeddings. There are a lot of approaches that deal with combining multiple modalities in a joint embedding space. Zhou et al. [30] propose a simple VQA architecture, which concatenates image and question modalities. Other models use simple element-wise multiplication of question and image features [2, 24]. Fukui et al. [7] state that the outer product between question and image modalities are more expressive than a vector concatenation or an element-wise product and introduce a technique called Multimodal Compact Linear pooling. However, the outer product is infeasible due to its high dimensionality, hence they project the outer product into a lower dimensional space. Yu et al. [28] also use a bilinear pooling model to project the image and question into a joint embedding space (see Section 5.3).

VQA architectures. For the original VQA [2] task, many architectures have been presented. For example, Zhou et al. [30] proposed a simple architecture, that uses a simple bag-of-words model as question features and image feature vectors extracted by a CNN. The creators of the original VQA dataset themselves introduced a model that trains a classification model on the 1000 most frequent answers. They use an LSTM model for the question embedding and the VGGNet [22] as the image feature extractor DCNN. Finally, Fukui et al. [7] won the VQA challenge by using Multimodal Compact Linear pooling.
The VQA v2 [9] dataset, which is a balanced version of the VQA dataset (see Section 3 for details), makes it harder to achieve high scores. In their analysis, Goyal et al. found out that many VQA models take advantage of language priors to predict the target answers. Teney et al. [24] present an architecture that uses soft scores as ground truth targets instead of using one-hot targets as used in traditional classification. They also implement a bottom-up attention to attend to specific regions of the images. With those and other findings they won the 2017 VQA challenge. After the challenge has ended, Yu et al. [28] even surpassed Teney et al. on the VQA-v2 open ended challenge leaderboard by using the Multimodal Factorized Bilinear pooling (MFB) approach.

3 DATASET

We train and test our model on the VQA-v2 [9] dataset, which is a balanced version of the original VQA [2] dataset. The VQA dataset is built upon the MSCOCO [18] dataset and contains (question, answer) pairs for a subset of the MSCOCO images. Goyal et al. [9] balanced the VQA dataset in such a way, that for every question there are two similar images that have differing answers to that question and, therefore, containing about twice the number of questions. They also found out that models trained on the first version of the dataset exploit language priors, thus, performing worse on the VQA-v2 dataset. Their dataset contains 443K, 214K and 453K questions in the train split, validation split and test split, respectively. The test split is divided into four subsplits: test-dev, test-standard, test-challenge and test-reserve. There is an online evaluation server[1] for generated answers on the test-dev and test-standard split known as the *VQA Real Image Challenge 2017 (Open-Ended)*. On average, the VQA-v2 dataset contains 5.34 questions per image and 53.4 answers per image, i.e., every question was answered by 10 different annotators. Every question has a ground-truth of 10 answers, whereas every answer is flagged, whether the annotator was confident to

[1] https://evalai.cloudcv.org/web/challenges/challenge-page/1/overview, test-dev allows 10 submissions per day, while test-standard is limited to 5 submissions in total.

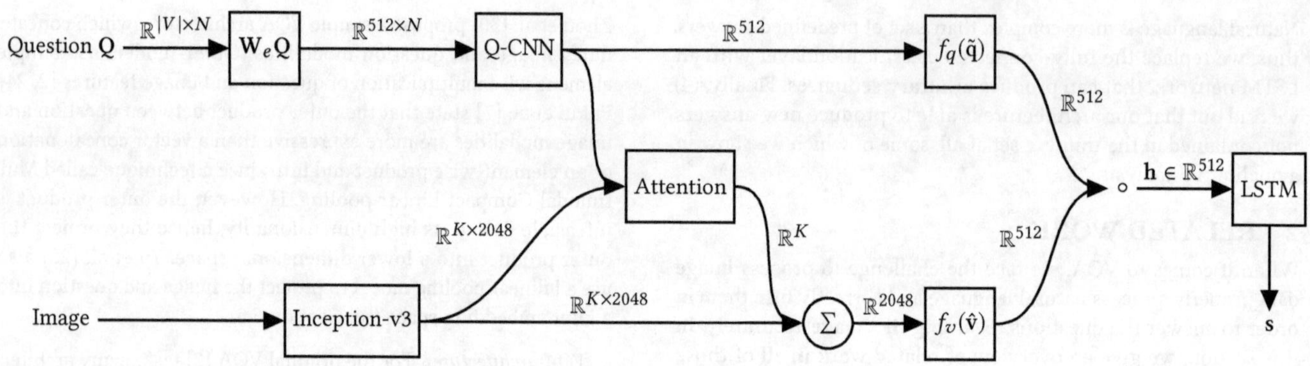

Figure 1: Architecture of our VQA model. We embed the question Q via the word embedding matrix $\mathbf{W}_e$ and extract the question features with a residual CNN. We attend to the image feature maps produced by the *Inception-v3* network with an attention mechanism producing a single weighted feature vector. We feed the image and question features through non-linear layers f and extract a joint multimodal feature vector h by element-wise multiplication.

answer the question correctly. We only use confident answers, i.e., every question has 8.11 confident answers on average.

For our studies we rebalance the train and validation splits, so we use the train split and 90% of the validation split as training set and the remaining 10% of the validation split as the validation set. We do this to have a larger training corpus available. For evaluating the performance of our models, we use the standard VQA script by Antol et al. [2]. This script calculates the overall accuracy and the accuracies over three different answer categories. These are yes/no answers (Y/N), number answers and other answers.

For some of our experiments, we extend the dataset by the popular Visual Genome [16] dataset, which contains an additional 1.7 million Visual Question Answers on 108,077 images.

4 MODEL

Our VQA model is composed of multiple components. We embed the question into a feature vector via a CNN and extract a feature vector from the corresponding image via a DCNN (*Inception-v3* [23] network in our case). We attend to the features of the input image via the question and combine both feature vectors via multimodal fusion into a single representation of the image-question pair. Instead of modeling the answering part as a classification task, we generate the answer with an LSTM network. We depict our architecture with the decoder LSTM in Figure 1. In the following, we describe each part of our architecture.

4.1 Question embedding

We add a start word <S> at the beginning and an end word </S> to the end of each question. Additionally, we tokenize each question by splitting it up into single words. We allow questions to be of any length and construct our vocabulary V from all words contained in the questions and answers (we tokenize answers the same way as we do with the questions). Each word in the question $\mathbf{Q} = (\mathbf{q}_0, \ldots, \mathbf{q}_N)$ of length N is represented by a one-hot vector $\mathbf{q}_t$, where t is the time-step or the index of the current word in the input question. We embed each word of the question into vectors

$$\hat{\mathbf{q}}_t = \mathbf{W}_e \mathbf{q}_t, t \in 0 \ldots N-1 \tag{1}$$

of dimenstion $m = 512$, where $\mathbf{W}_e \in \mathbb{R}^{512\times|V|}$.

For getting a feature representation of the whole sentence, we feed the sentence through a couple of convolutional layers. We use gated convolutions in a residual architecture like Dauphin et al. [5]. In particular, they state that CNNs do not suffer from vanishing and exploding gradients like RNNs do and, therefore, a forget gate used in RNNs like LSTMs is not required in CNNs, which process language. However, they find that allowing the network to control what information should be propagated through the layers via output gates is useful for language modeling and introduce the gated linear unit (GLU), which learns which information should be forwarded to the next layer. For each GLU we learn parameters for two convolution operations ($*$) with the same number of output feature maps m and calculate its result as

$$GLU(\mathbf{X}) = (\mathbf{X} * \mathbf{W}_{c1} + \mathbf{b}_{c1}) \circ \sigma(\mathbf{X} * \mathbf{W}_{c2} + \mathbf{b}_{c2}) \tag{2}$$

where $\mathbf{X} \in \mathbb{R}^{N\times m}$ is the input of the GLU and $\mathbf{W}_{c1} \in \mathbb{R}^{k\times m\times n}$, $\mathbf{b}_{c1} \in \mathbb{R}^n$, $\mathbf{W}_{c2} \in \mathbb{R}^{k\times m\times n}$, $\mathbf{b}_{c2} \in \mathbb{R}^n$ are learned parameters. Note that k is the kernel size of the convolution, $n = 512$ are the number of outputs and $\circ$ is the elementwise multiplication, so the output of the GLU is of dimensionality $\mathbb{R}^{N\times n}$. We visualize the architecture of a GLU in Figure 2.

We feed our embedded question through a GLU with $n = 512, k = 5$ followed by two residual blocks, each consisting out of two GLUs with a skip connection from the input to the output. We depict our question embedding architecture in Figure 3. Finally, we use global average pooling across the question length N to reduce the dimensionality of each question feature representation from $\mathbb{R}^{N\times n}$ to $\tilde{\mathbf{q}} \in \mathbb{R}^n$.

4.2 Image embedding

We also extract a feature representation from each input image with a DCNN, namely, we use the *Inception-v3* [23] architecture. We obtain a feature vector of size $K \times 2048$, where $K = 8 \times 8 = 64$

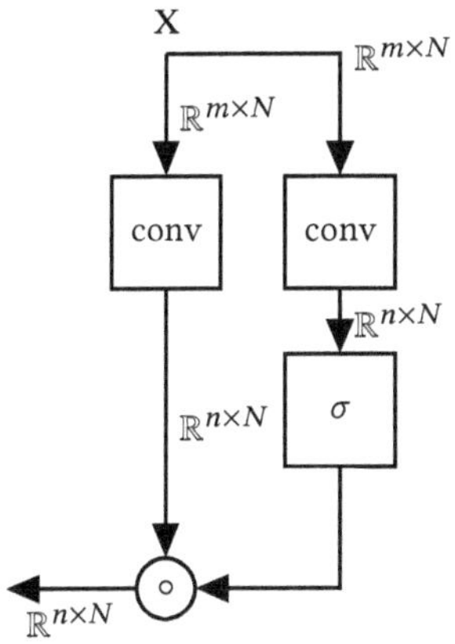

Figure 2: A gated linear unit (GLU). Inputs X are fed through a convolution layer twice with different parameter sets. One convolution layer has a sigmoid activation function while the other has no activation function. Their outputs are multiplied pointwise.

from the *Mixed_7c* layer in the case of the *Inception-v3* network. For our experiments we use (a) a global average pooled feature representation of size 2048 or (b) the feature vector of size $K \times 2048$ in the case of image attention (see Section 4.3).

4.3 Image attention

Similarly to Teney et al. [24], we use a simple form of image attention that attends to certain areas of the image. We do not use features from image regions extracted by a object detection pipeline like Faster-RCNN [20], but only attend to spatial locations on the feature map of the image. The feature map has a size of 8×8 with 2048 dimensions each, which corresponds to $K = 64$ image locations. We denote each location $i = 1 \ldots K$ by $\mathbf{v}_i$ and concatenate it with the question representation $\tilde{\mathbf{q}}$ and feed them through a non-linear layer f_a (see Section 4.4) to learn a scalar attention weight α_i for each image location.

$$\mathbf{a}_i = \mathbf{W}_a f_a([\mathbf{v}_i, \tilde{\mathbf{q}}]) \quad (3)$$
$$\boldsymbol{\alpha} = \text{softmax}(\mathbf{a}) \quad (4)$$
$$\hat{\mathbf{v}} = \sum_{i=1}^{K} \alpha_i \mathbf{v}_i, \quad (5)$$

where $\mathbf{W}_a \in \mathbb{R}^{K\times 2560}$ is a learned parameter matrix. In the case (b) of no image attention, we use global average pooled feature map as described in Section 4.2 ($\hat{\mathbf{v}} = \text{avg\_pool}(\mathbf{v})$).

4.4 Multimodal fusion

We need to project the question embedding and image embedding into a joint semantic space to be able to produce answers dependent both on the input image and the question. To do this, we first reduce the dimensionality of the image embedding to match the question embedding size of $n = 512$. Again, we use the non-linear layer f from [24], which is defined as a function $f_\theta : \mathbf{x} \in \mathbb{R}^\mu \rightarrow \mathbf{y} \in \mathbb{R}^\nu$

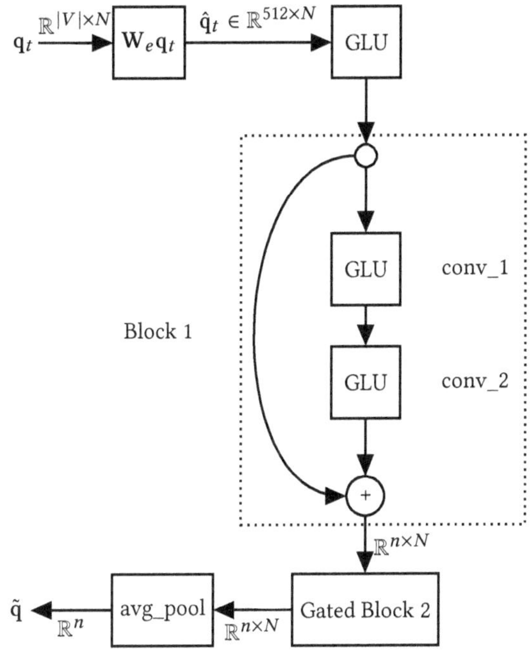

Figure 3: We extract a feature representation out of the input questions with a convolutional architecture. First, we embed each word of the question $\mathbf{q}_t$ into a lower-dimensional representation, which we feed through a GLU followed by two post-activation residual blocks. After those blocks, we use global average pooling to get one vector describing the question.

$$\tilde{\mathbf{y}} = \tanh(\mathbf{W}_\theta \mathbf{x} + \mathbf{b}_\theta) \quad (6)$$
$$\mathbf{g} = \sigma(\mathbf{W}_{\theta'} \mathbf{x} + \mathbf{b}_{\theta'}) \quad (7)$$
$$\mathbf{y} = \tilde{\mathbf{y}} \circ \mathbf{g}, \quad (8)$$

where $\mathbf{W}_\theta, \mathbf{W}_{\theta'} \in \mathbb{R}^{\nu\times\mu}$ are learned weight matrices and $\mathbf{b}_\theta, \mathbf{b}_{\theta'} \in \mathbb{R}^\nu$ are learned biases.

In particular, we use $f_v(\hat{\mathbf{v}})$ with $\nu = 512$ to reduce the dimensionality to the dimensionality of the question embedding. As common practice in the VQA community [2, 24], we then use the element-wise product to fuse image and question features with

$$\mathbf{h} = f_q(\tilde{\mathbf{q}}) \circ f_v(\hat{\mathbf{v}}). \quad (9)$$

Note, that we also apply the non-linearity function to the question embedding, where we set $\nu = \mu = 512$. We depict our model including the multimodal fusion in Figure 1.

4.5 Output LSTM

As we pointed out, most other VQA models have the drawback of leaving out the less common answers and model the problem of predicting the answer to an (image, question) pair as a classification task. To do otherwise, we use a classical approach coming from image captioning models [25] and machine translation networks. Generally speaking, those kind of models use an encoder-decoder structure, which encodes inputs (e.g. source language sentence or input image) into a fixed-length vector representation and decodes this feature vector into the target sentence.

In our case the input is the combination of question and input image and is encoded in the vector **h** and the target is the answer described by a sentence $S = (s_0, \ldots, s_M)$, where s_t is the word at time step t and M the length of the answer. Our model then maximizes the probability p of the correct answer S, given **h**

$$\Theta^* = \arg\max_{\theta} \sum_{(\mathbf{h},S)} \log p(S|\mathbf{h}; \Theta), \tag{10}$$

where Θ are all variables of our model and Θ^* is the optimal parameter set. Of course, each answer S consists of a variable number of words and the model is optimized for each (question, image, answer) triple. Therefore, for each training triple, the joint log probability

$$\log(S|\mathbf{h}) = \sum_{t=0}^{M} \log p(s_t|\mathbf{h}, s_0, \ldots, s_{t-1}) \tag{11}$$

is maximized.

We can model the log probability $p_t = \log p(s_t|\mathbf{h}, s_0, \ldots, s_{t-1})$ by using an RNN, where the probability p_t is the output of the RNN at time step t. In particular, we use an LSTM network as the decoder network, where we initialize the hidden state at time step $t = -1$ with the multimodal feature representation **h** of the question and image. Note, that we only feed **h** once into the LSTM network. The loss that defines the error signal is then given by the sum over the log likelihoods of the correct word at each position, where log is the natural logarithm applied element-wise to the vector p_t:

$$L(\mathbf{h}, S) = -\sum_{t=1}^{M} [\log p_t] \cdot s_t. \tag{12}$$

4.6 Training

In all experiments, we use a stochastic gradient descent (SGD) solver with a base learning rate of $\eta_b = 2.0$. The base learning rate applies to the decoder LSTM network, while we use a reduced learning rate for other parts of our model. For the question encoder CNN, the image attention and the multimodal fusion, we use a learning rate of $\eta_{\text{Q-CNN}} = 0.005 \cdot \eta_b$, $\eta_{\text{att}} = 0.05 \cdot \eta_b$ and $\eta_{\text{fusion}} = 0.05 \cdot \eta_b$, respectively. At a varying number ϵ of epochs, we halve the learning rate. When finetuning the *Inception-v3* network in an end-to-end fashion we set all learning rates to $\eta = 0.0005$. We use a batch-size of $\beta = 128$ in most of our experiments and reduce the batch-size to $\beta = 32$ when finetuning the *Inception-v3* network. All experiments were conducted on a single NVIDIA Titan X Pascal GPU.

For training we use each input (image, question, answer) triple as one training example. Note, that we sample multiple training examples from one (image, question) pair with multiple possible answers to model the uncertainty between the annotators. Thus, we get a slightly richer training signal because the model learns that multiple answers could be correct.

Depending on the model, we halve the learning rate 2 to 4 times and train for $\epsilon = 2$ to $\epsilon = 4$ epochs per learning rate. When using a lower learning rate, we increase the number of epochs per learning rate to 6. In the finetuning stage, we train until convergence for a total of up to $\epsilon = 35$ epochs. On our GPU, training in the first stage with precomputed features takes 2 to 4 days. The finetuning stage takes 8 to 10 additional days.

4.7 Implementation

We implemented our model in Tensorflow [1] and used the slim module for a prebuilt *Inception-v3* DCNN. Our model shares code with the Show and Tell [25] model, which is publicly available as a Tensorflow implementation.

5 EVALUATION

We conducted a series of experiments to conclude an architecture producing best results for our scenario (see Table 1). In the following we list some of our ablation experiments in order to justify our hyperparameter selection. All models build upon an *Inception-v3* DCNN pretrained on the ILSVRC 2012 corpus. We precomputed the *Inception-v3* features of the input images, since every image is used multiple times and, thus, training is sped up. Except stated otherwise, we report accuracies on our validation split of the VQA-v2 dataset.

5.1 Question feature extraction

As we described in Section 4.1, we used a convolutional architecture to extract a single feature vector out of a given question. In addition to the post-activation layers we also conducted experiments with pre-activation layers (similar to ResNet-v2 [11]), which performed a little worse in our case. We also compared classification accuracies for different number of residual blocks (see column # blocks). Here we see that a larger number of residual blocks (4) does not improve performance in comparison to our choice of using only 2 blocks. Furthermore, in the first column of the feature extraction columns, we show our different choices for the kernel size k of the question convolutions. As a comparison, we also extract the question features with a simple LSTM network (one LSTM cell with 512 units), which decreases the validation accuracy about an absolute of 10 %. Note, that we used GLUs for every model except for model 6. Therefore, for the question feature extraction part of our model, we chose to use 2 post-activation residual blocks with a kernel size of $k = 5$.

5.2 Image attention

We then added a simple image attention model (see Section 4.3) to our model. As we still precompute the feature maps of the *Inception-v3* network, we cannot use the global average pooled feature maps anymore, but precompute the direct output of the *Mixed_7c* layer. In the table we mark models, that use attention with a checkmark in the second column. In the results, we notice that our model also profits by adding a simple form of attention. Attention improves the accuracy by about 1% and applying the non-linear layer f_q (see Section 4.4) to the question features ($\tilde{\mathbf{q}}$) also has a small positive effect on the validation accuracy. If we also optimize parameters of the *Inception-v3* DCNN, we get an additional improvement of about 3%.

5.3 Multimodal Factorized Bilinear pooling

In addition of fusing the question and image features simply by calculating the element-wise product (see Section 4.4), we also

Table 1: Studies on our test and validation splits of the VQA-v2 dataset. We analyze different combinations of hyperparamters in our model. The first column states the kind of model, Att stands for Attention, FT for finetuning of all parameters (including the *Inception-v3* image feature extraction DCNN), MM-Fuse describes the kind of multimodal fusion used and decoder specifies whether we used an LSTM or a fully-connected (FC) layer for generating the answers. The columns for validation performance give the accuracies on our validation split (10 % of the VQA-v2 validation split).

				Feature extraction Q				MM-Fuse	Decoder	Validation Performance			
Name	Att	FT	VG	k	# blocks	act	$f_q(\tilde{q})$			All	Y/N	Num	Other
1				4	4	pre		eltwise	LSTM	52.02	71.69	34.82	41.38
2				4	4	post		eltwise	LSTM	52.42	71.57	35.98	42.05
3				4	1	pre		eltwise	LSTM	50.65	69.07	31.34	41.62
4				4	2	post		eltwise	LSTM	52.44	71.52	35.48	42.28
5		✓		4	2	post		eltwise	LSTM	54.67	72.63	37.04	45.55
6				-	LSTM	-		eltwise	LSTM	41.48	63.69	28.18	27.95
7	✓			5	2	post		eltwise	LSTM	53.54	73.33	34.81	43.34
8	✓			5	2	post	✓	eltwise	LSTM	53.71	73.62	35.12	43.38
9	✓		✓	5	2	post	✓	eltwise	LSTM	53.97	73.69	36.83	43.42
10	✓	✓		5	2	post	✓	eltwise	LSTM	56.62	75.45	39.33	46.79
11	✓			5	2	post	✓	eltwise	FC	49.16	72.82	33.41	35.26
12	✓			5	2	post		MFB	LSTM	51.94	72.44	33.54	41.13
13	✓		✓	5	2	post		MFB	LSTM	52.20	71.45	35.40	41.90

implemented the Multimodal Factorized Bilinear Pooling (MFB) approach by Yu et al. [28, 29], which is currently ranked first in the VQA-v2 open-ended challenge. They project the image features and question features into a larger embedding space, i.e., our embedding space is $\in \mathbb{R}^{5 \cdot 512}$. These larger embedding spaces are combined via an element-wise product and then reduced to $\mathbb{R}^{512}$ via sum-pooling, i.e., blocks of 5 values are summed up. This vector is then power normalized ($z \leftarrow sign(z)|z|^{0.5}$) and L_2 normalized ($z \leftarrow z/||z||_2$). Yu et al. propose that MFB supports the exploitation of more complex correlations between multimodal features. As we can see in the *MM-Fuse* column of Table 1, using the MFB approach (Models 12 and 13) does not increase overall accuracy in our case and we stick with using the simple fusing approach described in Section 4.4.

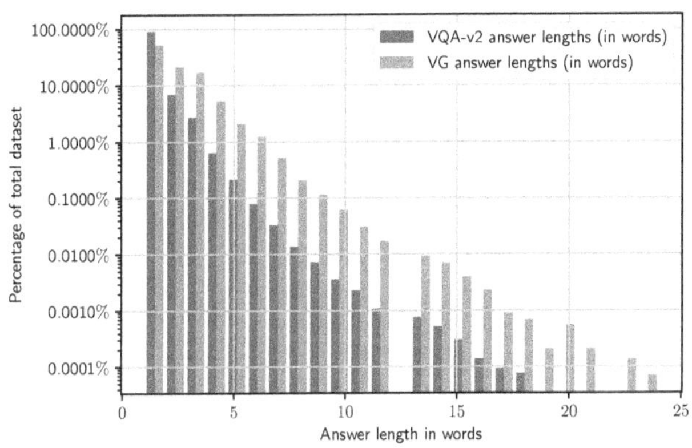

Figure 4: The VQA-v2 dataset contains many short answers (89.41% and 6.92% of all answers are of length 1 and 2 words, respectively), while the the VG dataset contains more answers with more words (52.47%, 21.86% and 16.70% of all answers are of length 1, 2 and 3 words, respectively).

5.4 Classical VQA approach

As we use an LSTM network as the decoder instead of a fully connected layer (FC) with a softmax cross-entropy loss function, we still want to compare our architecture to the classical VQA classification approach. For this reason, we extended our model to be able to classify the 3000 most common answers of the train split. When we evaluate this approach on our test set, accuracies drastically decrease compared to the LSTM decoder (53.71 vs. 49.61). This may be an indicator that the classification approach performs worse than an LSTM decoder network.

5.5 Dataset extension

We also examine, whether the validation accuracy can be improved by extending the dataset with the Visual Genome (VG) dataset. Because we do not evaluate on the VG dataset, we include the whole dataset into our train split. Models trained with the extended dataset are indicated by the VG column. In contrast to models that use the classification approach, we use the whole VG instead of only using the part, which contains the same top answers as the VQA-v2 dataset. In both experiments, in which we extended our dataset by VG, we notice a slight improvement in the scores. This is due to the fact that the VG dataset contains longer answers than the VQA-v2 dataset, which mainly consists of one to two word answers and we measure the performance on the validation split of the VQA-v2 dataset. We depict the distribution of answer lengths in Figure 4.

Table 2: Fractions of unique answers generated by our models. LCA are less common answers left out altogether by classification models, MCA are most common answers, which are the only answers generateable by classification models and new answers are newly generated sentences by our models not contained in the train split. The LCA accuracy describes the percentage of correctly generated answers out of the LCA set, i.e., these are correct answers given by our model, which classification models are not able to produce.

Name	LCA	LCA accuracy	MCA	new answers
9	14.97 %	11.91 %	62.73 %	22.30%
13	14.70 %	9.47 %	63.62 %	21.68 %
10	19.49 %	8.10 %	69.74 %	10.77 %
7	24.52 %	9.91 %	64.22 %	11.26 %

5.6 Less common answers

We use an LSTM network to generate answers, thus, in contrast to classification models, we are able to generate answers which are not part of the 3000 most common answers. Our train set contains 190,677 unique answers and the 3000 most common answers (MCA) comprise 90.5% of all answers in the dataset. Thus, classification models with 3000 logits are unable to produce 9.5% of the less common answers (LCA) of the train set. In contrast, our LSTM model is able to produce every answer and even new answers. In an experiment, we determined the fraction of MCA, LCA and new answers of all uniquely generated answers of some of our models. Our models generate between 14.70% and 24.52% LCA and between 11.26% and 22.30% new answers. With the official evaluation tool, we also find that the accuracy of LCA is up to 11.91%. We visualize these findings in Table 2. In qualitative analysis we depict some of the new answers generated by our model in Figure 5. The first row shows correct answers not detected by the official evaluation script. The second row depicts incorrect answers, e.g. (e) and (f) show answers being too short (due to the short answer bias of the dataset) and (g) and (h) show wrong answers, even though the answers are plausible given the scene.

5.7 Performance on the test set

In Table 3, we compare our model to other models on the test-dev as well as on the test-std dataset split. We compare our model to the MCB [7] approach as reported in [9] and the single network model by Teney et al. [24]. We did not train an ensemble of networks and did not implement attention on image regions by a object detection model. Our models surpass the d-LSTM+n approach but are worse than the best scoring approaches, since we focus more on generating less common answers. Furthermore, our model can produce more complex answers due to the LSTM decoder network and could be seen as an approach for more complex VQA datasets to come.

6 CONCLUSION AND FUTURE WORK

We presented an end-to-end architecture for the VQA task. In contrast to other approaches, we use an LSTM network to generate the answers for the (image, question) pairs. We conducted a series of experiments to find a good combination of hyperparameters for our architecture. Competing approaches model the VQA task as a classification task, where a fixed number of most common answers are the possible classes, hence, they are not able to produce less common answers. With our approach, we were able to generate such less common answers with an accuracy of 11.91% and also showed that our model generates answers not contained in the training set. Some of these produced sentences answer questions correctly. We also find out that the ground-truth answers of current VQA datasets are biased towards a short number of words, i.e., more than 90% of the answers have a maximum length of two words. For datasets containing more complex answers, our model is more suitable than models using the classification approach. Hence, we want to focus our future research on finding a performance measure to evaluate longer and more complex answers and extending the datasets by more complex sentences.

REFERENCES

[1] Martín Abadi, Paul Barham, Jianmin Chen, Zhifeng Chen, Andy Davis, Jeffrey Dean, Matthieu Devin, Sanjay Ghemawat, Geoffrey Irving, Michael Isard, et al. 2016. TensorFlow: A System for Large-Scale Machine Learning.. In *OSDI*, Vol. 16. 265–283.

[2] Stanislaw Antol, Aishwarya Agrawal, Jiasen Lu, Margaret Mitchell, Dhruv Batra, C Lawrence Zitnick, and Devi Parikh. 2015. Vqa: Visual question answering. In *Proceedings of the IEEE International Conference on Computer Vision*. 2425–2433.

[3] Kobus Barnard and David Forsyth. 2001. Learning the semantics of words and pictures. In *Computer Vision, 2001. ICCV 2001. Proceedings. Eighth IEEE International Conference on*, Vol. 2. IEEE, 408–415.

[4] Xinlei Chen, Hao Fang, Tsung-Yi Lin, Ramakrishna Vedantam, Saurabh Gupta, Piotr Dollár, and C Lawrence Zitnick. 2015. Microsoft COCO captions: Data collection and evaluation server. *arXiv preprint arXiv:1504.00325* (2015).

[5] Yann N Dauphin, Angela Fan, Michael Auli, and David Grangier. 2016. Language modeling with gated convolutional networks. *arXiv preprint arXiv:1612.08083* (2016).

[6] Ali Farhadi, Mohsen Hejrati, Mohammad Amin Sadeghi, Peter Young, Cyrus Rashtchian, Julia Hockenmaier, and David Forsyth. 2010. Every picture tells a story: Generating sentences from images. In *European conference on computer vision*. Springer, 15–29.

[7] Akira Fukui, Dong Huk Park, Daylen Yang, Anna Rohrbach, Trevor Darrell, and Marcus Rohrbach. 2016. Multimodal compact bilinear pooling for visual question answering and visual grounding. *arXiv preprint arXiv:1606.01847* (2016).

[8] Jonas Gehring, Michael Auli, David Grangier, Denis Yarats, and Yann N Dauphin. 2017. Convolutional Sequence to Sequence Learning. *arXiv preprint arXiv:1705.03122* (2017).

[9] Yash Goyal, Tejas Khot, Douglas Summers-Stay, Dhruv Batra, and Devi Parikh. 2016. Making the V in VQA matter: Elevating the role of image understanding in Visual Question Answering. *arXiv preprint arXiv:1612.00837* (2016).

[10] Kaiming He, Xiangyu Zhang, Shaoqing Ren, and Jian Sun. 2016. Deep residual learning for image recognition. In *Proceedings of the IEEE conference on computer vision and pattern recognition*. 770–778.

[11] Kaiming He, Xiangyu Zhang, Shaoqing Ren, and Jian Sun. 2016. Identity mappings in deep residual networks. In *European Conference on Computer Vision*. Springer, 630–645.

[12] Sepp Hochreiter and Jürgen Schmidhuber. 1997. Long short-term memory. *Neural computation* 9, 8 (1997), 1735–1780.

[13] Justin Johnson, Andrej Karpathy, and Li Fei-Fei. 2016. Densecap: Fully convolutional localization networks for dense captioning. In *Proceedings of the IEEE Conference on Computer Vision and Pattern Recognition*. 4565–4574.

[14] Andrej Karpathy. 2016. *CONNECTING IMAGES AND NATURAL LANGUAGE*. Ph.D. Dissertation. STANFORD UNIVERSITY.

[15] Andrej Karpathy and Li Fei-Fei. 2015. Deep visual-semantic alignments for generating image descriptions. In *Proceedings of the IEEE Conference on Computer Vision and Pattern Recognition*. 3128–3137.

[16] Ranjay Krishna, Yuke Zhu, Oliver Groth, Justin Johnson, Kenji Hata, Joshua Kravitz, Stephanie Chen, Yannis Kalantidis, Li-Jia Li, David A Shamma, et al. 2017. Visual genome: Connecting language and vision using crowdsourced dense image annotations. *International Journal of Computer Vision* 123, 1 (2017), 32–73.

[17] Siming Li, Girish Kulkarni, Tamara L Berg, Alexander C Berg, and Yejin Choi. 2011. Composing simple image descriptions using web-scale n-grams. In *Proceedings of the Fifteenth Conference on Computational Natural Language Learning*. Association for Computational Linguistics, 220–228.

(a) Q: Where is the man?
A: in a restaurant

(b) Q: Where are the trees?
A: behind the elephants

(c) Q: Where is the bus?
A: on the street

(d) Q: Where is the red carpet?
A: on the ground

(e) Q: Who wears a cowboy hat?
A: the man on the

(f) Q: What is the woman doing?
A: feeding the

(g) Q: Where is the photo taken?
A: in a kitchen

(h) Q: Where is the boy looking?
A: at the beach

Figure 5: Images associated with question and generated answers by our model. All answers shown are new ones not contained in the training set. Figures (a) - (d) show correct answers not detected by the official evaluation script. The second row shows wrong answers. Especially, (e) and (f) show sentences, where the end of sentence token was generated to early (dataset bias of short answers). (g) and (h) show wrong answers.

Table 3: One of our models (model 10) compared to state-of-the-art models on the test-dev and test-std dataset splits.

	VQA-v2 test-dev				VQA-v2 test-std			
	All	Y/N	Num	Other	All	Y/N	Num	Other
MCB [7, 9]	-	-	-	-	62.27	78.82	38.28	53.36
d-LSTM+n [9, 19]	-	-	-	-	54.22	73.46	35.18	41.83
Teney et al. Single Network [24]	62.07	79.20	39.46	52.62	62.27	79.32	39.77	52.59
10 (Ours)	56.32	75.64	36.21	44.36	56.68	76.02	36.56	44.46

[18] Tsung-Yi Lin, Michael Maire, Serge Belongie, James Hays, Pietro Perona, Deva Ramanan, Piotr Dollár, and C Lawrence Zitnick. 2014. Microsoft coco: Common objects in context. In *European Conference on Computer Vision.* Springer, 740–755.

[19] Jiasen Lu, Xiao Lin, Dhruv Batra, and Devi Parikh. 2015. Deeper LSTM and normalized CNN Visual Question Answering model. https://github.com/VT-vision-lab/VQA_LSTM_CNN. (2015).

[20] Shaoqing Ren, Kaiming He, Ross Girshick, and Jian Sun. 2015. Faster R-CNN: Towards real-time object detection with region proposal networks. In *Advances in neural information processing systems.* 91–99.

[21] Olga Russakovsky, Jia Deng, Hao Su, Jonathan Krause, Sanjeev Satheesh, Sean Ma, Zhiheng Huang, Andrej Karpathy, Aditya Khosla, Michael Bernstein, et al. 2015. Imagenet large scale visual recognition challenge. *International Journal of Computer Vision* 115, 3 (2015), 211–252.

[22] Karen Simonyan and Andrew Zisserman. 2014. Very deep convolutional networks for large-scale image recognition. *arXiv preprint arXiv:1409.1556* (2014).

[23] Christian Szegedy, Vincent Vanhoucke, Sergey Ioffe, Jon Shlens, and Zbigniew Wojna. 2016. Rethinking the inception architecture for computer vision. In *Proceedings of the IEEE Conference on Computer Vision and Pattern Recognition.* 2818–2826.

[24] Damien Teney, Peter Anderson, Xiaodong He, and Anton van den Hengel. 2017. Tips and Tricks for Visual Question Answering: Learnings from the 2017 Challenge. *arXiv preprint arXiv:1708.02711* (2017).

[25] Oriol Vinyals, Alexander Toshev, Samy Bengio, and Dumitru Erhan. 2015. Show and tell: A neural image caption generator. In *Proceedings of the IEEE conference on computer vision and pattern recognition.* 3156–3164.

[26] Oriol Vinyals, Alexander Toshev, Samy Bengio, and Dumitru Erhan. 2016. Show and tell: Lessons learned from the 2015 mscoco image captioning challenge. *IEEE transactions on pattern analysis and machine intelligence* (2016).

[27] Yonghui Wu, Mike Schuster, Zhifeng Chen, Quoc V Le, Mohammad Norouzi, Wolfgang Macherey, Maxim Krikun, Yuan Cao, Qin Gao, Klaus Macherey, et al. 2016. Google's Neural Machine Translation System: Bridging the Gap between Human and Machine Translation. *arXiv preprint arXiv:1609.08144* (2016).

[28] Zhou Yu, Jun Yu, Jianping Fan, and Dacheng Tao. 2017. Multi-modal factorized bilinear pooling with co-attention learning for visual question answering. In *Proc. IEEE Int. Conf. Comp. Vis*, Vol. 3.

[29] Zhou Yu, Jun Yu, Chenchao Xiang, Jianping Fan, and Dacheng Tao. 2017. Beyond Bilinear: Generalized Multi-modal Factorized High-order Pooling for Visual Question Answering. *arXiv preprint arXiv:1708.03619* (2017).

[30] Bolei Zhou, Yuandong Tian, Sainbayar Sukhbaatar, Arthur Szlam, and Rob Fergus. 2015. Simple baseline for visual question answering. *arXiv preprint arXiv:1512.02167* (2015).

Searching and Matching Texture-free 3D Shapes in Images

Shuai Liao
QUVA Lab, University of Amsterdam
s.liao@uva.nl

Efstratios Gavves
QUVA Lab, University of Amsterdam
egavves@uva.nl

Cees G. M. Snoek
QUVA Lab, University of Amsterdam
cgmsnoek@uva.nl

ABSTRACT

The goal of this paper is to search and match the best rendered view of a texture-free 3D shape to an object of interest in a 2D query image. Matching rendered views of 3D shapes to RGB images is challenging because, 1) 3D shapes are not always a perfect match for the image queries, 2) there is great domain difference between rendered and RGB images, and 3) estimating the object scale versus distance is inherently ambiguous in images from uncalibrated cameras. In this work we propose a deeply learned matching function that attacks these challenges and can be used for a search engine that finds the appropriate 3D shape and matches it to objects in 2D query images. We evaluate the proposed matching function and search engine with a series of controlled experiments on the 24 most populated vehicle categories in PASCAL3D+. We test the capability of the learned matching function in transferring to unseen 3D shapes and study overall search engine sensitivity w.r.t. available 3D shapes and object localization accuracy, showing promising results in retrieving 3D shapes given 2D image queries.

KEYWORDS

3D-2D Matching; 3D Shape Retrieval; Texture-free

ACM Reference Format:

Shuai Liao, Efstratios Gavves, and Cees G. M. Snoek. 2018. Searching and Matching Texture-free 3D Shapes in Images. In *ICMR '18: 2018 International Conference on Multimedia Retrieval, June 11–14, 2018, Yokohama, Japan.* ACM, New York, NY, USA, 9 pages. https://doi.org/10.1145/3206025.3206057

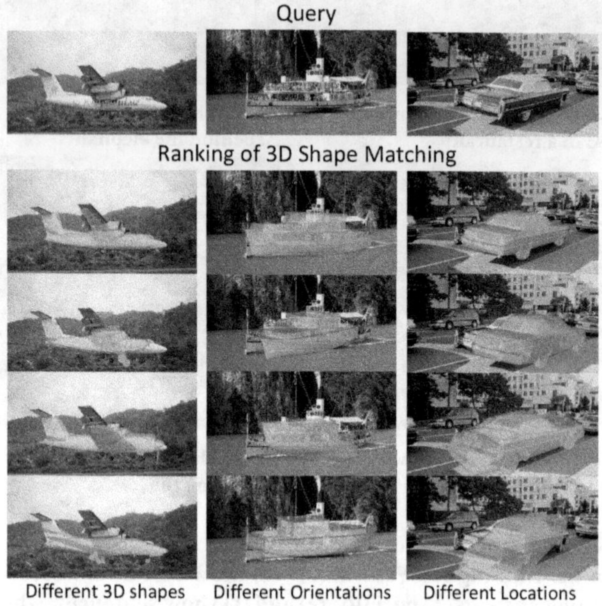

Figure 1: This paper strives to find the rendered view of a texture-free 3D shape that best matches an object of interest in a 2D query image. This matching is challenging because the 3D shapes are not always perfect for the image query (aeroplane, boat, car), there is an obvious domain difference between the appearance of the RGB object and the texture-free rendered image, and the intrinsic camera parameters are unknown. We propose and evaluate a deeply learned matching function that attacks these challenges and can be used as a search engine that finds and matches 3D shapes to objects in 2D images.

1 INTRODUCTION

The goal of this paper is to search and match the rendered view of a texture-free 3D shape to an object of interest in a 2D image. Matching shapes to image content has a long tradition in content-based image retrieval, *e.g.* [17, 27], where queries have been entered by sketching [13], by combining sketch and keywords [8], or by a provided 3D shape [1]. We build on this heritage and query a dataset of 3D shapes based on an image, but we also recognize and localize an object of interest in the image and match the object to its corresponding 3D model, so as to arrive at an alignment of the 3D shape in the 2D image as precise as possible, see Fig. 1.

Searching and matching a 3D shape to an object in a real-world 2D image is challenging because: *(a)* finding the 3D shape that has the exact shape as the objects in the image is not always possible, even when large 3D shape libraries, *e.g.* [4], are available, *(b)* matching a rendered image from a 3D shape with a real image is known to suffer from domain shift: the real image may have different texture, lighting condition, shadow and complex natural background, and *(c)* estimating the object scale versus distance is inherently ambiguous in images taken from uncalibrated cameras, where the camera intrinsic matrix is unknown. In this paper we study the influence of these challenges with respect to the searching and matching of 3D shapes in images.

ICMR '18, June 11–14, 2018, Yokohama, Japan

ACM ISBN 978-1-4503-5046-4/18/06...$15.00
https://doi.org/10.1145/3206025.3206057

1.1 Related Work

We are inspired by recent progress, mostly reported in computer vision venues, were several sophisticated methods for 3D to 2D object matching have been presented, *e.g.* [2, 3, 9]. Most methods rely their matching on exemplar classifiers, which are trained to learn an absolute relation between particular 3D model views and particular RGB appearances via texture-sensitive features, such as HOG [2, 3]. In the seminal work of [2], for example, Aubry *et al.* rely on 3D models of chairs from image search engines to align 3D models to 2D objects. The authors propose an LDA-based exemplar classifier trained on HOG features of textured 3D models to detect the 3D model and the pose that best matches real chair images. Unfortunately, the exemplar classifiers are trained for specific models, textures, and specific poses, namely they learn a specific classifier for each 3D model, its different poses and RGB appearances separately. Hence, novel 3D models or poses cannot be accommodated without retraining, limiting the applicability of the learned model for general-purpose 3D shape retrieval.

In [18] a method is described for aligning perfectly matched 3D shapes of IKEA furniture on RGB living room images, be it they rely on parts that must be defined and annotated a priori on the perfect matched 3D shapes. In [21] 3D models are reduced to 3D cuboids, for object categories with box-like geometry, like cars, thus making inference easier. These methods learn absolute relations between *textured* 3D models and the respective 2D objects available at training. Having textured 3D models can be beneficial, *e.g.* if the texture of the object in the 2D image happens to be similar. But it can also limit the algorithm, by biasing it to retrieving 3D models that only share similar textures regardless of apparent differences in shape geometry. Even with large-scale 3D shape datasets such as [4], finding similar textured 3D models that match objects as they appear in images in the wild is still limited by the stored variation in the dataset. What is more, the texture quality and style is not necessarily consistent, as they are typically designed by different 3D artists. Consequently, texture-based methods are constrained to textures already observed, and they are unable, nor intended, to transfer their knowledge to new 3D models or poses at test time. An alternative [3] is to rely on depth RGB images to learn the 3D-to-2D matching function, limiting, however, the applicability of the algorithm to RGB-D cameras only. Unlike these approaches, our focus is a search engine of the best matching 3D shapes given an object in a 2D images. Thus, we are also interested in transferability, even for unseen 3D shapes. In this work we focus on texture-free 3D shapes and standard RGB images as queries.

To alleviate the dependence on texture appearance, Choy *et al.* [5] first render textured 3D models into background-free images from a set of discretized viewpoints. Then, they compute synthesized detection templates from the extracted HOG features from these rendered views. At inference time, a detector is applied to 2D images in a sliding window fashion with multiple scales. When the detector is activated, the pose of 3D shape as well as its 2D location is transferred to the target object. Similar to [5] we also aim for localization and matching of objects in images, but rather than striving to limit the dependence on texture, we prefer to exclude texture completely.

In a recent work from the multimedia retrieval community, Junkert *et al.* [11] limit the dependency on domain shift of the generated textures of 3D shapes by relying on a neural transfer learning scheme rather than HOG descriptors. Their synthesized high quality image renderings of 3D shapes with texture, background and casted shadows. Once these synthesized images are obtained, they extract intermediate feature from an Inception [26] model pre-trained on ImageNet. Given a real image at test time, also represented by the same features, they search for the best matching 3D model by a k nearest neighbor search. As they assume all real and rendered objects have been centralized in the image, they are only able to return viewpoint angles without the location of objects. Similar to [11] we also exploit the transfer abilities of neural networks. Rather than matching the feature representations of textured 3D model renderings and the query image as is, we prefer to learn the matching function between an image and a texture-free 3D shape.

1.2 Contributions

We propose a search engine that given a query object image, localizes and matches the object to the appropriate 3D shape. Different from related approaches, we directly operate on texture-free 3D shapes, enabled by a novel learned matching function. The learned function is a shallow convolutional neural network, merged from a deep two-stream network, encapsulating the relative differences between texture-free 3D shape views and RGB objects. As we are interested in understanding the possibilities as well as the limitations of searching and matching texture-free 3D shapes in images, we rely on a controlled experimental setup on a large and diverse set of texture-free vehicle categories and sub-categories from PASCAL3D+ [29], where we evaluate its sensitivity w.r.t. available 3D shapes and object localization accuracy.

2 TOWARDS A 3D-TO-2D SEARCH ENGINE

We cast the problem of searching and matching a 3D shape to a 2D object in an image as a supervised optimization problem. In the offline phase, we assume we have a library of 3D shapes $g^{train} = \{g_1, ..., g_K\}$ describing a variety of object categories and their fine-grained sub-categories, where K is the total number of fine-grained categories. At query time, we start from a single RGB image containing an object of interest, that is either provided or detected automatically. We denote the appearance of the object with x, and in practice it can be the feature activations from one of the layers of a deep convolutional neural network. For the object of interest we assume there is an optimal, albeit hypothetical texture-free 3D model g_x^*. Given a previously unseen image x at query time, our goal is to search among the set of possible 3D shapes and their poses, g^{test}, ϕ^{test}, and place the optimal (g_x^*, ϕ_x^*) on top. To match an RGB image with a texture-free rendering, we introduce a geometric compatibility function $G(\cdot)$, which we want to maximize:

$$\phi_x = \arg\max_{\phi} G(\phi; x, x_{CAD}, g_k^{test}, \phi_{CAD}^{test}) \ , \qquad (1)$$

where x_{CAD} is the rendered image given a texture-free 3D shape g_k^{test} and pose transformation ϕ_{CAD}. The $g_k^{test}, \phi_k^{test}$ can be equivalent to the shapes observed at training, or expanded to contain more 3D shapes or their poses, $g_k^{train} \subseteq g_k^{test}, \phi_k^{train} \subseteq \phi_k^{test}$. We summarize the data flow of our search engine in Fig. 2 and detail its main components next.

2.1 Searching and Matching 3D Shapes

Object Recognition and Localization In the literature on 3D to 2D matching, the recognition and localization of the object is often provided in the form of ground truth, *e.g.* [5]. The rationale

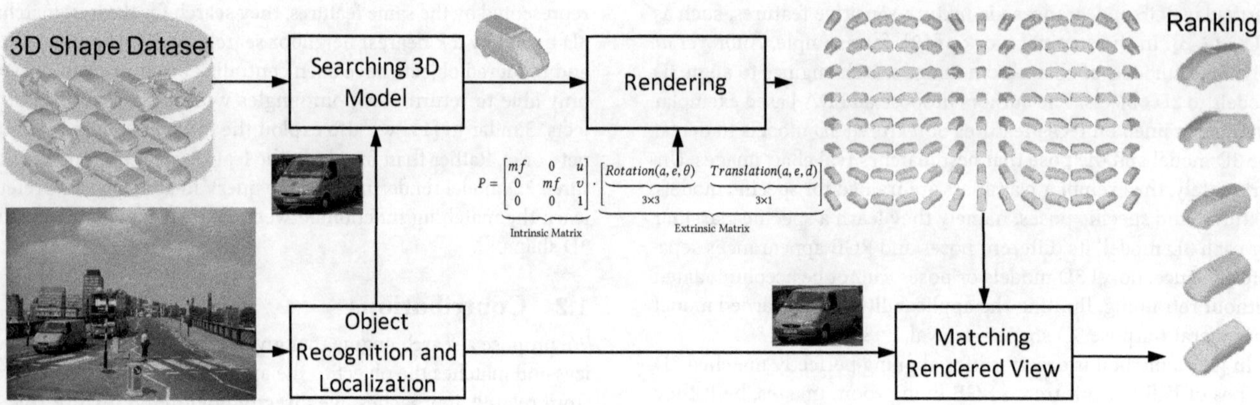

Figure 2: Dataflow for searching and matching texture-free 3D shapes in images. Our main innovation is in matching the rendered view, where we learn to match a texture-free rendering with an RGB image patch.

being that good object detectors are available [20, 22, 23]. Relevant to object recognition and localization, especially for 3D shape matching, are also the so-called amodal bounding boxes [12, 21]. Amodal boxes aim at detecting the full extent of the object, even if the bounds of the surrounding box extent the boundaries of the image. Amodal boxes capture the object centre location (u, v) and corresponding scale d, also including parts that might be not visible because of occlusion or truncation. In our experiments we quantify the sensitivity of our approach w.r.t. the quality of the (amodal) object recognition and localization using both (perturbed) groundtruth as well as a automatic object detection.

Searching 3D Model Once we have obtained the (fine-grained) object category and its enclosing box, we simply query the database of texture-free 3D shapes and forward the selected 3D shape to the rendering stage.

Rendering Each of the 3D shapes g_k can undergo various viewpoint transformations and 3D-to-2D projection. The viewpoint transformation includes rotation and translation that is controlled by extrinsic parameters, *i.e.* azimuth a, elevation e, in-plane rotation θ, camera distance d, whereas intrinsic parameters, *i.e.* principle offset (u, v), focal length f and viewport m, define the camera intrinsic matrix for 3D-to-2D projection. We aggregate the pose transformation parameters to $\phi_{CAD}^{train} = \{\phi_{CAD}^{1}, ..., \phi_{CAD}^{M}\}$, where M is the number of poses seen during training. In the following, to reduce notation clutter we drop the superscript *"train"* whenever it can be derived from the context.

Following [10], the formulation of the projection matrix takes the following form:

$$P = \underbrace{\begin{bmatrix} mf & 0 & u \\ 0 & mf & v \\ 0 & 0 & 1 \end{bmatrix}}_{\text{Intrinsic Matrix}} \cdot \underbrace{\begin{bmatrix} \underbrace{Rotation(a,e,\theta)}_{3\times3} & \underbrace{Translation(a,e,d)}_{3\times1} \end{bmatrix}}_{\text{Extrinsic Matrix}} ,$$

where we assume a calibrated camera, namely the focal length and viewport are fixed to $f = 1, m = 2,000$ respectively [29]. Each set of ϕ_{CAD} values produces a new *3D model rendering*. Similarly, for the hypothetical 3D model g_x^* there exists an optimal transformation vector ϕ_x^*.

Matching Rendered View Ideally, we want to avoid learning an explicit mapping from the appearance modality to the geometric modality. The reason is that an explicit mapping would function well for the 3D model rendering that are observed during training but not generalize well for new 3D models. To this end we define the geometric compatibility function as a differential on the geometric modality.

During training we have two images, x and x_{CAD}, as well as two rotation matrices, R_x and R_{CAD}, one from the real and one from the rendered image. We define our geometric compatibility function as:

$$G_{rel}^* \propto \partial\phi = g(R_x - R_{CAD}) \ . \quad (2)$$

According to eq. (2) $\partial\phi \propto g(R_x - R_{CAD})$ is a function of difference between two geometries expressed by R_x and R_{CAD}. Unfortunately, at testing time we cannot have R_x, as this is what we are looking for. To this end we propose to approximate the geometric compatibility with an approximate geometric compatibility function, which receives as inputs the appearance features of the RGB and the CAD rendering, namely:

$$G_{rel}^* \approx G_{rel} \propto \partial x = f(x - x_{CAD}) \ , \quad (3)$$

In the spirit of [14], we define the approximate geometric compatibility function $f(\cdot)$ in eq. (3) to be a separate neural network module, which we coin *geometric differential module*. A geometric differential module is implemented as a shallow convolutional neural network composed of two layers. The first layer is convolutional with kernel size 1×1 and is fusing the activations from the two streams. The second layer is a fully connected layer with a single output, which approximates $\partial\phi$. Unlike the typical fully connected layer which operates as a function approximator, the geometric differential module approximates a function differential, see Fig. 3.

The geometric differential module does not output directly any rotation matrices R_x nor any 3D model rendering ϕ_x. Instead, it returns relative geometric compatibility values. They are relative, because they are supposed to capture the difference of the R_{CAD} from R_x, and by extension the difference of ϕ_{CAD} from ϕ_x, solely on the basis of the appearance features x and x_{CAD}. Effectively, the network learns to estimate directly the matching between an RGB image and any 3D shape rendering, avoiding to compute the object's rotation matrix first. This has two advantages.

First, the network does not directly associate the compatibility score function in eq. (3) with the appearance of the particular renderings at training time. In fact, the network does not even make any strict assumptions regarding either the texture appearance of the 3D shape rendering, or the geometric precision of the 3D model for the given RGB object. Thus, even if the 3D model is not a perfect fit to the RGB object, either because the set of viewpoint was limited, or because the geometry of the 3D model is not exactly right for the object of interest, as in Fig. 1, the network can still predict the 3D model parameters ϕ_x that match the object of interest. For instance, assume our 3D shape library has models only of a *Boeing 707* and a *Boeing 717*, while our image depicts a *Boeing 747*. Obviously, none of the two available shapes are perfect for our image. Nonetheless, our network returns the best possible fit, as the matching maximizes the matching similarity with the available models, instead of directly classifying the object appearance [2, 5, 18].

Second, since the inference returns only a compatibility score for each provided 3D model rendering, there is no limit to the type of 3D models permissible at test time. The proposed network can return a compatibility score even for 3D models that were not observed during training. As expected, the accuracy of the compatibility score in these cases might be lower, since the network matches 3D shapes and RGB images of object categories it has never seen. Still, the approximate geometric compatibility function has learned *how to match at inference time* on the basis of any 3D model rendering provided at test time. Hence, in theory, the proposed network can cope with 3D shape rendering expanded dynamically, either by adding new 3D shapes or considering a finer discretization of the viewpoints.

An important choice for the geometric differential module is what distance measure it learns to imitate. Although any geometric distance can be used, in this work we opt for approximating the geodesic distance between two rotation matrices of the real object and the rendered image respectively, R, R_{CAD}. Namely, eq. (2) becomes

$$G^*_{rel} = \frac{\| \log(R_x^T R_{CAD}) \|_F^2}{\sqrt{2}} \quad . \tag{4}$$

Thereafter, a Euclidean loss is used to measure how accurately the geodesic differential module predicts G_{rel} by relying only on the appearance features x, x_{CAD}.

2.2 Learning to Match

We implement the matching of rendered views as a two-stream architecture [24] with non-shared weights, where each stream is a convolutional network. The first stream receives as an input the cropped RGB images of the object of interest. The second stream receives as an input a cropped rendering from a particular texture-free 3D shape and essentially, describes the object's candidate geometry.

For both streams we adopt the convolutional layers 1 to 5 from AlexNet [16]. The geometric differential module is composed of a convolutional pooling layer [7] with kernel size 1×1, that fuses the

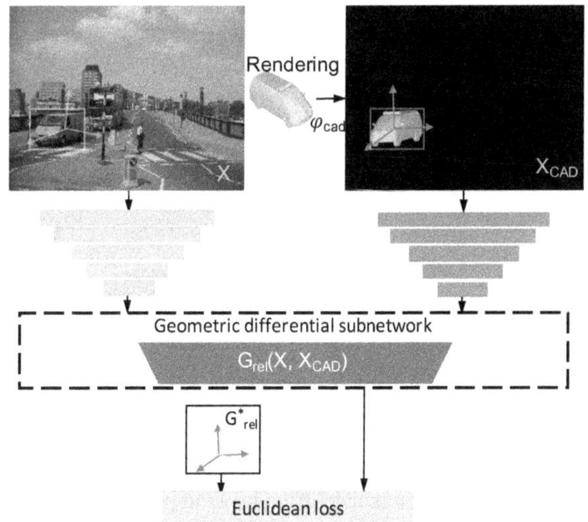

Figure 3: Matching a 3D model rendering to a 2D object in an image with geometric differentials. Starting from an image depicting a fine-grained object category and a texture-free 3D shapes, we derive a 3D model rendering and learn to match them to the localized object of interest. The network is composed of two streams. The first one processes the RGB input. The second one processes the rendered image produced by a candidate 3D model instantiation. The feature maps of the two inputs are fused together and then the geometric differential module estimates the geodesic distance between the two inputs based only on the appearances. It results in a ranking of the 3D model renderings for the localized object, ideally matching the pose of the object.

two streams, followed by a fully connected module with a single output, predicting the geometric compatibility score between the RGB and the rendering streams. We initialize the weights for convolutional layers 1-5 from AlexNet, while we initialize the remaining layers with a Gaussian distribution with standard deviation 0.005. The network is trained with SGD for 70000 iterations at a learning rate of 0.0001.

Data Preparation. The first stream receives a real image as input, while the second stream a rendered image from a 3D shape. We first create a rendering canvas with the same size as the real image. Given the selected 3D model and viewpoint annotation, we render it onto canvas. This results in a rendered image and a projected bounding box for the 3D model. We crop the real image and rendered image with the projected bounding box to obtain the input data for 2-stream network (see Fig. 3).

Training. During training we first sample a real image, for which we have the ground truth 3D model instantiation. As we want to learn to estimate the geodesic distance between different rotation matrices, we must give good estimates for both when the objects are close as well as far away, geometrically speaking. As our network is a regression model, there exist no positive or negative samples. However, to make sure that our regression model learns to approximate accurately enough across the whole spectrum of geodesic distances, we opt for a stratified sampling of the space of

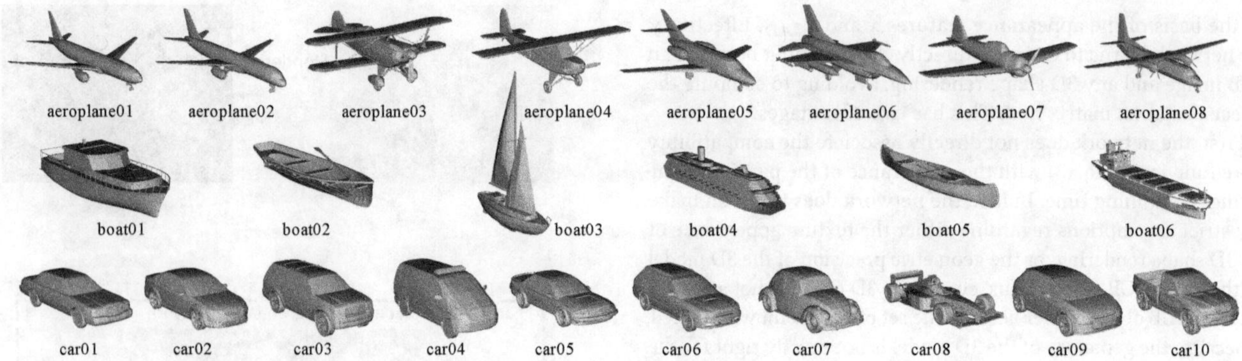

Figure 4: Texture-free 3D shapes for the 24 fine-grained *aeroplane, boat,* and *car* objects used in our experiments.

the rotation matrices to collect training examples. Specifically, per training image we sample (*i*) rotation matrices that are almost equal to the ground truth one, (*ii*) rotation matrices that are close enough but not equal, (*iii*) as well as rotation matrices that are far from the ground truth rotation matrix. In total, we end up with 30 rotation matrices per object of interest in training images. We then proceed with the training as usual, relying on SGD for backpropagation.

Inference. During inference and given one image, we traverse over possible renderings. Namely, we render all available 3D shapes in all desired viewpoints. We retain the most confident 3D model instantiation, namely, the 3D shape and viewpoint, whose rendering generates the smallest geodesic distance to the input RGB image.

3 EXPERIMENTAL SETUP

3.1 Texture-free 3D Shape Dataset

We evaluate our approach on the PASCAL3D+ dataset [29]. PASCAL3D+ extends the PASCAL VOC 2012 [6] by matching to every object location a corresponding texture-free 3D shape in its specific pose. As the 3D shapes are category- and not instance-specific and the size of the 3D shape library is finite, the matching quality varies across categories. We perform our experiments on the three vehicle categories with the most examples, namely *aeroplane, boat,* and *car,* for which 24 texture-free shapes exist in total, see Fig. 4. While this dataset is typically used for the problem of viewpoint estimation [25, 28], we rely on the texture-free 3D shapes for searching and matching. We follow the provided train/test splits. The statistics on the image/object data used in our experiments are summarized in Table 1.

3.2 Experiments

Experiment 1: Search and match the best rendered view given a specific 3D shape. In our first experiment, we assume the object is perfectly localized in the 2D image and the sub-category of the corresponding 3D shape is known. Thus we simply need to match the object of interest in the real image to a set of rendered views of the corresponding shape. Naturally this is an idealized setting, nonetheless it provides us with the opportunity to establish an upper-bound for our matching network to compare against in follow-up experiments.

Experiment 2: Search and match the best rendered view among a collection of 3D shapes. Although fine-grained object recognition approaches, *e.g.* [19], can be used for 3D shape selection directly, the matching module of our system should also be able to do this. In this experiment we study the performance of our system doing 3D shape search and rendered view matching at the same time. To be more specific, given a test object of interest in a 2D image, we only know the super category it belongs to (*e.g.* aeroplane), but without knowledge of whether it is an airliner or jet fighter. Hence, for each test object of interest, we have to match it with respect to all possible rendered views and all available fine-grained sub-category 3D shapes. This potentially add difficulties to our approach in distinguishing the best match especially when a few 3D shape candidates are of similar shape (*e.g.* car01, car02 and car05 in Fig. 4).

Experiment 3: Search and match the best rendered view from unseen 3D shapes Despite the discrepancy amongst 3D shapes under each category in experiment 1 and 2, all of them are seen both at training and test time. Thus, one interesting question is whether our approach is able to find and match unseen 3D shapes within one super category. Specifically, we consider using only half of the three super categories, aeroplane, boat and car, for training. At test time, we apply the trained network on an unseen sub-category to study whether our network is able to transfer the knowledge from the set of seen sub-categories. Note that, as an ablation study, we continue the setting from experiment 1, where location and scale of the 2D object is known.

Experiment 4: Search and match the best rendered view when object location and scale are imperfect.

In this experiment, we investigate how much localization noise our system can tolerate. We first study imperfect object location and scale separately. To simulate the object location error, we perturb the ground truth annotation (u, v) by adding random noise $(\Delta u, \Delta v)$ proportional to the size of ground truth amodal bounding box (width, height). We further evaluate inaccurate detection of object scale in terms of the camera distance d, by randomly scaling it down/up to a maximum of $\{80\%, 90\%, 100\%, 110\%, 120\%\}$ of the original value. This results in the 3D shape being rendered smaller/bigger than the object in the real image. Note that scaling down camera distance d means bringing an object closer to the camera and thus a larger amodal bounding box on the 2D space.

In the third sub-experiment, we perturb (u, v) and d at the same time, keeping the noise of $(\Delta u, \Delta v)$ at a level of 10% , while randomly varying the scale d to {90%, 100%, 110%} of the original. Note that the fine-grained shape is given in this experiment for a better understanding of the effect of noise on our system.

Experiment 5: Search engine comparison. In our last experiment, we compare our system with Choy *et al.* [5]. The comparisons are conducted with two settings: (1) search and match given the ground truth object location and (2) fully automatic search and match. As an object detector returns the bounding box coordinates, but not the full object extent in terms of principle point u, v and distance d, we simply choose the center of the bounding box provided by [20] and a scale value d that best matches the bounding box. In contrast, [5] relies on the detected bounding box and a local search is conducted with a multi-scaled detector template. For a fair comparison with [5], we run their software on our rendered images from the 24 texture-free 3D shapes and train both methods in the same way.

3.3 Evaluation Criteria

To test the searching and matching accuracy of our network, we first discretize the rotation parameter space of azimuth a, elevation e and in-plane rotation θ uniformly into 21, 11, 11 bins respectively. This results in 2,541 rendering views in total. At test time we report results when considering the ground truth rendering as well, resulting in 2,542 rendering views and thus 2,542 predictions of the matching score. We report the *precision*@5, namely a prediction is correct if it contains the ground truth 3D shape in the top-5 ranked positions. On top of the alignment precision at 5 we also measure the *amodal intersection over union (AIOU)*, see Fig. 5, to quantify the shape disagreement given a 2D object of interest and a 3D shape. To compute the AIOU we measure the intersection over union overlap between the 2D ground truth bounding box and the amodal bounding box[12] derived by the optimal 3D shape from the annotators. A perfectly fitting 3D shape will have very high IOU with the 2D box, while a poor fitting 3D shape will return a very different amodal bounding box and thus low AIOU. We also report the mean over all test queries, indicated by Query Mean.

For the comparison with Choy *et al.* [5], we follow their setup and report accuracy at θ ($ACC@\theta$) when the ground truth bounding box is given. This metric evaluates the fraction of viewpoint predictions that are within a fixed threshold (θ) of its ground truth. When incorporating automatic objection detection, we report Average Viewpoint Precision (AVP) for evaluation. It is similar to Average Precision (AP) in object detection, but it only counts detections as correct when the bounding box overlap ratio exceeds 0.5 and when the prediction of the discretized azimuth angle is in the right bin. We report performance on different levels of azimuth angle discretization, {4,8,16,24} bins. As discretization goes finer, the more difficult this task becomes.

4 RESULTS

4.1 Search and match specific 3D shape

We present the matching accuracy and AIOU results in Table 1. Cars are matched the best, as cars generally have a simple box-like shape. In contrast, boats are more challenging . For one, boats exhibit large variation in shape and object size/scale: a boat includes sub-categories from tanker to canoes, see Fig. 4. Moreover, for boats occlusion exists naturally since half of the boat is almost always underwater, thus confusing the matching network that expects the object to be fully visible. When excluding the ground truth pose from the rendered view search space, the *precision*@5 drops from 0.64 to 0.48 for aeroplanes, from 0.44 to 0.27 for boats and from 0.75 to 0.68 for cars. In this scenario, a poor-fitted amodal bounding box hurts even more. To decouple the matching from the rendered view search strategy, we include the ground truth rendering in the rendering search space in the remaining experiments.

When considering individual sub-categories we observe that apart from having a sufficient number of examples available for training, the consistency in shape appearance is important. For example, boat03 is relatively hard. This is due to the fact that sailing boats can have large shape variance and the sail may have different orientation from its body. In contrast, boat04 and boat06 are relatively easy because both of them are big ships resembling a 3D box floating on the water, which facilitates the matching. Similar observations hold for airplanes. Cars generally have more consistent accuracy. Interesting cases are car07 and car04, with car07 being better matched than car04 despite having fewer training samples. The reason is the frontal and rear view of car07 are quite distinguishable, whereas car04 looks like a box, with front and rear poses being often confused.

4.2 Search and match among 3D shapes

We show results in Table. 2. When the fine-grained sub-category of the object is unknown the network must iterate over all possible 3D shapes. This amounts to an N-fold increase of possible 3D shape instantiations, where N is the number of possible sub-categories. Despite this N-fold increase, we observe that the matching network accuracy drops only 2-fold, approximately. As a reference, a random baseline is about $2 \cdot 10^{-4}$ for aeroplanes, where our matching network scores 0.32. Loosely inspired by the work of Junkert *et al.* [11], intended for textured renderings, we also report a baseline based on a nearest neighbor search strategy. Specifically, we

Figure 5: 2D annotation bounding box (dashed blue) vs amodal bounding box (solid green). The difference of the two bounding boxes indicates the shape disagreement between a 3D model to the 2D object in image. For the car the two boxes align almost perfectly, while for the sailing boat there is a noticeable discrepancy. In general, in the PASCAL3D+ dataset, the 3D shapes of cars have the best agreement with the 2D object in an image, while boats have the worst. We show statistics of the amodal intersection over union (AIOU) in Table 1.

Table 1: Experiment 1: Search and match the best rendered view given a specific 3D shape. Note the correlation between precision at 5 and quality of the amodal bounding box per category measured by AIOU.

aeroplane					**boat**					**car**				
Subtype	#Train	#Queries	AIOU	p@5	Subtype	#Train	#Queries	AIOU	p@5	Subtype	#Train	#Queries	AIOU	p@5
aeroplane01	761	128	0.80	0.73	boat01	572	123	0.60	0.51	car01	696	97	0.84	0.78
aeroplane02	105	0	0.81	-	boat02	363	24	0.73	0.25	car02	729	37	0.87	0.73
aeroplane03	80	11	0.75	0.36	boat03	519	46	0.68	0.22	car03	932	35	0.87	0.63
aeroplane04	82	26	0.75	0.50	boat04	530	16	0.78	0.62	car04	141	24	0.82	0.54
aeroplane05	88	45	0.76	0.64	boat05	40	11	0.66	0.55	car05	139	17	0.82	0.76
aeroplane06	478	44	0.76	0.50	boat06	492	12	0.69	0.58	car06	1261	18	0.85	0.83
aeroplane07	392	21	0.73	0.62						car07	137	5	0.79	1.00
aeroplane08	88	0	0.80	-						car08	107	8	0.83	0.75
										car09	884	42	0.82	0.98
										car10	641	25	0.86	0.56
Query Mean			0.78	0.64	Query Mean			0.69	0.44	Query Mean			0.85	0.75

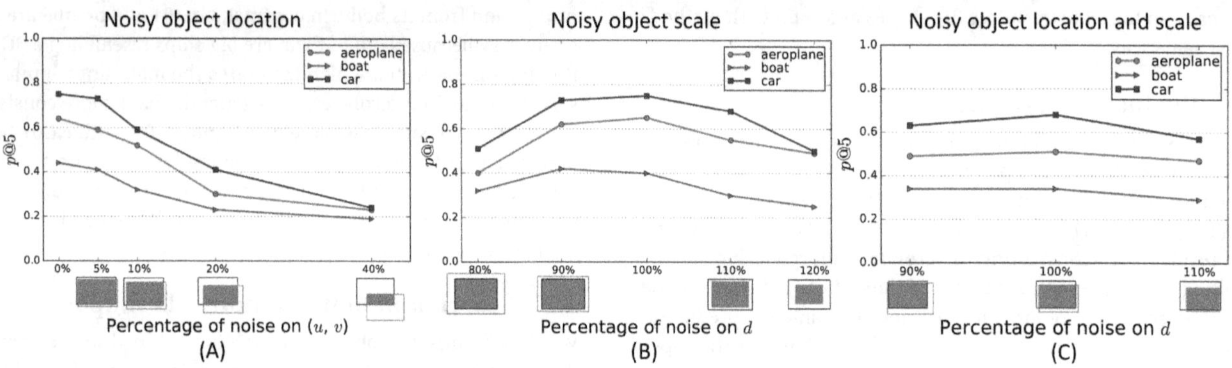

Figure 6: Experiment 4: Search and match the best rendered view when object location (u, v) and d scale are imperfect. On the x axis we visualize the indicative overlap displacement with respect to the perfect box. For moderate noise (5-10%) the model recovers a good match.

extract fc7 features of a pre-trained AlexNet [16] from the object of interest in both the real and rendered images with $K = 2,542$ different viewpoints, and rank them based on cosine similarity. The results show this approach does not work well in our setting, with p@5 around 0.07, as the domain shift from real images to rendered images without texture and background context is simply too large.

4.3 Search and match unseen 3D shapes

We report the performance of our network trained on both seen and unseen sub-categories in Table 3. The network is able to transfer its matching knowledge to unseen shapes to some extent. Note that this experimental setting is quite close to zero-shot image classification [15] where one classifies a category without having seen its visual examples, a challenging task where accuracy drops are generally high. Focusing on sub-categories, aeroplane05 is matched best, while aeroplane06 is affected more. Likely because aeroplane05 looks similar to both aeroplane01 and aeroplane02, while aeroplane06 (jet fighter) is more different. Similarly, boat05 is well matched because it resembles boat02. However, boat04 and boat06 refer to big ships, and transferring the matching knowledge from the considerably smaller boats (yachts, canoes and sailing boats) is harder. For cars, where all sub-categories are quite similar we observe a good matching accuracy. We conclude that if new 3D

Table 2: Experiment 2: Search and match the best rendered view among a collection of 3D shapes. Per super-category, we go over all N 3D shapes per sub-category, namely $N \cdot 2,542$ 3D shape hypotheses. Matching is feasible even when the sub-categories are unknown (compare with Table 1).

aeroplane		**boat**		**car**	
Subtype	p@5	Subtype	p@5	Subtype	p@5
aeroplane01	0.35	boat01	0.15	car01	0.46
aeroplane02	-	boat02	0.00	car02	0.27
aeroplane03	0.27	boat03	0.22	car03	0.23
aeroplane04	0.31	boat04	0.44	car04	0.08
aeroplane05	0.24	boat05	0.09	car05	0.35
aeroplane06	0.34	boat06	0.42	car06	0.28
aeroplane07	0.33			car07	0.40
aeroplane08	-			car08	0.25
				car09	0.69
				car10	0.16
Query Mean	0.32	Query Mean	0.18	Query Mean	0.37

Table 3: Experiment 3: Search and match the best rendered view from unseen 3D shapes. Intra-category knowledge transfer can be performed when new 3D shapes added at test time are somewhat similar to the ones seen during training (marked in gray).

aeroplane		boat		car	
Subtype	p@5	Subtype	p@5	Subtype	p@5
aeroplane01	0.67	boat01	0.43	car01	0.85
aeroplane02	-	boat02	0.29	car02	0.84
aeroplane03	0.45	boat03	0.37	car03	0.57
aeroplane04	0.62			car04	0.62
				car05	0.71
aeroplane05	0.40	boat04	0.06	car06	0.61
aeroplane06	0.14	boat05	0.55	car07	1.00
aeroplane07	0.33	boat06	0.00	car08	0.25
aeroplane08	-			car09	0.88
				car10	0.44

Table 4: Experiment 5: Search engine comparison with Choy *et al.* [5] using ground truth object location, where we run the software of Choy *et al.* on our texture-free setting. In terms of *ACC@θ* our approach is especially beneficial for 3D shapes that have sufficient training samples, where Choy *et al.* profit from limited example regimes (see Table 1). For boats both approaches perform modestly.

aeroplane			boat			car		
Subtype	Choy *et al.*	This paper	Subtype	Choy *et al.*	This paper	Subtype	Choy *et al.*	This paper
aero01	0.48	0.59	boat01	0.32	0.36	car01	0.39	0.62
aero02	-	-	boat02	0.48	0.21	car02	0.62	0.60
aero03	0.55	0.46	boat03	0.33	0.26	car03	0.54	0.57
aero04	0.39	0.31	boat04	0.19	0.19	car04	0.42	0.50
aero05	0.40	0.56	boat05	0.50	0.09	car05	0.35	0.71
aero06	0.39	0.57	boat06	0.42	0.25	car06	0.83	0.61
aero07	0.33	0.52				car07	0.40	0.80
aero08	-	-				car08	0.63	0.50
						car09	0.76	0.74
						car10	0.60	0.48
Query Mean	0.35	0.54	Query Mean	0.22	0.29	Query Mean	0.29	0.61

Table 5: Experiment 5: Search engine comparison with Choy *et al.* [5] with automatically detected object location, using their public software on our texture-free setting. The proposed system achieves better performance in terms of *AVP* for aeroplane and car and worse for boat.

	aeroplane				boat				car			
#Bins	4	8	16	24	4	8	16	24	4	8	16	24
Choy *et al.*	0.35	0.22	0.10	0.05	0.14	0.06	0.02	0.01	0.23	0.17	0.10	0.07
This paper	0.44	0.24	0.10	0.05	0.07	0.04	0.01	0.01	0.30	0.26	0.19	0.11

shapes added at test time are somewhat similar to the seen ones, our network can match them reasonably well.

4.4 Search and match under noisy conditions

Noisy object location. We first look at the effect of noise on the object location (u, v), see Fig. 6 (A). For a limited amount of 5% noise the impact on the network is modest, when averaged over categories the loss is 0.59 for aeroplane, 0.41 for boat and 0.73 for car. When we add more noise performance starts to suffer, with 10% noise the numbers drop to 0.52, 0.32 and 0.59 respectively. Unsurprisingly the performance drops as more and more noise is added, be it that the drop is less pronounced after 20%.

Noisy object scale. Next, we investigate the sensitivity when adding noise to the camera distance d, which relates to the detected object scale (smaller $d \longrightarrow$ larger object scale), see Fig. 6 (B). As before, the larger the deviation the larger the drop in performance and any noise in the range $\pm 10\%$ leads to an acceptable matching accuracy. Interestingly, when scaling d down to 90% it leads to a slight increase in performance for boats. The reason is that scaling down the camera distance d results in a bigger amodal bounding box that often is a better fit to the actual object.

Noisy object location and scale. Last, we assess the impact of having noise in both the location and the scale. Results are shown in Fig. 6 (C). We observe the accuracy remains stable for all categories, indicating the two different types of noise do not reinforce each other too much.

4.5 Search engine comparison

Results for given ground truth object location are shown in Table 4. In terms of the mean over all queries, we obtain better $ACC@\theta$ than [5] for all 3 categories. The boat category has relatively low performance for both methods, because of the low AIOU rate (see Table 1) that indicates large shape discrepancies. Looking into the sub-category comparisons, Choy *et al.* is better in some cases (e.g. aeroplane03, aeroplane04, boat02-boat06), mostly when less training examples are provided which results in our two-stream network being underfitting. Table 5 reports results of joint object detection and 3D-to-2D matching. In terms of AVP we outperform Choy *et al.* also in this setting. As expected, performance for both search engines suffers when azimuth angle discretization becomes finer. While aeroplanes and cars are again matched better, now aeroplane are easier to match than cars, presumably due to their easier detection of typically simpler backgrounds. We conclude that our system with a learned matching function is beneficial over hand-engineered feature matching approaches when sufficient (>80) training samples are available. At the same time there is still a lot of work needed before we arrive at generic and precise searching and matching of 3D shapes in images.

5 CONCLUSION

This paper focuses on searching and matching the best rendered view of a texture-free 3D shape to an object of interest in a 2D image. Matching rendered views of 3D shapes to RGB images is challenging because of imperfect 3D shapes and domain shift in appearance due to texture mismatch. We propose a deeply learned matching function that attacks these challenges and can be used as a search engine of 3D shapes to objects in 2D. We evaluate the proposed search engine on the most populated PASCAL3D+ vehicle categories, testing the capabilities of transferring the learnt function to unseen 3D shapes and its sensitivity to imperfect 3D shapes and localization. We also identify the need for accurate amodal bounding box detection in 2D images as an important 3D-to-2D matching topic for further investigation.

REFERENCES

[1] Jurgen Assfalg, Alberto Del Bimbo, and Pietro Pala. 2004. Retrieval of 3D Objects by Visual Similarity. In *MIR*.

[2] Mathieu Aubry, Daniel Maturana, Alexei Efros, Bryan Russell, and Josef Sivic. 2014. Seeing 3D chairs: exemplar part-based 2D-3D alignment using a large dataset of CAD models. In *CVPR*.

[3] Aayush Bansal, Bryan Russell, and Abhinav Gupta. 2016. Marr Revisited: 2D-3D Alignment via Surface Normal Prediction. In *CVPR*.

[4] Angel X. Chang, Thomas A. Funkhouser, Leonidas J. Guibas, Pat Hanrahan, Qi-Xing Huang, Zimo Li, Silvio Savarese, Manolis Savva, Shuran Song, Hao Su, Jianxiong Xiao, Li Yi, and Fisher Yu. 2015. ShapeNet: An Information-Rich 3D Model Repository. *CoRR* (2015).

[5] Christopher Bongsoo Choy, Michael Stark, Sam Corbett-Davies, and Silvio Savarese. 2015. Enriching Object Detection with 2D-3D Registration and Continuous Viewpoint Estimation. In *CVPR*.

[6] Mark Everingham, SM Ali Eslami, Luc Van Gool, Christopher KI Williams, John Winn, and Andrew Zisserman. 2015. The pascal visual object classes challenge: A retrospective. *IJCV* 111, 1 (2015), 98–136.

[7] Christoph Feichtenhofer, Axel Pinz, and Andrew Zisserman. 2016. Convolutional two-stream network fusion for video action recognition. In *CVPR*.

[8] Thomas Funkhouser, Patrick Min, Michael Kazhdan, Joyce Chen, Alex Halderman, David Dobkin, and David Jacobs. 2003. A Search Engine for 3D Models. *ACM Trans. Graph.* 22, 1 (2003), 83–105.

[9] Saurabh Gupta, Pablo Arbelaez, Ross Girshick, and Jitendra Malik. 2015. Aligning 3D models to RGB-D images of cluttered scenes. In *CVPR*.

[10] Richard Hartley and Andrew Zisserman. 2003. *Multiple View Geometry in Computer Vision* (2 ed.). Cambridge University Press, New York, NY, USA.

[11] Fabian Junkert, Markus Eberts, Adrian Ulges, and Ulrich Schwanecke. 2017. Cross-modal Image-Graphics Retrieval by Neural Transfer Learning. In *ICMR*. 330–337.

[12] Abhishek Kar, Shubham Tulsiani, Joao Carreira, and Jitendra Malik. 2015. Amodal completion and size constancy in natural scenes. In *ICCV*.

[13] Toshikazu Kato, Takio Kurita, Nobuyuki Otsu, and Kyoji Hirata. 1992. A sketch retrieval method for full color image database-query by visual example. In *ICPR*. IEEE, 530–533.

[14] Diederik P. Kingma and Max Welling. 2014. Auto-Encoding Variational Bayes. In *ICLR*.

[15] Svetlana Kordumova, Thomas Mensink, and Cees G. M. Snoek. 2016. Pooling Objects for Recognizing Scenes without Examples. In *ICMR*.

[16] Alex Krizhevsky, Ilya Sutskever, and Geoffrey E Hinton. 2012. ImageNet Classification with Deep Convolutional Neural Networks. In *NIPS*.

[17] Michael S Lew, Nicu Sebe, Chabane Djeraba, and Ramesh Jain. 2006. Content-based multimedia information retrieval: State of the art and challenges. *ACM TOMCCAP* 2, 1 (2006), 1–19.

[18] Joseph J Lim, Aditya Khosla, and Antonio Torralba. 2014. FPM: Fine pose parts-based model with 3d cad models. In *ECCV*.

[19] Tsung-Yu Lin, Aruni RoyChowdhury, and Subhransu Maji. 2015. Bilinear cnn models for fine-grained visual recognition. In *ICCV*.

[20] Wei Liu, Dragomir Anguelov, Dumitru Erhan, Christian Szegedy, Scott Reed, Cheng-Yang Fu, and Alexander C Berg. 2016. Ssd: Single shot multibox detector. In *ECCV*.

[21] Arsalan Mousavian, Dragomir Anguelov, John Flynn, and Jana Kosecka. 2016. 3D Bounding Box Estimation Using Deep Learning and Geometry. *arXiv preprint arXiv:1612.00496* (2016).

[22] Joseph Redmon, Santosh Divvala, Ross Girshick, and Ali Farhadi. 2016. You only look once: Unified, real-time object detection. In *CVPR*.

[23] Shaoqing Ren, Kaiming He, and Ross Girshick. 2015. Faster R-CNN_ Towards Real-Time Object Detection with Region Proposal Networks. In *NIPS*.

[24] Karen Simonyan and Andrew Zisserman. 2014. Two-stream Convolutional Networks for Action Recognition in Videos. In *NIPS*.

[25] Hao Su, Charles R Qi, Yangyan Li, and Leonidas J Guibas. 2015. Render for cnn: Viewpoint estimation in images using cnns trained with rendered 3d model views. In *ICCV*.

[26] Christian Szegedy, Wei Liu, Yangqing Jia, Pierre Sermanet, Scott Reed, Dragomir Anguelov, Dumitru Erhan, Vincent Vanhoucke, Andrew Rabinovich, et al. 2015. Going deeper with convolutions. In *CVPR*.

[27] Johan W. H. Tangelder and Remco C. Veltkamp. 2007. A survey of content based 3D shape retrieval methods. *MTAP* 39, 3 (2007), 441.

[28] Shubham Tulsiani and Jitendra Malik. 2015. Viewpoints and Keypoints. In *CVPR*.

[29] Yu Xiang, Roozbeh Mottaghi, and Silvio Savarese. 2014. Beyond PASCAL: A Benchmark for 3D Object Detection in the Wild. In *WACV*.

Challenges and Opportunities within Personal Life Archives

Duc-Tien Dang-Nguyen
Dublin City University
Dublin, Ireland
duc-tien.dang-nguyen@dcu.ie

Michael Riegler
Simula Metropolitan Center for Digital Engineering
Oslo, Norway
michael@simula.no

Liting Zhou
Dublin City University
Dublin, Ireland
zhou.liting2@dcu.ie

Cathal Gurrin
Dublin City University
Dublin, Ireland
cgurrin@computing.dcu.ie

ABSTRACT

Nowadays, almost everyone holds some form or other of a personal life archive. Automatically maintaining such an archive is an activity that is becoming increasingly common, however without automatic support the users will quickly be overwhelmed by the volume of data and will miss out on the potential benefits that lifelogs provide. In this paper we give an overview of the current status of lifelog research and propose a concept for exploring these archives. We motivate the need for new methodologies for indexing data, organizing content and supporting information access. Finally we will describe challenges to be addressed and give an overview of initial steps that have to be taken, to address the challenges of organising and searching personal life archives.

CCS CONCEPTS

• **Information systems → Digital libraries and archives**; **Personalization**; *Users and interactive retrieval*; *Evaluation of retrieval results*;

KEYWORDS

Search Engine, Lifelogging, Personal Life Archive

ACM Reference Format:

Duc-Tien Dang-Nguyen, Michael Riegler, Liting Zhou, and Cathal Gurrin. 2018. Challenges and Opportunities within Personal Life Archives. In *ICMR '18: 2018 International Conference on Multimedia Retrieval, June 11–14, 2018, Yokohama, Japan.* ACM, New York, NY, USA, 9 pages. https://doi.org/10.1145/3206025.3206040

1 INTRODUCTION

New devices such as mobiles, tablets, wearables, in addition to the various social media platforms such as Facebook, Instagram or Snapchat, have became a normal part of everyday life. Consequently, users end up passively collecting large volumes of data about themselves (typically non-indexed) in their own personal life archives, which are currently spread across multiple devices and services. These personal life archives can contain information about every activity an individual participates in, such as where they go, how they get there, who they speak with, what they see and what information they access. In effect, a multi-source, detailed, digital life diary is being generated for every individual who chooses to do use such technologies. The key enabling technology is the ready availability of power-efficient sensing devices, which are embedded in the modern cell-phones and wearables. It is our conjecture that it is only a short step to move from sensing life to searching through the resultant personal life archives.

Furthermore, we believe that there is a clear coverage-gap between the indexed online content and the non-indexed personal life archive content. While conventional search engines provide retrieval facilities over online data, the integration of personal data in the search process has not yet occurred, apart from some limited personalisation of search results (which is more limiting than helpful). It is our conjecture that a new generation of search engine should be able to "zoom" in and out to give users information based on their friends and families (i.e., via social network platforms, from people having the same habits, etc.), and continue to go deeper and must give the insights from the users themselves (from the quantified-self information). Given the right capture technologies, coupled with a new generation of data organisation techniques and semantic multimedia annotation, new ways of interacting with our own personal life archives will emerge and change the way we view ourselves and our activities.

What is needed as a next step of development and to unlock the potential of these data, are new ways of organizing, annotating, indexing and interacting with personal life archives. Being able to interact with the collected data with the same ease as one executes a Google search nowadays, will enable a new level of insight for the users that helps them to get a complete picture of their data and information. This can happen on different granularities such as a phone number, a location, an entire event in great multimedia detail, or even perform an analysis of lifestyle trends over many years.

Providing insights from personal life archives can help to improve healthcare, working lives, education and social activities [5] and can give new levels of self-awareness. Some obvious benefits for the users can be for example, an easy way of sharing natural life experiences, prospective memory feedback to enhance productivity, personalised wellness feedback, better understanding the

ACM ISBN 978-1-4503-5046-4/18/06...$15.00
https://doi.org/10.1145/3206025.3206040

functioning of the human memory system, and a better understanding of the associations between lifestyle, environmental context and mortality.

Nevertheless, there are many challenges to be overcome like optimised, semantically rich data capture, efficient data mining, knowledge extraction and retrieval tools and the provision of appropriate interaction methodologies. In this work we focus on identifying the opportunity and the challenges and then suggesting the mix of technologies that have the most potential to tackle these challenges in the future.

Consequently, the aims of this paper are:

- To provide an overview of past efforts to capture personal life archives in the research community;
- To inspire and motivate researchers in the multimedia community to use their know-how in this new emerging and societal important area;
- To propose how future personal life archive data should be stored and organised, and therefore made easy for a user to access via an appropriate search mechanism;
- To discuss the challenges in providing retrieval and access to personal life archives;

In the rest of this paper we will briefly describe the overall challenges before discussing the particular requirements for data capture, organisation, retrieval and presentation. Finally we will motivate the benefits of personal life archives and introduce our implementations to address these challenges .

2 CURRENT STATE AND PERSONAL LIFE ARCHIVES

In the 1940s Vannevar Bush introduced the world to the Memex, a life knowledge organisation hypermedia system operating as a desk-based device [6]. Memex introduced new concepts such as information links or trails which are created by the individual or by others. Memex was described as an *"enlarged intimate supplement to ones memory"*. In these words, Bush had identified some of the key issues for maintaining personal life archives, that they be enlarged (store as much information as feasible), intimate (private to the owner) and supplemental (working in synergy with ones memory). The Memex provided an inspiration for the Xanadu system [34] by Ted Nelson which introduced the terms hypertext and hypermedia and was a precursor to the WWW, though with different aims and goals. In 2006, Bell and Gemmel's work on developing the MyLifeBits [20] personal life experience archiving tool digital memories [4, 5], and their book Total Recall [5] introduced the public to the concept of maintaining personal life archives of all information encountered and developed the first database focused retrieval technologies.

Lifelogging has appeared to be an extreme activity carried out only by a small number of pioneering enthusiasts e.g., Steve Mann [32], Gordon Bell [4], and Cathal Gurrin [14, 26]. If one explores the reasons why only few pioneers had gathered these personal life archives automatically are many and varied and pose a set of challenges for the community to consider. One of the most important challenges is the privacy and ethical concerns [13, 35]. It is our conjecture that personal life archives are likely to follow the experiences of cell phone cameras, social networking sites, and location tracking services. Once the personalised experience, wellness, and memory capture and sharing provide a wide range of benefits to end users; these concerns become of secondary importance. In other words, society develops an acceptable usage policy and embraces a new technology as the benefits become apparent. Another challenge comes with the overwhelming amounts of data [41] that personal life archives naturally generate. Research has indicated that lifelog data can be summarised into useful knowledge through i) segmenting it into a series of distinct events or activities [15], ii) automatically labelling those events from both the content [14] and context [29], iii) automatically detecting faces and event novelty to identify those events that are more interesting to reflect on [16], iv) presenting segments of this personal life archive to the user as required and v) analysing this data to provide new knowledge to the user.

Another challenge is that personal life archives attract life activity data at varying degrees of fidelity. A single sensor (e.g., an odometer or pedometer) operates at a very low-fidelity whereas the wearable video technique moves towards high-fidelity total capture which digitises a much richer snapshot of life activities. All such data has sometimes been referred to as memories, yet this should not be considered as an actual memory capture technique, rather a multimedia sampling of a representation of a life activity, which, when located and presented by appropriate software to a user would help to trigger wet-ware memory recall.

Consequently, and in agreement with Bush's vision of the 'enlarged intimate supplement to ones memory', we refer to these lifelogs or e-memories as Personal Life Archives of sampled life experience data that can be analysed in real-time and work with the person's memory to enhance life experience. *Personal*, in the sense that they are intensely private archives that are gathered by the individual for the individual, though of course they may be stored and processed remotely and aspects of the archive may be shared with other people or organisations. *Life* in the sense that they are enlarged archives of life activity data and as such should aim for the target of total capture of life experience. *Archives* in that they will be historically stored and analysed throughout the life of the individual and potentially even longer. While real-time access will provide for life enriching contextual access to past activities (in synergy with the individual's natural memory), there is also enormous potential for long-term analysis and understanding of the life archive data.

3 CHALLENGES

Search and ranking is only one aspect of the challenge that information retrieval systems have to tackle. When we are developing retrieval systems, whether for personal life archives or simply for WWW pages, to find a starting point, we need to understand how the personal life archive will be accessed. To begin our consideration, contemplate how people access their own digital photo or video archives. For sufficiently small archives, a browsing mechanism (manually or automatic organisation into clusters based on folders or events) is acceptable, where the selection of an axis of browsing results in the generation of a manageable set of result documents. Consider browsing a photo archive using date or location. However, when the archives become larger and less organised, a search or search/browse metaphor is normally chosen to support fast and effective access.

Contemplating personal life archives, the sheer scale of these multi-year or multi-decade archives suggests that a browsing methodology is not sufficient from the outset. The initial (and the only) experiments into multi-year multimodal personal life archive search suggests that even a basic search methodology increases the possibility of a user locating desired content by a factor of three in a third of the time [16]. When considering search, there are a number of alternative search methodologies that could be considered. Firstly keyword based search can be processed over textual narratives generated from the sampled life experience. Another alternative approach is to support the user in generating a new type of multi-axes query in an efficient manner; for example, I know that my friends Paul and Jack were there, it was a Sunday evening, and we were in Barcelona watching a football game in a bar. A third option is the real-time context-driven automatic querying that is somewhat of a holy grail of this research area. The realtime sampling of life experience can trigger contextual queries to support recollection, retrieval of information and remembering intentions, which, if presented to the user in a suitable manner, can provide for truly novel and currently unknown applications for personal life archives. Applications that can remind you that the person you have just met is having a birthday today or that the last time you bought this type of soup, you felt ill the following day.

While there has been an explosion in the amount of consumer-sensed and -generated data now being created, stored and shared, the ability to organize and provide useful retrieval facilities over this data is still limited. There are many domain-specific solutions for uses such as sensing the level of exercise or sharing a user's location, however, there are still few attempts to fully grasp the full potential of sensing the person, the quantified self [33]. As we progress towards more enhanced sensing of the person (total capture), this coming world of personal life archives will pose new challenges for the areas of multimedia contextual sensor capture, multimedia data organisation, multimedia search and retrieval as well as the human factors that define how we can interact with these personal life archives, not to mention the outstanding issues such as privacy, security of data and supporting the important human need to forget.

We can point out that the key challenges are to gather rich archives in real-time in a non-intrusive manner, to organise these archives into meaningful experiences and generate descriptive metadata, to provide retrieval and recommendation facilities and to support omnipresence of access.

In order to more clearly define the interaction challenges and help to articulate our vision, let us again refer to the five R's of memory access from Sellen & Whittaker [41]. The five R's are recollecting, reminiscing, retrieving, reflecting and remembering intentions. Each of the five Rs define a different reason why people access their memories, and by inference, why people would wish to access their personal life archives. Since each R defines a different way that people are able to interact with their memories, and until such time as we have sufficient numbers of people maintaining personal life archives to get real-world usage data, they serve as a the only source of different proposed interaction scenarios available.

- *Recollecting* is concerned with reliving past experiences for various reasons. For example, we may want to recall who was at an event, or where we parked the car.
- *Reminiscing*, which is a form of recollecting, is about reliving past experiences for emotional or sentimental reasons. It is often concerned with story-telling or sharing of life experiences with others.
- *Retrieving (information)*, is a more specific form of recollecting in which we seek to retrieve specific information from the personal life archive, such as an address, a document or a piece of information.
- *Reflecting*, is a form of quantified self-analysis over the life archive data to discover knowledge and insights that may not be immediately obvious.
- *Remembering Intentions*, which is more about prospective (remembering plans) memory than episodic memory (past experiences). This is a form of planning future activities which is a life activity that everyone engages in.

These provide valuable clues how to develop the organisation, search and presentation elements of Personal Life archives and will be the focus of the remainder of this paper.

3.1 Life Archive Capture & Storage

The starting point in generating personal life archives is gathering the data in a non-intrusive manner. Prior work [41] has suggested that focused capture of only the information that the individual needs at a point in time is the best approach for supporting human memory; however we suggest that such an approach is not in keeping with the Memex vision and would significantly limit the potential of Personal Life Archives. The idea of 'total capture' [20], sampling life experience in high-fidelity, is that all life experience, whether considered important or useful at the time would be captured. This will provide for a more useful, future-proof and flexible personal life archive. As an analogy, WWW search engines index all the WWW; a search engine that selectively indexes only the important or popular content would fail to catch trends, hot-topics or the long-tail of user queries. Total capture of every aspect and moment of life experience, whether it is every heart beat, our locations and motion, or everything we see and do, provides us with new and potentially valuable information about ourselves.

Inspired by the work of Gurrin et al. in [21], we list different categories of life archiving tools which can be applied at the time of writing:

- Passive visual capture. Utilising wearable devices such as Narrative Clip [1], the Microsoft SenseCam [27], or first-generation Augmented Reality glasses, will allow for the continuous and automatic capture of life activities as a visual sequence of digital images.
- Passive audio capture. Audio capture could allow for the identification of events or identification people who was speaking. It is normally can be done via any smartphone.
- Personal biometrics. Sensing devices are becoming more common and widely used by the quantified self community, which allow wearer monitor their sleep duration, distance traveled, caloric output, and other biometrics information.

[1] http://getnarrative.com

- Mobile device context. This refers to using the phone to continuously and passively capture the users context (e.g., location, movement, or acceleration), coupled with smart watches, these devices are able to capture much of the activities of life.
- Communication activities. This refers to the phone or PC passively logs messages, emails, phone calls, or other contents of communications.
- Data creation/access activities. Logging data consumed and created, for example, the words typed, web pages visited, videos watched and so on.
- Environmental context and media. According to [21], lifelogging is mostly, but not exclusively about recording using wearable technology, they could be logged (and accessed) by other sensors, such as surveillance cameras.
- Manual logging life activities. This refers to the indirect or direct logging of activity that is initiated by the user, for example, video recording, personal logs and diary.

Once sensed data has been captured, it needs to be stored, which is one of the key challenges that needs to be addressed. In order to support any of the five R's (especially reflection) the personal life archive should not be time-limited, i.e., should extend back indefinitely and life experiences (unless expressly requested by the user) should not be deleted for reasons of storage capacity or processing overhead. However some form of summarisation may be necessary.

A typical lifelogging camera wearer will generate about 1TB of data per year. For an individual, this is reasonable to assume storage on a single computer and the assumption of Kryder's law, that hard drive densities will continue to increase, should see the storage capacity keep pace with data storage requirements. However, storage capacity that is sufficient for periodic photo capture will not necessarily keep pace with continuous video capture, which will require many tens of TBs per year. Notwithstanding the relatively low cost of digital storage, once data services scale to thousands or millions of people, then local storage solutions would tend to be replaced by cloud-hosting. However in the case of the data storage requirements of personal life archives, (at current pricing models) the data storage cost for cloud-hosting is likely to be prohibitive. An alternative solution needs to be found that merges the convenience and data security of a cloud-hosting service with the low cost of individual storage solutions.

Over the coming sections we will describe a typical technique to automatically organise personal life archives.

3.2 Life Archive Organisation

The human memory system has evolved over thousands of years to store autobiographical memories, and we believe that personal digital archives should mimic how human memory operates. Past literature suggests that human memory stores information in distinct events or episodes, that similar episodes are associated with each other, and that more important episodes are more strongly remembered [16]. However in addition to this, given the range of data streams associated with a given important episode of interest, a short descriptive summary narrative of that episode is required. As a starting point, the personal digital archive information could be arranged as follows:

- *Raw data should be hierarchically arranged and stored:* Typically in information retrieval (IR), there is a single basic unit for indexing and retrieval, typically called the document. For many IR tasks, this basic unit is the preferred unit of retrieval and choosing the basic unit is usually trivial. With lifelog data, this is not the case, since lifelogs are multimodal in nature with different modes captured at different frequencies (1 second to potentially 1 day, or longer) [13]. In order to deal with this problem, a typical approach would be to sort the data in chronological order [13], and use the minute as the basic unit of retrieval.
Building up from the basic unit, it becomes possible to organise the data at higher level which can produce more useful information systems. Typically, in a full day, we know that a person encounters anything upwards of 20 individual *episodes or events*, with each lasting on average about 30 minutes, though there is a lot of variety [17, 30] and agreement on 'what constitutes an event' does not yet exist. Prior work on episode segmentation analyses sensor streams from wearable cameras to segment of life-experience into events in a pre-indexing process [15], however this poses a problem. Human memory operates in real-time, so any personal life archive, that is designed to work in synergy with human memory, should also work in real-time. Hence, we propose that processing should occur in real-time and that this entails data analysis 'at the edge', both the smartphone, wearable devices and a cloud-based server, to operate in real-time and upload *events* to the personal life archive as they happen. Such event segmentation techniques have been extensively evaluated on uploaded data [15]. However future challenges remain in developing real-time episode segmentation on the devices, or some form of topic-focused query-time segmentation.
- *Episodes should be semantically described:* To support both post-hoc review and real-time analysis of episodes, both server-side and device-based semantic analysis tools are needed. These act as software sensors to enrich the raw sensor streams with semantically meaningful annotations; such software sensors are multi-layered to allow for additional derivations to be minded from existing sensor outputs the personal life archives. For example, raw accelerometer values on a smartphone can identify the physical activities of a user [3], bluetooth and GPS sensors or audio could facilitate the determination of where and with whom people are with [8]. Meanwhile automatic detection of concepts is possible from images [14] using deep-learning based computer vision. These user activities combined with event ontologies can help to infer higher-level semantics on the lifestyle of individuals. We currently utilise the following virtual sensors in our personal digital archiving research; semantic date/time, meaningful location, personal physical activity, social interactions (via bluetooth), environmental context (via GPS and crowd-sourcing of relevant tags [19]), semantic visual concepts automatically identified from the photos and personal context of the user's life pattern. Together, these generate a detailed description of user activities and behaviours. In addition the relative importance or potential memorability of each episode can be determined via a combination of image face detection and bluetooth people recognition, in conjunction with the relative uniqueness of the situation the user is in (relative to their normal lifestyle) [18].

- *A simple narrative summary of each episode should be generated:* Individuals desire quick and simple episode summaries that are easy to understand. For example, Xu explains why such simple summaries are desired on a cognitive functioning level [46], *"The mental representation or situation model clearly depends upon interactions between the language system and complementary, extra-linguistic cognitive processes . . . the situation model is created by connecting the text with knowledge derived from the reader's long-term memory, and involves additional demands upon attention (e.g., the ability to shift points of view and parse sequences of events), working memory (the ability to retain longer term, anaphoric references), and the contribution of emotional knowledge, visual imagery, empathy, and abstraction"* [46]. Concise narratives are an important building block for personal life archives in that they are shown to produce emotional responses to autobiographical memories and help support many of the 5 Rs of memory access. This therefore motivates the needs to summarise the range of sensor stream semantic annotations into a meaningful and engaging descriptive narrative. A secondary benefit of such narrative generation is that the textual narratives can also be used to support keyword text search [38].

3.3 Life Archive Indexing and Annotation

To be able to retrieve life experiences for search or recommendation from personal life archive, either later or in real-time, the experiences and their annotations need to be indexed. An initial assumption would be to employ state-of-the-art techniques from artificial intelligence, database search and information retrieval to scalably index the life-experience events and provide omnipresent access via keyword/database search, ranking, recommending and presenting the multimedia rich life experience archive through multimodal interfaces. However, we contend that to better understand how to develop lifelogging solutions and how to support effective access to these data, it becomes necessary not simply to view this as a new form of multimedia retrieval challenge. Rather, it is important to understand how people will use and access their life archives. As a starting point, we turn again to the five R's of memory access from Sellen & Whittaker [41]. Each of the five Rs define a different reason why people want to access their memories, and by inference, their personal life archives. They provide valuable clues as to how to develop the organisation, search and presentation elements of Personal Life archives.

- Recollecting is concerned with reliving past experiences for various reasons. To take an analogy from cognitive science, Recollecting is concerned with accessing episodic memories. Recollecting will require highly accurate search engines that semantically rank content and extract just the nugget of information that is most pertinent to the user and represent this event in as much detail as possible to as to aid recollection. This will require conventional information retrieval, coupled with query-specific experience segmentation (somewhat similar to the Shot Boundary Detection [43] of digital video. This in itself is a motivation for 'total capture'.
- Reminiscing, which is a form of recollecting, is about reliving past experiences for emotional or sentimental reasons, sometimes alone, often with others. From information Retrieval, it will require new techniques for narrative generation [9], storytelling [7], topic detection and tracking [1] and novelty detection [47] from single (and potentially from multiple individual's archives), all operating in conjunction with conventional multimedia document ranking techniques, as required for Retrieving (below).
- Retrieving (information), is a more specific form of recollecting in which we seek to retrieve specific nuggets of information from the personal life archive. Retrieval will require highly accurate text, multimedia and sensor data search engines that semantically rank content and extract just the nugget of information that is most pertinent to the user. The conventional Information Retrieval concept of top N ranked lists does not successfully operate for personal life archives (unless N = 1); after all, there is marginal benefit in a system that provides a ranked list of locations for where the car has been left. The query will define the type of knowledge that is required; it is unlikely that a whole document would be expected in response to a query, as is the norm for WWW search. Rather the personal life archive is more akin to question answering in Wolfram Alpha than to whole document retrieval in Google.
- Reflecting, is a form of quantified self analysis over the life archive data to discover knowledge and insights. It includes information summarisation from lifelog streams [36], event detection [19] and various forms of data analysis to infer and evaluate the importance of new semantic knowledge [8, 14, 37, 44] from the personal life archive. Typically such data analysis approaches rely on artificial intelligence, machine learning and various forms of statistical analysis and should proactively recommend new knowledge, not solely relying on a human information need as input, due to the fact that reflecting from a personal life archive brings the potential for new knowledge discovery.
- Remembering Intentions, is a form of planning future activities which is a life activity that everyone engages in. This assists people to remind or prompt them on tasks they would like to do (*e.g. post that letter*), or real-time prompts on who they are talking to (*e.g. this is Paul*), or giving prompts on conversation cues (*e.g. last time here together, you had just come away from seeing the new Batman film*). Past lifelogging efforts were exclusively focused on episodic memory as it was always a post-hoc analysis (i.e. constrained by technology); however now with real-time technology available we can now consider situational awareness (and past history of user) to provide prospective memory prompts.

Taking the five Rs as a guide, it becomes possible to propose efficient methods that can effectively provide insights from the life archive, not simply in response to an explicit user query, but also in response to real-time contextual cues.

4 POTENTIAL APPLICATIONS

Getting insights from personal live archives will very soon be a phenomenon available to everyone and exploiting the personal life archives will positively impact on everyone who uses the technology. Through integration with other wearable sensors (e.g. 360 degree cameras) new opportunities are presented, namely:

- **Easy sharing of natural life experiences:** There has been an increased prevalence of photo sharing on social networking sites such as Facebook, Instagram or Flickr. In particular uploads from mobile devices are becoming ever more common, e.g., the Instagram website has 800 million monthly active users at the time of writing, who produce images, videos and stories of life experience. However at present, the user has had to make a conscious decision to capture every image or photo. This has meant that any experience a user wants to capture had to be interrupted to take a photograph. The lifelogging platform of passive life experience capture now allows users to enjoy their experiences, safe in the knowledge that the media rich experience can easily be reviewed and shared after the experience has ended.

- **Prospective memory feedback to enhance productivity:** Most memory research exploiting visual lifelogging has focused on retrospective episodic memory tasks [10]. However as real-time upload of the visual field-of-view becomes feasible, we can now begin to support human prospective memory [2]. Given a user's prior set of experiences and preferences (historical lifelog data), and their current situation (gathered via on-board mobile device and wearable sensors), prospective memory prompts can be provided.
- **Personalised wellness feedback:** Poor diet and physical activity lifestyle choices are strongly associated with the early death of millions of people [45]. Passive capture lifelogging devices offer the potential to automatically identify episodes of physical activity [31] and diet [39]. Through learning the extent of the user's current physical activity and diet levels, in addition to setting some targets, an individual can be automatically relayed prompts to help them make the healthy lifestyle choice.
- **A greater knowledge of self:** Coupled with the concept of personal wellness, the era of personal life archives will provide information to the individual about their own life activities and performance; information that otherwise would go unnoticed. One can identify trends and pattern in lifestyle and wellness over an extended period of time.
- **A memory assistant:** Neurodegerative disease affects a large proportion of an aging population and maintaining a personal life archive has been shown in initial small-scale studies to help offset some of the debilitating effects of memory impairment [27]. Even for individuals with fully functional memories, the ability to refer back to the personal life archive will allow for disambiguation of faded memories and more accurate recall of the past, when such accuracy is needed.
- **An opportunity to better understand the functioning of the human memory system:** Given that self-reporting is notoriously prone to error [31], visual lifelogs offer the opportunity to verify the contextual details of episodic memories recalled by individuals and can play an important part of modern studies into human memory.
- **A new source of evidence for epidemiological studies on a large-scale:** Understanding the determinants and barriers to human behaviours is important in designing interventions to assist humans [40]. Personal life archives, if shared with trusted parties, using some privacy-supporting legally compliant process has the potential to open new sources of population-wide behavioural and activity data. Some prior work in this area is the Kidscam project [42] which reports on a new methodology (using personal life archives of over a hundred children) to objectively study the world in which children live in terms of their exposure to fast-food advertising, alcohol, smoking, âĂIJblueâĂİ space and gambling, and their use of âĂIJgreenâĂİ space, transport, and sun protection.

The potential for personal life archives is enormous. We do acknowledge that there are challenges to be overcome, such as privacy concerns, data storage, security of data, and the development of a new generation of search and organisation tools, but we believe that these will be overcome and that we are on the cusp of a positive turning point for society; the era of the quantified individual who knows more about the self than ever before, has more knowledge to improve the quality of their own life and can share life events and experiences in rich detail with friends and contacts.

5 INITIAL IMPLEMENTATION

This section presents our first implementations to tackle the challenges mentioned earlier as well as to inspire and motivate researchers in the multimedia analysis and retrieval community to use their expertise in this new emerging and societal important area.

5.1 Building Personal Life Archive Datasets

Researchers usually need data to evaluate their methods, and there is no exception for researchers in personal life archive organisation and retrieval. To support such research efforts, large volumes of lifelog data have been gathered from several volunteer lifeloggers and organized, annotated and published them for researchers as the two lifelogging tasks in NTCIR 12 - Lifelog [24, 25] and NTCIR 13 - Lifelog 2[2]. To the best of our knowledge, these collections are the largest (in terms of number of days and the size of the collection) and richest (in terms of types of information) datasets on personal life archives ever shared. These datasets are summarised in Table 1.

Moreover, over the last decade, we identified the challenges for building a shared personal life archive dataset [22], proposed principles, built and described the whole processes from data gathering to determining the roles for the people who are building, sharing and exploiting such kind of data [13]. These principles can be considered as references for systems that collect personal life archives.

Table 1: Statistics of the Datasets.

	NTCIR-12	NTCIR-13
Number of Lifeloggers	**3**	**2**
Number of days	**87**	**90**
Size of the Collection (GB)	**18.18**	**26.6**
Size of the Collection (Images)	**88,124**	**114,547**
Size of the Collection (Locations)	**130**	**138**

[2] http://ntcir-lifelog.computing.dcu.ie/

5.2 Benchmarking Initiatives and Workshops on Life Archive Analytics

As the first step of building the community working on personal life archives, we increasingly organize related workshops and panels: iConf 2016[3], Lifelogging Tools and Applications in ACM MM 2016 [23] and ACM MM 2017[4].

Together with these, we organize rigorous comparative benchmarking initiatives: NTCIR 12 - Lifelog [24, 25], NTCIR 13 - Lifelog 2, and the LifeLog task [12] at ImageCLEF 2017 [28], which aim to bring the attention of personal live archive analytics to a wide audience and to motivate research into some of the key challenges of the field.

Table 2: Statistics of the Benchmarking Campaigns.

	NTCIR-12 (2016)	NTCIR-13 (2017)	ImageCLEF (2017)
Number of Tasks	**2**	**4**	**2**
Number of Topics	**58**	**59**	**51**
Number of Submissions	**14**	**21**	**18**

Typically, for each benchmarking initiative, together with the dataset, we introduced several tasks which aims to advance the state-of-the-art research in lifelogging as an application of information retrieval. For example, in ImageCLEFlifelog 2017 edition[12], we introduce two tasks: Lifelog Retrieval Task (LRT) and Lifelog Summarisation Task (LS). In LRT, the participants had to analyse the lifelog data and for several specific queries, return the correct answers, for example *"In a Meeting: Find the moment(s) in which the user was in a meeting at work with 2 or more people"*. In LST, the participants had to analyse all the images and summarize them according to specific requirements. For instance: *"Shopping: Summarize the moment(s) in which user doing shopping. To be relevant, the user must clearly be inside a supermarket or shopping stores (includes book store, convenient store, pharmacy, etc). Passing by or otherwise seeing a supermarket are not considered relevant if the user does not enter the shop to go shopping. Blurred or out of focus images are not relevant. Images that are covered (mostly by the lifelogger's arm) are not relevant."*

Table 2 summarises our evaluation benchmarking campaigns. According to the results, we can confirm that the proposed dataset is enough for the proposed topics, in which the answers can be achieved by exploiting the provided multimodal data. For more details of these campaigns, please see in [12, 24, 25].

5.3 A Base-line Search Engine for Life Archives

Another means of supporting the research community, besides constructing datasets, organizing benchmarking initiatives and workshops, is building a baseline search engine for personal life archives. This baseline engine serves as a basic retrieval system where the query is made up from basic information needs, where each of them is asking for a single piece of information, which are already extracted and indexed. Queries were submitted that generate ranked lists based on faceted queries, by userID, location visual concept and/or physical activity. A preliminary version of this search engine can be obtained via: `http://search-lifelog.computing.dcu.ie/`, which provides a basic retrieval model for the lifelog datasets (other details of the data used in this baseline search engine are summarised in Table 3).

[3]http://irlld2016.computing.dcu.ie/index.html

[4]http://lta2017.computing.dcu.ie

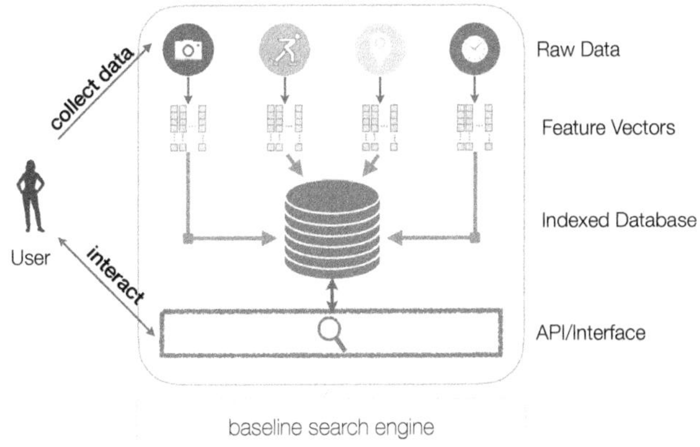

Figure 1: The baseline search engine architecture

Table 3: Statistics of the Data Used in the Baseline Search Engine.

Number of Lifeloggers	**1**
Number of Days	**90** days
Size of the Collection	**12.2** GB
Number of Images	**51,209** images
Number of Locations	**24** locations

Figure 1 summarises how we designed the baseline search engine system [48], as follows: from the raw lifelog data, we extract locations, visual concepts, time, and activities and transformed this raw data into indexable feature vectors. These feature vectors are then indexed and hierarchically organized. Finally, a user or other system can define a faceted query and retrieve ranked moments via the interface.

5.3.1 Data Organisation and Retrieval Process. To organise and index the data, we arrange features in chronological order, and use the minute as the basic unit of indexing and retrieval. Building up from these minutes, we organize the data at higher level which can be turned into more useful information, the minutes are hierarchically grouped into event nodes (typically, in a full day, a person encounters anything upwards of 20 individual events, with each lasting (on average) 30 minutes [17, 30]), then ultimately leading to larger units such as days and multi-day events (e.g. holidays).

In order to turn a query into specific criteria, i.e., to make the baseline search engine able to extract insights from the personal life archive, we apply two approaches: firstly, automatic query generation by considering the terms in the query as identifiers of concepts and then searching for all images that contain those concepts, and secondly, a fine-tunning method by manually generating a query string i.e., the researcher (we) will read the topic and "translate" it into the search criteria. For example, with the query:

(a) 20160818_Taking a train (b) 20160827_Taking an airplane (c) 20160829_Taking a bus

(d) 20160830_Taking a taxi (e) 20160906_Taking a coach (e) 20160906_Taking a bus

Figure 2: Examples of the results retrieved by the proposed baseline search engine for the query "Find the moment when I was taking public transportation or taxi at sunset."

`"Find the moments when user u1 was using public transportation or taxi at sunset."`

We follow the study methodology proposed in [49] and "translate" that query into specific required pieces of information, as follows:

- `User = {u1},`
- `Concepts = {sunset},`
- `Activity = {transport, airplane},`
- `time = {16:00-21:00}`
- `Location = {n/A}`

5.3.2 Ranking. To refine the results, i.e., to increase the precision of the top retrieved images, we use a hierarchical agglomerative clustering algorithm (see [11]) to group similar images into the same cluster based on all of their features. The clusters are then sorted based on the number of images, in decreasing rank order. Finally, we produce the ranked list by selecting representative images from the clusters by choosing the images closest to the center of each cluster.

5.3.3 Results. We applied the baseline search engine to the benchmarking campaigns mentioned in Section 5.2, serving as a baseline for the comparison. For some topics, the scores were 1.00 and 0.92 for precision and recall, which shows the potential of this baseline search engine. Consequently, this engine was added as a part of the campaigns, allowing participant to obtain baseline results and develop more complex retrieval systems on-top of this baseline search engine. Some other examples can be seen in Figure 2.

6 CONCLUSIONS

In this paper we presented a set of possible challenges and opportunities from personal life archives. We identified methods and technologies that can aid users to get insights in their data, from public resources to their social connections and closer intimacy, and moreover, from their personal life archive, including different granularities of information from their past experiences. We presented the current state of the field and provided a number of potential benefits. Furthermore, we identified and proposed solutions to the challenges that arise with such data. This will be increasingly important over the coming years as we learn more about ourselves and have access to technologies that will help us in many aspects of everyday life. We also showed that there are several research challenges to address in the fields of Artificial Intelligence, Cognitive Science and Information Retrieval. Starting with security and privacy, human computer interaction, and memory science, valuable insights into how to address these challenges can be obtained. Finally we presented a baseline search enginge that achieves reasonable results that can be useful for other researchers interested in the field.

REFERENCES

[1] James Allan. 2002. Topic detection and tracking. Kluwer Academic Publishers, Norwell, MA, USA, Chapter Introduction to topic detection and tracking, 1–16.

[2] Alan Baddeley (Ed.). 2004. *Your Memory: A User's Guide.* Carlton Books.

[3] Ling Bao and Stephen Intille. 2004. Activity Recognition from User-Annotated Acceleration Data. In *Pervasive Computing*, Alois Ferscha and Friedemann Mattern (Eds.). Lecture Notes in Computer Science, Vol. 3001. Springer Berlin / Heidelberg, 1–17.

[4] Gordon Bell and Jim Gemmell. 2007. A Digital Life. *Scientific American* (2007).

[5] Gordon Bell and Jim Gemmell (Eds.). 2009. *Total Recall: How the E-Memory Revolution Will Change Everything.* Penguin Books.

[6] Vannevar Bush. 1945. As We May Think. *The Atlantic Monthly* 176, 1 (Jul 1945), 101–108.

[7] Daragh Byrne, Aisling Kelliher, and Gareth J. F. Jones. 2011. Life editing: third-party perspectives on lifelog content.. In *CHI*, Desney S. Tan, Saleema Amershi, Bo Begole, Wendy A. Kellogg, and Manas Tungare (Eds.). ACM, 1501–1510.

[8] Daragh Byrne, Barry Lavelle, Aiden Roger Doherty, Gareth J.F. Jones, and Alan F. Smeaton. 2007. Using Bluetooth and GPS Metadata to Measure Event Similarity in SenseCam Images. In *IMAI'07 - 5th International Conference on Intelligent Multimedia and Ambient Intelligence.* 1454–1460.

[9] Charles B. Callaway and James C. Lester. 2002. Narrative prose generation. *Artif. Intell.* 139, 2 (Aug. 2002), 213–252.

[10] Martin A. Conway and Catherine Loveday. 2011. SenseCam: The Future of Everyday Memory Research. *Memory* 19, 7 (Oct 2011), 685–807.

[11] Duc-Tien Dang-Nguyen, Luca Piras, Giorgio Giacinto, Giulia Boato, and Francesco GB DE Natale. 2017. Multimodal retrieval with diversification and relevance feedback for tourist attraction images. *ACM Transactions on Multimedia Computing, Communications, and Applications (TOMM)* 13, 4 (2017), 49.

[12] Duc-Tien Dang-Nguyen, Luca Piras, Michael Riegler, Giulia Boato, Liting Zhou, and Cathal Gurrin. 2017. Overview of ImageCLEFlifelog 2017: Lifelog Retrieval and Summarization. In *CLEF2017 Working Notes (CEUR Workshop Proceedings).* CEUR-WS.org <http://ceur-ws.org>, Dublin, Ireland.

[13] Duc-Tien Dang-Nguyen, Liting Zhou, Rashmi Gupta, Michael Riegler, and Cathal Gurrin. 2017. Building a Disclosed Lifelog Dataset: Challenges, Principles and Processes. In *Content-Based Multimedia Indexing (CBMI).*

[14] Aiden Roger Doherty, Niamh Caprani, Ciaran O Conaire, Vaiva Kalnikaite, Cathal Gurrin, Alan F. Smeaton, and Noel E. O Connor. 2011. Passively recognising human activities through lifelogging. *Computers in Human Behavior* 27, 5 (2011), 1948–1958.

[15] Aiden Roger Doherty, Chris J.A. Moulin, and Alan F. Smeaton. 2011. Automatically assisting human memory: A SenseCam browser. *Memory* 7, 19 (2011), 785–795.

[16] Aiden Roger Doherty, K Pauly-Takacs, N Caprani, Cathal Gurrin, C J A Moulin, N E OÊijConnor, and Alan F. Smeaton. 2012. Experiences of Aiding Autobiographical Memory Using the SenseCam. *Human-Computer Interaction* 27, 1-2 (2012), 151–174.

[17] Aiden Roger Doherty and Alan F. Smeaton. 2008. Automatically segmenting lifelog data into events. In *Ninth International Workshop on Image Analysis for Multimedia Interactive Services.* IEEE, 20–23.

[18] Aiden Roger Doherty and Alan F. Smeaton. 2008. Combining Face Detection and Novelty to Identify Important Events in a Visual Lifelog. In *CIT: 8th International Conference on Computer and Information Technology, Workshop on Image- and Video-based Pattern Analysis and Applications.* IEEE Computer Society, Washington, DC, USA.

[19] Aiden Roger Doherty and Alan F. Smeaton. 2010. Automatically augmenting lifelog events using pervasively generated content from millions of people. *Sensors (Peterboroug* 10, 3 (2010), 1423–1446.

[20] Jim Gemmell, Gordon Bell, and Roger Lueder. 2006. MyLifeBits: a personal database for everything. *Commun. ACM* 49, 1 (2006), 88–95.

[21] Cathal Gurrin, Rami Albatal, Hideo Joho, and Kaori Ishii. 2014. A privacy by design approach to lifelogging. *Digital Enlightenment Yearbook 2014* (2014), 49–73.

[22] Cathal Gurrin, Daragh Byrne, Noel O'Connor, Gareth JF Jones, and Alan F. Smeaton. 2008. Architecture and challenges of maintaining a large-scale, context-aware human digital memory. In *International Conference on Visual Information Engineering.* 158–163.

[23] Cathal Gurrin, X. Giró-i Nieto, Petia Radeva, M. Dimiccoli, H. Johansen, H. Joho, and Vivek K Singh. 2016. LTA 2016 - The First Workshop on Lifelogging Tools and Applications. (10/2016 2016).

[24] Cathal Gurrin, Hideo Joho, Frank Hopfgartner, Liting Zhou, and Rami Albatal. 2016. NTCIR Lifelog: The First Test Collection for Lifelog Research. (2016), 705–708.

[25] Cathal Gurrin, Hideo Joho, Frank Hopfgartner, Liting Zhou, and Rami Albatal. 2016. Overview of NTCIR-12 Lifelog Task. , 354–360 pages.

[26] Cathal Gurrin, Alan F. Smeaton, and Aiden Roger Doherty. 2014. LifeLogging: Personal Big Data. *Foundations and Trends in Information Retrieval* 8, 1 (2014), 1–125.

[27] Steve Hodges, Emma Berry, and Ken Wood. 2011. SenseCam: A wearable camera that stimulates and rehabilitates autobiographical memory. *Memory* 7, 19 (2011), 685–696.

[28] Bogdan Ionescu, Henning Müller, Mauricio Villegas, Helbert Arenas, Giulia Boato, Duc-Tien Dang-Nguyen, Yashin Dicente Cid, Carsten Eickhoff, Alba Garcia Seco de Herrera, Cathal Gurrin, Kovalev Vassili Islam, Bayzidul and, Vitali Liauchuk, Josiane Mothe, Luca Piras, Michael Riegler, and Immanuel Schwall. 2017. Overview of ImageCLEF 2017: Information extraction from images. In *CLEF 2017 Proceedings.* Springer, Dublin, Ireland.

[29] Ramesh Jain and Pinaki Sinha. 2010. Content without context is meaningless. In *Proceedings of the international conference on Multimedia (MM '10).* ACM, New York, NY, USA, 1259–1268.

[30] Daniel Kahneman, Alan B. Krueger, David A. Schkade, Norbert Schwarz, and Arthur A. Stone. 2004. A Survey Method for Characterizing Daily Life Experience: The Day Reconstruction Method. *Science* 306 (2004), 1776–1780.

[31] Paul Kelly, Aiden Roger Doherty, Emma Berry, Steve Hodges, Alan M. Batterham, and charlie Foster. 2011. Can we use digital life-log images to investigate active and sedentary travel behaviour? Results from a pilot study. *Intnational Journal Behavioural Nutrition Physical Activity* 8 (2011), 44.

[32] S. Mann. 1997. Wearable computing: A first step toward personal imaging. *Computer* 30, 2 (1997), 25–32.

[33] Jochen Meyer, Steven Simske, Katie A. Siek, Cathal G. Gurrin, and Hermie Hermens. 2014. Beyond Quantified Self: Data for Wellbeing. In *CHI '14 Extended Abstracts on Human Factors in Computing Systems (CHI EA '14).* ACM, New York, NY, USA, 95–98. https://doi.org/10.1145/2559206.2560469

[34] Theodor H. Nelson. 1988. Managing immense storage. *BYTE* 13, 1 (Jan. 1988), 225–238.

[35] David H. Nguyen, Gabriela Marcu, Gillian R. Hayes, Khai N. Truong, James Scott, Marc Langheinrich, and Christof Roduner. 2009. Encountering SenseCam: personal recording technologies in everyday life. In *Ubicomp '09: Proceedings of the 11th international conference on Ubiquitous computing.* 165–174.

[36] Y. Ogras and Hakan Ferhatosmanoglu. 2006. Online summarization of dynamic time series data. *The VLDB Journal* 15, 1 (Jan. 2006), 84–98.

[37] Zhengwei Qiu, Aiden Roger Doherty, Cathal Gurrin, and Alan F. Smeaton. 2011. Mining user activity as a context source for search and retrieval. In *Semantic Technology and Information Retrieval (STAIR), 2011 International Conference on.* 162 -166.

[38] Z.W. Qiu, Cathal Gurrin, and Alan F. Smeaton. 2016. Evaluating Access Mechanisms for Multimodal Representations of Lifelogs. In *International Conference on Multimedia Modelling.* I: 574–585.

[39] Sasank Reddy, Andrew Parker, Josh Hyman, Jeff Burke, Deborah Estrin, and Mark Hansen. 2007. Image browsing, processing, and clustering for participatory sensing: lessons from a DietSense prototype. In *EmNets '07: Proceedings of the 4th workshop on Embedded networked sensors.* ACM, New York, NY, USA, 13–17.

[40] J. F. Sallis, N. Owen, and M. J. Fotheringham. 2000. Behavioral epidemiology: a systematic framework to classify phases of research on health promotion and disease prevention. *Ann Behav Med* 22 (2000), 294–298.

[41] Abigail J. Sellen and Steve Whittaker. 2010. Beyond total capture: a constructive critique of lifelogging. *Comm. ACM* 53, 5 (2010), 70–77.

[42] Louise N. Signal, Moira B. Smith, Michelle Barr, James Stanley, Tim J. Chambers, Jiang Zhou, Aaron Duane, Gabrielle L.S. Jenkin, Amber L. Pearson, Cathal Gurrin, Alan F. Smeaton, Janet Hoek, and Cliona Ni Mhurchu. 2017. KidsâĂŽCam: An Objective Methodology to Study the World in Which Children Live. *American Journal of Preventive Medicine* 53, 3 (2017), e89 – e95. https://doi.org/10.1016/j.amepre.2017.02.016

[43] Alan F. Smeaton, Paul Over, and Aiden Roger Doherty. 2010. Video shot boundary detection: Seven years of TRECVid activity. *Computer Vision and Image Understanding* 114, 4 (2010), 411 – 418.

[44] D. Tancharoen, T. Yamasaki, and K. Aizawa. 2006. Practical Life Log Video Indexing Based on Content and Context. In *Multimedia Content Analysis, Management, and Retieval ï£¡ In Proceedings of SPIE-IST Electronic Imaging.*

[45] WHO. 2007. *A guide for population based approaches to increasing levels of physical activity: Implementation of the WHO global strategy on diet, physical activity and health.* World Health Organisation.

[46] J. Xu, S. Kemeny, G. Park, C. Frattali, and A. Braun. 2005. Language in context: emergent features of word, sentence, and narrative comprehension. *Neuroimage* 25, 3 (2005), 1002–1015.

[47] Le Zhao, Min Zhang, and Shaoping Ma. 2006. The nature of novelty detection. *Inf. Retr.* 9, 5 (Nov. 2006), 521–541.

[48] Liting Zhou, Duc-Tien Dang-Nguyen, and Cathal Gurrin. 2017. A Baseline Search Engine for Personal Life Archives. In *Proceedings of the 2nd Workshop on Lifelogging Tools and Applications (LTA '17).* 21–24.

[49] Liting Zhou, Luca Piras, Michael Rieger, Giulia Boato, Duc-Tien Dang-Nguyen, and Cathal Gurrin. 2017. Organizer Team at ImageCLEFlifelog 2017: Baseline Approaches for Lifelog Retrieval and Summarization. *CLEF working notes, CEUR* (September 11-14 2017).

Object Trajectory Proposal via Hierarchical Volume Grouping

Xu Sun[1], Yuantian Wang[1], Tongwei Ren[1,*], Zhi Liu[2], Zheng-Jun Zha[3], and Gangshan Wu[1]
[1] State Key Laboratory for Novel Software Technology, Nanjing University, Nanjing, China
[2] School of Communication and Information Engineering, Shanghai University, Shanghai, China
[3] University of Science and Technology of China, China
sunx@smail.nju.edu.cn, wangyt@smail.nju.edu.cn, rentw@nju.edu.cn, liuzhi@staff.shu.edu.cn, zhazj@ustc.edu.cn, gswu@nju.edu.cn

ABSTRACT

Object trajectory proposal aims to locate category-independent object candidates in videos with a limited number of trajectories, *i.e.*, bounding box sequences. Most existing methods, which derive from combining object proposal with tracking, cannot handle object trajectory proposal effectively due to the lack of comprehensive objectness measurement through analyzing spatio-temporal characteristics over a whole video. In this paper, we propose a novel object trajectory proposal method using hierarchical volume grouping. Specifically, we first represent a given video with hierarchical volumes by mapping hierarchical regions with optical flow. Then, we filter the short volumes and background volumes, and combinatorially group the retained volumes into object candidates. Finally, we rank the object candidates using a multi-modal fusion scoring mechanism, which incorporates both appearance objectness and motion objectness, and generate the bounding boxes of the object candidates with the highest scores as the trajectory proposals. We validated the proposed method on a dataset consisting of 200 videos from ILSVRC2016-VID. The experimental results show that our method is superior to the state-of-the-art object trajectory proposal methods.

CCS CONCEPTS

• **Artificial intelligence → Computer vision**; *Hierarchical representations*;

KEYWORDS

Object trajectory proposal, hierarchical volume representation, volume combinatorial grouping, multi-modal fusion scoring

ACM Reference Format:
Xu Sun[1], Yuantian Wang[1], Tongwei Ren[1,*], Zhi Liu[2], Zheng-Jun Zha[3], and Gangshan Wu[1]. 2018. Object Trajectory Proposal via Hierarchical Volume Grouping. In *ICMR'18: 2018 International Conference on Multimedia Retrieval, June 11–14, 2018, Yokohama, Japan.* ACM, New York, NY, USA, 9 pages. https://doi.org/10.1145/3206025.3206059

ICMR'18, June 11–14, 2018, Yokohama, Japan

ACM ISBN 978-1-4503-5046-4/18/06...$15.00
https://doi.org/10.1145/3206025.3206059

Figure 1: An example of object trajectory proposal using object proposal and tracking combination and our grouping method.

1 INTRODUCTION

Object trajectory proposal aims to locate category-independent object candidates in videos with a limited number of bounding box sequences named *trajectory* [29]. These generated trajectory proposals provide spatio-temporal characteristics of object candidates, which can be extracted and analyzed in numerous multimedia applications, such as object detection [17], action recognition [34], visual relation detection [28], object segmentation [35] and content-based video retrieval [8].

A primary strategy for object trajectory proposal is to take advantage of the advances in object proposal, which is studied to locate category-independent object candidates in images with a limited number of bounding boxes. Most existing object trajectory proposal methods apply object proposal on one or several selected video frames, and track the generated bounding boxes on other frames to generate trajectory proposals [12, 21, 30, 39]. Nevertheless, it is intractable to automatically select one or few video frames that contain all the objects appearing in a given video. As shown in the top row of Figure 1, two objects are omitted because the object proposal is only applied on the middle frame but these two objects do not appear in this frame. As the state-of-the-art object proposal methods like [10, 43] and object detection methods like [7, 26] can process images in real-time, some works apply object proposal densely or even on all the frames to avoid object omission. Different to specific object detection, such as pedestrian[2, 7], this kind of trajectory proposal methods can easily obtain excessive candidates, because the features of category-independent objects are much more general than those in particular categories. It will lead to high time consumption in object tracking and candidate merging. To make matters worse, these methods only measure objectness on video frames with appearance characteristics, but ignore the characteristics of object candidates on other modalities, such as motion.

Recently, Shang *et al.* [29] improve this strategy by traversing all the video frames with bounded computational cost and partially incorporating object motion in objectness measurement. However, they still conduct objectness measurement independently on each frame instead of generating object candidates through analyzing spatio-temporal characteristics over the whole video.

To overcome these drawbacks, we learn from the advances in object proposal on images. There are two strategies mainly used in object proposal: window scoring and grouping. The former samples sufficient bounding boxes and selects the ones with high objectness scores as proposals, while the latter segments images into regions and merges them into proposals. Considering there exist enormous possible trajectories in a video which cannot be sufficiently sampled, we choose grouping strategy for conducting object trajectory proposal in a whole video. Similar to grouping-based object proposal methods, there are three key issues which should be addressed in grouping-based object trajectory proposal methods: First, how to define a type of basic unit that facilitates grouping to represent various video content? Second, how to group the basic units into object candidates even they have complex compositions? Third, how to score the object candidates with the spatio-temporal characteristics of the video?

In this paper, we propose a novel object trajectory proposal method based on hierarchical volume grouping. Figure 2 shows an overview of the proposed method. Given a video, we first represent it with hierarchical volumes by mapping hierarchical regions with optical flow. Then, we filter the short volumes and the background volumes, and group the retained volumes into object candidates. Finally, we rank the object candidates by fusing appearance objectness and motion objectness, and generate the bounding boxes for the object candidates with the highest scores as the trajectory proposals. A grouping-based method with a similar framework was proposed in [13]. However, it has obvious limitations in addressing the aforementioned key issues of grouping-based object trajectory proposal (refer to Section 2.2) which leads to its unsatisfactory performance (refer to Section 4.3) as compared to that of our method. We validated the proposed method on a dataset consisting of 200 videos from ILSVRC2016-VID [27]. It shows that our method outperforms the state-of-the-art object trajectory proposal methods.

Our contributions mainly include:

- We propose a grouping-based object trajectory proposal method, which generates trajectory proposals by analyzing the spatio-temporal characteristics over a whole given video.
- We present multiple key techniques, namely hierarchical volume representation, volume combinatorial grouping, and multi-modal fusion scoring, which can effectively address the key issues in grouping-based object trajectory proposal.
- We construct a dataset with 200 videos from ILSVRC2016-VID to validate the performance of the proposed method. The experimental results show that our method is superior to the state-of-the-art methods.

2 RELATED WORK

2.1 Object proposal

The existing object proposal methods can be roughly classified into two categories: window scoring-based methods and grouping-based methods.

Window scoring-based methods measure the objectness of sufficiently sampled bounding boxes and select the bounding boxes with high scores as proposals on RGB images [1, 10, 40, 43] and RGB-D images [19]. Generally speaking, window scoring-based methods are efficient in object proposal, but they easily fail to generate the proposals with high Intersection of Union (IoU) to the groundtruths of objects.

Grouping-based methods segment images into regions and merge them into proposals on RGB images [20, 23, 33] and RGB-D images [36]. In contrast, grouping-based methods can generate accurate proposals against the groundtruths, but they usually have low efficiency because of the time-consuming bottom-up merging.

2.2 Object trajectory proposal

Most existing object trajectory methods derive from combining object proposal with tracking. Some methods mainly focuses on salient objects [30, 38] or moving objects [15, 22], while other methods extract objects in a unified objectness strategy [9, 12, 18, 21, 29, 39]. As mentioned above, these methods cannot handle object trajectory proposal effectively due to the lack of comprehensive objectness measurement through analyzing spatio-temporal characteristics over the whole video.

Dan *et al.* [13] first propose a grouping-based object trajectory proposal method using supervoxel clustering. Though Dan's method is similar in overview as compared to our method, it has some obvious limitations in addressing the key issues of grouping-based object trajectory proposal. First, Dan's method uses the supervoxels generated by hierarchical clustering as the basic units in grouping. These supervoxels on the coarsest level may not contain the detailed object portions because of the inaccuracy of clustering. In contrast, our method represents the video with hierarchical volume, which contains all the levels for the subsequent grouping. Second, Dan's method only merges the supervoxels with high similarities in grouping, which cannot group the object parts with different appearances. In contrast, our method uses combinatorial grouping, which can combine the neighboring volumes with significant differences. Third, Dan's method does not provide an effective scoring strategy, which directly treats the clustering result as the proposals. Our method presents a multi-modal fusing scoring mechanism to measure appearance objectness and motion objectness together.

2.3 Object tracking

Object tracking aims to estimate the existence and locations of target objects in the subsequent frames. Numerous object tracking methods have been proposed. For example, sparse representation based methods utilize local sparse representations and collaborative representations to determine the target locations [6, 41]; color histogram based methods track target objects via pixel level statistics [11, 25] and edge information [24, 32]; discriminative

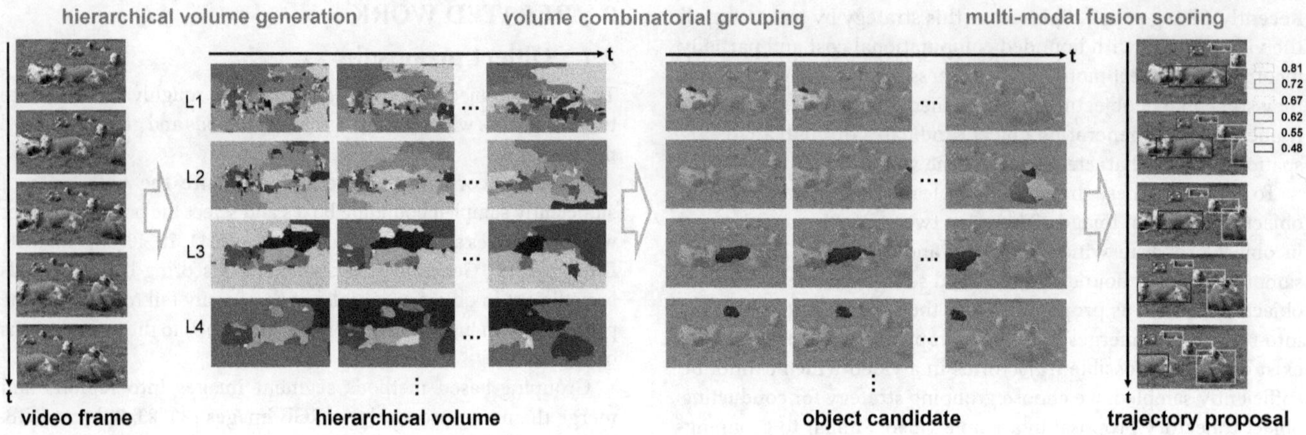

Figure 2: An overview of the proposed method.

model based methods utilize learned binary classifiers to segment the target objects from background [4, 5]. Although both tracking and trajectory proposal generate bounding box sequences as their outputs, they are significantly different. First, object tracking requires one or several manually labeled bounding boxes on the first frame for initialization while trajectory proposal searches for object candidates on all the frames automatically. Second, tracking only searches for similar regions through adjacent frames while trajectory proposal requires to measure objectness for trajectory candidates and eliminates those with low objectness. Third, the number of the trajectories extracted by trajectory proposal is much larger than the number of those generated by tracking, which means that trajectory proposal has stricter computational cost limitation in trajectory generation.

3 OUR METHOD

3.1 Hierarchical volume representation

Hierarchical volume is the basic unit of combinatorial grouping in our method. A volume is a spatio-temporal component within a given video, which is composed of a sequence of ordered regions. In effective hierarchical volume representation, each volume covers the regions with the same content on consecutive frames with coherent boundaries and accurate duration on different levels. Such hierarchical volume representation retains both the principal components and partial details of objects, and helps to generate object candidates.

Hierarchical region representation of video frame. To obtain the hierarchical volume representation of a video, we first represent each video frame with hierarchical regions referring to [23]. Specifically, we detect the contours in a given video frame and weight them in the value range of $[0, 1]$ using ultra-metric contour map [3], in which color, brightness and texture gradient are combined to provide indexed contours for hierarchical regions. Based on these contours, we obtain the finest region representation of the video frame. Then, we merge these regions iteratively by removing the contours whose strengths are lower than an incremental threshold from a set of trained thresholds. The regions surrounded with the rest of closed contours in each iteration are constructed as the hierarchical regions.

To each frame f^t, assume the number of leaf regions (*i.e.*, the regions on the finest level), is N_L^t and the number of the regions on all the levels is N_R^t. We construct a binary matrix $\mathbf{C}^t$ in size of $N_R^t \times N_L^t$ to denote the coverage relationships between hierarchical regions and leaf regions. Here, $\mathbf{C}_{i,j}^t$ equals 1 if the ith hierarchical region covers the jth leaf region; otherwise, it equals 0.

Volume generation by region mapping. We map the hierarchical regions on adjacent video frames to generate hierarchical volumes. Rather than directly searching the most similar region for each region in the subsequent frame, which is very time consuming, we utilize optical flow to establish the mapping relationships between regions on adjacent frames, because optical flow estimation is only required to conduct once for a whole frame and it can be used for the mapping of all the regions in the frame.

We first estimate bidirectional dense optical flow using Deepflow [37], which effectively handles large displacements in videos via dense correspondences matching. To two adjacent video frames f^t and f^{t+1}, we construct two matrices $\mathbf{O}^{t\to t+1}$ in size of $N_L^t \times N_L^{t+1}$ and $\mathbf{O}^{t+1\to t}$ in size of $N_L^{t+1} \times N_L^t$ to denote the mapping relationships between the leaf regions in f^t and f^{t+1}. Specifically, $\mathbf{O}_{i,j}^{t\to t+1}$ denotes the number of the pixels in the ith leaf region in f^t whose corresponding pixels mapped with the optical flow from f^t to f^{t+1} belong to the jth leaf region in f^{t+1}:

$$\mathbf{O}_{i,j}^{t\to t+1} = |P_i^{t\to t+1} \cap P_j^{t+1}|, \tag{1}$$

where $P_i^{t\to t+1}$ is the set of the pixels in f^{t+1} which are mapped with optical flow from the pixels in the ith leaf region in f^t; P_j^{t+1} denotes the set of the pixels belonging to the jth leaf region in f^{t+1}; $|\cdot|$ denotes the cardinality of a set, *i.e.*, the number of pixels within a set. The elements in $\mathbf{O}^{t+1\to t}$ are defined in a similar manner.

Based on the region coverage matrix and the leaf region mapping matrix, we map the hierarchical regions between the adjacent frames. To f^t and f^{t+1}, we construct two matrices $\mathbf{M}^{t\to t+1}$ in size of $N_R^t \times N_R^{t+1}$ and $\mathbf{M}^{t+1\to t}$ in size of $N_R^{t+1} \times N_R^t$ to denote the mapping relationships between the hierarchical regions in f^t and

f^{t+1}:

$$\mathbf{M}^{t\to t+1} = \mathbf{C}^t\mathbf{O}^{t\to t+1}(\mathbf{C}^{t+1})^{\mathrm{T}}, \quad (2)$$
$$\mathbf{M}^{t+1\to t} = \mathbf{C}^{t+1}\mathbf{O}^{t+1\to t}(\mathbf{C}^{t})^{\mathrm{T}}. \quad (3)$$

where each element $\mathbf{M}_{i,j}^{t\to t+1}$ in $\mathbf{M}^{t\to t+1}$ denotes the number of the pixels in the ith region in f^t whose corresponding pixels mapped with the optical flow from f^t to f^{t+1} belong to the jth region in f^{t+1}. The elements in $\mathbf{M}^{t+1\to t}$ are defined in a similar manner.

We normalize the elements in $\mathbf{M}^{t\to t+1}$ to construct a matrix $\Psi^{t\to t+1}$ as follows:

$$\Psi_{i,j}^{t\to t+1} = \mathbf{M}_{i,j}^{t\to t+1}/|Q_i^t|, \quad (4)$$

where Q_i^t denotes the set of the pixels belong to the ith hierarchical region in f^t; $|\cdot|$ denotes the cardinality of a set. We can construct a matrix $\Psi^{t+1\to t}$ from $\mathbf{M}^{t+1\to t}$ in a similar manner.

To each hierarchical region in f^t, we search its mapping region in f^{t+1} by checking the elements in the ith row in $\Psi^{t\to t+1}$ and the ith column in $\Psi^{t+1\to t}$. If both $\Psi_{i,j}^{t\to t+1}$ and $\Psi_{j,i}^{t+1\to t}$ are larger than a predefined threshold, which equals 0.5 in our experiments, we consider the ith region in f^t is mapped to the jth region in f^{t+1} successfully and merge them into a volume. If a region in f^t is mapped to more than one regions in f^{t+1}, we select the one with the highest mapping score, *i.e.*, the sum of $\Psi_{i,j}^{t\to t+1}$ and $\Psi_{j,i}^{t+1\to t}$. We repeat the above procedure from the first frame to the last one, and generate hierarchical volumes by merging the mapped regions.

Note here, we map the hierarchical regions and retain the volumes on all the levels for the subsequent grouping, *i.e.*, one volume generated by our method may contain another volume or its portions. In contrast, supervoxels in [13] are generated by hierarchical clustering of single level superpixels, which only consist of the coarsest regions and have no overlap between each other.

There are two advantages of our hierarchical volume representation as compared to hierarchical supervoxel in [13]. On the one hand, it is difficult to find appropriate relationships when directly mapping the regions in the adjacent frames on superpixel level. In fact, we cannot generate the volumes with long lengths (the length of a volume denotes the number of the regions belonging to the volume) by mapping the leaf regions in the experiments unless we relax the mapping threshold to a small value. It leads to the generated supervoxels with low cohesion and prevents the effectiveness of the supervoxel representation in [13]. On the other hand, both the generation of hierarchical volume and supervoxel are only based on low-level features, which inevitably brings in inaccuracy. If only using the supervoxels composed of the coarsest regions [13], the detailed object portions lost in clustering cannot be obtained in grouping. It will further cause the inaccuracy of generating trajectory proposals. As comparison, our method generates the volumes in different levels and retains most of them, which will provide more comprehensive candidates in grouping.

Broken volume connection. Our hierarchical volume representation maps the regions based on optical flow, but optical flow only represents the low-level similarity between pixels in adjacent frames. It is easy to generate broken volumes because optical flow is sensitive to partial occlusion and illumination variation. These broken volumes increase the complexity of grouping them into the object candidates. Hence, we connect the volumes, which may represent the same content, based on their high-level appearance similarities.

Assume v_i and v_j are two volumes, and v_i ends before v_j starts. We track the bounding box of the region, which belongs to v_i in its end frame, using kernelized correlation filter tracker [16]. If the tracked bounding box in the start frame of v_j has large enough IoU to the bounding box of the region belonging to v_j in the same frame, we consider that v_i and v_j can be connected.

In our implementation, we filter the volumes with extremely short lengths for efficiency, which are less than 10 frames in our experiments, and sort all the retained volumes into two queues $\boldsymbol{q}_s$ and $\boldsymbol{q}_e$ based on their start frames and end frames. To each volume v in $\boldsymbol{q}_e$, we check whether exist volumes starting in a short temporal interval after v ends, which equals 4 frames in our experiments. If so, we greedily connect v to these volumes by tracking, *i.e.*, we only connect a volume to the first volume which can be connected to it. The IoU threshold for connection in our experiments is set to 0.6. Because the number of volumes that start in a short temporal interval after each volume can be treated as a constant and only once traversal is required for $\boldsymbol{q}_e$, the time complexity of volume connect is $O(N_V \log N_V)$, here N_V is the number of volumes after filtering.

3.2 Volume combinatorial grouping

Adaptive short volume filtering. Considering most objects are visible for relatively long durations in videos, the volumes with short lengths are usually useless for generating object candidates. Preliminary filtering of such short volumes can decrease the number of volumes and effectively reduce the computational complexity of volume grouping.

Considering the variation of video lengths, we use an adaptive threshold in short volume filtering. On the one hand, we consider that the volumes contributive to object candidate generation should be visible for more than a certain duration, for example, one second (20 frames) in our experiments. On the other hand, to avoid too strict filtering for short videos, we require that the length of the filtered volumes should be no larger than a certain ratio of the length of the whole video, such as 20% in our experiments. Hence, the final threshold κ for short volume filtering is calculated as:

$$\kappa = \min(20, 0.2 \cdot ||V||), \quad (5)$$

where $||V||$ denotes the length of the whole video.

Background volume elimination. The volumes containing background content usually have long lengths because the stability in background appearance helps to region mapping in hierarchical volume generation. These background volumes cannot be removed in short volume filtering, but they hamper trajectory proposal because they are easy to be grouped with other volumes in combinatorial grouping and generate many object candidates covering no objects.

To eliminate the background volumes, we calculate the boundary connectivity of each volume based on that of the regions belonging to this volume. Assume v_i is a volume composed of a region sequence $\{r_i^{t_k}\}_{k=1,\cdots,||v_i||}$. Here, v_i starts in frame f^{t_1} and ends in frame $f^{t_{||v_i||}}$, and $||v_i||$ denotes the length of v_i. To each region

$r_i^{t_k}$, we calculate its boundary connectivity $B(r_i^{t_k})$ by measuring the extent of its connection to frame boundary [42] as follows:

$$B(r_i^{t_k}) = \frac{|C(r_i^{t_k})|}{\sqrt{|r_i^{t_k}|}}, \quad (6)$$

where $C(r_i^{t_k})$ denotes the set of pixels which are on both the boundaries of $r_i^{t_k}$ and frame f^{t_k}; $|\cdot|$ denotes the cardinality of a set, *i.e.*, the number of pixels within a set or a region.

Based on the boundary connectivity of all the regions belonging to v_i, we calculate the boundary connectivity of v_i as follows:

$$B(v_i) = \frac{|\{r_i^{t_k} | B(r_i^{t_k}) > \theta, k = 1, \cdots, ||v_i||\}|}{||v_i||}, \quad (7)$$

where θ is a boundary connectivity threshold, which equals 1 in our experiments referring to [42].

To avoid eliminating the volumes covering the objects that appear in frame boundaries, we use a high threshold in background volume elimination. In our experiments, only the volumes whose boundary connectivity is larger than 0.9 will be eliminated as background.

Candidate generation by volume grouping. Based on the retained volumes, we generate the object candidates by grouping these volumes. Most exiting methods conduct grouping based on volume similarity, such as [13]. However, such grouping strategies usually fail in generating object candidates effectively, because the parts of an object usually have significant differences in appearance and/or motion. Inspired by [23], we adopt a combinatorial grouping strategy in volume grouping, which only measures the neighborhood relationships between volumes while taking no account of volume similarity.

Considering the neighborhood relationship between two volumes is more complex than that between two regions, *e.g.*, two volumes may be overlapping, adjacent and disjointed in different frames, we relax the combination condition in volume grouping from adjacent in [23] to overlapping or adjacent, in order to generate sufficient object candidates. Specifically, we first construct a binary matrix $\mathbf{A}^t$ in size of $N_L^t \times N_L^t$ to represent the neighborhood relationship between the leaf regions in frame f^t, in which $\mathbf{A}_{i,j}^t$ equals 1 if the ith leaf region and the jth leaf region in f^t are adjacent and 0 otherwise. Then, we represent the neighborhood relationships between the hierarchical regions in f^t by a matrix Λ^t in size of $N_R^t \times N_R^t$:

$$\Lambda^t = \mathbf{C}^t \mathbf{A}^t (\mathbf{C}^t)^{\mathrm{T}}, \quad (8)$$

where $\mathbf{C}^t$ is the coverage relationship matrix defined in Section 3.1. Here, $\Lambda_{i,j}^t$ is larger than 0 if the ith region and the jth region in f^t are overlapping or adjacent, and $\Lambda_{i,j}^t$ equals 0 if they are disjointed.

Assuming that two volumes v_i and v_j appear in a video with the common duration from f^{t_1} to f^{t_K}, we measure the neighborhood relationship between these two volumes as follows:

$$\Theta(v_i, v_j) = \frac{\sum_{t=t_1}^{t_K} \eta(r_i^t, r_j^t)}{\min(||v_i||, ||v_j||)}, \quad (9)$$

where r_i^t and r_j^t are the regions belonging to v_i and v_j in f^t, respectively; $\eta(,)$ equals 1 if two regions are overlapping or adjacent in f^t and 0 otherwise, which can refer to Λ^t in Eq. (8); $||\cdot||$ denotes the length of a volume. If $\Theta(v_i, v_j)$ is larger than a threshold, which equals 0.3 in our experiments, v_i and v_j are allowed to group.

Based on the constraint in Eq. (9), we group the volumes into the candidates containing from one to four volumes. Similar to [23], we constrain the number of object candidates using Pareto front optimization [14] to avoid the combinatorial explosion. In our experiments, volume grouping will terminate if all volume combinations are exhausted or the number of object candidates reaches 10,000.

3.3 Multi-modal fusion scoring

We measure the objectness of the object candidates, and select the ones with high scores to generate the final trajectory proposal. In objectness measurement, we analyze both appearance objectness and motion objectness of each candidate. The former has been widely used in image proposal [10, 43], and the latter has been validated its effectiveness in trajectory proposal [29].

As for appearance objectness, we adopt the scoring model provided in [23], which is a regressor trained on multi-modal features including shape, edges, size and location. To each candidate c_k, which appears from frame f^{t_1} to f^{t_K}, we measure the appearance objectness of the grouped regions belonging to c_k on each frame, and calculate the appearance objectness score of c_k as follows:

$$s^A(c_k) = \frac{\sum_{t=t_1}^{t_K} s^A(g_k^t)}{||c_k||}, \quad (10)$$

where $s^A(\cdot)$ denotes appearance objectness score; g_k^t denotes the grouped regions belonging to c_k in frame f^t; $||\cdot||$ denotes the length of a candidate, *i.e.*, the number of the frames that the candidate appears in.

As for motion objectness, we measure the motion contrast of an object candidate to background. We calculate the average motion strength of all the regions belonging to background volumes (refer to Section 3.2) on each frame as the motion strength of background. If no background volume is detected in some frame, we use the average motion strength of the whole frame to instead. To each candidate c_k, which appears from frame f^{t_1} to f^{t_K}, we calculate the distance between the average motion strength of the grouped regions belonging to c_k and that of background, and calculate the motion objectness score of c_k as follows:

$$s^M(c_k) = \frac{\sum_{t=t_1}^{t_K} |m_k^t - m_B^t|}{||c_k||}, \quad (11)$$

where $s^M(.)$ denotes motion objectness score; m_k^t denotes the average motion strength of the grouped regions belonging to c_k in frame f^t; m_B^t denotes the average motion strength of background in frame f^t.

We normalize the appearance objectness score and the motion objectness score of each candidate c_k to the value range of [0, 1], and fuse them with linear combination as the total objectness score of c_k:

$$s(c_k) = \lambda \cdot s^A(c_k) + (1 - \lambda) \cdot s^M(c_k), \quad (12)$$

where λ is a weight parameter, which equals to 0.7 in our experiments to handle the inaccuracy of motion contrast in motion objectness measurement.

We rank all the candidates according to their objectness scores, generate the bounding boxes of the top selected candidates as the trajectory proposals, and preferentially return the proposals composed with less volumes.

4 EXPERIMENTS

4.1 Dataset and experiment settings

We validated the performance of the proposed method on a dataset consisting of 200 videos, which are randomly selected from ILSVRC2016-VID [27]. These videos have various content and contain 3.26 objects on average. The average object number of our dataset is larger than the one of the whole ILSVRC2016-VID dataset, which is only 2.06. The manually labeled object trajectories in ILSVRC2016-VID were used as the groundtruths in our experiments. To the best of our knowledge, it is the largest dataset for object trajectory proposal.

We used the evaluation criteria proposed in [29], namely *mean Trajectory IoU* (mT-IoU) and *recall*, on the top 500 trajectory proposals for each video. These criteria are defined as follows:

$$mT\text{-}IoU = \frac{1}{N_V}\sum_{k=1}^{N_V}\frac{1}{N_G^k}\sum_{j=1}^{N_G^k}\max_i\{T\text{-}IoU_{i,j}\}, \tag{13}$$

$$recall = \frac{1}{N_V}\sum_{k=1}^{N_V}\frac{1}{N_G^k}\sum_{j=1}^{N_G^k}\delta\big(\max_i\{T\text{-}IoU_{i,j}\} - \tau\big), \tag{14}$$

where $T\text{-}IoU_{i,j}$ denotes the trajectory IoU between a trajectory proposal $\mathcal{T}_i$ and a trajectory groundtruth $\mathcal{G}_j$; N_V is the number of videos; N_G^k is the number of groundtruths in the kth video; δ is a function that outputs 1 if the input is positive, and 0 otherwise; τ is a threshold, which equals to 0.5 in our experiments.

All the experiments were conducted on a computer with i7 3.5GHz CPU and 32GB memory. For all the methods in comparison, we used their default settings suggested by the authors.

4.2 Component analysis

There are several key techniques incorporated in our method: region mapping, volume representation, volume filtering and candidate scoring. We validated their influences to the performance of our method.

Region mapping. We use bidirectional optical flow in region mapping to construct the mapping relationship between the regions in adjacent frames (refer to Section 3.1), which has high computational cost. To evaluate the necessity of bidirectional optical flow, we generate a baseline only using forward optical flow (FOF), which requires half computational cost in optical flow estimation as compared to our method.

Figure 3 shows the performance of our method using different optical flow in region mapping. We can see that the performance declines on both mT-IoU and recall when replacing bidirectional optical flow with forward optical flow. The reason is that optical flow estimation only focuses on pixel-level similarity measurement even using global consistency constraint, which is sensitive to variable video content. Once using bidirectional optical flow, we can diminish the influence of optical flow inaccuracy and map the regions more effectively.

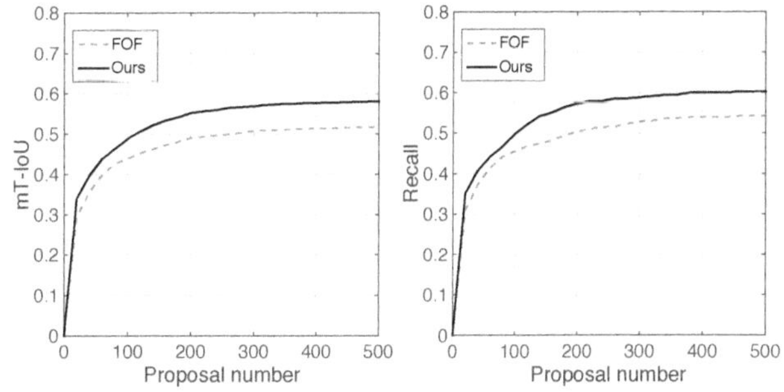

Figure 3: Evaluation of our method using different optical flow in region mapping on mT-IoU and recall.

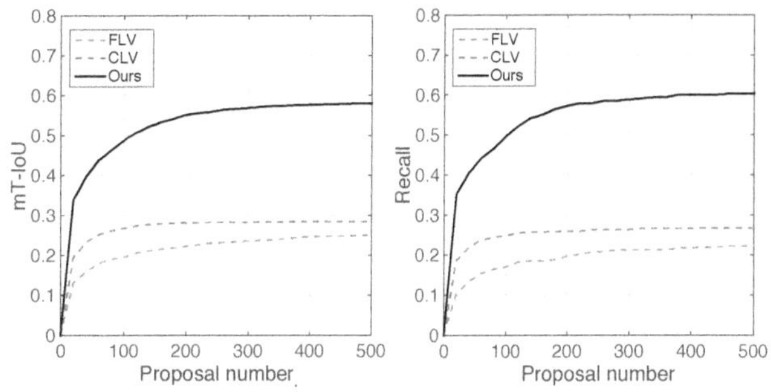

Figure 4: Evaluation of our method using different volume representation on mT-IoU and recall.

Volume representation. We represent video content with hierarchical volumes on all the levels, *i.e.*, one volume may contain another volume or its portions (refer to Section 3.1). Such a volume representation can represent both the principal components and the details of objects. To illustrate the superiority of our hierarchical volume representation, we generate two baselines: using the finest level volumes (FLV), which are generated by the finest level regions on each video frame, and using the coarsest level volumes (CLV), which merges the regions on each video frame until the number of regions is no more than 30% of the one of the finest regions and maps these regions to generate the volumes.

Figure 4 shows the performance of our method using different volume representations. We can see that both FLV and CLV have dramatic drops on mT-IoU and recall. For example, the mT-IoU and recall values obtained by CLV on 500 proposals are only half of the ones obtained by our method. It shows that only the coarsest level volumes, which represent the principal components of objects, cannot effectively support trajectory proposal because all the object details are lost. Moreover, FLV has worse performance than CLV, which is caused by two reasons: 1) The leaf regions are difficult to be mapped into long-duration finest level volumes due to the inaccuracy of optical flow, which increases the complexity of volume grouping. 2) Our method only groups at most four volumes into a candidate to avoid combinatorial explosion, which leads to the candidate grouped by the finest level volumes are usually seriously incomplete against objects. It validates the effectiveness of hierarchical volume for video content representation.

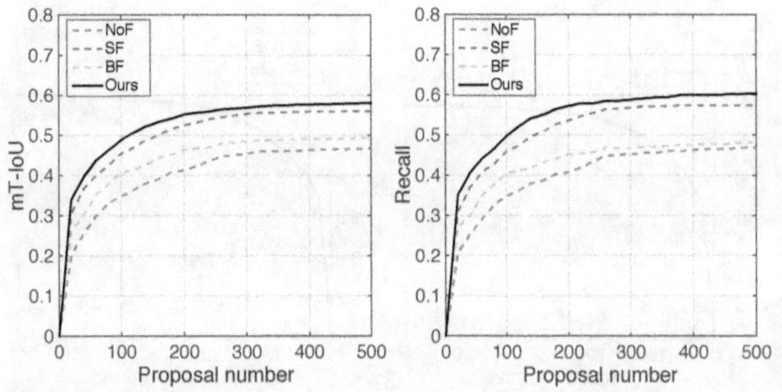

Figure 5: Evaluation of our method using different volume filtering strategies on mT-IoU and recall.

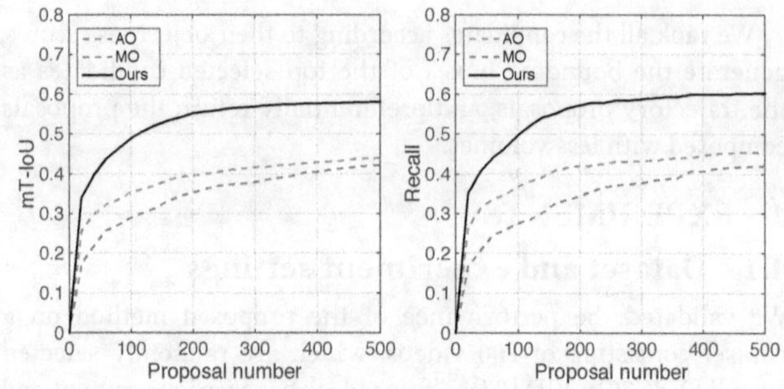

Figure 6: Evaluation of our method using different candidate scoring mechanisms on mT-IoU and recall.

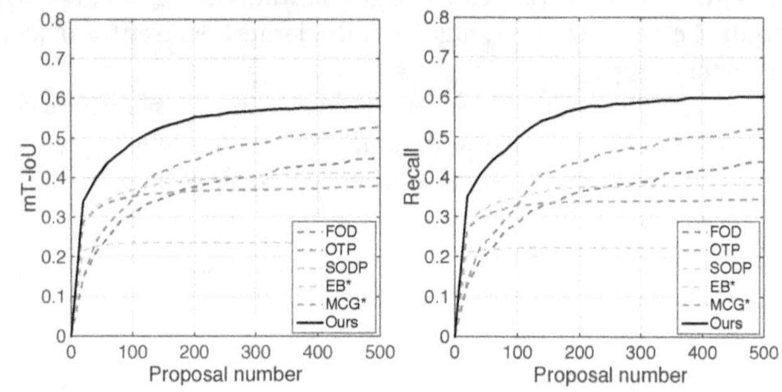

Figure 7: Evaluation of different trajectory proposal methods on mT-IoU and recall.

Volume filtering. We consider the short volumes and the background volumes are useless in object representation, and filter them to reduce the complexity of volume grouping (refer to Section 3.2). To illustrate the necessity of volume filtering, we generate three baselines: without short volume filtering or background volume filtering (NoF), only filtering short volumes (SF), and only filtering background volumes (BF).

Figure 5 shows the performance of our method using different volume filtering strategies. We can see that the performance of NoF is worse than that using other volume filtering strategies. Note here, in broken volume connection (refer to Section 3.1), we have filtered the volumes whose lengths are less than 10 frames for efficiency. It means that NoF actually uses the volume filtering strategy by removing the extremely short volumes (less than 10 frames) rather than filters nothing. Once increasing the filtering threshold on volume length from 10 frames to 20 frames, the performance of SF is improved significantly as compared to NoF. It shows the effectiveness of short volume filtering. Moreover, we can see that the performance will be improved when filtering background volumes, no matter on NoF (*i.e.*, BF) and on SF (*i.e.*, Ours). It shows that background volume elimination is beneficial to trajectory proposal.

Candidate scoring mechanism. We use a multi-modal fusion scoring mechanism in ranking object candidates, which fuses both appearance objectness and motion objectness (refer to Section 3.3). To validate the effectiveness of our multi-modal fusion scoring mechanism, we generate two baselines: scoring with appearance objectness (AO), and scoring with motion objectness (MO).

Figure 6 shows the performance of our method using different scoring strategies. We can see that the performance of both AO and MO is significantly worse than that of our method on mT-IoU and recall, which illustrates the effectiveness of fusing appearance objectness and motion objectness in scoring. Moreover, the performance of MO is only slightly worse than that of AO. Because objects usually have different motions against background, motion objectness contributes to trajectory proposal especially when object appearance is complex.

4.3 Comparison with the state-of-the-arts

To validate the performance of our method, we compared it with three state-of-the-art video object proposal methods, namely free object discovery (FOD) [12], object trajectory proposal (OTP) [29], and spatio-temporal object detection proposal (SODP) [13]. In the same way as [29], we generate two baselines EB* and MCG*, which generate object proposals on the middle frame of each video and track the proposals with KCF tracker [16] bidirectionally to generate trajectory proposals.

Figure 7 shows the performance of our method and five compared methods. We have: 1) Our method is superior to all the compared methods on both mT-IoU and recall, which illustrates the effectiveness of our method. 2) Though SODP has a similar framework to our method, its performance is dramatically worse than that of our method and other methods. It shows the effectiveness of the key techniques in our methods, namely hierarchical volume representation, volume combinatorial grouping, and multi-modal fusion scoring. 3) The performance of EB* and MCG* is worse than other methods except SODP, though EB and MCG are the best object proposal methods on images. It is because they cannot propose the object trajectories which do not appear on the middle frames of videos (or any other selected frames as the start of trajectory generation). It illustrates the drawbacks of object trajectory proposal by combining image object proposal and tracking. 4) Though FOD and OTP aim to address the start frame problem by traversing all the video frames, their performance is still worse than ours. It is because they cannot effectively measure objectness based on spatio-temporal characteristics, and propose objects independently on each frame.

Figure 8 illustrates several examples of our results. In each video example, the trajectory proposal with the highest mT-IoU to each trajectory groundtruth from the top 500 proposals is shown. It

Figure 8: Qualitative examples of object trajectory proposal using our method. In each video example, the bounding boxes with the same color indicate a trajectory proposal, and the trajectory proposal with the highest mT-IoU to each trajectory groundtruth from the top 500 proposals is shown.

Table 1: Comparison with the state-of-the-art methods and the baselines on time cost per frame.

Method	Language	Time (s)
FOD	C++ & Python	3.4
OTP	C++ & Python	3.4
SODP	C++ & Matlab & Python	6.7
EB*	C++ & Matlab	5.5
MCG*	C++ & Matlab	3.5
Ours	C++ & Matlab	7.5

shows that our method can handle the videos with multiple objects in various content.

We also validated the efficiency of our method. Table 1 shows the time cost per frame of our method and the compared methods. It shows that our method is comparable to other grouping-based object trajectory proposal methods, such as SODP. The most time consuming component in our method is bidirectional optical flow estimation. It can be accelerated by GPU [31] to make our method more efficient.

4.4 Discussion

In the experiments, we found some limitations of our method. As shown in the top row of Figure 9, one goat is omitted because it is occluded by two other goats with similar appearances, which leads to serious inaccuracy in volume representation. Another failure example shown in the bottom row of Figure 9. There are many motorcycles and cars with small sizes are omitted. It is because these small objects are composed of multiple small volumes, which are easily filtered in volume grouping. Moreover, as shown in Table 1, the time costs of our method and other existing trajectory proposal methods are still high, which prevents their application in real-time conditions.

5 CONCLUSION

In this paper, we proposed an object trajectory proposal method based on hierarchical volume grouping. Three techniques, namely hierarchical volume representation, volume combinatorial grouping and multi-modal fusion scoring, were presented to address the key

Figure 9: Our failure examples influenced by object occlusion and small objects.

issues in grouping-based object trajectory proposal. Benefiting from measuring objectness through analyzing spatio-temporal characteristics over a whole video, our method can effectively generate the trajectory proposals on the videos with multiple objects in various content. We constructed a dataset consisting of 200 videos from ILSVRC2016-VID dataset. The experimental results on the dataset show that our method outperforms the state-of-the-art object trajectory proposal methods.

6 ACKNOWLEDGEMENTS

This work is supported by National Science Foundation of China (61321491, 61771301, 61202320), and Collaborative Innovation Center of Novel Software Technology and Industrialization.

REFERENCES

[1] Bogdan Alexe, Thomas Deselaers, and Vittorio Ferrari. 2012. Measuring the Objectness of Image Windows. *IEEE Transactions on Pattern Analysis and Machine Intelligence* 34 (2012), 2189–2202.
[2] Mykhaylo Andriluka, Stefan Roth, and Bernt Schiele. 2008. People-tracking-by-detection and People-detection-by-tracking. In *IEEE Conference on Computer Vision and Pattern Recognition*. 1–8.
[3] Pablo Arbelaez. 2006. Boundary Extraction in Natural Images Using Ultrametric Contour Maps. In *IEEE Conference on Computer Vision and Pattern Recognition Workshops*. 182–182.
[4] Shai Avidan. 2007. Ensemble Tracking. *IEEE Transactions on Pattern Analysis and Machine Intelligence* 29, 2 (2007), 261–271.
[5] Boris Babenko, Ming Hsuan Yang, and Serge Belongie. 2011. Robust Object Tracking with Online Multiple Instance Learning. *IEEE Transactions on Pattern Analysis and Machine Intelligence* 33, 8 (2011), 1619–1632.

[6] Chenglong Bao, Yi Wu, Haibin Ling, and Hui Ji. 2012. Real Time Robust L1 Tracker using Accelerated Proximal Gradient Approach. In *IEEE Conference on Computer Vision and Pattern Recognition*. 1830–1837.

[7] Rodrigo Benenson, Markus Mathias, Radu Timofte, and Luc Van Gool. 2012. Pedestrian Detection at 100 Frames per Second. In *IEEE Conference on Computer Vision and Pattern Recognition*. 2903–2910.

[8] Rachid Benmokhtar and Benoit Huet. 2007. Multi-level Fusion for Semantic Video Content Indexing and Retrieval. In *International Workshop on Adaptive Multimedia Retrieval*. 160–169.

[9] Michael Van Den Bergh, Gemma Roig, Xavier Boix, Santiago Manen, and Luc Van Gool. 2013. Online Video SEEDS for Temporal Window Objectness. In *IEEE International Conference on Computer Vision*. 377–384.

[10] Ming-Ming Cheng, Ziming Zhang, Wen-Yan Lin, and Philip H. S. Torr. 2014. BING: Binarized Normed Gradients for Objectness Estimation at 300fps. In *IEEE Conference on Computer Vision and Pattern Recognition*. 3286–3293.

[11] Dorin Comaniciu, Visvanathan Ramesh, and Peter Meer. 2003. Kernel-Based Object Tracking. *IEEE Transactions on Pattern Analysis and Machine Intelligence* 25, 5 (2003), 564–575.

[12] Giovanni Cuffaro, Federico Becattini, Claudio Baecchi, Lorenzo Seidenari, and Alberto Del Bimbo. 2016. Segmentation Free Object Discovery in Video. In *European Conference on Computer Vision workshops*. 25–31.

[13] Oneata Dan, Jerome Revaud, Jakob Verbeek, and Cordelia Schmid. 2014. Spatio-temporal Object Detection Proposals. In *European Conference on Computer Vision*. 737–752.

[14] Matthias Ehrgott. 2005. *Multicriteria Optimization*. Vol. 491. Springer Science and Business Media. 222–231 pages.

[15] Katerina Fragkiadaki, Pablo Arbelaez, Panna Felsen, and Jitendra Malik. 2015. Learning to Segment Moving Objects in Videos. In *IEEE Conference on Computer Vision and Pattern Recognition*. 4083–4090.

[16] JoÃčo F. Henriques, Caseiro Rui, Pedro Martins, and Jorge Batista. 2015. High-Speed Tracking with Kernelized Correlation Filters. *IEEE Transactions on Pattern Analysis and Machine Intelligence* 37, 3 (2015), 583–596.

[17] Kai Kang, Wanli Ouyang, Hongsheng Li, and Xiaogang Wang. 2016. Object Detection from Video Tubelets with Convolutional Neural Networks. In *IEEE Conference on Computer Vision and Pattern Recognition*. 817–825.

[18] Jianwu Li, Tianfei Zhou, and Yao Lu. 2017. Learning to Generate Video Object Segment Proposals. In *IEEE International Conference on Multimedia and Expo*. 787–792.

[19] Jing Liu, Tongwei Ren, Yuantian Wang, Sheng hua Zhong, Jia Bei, and Shengchao Chen. 2017. Object Proposal on RGB-D Images via Elastic Edge Boxes. *Neurocomputing* 236 (2017), 134–146.

[20] Santiago Manen, Matthieu Guillaumin, and Luc J. Van Gool. 2013. Prime Object Proposals with Randomized Prim's Algorithm. In *IEEE International Conference on Computer Vision*. 2536–2543.

[21] Liang Peng and Xiaojun Qi. 2016. Temporal objectness: Model-free learning of object proposals in video. In *IEEE International Conference on Image Processing*. 3663–3667.

[22] Federico Perazzi, Oliver Wang, Markus Gross, and Alexander Sorkine-Hornung. 2015. Fully Connected Object Proposals for Video Segmentation. In *IEEE International Conference on Computer Vision*. 3227–3234.

[23] Jordi Ponttuset, Pablo Arbelaez, Jonathan Barron, Ferran Marques, and Jitendra Malik. 2016. Multiscale Combinatorial Grouping for Image Segmentation and Object Proposal Generation. *IEEE Transactions on Pattern Analysis and Machine Intelligence* 39, 1 (2016), 128–140.

[24] Fatih Porikli. 2005. Integral Histogram: A Fast Way To Extract Histograms in Cartesian Spaces. In *IEEE Conference on Computer Vision and Pattern Recognition*. 829–836.

[25] P. PÃľrez, C. Hue, J. Vermaak, and M. Gangnet. 2002. Color-Based Probabilistic Tracking. In *European Conference on Computer Vision*. 661–675.

[26] Joseph Redmon and Ali Farhadi. 2016. YOLO9000: Better, Faster, Stronger. In *IEEE Conference on Computer Vision and Pattern Recognition*. 6517–6525.

[27] Olga Russakovsky, Jia Deng, Hao Su, Jonathan Krause, Sanjeev Satheesh, Sean Ma, Zhiheng Huang, Andrej Karpathy, Aditya Khosla, and Michael Bernstein. 2015. ImageNet Large Scale Visual Recognition Challenge. *International Journal of Computer Vision* 115, 3 (2015), 211–252.

[28] Xindi Shang, Tongwei Ren, Jingfan Guo, Hanwang Zhang, and Tat-Seng Chua. 2017. Video Visual Relation Detection. In *ACM International Conference on Multimedia*. 1300–1308.

[29] Xindi Shang, Tongwei Ren, Hanwang Zhang, Gangshan Wu, and Tat-Seng Chua. 2017. Object Trajectory Proposal. In *IEEE International Conference on Multimedia and Expo*. 331–336.

[30] Gilad Sharir and Tinne Tuytelaars. 2012. Video Object Proposals. In *IEEE Conference on Computer Vision and Pattern Recognition Workshops*. 9–14.

[31] Narayanan Sundaram, Thomas Brox, and Kurt Keutzer. 2010. Dense Point Trajectories by GPU-accelerated Large Displacement Optical Flow. In *European Conference on Computer Vision*. 438–451.

[32] Feng Tang, S Brennan, Qi Zhao, and Hai Tao. 2007. Co-Tracking Using Semi-Supervised Support Vector Machines. In *IEEE International Conference on Computer Vision*. 1–8.

[33] Jasper R. R. Uijlings, Koen E. A. van de Sande, Theo Gevers, and Arnold W. M. Smeulders. 2013. Selective Search for Object Recognition. *International Journal of Computer Vision* 104, 2 (2013), 154–171.

[34] Heng Wang, A. Klaser, C. Schmid, and Cheng Lin Liu. 2011. Action Recognition by Dense Trajectories. In *IEEE Conference on Computer Vision and Pattern Recognition*. 3169–3176.

[35] Wenguan Wang, Jianbing Shen, and F Porikli. 2015. Saliency-aware Geodesic Video Oject Segmentation. In *IEEE Conference on Computer Vision and Pattern Recognition*. 3395–3402.

[36] Yuantian Wang, Lei Huang, Tongwei Ren, Sheng-Hua Zhong, Yan Liu, and Gangshan Wu. 2017. Object Proposal via Depth Connectivity Constrained Grouping. In *Pacific-Rim Conference on Multimedia*. 1–10.

[37] Philippe Weinzaepfel, Jerome Revaud, Zaid Harchaoui, and Cordelia Schmid. 2014. DeepFlow: Large Displacement Optical Flow with Deep Matching. In *IEEE International Conference on Computer Vision*. 1385–1392.

[38] Fanyi Xiao and Jae Lee Yong. 2016. Track and Segment: An Iterative Unsupervised Approach for Video Object Proposals. In *IEEE Conference on Computer Vision and Pattern Recognition*. 933–942.

[39] Jae Lee Yong, Jaechul Kim, and Kristen Grauman. 2011. Key-segments for Video Object Segmentation. In *IEEE International Conference on Computer Vision*. 1995–2002.

[40] Ziming Zhang, Yun Liu, Xi Chen, Yanjun Zhu, Ming Ming Cheng, Venkatesh Saligrama, and Philip H. S. Torr. 2018. Sequential Optimization for Efficient High-Quality Object Proposal Generation. *IEEE Transactions on Pattern Analysis and Machine Intelligence* 40, 5 (2018), 1209–1223.

[41] Wei Zhong, Huchuan Lu, and Ming-Hsuan Yang. 2014. Robust Object Tracking via Sparse Collaborative Appearance Model. *IEEE Transactions on Image Processing* 23, 5 (2014), 2356–2368.

[42] Wangjiang Zhu, Shuang Liang, Yichen Wei, and Jian Sun. 2014. Saliency Optimization from Robust Background Detection. In *IEEE Conference on Computer Vision and Pattern Recognition*. 2814–2821.

[43] C. Lawrence Zitnick and Piotr Dollár. 2014. Edge Boxes: Locating Object Proposals from Edges. In *European Conference on Computer Vision*. 391–405.

CBVMR: Content-Based Video–Music Retrieval Using Soft Intra-Modal Structure Constraint

Sungeun Hong
SK T-Brain
Republic of Korea
csehong@sktbrain.com

Woobin Im
School of Computing, KAIST
Republic of Korea
iwbn@kaist.ac.kr

Hyun S. Yang
School of Computing, KAIST
Republic of Korea
hsyang@kaist.ac.kr

ABSTRACT

Up to now, only limited research has been conducted on cross-modal retrieval of suitable music for a specified video or vice versa. Moreover, much of the existing research relies on metadata such as keywords, tags, or description that must be individually produced and attached posterior. This paper introduces a new content-based, cross-modal retrieval method for video and music that is implemented through deep neural networks. We train the network via inter-modal ranking loss such that videos and music with similar semantics end up close together in the embedding space. However, if only the inter-modal ranking constraint is used for embedding, modality-specific characteristics can be lost. To address this problem, we propose a novel soft intra-modal structure loss that leverages the relative distance relationship between intra-modal samples before embedding. We also introduce reasonable quantitative and qualitative experimental protocols to solve the lack of standard protocols for less-mature video–music related tasks. All the datasets and source code can be found in our online repository (https://github.com/csehong/VM-NET).

CCS CONCEPTS

• **Information systems → Multimedia and multimodal retrieval**; • **Computer systems organization → Neural networks**;

KEYWORDS

Content-based video–music retrieval (CBVMR), Multimodal embedding, Cross-modal retrieval, Music recommendation, YouTube-8M

ACM Reference Format:

Sungeun Hong, Woobin Im, and Hyun S. Yang. 2018. CBVMR: Content-Based Video–Music Retrieval Using Soft Intra-Modal Structure Constraint. In *ICMR '18: 2018 International Conference on Multimedia Retrieval, June 11–14, 2018, Yokohama, Japan.* ACM, New York, NY, USA, 9 pages. https://doi.org/10.1145/3206025.3206046

1 INTRODUCTION

Music, images, and videos are widely used in everyday life and as a result, various studies on these fields have been actively conducted over recent decades [3, 14, 21, 27, 28]. However, to date, the relation between music and visual modalities (e.g., image or video) has not been adequately investigated. Some pioneering approaches that have explored the relation between music and visual modalities have been developed [2, 4, 5, 25, 40]. However, these techniques mainly use metadata, which is separately attached to each individual item, rather than content-based information that can be derived directly from the music or visual data itself.

ICMR '18, June 11–14, 2018, Yokohama, Japan

ACM ISBN 978-1-4503-5046-4/18/06...$15.00
https://doi.org/10.1145/3206025.3206046

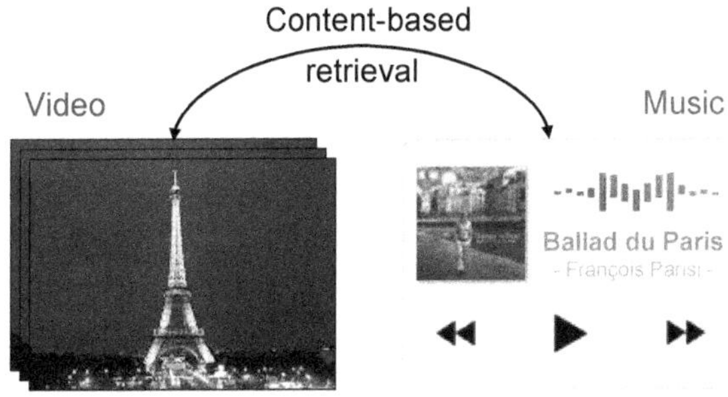

Figure 1: Content-based video–music retrieval (CBVMR): Unlike existing methods use metadata (e.g., keywords, mood tags, and description), our model only uses image frames for the video part and audio signals for the music part.

We argue that content-based approaches are more appropriate than metadata-based approaches for several reasons. First, metadata-based systems require writing the meta-information for each data item individually, and this can be impractical for large-scale datasets. Moreover, in this situation, as mentioned in [34], unpopular multimedia items can be neglected because their meta-information is scarce or difficult to obtain. Second, metadata-based approaches often rely on a hard-coded mapping function that links concepts from a visual modality to music templates, and this imposes limitations on their various applications.

In this study, we undertook the task of finding music that suits a given video and vice versa using a content-based approach as shown in Fig. 1. The main challenge in this task is to design a cross-modal model that has no requirements for metadata and, additionally, has no hard-coded mapping functions. The second, practical challenge is the difficulty of obtaining well-matched video–music pairs that are essential for data-driven learning such as deep learning. The matching criteria between video and music are more ambiguous than that of other cross-modal tasks such as image-to-text retrieval.

Our key insight is that if the large-scale video–music pair dataset is obtainable, then the relationship between video and music can be learned through deep neural networks. To obtain video–music pairs, we leverage a huge amount of music videos by treating each audio and visual signal from the same music video as a ground truth pair. Concretely, the contributions of this study are three-fold:

1) **Content-based, cross-modal embedding network.** We introduce VM-NET, two-branch neural network that infers the latent alignment between videos and music tracks using only their contents. We train the network via inter-modal ranking loss, such that videos and music with similar semantics end up close together in the embedding space. However, if only the inter-modal ranking constraint for embedding is considered, modality-specific characteristics (e.g., rhythm or tempo for music and texture or color for image) may be lost. To solve this problem, we devise a novel soft intra-modal structure constraint that takes advantage of the relative distance relationship of samples within each modality.

2) **Large-scale video–music pair dataset.** Owing to the lack of video–music pair datasets, we have compiled a large-scale benchmark called Hong & Im Music–Video 200K (HIMV-200K) composed of 200,500 video–music pairs. While most previous studies have used only official music videos, which limit the musical style or amount of data, our HIMV-200K includes official music videos, parody music videos, and user-generated videos.

3) **Reasonable experimental protocols.** Existing video–music related approaches have few standard protocols for evaluation, and even most of them mainly performed subjective user evaluation. For quantitative evaluation, we use Recall@K, which can give a baseline for subsequent CBVMR studies. We also suggest and conduct a reasonable subjective test that examines user preferences for videos that suit given music and, vice versa. Finally, we present a qualitative investigation of the retrieval results using our model.

2 RELATED WORK

2.1 Video–Music Related Tasks

For music genre classification, Libeks et al [22] proposed a framework that use promotional photos of artists as well as album covers. They predict music genre tags based on content-based image analysis using color and texture features. A set of color features and affective features extracted from music videos has also been proposed for music genre classification [30]. To capture different types of features, they use various psychological or perceptive models.

To match videos and music, Chao et al. [5] introduced a technique to recommend suitable music for photo albums. They utilized a cross-modal graph in which synsets of mood tags obtained from images and music are used as vertices, and relations between synsets are expressed as edges. Recently, Sasaki et al. [29] proposed a one-directional video-to-music recommendation by using the valence arousal plane. The approach most closely related to our study is that proposed by Wu et al. [40]. To connect music and images, the authors used text from lyrics as a go-between media (i.e., metadata) and applied canonical correlation analysis [32].

Overall, most of the existing methods use metadata (e.g., keywords, mood tags, and associated description) [23, 31, 40] to associate music with visual modalities. In contrast to these approaches, we directly connect items from the music and visual modalities using only the contents of each modality.

2.2 Two-branch Neural Networks

Over the past decade, deep neural networks have shown promising results over various fields [12, 13]. From the viewpoint of architecture, our approach is similar to the existing two-branch neural networks for image–text related tasks. In this section, we discuss the similarities and differences between our method and conventional approaches.

Most studies investigating cross-modal matching have been carried out on MSCOCO [24] and Flickr30K [41] in which each image in the datasets is described independently by five captions. Early works based on two-branch neural networks have involved WSABIE [39] and DeVISE [7]. They learn linear transformations of features from visual and textual modalities to the shared embedding space using a single-directional ranking loss. To better understand the relationship between visual and textual modalities, a few other works have proposed a bidirectional ranking loss [16, 17, 20].

In considering the intra-modal structure, image–text embedding networks [35] and similarity networks [36] are most related to our method. They propose a structure-preserving constraint that uses ground truth pair information within individual modality resulting in an embedding space where the five captions corresponding to a particular image are close together. However, our approach does not use pair information within individual modality, which can be applied in more general situations.

In addition to the techniques employed for image–text matching, some works based on the two-branch neural network for music and visual modalities have also been proposed. Among them, the work by Acar et al. [2] is closely related to our approach. They presented a framework for the affective labeling of music videos in which higher-level representations are learned from low-level audio-visual features using a convolutional neural network (CNN). However, unlike our model, they use deep architecture only as a mid-level feature extractor for music and images and do not learn inter-modal relationships.

3 THE PROPOSED METHOD

Our goal is to design a model that infers the latent alignment between video and music as shown in Fig. 2, enabling the retrieval of music that suits a given video and vice versa.

3.1 Music Feature Extraction

We first decompose an audio signal into harmonic and percussive components. We then slice the components into shorter segments called local frames (or windowed excerpts) and extract multiple features from each component of each frame.

Frame-level features. (1) Spectral features: We first apply the fast Fourier transform and the discrete wavelet transform to the windowed signal in each local frame. From the magnitude spectral results, we compute summary features including the spectral centroid, the spectral bandwidth, the spectral rolloff, and the polynomial features of a spectrogram [8]. (2) Mel-scale features: We also compute the Mel-scale spectrogram of each frame as well as the Mel-frequency Cepstral Coefficients (MFCC). Further, to capture variations of timbre over time, we also use delta-MFCC features. (3) Chroma features: While Mel-scaled representations efficiently capture timbre, they provide poor resolution of pitches and pitch classes. To rectify this issue, we use chroma short-time Fourier transform [18] as well as chroma energy normalized [26]. (4) Etc.: We use the number of time domain zero-crossings as an audio feature in order to detect the amount of noise in the audio signal.

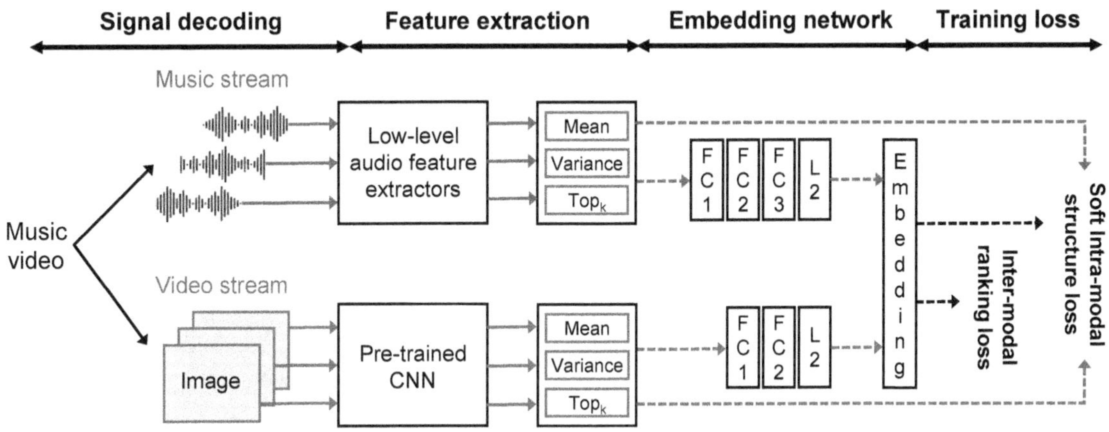

Figure 2: Framework for the proposed method. For each modality, the features are extracted and fed into a two-stream neural network. The embedding network is trained by two losses with different purposes. Each dotted arrow indicates a flow that can be trainable, while the solid arrows indicate flows that does not.

We also use the root-mean-square energy for each frame. Table 1 summarizes the audio features utilized in our approach.

Music-level features. For each frame-level feature, we calculate three music-level features that capture properties of the entire music signal. In particular, we calculate first- and second-order statistics of each frame-level feature as well as maximum top K ordinal statistics, which provide vectors consisting of the K largest values for each dimension of frame-level features. Finally, all the calculated features are concatenated.

3.2 Video Feature Extraction

Frame-level features. Because our proposed HIMV-200K dataset contains a large number of videos, it is impractical to train the deep network from scratch. Instead, following the work in [1], we extract frame-level features from the individual frames using an Inception network [33] trained on the large-scale ImageNet dataset [6]. We then apply a whitened principal component analysis (WPCA) so that the normalized features are approximately multivariate Gaussian with zero mean and identity covariance.

Video-level features. Once frame-level features are obtained, we apply feature aggregation techniques and then perform concatenation as in the process of obtaining the music-level features. We then apply a global normalization process, which subtracts the mean of vectors from all the features, and we apply principal component analysis (PCA) [15]. Finally, we perform L2 normalization to obtain video-level features.

Table 1: Low-level audio features used in our approach.

Type	Audio features
Spectral	spectral centroid, spectral bandwidth, spectral rolloff, poly-feature (*1st* and *2nd*)
Mel-scale	MFCC, Mel-spectrogram, delta-MFCC (*1st* and *2nd*)
Chroma	chroma-cens, choroma-STFT
Etc.	zero-crossing, root-mean-square energy

3.3 Multimodal Embedding

Inter-modal ranking constraint. The music and video features obtained via the processes in Sec. 3.1 and Sec. 3.2 are fed into a two-branch neural network. For cross-modal matching, we wish to ensure that a video is closer to suitable music than unsuitable music, and vice versa. Inspired by the triplet ranking loss [38], we used the inter-modal ranking constraint in which similar cross-modal input items are mapped to nearby feature vectors in the multimodal embedding space. Assume triplets of items consisting of an arbitrary anchor, a positive cross-modal sample that is a ground truth pair item separated from the same music video, and a negative sample that is not paired with the anchor as shown in Fig. 3 (a). The purpose of the inter-modal ranking constraint is to minimize the distance between an anchor and a positive sample while maximizing the distance between an anchor and a negative sample in the multimodal embedding space.

In the triplet selection process, calculating the loss for all possible triplets requires a considerable amount of computation. Therefore, in our experiments, we select top Q most violated cross-modal matches in each mini-batch.

Soft intra-modal structure constraint. If we only use the inter-modal ranking constraint for training the whole embedding network, modality-specific characteristics can be lost as can be seen from the bottom left of Fig. 3 (b). Here, the modality-specific characteristics can include rhythm, tempo, or timbre in music, and brightness, color, or texture in videos. To solve the problem of collapsing the structure within each modality, we devised a novel soft intra-modal structure loss.

Suppose that three intra-modal features are extracted from different music videos using the process described in Sec. 3.1 or Sec. 3.2. As these features have not yet been fed into the embedding network, they can maintain modality-specific characteristics. In Fig. 3 (b), from the perspective of video, blue is more similar to purple than green. From the perspective of music, blue is more similar to sky blue than yellow. By leveraging this relative distance relationship to remain in the embedding space, we can preserve modality-specific characteristics even after the embedding process. The expression

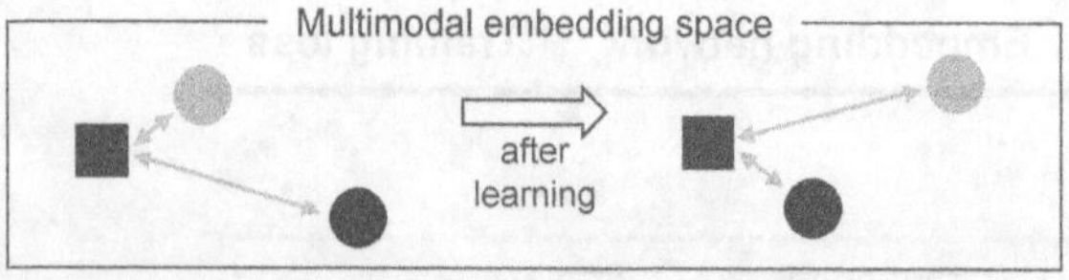

(a) Embedding with inter-modal ranking constraint. Videos and music with similar semantics are close together in embedding space.

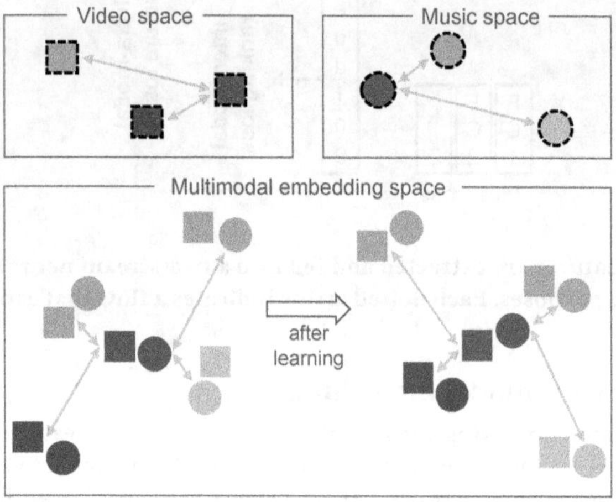

(b) Embedding with (right) and without (left) soft intra-modal structure constraint. If only inter-modal ranking constraint is used for embedding, the modality-specific characteristics can be lost. By leveraging the relative distance relationship between intra-modal samples to be maintained in the embedding space, we can maintain the modality-specific characteristics in the embedding space.

Figure 3: Two constraints for multimodal embedding. Identical shapes signify feature vectors obtained from the same modality. The same color means that they come from the same music video. Shapes with dotted outlines represent intra-modal samples before embedding.

of our proposed soft intra-modal ranking constraint for a given situation of visual input is as follows:

$$d(v_i, v_j) < d(v_i, v_k) \quad \text{if } d(\widetilde{v}_i, \widetilde{v}_j) < d(\widetilde{v}_i, \widetilde{v}_k) \tag{1}$$

where v_i, v_j, v_k are the video features in multimodal space from the i-th, j-th, and k-th music videos, respectively. $\widetilde{v}_i, \widetilde{v}_j, \widetilde{v}_k$ are also the video features from the i-th, j-th, and k-th music videos, but they have not yet passed through the embedding network. Unlike the conventional image–text embedding approaches [35, 36] that leverage five captions corresponding to one image (relatively hard structure or relationship), the relative distance relationship between samples is a soft relationship; thus, we do not use the margin constant when defining the soft intra-modal structure constraint.

Embedding network loss. Finally, we can combine the inter-modal ranking constraint with our proposed soft intra-modal structure constraint to construct an unified embedding network. Given a mini-batch of N music videos, we can obtain N pairs of embedded features of the form (v_i, m_i), where i ranges over the mini-batch. Here, v_i and m_i are the features from the video and music of the i-th music video, after passing through the two-stream embedding network. In this scenario, for the inter-modal ranking constraint, we can build two types of triplets (v_i, m_i, m_j) and (m_i, v_i, v_j), where $i \neq j$ are two different indices of music videos. For the soft intra-modal structure constraint, we used two types of triplets (v_i, v_j, v_k) and (m_i, m_j, m_k), where $i \neq j \neq k$ are three different indices of music videos. Taking into consideration all these triplets, we set the network loss as

$$\begin{aligned} L = {} & \lambda_1 \sum_{i \neq j} max(0, v_i^T m_j - v_i^T m_i + e) \\ & + \lambda_2 \sum_{i \neq j} max(0, m_i^T v_j - m_i^T v_i + e) \\ & + \lambda_3 \sum_{i \neq j \neq k} C_{ijk}(v)(v_i^T v_j - v_i^T v_k) \\ & + \lambda_4 \sum_{i \neq j \neq k} C_{ijk}(m)(m_i^T m_j - m_i^T m_k) \end{aligned} \tag{2}$$

Here, λ_1 and, λ_2 balance the impact of inter-modal ranking loss from video-to-music and music-to-video matching. Recall that both video and music features are L2 normalized; therefore, as a distance measure, we use the negative value of the dot product between the video feature and the music feature. The impact of soft intra-modal structure loss within each modality was balanced by λ_3 and, λ_4, respectively. The function $C(\cdot)$ in Eq. 2 is defined as follows:

$$C_{ijk}(x) = sign(x_i^T x_k - x_i^T x_j) - sign(\widetilde{x}_i^T \widetilde{x}_k - \widetilde{x}_i^T \widetilde{x}_j) \tag{3}$$

where x_i, x_j, and x_k are the trainable features in multimodal space and $\widetilde{x}_i$, $\widetilde{x}_j$, and $\widetilde{x}_k$ are intra-modal features before passing through the embedding network. $sign(x)$ is a function that returns one if x is a positive value, zero if x is equal to zero, and -1 if x is a negative value. As we mentioned, the intra-modal structure is not rigid (or hard); thus, instead of using real distance values, we apply the *sign* function when converting the intra-modal structure constraints to our training objective (i.e., loss function).

4 IMPLEMENTATION DETAILS

4.1 Construction of the Dataset

The practical challenge of CBVMR using data-driven learning such as deep learning is the difficulty of obtaining well-matched video–music pairs. Until now, public datasets consisting of music and visual modality (e.g., images or videos) have been rare. Hence, we compiled a Hong & Im Music–Video 200K (HIMV-200K) benchmark dataset, composed of 200,500 video–music. We obtained these video–music pairs from the YouTube-8M, a large-scale labeled video dataset that consists of millions of YouTube video IDs and associated labels [1]. Once all videos with a "music video" label were downloaded, they were separated into video and audio components. As a result, we obtained 205,000 video–music pairs, and the sets for training, validation, and test comprised 200K, 4K, and 1K pairs, respectively.

4.2 Network Structure

The details of our two-branch embedding network is as follows. Given that high-level video features are extracted from the pre-trained CNN, we stacked only two FC layers with 2048 and 512 nodes for the video branch. On the other hand, after high-level music features are obtained from various low-level audio features, we stacked three FC layers with 2048, 1024, and 512 nodes. Finally, to solve the scale imbalance between music and image features, we apply batch normalization before the embedding loss layer in both video and audio part. Our approach used the ADAM optimizer [19] with learning rate 0.0003, and a dropout scheme with probability 0.9 is used. We selected a mini-batch size for training of 2,000 video–music pairs.

5 EXPERIMENTAL RESULTS

5.1 The Recall@K Metric

The protocol. Conventional video–music related approaches has few standard protocols for evaluation, and even most of them mainly performed subjective user evaluation. To address this issue we apply Recall@K, a standard protocol for cross-modal retrieval, especially in image–text retrieval [16, 35] to our CBVMR task. For a given value of K, it measures the percentage of queries in a test set for which at least one correct ground truth match was ranked among the top K matches. For example, if we consider video queries that request suitable music, then Recall@10 tells us the percentage of video queries for which the top ten results include a ground truth music match. To our knowledge, our study is the only work using Recall@K to quantitatively evaluate the performance of bidirectional video–music retrieval.

Key factors. Motivated by [16, 35, 36], we used a test set of 1,000 videos and their corresponding music tracks. Several key factors affected the performance of our model under the Recall@K protocol as shown in Table 2. As a baseline, we provide the expected value for Recall@K using random retrieval from 1,000 video–music pairs. All experimental results in this table were obtained from our model using only inter-modal ranking loss (i.e., λ_3 and λ_4 were set to zero)

The first section of the table shows the influence of the constraint weights. It is apparent that the performance can be generally improved by relatively giving more weight to λ_1 than λ_2. However, empirically, we confirmed that setting λ_1 to five or more does not improve Recall@K.

We also analyzed the results by changing the number of layers in the music and video branches of the embedding network. Using only one layer for each modality resulted in low performance, and it can be inferred that a deeper network is needed to generate an effective embedding. As the number of layers increases, the performance tends to be higher. We also confirmed that when the number of layers for the video part is more than three, the network weights do not converge in training. This appears to be due to degradation that often occurs in deep networks, as mentioned in [11].

Finally, we also analyzed the results by changing the number of top violations, Q (see Sec. 3.3). From the table, it is clear that there is a tendency for the performance to increase as Q increases. In particular, the use of top 1000 violations results in a high retrieval rate of 9.1% in the music-to-video task. We also performed experiments on the entire training mini-batch (i.e., K=2000) but could not confirm any additional performance improvements.

Comparison with other methods. Table 3 presents the comparisons of our VM-NET with previous work. As a baseline, we present the result from linear models such as PCA [15] and techniques based on partial least squares (PLS) [37]. We also present the result of canonical correlation analysis (CCA) [10], which finds linear projections that maximize the correlation between projected vectors from the two modalities. To fairly compare the conventional linear models to our own using bidirectional loss (i.e., inter-modal ranking loss), we evaluated the performance of our model without ReLU nonlinearities. We also present the results of our linear model using one-directional loss (i.e., λ_1, λ_3, and λ_4 were set to zero), and our model is very similar to the WSABIE image–text model [39]. Inspired by a technique [27] that applied the domain-adversarial neural network (DANN) [9] to image–text retrieval, we also applied DANN to our model.

From the experiment, it is clear that obtaining a good retrieval performance with conventional linear models is difficult. In nonlinear models, using bidirectional constraints instead of one-directional constraints improves the retrieval results by 2-3% for R@1 and by a larger amount for the R@10 and R@25 protocols.

As the matching criteria between video and music are ambiguous than that of other cross-modal tasks such as image-to-text retrieval, the result of R@10 and R@25 may be more appropriate evaluation criteria than that of R@1 in CBVMR tasks. It is apparent from Table 3 that using both inter-modal and intra-modal loss results in a significant performance improvement over using only inter-modal loss, especially in the performance of R@10 and R@25. This result suggests that the proposed soft intra-modal structure that preserves modality-specific characteristics is helpful for inferring the latent alignment between videos and music tracks.

5.2 A Human Preference Test

Applying Recall@K to the relatively subjective cross-modal video–music retrieval is one way to evaluate performance, but it might not be the most appropriate protocol. Therefore, we suggest and conduct a reasonable subjective evaluation protocol using humans.

Outline. We developed a web-based application in which test subjects were asked to pick one of two cross-modal items that the user thought was the best match to a given query. Fig. 4 shows the overall flow diagram of the human preference test for video-to-music and music-to-video selection.

Selection pairs. To analyze the users' subjectivity in detail, we used three different types of answer pairs. In some queries, the user was required to choose between a ground truth match and a randomly chosen match (**G-R**). Other queries required a choice between a ground truth match and a search match (**G-S**); still other queries had a choice between a search match and a random match (**S-R**). Here, "ground truth" indicates the cross-modal item extracted from the music video from which the query item was also extracted; "random" means a randomly selected item; and "search" indicates the closest cross-modal item to the query in the embedding space of our VM-NET model.

Analysis. Table 4 presents the results of the preference test, where each row (such as G>R) indicates the percent of answers where the subject preferred one match to another (such as preferring ground truth over random). Note that the human subjects' preference for G>R is over 80%, which is much higher than the expected value of a random answer (i.e., 50%). It follows that a human's preference for selecting video and music obtained from the same music video is fairly high, and this supports the validity of using video and music pairs from music videos for learning.

Compared to G>R, G>S shows a clear decrease in human preference. In other words, humans had a very clear preference for ground

Table 2: Retrieval results on HIMV-200K with respect to the key factors of VM-NET.

Parameter		Music-to-video			Video-to-music		
		R@1	R@10	R@25	R@1	R@10	R@25
Expected value of R@K		0.1	1.0	2.5	0.1	1.0	2.5
Constraint weight (λ_1, λ_2)	(1, 3)	6.1	12.3	18.8	5.8	11.4	17.3
	(1, 5)	5.2	12.0	17.5	4.7	11.6	16.9
	(1, 1)	8.4	**19.3**	28.6	7.3	17.6	29.2
	(3, 1)	8.5	19.2	**29.1**	7.2	**20.5**	27.5
	(5, 1)	**8.7**	18.7	27.4	**7.7**	18.0	**29.3**
Number of layers (N_{music}, N_{video})	(1, 1)	4.3	16.1	25.6	2.9	15.0	24.9
	(2, 2)	7.5	16.5	27.3	7.3	16.0	26.4
	(2, 3)	7.4	16.8	26.4	6.7	16.2	25.9
	(3, 2)	**8.5**	**19.2**	**29.1**	7.2	**20.5**	**27.5**
	(4, 2)	8.2	18.5	27.3	**7.5**	16.5	25.5
Number of top violations Q	10	4.4	8.5	13.8	4.5	6.5	9.1
	50	8.0	17.3	25.7	7.4	16.5	25.4
	100	8.5	19.2	29.1	7.2	20.5	27.5
	500	8.4	21.2	31.7	**7.6**	19.4	**32.0**
	1000	**9.1**	**22.5**	**32.6**	**7.6**	**20.1**	31.8

Table 3: Comparison of results on HIMV-200K using different methods.

Method		Music-to-video			Video-to-music		
		R@1	R@10	R@25	R@1	R@10	R@25
Linear	PCA [15]	0.0	0.5	2.1	0.1	1.1	2.7
	PLSSVD [37]	0.7	5.9	13.0	0.8	6.8	14.1
	PLSCA [37]	0.8	6.3	13.7	0.4	7.1	14.1
	CCA [10]	2.7	14.0	25.8	1.8	14.3	26.6
	Ours (one-directional setting)	4.2	15.3	24.4	3.9	15.7	5 26.4
	Ours (inter)	4.3	16.3	27.0	3.5	15.3	26.9
	Ours (inter + intra)	4.0	16.7	26.5	3.4	14.3	25.9
Nonlinear	Ours (one-directional setting)	6.5	13.5	19.9	5.2	12.0	18.6
	Ours (inter)	**9.1**	22.5	32.6	7.6	20.1	31.8
	Ours (inter + soft intra)	8.9	**25.2**	**37.9**	**8.2**	**23.3**	**35.7**
	Ours (inter + DANN [9])	7.7	19.7	28.6	8.0	19.9	29.8
	Ours (inter + soft intra + DANN [9])	8.5	24.0	**37.9**	6.7	22.9	35.4

inter: inter-modal ranking loss, soft intra: soft intra-modal structure loss

Table 4: Results of the human preference test, showing the percentage of subjects preferring one possible match to another. The type of pairs, (G-R), (G-S), (S-R), were not informed to the subjects in this test.

Subject	Preference	V2M	M2V	Total
Human	G>R	81.98	81.98	81.98
	G>S	65.57	64.62	65.09
	S>R	71.79	74.25	73.02
Machine	G>R	78.45	78.50	78.48

G: ground truth, R: random, S: search result.
V2M: Video-to-Music, M2V: Music-to-Video.

truth over random matches, but that preference for ground truth decreases when the provided alternative is the search result from our model. This indicates that our model's results are better than the randomly selected results. That is, the retrieved results from our model are similar to ground truth items, which make it difficult for the subjects to choose. We can also see that the preference for S>R is over 70%, which validates the effectiveness of our method in this subjective task. To show the distribution of preferences in each task in more detail, we also present a box plot in Fig. 5.

To compare the performance with human subjects and the machine (i.e., our model), we also experimented with what the machine preferred between ground truth items (G) and randomly selected items (R). In this experiment, we assumed that the machine always selected the item closer to the query in the embedding space. From Table 4, interestingly, we can see that the performance of our model in the G>R task is similar to human performance. This suggests a correlation between video and music regardless whether the judgment is by a human or the machine.

5.3 A Video–Music Qualitative Experiment

We also investigated the quality of the retrieval results for CBVMR tasks by using a test set comprising 1,000 video–music pairs as

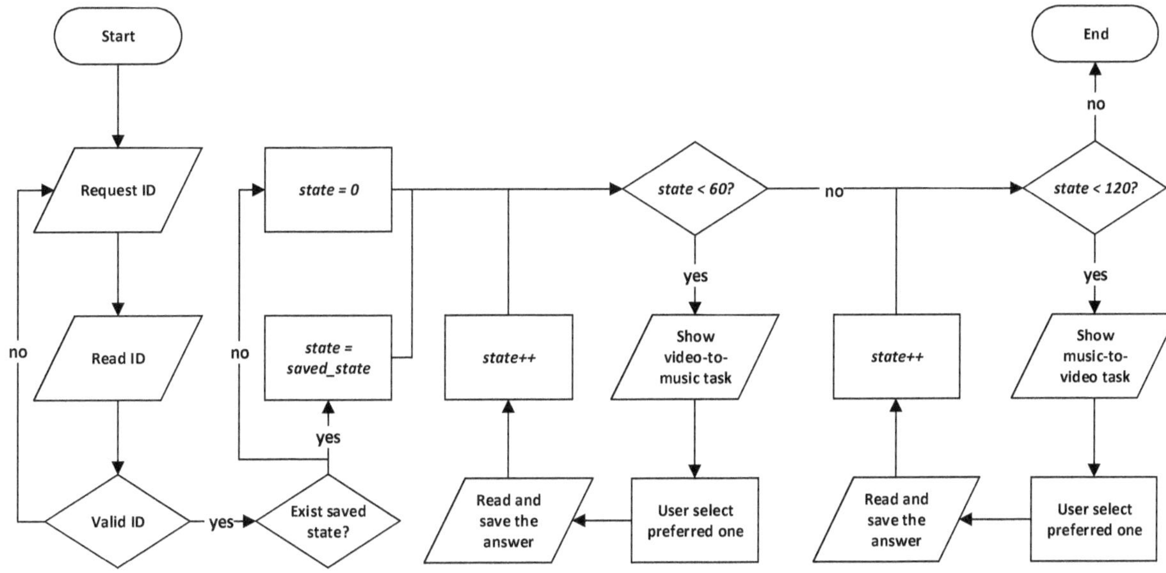

Figure 4: Flowchart of the human preference test. Fifty-three people participated in this test. We gave each subject 120 questions containing 60 video-to-music and 60 music-to-video selection tasks. We sent a unique ID to every subject. When they had access to the address by web browsers on their computers, they performed video-to-music and music-to-video tasks.

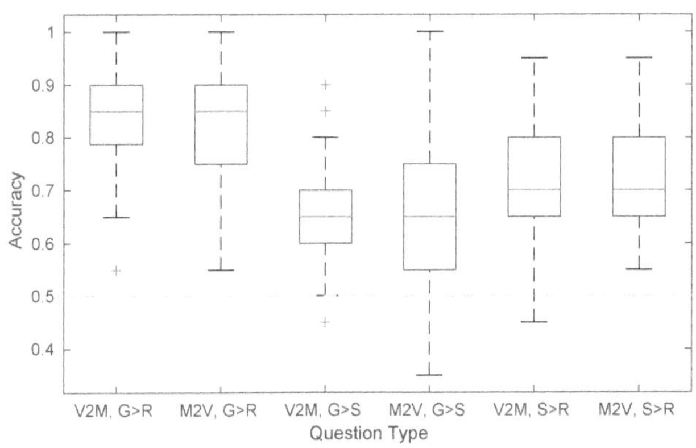

Figure 5: Box plot showing the range of individual differences in preferences.

shown in Fig. 6. In the figure, pictures with the purple outlines represent the video items. Blue boxes represent music items. Because it is very difficult to express music or video itself only with figures, in both cases, we use just one key frame of the music video to represent its video item or the music item. Although the retrieval task was performed based only on content, we present in the figure a single piece of genre meta-information for each item to better convey the music or video content characteristics. Overall, the figure shows the results of each query in order from best match (on the left) to worst match (on the right). Even with the few examples shown in Fig. 6, it is clear that the retrieved results accurately reflect characteristics of music or videos.

Finally, to demonstrate the flexibility of VM-NET, we performed additional experiments using video and music that had been assigned by YouTube-8M to a general category (e.g., "boxing," "motorsport," and "U.S. army") rather than just "music video." (See Fig. 7.) Once again, the query results appear to be meaningful with respect to aspects such as gender and race of the characters.

6 CONCLUSION

In this paper, we introduced VM-NET, a two-branch deep network that associates videos and music considering inter- and intra-modal relationships. We showed that inter-modal ranking loss widely used in other cross-modal matching is effective for the CBVMR task. We also demonstrated that our newly proposed soft intra-modal structure preserving modality-specific characteristics significantly improves performance. In the CBVMR task measured by Recall@K, our model outperformed conventional cross-modal approaches and this can be a quantitative baseline for subsequent CBVMR studies. To evaluate how well our model relates the two cross-modal sources qualitatively, we also conducted a novel reasonable evaluation with human subjects. Finally, the quality of the bidirectional CBVMR results suggests that the genre of music or gender or nationality of the singer can be learned by our model.

ACKNOWLEDGMENTS

This work was supported by the ICT R&D program of MSIP/IITP [2017-0-00162. Development of Human-care Robot Technology for Aging Society]. This work was also supported by Institute for Information & Communications Technology Promotion(IITP) grant funded by the Korea government(MSIT) (R0124-16-0002, Emotional Intelligence Technology to Infer Human Emotion and Carry on Dialogue Accordingly). The authors would like to thank Seokhyun Oh and Seokkyung Oh for their valuable seed ideas and helpful suggestions.

Figure 6: Bidirectional video–music retrieval results for the HIMV-200K: Note that the genre information written below each item was not used during the content-based retrieval, but that information aids in a qualitative assessment of the retrievals.

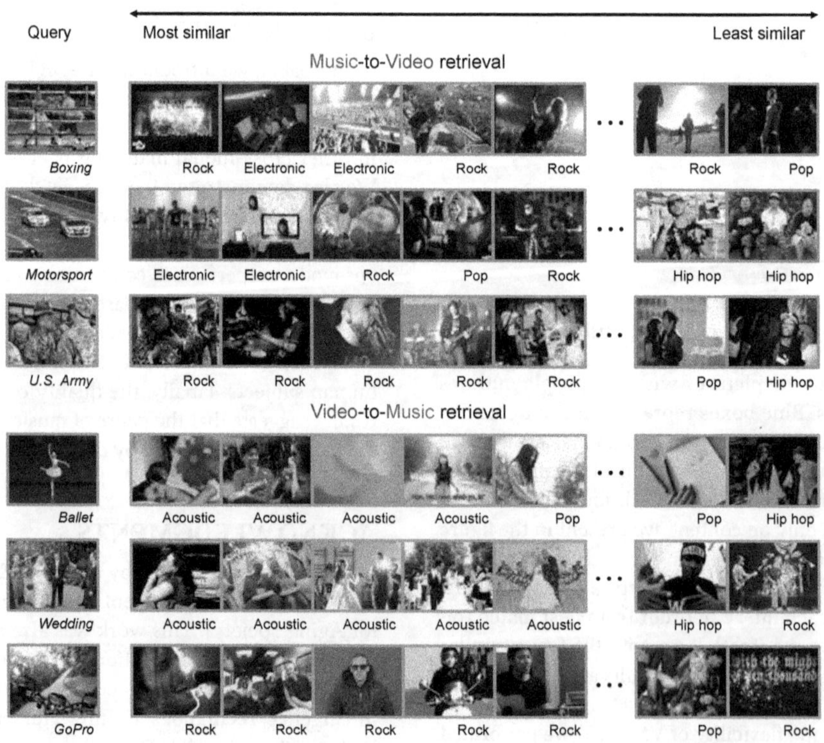

Figure 7: Additional bidirectional video–music retrieval results using queries from videos and music that had been assigned by YouTube-8M to a general category: the general category metadata written below each item was not used during retrieval.

REFERENCES

[1] Sami Abu-El-Haija, Nisarg Kothari, Joonseok Lee, Paul Natsev, George Toderici, Balakrishnan Varadarajan, and Sudheendra Vijayanarasimhan. 2016. Youtube-8m: A large-scale video classification benchmark. *arXiv preprint arXiv:1609.08675* (2016).

[2] Esra Acar, Frank Hopfgartner, and Sahin Albayrak. 2014. Understanding affective content of music videos through learned representations. In *International Conference on Multimedia Modeling*. Springer, 303–314.

[3] Sujung Bae, Sungeun Hong, Yeongjae Choi, and Hyun S Yang. 2013. Recursive Bayesian fire recognition using greedy margin-maximizing clustering. *Machine vision and applications* 24, 8 (2013), 1605–1621.

[4] Eric Brochu, Nando De Freitas, and Kejie Bao. 2003. The sound of an album cover: Probabilistic multimedia and IR. In *Workshop on Artificial Intelligence and Statistics*.

[5] Jiansong Chao, Haofen Wang, Wenlei Zhou, Weinan Zhang, and Yong Yu. 2011. Tunesensor: A semantic-driven music recommendation service for digital photo albums. In *Proceedings of the 10th International Semantic Web Conference. ISWC2011 (October 2011)*.

[6] Jia Deng, Wei Dong, Richard Socher, Li-Jia Li, Kai Li, and Li Fei-Fei. 2009. Imagenet: A large-scale hierarchical image database. In *Computer Vision and Pattern Recognition, 2009. CVPR 2009. IEEE Conference on*. IEEE, 248–255.

[7] Andrea Frome, Greg S Corrado, Jon Shlens, Samy Bengio, Jeff Dean, Tomas Mikolov, et al. 2013. Devise: A deep visual-semantic embedding model. In *Advances in neural information processing systems*. 2121–2129.

[8] Zhouyu Fu, Guojun Lu, Kai Ming Ting, and Dengsheng Zhang. 2011. A survey of audio-based music classification and annotation. *IEEE transactions on multimedia* 13, 2 (2011), 303–319.

[9] Yaroslav Ganin, Evgeniya Ustinova, Hana Ajakan, Pascal Germain, Hugo Larochelle, François Laviolette, Mario Marchand, and Victor Lempitsky. 2016. Domain-adversarial training of neural networks. *Journal of Machine Learning Research* 17, 59 (2016), 1–35.

[10] David R Hardoon, Sandor Szedmak, and John Shawe-Taylor. 2004. Canonical correlation analysis: An overview with application to learning methods. *Neural computation* 16, 12 (2004), 2639–2664.

[11] Kaiming He, Xiangyu Zhang, Shaoqing Ren, and Jian Sun. 2016. Deep residual learning for image recognition. In *Proceedings of the IEEE Conference on Computer Vision and Pattern Recognition*. 770–778.

[12] Sungeun Hong, Woobin Im, Jongbin Ryu, and Hyun S Yang. 2017. SSPP-DAN: Deep Domain Adaptation Network for Face Recognition with Single Sample Per Person. *arXiv preprint arXiv:1702.04069* (2017).

[13] Sungeun Hong, Jongbin Ryu, Woobin Im, and Hyun S Yang. 2017. Recognizing Dynamic Scenes with Deep Dual Descriptor based on Key Frames and Key Segments. *arXiv preprint arXiv:1702.04479* (2017).

[14] Sungeun Hong, Jongbin Ryu, and Hyun S Yang. 2018. Not all frames are equal: aggregating salient features for dynamic texture classification. *Multidimensional Systems and Signal Processing* 29, 1 (2018), 279–298.

[15] Ian Jolliffe. 2002. *Principal component analysis*. Wiley Online Library.

[16] Andrej Karpathy and Li Fei-Fei. 2015. Deep visual-semantic alignments for generating image descriptions. In *Proceedings of the IEEE Conference on Computer Vision and Pattern Recognition*. 3128–3137.

[17] Andrej Karpathy, Armand Joulin, and Fei Fei F Li. 2014. Deep fragment embeddings for bidirectional image sentence mapping. In *Advances in neural information processing systems*. 1889–1897.

[18] Maksim Khadkevich and Maurizio Omologo. 2013. Reassigned spectrum-based feature extraction for gmm-based automatic chord recognition. *EURASIP Journal on Audio, Speech, and Music Processing* 2013, 1 (2013), 15.

[19] Diederik Kingma and Jimmy Ba. 2014. Adam: A method for stochastic optimization. *arXiv preprint arXiv:1412.6980* (2014).

[20] Ryan Kiros, Ruslan Salakhutdinov, and Richard S Zemel. 2014. Unifying visual-semantic embeddings with multimodal neural language models. *arXiv preprint arXiv:1411.2539* (2014).

[21] Sangeun Kum, Changheun Oh, and Juhan Nam. 2016. Melody Extraction on Vocal Segments Using Multi-Column Deep Neural Networks. In *The International Society for Music Information Retrieval (ISMIR), 2016*. ISMIR.

[22] Janis Libeks and Douglas Turnbull. 2011. You can judge an artist by an album cover: Using images for music annotation. *IEEE MultiMedia* 18, 4 (2011), 30–37.

[23] Cynthia Liem, Alessio Bazzica, and Alan Hanjalic. 2012. MuseSync: standing on the shoulders of Hollywood. In *Proceedings of the 20th ACM international conference on Multimedia*. ACM, 1383–1384.

[24] Tsung-Yi Lin, Michael Maire, Serge Belongie, James Hays, Pietro Perona, Deva Ramanan, Piotr Dollár, and C Lawrence Zitnick. 2014. Microsoft coco: Common objects in context. In *European conference on computer vision*. Springer, 740–755.

[25] Rudolf Mayer. 2011. Analysing the similarity of album art with self-organising maps. In *International Workshop on Self-Organizing Maps*. Springer, 357–366.

[26] Meinard Müller and Sebastian Ewert. 2011. Chroma Toolbox: MATLAB implementations for extracting variants of chroma-based audio features. In *Proceedings of the 12th International Conference on Music Information Retrieval (ISMIR), 2011. hal-00727791, version 2-22 Oct 2012*. Citeseer.

[27] Gwangbeen Park and Woobin Im. 2016. Image-Text Multi-Modal Representation Learning by Adversarial Backpropagation. *arXiv preprint arXiv:1612.08354* (2016).

[28] Jongbin Ryu, Sungeun Hong, and Hyun S Yang. 2015. Sorted consecutive local binary pattern for texture classification. *IEEE Transactions on Image Processing* 24, 7 (2015), 2254–2265.

[29] Shoto Sasaki, Tatsunori Hirai, Hayato Ohya, and Shigeo Morishima. 2015. Affective Music Recommendation System Based on the Mood of Input Video. In *International Conference on Multimedia Modeling*. Springer, 299–302.

[30] Alexander Schindler and Andreas Rauber. 2015. An audio-visual approach to music genre classification through affective color features. In *European Conference on Information Retrieval*. Springer, 61–67.

[31] Rajiv Ratn Shah, Yi Yu, and Roger Zimmermann. 2014. Advisor: Personalized video soundtrack recommendation by late fusion with heuristic rankings. In *Proceedings of the 22nd ACM international conference on Multimedia*. ACM, 607–616.

[32] John Shawe-Taylor and Nello Cristianini. 2004. *Kernel methods for pattern analysis*. Cambridge university press.

[33] Christian Szegedy, Wei Liu, Yangqing Jia, Pierre Sermanet, Scott Reed, Dragomir Anguelov, Dumitru Erhan, Vincent Vanhoucke, and Andrew Rabinovich. 2015. Going deeper with convolutions. In *Proceedings of the IEEE Conference on Computer Vision and Pattern Recognition*. 1–9.

[34] Aaron Van den Oord, Sander Dieleman, and Benjamin Schrauwen. 2013. Deep content-based music recommendation. In *Advances in neural information processing systems*. 2643–2651.

[35] Liwei Wang, Yin Li, and Svetlana Lazebnik. 2016. Learning deep structure-preserving image-text embeddings. In *Proceedings of the IEEE Conference on Computer Vision and Pattern Recognition*. 5005–5013.

[36] Liwei Wang, Yin Li, and Svetlana Lazebnik. 2017. Learning Two-Branch Neural Networks for Image-Text Matching Tasks. *arXiv preprint arXiv:1704.03470* (2017).

[37] Jacob A Wegelin et al. 2000. A survey of Partial Least Squares (PLS) methods, with emphasis on the two-block case. *University of Washington, Department of Statistics, Tech. Rep* (2000).

[38] Kilian Q Weinberger and Lawrence K Saul. 2009. Distance metric learning for large margin nearest neighbor classification. *Journal of Machine Learning Research* 10, Feb (2009), 207–244.

[39] Jason Weston, Samy Bengio, and Nicolas Usunier. 2011. Wsabie: Scaling up to large vocabulary image annotation. In *IJCAI*, Vol. 11. 2764–2770.

[40] Xixuan Wu, Yu Qiao, Xiaogang Wang, and Xiaoou Tang. 2016. Bridging Music and Image via Cross-Modal Ranking Analysis. *IEEE Transactions on Multimedia* 18, 7 (2016), 1305–1318.

[41] Peter Young, Alice Lai, Micah Hodosh, and Julia Hockenmaier. 2014. From image descriptions to visual denotations: New similarity metrics for semantic inference over event descriptions. *Transactions of the Association for Computational Linguistics* 2 (2014), 67–78.

Multi-Scale Spatiotemporal Conv-LSTM Network for Video Saliency Detection

Yi Tang
College of Information Engineering, Shenzhen University
Shenzhen, Guangzhou, P.R.China
yitang@szu.edu.cn

Wenbin Zou*
College of Information Engineering, Shenzhen University
Shenzhen, Guangzhou, P.R.China
zouszu@sina.com

Zhi Jin
College of Information Engineering, Shenzhen University
Shenzhen, Guangzhou, P.R.China
jinzhi_126@163.com

Xia Li
Chinese University of Hong Kong
Shenzhen, Guangzhou, P.R.China
lixia@cuhk.edu.cn

ABSTRACT

Recently, deep neural networks have been crucial techniques for image salient detection. However, two difficulties prevent the development of deep learning in video saliency detection. The first one is that the traditional static network cannot conduct a robust motion estimation in videos. The other is that the data-driven deep learning is in lack of sufficient manually annotated pixel-wise ground truths for video saliency network training. In this paper, we propose a multi-scale spatiotemporal convolutional LSTM network (MSST-ConvLSTM) to incorporate spatial and temporal cues for video salient objects detection. Furthermore, as manually pixel-wised labeling is very time-consuming, we sign lots of coarse labels, which are mixed with fine labels to train a robust saliency prediction model. Experiments on the widely used challenging benchmark datasets (e.g., FBMS and DAVIS) demonstrate that the proposed approach has competitive performance of video saliency detection compared with the state-of-the-art saliency models.

CCS CONCEPTS

• **Computing methodologies → Interest point and salient region detections**; *Machine learning approaches*; *Neural networks*;

KEYWORDS

Video Saliency, Deep Learning, Spatiotemporal Fusion

*Wenbin Zou is the corresponding author.

ICMR'18, June 11–14, 2018, Yokohama, Japan
© 2018 Association for Computing Machinery.
ACM ISBN 978-1-4503-5046-4/18/06...$15.00
https://doi.org/10.1145/3206025.3206052

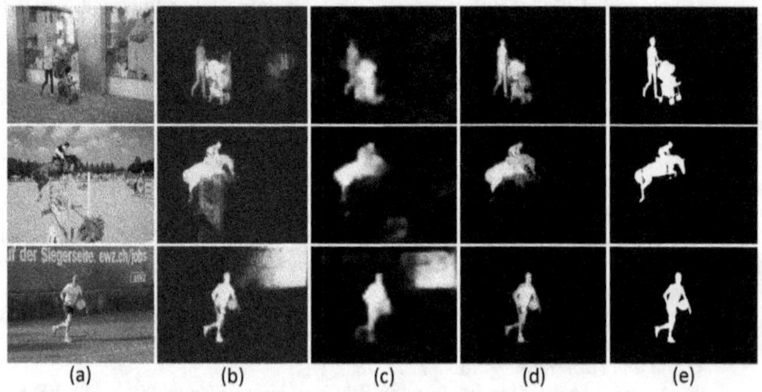

Figure 1: Saliency detection by different deep learning models. (a) Video frame. (b) Saliency maps by image saliency detection [15]. (c) Saliency maps by video saliency detection [31]. (d) Saliency maps by the proposed network. (e) Ground truths.

ACM Reference Format:
Yi Tang, Wenbin Zou, Zhi Jin, and Xia Li. 2018. Multi-Scale Spatiotemporal Conv-LSTM Network for Video Saliency Detection. In *Proceedings of 2018 International Conference on Multimedia Retrieval (ICMR'18)*. ACM, New York, NY, USA, 8 pages. https://doi.org/10.1145/3206025.3206052

1 INTRODUCTION

Saliency detection, whose purpose is accurately and uniformly highlighting the regions that draw human attention in an image or video, has become a very active research field in computer vision because of its importance to support high-level computer vision tasks, such as video classification [22, 36], action recognition [6, 19] and content-based image retrieval [33]. According to the type of input data, saliency detection can be classified into image saliency detection and video saliency detection. In this paper, we focus on video saliency detection.

Recently, deep learning models, especially the fully convolutional network (FCN), have widely been employed to detect salient objects and substantially improved the accuracy of saliency detection in static images. However, these deep learning models cannot adapt directly to the video saliency detection, even if the transfer learning has been introduced to fine-tune the deep networks. The difficulties behind this phenomenon may be two-fold:

One of the difficulties is that the traditional networks in static images cannot capture motion cues in a single frame. These networks learn the features only in an image space, which leads to detect some extra objects in complex video scenes (e.g., Figure.1 (b)). In order to integrate the static and motion cues, [31] tries to train a suitable deep network to complete the task. Their deep model mainly exploits the motion cues between two consecutive frames, but it cannot learn sufficient motion information to completely eliminate non-salient regions in some videos (e.g., Figure.1 (c)).

The other issue is the lack of sufficient pixel-wise labeled video data to train the deep learning network. To obtain robust deep networks, large-scale labeled data are needed. Unfortunately, current datasets for video saliency detection have very limited pixel-wise ground truths. The total number of labeled data in the widely used video datasets (e.g., SegTrackV2 [14], FBMS [1], DAVIS [24]) is less than 5000 frames (including the data for testing). Moreover, the pixel-wise labels of some video sequences are discontinuous. Therefore, insufficient data makes the deep network hardly learn robust motion features, thus reducing the accuracy of video saliency detection.

Based on the aforementioned issues above, we, on the one hand, try to find a desirable deep network architecture which can incorporate spatial and temporal cues to accurately detect salient objects in video sequences. On the other hand, we expect to obtain adequate pixel-wise labeled video data to train the proposed network. Hence, we propose a multi-scale spatiotemporal convolutional LSTM network (MSST-ConvLSTM) for video saliency detection and train this network with a amount of coarse pixel-wise labels. The proposed network consists of two FCN-based sub-networks, spatial sub-network and temporal sub-network. First, we exploit the spatial sub-network, whose input is a static frame, to extract spatial features. Second, we extract the motion features from two aspects. One is the optical flow. A motion prior map generated by optical flow is fed into the temporal sub-network to extract temporal features. The other is the proposed MSST-ConvLSTM. The multi-scale feature maps of several consecutive frames are produced from both sub-networks, and then the recurrent-based model exploits these feature maps to further extract the sequential motion features. Third, the spatial and temporal features are effectively fused at the top of the proposed network to generate fine-grained video saliency prediction (e.g., Figure.1 (d)). Besides, we introduce a coarse labeling strategy, which fuses saliency maps from different saliency models, and then manually erases the error detection regions from the fusing saliency maps. Through this strategy, a number of coarse pixel-wise labels are rapidly generated to support the training of the proposed network.

To summarize, the main contributions of this paper are as follows:

1. We propose a multi-scale spatiotemporal convolutional LSTM network for video saliency detection. This architecture not only retains original spatial cue, but also effectively integrates temporal cue from optical flow map and the structure of LSTM.
2. Following the labeling criteria of [1], we choose some videos in FBMS dataset and label the frames in a coarse pixel-wise way, which makes our deep network learn more robust salient features.
3. We demonstrate that our proposed approach substantially outperforms the state-of-the-art salient object detection models.

2 RELATED WORKS

Over the recent years, a large number of approaches have been proposed in the field of saliency detection. Especially, with the raise of deep learning architecture, the performance of saliency detection obtains a significant improvement. In this section, we give a brief overview of recent saliency detection works in two categories: traditional modeling-based approaches and deep learning-based approaches.

2.1 Modeling-based saliency detection

Saliency detection can be further divided into image saliency and video saliency according to their inputs. The traditional modeling-based approaches in image saliency detection contain low-rank matrix recovery [39], spatial prior [32], regional contrast [38, 40], and graphical modeling [4]. These models are built in the image space and cannot be directly adapted to video saliency. Therefore, some spatiotemporal fusing models [34, 37] have been proposed to incorporate the spacial and temporal cues. In [2], the global motion clues are firstly exploited to generate an initial saliency, and then the low-rank coherency clues are employed to guide the spatial-temporal saliency diffusion. By incorporating the spatial transition matrix and the temporal restarting distribution, Kim et al. [12] propose a novel saliency detection algorithm based on the random walk to estimate saliency distribution. In [25], a statistical framework is proposed for saliency prediction by using motion, illumination and color information. Moreover, as the estimation of moving pixels, optical flow has been widely used in video saliency detection [29, 30]. Although the computation of optical flow is time-consuming, it can extract robust motion features to detect salient objects. Meanwhile, some other methods have been proposed to adopt some optimization mechanisms, such as center-surrounding hypothesis [9], motion attention cue [8], motion boundaries [21], and nonparametric kernel density feature [26].

2.2 Deep learning-based saliency detection

Compared with traditional modeling-based methods, the development of deep learning-based methods can be classified into two phases. In the first phase, convolutional neural network (CNN) is exploited as a feature extractor. The handcrafted features are replaced by the deep features from CNNs

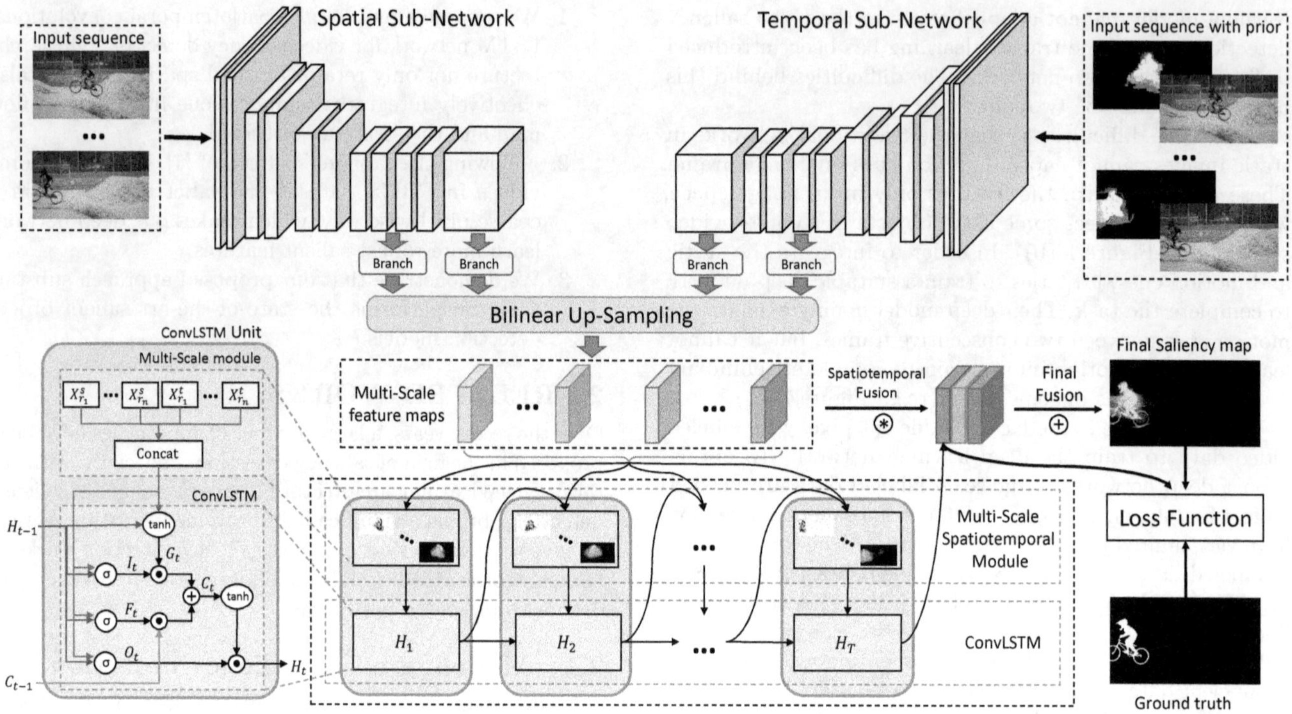

Figure 2: The framework of the proposed network. The multi-scale feature maps are generated from spatial sub-network and temporal sub-network, which are trained by video frames and video frames with the corresponding motion prior, respectively. Along with the modified ConvLSTM units to refine motion information, all of feature maps are fused to generate saliency map.

to detect salient objects in an image. In [16], the multi-scale deep features are combined with multi-region decomposition to detect salient regions. In [35], the deep features of image superpixels are extracted to generate saliency maps. Besides, the integration of region proposal and deep features are adopted for local estimation and global search [27]. In the second phase, an end-to-end FCN [20] has been employed into saliency detection field. Based on the FCN, a series of approaches have been proposed. In order to exploit multi-level feature maps, DHSN [18] proposes a hierarchical FCN to estimate visual saliency. RFCN [28] incorporates saliency prior knowledge, recurrent neural network (RNN) and FCN to perform a full saliency prediction. DCL [15] considers the reduction of receptive field with excessive pooling layers, so the dilated convolutional operation [3] is introduced into FCN. DSMT [17] designs a multi-task convolutional neural network to optimize FCN. Considering a more suitable up-sampling structure, DSS [10] introduces a short connection into FCN.

Due to the shortage of consecutive pixel-wise ground truths, the approaches of video saliency detection by deep learning are not much. Recently, with a novel data augmentation techniques, SFCN [31] proposes an effective deep learning architecture, which fuses spatial and temporal saliency stimuti well. However, their extracted motion information from two consecutive frames is not robust enough. We expect to design more suitable network structure to further extract the motion features.

3 MSST-CONVLSTM FOR VIDEO SALIENCY DETECTION

As shown in Figure.2, the proposed framework is composed of three components, spatial sub-network, temporal sub-network and ConvLSTM units. The spatial sub-network is a modified VGG-based FCN, which introduces dilated convolutional layers in the last two convolutional blocks. This sub-network processes static frames to extract the feature maps with spatial information. The temporal sub-network has almost the same structure with the spatial one. The only difference is that a four-channel image, which consists of a RGB frame and corresponding motion prior (described in section 3.1), is fed into temporal sub-network to generate the feature maps with temporal information. We design serval branches after pooling layers to produce multi-scale feature maps in both sub-networks. Then, the feature maps are fed into the ConvLSTM units to further refine motion information. At last, the feature maps from spatial sub-network, temporal sub-network and ConvLSTM units are fused at the top of network through a convolutional layer (1×1 kernel) to produce the final saliency maps.

3.1 The generation of motion prior

In the temporal sub-network, we aim to obtain robust motion features from the video sequences. Instead of solely relying on optical flow map, we feed a four-channel image into the temporal sub-network, which can ensure that the sub-network learns robust motion information even if the optical flow map is serious fault. In the generation of motion prior, we firstly conduct $\mathcal{M}$ segmentations on the optical flow map by using [7] to obtain multi-scale superpixels. Secondly, the deep features [16] are extracted for each superpixel $r_i^j (j = 1, 2, ..., \mathcal{M})$, where i denotes the superpixel index in the j-level segmentation. Thirdly, a binary classifier based on a three-layer neural network (300 neurons) is trained for salient superpixel prediction. Finally, a linear fusion is employed to generate the motion prior $\mathcal{P}_m$ from different segmentation levels as below:

$$\mathcal{P}_m(r_i) = \frac{1}{\mathcal{M}} \sum_{j=1}^{\mathcal{M}} \mathcal{S}^j(\mathcal{D}(r_i^j)) \tag{1}$$

where $\mathcal{D}(\cdot)$ and $\mathcal{S}^j(\cdot)$ represent the deep features of the superpixel r_i^j and saliency value predicted by the classifier, respectively.

3.2 The proposed architecture

The VGG-based FCN contains five pooling layers, which gradually increase the receptive field and separate the network into six convolutional blocks. In order to retain fine semantic context, the last pooling layer is removed and the dilated convolutional layers are introduced into the last two convolutional blocks in modified FCN. Meanwhile, we add several branches after these pooling layers. Each of the branches contains a 128-channel convolutional layer (3 × 3 kernel) and a 1-channel convolutional layer (1 × 1 kernel). With the bilinear up-sampling layers, the multi-scale feature maps are generated from these branches in both spatial and temporal sub-networks. These feature maps are fed into the ConvLSTM units to further refine the motion information.

The bottom-left part of Figure.2 shows the specific structure of ConvLSTM unit, which is composed of a multi-scale spatiotemporal module and a ConvLSTM module. Assume I^s and I^t denote the inputs of both sub-networks, the processing steps of the MSST-ConvLSTM network can be demonstrated as follows:

$$X^{\tau} = \mathbf{Cat}(X_{r_1}^s, ..., X_{r_n}^s, X_{r_1}^t, ..., X_{r_n}^t) \tag{2}$$

where

$$\begin{aligned} X_{r_i}^s &= \mathcal{U}_{r_i}^s(\mathcal{F}_{r_i}^s(I^s; \theta_{r_i}^s)) \\ X_{r_i}^t &= \mathcal{U}_{r_i}^t(\mathcal{F}_{r_i}^t(I^t; \theta_{r_i}^t)), i \in \{1, 2, ..., n\} \end{aligned} \tag{3}$$

The spatial feature maps $X_{r_i}^s$ and temporal feature maps $X_{r_i}^t$ at different scale r_i are extracted through a series of convolutional operations $\mathcal{F}_{r_i}^s(\cdot)$ and $\mathcal{F}_{r_i}^t(\cdot)$, and up-sampling operations $\mathcal{U}_{r_i}^s(\cdot)$ and $\mathcal{U}_{r_i}^s(\cdot)$. Then, a cross-channel concatenation operation **Cat** is introduced to stack the feature maps.

After that, the sequence of concatenated feature maps $X^1, ..., X^T$ is fed into the ConvLSTM $\mathcal{M}$, where T is the timesteps, which is set to four in our experiment; θ_m is the parameters. As we select a many-to-one model, the output of these operations is a 2-d refined spatiotemporal feature map O^T:

$$O^T = \mathcal{M}(X^1, ..., X^T; \theta_m) \tag{4}$$

At the top of the proposed network, the feature maps from spatial sub-network, temporal sub-network and ConvLSTM units are fused to produce the final prediction map. To retain relative semantic context, a hierarchical structure is exploited to fuse the spatial, temporal and historical semantic information:

$$\mathcal{S} = W^s * X^s + W^t * X^t + O^T \tag{5}$$

where

$$\begin{aligned} X^s &= \mathbf{Cat}(X_{r_1}^s, ..., X_{r_n}^s) \\ X^t &= \mathbf{Cat}(X_{r_1}^t, ..., X_{r_n}^t), i \in \{1, 2, ..., n\} \end{aligned} \tag{6}$$

X^s and X^t are concatenated multi-scale feature maps from spatial and temporal sub-network, respectively; W^s and W^t are their corresponding convolutional parameters; O^T is the spatiotemporal feature map from ConvLSTM units; $\mathcal{S}$ denotes the final prediction map. We firstly use two convolutional layers (1 × 1 kernel) to fuse the feature maps from spatial and temporal sub-network. Then, a element-wise sum is employed to fuse all of the feature maps.

To optimize the whole network, a loss function is applied to compute the errors between the final prediction map $\mathcal{S} \in [0, 1]^{h*w*1}$ and the pixel-wise label $\mathcal{G} \in [0, 1]^{h*w*1}$, where h and w represent the height and width of the input video frame, respectively. Considering the unbalance between salient pixels and non-salient pixels, we employ a weighted sigmoid cross-entropy loss function $\mathcal{L}_f$ as follow:

$$\begin{aligned} \mathcal{L}_f(\mathcal{S}, \mathcal{G}) = &- \alpha \sum_{i=1}^{h*w} g_i \log P(s_i = 1 | I_i^s, I_i^t; \mathcal{W}) \\ &- (1 - \alpha) \sum_{i=1}^{h*w} (1 - g_i) \log P(s_i = 0 | I_i^s, I_i^t; \mathcal{W}) \end{aligned} \tag{7}$$

where $s_i \in \mathcal{S}$ and $g_i \in \mathcal{G}$ demonstrate the saliency value and the label of ground truth for a pixel, respectively; $\mathcal{W}$ is the parameter of the proposed network; $P(\cdot|\cdot)$ denotes the confidence score of the prediction; α is the balance factor.

To speed up the training of the ConvLSTM units, we set another auxiliary loss function $\mathcal{L}_r$ after the ConvLSTM units. This loss function is also a weighted sigmoid cross-entropy loss, but the parameters do not include the fusing operations. Therefore, the final joint loss function for the whole network is defined as below:

$$\mathcal{L} = \mathcal{L}_f(\mathcal{S}, \mathcal{G}) + \beta \mathcal{L}_r(\mathcal{R}, \mathcal{G}) \tag{8}$$

where $\mathcal{R}$ is the feature map from ConvLSTM units; β is the loss weight. Here, it is set to 0.1.

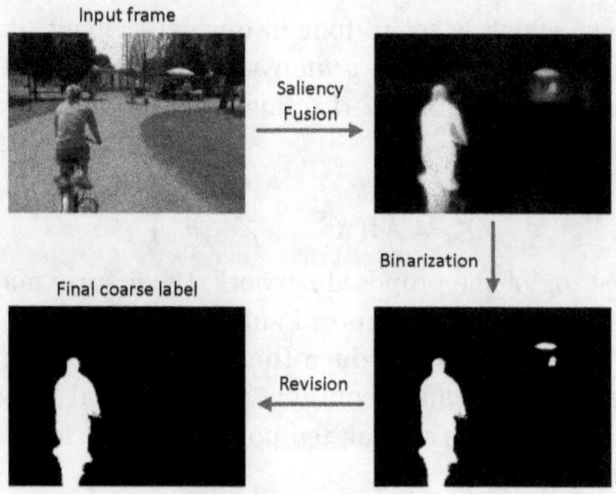

Figure 3: The generation of coarse pixel-wise labels.

3.3 The coarse pixel-wise labeling

Due to the shortage of pixel-wise labeled video data, the proposed network is hard to train. The best solution is labeling sufficient and fine pixel-wise labels, but it is very time-consuming. Therefore, instead of the fine labels, we sign video data with coarse pixel-wise labels, which retain the rough outline but ignore the details of salient objects. The generation pipeline is displayed in Figure.3. Firstly, given the video sequences in the training set of FBMS dataset, the fused saliency maps of video frames are generated by a weighted linear combination [11] of three image saliency detection methods (i.e., DCL [15], RFCN [28], DSMT [17]), which are the recent deep learning models and achieve competitive performance in image saliency detection. Although some background regions are highlighted in the complex scenes, these approaches are able to detect the main salient objects. Besides, we employ the weighted linear combination to fuse these saliency maps, which can make these saliency maps compensate for each other and generate more accurate ones. Then, with the fusing saliency maps, the binary pixel-wise labels are generated by Otsu thresholding method. Finally, we manually erase the error detection regions and produce the final coarse pixel-wise labels. In our approach, we totally obtain 3,326 coarse pixel-wise labels, which are mixed with the original labeled ones to train the proposed network.

4 EXPERIMENTS

4.1 Experimental Setup

Datasets. Three datasets, SegTrackV2 [14], FBMS [1], and DAVIS [24], are used for evaluating our experiments.

In our experiments, the training data (totally 51 sequences, 6,098 frames) includes the half of DAVIS, the training set of FBMS (with generated coarse pixel-wise labels) and all of SegTrackV2 videos. The testing set is the remaining video sequences of DAVIS and the testing set of FBMS (with ground truths).

Evaluation criteria. In our experiments, the standard precision-recall (PR) curve and mean absolute error (MAE) are adopted. In PR curve, the binary mask is converted from the saliency map with a integer threshold. Then, the precision and recall is computed by comparing the binary mask against the ground-truth. In addition, MAE is introduced as a complemental measure. MAE measures the average absolute difference between a saliency map and its corresponding ground truth in pixel level.

Implementation. To better fuse spatial and temporal cues and obtain robust feature maps, the network training follows next several settings:

- Before the network training, both spatial and temporal sub-networks are initialized by the same pre-trained VGG-based FCN from ImageNet [5]. In order to match the input of the temporal sub-network, the first convolutional layer is re-initialized by Gaussian distribution.
- In the proposed network, we design several branches to extract the multi-scale feature maps. Specifically, there are two branches in each sub-network, one is after the fourth pooling layers, the other is after the last convolutional layer.
- As the application of FCN, the input size of images is arbitrary. To make the network to learn more fine-grained features, two resolution images (321×321 and 512×512) are used for training.
- In the testing stage, to improve spatial coherence, a dense CRF [3] is employed as a post-processing method to refine the generated saliency maps.
- In the entire training process, the Adaptive Moment Estimation (Adam) [13] is chosen to optimize the network. The initial learning rate is 10^{-3} for the proposed network training.

The PC configuration is an Intel(R) i7-5820 CPU (3.3GHz), 64G RAM and a Nvidia Geforce TITAN X GPU. The proposed method costs 2.9 seconds to process a sequence (4 frames with 512×512 resolution). The network forwarding operation takes 2.1 seconds and the post-processing costs 0.8 seconds.

4.2 Comparison to the State-of-the-art Methods

In this section, 6 video saliency detection methods and 8 image saliency detection methods are compared with the proposed approach. The video saliency detection methods include ST [37], CS [8], SS [25], CG [30], SA [29] and SFC-N [31]. The image saliency detection methods include SF [23], MDF [16], DCL [15], RFCN [28], DSMT [17], LEGS [27], DSS [10] and DHSN [18].

As shown in Figure.4, the proposed method outperforms the existing approaches in term of both PR curve and MAE criteria. Notice that the PR curves demonstrate that the proposed method achieves the competitive performance. At the same time, the MAEs are decreased to 8.2% and 4.5% on the FBMS and DAVIS, respectively. The proposed method obtains the lowest MAE among all the state-of-the-art methods.

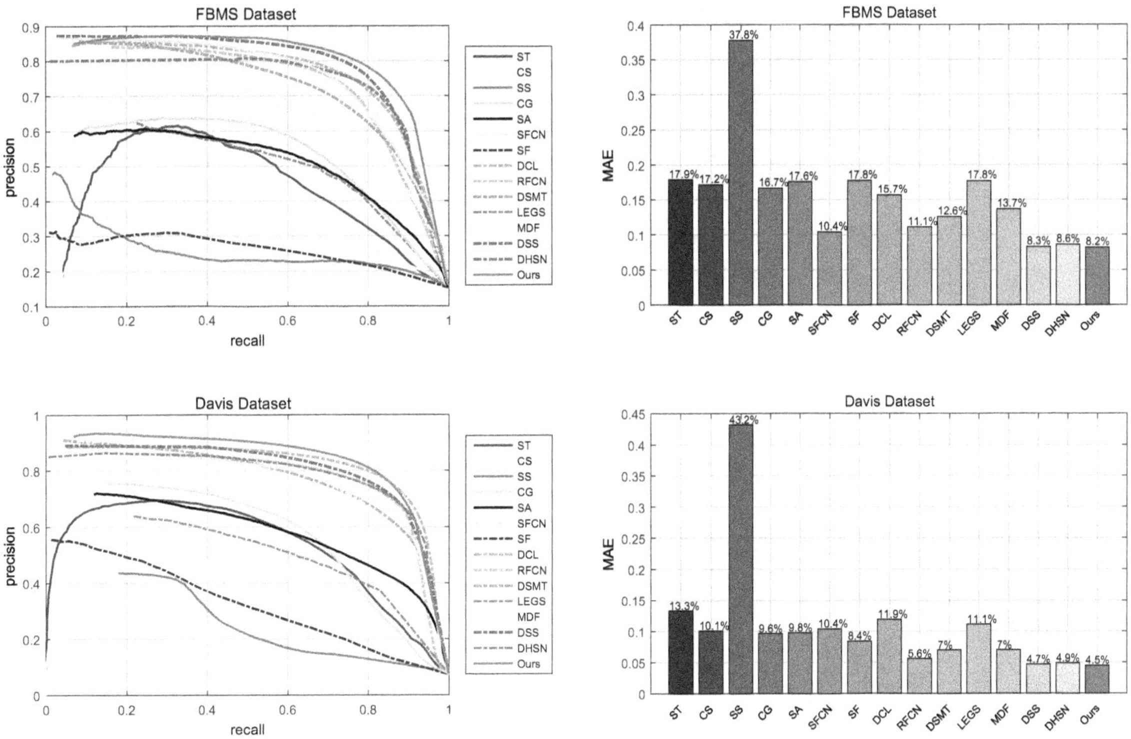

Figure 4: Comparison with 14 different saliency detection methods including 6 video saliency detection methods (solid lines) and 8 image saliency detection methods (dashed lines) by using FBMS dataset (top) and DAVIS dataset (bottom). The left two figures are PR curves and the right two are MAEs of different methods.

In qualitative comparison, Figure.5 shows the saliency maps generated by different saliency detection models. Based on these examples, serval observations are obtained as follows:

Multiple salient objects: In the *horse04* sequence (the third row), there are three salient objects in the ground truth. Previous models cannot highlight all of them. Our model by fusing spatial and temporal features successfully detects all of the salient objects in this video.

Tiny salient objects: For some video scenes containing tiny saliency (e.g., the fifth row), previous models can detect the moving soccer ball, but some other regions also are detected at the same time. On the contrary, the proposed approach with multi-scale spatiotemporal features is able to pop out the tiny object from background regions.

Motion features: Our network effectively extracts motion features from two aspects (optical flow and RNNs). These features are robust enough to make the moving objects more salient and eliminate extra background regions (e.g., the bench in *lucia* sequence).

4.3 Ablation Studies

The proposed deep learning architecture consists of spatial sub-network, temporal sub-network and MSST-ConvLSTM. In order to validate the effectiveness of these components, we report the saliency performance by different configurations of network.

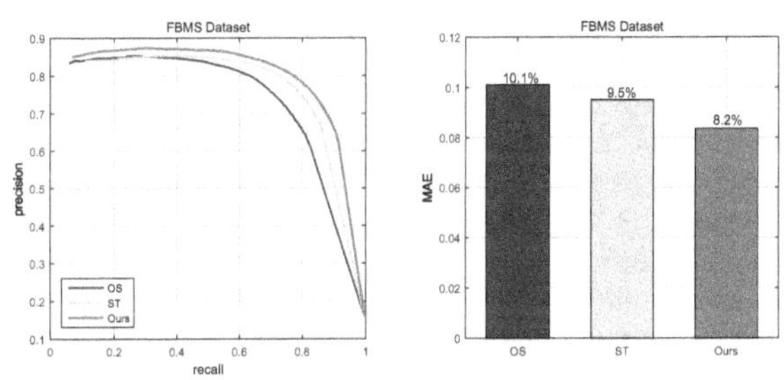

Figure 6: PR curves and MAEs by using different configurations on FBMS dataset.

- *OS*: This architecture only contains a spatial sub-network, which is extended by modified VGGNet. We train this network only with video frames and do not introduce any temporal information.
- *ST*: This network combines spatial and temporal sub-networks. The feature maps generated from both sub-networks are integrated into the final saliency map at the top of the network.
- *MSST-ConvLSTM*: Based on the integration of spatial and temporal sub-network, the proposed MSST-ConvLSTM architecture is introduced to make the network further learn motion features.

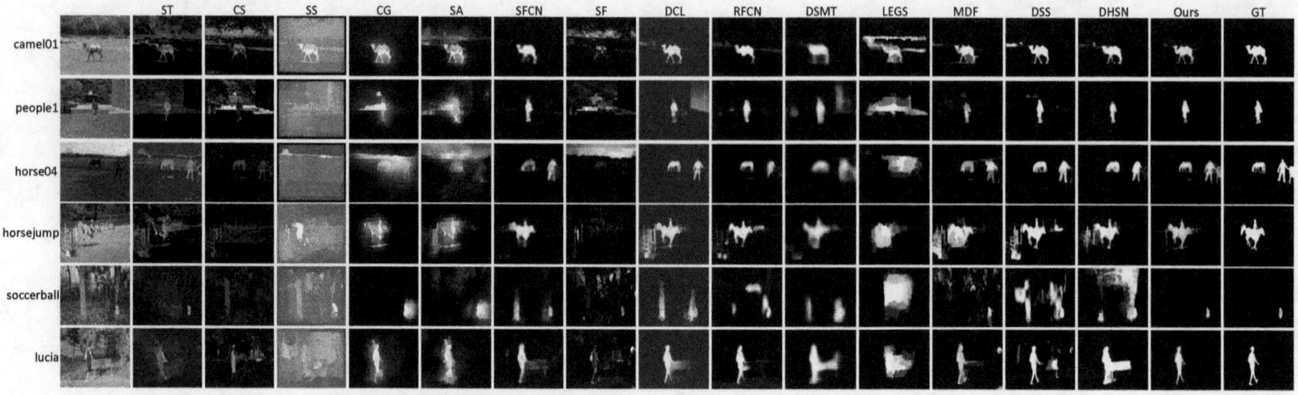

Figure 5: The saliency maps are generated from different saliency detection approaches. Top and bottom three rows are the video frames from FBMS and DAVIS datasets, respectively

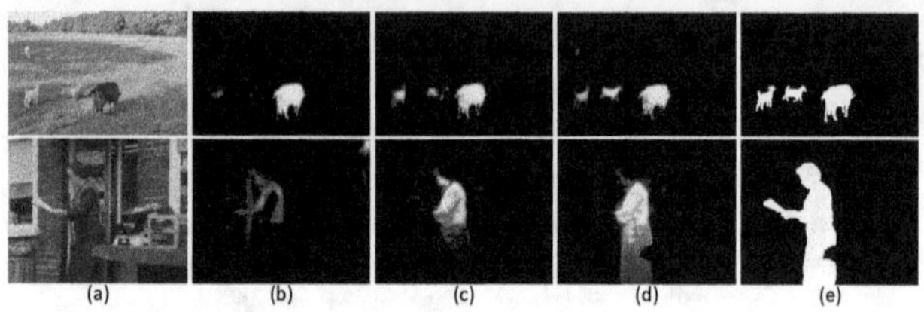

Figure 7: Saliency maps generated by networks with different architectures. (a) Input video frames. (b) Results of only spatial network (c) Results of spatiotemporal network. (d) Results of MSST-ConvLSTM. (e) Ground truths.

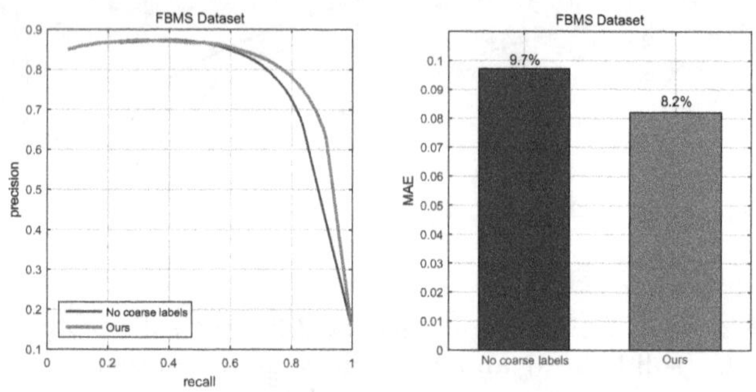

Figure 8: Comparison of PR curves and MAEs with and without coarse pixel-wise labels

As shown in Figure.6, the proposed MSST-ConvLSTM model achieves the best performance in both PR curve and MAE criteria. At the beginning, the network only uses the single frame as training samples, which leads to the failure detection of moving objects (e.g., Figure.7 (b)). With the employment of temporal sub-network, the moving objects are obviously highlighted (e.g., Figure.7 (c)). After the proposed MSST-ConvLSTM step, the saliency maps are closer to the ground truths (e.g., Figure.7 (d))

In order to validate the effectiveness of the generated coarse pixel-wise labels, we report the saliency performance of training the proposed network with and without coarse pixel-wise labels. As the Fig.8 shown, this experiment proves that the generated coarse pixel-wise labels have positive effect on saliency prediction. The training data increases from 2,772 frames to 6,098 frames. Besides, these training data contains many complex video scenes, which can make the network learn more robust salient features, thus improve the accuracy of the saliency detection.

5 CONCLUSION

In this paper, we propose a multi-scale spatiotemporal convolutional LSTM network (MSST-ConvLSTM) for video saliency detection. Our network consists of the complementary components, a spatial sub-network and a temporal sub-network. The network not only commendably retains the spatial features but also learns the temporal features. Moreover, the proposed MSST-ConvLSTM can further fuse the spatial and temporal cues to generate final spatiotemporal saliency maps. Meanwhile, to train the data-driven network, we produce an amount of coarse pixel-wise labels, which effectively improve robustness of the proposed network. Finally, the experimental results on the two datasets, FBMS and DAVIS, demonstrate that the proposed network can outperform the-state-of-the-arts in term of both PR curve and MAE criteria.

6 ACKNOWLEDGEMENT

This work is supported by the NSFC Project under Grant 61771321, Grant 61701313, Grant 6171101606 and Grant 61472257, in part by the Natural Science Foundation of Shenzhen under Grant KQJSCX20170327151357330, Grant JCYJ20170818091621856, Grant JCYJ20160307154003475, Grant JCYJ20160506172651253 and Grant JCYJ2017030214-5906843, in part by the Interdisciplinary Innovation Team of Shenzhen University, and in part by the Natural Science Foundation of SZU under Grant 827-000152.

REFERENCES

[1] Thomas Brox and Jitendra Malik. 2010. Object segmentation by long term analysis of point trajectories. In *Proceedings of the European Conference on Computer Vision*. Springer, 282–295.

[2] Chenglizhao Chen, Shuai Li, Yongguang Wang, Hong Qin, and Aimin Hao. 2017. Video Saliency Detection via Spatial-Temporal Fusion and Low-Rank Coherency Diffusion. *IEEE Transactions on Image Processing* 26, 7 (2017), 3156–3170.

[3] Liang-Chieh Chen, George Papandreou, Iasonas Kokkinos, Kevin Murphy, and Alan L Yuille. 2014. Semantic image segmentation with deep convolutional nets and fully connected crfs. *arXiv preprint:1412.7062* (2014).

[4] Ming-Ming Cheng, Niloy J Mitra, Xiaolei Huang, Philip HS Torr, and Shi-Min Hu. 2015. Global contrast based salient region detection. *IEEE Transactions on Pattern Analysis and Machine Intelligence* 37, 3 (2015), 569–582.

[5] Jia Deng, Wei Dong, Richard Socher, Li Jia Li, Kai Li, and Fei Fei Li. 2009. ImageNet: A large-scale hierarchical image database. In *Proceedings of the IEEE Conference on Computer Vision and Pattern Recognition*. 248–255.

[6] Ionut C. Duta, Bogdan Ionescu, Kiyoharu Aizawa, and Nicu Sebe. 2017. Simple, Efficient and Effective Encodings of Local Deep Features for Video Action Recognition. In *Proceedings of the 2017 ACM on International Conference on Multimedia Retrieval*. ACM, 218–225.

[7] Pedro F. Felzenszwalb and Daniel P. Huttenlocher. 2004. Efficient Graph-Based Image Segmentation. *International Journal of Computer Vision* 59, 2 (2004), 167–181.

[8] Huazhu Fu, Xiaochun Cao, and Zhuowen Tu. 2013. Cluster-based co-saliency detection. *IEEE Transactions on Image Processing* 22, 10 (2013), 3766–3778.

[9] Dashan Gao, Vijay Mahadevan, and Nuno Vasconcelos. 2008. The discriminant center-surround hypothesis for bottom-up saliency. In *Proceedings of the Advances in Neural Information Processing Systems*. 497–504.

[10] Qibin Hou, Ming-Ming Cheng, Xiaowei Hu, Zhuowen Tu, and A Borji. 2017. Deeply supervised salient object detection with short connections. In *Proceedings of the IEEE Conference on Computer Vision and Pattern Recognition*. IEEE.

[11] Huaizu Jiang, Jingdong Wang, Zejian Yuan, Yang Wu, Nanning Zheng, and Shipeng Li. 2013. Salient object detection: A discriminative regional feature integration approach. In *Proceedings of the IEEE Conference on Computer Vision and Pattern Recognition*. IEEE, 2083–2090.

[12] Hansang Kim, Youngbae Kim, Jae-Young Sim, and Chang-Su Kim. 2015. Spatiotemporal saliency detection for video sequences based on random walk with restart. *IEEE Transactions on Image Processing* 24, 8 (2015), 2552–2564.

[13] Diederik P Kingma and Jimmy Ba. 2014. Adam: A Method for Stochastic Optimization. *Computer Science* (2014).

[14] Fuxin Li, Taeyoung Kim, Ahmad Humayun, David Tsai, and James M Rehg. 2013. Video segmentation by tracking many figure-ground segments. In *Proceedings of the IEEE International Conference on Computer Vision*. IEEE, 2192–2199.

[15] Guanbin Li and Yizhou Yu. 2016. Deep contrast learning for salient object detection. In *Proceedings of the IEEE Conference on Computer Vision and Pattern Recognition*. IEEE, 478–487.

[16] Guanbin Li and Yizhou Yu. 2016. Visual saliency detection based on multiscale deep CNN features. *IEEE Transactions on Image Processing* 25, 11 (2016), 5012–5024.

[17] Xi Li, Liming Zhao, Lina Wei, Ming-Hsuan Yang, Fei Wu, Yueting Zhuang, Haibin Ling, and Jingdong Wang. 2016. DeepSaliency: Multi-Task deep neural network model for salient object detection. *IEEE Transactions on Image Processing* 25, 8 (2016), 3919–3930.

[18] Nian Liu and Junwei Han. 2016. Dhsnet: Deep hierarchical saliency network for salient object detection. In *Proceedings of the IEEE Conference on Computer Vision and Pattern Recognition*. 678–686.

[19] Wu Liu, Cheng Zhang, Huadong Ma, and Shuangqun Li. 2018. Learning Efficient Spatial-Temporal Gait Features with Deep Learning for Human Identification. *Neuroinformatics* (2018), 1–15.

[20] Jonathan Long, Evan Shelhamer, and Trevor Darrell. 2015. Fully convolutional networks for semantic segmentation. In *Proceedings of the IEEE Conference on Computer Vision and Pattern Recognition*. IEEE, 3431–3440.

[21] Anestis Papazoglou and Vittorio Ferrari. 2013. Fast object segmentation in unconstrained video. In *Proceedings of the IEEE International Conference on Computer Vision*. IEEE, 1777–1784.

[22] Yuxin Peng, Yunzhen Zhao, and Junchao Zhang. 2017. Two-stream Collaborative Learning with Spatial-Temporal Attention for Video Classification. *arXiv preprint arXiv:1711.03273* (2017).

[23] Federico Perazzi, Philipp Krähenbühl, Yael Pritch, and Alexander Hornung. 2012. Saliency filters: Contrast based filtering for salient region detection. In *Proceedings of the IEEE Conference on Computer Vision and Pattern Recognition*. IEEE, 733–740.

[24] Federico Perazzi, Jordi Pont-Tuset, Brian McWilliams, Luc Van Gool, Markus Gross, and Alexander Sorkine-Hornung. 2016. A benchmark dataset and evaluation methodology for video object segmentation. In *Proceedings of the IEEE Conference on Computer Vision and Pattern Recognition*. IEEE, 724–732.

[25] Esa Rahtu, Juho Kannala, Mikko Salo, and Janne Heikkilä. 2010. Segmenting salient objects from images and videos. In *Proceedings of the European Conference on Computer Vision*. Springer, 366–379.

[26] Hae Jong Seo and Peyman Milanfar. 2009. Static and space-time visual saliency detection by self-resemblance. *Journal of vision* 9, 12 (2009), 15–15.

[27] Lijun Wang, Huchuan Lu, Xiang Ruan, and Ming-Hsuan Yang. 2015. Deep networks for saliency detection via local estimation and global search. In *Proceedings of the IEEE Conference on Computer Vision and Pattern Recognition*. IEEE, 3183–3192.

[28] Linzhao Wang, Lijun Wang, Huchuan Lu, Pingping Zhang, and Xiang Ruan. 2016. Saliency detection with recurrent fully convolutional networks. In *Proceedings of the European Conference on Computer Vision*. Springer, 825–841.

[29] Wenguan Wang, Jianbing Shen, and Fatih Porikli. 2015. Saliency-aware geodesic video object segmentation. In *Proceedings of the IEEE Conference on Computer Vision and Pattern Recognition*. IEEE, 3395–3402.

[30] Wenguan Wang, Jianbing Shen, and Ling Shao. 2015. Consistent video saliency using local gradient flow optimization and global refinement. *IEEE Transactions on Image Processing* 24, 11 (2015), 4185–4196.

[31] Wenguan Wang, Jianbing Shen, and Ling Shao. 2018. Video salient object detection via fully convolutional networks. *IEEE Transactions on Image Processing* 27, 1 (2018), 38–49.

[32] Yichen Wei, Fang Wen, Wangjiang Zhu, and Jian Sun. 2012. Geodesic saliency using background priors. In *Proceedings of the European Conference on Computer Vision*. Springer, 29–42.

[33] Dayan Wu, Zheng Lin, Bo Li, Mingzhen Ye, and Weiping Wang. 2017. Deep Supervised Hashing for Multi-Label and Large-Scale Image Retrieval. In *Proceedings of the 2017 ACM on International Conference on Multimedia Retrieval*. ACM, 150–158.

[34] Yun Zhai and Mubarak Shah. 2006. Visual attention detection in video sequences using spatiotemporal cues. In *Proceedings of the ACM international conference on Multimedia*. ACM, 815–824.

[35] Rui Zhao, Wanli Ouyang, Hongsheng Li, and Xiaogang Wang. 2015. Saliency detection by multi-context deep learning. In *Proceedings of the IEEE Conference on Computer Vision and Pattern Recognition*. IEEE, 1265–1274.

[36] Yunzhen Zhao and Yuxin Peng. 2017. Saliency-guided video classification via adaptively weighted learning. In *Proceedings of the IEEE International Conference on Multimedia and Expo*. IEEE, 847–852.

[37] Feng Zhou, Sing Bing Kang, and Michael F Cohen. 2014. Time-mapping using space-time saliency. In *Proceedings of the IEEE Conference on Computer Vision and Pattern Recognition*. IEEE, 3358–3365.

[38] Wenbin Zou and Nikos Komodakis. 2015. HARF: Hierarchy-Associated Rich Features for Salient Object Detection. In *Proceedings of the IEEE International Conference on Computer Vision*. IEEE, 406–414.

[39] Wenbin Zou, Kidiyo Kpalma, Zhi Liu, and Joseph Ronsin. 2013. Segmentation driven low-rank matrix recovery for saliency detection. In *Proceedings of the British Machine Vision on Conference*. 1–13.

[40] Wenbin Zou, Zhi Liu, Kidiyo Kpalma, Joseph Ronsin, Yong. Zhao, and Nikos Komodakis. 2015. Unsupervised Joint Salient Region Detection and Object Segmentation. *IEEE Transactions on Image Processing* 24, 11 (2015), 3858–3873.

Supervised Nonparametric Multimodal Topic Modeling Methods for Multi-class Video Classification

Jianfei Xue
Graduate School of System Informatics
Kobe University, Japan
xjfxjf008@gmail.com

Koji Eguchi
Graduate School of System Informatics
Kobe University, Japan
eguchi@port.kobe-u.ac.jp

ABSTRACT

Nonparametric topic models such as hierarchical Dirichlet processes (HDP) have been attracting more and more attentions for multimedia data analysis. However, the existing models for multimedia data are unsupervised ones that purely cluster semantically or characteristically related features into a specific latent topic without considering side information such as class information. In this paper, we present a novel supervised sequential symmetric correspondence HDP (Sup-SSC-HDP) model for multi-class video classification, where the empirical topic frequencies learned from multimodal video data are modeled as a predictor of video class. Qualitative and quantitative assessments demonstrate the effectiveness of Sup-SSC-HDP.

KEYWORDS

Bayesian nonparametric models; multimedia content classification; hierarchical Dirichlet processes; topic models

ACM Reference Format:

Jianfei Xue and Koji Eguchi. 2018. Supervised Nonparametric Multimodal Topic Modeling Methods for Multi-class Video Classification. In *ICMR '18: 2018 International Conference on Multimedia Retrieval, June 11–14, 2018, Yokohama, Japan.* ACM, New York, NY, USA, 9 pages. https://doi.org/10.1145/3206025.3206036

1 INTRODUCTION

Nonparametric topic models, such as hierarchical Dirichlet processes (HDP) [13], provide an effective way to learn latent properties from data. For text mining, they assume that the words in each document are generated from a mixture of latent topics, where each latent topic is represented as a word distribution. HDP models a collection of documents with multiple infinite Dirichlet processes (DP), which are connected through sharing the same mixture of components. Compared with parametric topic models, such as latent Dirichlet allocation (LDA) [2], nonparametric HDP has a significant advantage in that it can automatically learn the necessary number of topics during training, which is manually predefined when learning with LDA. This makes HDP more flexible and efficient than other parametric topic models, especially for certain applications in data mining.

Many researchers have tried to extend HDP models to numerous specific and complex applications. One of the most popular applications is multimedia data analysis. Unlike text data, multimedia data have their own peculiarities, such as time dependency for sequential data and data multimodality, which need to be properly taken into consideration when modeling such data. Ren et al. [11], Kuettel et al. [6] and Xue et al. [14] presented three different solutions to handle the time dependency issue on multimedia data by linking local measures within the HDP conditioned on the Markovian assumption. On the other hand, inspired by previous studies [1, 5] on multimodal data modeling issue with LDA, a sequential correspondence HDP (Seq-cHDP) [14] model and a sequential symmetric correspondence HDP (Seq-Sym-cHDP) [15] model have been proposed for video data analysis, whose incorporated correspondence mechanism can simultaneously handle both visual words and speech words drawn from videos, and make them share the same mixture of latent topics in a unified model.

However, all the above models are unsupervised ones, which cluster semantically or characteristically related features into a specific latent topic, such a topic is hard to interpret or map to a real class. In this paper, we thus seek a supervised learning method for multi-class video classification. Regarding the previous studies, Blei et al. [10] firstly proposed a supervised topic model (sLDA) to regard document-level numerical rating as a regression response. Lacoste-Julien et al. [7] presented a discriminative LDA (DiscLDA) that introduced a class-dependent linear transformation on the topic mixture proportions. Zhu et al. [16] developed a maximum entropy discrimination LDA (MedLDA) that can make more effective use of side information by leveraging the maximum margin principle during topic learning. Recently, Dai et al. [3] attempted to develop such a supervised method in an HDP-based model, named supervised HDP (sHDP), it can learn topics that are predictive of document responses without having to preset a fixed number of topics. However, all these supervised topic models focused on static unimodal data (such as text data) modeling. Furthermore, there is still no proper HDP-based supervised model for multi-class classification.

In this paper, we propose a novel supervised topic model called supervised sequential symmetric correspondence

ICMR '18, June 11–14, 2018, Yokohama, Japan

ACM ISBN 978-1-4503-5046-4/18/06...$15.00
https://doi.org/10.1145/3206025.3206036

HDP (Sup-SSC-HDP) for multi-class video classification, which can directly capture discrete video classes as classification response. Sup-SSC-HDP is a video data oriented topic model that incorporates a time-dependency mechanism [14] (for modeling the relationship among video frames) and a symmetric correspondence mechanism [5, 15] (for modeling multimodal data from videos) to offer a suitable learning for videos. A generalized linear model (GLM) is used to model the relationship between empirical topic frequencies over multimodal data and video class, and a softmax regression algorithm is used to learn their regression coefficients. We infer the Sup-SSC-HDP via a posterior representation sampler, and implement it by developing a cascaded Gibbs sampling method. We conduct multi-class video classification experiments on Sup-SSC-HDP and baseline models to assess the effectiveness of our model.

2 PRELIMINARY WORK

A three-layer sequential HDP (Seq-HDP) [14] model was proposed for handling the time dependencies between neighboring video frames within a video. Here, we give a brief review to show the structure of Seq-HDP and how Seq-HDP generates data samples in an unsupervised manner.

In this three-layer Seq-HDP model, we define three different probability measures G, G_0^f and G_j^f to construct generative processes corresponding to different layers in Seq-HDP. G located on the top layer of Seq-HDP stands for an overall measure among all videos. Next, G_0^f represents the global measure reflecting the f-th video on the second layer of Seq-HDP. On the third layer, G_j^f indicates the local measure corresponding to the j-th frame in the f-th video. Since video frames in the same video are sequential and time dependent, a Markovian transfer link with a transfer weight w_j^f is thus established between two adjacent local measures G_{j-1}^f and G_j^f in Seq-HDP. The detailed generative process of Seq-HDP is described as follows.

- **Step 1:** The overall measure G is drawn from a Dirichlet process as $G \sim DP(\xi, H)$, where H is a base measure, and ξ is a concentration parameter for generating G.
- **Step 2:** Similarly, the global measure G_0^f for each video is drawn from $G_0^f \sim DP(\gamma^f, G)$, where γ^f is a concentration parameter for generating G_0^f.
- **Step 3:** The generative process for each local measure G_j^f is affected by both the global measure G_0^f and previous local measure G_{j-1}^f because of the time-dependency mechanism. Hence, G_j^f is drawn from $G_j^f \sim DP(\alpha_0^f, w_{j-1}^f G_{j-1}^f + (1 - w_{j-1}^f)G_0^f)$, where α_0^f is a concentration parameter, and w_{j-1}^f is the transfer weight mentioned above.
- **Step 4:** Each data sample x_{fji} in the j-th frame of the f-th video is drawn from $x_{fji} \sim F(x|\theta_{fji})$, where $F(\cdot|\theta_{fji})$ indicates a conditional probability distribution conditioned on a component density θ_{fji}, i is the index of the data sample, and θ_{fji} is directly drawn from the local measure G_j^f.

To make the model more understandable and applicable, it is reformulated with a stick-breaking construction (SBC) method as shown in Fig. 1, where measures extracted from a DP can be expressed by using independent sequences of *i.i.d.* random variables. We respectively use component weight variables $\boldsymbol{\nu}$, $\boldsymbol{\beta^f}$, and $\boldsymbol{\pi_j^f}$ to construct corresponding measures in the different layers of Seq-HDP, the process is described as:

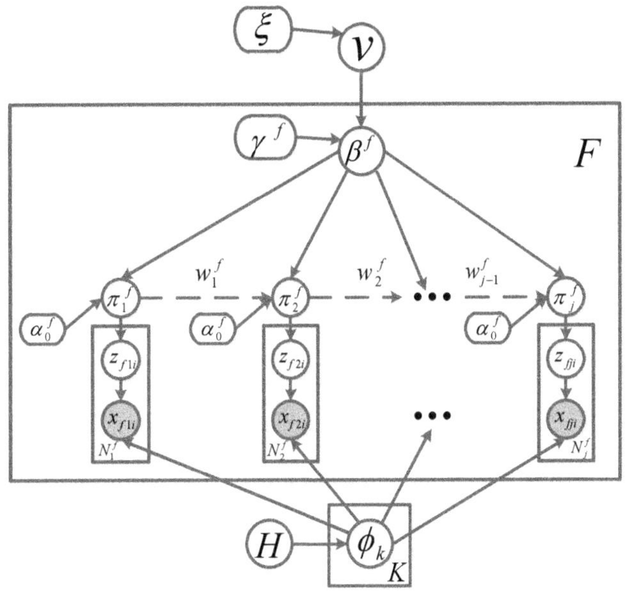

Figure 1: Graphical model representation for SBC of Seq-HDP.

$$G = \sum_{k=1}^{\infty} \nu_k \delta_{\phi_k},\ G_0^f = \sum_{k=1}^{\infty} \beta_k^f \delta_{\phi_k},\ G_j^f = \sum_{k=1}^{\infty} \pi_{jk}^f \delta_{\phi_k} \quad (1)$$

where each component weight vector comprises an infinite number of corresponding component weights, *i.e.*, $\boldsymbol{\nu} = \{\nu_1, \nu_2, ..., \nu_k, ...\}$, $\boldsymbol{\beta^f} = \{\beta_1^f, \beta_2^f, ..., \beta_k^f, ...\}$, and $\boldsymbol{\pi_j^f} = \{\pi_{j1}^f, \pi_{j2}^f, ..., \pi_{jk}^f, ...\}$. δ_{ϕ_k} is a probability measure concentrated at component ϕ_k.

Following the hierarchical structure in Seq-HDP, we can successively draw these component weight variables with:

$$\boldsymbol{\nu} \sim GEM(\xi),\ \boldsymbol{\beta^f} \sim DP(\gamma^f, \boldsymbol{\nu}),\ \boldsymbol{\pi_j^f} \sim DP(\alpha_0^f, \boldsymbol{\pi'}_j^f) \quad (2)$$

where GEM represents a GEM process, which is formed by such a process: $\hat{\nu}_k \sim Beta(1, \xi)$, $\nu_k = \hat{\nu}_k \Pi_{i=1}^{k-1}(1 - \hat{\nu}_i)$. Note that the generation of $\boldsymbol{\pi_j^f}$ is influenced by both $\boldsymbol{\beta^f}$ and $\boldsymbol{\pi_{j-1}^f}$ because of the time dependency. Hence, $\boldsymbol{\pi'}_j^f$ is expressed as $\boldsymbol{\pi'}_j^f = w_{j-1}^f \boldsymbol{\pi_{j-1}^f} + (1 - w_{j-1}^f)\boldsymbol{\beta^f}$.

Then, for each data sample, we directly draw z_{fji} from π_{jk}^f. The data sample x_{fji} is generated conditioned on the sampled z_{fji} and ϕ_k. In the case of a real application, z_{fji} can be considered to be a sampled latent topic, and x_{fji} is a generated word.

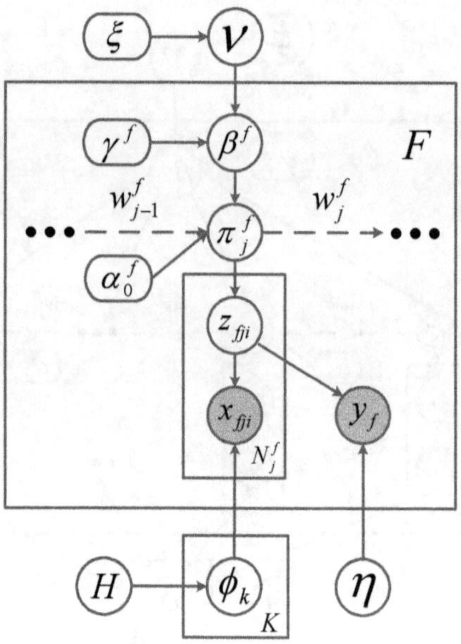

Figure 2: Graphical model representation of supervised Seq-HDP.

3 SUPERVISED METHODS

3.1 Supervised Sequential HDP

Although latent topics learned with unsupervised topic models are adequately expressive, they are not appropriate for a classification task, since the observed class information for each document is not exploited during training. Supervised topic models can overcome such problems by jointly learning topics and their regression coefficients for the document responses. In this section, we present a novel supervised method for Seq-HDP based on the SBC structure.

To model the relationship between covariates and response, a generalized linear model (GLM) is widely used, which is still available even if the covariates and the response are non-linearly related or the response is not based on a Gaussian assumption. For the supervised Seq-HDP model, we thus use GLM to model the relationship between the empirical frequencies of the topics in the f-th video $\bar{\mathbf{z}}_f$ and the video response y_f, where we define a linear predictor $\varpi = \boldsymbol{\eta}^\top \bar{\mathbf{z}}_f$, $\boldsymbol{\eta}$ denotes regression coefficients corresponding to the empirical frequencies of the topics $\bar{\mathbf{z}}_f$, and we consider that the video response y_f obeys an exponential family distribution. Then, a canonical link function $g^{-1}(\cdot)$ is used to relate ϖ to the mean $E[y_f|\cdot]$ of y_f, which is expressed as $E[y_f|\cdot] = g^{-1}(\varpi)$.

A simplified graphical model representation of the SBC of supervised Seq-HDP is depicted in Fig. 2. Its generative process is as follows.

- **Step 1:** Successively draw component weight variables $\boldsymbol{\nu}$, $\boldsymbol{\beta}^f$, and $\boldsymbol{\pi}_j^f$ based on Eq. (2).
- **Step 2:** For each word, draw its topic z_{fji} from $\boldsymbol{\pi}_j^f$, then sample the word x_{fji} conditioned on both z_{fji} and ϕ_k.
- **Step 3:** For each video, draw the video response with $y_f \sim ExpFam(g^{-1}(\boldsymbol{\eta}^\top \bar{\mathbf{z}}_f), \varrho)$, where $ExpFam$ is a distribution from the exponential family, and ϱ is the dispersion parameter of the distribution.

For GLM, the distribution of response can have different specific forms due to the different applications, such as Gaussian, Bernoulli or multinomial. Here, we focus on multi-class video classification and thus model y_f as being distributed according to a multinomial distribution (the number of trials $n = 1$), and $y_f \in \{1, 2, ..., R\}$, where R is the total number of classes. Because of GLM, we express this distribution with an exponential family representation:

$$P(y_f = c|\boldsymbol{\eta}, \bar{\mathbf{z}}_f) = \frac{exp(\boldsymbol{\eta}^{c\top} \bar{\mathbf{z}}_f)}{\sum_{r=1}^{R} exp(\boldsymbol{\eta}^{r\top} \bar{\mathbf{z}}_f)} \tag{3}$$

where $\boldsymbol{\eta}$ is an $R \times K(\infty)$ regression coefficient matrix, and $\boldsymbol{\eta}^c$ is a coefficient vector extracted from the c-th row of $\boldsymbol{\eta}$. Note that this multi-class supervised learning process is also known as softmax regression.

3.2 Multimodality Modeling on Supervised Seq-HDP

Different from unimodal data such as text data, video data have more complex data components, which are generally enriched with image and speech information, *i.e.*, video can be deemed as a type of multimodal data. To handle such data, Xue et al. [14] proposed a sequential correspondence HDP (Seq-cHDP) model, whose correspondence mechanism models the multimodal data by establishing a unidirectional dependency among them. However, the major drawback of Seq-cHDP is that the pivot data type (modality) needs to be manually predefined. To make the correspondence mechanism more flexible, Xue et al. [15] later proposed a sequential symmetric correspondence HDP (Seq-Sym-cHDP, where the pivot data type among multimodal data is spontaneously selected by using a pivot flag generator when generating each topic. We incorporate this symmetric correspondence mechanism into the supervised Seq-HDP framework, and then devise a novel supervised sequential symmetric correspondence HDP (Sup-SSC-HDP) model for multi-class video classification. Note that data in each modality of videos need to be converted into independent characteristic words according to the generative process of Sup-SSC-HDP, which will be specified in Section 5.1.

A simplified graphical model representation of Sup-SSC-HDP is shown in Fig. 3, where we use l to represent the index of the data type (modality), and $l \in \{1, ..., L\}$, and $N_{fj}^{(l)}$ is the total count for the words of data type l in frame j of video f, and all the $\{\phi_k^{(l)}\}_{l=1}^{L}$ drawn from H share the same $K(\infty)$ topics. The detailed generative process of Sup-SSC-HDP is as follows.

- **Step 1:** Successively draw component weight variables $\boldsymbol{\nu}$, $\boldsymbol{\beta}^f$, and $\boldsymbol{\pi}_j^f$ based on Eq. (2).
- **Step 2:** Draw a multinomial pivot flag generator $\boldsymbol{\sigma}_{fj}$ from $Dir(\lambda)$.

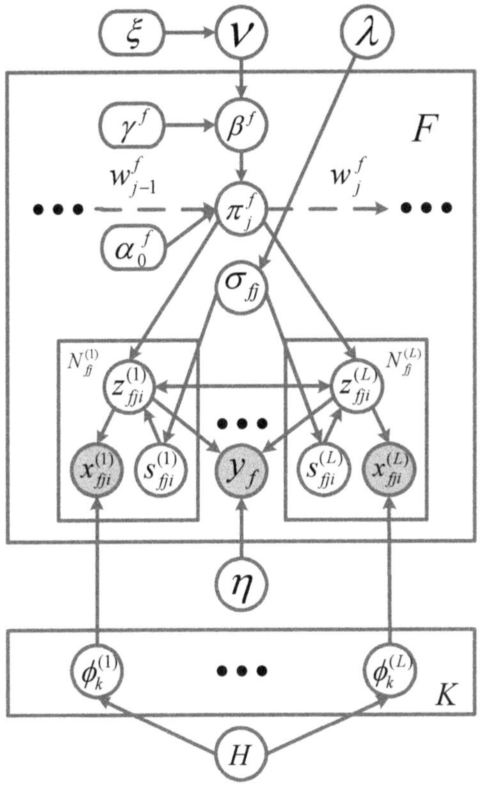

Figure 3: Graphical model representation of Sup-SSC-HDP.

- **Step 3-a:** For each word of data type l in frame j of video f, draw a pivot flag $s_{fji}^{(l)}$ from $\boldsymbol{\sigma_{fj}}$.
- **Step 3-b:** If $s_{fji}^{(l)} = l$, draw a topic $z_{fji}^{(l)}$ from $\boldsymbol{\pi_j^f}$. Otherwise if $s_{fji}^{(l)} = h \neq l$, draw a topic $z_{fji}^{(l)}$ from $Uniform(z_{fj1}^{(h)}, ..., z_{fjH_{fj}^{(h)}}^{(h)})$.
- **Step 3-c:** Conditioned on sampled $z_{fji}^{(l)}$, draw a word $x_{fji}^{(l)}$ from $f(x_{fji}^{(l)} | \phi_k^{(l)}, k = z_{fji}^{(l)})$.
- **Step 4:** For each video, draw a video class y_f from a distribution $P(y_f | \boldsymbol{\eta}, \bar{\mathbf{z}}_f)$.

Here, $Dir(\lambda)$ indicates a Dirichlet distribution with a hyperparameter λ. $f(x_{fji}^{(l)} | \phi_k^{(l)})$ denotes a word distribution conditioned on $\phi_k^{(l)}$. $\boldsymbol{\eta}$ is the regression coefficient, and $\bar{\mathbf{z}}_f$) is the empirical frequencies of the topics within video f.

In this method, the way of generating the topic is chosen using a sampled pivot flag, which determines the current pivot data type. To be specific, for the word $x_{fji}^{(l)}$ with data type l, if its sampled pivot flag points to the same data type (*i.e.*, $s_{fji}^{(l)} = l$), its topic assignment will be independent from other topic assignments and only associated with $\boldsymbol{\pi_j^f}$. However, if its sampled pivot flag points to the other data type h (*i.e.*, $s_{fji}^{(l)} = h \neq l$), its topic will be drawn from a uniform distribution, which is parameterized with all the topics assigned to $H_{fj}^{(h)}$ words with data type h. Different from $N_{fj}^{(h)}$, $H_{fj}^{(h)}$ represents the number of words that have already been assigned topics in the current step, which means $H_{fj}^{(h)} \leq N_{fj}^{(h)}$. Through this method, the generative processes for different multimodal data can be modeled in a symmetric way, and the dependencies among all the multimodal data can be appropriately taken into account.

4 INFERENCE AND CLASS PREDICTION

4.1 Posterior Representation

Based on posterior representation sampler [12], we provide a inference scheme for inferring the Sup-SSC-HDP.

a) Sampling Component Weight Variables

Because of the posterior representation sampler [12], every original infinite component weight vector is reformulated with a new augmentable finite vector that consists of K components and a promising component u. Below, we give the new representation of $\boldsymbol{\nu}$ and its sampling procedure:

$$\boldsymbol{\nu} = (\nu_1, ..., \nu_K, \nu_u) \sim Dir(M_1^{\cdot}, ..., M_K^{\cdot}, \xi) \tag{4}$$

where a new variable M_k^f used for sampling $\boldsymbol{\nu}$ denotes the metatable counts in the Chinese restaurant franchise (CRF) [13] process of three-layer HDP, which is explained in [14]. $M_k^{\cdot}$ is the marginal form of M_k^f (*i.e.*, $M_k^{\cdot} = \sum_f M_k^f$).

Similarly, $\boldsymbol{\beta^f}$ can be represented and sampled using:

$$\boldsymbol{\beta^f} = (\beta_1^f, ..., \beta_K^f, \beta_u^f) \sim Dir(\tilde{\beta}_1^f, ..., \tilde{\beta}_K^f, \tilde{\beta}_u^f) \tag{5}$$

where $\tilde{\beta}_k^f = \gamma^f \nu_k + T_{fk}^{0\rightarrow\cdot}$ and $\tilde{\beta}_u^f = \gamma^f \nu_u$. The variable $T_{fk}^{0\rightarrow j}$ denotes the table counts of CRF yielded by β_k^f in the video frame j, and $T_{fk}^{0\rightarrow\cdot}$ is the marginal form of $T_{fk}^{0\rightarrow j}$ (*i.e.*, $T_{fk}^{0\rightarrow\cdot} = \sum_j T_{fk}^{0\rightarrow j}$).

For the local component weight, $\boldsymbol{\pi_j^f}$ can be represented and sampled as:

$$\boldsymbol{\pi_j^f} = (\pi_{j1}^f, ..., \pi_{jK}^f, \pi_{ju}^f) \sim Dir(\tilde{\pi}_{j1}^f, ..., \tilde{\pi}_{jK}^f, \tilde{\pi}_{ju}^f) \tag{6}$$

where two estimators $\tilde{\pi}_{jk}^f$ and $\tilde{\pi}_{ju}^f$ can be linearly formulated with both β_k^f (or β_u^f) and $\pi_{(j-1)k}^f$ (or $\pi_{(j-1)u}^f$) because of the time-dependency mechanism, as follows:

$$\begin{aligned} \tilde{\pi}_{jk}^f &= \alpha_0^f w_{j-1}^f \pi_{(j-1)k}^f + \alpha_0^f (1 - w_{j-1}^f) \beta_k^f + C_{fjlk}^{(\cdot)} + T_{fk}^{j\rightarrow j+1} \\ \tilde{\pi}_{ju}^f &= \alpha_0^f w_{j-1}^f \pi_{(j-1)u}^f + \alpha_0^f (1 - w_{j-1}^f) \beta_u^f \end{aligned} \tag{7}$$

where $C_{fjlk}^{(l)}$ denotes the counts for the word with data type l in frame j of video f possessing the pivot flag with the same data type l when the sampled topic is k, and $C_{fjlk}^{(\cdot)} = \sum_{(l)} C_{fjlk}^{(l)}$. $T_{fk}^{j\rightarrow j+1}$ denotes another table counts of CRF that occurs because of the time-dependency mechanism (from π_{jk}^f to $\pi_{(j+1)k}^f$).

b) Sampling Table Counts of CRF

Because of the CRF of a three-layer HDP [14], the metatable counts M_k^f can quantitatively reflect the generative process from ν_k to β_k^f. T_{jk}^f indicates the total table counts comprised of $T_{fk}^{j-1\rightarrow j}$ and $T_{fk}^{0\rightarrow j}$ (*i.e.*, $T_{jk}^f = T_{fk}^{j-1\rightarrow j} + T_{fk}^{0\rightarrow j}$), where $T_{fk}^{j-1\rightarrow j}$ quantitatively reflects the generative process from $\pi_{(j-1)k}^f$ to π_{jk}^f, and $T_{fk}^{0\rightarrow j}$ quantitatively reflects the generative process from β_k^f to π_{jk}^f. In this paper, we utilize a Bernoulli trial method to sample these counts, and its probability of getting a value of 1 is defined as $P(n|a,b) = \frac{ab}{ab+n-1}$. Then, T_{jk}^f can be sampled with:

$$T_{jk}^f = \sum_{n=1}^{C_{fjlk}^{(\cdot)}} m_n, \quad m_n \sim Bern(P(n|a,b)) \tag{8}$$

where $Bern(\cdot)$ denotes a Bernoulli distribution, $a = \alpha_0^f$, and $b = w_{j-1}^f \pi_{(j-1)k}^f + (1 - w_{j-1}^f)\beta_k^f$.

Then, $T_{fk}^{j-1\to j}$ and $T_{fk}^{0\to j}$ can be sampled based on a binomial distribution with T_{jk}^f.

$$(T_{fk}^{j-1\to j}, T_{fk}^{0\to j}) \sim Binomial(T_{jk}^f, [P_T, 1 - P_T])$$
$$P_T = \frac{w_{j-1}^f \pi_{(j-1)k}^f}{(1 - w_{j-1}^f)\beta_k^f + w_{j-1}^f \pi_{(j-1)k}^f} \tag{9}$$

Similarly, M_k^f can be sampled with:

$$M_k^f = \sum_{n=1}^{T_{\cdot k}^f} m_n, \quad m_n \sim Bern(P(n|a,b)) \tag{10}$$

where we can obtain $T_{\cdot k}^f$ via $T_{\cdot k}^f = \sum_j T_{jk}^f$, $a = \gamma^f$, and $b = v_k$.

c) Sampling Topics and Pivot Flags for Words

In Sup-SSC-HDP, a full conditional joint likelihood is derived for sampling both the topic $z_{fji}^{(l)}$ and pivot flag $s_{fji}^{(l)}$ for each word.

$$P(z_{fji}^{(l)} = k, s_{fji}^{(l)} = m | x_{fji}^{(l)}, \lambda, \boldsymbol{\eta}, ...) \propto$$
$$P(s_{fji}^{(l)} = m|\lambda) P(z_{fji}^{(l)} = k|\cdot) P(x_{fji}^{(l)}|\phi_k^{(l)}) P(y_{fj}|z_{fji}^{(l)} = k, \boldsymbol{\eta}) \tag{11}$$

We describe these expanded likelihoods in the following. $P(s_{fji}^{(l)} = m|\lambda)$ denotes the pivot flag likelihood, which is formulated as:

$$P(s_{fji}^{(l)} = m|\lambda) = \frac{C_{fjm}^{-fjli} + \lambda}{C_{fjm}^{-fjli} + \sum_{m' \neq m} C_{fjm'} + L\lambda} \tag{12}$$

where C_{fjm} denotes the counts for the pivot flag pointing to data type m over all the multimodal data in frame j of video f, and the superscript $-fjli$ for a variable denotes the terms excluding the $fjl i$th term.

$P(z_{fji}^{(l)} = k|\cdot)$ denotes the conditional likelihood for topic k, if $s_{fji}^{(l)} = l$, $P(z_{fji}^{(l)} = k|\boldsymbol{\pi}_j^f)$ is equal to π_{jk}^f (or π_{ju}^f when k is newborn), if $s_{fji}^{(l)} = h \neq l$, there is $P(z_{fji}^{(l)} = k|\boldsymbol{Z}_{fj}^{(h)}) = \frac{n_{fjk}^{(h)}}{N_{fj}^{(h)}}$ where $\boldsymbol{Z}_{fj}^{(h)}$ is a vector that records all the topic assignments for the words of data type h in frame j of video f, and $n_{fjk}^{(h)}$ is the count for the assigned topic k in the same domain.

$P(x_{fji}^{(l)}|\phi_k^{(l)})$ denotes the conditional word likelihood, if the topic k is previously used, there is:

$$P(x_{fji}^{(l)}|\phi_k^{(l)}) = \frac{n_{kv^{(l)}}^{-fjli} + \tau}{\sum_{v'^{(l)}} n_{kv'^{(l)}}^{-fjli} + V^{(l)}\tau} \tag{13}$$

if k is a newborn topic, the likelihood is $1/V^{(l)}$, where $v^{(l)}$ is the index of words in terms of the vocabulary in data type l, $n_{kv^{(l)}}$ is the counts for the word $v^{(l)}$ assigned to topic k, $V^{(l)}$ is the vocabulary size of data type l, τ is a hyperparameter for a Dirichlet distribution, and $H = Dir(\tau)$.

$P(y_{fj}|z_{fji}^{(l)} = k, \boldsymbol{\eta})$ denotes the conditional class likelihood, which is formulated by:

$$P(y_{fj} = c | z_{fji}^{(l)} = k, \boldsymbol{\eta}) = \frac{exp(\sum_{k'} \eta_{k'}^c \bar{z}_{fjk'}^{-fjli} + \frac{\eta_k^c}{\sum_l N_{fj}^{(l)}})}{\sum_{r=1}^{R} exp(\sum_{k'} \eta_{k'}^r \bar{z}_{fjk'}^{-fjli} + \frac{\eta_k^r}{\sum_l N_{fj}^{(l)}})} \tag{14}$$

where we assume $y_{fj} = y_f$ during training, If k is newborn, we reformulate each $\boldsymbol{\eta}^r$ with $\boldsymbol{\eta}^r = (\boldsymbol{\eta}^r, \eta_{knew}^r)$, where η_{knew}^r is drawn from a Gaussian prior.

d) Sampling Other Parameters

We sample the hyperparameters ξ, γ^f and α_0^f corresponding to ν, β^f and π_j^f from a gamma prior. The hyperparameter λ is another controlling parameter that will be discussed in the experimental section, and the hyperparameter τ is a constant parameter in this paper. During training, the regression coefficients $\boldsymbol{\eta}$ can be updated with a gradient descent algorithm, which will be described in Section 4.3.

Algorithm 1: Inference Scheme with CGS

```
Parameter Initialization
for f = 1 to F do
  for j = J^f to 1 do
    for l = 1 to L do
      Sample pivot flags S_fj^(l) and topics Z_fj^(l)
    end for
    for k = 1 to K do
      Sample table counts T_jk^f, T_fk^(j-1→j) and T_fk^(0→j)
    end for
  end for
  for k = 1 to K do
    Sample metatable counts M_k^f
  end for
end for
Update regression coefficients η
Sample hyperparameters ξ, γ^f and α_0^f
Sample overall component weights ν
for f = 1 to F do
  Sample global component weights β^f
  for j = 1 to J^f do
    Sample local component weights π_j^f
  end for
end for
```

4.2 Cascaded Gibbs Sampling

Here, we derive a cascaded Gibbs sampling (CGS) method for implementing the inference scheme of Sup-SSC-HDP based on the posterior representation sampler, which is summarized as Algorithm 1.

In the initialization phase, words are randomly allocated to pivot flags and topics, and the regression coefficients $\boldsymbol{\eta}$ are drawn from a Gaussian prior. During the Gibbs sampling

Table 1: Summary of Experimental Dataset.

the number of videos[1]	1726
the number of classes	26
the number of key frames	40588
the vocabulary size of visual words	1000
the vocabulary size of speech words	17596

[1] Only *test_data* dataset of MEGTT is used in this experiments.

phase, the total number of topics K increases if the promising component is triggered to sample a newborn topic when sampling $z_{fji}^{(l)}$. All the component weight parameters are thus required to augment their components with this newborn topic in the sampler [13]. In the testing phase, the posterior of $\overline{\mathbf{z}}_f$ is necessary over the test videos for class prediction. Hence, we remove the $P(y_{fj}|\cdot)$ term from the full conditional joint likelihood for sampling $z_{fji}^{(l)}$ and $s_{fji}^{(l)}$ in the testing period, which makes that the inference on the test videos is identical to unsupervised learning.

4.3 Softmax Regression and Class Prediction

During the training period, the regression coefficients $\boldsymbol{\eta}$ need to be updated for each iteration (or a number of iterations) of CGS. As we mentioned in Section 3.1, this can be considered a softmax regression problem because of the multi-class video classification task.

Based on the learned $\overline{\mathbf{z}}_f$ and observed y_f for each video, the cost function is expressed as:

$$J(\boldsymbol{\eta})=-\frac{1}{F}\left[\sum_{f=1}^{F}\sum_{r=1}^{R}1\{y_f=r\}logP(y_f=r|\boldsymbol{\eta},\overline{\mathbf{z}}_f)\right]+\frac{\varepsilon}{2}\sum_{r=1}^{R}\boldsymbol{\eta}^{r\top}\boldsymbol{\eta}^r \tag{15}$$

where F is the total number of videos, $1\{\cdot\}$ is an indicator function that takes on a value of 1 if its argument is true. $P(y_f = r|\boldsymbol{\eta}, \overline{\mathbf{z}}_f)$ is the class probability defined in Eq. (3). Note that we add a weight decay term $\frac{\varepsilon}{2}\sum_{r=1}^{R}\boldsymbol{\eta}^{r\top}\boldsymbol{\eta}^r$ in this cost function to make $J(\boldsymbol{\eta})$ strictly convex, and $\varepsilon > 0$. To minimize the $J(\boldsymbol{\eta})$, we use a gradient descent algorithm and then find the optimized $\boldsymbol{\eta}$. The gradient for each $\boldsymbol{\eta}^r$ is expressed as follows.

$$\nabla_{\boldsymbol{\eta}^r}J(\boldsymbol{\eta})=-\frac{1}{F}\sum_{f=1}^{F}\left[\overline{\mathbf{z}}_f(1\{y_f=r\}-P(y_f=r|\boldsymbol{\eta},\overline{\mathbf{z}}_f))\right]+\varepsilon\boldsymbol{\eta}^r \tag{16}$$

During testing, the empirical frequencies of topics $\overline{\mathbf{z}}_f$ for each video are computed over a number of iterations. We average these $\overline{\mathbf{z}}_f$, and obtain $E[\overline{\mathbf{z}}_f]$. Based on the $E[\overline{\mathbf{z}}_f]$ and the $\boldsymbol{\eta}$ learned from training, we predict a class $\widetilde{c}_f$ for each test video as follows.

$$\widetilde{c}_f = \underset{c\in(1,\ldots,R)}{\arg\max} \quad \frac{exp(\boldsymbol{\eta}^{c\top}E[\overline{\mathbf{z}}_f])}{\sum_{r=1}^{R}exp(\boldsymbol{\eta}^{r\top}E[\overline{\mathbf{z}}_f])} \tag{17}$$

5 EXPERIMENTATIONS

5.1 Experimental Setup

We conducted the experiments on the video dataset provided by *MediaEval-2011 Genre Tagging Task* [8] (MEGTT), where two types of data were drawn from videos. For each video, a sequence of key frames were extracted as image data, meanwhile a number of speech transcript words considered to be speech data were allocated to each key frame via an automatic speech recognition (ASR) [8]. Because of the topic models, these image data and speech data need to be processed to independent visual words and speech words, respectively. For each key frame image within each video, we first computed its SIFT descriptor [4] for every 10×10 pixel grid conditioning in which the patch size is randomly sampled between scales of 10 to 30 pixels. Then, we clustered all the extracted SIFT descriptors over all the videos into V types of visual words (*i.e.*, visual words with vocabulary size V) via a k-means method. For the speech transcript, we removed standard stop words and rare words (which appeared in less than five videos) and consider the rest of the general words to be speech words. The details of the experimental dataset is summarized in Table 1.

To evaluate the performance of Sup-SSC-HDP, four different multimodal topic models, *i.e.*, Seq-Sym-cHDP, sequential conditionally independent HDP (Seq-CI-HDP), Seq-cHDP and symmetric correspondence HDP (Sym-cHDP) were chosen as baseline models (they are briefly described in Section 5.3). For the initializations on these topic models, the hyperparameters ξ, γ^f, and α_0^f were sampled from a gamma prior $Gamma(1.0, 1.0)$. Referring to the previous work [14], we set all the transfer weights w_j^f to a constant, 0.5. In addition, τ was set to 1.0. The controlling parameter λ was tuned with different values, which is described in Section 5.3. The CGS system totally ran 1000 iterations for each training or testing task so as to let all the variables in the model fully converge.

5.2 Qualitative Evaluation

To demonstrate intuitively how Sup-SSC-HDP performed in the experiments, we utilized the t-SNE stochastic neighborhood embedding [9] method to depict the 2D embedding of the learned topic frequencies $\overline{\mathbf{z}}_f$ by Sup-SSC-HDP and unsupervised Seq-Sym-cHDP, respectively, as shown in Fig. 4. In this figure, clustering phenomenon with respect to dots of the same color occurred in both 2D embedding graphs, which demonstrate that some of the videos within the same class were successfully grouped after learning via Sup-SSC-HDP and Seq-Sym-cHDP. Furthermore, Sup-SSC-HDP performed better than Seq-Sym-cHDP in clustering and separating the videos into different classes, which means that the supervised modeling method learns better how to map topics to different classes. However, we also noticed that there a number of videos were not well grouped or were grouped into incorrect clusters. The causes of these failures are explained in the following.

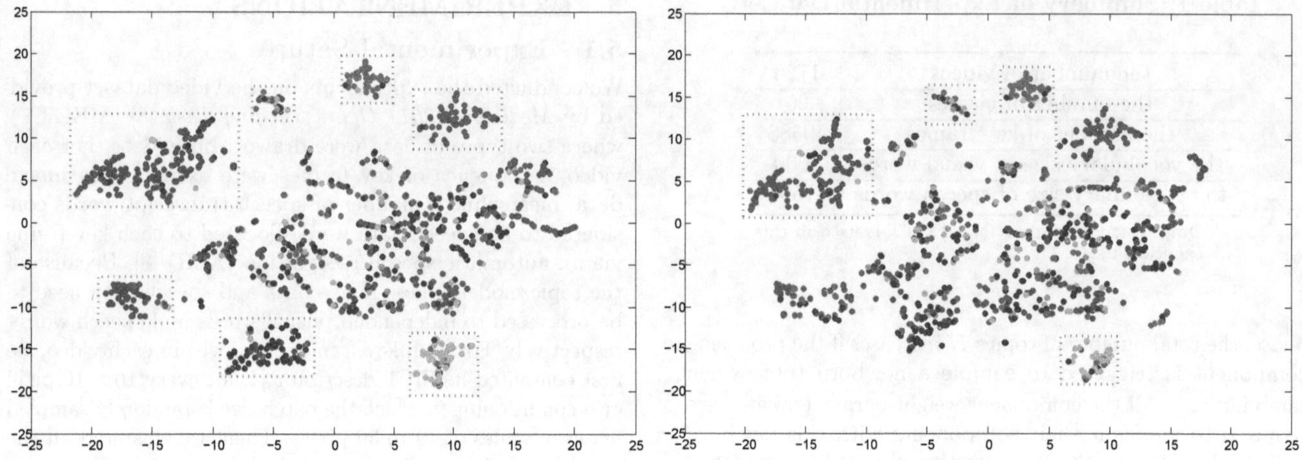

(a) Sup-SSC-HDP (b) Seq-Sym-cHDP

Figure 4: t-SNE 2D embedding of topic frequencies. Each dot stands for a video, and each type of color superimposed on the dot stands for a specific class for videos. Each box plotted with a red dotted line stands for a visually observed cluster.

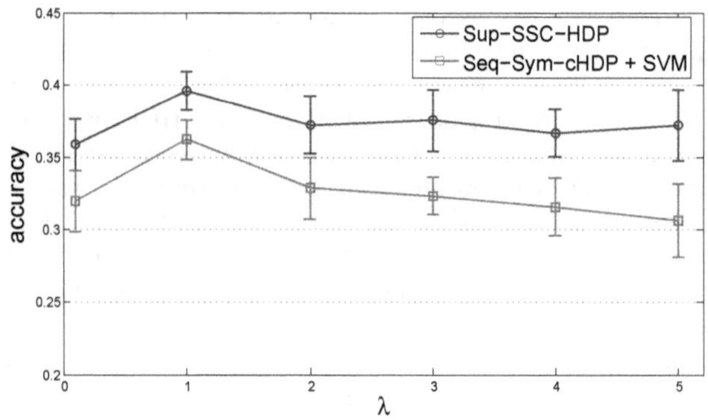

Figure 5: Performance of video classification with different λ.

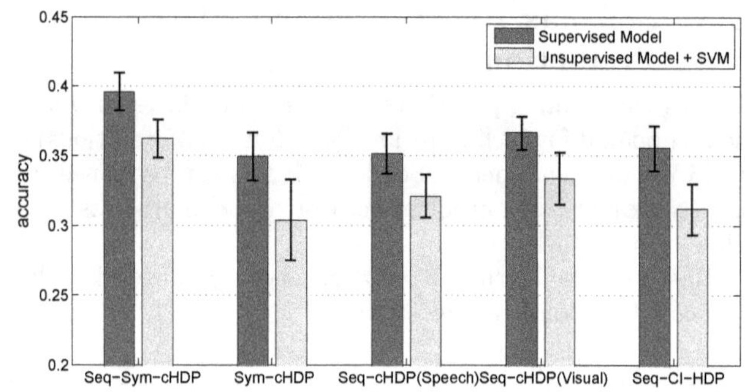

Figure 6: Video classification performance of Sup-SSC-HDP and baseline models. Sup-SSC-HDP is referred to as the supervised model of Seq-Sym-cHDP in the figure.

1) The video counts for different classes are imbalanced in this dataset, some of the major classes have more than 100 videos per class, while some of the minor classes have less than 20 videos per class. This imbalance especially affects the learning for videos in the minor class.

2) The ranges of definition for some of the classes overlap. For instance, two classes *science* and *educational* exist in our dataset, however, sometimes, scientific video can be regarded as educational video. Such ambiguous cases are problematic for video learning.

5.3 Quantitative Evaluation

Here, we focus on evaluating the performance of multi-class video classification with topic models. To comprehensively assess our model, the comparisons were made of: (1) supervised and unsupervised methods, (2) symmetric correspondence and other multimodal modeling methods, and (3) sequential and nonsequential methods. Note that the unsupervised topic model cannot directly classify videos, so we needed to input its learned topic frequencies into an extra classifier (such as SVM) to conduct the classification. In addition, we used a five-fold cross-validation scheme in the experiments.

The hyperparameter λ in Sup-SSC-HDP is a controlling parameter that influences the generation of pivot flags. Here, we were interested in examining the performance of classification on Sup-SSC-HDP while varying λ. The results for Sup-SSC-HDP and an unsupervised version of Sup-SSC-HDP (*i.e.*, Seq-Sym-cHDP) with λ manually set at $\{0.1, 1, 2, 3, 4, 5\}$ in Fig. 5, and find that the models performed the best when $\lambda = 1$. In addition, Sup-SSC-HDP outperformed Seq-Sym-cHDP in each experiment of selecting λ.

Fig. 6 shows a comprehensive comparison of Sup-SSC-HDP and the baseline models, where Sym-cHDP is a nonsequential

Table 2: Example Results on Video Classification with Sup-SSC-HDP.

	Video Title	Key Frames	Main Speech Words	Topic Frequency	True Class	Predicted Class
Successful Cases	Insight With Tariq Ali On Pakistan (©*Frontline Club*)	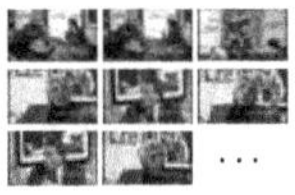 ...	war, political, military, weapons, Pakistan, power, army, government, national, country...	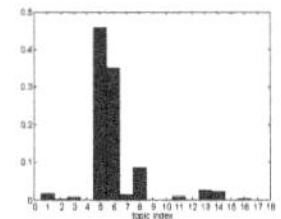	politics	politics
	Web Expo - Things That Matter (©*O'Reilly Media*)	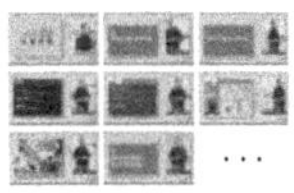 ...	developers, technology, work, eBay, ecommerce, iPhone, online, PayPal, platform, Internet...	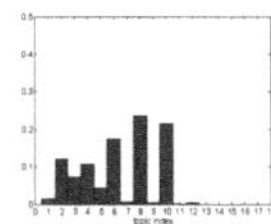	technology	technology
	Why We Don't Watch Soccer (©*That Sports Show*)	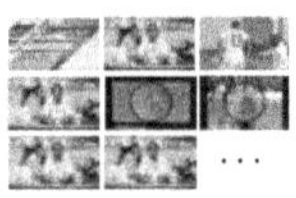 ...	sports, game, teams, soccer, play, cup, matches, run, lead, catch...	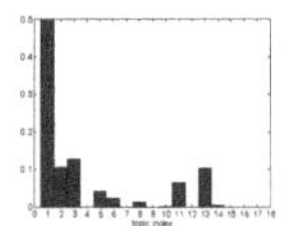	sports	sports
Failure Case	How Data Can Improve Health Care (©*O'Reilly Media*)	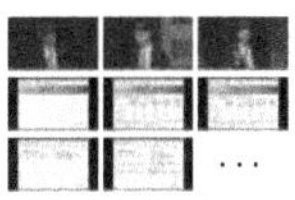 ...	health, medical, care, system, improve, measures, physicians, study, technical, hospital...	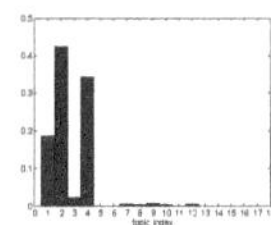	technology	health

version of Seq-Sym-cHDP (*i.e.*, $w_j^f = 0$), and Seq-CI-HDP is a non-correspondence[1] version of Seq-cHDP or Seq-Sym-cHDP. Seq-cHDP had two forms, one setting speech data as the pivot data type, the other setting visual data as the pivot data type. We can see that supervised method outperformed the unsupervised one in terms of classification accuracy for each HDP-based model, which demonstrates that learning the topics in such a supervised manner (relating topics to observed classes in training) improves the accuracy of classifying videos. Compared with other supervised baseline models, Sup-SSC-HDP achieved the best performance with the accuracy of 0.396 ± 0.013. We thus infer that the time-dependency mechanism (in contrast to Sym-cHDP) and the symmetric correspondence mechanism (in contrast to Seq-cHDP and Seq-CI-HDP) incorporated in Sup-SSC-HDP contribute to a more precise video classification, as they can offer the best suitable modeling solution for video data.

We list four video classification examples (three successes and one failure) in Table 2. Here, Sup-SSC-HDP predicted the correct classes for videos expressing class-related visual and speech content, and the learned topic frequencies behaved discriminatively as well. But, the videos were sometimes hard to classify when their content was vague. The failure in Table 2, *i.e.*, the video titled "*How Data Can Improve Health Care*", belongs to the class of *technology*, whereas its speech words include lots of *health*-related words, this made Sup-SSC-HDP misclassify this video as a *health* video. This problem is also discussed in Section 5.2 about the reasons of incorrect video clustering.

[1] Seq-CI-HDP assumes that all data types are conditionally independent when generating their data samples.

6 CONCLUSIONS

This paper presented a supervised sequential symmetric correspondence HDP (Sup-SSC-HDP) model for multi-class video classification, where a generalized linear model (GLM) was used to model the relationship between empirical topic frequencies over multimodal video data and video class. We inferred Sup-SSC-HDP with a posterior representation sampler, and implemented it by using a cascaded Gibbs sampling method. We conducted comprehensive experiments demonstrating that our method outperformed a number of baseline methods. Future work will focus on incorporating a more effective supervised learning approach such as maximum entropy discrimination [16].

ACKNOWLEDGMENTS

This work was supported in part by the Grant-in-Aid for Scientific Research (#15H02703) from JSPS, Japan.

REFERENCES

[1] David M Blei and Michael I Jordan. 2003. Modeling annotated data. In *Proceedings of the 26th annual international ACM SIGIR conference on Research and development in informaion retrieval*. ACM, 127–134.

[2] David M Blei, Andrew Y Ng, and Michael I Jordan. 2003. Latent Dirichlet allocation. *the Journal of machine Learning research* 3 (2003), 993–1022.

[3] Andrew M Dai and Amos J Storkey. 2015. The supervised hierarchical Dirichlet process. *IEEE transactions on pattern analysis and machine intelligence* 37, 2 (2015), 243–255.

[4] Li Fei-Fei and Pietro Perona. 2005. A Bayesian hierarchical model for learning natural scene categories. In *IEEE Computer Society Conference on Computer Vision and Pattern Recognition, 2005.*, Vol. 2. IEEE, 524–531.

[5] Kosuke Fukumasu, Koji Eguchi, and Eric P Xing. 2012. Symmetric correspondence topic models for multilingual text analysis. In *Advances in Neural Information Processing Systems*. 1286–1294.

[6] Daniel Kuettel, Michael D Breitenstein, Luc Van Gool, and Vittorio Ferrari. 2010. What's going on? Discovering spatio-temporal dependencies in dynamic scenes. In *IEEE Conference on Computer Vision and Pattern Recognition, 2010. CVPR 2010*. IEEE, 1951–1958.

[7] Simon Lacoste-Julien, Fei Sha, and Michael I Jordan. 2009. DiscLDA: Discriminative learning for dimensionality reduction and classification. In *Advances in neural information processing systems*. 897–904.

[8] Martha Larson, Maria Eskevich, Roeland Ordelman, Christoph Kofler, Sebastian Schmiedeke, and Gareth JF Jones. 2011. Overview of MediaEval 2011 rich speech retrieval task and genre tagging task. CEUR Workshop Proceedings.

[9] Laurens van der Maaten and Geoffrey Hinton. 2008. Visualizing data using t-SNE. *Journal of Machine Learning Research* 9, Nov (2008), 2579–2605.

[10] Jon D Mcauliffe and David M Blei. 2008. Supervised topic models. In *Advances in neural information processing systems*. 121–128.

[11] Lu Ren, David B Dunson, and Lawrence Carin. 2008. The dynamic hierarchical Dirichlet process. In *Proceedings of the 25th international conference on Machine learning*. ACM, 824–831.

[12] Yee Whye Teh and Michael I Jordan. 2010. Hierarchical Bayesian nonparametric models with applications. *Bayesian nonparametrics* 1 (2010).

[13] Yee Whye Teh, Michael I Jordan, Matthew J Beal, and David M Blei. 2006. Hierarchical Dirichlet processes. *Journal of the american statistical association* 101, 476 (2006).

[14] Jianfei Xue and Koji Eguchi. 2016. Sequential correspondence hierarchical Dirichlet processes for video data analysis. In *Proceedings of the 2016 ACM on International Conference on Multimedia Retrieval*. ACM, 229–233.

[15] Jianfei Xue and Koji Eguchi. 2016. Sequential Symmetric Correspondence Hierarchical Dirichlet Processes for Video Data Analysis. In *NIPS Workshop on Practical Bayesian Nonparametrics*.

[16] Jun Zhu, Amr Ahmed, and Eric P Xing. 2012. MedLDA: maximum margin supervised topic models. *Journal of Machine Learning Research* 13, Aug (2012), 2237–2278.

Dense Dilated Network for Few Shot Action Recognition

Baohan Xu*
ZhongAn Technology
Shanghai, China
xubaohan@zhongan.io

Hao Ye*
Shanghai Advanced Research Institute, CAS, China
yeh@sari.ac.cn

Yingbin Zheng
Shanghai Advanced Research Institute, CAS, China
zhengyb@sari.ac.cn

Heng Wang
ZhongAn Technology
Shanghai, China
wangheng@zhongan.io

Tianyu Luwang†
ZhongAn Technology
Shanghai, China
luwangtianyu@zhongan.io

Yu-Gang Jiang
Fudan University
Shanghai, China
ygj@fudan.edu.cn

ABSTRACT

Recently, video action recognition has been widely studied. Training deep neural networks requires a large amount of well-labeled videos. On the other hand, videos in the same class share high-level semantic similarity. In this paper, we introduce a novel neural network architecture to simultaneously capture local and long-term spatial temporal information. The dilated dense network is proposed with the blocks being composed of densely-connected dilated convolutions layers. The proposed framework is capable of fusing each layer's outputs to learn high-level representations, and the representations are robust even with only few training snippets. The aggregations of dilated dense blocks are also explored. We conduct extensive experiments on UCF101 and demonstrate the effectiveness of our proposed method, especially with few training examples.

KEYWORDS

Action recognition; dilated convolution; few-shot learning; video analysis

ACM Reference Format:
Baohan Xu, Hao Ye, Yingbin Zheng, Heng Wang, Tianyu Luwang, and Yu-Gang Jiang. 2018. Dense Dilated Network for Few Shot Action Recognition. In *Proceedings of 2018 International Conference on Multimedia Retrieval, Yokohama, Japan, June 11–14, 2018 (ICMR '18)*, 9 pages.
https://doi.org/10.1145/3206025.3206028

Figure 1: Some example frames of video action dataset UCF101 [26]. Although the same class of videos contain high-level semantic correlations, different backgrounds and lack of quality control makes few-shot learning more challenging.

1 INTRODUCTION

Video analysis is one of the most fundamental computer vision tasks, and has drawn a significant amount of attention with the popularity of video capture devices and the surge of Internet [10, 18, 19, 24, 28, 30]. Recently, deep neural networks achieved state-of-the-arts on many computer vision benchmarks, such as image classification and object detection [6, 8, 12, 25]. But the data volume for training the video analysis system is orders of magnitude larger than images. Annotating these large and varying kind of videos is labor intensive and time consuming due to their complexity and diversity. Therefore, the data scarcity problem is a common issue for newly emerged action categories. This impedes the neural networks from learning discriminative features. Figure 1 shows some example frames in video action datasets. The actions in the same category have variety of backgrounds, which requires sufficient amount of annotated video data for training a deep neural network. It would be better if we can find a way to learn new action categories with few examples.

Few-shot learning aims to fully make use of knowledges that have been obtained so far from pre-training rather than to start from scratch when new action categories need to be learned. A recent highly effective prototype-based learning paradigm on few-shot learning attempts to resolve the data scarcity problem by using a pre-trained deep neural network as a starting point [3]. In action recognition, many different kinds of actions share similar spatial or motion primitives, whereas a new classifier, referred to as prototype, may be reconstructed by taking these shared primitives and the additional examples into account. It is widely acknowledged that

*These authors contributed equally to this work.
†Corresponding author.

ICMR '18, June 11–14, 2018, Yokohama, Japan

ACM ISBN 978-1-4503-5046-4/18/06...$15.00
https://doi.org/10.1145/3206025.3206028

deep neural networks provide a promising capability of keeping and reusing these primitives.

In this paper, we propose a dilated dense connection based deep network architecture that deals with the few-shot action recognition by framing the problem within the prototype learning settings. The densely connected blocks capture not only the spatial information within the layer-wise concatenation, but also the long-term context through the dilated temporal convolution. Rather than retraining the action recognizer by replacing the classifier in an incremental manner, we regard the existing networks trained on seen data as action primitive extractors. Our proposed networks take these primitives as inputs so that they can adapt to those never-before-seen actions easily.

In this dilated dense connection based framework, two basic ConvNets are pre-trained on frames and stacked optical flows respectively. The spatial and motion primitives extracted from these two pathways are sent to the consecutive densely connected architecture where each layer receives additional inputs from all preceding layers except the basic ConvNet and pass its features to the subsequent layers. Thereon, a compact flow of information is fully employed to aggregate the spatial and temporal features from the few training video snippets. Under this point of view, densely connected blocks and temporal dilated convolutions are capable of mining few action examples by unleashing the potential of densely connected blocks.

Our contributions are summarized as follows:

- We propose a novel deep neural network architecture combing dilated temporal convolution and densely layer connection to perform video action recognition. Our framework can generate new class prototypes where only a small number of new action videos are needed.
- The dilated dense blocks in our framework are able to capture spatial-temporal information from both snippet-level and long-term context.
- We achieve the state-of-the-art action recognition performance on UCF101 by only using part of the training videos and then reveal the effectiveness of dense connection blocks on few-shot action recognition.

The rest of our paper is arranged as follows. We begin with a brief review of literatures on action recognition and few shot learning in Section 2. In Section 3, we give the details of our framework structure, and implementation stages of the densely connection configuration. We show a variety of experimental results conducted on UCF-101 to demonstrate the effectiveness in Section 4. Section 5 concludes the paper.

2 RELATED WORKS

2.1 Video Action Recognition

Video action recognition has been widely studied during last few years. A detailed survey can be found in [2]. Early researchers focused on hand-crafted feature extractions. Various features have been explored, such as space-time interest points (STIP) [14], histogram of gradient (HoG) and histogram of optical flow (HOF) [15]. Knowledge from image domain is extended to capture the temporal information. Further more, Wang et al. proposed dense trajectory features to densely sample and track local patches from each field in a dense optical flow field [28]. However, these hand-crafted features still have some limitations for further improvements, especially when dealing with large scale of video data.

Recent years, convolutional neural networks gained more and more attention. It showed great success in image classification and detection. In 2012, AlexNet [12] won ImageNet Challenge [23] with convolutional neural network. With ConvNets becoming more popular in computer vision field, a number of attempts have been made to improve performance. Simonyan et al. [25] proposed a deeper network by adding more convolutional layers. More recently, He et al. [6] developed a residual function with reference to the layer inputs. The residual nets, which have a total of 152 layers, are still able to increase accuracy gained from greatly increased depth. Huang et al. proposed DenseNet [8], which focuses on feature reuse and learns a variation in the input of different layers. These state-of-the-art networks were designed for static image classification. Directly using these frameworks on video action recognition tasks will lose lots of discriminative information such as temporal contexts and motions.

To tackle these problems, Simonyan et al. [24] proposed a fusion network which combines both static frames and motion optical flows. Ye et al. [32] evaluated important implementation options on two-stream CNN. Competitive results were attained on popular video classification benchmarks, such as HMDB51 [13], UCF101 [26] and ActivityNet [7]. While treating videos as frames or optical flow images separately will leave the temporal relations not fully explored.

Many studies also paid attentions to how to use temporal information in order to achieve multi-modality recognition. Tran et al. [27] adopted 3D CNN (C3D) for joint learning spatial-temporal representations in video datasets. Later in [21], Qiu constructed 2D spatial convolutions and 1D temporal connections to stimulate 3D convolutions. The deep residual learning framework also designed for efficiently training a deeper neural network. Instead of using traditional convolutions, Lea et al. [29] explored temporal convolutions for action segmentation tasks. Encoder-decoder temporal convolutional network (TCN) and dilated TCN were used to capture long-range temporal patterns. However, these approaches still require large amount of data and resources to get a satisfactory result.

2.2 Few Shot Learning

In early studies, few shot video action recognition mainly focused on datasets like KTH and Weizmann [20, 31]. These datasets consist of actors performing scripted "atomic" actions, such as walking, jogging and running, which are easy to recognize using only a small percentage of the training data. Hidden markov model (HMM) combined with encoding methods demonstrated some effectiveness [22]. However, when facing large scale unconstrained data, the performance of these methods are not very encouraging.

Recently, some researchers transfered pretrained image domain models to video action recognition on unconstrained video datasets [3], such as UCF101 [26]. Since these videos are generated by users with little quality control, it makes few shot recognition more challenging. Li et al. mapped videos into low-dimensional feature space using spatial attention map [17]. These domain adaptive methods

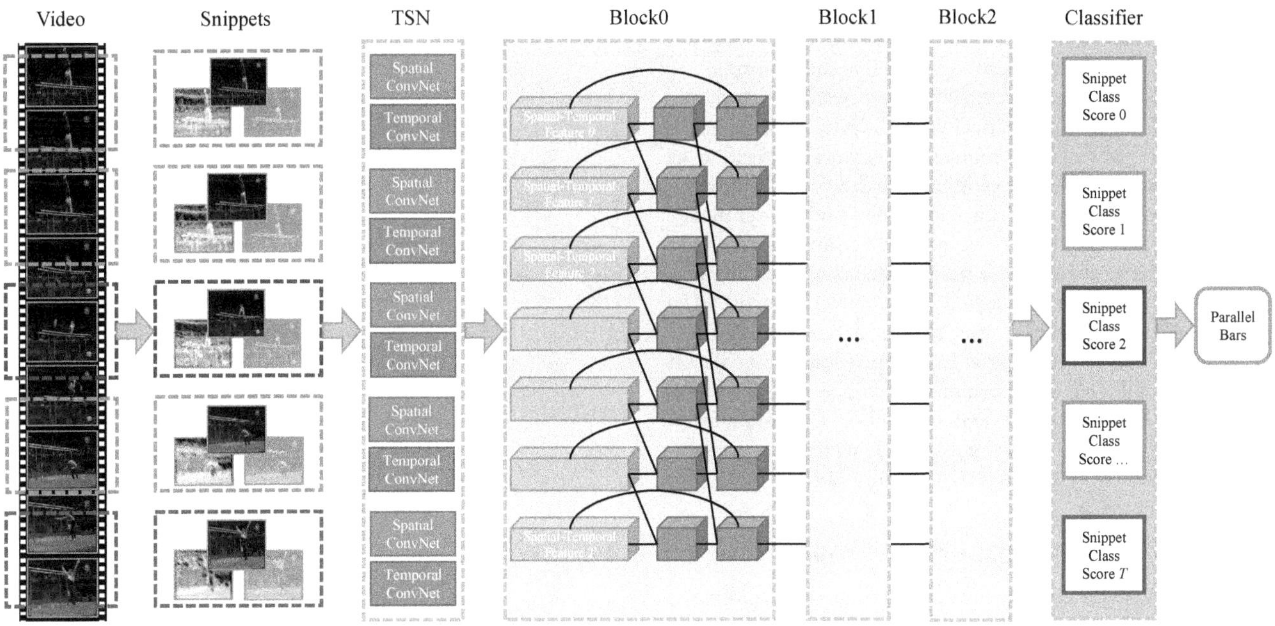

Figure 2: The framework of our proposed dense dilated network. Videos are divided into n snippets. Temporal segment network (TSN) is used to extract spatial-temporal features of every snippets. Dense dilated blocks are utilized to densely connect channel wise features. The dilated convolutions help explore temporal relations between different snippets. Prediction scores are made based on all the feature-maps in the network. The scores of all the snippets are leveraged to perform video-level prediction.

need auxiliary images or other heterogeneous information to transfer knowledge. Temporal and motion clues are neglected. Instead of using auxiliary information, few scholars focused on modifying the structure of the network to perform few-shot learning.

Inspired by previous researches, we propose a dense dilated temporal convolution network instead of constructing deep or complicated architectures. With only few training examples, actions in the same class could share some common high-level semantic attributions. We explore how to fully utilize local and global temporal information to learn inner-class semantic representations. First of all, the dilated temporal convolution provides wide receptive fields for each layer. Then concatenating different feature maps in each layer helps the model to learn long-range temporal representations, especially when the training data is limited. In addition, the densely connected architecture makes the whole network easier to train and more efficient.

3 METHOD

In this section, we introduce our proposed framework. Recent proposed DenseNet [8] is found useful in image classification tasks. Rather than traditional feed-forward architectures, DenseNet investigates a novel and simple connectivity pattern to allow maximum information flow between layers. The dense connections across channels help to achieve significant improvement of image tasks, especially on a small dataset.

Inspired by DenseNet, our proposed framework aims to fully utilize spatial-temporal information of the entire video using dense connections. As illustrated in Figure 2, for each snippet of videos, dense dilated blocks are designed to concatenate all feature maps, which provide both local and global spatial-temporal features to subsequent layers.

Formally, suppose we extracted n frames and optical flow images of each video. The temporal segment network (TSN) [29] is utilized to extract RGB features and flow features separately. The basic network of TSN is Google Inception network [9]. The TSN is trained on Kinetics dataset [11], which contains about 300,000 video action clips among 400 classes. Specifically, we use the 1024 dimensions of global pool features before the softmax layer.

The temporal dilated convolutions use different dilation parameters to get different views of temporal information, which has been shown to be effective in many tasks such as video action detection [16], semantic segmentation [1, 33], RGB-D [34], and DNA modeling [5]. Densely connection inside the blocks on channel level can give more variations to the input of subsequent blocks. Aggregation of each dense dilated block can leverage the global features of whole videos and the specific snippets, which is useful for recognition. We will explain each part in following subsections.

3.1 Dense Dilated Blocks

The advantage of DenseNet is not only to prevent gradient dispersion, but also to reduce the number of parameters. The layer of DenseNet is often very narrow, such as 12 filters per layer, which makes the whole network easy to train and converge. It's also worth noticing that dense connections have a regularizing effect [8]. It can reduce overfitting, especially with smaller amount of training data. We propose dense dilated framework not only to improve video action recognition but also to enable few shot learning.

Figure 3 demonstrates the detailed information in each dilated convolutional block. We empirically set 3 layers as example, the performance of varying layer number are explored in Section 4.4. Every layer consists of three operations: a batch normalization [9], a dilated convolution, and a rectified linear uint (ReLU) [4] function.

Specifically, every block has a sequence of L layers. Every layer contains a batch normalization, a set of dilated convolutions with a rate parameter s, and a ReLU function. The dilation rate increases for consecutive layers in the block as $s_l = 2^l$. Compared to traditional convolutions, dilated convolution can capture long-range dependencies. This will give the discriminative snippets more weights to make contributions to the overall recognition. Convolutions are applied over two time steps, t and $t - s$. Thus the filters can be represented as $W = \{W^{(1)}, W^{(2)}\}$. Therefore, we can define the dilated convolution as

$$x_t^l = f(W^{(1)}x_{t-s}^{l-1} + W^{(2)}x_t^{l-1} + b), \tag{1}$$

where x_t^l refers to the dilated convolution results on time t in layer l and b is the bias vector.

To further improve our framework, we consider the dense connection within each block. Concatenating feature maps learned by different layers can provide more variations to the input of subsequent layers. Inner-class representations can be learned more easily, especially when the training data is limited. Layers in each temporal dilated convolution (TDC) block i have the same number of filters k^i, which could also be regarded as growth rate in DenseNet. The dense connection combines all layers in channel-wise manner.

More specifically, we define the output of every block B^i on time t as S_t^i,

$$S_t^i = [x_t^l, x_t^{(l-1)}, \ldots, x_t^0], \tag{2}$$

where S_t^i concatenate all the outputs into a single tensor.

Transition layers. We also add transition layers between blocks. It consists of a batch normalization layer followed by an 1×1 convolutional layer to down sample the feature maps.

Growth rate. We refer k as growth rate of different blocks. Each layer produce k^i feature-maps in the i-th block, then the filters of different blocks can write down as

$$k^i = k^{i-1} \times (l-1) + k^0, \tag{3}$$

where k^0 refer to the number of channels in the input layer, l is the number of layers in each block. On limited training data, we show that a relatively small growth rate and small number of layers and blocks are sufficient to get a high accuracy.

3.2 Dense Dilated Aggregation

We explore different connection structures to build dense dilated network, we set 3 blocks as the basic structure of all the aggregations. Figure 4 illustrates 3 aggregation strategies, including adding all the TDC blocks, concatenating blocks and extracting features of different blocks. Utilize the information of all the blocks may provide more knowledge of the whole video, while the output of blocks from a simpler network could give different scales of information. We'll explain each way in detail as follows.

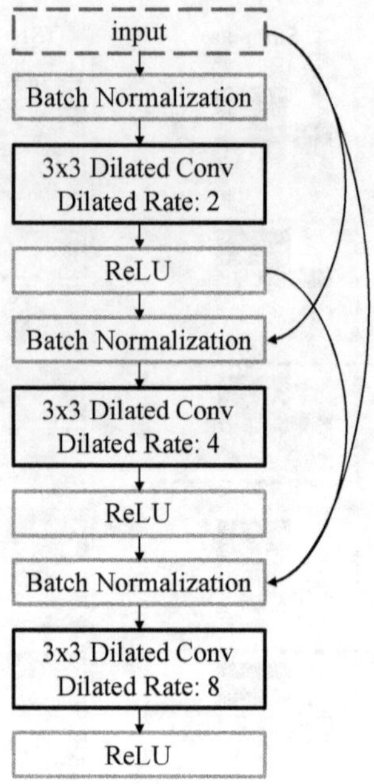

Figure 3: The framework of temporal dense convolution with 3 layers. Every layer consists of a batch normalization, a dilated convolution, and an activation function. Different layers are concatenated in a dense way.

Adding layers Naturally, we first tried adding the output of all layers together. Due to different shapes of filters in different blocks, we apply 1×1 convolutions to align all the output tensors. The output layer can be defined as:

$$Z_t = ReLU(V \sum_{i=0}^{B-1} S_t^i + e), \tag{4}$$

where V is the weight matrix and e is the bias. We refer this architecture as dense dilated adding (DDA) aggregation as (a) in Figure 4.

Concatenating layers Further more, in order to make receptive fields wider, we explore concatenating the output of different layers. The final layer has wider range of channels than other connection methods.

$$Z_t = ReLU([S_t^{B-1}, S_t^{B-2}, \ldots, S_t^0] + e). \tag{5}$$

This way we call it dense dilated concatenation (DDC) connection as (b) in Figure 4.

Output features of different blocks More straightforwardly, we extracted the output of different blocks to perform recognition of video actions. Considering the output as snippet-level representations helps us get more insights of the proposed architecture. This will also provide useful information when tuning the hyper-parameters. As illustrate as (c) in Figure 4, we refer the output features of each block as DD1, DD2, and DD3 respectively.

Compared to extracting features, the adding and concatenating ways maybe redundant, which produce unnecessary information not only make the network more complicated, but also make it harder to converge on small datasets.

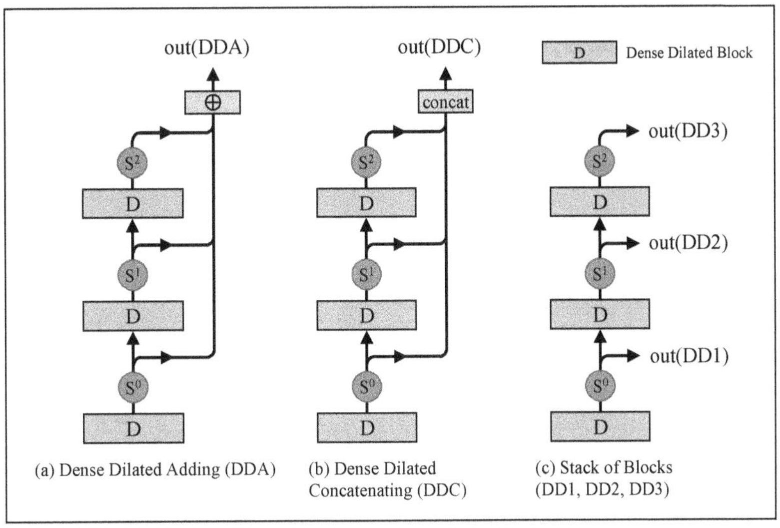

Figure 4: Different layer aggregation strategies. (a) is summed using a set of skip connections. (b) is concatenated over the output of different output blocks. (c) are more straightforward to extract every block as snippet-level representation.

3.3 Classification

We extract the last layer before softmax as output of all dense dilated networks. The output consists of n snippets $\times$ d-dimension features. A support vector machine (SVM) is used as the predictor $\mathcal{P}(\cdot)$ to predict the class label for every snippet. Majority vote is applied to decide the video-level prediction.

4 EVALUATIONS

In this section, we first introduce the experimental settings, and then validate the effectiveness of our framework using both whole data and few shot settings. Varying the hyper parameters are also fully explored in our experiments.

4.1 Dataset and Settings

We utilize popular video action recognition dataset UCF101 [26]. It consists of 101 action classes, 13,320 clips and 27 hours of unconstrained videos collected from YouTube. The large variations in camera motion, different background and illumination conditions makes it a challenge video action dataset. Figure 5 shows some example frames of different categories in UCF101. In order to enable few shot learning, we randomly sample 10%, 20%, 33%, and 50% videos from the training set. The experiments are separately done on the three public train/test splits for comparision, and the result is averaged across three test splits.

We extract global pool features from temporal segment network (TSN) with pretrained model on Kinetics. Each video contains 25 snippets as the default setting in TSN. RGB and Optical flow features are concatenated as snippet-level features for every video. The concatenating spatio-temporal features are regarded as the input of our frameworks. The growth rate K of all the block is set as 12 to leverage the accuracy and the computation cost.

Figure 5: Example frames of UCF101.

As illustrated in Figure 4 and Section 3.2, we compare some state-of-the-art methods as baselines with 3 different layer aggregation frameworks that we proposed.

4.2 Video Action Recognition

To evaluate our algorithm, we compare with different video action recognition methods. First four baseline methods make use of spatial-temporal features, which is similar to our method. **(1) C3D [27].** This method proposes an effective approach for spatial-temporal feature learning using deep 3-dimensional convolutional networks. **(2) P3D [21].** Spatial and temporal information in videos are combined to build a bottleneck block, which can simulate 3D

Table 1: Comparison with state-of-the-art methods on UCF101 using all data. The result of dilated TCN is computed by ourself, while other baseline results are reported in the papers.

Method	Accuracy(%)
C3D[27]	85.2
P3D[21]	88.60
Temporal Segment Network[29]	93.50
Dilated TCN[16]	92.31
EnergyNet[17]	88.00
DDA	94.74
DDC	95.30
DD1	95.17
DD2	**96.15**
DD3	95.48

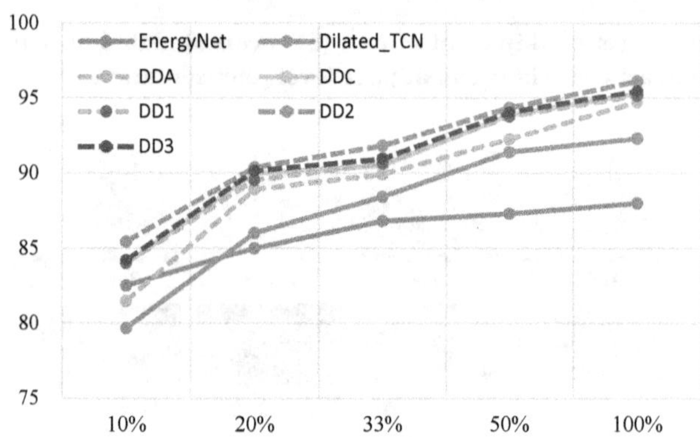

Figure 6: Few shot video action recognition results.

Table 2: Few shot results with only 20% training videos.

Method	Accuracy(%)
Dilated TCN [16]	86.02
EnergyNet [17]	85.00
DDA	88.92
DDC	89.98
DD1	89.54
DD2	**90.38**
DD3	90.15

Table 3: The accuracy of DDA and DDC with 2 dense dilated blocks using 20% training data and 100% training data.

Method	20%	100%
DDA	89.56	95.47
DDC	**90.45**	**95.76**

convolutions in an effective way. **(3) Temporal segment network [29].** This method combines a sparse temporal sampling strategy and video-level supervision to enable efficient and effective learning using the whole action video. **(4) Dilated TCN [16].** Dilated TCN is most related to our method. Residual connections and dilated convolutions are used to perform video segmentation and detection. **(5) EnergyNet [17].** While EnergyNet use web images to learn attention maps, which is also helpful in few shot learning. We'll discuss more detail in Section 4.3.

Table 1 shows the results for video action recognition using whole training set. It clearly shows that all our proposed frameworks outperform state-of-the-art methods on UCF101 when using all data. These results demonstrate that adding dense connection can not only retrieve features from action snippets but also capture high-level semantics of the whole video. The improvement of DDC over DDA shows that concatenating channels expands the reception fields, which helps action recognition. While among the three feature extraction frameworks, DD2 surprisingly achieves best performance. DD1 performs even worse than DDC. This indicates that the representation of two dense dilated blocks are enough for our task. The pooling operation between DD2 and DD3 may lose some significant spatial-temporal features.

4.3 Few Shot Recognition

We mainly compare our few shot learning methods with [17], which reported few shot results using auxiliary image datasets. They proposed an EnergyNet transferring knowledge from web images to videos. The transfer learning method can adapt to the target domain with limited amount of training data. However, EnergyNet only considers the attention information of static images. This framework is difficult to be expanded to use multi-modal information. While our framework enables the network to learn high-level semantics of each class without auxiliary images or other information. Image and optical flow are both utilized in our framework as multi-modal features.

The comparison results are reported in Table 2. It suggests that our dense dilated methods outperform our baseline methods using 20% training data. Figure 6 illustrates the accuracy when different amounts of training videos are used. DD2 still outperforms all other methods. Our proposed frameworks can also achieve better performance using fewer videos compared with the baseline methods. Using only 20% training videos, they all outperform EnergyNet which uses 100% training data. While with 50% videos, DD2 outperforms dilated TCN with whole training data. One interesting finding is that dense dilated methods get more improvements with less training data. Using 10% training videos, DD2 outperforms dilated TCN by 4.54%, compared with 2.46% when using 50% training data. This finding demonstrates our proposed method can preserve more intra-class relationship than baseline methods giving little training data.

To further evaluate the complimentary of different blocks, we also conduct experiments on DDA and DDC using 2 dense dilated blocks. Table 3 reported the accuracy for each architecture. The result of DDC outperforms other dense dilated structures, which proves the complementary of first 2 blocks. It also shows that adding the third block may not be a good choice.

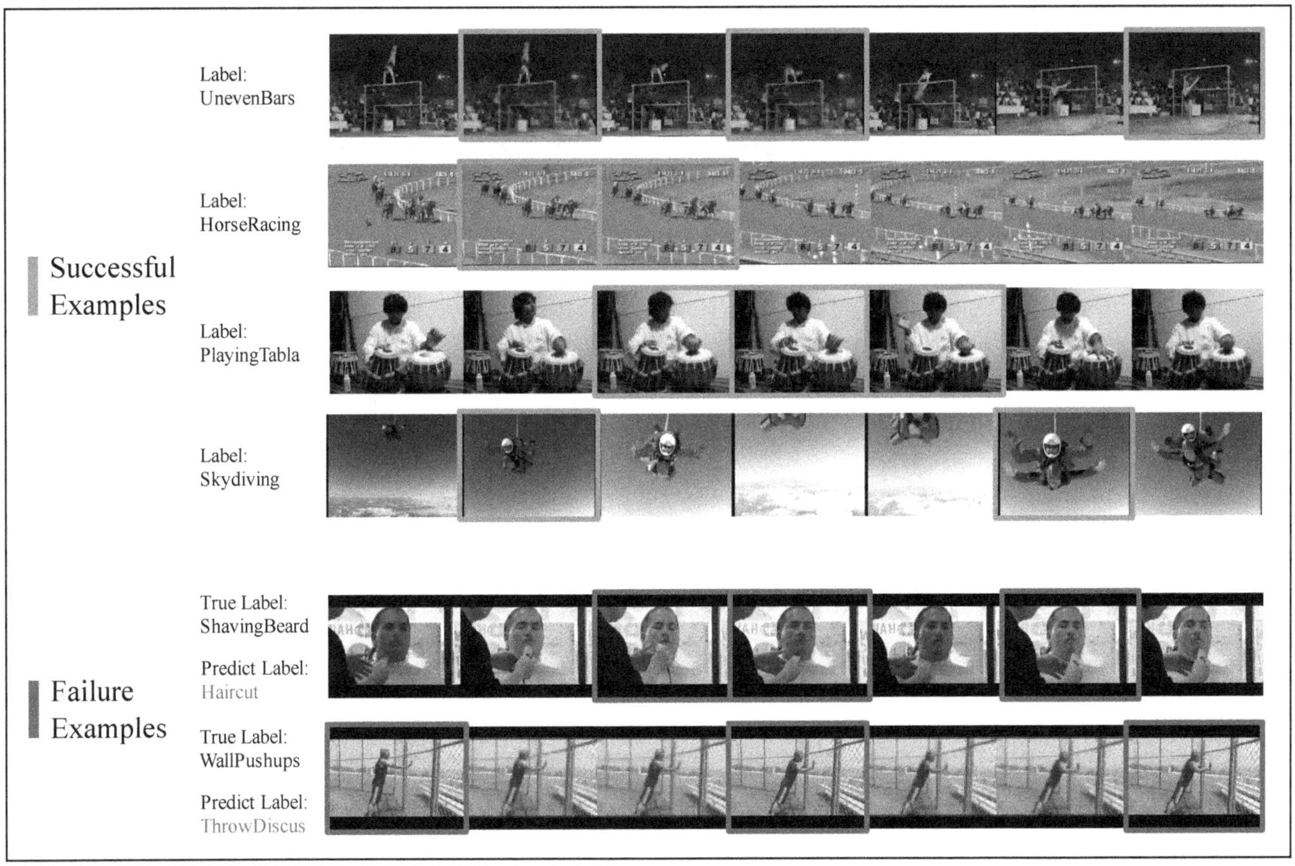

Figure 7: Quantitive examples of successful and failure examples. 20% training data are used by DD2 model.

Figure 7 demonstrates some quantitive examples for successful and failure cases. The top four examples are the successfully recognized examples. Even with few training data, our methods can successfully classify most of the classes with different backgrounds and qualities. The green frames refer to the snippets that our frameworks are more confident, which also illustrates that the proposed method can identify important movements for recognition. The last two rows show some failure examples. The similar backgrounds and the unclear movements make the system misclassified these videos into Haircut and ThrowDiscus.

4.4 Hyper Parameter Tuning

The hyper-parameters in our frameworks include the number of layers and the growth rate. The changing of these hyper-parameters may affect the performance. In this subsection, we explore the influence of different choices of these settings. 20% training data are used in all the experiments.

Varying different layers. We compare the performance of our frameworks with varying number of layers L in the dense dilated block. In Figure 8, lines show accuracy for L from 2 to 4 . All the methods perform best with $L = 3$. Compared to $L = 2$, more layers in each block can boost the performance. However, when L gets larger, the performances for both algorithms are decreased. This is because complicated neural networks lead to under fitting when the scale of training data is small.

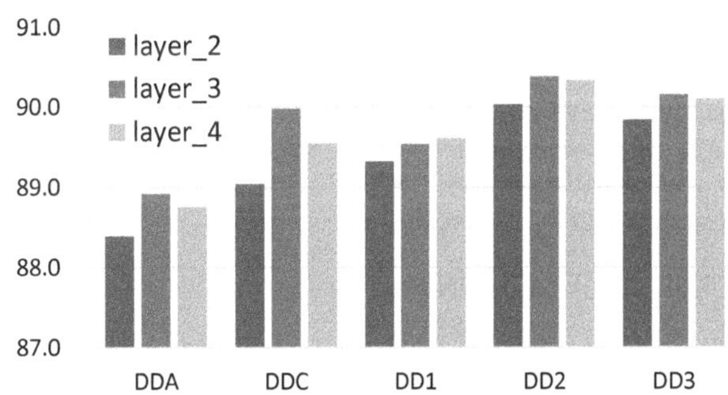

Figure 8: Performance of varying layer count L.

Varying growth rate. Figure 9 shows how different growth rates affect the accuracy. Due to limited data, our dense dilated architecture can converge with relatively small growth rate. When $K = 12$ and $K = 16$, we can achieve a relatively high accuracy without drastically increasing the number of parameters for all the frameworks.

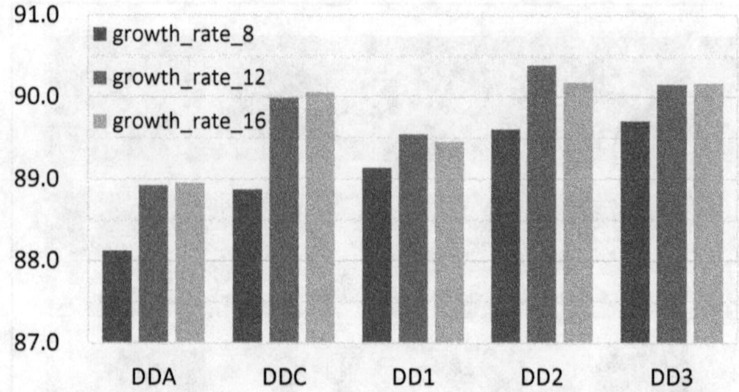

Figure 9: Performance of varying growth rate K.

The influence of Kinetics. To further validate whether the performance of our proposed methods is affected by the original training dataset Kinetics [11], we add another simple experiment to recognize the classes in UCF101 but not in Kinetics. According to manual visual inspection, about 45 classes in UCF101 are not the same as the classes in Kinetics. We use DD2 to train 20% of training videos in the 45 classes and do the evaluation. The accuracy is 86.23% of 45 classes. This shows our model can recognize video categories other than those in the pretrained models.

5 CONCLUSIONS

We introduce a novel dense dilated framework to perform video action recognition and few shot learning. The receptive fields include both local and global features via dense connections. The experiments show the effectiveness of our proposed framework compared to baseline metods. Our proposed framework also achieves state-of-the-art performance when facing limited data. We further explore the different strategies for layer aggregation among dense dilated blocks. The concatenating way is better than adding up all the blocks. The features of the second layer of blocks achieve best results under all conditions.

For further improvements, we will explore learning from scratch to perform video action recognition on more variety of videos. Video segmentation and action detection are also important topics that we leave for further investigation.

ACKNOWLEDGMENTS

This work was supported in part by the National Natural Science Foundation of China under Grants 61602459, 61622204, and 61572134, and in part by the Science and Technology Commission of Shanghai Municipality under Grant 16QA1400500.

REFERENCES

[1] Liang-Chieh Chen, George Papandreou, Iasonas Kokkinos, Kevin Murphy, and Alan L Yuille. 2017. Deeplab: Semantic image segmentation with deep convolutional nets, atrous convolution, and fully connected crfs. *IEEE Transactions on Pattern Analysis and Machine Intelligence* (2017).

[2] Guangchun Cheng, Yiwen Wan, Abdullah N Saudagar, Kamesh Namuduri, and Bill P Buckles. 2015. Advances in human action recognition: A survey. *arXiv:1501.05964* (2015).

[3] Chuang Gan, Chen Sun, Lixin Duan, and Boqing Gong. 2016. Webly-supervised video recognition by mutually voting for relevant web images and web video frames. In *European Conference on Computer Vision (ECCV)*. 849–866.

[4] Xavier Glorot, Antoine Bordes, and Yoshua Bengio. 2011. Deep sparse rectifier neural networks. In *International Conference on Artificial Intelligence and Statistics (AISTATS)*. 315–323.

[5] Ankit Gupta and Alexander M Rush. 2017. Dilated Convolutions for Modeling Long-Distance Genomic Dependencies. *arXiv:1710.01278* (2017).

[6] Kaiming He, Xiangyu Zhang, Shaoqing Ren, and Jian Sun. 2016. Deep residual learning for image recognition. In *IEEE Conference on Computer Vision and Pattern Recognition (CVPR)*. 770–778.

[7] Fabian Caba Heilbron, Victor Escorcia, Bernard Ghanem, and Juan Carlos Niebles. 2015. Activitynet: A large-scale video benchmark for human activity understanding. In *IEEE Conference on Computer Vision and Pattern Recognition (CVPR)*. 961–970.

[8] Gao Huang, Zhuang Liu, Kilian Q Weinberger, and Laurens van der Maaten. 2016. Densely connected convolutional networks. *arXiv:1608.06993* (2016).

[9] Sergey Ioffe and Christian Szegedy. 2015. Batch normalization: Accelerating deep network training by reducing internal covariate shift. In *International Conference on Machine Learning (ICML)*. 448–456.

[10] Yu-Gang Jiang, Yanran Wang, Rui Feng, Xiangyang Xue, Yingbin Zheng, and Hanfang Yang. 2013. Understanding and Predicting Interestingness of Videos. In *AAAI Conference on Artificial Intelligence (AAAI)*.

[11] Will Kay, Joao Carreira, Karen Simonyan, Brian Zhang, Chloe Hillier, Sudheendra Vijayanarasimhan, Fabio Viola, Tim Green, Trevor Back, Paul Natsev, Mustafa Suleyman, and Andrew Zisserman. 2017. The Kinetics Human Action Video Dataset. *arXiv:1705.06950* (2017).

[12] Alex Krizhevsky, Ilya Sutskever, and Geoffrey E Hinton. 2012. ImageNet classification with deep convolutional neural networks. In *Neural Information Processing Systems (NIPS)*.

[13] Hildegard Kuehne, Hueihan Jhuang, Estíbaliz Garrote, Tomaso Poggio, and Thomas Serre. 2011. HMDB: a large video database for human motion recognition. In *International Conference on Computer Vision (ICCV)*. 2556–2563.

[14] Ivan Laptev. 2005. On space-time interest points. *International Journal of Computer Vision* 64, 2-3 (2005), 107–123.

[15] Ivan Laptev, Marcin Marszalek, Cordelia Schmid, and Benjamin Rozenfeld. 2008. Learning realistic human actions from movies. In *IEEE Conference on Computer Vision and Pattern Recognition (CVPR)*.

[16] Colin Lea, Michael Flynn, Rene Vidal, Austin Reiter, and Greg Hager. 2017. Temporal Convolutional Networks for Action Segmentation and Detection. In *IEEE Conference on Computer Vision and Pattern Recognition (CVPR)*.

[17] Junnan Li, Yongkang Wong, Qi Zhao, and Mohan S Kankanhalli. 2017. Attention Transfer from Web Images for Video Recognition. In *ACM International Conference on Multimedia (MM)*.

[18] Yao Lu, Aakanksha Chowdhery, and Srikanth Kandula. 2016. Optasia: A relational platform for efficient large-scale video analytics. In *ACM Symposium on Cloud Computing (SoCC)*.

[19] Joe Yue-Hei Ng, Matthew Hausknecht, Sudheendra Vijayanarasimhan, Oriol Vinyals, Rajat Monga, and George Toderici. 2015. Beyond Short Snippets: Deep Networks for Video Classification. In *IEEE Conference on Computer Vision and Pattern Recognition (CVPR)*.

[20] Carlos Orrite, Mario Rodríguez, and Miguel Montañés. 2011. One-sequence learning of human actions. In *International Workshop on Human Behavior Understanding*. Springer, 40–51.

[21] Zhaofan Qiu, Ting Yao, and Tao Mei. 2017. Learning spatio-temporal representation with pseudo-3d residual networks. In *International Conference on Computer Vision (ICCV)*. 5534–5542.

[22] Mario Rodriguez, Carlos Orrite, Carlos Medrano, and Dimitrios Makris. 2017. Fast Simplex-HMM for one-shot learning activity recognition. In *CVPR Workshops*. 41–48.

[23] Olga Russakovsky, Jia Deng, Hao Su, Jonathan Krause, Sanjeev Satheesh, Sean Ma, Zhiheng Huang, Andrej Karpathy, Aditya Khosla, Michael Bernstein, Alexander C. Berg, and Li Fei-Fei. 2015. ImageNet Large Scale Visual Recognition Challenge. *International Journal of Computer Vision* 115, 3 (2015), 211–252.

[24] Karen Simonyan and Andrew Zisserman. 2014. Two-stream convolutional networks for action recognition in videos. In *Neural Information Processing Systems (NIPS)*. 568–576.

[25] Karen Simonyan and Andrew Zisserman. 2015. Very Deep Convolutional Networks for Large-Scale Image Recognition. In *International Conference on Learning Representations (ICLR)*.

[26] Khurram Soomro, Amir Roshan Zamir, and Mubarak Shah. 2012. UCF101: A dataset of 101 human actions classes from videos in the wild. *arXiv:1212.0402* (2012).

[27] Du Tran, Lubomir Bourdev, Rob Fergus, Lorenzo Torresani, and Manohar Paluri. 2015. Learning spatiotemporal features with 3d convolutional networks. In *International Conference on Computer Vision (ICCV)*. 4489–4497.

[28] Limin Wang, Yu Qiao, and Xiaoou Tang. 2015. Action recognition with trajectory-pooled deep-convolutional descriptors. In *IEEE Conference on Computer Vision and Pattern Recognition (CVPR)*. 4305–4314.

[29] Limin Wang, Yuanjun Xiong, Zhe Wang, Yu Qiao, Dahua Lin, Xiaoou Tang, and Luc Van Gool. 2016. Temporal segment networks: Towards good practices for deep action recognition. In *European Conference on Computer Vision (ECCV)*. 20–36.

[30] Baohan Xu, Yanwei Fu, Yu-Gang Jiang, Boyang Li, and Leonid Sigal. 2016. Video emotion recognition with transferred deep feature encodings. In *ACM International Conference on Multimedia Retrieval (ICMR)*. 15–22.
[31] Yang Yang, Imran Saleemi, and Mubarak Shah. 2013. Discovering motion primitives for unsupervised grouping and one-shot learning of human actions, gestures, and expressions. *IEEE Transactions on Pattern Analysis and Machine Intelligence* 35, 7 (2013), 1635–1648.
[32] Hao Ye, Zuxuan Wu, Rui-Wei Zhao, Xi Wang, Yu-Gang Jiang, and Xiangyang Xue. 2015. Evaluating two-stream CNN for video classification. In *ACM International Conference on Multimedia Retrieval (ICMR)*. 435–442.
[33] Fisher Yu, Vladlen Koltun, and Thomas Funkhouser. 2017. Dilated residual networks. In *IEEE Conference on Computer Vision and Pattern Recognition (CVPR)*.
[34] Yingbin Zheng, Hao Ye, Li Wang, and Jian Pu. 2018. Learning Multiviewpoint Context-Aware Representation for RGB-D Scene Classification. *IEEE Signal Processing Letters* 25, 1 (2018), 30–34.

Precise Temporal Action Localization by Evolving Temporal Proposals

Haonan Qiu*
East China Normal University
Shanghai, China
hnqiu@ica.stc.sh.cn

Yingbin Zheng*
Shanghai Advanced Research Institute, CAS, China
zhengyb@sari.ac.cn

Hao Ye†
Shanghai Advanced Research Institute, CAS, China
yeh@sari.ac.cn

Yao Lu
University of Washington
Seattle, WA, USA
luyao@cs.washington.edu

Feng Wang
East China Normal University
Shanghai, China
fwang@cs.ecnu.edu.cn

Liang He
East China Normal University
Shanghai, China
lhe@cs.ecnu.edu.cn

ABSTRACT

Locating actions in long untrimmed videos has been a challenging problem in video content analysis. The performances of existing action localization approaches remain unsatisfactory in precisely determining the beginning and the end of an action. Imitating the human perception procedure with observations and refinements, we propose a novel three-phase action localization framework. Our framework is embedded with an Actionness Network to generate initial proposals through frame-wise similarity grouping, and then a Refinement Network to conduct boundary adjustment on these proposals. Finally, the refined proposals are sent to a Localization Network for further fine-grained location regression. The whole process can be deemed as multi-stage refinement using a novel non-local pyramid feature under various temporal granularities. We evaluate our framework on THUMOS14 benchmark and obtain a significant improvement over the state-of-the-arts approaches. Specifically, the performance gain is remarkable under precise localization with high IoU thresholds. Our proposed framework achieves mAP@IoU=0.5 of 34.2%.

KEYWORDS

Action localization; temporal proposal; deep neural network

ACM Reference Format:
Haonan Qiu, Yingbin Zheng, Hao Ye, Yao Lu, Feng Wang, and Liang He. 2018. Precise Temporal Action Localization by Evolving Temporal Proposals. In *Proceedings of 2018 International Conference on Multimedia Retrieval, Yokohama, Japan, June 11–14, 2018 (ICMR '18)*, 9 pages. https://doi.org/10.1145/3206025.3206029

*These authors contributed equally to this work.
†Corresponding author.

ICMR '18, June 11–14, 2018, Yokohama, Japan

ACM ISBN 978-1-4503-5046-4/18/06...$15.00
https://doi.org/10.1145/3206025.3206029

Figure 1: Localization of precise action boundary is challenging. We demonstrate an example from the THUMOS14 dataset [11], and the middle frame is the annotated ending of the action "FrisbeeCatch".

1 INTRODUCTION

With the ubiquitous video capture devices, a huge amount of videos are producted, which brings a great demand for automatic video content analysis [7, 14, 20, 32–34, 44–49]. Action localization and recognition answer *where* and *what* an action is in the video. Since most collected videos are untrimmed, action localization becomes, undoubtedly, the first and the foremost steps in video action analysis. On common image object detection, the "*Proposal + Classification*" framework demonstrates its capability [8, 19, 27, 28], and is easy to be transferred to other detection tasks, such as detecting the face [13], text [24] and vehicle [38]. For the video action localization task, the high-quality temporal proposals are also crucial following this paradigm. A promising temporal proposal candidate in action localization should contain the action of interest in accordance with high Intersection-over-Union (IoU) overlap with the groundtruth.

Recently, training deep neural networks to extract the spatial-temporal features of the proposals is widely used in action localization. Both the regressor and the classifier are trained to determine the fidelity of the boundary and the completeness of an action based on these proposal features. Nevertheless, regressing the boundary and judging the completeness of an action are nontrivial tasks due to two difficulties. First, compared to the object proposals which have solid internal consistency, the boundary between an action and the background is vague, because the variations of the consecutive video frames are subtle. This may lead to an unsteady or even incorrect boundary regression, especially under frame-level granularity. Second, it is very subjective to judge the completeness of an action from the background. The action is usually complex and diverse, which makes it hard to discern action snippets from backgrounds. Figure 1 illustrates an example of the unclear boundary between the action and the background in some action videos. These two issues impede the accuracy of action localization in the long untrimmed videos.

To precisely detect the actions in the untrimmed videos, many efforts have been made to generate well-anchored temporal proposals and to judge the actionness of the proposals. Grouping sampled snippets of various granularities in a bottom-up manner can generate proposals with vastly varying lengths (*e.g.*, in [42, 47]). However, snippets grouping is much dependent on the selections of the similarity metrics and the threshold, which decides the clearness of the action boundaries. In this paper, we propose an evolving framework in which the boundary of temporal proposals is precisely predicted with a three-phase algorithm. The first phase generates temporal proposals by an Actionness Network (AN) which employs frame-level features. The goal is to discern the actionness of the proposals. The second phase refines the boundaries of these proposals through a Refinement Network (RN) to improve the fidelity of the proposal boundaries. It turns out that coarse-grained temporal boundary regression is more effective and stable. That is, by segmenting a proposal into smaller units, RN adjusts the boundary on these unit-based features. Finally, the adjusted proposals are sent to the third phase, namely Localization Network (LN), to precisely refine the action boundary. With our evolving framework, we demonstrate a significant improvement over those regressed directly from the original proposals.

Our contributions are summarized as follows.

- We propose a novel three-phase evolving temporal proposal framework for action localization using multi-stage temporal coordinate regression under various temporal granularities.
- We exploit unit-based temporal coordinate regression to the boundaries of the proposals to precisely locate the action.
- We use non-local pyramid features to effectively model an action, which is capable of discriminating between completeness and incompleteness of a proposal.
- Our proposed framework outperforms the state-of-the-arts approaches, especially in precise action localization.

The remaining of this paper is organized as follows. Section 2 briefly reviews the literature on temporal action localization and the related topics. Section 3 presents the details of the evolving architecture of our framework. We empirically evaluate our proposed framework in Section 4. Finally, Section 5 concludes this paper.

2 RELATED WORKS

2.1 Action Recognition

Action recognition has been widely studied during last few years. Early works focus on hand-crafted feature engineering. Various features have been invented, for instance, space-time interest points (STIP) [16] and histogram of optical flow (HOF) [17]. With the development of deep neural network, more effective features are extracted using various deep neural networks. Multi-stream features are fused for action recognition and show remarkable performance [34, 41, 45].

2.2 Temporal Action Proposal

Temporal action proposal is the elementary factor in the "*Proposal + Classification*" paradigm. Escorcia *et al.* use LSTM networks to encode a video stream and produce the proposals inside the video stream [5]. Buch *et al.* develop a new effective deep architecture to generate single-stream temporal proposals without dividing the video into short snippets [2]. Gao *et al.* use unit-level temporal coordinate regression to predict the temporal proposals and refine the proposal boudnaries [7]. Gao *et al.* exploit cascaded boundary regression to refine the sliding windows as class-agnostic proposals [6]. Xiong *et al.* propose a learning-based bottom-up proposal generation scheme called temporal actionness grouping (TAG) [42].

2.3 Temporal Action Localization

Action localization aims to predict where an action begins and ends in the untrimmed videos. Shou *et al.* propose a Segment-CNN (S-CNN) proposal network and address temporal action localization by using 3D ConvNets (C3D) features, which involve two stages, namely proposal network and localization network [33]. Xu *et al.* introduce the regional C3D model which uses a three-dimensional fully convolutional network to generate the temporal regions for activity detection [43]. Yeung *et al.* propose an end-to-end learning framework using LSTM and CNN features separately, and reinforcement learning for action localization. However, each module is sub-optimal and the action boundaries are not predicted accurately [46]. Shao *et al.* extend two-stream framework to multi-stream network and uses bi-directional LSTM network to encode temporal information for fine-grained action detection [35]. Ma *et al.* address the problem of early action detection. That is, to train an LSTM network with ranking loss and merge the detection spans based on the frame-wise prediction scores generated by LSTM [25]. Yang *et al.* propose temporal preservation convolutional network (TPC) which preserves temporal resolution but down-samples the spatial resolution simultaneously to detect the activities [44]. Zhao *et al.* propose structured segment network to model activities via structured temporal pyramid [48]. Yuan *et al.* introduce a pyramid of score distribution feature to capture the motion information for action detection [47].

3 EVOLVING TEMPORAL PROPOSALS

We illustrate the evolving architecture and networks of our deep learning framework in Figure 2, which are composed of the following components.

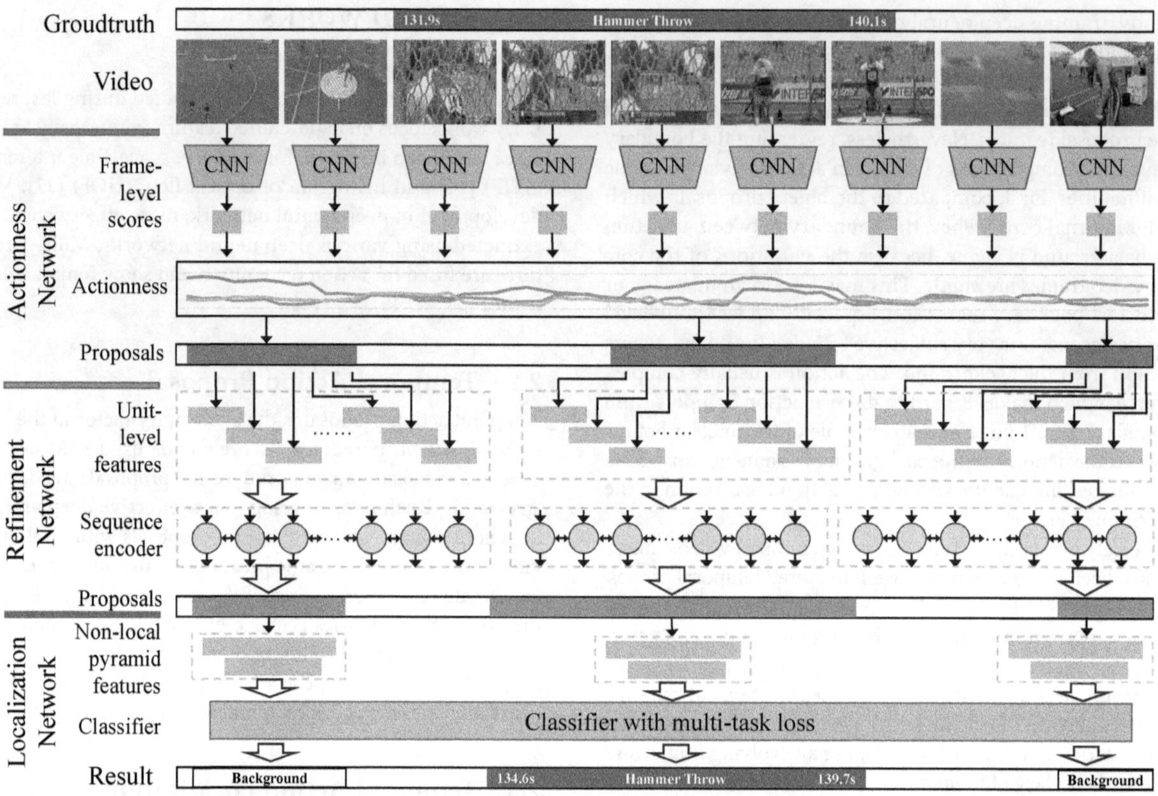

Figure 2: The evolving architecture of our framework. Given a video, we use the Actionness Network to generate initial temporal action proposals. For each proposal, a few video units are extracted and represented by the unit-level features. The features are input to the GRU-based sequence encoder, which produces a refined temporal proposal. The predictions of all proposals are computed in the Localization Network with the non-local pyramid features.

- *Actionness Network* (AN). Each frame of the videos is firstly fed to the network to compute frame-level scores. These actionness scores are used to generate initial proposals.
- *Refinement Network* (RN). This network takes the proposals from AN as input. For a single proposal, several video units are cropped with a fixed stride and length. The unit-level features are extracted and fed into a GRU-based sequence encoder. After connecting to a fully connected layer with the target of proposal position, the corresponding refined temporal proposals are produced.
- *Localization Network* (LN). The LN takes the refined proposals from the previous network as input. Non-local pyramid features are extracted from the proposals and are sent to the classifier with a multi-task loss. The final outputs are the position of evolved temporal proposals and the appropriate scores.

We describe below each individual component in detail.

3.1 Actionness Network

Initial temporal action proposals are produced by this network. *Actionness* is introduced and discussed in [42] as the measure of possibility of a video snippet residing in any activity instance. The concept of actionness is similar to the saliency measurement that indicates the salient visual stimuli for a given image [1, 4, 9, 12, 21–23]. Features used for learning a model of saliency include the low-level features (*e.g.*, orientation and color), mid-level features (*e.g.*, surface and horizon line), and high-level features (*e.g.*, face and objects). The saliency can be divided into *generic* saliency (the degree of uniqueness of the neighborhood w.r.t. entire image) or *class-specific* saliency (the visual characteristics that best distinguish a particular object class from others). For the actionness, previous work [42] handles the generic case by learning the binary classifier. Due to the limited size of the video dataset versus the complexity of the concept actionness, only using a binary classifier may not achieve ideal classification results. Therefore, in this paper we focus on the frame-level class-specific actionness. A classification network is trained based on the frames from the UCF101 dataset [36]. This step accepts arbitrary networks designed for image classification task, and actionness results may benefit from an effective structure. Here we leverage the ResNet architecture [10] by first loading the weights pre-trained on the ImageNet dataset [30] and then fine-tuning on the UCF101 dataset [36]. We denote a video as $X_v = \{x_t | t = 1, ..., T\}$, where T is the number of frames and x_t is the t-th frame. x_t id fed to the classifier to get the action prediction score. The predicted scores from all the frames are stacked and

Algorithm 1 Proposal generation in AN

```
1: Input: Action predict score vectors S^1, S^2, ..., S^K, minimum
   (maximum) length min (max), threshold t
2: Output: Candidate Proposals Set CPSet
3: function PROPOSAL((S^1, S^2, ..., S^K), min, max, t)
4:     Average score vector S^{K+1} = (1/K) Σ_{i=1}^{K} S^i
5:     for k ∈ 1:K + 1 do
6:         PSet_k ←CONNCOMPONENT(S^k, min, max, t)
7:         Ŝ^k ←Smooth(S^k)
8:         PSet'_k ←CONNCOMPONENT(Ŝ^k, min, max, t)
9:         Merge PSet_k, PSet'_k into CPSet
10:    end for
11:    CPSet ← NMS(CPSet)
12:    return CPSet
13: end function
14: function CONNCOMPONENT(S, min, max, t)
15:    Candidate Set CSet ← {{i}|S_i ≥ t}
16:    Proposal Set PSet ← ∅
17:    while |CSet| > 1 do
18:        for C_i ∈ CSet (C_i = {p, ..., q}) do
19:            C_i = {p − 1, p, ..., q, q + 1}
20:        end for
21:        for each pair (C_i, C_j) ∈ CSet do
22:            if C_i ∩ C_j ≠ ∅ then
23:                Remove C_i, C_j from CSet
24:                Expand C_i ∪ C_j to CSet
25:            end if
26:        end for
27:        for C ∈ CSet do
28:            Move C to PSet, if min < |C| < max
29:        end for
30:    end while
31:    return PSet
32: end function
```

form the action score vectors $S^1, S^2, ..., S^K$, where $S^k = [s_1^k, ..., s_T^k]$ and s_t^k is the score of action k for frame t.

To generate initial proposals from these actionness vectors, Algorithm 1 is used. Our basic assumption is that a snippet containing action should consist of frames with the actionness score higher than a threshold. Meanwhile, we observe that action snippets usually have limited durations, therefore the minimum and maximum frame lengths are used. Given the scores, a connected component scheme is devised to merge the neighboring regions with high scores (Line 14-32). Besides the original curve from the action scores, the smooth curve is also applied with Gaussian kernel density estimation (Line 8-9). After that, the proposal set is generated by the non-maximum suppression (NMS) of the candidate snippets.

3.2 Refinement Network

Refining the proposals is important to build an efficient action localization system. While the Actionness Network uses the frame-level information, the Refinement Network considers the context of the short video unit. A unit is represented as $U(s, d) = \{x_i | i = s, s+1, ..., s+d\}$, where X represents the video, s is the starting

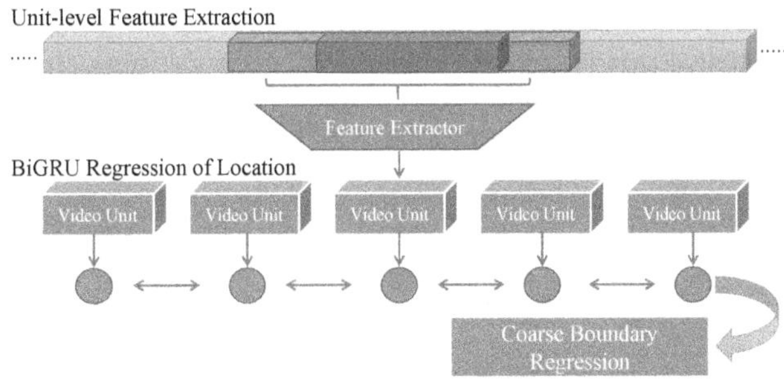

Figure 3: Architecture of Refinement Network. The frame-level features are aggregated to get unit-level feature. Refinement Network walks through the unit-level features of the proposal to regress the coarse boundary.

frames and d is unit length. The borders of the actions are usually vague. As a result, it is hard to train the model for the precise boundary regression. For each video, we generate units by cropping the proposal with a fixed length and stride. Any spatial or temporal features can be used to represent the unit. Here we employ the non-local pyramid features, which will be described in Section 3.3.

Context information will help the network to know how to start and where to end. To keep context information, we follow the pipeline in [48] and augment the range of unit U from $[s, s+d]$ to $[s - \frac{d}{2}, s + d + \frac{d}{2}]$. As actions are usually composed by a set of motions, modeling the unit sequence is essential to the success of Refinement Network. To this end, we leverage an RNN-based sequence encoder. Specifically, we use Bi-directional Gated Recurrent Unit(BiGRU) [31] as the RNN unit to encode the context information.

GRU is the of architecture of recurrent unit that learns to encode a variable-length sequence into a fixed-length code. Figure 3 illustrates the architecture of RN based on GRU. Rather than using five gates in LSTM, GRU has only two gates to control the updates of the hidden units, *i.e.*, *reset* gate r and *update* gate z.

The i-th hidden unit of *reset* gate r_j is computed by:

$$r_j = \sigma([\mathrm{W}_r x]_j + [\mathrm{U}_r h^{\langle t-1 \rangle}]_j) \tag{1}$$

where σ is sigmoid function and $[.]_j$ denotes the j-th element of a vector. The inputs are x and previous state $h^{\langle t-1 \rangle}$, and W_r and U_r are *reset* gate weights.

The computation of *update* gate z is similar, which is:

$$z_j = \sigma([\mathrm{W}_z x]_j + [\mathrm{U}_z h^{\langle t-1 \rangle}]_j) \tag{2}$$

The activation of hidden unit h_j is computed by

$$h_j^{\langle t \rangle} = z_j h_j^{\langle t-1 \rangle} + (1 - z_j)\hat{h}_j^{\langle t \rangle} \tag{3}$$

where

$$\hat{h}_j^{\langle t \rangle} = \phi([\mathrm{W}x]_j + [\mathrm{U}(r \odot h^{\langle t-1 \rangle}]_j)$$

We define three types of proposals based on Intersection-over-Union (IoU) with its groundtruth: positive proposals with IoU > 0.7, incomplete proposals with $0.3 \leq$ IoU < 0.7, and background proposals with IoU<0.1. During training, both input proposals and the target boundary coordinates are first fit to the applicable video unit. The unit-level features are encoded one by one through the

BiGRU network. A full-connected layer then receives the output from BiGRU and is used to regress the localization. Parameter coordinate offset is used for regression. The Refinement Network regresses both interval center and proposal span. The regression loss is defined as

$$L_{loc} = \frac{1}{N}\sum_{i=1}^{N} \text{smooth}_{L_1}(c) + \text{smooth}_{L_1}(s), \quad (4)$$

where $c = \frac{c_{gt}-c_{unit}}{l_{unit}}$ is the interval center, $s = log\frac{l_{gt}}{l_{unit}}$ is the proposal span, $N = N_{pos} + N_{inc}$ (positive and incomplete proposals are considered), and $\text{smooth}_{L_1}(\cdot)$ is the smooth-L_1 loss. Here c_y and l_y are the center frame and length of the groundtruth ($y = gt$) or video snippet ($y = unit$).

3.3 Localization Network

Localization Network is responsible for producing the evolved temporal proposals and the scores. Ideally, the network not only finds the recognized action and the precise action proposals, but also decides whether an proposal is the action or the background. To this end, we adopt the structured segment networks (SSN) [48] as the backbone. Specifically, the temporal proposals from Refinement Network are augmented with three stages, *i.e.*, *starting*, *course*, and *ending*. The structured temporal pyramid features are then calculated in the SSN framework. Inspired by the application of non-local neural network for video classification [40], we extend the representation by adding a non-local block before the last layer. The non-local operation is defined as:

$$\mathbf{y}_i = \frac{1}{C(\mathbf{x})}\sum_{\forall j} f(\mathbf{x}_i, \mathbf{x}_j)g(\mathbf{x}_j), \quad (5)$$

where $\mathbf{x}$ and $\mathbf{y}$ are the input and the output signals respectively, $\forall j$ indicates the non-local behaviour for all positions in the frame, $g(\cdot)$ is the representation, and $f(\mathbf{x}_i, \mathbf{x}_j) = \theta(\mathbf{x}_i)^T\phi(\mathbf{x}_j)$ is the dot-product similarity function between $\mathbf{x}_i$ and $\mathbf{x}_j$. To avoid breaking the existing models, the non-local block is added with the residual connection [10]. We denote the representations as *non-local pyramid features*. We will show in our experiments that this feature is superior to directly extracting the structured temporal pyramid features. Based on the features, the multi-task loss is used to train the Localization Network.

Action Classification. Positive and background proposals are used to train a classifier with K classes for actions and 1 for background. We randomly sample the positive and background proposals to make the ratio around 1:1 to avoid data imbalance. Cross entropy loss is used as follows,

$$L_{cls} = \frac{1}{N_{tr}}\sum_{i=1}^{N_{tr}} -log(p_i^k) \quad (6)$$

$$p_i^k = \exp(s_i^k)/\sum_j \exp(s_i^j). \quad (7)$$

where N_{tr} is the number of training samples, and s_i^j is the score of action j for proposal i.

Completeness Evaluation. Only a few proposals will match the groundtruth instance. A binary classifier is used to predict a value s_{comp} to represent whether the proposal is background or an action component, which plays an important role during evaluation in ranking the proposals. Positive and incomplete proposals are used to train this task. we use the online hard example mining strategy to overcome imbalance of dataset and improve classifier performance. We put positive proposals and incomplete proposals with a ratio of 1:4. During the training we only choose the first 1/4 incomplete proposal examples according to loss value to train loss with positive proposals. The Hinge loss is applied:

$$L_{comp} = \frac{1}{N_{tr}}\sum_{i=1}^{N_{tr}} \max(0, 1 - c_i \cdot p_i) \quad (8)$$

where c_i indicates whether the i-th proposal is positive proposal ($c_i = 1$) or incomplete proposal ($c_i = -1$), and p_i is the probability that proposal i is an action component.

Localization Regression. The loss function in Equation (4) is used. Different from Refinement Network, this step only uses the positive proposals for boundary fine-tuning. Therefore, $N = N_{pos}$ is set for Equation (4).

The overall multi-task loss function in Localization Network is defined as

$$L = L_{cls} + \alpha L_{comp} + \beta L_{loc}. \quad (9)$$

We set α and β to 0.1 in our experiments. Based on the multi-task loss, the normalized classification score p_{cls}^k (see Equation (7)) and completeness score s_{comp} are computed for a given proposal. The final ranking score for action k is $s^k = p_{cls}^k \cdot \exp(s_{comp})$.

4 EXPERIMENTS

In this section, we evaluate the effectiveness of the proposed framework on the action localization benchmarks. We first introduce the evaluation datasets and the experimental setup, and then evaluate the performance of the proposed framework and compare it with several state-of-the-art approaches. Finally, we discuss the effect of parameters and components. We denote our approach as **ETP** (**E**volving **T**emporal **P**roposals).

4.1 Dataset and Evaluation Metric

We conduct the experiments on the THUMOS Challenge 2014 dataset (THUMOS14) [11]. The whole dataset contains 1010 videos for validation and 1,574 videos for testing. For the temporal action localization task, only 200 validation-set videos and 213 testing-set videos with temporal annotations of 20 action classes are provided. The UCF101 dataset [36] is appointed as the official training set. As the videos in UCF101 are trimmed, we train our framework on the THUMOS14 validation set and then evaluate on the testing set.

The mean average precision (mAP) at different IoU thresholds α are reported. Following recent works for precise temporal action localization [32, 44], we consider the thresholds α of {0.3, 0.4, 0.5, 0.6, 0.7}, and the mAP at $\alpha = 0.5$ is used for comparing different approaches.

Figure 4: Visualization of the action instances by our proposed approach on THUMOS14 dataset.

4.2 Experimental Settings

Training. We implment our approach based on PyTorch[1]. In the Actionness Network, we use the ResNet-34 [10] to extract the frame-level class-specific actionness scores. The ResNet-34 network is pre-trained on ImageNet dataset and then fine-tuned on the UCF101 dataset. Random horizontal flip and random center crop are used for data augmentation.

We use 2 BiGRU cells with 512 hidden values as RNN units to build the Refinement Network. The training batch size is 128 and it has $20K$ iterations. Only the positive and incomplete proposals are used as the training samples. We use SGD as the optimizer to train the network with momentum 0.9. The base learning rate of the network is 0.1 with the decay rate 0.1 to decrease the learning rate at every $5K$ iterations.

In Localization Network, the feature extraction is based on Inception V3 [37] with batch normalization pre-trained on Kinetics Human Action Video dataset [15]. Both spatial and temporal flow networks are trained using SGD with momentum 0.9. The network is trained for $90K$ iterations with the learning rate of 0.1 and scaled down by 0.1 every $5K$ iterations until the learning rate is less than 10^{-5}.

Inference. During testing phase, the initial proposals are generated by Algorithm 1. The Refinement Network is then used for coarse regression of the proposals, which are sent to Localization Network to enhance the boundary regression and predicted action classes. The choice of NMS threshold has important influences on testing results. To achieve precise localization results with higher IoU thresholds, we empirically set the NMS threshold to 0.36.

[1] http://pytorch.org/

4.3 Comparison with State-of-the-arts

We first evaluate the overall results of our proposed framework for action localization and compare them with several state-of-the-art approaches. There are a few parameters in ETP, including the lengths of units in the Refinement Network, and feature types in the Actionness Network and the Localization Network. In our experiments, we set 64 frames for unit length, and extract the non-local pyramid features. The effects of these parameters, as well as the components of the framework, will be evaluated in Section 4.4.

Table 1 summarizes the mAPs of all action classes in THUMOS14. We compare ETP with the results during the challenge [26, 39] and state-of-the-art approaches. From Table 1 we can see that when $\alpha = 0.5$, ETP outperforms all the challenge results as well as the state-of-the-art approaches shown in the middle part of Table 1, including the actionness based approach TAG [42], the Convolutional-De-Convolutional Networks [32], the Cascaded Boundary Regression models [6], and a very recent Temporal Preservation Networks [44]. The substantial performance gains over the previous works under different IoU thresholds confirm the effectiveness of our evolving temporal proposals for precise temporal action localization. Table 2 further shows the per-class results at $\alpha = 0.5$ for our approach and several previous works (Yeung *et al.* [46], S-CNN [33],

Table 1: Action detection results on THUMOS14 (in %). mAP at different IoU thresholds α are reported. The results are sorted in ascending order of the performances at $\alpha = 0.5$. '-' indicates the results are not available in the corresponding papers. Bold faces are the top results while underlines correspond to the second runners-up.

IoU thresholds α	0.3	0.4	0.5	0.6	0.7
Wang *et al.* [39]	14.6	12.1	8.5	4.7	1.5
Oneata *et al.* [26]	28.8	21.8	15.0	8.5	3.2
Heilbron *et al.* [3]	-	-	13.5	-	-
Escorcia *et al.* [5]	-	-	13.9	-	-
Richard and Gall [29]	30.0	23.2	15.2	-	-
Yeung *et al.* [46]	36.0	26.4	17.1	-	-
PSDF [47]	33.6	26.1	18.8	-	-
S-CNN [33]	36.3	28.7	19.0	10.3	5.3
Conv & De-conv [32]	38.6	28.2	22.4	12.0	7.5
CDC [32]	40.1	29.4	23.3	13.1	7.9
SSAD [18]	43.0	35.0	24.6	-	-
TPC+S-CNN [44]	41.9	32.5	25.3	14.7	9.0
TURN TAP [7]	44.1	34.9	25.6	-	-
TPC+FGM [44]	44.1	37.1	28.2	20.6	12.7
TAG [42]	48.7	39.8	28.2	-	-
R-C3D [43]	44.8	35.6	28.9	-	-
SSN [48]	**51.9**	41.0	29.8	-	-
CBR [6]	50.1	41.3	31.0	19.1	9.9
ETP [ours]	48.2	**42.4**	**34.2**	**23.4**	**13.9**

Table 2: Per-class AP at $\alpha = 0.5$ on THUMOS14 (in %).

	[46]	[33]	[43]	Ours
BaseballPitch	14.6	14.9	**26.1**	22.5
BasketballDunk	6.3	20.1	**54.0**	30.3
Billiards	**9.4**	7.6	8.3	8.1
CleanAndJerk	**42.8**	24.8	27.9	40.9
CliffDiving	15.6	27.5	**49.2**	16.7
CricketBowling	10.8	15.7	**30.6**	16.3
CricketShot	3.5	**13.8**	10.9	7.2
Diving	10.8	17.6	26.2	**50.9**
FrisbeeCatch	10.4	15.3	**20.1**	2.3
GolfSwing	13.8	18.2	16.1	**44.4**
HammerThrow	28.9	19.1	43.2	**71.7**
HighJump	33.3	20.0	30.9	**51.2**
JavelinThrow	20.4	18.2	47.0	**47.3**
LongJump	39.0	34.8	57.4	**81.9**
PoleVault	16.3	32.1	42.7	**56.5**
Shotput	16.6	12.1	19.4	**32.0**
SoccerPenalty	8.3	19.2	15.8	**19.7**
TennisSwing	5.6	19.3	16.6	**29.1**
ThrowDiscus	29.5	24.4	29.2	**39.1**
VolleyballSpiking	5.2	4.6	5.6	**14.0**
mAP@0.5	17.1	19.0	28.9	**34.2**

and R-C3D [43]). Notably, our approach performs the best on 12 action classes and shows significant improvement (by more than 20% absolute AP over the next best) for 10 actions such as Diving, High Jump, Pole Vault, and Long Jump. Figure 4 illustrates some prediction results for these actions respectively.

Table 3: mAP from different modalities.

IoU thresholds α	0.3	0.4	0.5	0.6	0.7
RGB	39.9	33.7	25.3	16.1	8.6
Flow	34.8	30.4	25.0	18.0	10.7
RGB+Flow	**48.2**	**42.4**	**34.2**	**23.4**	**13.9**

4.4 Ablation Study

In this part, the control experiments of switching off different components of the proposed framework are conducted.

Effect of Refinement Network We first evaluate the effect of the Refinement Network over the whole framework. Figure 5 gives the comparison of all the action classes with the pipeline that the outputs of Actionness Network are directly sent to Localization Network. There are 13 categories with performance gains after incorporating with Refinement Network and the overall AP is increased by 1.3%.

Unit Length in RN. We also evaluate the setting of the video unit length in the Refinement Network. The lengths of {16,32,64,128} are tested, and the stride is set to half of the length. In Figure 7 we plot the localization results versus the video unit length and the IoU thresholds α. Using the length of 16 frames per video unit, we can already get the mAP of 32.6% when IoU threshold $\alpha = 0.5$, which already outperforms previous works. We observe significant performance gains when the length increases from 16 to 32, after which the performance tends to be saturated. There is a performance drop when the unit length is 128, and we conjecture that a larger unit length may not be the one at which the GRU-based sequence encoder responds with optimal context information.

Non-local Pyramid Features. Recall that the non-local pyramid features by adding a non-local residual block, based on the non-local operation shown in Equation (5). In Figure 6 we report the detailed localization results for each action learned using the non-local pyramid features as well as the structured temporal pyramid features in [48]. For 16 action classes we achieve higher AP values, which is consistent with the observations from previous work [40].

Video Modality. Our last experiment evaluates the effect of different modalities for temporal action localization. The results are shown in Table 3. The RGB modality achieves a higher mAP when the IoU threshold α is smaller, and the Flow modality tends to be better after increasing α. As shown in Table 3, using both modalities leads to performance gains for all IoU thresholds.

5 CONCLUSIONS

In this paper, we have proposed the Evolving Temporal Proposals (ETP), a framework with three components (*i.e.*, Actionness Network, Refinement Network, and Localization Network) to generate temporal proposals for precise action localization in the untrimmed videos. Through empirical temporal action localization experiments,

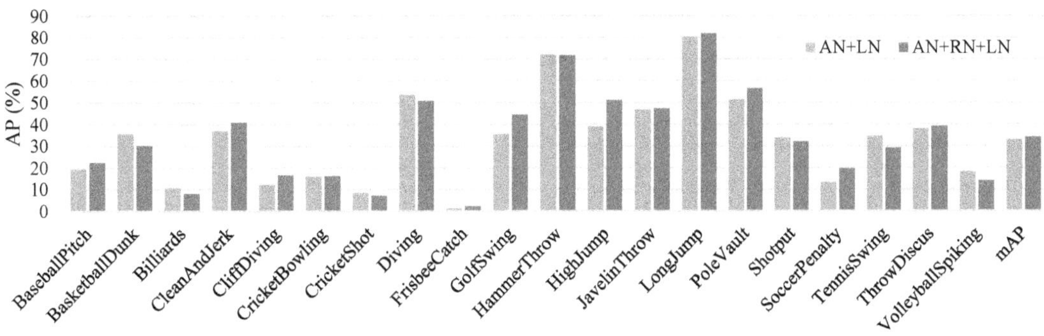

Figure 5: Per-class AP@α = 0.5 with incorporating of Refinement Network.

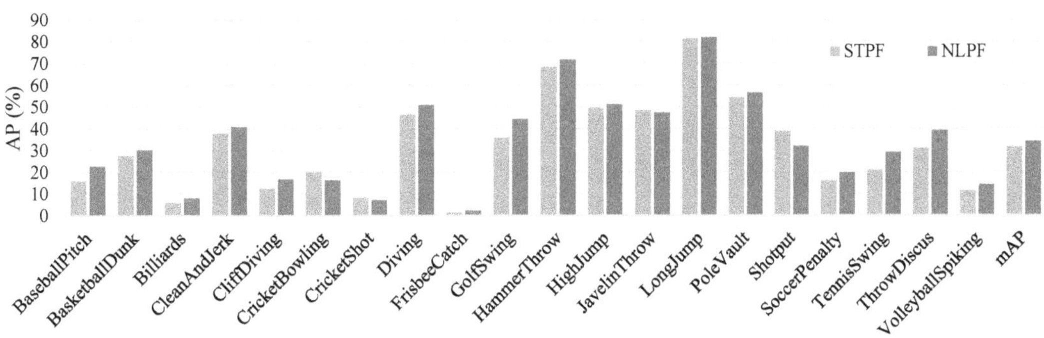

Figure 6: Per-class AP@α = 0.5 w.r.t. various features (STPF: structured temporal pyramid features; NLPF: non-local pyramid features).

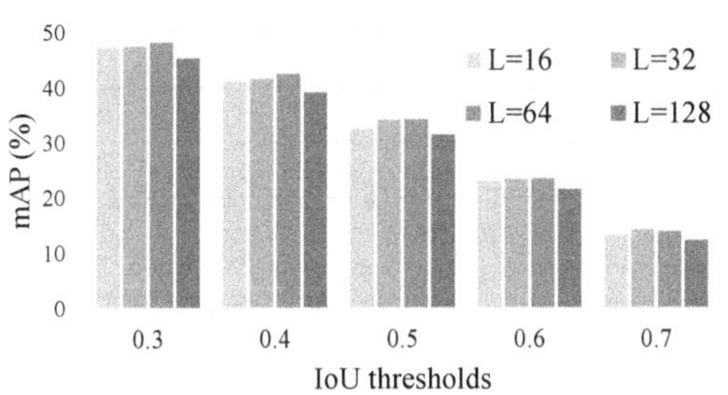

Figure 7: Evaluation of the ETP framework with different video unit lengths in Refinement Network on THUMOS14.

we have shown that ETP is more effective than previous systems by generating very competitive results on the THUMOS14 dataset. We leverage the non-local pyramid features to effectively model the activity, which improves the discriminative ablity between completeness and incompleteness of a proposal. For future work, we plan to optimize the inference procedure of the proposed framework, and explore the one-stream video action localization.

ACKNOWLEDGMENTS

This work was supported in part by the National Natural Science Foundation of China under Grants 61602459 and 61375016, and in part by the Science and Technology Commission of Shanghai Municipality under Grant 17511101902.

REFERENCES

[1] Bogdan Alexe, Thomas Deselaers, and Vittorio Ferrari. 2010. What is an object?. In *IEEE Conference on Computer Vision and Pattern Recognition (CVPR)*.

[2] Shyamal Buch, Victor Escorcia, Chuanqi Shen, Bernard Ghanem, and Juan Carlos Niebles. 2017. SST: Single-Stream Temporal Action Proposals. In *IEEE Conference on Computer Vision and Pattern Recognition (CVPR)*.

[3] Fabian Caba Heilbron, Juan Carlos Niebles, and Bernard Ghanem. 2016. Fast Temporal Activity Proposals for Efficient Detection of Human Actions in Untrimmed Videos. In *IEEE Conference on Computer Vision and Pattern Recognition (CVPR)*.

[4] Ming-Ming Cheng, Ziming Zhang, Wen-Yan Lin, and Philip Torr. 2014. BING: Binarized Normed Gradients for Objectness Estimation at 300fps. In *IEEE Conference on Computer Vision and Pattern Recognition (CVPR)*. 3286–3293.

[5] Victor Escorcia, Fabian Caba Heilbron, Juan Carlos Niebles, and Bernard Ghanem. 2016. DAPs: Deep Action Proposals for Action Understanding. In *European Conference on Computer Vision (ECCV)*.

[6] Jiyang Gao, Zhenheng Yang, and Ram Nevatia. 2017. Cascaded Boundary Regression for Temporal Action Detection. *arXiv:1705.01180* (2017).

[7] Jiyang Gao, Zhenheng Yang, Chen Sun, Kan Chen, and Ram Nevatia. 2017. TURN TAP: Temporal Unit Regression Network for Temporal Action Proposals. In *International Conference on Computer Vision (ICCV)*. 3648–3656.

[8] Ross Girshick, Jeff Donahue, Trevor Darrell, and Jitendra Malik. 2014. Rich feature hierarchies for accurate object detection and semantic segmentation. In *IEEE Conference on Computer Vision and Pattern Recognition (CVPR)*. 580–587.

[9] Jonathan Harel, Christof Koch, and Pietro Perona. 2006. Graph-Based Visual Saliency. In *Neural Information Processing Systems (NIPS)*.

[10] Kaiming He, Xiangyu Zhang, Shaoqing Ren, and Jian Sun. 2016. Deep residual learning for image recognition. In *IEEE Conference on Computer Vision and Pattern Recognition (CVPR)*. 770–778.

[11] Haroon Idrees, Amir R Zamir, Yu-Gang Jiang, Alex Gorban, Ivan Laptev, Rahul Sukthankar, and Mubarak Shah. 2017. The THUMOS challenge on action recognition for videos "in the wild". *Computer Vision and Image Understanding* 155 (2017), 1–23.

[12] Laurent Itti and Christof Koch. 2001. Computational modelling of visual attention. *Nature Reviews Neuroscience* 2, 3 (2001), 194.

[13] Huaizu Jiang and Erik Learned-Miller. 2017. Face Detection with the Faster R-CNN. In *IEEE International Conference on Automatic Face Gesture Recognition (FG)*. 650–657.

[14] Yu-Gang Jiang, Yanran Wang, Rui Feng, Xiangyang Xue, Yingbin Zheng, and Hanfang Yang. 2013. Understanding and Predicting Interestingness of Videos. In *AAAI Conference on Artificial Intelligence (AAAI)*.

[15] Will Kay, Joao Carreira, Karen Simonyan, Brian Zhang, Chloe Hillier, Sudheendra Vijayanarasimhan, Fabio Viola, Tim Green, Trevor Back, Paul Natsev, Mustafa Suleyman, and Andrew Zisserman. 2017. The kinetics human action video dataset. *arXiv:1705.06950* (2017).

[16] Ivan Laptev. 2005. On space-time interest points. *International Journal of Computer Vision* 64, 2-3 (2005), 107–123.

[17] Ivan Laptev, Marcin Marszalek, Cordelia Schmid, and Benjamin Rozenfeld. 2008. Learning realistic human actions from movies. In *IEEE Conference on Computer Vision and Pattern Recognition (CVPR)*.

[18] Tianwei Lin, Xu Zhao, and Zheng Shou. 2017. Single Shot Temporal Action Detection. In *ACM International Conference on Multimedia (MM)*.

[19] Wei Liu, Dragomir Anguelov, Dumitru Erhan, Christian Szegedy, Scott Reed, Cheng-Yang Fu, and Alexander C Berg. 2016. Ssd: Single shot multibox detector. In *European Conference on Computer Vision (ECCV)*. 21–37.

[20] Yao Lu, Aakanksha Chowdhery, and Srikanth Kandula. 2016. Optasia: A relational platform for efficient large-scale video analytics. In *ACM Symposium on Cloud Computing (SoCC)*.

[21] Yao Lu and Linda G Shapiro. 2017. Closing the Loop for Edge Detection and Object Proposals. In *AAAI Conference on Artificial Intelligence (AAAI)*. 4204–4210.

[22] Yao Lu, Wei Zhang, Cheng Jin, and Xiangyang Xue. 2012. Learning attention map from images. In *IEEE Conference on Computer Vision and Pattern Recognition (CVPR)*. 1067–1074.

[23] Yao Lu, Wei Zhang, Hong Lu, and Xiangyang Xue. 2011. Salient object detection using concavity context. In *International Conference on Computer Vision (ICCV)*. 233–240.

[24] Jianqi Ma, Weiyuan Shao, Hao Ye, Li Wang, Hong Wang, Yingbin Zheng, and Xiangyang Xue. 2018. Arbitrary-Oriented Scene Text Detection via Rotation Proposals. *IEEE Transactions on Multimedia* (2018).

[25] Shugao Ma, Leonid Sigal, and Stan Sclaroff. 2016. Learning activity progression in lstms for activity detection and early detection. In *IEEE Conference on Computer Vision and Pattern Recognition (CVPR)*. 1942–1950.

[26] Dan Oneata, Jakob Verbeek, and Cordelia Schmid. 2014. The LEAR submission at Thumos 2014. In *ECCV THUMOS Workshop*.

[27] Joseph Redmon, Santosh Divvala, Ross Girshick, and Ali Farhadi. 2016. You only look once: Unified, real-time object detection. In *IEEE Conference on Computer Vision and Pattern Recognition (CVPR)*. 779–788.

[28] Shaoqing Ren, Kaiming He, Ross Girshick, and Jian Sun. 2015. Faster R-CNN: Towards real-time object detection with region proposal networks. In *Neural Information Processing Systems (NIPS)*. 91–99.

[29] Alexander Richard and Juergen Gall. 2016. Temporal Action Detection Using a Statistical Language Model. In *IEEE Conference on Computer Vision and Pattern Recognition (CVPR)*.

[30] Olga Russakovsky, Jia Deng, Hao Su, Jonathan Krause, Sanjeev Satheesh, Sean Ma, Zhiheng Huang, Andrej Karpathy, Aditya Khosla, Michael Bernstein, Alexander C. Berg, and Li Fei-Fei. 2015. ImageNet Large Scale Visual Recognition Challenge. *International Journal of Computer Vision* 115, 3 (2015), 211–252.

[31] Mike Schuster and Kuldip K Paliwal. 1997. Bidirectional recurrent neural networks. *IEEE Transactions on Signal Processing* 45, 11 (1997), 2673–2681.

[32] Zheng Shou, Jonathan Chan, Alireza Zareian, Kazuyuki Miyazawa, and Shih-Fu Chang. 2017. CDC: Convolutional-De-Convolutional Networks for Precise Temporal Action Localization in Untrimmed Videos. In *IEEE Conference on Computer Vision and Pattern Recognition (CVPR)*.

[33] Zheng Shou, Dongang Wang, and Shih-Fu Chang. 2016. Temporal Action Localization in Untrimmed Videos via Multi-Stage CNNs. In *IEEE Conference on Computer Vision and Pattern Recognition (CVPR)*.

[34] Karen Simonyan and Andrew Zisserman. 2014. Two-stream convolutional networks for action recognition in videos. In *Neural Information Processing Systems (NIPS)*. 568–576.

[35] Bharat Singh, Tim K Marks, Michael Jones, Oncel Tuzel, and Ming Shao. 2016. A multi-stream bi-directional recurrent neural network for fine-grained action detection. In *IEEE Conference on Computer Vision and Pattern Recognition (CVPR)*. 1961–1970.

[36] Khurram Soomro, Amir Roshan Zamir, and Mubarak Shah. 2012. UCF101: A dataset of 101 human actions classes from videos in the wild. *arXiv:1212.0402* (2012).

[37] Christian Szegedy, Vincent Vanhoucke, Sergey Ioffe, Jon Shlens, and Zbigniew Wojna. 2016. Rethinking the inception architecture for computer vision. In *IEEE Conference on Computer Vision and Pattern Recognition (CVPR)*. 2818–2826.

[38] Li Wang, Yao Lu, Hong Wang, Yingbin Zheng, Hao Ye, and Xiangyang Xue. 2017. Evolving Boxes for fast Vehicle Detection. In *IEEE International Conference on Multimedia & Expo (ICME)*. 1135–1140.

[39] Limin Wang, Yu Qiao, and Xiaoou Tang. 2014. Action Recognition and Detection by Combining Motion and Appearance Features. In *ECCV THUMOS Workshop*.

[40] Xiaolong Wang, Ross Girshick, Abhinav Gupta, and Kaiming He. 2017. Non-local Neural Networks. *arXiv:1711.07971* (2017).

[41] Zuxuan Wu, Yu-Gang Jiang, Xi Wang, Hao Ye, and Xiangyang Xue. 2016. Multi-stream multi-class fusion of deep networks for video classification. In *ACM International Conference on Multimedia (MM)*. 791–800.

[42] Yuanjun Xiong, Yue Zhao, Limin Wang, Dahua Lin, and Xiaoou Tang. 2017. A Pursuit of Temporal Accuracy in General Activity Detection. *arXiv:1703.02716* (2017).

[43] Huijuan Xu, Abir Das, and Kate Saenko. 2017. R-C3D: Region Convolutional 3D Network for Temporal Activity Detection. In *International Conference on Computer Vision (ICCV)*.

[44] Ke Yang, Peng Qiao, Dongsheng Li, Shaohe Lv, and Yong Dou. 2017. Exploring Temporal Preservation Networks for Precise Temporal Action Localization. *arXiv:1708.03280* (2017).

[45] Hao Ye, Zuxuan Wu, Rui-Wei Zhao, Xi Wang, Yu-Gang Jiang, and Xiangyang Xue. 2015. Evaluating two-stream CNN for video classification. In *ACM International Conference on Multimedia Retrieval (ICMR)*. 435–442.

[46] Serena Yeung, Olga Russakovsky, Greg Mori, and Li Fei-Fei. 2016. End-To-End Learning of Action Detection From Frame Glimpses in Videos. In *IEEE Conference on Computer Vision and Pattern Recognition (CVPR)*.

[47] Jun Yuan, Bingbing Ni, Xiaokang Yang, and Ashraf A Kassim. 2016. Temporal Action Localization with Pyramid of Score Distribution Features. In *IEEE Conference on Computer Vision and Pattern Recognition (CVPR)*.

[48] Yue Zhao, Yuanjun Xiong, Limin Wang, Zhirong Wu, Xiaoou Tang, and Dahua Lin. 2017. Temporal Action Detection With Structured Segment Networks. In *International Conference on Computer Vision (ICCV)*.

[49] Yingbin Zheng, Renzhong Wei, Hong Lu, and Xiangyang Xue. 2010. Semantic Video Indexing by Fusing Explicit and Implicit Context Spaces. In *ACM International Conference on Multimedia (MM)*. 967–970.

Image Selection in Photo Albums

Dmitry Kuzovkin
Technicolor, IRISA,
University of Rennes 1
Rennes, France
dmitry.kuzovkin@technicolor.com

Tania Pouli
Technicolor
Rennes, France
tania.pouli@technicolor.com

Rémi Cozot
IRISA, University of Rennes 1
Rennes, France
remi.cozot@irisa.fr

Olivier Le Meur
IRISA, University of Rennes 1
Rennes, France
olivier.le_meur@irisa.fr

Jonathan Kervec
Technicolor
Rennes, France
jonathan.kervec@technicolor.com

Kadi Bouatouch
IRISA, University of Rennes 1
Rennes, France
kadi.bouatouch@irisa.fr

ABSTRACT

The selection of the best photos in personal albums is a task that is often faced by photographers. This task can become laborious when the photo collection is large and it contains multiple similar photos. Recent advances on image aesthetics and photo importance evaluation has led to the creation of different metrics for automatically assessing a given image. However, these metrics are intended for the independent assessment of an image, without considering the possible context implicitly present within photo albums. In this work, we perform a user study for assessing how users select photos when provided with a complete photo album⊠ a task that better reflects how users may review their personal photos and collections. Using the data provided by our study, we evaluate how existing state-of-the-art photo assessment methods perform relative to user selection, focusing in particular on deep learning based approaches. Finally, we explore a recent framework for adapting independent image scores to collections and evaluate in which scenarios such an adaptation can prove beneficial.

KEYWORDS

Photo selection, Image aesthetics, Image quality

ACM Reference Format:
Dmitry Kuzovkin, Tania Pouli, Rémi Cozot, Olivier Le Meur, Jonathan Kervec, and Kadi Bouatouch. 2018. Image Selection in Photo Albums. In *ICMR ⊠18: 2018 International Conference on Multimedia Retrieval, June 11⊠14, 2018, Yokohama, Japan.* ACM, New York, NY, USA, 8 pages. https://doi.org/10.1145/3206025.3206077

1 INTRODUCTION

Casual photography has in recent years become an essential part of everyday life, where people tend to document each moment of their life through a photo. Not restricted by storage limitations or camera availability, users often take numerous photos of the same life moment. This is further exaggerated by functionalities such as the burst mode available on most modern smartphones, which produce dozens of nearly identical images to ensure that the perfect moment or expression is optimally captured. As a result, users often evade the responsibility of taking one best shot during the action of photo capture itself. Eventually, they might obtain an extremely large collection of photos, where for each significant moment, the best shot has to be chosen among many similar photos.

Assessment of photographs in a photo album is a non-trivial task. The selection of the best photos is a subjective process that is also highly affected by the photo album context. For instance, a particular photo might appear of low quality when observed in an isolated manner, while inside the belonging album, the same photo may be the best candidate when compared with other similar photos. Thus, the selection of photos in the album is, to a large extent, a comparison-based process.

To facilitate and eventually automate this time-consuming task, computational modelling of these human decisions would be necessary. Recent progress in computer vision and machine learning techniques has led to a wealth of image assessment techniques [8, 20, 26, 28, 29, 31], where an image is usually assigned a ranking score, or a label of high or low aesthetics. Going a step further, certain works have attempted to analyze and understand the image features and general characteristics that affect people's decisions regarding aesthetic quality or beauty of a photograph [16, 30, 41]. Among other applications, automatic image assessment can be used to assist different tasks, such as image retrieval [12, 15] or automatic video thumbnailing [37].

Although such approaches could help guide automatic photo selection or rating decisions, a few major drawbacks limit their usefulness when applied to users' photo collections. By their nature, such methods are typically trained or optimized on large, general collections accumulating photographs from multiple users. As such, they inherently represent average user preferences modeled over a large variety of content. Further, the models or features learned in such methods are often biased towards professional level photographs, as these types of images are likely to be preferred by the average user when faced with a varied selection of photographs. Finally, the evaluation of each photo is performed independently, where possible connections to other similar photos in the collection are not taken into account.

ICMR ⊠18, June 11⊠14, 2018, Yokohama, Japan

ACM ISBN 978-1-4503-5046-4/18/06...$15.00
https://doi.org/10.1145/3206025.3206077

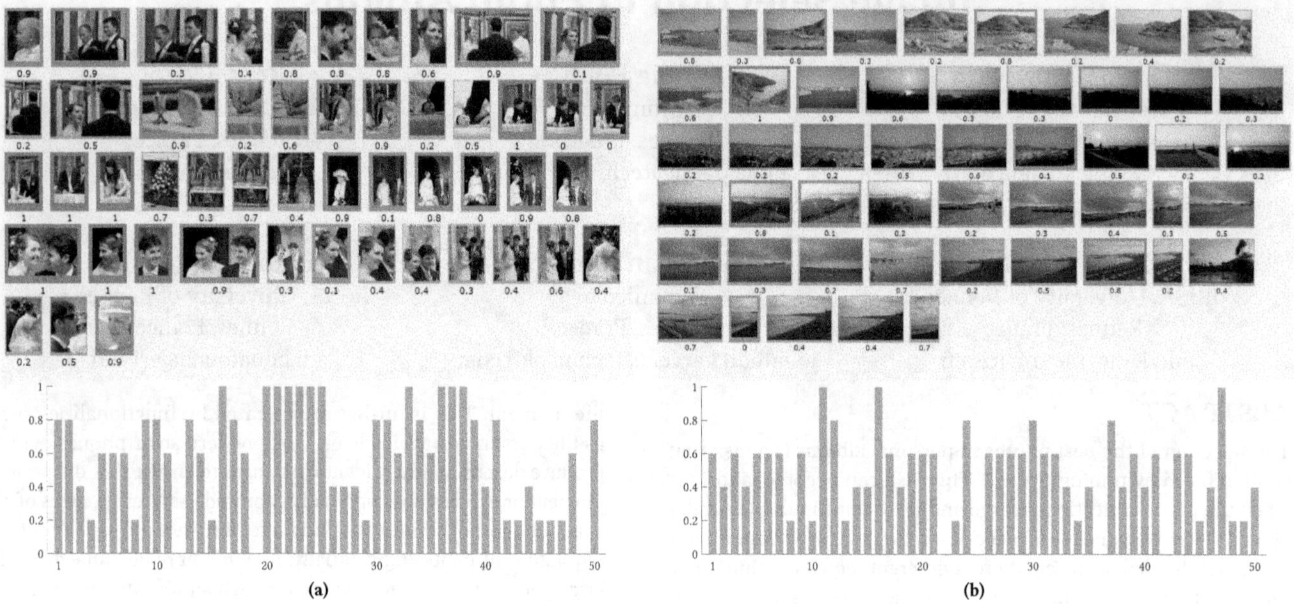

Figure 1: Demonstration of two albums from our user study (*Family event 1* and *Travel album 2*), with a visualization of user preferences shown around each image and confidence bar charts, which indicate confidence of user preferences. (a) Family event with high confidence of user selections. As it can be seen, in the albums with people's photos, users tend to agree more in their selections. (b) Travel album with lower confidence of user selections. In the albums with landscape photos, users tend to agree less.

Given the above limitations, classic approaches for photo aesthetics assessment can be directly applied to more general tasks, such as image retrieval, but may be less capable to reproduce user selections within a photo album, which is the focus of our work. A framework was recently proposed for adapting a general image quality or aesthetics score to the context of a collection [23]. By clustering images according to their degree of similarity, individual image scores could be scaled, such that final selection preferred images that were the best in their cluster, even if they were assessed as being low quality independently. Nevertheless, this framework was demonstrated only using a sharpness metric as an independent assessment criterion, which covers only one of a multitude of image characteristics considered both by users and image aesthetics models [30, 43].

To better define how to assess images within the context of their surrounding collection, a deeper understanding of the behavior of users when faced with this task is necessary. To that end, we perform a user study, where, for a variety of photo albums, users have to place themselves in the role of the photographer and identify the images they would like to keep. Our study considers photo albums covering typical scenarios from vacation albums to specific events such as weddings or birthday parties, allowing us to analyze user behavior and cross-user agreement across different situations. Based on this data, we evaluate existing approaches to assess their suitability for selecting photos within collections in a manner consistent with user preferences. Our evaluation considers several state-of-the-art deep-learning methods for image assessment applied to images independently, as well as their adaption with a clustering-based framework [23].

2 RELATED WORK

Photo selection is a complex task, where a selection decision depends on objective characteristics of image quality (e.g. sharpness, dynamic range and presence of artifacts), on subjectively perceived attributes, which make an image attractive (e.g. photo composition and color style), and on semantic aspects, such as presence of important people in a photo and their face expressions [2, 30, 41].

To model human preferences in image evaluation, machine learning techniques are often used as they can learn from pre-evaluated data. Hand-crafted features and different types of image descriptors have been used by several approaches to guide the image analysis and evaluation [8, 28, 31, 32, 35, 36, 39]. Similar to the factors that affect user decisions, such hand-crafted features may be inspired by photography practices or can take the form of more objective quality metrics. However, these features are not fully capable of modeling and predicting the complex and highly subjective notion of aesthetics, which tends to limit their performance in image evaluation.

To encompass higher level concepts that may influence how people evaluate images, methods for assessing image memorability and interestingness were proposed. The term of memorability is linked with the likelihood that a user will recognize the same photograph after a certain time delay [16, 19]. The term of interestingness is linked with the ability of a certain image or video to draw attention of a user to its content and keep this attention for an extent of time [9, 13]. Such methods are primarily concerned with evaluating the effect a new, unseen image might have to a user, and hence, they might be not directly applicable to the image selection task.

A more recent trend in photo aesthetics assessment is represented by the wealth of deep learning based methods [4, 17, 20, 26, 27, 29, 38, 42], since the task of photo assessment can largely benefit from the abstract feature modeling achieved by convolutional neural networks (CNN). The first CNN-based methods were representing the entire image by a fixed-size cropped patch [26] or multi-patch aggregation models [27], while providing a binary label of low or high aesthetics as an output. Later proposals were able to handle the input images directly, while preserving their aspect ratio, providing a ranking score to an image [17, 29] instead of a binary label. Certain methods combine the estimation of technical image quality along with aesthetics, such as the proposal by Talebi et al. [38]. The model proposed by Kong et al. [20] can assess multiple meaningful photographic attributes from the content, and then estimate an overall ranking score from them.

Despite the number of studies conducted in the area of independent image assessment, little attention has been paid to context-dependent and personalized assessment of images. While the majority of automatic approaches assess the analyzed photo against non-related photos (or features) from the learned dataset, in a real-life scenario each photo is usually evaluated in comparison with similar photos from the same album. In addition, the actual process of photo selection in photo albums is largely affected by individual preferences, the capturing conditions and other properties associated with a particular album and a particular user.

The usage of individual preferences for image aesthetics assessment was demonstrated in a few recent works. In the work of Yeh et al. [44], the influence of each extracted feature is weighted by the user's adjustments, either provided manually or learned from a photo example. Adaptation of the general photo assessment model was also proposed by Park et al. [33], where a ranking model for personal preferences is learned from a subset of test images assessed by users, and is then used for adaptation. However, existing user-adaptive methods still require some amount of user interaction to be able to model specific preferences. In absence of such information we can still discover and employ useful patterns in photo albums, such as relations between similar photos taken in the same scene and characteristics of other photos from the entire album.

The characteristics of the associated photo context can be extracted by considering and comparing photos within coherent clusters [3, 25], which are typically constructed by detecting the natural boundaries in the caputured image series. Existing approaches for collection clustering are usually based on temporal information [7, 34] or image similarity [3, 5, 23, 25]. A versatile technique for clustering data where the number of clusters is unknown is hierachical clustering, which was demonstrated as advantageous in photo collection based applications [10, 22, 23].

Once a clustering is obtained, several approaches may be considered for analyzing the cluster contents and assessing images in their newly defined context. The method proposed by Ceroni et al. [3] utilizes the features collected both on intra- and inter-cluster levels, where a Support Vector Machine based prediction model is learned to predict the selection probabilities for unseen photos. Although their method takes the characteristics of each cluster into account, the learned model is not completely album-adaptive, as it is learned over numerous non-related albums and users. The nature of selection decisions within a given group of similar photos taken in the same scene was studied in the recent work by Chang et al. [4]. In their proposed method, pairwise comparisons are learned with a Siamese CNN, and a relative ranking of images in the group is produced. To handle a similar problem on the album-wise level, the method by Wang et al. [42] complements their Siamese CNN architecture with event type information. Another approach to the context assessment was proposed by Kuzovkin et al. [23], where an independent score provided by an external method is adapted to the multi-level photo context extracted with hierarchical clustering.

Although the problem of automatic photo assessment has attracted a lot of attention in recent years, it has been difficult to evaluate the relative merits of the proposed methods in real-life scenarios, such as image selection in complete photo albums. In part, this is due to the absence of appropriate ground truth data for image selection within albums, and, from the other side, due to the lack of knowledge on how users perform this task themselves. In this work, we attempt to address these matters through a user study, which allows us to compare different methods and provides useful insights on the user decision patterns.

3 USER PHOTO SELECTION ASSESSMENT

To better understand how users select their preferred photographs within a collection, we perform a user study evaluating user selection decisions on a series of different photo collections. For each album, average *user preference scores* are calculated, indicating how often a particular image was chosen by the study participants, as well as *user confidence scores*, giving an indication of user agreement for each decision.

Figure 2: Interface of the conducted selection user study. User can freely browse through the entire collection and perform an image selection on key press.

Kong et al. [20]	0.55	0.58	0.54	0.53
Jin et al. [17]	3.13	4.59	4.86	5.06
NIMA [38]	4.87	5.01	4.76	4.54

Table 1: Scoring of different photos in the same album by the analyzed image assessment methods. In this case, one pair of similar images is always scored higher than another pair, by each tested method. Thus, a global ranking of photos in an album would not provide an expected selection, if the presence of different scenes is not taken into account.

3.1 User Study Design

Photo Album Data: For the purpose of this user study, we selected six photo albums covering a variety of typical scenarios where amateur photographers may opt to take a large number of photos. Photo albums were selected from several different sources, including PEC dataset [1], YFCC100M dataset [40], CUFED dataset [42] and personal albums of the authors. We have limited our search to collections that were not altered by image processing software, and where no evident pre-selection was applied before, thus possibly containing multiple similar and near-duplicate photos, and reflecting a typical modern photo album taken with a digital camera or a smartphone. As the initial collections vary in the number of photos, and to limit the duration of the experiment, we have extracted 50 photos from each album, in their original consecutive order.

Each user was presented with a pair of albums, where one given album represented a typical family event, such as wedding or birthday, while the second represented a travel photo collection. Two example albums are shown in Figure 1.

The analyzed albums demonstrate different characteristics, which allow us to study various real-life scenarios and also identify particular behavior of assessed methods:

- *Family Event 1* is a wedding photo album, with a moderate number of repetitive photos (from 1 to 3 photos for each captured moment on average), where the pictures are taken with a semi-professional camera.
- *Family Event 2* is another wedding photo album captured with a semi-professional camera, but with a higher number of repetitive photos (in some cases, more than 5 photos for each same moment).
- *Family Event 3* album represents a family birthday gathering taken mostly indoors, with a point-and-shoot camera. This collection presents a large number of fuzzy shots, where the points of interest are not well defined, with a moderate-to-high number of repetitive photos (from 3 to 6 photos on average).
- *Travel Album 1* represents a common scenario of vacation photos, where photos of landscapes are mixed together with photos of people posing in front of a landscape. The photos are taken with a semi-professional camera, and multiple highly similar photos of the same moment are taken (more than 5 photos on average).
- *Travel Album 2* consists only of landscape photos, taken with a semi-professional camera, and the number of repetitions is moderate: 2 to 3 photos are taken for each captured moment.
- *Travel Album 3* represents photographs taken during an amusement park visit. In this album, no people are present: it consists of multiple pictures of architecture, landscapes and objects (usually from 2 to 5 photos per same scene). The photos are taken with a point-and-shoot camera and various cases of blurred or under-exposed photos are present.

Participants: In total, 30 participants took part in our study (7F/23M), with ages ranging between 24 and 55 years. Each pair of albums was evaluated by 10 different users. All participants could be characterized as amateur or casual photographers, with varying levels of photographic experience and interest.

Task: For each shown photo album, users were presented with a browser-based interface as shown in Figure 2, and were tasked with putting themselves in the role of the photographer of that collection to select the *best, more representative, or most important photos* in their opinion. No limit was placed on the number of photos selected in each album. Before the start of the experiment, each user was presented with two practice collections of 12 photos each, in order to get familiar with a task and the interface. Then, once the user was ready, they could proceed to selecting photos in the two complete collections assigned to them.

All photos of each album were simultaneously visible as thumbnails, while a larger version of the examined photo was also shown. Users could navigate within the collection freely, with a possibility of viewing all photos before making any selection. Each album had to be completed before moving to the next one. Overall, users took around 20 minutes to complete the entire task.

	Travel album 2	Travel album 3	Family event 2	Family event 3	Family event 1	Travel album 1
Kappa agreement	0.179	0.210	0.334	0.351	0.393	0.472
Kong et al. [20]	0.302	0.120	0.175	0.263	0.384	0.397
Jin et al. [17]	0.258	0.009	0.080	0.075	0.236	0.721
NIMA [38]	0.269	0.196	0.115	0.044	0.128	0.260

Table 2: User selections agreement and performance comparison for analyzed methods. The kappa agreement values are given in the first row (the albums are sorted from the lowest to the highest user agreement). The performance values for each method are computed as the Pearson correlation coe cient between user preferences and scores provided by analyzed methods.

3.2 Analysis of User Selection Results

User selections were recorded and averaged across the ten users assessing each album, obtaining a normalized *user preference score* for each image. Higher values in this case indicate that an image was selected more often, with a value of one identifying images that were selected by all users. The user preference score for an image i is computed as

$$s_{u_i} = \frac{N_{sel_i}}{N_{users}}, \tag{1}$$

where N_{sel_i} is the number of times image i was selected, and N_{users} is the total number of users.

To better visualize agreement between users, we additionally compute a *user con dence score* which indicates how decisive the preference score for the particular image. The confidence score is calculated using the inverse of the triangular function over the preference score

$$c_{u_i} = \frac{1}{\text{tri}(2s_{u_i} - 1)}, \tag{2}$$

which produces higher confidence when the preference is closer to 1 (every user has selected the image) or to 0 (no user has selected the image). The per-image preference and confidence scores for two example albums used in our study can be seen in Figure 1.

As photo selection is a subjective process, the provided user selections can and do vary between users for each album. To assess the consistency of the selections of different users, the inter-agreement between observers for such data can be computed in different ways. A common choice to estimate the inter-rater agreement is the Kendall's W coefficient [18] or Cohen's kappa statistics [6]. The Kendall's W coefficient is generally used for ordinal ratings, while kappa statistics are applied for nominal ratings, which is our case (*selected/not selected* labels). As in our case ten users rate each album, we employ the modified Fleiss' kappa measure [11], which is a generalization of the original kappa for more than two raters. Values for this measure can be interpreted as follows according to [24]: $\kappa < 0.2$ indicates slight agreement, $0.2 \leq \kappa < 0.4$ indicates fair agreement, $0.4 \leq \kappa < 0.6$ indicates moderate agreement. The computed Fleiss' kappa values for each album are given in the first row of Table 2.

Most albums assessed lead to a fair to moderate agreement between users, with the exception of two albums where slight agreement was found (*Travel album 2* and *Travel album 3*). Looking at the content of the albums, several interesting conclusions may be drawn. We observe that albums with higher agreement contain a larger number of people portraits, with repetitive similar photos of the same person or group (including *Travel album 1*, which contains multiple people portraits taken in front of landscapes). At the same time, *Travel album 2* and *Travel album 3* do not contain people's photos and consist mostly of landscapes and architecture photos. These latter albums demonstrate a larger variance in user selections: the notion of an attractive landscape appears to vary much more than the understanding of a well-captured portrait or group photo.

This suggests that for users it may be easier to perform photo selection of people's photos within an album, even when the presented people are unknown. In fact, closer observation of users' selections during the study reveals that facial expressions were a critical factor guiding their decisions when multiple photos of the same people were present. On the other hand, unique photos of people were almost always selected, irrespective of the quality or expression present.

Further, in *Travel album 2* we find a particular example of a photo sequence, where the concept of best photo selection may not be directly applicable: this photo sequence present a panoramic-like capture of the surrounding landscape (seen in the second and third rows of the second album in Figure 1). In this scenario, it is unlikely that a user would want to keep a single photo, as the series is intended for a particular type of post-processing. Indeed in this case we note that users have shared their selection across the series with no particular photo showing higher selection preference. Another similar scenario could occur when capturing a bracketed series for later construction of a high dynamic range image. Such use cases can frequently occur given the general availability of advanced photo processing tools even on mobile devices.

Another challenging example where user selections become divided is when nearly identical photos are present, with no discernible differences in quality. In such cases, we found that user votes were approximately equally shared between the photos in question, meaning that no single image led to a higher preference, despite users wanting to keep at least one representative image of such scenes.

4 EVALUATION OF IMAGE ASSESSMENT METHODS

As discussed in the previous section, photo selection is a highly subjective task, where, depending on the type of images and collections assessed, even user agreement may be low. As such, automating this task is a daunting challenge. Although a wealth of approaches exist for rating or assessing images, it is unclear how well they

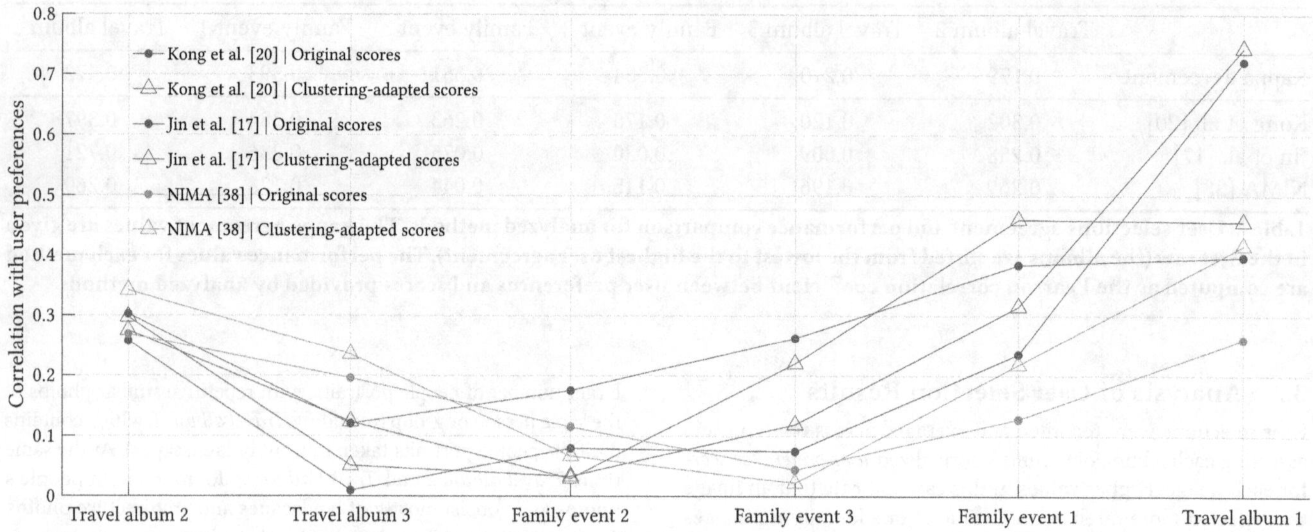

Figure 3: Per-album correlation between computed scores and user preferences, given for the original independent scores and the scores after clustering-based adaptation. The albums are sorted from the lowest to the highest kappa user agreement.

perform for selecting images within a photo collection. To evaluate the applicability of different methods for this task, we compare their assigned image scores with our experimental findings.

Given the promising advances in this field with recent deep learning based methods, we opt for evaluating the following, CNN-based methods, which were mentioned in Section 2:

- The approach by Kong et al. [20], which has recently shown the state-of-the-art performance in the independent image aesthetics assessment. In their method, different photographic attributes are estimated and weighted by the image content, giving proper relevance to what should be considered important in an image. It is possible that their proposed content adaptation might be applicable in photo albums as well.
- The method proposed by Jin et al. [17], which introduced another fine-tuning scheme with sample weights that should allow to assess images spanning a wide range of aesthetic quality. In addition, it was demonstrated that their method can be applied for automatic image cropping, therefore we can expect it to cope better with similar repetitive images often present in photo albums.
- The NIMA method proposed by Talebi et al. [38], which was designed to estimate both technical image quality and aesthetic attractiveness of an image. In our analysis, we use their NIMA MobileNet [14] version of the CNN architecture.

4.1 Performance of Analyzed Methods

The methods assessed provide a ranking score for each processed image, which we compare against the average user preference scores determined in our experiment. To estimate the performance of each analyzed method, we compute the Pearson correlation coefficient between the method's photo assessment scores and the user preference scores. With this approach, even if the scores from each method are not computed on the same scale, we can estimate the extent of correlation between the computed independent image scores and the user evaluations. The computed correlation values are detailed in Table 2 and visualized in Figure 3.

Several observations arise from this correlation analysis. The method by Jin et al. [17] often performs poorly in the complete photo albums, despite its potential for dealing with image crops. Nevertheless, for *Travel album 1* it shows the best correlation with the user preferences, among all the methods. This album consists of a number of very similar photos of landscapes and landscapes with people, which is possibly the scenario where the approach by Jin et al. [17] demonstrates its best performance. In addition, their approach appears to respond to the presence of blur in images, and our observations show that in this album the users often selected the most sharp photos among similar ones.

The NIMA method [38] performs worse in the albums where people's photos are present, but it shows its best performance in landscape-focused *Travel album 2* and *Travel album 3*. However, the degree of inter-observer agreement is relatively low for these collections, therefore no certain conclusions can be made.

On average, the highest performance is demonstrated by the approach of Kong et al. [20]. Despite their primary aim of addressing general aesthetics scoring of photos, their produced score demonstrates a noticeable correlation with the user preferences. Possibly, this is due to their proposed content-dependent weighting scheme, which provides better estimation of different type of the image content. Thus, their approach could be potentially suitable for aiding the selection process as well.

5 CLUSTERING-BASED SCORE ADAPTATION

As it was shown in the previous section, the applicability of independent image assessment methods is limited in complete photo collections. Although in some cases this could be explained by the method's occasional failure on certain images with complex content, another important reason is that the photo context is not considered by such methods. The illustration of this point is given in Table 1: it can be observed that photos from different scenes in the same album often receive non-comparable scores, which can lead to inaccurate ranking of photos in the album, if it is performed in a global manner.

The direct approach of using independent image scores in a photo album would be to rescale and normalize the scores linearly, in accordance with other scores computed in the album. However, we have observed earlier that the original scores given by methods are often poorly correlated with user preferences. One reason for this could be the elimination of the context present in photo albums, as each photo is assessed independently, without consideration of its surrounding photos. For example, even if multiple pictures of the same scene were taken, suggesting that the user found that scene important, each picture from the scene could receive a low score and be potentially rejected. For this reason, we attempt to utilize the notion of context in the photo assessment within an album.

As discussed in Section 2, a possible approach to define the photo context is through album clustering, where the entire collection is clustered into groups of similar photos. For this purpose, we apply the framework proposed in the approach of Kuzovkin et al. [23], where the entire photo collection is clustered into clusters of different similarity levels to define the relevant context for each photo.

The context of a photo is modeled using three enclosed hierarchical levels: collection level (containing the whole collection), scene cluster level (containing photos depicting the same scene), and near-duplicate cluster level (reflecting very similar images). This context hierarchy is obtained by combining time-based clustering together with similarity clustering based on the SIFT descriptors.

To evaluate how the presence of context affects the performance of the state-of-the art methods tested in the previous section, each album from our user study was clustered and its scores were adapted, according to [23]. To adapt an image-based score to its associated context, z-scores [21] are computed for each image and for each clustering level, considering both the image score and statistics of the cluster, as follows:

$$z_{I_L} = \frac{s_I - \mu_L}{\sigma_L}, \tag{3}$$

where μ_L and σ_L denote mean and standard deviation of the scores, computed on one of three levels $L \in C, SC, ND$, which define collection level, scene cluster level and near-duplicate cluster level, respectively. After z-scores for each level are computed, they are combined into the global score Z_I, as an average of the adapted scores from three levels.

In Figure 3, we also demonstrate the result of the z-score context adaptation for the analyzed methods. It can be seen that for the methods by Jin et al. [17] and NIMA method [38] the correlation with user preferences increases for the most of the albums, after the performed adaptation. Especially noticeable increase in performance can be observed for NIMA method [38], which is also reflected in the average correlation increase, shown in Table 3. For the method of Kong et al. [20], the performance gain is not particularly evident. In this case, the performance has increased for the albums where similar repetitive sequences of photos are largely present, such as *Family event 1* and *Travel album 1* (also the kappa user agreement is the highest for these albums). However, for other albums the effect of adaptation is opposite, with a decrease in the correlation. This could be also due to the nature of these albums, as some of them contain a lower number of repetitive photos.

	Original scores	Clustering-adapted scores [23]
Kong et al. [20]	0.274	0.261
Jin et al. [17]	0.230	0.260
NIMA [38]	0.169	0.217

Table 3: Average correlation across all albums for original scores and scores after clustering-based adaptation.

It is also important to note that the utilized clustering is less robust in *Travel album 2* and *Travel album 3*, due to occasional large viewpoint changes for the same captured scenes and presence of severe blur in some photos. Additionally, the album *Family Event 2* represents a special case for all methods, where the correlation before and after adaptation is rather low, even in presence of multiple similar photos. We found that the number of low-quality photos (such as blurred ones) is smaller in this album, while, as we previously observed, the user preferences in this album were often guided by more complex factors, such as face expressions or people's poses. Due to this, the original scores may not always be accurate, which can in turn lead to an unreliable adaptation. Moreover, the employed adaptation approach sometimes may be too simplistic to model the subtleties of user employed criteria.

6 CONCLUSION

Our work studies the performance of image assessment methods when applied to the task of photo selection in photo albums. Despite the wealth of work available for assessing the quality or aesthetics of images, most existing methods consider images independently, without knowledge of their surrounding collection or context. To understand how users perform this task, we have collected a selection of photo albums covering different events and quality levels, and conducted a user study on them where users were asked to select which photos they would like to keep in each collection. Our findings suggest that users consider several elements in their decisions, varying from the quality of images, to the depicted scene or people. More interestingly, we find that users often show very different selection decisions between them, highlighting the difficulty of this task for an automated method. The low agreement for some albums also confirms that in certain cases a personalized user preferences modeling would be necessary.

Our comparisons of image evaluation scores from several state-of-the-art methods relative to the results of our user study show that, in most cases, independent image assessment solutions correlate to a limited degree with user selections. At the same time, most methods performed better for albums where user agreement was higher. To assess whether additional knowledge of the context of images could improve the results of automatic image evaluation approaches, we adapted independent image scores using an album clustering approach [23]. Although this adaptation showed some benefit in higher user-agreement albums, no clear conclusions could be drawn in lower agreement cases.

Given the large quantities of photographs captured for any key event in our lives, efficient solutions that can aid users in the cumbersome task of photo selection are likely to become increasingly necessary. In this work, we show that existing methods can work for some scenarios, but are globally far from being able to predict user decisions in the context of their own albums and photo collections. Nevertheless, our study provides some insights in user behavior that we hope may serve as a basis for future work, such as further computational analysis which image features affect user selection decisions within photo albums.

REFERENCES

[1] Lukas Bossard, Matthieu Guillaumin, and Luc Van. 2013. Event Recognition in Photo Collections with a Stopwatch HMM. In *2013 IEEE International Conference on Computer Vision.* 1193⊠1200.

[2] Andrea Ceroni, Vassilis Solachidis, Mingxin Fu, Nattiya Kanhabua, Olga Papadopoulou, Claudia Niederee, and Vasileios Mezaris. 2015. Investigating human behaviors in selecting personal photos to preserve memories. *2015 IEEE International Conference on Multimedia and Expo Workshops (ICMEW)* (2015).

[3] Andrea Ceroni, Vassilios Solachidis, Claudia Niederée, Olga Papadopoulou, Nattiya Kanhabua, and Vasileios Mezaris. 2015. To Keep or Not to Keep: An Expectation-oriented Photo Selection Method for Personal Photo Collections. In *Proceedings of the 5th ACM on International Conference on Multimedia Retrieval (ICMR ⊠15).* 187⊠194.

[4] Huiwen Chang, Fisher Yu, Jue Wang, Douglas Ashley, and Adam Finkelstein. 2016. Automatic triage for a photo series. *ACM Transactions on Graphics (TOG)* 35, 4 (2016), 148.

[5] Wei-Ta Chu and Chia-Hung Lin. 2008. Automatic Selection of Representative Photo and Smart Thumbnailing Using Near-duplicate Detection. In *Proceedings of the 16th ACM International Conference on Multimedia (MM ⊠08).* 829⊠832.

[6] Jacob Cohen. 1960. A coefficient of agreement for nominal scales. *Educational and psychological measurement* 20, 1 (1960), 37⊠46.

[7] Matthew Cooper, Jonathan Foote, Andreas Girgensohn, and Lynn Wilcox. 2005. Temporal Event Clustering for Digital Photo Collections. *ACM Trans. Multimedia Comput. Commun. Appl.* 1, 3 (Aug. 2005), 269⊠288.

[8] Ritendra Datta, Dhiraj Joshi, Jia Li, and James Z. Wang. 2006. Studying Aesthetics in Photographic Images Using a Computational Approach. *Computer Vision ⊠ ECCV 2006* (2006), 288⊠301.

[9] Claire-Hélène Demarty, Mats Sjöberg, Mihai Gabriel Constantin, Ngoc Q. K. Duong, Bogdan Ionescu, Thanh-Toan Do, and Hanli Wang. 2017. Predicting Interestingness of Visual Content. In *Visual Content Indexing and Retrieval with Psycho-Visual Models.* Springer, 233⊠265.

[10] Boris Epshtein, Eyal Ofek, Yonatan Wexler, and Pusheng Zhang. 2007. Hierarchical Photo Organization Using Geo-relevance. In *Proceedings of the 15th annual ACM international symposium on Advances in geographic information systems.* ACM, 18.

[11] Joseph L Fleiss and Jacob Cohen. 1973. The equivalence of weighted kappa and the intraclass correlation coefficient as measures of reliability. *Educational and psychological measurement* 33, 3 (1973), 613⊠619.

[12] Bo Geng, Linjun Yang, Chao Xu, Xian-Sheng Hua, and Shipeng Li. 2011. The role of attractiveness in web image search. In *Proceedings of the 19th ACM international conference on Multimedia.* ACM, 63⊠72.

[13] Michael Gygli, Helmut Grabner, Hayko Riemenschneider, Fabian Nater, and Luc Van Gool. 2013. The Interestingness of Images. In *2013 IEEE International Conference on Computer Vision.* 1633⊠1640.

[14] Andrew G Howard, Menglong Zhu, Bo Chen, Dmitry Kalenichenko, Weijun Wang, Tobias Weyand, Marco Andreetto, and Hartwig Adam. 2017. Mobilenets: Efficient convolutional neural networks for mobile vision applications. *arXiv preprint arXiv:1704.04861* (2017).

[15] Bogdan Ionescu, Adrian Popescu, Anca-Livia Radu, and Henning Müller. 2016. Result diversification in social image retrieval: a benchmarking framework. *Multimedia Tools and Applications* 75, 2 (2016), 1301⊠1331.

[16] Phillip Isola, Jianxiong Xiao, Antonio Torralba, and Aude Oliva. 2011. What makes an image memorable? *Proceedings of the IEEE Computer Society Conference on Computer Vision and Pattern Recognition (CVPR)* (2011), 145⊠152.

[17] Bin Jin, Maria V Ortiz Segovia, and Sabine Süsstrunk. 2016. Image aesthetic predictors based on weighted CNNs. In *2016 IEEE International Conference on Image Processing (ICIP).* 2291⊠2295.

[18] Maurice G Kendall and B Babington Smith. 1939. The problem of m rankings. *The annals of mathematical statistics* 10, 3 (1939), 275⊠287.

[19] Aditya Khosla, Akhil S Raju, Antonio Torralba, and Aude Oliva. 2015. Understanding and Predicting Image Memorability at a Large Scale. *2015 IEEE International Conference on Computer Vision (ICCV)* (Dec. 2015), 2390⊠2398.

[20] Shu Kong, Xiaohui Shen, Zhe Lin, Radomir Mech, and Charless Fowlkes. 2016. Photo Aesthetics Ranking Network with Attributes and Content Adaptation. In *Computer Vision ⊠ ECCV 2016.* Springer, 662⊠679.

[21] Erwin Kreyszig. 2007. *Advanced engineering mathematics.* Wiley publishing.

[22] Santhana Krishnamachari and Mohamed Abdel-Mottaleb. 1999. Image browsing using hierarchical clustering. In *Proceedings IEEE International Symposium on Computers and Communications.* 301⊠307.

[23] Dmitry Kuzovkin, Tania Pouli, Rémi Cozot, Olivier Le Meur, Jonathan Kervec, and Kadi Bouatouch. 2017. Context-aware Clustering and Assessment of Photo Collections. In *Proceedings of the Symposium on Computational Aesthetics (CAE ⊠17).* ACM, 6:1⊠6:10.

[24] J Richard Landis and Gary G Koch. 1977. The Measurement of Observer Agreement for Categorical Data. *Biometrics* 33, 1 (1977), 159⊠174.

[25] Alexander C Loui and Andreas Savakis. 2003. Automated event clustering and quality screening of consumer pictures for digital albuming. *IEEE Transactions on Multimedia* 5, 3 (Sept. 2003), 390⊠402.

[26] Xin Lu, Zhe Lin, Hailin Jin, Jianchao Yang, and James Z. Wang. 2014. RAPID: Rating Pictorial Aesthetics Using Deep Learning. *Proceedings of the ACM International Conference on Multimedia - MM ⊠14* (2014), 457⊠466.

[27] Xin Lu, Zhe Lin, Xiaohui Shen, Radomir Mech, and James Z Wang. 2015. Deep Multi-patch Aggregation Network for Image Style, Aesthetics, and Quality Estimation. In *2015 IEEE International Conference on Computer Vision (ICCV).* 990⊠998.

[28] Yiwen Luo and Xiaoou Tang. 2008. Photo and Video Quality Evaluation: Focusing on the Subject. In *Computer Vision ⊠ ECCV 2008.* Springer, 386⊠399.

[29] Long Mai, Hailin Jin, and Feng Liu. 2016. Composition-Preserving Deep Photo Aesthetics Assessment. In *2016 IEEE Conference on Computer Vision and Pattern Recognition (CVPR).* 497⊠506.

[30] Luca Marchesotti and Florent Perronnin. 2013. Learning beautiful (and ugly) attributes. *British Machine Vision Conference (BMVC)* 7 (2013), 1⊠11.

[31] Luca Marchesotti, Florent Perronnin, Diane Larlus, and Gabriela Csurka. 2011. Assessing the aesthetic quality of photographs using generic image descriptors. *2011 International Conference on Computer Vision (ICCV)* (Nov. 2011), 1784⊠1791.

[32] Eftichia Mavridaki and Vasileios Mezaris. 2015. A comprehensive aesthetic quality assessment method for natural images using basic rules of photography. In *2015 IEEE International Conference on Image Processing (ICIP).* 887⊠891.

[33] Kayoung Park, Seunghoon Hong, Mooyeol Baek, and Bohyung Han. 2017. Personalized Image Aesthetic Quality Assessment by Joint Regression and Ranking. *2017 IEEE Winter Conference on Applications of Computer Vision (WACV)* (March 2017), 1206⊠1214.

[34] John C. Platt, Mary Czerwinski, and Brent A. Field. 2003. PhotoTOC: automatic clustering for browsing personal photographs. *Proceedings of the 2003 Joint Conference of the 4th International Conference on Information, Communications and Signal Processing and 4th Pac⊠c-Rim Conference on Multimedia* 1 (Dec. 2003), 6⊠10 Vol.1.

[35] Miriam Redi, Nikhil Rasiwasia, Gaurav Aggarwal, and Alejandro Jaimes. 2015. The beauty of capturing faces: Rating the quality of digital portraits. In *11th IEEE International Conference and Workshops on Automatic Face and Gesture Recognition (FG)*, Vol. 1. 1⊠8.

[36] Philipp Sandhaus, Mohammad Rabbath, and Susanne Boll. 2011. Employing aesthetic principles for automatic photo book layout. In *International Conference on Multimedia Modeling.* Springer, 84⊠95.

[37] Yale Song, Miriam Redi, Jordi Vallmitjana, and Alejandro Jaimes. 2016. To click or not to click: Automatic selection of beautiful thumbnails from videos. In *Proceedings of the 25th ACM International on Conference on Information and Knowledge Management.* ACM, 659⊠668.

[38] Hossein Talebi and Peyman Milanfar. 2017. NIMA: Neural Image Assessment. *arXiv preprint arXiv:1709.05424* (2017).

[39] Xiaoou Tang, Wei Luo, and Xiaogang Wang. 2013. Content-Based Photo Quality Assessment. *IEEE Transactions on Multimedia* 15, 8 (Dec. 2013), 1930⊠1943.

[40] Bart Thomee, David A. Shamma, Gerald Friedland, Benjamin Elizalde, Karl Ni, Douglas Poland, Damian Borth, and Li-Jia Li. 2016. YFCC100M: The New Data in Multimedia Research. *Commun. ACM* 59, 2 (Jan. 2016), 64⊠73.

[41] Tina Caroline Walber, Ansgar Scherp, and Steffen Staab. 2014. Smart Photo Selection: Interpret Gaze As Personal Interest. (2014), 2065⊠2074.

[42] Yufei Wang, Zhe Lin, Xiaohui Shen, Radomir Mech, Gavin Miller, and Garrison W Cottrell. 2016. Event-specific image importance. In *Proceedings of the IEEE Conference on Computer Vision and Pattern Recognition.* 4810⊠4819.

[43] Maria K. Wolters, Elaine Niven, and Robert H. Logie. 2014. The Art of Deleting Snapshots. In *CHI ⊠14 Extended Abstracts on Human Factors in Computing Systems (CHI EA ⊠14).* ACM, 2521⊠2526.

[44] Che-Hua Yeh, Yuan-Chen Ho, Brian A. Barsky, and Ming Ouhyoung. 2010. Personalized Photograph Ranking and Selection System. In *Proceedings of the 18th ACM International Conference on Multimedia (MM ⊠10).* 211⊠220.

Feature Selection and Multimodal Fusion for Estimating Emotions Evoked by Movie Clips

Yasemin Timar
Computer Eng. Dept., Bogazici University
Istanbul, Turkey
yasemin.timar@boun.edu.tr

Nihan Karslioglu
Computer Eng. Dept., Bogazici University
Istanbul, Turkey
nihan.karslioglu@boun.edu.tr

Heysem Kaya
Computer Eng. Dept., Namik Kemal University
Corlu, Tekirdag, Turkey
hkaya@nku.edu.tr

Albert Ali Salah
Computer Eng. Dept., Bogazici University
Istanbul, Turkey
Future Value Creation Research Center, Nagoya University
Nagoya, Japan
salah@boun.edu.tr

ABSTRACT

Perceptual understanding of media content has many applications, including content-based retrieval, marketing, content optimization, psychological assessment, and affect-based learning. In this paper, we model audio visual features extracted from videos via machine learning approaches to estimate the affective responses of the viewers. We use the LIRIS-ACCEDE dataset and the MediaEval 2017 Challenge setting to evaluate the proposed methods. This dataset is composed of movies of professional or amateur origin, annotated with viewers' arousal, valence, and fear scores. We extract a number of audio features, such as Mel-frequency Cepstral Coefficients, and visual features, such as dense SIFT, hue-saturation histogram, and features from a deep neural network trained for object recognition. We contrast two different approaches in the paper, and report experiments with different fusion and smoothing strategies. We demonstrate the benefit of feature selection and multimodal fusion on estimating affective responses to movie segments.

CCS CONCEPTS

• **Information systems → Content analysis and feature selection; Sentiment analysis; Multimedia and multimodal retrieval;**

KEYWORDS

Affective computing, multimodal interaction, emotion estimation, audio-visual features, movie analysis, face analysis

ACM Reference Format:
Yasemin Timar, Nihan Karslioglu, Heysem Kaya, and Albert Ali Salah. 2018. Feature Selection and Multimodal Fusion for Estimating Emotions Evoked by Movie Clips. In *ICMR'18: 2018 International Conference on Multimedia Retrieval, June 11–14, 2018, Yokohama, Japan.* ACM, New York, NY, USA, Article 4, 8 pages. https://doi.org/10.1145/3206025.3206074

ICMR'18, June 11–14, 2018, Yokohama, Japan
© 2018 Association for Computing Machinery.
ACM ISBN 978-1-4503-5046-4/18/06...$15.00
https://doi.org/10.1145/3206025.3206074

1 INTRODUCTION

Affective video content analysis focuses on perceptual understanding of emotions of viewers for emotion based media content delivery, summarization, and protection of younger viewers from harmful content. Emotional engagement of the viewer is driven by audio-visual media content, typically generated professionally, with powerful presentation and composition techniques. To investigate perceptual effects of multimedia content, methods of computer vision, machine learning, and cognitive science are used [31]. This work proposes multimodal fusion approaches for the prediction of affective content of video clips denoted by valence, arousal, and fear scores. We have used the MediaEval LIRIS-ACCEDE dataset [3], and evaluated a range of features, classifiers, and their combinations.

We contrast two approaches in this paper. The first approach applies PCA for dimensionality reduction, followed by Fisher vector encoding, and feature selection prior to classification. We computed Mel-frequency Cepstral Coefficients as audio features and three types of visual features, namely, the Hue Saturation Histogram, Dense SIFT, and deep neural network based features, respectively. Extreme Learning Machine (ELM) classifiers and score fusion were applied for both arousal and valence prediction tasks. Our second approach uses audio and visual features without any dimensionality reduction, and adds low level scene features and facial features for emotion estimation. Early fusion of the visual features are fed to a Random Forest classifier and to Support Vector Regressors, whose hyper parameters are explored with grid search. The audio and visual subsystem scores are fused with simple averaging, and the scores for a given movie are smoothed with Holt-Winters exponentially weighted moving average method.

An initial version of this work was published as a short report for our team's official MediaEval 2017 "Emotional Impact of Movies Task" Challenge contribution [15]. This paper extends our analysis, and reports new results, including the combination of the two approaches. Section 2 reports related work on affect estimation from movies. The MediaEval Challenge is described in Section 3. The proposed approaches are in Section 4, followed by results and discussion in Section 5, and conclusions in Section 6.

2 RELATED WORK

Affective video content analysis and multimedia studies on content indexing and retrieval involve describing, storing, and organizing multimedia information and assisting users to conveniently and quickly look up multimedia resources [19]. The main components of a multimedia indexing and retrieval system are structural analysis, feature extraction, data mining, classification and annotation, query and retrieval [12]. Structural analysis aims to segment a video into several semantic structural elements, including shot boundary detection, key frame extraction, and scene segmentation. These structural elements may play a significant role in evoking emotions in the audience. Furthermore, the quality and aesthetic properties of the images are very important. A number of works have investigated quality assessment of images and videos , as well as of paintings and photographs [9, 20].

The "Affective Impact of Movies Task" was a part of the Medieval Benchmarking Initiative in 2015, and "Emotional Impact of Movies Task" is a part of the Medieval 2016 and 2017 challenges [10, 24]. The overall use case scenario of the task is defined as to design a video search system that uses automatic tools to help users find videos that fit their particular mood, age, or preferences. Audio descriptors and visual features are extracted from the videos with several tools. Support Vector Regression and Random Forest models, Least Square Boosting, Moving Average Smoothing, convolutional neural network (CNN) and long-short-term memory (LSTM) networks have been studied in the challenges by the participants. Dense SIFT, improved dense trajectories (IDT), histogram of gradients (HOG), histogram of optical flow (HOF) and motion boundary histograms (MBH) feature descriptors with Fisher Vectors, which are successful in activity recognition, are also applied in emotion estimation to model the motion in the movie clips to estimate the response of the viewer [18, 29]. For audio, Mel-frequency Cepstral Coefficients (MFCC) is a popular choice as audio feature, as it models the human voice well.

Recent studies on affective movie analysis include cinematographic features with machine learning and pattern recognition techniques executed on specific fiction movies [6, 7]. Canini et al. argue that since the distance between the camera and the subject greatly affects the narrative power of the shot, investigating the characteristics of the shot type would contain indirect information about the distance. In their work on classification of cinematographic shot types [7], 2D scene geometric composition, frame color intensity properties, motion distribution, spectral amplitude and shot content are considered for classifying shots, using C4.5 Decision Trees and Support Vector Machines (SVM). The features defined for the scene/shot are (1) color intensity distribution on local regions in the frames, (2) motion activity maps [30] for motion distribution, (3) the geometry of the scene, through the measurement of the angular aperture of perspective lines found by Hough transform, (4) detecting subjects in the frame by their faces and face dimensions and (5) the spectral amplitude of the scene and its decay.

According to Smith [25], if a film structure aims to elicit an emotion, the priority of movie makers should be to create a mood. Although mood is not as strong as emotion, it is long-lasting. Being in a mood stimulates our emotion system again and again. As an example, a fearful mood alerts our fear system and drives us to perceive dark shadows and scary objects. This mood orients the viewer towards a particular frightening feeling in the future, and continues until fear emerges [25].

Filmic cues providing emotional information can help to elicit mood or strong emotions. Some of them are facial expressions, dialogue, vocal expression and tone, costume, sound, music, lighting, mise-en-scene, set design, editing, and camera usage [26]. Using a single filmic cue is not enough to arouse a mood. Emotion systems of audiences are very diverse and a single cue can be received by some viewers, but other viewers may miss it. For this reason, redundant filmic cues are used in films and that helps to increase chances of reaching the targeted emotion for many viewers [26]. Accordingly in this work, we have investigated multiple cues, and their fusion for estimating the affective content for movies.

3 THE MEDIAEVAL CHALLENGE AND THE DATASET

We use the LIRIS-ACCEDE dataset, which is designed for training and benchmarking of computational models for machine-based emotion understanding [2, 3]. This dataset is publicly available at: http://liris-accede.ec-lyon.fr/. The part that is used for training purposes in the Challenge includes 30 movies, from which consecutive ten-seconds segments sliding over the whole movie with a shift of 5 seconds are considered and provided with annotations. The test set is different, and its annotations are sequestered. It includes clips from 14 movies for a total duration of about 8 hours.

The audio features available in the dataset have been extracted using the openSMILE toolbox with "emobase2010.conf" configuration [11]. 1582 features are computed, which result from a base of 34 low-level descriptors (LLD) with 34 corresponding delta coefficients appended, and 21 functionals applied to each of these 68 LLD contours (1428 features). In addition, 19 functionals are applied to the 4 pitch-based LLD and their four delta coefficient contours (152 features). Finally the number of pitch onsets (pseudo syllables) and the total duration of the input are appended (2 features).

The visual features are extracted for each of the 30 movies, at a rate of one frame per second. For each of the frames, several general purpose visual features are provided using the LIRE library (http://www.lire-project.net/). Convolutional neural network (CNN) features (VGG16 [23] FC6 layer output) are extracted using the MatConvNet library [27]. The visual features are the following: Auto Color Correlogram, Color and Edge Directivity Descriptor (CEDD), Color Layout, Edge Histogram, Fuzzy Color and Texture Histogram (FCTH), Gabor, Joint descriptor joining CEDD and FCTH in one histogram, Scalable Color, Tamura, Local Binary Patterns, deep neural network based features (VGG16 FC6 layer), respectively.

The Challenge defines two tasks, namely, valence - arousal prediction, and fear prediction, respectively. In the first task, the submitted systems are expected to predict a score of induced valence (negative-positive) and induced arousal (calm-excited) for each consecutive ten-seconds segments. In the second, related task, the purpose is to predict, for each consecutive ten-seconds segment, whether they are likely to induce fear or not. The targeted use case is the prediction of frightening scenes to help systems protecting children from potentially harmful video content.

As we examine the annotations of arousal, valence, and fear annotations of 30 movies clips, we can clearly see that most of the fear annotations exist when there is an increase in arousal and decrease in valence. We also know that fear is located in the negative valence, positive arousal quadrant in the Circumplex Model of Affect [22]. On the other hand, some of the fear annotations are contrary to this assumption (e.g. the movie "Norm or Full Service"). It is important to observe the trend in the valence and arousal scores, which gives the most important clue about fear. However, fear annotations are labeled by different annotators, whose emotional responses show a high variance. Subsequently, it is challenging to produce emotion estimators that will consistently and accurately predict the viewer responses.

4 SYSTEM DEVELOPMENT

We contrast two different approaches to the problem of affect estimation from movies. They highlight different aspects of the problem. We describe them in two separate subsections here.

4.1 First approach: Audio-Visual Features with Dimensionality Reduction

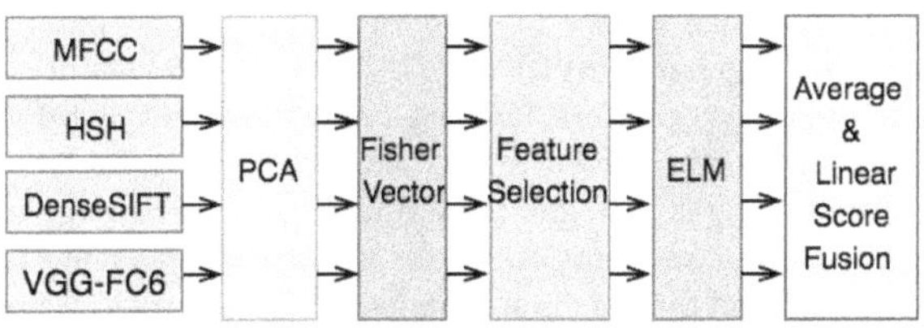

Figure 1: Audiovisual pipeline in the first approach.

Our first pipeline, given in Fig. 1, is an investigation into feature extraction and selection for this problem. The proposed method extracts a number of features, reduces their dimension with PCA, summarizes them with Fisher vector encoding, and further applies a feature selection stage prior to classification. As audio features, we computed Mel-frequency Cepstral Coefficients (MFCC 0-12), from 32ms windows (with 50% overlap). First and second derivatives were added, resulting in a 39-dimensional feature vector. We used three types of visual features in addition to these audio features. The Hue Saturation Histogram (HSH) feature is a 1023-dimensional histogram of color pixels, in 33 Hue and 31 saturation levels. They were sampled from one frame per second, and frames were resized to 240x320. For the Dense SIFT feature, the frames were further resized to 120x160, and Dense SIFT features [4] were extracted at scales {4,6,8}, at 5 pixel intervals and once for every 30 frames of video. Finally, we used the VGG16 FC6 feature available in the dataset, which is extracted from a deep neural network trained for object recognition [23]. We normalized the features with signed square root and L2 normalization. After reducing their dimensionality by 50% via PCA, we encoded them with Fisher vectors (FV) [21], which measures how much the features deviate from a background probability model, in this case a mixture of Gaussians. In other words, FV encoding quantifies the amount of parameter shift needed to best fit the new coming data in the probability model. The number of GMM components were selected as 32 for DenseSIFT and MFCC, and a single Gaussian was used for HSH and VGG16 FC6.

A ranking based feature selection approach was applied using Random Samples versus Labels Canonical Correlation Analysis Filter (SLCCA-Rand) method [16]. The main idea is to apply CCA between features and target labels, then sort the absolute value of the projection weights to get a ranking. Features that sum up to 99% of the total weight for each modality are selected in this approach.

For regression, Extreme Learning Machines (ELM) were applied for both arousal and valence prediction tasks [13]. Grid search is applied to find the best parameters of ELM. Regularization coefficient was searched from the range of [0.01,1000] with exponential steps. Radial basis function (RBF) and linear kernels were tested. The RBF kernel scale parameter is optimized in the range of [0.01,1000], also with exponential steps. Pearson Correlation Coefficient (PCC) is taken as performance measure, and optimized over 5-fold cross validation on the development partition. Results in Table 1 are obtained on the test set, for which the ground truth was sequestered.

Table 1 and 2 contain a number of further experiments with features. In one experiment, we normalized features with min-max normalization, and summarized them with their mean, geometric mean, standard variation, maximum, and minimum. PCA is then used to reduce the dimensionality, by selecting features to explain 95% of the variance. Min-max normalization is again applied to the output of PCA, before applying ELM as a classifier. These systems (denoted with Stats in Table 1) did not perform well. We have also tried to incorporate facial features, by using the OpenFace tool [1] to extract a set of facial action units. This also did not improve the error rates. For the imbalanced fear task, we have experimented with weighted ELM [33], but the main problem here is the small number of positive examples, and unless the data issue is solved, improvements based on the classifier will be limited.

4.2 Second Approach: Audio-Visual Feature Performances in Emotion Estimation

Our second approach used baseline audio and visual features, as well as extracted face and low level features without any dimensionality reduction. Dimensions are 1.582 for audio, and 1.271 for visual features. Additionally, we have extracted low level features and face geometric features, which have different pipelines before fusion. Early fusion of the visual features (except FC6) are fed to Random Forest and support vector regressors (SVR). For the binary fear classification task, we use support vector classifiers (SVC) instead of regressors. Hyper parameters are explored with grid search. Additionally, deep neural network features were used, obtained from the FC6 layer of the VGG19 network, as in the previous subsection.

4.2.1 Faces of Characters. A very important feature in a scene is the human presence, which is related to the main characters in the movie. The physical properties seen on the screen of the characters are perceived by the viewer to understand the dynamics of the scene in a general sense. The face of a character is an important clue, as the viewer has some intrinsic knowledge on human body proportions with regards to the surroundings. We have employed the dlib [17] face recognition system to detect faces, and used the face geometry to derive the shot scale as a scene feature, as well as for a basic emotional evaluation of the face in the scene. A closer

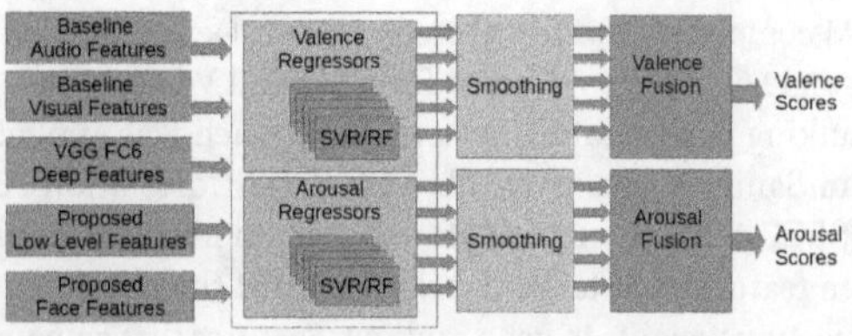

Figure 2: Valence/Arousal Regression in the second approach

shot of the character signifies stronger affect in the scene, while the relative dimensions of the faces in a group can suggest relations between the characters.

4.2.2 Low Level Features of Scenes. Various color spaces are studied in computer vision research. However hue-saturation-value HSV space is very popular in the domain of human visual perception modeling. In general terms, *hue* refers to the color itself, *saturation* represents the boldness of the color, and *value* gives the brightness level. As an example pastel blue would be less saturated than a very bold blue. Saturated colors are more preferred by humans over non-saturated colors [5]. According to recent studies, since 1940s when the color film became the standard, saturation in films has been steadily increasing. Hue, which tends to be the more easily identifiable color dimension, also plays a significant part in our narrative understanding. The average hue of the whole movie may not be particularly useful, but the average hue of a shot can be very important [5].

Luminance is a measurement of how much light is present in an image or a series of images. Luminance is controlled not only during shooting but also in post production by manipulating the contrast and exposure of the film. Well-known concepts of "low-key" and "high-key" in the photography are also used in movies. The histogram of the key frames image can be used as the features of a shot. However, as Brunick et al. state, most films are composed of slighter luminance changes [5]. So a luminance indicator of the movie can be estimated by first calculating the median luminance for each frame of the film and then averaging across the entire film. We propose the same approach to estimate the luminance of each shot by transforming the key frame to gray scale and calculating the median value.

Within a movie, two basic on-screen activities are defined; (1) *motion* refers to the actions of an agent in front of the camera, and (2) *camera movement* refers to results of change in camera position or lens length, like pans, tilts and zooms. However, people generally do not consciously realize the distinction between these two activities when processing visual information [5]. Cutting et al. proposed to combine both motion and movement into a *visual activity* descriptor [8]. We propose to measure the visual activity by using background models and background subtraction. One of the commonly used approaches for this is applying probability density functions and estimators for the variance of each pixel in the scene model. The method we have used is the Gaussian Mixture-based Background/Foreground Segmentation Algorithm, implementing the improved Gaussian mixture model background subtraction proposed by Zivkovic et al. [32]. In this model, the scene has a history of frames which affect the background model, and there is a threshold on the squared Mahalanobis distance between the scene pixel and the model to decide whether a pixel is well described by the background model. We have set the history to 500 (frames). We assume the background model generated at the end of each shot includes all the visual activity occurred during the shot. We calculate the mean intensity to summarize this information to be used as a low level feature of the scene.

4.2.3 Regressors. Support Vector Regression models are widely used in affective content analysis. Two parameters are used to control learning in SVR with radial basis kernels. The γ parameter controls the kernel size around the support vector, and larger values limit the influence of support vectors. The C parameter controls model fit by providing weighted penalties for misclassified samples. If it is too small, we may have underfitting. We use grid search to optimize these parameters.

The second approach we use is the Random Forest, which is a widely used ensemble learning method in affective computing. A random forest fits a number of decision trees on various sub-samples of input data and uses averaging to improve the predictive accuracy and to avoid over-fitting.

In our approach, we use early fusion of visual features (except VGG FC6), which are fed to Random Forest classifiers and support vector regressors (SVR). CNN (i.e. VGG16 FC6) features are fed to separate regressors. Hyper parameters are explored with grid search. In our pipeline evaluation with grid search, for SVR, standard scaling is used and the C and γ parameters range from 0.001 to 100. For Random Forests, the number of trees range from 100 to 1000, and the maximum number of features per tree from 3 to 20. Five train and test folds (balanced according to duration and fear labels) are defined to ensure that each movie appears in either in the train set or the validation set, but not in both. The best regressors were chosen via grid search, and tested on each fold to evaluate the performance on a subset of the development set. According to MSE and PCC scores on each fold, the regressors are trained with the best group. The audio and visual subsystem scores are fused with simple averaging, and the scores for a given movie are smoothed with Holt-Winters exponentially weighted moving average method [28]. The pipeline is visually presented in Fig. 2.

4.3 Fusion of Two Approaches

After the predictions of different regressors are generated, we have executed a decision level fusion algorithm with average and weighted average methods. We have submitted 5 official runs to the Mediaeval 2017, Emotional Impact Challenge. Runs 1 to 4 are generated by the first approach. Run 5 is generated by the second approach, with a similar set of visual features. The fusion of both approaches produces a better result in valence/arousal prediction. The results are presented in the following section and in Tables 5-7.

5 RESULTS AND DISCUSSION

To quantify the performance of the two pipelines, mean-squared error (MSE) and Pearson's r are computed. The MSE for regression models is widely used to quantify the difference between estimated values and the true values, while the Pearson product-moment correlation coefficient (or Pearson's r) is a measure of the linear

(a) t=10

(b) t=11

(d) t=30

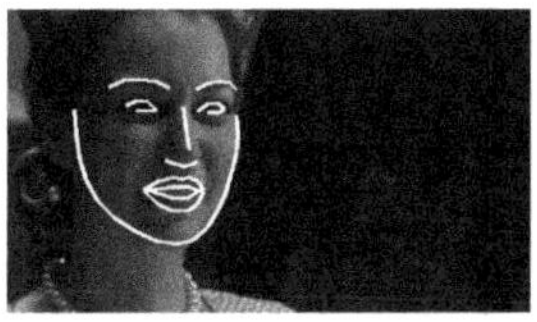

(e) t=31

(f) t=50

(g) t=51

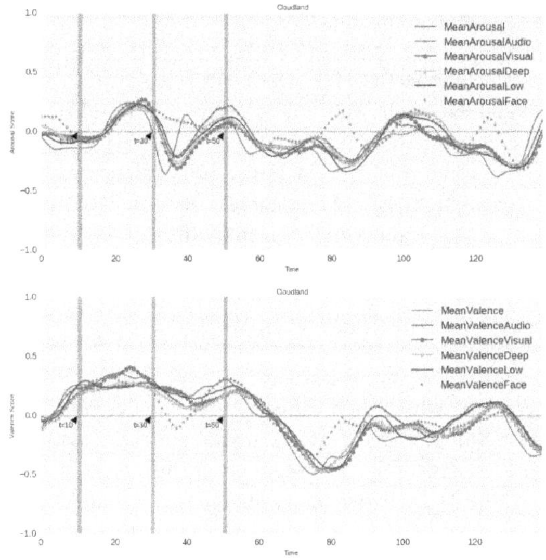

(c) Prediction

Figure 3: "Cloudland" faces in dual-frames t=10, 30, 50

(a) t=56

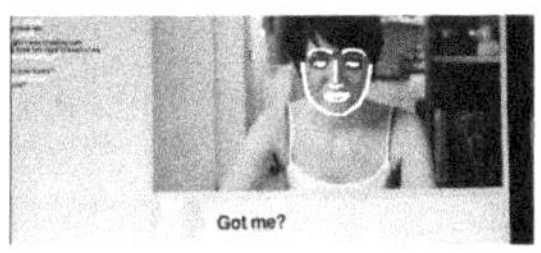

(b) t=57

(d) t=73

(e) t=74

(f) t=83

(g) t=84

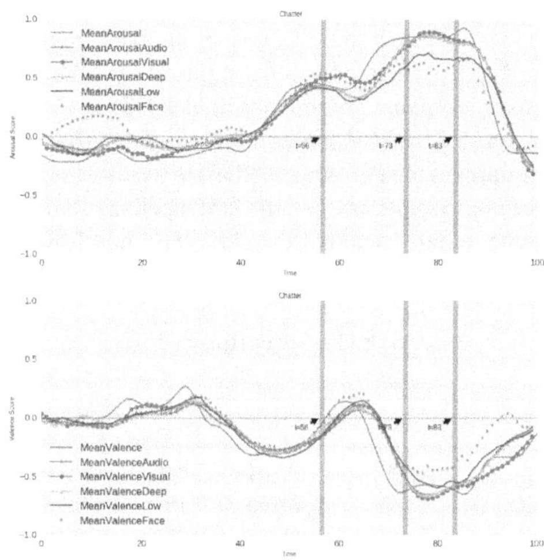

(c) Prediction

Figure 4: "Chatter" faces in dual-frames t=56, 73, 83

correlation between estimated and true values. The measurements on the test set provided by the organizers are used to evaluate the pipelines separately. The results of the first approach are presented in Table 1. The first run is the average scores of MFCC, HSH, Dense SIFT and VGG FC6 subsystems. The second run is a linear weighted combination of the predictions used in the first run. In the third run, while an average of MFCC and FC6 are computed for valence, the average of MFCC, HSH and FC6 are computed for arousal. In the fourth run, linear combination scores of MFCC, Dense SIFT and FC6 are computed for valence, and linear combination scores of MFCC, HSH and FC6 are computed for arousal. Results using statistical feature summarization methods of action units, Dense SIFT, HSH, FC6 and MFCC are also in Table 1.

For the arousal task, action units have the best PCC results in the first approach. While Dense SIFT, FC6, HSH and MFCC have very low results for PCC according to Table 1, their average score fusion is promising for the arousal task. For the valence task, dense SIFT seems to work best alone. Score fusion of MFCC, HSH, Dense SIFT, FC6 provide better results.

Table 3 presents the results of the tests conducted with the second approach, on the sequestered test set of the challenge. Regarding the valence predictions in Table 3, the visual and VGG FC6 features

Table 1: Results of the first approach

Run	Arousal MSE	Arousal PCC	Valence MSE	Valence PCC
avg: MFCC, HSH, Dense SIFT and FC6	**0.123**	**0.129**	**0.186**	0.026
weighted comb.: MFCC, HSH, Dense SIFT and FC6	0.143	0.099	0.225	**0.046**
selective avg: MFCC and FC6 (valence) + HSH (arousal)	**0.123**	0.105	**0.189**	0.039
linear selective comb.: MFCC, FC6, Dense SIFT (valence),HSH (arousal)	0.143	0.099	0.225	**0.046**
Stats + PCA (Statistical Feature Summarization with PCA): Action Units	0.165	**0.230**	0.208	-0.280
Stats + PCA: Dense SIFT	0.255	0.052	0.247	-0.028
Stats + PCA: FC6	0.176	0.026	0.209	**0.055**
Stats + PCA: HSH	0.173	-0.075	0.228	-0.005
Stats + PCA: MFCC	0.166	-0.006	0.221	-0.010

are more successful, while fused values produce an average MSE and Pearson's r. Still, low level features are not quite successful as the visual features. Regarding the arousal results in Table 3, we see that the fused results are better than individual visual and audio features. On the other hand, if the results are poor, as in the case of low level features, smoothing degrages them further.

Face geometry is not quite successful, compared to the other features. One of the reasons is that the face is not being recognized in most of the shots. For example, in the movie "Island" there is a human in most of the frames, but since the character is shot from the back, we can not see her face most of the time. As a result, human detection fails in those frames and this creates an inaccuracy.

For the second approach, late fusion is applied to results of the pipelines. The fused scores are presented in Tables 4. The minimum MSE scores and maximum PCC scores are highlighted. It is clear that smoothing improves the PCC score of the late fusion of separate pipelines. We see improvements when the face pipeline predictions are combined with other visual features, like FC6 and low level features.

Table 2: Fear task classification results.

Feature	Accuracy	Precision	Recall	F1 Score
MFCC	0.539	0.161	0.340	0.192
Action Units	0.505	0.150	0.351	0.187
Dense SIFT	0.590	0.152	0.255	0.166
HSH	0.707	0.121	0.093	0.090
FC6	0.836	0.017	0.014	0.015

Table 2 shows the performance of individual features for the fear classification task. This is a very challenging task, with a very unbalanced training and test set. The F1 scores are low on the overall, with MFCC achieving the best F1 with a small margin.

To understand the effects of various features, we have visualized the prediction scores. We have displayed the emotion predictions for two movies in Figs. 3 and 4, namely "Cloudland" and "Chatter" respectively. We have selected sample scenes with human presence and annotated the corresponding approximate time in the prediction curve. As one can see, visual features and CNN features with SVR regression have the lowest error. Face features change more rapidly compared to the low level features such as color, lighting, and motion of the scene. This suggests that there should be a more elaborate approach to detect humans in the scene.

Decision level fusion of the two approaches produces better scores as it is presented in the Table 5. Averaging of run 1 (average score of MFCC, HSH, Dense SIFT and FC6 features with PCA, FV and ELM pipelines) and run 5 (average of the scores generated with the audio and visual features with SVM regressors) produces the best results, suggesting that these approaches complement each other. This is also valid for the combination of run 3 and run 5. However fusing the run 2 and 4 with run 5 renders a poorer performance.

The valence and arousal predictions of our models are very similar to the top results of the Mediaeval 2017 Emotion Impact challenge, which are presented in Figures 5 and 6. Among the models of the participants, the system with the best PCC for valence prediction used VGG features with SVR regressors, while the best MSE scores were produced with fusion of custom audio features, VGG and visual features fed to 2-layer LSTM networks [14]. We have produced the best MSE scores in arousal with audio visual regression and late fusion. On the other hand, we have obtained the best PCC scores using VGG features with SVR. The variance of MSE scores in the challenge is low, despite the fact that PCC scores vary noticeably, mostly because the cost functions of the regressors favor minimizing the error over maximizing the correlation.

6 CONCLUSIONS

In this work, we have investigated various approaches to predict viewer emotions while watching movies. In the first approach, MFCC and various visual features, different feature summarization methods, score fusions and single feature runs are performed for arousal and valence task. From these experiments, representations based on single features can sometimes work well, but typically, fusion of features result in better models. This conclusion echoes the principle that multiple emotional cues should be used in a movie to elicit emotions from the viewers.

As it is shown in our second approach, grid search enables models with a high performance with traditional regressors, without any further need for feature selection. Additional visual cinematographic features and face features produce promising results, indicating room for improvement through stylistic features. Post-processing is also very helpful; the positive effect of smoothing is clearly observed in the arousal results. In fact, the best performance

Table 3: Valence and Arousal evaluations of second approach

Features	Regressors	Smoothing	Valence MSE	Valence PCC	Arousal MSE	Arousal PCC
Visual	SVR	yes	**0.181**	0.107	0.136	0.122
FC6	SVR	yes	**0.183**	**0.339**	**0.126**	**0.150**
FC6	SVR	no	0.185	0.207	0.128	0.073
Visual	SVR	no	0.185	0.061	0.140	0.070
avg Audio-Visual	SVR	yes	0.188	0.090	**0.113**	**0.219**
Face	RF	yes	0.206	-0.058	0.136	0.031
Face	RF	no	0.213	0.010	0.142	-0.017
Low Level	RF	no	0.240	-0.061	0.139	-0.004
Low Level	RF	yes	0.242	**-0.223**	0.132	-0.027
Audio	SVR	yes	0.243	-0.025	0.147	0.018
Audio	SVR	no	0.245	0.013	0.152	-0.044

Table 4: Fusion of smoothed scores in 2nd approach

Run with Smoothing	Valence MSE	Valence PCC	Arousal MSE	Arousal PCC
FC6, Low Level	0.202	0.032	**0.127**	-0.084
FC6, Low Level, Visual	0.191	0.084	**0.128**	0.030
FC6, Visual	**0.178**	**0.263**	0.128	**0.159**
Low Level, Visual	0.201	-0.065	0.131	-0.031
FC6, Visual, Audio	0.194	0.196	0.132	0.123
FC6, Visual, Face	**0.186**	0.222	0.133	**0.136**
FC6, Visual, Audio, Face, Low Level	0.202	0.047	0.133	-0.016

Table 5: Decision Level Fusion (Average) of 1st and 2nd approaches

Fusion Run	Valence MSE	Valence PCC	Arousal MSE	Arousal PCC
fused_1_5	**0.186**	**0.091**	**0.116**	**0.233**
fused_3_5	**0.187**	0.087	**0.116**	**0.227**
me17ei_BOUN-NKU_5	0.188	**0.090**	**0.113**	0.219
fused_4_5	0.200	0.075	0.120	0.160
fused_2_5	0.200	0.075	0.120	0.159
me17ei_BOUN-NKU_1	0.186	0.026	0.123	0.129
me17ei_BOUN-NKU_3	0.189	0.039	0.124	0.105
me17ei_BOUN-NKU_4	0.225	0.046	0.143	0.099
me17ei_BOUN-NKU_2	0.225	0.046	0.143	0.099

Table 6: Weighted Average Fusion of Valence scores in 1st and 2nd approach

weighted average fusion	alpha	MSE	PCC
run_1_5_valence_minMSE	**0.34**	**0.186**	**0.083**
run_1_5_valence_maxPCC	**0.66**	**0.186**	**0.092**
run_3_5_valence_minMSE	**0.58**	**0.187**	**0.090**
run_3_5_valence_maxPCC	**0.76**	**0.187**	**0.093**
run_2_5_valence_maxPCC	0.00	0.188	0.090
run_2_5_valence_minMSE	0.00	0.188	0.090
run_4_5_valence_maxPCC	0.98	0.188	0.090
run_4_5_valence_minMSE	0.98	0.188	0.090

Table 7: Weighted Average Fusion of Arousal scores in 1st and 2nd approach

weighted average fusion	alpha	MSE	PCC
run_2_5_arousal_minMSE	0.00	0.113	0.219
run_4_5_arousal_minMSE	0.98	0.113	0.221
run_1_5_arousal_minMSE	0.98	0.113	0.219
run_3_5_arousal_minMSE	0.98	0.113	0.219
run_1_5_arousal_maxPCC	**0.48**	**0.186**	**0.233**
run_3_5_arousal_maxPCC	**0.60**	**0.187**	**0.229**
run_2_5_arousal_maxPCC	0.08	0.189	0.225
run_4_5_arousal_maxPCC	0.92	0.189	0.225

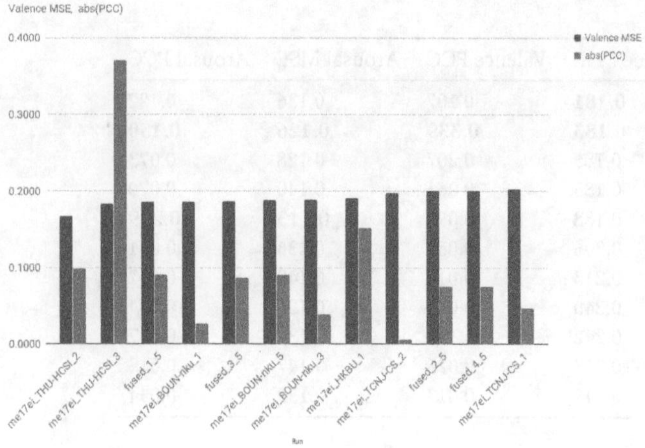

Figure 5: Mediaeval 2017 Valence scores. "me17ei_" prefix denotes challenge submissions by different teams.

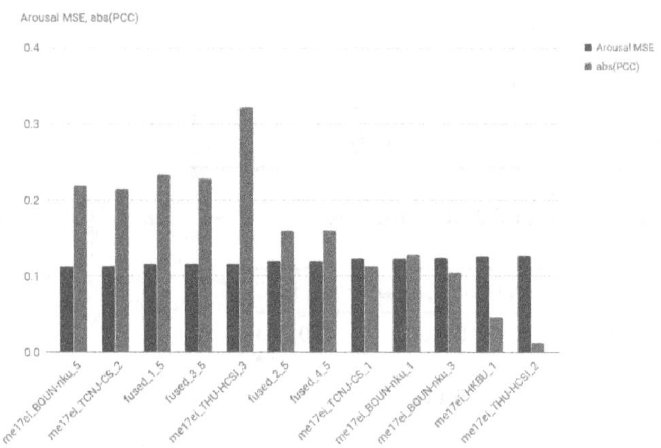

Figure 6: Mediaeval 2017 Arousal scores. "me17ei_" prefix denotes challenge submissions by different teams.

scores for valence are produced by CNN features with SVR models and arousal prediction is generally better than valence prediction, which is consistent with the literature and MediaEval Emotional Impact challenge results. The high subjectivity of emotions is the main challenge, for which we will continue to develop more accurate emotion estimators for movie viewers. In our future works, we plan to analyze the features of speech, music and sound effects separately in the audio domain. Each modality has a different effect on the viewer, which we hope to observe in the dataset.

REFERENCES

[1] Tadas Baltrušaitis, Marwa Mahmoud, and Peter Robinson. 2015. Cross-dataset learning and person-specific normalisation for automatic action unit detection. In *IEEE FG*.

[2] Yoann Baveye, Emmanuel Dellandréa, Christel Chamaret, and Liming Chen. 2015. Deep learning vs. kernel methods: Performance for emotion prediction in videos. In *Proc. ACII*. IEEE, 77–83.

[3] Yoann Baveye, Emmanuel Dellandrea, Christel Chamaret, and Liming Chen. 2015. LIRIS-ACCEDE: A video database for affective content analysis. *IEEE Transactions on Affective Computing* 6, 1 (2015), 43–55.

[4] Anna Bosch, Andrew Zisserman, and Xavier Munoz. 2007. Image classification using random forests and ferns. In *ICCV*.

[5] KL Brunick, JE Cutting, and JE DeLong. 2013. Low-level features of film: What they are and why we would be lost without them. *Psychocinematics: Exploring cognition at the movies* (2013), 133–148.

[6] Luca Canini, Sergio Benini, and Riccardo Leonardi. 2013. Affective recommendation of movies based on selected connotative features. *Circuits and Systems for Video Technology, IEEE Transactions on* 23, 4 (2013), 636–647.

[7] Luca Canini, Sergio Benini, and Riccardo Leonardi. 2013. Classifying cinematographic shot types. *Multimedia tools and applications* 62, 1 (2013), 51–73.

[8] James E Cutting, Kaitlin L Brunick, Jordan E DeLong, Catalina Iricinschi, and Ayse Candan. 2011. Quicker, faster, darker: Changes in Hollywood film over 75 years. *i-Perception* 2, 6 (2011), 569–576.

[9] Ritendra Datta, Dhiraj Joshi, Jia Li, and James Z Wang. 2006. Studying aesthetics in photographic images using a computational approach. In *ECCV*. 288–301.

[10] Emmanuel Dellandréa, Liming Chen, Yoann Baveye, Mats Viktor Sjöberg, Christel Chamaret, et al. 2016. The mediaeval 2016 emotional impact of movies task. In *MediaEval 2016 Multimedia Benchmark Workshop Working Notes*.

[11] Florian Eyben and Björn Schuller. 2015. openSMILE: the Munich open-source large-scale multimedia feature extractor. *Proc. ACM Multimedia* 6, 4 (2015), 4–13.

[12] Weiming Hu, Nianhua Xie, Li Li, Xianglin Zeng, and Stephen Maybank. 2011. A survey on visual content-based video indexing and retrieval. *IEEE Trans. Systems, Man, and Cybernetics, Part C* 41, 6 (2011), 797–819.

[13] Guang-Bin Huang, Hongming Zhou, Xiaojian Ding, and Rui Zhang. 2012. Extreme learning machine for regression and multiclass classification. *IEEE Transactions on Systems, Man, and Cybernetics, Part B (Cybernetics)* 42, 2 (2012), 513–529.

[14] Zitong Jin, Yuqi Yao, Ye Ma, and Mingxing Xu. 2017. THUHCSI in MediaEval 2017 Emotional Impact of Movies Task. In *Proc. MediaEval*.

[15] Nihan Karslioglu, Yasemin Timar, Albert Ali Salah, and Heysem Kaya. 2017. BOUN-NKU in MediaEval 2017 Emotional Impact of Movies Task. In *Proc. MediaEval*.

[16] Heysem Kaya, Tuğçe Özkaptan, Albert Ali Salah, and Fikret Gürgen. 2015. Random discriminative projection based feature selection with application to conflict recognition. *IEEE Signal Processing Letters* 22, 6 (2015), 671–675.

[17] Davis E King. 2009. Dlib-ml: A machine learning toolkit. *Journal of Machine Learning Research* 10, Jul (2009), 1755–1758.

[18] Vu Lam, Sang Phan Le, Duy-Dinh Le, Shin'ichi Satoh, and Duc Anh Duong. 2015. NII-UIT at MediaEval 2015 Affective Impact of Movies Task. In *Proc. MediaEval*.

[19] Michael S Lew, Nicu Sebe, Chabane Djeraba, and Ramesh Jain. 2006. Content-based multimedia information retrieval: State of the art and challenges. *ACM TOMCCAP* 2, 1 (2006), 1–19.

[20] Weisi Lin and C-C Jay Kuo. 2011. Perceptual visual quality metrics: A survey. *Journal of Visual Communication and Image Representation* 22, 4 (2011), 297–312.

[21] Florent Perronnin and Christopher Dance. 2007. Fisher kernels on visual vocabularies for image categorization. In *CVPR*.

[22] James A Russell. 1980. A circumplex model of affect. *Journal of personality and social psychology* 39, 6 (1980), 1161–1178.

[23] Karen Simonyan and Andrew Zisserman. 2014. Very deep convolutional networks for large-scale image recognition. *arXiv preprint arXiv:1409.1556* (2014).

[24] Mats Sjöberg, Yoann Baveye, Hanli Wang, Vu Lam Quang, Bogdan Ionescu, Emmanuel Dellandréa, Markus Schedl, Claire-Hélène Demarty, and Liming Chen. 2015. The MediaEval 2015 Affective Impact of Movies Task.. In *Proc. MediaEval*.

[25] Greg M Smith. 1999. Local emotions, global moods, and film structure. *Passionate views: Film, cognition, and emotion* (1999), 103–26.

[26] Greg M Smith. 2003. *Film structure and the emotion system*. Cambridge University Press.

[27] A. Vedaldi and K. Lenc. 2015. MatConvNet – Convolutional Neural Networks for MATLAB. In *Proceeding of the ACM Int. Conf. on Multimedia*.

[28] Peter R Winters. 1960. Forecasting sales by exponentially weighted moving averages. *Management science* 6, 3 (1960), 324–342.

[29] Yun Yi, Hanli Wang, Bowen Zhang, and Jian Yu. 2015. MIC-TJU in MediaEval 2015 Affective Impact of Movies Task. In *Proc. MediaEval*.

[30] Wei Zeng, Wen Gao, and Debin Zhao. 2002. Video indexing by motion activity maps. In *Proc. ICIP*, Vol. 1. I–912.

[31] Zhihong Zeng, Maja Pantic, Glenn I Roisman, and Thomas S Huang. 2009. A survey of affect recognition methods: Audio, visual, and spontaneous expressions. *IEEE transactions on pattern analysis and machine intelligence* 31, 1 (2009), 39–58.

[32] Zoran Zivkovic and Ferdinand van der Heijden. 2006. Efficient adaptive density estimation per image pixel for the task of background subtraction. *Pattern recognition letters* 27, 7 (2006), 773–780.

[33] Weiwei Zong, Guang-Bin Huang, and Yiqiang Chen. 2013. Weighted extreme learning machine for imbalance learning. *Neurocomputing* 101 (2013), 229–242.

Multimodal Continuous Prediction of Emotions in Movies using Long Short-Term Memory Networks

Sarath Sivaprasad
TCS Research, Tata Consultancy Services Ltd.
Pune, India
sarath.s7@tcs.com

Tanmayee Joshi
TCS Research, Tata Consultancy Services Ltd.
Pune, India
tanmayee.joshi@tcs.com

Rishabh Agrawal
TCS Research, Tata Consultancy Services Ltd.
Pune, India
rishabh.agrawal@tcs.com

Niranjan Pedanekar
TCS Research, Tata Consultancy Services Ltd.
Pune, India
n.pedanekar@tcs.com

ABSTRACT

Predicting emotions that movies are designed to evoke, can be useful in entertainment applications such as content personalization, video summarization and ad placement. Multimodal input, primarily audio and video, helps in building the emotional content of a movie. Since the emotion is built over time by audio and video, the temporal context of these modalities is an important aspect in modeling it. In this paper, we use Long Short-Term Memory networks (LSTMs) to model the temporal context in audio-video features of movies. We present continuous emotion prediction results using a multimodal fusion scheme on an annotated dataset of Academy Award winning movies. We report a significant improvement over the state-of-the-art results, wherein the correlation between predicted and annotated values is improved from 0.62 vs 0.84 for arousal, and from 0.29 to 0.50 for valence.

CCS CONCEPTS

• **Computing methodologies** → **Neural networks**; • **Applied computing** → **Media arts**;

KEYWORDS

Emotion prediction; Multimodal; Movies; LSTM; Deep learning

ACM Reference Format:
Sarath Sivaprasad, Tanmayee Joshi, Rishabh Agrawal, and Niranjan Pedanekar. 2018. Multimodal Continuous Prediction of Emotions in Movies using Long Short-Term Memory Networks. In *ICMR '18: 2018 International Conference on Multimedia Retrieval, June 11–14, 2018, Yokohama, Japan.* ACM, New York, NY, USA, 7 pages. https://doi.org/10.1145/3206025.3206076

1 INTRODUCTION

Movies generate a multitude of emotions in viewers. Creators of movies employ a set of moving images, music, sounds and speech to evoke certain emotions in viewers' minds. Predicting or profiling emotions that movies are designed to invoke in viewers can be useful in a number of affective computing applications in entertainment. For example, Canini et al. [4] predicted values of intended emotions in movie scenes using visual, audio and film grammar-related features to recommend video content. Yadati et al. [17] predicted emotion profile of YouTube videos using motion, cut density and audio energy, and used it to optimize advertisement placement in videos. Zhang et al. [18] used multimodal features to index, retrieve and visualize music videos. Goyal et al. [8] suggested that an emotional profile of a movie could also serve as an input to a model predicting the success of a movie. If the emotional profile of a movie can be predicted continuously over time, it can not only provide a more granular input to the aforementioned applications, but can also be useful for newer applications such as semi-automated editing and novel methods to rate movies [5].

Continuous emotion prediction can be defined as prediction of emotions that entertainment media are designed to evoke in viewers, over continuous time and over a continuous dimensional space representing emotions. Such prediction for movies is a challenging task given the dynamic interplay of audio, visual and textual information [8]. Hanjalic and Xu [10] introduced the concept of mapping movies using their audio-visual features onto the continuous, two-dimensional emotion space of valence and arousal. *Valence* characterizes the positivity or negativity of an emotion, while *arousal* indicates its intensity [14]. The valence-arousal model is typically found to describe human emotional response to videos adequately [6, 9].

Most of the existing literature on movie emotion prediction has considered scenes or small segments of movies rather than a large contiguous movies, or a limited number of emotion classes rather than a continuous emotion scale. Baveye et al. [2] contributed a dataset called LIRIS-ACCEDE consisting of continuous valence and arousal annotations for 30 short films. In another work [1], they also predicted continuous valence and arousal profiles for this dataset using kernel methods and deep learning, but without incorporating a temporal context. Malandrakis et al. [12] contributed an annotated dataset of 30 minute clips of 12 Academy Award winning movies, and predicted continuous valence and arousal profiles using hand-crafted audio-visual features with Hidden Markov Models to provide temporal context. Goyal et al. [8] reported an improvement over these results using a Mixture-of-Experts (MoE) model to

ICMR '18, June 11–14, 2018, Yokohama, Japan

ACM ISBN 978-1-4503-5046-4/18/06...$15.00
https://doi.org/10.1145/3206025.3206076

fuse the results of audio and visual emotion prediction. They incorporated the temporal context using a temporal Gaussian smoothing over the predicted values of valence and arousal, and optimized the length of the smoothing window such that it provided the best correlation with the annotated values.

Long Short-Term Memory (LSTM) networks [7] are neural networks commonly used to model the temporal context of multi-dimensional data such as music, speech, language and time series. They have also been used in continuous prediction of emotions for videos of human interactions with operators [13] and with artificially intelligent agents [16]. In this paper, we use LSTMs to model the temporal context of audio-visual data extracted from 12 Academy Award winning movies using the annotated dataset provided by Malandrakis et al. [12] and later used by Goyal et al. [8]. We chose this dataset over the LIRIS-ACCEDE dataset, since the movies referred to in the dataset, being popular Academy Award winning movies, were more likely to evoke the intended emotions in viewers [12]. We used the same set of hand-crafted features used by Goyal et al. [8], modeled their temporal context using two LSTMs, and used a late fusion model to combine the LSTM outputs.

Our contribution in this paper is that, using LSTMs to model the temporal context for this mainstream movie dataset, we report a significant improvement over the current state-of-the-art results reported by Goyal et al. [8].

2 DATASET AND FEATURES

We used the dataset described by Malandrakis et al. [12] containing continuous annotations of *intended* arousal and valence by experts for clips from 12 Academy award winning movies. The dataset also contained continuous annotations of *expected* arousal and valence as reported by viewers. Malandrakis et al. [12] reported a high correlation of 0.74 for arousal and 0.70 for valence between the intended and expected annotations. For the work described in this paper, we used the intended annotations as ground truth, since Goyal et al. [8] used the same as ground truth while reporting the performance of their arousal and valence prediction models. The mean length of the clips in the aforementioned dataset was 30.6 2.55 minutes. The range of arousal and valence annotations was from -1 to +1.

As per Hanjalic and Xu [10], a typical 2-D emotion space that humans encounter with valence and arousal as dimensions, is a parabolic contour with most emotions lying within this contour as shown in Fig. 1 (a). Fig. 1 also shows typical scenes from *Crash*[1], an Academy award-winning movie from the dataset. Fig. 1 (b) shows a high-arousal, positive valence case where the character realises that his child is safe despite a shot being fired at her. Fig. 1 (c) shows a high-arousal, negative valence case where a car crash has just occurred and a policeman is rushing away from an impending explosion. Fig. 1 (d) shows a low-arousal, neutral valence case where the police officers are meeting in a government office.

As suggested by Goyal et al. [8], we sampled the annotations of intended arousal and valence at 5-second intervals, since the annotated emotions did not show a very rapid variation. We divided the movies into non-overlapping 5-second clips of audio and video data corresponding to each one of the annotation samples. For

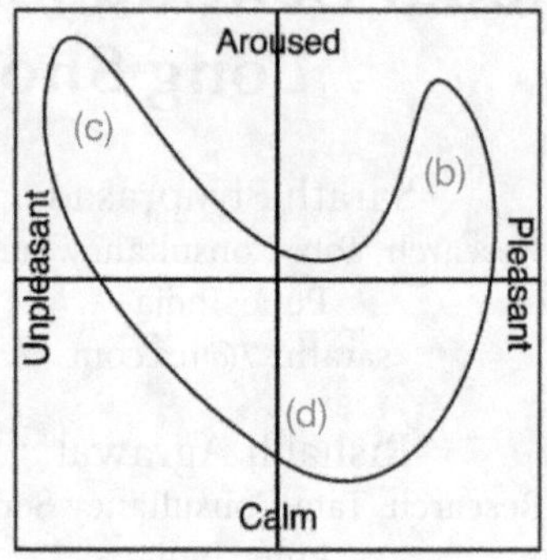

(a) 2-D emotion space as suggested by Hanjalic and Xu [10]

(b) High arousal, positive valence scene

(c) High arousal, negative valence scene

(d) Low arousal, neutral valence scene

Figure 1: (a) shows a typical 2-D emotion space as suggested by Hanjalic and Xu [10], while (b)-(d) show frames from the 2004 movie *Crash* occurring in different parts of the emotion space according to intended annotations.

[1]Lionsgate Films.

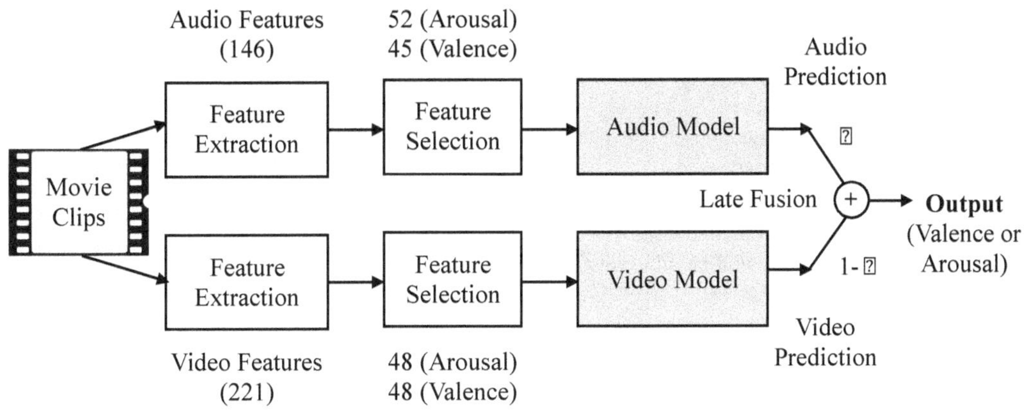

(a) Schematic diagram

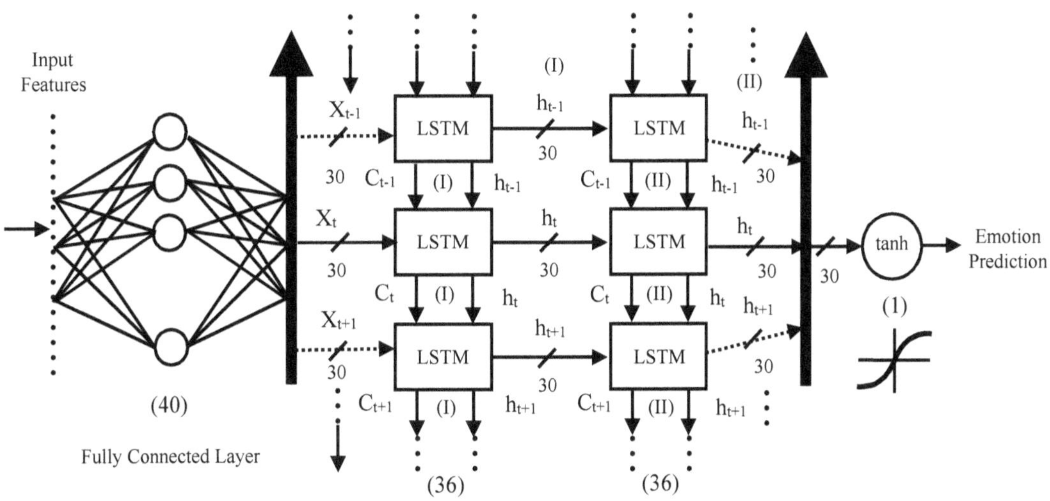

(b) Model Architecture

Figure 2: (a) shows a schematic diagram of the proposed architecture for continuous prediction of arousal and valence using late fusion. Audio and video features serve as inputs to two separate deep networks with two LSTMs in each. (b) shows the architecture for the LSTM-based model. X denotes the input feature vector, C, the cell state or long-term memory, and h, the hidden state or working memory.

each clip, we calculated the following hand-crafted audio and video features as described by Goyal et al. [8]:

(1) **Audio Features** (size 146): Mel frequency spectral coefficients (MFCC), their derivatives and statistics (min, max, mean); Chroma, its derivatives and statistics (min, max, mean); Audio compressibility; Harmonicity.
(2) **Video Features** (size 221): Shot frequency; Histogram of optical flow (HOF) and statistics (min, max, mean); Histogram of 3D hue saturation value (HSV) and statistics (min, max, mean); Video compressibility; Histogram of facial area.

The motivation behind using each of these features is described in detail by Goyal et al. [8]. We created separate input feature vectors for audio and video. Since we wanted to examine the effectiveness of LSTMs to model context, we used the same hand-crafted features as given by Goyal et al. [8] as input to the model. In principle, a deep network can learn appropriate features from input data and may not need separate feature selection. But since the dataset used was relatively small and sparse for training a deep learning model such as LSTM, it could prove difficult to train with a high number of input features. Also, Wöllmer et al. [16] reported a gain in emotion prediction accuracy using LSTMs for conversation videos using a correlation-based feature selection (CFS) prescribed by Witten and Frank [15]. Therefore, using CFS, we selected only the audio and video features that showed a correlation above a certain threshold with the annotated arousal and valence values. Thus, we formed the following input feature vectors:

(1) Audio arousal model: 52 audio features,
(2) Audio valence model: 45 audio features,
(3) Video arousal model: 48 video features, and
(4) Video valence model: 48 audio features.

As suggested by Goyal et al. [8], we did not calculate visual features for two animated movies from the dataset, as certain visual features typically extracted for animated movies would be different than those for non-animated movies.

3 PROPOSED PREDICTION MODEL

Fig. 2 (a) shows the LSTM-based continuous emotion prediction model proposed in this paper. It consists of separate models for audio and video prediction, denoted by gray boxes followed by a late fusion over these predictions, and is constructed separately for arousal and valence.

3.1 LSTM-based Model

LSTM is a recurrent neural network that allows learning context from sequential inputs [7]. It consists of memory cells where an input sequence is scaled by the activation of an input gate, output by the activation of an output gate, and past values by the activation of a forget gate. Given input sequences and corresponding output, the neural network learns parameters of all the activations using back propagation. This allows the memory cells to use past information over long periods of time. Fig. 2 (b) shows the architecture of the LSTM-based models, each shown in a gray box in Fig. 2 (a). We used two LSTMs inside each model, first to build a context around a representation of input (audio-video features) and second to model the context for the output (arousal or valence). For the audio-based arousal model, we first fed the input feature vector (length 52) to a fully connected layer with 40 nodes. We used a piece-wise differentiable Rectifier Linear Unit (ReLU) activation in this layer to transform the input into a representation suitable for LSTMs. We connected the output of the fully connected layer to LSTM I with 30 hidden layers. We connected the output of LSTM I to LSTM II with 30 hidden layers. We then subjected the output of LSTM II to a linear transformation, and used a *tanh* activation function to limit the predicted arousal values to the range of the annotated values (-1 to +1). We used the same model architecture for audio-based valence, video-based arousal and video-based valence prediction models.

We trained the aforementioned model by back propagating errors and learning weights of fully connected layers, LSTM cells and *tanh* activation function using Gradient Descent, such that the loss function L was minimized. We defined L to be the Mean Squared Error (MSE) for prediction as

$$L = \frac{1}{n}\sum_{i=1}^{n}(Y_{out,i} \quad Y_{true,i})^2 \tag{1}$$

where n was the total number of input samples, $Y_{out,i}$ was the predicted value for i^{th} sample, and $Y_{true,i}$ was the annotated value for i^{th} sample. We had a total of 17991 trainable parameters in the network. Since most (88%) of the trainable parameters were in LSTMs, we used a dropout (0.3) on LSTMs to further avoid overfitting. Since, LSTMs require a large amount of data to learn effectively, we trained them by using random batches of input features and their corresponding annotated arousal or valence values. We used a batch size of 40. Thus each batch got to optimize over a different context, in effect increasing the amount and variety of data seen by the network. We used a learning rate of 0.001 for all the models in the beginning for all parameters. We increased the rate further with a momentum of 0.05, whenever the solution moved into a particular direction in the search space for a number of iterations. We allowed the network to train for a maximum of 800 epochs. If L saturated with a zero slope for 150 iterations, we stopped the training assuming that the network had reached an optimum.

Bordwell [3] reported that typical scene lengths in modern movies were 1.5 to 3 minutes. Using this insight, we used a context of 3 minutes while training the LSTM. Given that we sampled data at 5 seconds and context required was 180 seconds, we unrolled the LSTMs 36 units in time step.

3.2 Late Fusion Model

We implemented a late fusion model to combine audio prediction $Y_{pred_{aud}}$ and video prediction $Y_{pred_{vid}}$ using their weighted average as

$$Y_{pred} = \alpha Y_{pred_{aud}} + (1 \quad \alpha) Y_{pred_{vid}} \tag{2}$$

as per Goyal et al. [8]. We selected a single value of α that maximized correlation of model predictions with annotated values for all validation folds as described in Sec. 3.4.

3.3 Early Fusion Model

For comparison, we also constructed an early fusion model for both arousal and valence, which resembled the aforementioned audio arousal model. The only differences were: (1) The input feature vector was a concatenation of the selected audio and video features, and (2) we used two fully connected layers (90 and 50 nodes each) instead of one.

3.4 Model Validation and Performance

We used a leave one out strategy for cross validation as described by Goyal et al. [8]. We trained each model using features for $m \quad 1$ movies, and validated the model by predicting arousal and valence values for the remaining one movie, where m was the total number of movies. We also calculated two model performance metrics: ρ, mean of absolute values of Pearson Correlation Coefficients (PCC) and MSE, mean of Mean Squared Error between predicted and annotated values for all m validation folds. We used features for all 12 movies for evaluation of audio-based models, and for 10 non-animated movies for evaluation of video-based and fusion models.

4 EXPERIMENTS

We replicated all scenarios reported by Goyal el al. in [8] except MoE. In specific, we ran the following experiments to evaluate the performance of the proposed model:

E1: LSTM-based model using audio features only, for all 12 movies (Audio only$_1$),

Experiment	$\rho_{ar,baseline}$		ρ_{ar}		MSE_{ar}		$\rho_{vl,baseline}$		ρ_{vl}		MSE_{vl}	
Baseline - MoE from [8])	0.62	0.16	–		–		0.29	0.16	–		–	
E1 - Audio only$_1$	0.56	0.23	**0.81**	**0.07**	0.09	0.04	0.24	0.15	**0.49**	**0.13**	0.24	0.13
E2 - Audio only$_2$	0.54	0.23	**0.80**	**0.07**	0.10	0.03	0.24	0.15	**0.49**	**0.14**	0.21	0.06
E3 - Video only	0.49	0.18	**0.70**	**0.11**	0.14	0.05	0.16	0.12	**0.40**	**0.11**	0.25	0.09
E4 - Early Fusion	0.58	0.17	**0.69**	**0.12**	0.13	0.06	0.22	0.12	**0.45**	**0.11**	0.32	0.12
E5 - Late Fusion	0.59	0.2	**0.84**	**0.06**	0.08	0.04	0.24	0.14	**0.50**	**0.14**	0.21	0.06

Table 1: A comparison of mean absolute Pearson Correlation Coefficients ρ while predicting arousal and valence using LSTM models with those for baseline results $\rho_{baseline}$ reported by Goyal et al. [8]. We also report *MSE* for arousal and valence.

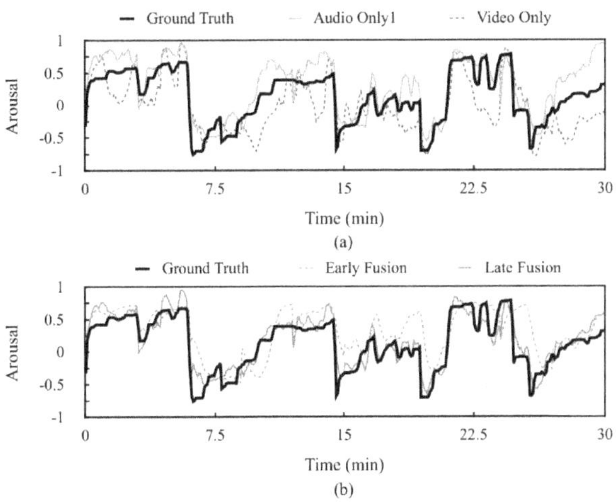

Figure 3: Prediction of arousal for the movie *Chicago* (ρ = 0.91).

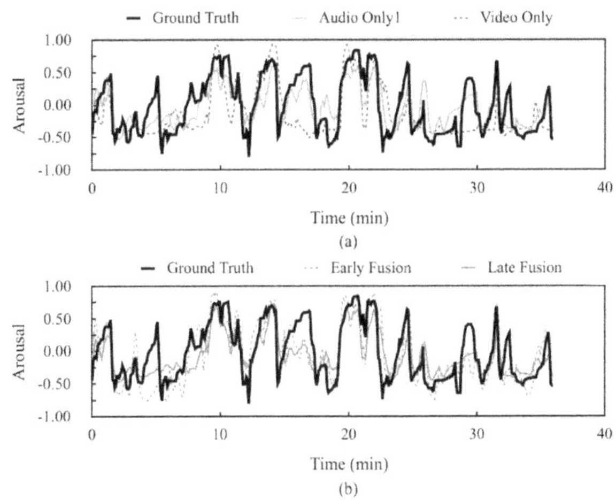

Figure 4: Prediction of arousal for the movie *Lord of The Rings: Return of the King* (ρ = 0.76).

E2: LSTM-based model using audio features only, evaluated for 10 non-animated movies (Audio only$_2$),
E3: LSTM-based model using video features only,
E4: Early fusion,
E5: Late fusion.

5 RESULTS AND DISCUSSION

Table 1 compares ρ values obtained using our prediction models with those reported by Goyal et al. [8], treated as our baseline. We observed that in all experimental cases, our corresponding models performed significantly better than [8]. Our best result was with the late fusion model (ρ_{ar} = 0.84, ρ_{vl} = 0.50), which was significantly higher that the best baseline result ($\rho_{ar,baseline}$ = 0.62, $\rho_{vl,baseline}$ = 0.24) obtained using a Mixture-of-Experts (MoE) approach. In addition, we made the following observations:

(1) We found that the LSTM-based models could handle arousal better than valence. This was consistent with results reported by Goyal et al. [8]. Since feeling good or bad while watching a movie involves more cognitive thinking related to plot and characters, valence is more difficult to capture using audio-visual cues and context than arousal.
(2) We found that the optimal weight for audio prediction, α, in the late fusion model was 0.71 for arousal and 0.97 for valence. Goyal et al. [8] reported these values to be 0.56 and 0.91 respectively. Higher α in our models is due to better performance of the LSTM-based models in capturing the audio context as seen in Table 1. The observed importance of audio in predicting emotion is consistent with the observation by Lipscomb and Kendall [11] that music in movies "*exercises a strong and consistent influence over the subject responses to an audiovisual composite, regardless of visual stimulus*".
(3) Fig. 3 shows predicted arousal using different models for the movie *Chicago*[2] against the annotation. We observed that the late fusion predictions (ρ = 0.91) closely matched the ground truth. We also observed that the audio only model (ρ = 0.88) was also able to capture the arousal well, as compared to the video only model (ρ = 0.74). This is consistent with the fact that a lot of emotion in musicals such as *Chicago* are conveyed through music, while the visuals show a darker, theatrical setting conveying less arousal than intended.
(4) Fig. 4 shows predicted arousal using different models for the movie *Lord of The Rings: Return of the King*[3] against the annotation. We observed that the late fusion predictions (ρ = 0.76) performed better than the other models. We also observed that the arousal predicted in the region between 4 to 6 minutes of the clip was flatter than the intended. We found

[2]Miramax Films.
[3]Warner Brothers.

that this was a conversational scene between the characters *Gandalf* and *Denethor* where tension was intended to rise to a high value, but the model did not seem to find audio-visual cues and context to predict the tension to the intended level. We also found that the arousal predicted in the region between 20 to 22 minutes matched the intended arousal closely. This was a battle scene at *Gondor* where high arousal was built through audio-visual cues such as music, loudness, close-ups and high optical flow, which was captured by the model well.

(5) Fig. 5 shows predicted valence using different models for the movie *American Beauty*[4] against the annotation. We observed that the late fusion predictions ($\rho = 0.67$) performed better than the other models. But despite the relatively high correlation, we found several areas where the prediction was not adequately matching the ground truth. In general, we found the valence models did not provide consistent and usable prediction, though they were an improvement over the state-of-the-art [8].

(6) The positive valence part of the scene shown in Fig.1 (b) in the movie *Crash* was not captured by the valence model, though the high arousal was captured by the arousal model. This could be mainly because it involved a high arousal scene where a shooting takes place (negative valence) followed by the realization by the father than his child is safe (positive valence). Such a perceived reversal of valence requires understanding of the plot, especially in absence of audio-visual cues to depict the change.

(7) The high arousal and negative valence components for the scene shown in Fig.1 (c) was captured by the models. This was probably because the model could capture visual cues such as fire and high optical flow, and audio cues such as high-intensity music and loud shouts.

(8) The low arousal in the scene shown in Fig.1 (d) was captured by the model, but the valence was predicted to be negative. This could be because of the dimly lit office room, dark surroundings and low voices.

(9) We also found some negative correlations in valence predictions. This may be due to cinematic grammar used by some movies not being followed by other movies, e.g. dark visuals for a scene with positive emotions, or happy music for a scene with negative emotions.

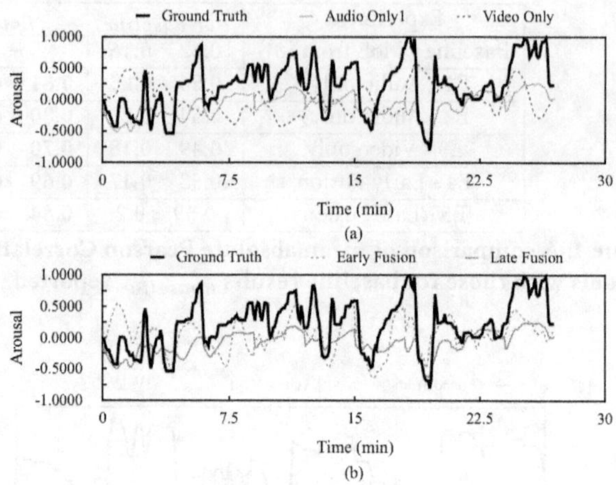

Figure 5: Prediction of valence for the movie *American Beauty* ($\rho = 0.67$).

Experiment	LSTM		SVR	
	$\Delta\rho_{ar}$	$\Delta\rho_{vl}$	$\Delta\rho_{ar}$	$\Delta\rho_{vl}$
E1 - Audio only$_1$	0.01	0.03	0.04	0.07
E2 - Audio only$_2$	0.01	0.02	0.03	0.07
E3 - Video only	0.01	0.04	0.08	0.12
E4 - Early Fusion	0.02	0.04	–	–
E5 - Late Fusion	0.00	0.02	–	–

Table 2: Change in Pearson Correlation Coefficients, $\Delta\rho$, for arousal and valence LSTM models after filtering predictions using an optimal Gaussian window. The table also shows such change using a Support Vector Regression (SVR) model.

5.1 Effectiveness in Modeling Context

Goyal et al. [8] used a Gaussian smoothing to incorporate context in predicted values and prescribed using length of the smoothing window that maximized ρ. We found no significant difference in ρ for our model predictions after we applied optimal Gaussian filtering. For example, we found that ρ_{ar} for LSTM prediction as well as for the filtered prediction were the same (0.84). Table 2 shows the improvement in correlation, $\Delta\rho$, obtained after filtering the predictions using optimal Gaussian filtering. For comparison with the LSTM-based models, we also used Support Vector Regression (SVR) for prediction as employed by [8], and found that there was a marked improvement in ρ with filtering[5]. For example, ρ_{ar} for **E3** (video only) increased from 0.40 to 0.48 for SVR, while it increased only from 0.70 to 0.71 for the corresponding LSTM model. This indicated that LSTMs were already capturing the context information, and there was no need for an external filter to be used. We also found that the LSTM-based valence models had not done as well as the arousal models in capturing the context, as seen from the larger improvement obtained after optimal filtering.

5.2 Additional Validation

In general, we observed that though we had trained the model with MSE as the loss function, the late fusion prediction had high correlation with the ground truth. To further ensure that we were not overfitting, we evaluated the performance of audio only$_1$ arousal model using one half of each test movie for testing and the other for validation. We obtained $\rho_{ar} = 0.85 \quad 0.05$ for test data and $\rho_{ar} = 0.75 \quad 0.14$ for validation data, indicating that the model could generalize on unseen data.

[4]DreamWorks Pictures.

[5]We did not carry out the SVR experiment for E4 and E5.

6 CONCLUSION AND FUTURE WORK

In this paper, we presented a continuous emotion prediction model for movies. We used LSTMs to model context information, while using hand-crafted audio-video features as input. We presented significant improvements over the state-of-the-art results, while establishing that LSTMs could effectively model context information in movies. We found encouraging and usable results while predicting arousal. For predicting valence, we believe that there is a need to incorporate more semantic information about the plot and the characters for better predictions.

In future, we intend to train LSTM-based models which incorporate late fusion estimating α at every time step. This might be useful in localized scenes where video helps in predicting emotions better than audio, as opposed to using a single value of optimized *alpha* reported in this paper. We also intend to test the model on different datasets such as LIRIS-ACCEDE [2] to test its efficacy. Though we have used random batching of input data to increase the context data seen by LSTMs, they would benefit from a larger annotated dataset. One direction of research could be creating such a dataset using crowdsourcing and wearables. We believe that the model can be used in a variety of entertainment applications once it is trained on larger and more varied datasets.

7 ACKNOWLEDGMENTS

We thank Nikos Malandrakis from University of Southern California and Nancy Zlatintsi from National Technical University of Athens for sharing the annotation data, and Rohit Saxena, Savita Bhat and Shirish Karande from TCS Research for discussions and reviews.

REFERENCES

[1] Yoann Baveye, Christel Chamaret, Emmanuel Dellandréa, and Liming Chen. 2017. Affective Video Content Analysis: A Multidisciplinary Insight. *IEEE Transactions on A⊠ective Computing* (2017).

[2] Yoann Baveye, Emmanuel Dellandrea, Christel Chamaret, and Liming Chen. 2015. Liris-accede: A video database for affective content analysis. *IEEE Transactions on A⊠ective Computing* 6, 1 (2015), 43–55.

[3] David Bordwell. 2006. *The way Hollywood tells it: Story and style in modern movies.* Univ of California Press.

[4] Luca Canini, Sergio Benini, and Riccardo Leonardi. 2013. Affective recommendation of movies based on selected connotative features. *IEEE Transactions on Circuits and Systems for Video Technology* 23, 4 (2013), 636–647.

[5] Ho-Seung Cha, Won-Du Chang, Young Seok Shin, Dong Pyo Jang, and Chang-Hwan Im. 2015. EEG-based neurocinematics: challenges and prospects. *Brain-Computer Interfaces* 2, 4 (2015), 186–192.

[6] Richard Dietz and Annie Lang. 1999. Affective agents: Effects of agent affect on arousal, attention, liking and learning. In *Proceedings of the Third International Cognitive Technology Conference, San Francisco.*

[7] Felix A Gers, Jürgen Schmidhuber, and Fred Cummins. 1999. Learning to forget: Continual prediction with LSTM. (1999).

[8] Ankit Goyal, Naveen Kumar, Tanaya Guha, and Shrikanth S Narayanan. 2016. A multimodal mixture-of-experts model for dynamic emotion prediction in movies. In *Acoustics, Speech and Signal Processing (ICASSP), 2016 IEEE International Conference on.* IEEE, 2822–2826.

[9] Mark K Greenwald, Edwin W Cook, and Peter J Lang. 1989. Affective judgment and psychophysiological response: Dimensional covariation in the evaluation of pictorial stimuli. *Journal of psychophysiology* 3, 1 (1989), 51–64.

[10] Alan Hanjalic and Li-Qun Xu. 2005. Affective video content representation and modeling. *IEEE Transactions on multimedia* 7, 1 (2005), 143–154.

[11] Scott D Lipscomb and Roger A Kendall. 1994. Perceptual judgement of the relationship between musical and visual components in film. *Psychomusicology: A Journal of Research in Music Cognition* 13, 1-2 (1994), 60.

[12] Nikos Malandrakis, Alexandros Potamianos, Georgios Evangelopoulos, and Athanasia Zlatintsi. 2011. A supervised approach to movie emotion tracking. In *Acoustics, Speech and Signal Processing (ICASSP), 2011 IEEE International Conference on.* IEEE, 2376–2379.

[13] Mihalis A Nicolaou, Hatice Gunes, and Maja Pantic. 2011. Continuous prediction of spontaneous affect from multiple cues and modalities in valence-arousal space. *IEEE Transactions on A⊠ective Computing* 2, 2 (2011), 92–105.

[14] James A Russell and Albert Mehrabian. 1977. Evidence for a three-factor theory of emotions. *Journal of research in Personality* 11, 3 (1977), 273–294.

[15] Ian H Witten, Eibe Frank, Mark A Hall, and Christopher J Pal. 2016. *Data Mining: Practical machine learning tools and techniques.* Morgan Kaufmann.

[16] Martin Wöllmer, Moritz Kaiser, Florian Eyben, Björn Schuller, and Gerhard Rigoll. 2013. LSTM-Modeling of continuous emotions in an audiovisual affect recognition framework. *Image and Vision Computing* 31, 2 (2013), 153–163.

[17] Karthik Yadati, Harish Katti, and Mohan Kankanhalli. 2014. CAVVA: Computational affective video-in-video advertising. *IEEE Transactions on Multimedia* 16, 1 (2014), 15–23.

[18] Shiliang Zhang, Qingming Huang, Shuqiang Jiang, Wen Gao, and Qi Tian. 2010. Affective visualization and retrieval for music video. *IEEE Transactions on Multimedia* 12, 6 (2010), 510–522.

Learning Perceptual Embeddings with Two Related Tasks for Joint Predictions of Media Interestingness and Emotions

Yang Liu
Department of Computer Science
Hong Kong Baptist University
Hong Kong SAR, China
IRACE, HKBU, Shenzhen, China
csygliu@comp.hkbu.edu.hk

Zhonglei Gu
Department of Computer Science
Hong Kong Baptist University
Hong Kong SAR, China
cszlgu@comp.hkbu.edu.hk

Tobey H. Ko
Department of Industrial and Manufacturing Systems Engineering
The University of Hong Kong
Hong Kong SAR, China
tobeyko@hku.hk

Kien A. Hua
Department of Computer Science
University of Central Florida
Orlando, Florida, USA
kienhua@cs.ucf.edu

ABSTRACT

Integrating media elements of various medium, multimedia is capable of expressing complex information in a neat and compact way. Early studies have linked different sensory presentation in multimedia with the perception of human-like concepts. Yet, the richness of information in multimedia makes understanding and predicting user perceptions in multimedia content a challenging task both to the machine and the human mind. This paper presents a novel multi-task feature extraction method for accurate prediction of user perceptions in multimedia content. Differentiating from the conventional feature extraction algorithms which focus on perfecting a single task, the proposed model recognizes the commonality between different perceptions (e.g., interestingness and emotional impact), and attempts to jointly optimize the performance of all the tasks through uncovered commonality features. Using both a media interestingness dataset and a media emotion dataset for user perception prediction tasks, the proposed model attempts to simultaneously characterize the individualities of each task and capture the commonalities shared by both tasks, and achieves better accuracy in predictions than other competing algorithms on real-world datasets of two related tasks: MediaEval 2017 Predicting Media Interestingness Task and MediaEval 2017 Emotional Impact of Movies Task.

ICMR '18, June 11–14, 2018, Yokohama, Japan

ACM ISBN 978-1-4503-5046-4/18/06...$15.00
https://doi.org/10.1145/3206025.3206071

KEYWORDS

Perceptual embedding, multi-task feature extraction, multimedia interestingness prediction, multimedia emotional impact prediction

ACM Reference Format:
Yang Liu, Zhonglei Gu, Tobey H. Ko, and Kien A. Hua. 2018. Learning Perceptual Embeddings with Two Related Tasks for Joint Predictions of Media Interestingness and Emotions. In *ICMR '18: 2018 International Conference on Multimedia Retrieval, June 11–14, 2018, Yokohama, Japan.* ACM, New York, NY, USA, 8 pages. https://doi.org/10.1145/3206025.3206071

1 INTRODUCTION

Multimedia is created by integrating media elements in various mediums to form a representation of information alluring to the audience. By mixing together different medium (such as text, images, audios, videos), multimedia has the capability of delivering a large volume of information in a small space. Such characteristics make multimedia ideal for delivering the difficult and complex information, fueling multimedia to gain in popularity in a diversity of applications, ranging from advertising to education and entertainment, ever since its conception hundreds of years ago. Alongside technological advancements which bring increasing complexity to multimedia content, multimedia expression has gone through some major evolutions over the years. For instance, the use of color and structure in images, the choice of tone and tempo in music, the utilization of audio/visual effect and editing in movies, etc., have all experienced drastic changes in the history of multimedia. Multimedia content evolved as content creators attempt to search for more effective ways to interest the targeted audience and deliver complex message in a compact manner. The study of user perception of multimedia content is therefore conceived.

The study of user perception is, in essence, a study of information processing. Psychologists see perception as the processing of information to create a mapping between the separate sensory presentations and the re-presentation by the mind [8]. Under this framework, vague concepts such as interestingness, affective values and emotions, aesthetic values, memorability in a certain multimedia content can be inferred by discovering the mapping between information in the multimedia content and these human-like concepts. For example, the psychology of color associates color of different hues and tones with a range of emotional responses [38], whereas varying the tempi, pitches, and rhythms of a musical piece can convey a multitude of feelings to the listener [37]. In this sense, a content creator can theoretically convey a certain human-like concept to the audience by simply incorporating the corresponding mapped multimedia element into the content. In practice, the understanding and prediction of user perception is, however, an entirely different story. Since the multimedia content is complex and multifaceted, understanding the impacts from individual multimedia elements is no longer sufficient, the accurate understanding and prediction of user perception on a given multimedia content thus requires careful analysis from experts.

Fast-forward to today's social media era, where individuals are accustomed to attaining information in the online arena, the multimedia content creators face the challenge of creating engaging contents to steal the viewers' limited attention span. With an ocean of raw multimedia resources accessible by the content creator, choosing the right resources for production through examining the pieces individually is nearly impossible and extremely cost-ineffective. The need to develop more effective analytic tools through computational techniques thus arise. Due to the high dimensionality of multimedia content, performing user perception analytics using the high dimensional data is inefficient and often yields unreliable results, so computational techniques typically employ a feature extraction mechanism to improve efficiency and accuracy of such techniques. In this paper, we propose a novel multi-task feature extraction model named Multi-Task Perceptual Embedding (MTPE) for effective prediction of user perceptions on multimedia data. Unlike the conventional feature extraction algorithms which attempt to perfect the performance of the model for a single task, the proposed model aims at optimizing the performance of multiple related user perception tasks by recognizing the commonalities among them.

Figure 1 illustrates the concept of the proposed MTPE. Given datasets ($\mathbf{X}^1$ and $\mathbf{X}^2$) from different tasks (which may be different in dimensions as well as in number of data samples), the proposed MTPE aims to capture the individualities of each task (with $\mathbf{U}^1$ and $\mathbf{U}^2$, respectively) and the commonalities of both tasks (with $\mathbf{V}$). Then the high-dimensional dataset $\mathbf{X}^1$ and $\mathbf{X}^2$ can be mapped to the low-dimensional representations $\mathbf{Y}^1$ and $\mathbf{Y}^2$ by $\mathbf{W}_1(=\mathbf{U}_1\mathbf{V})$ and $\mathbf{W}_2(=\mathbf{U}_2\mathbf{V})$, respectively[1].

Apart from learning the commonalities between multiple tasks, another key aspect which differentiates the proposed

[1]Note that although the proposed method is demonstrated using two related tasks, it can be extended to the multi-task scenarios in a straightforward manner.

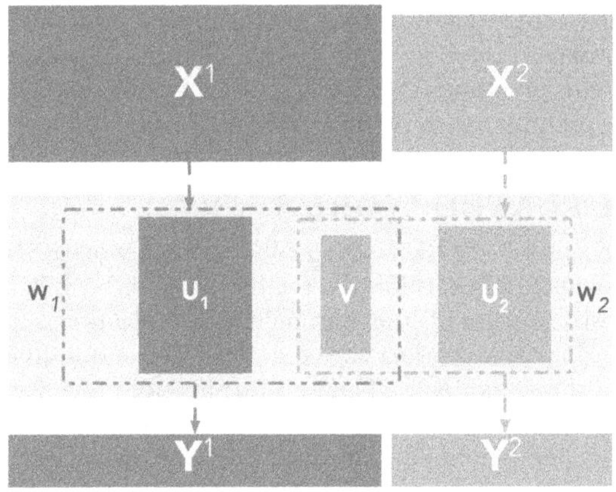

Figure 1: Illustration of the idea of Multi-Task Perceptual Embedding (MTPE).

method with conventional techniques is the consideration of an imbalance of emphasis between items among different levels of perceptions (e.g., interestingness and emotional impact) within each task. Using the dataset for MediaEval 2017 Predicting Media Interestingness Task and the LIRIS-ACCEDE dataset for MediaEval 2017 Emotional Impact of Movies Task as an example, in both interestingness and emotional impact predictions, we observe that the users' attention is generally focusing on data samples with higher interestingness levels or those with stronger emotional impacts. Therefore, we formulate a weighted discrimination maximization criterion to take the aforementioned imbalanced interests into consideration.

The contributions of this paper are summarized as follows:

- We investigate the problem of making predictions on media interestingness and emotional impacts from the perspective of multi-task feature extraction, which aims to simultaneously find compact and discriminative features for both tasks. To the best of our knowledge, there is no existing work attempting to explore this challenging problem via multi-task feature extraction.
- We propose a novel method named Multi-Task Perceptual Embedding (MTPE) to learn the low-dimensional discriminative representations for two related tasks. The individualities of each task and the commonalities shared by both tasks are modeled in MTPE. A weighted discrimination maximization criterion is proposed to take special care on more important data samples (e.g., the media data of keener interests or the media data that express/invoke stronger emotions).
- We perform extensive experiments on real-world datasets of two related tasks, i.e., the MediaEval 2017 Predicting Media Interestingness Task and the MediaEval 2017 Emotional Impact of Movies Task, showing the effectiveness of the proposed method.

The rest of the paper is organized as follows. In Section 2, we briefly review some related works on feature extraction for predicting interestingness and emotional impact of multimedia content and multi-task feature extraction. The proposed method is introduced in Section 3. The evaluation results of the proposed method on real-world datasets of two related tasks are presented in Section 4. Finally, we conclude our paper and discuss the future works in Section 5.

2 RELATED WORKS

The proposed MTPE aims to collaboratively learn the feature transformations for two related tasks, i.e., multimedia interestingness prediction and multimedia emotional impact prediction, by exploring the commonalities and individualities of these two tasks. This section therefore reviews some related works on feature extraction for multimedia interestingness and emotional impact predictions, as well as those on multi-task feature extraction.

2.1 Feature Extraction for Predicting Interestingness of Multimedia Content

Existing computational models predicted media content interestingness based on different kinds of features, such as low-level visual features [43], high-level image features [12], a combination of low-level and high-level features [24], and perceptual features [18, 19]. With these high-dimensional features, some feature extraction algorithms have been proposed to extract informative features for better prediction. For instance, several studies used the classical feature extraction algorithm, principal component analysis (PCA) [21], to reduce the high-dimensionality [40, 41]. Shen et al. [42] and Berson et al. [4] proposed deep learning models to extract multi-modal features for media interestingness prediction. Ben-Ahmed et al. inferred the media genres from the audio-visual deep features extracted from a deep neural network for media interestingness prediction [3]. Liu et al. presented several supervised dimensionality reduction methods to learn discriminative features from the high-dimensional multimedia data for interestingness prediction [28, 29, 31].

2.2 Feature Extraction for Predicting Emotional Impacts of Multimedia Content

Similar to the task of media interestingness prediction, feature extraction also plays an important role in the task of emotion prediction. Several works recently have devised algorithms with feature extraction techniques on various applications. Fewzee and Karray utilized PCA and its variants to reduce the dimensionality of speech features for emotional speech recognition [13]. Jenke et al. compared some feature extraction and selection methods for emotion recognition on EEG data [22]. Ma et al. used PCA and convolutional neural network (CNN) to extract visual features for predicting emotional impacts of movies [36]. Liu et al. developed several supervised feature extraction algorithms for multimedia emotion classification and prediction [30, 32]. Gaikwad et al. employed dimensionality reduction to extract facial features to recognize emotion states [39].

2.3 Multi-task Feature Extraction

Although seldom applied to the context of multimedia interestingness and emotional impact predictions, studies exploring multi-task feature extraction techniques to enhance the learning performance have gained momentum in recent years. Yamane et al. [45] and Zhang et al. [47] extended the classical PCA [21] and linear discriminant analysis (LDA) [14], to their multi-task versions, respectively. Yan et al. further extended the multi-task LDA for view-invariant action recognition [46]. Argyriou et al. presented a method to learn a low-dimensional representation shared across multiple related tasks [1]. Gong et al. introduced several multi-task feature learning strategies to capture a common set of features among relevant tasks [15–17]. Zuo et al. proposed a multi-view multi-task feature extraction method for web image classification [48]. Jin et al. explored several algorithms to learn the common subspace for multiple feature spaces from different tasks [26, 27]. Lu et al. presented a multilinear factorization machine for multi-task multi-view learning [33]. Luo et al. exploited a large margin multi-modal multi-task feature extraction algorithm to explore the complementary nature of different modalities obtained from multiple tasks [35]. They further developed a tensor based heterogeneous multi-task feature learning framework to exploit high-order information among different tasks [34].

3 PROPOSED METHOD

3.1 Problem Definition

Suppose we are given two related learning tasks, multimedia interestingness prediction (denoted as $\mathcal{T}_1$) and multimedia emotional impact prediction (denoted as $\mathcal{T}_2$). The training set $\mathcal{S}_i = \{(\mathbf{x}_j^i, \mathbf{l}_j^i)\}_{j=1}^{n_i}$ $(i = 1, 2)$ for $\mathcal{T}_i$ contains n_i data samples with $\mathbf{x}_j^i \in \mathbb{R}^{D_i}$ and its corresponding label $\mathbf{l}_j^i$, where D_i is the original dimensionality of the data samples in $\mathcal{S}_i$. In our problem, we have $l_j^1 \in [0, 1]$, with 1 indicating extremely interesting and 0 indicating extremely non-interesting. Meanwhile, we have $\mathbf{l}_j^2 = [l_{j(1)}^2, l_{j(2)}^2]^T$ being the emotion label vector of $\mathbf{x}_j^2$, where $l_{j(1)}^2, l_{j(2)}^2 \in [-1, 1]$ denote the arousal value and valence value, respectively.

Given the above training datasets, the proposed Multi-Task Perceptual Embedding (MTPE) aims to learn two transformation matrices $\mathbf{W}_i \in \mathbb{R}^{D_i \times d}$ $(d < D_i, i = 1, 2)$, which are capable of projecting the original high-dimensional data in $\mathcal{S}_i$ to a low-dimensional subspace $\mathcal{Y} = \mathbb{R}^d$ by $\mathbf{y}_j^i = \mathbf{W}_i^T \mathbf{x}_j^i$, where the commonalities and individualities of $\mathcal{S}_1$ and $\mathcal{S}_2$ could be preserved.

3.2 Objective Function

3.2.1 *Maximizing Weighted Discrimination.*

To improve the accuracy of predictions, we aim to maximize the discrimination of the learned subspace. An interesting observation in both interestingness and emotional impact predictions is that we generally do not pay equal attention to the data samples with different labels. For instance, in the task of multimedia interestingness prediction, we probably

$$\{\mathbf{W}_i\}_{i=1,2} = \underset{\{\mathbf{W}_i\}_{i=1,2}}{\arg\max} \frac{tr\Big(\sum_{i=1}^{2}\big(\sum_{j,k=1}^{n_i} B_{jk}^i(\mathbf{W}_i^T\mathbf{x}_j^i - \mathbf{W}_i^T\mathbf{x}_k^i)(\mathbf{W}_i^T\mathbf{x}_j^i - \mathbf{W}_i^T\mathbf{x}_k^i)^T\big)\Big)}{tr\Big(\sum_{i=1}^{2}\big(\sum_{j,k=1}^{n_i} A_{jk}^i(\mathbf{W}_i^T\mathbf{x}_j^i - \mathbf{W}_i^T\mathbf{x}_k^i)(\mathbf{W}_i^T\mathbf{x}_j^i - \mathbf{W}_i^T\mathbf{x}_k^i)^T\big)\Big)}. \tag{1}$$

pay more attention to the interesting media data than those non-interesting ones; in the task of multimedia emotional impact prediction, we might be more interested in the media data that express/invoke stronger emotions.

Taking the aforementioned imbalanced interests into consideration, we propose the objective function for weighted discrimination maximization in Eq. (1). In the objective function, $tr(\cdot)$ denotes the trace operation, and

$$B_{jk}^i = ||\mathbf{l}_j^i - \mathbf{l}_k^i||_2 \times \frac{||\mathbf{l}_j^i||_2 + ||\mathbf{l}_k^i||_2}{2} \times N_{jk}^i, \tag{2}$$

$$A_{jk}^i = \big(\max_{j,k}\{||\mathbf{l}_j^i - \mathbf{l}_k^i||_2\} - ||\mathbf{l}_j^i - \mathbf{l}_k^i||_2\big) \times \frac{||\mathbf{l}_j^i||_2 + ||\mathbf{l}_k^i||_2}{2} \times N_{jk}^i, \tag{3}$$

where $||\cdot||_2$ denotes the L_2 norm, $N_{jk}^i = exp(-||\mathbf{x}_j^i - \mathbf{x}_k^i||^2/2\sigma_i)$ indicates the closeness of two samples in the original feature space of $\mathcal{S}_i$, and σ_i is empirically set by $\sigma_i = \sum_{j=1}^{n_i}||\mathbf{x}_j^i - \mathbf{x}_{j(K)}^i||_2^2/n_i$ with $\mathbf{x}_{j(K)}^i$ being the K-th nearest neighbor of $\mathbf{x}_j^i$ [29].

On the right-hand side of Eq. (2) and Eq (3), the first term denotes the dissimilarity (for Eq. (2)) or similarity (for Eq. (3)) between two labels; the second term represents the magnitude of two labels, which indicates the importance of the corresponding data samples; and the last term measures the similarity between two data samples in the original feature space.

The motivation of the first term in Eq. (2) and Eq (3) is that, the more distinct two labels from each other, the more effort we have to put on to differentiate the corresponding data samples in the learned subspace; the more similar two labels are, the more effort we should put on to pull them together. The rationale of the second term is to pay more attention to the data samples with higher importance, which is consistent with our emphasis on more interesting media data in the task of interestingness prediction and the data with stronger emotional impacts in the task of emotional impact prediction. The purpose of the last term is to maintain the neighbor relations for nearby data samples with similar labels in the learned subspace while differentiating neighboring data with different labels as much as possible. With the above settings in Eq. (1) - Eq. (3), the objective of weighted discrimination maximization is achieved and thus the label of a new data sample is expected to be more reliably predicted.

3.2.2 *Learning Commonalities and Individualities.*

In order to capture the commonalities between $\mathcal{S}_1$ and $\mathcal{S}_2$ while characterizing the individualities of $\mathcal{S}_1$ and $\mathcal{S}_2$, we represent $\mathbf{W}_i$ $(i = 1, 2)$ as:

$$\mathbf{W}_i = \mathbf{U}_i\mathbf{V}, \tag{4}$$

where $\mathbf{U}_1 \in \mathbb{R}^{D_1\times D}$ and $\mathbf{U}_2 \in \mathbb{R}^{D_2\times D}$ are the interestingness-specific and emotion-specific transformation matrices to extract the individual features from $\mathcal{S}_1$ and $\mathcal{S}_2$, respectively, while $\mathbf{V} \in \mathbb{R}^{D\times d}$ is introduced to mine the common perceptual features shared by $\mathcal{S}_1$ and $\mathcal{S}_2$. Here D is the intermediate dimensionality.

Based on Eq. (4), the objective function in Eq. (1) could be rewritten as:

$$\{\mathbf{U}_i\}_{i=1,2}, \mathbf{V} = \underset{\substack{\{\mathbf{U}_i\}_{i=1,2},\mathbf{V}\\ \mathbf{U}_i^T\mathbf{U}_i=\mathbf{I}_D\\ \mathbf{V}^T\mathbf{V}=\mathbf{I}_d}}{\arg\max} \frac{tr\Big(\sum_{i=1}^{2}\mathbf{V}^T\mathbf{U}_i^T\mathbf{B}^i\mathbf{U}_i\mathbf{V}\Big)}{tr\Big(\sum_{i=1}^{2}\mathbf{V}^T\mathbf{U}_i^T\mathbf{A}^i\mathbf{U}_i\mathbf{V}\Big)}, \tag{5}$$

where

$$\mathbf{B}^i = \sum_{j,k=1}^{n_i} B_{jk}^i(\mathbf{x}_j^i - \mathbf{x}_k^i)(\mathbf{x}_j^i - \mathbf{x}_k^i)^T, \tag{6}$$

$$\mathbf{A}^i = \sum_{j,k=1}^{n_i} A_{jk}^i(\mathbf{x}_j^i - \mathbf{x}_k^i)(\mathbf{x}_j^i - \mathbf{x}_k^i)^T. \tag{7}$$

Moreover, we introduce two constraints $\mathbf{U}_i^T\mathbf{U}_i = \mathbf{I}_D$ and $\mathbf{V}^T\mathbf{V} = \mathbf{I}_d$ to remove the scaling factor in the learning process and eliminate the redundancy between different projection directions, where $\mathbf{I}_D$ and $\mathbf{I}_d$ denote the D-dimensional and d-dimensional identity matrices, respectively.

3.3 Optimization Procedure

To the best of our knowledge, there is no closed-form solution for the optimization problem in Eq. (5). Therefore, we utilize an alternating strategy to solve it. First we fix $\mathbf{U}_2$ and $\mathbf{V}$, and find the optimal $\mathbf{U}_1$. Then we fix $\mathbf{U}_1$ and $\mathbf{V}$, and find the optimal $\mathbf{U}_2$. Finally, we fix $\mathbf{U}_1$ and $\mathbf{U}_2$, and find the optimal $\mathbf{V}$. We repeat the above procedure until convergence. Specifically, we introduce the optimization details as follows.

3.3.1 *Optimizing $\mathbf{U}_1$ with fixed $\mathbf{U}_2$ and $\mathbf{V}$.*

We rewrite Eq. (5) as follows:

$$\mathbf{U}_1 = \underset{\substack{\mathbf{U}_1\\ \mathbf{U}_1^T\mathbf{U}_1=\mathbf{I}_D}}{\arg\max} \frac{tr(\mathbf{V}^T\mathbf{U}_1^T\mathbf{B}^1\mathbf{U}_1\mathbf{V}) + tr(\mathbf{V}^T\mathbf{U}_2^T\mathbf{B}^2\mathbf{U}_2\mathbf{V})}{tr(\mathbf{V}^T\mathbf{U}_1^T\mathbf{A}^1\mathbf{U}_1\mathbf{V}) + tr(\mathbf{V}^T\mathbf{U}_2^T\mathbf{A}^2\mathbf{U}_2\mathbf{V})}. \tag{8}$$

As both $\mathbf{U}_2$ and $\mathbf{V}$ are fixed, the second term of the numerator and that of the denominator are two constants. Moreover, according to the given constraints $\mathbf{U}_2^T\mathbf{U}_2 = \mathbf{I}_D$ and $\mathbf{V}^T\mathbf{V} = \mathbf{I}_d$, we have $\mathbf{V}^T\mathbf{U}_2^T\mathbf{U}_2\mathbf{V} = \mathbf{V}^T\mathbf{V} = \mathbf{I}_d$, and thus $tr(\mathbf{V}^T\mathbf{U}_2^T\mathbf{U}_2\mathbf{V}) = tr(\mathbf{I}_d) = d$. Then we can rewrite Eq. (8) as:

$$\mathbf{U}_1 = \underset{\substack{\mathbf{U}_1\\ \mathbf{U}_1^T\mathbf{U}_1=\mathbf{I}_D}}{\arg\max} \frac{tr(\mathbf{V}^T\mathbf{U}_1^T\tilde{\mathbf{B}}^1\mathbf{U}_1\mathbf{V})}{tr(\mathbf{V}^T\mathbf{U}_1^T\tilde{\mathbf{A}}^1\mathbf{U}_1\mathbf{V})}, \tag{9}$$

Algorithm 1: Optimizing $\mathbf{U}_1$ with fixed $\mathbf{U}_2$ and $\mathbf{V}$

Input: Training datasets $\mathcal{S}_1, \mathcal{S}_2$ and existing $\mathbf{U}_1, \mathbf{U}_2, \mathbf{V}$
Output: Updated $\mathbf{U}_1$

$\mathbf{U}_1^{(0)} \leftarrow \mathbf{U}_1$;
Compute $\tilde{\mathbf{B}}^1$ using Eq. (10);
Compute $\tilde{\mathbf{A}}^1$ using Eq. (11);
for $m \leftarrow 1, ..., M$ **do**
  $r_{1(m)} \leftarrow \frac{tr(\mathbf{V}^T(\mathbf{U}_1^{(m-1)})^T\tilde{\mathbf{B}}^1\mathbf{U}_1^{(m-1)}\mathbf{V})}{tr(\mathbf{V}^T(\mathbf{U}_1^{(m-1)})^T\tilde{\mathbf{A}}^1\mathbf{U}_1^{(m-1)}\mathbf{V})}$;
  $\mathbf{P}_1^{(m)} \leftarrow$ the top D eigenvectors of $(\tilde{\mathbf{B}}^1 - r_{1(m)}\tilde{\mathbf{A}}^1)$;
  $\mathbf{Q} \leftarrow$ the eigenvector matrix of $\mathbf{V}\mathbf{V}^T$;
  $\mathbf{U}_1^{(m)} \leftarrow \mathbf{P}_1^{(m)}\mathbf{Q}^T$;
  $\tilde{\mathbf{A}}_U^1 \leftarrow \mathbf{U}_1^{(m)}(\mathbf{U}_1^{(m)})^T\tilde{\mathbf{A}}^1\mathbf{U}_1^{(m)}(\mathbf{U}_1^{(m)})^T$;
  $\mathbf{U}_1^{(m)} \leftarrow$ the top D eigenvectors of $\tilde{\mathbf{A}}_U^1$;
  if $||\mathbf{U}_1^{(m)} - \mathbf{U}_1^{(m-1)}||_F \leq \epsilon$ **then**
    Break;
  end
end
$\mathbf{U}_1 \leftarrow \mathbf{U}_1^{(m)}$;

Algorithm 2: Optimizing $\mathbf{U}_2$ with fixed $\mathbf{U}_1$ and $\mathbf{V}$

Input: Training datasets $\mathcal{S}_1, \mathcal{S}_2$ and existing $\mathbf{U}_1, \mathbf{U}_2, \mathbf{V}$
Output: Updated $\mathbf{U}_2$

$\mathbf{U}_2^{(0)} \leftarrow \mathbf{U}_2$;
Compute $\tilde{\mathbf{B}}^2$ using Eq. (13);
Compute $\tilde{\mathbf{A}}^2$ using Eq. (14);
for $m \leftarrow 1, ..., M$ **do**
  $r_{2(m)} \leftarrow \frac{tr(\mathbf{V}^T(\mathbf{U}_2^{(m-1)})^T\tilde{\mathbf{B}}^2\mathbf{U}_2^{(m-1)}\mathbf{V})}{tr(\mathbf{V}^T(\mathbf{U}_2^{(m-1)})^T\tilde{\mathbf{A}}^2\mathbf{U}_2^{(m-1)}\mathbf{V})}$;
  $\mathbf{P}_2^{(m)} \leftarrow$ the top D eigenvectors of $(\tilde{\mathbf{B}}^2 - r_{2(m)}\tilde{\mathbf{A}}^2)$;
  $\mathbf{Q} \leftarrow$ the eigenvector matrix of $\mathbf{V}\mathbf{V}^T$;
  $\mathbf{U}_2^{(m)} \leftarrow \mathbf{P}_2^{(m)}\mathbf{Q}^T$;
  $\tilde{\mathbf{A}}_U^2 \leftarrow \mathbf{U}_2^{(m)}(\mathbf{U}_2^{(m)})^T\tilde{\mathbf{A}}^2\mathbf{U}_2^{(m)}(\mathbf{U}_2^{(m)})^T$;
  $\mathbf{U}_2^{(m)} \leftarrow$ the top D eigenvectors of $\tilde{\mathbf{A}}_U^2$;
  if $||\mathbf{U}_2^{(m)} - \mathbf{U}_2^{(m-1)}||_F \leq \epsilon$ **then**
    Break;
  end
end
$\mathbf{U}_2 \leftarrow \mathbf{U}_2^{(m)}$;

where

$$\tilde{\mathbf{B}}^1 = \mathbf{B}^1 + \frac{\mathbf{I}_{D_1}}{d} tr(\mathbf{V}^T\mathbf{U}_2^T\mathbf{B}^2\mathbf{U}_2\mathbf{V}), \tag{10}$$

$$\tilde{\mathbf{A}}^1 = \mathbf{A}^1 + \frac{\mathbf{I}_{D_1}}{d} tr(\mathbf{V}^T\mathbf{U}_2^T\mathbf{A}^2\mathbf{U}_2\mathbf{V}). \tag{11}$$

According to the theorems in [47], the optimization problem in Eq. (9) can be solved in an iterative way. The detailed procedure is listed in Algorithm 1, where M is the maximum iteration number.

3.3.2 Optimizing $\mathbf{U}_2$ with fixed $\mathbf{U}_1$ and $\mathbf{V}$.
Similar to the objective function in Eq. (9), the optimal $\mathbf{U}_2$ can be obtained by maximizing the following objective function:

$$\mathbf{U}_2 = \underset{\substack{\mathbf{U}_2 \\ \mathbf{U}_2^T\mathbf{U}_2 = \mathbf{I}_D}}{\arg\max} \frac{tr(\mathbf{V}^T\mathbf{U}_2^T\tilde{\mathbf{B}}^2\mathbf{U}_2\mathbf{V})}{tr(\mathbf{V}^T\mathbf{U}_2^T\tilde{\mathbf{A}}^2\mathbf{U}_2\mathbf{V})}, \tag{12}$$

where

$$\tilde{\mathbf{B}}^2 = \mathbf{B}^2 + \frac{\mathbf{I}_{D_2}}{d} tr(\mathbf{V}^T\mathbf{U}_1^T\mathbf{B}^1\mathbf{U}_1\mathbf{V}), \tag{13}$$

$$\tilde{\mathbf{A}}^2 = \mathbf{A}^2 + \frac{\mathbf{I}_{D_2}}{d} tr(\mathbf{V}^T\mathbf{U}_1^T\mathbf{A}^1\mathbf{U}_1\mathbf{V}). \tag{14}$$

The procedure for optimizing $\mathbf{U}_2$ with fixed $\mathbf{U}_1$ and $\mathbf{V}$ is described in Algorithm 2.

3.3.3 Optimizing $\mathbf{V}$ with fixed $\mathbf{U}_1$ and $\mathbf{U}_2$.
When $\mathbf{U}_1$ and $\mathbf{U}_2$ are fixed, the optimization problem in Eq. (5) becomes

$$\mathbf{V} = \arg\max_{\mathbf{V}} \frac{tr\Big(\mathbf{V}^T\big(\sum_{i=1}^2 \mathbf{U}_i^T\mathbf{B}^i\mathbf{U}_i\big)\mathbf{V}\Big)}{tr\Big(\mathbf{V}^T\big(\sum_{i=1}^2 \mathbf{U}_i^T\mathbf{A}^i\mathbf{U}_i\big)\mathbf{V}\Big)}. \tag{15}$$

We then utilize the decomposed Newton's method (DNM) introduced in [23] to solve the above trace ratio optimization problem [23, 44].

Algorithm 3: Multi-Task Perceptual Embedding (MTPE)

Input: The training datasets $\mathcal{S}_1, \mathcal{S}_2$
Output: $\mathbf{U}_1, \mathbf{U}_2, \mathbf{V}$

Initialize $\mathbf{U}_1^{(0)}, \mathbf{U}_2^{(0)}, \mathbf{V}^{(0)}$ as arbitrary column orthogonal matrices;
for $i \leftarrow 1, 2$ **do**
  for $j, k \leftarrow 1, ..., n_i$ **do**
    Compute B_{jk}^i using Eq. (2);
    Compute A_{jk}^i using Eq. (3);
  end
  Compute $\mathbf{B}^i$ using Eq. (6);
  Compute $\mathbf{A}^i$ using Eq. (7);
end
while *not converge* **do**
  Optimize $\mathbf{U}_1$ using Algorithm 1;
  Optimize $\mathbf{U}_2$ using Algorithm 2;
  Optimize $\mathbf{V}$ using DNM [23];
end

In the above alternating strategy, we can obtain a globally optimal solution at each step [23, 44, 47]. Therefore, the proposed method can be guaranteed to converge to a locally optimal solution [5]. The entire procedure of the proposed MTPE is summarized in Algorithm 3.

4 EXPERIMENTAL VALIDATION

In this section, we evaluate the performance of the proposed method on real-world datasets of two related tasks: 1) the dataset for MediaEval 2017 Predicting Media Interestingness

Task [11]; and 2) the LIRIS-ACCEDE dataset for MediaEval 2017 Emotional Impact of Movies Task [2, 9].

4.1 Dataset Description

4.1.1 Dataset for Media Interestingness Prediction. The dataset for MediaEval 2017 Predicting Media Interestingness Task [11] is extracted from Hollywood-like videos under the Creative Commons license. In particular, 103 movie trailers and 4 continuous extracts of ca. 15min from full-length movies are included in the dataset. The entire dataset contains $9,831$ shots, $7,396$ of which are used for training and the remaining $2,435$ shots are used for test in our experiments. For each shot, the middle frame is extracted as its key frame and a set of low-level features of this key frame is computed as the original feature representation of the corresponding shot [10]. In our experiments, we utilize five types of features, i.e., 300-D dense Scale Invariant Feature Transform (dense SIFT) features, 300-D HoG 2×2 features, 59-D Local Binary Patterns (LBP) features, 512-D GIST features, and 128-D color histogram features. The total dimension of the feature set is therefore $1,299$. All data are manually annotated in terms of interestingness ranging from 0 to 1 by human assessors.

4.1.2 Dataset for Emotional Impact Prediction. The dataset for MediaEval 2017 Emotional Impact of Movies Task is the LIRIS-ACCEDE dataset (liris-accede.eclyon.fr), which contains videos from a set of 160 professionally made and amateur movies, shared under Creative Commons licenses that allow redistribution [2]. The entire dataset contains $10,984$ ten-second shots, $5,274$ of which are used for training and the remaining $5,710$ shots are used for test in our experiments. For each ten-second shot, we further partition it to 10 one-second segment, and extract ten types of feature for this one-second segment, i.e., 256-D Auto Color Correlogram (ACC) features, 144-D Color and Edge Directivity Descriptor (CEDD) features, 33-D Color Layout (CL) features, 80-D Edge Histogram (EH) features, 192-D Fuzzy Color and Texture Histogram (FCTH) features, 60-D Gabor features, 168-D Joint descriptor joining CEDD and FCTH in one histogram features, 256-D LBP features, 64-D Scalable Color (SC) features, and 18-D Tamura features. The total dimension of the feature vector for the one-second segment is therefore $1,271$. We then calculate the mean and standard deviation over the feature vectors of 10 one-second segments, and concatenate these two $1,271$-D vectors as the feature representation of each ten-second shot. Therefore, the original dimension of the data is $2,542$ in our experiments. All data are manually annotated in terms of arousal and valence ranging from -1 to 1 by human assessors.

4.2 Experimental Results

In order to validate the effectiveness of the proposed method, we compare it with six representative feature extraction algorithms, including PCA [21], LDA [14], locality preserving projection (LPP) [20], supervised manifold regression (SMR) [28], biased discriminant embedding (BDE) [30], and multi-task discriminant analysis (MTDA) [47]. We also include the performance of original data (without feature extraction) as the baseline.

For both datasets, we normalize each dimension of the training data to the range $[0,1]$ by $\hat{x} = \frac{x - x_{min}}{x_{max} - x_{min}}$ before feature extraction, where x_{min} and x_{max} denote the minimum and maximum values in the corresponding dimension, respectively. After feature extraction, we use ϵ-SVR [6] with an RBF kernel to predict the continuous value of interestingness, arousal, and valence. We set $cost = 1$, $\epsilon = 0.001$, and $\gamma = \frac{1}{1,299}$ for interestingness dataset and $\gamma = \frac{1}{2,542}$ for emotion dataset.

In order to reflect different importance levels of various data samples, in our experiments, we use the Weighted Root-Mean-Square Error (W-RMSE) and the Weighted Mean Absolute Error (W-MAE) [7] to evaluate the performance of different algorithms. Specifically, the W-RMSE and W-MAE in our experiments are defined as follows:

$$\text{W-RMSE} = \sqrt{\sum_{j=1}^{n} \frac{|l_j|}{n} (\hat{l}_j - l_j)^2}, \tag{16}$$

$$\text{W-MAE} = \frac{\sum_{j=1}^{n} (|l_j| \cdot |\hat{l}_j - l_j|)}{\sum_{j=1}^{n} |l_j|}, \tag{17}$$

where l_j and $\hat{l}_j$ denote the ground truth label and the predicted label, respectively, and $|\cdot|$ denotes the absolute value. By utilizing the weighted criteria, we put heavy penalty on the mis-predicted samples with large value of $|l_j|$ (i.e., media data of high interest or those with high emotional intensity), which is consistent with our intention of making accurate predictions on data with great emphasis.

Table 1 shows the performance of aforementioned seven feature extraction methods (as well as the baseline) on the dataset for MediaEval 2017 Predicting Media Interestingness Task (predicting interestingness level) and the LIRIS-ACCEDE dataset for MediaEval 2017 Emotional Impact of Movies Task (predicting arousal and valence values). By simultaneously characterizing the individualities of each task and capturing the commonalities shared by both tasks, MTPE achieves better performance than PCA, LDA, LPP, SMR, BDE, as well as the baseline. By maximizing the weighted discrimination, the MTPE also performs better than another typical multi-task feature extraction algorithm, MTDA, in most of the situations.

After having demonstrated the effectiveness of the proposed method, we further demonstrate the contribution of original features on both the interestingness prediction dataset (task 1) and the emotional impact prediction dataset (task 2). For task i ($i = 1, 2$), we define the contribution of the s-th feature ($s = 1, ..., D_i$) as:

$$Contribution_{(i)s} = \sum_{t=1}^{d} |w_{(i)st}|, \tag{18}$$

where $w_{(i)st}$ denotes the (s,t)-th element of $\mathbf{W}_i$. For each $\mathbf{w}_{(i)t}$ (i.e., the t-th column of $\mathbf{W}_i$), the magnitude of its s-th component $w_{(i)st}$ serves as the weight of the s-th dimension

Table 1: Performance evaluation (in terms of weighted RMSE and weighted MAE) of the proposed MTPE and six competing feature extraction algorithms on the dataset for MediaEval 2017 Predicting Media Interestingness Task (predicting interestingness level) and the LIRIS-ACCEDE dataset for MediaEval 2017 Emotional Impact of Movies Task (predicting arousal and valence values). The corresponding optimal reduced dimension (i.e., d) of each method on each prediction task is listed in the bracket.

	Weighted RMSE			Weighted MAE		
	Interestingness	Arousal	Valence	Interestingness	Arousal	Valence
Original	0.1581 (1299)	0.1965 (2542)	0.2110 (2542)	0.2433 (1299)	0.3821 (2542)	0.4718 (2542)
PCA [1933]	0.1586 (7)	0.2121 (10)	0.2307 (5)	0.2301 (6)	0.3687 (8)	0.4715 (10)
LDA [1936]	0.1703 (2)	0.1970 (2)	0.2142 (2)	0.2386 (2)	0.3712 (2)	0.4691 (2)
LPP [2003]	0.1592 (8)	0.2248 (4)	0.2178 (6)	0.2222 (16)	0.3751 (10)	0.4663 (12)
SMR [2016]	0.1643 (8)	0.1792 (10)	0.2213 (9)	0.2101 (9)	0.3412 (7)	0.4518 (11)
BDE [2017]	0.1686 (7)	0.1715 (8)	0.2101 (10)	0.2073 (10)	0.3522 (6)	0.4478 (13)
MTDA [2011]	0.1601 (19)	0.1587 (12)	**0.1950** (13)	0.1813 (15)	0.3396 (19)	0.4381 (16)
MTPE [proposed]	**0.1578** (20)	**0.1480** (13)	0.1970 (16)	**0.1594** (17)	**0.3311** (20)	**0.4250** (11)

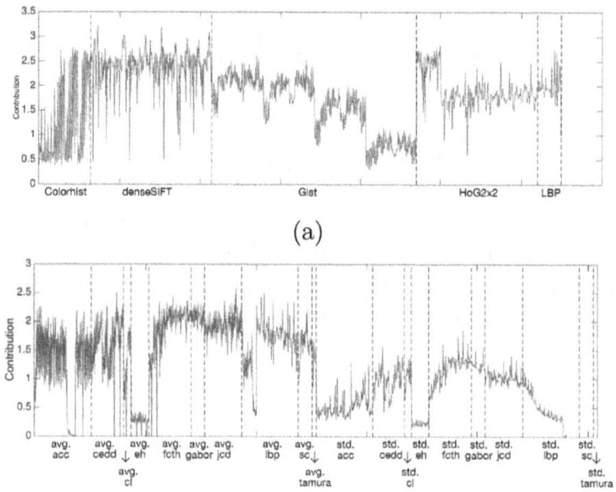

(a)

(b)

Figure 2: Analysis of feature contribution on both datasets. (a) Contribution of each feature of data in interestingness prediction dataset. (b) Contribution of each feature of data in emotional impact prediction dataset

in the original space when mapping the data sample to the low-dimensional space. By summating $|w_{(i)st}|$ over t, the overall contribution of the s-th dimension is obtained.

Figure 2 shows the contribution of each feature on both datasets. From Figure 2(a), we can observe that the denseSIFT and HoG features play the most important role in the media interestingness prediction. This observation is consistent with the conclusion drawn in [25] on a different dataset, pointing out the denseSIFT and HoG features consistently outperform the other visual features in the task of video emotion prediction. Provided that the contributions of these features were not significant in single-task feature extraction methods (SMR and BDE) on media interestingness prediction task [31], it implies the enhanced dominance is captured from the commonalities of the two related tasks, in which the proposed method uncovered the features that are important to both tasks, even though the denseSIFT and HoG features were not included in our emotional impact prediction dataset.

5 CONCLUSIONS AND OUTLOOK

This paper presented a novel feature extraction method dubbed Multi-Task Perceptual Embedding (MTPE) to learn the low-dimensional discriminative representations for two related tasks, i.e., predicting interestingness and predicting emotional impacts of multimedia content. By simultaneously characterizing the individualities of each task and capturing the commonalities shared by two tasks, the proposed method achieved better performance than other competing algorithms on both the dataset for MediaEval 2017 Predicting Media Interestingness Task and the LIRIS-ACCEDE dataset for MediaEval 2017 Emotional Impact of Movies Task.

The future work will be investigated from the following three aspects. First, although MTPE outperformed the other methods, the linear mapping mechanism limits the discriminative ability of the learned subspace and there is still room for improvement. We therefore plan to extend the proposed method to nonlinear versions by exploring powerful nonlinear learning mechanisms such as deep neural nets and kernel methods. Moreover, in the current formulation, we used a transformation matrix $\mathbf{V}$ to extract the common features shared by two tasks. We are interested in exploiting other manners to capture the relations between different tasks. Last but not least, as both interestingness and emotion are the perceptual concepts originated from psychology, we are going to further examine the physical meaning of the extracted features by referring the domain-knowledge in psychology, which can help us improve the interpretability of the proposed method.

ACKNOWLEDGMENTS

This work was supported in part by the National Natural Science Foundation of China under Grant 61503317, in part by the Grant from the Research Grant Council of Hong Kong SAR under Project RGC/HKBU12202417, in part by the Science and Technology Research and Development Fund of Shenzhen with Project Code JCYJ20170307161544087, and in part by the Faculty Research Grant of Hong Kong Baptist University (HKBU) under Project FRG2/16-17/032.

REFERENCES

[1] A. Argyriou, T. Evgeniou, and M. Pontil. 2007. Multi-Task Feature Learning. In *NIPS 19*. 41–48.

[2] Y. Baveye, E. Dellandréa, C. Chamaret, and L. Chen. 2015. LIRIS-ACCEDE: A Video Database for Affective Content Analysis. *IEEE Trans. Affect. Comput.* 6, 1 (2015), 43–55.

[3] O. Ben-Ahmed, J. Wacker, A. Gaballo, and B. Huet. 2017. EURECOM MediaEval 2017: Media Genre Inference for Predicting Media Interestingness. In *Proc. of the MediaEval 2017 Workshop*. Dublin, Ireland, Sept. 13–15, 2017.

[4] E. Berson, C.-H. Demarty, and N. Q. K. Duong. 2017. Multimodality and Deep Learning when Predicting Media Interestingness. In *Proc. of the MediaEval 2017 Workshop*. Dublin, Ireland, Sept. 13–15, 2017.

[5] D.P. Bertsekas. 1999. *Nonlinear Programming*. Athena Scientific.

[6] Chih-Chung Chang and Chih-Jen Lin. 2011. LIBSVM: A library for support vector machines. *ACM Transactions on Intelligent Systems and Technology* 2 (2011), 27:1–27:27. Issue 3.

[7] S. Cleger-Tamayo, J. M. Fernandez-Luna, and J. F. Huete. 2012. On the use of Weighted Mean Absolute Error in Recommender Systems. In *Proceedings of the Workshop on Recommendation Utility Evaluation (RUE 2012)*. 24–26.

[8] J. E. Cutting. 1987. Perception and information. *Annual review of psychology* 38, 1 (1987), 61–90.

[9] E. Dellandrea, M. Huigsloot, L. Chen, Y. Baveye, and M. Sjoberg. 2017. The MediaEval 2017 Emotional Impact of Movies Task. In *Mediaeval 2017 Workshop*. Dublin, Ireland, Sept. 13–15, 2017.

[10] C.-H. Demarty, M. Sjöberg, B. Ionescu, T.-T. Do, H. Wang, N. Q. K. Duong, and F. Lefebvre. 2016. MediaEval 2016 Predicting Media Interestingness Task. In *Proc. of the MediaEval 2016 Workshop*. Hilversum, Netherlands, Oct. 20–21, 2016.

[11] C.-H. Demarty, M. Sjoberg, B. Ionescu, T.-T. Do, M. Gygli, and N. Q. K. Duong. 2017. MediaEval 2017 Predicting Media Interestingness Task. In *Proc. of the MediaEval 2017 Workshop*. Dublin, Ireland, Sept. 13–15, 2017.

[12] S. Dhar, V. Ordonez, and T. L. Berg. 2011. High level describable attributes for predicting aesthetics and interestingness. In *CVPR 2011*. 1657–1664.

[13] P. Fewzee and F. Karray. 2012. Dimensionality Reduction for Emotional Speech Recognition. In *2012 International Conference on Privacy, Security, Risk and Trust and 2012 International Confernece on Social Computing*. 532–537.

[14] R. A. Fisher. 1936. The Use of Multiple Measurements in Taxonomic Problems. *Ann. Eugen.* 7 (1936), 179–188.

[15] P. Gong, J. Ye, and C. Zhang. 2012. Multi-Stage Multi-Task Feature Learning. In *NIPS 25*. 1988–1996.

[16] P. Gong, J. Ye, and C. Zhang. 2012. Robust Multi-task Feature Learning. In *Proc. 18th SIGKDD*. 895–903.

[17] P. Gong, J. Ye, and C. Zhang. 2013. Multi-stage Multi-task Feature Learning. *J. Mach. Learn. Res.* 14, 1 (2013), 2979–3010.

[18] H. Grabner, F. Nater, M. Druey, and L. Van Gool. 2013. Visual Interestingness in Image Sequences. In *Proc. 21st ACM Multimedia*. 1017–1026.

[19] M. Gygli, H. Grabner, H. Riemenschneider, F. Nater, and L. V. Gool. 2013. The Interestingness of Images. In *Proc. ICCV*. 1633–1640.

[20] X. He and P. Niyogi. 2004. Locality Preserving Projections. In *NIPS 16*.

[21] H. Hotelling. 1933. Analysis of a complex of statistical variables into principal components. *J. Educ. Psychol.* 24, 6 (1933), 417–441.

[22] R. Jenke, A. Peer, and M. Buss. 2014. Feature Extraction and Selection for Emotion Recognition from EEG. *IEEE Trans. Affect. Comput.* 5, 3 (2014), 327–339.

[23] Y. Jia, F. Nie, and C. Zhang. 2009. Trace Ratio Problem Revisited. *IEEE Trans. Neural Netw.* 20, 4 (2009), 729–735.

[24] Y.-G. Jiang, Y. Wang, R. Feng, X. Xue, Y. Zheng, and H. Yang. 2013. Understanding and Predicting Interestingness of Videos. In *Proc. 27th AAAI*.

[25] Y.-G. Jiang, B. Xu, and X. Xue. 2014. Predicting Emotions in User-Generated Videos. In *Proc. 28th AAAI*. 73–79.

[26] X. Jin, F. Zhuang, S. J. Pan, C. Du, P. Luo, and Q. He. 2015. Heterogeneous Multi-task Semantic Feature Learning for Classification. In *Proc. 24th CIKM*. 1847–1850.

[27] X. Jin, F. Zhuang, H. Xiong, C. Du, P. Luo, and Q. He. 2014. Multi-task Multi-view Learning for Heterogeneous Tasks. In *Proc. 23rd CIKM*. 441–450.

[28] Y. Liu, Z. Gu, and Y.-M. Cheung. 2016. Supervised Manifold Learning for Media Interestingness Prediction. In *Proc. of the MediaEval 2016 Workshop*. Hilversum, Netherlands, Oct. 20–21, 2016.

[29] Y. Liu, Z. Gu, Y.-M. Cheung, and K. A. Hua. 2017. Multi-view Manifold Learning for Media Interestingness Prediction. In *Proc. ICMR*. 308–314.

[30] Y. Liu, Z. Gu, and T. H. Ko. 2017. HKBU at MediaEval 2017 - Emotional Impact of Movies Task. In *Mediaeval 2017 Workshop*. Dublin, Ireland, Sept. 13–15, 2017.

[31] Y. Liu, Z. Gu, and T. H. Ko. 2017. Predicting Media Interestingness via Biased Discriminant Embedding and Supervised Manifold Regression. In *Proc. of the MediaEval 2017 Workshop*. Dublin, Ireland, Sept. 13–15, 2017.

[32] Y. Liu, Y. Liu, Y. Zhao, and K.A. Hua. 2015. What Strikes the Strings of Your Heart? – Feature Mining for Music Emotion Analysis. *IEEE Trans. Affect. Comput.* 6, 3 (2015), 247–260.

[33] C.-T. Lu, L. He, W. Shao, B. Cao, and P. S. Yu. 2017. Multilinear Factorization Machines for Multi-Task Multi-View Learning. In *Proc. 10th WSDM*. 701–709.

[34] Y. Luo, D. Tao, and Y. Wen. 2017. Exploiting High-Order Information in Heterogeneous Multi-Task Feature Learning. In *Proc. 26th IJCAI*. 2443–2449.

[35] Y. Luo, Y. Wen, D. Tao, J. Gui, and C. Xu. 2016. Large Margin Multi-Modal Multi-Task Feature Extraction for Image Classification. *IEEE Trans. Image Process.* 25, 1 (2016), 414–427.

[36] Y. Ma, Z. Ye, and M. Xu. 2016. THU-HCSI at MediaEval 2016: Emotional Impact of Movies Task. In *Proc. of the MediaEval 2016 Workshop*. Hilversum, Netherlands, Oct. 20–21, 2016.

[37] L. B. Meyer. 1961. *Emotion and Meaning in Music*. University of Chicago Press.

[38] L.-C. Ou, M. R. Luo, A. Woodcock, and A. Wright. 2004. A study of colour emotion and colour preference. Part I: Colour emotions for single colours. *Color Research and Application* 29, 3 (June 2004), 232–240.

[39] K. P. Gaikwad, C. M. Sheela Rani, S. B. Mahajan, and P. Sanjeevikumar. 2018. Dimensionality Reduction of Facial Features to Recognize Emotion State. In *Advances in Systems, Control and Automation*, A. Konkani, R. Bera, and S. Paul (Eds.). Springer Singapore, 719–725.

[40] J. Parekh, H. Tibrewal, and S. Parekh. 2017. The IITB Predicting Media Interestingness System for MediaEval 2017. In *Proc. of the MediaEval 2017 Workshop*. Dublin, Ireland, Sept. 13–15, 2017.

[41] R. A. Permadi, S. G. P. Putra, Helmiriawan, and C. C. S. Liem. 2017. DUT-MMSR at MediaEval 2017: Predicting Media Interestingness Task. In *Proc. of the MediaEval 2017 Workshop*. Dublin, Ireland, Sept. 13–15, 2017.

[42] Y. Shen, C. H. Demarty, and N. Q. K. Duong. 2017. Deep learning for multimodal-based video interestingness prediction. In *Proc. 18th ICME*. 1003–1008.

[43] M. Soleymani. 2015. The Quest for Visual Interest. In *Proc. 23rd ACM Multimedia*. 919–922.

[44] H. Wang, S. Yan, D. Xu, X. Tang, and T. Huang. 2007. Trace Ratio vs. Ratio Trace for Dimensionality Reduction. In *Proc. CVPR*. 1–8.

[45] I. Yamane, F. Yger, M. Berar, and M. Sugiyama. 2016. Multitask Principal Component Analysis. In *Proc. 8th ACML*, Vol. 63. 302–317.

[46] Y. Yan, E. Ricci, R. Subramanian, G. Liu, and N. Sebe. 2014. Multitask Linear Discriminant Analysis for View Invariant Action Recognition. *IEEE Tran. Image Process.* 23, 12 (2014), 5599–5611.

[47] Y. Zhang and D.-Y. Yeung. 2011. Multi-Task Learning in Heterogeneous Feature Spaces. In *Proc. 25th AAAI*. 574–579.

[48] Z. Zuo, Y. Luo, D. Tao, and C. Xu. 2014. Multi-view Multi-task Feature Extraction for Web Image Classification. In *Proc. 22nd ACM Multimedia*. 1137–1140.

Deep Pairwise Classification and Ranking for Predicting Media Interestingness

Jayneel Parekh
Indian Institute of Technology Bombay
Mumbai, India
jayneelparekh@gmail.com

Harshvardhan Tibrewal
Indian Institute of Technology Bombay
Mumbai, India
hrtibrewal@gmail.com

Sanjeel Parekh
LTCI, Télécom ParisTech and Technicolor R&I
France
sanjeelparekh@gmail.com

ABSTRACT

With the explosive increase in the consumption of multimedia content in recent years, the field of media interestingness analysis has gained a lot of attention. This paper tackles the problem of image interestingness in videos and proposes a novel algorithm based on pairwise-comparisons of frames to rank all frames in a video. Experiments performed on the Predicting Media Interestingness dataset, affirm its effectiveness over existing solutions. In terms of the official metric i.e. Mean Average Precision at 10, it outperforms the previous state-of-the-art (to the best of our knowledge) on this dataset. Additional results on video interestingness substantiate the flexibility and performance reliability of our approach.

KEYWORDS

Media Interestingness, Image Interestingness, Pairwise Comparisons, Artificial Neural Network

ACM Reference Format:

Jayneel Parekh, Harshvardhan Tibrewal, and Sanjeel Parekh. 2018. Deep Pairwise Classification and Ranking for Predicting Media Interestingness. In *ICMR '18: 2018 International Conference on Multimedia Retrieval, June 11–14, 2018, Yokohama, Japan.* ACM, New York, NY, USA, 6 pages. https://doi.org/10.1145/3206025.3206078

1 INTRODUCTION

Due to an outburst of internet usage and cheaper data transmission, recent years have observed a huge increase in the consumption of multimedia content. The content's interestingness is an important concern for both, its consumers and creators. This has led to an increased effort towards building systems that automatically predict media interestingness. Quantifying this notion finds interesting applications in areas such as personalized retrieval and recommendation of multimedia.

Interestingness is a subjective property and varies depending upon personal preferences. Despite these variations, it has been observed that individuals tend to largely agree on image interestingness [14, 25]. The possibility of building its computational models was demonstrated in some early works by Dhar et al. [12] and Gygli et al. [14]. While the former predicts interestingness on Flickr dataset using high-level aesthetic features, the authors of latter use aesthetics, unusualness and general preferences as cues for the task.

The ambiguity involved in defining the notion of interestingness can be reduced by collecting and annotating data with a specific use case in mind. The Predicting Media Interestingness Task [10, 11], organized as part of MediaEval benchmark initiative, attempts to do so in the context of a real-world use case provided by Technicolor, which involves helping professionals to illustrate a Video on Demand (VOD) web site by selecting some interesting frames and/or video excerpts for the posted movies [11]. Specifically, an image/video was defined to be interesting *in the context of helping a user to make his/her decision about whether he/she is interested in watching the movie it represents* [9]. In this work, we tackle the image interestingness subtask which requires to automatically identify images from a given set of key-frames (extracted from a movie trailer) that viewers report to be the most interesting with respect to the above definition. While we focus on image interestingness, to demonstrate the flexibility of our method, we also show the results on the video interestingness subtask. This subtask involves automatically identifying video shots from a given set of shots of a movie trailer, that viewers report to be the most interesting.

In contrast to prior work, where datasets relied on social popularity cues such as comments and views for labeling [9], this task adopted for a more content-specific and task-centric annotation procedure. In particular, labeling was done using a pair-wise comparison protocol [4], wherein annotators were provided with a pair of images at a time (taken from same trailer) and asked to tag the more "interesting" one. It is worth noting that here, interestingness, as a property of an image, is local to the trailer it is taken from and is in general less subjective when seen relative to other images coming from similar context, in this case, the same trailer. This motivates us to design a system which can learn to *compare* interestingness of images from the same trailer. In general such relative attribute modelling has been applied to various visual recognition tasks [20].

Inspired by this annotation protocol and use case, we propose a two-step approach to image interestingness prediction. Our contributions are three-fold: (i) We design a novel deep architecture for pair-wise interestingness classification, that closely simulates

ICMR '18, June 11–14, 2018, Yokohama, Japan

ACM ISBN 978-1-4503-5046-4/18/06...$15.00
https://doi.org/10.1145/3206025.3206078

the annotation process, (ii) we experiment with different ranking algorithms for arranging the pairwise results, and (iii) demonstrate the effectiveness of our system through experimental validation. It is worth mentioning that we achieve state-of-the-art results on MediaEval task's benchmark dataset. Moreover, as shown through its application to videos, the presented approach can be generally applied to other forms of multimedia.

The rest of this work is organized as follows: in Section 2 we discuss related works and Section 3 describes our system in more detail along with the different ranking algorithms. Section 4 details the experimental setup, followed by results and discussion in Section 5.

2 RELATED WORK

Our previous work [19] adopted two different kinds of approaches to interestingness prediction. The first one treated this as a typical classification problem where the classifier was trained to classify any given image as interesting/non-interesting. The second approach, which is closely related to our current work, consisted of pairwise classification followed by ranking. The input image representation was obtained after running principal component analysis on fc7 (of AlexNet [15]) features. However, this did not yield good results. We hypothesize that this occurred because (i) the input was processed using a linear classifier which did not allow adaptation to the task at hand and (ii) poor parameter tuning. We alleviate these shortcomings by employing a deep architecture and carefully experimenting with hyperparameters on a randomly chosen validation set. Our claims are well supported through experiments detailed in Section 4.

RUC team's submission [26] to MediaEval Interestingness Task is another closely related work. The authors approach this as a deep ranking problem, using image pairs with a ranking loss. There are key differences with our current work with regard to the network architecture, training, and ranking methods (discussed in Section 3.2). Moreover, we investigate a two-step procedure where ranking is performed separately with different algorithms. As we show through experimental validation, we outperform this method by a significant margin.

We acknowledge that a lot of research has been done in computer vision and machine learning community on siamese networks for measuring similarity in images and producing a ranking. The proposed architecture is reminiscent of siamese networks, introduced in 1990's by Bromley and LeCun [5]. In other domains, such as urban perception understanding, siamese convolutional neural networks with motivations similar to ours have been utilized for studying relationship between a city's physical appearance and health of its residents [13]. However as per our knowledge, this has not been extensively explored for the task of interestingness.

Lastly, we discuss some recent works achieving top results in the image interestingness subtask at MediaEval 2017:

(1) DUT-MMSR [21]: Proposed a late fusion strategy combining classifiers from different features by stacking them using logistic regression. They have used both low level and deep features (fc7) in addition to a contextual feature (mean of local binary patterns over the whole video). This approach gave the best MAP@10 for the image subtask.
(2) HKBU [17]: Present a new algorithm based on supervised dimensionality reduction of original features space to extract discriminant features with discrete and continuous labels. They use BDE and SMR algorithms mentioned in their paper and use an SVM classifier to get the final interestingness.
(3) GIBIS [1]: They focus their approach on ranking algorithms rather than classifiers. First they train different learning-to-rank algorithms creating 'rankers' capable of predicting interestingness. Later these results are combined using rank aggregation methods yielding better predictions.

3 OUR APPROACH

3.1 System Details

The proposed system is depicted in Fig. 1. We represent each image as a feature vector composed of fc7 features from AlexNet [15], officially provided by the task organizers [10]. Given a pair of images, we train a classifier to predict which image is more interesting. Specifically, the classifier takes as input for training, the concatenated fc7 representation of two images, i.e. an ordered pair (I_1, I_2), $I_1, I_2 \in \mathbb{R}^{4096}$, with the output label y assigned as follows:

$$y = \begin{cases} 1, & I_1 \text{ is more interesting than } I_2 \\ 0, & \text{otherwise} \end{cases} \tag{1}$$

The precise algorithm of training is specified in Section 4.

Classifier. The major difference in this work as compared to our previous attempt [19] is in the classifier used. Since the representation used for images is fc7 from AlexNet, which is an object recognition network, we chose to use hidden layers after concatenation of the fc7 features to tune the system for this task. Thus, the classifier used here is a neural network. The final architecture is as shown in figure 1, consisting of two fully connected hidden layers (with dropouts after input and hidden layers) and an output unit. In Section 4, we describe in greater detail the experiments carried out to arrive at this architecture.

Prediction. After training the classifier to predict the more interesting image from a given pair, we tackle the task of ranking all the images of a given video. This is carried out by first obtaining the prediction of our network on all the possible pairs images within the video and subsequently ranking them based on the results. The ranking algorithms we experiment with are described next.

3.2 Ranking Algorithms

Consider N images in any particular video, with the pairwise comparison results for (I_j, I_k) denoted by $r_{jk} \in \{0, 1\} \forall \{1 \leq j, k \leq N, j \neq k\}$. r_{jk} is equal to 1 when I_j is predicted more interesting than I_k by the classifier and 0 otherwise.

(1) **Simple Penalty** (SP) : This algorithm calculates penalties for all images and then ranks them in ascending order. Penalty of image I_j is defined as:

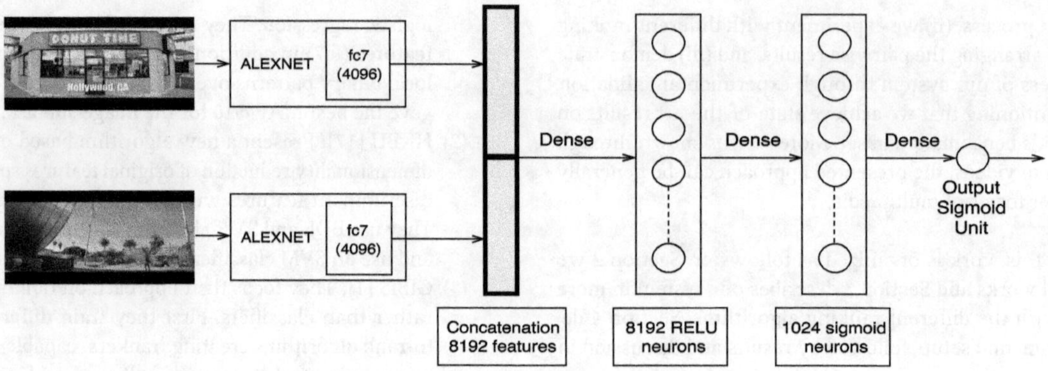

Figure 1: Pairwise comparison based Training: Concatenated images features (fc7 of AlexNet) of pairs of frames from same trailer are fed to the classifier and it learns to predict the more interesting image

$$\text{Penalty } (I_j) = \sum_{k=1, k \neq j}^{k=N} \mathbb{I}\{r_{jk} = 0\}$$

where $\mathbb{I}(.)$ denotes the indicator function. Essentially, the penalty for an image is the number of images more interesting than it, as predicted by the classifier. No special steps are taken in case of ties, and the image that appears first in the video is ranked above.

(2) **Probabilistic Penalty** (PP) :
The classifier predicts a pair of images (I_j, I_k) as r_{jk} with a confidence associated to it. Let the probability that the classifier classifies I_j more interesting be p_{jk}. That is, $p_{jk} = Pr(r_{jk} = 1)$.
Here, we define the penalty of image I_j as:

$$\text{Penalty } (I_j) = \sum_{k=1, k \neq j}^{k=N} (1 - 2 * p_{jk}) \mathbb{I}\{r_{jk} = 0\}$$

where $\mathbb{I}(.)$ denotes the indicator function. The term $(1 - 2 * p_{jk})$ is the penalty incurred whenever I_j is not predicted as more interesting. No special steps are taken in case of ties, and the image that appears first in the video is ranked above.

(3) **Minimum Inversions Heuristic** (MIH) :

Definition 3.1. An *inverted pair* in a pairwise-comparison based ranking is an ordered pair of images (I_j, I_k) such that $rank(I_j) < rank(I_k)$ but $r_{jk} = 0$. This is counted as a single inversion.

In other words, I_j has a better rank than I_k but classifier predicts I_k as more interesting. The total number of inversions in a ranking then, is the number of inverted pairs.

Definition 3.2. Optimal Ranking: A ranking is considered optimal if it minimizes the total number of inversions.

Finding such an optimal ranking is a NP-complete problem [7, 16]. However, we can arrive at the heuristic ranking method presented in Algorithm 1 by answering the following simpler question: Given k ranked images and a candidate image I, at which location should image I be placed in the ranking order so that minimum additional inversions are incurred?
We observe that the aforementioned problem, which can be solved in a brute force manner, yields a ranking of $k + 1$ images. Thus, a complete ranking can be generated by solving these sub-problems in a bottom-up fashion. The candidate image at each iteration can be chosen either according to their temporal order or randomly.
It is interesting to note that although the algorithm does not yield an optimal ranking, it does yield a "locally" optimal ranking (Please refer to the appendix for more details on this).

It is important to note that these algorithms are *not* guaranteed to produce an optimal ranking given the pairwise comparison of images but are heuristics that act as reasonable ranking algorithms. The SP & PP algorithms were also used in our previous attempt [19].

4 EXPERIMENTAL SETUP

4.1 Data

We use the Predicting Media Interestingness dataset [10], provided by the organizers at MediaEval 2017. The development data consists of 78 trailers/videos with a total of 7396 key-shots/images and the test set consists of 30 trailers/videos with 2435 key-shots/frames. Number of images in the trailer ranged from 25 to 169 (only in perfect squares). More details about the task can be found out in [10]. We randomly split the development data in two parts, training (60 videos) and validation (18 videos) sets. These two were then fixed for all the subsequent experiments. All the experiments related to different architectures and training parameters were performed using these sets, and the results on them were used to narrow down to the final architecture and training parameters. The final training for the selected architecture was done on all the development data.

4.2 Architecture

With regard to the architecture of our classification unit, we experimented with the parameters given below. The final experiments

```
Function Mininum Inversions Ranking (P_N)
    Data: Matrix P_N containing predictions of
          pairwise-comparisons
    Result: Ranking of N images
    if N = 1 is true then
        return [1];
    else
        Select a candidate image I;
        P_{N-1} = P_N - information related to I;
        rank = Mininum Inversions Ranking (P_{N-1});
        pos = -1; inv = ∞;
        for j = 1 to N do
            extra_inv = Extra inversions for ranking I at j;
            if extra_inv < inv then
                pos = j; inv = extra_inv;
            else
                continue;
            end
        end
        final_rank = Insert I in rank at pos and update rank;
        return final_rank
    end
```

Algorithm 1: Ranking images through minimum inversions heuristic. "information related to I" refers to all pairwise-comparison predictions where one of the image is I. "Removing" this information essentially corresponds to deletion of a row & column from P_N. "Extra inversions for ranking I at j" refers to increase in number of inversions, after image I is inserted at position j. Please refer to the text for more details

were carried out with settings which gave us the best results. However, we briefly discuss here our experience and conclusions to aid further research.

(1) **Number of hidden layers**: We investigated with up to 3 hidden layers before the output unit. Improvements were seen in increasing the number of hidden layers from one to two, but little to no improvement (MAP & MAP@10) was observed in increasing from two to three. Hence, we chose to go ahead with two hidden layers for its lesser training time.
(2) **Number of neurons**: We typically tried different number of neurons in exponents of two (e.g. 1024, 2048, 8192). The architecture with 8192 neurons in first hidden layer and 1024 neurons in the second generally performed better than others.
(3) **Type of neurons**: We mostly experimented with Rectified Linear Units (ReLU) [18] and Sigmoid activation units. Experiments with ReLU activation in the first and sigmoid activation in the second hidden layer performed better than all other combinations. The output unit is fixed to have sigmoid activation.
(4) **Dropout** To avoid overfitting, dropouts are added after input layer and both hidden layers. Dropout rates are kept at 50% after each layer. We observed that any variation around this value did not affect the results much.

System	MAP	MAP@10
DUT-MMSR ([21])	0.3075	0.1385
HKBU ([17])	0.2910	0.1369
GIBIS ([1])	0.2710	0.1129
RUC ([26])	0.2655	0.0940
Logistic Regression + SP [19]	0.2054	0.0521
Best run from [19]	0.2570	0.0911
Ours-MSE + SP	0.2993	0.1401
Ours-BCE + SP	0.3029	0.1513
Ours-BCE + PP	0.2932	0.1391
Ours-BCE + MIH (TO)	**0.3125**	**0.1560**
Ours-BCE + MIH (RO)	0.3023	0.1442

Table 1: Results for Image Subtask: Approaches from first block are results from prior works submitted to MediaEval 2017 Interestingness Task. The second block illustrates our submission to the same task. The third block reports results of our proposed approach in different configurations. Please refer to the text for more details.

4.3 Training details

(1) **Loss function & Optimizer**: We experimented with binary cross-entropy (BCE) and mean squared error (MSE) [27]. BCE performed better than MSE for a fixed architecture always and so we chose BCE as our loss function. Stochastic gradient descent (SGD) [23] was our optimizer in all the experiments.
(2) **Pairwise Sampling**: An epoch consisted of two iterations over each video from the training set. The batch for each iteration consisted of randomly selecting 25 images from the video, forming all the 300 pairs of concatenated fc7 feature vectors between them, with each pair randomly ordered. Random ordering is important to prevent the classifier being biased towards any particular input.

After deciding on our architecture as described in 4.2, we trained our classifier for 100 epochs. After observing the results on the validation set, for the final training (on complete development set), we decided to train our models for 35-40 epochs. We'll make our code and models publicly available.

5 RESULTS & DISCUSSION

Mean average precision at 10 (MAP@10) was used as the official metric for the MediaEval 2017 Interestingness task, since it reflects the Video-on-Demand (VOD) use case closely [10]. Thus it is used as our main metric along with Mean Average Precision (MAP).

Table 1 reports performances of various systems on the test set. It compares our performance with the best known benchmarks on this dataset for the image subtask ([21], [17], [1]) and systems similar to ours ([26], our previous attempt [19]). Each of the works mentioned in the first block of Table 1 has been briefly described in Section 2. For convenience we use following acronyms in Table 1:

(1) BCE denotes binary cross-entropy loss function and MSE denotes mean squared error loss function.

(2) SP denotes simple penalty, PP denotes probabilistic penalty, MIH denotes Minimum Inversions Heuristic. These are the ranking algorithms used, and are explained in Section 3.2
(3) In MIH, the selection of candidate images as described earlier can be made in two ways, either by selecting images in temporal order (denoted by TO), or in random order (denoted by RO).
(4) Note that "Logistic Regression + SP" denotes our previous pairwise-comparison based system [19]. This system after concatenation of fc7 features directly applies logistic regression for classification. The best run from our previous attempt is a non-pairwise classification strategy which treats this task as a binary classification problem on images, with logistic regression (l1-penalty) as the classifier.

5.1 Discussion

It is clear from the results that we outperform all the other systems on both the metrics. In particular, when compared to our previous attempt, we show significant improvement. This can be partly attributed to the use of a deep classification unit. We believe that this helps the classifier, which takes the input from an object recognition network, to adapt itself to predicting interestingness. The results for pairwise approaches in [19] are possibly also affected by poor parameter tuning.

Importance of classifier. It is worth highlighting that however good the ranking algorithm may be, the performance depends primarily on classification results. For instance, if a classifier preserves transitivity and anti-symmetry in its predictions, it would automatically define an order over the images, making ranking trivial. This supports our motivation to keep the ranking algorithms simple. Though we use heuristics to tackle the ranking problem, results in Table 1 validate their effectiveness.

Possible modifications to our system. It is worth mentioning that the experiments were carried out on a CPU (core i7, 2.4GHz, 8GB RAM), running Keras with tensorflow back-end [6]. We believe the results can be further improved through more computationally extensive experimentation on GPUs. Some of these are listed below

(1) We have used AlexNet's fc7 features as a representation of an image. There are several other networks which have been shown to give a better feature representation of an image VGG-16, ResNet, InceptionV3. On using features from such networks might improve the classifier. Also more general layers of AlexNet can be used for input representation.
(2) Instead of using two fully connected layers, more improvisations can be done in the classification unit architecture.

5.2 Additional Results on Video Interestingness

For completeness, we apply the same model with 75% dropout to the video interestingness subtask. Here the input representation is C3D features [24] extracted from video shots. We report our results in Table 2. For the third block our system variants were selected based on their performance in the image subtask. It must be noted that the best competing method [3] is a multimodal approach, utilizing various visual and audio features from pre-trained deep architectures such as VGG-16 [22] and SoundNet [2]. These are used in conjunction with neural network and SVM classifiers. The LAPI [8] team employs early and late fusion strategies using various content descriptors and SVM classifiers.

System	MAP	MAP@10
EURECOM ([3])	**0.2094**	**0.0827**
LAPI ([17])	0.2028	0.0732
Logistic Regression + SP [19]	0.1675	0.0445
Logistic Regression + PP [19]	0.1700	0.0474
Best run from [19]	0.1795	0.0525
Ours-BCE + SP	0.1979	0.0724
Ours-BCE + MIH (TO)	0.1970	0.0708
Ours-BCE + MIH (RO)	0.1982	0.0729

Table 2: Results for Video Subtask: In the first block we present the best runs from the top two teams participating in MediaEval 2017 Interestingness Task. The second block reports our submission for the same task and the last block reports selected variants of our system

We observe significant improvements over our previous attempt, and achieve results comparable to the competing methods. Our previous best method treated this as a binary classification problem on video-shots, and used SVM as the classifier. These results serve to show that our proposed technique is flexible enough when applied to different forms of multimedia without loss in performance. We realize that, as done for competing systems, with multimodal features and fusion strategies, we could further improve the results.

6 CONCLUSION

In summary, we propose a system consisting of pairwise classification and ranking to predict media interestingness. This system captures interestingness in a local environment with respect to other images/shots from the same video and tries to simulate the process of human annotation of the data. We validate the idea of using adaptive layers to tune features for the task. The combination of deep network classifier and heuristic ranking gives best results on the data in comparison to other systems known to us for the image subtask. The system generalizes to inputs of different kinds, as highlighted by its application to videos.

REFERENCES

[1] Jurandy Almeida and Ricardo M Savii. 2017. GIBIS at MediaEval 2017: Predicting Media Interestingness Task. In *Proc. of the MediaEval 2017 Workshop, Dublin, Ireland.*
[2] Yusuf Aytar, Carl Vondrick, and Antonio Torralba. 2016. Soundnet: Learning sound representations from unlabeled video. In *Advances in Neural Information Processing Systems.* 892–900.
[3] Olfa Ben-Ahmed, Jonas Wacker, Alessandro Gaballo, and Benoit Huet. 2017. EURECOM@ MediaEval 2017: Media Genre Inference for Predicting Media Interestingnes. In *Proc. of the MediaEval Workshop, Dublin, Ireland.*
[4] Ralph Allan Bradley and Milton E Terry. 1952. Rank analysis of incomplete block designs: I. The method of paired comparisons. *Biometrika* 39, 3/4 (1952), 324–345.

[5] Jane Bromley, Isabelle Guyon, Yann LeCun, Eduard Säckinger, and Roopak Shah. 1994. Signature verification using a siamese time delay neural network. In *Advances in Neural Information Processing Systems*. 737–744.
[6] François Chollet et al. 2015. Keras. (2015).
[7] William W Cohen, Robert E Schapire, and Yoram Singer. 1998. Learning to order things. In *Advances in Neural Information Processing Systems*. 451–457.
[8] Mihai Gabriel Constantin, Bogdan Boteanu, and Bogdan Ionescu. 2017. LAPI at MediaEval 2017-Predicting Media Interestingness. In *Proc. of the MediaEval Workshop, Dublin, Ireland*.
[9] Claire-Helène Demarty, Mats Sjöberg, Mihai Gabriel Constantin, Ngoc QK Duong, Bogdan Ionescu, Thanh-Toan Do, and Hanli Wang. 2017. Predicting Interestingness of Visual Content. In *Visual Content Indexing and Retrieval with Psycho-Visual Models*. Springer, 233–265.
[10] C.-H. Demarty, Mats Sjöberg, Bogdan Ionescu, Thanh-Toan Do, Michael Gygli, and Ngoc Q.K. Duong. 2017. MediaEval 2017 Predicting Media Interestingness Task. In *Proc. of the MediaEval Workshop, Dublin, Ireland*.
[11] Claire-Hélène Demarty, Mats Viktor Sjöberg, Bogdan Ionescu, Thanh-Toan Do, Hanli Wang, Ngoc QK Duong, Frédéric Lefebvre, et al. 2016. Mediaeval 2016 predicting media interestingness task. In *Proc. of the MediaEval Workshop, Hilversum, Netherlands*.
[12] Sagnik Dhar, Vicente Ordonez, and Tamara L Berg. 2011. High level describable attributes for predicting aesthetics and interestingness. In *IEEE Conference on Computer Vision and Pattern Recognition (CVPR)*. 1657–1664.
[13] Abhimanyu Dubey, Nikhil Naik, Devi Parikh, Ramesh Raskar, and César A Hidalgo. 2016. Deep learning the city: Quantifying urban perception at a global scale. In *European Conference on Computer Vision*. Springer, 196–212.
[14] Michael Gygli, Helmut Grabner, Hayko Riemenschneider, Fabian Nater, and Luc Van Gool. 2013. The interestingness of images. In *IEEE International Conference on Computer Vision (ICCV)*. IEEE, 1633–1640.
[15] Alex Krizhevsky, Ilya Sutskever, and Geoffrey E Hinton. 2012. Imagenet classification with deep convolutional neural networks. In *Advances in Neural Information Processing Systems*. 1097–1105.
[16] Tie-Yan Liu et al. 2009. Learning to rank for information retrieval. *Foundations and Trends® in Information Retrieval* 3, 3 (2009), 225–331.
[17] Yang Liu, Zhonglei Gu, and Tobey H Ko. 2017. Predicting Media Interestingness via Biased Discriminant Embedding and Supervised Manifold Regression. In *Proc. of the MediaEval Workshop, Dublin, Ireland*.
[18] Vinod Nair and Geoffrey E Hinton. 2010. Rectified linear units improve restricted boltzmann machines. In *Proc. of the 27th International Conference on Machine Learning (ICML)*. 807–814.
[19] Jayneel Parekh, Harshvardhan Tibrewal, and Sanjeel Parekh. 2017. The IITB Predicting Media Interestingness System for MediaEval 2017. In *Proc. of the MediaEval Workshop, Dublin, Ireland*.
[20] Devi Parikh and Kristen Grauman. 2011. Relative attributes. In *Computer Vision (ICCV), 2011 IEEE International Conference on*. IEEE, 503–510.
[21] Reza Aditya Permadi, Septian Gilang Permana Putra, Cynthia Helmiriawan, and CS Liem. 2017. DUT-MMSR at MediaEval 2017: Predicting Media Interestingness Task. In *Proc. of the MediaEval Workshop, Dublin, Ireland*.
[22] K. Simonyan and A. Zisserman. 2014. Very Deep Convolutional Networks for Large-Scale Image Recognition. *CoRR* abs/1409.1556 (2014).
[23] Ilya Sutskever, James Martens, George Dahl, and Geoffrey Hinton. 2013. On the importance of initialization and momentum in deep learning. In *International Conference on Machine Learning (ICML)*. 1139–1147.
[24] Du Tran, Lubomir Bourdev, Rob Fergus, Lorenzo Torresani, and Manohar Paluri. 2015. Learning spatiotemporal features with 3d convolutional networks. In *IEEE International Conference on Computer Vision (ICCV)*. IEEE, 4489–4497.
[25] Edward A Vessel and Nava Rubin. 2010. Beauty and the beholder: highly individual taste for abstract, but not real-world images. *Journal of Vision* 10, 2 (2010), 18–18.
[26] Shuai Wang, Shizhe Chen, Jinming Zhao, Wenxuan Wang, and Qin Jin. 2017. RUC at MediaEval 2017: Predicting Media Interestingness Task. In *Proc. of the MediaEval Workshop, Dublin, Ireland*.
[27] Guoqiang Peter Zhang. 2000. Neural networks for classification: a survey. *IEEE Transactions on Systems, Man, and Cybernetics, Part C (Applications and Reviews)* 30, 4 (2000), 451–462.

A APPENDIX

We now prove a property to show a form of local optimality that the Minimum Inversion Heuristic (MIH) ranking algorithm (described in section 3.2) exhibits.

Definition A.1. $S(n)$: Interchanging the rank of any two frames ranked $t, t+1, \forall 1 \leq t \leq n-1$, in a ranking of n frames as produced by Algorithm 1 strictly increases the number of inversions.

THEOREM A.2. *$S(n)$ is true* $\forall\ n \in \mathbb{Z}^+$

PROOF. This can be easily proved using induction on n. $S(1)$ is vacuously true and $S(2)$ is obviously true since for any two frames, the frame predicted more interesting by the classifier is ranked higher by Algorithm 1. Now, we need to show $S(k)$ true $\implies S(k+1)$ true. Let F_k denote the set of k frames with their corresponding ranking as produced by algorithm 1, $Inv(F_k)$ denote the total number of inversions in this ranked set of frames, $Inv(F_k, f), f \in F_k$ denote number of inversions in F_k involving f. Now for any pair of consecutively ranked frames (I_1, I_2), we have

$$Inv(F_{k+1}) = Inv(F_{k+1} - \{I_2\}, I_1) + Inv(F_{k+1} - \{I_1\}, I_2) \\ + Inv(F_{k+1} - \{I_1, I_2\}) + Inv(\{I_1, I_2\})$$

Exchanging rank of I_1, I_2 changes only the last term on the right hand side, $Inv(\{I_1, I_2\})$ which is either 1 or 0 depending upon whether ranks of the two frames agree with the prediction of classifier or not and becomes 0 or 1 respectively after the exchange. If the candidate image at $(k+1)th$ stage $I \notin \{I_1, I_2\}$, then $S(k)$ true $\implies$ exchanging the ranks of I_1, I_2, strictly increases $Inv(\{I_1, I_2\})$. If instead $I \in \{I_1, I_2\}$, then we know that exchanging ranks of I_1, I_2 can't decrease the last term because that would give a more optimal position of I which is not possible. Since this term has to change upon exchanging the ranks, it means that it will increase, implying that the total number of inversions will also increase. This proves the theorem. □

Perceptually-guided Understanding of Egocentric Video Content: Recognition of Objects to Grasp

Iván González-Díaz
Universidad Carlos III de Madrid
Leganés (Madrid), Spain
igonzalez@tsc.uc3m.es

Jenny Benois-Pineau
LaBRI - UMR 5800 - CNRS Université de Bordeaux
Talence, France
jenny.benois-pineau@u-bordeaux.fr

Jean-Philippe Domenger
LaBRI - UMR 5800 - CNRS Université de Bordeaux
Talence, France
domenger@labri.fr

Aymar de Rugy
INCIA - UMR 5287 - CNRS Université de Bordeaux
Bordeaux, France
aymar.derugy@u-bordeaux.fr

ABSTRACT

Incorporating user perception into visual content search and understanding tasks has become one of the major trends in multimedia retrieval. We tackle the problem of object recognition guided by user perception, as indicated by his gaze during visual exploration, in the application domain of assistance to upper-limb amputees. Although selecting the object to be grasped represents a task-driven visual search, human gaze recordings are noisy due to several physiological factors. Hence, since gaze does not always point to the object of interest, we use video-level weak annotations indicating the object to be grasped, and propose a video-level weak loss in classification with Deep CNNs. Our results show that the method achieves notably better performance than other approaches over a complex real-life dataset specifically recorded, with optimal performance for fixation times around 400-800ms, producing a minimal impact on subjects' behavior.

CCS CONCEPTS

• **Computing methodologies → Object recognition**; *Activity recognition and understanding*;

KEYWORDS

Human perception, video object recognition

ACM Reference Format:
Iván González-Díaz, Jenny Benois-Pineau, Jean-Philippe Domenger, and Aymar de Rugy. 2018. Perceptually-guided Understanding of Egocentric Video Content: Recognition of Objects to Grasp. In *ICMR '18: 2018 International Conference on Multimedia Retrieval, June 11–14, 2018, Yokohama, Japan.* ACM, New York, NY, USA, 9 pages. https://doi.org/10.1145/3206025.3206073

ACM ISBN 978-1-4503-5046-4/18/06...$15.00
https://doi.org/10.1145/3206025.3206073

1 INTRODUCTION

Incorporating user perception into visual content search and understanding tasks has become one of the major trends in multimedia retrieval. The application domains of these methods move from classical content-based search in multimedia databases to a great variety of tasks of human instrumentation and human-machine interfaces. In these scenarios, fusing visual data and gaze capturing devices (eye-trackers) provides a deep insight into human perception as they show exactly what a person is looking at while moving freely in any real-world setting. In the context of active perception [14], the visual searches expressed by occular saccades can be viewed and modeled as active experiments that generate the sensory data necessary to perception itself [13]. Hence, gaze information is an important cue of the user intention in scenarios like collaborative information search [9], gaze-based image retrieval [24] or meal preparation [20, 36]. We propose to use gaze to guide object detection to the element of interest, *the active object*, in egocentric video.

Our target application is assistance to upper-limb amputees wearing neuro-prostheses. Although there have been several recent attempts to use computer vision to assist prothesis control, such as in adjusting a robotic or prosthetic grasp to a recognized object [26, 35], they were typically conducted in too simple visual environments. A critical aspect of our contribution is to enable robust object identification in challenging and realistic visual scenarios containing clutter, occlusions and many objects present in the scene. Addressing this task appropriately would also be relevant to an enormous range of scenarios where identifying the object-of-interest in a scene becomes a key step for subsequent visual indexing tasks as activity recognition [17] or video summarization [22].

The use of gaze as a guiding signal for detection of objects-of-interest is very promising. User's foveation can be used to restrict recognition process to the area-of-interest. Furthermore, in contrast to the traditional annotation with bounding boxes requiring a strong human effort, gaze can be used to efficiently generate weak annotations yet useful to learn object

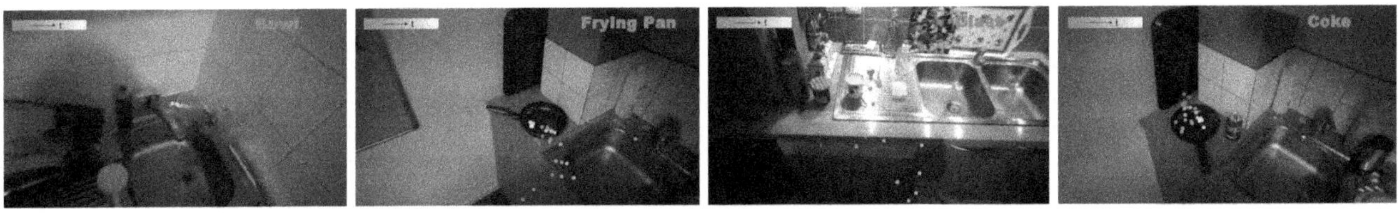

Figure 1: Examples of sequences of geometrically aligned gaze points shown in one frame of the video sequence. Points are labeled in color from the frame in which the user starts to fixate the object being grasped (red point) until the moment before the object is grasped (yellow point). Active object is indicated in the top-right corner of the images. (left) Easy case with active object fixated, (middle-left, middle-right) cases with partial distractions, (right) hard case with distracting objects and use of peripheral vision. Although color images were used in our framework, graylevel frames are used here to improve visualization.

detectors [1]. However, despite these advantages, it remains an open problem as many challenges arise in realistic environments. First, active object detection requires to identify which of the many elements in the scene is the 'active' one for every particular action. This task goes beyond the traditional object detection problem and requires to fuse object recognition techniques with automatic algorithms understanding user perception. In contrast to previous works where the active object is actually manipulated during tasks requiring eye-hand interactions [10, 23, 25], our scenario implies that the objects of interest are those that the subject wishes to grasp in an immediate future. This causes an important loss of visual support as the detection must be performed before actions are carried out. Second, gaze measurements are particularly noisy in our scenario due to many factors. For instance, the presence of distractors in a cluttered natural environment, microsaccades, or the use of peripheral vision, represent artifacts that are much more common when a subject is identifying the object to be grasped than while it is already being manipulated. This issue is illustrated in Figure 1. Third, gaze provides only partial information about the object location, which is limited to a simple point within the object, and prevents from generating ground truth bounding boxes as those required for learning in traditional supervised object detection.

All these observations lead to our particular scenario, where the granularity of the annotations moves away from the desired frame-by-frame bounding boxes to the set of clip-level object labels and noisy sequences of gaze fixations. In particular, our labels state which object is active (will be grasped in a near future) in a short video clip/temporal segment, even if the object is not fixated in all frames (see Figure 1). To address our challenging problem we present several contributions in this paper: a) A gaze-driven detection model for objects to be grasped in egocentric video. We train this model using only gaze fixations and weak video clip-level annotations. b) Two alternative methods for noise handling: one that reduces the level of noise, and another that estimate confidence measures over the gaze points. c) A new public dataset, *Grasping In The Wild (GITW)* that, in contrast to previous databases, addresses the detection of active objects in natural environments before they are actually manipulated.

The remainder of this paper is organized as follows: in section 2 we discuss related works, in section 3 a detailed description of our approach is provided, in section 4 we show our experiments and results to draw conclusions and perspectives of research in section 5.

2 RELATED WORK

Although scene analysis based on weak labels allows reducing the human effort devoted to annotate training datasets [24], it is yet a challenging and open problem due to the distinct granularity of data and labels. In our particular case, whereas object detection networks provide object scores at bounding boxes in images, our active object labels are given for short video clips associated to moments in which a subject fixates an object to be grasped. In consequence, aggregation methods are required to bridge the gap between training data and labels. Many works formulate this problem using Multiple Instance Learning (MIL) principles and develop several aggregation operators: *avg* [31], *max* [6, 27], *Log-Sum-Exp (LSE)* [31], *global weighted rank-pooling* [21], *negative evidence models* [8], *weighted average* of regions with maximum and minimum scores [7], etc. Alternatively, other approaches incorporate aggregation methods into novel losses dealing with the different granularities of data and labels: in [29] the authors propose a latent model to generate this loss, in [30] a constrained weak loss with inequalities is proposed applied over the accumulated probabilities along pixels. We can also find works in which losses are implemented over latent SVMs so that the object localization becomes the latent variable: in [2] symmetry and mutual exclusion regularizations are applied to the network outputs, in [3] visual similarity is enforced between test locations and training exemplars.

Detecting the object to be grasped goes beyond traditional object recognition as it also requires to identify which of the objects in a cluttered visual scene is the active one. In this challenging scenario, well-known region proposal techniques such as [3, 4, 32], or even specialized CNNs proposing category-aware candidate boxes [6], do not perform well. They cannot identify which is the active object among those present in a scene. However, if gaze fixations are available, they become a valuable cue of the subject intention and might be used to predict the object location. The works in [28, 34] propose methods that, learning from sequences of fixations of subjects observing images, derive bounding boxes that can be used to train object detectors. Closely related to our scenario, some works drive active object detection in egocentric videos using gaze fixations [11] or automatically computed saliency [16].

However, none of these previous approaches have considered the noisy nature of gaze due to cognitive and physiological factors. We note that some attempts to reduce noise on the basis of attention models in natural scenes with toy objects have been done in egocentric video by just removing fragments of scene exploration, and filtering detection results in a temporal buffer [5]. Our proposal, instead, aims to reduce the noise present in a sequence of gaze fixations to recognize and localize objects-of-interest in video. It also incorporates confidence measures to a weak loss used in the learning process with the ultimate goal of learning better visual models for active objects.

3 PROPOSED MODEL FOR GAZE-DRIVEN ACTIVE OBJECT DETECTION

This section describes our model for gaze-driven detection of active objects in egocentric videos with weak annotations and noise. As we show in Fig. 2, our processing pipeline can be decomposed into two different blocks, namely: a) *Data Processing and Noise Handling in gaze fixations*, which aims at generating a set of *Regions of Interest* (ROIs) per video frame that are candidate to contain the object-of-interest, and incorporates several processing modules that estimate and reduce the level of noise present in the gaze points gathered by the acquiring eye-tracker; and b) *Gaze-driven Active Object Detection*, that evaluates the candidate ROIs and recognizes the object-of-interest within a video clip.

3.1 Data Processing and Noise Handling in gaze fixations

The final goal of this block is to generate a set of candidate ROIs to evaluate the presence of active objects. To do so, the system sequentially performs several operations: first, it decouples camera and eye movements using a geometric alignment module; second, it deals with noise present in the sequence of gaze fixations due to distractors, microsaccades and peripheral vision, by following one of two alternatives: 1) reducing fixation noise or 2) estimating a confidence measure associated to each fixation; finally, it provides a set of candidate ROIs to contain the active object.

3.1.1 Geometric Alignment module: In our egocentric scenario, in which the subject wears a camera (mounted in his/her glasses), there is some motion between consecutive frames caused by the natural movement of the subject's body and head. Even if the subject is looking at the same point in the scene (e.g. the active object), the projected gaze coordinates in images will vary between two consecutive frames due to this camera motion. This issue makes that measured gaze locations in two frames cannot be directly compared unless camera and eye motions are first decoupled.

To do this we need to first estimate and compensate the ego-motion between every two consecutive frames. Given a short video clip with N frames and a sequence of gaze points $\mathbf{g}_n = \{(g_{xn}, g_{yn}), n = 1...N$, our system operates as follows: for each pair of consecutive frames, it detects and describes local features, establishes an initial set of matches, and applies a robust estimation algorithm to compute a projective transformation H (3x3 homography) between frames (e.g. DLT algorithm [18] and RANSAC [12]). Let us note that our projective homography only explains transformations of planar surfaces and cannot be applied with generality to content including volumetric surfaces. Hence, we restrict the process to a circular area surrounding the gaze point, in which depth variations can be neglected without too much error. The radius of this area is initially set to 100px and then increased if not enough local features are detected that ensure stability in the homography computation.

Once we have computed the sequence of geometric transformations $H_{n,n-1}$ between consecutive frames in the video clip, we generate an aligned sequence of fixations. For that end, we first define a common reference frame r (in our case $r = \lfloor \frac{N}{2} \rfloor$ is the central frame of the video clip), accumulate homographies to compute transformations H_{nr} between every frame n and the reference one, and generate the *aligned sequence of gaze points* $\hat{\mathbf{g}}_n$. Examples of aligned gaze sequences are shown in Fig. 1 (red-to-yellow sequences of points).

3.1.2 Noise Handling. This block constitutes one of the key elements in our proposal as it implements the two techniques that deal with noise present in the sequence of gaze fixations. In particular, we use the sequence of geometric transforms $H_{n,n-1}$ and the aligned sequence of gaze points $\hat{\mathbf{g}}_n$ to predict the most probable location of the active object in a training scene. To do so, we use Kernel Density Estimation (KDE) with 2D Gaussian kernels [33] over the sequence $\hat{\mathbf{g}}_n$ to estimate a 2-dimensional probability distribution modeling the active object location. The global maximum of this distribution becomes our prediction of the object location in the reference frame $\mathbf{o}_r = (o_{rx}, o_{ry})$. Figure 3 contains two examples of the KDE prediction (in blue).

The final goal of this module is to define a set of triplets $(\mathbf{x}_n, w_n) = (x_n, y_n, w_n)$ that will represent our weak annotations of the active object location along the frames in the video clip. Here x_n, y_n are the coordinates of the points and w_n stands for a confidence measure about the quality of the point. We have developed two complementary methods to compute these triples:

1. ***Noise Reduction***: with this method, we apply the inverse accumulated homographies $H_{n,r}^{-1}$ over the predicted object location $\mathbf{o}_r$ to generate the final sequence of points $\mathbf{o}_n$ in the video clip. Hence, the final set of points used as weak annotations is $\mathbf{x}_n = \mathbf{o}_n$, and $w_n = 1$ for every frame n in the clip. It is easy to see that this method strongly reduces the level of noise in the training data as it associates every frame to the same element in the scene (the location

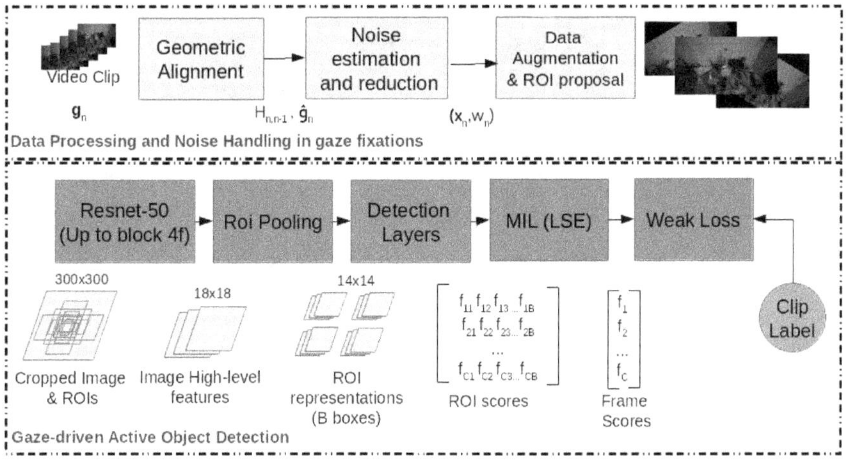

Figure 2: Proposed scheme to detect active objects under weakly supervised and noisy scenarios using gaze. A detailed description of each of the modules shown in the scheme is provided in text.

predicted by the KDE). In Figure 4 we show two examples of the original sequences of candidate ROIs (top row) and the ones generated by the method (bottom row). We can perceive how this method strongly reduces the amount of noise in the training data.

2. ***Estimation of confidence in gaze fixations***: in this second approach, we keep the original captured gaze points as weak annotations $\mathbf{x}_n = \mathbf{g}_n$ and, alternatively, estimate some weights w_n that represent our confidence in each gaze point. The weights w_n are inversely proportional to the distance between the aligned gaze point $\hat{\mathbf{g}_n}$ and the prediction of the active object location $\mathbf{o}_r$:

$$w_n \propto \exp(-\gamma d(\hat{\mathbf{g}}_n, \mathbf{o}_r)) \qquad (1)$$

where $d(\cdot)$ stands for the euclidean distance, and γ is a parameter of the model set to $\gamma = 0.01$ in some preliminary tests. Hence, gaze fixations that, when aligned to the reference frame, are close to the predicted location, are considered as good samples and receive a high weight, whereas points that are far from the object location receive lower weights. In this second approach, we are not explicitly removing noise (we are keeping the original gaze points) but, instead, estimate a metric of confidence that will be used to train our model for active object detection (see section 3.2). The rationale behind is that keeping the original gaze points may provide more diversity than generating all the annotation points as projections of the same location.

To end up, it is worth noting that these two complementary processes are performed in training, when we have access to the whole sequence of frames in each video clip. During test, the algorithm performs on a frame-by-frame basis, using the original set of gaze points $\mathbf{x}_n = \mathbf{g}_n$ with no weights.

3.1.3 Data Augmentation and ROI proposal: In order to gain diversity in the training data and account for potential transformations that may happen in test samples, we have also included a Data Augmentation module. We first rotate input images using angles in the range $[-45, 45]^\circ$, which produce quite realistic images of subjects rotating their head

Figure 3: Two examples of object prediction (coke and glass) using KDE over aligned gaze points. Images show aligned gaze points (red-to-yellow indicating time along the video clip) and the predicted object location (blue).

when scanning the scene. Next, for each image and annotation point, we adapt to the varying scale and shape of objects, proposing Regions Of Interest (ROIs) at 3 scales $s = (78, 125, 200)$ px and 3 aspect ratios $r = (0.8, 1, 1.25)$. We therefore use B=9 bounding boxes of size $w \times h$, with $w = s/\sqrt{r}$ and $h = s\sqrt{r}$, centered on random shifts around the annotation point $\mathbf{x}_n$ of the frame. Fig. 4 shows several examples of our ROI candidate set.

Let us note that our proposal might also be combined with modern region proposal algorithms, such as [32], taking those proposed boxes that contain the annotation point $\mathbf{x}_n$. However, in the experimental section we will show how using these region proposals is not enough to achieve good performance due to the noisy nature of gaze points.

3.2 Gaze-driven Active Object Detection using weak annotations

This block aims to perform a robust detection of active objects using gaze as a weak and noisy guiding signal. The system is depicted in the bottom row in Fig. 2 and involves several building blocks. It builds over the well-known Resnet-50 CNN [19] and incorporates several new layers on the top to perform the object detection in our weakly-annotated scenario.

We initialize our network with the original weights up to the layer *res4f*, and discard the remaining layers, which are instead substituted by our own blocks towards the detection

Figure 4: An illustration of the behavior of our Noise Reduction technique, which corresponds with the first example in Fig. 3. (Top) Frames with candidate ROIs computed over the original sequence of gaze points. (Bottom) Noise-free candidate ROIs by back-projecting the predicted object location to the frame sequence.

of object with weak annotations. Furthermore, we use Batch Gradient Descent algorithm for training, where each batch contains frames of the same video clip in order to apply our weak loss at the video level.

3.2.1 ROI pooling and detection layers: The output of the resnet-50 subnet is a high-level representation of the input image. In practice, for an input crop of 300×300 (centered on the gaze point) we generate a tensor of size $18 \times 18 \times 2048$, with a reduced spatial dimension (18×18) and a extended set of 2048 high-level feature channels. A nice consequence of our approach is that all this processing is made just once as it is common for every evaluated ROI in the frame.

Then, we need to generate individual representations for each considered candidate ROI, for which we use the efficient ROI Pooling method described in [15], and produce a set of B $14 \times 14 \times 2048$ tensors associated to each of the candidate ROIs. Once we have an independent representation of each ROI, we can therefore compute a detection score for each object category. For that end, the so-called *detection layer* is a fully-connected layer that transforms the $14 \times 14 \times 2048$ input tensors into a C-length vector $f_{c,b}$ with the scores of the different classes c in the ROI b. Finally, concatenating the vectors of all ROIs we can generate the matrix of ROI scores $\{f_{c,b}\}$ shown in Fig. 2, where c stands for the object class and b for the bounding box.

3.2.2 MIL aggregation: Given the matrix with the ROI scores $\{f_{c,b}\}$, we generate a vector of frame-level predictions using Multiple Instance Learning, considering that there exists at least one candidate ROI that is tight with the object being detected. In particular, we have used Log-Sum-Exp (LSE) aggregation developed for MIL [31]. Given a set of class scores $f_{c,b}$ for the B ROIs in a frame, the *aggregated score at the frame level* f_c is computed as:

$$f_c = \frac{1}{\gamma} \log \left(\frac{1}{B} \sum_{b=1}^{B} \exp\left(\gamma f_{c,b}\right) \right) \quad (2)$$

This aggregation will produce the vector of frame-level scores for the object categories. This vector can be finally transformed into a set of *object probabilities* using a simple softmax operator: $p_c = softmax(f_c)$.

3.2.3 Weak loss: Although the previous layer provides active object detections at ROI level, our training process requires an additional step as the weak labels indicating the presence of an active object are given for each short video clip. Indeed, due to distracting objects, use of peripheral vision and noise during gaze capturing process, some of the frames may not even show the active object at the gaze location. This prevents from using labels at frame level and rises the need of an additional layer aggregating the information at the video level and learning from a loss at this granularity.

To cope with all these requirements, we have adopted a constrained loss for learning under weakly annotated scenarios [30], which was initially developed for pixel-wise weak semantic segmentation. In our work, instead, it has been adapted for active object detection in weakly annotated video, defining our constraints over the accumulated scores along frames, and incorporating the weights w_n modeling the confidence over each frame. Considering marginal independence between frames, the probability distribution of a video clip with N frames can be factorized as:

$$P(C|\theta) = \prod_{n}^{N} p_n(c_n|\theta)^{w_n} \quad (3)$$

where C is a random variable of the active object classes, θ stands for the parameters (weights) of the CNN, $p_n(c_n|\theta) = p^n_{c_n}$ stands here for the probability of the class c_n associated in the frame n, and w_n is the weight associated to each training frame in the video (as defined in section 3.1.2). This leads to an optimization problem with inequality constraints:

$$\text{find} \quad \theta; \quad \text{subject to} \quad A\vec{P} \geq \vec{b} \quad (4)$$

where $\vec{P}$ is the vectorized version form of the network output $P(C|\theta)$, and $A \in \mathbb{R}^{K \times PN}$ and $\vec{b} \in \mathbb{R}^K$ define K linear constraints over the output distribution P. Since this problem is not convex with respect to the network parameters θ, the authors in [30] defined a variational latent probability distribution $Q(C)$ over the object categories, independent from the CNN parameters θ, applied the constraints to this new distribution rather than to the original network output $P(C|\theta)$, and enforced $Q(C)$ to be similar to $P(C|\theta)$ by minimizing their Kullback-Leibler divergence. The interested reader is referred to the original paper [30] for an in-depth derivation

Table 1: GITW details and experimental set-up.

Total videos/frames/valid frames	404/93548/11458
Avg Fold videos/frames/valid frames	80.8/18709.5/2291.6
Object Categories	16
Training time (training set 4-folds)	~ 10 hr
Test time (per frame)	25ms

of the equations (let us note that the set of weights w_n was not included in the original approach).

By setting proper values of the parameters A and $\overrightarrow{b}$, we can impose constraints over the object class probabilities along each video clip. In particular, given a category c, we impose the following constraint:

$$K_{c,min} \leq \frac{1}{\sum_n w_n} \sum_{n=1}^{N} w_n p_c^n \leq K_{c,max} \quad (5)$$

where p_c^n is the probability score of the class c in the frame n, $K_{c,min}, K_{c,max} \in [0, 1]$ are model parameters that stand for the minimum and maximum percentage of accumulated probability that correspond with the category c in the video segment, respectively. Intuitively, we are imposing that the percentage of the frames that show the object c in the fixation area should range between $K_{c,min}$ and $K_{c,max}$. Setting appropriate values for these parameters allows to deal with the presence of noise, and the existence of frames showing background or even other non-active objects. In particular, we have considered the following cases that yielded reasonable results: a) if c represents the *active object* in a video clip, then $K_{ao,min} = 0.85$, and $K_{ao,max}$ is deactivated; b) for those classes c that are considered as *non-active* in a video segment, $K_{nao,max} = 0.01$, whereas $K_{nao,min}$ is deactivated; and c) for the *background class* $c = 0$, $K_{0,min} = 0$ and $K_{0,max} = 1 - K_{ao,min} = 0.15$.

4 EXPERIMENTS AND RESULTS

4.1 Dataset and experimental set-up

We run our experiments using a new recorded egocentric dataset: *Grasping In The Wild (GITW)*[1]. We had designed a new dataset as previous ones focused on the detection of active objects during their manipulation [10, 11, 23] and therefore did not fit with our goal of to-be-grasped object detection. GITW has been recorded by Tobii Glasses 2 worn by subjects performing activities of everyday life in an ecological environment (7 kitchens), contains 404 egocentric videos and includes 16 active object categories. The recording process was as follows: after hearing the name of an object, a subject scans the scene, identifies its location, and grasps it. To fit our goal, we have annotated the dataset labeling the temporal segment starting when the user fixates the active object and ending at the instant just before the object is grasped. This segment corresponds with the moment during which we aim to detect the object to-be-grasped. Hence, GITW dataset is very challenging because active objects should be recognized *before* they are manipulated (the subject is still looking at them) and scenes usually contain many objects that are not active. As we have already discussed, both facts lead to an increase of the noise present in the gaze sequence.

[1] www.labri.fr/projet/AIV/dossierSiteRoBioVis/GraspingInTheWildV2.htm

Table 2: Results of our proposals and several compared methods in GITW dataset, given in mean AP and Acc % with standard deviations.

Algorithm	$mAP \pm std$	$mAcc \pm std$
Strong	75.0 ± 1.8	68.4 ± 3.9
MIL-AVG	72.2 ± 3.1	66.7 ± 6.1
MIL-LSE	78.0 ± 3.3	71.0 ± 2.5
DEEPMASK	67.0 ± 5.2	60.5 ± 6.4
CCNN	78.2 ± 2.8	69.4 ± 3.8
GDOD-CE	80.5 ± 4.3	73.5 ± 4.4
GDOD-NR	81.6 ± 2.5	74.7 ± 2.9
GDOD-COMB	$\mathbf{81.9 \pm 3.7}$	$\mathbf{75.3 \pm 3.3}$

As we show in Table 1, we have divided our dataset into 5 folds, ensuring that all frames of a video are not split into different folds. Each fold contains 80-81 video clips and around 2290 valid frames (frames associated to the aforementioned temporal segment of interest). In order to obtain statistically significant results, we have followed a 5-fold cross-validation approach, repeating the experiments 5 times and leaving each time one fold for test. We have used *mean Average Precision* (mAP) and *mean Accuracy* (mAcc) as our performance metrics, computed over all the object categories (after background class removal) and experiments, and using video clip labels. This means that, even in test, we need to aggregate our scores to produce a unified score for the whole video clip.

4.2 Results for active object detection

We have compared our approach with other weakly-supervised object detection methods (those that are not intended for manipulated objects, which could not be applied to our scenario), as well as with some reference models:

- Baseline Strong (Strong): a strongly supervised system that considers each candidate ROI in a frame as a positive sample of the active object in the video clip.

- Multiple Instance Learning methods: including Average aggregation (MIL-AVG), and LSE aggregation (MIL-LSE) [31]: used both to generate frame and video-level outputs from ROI scores. We have not included Max aggregation [6, 27] as it yielded very poor performance due to the usual presence of distracting objects which are fixated in some frames of the video.

- Deepmask [32]: it uses, from the set of candidate boxes proposed by Deepmask region proposal algorithm [32], those that contain the gaze point. If several boxes are available MIL-LSE is used to generate frame-level scores.

- Constrained CNN (CCNN) [30]: a constrained weak loss over the video accumulated object probabilities. It is similar to our approach, removing the weights in the loss functions, and does not include any method to deal with noise.

To establish a fair comparison, we use gaze points to guide the detection process of every method, and the same detection network in except of the noise handling, aggregations

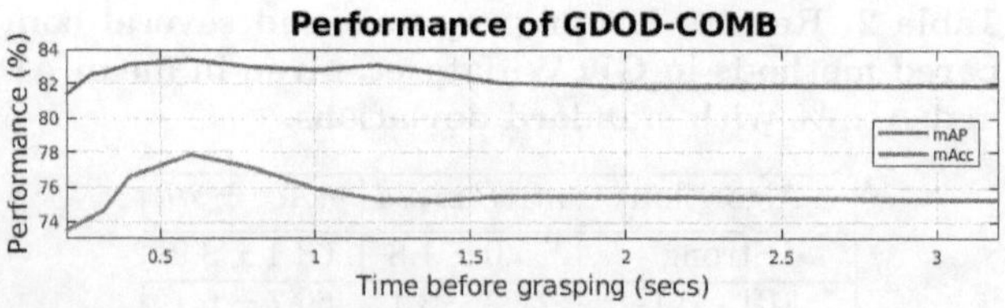

Figure 5: Performance of our system as a function of the time before grasping considered during test

methods and the learning losses. We include three versions of our *Gaze-Driven Object Detection (GDOD)* approach in the comparison: one that employs our Noise Reduction mechanism (GDOD-NR), another with our Confidence Estimation method (GDOD-CE), and a one that combines the ROIs and weights proposed by the previous methods (GDOD-COMB).

Results of our experiments in GITW dataset are shown in Table 2. We can see that both our techniques for noise handling notably improve the system performance and outperform the baseline strong approach and every other compared method for weak learning. Particularly, region proposals as Deepmask [32] fail in our problem as, when the gaze does not point to a particular object but to intermediate areas, they tend to propose boxes over non-active objects, which seriously harms learning. In all cases, the low standard deviation values show the statistical significance of the improvements.

Finally, although individual results show that reducing noise in gaze fixation might be preferable than using confidence measures over the original gaze points, our combined version (GDOD-COMB) takes the best of the two approaches and achieves the top performance in our dataset.

4.3 System usability assessment

In this section we aim to evaluate the usability of our system in the task of automatizing the control of prosthetic arms using gaze. For that end we aim at answering the three questions stated in the next paragraphs.

a) *Are the fixation times reasonable for a user operating with our system?:* First, let us note that the results in Table 2 were computed averaging object scores along all video frames for each short video-clip. The length of these clips varies in our dataset from 280 ms to 3 seconds, covering the segment between the moment when a subject fixates the object until he grasps it. Although this length is very useful during training, showing active objects under different viewpoints and scales, fixating the object of interest during seconds is not realistic and would prevent the final adoption of our system. Hence, we have evaluated the performance of our best solution GDOD-COMB as a function of the time before grasping considered during test. Fig. 5 shows good performance for segments between 400ms and 800ms, and optimal results of **mAP** = **83.4** and **mAcc** = **77.9** at 600ms. From our point of view, these values are reasonable and would help to amputees with minimal adjustments in their behavior. The slight drop in performance for larger values is due to the inclusion of early frames (more distant to the grasping action), which are in general more noisy and lead to the apparition of distractors.

b) *Is the performance of our system good enough to be usable?*: To give an answer, we have asked a subject to predict the active object looking at the sequence of aligned gaze points shown in Fig. 1. We obtained a **mAP** = **83.0** and **mAcc** = **79.0**, performance that is very close to that of our automatic method (see optimal performance in the previous point). This result demonstrates that errors come on sequence where a user grasps an object using peripheral vision, preventing both manual and automatic detection. Hence, looking at the active object is a crucial requierement of our system.

c) *Is the system efficient enough to be used in real environments?*: To answer this question we have measured the execution time of our system in test. As shown in Table 1, running our detection system using a NVIDIA TITAN X GPU with our implementation over Caffe learning framework takes 25 ms per frame. Hence, our method is very efficient, mainly because processing is concentrated around the fixation point, and meets our real-time requirements of 25 fps.

5 CONCLUSION

We have presented a system for perceptually-guided recognition of objects to be grasped in egocentric video, exploiting gaze information produced by visual search during natural behaviors. Our scenario is particularly challenging as detecting objects before they are manipulated introduces several artifacts in gaze sequences related to the physiology of human perception: deviation by distractors, microssaccades, and acquisition noise. Furthermore, there is an imposed change in the granularity of the annotation, which is in our case associated with video clips rather than with frames or bounding boxes. Under such scenario, dealing with noise becomes an essential step for any object detection system. In this work, we have introduced two alternative methods, one that reduces noise in gaze sequences and another that estimates confidence measures over gaze fixations, and incorporated them into a system for weakly-labeled active object detection. We showed that our methods achieve substantially better results than other related approaches, including aggregation blocks, region proposal algorithms and weak losses, on a dataset specifically designed to fit our goal. Furthermore, we have also shown that the method is efficient and has a minimal impact on user's behavior in our scenario of interest: automatic control of prosthetic arms based on gaze information. In the future, this method will be combined with recurrent networks in order to model gaze-dynamics and explicitly predict the grasping action.

6 ACKNOWLEDGMENTS

This work was partially supported by French National Center of Scientific research with grant Suvipp PEPS CNRS-Idex 215-2016, by French National Center of Scientific research with Interdisciplinary project CNRS RoBioVis 2017-2019, the Scientific Council of Labri, University of Bordeaux, and the Spanish Ministry of Economy and Competitiveness under the National Grant TEC2014-61729-EXP.

REFERENCES

[1] J. Benois-Pineau, M. S. Garcia-Vazquez, L. A. Oropesa Morales, and A. A. Ramirez Acosta. 2017. Semi-Automatic Annotation with Predicted Visual Saliency Maps for Object Recognition in Wearable Video. In *Proceedings of the 2017 Workshop on Wearable MultiMedia (WearMMe '17)*. ACM, New York, NY, USA, 10–14. https://doi.org/10.1145/3080538.3080541

[2] Hakan Bilen, Marco Pedersoli, and Tinne Tuytelaars. 2014. Weakly Supervised Object Detection with Posterior Regularization. In *British Machine Vision Conference 2014*.

[3] Hakan Bilen, Marco Pedersoli, and Tinne Tuytelaars. 2015. Weakly supervised object detection with convex clustering.. In *CVPR*. IEEE Computer Society, 1081–1089.

[4] H. Bilen and A. Vedaldi. 2016. Weakly Supervised Deep Detection Networks. In *IEEE Conference on Computer Vision and Pattern Recognition*.

[5] Philippe Prez de San Roman, Jenny Benois-Pineau, Jean-Philippe Domenger, Florent Paclet, Daniel Cataert, and Aymar de Rugy. 2017. Saliency Driven Object recognition in egocentric videos with deep CNN: toward application in assistance to Neuroprostheses. *Computer Vision and Image Understanding* 164 (2017), 82 – 91. https://doi.org/10.1016/j.cviu.2017.03.001 Deep Learning for Computer Vision.

[6] Ali Diba, Vivek Sharma, Ali Pazandeh, Hamed Pirsiavash, and Luc Van Gool. 2017. Weakly Supervised Cascaded Convolutional Networks. In *The IEEE Conference on Computer Vision and Pattern Recognition (CVPR)*.

[7] Thibaut Durand, Taylor Mordan, Nicolas Thome, and Matthieu Cord. 2017. WILDCAT: Weakly Supervised Learning of Deep ConvNets for Image Classification, Pointwise Localization and Segmentation. In *The IEEE Conference on Computer Vision and Pattern Recognition (CVPR)*.

[8] T. Durand, N. Thome, and M. Cord. 2016. WELDON: Weakly Supervised Learning of Deep Convolutional Neural Networks. In *2016 IEEE Conference on Computer Vision and Pattern Recognition (CVPR)*. 4743–4752. https://doi.org/10.1109/CVPR.2016.513

[9] Susan E Brennan, Xin Chen, Christopher Dickinson, Mark Neider, and Gregory J Zelinsky. 2008. Coordinating cognition: The costs and benefits of shared gaze during collaborative search. 106 (04 2008), 1465–77.

[10] Alireza Fathi, Yin Li, and James M. Rehg. 2012. Learning to Recognize Daily Actions Using Gaze. In *12th European Conference on Computer Vision (ECCV'12)*. Springer-Verlag, Berlin, Heidelberg, 314–327. https://doi.org/10.1007/978-3-642-33718-5_23

[11] A. Fathi, X. Ren, and J. M. Rehg. 2011. Learning to recognize objects in egocentric activities. In *CVPR 2011*. 3281–3288. https://doi.org/10.1109/CVPR.2011.5995444

[12] Martin A. Fischler and Robert C. Bolles. 1981. Random Sample Consensus: A Paradigm for Model Fitting with Applications to Image Analysis and Automated Cartography. *Commun. ACM* 24, 6 (June 1981), 381–395. https://doi.org/10.1145/358669.358692

[13] Karl Friston, Rick Adams, Laurent Perrinet, and Michael Breakspear. 2012. Perceptions as Hypotheses: Saccades as Experiments. *Frontiers in Psychology* 3 (2012), 151. https://doi.org/10.3389/fpsyg.2012.00151

[14] James J. Gibson. 1979. *The Ecological Approach to Visual Perception*. Houghton Mifflin.

[15] Ross Girshick. 2015. Fast R-CNN. In *IEEE International Conference on Computer Vision (ICCV '15)*. IEEE Computer Society, Washington, DC, USA, 1440–1448. https://doi.org/10.1109/ICCV.2015.169

[16] Iván González-Díaz, Vincent Buso, and Jenny Benois-Pineau. 2016. Perceptual modeling in the problem of active object recognition in visual scenes. *Pattern Recognition* 56, Supplement C (2016), 129 – 141. https://doi.org/10.1016/j.patcog.2016.03.007

[17] Iván González-Díaz, Vincent Buso, Jenny Benois-Pineau, Guillaume Bourmaud, and Rémi Mégret. 2013. Modeling instrumental activities of daily living in egocentric vision as sequences of active objects and context for alzheimer disease research. In *ACM international workshop on Multimedia indexing and information retrieval for healthcare*. 11–14. https://doi.org/10.1145/2505323.2505328

[18] R. I. Hartley and A. Zisserman. 2004. *Multiple View Geometry in Computer Vision* (second ed.). Cambridge University Press, ISBN: 0521540518.

[19] Kaiming He, Xiangyu Zhang, Shaoqing Ren, and Jian Sun. 2016. Deep Residual Learning for Image Recognition. In *2016 IEEE Conference on Computer Vision and Pattern Recognition, CVPR 2016, Las Vegas, NV, USA, June 27-30, 2016*. 770–778. https://doi.org/10.1109/CVPR.2016.90

[20] Chien-Ming Huang, Sean Andrist, Allison Saupp, and Bilge Mutlu. 2015. Using gaze patterns to predict task intent in collaboration. *Frontiers in Psychology* 6 (2015), 1049. https://doi.org/10.3389/fpsyg.2015.01049

[21] Alexander Kolesnikov and Christoph H. Lampert. 2016. Seed, Expand and Constrain: Three Principles for Weakly-Supervised Image Segmentation. In *European Conference on Computer Vision (ECCV)*. Springer.

[22] Yong Jae Lee and Kristen Grauman. 2015. Predicting Important Objects for Egocentric Video Summarization. *Int. J. Comput. Vision* 114, 1 (Aug. 2015), 38–55. https://doi.org/10.1007/s11263-014-0794-5

[23] Y. Li, Zhefan Ye, and J. M. Rehg. 2015. Delving into egocentric actions. In *2015 IEEE Conference on Computer Vision and Pattern Recognition (CVPR)*. 287–295. https://doi.org/10.1109/CVPR.2015.7298625

[24] Stéphanie Lopez, Arnaud Revel, Diane Lingrand, and Frédéric Precioso. 2017. Handling Noisy Labels in Gaze-Based CBIR System. In *Advanced Concepts for Intelligent Vision Systems - 18th International Conference, ACIVS 2017, Antwerp, Belgium, September 18-21, 2017, Proceedings*. 396–405. https://doi.org/10.1007/978-3-319-70353-4_34

[25] M. Ma, H. Fan, and K. M. Kitani. 2016. Going Deeper into First-Person Activity Recognition. In *2016 IEEE Conference on Computer Vision and Pattern Recognition (CVPR)*. 1894–1903. https://doi.org/10.1109/CVPR.2016.209

[26] Marko Markovic, Hemanth Karnal, Bernhard Graimann, Dario Farina, and Strahinja Dosen. 2017. GLIMPSE: Google Glass interface for sensory feedback in myoelectric hand prostheses. *Journal of Neural Engineering* 14, 3 (2017), 036007. http://stacks.iop.org/1741-2552/14/i=3/a=036007

[27] Maxime Oquab, Léon Bottou, Ivan Laptev, and Josef Sivic. 2015. Is object localization for free? - Weakly-supervised learning with convolutional neural networks. *2015 IEEE Conference on Computer Vision and Pattern Recognition (CVPR)* (2015), 685–694.

[28] Dim P. Papadopoulos, Alasdair D. F. Clarke, Frank Keller, and Vittorio Ferrari. 2014. *Training Object Class Detectors from Eye Tracking Data*. Springer International Publishing, Cham, 361–376. https://doi.org/10.1007/978-3-319-10602-1_24

[29] George Papandreou, Liang-Chieh Chen, Kevin P. Murphy, and Alan L. Yuille. 2015. Weakly-and Semi-Supervised Learning of a Deep Convolutional Network for Semantic Image Segmentation. In *IEEE International Conference on Computer Vision (ICCV) (ICCV '15)*. Washington, DC, USA, 1742–1750. https://doi.org/10.1109/ICCV.2015.203

[30] Deepak Pathak, Philipp Krähenbühl, and Trevor Darrell. 2015. Constrained Convolutional Neural Networks for Weakly Supervised Segmentation. In *ICCV*.

[31] Pedro H. O. Pinheiro and Ronan Collobert. 2015. From image-level to pixel-level labeling with Convolutional Networks. In *IEEE Conference on Computer Vision and Pattern Recognition, CVPR 2015, Boston, MA, USA, June 7-12, 2015*. 1713–1721. https://doi.org/10.1109/CVPR.2015.7298780

[32] Pedro O. Pinheiro, Ronan Collobert, and Piotr Dollár. 2015. Learning to Segment Object Candidates. In *Proceedings of the 28th International Conference on Neural Information Processing Systems - Volume 2 (NIPS'15)*. MIT Press, Cambridge, MA, USA, 1990–1998.

[33] David W. Scott. [n. d.]. *Multivariate density estimation: theory, practice, and visualization* (second edition ed.). John Wiley & Sons, Inc.

[34] Xin Wang, Nicolas Thome, and Matthieu Cord. 2017. Gaze latent support vector machine for image classification improved by weakly supervised region selection. *Pattern Recognition* 72 (2017), 59 – 71. https://doi.org/10.1016/j.patcog.2017.07.001

[35] Jonathan Weisz, Peter Allen, Alexander G Barszap, and Sanjay S Joshi. 2017. Assistive grasping with an augmented reality user interface. 36 (05 2017).

[36] Weilie Yi and Dana Ballard. 2009. Recognizing behavior in hand-eye coordination patterns. *International Journal of Humanoid Robotics* 06, 03 (2009), 337–359. https://doi.org/10.1142/S0219843609001863

Towards Better Understanding of Player's Game Experience

Wenlu Yang
Sorbonne University, CNRS, LIP6
Paris, France
wenlu.yang@lip6.fr

Maria Rifqi
Université Panthéon-Assas - Paris 2, LEMMA
Paris, France
maria.rifqi@u-paris2.fr

Christophe Marsala
Sorbonne University, CNRS, LIP6
Paris, France
christophe.marsala@lip6.fr

Andrea Pinna
Sorbonne University, CNRS, LIP6
Paris, France
andrea.pinna@lip6.fr

ABSTRACT

Improving player's game experience has always been the common goal of video game practitioner. In order to get a better understanding of player's perception of game experience, we carry out experimental study for data collection and present game experience prediction model based on machine learning method. The model is trained on the proposed multi-modal database which contains: physiological modality, behavioral modality and meta-information to predict the player game experience in terms of difficulty, immersion and amusement. By investigating the model trained on separate and fusion feature sets, we show that physiological modality is effective. Moreover, better understanding is achieved with further analysis on the most relevant features in the behavioral and meta-information features set. We argue that combining the physiological modalities with behavioral and meta information can provide a better performance on the game experience prediction.

CCS CONCEPTS

• **General and reference** → **Empirical studies**; **Experimentation**; • **Applied computing** → **Computer games**; • **Human-centered computing** → *User models*;

KEYWORDS

User experience research; game experience; affective gaming; physiological signal; game events; machine learning; interpretability.

ACM Reference Format:
Wenlu Yang, Maria Rifqi, Christophe Marsala, and Andrea Pinna. 2018. Towards Better Understanding of Player's Game Experience. In *ICMR '18: 2018 International Conference on Multimedia Retrieval, June 11–14, 2018, Yokohama, Japan.* ACM, New York, NY, USA, 8 pages. https://doi.org/10.1145/3206025.3206072

1 INTRODUCTION

As part of the entertainment multimedia field, video games have developed from the initial entertainment purpose to wide range of applications such as serious game, effective learning [1]. No matter what specific application is, video game is designed to provide an engaging experience. Therefore, understanding of players' perception on the game experience is of vital importance. Game experience has been widely investigated in the game design domain. Traditional methods evaluates game experience relies on player's self-reported assessment. This is an efficient way to collect information on the player's perception of the game. However, this method is not applicable to the situation where automatic experience assessment is needed and it sometimes suffers from cognitive bias due to its subjectivity.

In order to create a model that can automatically assess the player's game experience, efforts should be made to deduce the game experience from a more objective measurable modalities. In this paper we propose to use the physiological modalities and behavioral modalities to assess the player's game experience. Recent years have seen a lot of studies that explore the interplay between physiological signals and affect during gameplay [2]. Physiological modalities provide continuous, objective, and quantitative measures. Even though there exist evidences for the relationship between physiology and emotion [3, 4], the exact relation between them is still controversy and vary from context to context [5–7]. Therefore, to understand the physiological response related to the game experience, a model should be created on the relevant data. Behavioral modality refers to the player behavior during game player. Game event is an important form of behavioral data, and have received more and more attention in the game research. Overall game evaluation cannot provide enough information to improve the game, assessment associated with game events provides more detailed information on the mechanisms that elicit player experience. Existing works exploit game event by searching for important play pattern [8, 9] using sequential analysis or clustering method. However, the question of how local game events and their related emotions affect the global experience has not been studied.

In this paper, we propose a method to investigate game experience based on more objective measurable physiological modalities and behavioral modalities as well as the meta-information related to player profile or game information. Our major contributions are 1) an experimental study that collects relevant physiological signals, behavioral data, meta-information, as well as self-reported game experience evaluation in a game context; 2) statistical analysis on the collected data concerning the relation between game events and associated emotions, relation among different game experience evaluation dimensions; 3) a method to create model that predicts

ACM ISBN 978-1-4503-5046-4/18/06...$15.00
https://doi.org/10.1145/3206025.3206072

player experience using machine learning techniques. The paper is organized as follows: Section 2 reviews the related work. Section 3 presents the experimental study. Section 4 presents the process to create the game experience prediction model. Section 5 discusses the limitation and some possible improvement. Conclusion and future work are presented in Section 6.

2 RELATED WORK

2.1 Player Experience

Modern game research has evolved from a focus on functionality toward creating a good player experience. Despite its popularity in the research field, the understanding of the meaning of player experience varies among researchers [10]. Some takes it as playability and game usability that focus on a low technological level [11]. Others focus more on the affective level specific to games, and states that it "describes the individual perception of the interaction process between player and game" [12] or argues that it shows how well the game supports and provides the type of fun the player wants to have [13]. Different frameworks have been proposed to characterize the game experience.

Framework based on people intrinsic motivation such as self-determination (SDT) [14] emphasizes that there are three basic needs: competence, autonomy and relatedness for people and so that these needs are important factors to produce good experience. Keller developed a model that includes four main strategies to elicit and maintain motivation: attention, relevance, confidence, and satisfaction (ARCS) [15]. Besides the framework that try to satisfy peoples intrinsic motivation, there are models aiming to find a connection between the player and the game. For example, the flow theory [16] and the more specific game flow framework [17] consist in eight elements: concentration, challenge, skills, control, clear goals, feedback, immersion, and social interaction; FUGA [18] framework investigates sensory and imaginative immersion, tension, competence, flow, negative affect, positive affect, and challenge.

These frameworks highlight important factors to take into account in the game design. Meanwhile, given a specific game, experiences of different players vary depending on what they encounter during the game. Therefore, being aware of the game events and the players' emotional state is also important to achieve game supports and provides the type of fun the player wants to have. The only framework that refers to the game events is the PPAX framework [9]. PPAX framework connects the game design pattern, player personality and subjective non-subjective measures to analyze game experience. It uses FP-growth algorithm [19] to find the frequent event sequence patterns and shows certain physiological signal is effective in characterizing some specific event. However, it doesn't show how the local game events influence the global game experience.

Concerning the evaluation method of player experience, methods such as interview or focus group [20] are flexible to gather information and cover participant's opinion, perception, attitudes, thoughts. However its processing is time-consuming and it is difficult to make quantitative analysis because of the unstructured nature of the data. Questionnaire is a common method for game experience evaluation. Immersive experience questionnaire (IEQ) [21], game engagement questionnaire (GEQ) [22] and player experience of need satisfaction (PENS) [23] are three of the prevailing questionnaire-based approaches. It has been shown a considerable convergence between these three questionnaires and the fact that there is room to refine them into a more widely applicable measure of general game engagement [24]. These questionnaires measure broader experiences, such as engagement or immersion in games which generally contains the item such as difficulty (challenge,competence), immersion (absorption,presence, etc.) and amusement (involvement, flow). By taking inspiration from these questionnaires, we measure the player experience on three simplified criteria: difficulty, immersion and amusement (DIA).

2.2 Using Physiological Signals for A⊠ective Gaming

Affective gaming (AG) refers to the new generation of games that not only react to player's control, but also take into account their behavioral cues and emotional states in order to adjust game plot accordingly. Physiological signals (PS) offer a continuous and objective measurement and prove to be an effective representation of inner feelings [25]. Most physiological modalities presented in the literatures are signals coming from PNS, which confirmes the popularity of using these signals in the affective game research. PNS modalities used are modalities related with cardiovascular system such as ECG, HR, BVP, HRV, Respiration, EDA and EMG. Generally, these studies apply the concepts and methodologies of traditional psychophysiology [26] and contribute to applications such as introducing novice game control [27, 28], game experience augmentation or dynamic difficulty adjustment (DDA) [29–31], player modelling [32]. For example, in order to realize a dynamic difficulty adjustment (DDA) schema [33], features from overt behavior (key-press force) and physiological responses (electro-dermal activity (EDA), heart rate (HR), respiration (RESP), electromyography (EMG)) are used for identifying various emotional states (bored / frustrated / enjoyed). In a first-person shooter (FPS) game [34], an affective game engine has been proposed that uses affective states to adapt characters, non-player character (NPCs) and the environment by using GSR signals.

Machine learning methods have been widely used to analyze affective element in affective gaming [30, 35, 36]. These data-driven approaches are able to investigate the non-linear multivariate relationship that may otherwise be neglected by traditional theoretical methods. Depending on the research purpose, the target of machine learning model for affective gaming can be divided into three main categories: representation based on the emotion theory, using categorical emotions such as critical emotion in game such as horror, anxiety [35, 37] or using dimensional representation such as arousal/valence score [38, 39] in which arousal represents the general excitation, ranging from deactivation to activation; valence means the intrinsic attractiveness/"good"-ness or averseness/"bad"-ness of an event, ranging from unpleasant to pleasant; representation based on the flow theory [16] such as boredom, engagement and frustration [29, 40]; and representation based on other dimensions such as preference or attention [36, 41] which represent specific characteristics that interest the researchers.

In this paper, our objective is to deduce the player's perception of game experience. We propose to use physiological signals as well as the behavior and meta-information as modalities to automatically predict the player's game experience. We highlight the effectiveness of using physiological signals in the game user research and emphasize the importance of integrating behavioral data (the game event and the associated emotion) in the framework as it provides better interpretability of how the local events influence the global game experience.

3 EXPERIMENTAL STUDY

We selected a football simulation game FIFA 2016 as emotion stimulation for the following reasons: 1) short repeated events in game can be used to generate different emotions and are easier to get significant analysis; 2) close relation between emotion and event can be used to provide emotion reference; 3) changeable difficulty level of the game can be used to provide different experiences. The experiment was conducted at INSEAD - Sorbonne University Multidisciplinary Centre for Behavioural Sciences[1]. In total, 58 participants (50 males, 8 females; mean age 25) of different skill levels took part in this study. The data has been made available online [2].

3.1 Modalities and measuring equipments

To analyse physiological responses during game playing, we recorded

(1) peripheral physiological signals: ECG, EDA, EMG, respiration and body movement with a 3-axis accelerometer,
(2) facial recording,
(3) game screen recording,
(4) meta-information such as player skill level, game difficulty level, and game resulting score.

Physiological signals were collected using the BioNomadix wireless sensors and physiology monitoring system Biopac MP150[3]. The sensors used were: an ECG sensor to measure electrocardiogram, an EDA sensor to measure electro-dermal activity, a respiration belt to estimate chest cavity expansion, two ElectroMyoGraphic (EMG) sensors to measure zygomaticus and corrugator muscles movement, an accelerometer sensor to measure body movements. All the used electrodes were Biopac pre-gelled electrodes. In order to reduce the artefacts caused by the movements of hands, the EDA signals have been taken from the arch of the foot.

The game screen output, webcam recording, and screen containing the physiological data were synchronized using a software ObserverXT[4] and visualized on the same screen (Figure 1) for experimenter.

3.2 Experimental Protocol

Participants played the game in an isolated environment. The procedure of the experiment is presented in Figure 2. Each experiment was composed of 4 phases: one training phase and 3 match phases. Each match began with 3 minutes of soft music, during which the participant return to neutral state (Figure 2, Baseline soft music

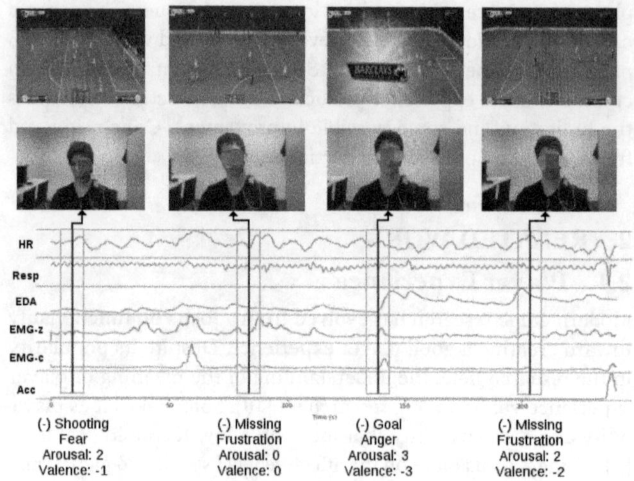

Figure 1: Experiment scene on one half-time match. The presented elements from top to bottom are: screen recording, player video, physiological signals (HR, Respiration, EDA, pre-processed EMG and pre-processed ACC), and annotations.

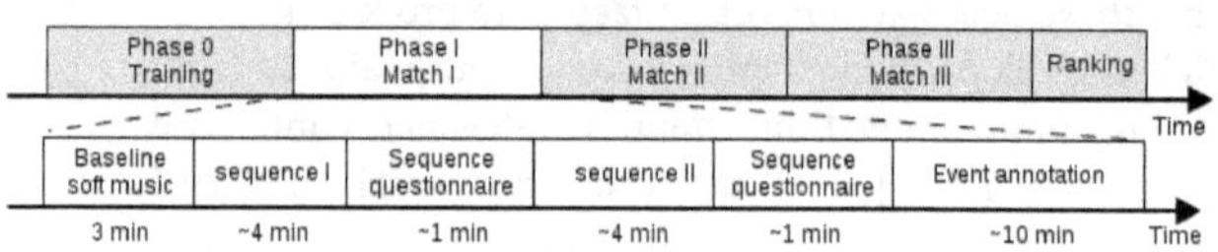

Figure 2: Protocol of experimentation.

phase). Then, the participant played two half-time (4 minutes for each) of game (Figure 2, 1st half-time and 2nd half-time phase).

After each half-time, the participants filled out a game experience questionnaire (Figure 2, Sequence questionnaire phase), in which they scored their experience in terms of DIA in a 5-point rating scale.

At the end of each match, the participant viewed the recording of match and annotated the emotions triggered by significant events during the game (Figure 2, Event annotation phase). To make the annotation easier, we offered participants a list of emotions and events. These lists drawn from the pre-questionnaires during the recruitment process contained the most frequent emotions and events in the game. The elements included in each annotation are:

- events: goal, penalty, shooting, interception of guard, foul, gesture, tackle, corner kick, free kick, arbitration, offside, missing and touch;
- emotions: happiness, frustration, proud, curious, angry, fear, boredom, sadness;
- arousal/ valence score: -3, -2, -1, 0, 1, 2, 3.

To speed-up the annotation process, the experimenter helped the participant to annotate with corresponding time-stamp using the software ObserverXT.

[1]http://centres.insead.edu/sorbonne-behavioural-lab/eng/index.cfm
[2]http://erag.lip6.fr
[3]https://www.biopac.com
[4]http://www.noldus.com/the-observer-xt

Table 1: Correlations of player perceived game experience in terms of difficulty, immersion, amusement and presenting order ,*p<0.05; **p<0.01

	Difficulty	Immersion	Amusement	order
Difficulty	1.00**	0.00	-0.13	0.03
Immersion		1.00	0.49**	0.22**
Amusement			1.00	0.20**
order				1.00

In the end, the participants ranked the 3 matches in terms of their perception of difficulty, immersion and amusement (DIA) (Figure 2, Ranking phase).

3.3 Statistical Analysis

3.3.1 Relation between game event and emotion. Concerning the local self-reported evaluation on in-game events, we calculate the frequency of each game event in different emotion category or arousal/valence scores. For the 5 types of game event, we distinguish them as positive/negative ones. Each event is beneficial either to the player (positive event) or to the adversary (negative event). For example, positive goal is a goal scored by the participant (noted as (+) *goal*), while negative goal represents a scoring by the adversary (noted as (−) goal). Figure 3 presents the frequencies of different emotions or arousal / valence scores for each event.

We observe a close relationship between the event type and the associated emotion. We notice that most positive events correspond to "happy" emotion, while most negative events result in negative emotion: "missing" and "goalkeeper's interception" are mostly associated to "frustration"; "goal" is mostly related to "anger" and "shooting" mostly related to "fear". These observations are consistent with our intuition. For arousal score, most positive events result in high arousal score. While for the negative events, even though the arousal scores are concentrated on the positive plan, its distribution is more disperse compared to the positive events. Concerning the valence score, positive events result in positive score, while the negative events result in negative score. Among them, (+)goal mostly yields the highest valence score while the (-)goal and (-)foul yields the lowest valence score.

3.3.2 Relation between game experience dimensions. Table 1 presents the correlation of the different self-assessed game experience ratings.

We notice that medium positive correlations were observed within the pair amusement and immersion, suggesting that participants tend to be more immersed in the game sequences that amuse them. This phenomenon can be explained by the ⊠flow theory" [42]: players in the flow state are more engaged in the game and acquire a higher level of enjoyment.

Small and positive correlations were observed between sequence presenting order and difficulty,implication, and amusement ratings, which implies that as time went by, the participants' evaluation on the experience did not suffer from effects of fatigue or habituation. No clear correlation were observed between the difficulty/immersion or difficulty/amusement pair.

4 METHODOLOGY

Player's game experience can be assessed from different modalities. Figure 4 presents the framework we used to train a machine learning model and predict player's perceived game experience. The model is alimented by 3 modalities: the physiological modalities which contain physiological features, the behavioral modalities which contains event features and associated emotion features, and meta information which contains information such as player's profile and game information.

The objective of the model is to predict the perceived ranking of the matches in the DIA dimensions. More specifically, for each DIA dimension, we take the subjective assessment of ranking of the three matches as ground truth, and create pairwise comparisons: (M1,M2), (M1,M3), (M2,M3). The ranking problem becomes: whether a match scores higher than another one in one of DIA dimensions. If it is true, the current instance belongs to the positive class, otherwise, it belongs to the negative class. Therefore, the ranking problem is transformed into a binary classification problem. In the following sections, we present the process to extract features in each modality and the method to train the model.

4.1 Feature extraction

4.1.1 Physiological features. The general process of feature extraction for physiological signals consists of 3 stages (Table 2):

(1) *signal pre-processing* cleans the signals to avoid noise or artefacts (such as spiking removing, signal baseline removing, filtering),
(2) *signal transformation* represents the characteristic of a signal in a different aspect (e.g. generating HR sequence from ECG signal),
(3) *feature calculation* extracts common/specific, linear/non-linear, time/frequency domain features on the pre-processed or transformed signal.

For the *feature calculation*, 2 common feature sets are considered:

(1) ***time-domain feature set (time)***
Common time-domain statistic features applied to the sequences are : mean, median, maximum, minimum, range, variance, standard deviation, average derivative, maximum derivative, absolute deviation, kurtosis and skewness. Time-domain feature set contains 12 features in total.

(2) ***frequency-domain feature set (freq)***
For feature in frequency domain, as no consensus has been found in the existing works [43, 44], we propose the frequency bands reflecting the main spectral characteristic by covering the principle spectral space. We calculate the band energy of 3 frequency bands in the frequency range [0,4.8] Hz. 4 band energy of the [0,1.6] Hz and the band energy ratios. Frequency-domain feature set contains 8 features in total.

For each segment of signals we obtain 173 features. In the following section, we present the classification tasks and results based on these features.

4.1.2 Behavioral and meta information features. Behavioral features include the features from game event log and the associated

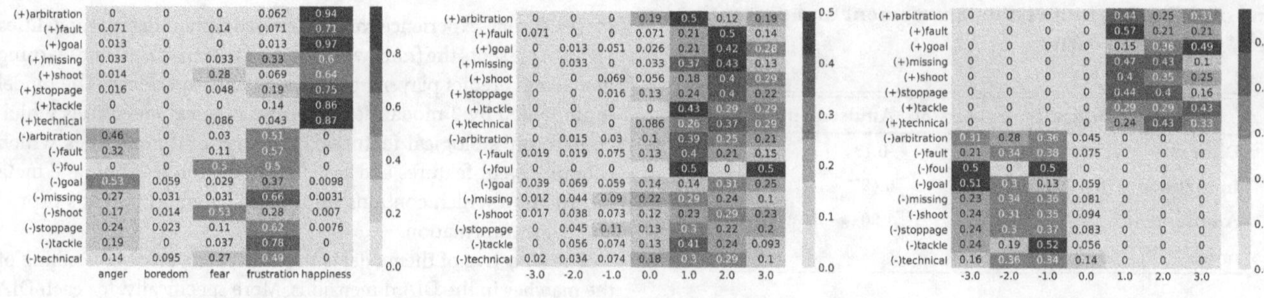

(a) Emotion (b) Arousal (c) Valence

Figure 3: Distribution of the annotated events in terms of emotions.

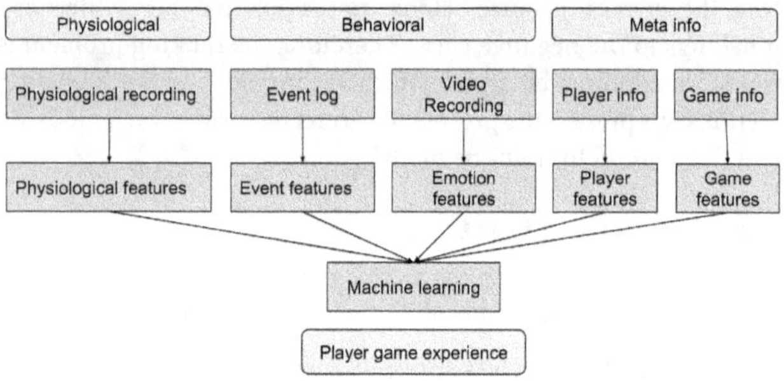

Figure 4: Framework

Table 2: Feature extraction process

Sig. (nb. fea.)	Preprocess.	Trans.	Feature calcu.
ECG (44)	baseline removing, filtering	raw IBI HRV HR	raw: *freq* IBI: *time.* HRV: *time.* HR: *time, freq.*
EDA (53)	spike removing, filtering, subsampling	raw phasic dephasic tonic	raw: *time, freq* phasic: *time* dephasic: *time* tonic: *time* specific: nb. of peaks
EMG (24)	RMS smoothing, aggregating, subsampling	raw	raw: *time*
Respiration (40)	spike removing, filtering, subsampling, baseline removing	raw RR amp.	raw: *time, freq* RR: *time* amp.: *time*
ACC (12)	baseline removeing, RMS smoothing, 3-axis aggregating, subsampling	raw	raw: *time*

raw - pre-processed signals, ***time*** - calculate time domain feature set, ***freq*** - calculate frequency domain feature set

emotion features. In the current study, these features derives from the manually collected event annotations. Game events play an important role in deciding the final evaluation of the game. Different events have different affective effects, by analyzing on event scale we can get better insight on how the emotions, triggered by game events, influence the final game experience. We infer the overall experience based on the game event sequence and the associated emotions sequence. Each match is represented by the event or emotion frequency vector. Besides the frequency of event and emotion, frequency of positive valence events (**posVa**), negative valence events (**negVa**), positive arousal events (**posAr**), negative arousal events (**negAr**), high score valence events (**hVa**), high score arousal events (**hAr**) are also extracted.

Meta-information contains features related to player and the game. In the current study, we record the *player's skill level* (**pLevel**) as the player feature. Concerning game information, *game level* and *game outcome* are widely known as important factors that can influence player's game experience. A proper setting of game difficulty level helps players to enter a "flow" state where the player immerses totally in the game as his/her ability matches with the challenge. A better game outcome can satisfy players, as it helps to improve their sense of accomplishment. Extracted features for **game level** are game difficulty level (**gLevel**), and game relative difficulty level with respect to the player's skill level(**rLevel**); features for **game outcome** are relative score of the match (**Goal**), difference of the score between the first and the second half-time (**diff Goal**).

Table 3 summarizes the feature extracted from the different modalities.

4.2 Model construction

The ranking of the 3 matches gives 6 match pairs. We extracted the difference of features in match pair as features and used machine learning method to predict which match in the pair ranks higher. Random Forests is a state of the art classifier for multi-modal data, moreover, it provides information on feature importance. For each of the DIA dimension, a random forest (N=50) is created using the feature sets from physiological, behavioral and meta-information modalities. All the models are validated using Leave-One-Out (LOO) schema and the performance of learning is presented in Table 4.

Table 3: Feature for game experience prediction model

Modality	Feature set	Number	Detail
Physiological	Signals	173	(Table 2)
Behavioral	Event	10	One for each event
	Emotion	5	One for each emotion
	Arousal/Valence	6	posVa, negVa, posAr, negAr, hVa, hAr
Meta info	Player	1	plevel
	Game	4	glevel, rlevel, Goal, diffGoal

In this table, each line presents the accuracy of learned model from corresponding feature set for each of the DIA dimension. The baseline row represents the accuracy when using a majority class classifier.

From the accuracy table we notice that, within each separate feature set, models created from physiological signals always achieve the best performances. Physiological-based recognition on the amusement achieves the best result, followed by difficulty. Being a totally objective modality, this result is promising, as it shows the effectiveness of using physiological signal to recognize the player's game experience. Besides the physiological modalities, behavioral and meta-information modalities also achieves significantly better result than the baseline.

When investigating the effect of feature fusion, the performance of models significantly improves compared to the model based on separate feature set. The combination of physiological and behavioral features achieves the best performance in all the DIA dimension. It should be mentioned that, despite the fact that behavioral and meta-info modalities provide much less features than the physiological modality, the fusion of them also greatly improves the performance of recognition, especially for the difficulty and amusement dimension. We may infer that immersion prediction relies more on the physiological modality. Fusion of all the modalities also achieves significantly better performance than the separate modalities. However, it doesn't achieve significantly better performance than the physiological and behavioral modality based models. This may be caused by the small number of features provided by the meta-information.

Table 4: Performance of game experience evaluation using physiological, behavioral and meta-information features.

	Difficulty	Immersion	Amusement
Physiological	0.767 (0.052)	0.743 (0.048)	0.793 (0.068)
Behavioral	0.624 (0.067)	0.577 (0.068)	0.583 (0.069)
Meta-info	0.628 (0.051)	0.572 (0.053)	0.603 (0.055)
Physio + Behavioral	0.782 (0.062)	0.766 (0.039)	0.803 (0.080)
Physio + Meta	0.743 (0.053)	0.736 (0.044)	0.803 (0.072)
Behavioral + Meta	0.701 (0.053)	0.589 (0.071)	0.616 (0.057)
All	0.774 (0.059)	0.775 (0.044)	0.815 (0.075)
Baseline	0.500 (0.000)	0.500 (0.000)	0.500 (0.000)

4.3 Feature importance

Game events are important factors that influence player's experience. By investigating the importance of features from behavioral and meta-information game experience prediction, we may get an insight on the most effective factors. Figure 5 presents the 3 most important features in each feature set.

For the *di⊠ culty* dimension, the most relevant features are: the number of scored goals (**Goal**) and the number of positive arousal events (**posAr**). The difficulty levels (**pLevel, gLevel, rLevel**) are much less important than the game result (**Goal**) feature. It reflects the fact that the proposed objective difficulty level is different than the perceived subjective difficulty level. Player's perception of the difficulty of match is closely related with the game outcome and high arousal moments.

For the immersion dimension, the most relevant features are: frequency of positive valence events (**posVa**), number of high arousal events (**hAr**), number of interceptions of guard by the adversary (**(-)Intercept.**), number of happy events (**happy**), number of scored goals (**Goal**). By reviewing the related games events and meta-information, we notice that the sense of immersion are both triggered by discriminant positive (such as **happy** and **posVa**) and negative (such as presence of **(-)Intercept.**).

For the amusement dimension, the most relevant features are: game outcome (**Goal,di⊠ Goal**) and number of high arousal (**hAr,posAr**) and high valence events (**hVa**). The sense of amusement is more related with game outcome as well as the improvement of game result. It also related with high arousal and high valence, this can be explained by the fact that amusement raises with the sense of accomplishment.

5 DISCUSSION

We have shown that physiological, behavioral and meta-information are effective for predicting and understanding the player's game experience. In the present study, the behavioral modalities is proposed by manual annotation. On the bright side, this method of annotation provides us a corpus to investigate the relationship between a game event and the associated self-reported emotion, which is rarely realized in the existing works. As shown in Figure 3, a close relationship can be found between them. Therefore, with a prior knowledge of event type and emotional response, we can get a better understanding of player's instant emotional state. Meanwhile, we also notice that not all the game events trigger emotional response, that is, they are neither reported by the player nor trigger a visible physiological response. This observation emphasizes the

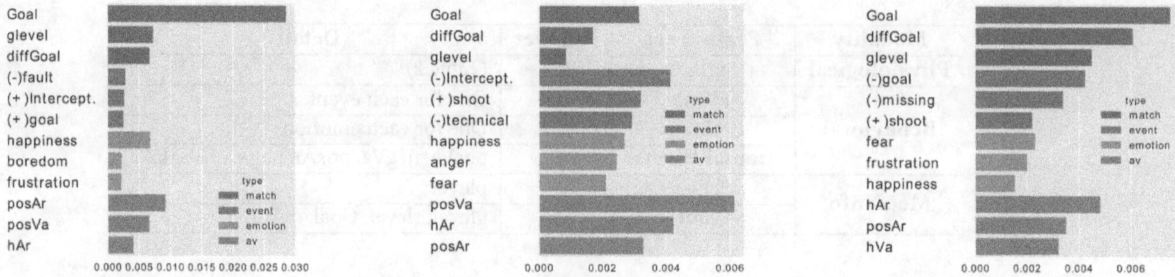

(a) Difficulty (b) Immersion (c) Amusement

Figure 5: Distribution of the annotated events in terms of emotions.

importance of physiological signals, that can be used as guideline to figure out the effective game event stimulation.

On the other side, manual event annotation is not applicable to practical use case. Therefore, we advocate the use of event log as a source of behavioral modality. Current work characterizes the game event or emotion sequence by their frequency. In the future work, efforts can be made to investigate the event sequence in more detail. For example, by using sequential analysis or clustering to determine discriminant event patterns as features [8, 9]. Another possibility is to view the event and emotion sequence as words in a sentence, and use method for sentiment analysis [45] to predict the game experience. Common method such as bags of word [46] using different N-grams or word embedding [47] can be applied to achieve better representation of the sequence in the target space. However, these methods require more data to tune the model and embedding on a different space result in lack of interpretability. Lastly, current dataset do not have good gender balance, so that the gender effects have not been investigated.

6 CONCLUSION

In this paper, we propose an approach to predict the player's perception of game experience. We first present a multi-modal dataset collected in the game context. The dataset contain physiological modality (ECG, EDA, respiration, EMG, ACC), behavioral modality (the game events and the associated emotion) and meta-information related to the player profile and game information. Statistical analysis on the collected data shows that there is a close relationship between the game event and the associated emotion and that there is a positive correlation between the players' perception of immersion and amusement in the game experience evaluation. Based on the collected data, we use machine learning method to predict the game experience in terms of difficulty, immersion and amusement based on separated and fused modalities. We show that physiological signal is an effective modality to predict the player's game experience and that the fusion of features from behavioral and meta-information modalities improves significantly the prediction performance. By investigating the relevant features from the behavioral and meta-information, we highlight the most important factors that influence the global game experience. In future, we aim to work on automatic collected behavioral data and experiment on a larger scale to validate the framework.

ACKNOWLEDGMENTS

This work was performed within the Labex SMART (ANR-11-LABX-65) supported by French state funds managed by the ANR within the Investissements d'Avenir programme under reference ANR-11-IDEX-0004-02. The experiment has been done thanks to the fund "Soutien au démarrage d'études comportementales" granted by the Centre Multidisciplinaire des Sciences Comportementales, Sorbonne Universités-INSEAD.

Furthermore, the authors gratefully thank Victor Billot for aiding carrying out the experiment and also members of INSEAD-Sorbonne Universités Behavioural Lab: Liselott Pettersson, Jean-Yves Mariette, Germain Dépetasse, Hoai Huong Ngo.

REFERENCES

[1] Brad Paras. Game, motivation, and effective learning: An integrated model for educational game design. 2005.
[2] Boyan Bontchev. Adaptation in affective video games: A literature review. *Cybernetics and Information Technologies*, 16(3):3–34, 2016.
[3] Sylvia D Kreibig. Autonomic nervous system activity in emotion: A review. *Biological psychology*, 84(3):394–421, 2010.
[4] Georgios N Yannakakis, Hector P Martinez, and Maurizio Garbarino. Psychophysiology in games. In *Emotion in Games*, pages 119–137. Springer, 2016.
[5] Lisa Feldman Barrett. Are emotions natural kinds? *Perspectives on psychological science*, 1(1):28–58, 2006.
[6] Robert W Levenson. The autonomic nervous system and emotion. *Emotion Review*, 6(2):100–112, 2014.
[7] Catharine Evers, Henrik Hopp, James J Gross, Agneta H Fischer, Antony SR Manstead, and Iris B Mauss. Emotion response coherence: A dual-process perspective. *Biological psychology*, 98:43–49, 2014.
[8] Guenter Wallner. Sequential analysis of player behavior. In *Proceedings of the 2015 Annual Symposium on Computer-Human Interaction in Play*, pages 349–358. ACM, 2015.
[9] Benjamin Cowley, Ilkka Kosunen, Petri Lankoski, J Matias Kivikangas, Simo Järvelä, Inger Ekman, Jaakko Kemppainen, and Niklas Ravaja. Experience assessment and design in the analysis of gameplay. *Simulation & Gaming*, 45(1):41–69, 2014.
[10] Josef Wiemeyer, Lennart Nacke, Christiane Moser, et al. Player experience. In *Serious Games*, pages 243–271. Springer, 2016.
[11] Lennart Nacke. From playability to a hierarchical game usability model. In *Proceedings of the 2009 Conference on Future Play on@ GDC Canada*, pages 11–12. ACM, 2009.
[12] Kathrin M Gerling, Matthias Klauser, and Joerg Niesenhaus. Measuring the impact of game controllers on player experience in fps games. In *Proceedings of the 15th International Academic MindTrek Conference: Envisioning Future Media Environments*, pages 83–86. ACM, 2011.
[13] Katherine Isbister and Noah Schaffer. *Game usability: Advancing the player experience*. CRC Press, 2015.
[14] Richard M Ryan and Edward L Deci. Self-determination theory and the facilitation of intrinsic motivation, social development, and well-being. *American psychologist*, 55(1):68, 2000.

[15] John M Keller. *Motivational design for learning and performance: The ARCS model approach.* Springer Science & Business Media, 2009.
[16] Mihaly Csikszentmihalyi. Das flow-erlebnis. *Jenseits von Angst und Langeweile: im Tun aufgehen. Stuttgart*, 1985.
[17] Penelope Sweetser and Peta Wyeth. Gameflow: a model for evaluating player enjoyment in games. *Computers in Entertainment (CIE)*, 3(3):3–3, 2005.
[18] K Poels, YAW de Kort, and WA IJsselsteijn. Fuga-the fun of gaming: measuring the human experience of media enjoyment. *Deliverable D3*, 3, 2008.
[19] Christian Borgelt. An implementation of the fp-growth algorithm. In *Proceedings of the 1st international workshop on open source data mining: frequent pattern mining implementations*, pages 1–5. ACM, 2005.
[20] Yubo Kou, Xinning Gui, and Yong Ming Kow. Ranking practices and distinction in league of legends. In *Proceedings of the 2016 Annual Symposium on Computer-Human Interaction in Play*, pages 4–9. ACM, 2016.
[21] Charlene Jennett, Anna L Cox, Paul Cairns, Samira Dhoparee, Andrew Epps, Tim Tijs, and Alison Walton. Measuring and defining the experience of immersion in games. *International journal of human-computer studies*, 66(9):641–661, 2008.
[22] Jeanne H Brockmyer, Christine M Fox, Kathleen A Curtiss, Evan McBroom, Kimberly M Burkhart, and Jacquelyn N Pidruzny. The development of the game engagement questionnaire: A measure of engagement in video game-playing. *Journal of Experimental Social Psychology*, 45(4):624–634, 2009.
[23] Scott Rigby and Richard Ryan. The player experience of need satisfaction (pens) model. 2007.
[24] Alena Denisova, A Imran Nordin, and Paul Cairns. The convergence of player experience questionnaires. In *Proceedings of the 2016 Annual Symposium on Computer-Human Interaction in Play*, pages 33–37. ACM, 2016.
[25] Margaret M Bradley and Peter J Lang. Measuring emotion: Behavior, feeling, and physiology. *Cognitive neuroscience of emotion*, 25:49–59, 2000.
[26] Stephen H Fairclough. Psychophysiological inference and physiological computer games. In *BRAINPLAY 07 Brain-Computer Interfaces and Games Workshop at ACE (Advances in Computer Entertainment)*, page 19, 2007.
[27] Sara Ilstedt Hjelm and Carolina Browall. Brainball-using brain activity for cool competition. In *Proceedings of NordiCHI*, volume 7, 2000.
[28] John Sharry, Matt McDermott, and Jim Condron. Relax to win treating children with anxiety problems with a biofeedback video game. *Eisteach*, 2:22–26, 2003.
[29] Tim Tijs, Dirk Brokken, and Wijnand IJsselsteijn. Creating an emotionally adaptive game. In *International Conference on Entertainment Computing*, pages 122–133. Springer, 2008.
[30] Guillaume Chanel, Cyril Rebetez, Mireille Bétrancourt, and Thierry Pun. Boredom, engagement and anxiety as indicators for adaptation to difficulty in games. In *Proceedings of the 12th international conference on Entertainment and media in the ubiquitous era*, pages 13–17. ACM, 2008.
[31] Zachary O Toups, Ross Graeber, Andruid Kerne, Louis Tassinary, Sarah Berry, Kyle Overby, and Maritza Johnson. A design for using physiological signals to affect team game play. *Foundations of Augmented Cognition*, pages 134–139, 2006.
[32] Pedro Alves Nogueira, Rúben Aguiar, Rui Amaral Rodrigues, Eugénio C Oliveira, and Lennart Nacke. Fuzzy affective player models: A physiology-based hierarchical clustering method. In *AIIDE*, 2014.
[33] Tim JW Tijs, Dirk Brokken, and Wijnand A IJsselsteijn. Dynamic game balancing by recognizing affect. In *Fun and Games*, pages 88–93. Springer, 2008.
[34] Faham Negini, Regan L Mandryk, and Kevin G Stanley. Using affective state to adapt characters, npcs, and the environment in a first-person shooter game. In *Games Media Entertainment (GEM), 2014 IEEE*, pages 1–8. IEEE, 2014.
[35] Changchun Liu, Pramila Agrawal, Nilanjan Sarkar, and Shuo Chen. Dynamic difficulty adjustment in computer games through real-time anxiety-based affective feedback. *International Journal of Human-Computer Interaction*, 25(6):506–529, 2009.
[36] Simone Tognetti, Maurizio Garbarino, Andrea Bonarini, and Matteo Matteucci. Modeling enjoyment preference from physiological responses in a car racing game. In *Computational Intelligence and Games (CIG), 2010 IEEE Symposium on*, pages 321–328. IEEE, 2010.
[37] Andrew Dekker and Erik Champion. Please biofeed the zombies: Enhancing the gameplay and display of a horror game using biofeedback. In *DiGRA Conference*, 2007.
[38] Pedro A Nogueira, Rui Rodrigues, and Eugénio Oliveira. Real-time psychophysiological emotional state estimation in digital gameplay scenarios. In *International Conference on Engineering Applications of Neural Networks*, pages 243–252. Springer, 2013.
[39] Avinash Parnandi and Ricardo Gutierrez-Osuna. A comparative study of game mechanics and control laws for an adaptive physiological game. *Journal on Multimodal User Interfaces*, 9(1):31–42, 2015.
[40] Stephen Fairclough and Kiel Gilleade. Construction of the biocybernetic loop: a case study. In *Proceedings of the 14th ACM international conference on Multimodal interaction*, pages 571–578. ACM, 2012.
[41] Lun-De Liao, Chi-Yu Chen, I-Jan Wang, Sheng-Fu Chen, Shih-Yu Li, Bo-Wei Chen, Jyh-Yeong Chang, and Chin-Teng Lin. Gaming control using a wearable and wireless eeg-based brain-computer interface device with novel dry foam-based sensors. *Journal of neuroengineering and rehabilitation*, 9(1):5, 2012.
[42] Mihaly Csikszentmihalyi. Flow and the psychology of discovery and invention. *New York: Harper Collins*, 1996.
[43] S. Koelstra, C. Muhl, M. Soleymani, J. S. Lee, A. Yazdani, T. Ebrahimi, T. Pun, A. Nijholt, and I. Patras. DEAP: A database for emotion analysis ;using physiological signals. *IEEE Transactions on A⊠ective Computing*, 3:18–31, Jan 2012.
[44] M. K. Abadi, R. Subramanian, S. M. Kia, P. Avesani, I. Patras, and N. Sebe. Decaf: Meg-based multimodal database for decoding affective physiological responses. *IEEE Transactions on A⊠ective Computing*, 6:209–222, July 2015.
[45] Bing Liu and Lei Zhang. A survey of opinion mining and sentiment analysis. In *Mining text data*, pages 415–463. Springer, 2012.
[46] Wen Zhang, Taketoshi Yoshida, and Xijin Tang. A comparative study of tf* idf, lsi and multi-words for text classification. *Expert Systems with Applications*, 38(3):2758–2765, 2011.
[47] Tomas Mikolov, Kai Chen, Greg Corrado, and Jeffrey Dean. Efficient estimation of word representations in vector space. *arXiv preprint arXiv:1301.3781*, 2013.

Multimodal Filtering of Social Media for Temporal Monitoring and Event Analysis

Po-Yao Huang
Carnegie Mellon University
Pittsburgh, PA
poyaoh@cs.cmu.edu

Junwei Liang
Carnegie Mellon University
Pittsburgh, PA
junweil@cs.cmu.edu

Jean-Baptiste Lamare
Carnegie Mellon University
Pittsburgh, PA
jlamare@cs.cmu.edu

Alexander G. Hauptmann
Carnegie Mellon University & Shandong Normal University
Pittsburgh, PA
alex@cs.cmu.edu

ABSTRACT

Developing an efficient and effective social media monitoring system has become one of the important steps towards improved public safety. With the explosive availability of user-generated content documenting most conflicts and human rights abuses around the world, analysts and first-responders increasingly find themselves overwhelmed with massive amounts of noisy data from social media. In this paper, we construct a large-scale public safety event dataset with retrospective automatic labeling for 4.2 million multimodal tweets from 7 public safety events occurred in 2013~2017. We propose a new multimodal social media filtering system composed of encoding, classification, and correlation networks to jointly learn shared and complementary visual and textual information to filter out the most relevant and useful items among the noisy social media influx. The proposed model is verified and achieves significant improvement over competitive baselines under the retrospective and real-time experimental protocols.

CCS CONCEPTS

• **Information systems → Document filtering**; **Multimedia and multimodal retrieval**;

KEYWORDS

Text Summary; Visual Summary; Event Detection

ACM Reference Format:
Po-Yao Huang, Junwei Liang, Jean-Baptiste Lamare, and Alexander G. Hauptmann. 2018. Multimodal Filtering of Social Media for Temporal Monitoring and Event Analysis. In *ICMR '18: 2018 International Conference on Multimedia Retrieval, June 11–14, 2018, Yokohama, Japan.* ACM, New York, NY, USA, 8 pages. https://doi.org/10.1145/3206025.3206079

ICMR '18, June 11–14, 2018, Yokohama, Japan

ACM ISBN 978-1-4503-5046-4/18/06...$15.00
https://doi.org/10.1145/3206025.3206079

Figure 1: As an event develops, most of the user-generated social media posts are unrelated or even rumors. Through the proposed multimodal filtering system, useful information can be obtained in a near real-time fashion.

1 INTRODUCTION

With the growing use of social media, user-generated content has become an increasingly important information source for conflict monitoring and public safety event analysis. People document their daily lives and broadcast events all over the world using their smartphones, recording with either videos, images or texts and posting to social media like Twitter and Facebook. When an event happens, especially for the public safety events involving a large crowd of people, tweets that include crucial information from multiple modalities are posted and shared, capturing the event from different times, locations and from different perspectives. For example,

Table 1: Statistics of the collected public safety event dataset

Year	Event	Tweets	Images	First day tweets	Vocabulary	Tweet length	Positive %
2013	Boston Marathon bombing	1,807,695	70,028 (3.87%)	522,696 (28.92%)	69,129	17.8 ± 6.3	2.0%
2013	Washington Navy Yard shooting	263,621	7,210 (2.74%)	128,069 (48.64%)	85,546	15.8 ± 5.4	2.2%
2015	Charleston massacre	435,051	48,667 (11.19%)	84,992 (19.54%)	79,617	16.9 ± 6.0	2.5%
2015	Paris attacks	400,254	80,976 (20.23%)	47,519 (11.87%)	55,314	15.2 ± 7.1	1.7%
2016	Orlando shooting	191,740	29,314 (15.29%)	76,919 (39.96%)	61,449	17.1 ± 5.9	2.0%
2016	Dallas shooting	291,935	26,340 (9.02%)	48,965 (16.77%)	40,982	16.8 ± 5.8	2.0%
2017	Las Vegas shooting	887,997	123,322 (13.89%)	464,488 (52.31%)	69,129	18.4 ± 6.9	2.1%

events like the Boston Marathon bombing and Las Vegas shooting all have hundreds of witnesses posted tweets of the event as the event developed. The collection of these data might enable the authority and first-responders to better address the situation timely.

A rising and inevitable challenge under such scenario is to handle the thrilling amount of noisy social media data. Figure 1 shows real tweets of the Las Vegas shooing event. As can be seen, a great portion social media content is irrelevant or even contains misleading information. Analysts have to not only search and retrieve the content, but also determine the veracity and extract relevant and useful information efficiently and effectively. In most of the cases, even with some heuristic techniques like keyword filtering, analysts still need to examine hundreds of thousands of noisy posts manually. For instance, more than 0.9 million related tweets were sent in the first week of the Las Vegas shooting. In our manual investigation over randomly sampled 10,000 tweets, we found that only 2% of them might considered as relevant or useful for the event under the criteria that it contains information which would contribute to the event summarization aftermath.

Concerning these challenges for better public safety, we respond by building the first public safety event dataset. We collect 4.2 million tweets along with their multimodal content for 7 events with severe causalities. The scale of the dataset makes manual labeling of all the instances for learning automatic models impractical. In this study, we choose an alternative approach for annotation. Since all the events have occurred, retrospectively, we utilize the event summarization publicly available as the reference for relevance and usefulness measurement to the tweets sent in the past. The result is a large-scale multi-event dataset that may speed up related research timely. Ultimately, finding efficient and accurate approaches to distill critical information under real-world scale has become the important step towards improved public safety.

As depicted in Figure 1, to help unravel the entangled event and distill important information for all the modalities available, our effort proposes a multimodal filtering of visual and textual information. With recent advances in neural network, the performance of conventional classification and retrieval tasks with single modality has been greatly pushed forward. For example, tasks related to text [29], image [6, 13], and video [9] classification all benefit from more sophisticated representations learned with deeper structure and larger amount of data. For filtering noisy tweets with text and/or image inputs, we propose a new deep correlation network tackling textual and visual representation learning for classification while being regularized by the joint embedding learning in parallel.

Our contribution is twofold: First, we construct a large-scale multi-event dataset which includes tweets with corresponding metadata, text, and images for 7 public-safety events resulting in severe causalities. For the 4.2 million tweet collections, we analyze the user-generated content and build a retrospective automatic labeling scheme to annotate the dataset for related research. Second, we develop a multimodal filtering system incorporates a classification model with joint embedding learning over encoded noisy parallel content. In the retrospective and real-time evaluations, we demonstrate that the proposed model outperforms other competitive baseline models and achieves the best performance.

2 RELATED WORKS

Conflict Monitoring in Social Media Recently, there has been a growth of research in building tools and algorithms for conflict monitoring in social media. Video dataset of the real-world event from social media [4] has been collected for video synchronization [16] and event reconstruction [15]. Webly supervised learning is utilized to automatically train detector to discover concepts and events in social media videos [18, 19]. A similar method has been applied to temporally localizing audio events [17]. Previous research in tweets has been focusing on text analysis, such as sentiment analysis [10, 23] and event detection [2, 30]. To the best of our knowledge, there has not been any prior work on multimodal tweet filtering for conflict event monitoring.

Multimodal Joint Embedding In recent years, multimodal joint embedding has been utilized for tasks with multimodal inputs. Two-dimensional encoding of regional visual feature and sequential textual feature has been introduced in [8] for multimodal machine translation. In [12, 28], canonical correlation analysis (CCA) with multi-layer perceptrons as encoders has been proposed to find joint embeddings that maximize the correlation between images and sentences. Wang et al. [27] further utilize max-margin loss to make joint embeddings more discriminative. Memory networks in [21] further allow the model to attend to image and text simultaneously. For real-world tweets, the image-text alignments are considerably more abstract and noisy in comparison to the conventional clean text-to-image retrieval dataset such as the Flickr30K dataset [7]. Therefore, instead of directly optimizing the joint embedding, we consider learning two classification tasks in parallel and utilize the joint embedding loss as the regularization signal for the encoders.

Time Series Modeling With the increasingly growing amount of social media posts, predicting events and activities based on such time-series data has become an important problem. A Probabilistic spatio-temporal model was introduced to predict natural disasters

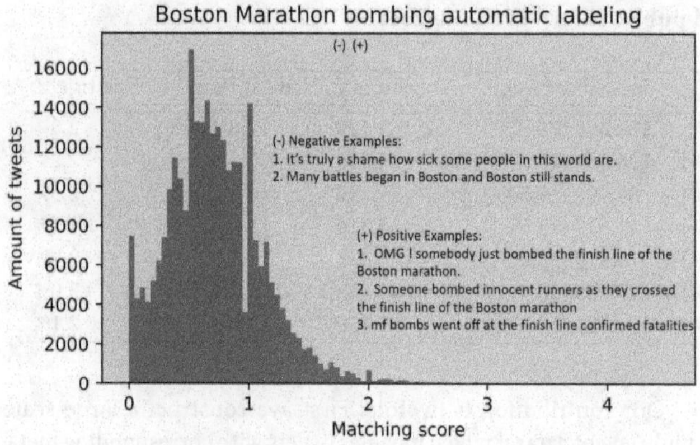

(a) Matching score distribution and automatic labeling example for the Boston Marathon bombing.

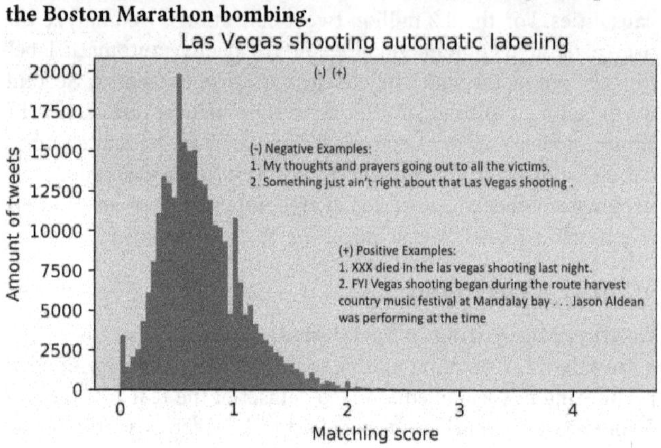

(b) Matching score distribution and automatic labeling example for the Las Vegas shooting.

Figure 2: Textual relevance labeling.

Text: "Who's that guy on the roof!?!?"
Post Time: Mon Apr 15 18:01:08 2013

(a) Example positive from auto labeling of the Boston Marathon bombing event. On the left is the video frame from event kit used to match to the tweet image on the right. Tweet text is shown on top.

Text: "Look at the window the shooting is from. Real or fake?"
Post Time: Tue Oct 03 10:51:19 2017

(b) Example positive from auto labeling of the Vegas shooting event. On the left is the video frame from event kit used to match to the tweet image on the right. Tweet text is shown on top.

Figure 3: Qualitative visual relevance labeling examples.

like earthquakes and typhoons in real time [25]. Continuous sentiment analysis has been used to predict the stock market [3]. Crime prediction system based on Twitter [5] utilized kernel density estimation to fit a two-dimensional spatial probability density function to a historical crime record. More recently, neural network approach was used in time-series forecasting of extreme rider demands from Uber data [14]. Our work tackles a more challenging scenario where instantaneous feedback may be noisy or even unavailable.

3 DATASET COLLECTION

We focus on the mass shooting events and the terrorist attacks occurred in recent years. We collect the corresponding tweets and its multimedia contents for the 7 events summarized in Table 1.

3.1 Collecting Event Tweets

We use event-specific keywords and hashtags to search the tweets sent in the first week of the event then download the available multimodal data. For example, *las vegas shooting, #lasvegasshooting...* etc., were used to search tweets related to the Las Vegas shooting event tweeted between October 1st and October 8th, 2017. The hashtags and keywords are first selected by manually inspecting the tweets at the corresponding dates when an event occurred. We sampled 100 tweets contains the event name and extract the most frequent phrases and hashtags up to 60% coverage, the exact number of them would vary for different events. Our objective being extracting relevant information of a specific public safety event, we focus on "factual" keywords and hashtags by further manually refine the searching term pool. In the collection phase we also perform heuristic keyword filtering which may also be done by analysts. Example are many tweets with hashtags "#prayforvegas" can be easily excluded since they usually not present any factual information. Additionally, analysts would also naively filter out all the tweets containing a news link within its text, for the tweet may just be a quote or restatement of the news content and contribute no additional information for the event of concern. The qualitative result is shown in the gray box in Figure 1.

Once we have determined the event-related searching terms, we mine the tweets within the corresponding dates with the twitter advanced search[1], and then extract the *tweet ID, text, date, user screen name, username, user ID, number of retweets* and *favorites*

[1] https://twitter.com/search-advanced

with BeautifulSoup[2]. Inside this collection, some tweets contain only textual information, while some additionally contain photos or videos which may be useful.

Following the process we collected 4.2 million multimodal tweets for 7 public safety events about mass shooting and terrorist attack occurred in 2013~2017. Though a rich amount of metadata, texts, images, videos are available for analysis, in this paper we focus on two events and compare models upon them: 1) the 2017 Las Vegas shooting and 2) the 2013 Boston Marathon bombing as they share largest amounts of tweets available.

3.2 Retrospective Automatic Labeling

The main challenge for constructing the public safety event dataset is to maintain the annotation quality at a scale of $10^5 \sim 10^6$ instances for each event. At this scale, labeling every tweet manually is infeasible considering the trade-off between the total time effort and the subjective variances among annotators. Alternatively, we choose a semi-automatic approach under the retrospective assumption: all events happened in the past.

In order to determine the relevance and usefulness of a tweet with the consistent criteria, we resort to the event summarization from some publicly available knowledge base as the event has occurred. A tweet is considered useful/relevant and labeled positive if its content would contribute to or is related to the retrospective event kit summarization. To get reliable and consistent automatic annotations for a specific event, we first manually construct the event kits as the reference. The event kit consists textual and visual parts and is constructed in a retrospective manner as the event has already occurred. After constructing the event kit, we then apply relevance matching to measure and label each tweet as a positive or negative instance.

Constructing Event Kits We construct event kits with textual event descriptions and unedited videos taken from that scene. For the textual description, we use the content on the Wikipedia as the ground truth summarization. We crawl the Wikipedia page of the event and remove its reference and external link part. To collect relevant videos, we search videos from major video sharing sites such as YouTube using event keywords. For the Boston Marathon bombing 2013, we utilize the videos from the Boston Dataset [4]. We apply shot segmentation and de-duplication to finalize the video pool for each event.

Relevance Matching We use the event kit to determine how relevant a tweet is then labeled it. For the textual relevance we apply weighted n−gram matching ($n = 1, 2, 3, w_n = 0.4, 0.3, 0.3$ respectively) between a tweet and the event specific Wikipedia content followed by tweet-length normalization. The matching scores are then used to rank the relevance of tweets. The matching score histogram the Boston marathon bombing and the Las Vegas shooting are depicted in Figure 2. As can be seen, tweets with higher matching scores imply more relevance to the event. Examples like *"FYI ... Jason Aldean was performing at that time"* is more useful as it provides the timing information about when the tragedy started. In contrast, tweets like *"My thoughts and prayers...,"* are less useful even if it is tagged with *#lasvegasshooting*. We observe that the majority of tweets are not useful. A preliminary analysis also shows

[2]https://www.crummy.com/software/BeautifulSoup/bs4/doc/

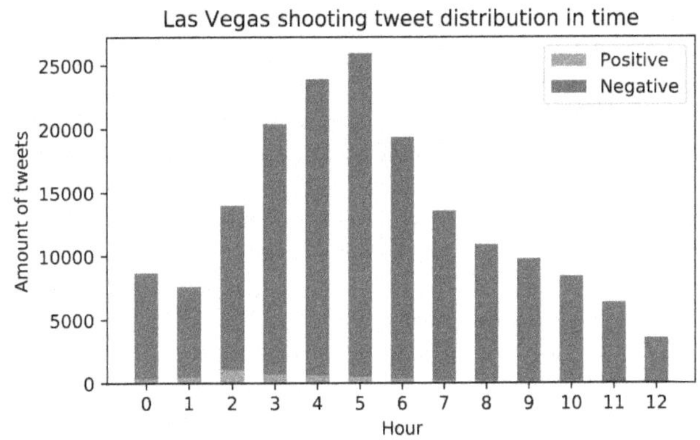

(a) Hourly tweets of the Las Vegas shooting.

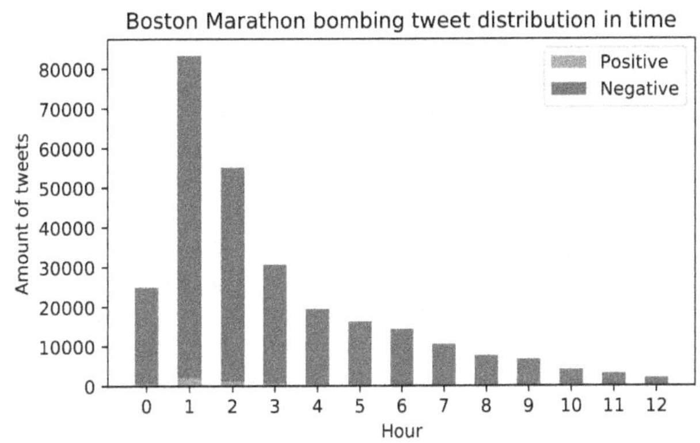

(b) Hourly tweets of the Boston Marathon bombing.

Figure 4: Evolution of amount of tweets in the two events of concern.

that there is no trivial feature would help infer the relevance of a tweet. For instance, the number of retweets is often biased towards celebrities instead of relevance to the event. We use a threshold to binarize positive/negative examples. After carefully investigating the quality of the matching score distribution of the two events, we manually set the threshold that incorporates roughly 2.0% of instances as relevant for each event.

For visual relevance, we only calculate such score on tweets with images. We first uniformly sample frames from the video pool and extract frame-level features as described in Section 5.1. The relevance score for each tweet is then calculated as the maximum cosine similarity between the tweet image feature to all video frames. Examples of positive tweets are shown in Figure 3a & 3b.

3.3 Dataset Analysis

Basic statistics of the collected events in the dataset is shown in Table 1. The union set of textually positive and visually positive tweets is considered as the final positive set while the rest are negative. The collected Tweets are very noisy, only 1.5~2.5% of them are relevant.

Retrospectively, one can treat an event as a whole without considering its temporal segmentation. Nevertheless, in practical applications, the first-responders or the police authority may concern more about how the event develops through time. For example, can the system identify when is the first time the suspect is mentioned or discussed in the social media? Can the system track how the authentic or fake information broadcast over time? How to utilize the temporal information will be the critical but still missing piece for practical deployment of a real-time event monitoring system.

Figure 4 shows the hourly dynamics of tweets in the first 13 hours of the Las Vegas shooting and the Boston marathon bombing. Unique user behaviors have been observed. For the Las Vegas shooting event, the tragedy gradually captured tweet users' attention most likely due to the shift of time zone. The peak of positive tweets locates at the 2nd hour and as it is loosely aligned with the time when the police arrested the gunman 72 minutes after the shooting occurred. More than 50% of the tweets were tweeted in the 24 hours of the Las Vegas shooting event.

For the Boston marathon bombing event, the initial explosions immediately captured tweet users' attention and result in the burst discussion. Without more information, the number of both positive and negative tweets shrinks in the following hours. There are multiple incidents over the development of the Boston Marathon bombing event. Around 30% of tweets were tweeted on the first day. While the second rise (not shown in the figure) happened 4 days later as the last gunman arrested by the law enforcement officers.

In both cases, we observe initial information bursts and high dynamics over time. In addition to treating an event as a whole for training and evaluation model, these facts make the temporal analysis of events more challenging but crucial.

4 MODEL

As shown in Figure 5, the proposed multimodal filtering system is composed of five components: 1) Textual encoding network 2) Textual classification network 3) Visual encoding network 4) Visual classification network 5) Multimodal joint embedding learning with deep canonical correlation analysis. The encoders are built upon a long short-term memory (LSTM) network (for sequential data such as text) and a residual network (for visual data). The multimodal joint embedding module would be viewed as the regularizer over encoded representations across different modalities. We jointly train the encoding, classification, and the joint embedding modules under a multi-task fashion.

4.1 Multimodal Joint Embedding Learning

Let $X \in \mathbb{R}^{d_t \times M}$ and $V \in \mathbb{R}^{d_v \times M}$ represents the set of textual and visual representations respectively. With $\Sigma_{xx}, \Sigma_{vv}, \Sigma_{xv}$ denoting the covariance and cross covariance matrices. Canonical correlation analysis(CCA) seek pairs of projection maximizing the correlation between two modalities:

$$(\mathbf{w}_x, \mathbf{w}_v) = \underset{\mathbf{w}_x, \mathbf{w}_v}{\text{argmax}} \quad corr(\mathbf{w}_x^T X, \mathbf{w}_v^T V) = \underset{\mathbf{w}_x, \mathbf{w}_v}{\text{argmax}} \quad \frac{\mathbf{w}_x^T \Sigma_{xv} \mathbf{w}_v^T}{\sqrt{\mathbf{w}_x^T \Sigma_{xx} \mathbf{w}_x \mathbf{w}_v^T \Sigma_{vv} \mathbf{w}_v}} \quad (1)$$

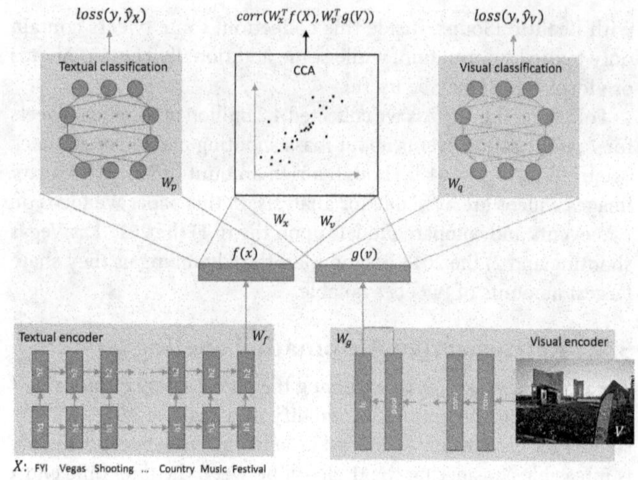

Figure 5: Multimodal tweet filtering

Let (W_x, W_v) denote the projection matrices composed of top un-correlated projections $(\mathbf{w}_x, \mathbf{w}_v)$. Since the objective should be scale-invariant of W_x, W_v, we constraint the projections to share unit variance in avoidance of trivial solution. The CCA objective then can be rewritten as:

$$\underset{W_t, W_v}{\text{argmax}} \quad tr(W_x^T \Sigma_{xv} W_v^T) \qquad \text{s.t.} \quad W_x^T \Sigma_{xx} W_x = W_v^T \Sigma_{yy} W_v = I \quad (2)$$

In [1], Andrew et al. propose a deeper version of CCA with deep neural network, i.e. DCCA, by encoding raw features with multi-layer perceptron ($f(X) \in \mathbb{R}^{d_{f(x)} \times M}$ and $g(V) \in \mathbb{R}^{d_{g(v)} \times M}$) followed by mini-batch training with size M.

Notably, under mini-batch training with a typical size $M = 10^2 \sim 10^3$, a regularization with parameter λ_x is often required to ensure non-singularity of covariance matrices estimated as $\Sigma_{xx} = \frac{1}{1-M} XX^T + \lambda_x I$. Formally, DCCA learns to solve:

$$\underset{W_t, W_v, W_f, W_g}{\text{argmax}} \quad tr(W_x^T f(X) g(V) W_v^T)$$
$$\text{s.t.} \quad W_x^T \left(\frac{1}{M-1} f(X) f(X)^T + \lambda_x I \right) W_x = I \quad (3)$$
$$W_v^T \left(\frac{1}{M-1} g(V) g(V)^T + \lambda_v I \right) W_v = I$$

Considering the fact that both textual and visual information of a tweet can be useful for event analysis, we propose a novel architecture jointly learns the textual and visual encoding/classification models bridged by CCA as shown in Figure 5.

We use an LSTM network as the textual encoder $f(.)$ and use a multi-layer perceptron with a residual link as the visual encoder $g(.)$. For the textual encoder, the padded word tokens of length L in a tweet are first mapped into word embeddings $w_i = W_{emb}^T x_i, i \in [1...L]$. The LSTM network then encodes the sequence to generate the outputs and corresponding hidden states as:$\mathbf{y}, \mathbf{h} = LSTM(\mathbf{w}; W_f)$. We use the last hidden state $f(\mathbf{x}) = h_L$ as the fixed length textual representation of the tweet.

The encoded vector $f(\mathbf{x})$ and $g(\mathbf{v})$ then be used for classification and CCA. For simplicity in network design, we use two independent multi-layer perceptron network with residual links as the textual and visual classification models ($p(.)$ and $q(.)$) parametrized by W_p and W_q respectively.

The two classification models and the joint embedding model are jointly learned under a multi-task learning fashion. Specifically, in addition to learn the joint embedding with DCCA as in Eq. 3, the proposed model also targets to minimize the weighted multi-modal classification losses. For example, the textual classification loss with the cross-entropy loss function is: $l(y, \hat{y}) = l(y, p(f(X); W_p)) = \sum_{i=1}^{M} \sum_{c=1}^{C} y_{ic} log(p_c(f(x_i); W_p))$. In this study our concern is the binary relevance of a tweet and therefore therefore $C = 2$. Let α, β, and γ denotes the weights for textual, visual classification loss and correlation respectively. The overall objective function is:

$$\begin{aligned} \underset{\substack{W_x, W_v, W_f, \\ W_g, W_p, W_q}}{\text{argmax}} \quad & \frac{\alpha}{M} \sum_{i=1}^{M} y_i log\left(p(f(x_i))\right) + (1 - y_i) log\left(1 - p(f(x_i))\right) \\ & + \frac{\beta}{M} \sum_{i=1}^{M} y_i log\left(q(g(v_i))\right) + (1 - v_i) log\left(1 - q(g(x_i))\right) \\ & + \gamma Tr(W_x^T f(X) g(V) W_v^T) \\ \text{s.t.} \quad & W_x^T \left(\frac{1}{M-1} f(X) f(X)^T + \lambda_x I \right) W_x = I \\ & W_v^T \left(\frac{1}{M-1} g(V) g(V)^T + \lambda_v I \right) W_v = I \end{aligned} \tag{4}$$

Similar to DCCA, we apply stochastic optimization to maximize the objective function in Eq. 4. The classification models and the encoder models are fully differentiable. For the gradient term of the correlation objective, first we define the estimation of the covariance matrix $\Sigma_{xx} = \frac{1}{M-1} f(x) f(x)^T + \lambda_x I$ and $\Sigma_{vv} = \frac{1}{M-1} g(v) g(v)^T + \lambda_v I$ (Note here we simplified the subscript $\Sigma_{f(x)f(x)}$ to Σ_{xx} for clearance in notation.) Set $T = \Sigma_{xx}^{-1/2} \Sigma_{xv} \Sigma_{vv}^{-1/2}$ and U_k and V_k be the first k left- and right- singular vector of T. As shown in [1], for $k = d_{f(x)} = d_{g(x)}$, then total correlation objective in Eq.4 becomes the matrix trace norm of T:

$$corr\left(W_x^T f(X), W_v^T g(V)\right) = ||T||_{tr} = tr(T^T T)^{1/2} \tag{5}$$

And the gradient of the total correlation with respect to X can be derived as:

$$\frac{\partial corr(f(X), g(V)}{f(X)} = \frac{1}{M-1} (2 \nabla_{xx} f(X) + \nabla_{xv} g(V)) \tag{6}$$

where

$$\begin{aligned} \nabla_{xx} &= \frac{-1}{2} \Sigma_{xx}^{-1/2} U D U^T \Sigma_{xx}^{-1/2} \\ \nabla_{xv} &= \Sigma_{xx}^{-1/2} U V^T \Sigma_{vv}^{-1/2} \end{aligned} \tag{7}$$

The gradients for V share the same form by swapping $f(X)$ and $g(V)$. The overall stochastic gradient is the aggregation of the gradient for the classification model and the gradient for the correlation term as in Eq. 6.

5 EXPERIMENTS

The efficacy of our system is verified on the two largest events in our collection: the 2013 Boston Marathon bombing event and the 2017 Las Vegas shooting event. We evaluate under two experimental protocols: 1) A retrospective setting in which we assume the event has already occurred and the target is to mine relevant tweet among a fixed collection. 2) A real-time scenario in which we assume the event is happening and a on-line model adapts and filters according to the hourly tweet influx.

5.1 Experimental Setup

Datasets, Features, Evaluation Metrics and baselines In order to keep our experiments closer to the real-world scenario, we limit the evaluation of the dataset to the first 36 hours of the events. We use automatic labels as the ground truth $\mathbf{y}$ for model regression. Average precision is used as our primary evaluation metrics. For SVM baselines, we utilize pre-trained GloVe [22] word vectors to extract sentence representation by average pooling. For a fair comparison, we also use the LSTM-encoded representations of tweets described in the following. We use chi-square kernel for SVM and the hyper-parameters are selected through cross-validation.

For neural-network-powered models, we encode the tweets with a two-layered stacked LSTM, where each layer is with 1200 units. The encoder parameters and word embeddings are pre-trained under the uni-directional self-supervised skip-thought scheme [11] with the BookCorpus [31]. During training, we fine-tuned the LSTM encoder under the collected dataset while fixing the embedding layer. All textual representations of a tweet is a fixed 2400-dim vector before feeding into the joint embedding network.

The visual features are extracted using the Inception-Resnet-V2 model [26] pre-trained on ImageNet dataset [24]. The flattened last pooling layer is concatenated with the final prediction layer, resulting in a 2537-dim dense vector for each image after l-2 normalization. For SVM baselines that involve multimodal features, we utilize late fusion to get the final scores.

Implementation Details The pre-processing step and hyperparameters for training the model are described as follows: For text pre-processing, after removing URLs, numbers, and hashtags in the tweet, we perform tokenization and lemmatization with NLTK [20]. Each tweet is then padded and truncated into sequences with a maximum length of 30 before feeding into the 2-layered stacked LSTM encoder with 1200 units in each layer. For the visual part, we apply a 2-layered (2048 neurons in each layer) MLP with residual links as the visual encoder.

$W_x \in \mathbb{R}^{2400 \times 256}$ and $W_v \in \mathbb{R}^{2537 \times 256}$ in DCCA are randomly initialized for mapping outputs of the textual and visual encoder into the 256-dim joint embedding vectors. The textual and visual classification models are both 2-layered MLPs with hidden size 1024 and 512. For training, we use mini-batches of size 512 and apply Adam optimizer with 0.001 learning rate and 0.3 dropout rate.

5.2 Retrospective Experiments

In the retrospective experiments, we compare our model with SVM using different features on the full dataset. The full dataset containing all tweets in the first 36 hours of the event is used in 5-fold cross-validation experiments, as shown in Table 2. Numbers are averaged across all folds. Visual only baselines are only measured on the subset of tweets that contain images. This setting is the most common setting for event analysis.

Table 2: Average precision under the retrospective setting. *V/T* stands for using visual/textual content.

Method	Boston Marathon bombing	Las Vegas shooting
Resnet+SVM (V)	0.5173	0.2282
GloVe+SVM (T)	0.3632	0.3750
LSTM+SVM (T)	0.6487	0.7707
LSTM/Resnet+SVM (T+V)	0.6491	0.7736
ours (T)	0.6683	0.8107
ours (T+V)	**0.6750**	**0.8157**

5.3 Real-Time Prediction Experiment

In the real-time prediction setting, we evaluate the models' ability to filter a massive amount of tweets efficiently and accurately as the event progresses, similar to the real-world scenario, where useful tweets should be selected for analysis as soon as possible, not after the event has happened. In the real-time prediction experiment, we partition the event tweet dataset into bins with equal length of time. To classify the tweets of k-th bin, tweets from $(1..k-1)$-th bins are used to train the model. We only utilize the ground truth labels of the first bin (the first one or two hours of the event), which usually only contains several thousands of tweets and is manageable in the real-world scenario, to train our initial model. Later models are trained using the combination of ground truth labels from the first bin and the prediction results of the previous model. The 2400 dimensional text embedding features and visual features are used.

5.4 Result and Discussion

Retrospective Results: From Table 2, while the average of pre-trained GloVe word embeddings results in the unsatisfactory average prevision, the models with a LSTM encoder demonstrate relatively strong performance. The results seems to imply that visual features are not as effective as textual features under the current event dataset collection and annotation criteria. However, after carefully investigating the event image collection, we found that there are clear event-wise social media users biases. Images in the Boston Marathon bombing is more convincing (and thus result in better performance) than images from the Las Vegas shooting mainly because the former happened during the daytime.

The textual and visual features are complementary to each other and result in better performance. However, we also observe that the improvement of textual+visual features over textual feature only is not very significant. A possible explanation is that only a small portion of tweets contains an image and a smaller portion of them contains complementary visual information.

The improvements provided by our proposed model is consistent with the two events. The model outperforms best SVM baselines by 2.6% and 4.2% in the Boston Marathon bombing and the Las Vegas shooting event respectively. We contribute the outperformance to the fact the proposed model considers not only the complementary

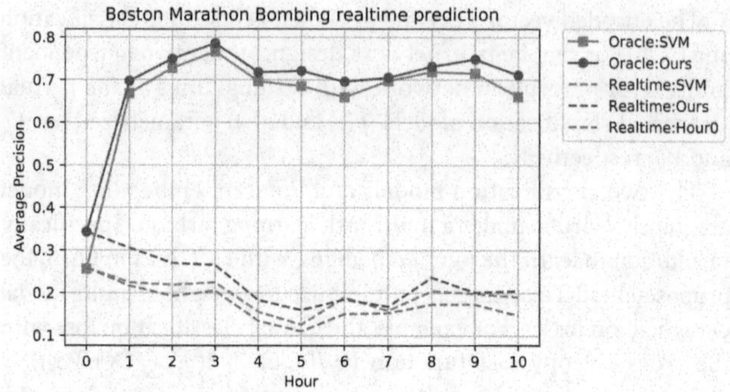

(a) Hourly rolling prediction for the Boston Marathon bombing.

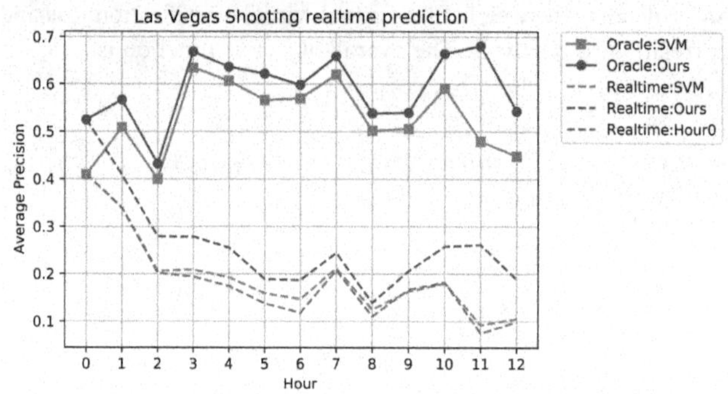

(b) Hourly rolling prediction for the Las Vegas shooting.

Figure 6: Real time average precision results. Oracle: Use ground truth labels in the past for training next-hour model. Realtime: Lowest 5% and top 0.05% of inferred instances are considered as negative/positive instances for training the next-hour model. The metric is AP on the next-hour bin

visual and textual features but also optimizes over the common part through canonical correlation analysis. The inevitable challenges of the real-world event data are the imbalance between tweets with text and tweets with images as well as the sparsity of high-quality parallel text and image within tweets.

Empirically we also found that the event-specific model is hard to generalize as every event is unique with its one content. Transferring of models from one model to another will result in faster convergence but similar classification performance.

Real-Time Results: Another practical scenario is to use the inferred instances and update the model on-the-fly. Figure 6b and Figure 6a show the experimental results of the two events under the real-time prediction setting. We first compare our model with SVM classifiers in the oracle setting with ground truth labels. In the oracle setting, when predicting on the k-th bin, ground truth labels from $(1..k-1)$-th bins are utilized. In the oracle experiment, our model performs better than SVM baseline in both events with an average improvement of 6.6% (Boston) and 12.9% (Las Vegas). The gap in real-time prediction is even larger, which is 16.6% and 42.5% relative improvement to the SVM, showing that the proposed model is more robust against real-world noise.

To investigate the effect of incorporating predicted labels from the previous model into training, we compare our model with SVM baseline trained only using the ground truth labels from Hour0. As we see, our model outperforms the Hour0 baseline by 31.6% and 55.3% relatively, which suggests the efficacy of our training method. We believe such big performance gap is caused by the fact that as time progresses, more diverse and useful information that is not included in the first hour will emerge and they are important for the model to learn to filter future information.

Furthermore, we find that the performance of our model can be boosted by more than 10% if we use model trained later to predict on earlier times during the first few hours. For example, using the model from Hour4 to predict on Hour1 to Hour3 is better than using Hour1 to Hour3 models separately. It is not surprising since the later model can utilize more training samples. However, it is not desirable if users desire instant results, suggesting that an accuracy-speed trade-off to be optimized. We leave this to future work.

6 CONCLUSION

We have addressed the problem of temporal monitoring and distillation of useful information with multimedia content from social media. A large-scale public safety event dataset with retrospective automatic labeling has been constructed as a new challenging research platform for event analysis. We have proposed a multimodal monitoring system with two encoding/classification networks and a joint representation learning network with CCA to leverage information from different modalities while jointly regularizing the encoded representations. In the retrospective and real-time evaluations, we have demonstrated the outperformance of the proposed model over other competitive baselines. In addition to improve the temporal robustness of event monitoring, we consider phase-by-phase event summarization and itemization with multimedia content as the interesting next step.

ACKNOWLEDGEMENT

This work was performed under the financial assistance award 60NANB17D156 from U.S. Department of Commerce, National Institute of Standards and Technology (NIST). Disclaimer: The views and conclusions contained herein are those of the authors and should not be interpreted as necessarily representing the official policies or endorsements, either expressed or implied, of NIST or the U.S. Government. The authors also gratefully acknowledge the support of Google Cloud with donation of the Google Cloud credits and the computing resource used for this research.

REFERENCES

[1] Galen Andrew, Raman Arora, Jeff Bilmes, and Karen Livescu. 2013. Deep canonical correlation analysis. In *International Conference on Machine Learning*. 1247–1255.
[2] Farzindar Atefeh and Wael Khreich. 2015. A survey of techniques for event detection in twitter. *Computational Intelligence* 31, 1 (2015), 132–164.
[3] Johan Bollen, Huina Mao, and Xiaojun Zeng. 2011. Twitter mood predicts the stock market. *Journal of computational science* 2, 1 (2011), 1–8.
[4] Jia Chen, Junwei Liang, Han Lu, Shoou-I Yu, and Alexander Hauptmann. 2016. Videos from the 2013 Boston Marathon: An Event Reconstruction Dataset for Synchronization and Localization. (2016).
[5] Matthew S Gerber. 2014. Predicting crime using Twitter and kernel density estimation. *Decision Support Systems* 61 (2014), 115–125.
[6] Kaiming He, Xiangyu Zhang, Shaoqing Ren, and Jian Sun. 2016. Deep residual learning for image recognition. In *Proceedings of the IEEE conference on computer vision and pattern recognition*. 770–778.
[7] Micah Hodosh, Peter Young, and Julia Hockenmaier. 2013. Framing image description as a ranking task: Data, models and evaluation metrics. *Journal of Artificial Intelligence Research* 47 (2013), 853–899.
[8] Po-Yao Huang, Frederick Liu, Sz-Rung Shiang, Jean Oh, and Chris Dyer. 2016. Attention-based Multimodal Neural Machine Translation. In *Proceedings of the First Conference on Machine Translation: Volume 2, Shared Task Papers*. Association for Computational Linguistics, 639–645. http://www.aclweb.org/anthology/W16-2360
[9] Po-Yao Huang, Ye Yuan, Zhen-Zhong Lan, Lu Jiang, and Alexander G. Hauptmann. 2017. Video Representation Learning and Latent Concept Mining for Large-scale Multi-label Video Classification. *CoRR* abs/1707.01408 (2017). arXiv:1707.01408
[10] Aamera ZH Khan, Mohammad Atique, and VM Thakare. 2015. Combining lexicon-based and learning-based methods for Twitter sentiment analysis. *International Journal of Electronics, Communication and Soft Computing Science & Engineering (IJECSCSE)* (2015), 89.
[11] Ryan Kiros, Yukun Zhu, Ruslan R Salakhutdinov, Richard Zemel, Raquel Urtasun, Antonio Torralba, and Sanja Fidler. 2015. Skip-thought vectors. In *Advances in neural information processing systems*. 3294–3302.
[12] Benjamin Klein, Guy Lev, Gil Sadeh, and Lior Wolf. 2015. Associating neural word embeddings with deep image representations using fisher vectors. In *Proceedings of the IEEE Conference on Computer Vision and Pattern Recognition*. 4437–4446.
[13] Alex Krizhevsky, Ilya Sutskever, and Geoffrey E Hinton. 2012. Imagenet classification with deep convolutional neural networks. In *Advances in neural information processing systems*. 1097–1105.
[14] Nikolay Laptev, Jason Yosinski, Li Erran Li, and Slawek Smyl. [n. d.]. Time-series extreme event forecasting with neural networks at uber.
[15] Junwei Liang, Desai Fan, Han Lu, Poyao Huang, Jia Chen, Lu Jiang, and Alexander G Hauptmann. 2017. An Event Reconstruction Tool for Conflict Monitoring Using Social Media.. In *AAAI*. 5097–5098.
[16] Junwei Liang, Poyao Huang, Jia Chen, and Alexander Hauptmann. 2017. Synchronization for multi-perspective videos in the wild. In *Acoustics, Speech and Signal Processing (ICASSP), 2017 IEEE International Conference on*. IEEE, 1592–1596.
[17] Junwei Liang, Lu Jiang, and Alexander Hauptmann. 2017. Temporal localization of audio events for conflict monitoring in social media. In *Acoustics, Speech and Signal Processing (ICASSP), 2017 IEEE International Conference on*. IEEE, 1597–1601.
[18] Junwei Liang, Lu Jiang, and Alexander G Hauptmann. 2017. Webly-Supervised Learning of Multimodal Video Detectors.
[19] Junwei Liang, Lu Jiang, Deyu Meng, and Alexander G Hauptmann. [n. d.]. Learning to Detect Concepts from Webly-Labeled Video Data.
[20] Edward Loper and Steven Bird. 2002. NLTK: The natural language toolkit. In *Proceedings of the ACL-02 Workshop on Effective tools and methodologies for teaching natural language processing and computational linguistics-Volume 1*. Association for Computational Linguistics, 63–70.
[21] Hyeonseob Nam, Jung-Woo Ha, and Jeonghee Kim. [n. d.]. Dual attention networks for multimodal reasoning and matching. ([n. d.]).
[22] Jeffrey Pennington, Richard Socher, and Christopher Manning. 2014. Glove: Global vectors for word representation. In *Proceedings of the 2014 conference on empirical methods in natural language processing (EMNLP)*. 1532–1543.
[23] Sara Rosenthal, Noura Farra, and Preslav Nakov. 2017. SemEval-2017 task 4: Sentiment analysis in Twitter. In *Proceedings of the 11th International Workshop on Semantic Evaluation (SemEval-2017)*. 502–518.
[24] Olga Russakovsky, Jia Deng, Hao Su, Jonathan Krause, Sanjeev Satheesh, Sean Ma, Zhiheng Huang, Andrej Karpathy, Aditya Khosla, Michael Bernstein, Alexander C. Berg, and Li Fei-Fei. 2015. ImageNet Large Scale Visual Recognition Challenge. *International Journal of Computer Vision (IJCV)* 115, 3 (2015), 211–252.
[25] Takeshi Sakaki, Makoto Okazaki, and Yutaka Matsuo. 2010. Earthquake shakes Twitter users: real-time event detection by social sensors. In *Proceedings of the 19th international conference on World wide web*. ACM, 851–860.
[26] Christian Szegedy, Sergey Ioffe, Vincent Vanhoucke, and Alexander A Alemi. 2017. Inception-v4, inception-resnet and the impact of residual connections on learning.
[27] Liwei Wang, Yin Li, and Svetlana Lazebnik. 2016. Learning deep structure-preserving image-text embeddings. In *Proceedings of the IEEE conference on computer vision and pattern recognition*. 5005–5013.
[28] Fei Yan and Krystian Mikolajczyk. 2015. Deep correlation for matching images and text. In *Computer Vision and Pattern Recognition (CVPR), 2015 IEEE Conference on*. IEEE, 3441–3450.
[29] Zichao Yang, Diyi Yang, Chris Dyer, Xiaodong He, Alex Smola, and Eduard Hovy. 2016. Hierarchical attention networks for document classification. In *Proceedings of the 2016 Conference of the North American Chapter of the Association for Computational Linguistics: Human Language Technologies*. 1480–1489.
[30] Xiangmin Zhou and Lei Chen. 2014. Event detection over twitter social media streams. *The VLDB journal* 23, 3 (2014), 381–400.
[31] Yukun Zhu, Ryan Kiros, Rich Zemel, Ruslan Salakhutdinov, Raquel Urtasun, Antonio Torralba, and Sanja Fidler. 2015. Aligning books and movies: Towards story-like visual explanations by watching movies and reading books. In *Proceedings of the IEEE international conference on computer vision*. 19–27.

A LiDAR Point Cloud Generator: from a Virtual World to Autonomous Driving

Xiangyu Yue, Bichen Wu, Sanjit A. Seshia, Kurt Keutzer and Alberto L. Sangiovanni-Vincentelli
EECS, University of California, Berkeley
{xyyue,bichen,sseshia,keutzer,alberto}@eecs.berkeley.edu

ABSTRACT

3D LiDAR scanners are playing an increasingly important role in autonomous driving as they can generate depth information of the environment. However, creating large 3D LiDAR point cloud datasets with point-level labels requires a significant amount of manual annotation. This jeopardizes the efficient development of supervised deep learning algorithms which are often data-hungry. We present a framework to rapidly create point clouds with accurate point-level labels from a computer game. To our best knowledge, this is the first publication on LiDAR point cloud simulation framework for autonomous driving. The framework supports data collection from both auto-driving scenes and user-configured scenes. Point clouds from auto-driving scenes can be used as training data for deep learning algorithms, while point clouds from user-configured scenes can be used to systematically test the vulnerability of a neural network, and use the falsifying examples to make the neural network more robust through retraining. In addition, the scene images can be captured simultaneously in order for sensor fusion tasks, with a method proposed to do automatic registration between the point clouds and captured scene images. We show a significant improvement in accuracy (+9%) in point cloud segmentation by augmenting the training dataset with the generated synthesized data. Our experiments also show by testing and retraining the network using point clouds from user-configured scenes, the weakness/blind spots of the neural network can be fixed.

CCS CONCEPTS

• **Computing methodologies** → **Simulation environments**; • **Information systems** → *Extraction, transformation and loading*; • **Software and its engineering** → *Software infrastructure*; *Simulator / interpreter*; Software verification;

KEYWORDS

LiDAR Point Cloud, Simulation Environment, Autonomous Driving, Neural Network Analysis, Neural Network Retraining

ACM Reference Format:
Xiangyu Yue, Bichen Wu, Sanjit A. Seshia, Kurt Keutzer and Alberto L. Sangiovanni-Vincentelli . 2018. A LiDAR Point Cloud Generator: from a Virtual World to Autonomous Driving. In *ICMR'18: 2018 International Conference on Multimedia Retrieval, June 11–14, 2018, Yokohama, Japan*, Jennifer B. Sartor, Theo D'Hondt, and Wolfgang De Meuter (Eds.). ACM, New York, NY, USA, Article 4, 7 pages. https://doi.org/10.1145/3206025.3206080

ACM ISBN 978-1-4503-5046-4/18/06...$15.00
https://doi.org/10.1145/3206025.3206080

1 INTRODUCTION

Autonomous driving requires accurate and reliable perception of the environment. As 3D data has some superiority in information representation over 2D data [9, 12, 27, 28], 3D LiDAR (Light Detection And Ranging) sensors are playing an increasingly important role of all the environment sensors for autonomous driving. On the one hand, 3D LiDAR sensors can provide direct distance measurements that allow detection of all kinds of obstacles, and their resolution and field of view exceed radar and ultrasonic sensors [17]. On the other hand, LiDAR sensors are robust under a variety of conditions: day or night, with or without glare and shadows [26]. While LiDAR point clouds contain accurate depth measurement of the environment, navigation of autonomous vehicles also relies on correct understanding of the semantics of the environment. Most of the LiDAR-based perception tasks, such as semantic segmentation [3, 4, 26] and drivable area detection [8, 16], require significant amount of point-level labels for training and/or validation. Such annotation, however, is usually very expensive.

To facilitate the manual annotation process, much work has been done on interactive annotation. Annotation methods have been proposed for labeling 3D point clouds of both indoor scenes [21] and outdoor driving scenes [10]. These methods utilize little computer assistance during the annotation process and thus need a significant amount of human effort. In [15, 23], approaches have been proposed to enhance the human-machine interaction to improve annotation efficiency. In [20, 25], annotation suggestions for indoor RGBD scenes are proposed by the system that are interactively corrected or refined by the user. In order to provide faster interactive labeling rates, Boyko *et al.* [2] proposed a group annotation approach for labeling objects in 3D LiDAR scans. Active learning has also been introduced in the annotation process to train a classifier with fewer interactions [14, 22], yet it requires users to interact with examples one-by-one. Other frameworks further take into account the risk of mislabeling and cost of annotation. In [24], Welinder *et al.* proposed a model of the labeling process and dynamically chooses which images will be labeled next in order to achieve a desired level of confidence.

Recently, video games have been used for creating large-scale ground truth data for training purposes. In [19], a video game is used to generate ground truth semantic segmentation for the synthesized in-game images. However, human effort is still required in the annotation process. In [13], the same game engine is used to generate ground truth 2D bounding boxes of objects in the images.

(a) (b) (c)

Figure 1: Sample data extracted from an in-game scene. (a): Image of the scene; (b): Extracted point cloud from the same scene; (c): Point cloud of car mapped to image after registration (Blue dots) matches car in image.

Richter *et al.* [18] further extended the work of [19] so that various ground truth information (e.g. semantic segmentation, semantic instance segmentation, and optical flow) can be extracted from the game engine. In addition, many driving simulation environments [1, 5, 11] have been built in order to obtain various kinds of labeled data for autonomous driving purposes. Many of these work [5, 13, 18, 19] show the effectiveness of synthetic data in image-based learning tasks by showing improved performance after training with additional synthetic data. However, little work has been done on extracting annotated 3D LiDAR point clouds from simulators, not to mention showing the efficacy of the synthetic point clouds during the training process of neural networks.

Note that even if we could provide large amounts of training data, it is still almost impossible for any algorithms to achieve 100% accuracy. For Cyber-Physical Systems used for safety critical purposes, such as autonomous driving, verifying neural networks is of extreme importance [6]. In [7], a framework is proposed to systematically analyze Convolutional Neural Networks (CNNs) used in objection detection in autonomous driving systems. However, the framework only takes into account cars from direct front/back view and thus has a very limited modification space. In addition, each background image needs to be manually annotated, making it expensive to generate a dataset with large diversity. To the best of our knowledge, no similar work has been done on LiDAR point clouds. In this paper, we propose an extraction-annotation-CNN testing framework based on a popular video game. The main contributions of this paper are as follows:

- This is the first publication on LiDAR point cloud simulation framework for autonomous driving.
- The framework can automatically extract point-cloud data with ground truth labels together with the corresponding image frame of the in-game scene, as shown in Figure 1.
- The framework can do automatic registration between collected point clouds and images which can then be used together for sensor fusion tasks, e.g. inferring depth information from RGB images.
- Users can construct specified scenarios in the framework interactively and the collected data (point clouds and images) can then be used to systematically test, analyze and improve LiDAR-based and/or image-based learning algorithms for autonomous driving.

We conduct experiments on a Convolutional Neural Network (CNN)-based model for 3D LiDAR point cloud segmentation using the data collected from the proposed framework. The experiments show 1) significantly improved performance on KITTI dataset [10] after retraining with additional synthetic LiDAR point clouds, and 2) efficacy of using the data collected from user-configured scenes in the framework to test, analyze and improve the performance of the neural network. The performance improvements come from the fact that the data collected in the rich virtual world contains a lot of information that the neural network failed to learn from the limited amount of original training samples.

2 TECHNICAL APPROACH

2.1 In-Game Simulation Setup and Method for Data Collection

We choose to utilize the rich virtual world in Grand Theft Auto V (GTA-V), a popular video game, to obtain simulated point clouds as well as captured in-game images with high fidelity[1]. Our framework is based on DeepGTAV[2], which uses Script Hook V[3] as a plugin.

In order to simulate realistic driving scenes, an ego car is used in the game with a virtual LiDAR scanner mounted atop, and it is set to drive autonomously in the virtual world with the AI interface provided in Script Hook V. While the car drives on a street, the system collects LiDAR point clouds and captures the game screen, simultaneously. We place the virtual LiDAR scanner and the game camera at the same position in the virtual 3D space. This set-up offers two advantages: 1) a sanity check can be easily done on the collected data, since point clouds and corresponding images must be consistent; 2) registration between the game camera and the virtual LiDAR scanner can be done automatically, and then collected point clouds and scene images can be combined together as training dataset for neural networks for sensor fusion tasks. Details of the proposed registration method will be described in Section 2.2.

Ray casting is used to simulate each laser ray emitted by the virtual LiDAR scanner. The ray casting API takes as input the 3D coordinates of the starting and ending point of the ray, and returns the 3D coordinates of the first point the ray hits. This point is used, with another series of API function calls, to calculate, among other

[1] The publisher of GTA-V allows non-commercial use of footage of gameplay [19].
[2] https://github.com/aitorzip/DeepGTAV
[3] http://www.dev-c.com/gtav/scripthookv/

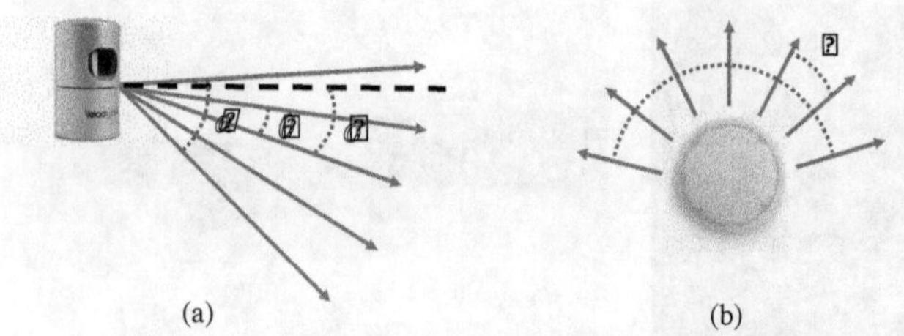

Figure 2: Sample configurable parameters of the virtual LiDAR. (a) shows front view of the virtual LiDAR: black dotted line is the horizontal line, α is the vertical field of view (FOV), θ is the vertical resolution, σ is the pitch angle; (b) shows top view of the virtual LiDAR, β is the horizontal FOV, and ϕ is the horizontal resolution.

data, the distance of the point, the category and instance ID of the object hit by the ray, thus allowing automatic annotation on the collected data.

In our framework, users can provide configurations of the LiDAR scanner including vertical field of view (FOV), vertical resolution, horizontal FOV, horizontal resolution, pitch angle, maximum range of laser rays, and scanning frequency. Some of the configurable parameters are shown in Figure 2.

2.2 Automatic Registration Method

The goal of the registration process is to find the corresponding pixel in the image for each LiDAR point. In our framework, the registration process can be done automatically by the system based on the parameters of the camera and LiDAR scanner. In addition, the centers of the camera and LiDAR scanner are set to the same position in the virtual world, making the registration projection similar to the camera perspective projection model, as shown in Figure 3.

The problem is formulated as follows: for a certain laser ray with *azimuth* angle ϕ and *zenith* angle θ, calculate the index (i, j) of the corresponding pixel on image. $\mathcal{F}_c$, $\mathcal{F}_o$, P, P and P_{far} are 3D coordinates of a) center of camera/LiDAR scanner, b) center of camera near clipping plane. c) point first hit by the virtual laser ray (in red), d) pixel on image corresponding to P, and e) a point far away in the laser direction (required as an input argument to the ray casting API), respectively. m and n are the width and height of the near clipping plane. γ is 1/2 vertical FOV of camera while ψ is 1/2 vertical FOV of the LiDAR scanner. Note that LiDAR scanner FOV is usually smaller than camera FOV, since there is usually no object in the top part of the image, and thus emitting laser to open space is not necessary. After a series of 3D geometry calculation, we can get:

$$
\begin{aligned}
i &= \frac{R_m}{m}\left(f \ \tan\gamma \ \frac{m}{n} - \frac{f}{\cos\theta} \ \tan\phi\right),\\
j &= \frac{R_n}{n}\left(f \ \tan\gamma + f \ \tan\theta\right),
\end{aligned}
\tag{1}
$$

where $f = \left\|\overline{\mathcal{F}_c\mathcal{F}_o}\right\|$, and (R_m, R_n) is the pixel resolution of the image/near clipping plane.

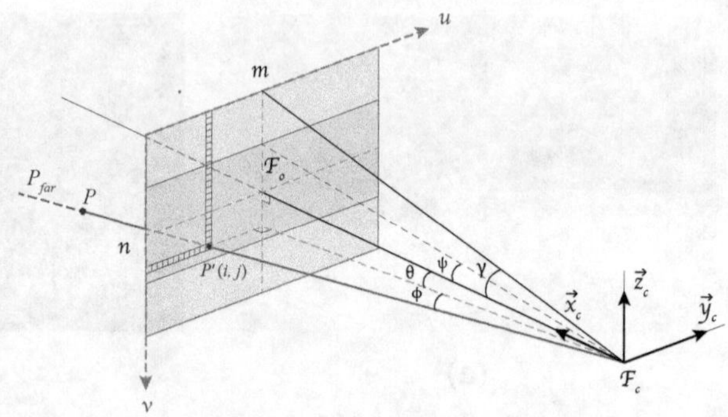

Figure 3: Projection for Registration. $\mathcal{F}_o$ is the center of the near clipping plane of the camera; $\mathcal{F}_c$ is the center of the camera and of the LiDAR scanner; the red line is the laser ray and P is the point hit by the ray; the calibrated on-image point has pixel index (i, j) and 3D coordinates P ; γ is 1/2 the camera vertical FOV and ψ is 1/2 the LiDAR vertical FOV; ϕ and θ are the *azimath* and *zenith* angles of the laser ray.

Further, as an input argument to the ray casting API, the 3D coordinates of P_{far} are also required. Using similar 3D geometry calculations, we obtain:

$$
\begin{aligned}
P &= \mathcal{F}_c + f \ \overline{x}_c - \frac{f}{\cos\theta} \ \tan\phi \ \overline{y}_c - f \ \tan\theta \ \overline{z}_c,\\
P_{far} &= \mathcal{F}_c + k \ (P - \mathcal{F}_c),
\end{aligned}
\tag{2}
$$

where k is a large coefficient, and $\overline{x}_c, \overline{y}_c, \overline{z}_c$ are unit vectors of the camera axis in the world coordinate system.

An example of the registration result is shown in Figure 1. After simulation, both image and point cloud of the specified in-game scene are collected by the framework (Figure 1 (a, b)). Then with the proposed registration method, we map all the points with category "Car" to the corresponding image. As shown in Figure 1 (c), the mapped car point cloud (blue dots) matches the car in the image fairly accurately.

2.3 Configurable In-game Scene

Besides the auto-driving mode for large-scale data collection, our framework offers a configurable mode, where the user can configure desired in-game scenes and collect data from them. One advantage of configurable scenes is generating training data of driving scenes that are dangerous or rare in real world. Another advantage is that we can systematically sample the modification space (e.g. number of cars, position and orientation of a car) of an in-game scene. The data can then be used to test a neural network, expose its vulnerabilities and improve its performance through retraining. Our framework offers a large modification space of the in-game scene. As shown in Figure 4, the user can specify and change 8 dimensions of in-game scene: car model, car location, car orientation, number of cars, scene background, color of car, weather, and time of day. The first 5 dimensions affect both LiDAR point cloud and scene image, while the last three dimensions affect only the scene image. An example of sampling is shown in Figure 5, where the scenes are only sampled from the spatial dimensions (X, Y) with only one car in each scene. X and Y are the location offset of the car relative to the camera/LiDAR location in the left-right and forward-backward

Figure 4: Modification dimensions of the framework with image in center showing the reference scene.

Figure 5: Scenes with one car sampled from spatial dimensions and corresponding point cloud. (a) shows the scene image while changing the location of the car on X (left-right) and Y (forward-backward) directions; (b) shows point clouds (red for car and blue for background) of scenes in (a).

Ground truth segmentation Predicted segmentation

Figure 6: LiDAR point cloud segmentation

directions. Figure5 (b) shows collected point cloud of the samples shown in Figure5 (a). The red points represent car points while the blue points represent the scene background. The collected point clouds match the scenes well thus allowing the use of the data to test neural networks systematically.

3 EXPERIMENTS AND RESULTS

We performed experiments to show the efficacy of our data synthesis framework: 1) Data collected by the framework can be used in the training phase and help improve the validation accuracy; 2) Collected data can be used to systematically test a neural network and improve its performance via retraining.

3.1 Evaluation Metrics

Our experiments are performed on the task of LiDAR point cloud segmentation; specifically, given a point cloud detected by a LiDAR sensor, we wish to perform point-wise classification, as shown in Figure 6. This task is an essential step for autonomous vehicles to perceive and understand the environment, and navigate accordingly.

To evaluate the accuracy of the point cloud segmentation algorithm, we compute *Intersection-over-Union* (IoU), *Precision* and *Recall* as:

$$IoU_c = \frac{\mathcal{P}_c \quad \mathcal{G}_c}{\mathcal{P}_c \quad \mathcal{G}_c}, Pr_c = \frac{\mathcal{P}_c \quad \mathcal{G}_c}{\mathcal{P}_c}, Recall_c = \frac{\mathcal{P}_c \quad \mathcal{G}_c}{\mathcal{G}_c}.$$

Here, $\mathcal{P}_c$ denotes the set of points that our model predicted to be of class-c, $\mathcal{G}_c$ denotes the ground-truth set of points belonging to class-c, and denotes the cardinality of a set. *Precision* and *Recall* measures accuracy with regard to false positives and false negatives, respectively; while *IoU* takes both into account. For this, ***IoU*** is used as the primary accuracy metric in our experiments.

3.2 Experimental Setup

Our analysis is based on SqueezeSeg [26], a convolutional neural network based model for point cloud segmentation. To collect the real-word dataset, we used LiDAR point cloud data from the KITTI dataset and converted its 3D bounding box labels to point-wise labels. Since KITTI dataset only provides reliable 3D bounding boxes for front-view LiDAR point clouds, we limit the horizontal field of view (FOV) to the forward-facing 90 . This way, we obtained 10,848 LiDAR scans with manual labels. We used 8,057 scans for training and 2,791 scans for validation. Each point in a KITTI LiDAR scan has 3 cartesian coordinates (x, y, z) and an intensity value, which measures the amplitude of the laser signal returned. Although the intensity measurement as an extra input feature is beneficial to improve the segmentation accuracy, simulating the intensity measurement is very difficult and not supported in our current framework. Therefore we excluded intensity as an input feature to the neural network for GTA-V synthetic LiDAR data. We use NVIDIA TITAN X GPUs for the experiments during both the training and validation phases.

Table 1: Segmentation Performance Comparison on the Car Category. Only data used in the first row has Intensity channel. All numbers are in percentage.

	Precision	Recall	**IoU**
KITTI w/ Intensity	66.7	95.4	64.6
KITTI w/o Intensity	58.9	95.0	57.1
GTA-V only	30.4	86.6	29.0
KITTI w/o Intensity + GTA-V	69.6	92.8	**66.0**

3.3 Experimental Results

Synthetic Data for Training: For the first set of experiments, we used our data synthesis framework to generate 8,585 LiDAR point cloud scans in autonomous-driving scenes. The generated data contain (x, y, z) measurements but do not contain intensity. The horizontal FOV of the collected point clouds are set to be 90 to match the setting of KITTI point clouds described in Section 3.2.

To quantify the effect of training the model with synthetic data, we first trained two models on the KITTI training set with intensity included and excluded, and validated on the KITTI validation set. The performance is shown in the first 2 rows of Table 1 as the baseline. The model with intensity achieved better result. Then we trained another model with only GTA-V synthetic data. As shown in the third row of Table 1, the performance drops a lot. This is mostly because the distributions of the synthetic dataset and KITTI dataset are quite different. Therefore, through training purely on synthetic dataset, it is hard for the neural network to learn all the required details for the KITTI dataset, which might be missing or insufficient in the synthetic training dataset. Finally, we combined the KITTI data and GTA-V data together as the training set and train another model. As shown in the last row of Table 1, the performance gets improved significantly, almost 9% better than the accuracy achieved only using real-world data. Despite the loss of the intensity channel, the GTA+KITTI dataset gives better accuracy (66.0%) than if intensity is included (64.6%). This demonstrates the efficacy of the synthetic data extracted in our framework.

Neural Network Testing and Robustness Enhancement: For the second set of experiments, we first used our framework to systematically test SqueezeSeg. As an illustrative experiment, we only performed sampling in the car location X-Y dimensions as in Figure 5, rather than the whole modification space. 555 scenes were sampled to test SqueezeSeg, with the IoU results shown in Figure 7. The blue and green dots show the car locations resulting in low IoU. Most of the "blind spot" are locations far from the LiDAR scanner, but there are also closer locations that result in low IoU scores. Close locations with low IoUs are dangerous in autonomous

Figure 7: IoU scatter with the change of car location

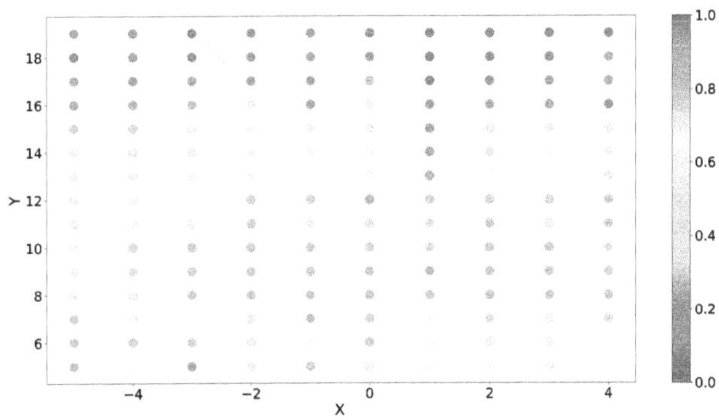

Figure 8: mIoU map of the validation set before retraining

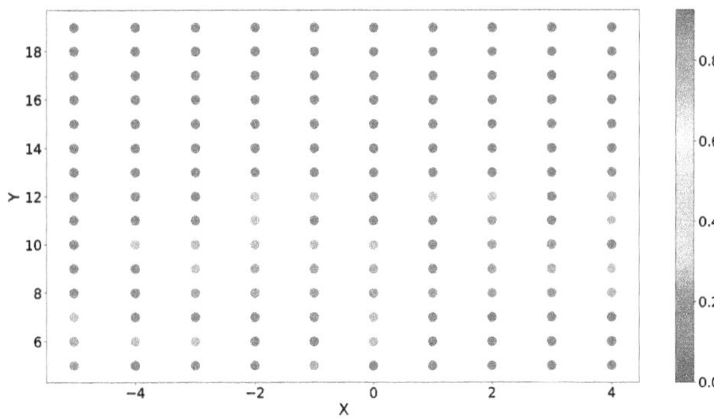

Figure 9: mIoU map of the validation set after selection with mIoU less than 0.65 set to 0. All the point clouds in the retraining set $\mathcal{R}$ corresponding to the blue positions in the new mIoU map will be added to the original training set.

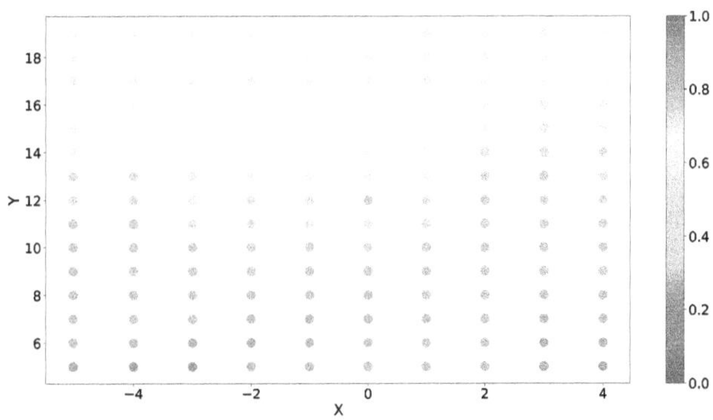

Figure 10: mIoU map of the validation set after retraining

driving, since they can mislead the decision-making system of the autonomous vehicles and result in immediate accident.

Further experiments are then done to show the efficacy of using generated synthetic data to possibly improve performance and robustness of the network in the modification space. We synthesized totally 2,250 LiDAR point cloud scans in 15 different scene backgrounds. In each scene background, only one car is placed with the same orientation as the camera view. We obtained 150 point cloud scans in each scene background by changing the position of the car (X, Y) in the sampled space: $S = (x, y) \quad x \quad -5, \quad ,4 \ ,y \quad 5, \quad ,19$, where X, Y are respectively the left-right and forward-backward offset relative to the position of the camera. For each scene background, the position and orientation of the camera were fixed.

We split the collected point cloud scans based on the scene background. 1200 point cloud scans in the first 8 backgrounds are used as validation set $\mathcal{V}$, and the rest 1050 scans from the other 7 backgrounds, which we call retraining set $\mathcal{R}$, are used for retraining purpose. First, we train a neural network with purely KITTI data and do evaluation on the synthetic 1200 scans in the validation set $\mathcal{V}$. We define *mean IoU (mIoU)* for each point in the 15 10 X-Y modification space as averaging IoUs over all the scene backgrounds in $\mathcal{V}$:

$$mIoU(i, j) = \frac{1}{n} \sum_{k=1}^{n} IoU(i, j, k),$$

where n is the number of scene backgrounds ($n = 8$ in this experiment), (i, j) is in $(i, j) \quad i \quad [-5, 4], j \quad [5, 19], i, j \quad \mathbb{Z}$ and $IoU(i, j, k)$ refers to the IoU of the point cloud scan sampled at (i, j) in the X-Y modification with the k_{th} scene background.

The mIoU map of the validation set is computed, as shown in Figure 8. We can see that the pre-trained network performs poorly on positions that are far away, at the boundary of the FOV. But more surprisingly, we also observed that on some positions that are fairly close to the ego-vehicle, e.g. (-3, 5), the mIoU scores are also very low. Detection errors at such near distance can be very dangerous.

Based on the mIoU map, we choose positions with an mIoU smaller than a threshod to form a retraining set, as shown in Figure 9. Then all the point clouds in the retraining set $\mathcal{R}$ with a selected position are added to the original training set. After the retraining process, we re-evaluate the validation set $\mathcal{V}$, with the new mIoU map shown in Figure 10. As the figure shows, at almost all the close-to-center positions originally with low mIoU, the neural network performs much better than before the retraining. In order to visualize the performance improvements better, we plot the mIoU improvement after the retraining process for each position. The mIoU improvements are sorted and plotted in Figure 11. We see that after retraining, performance on point clouds at most of the

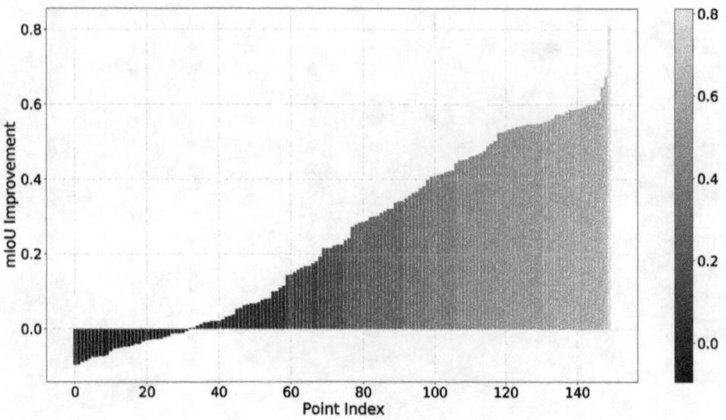

Figure 11: mIoU improvements in ascending order for all 150 positions

positions gets much better, with slightly degraded performance at only a small fraction of positions. Meanwhile, the performance on KITTI dataset remained almost the same with IoU changing from 60.8% to 60.6%. These experiments show the efficacy of using synthetic data from user-configured scenes of the proposed framework to test, analyze and improve the performance of neural networks through retraining.

4 CONCLUSIONS AND FUTURE WORK

In this paper, we proposed a framework that synthesizes annotated LiDAR point clouds from a virtual world in a game, with a method to automatically calibrate the point cloud and scene image. Our framework can be used to: 1) obtain a large amount of annotated point cloud data, which can then be used to help neural network training; 2) systematically test, analyze and improve performance of neural networks for tasks such as point cloud segmentation. Experiments show that for a point cloud segmentation task, synthesized data help improve the validation accuracy (IoU) by 9% on a real-world benchmark. Furthermore, the systematical sampling and testing framework can help us to identify potential weakness/blind spots of our neural network model and fix them. Our future works will focus on two directions: 1) Experiments show that the intensity channel in LiDAR point clouds is crucial for LiDAR-based perception tasks, but current framework does not support intensity synthesis. We plan to explore techniques to simulate realistic LiDAR intensity. 2) The effectiveness of using synthetic data to train perception algorithms is usually limited by domain shift. We plan to explore domain adaptation methods to diminish the gap between virtual world and real world.

ACKNOWLEDGEMENT

This work was partially supported by NSF, Award 1645964, together with Berkeley Deep Drive. We thank Kostadin Ilov for providing system assistance.

REFERENCES

[1] Daniel Biedermann, Matthias Ochs, and Rudolf Mester. 2016. Evaluating visual ADAS components on the COnGRATS dataset. In *IEEE Intelligent Vehicles Symposium*. 986–991.

[2] Aleksey Boyko and Thomas Funkhouser. 2014. Cheaper by the Dozen: Group Annotation of 3D Data. In *ACM Symposium on User Interface Software and Technology*. 33–42.

[3] Ayush Dewan, Gabriel L Oliveira, and Wolfram Burgard. 2017. Deep Semantic Classification for 3D LiDAR Data. *arXiv preprint arXiv:1706.08355* (2017).

[4] David Dohan, Brian Matejek, and Thomas Funkhouser. 2015. Learning hierarchical semantic segmentations of lidar data. In *International Conference on 3D Vision*. 273–281.

[5] Alexey Dosovitskiy, German Ros, Felipe Codevilla, Antonio Lopez, and Vladlen Koltun. 2017. CARLA: An Open Urban Driving Simulator. In *Proceedings of the 1st Annual Conference on Robot Learning*. 1–16.

[6] Tommaso Dreossi, Alexandre Donzé, and Sanjit A Seshia. 2017. Compositional Falsification of Cyber-Physical Systems with Machine Learning Components. In *NASA Formal Methods Symposium*. 357–372.

[7] Tommaso Dreossi, Shromona Ghosh, Alberto Sangiovanni-Vincentelli, and Sanjit A. Seshia. 2017. Systematic testing of convolutional neural networks for autonomous driving. *arXiv preprint arXiv:1708.03309* (2017).

[8] R. Fernandes, C. Premebida, P. Peixoto, D. Wolf, and U. Nunes. 2014. Road Detection Using High Resolution LIDAR. In *IEEE Vehicle Power and Propulsion Conference*. 1–6.

[9] Yue Gao, Meng Wang, Dacheng Tao, Rongrong Ji, and Qionghai Dai. 2012. 3-D object retrieval and recognition with hypergraph analysis. *IEEE Transactions on Image Processing* 21, 9 (2012), 4290–4303.

[10] Andreas Geiger, Philip Lenz, Christoph Stiller, and Raquel Urtasun. 2013. Vision meets Robotics: The KITTI Dataset. *International Journal of Robotics Research* 32, 11 (2013), 1231–1237.

[11] Vladimir Haltakov, Christian Unger, and Slobodan Ilic. 2013. Framework for generation of synthetic ground truth data for driver assistance applications. In *German Conference on Pattern Recognition*. 323–332.

[12] Rongrong Ji, Ling-Yu Duan, Jie Chen, Tiejun Huang, and Wen Gao. 2014. Mining compact bag-of-patterns for low bit rate mobile visual search. *IEEE Transactions on Image Processing* 23, 7 (2014), 3099–3113.

[13] Matthew Johnson-Roberson, Charles Barto, Rounak Mehta, Sharath Nittur Sridhar, Karl Rosaen, and Ram Vasudevan. 2017. Driving in the matrix: Can virtual worlds replace human-generated annotations for real world tasks?. In *IEEE International Conference on Robotics and Automation*. 746–753.

[14] Ashish Kapoor, Kristen Grauman, Raquel Urtasun, and Trevor Darrell. 2007. Active learning with gaussian processes for object categorization. In *IEEE International Conference on Computer Vision*. 1–8.

[15] Regis Kopper, Felipe Bacim, and Doug A Bowman. 2011. Rapid and accurate 3D selection by progressive refinement. In *IEEE Symposium on 3D User Interfaces*. 67–74.

[16] Ziyi Liu, Siyu Yu, Xiao Wang, and Nanning Zheng. 2017. Detecting Drivable Area for Self-driving Cars: An Unsupervised Approach. *arXiv preprint arXiv:1705.00451* (2017).

[17] Frank Moosmann, Oliver Pink, and Christoph Stiller. 2009. Segmentation of 3D lidar data in non-flat urban environments using a local convexity criterion. In *IEEE Intelligent Vehicles Symposium*. 215–220.

[18] Stephan R Richter, Zeeshan Hayder, and Vladlen Koltun. 2017. Playing for benchmarks. In *IEEE International Conference on Computer Vision*. 2232–2241.

[19] Stephan R Richter, Vibhav Vineet, Stefan Roth, and Vladlen Koltun. 2016. Playing for data: Ground truth from computer games. In *European Conference on Computer Vision*. 102–118.

[20] Tianjia Shao, Weiwei Xu, Kun Zhou, Jingdong Wang, Dongping Li, and Baining Guo. 2012. An Interactive Approach to Semantic Modeling of Indoor Scenes with an RGBD Camera. *ACM Transactions on Graphics* 31, 6 (2012), 136:1–136:11.

[21] Nathan Silberman, Derek Hoiem, Pushmeet Kohli, and Rob Fergus. 2012. Indoor segmentation and support inference from rgbd images. In *European Conference on Computer Vision*. 746–760.

[22] Andrew Top, Ghassan Hamarneh, and Rafeef Abugharbieh. 2011. Active learning for interactive 3D image segmentation. In *International Conference on Medical Image Computing and Computer-Assisted Intervention*. 603–610.

[23] Manuel Veit and Antonio Capobianco. 2014. Go'Then'Tag: A 3-D point cloud annotation technique. In *IEEE Symposium on 3D User Interfaces*. 193–194.

[24] Peter Welinder and Pietro Perona. 2010. Online crowdsourcing: rating annotators and obtaining cost-effective labels. In *IEEE Computer Society Conference on Computer Vision and Pattern Recognition Workshops*. 25–32.

[25] Yu-Shiang Wong, Hung-Kuo Chu, and Niloy J Mitra. 2014. Smartannotator: An interactive tool for annotating RGBD indoor images. *arXiv preprint arXiv:1403.5718* (2014).

[26] Bichen Wu, Alvin Wan, Xiangyu Yue, and Kurt Keutzer. 2018. SqueezeSeg: Convolutional Neural Nets with Recurrent CRF for Real-Time Road-Object Segmentation from 3D LiDAR Point Cloud. In *IEEE International Conference on Robotics and Automation*.

[27] Sicheng Zhao, Lujun Chen, Hongxun Yao, Yanhao Zhang, and Xiaoshuai Sun. 2015. Strategy for dynamic 3D depth data matching towards robust action retrieval. *Neurocomputing* 151 (2015), 533–543.

[28] Sicheng Zhao, Hongxun Yao, Yanhao Zhang, Yasi Wang, and Shaohui Liu. 2015. View-based 3D object retrieval via multi-modal graph learning. *Signal Processing* 112 (2015), 110–118.

3D Image-based Indoor Localization Joint With WiFi Positioning

Guoyu Lu
Chester F. Calson Center for Imaging Science
Rochester Institute of Technology, USA

Jingkuan Song
School of Computer Science and Engineering
University of Electronic Science and Technology of China

ABSTRACT

We realize a system that utilizes WiFi to facilitate the image-based localization system, which avoids the confusion caused by the similar decoration inside the buildings. While WiFi-based localization thread obtains the rough location information, the image-based localization thread retrieves the best matching images and clusters the camera poses associated with the images into different location candidates. The image cluster closest to the WiFi localization outcome is selected for the exact camera pose estimation. The usage of WiFi significantly reduces the search scope, avoiding the extensive search of millions of descriptors in a 3D model. In the image-based localization stage, we also propose a novel 2D-to-2D-to-3D localization framework which follows a coarse-to-fine strategy to quickly locate the query image in several location candidates and performs the local feature matching and camera pose estimation after choosing the correct image location by WiFi positioning. The entire system demonstrates significant benefits in combining both images and WiFi signals in localization tasks and great potential to be deployed in real applications.

CCS CONCEPTS

• **Information systems → Multimedia and multimodal retrieval**;

KEYWORDS

Image-based localization, WiFi positioning, 3D registration, Image retrieval, Camera pose estimation

ACM Reference Format:
Guoyu Lu and Jingkuan Song. 2018. 3D Image-based Indoor Localization Joint With WiFi Positioning. In *ICMR '18: 2018 International Conference on Multimedia Retrieval, June 11–14, 2018, Yokohama, Japan.* ACM, New York, NY, USA, 8 pages. https://doi.org/10.1145/3206025.3206070

1 INTRODUCTION

Indoor localization addresses the problem of "Where am I", which supports extensive applications, such as finding the exact store in a big shopping mall or searching an exhibition room in a museum. There are different solutions to realize the localization, for example Bluetooth, Satellite, Ultra-wideband, and ZigBee [23]. Most of these technologies require extra equipment and the localization accuracy is far from satisfactory. Among these technologies, WiFi is a promising method, which does not require sophisticated devices and WiFi signals are commonly accessible in most buildings, even if there is no mobile phone signal or satellite signals.

ICMR '18, June 11–14, 2018, Yokohama, Japan

ACM ISBN 978-1-4503-5046-4/18/06...$15.00
https://doi.org/10.1145/3206025.3206070

(a) (b) (c) (d)

Figure 1: Examples for similar appearance images from different places in indoor environments.

However, WiFi-based localization still suffers from several bottlenecks. The first deficiency is that the localization signal is usually affected and attenuated during the time of spreading. The layout change inside the building would also change the distribution of the signals, due to the complicated signal refraction. Even without any change of the building layout, the accuracy still cannot meet the demand. The WiFi localization error is usually several meters or even tens of meters. Another issue for WiFi-based localization is that it can only have 3 degrees of freedom. Through WiFi, we can only obtain the position information while the orientation information is missed, which is also essential in localization tasks. These deficiencies limit the reliability of WiFi in localization.

Image-based localization technology is developed to obtain precise position information. Like WiFi, image-based localization does not require complex facilities. Only a camera is sufficient to conduct the localization task. In addition, there is no need to install other devices in the building, reducing the cost of this method. Unlike WiFi, image-based localization is not significantly affected by the layout the building. With small environment changes, query images can still find sufficient matching areas within the image databases. Besides, the orientation information can be obtained during the process of camera pose estimation for the query images, which is not available for normal signal-based methods. Moreover, through pose estimation, image-based localization is able to achieve high accuracy, which can reduce the localization error to centimeters.

Nonetheless, image-based localization undergoes its own issues as well. Images obtain the location information through querying the image database for similar appearance in the building. This is generally effective for most areas which have distinct appearance. In reality, many buildings, especially in indoor environments, have similar decorations, resulting in the confusion of finding the exact corresponding location. Repetitive patterns usually happen in indoor buildings, such as stairs, doors and similar decorations, as shown in Fig. 1.

Previous solutions attempt to resolve the localization task by WiFi or images separately, which ignores the fact that these two approaches can compensate for each other. To overcome the deficiencies existed in each approach, we propose to utilize both images

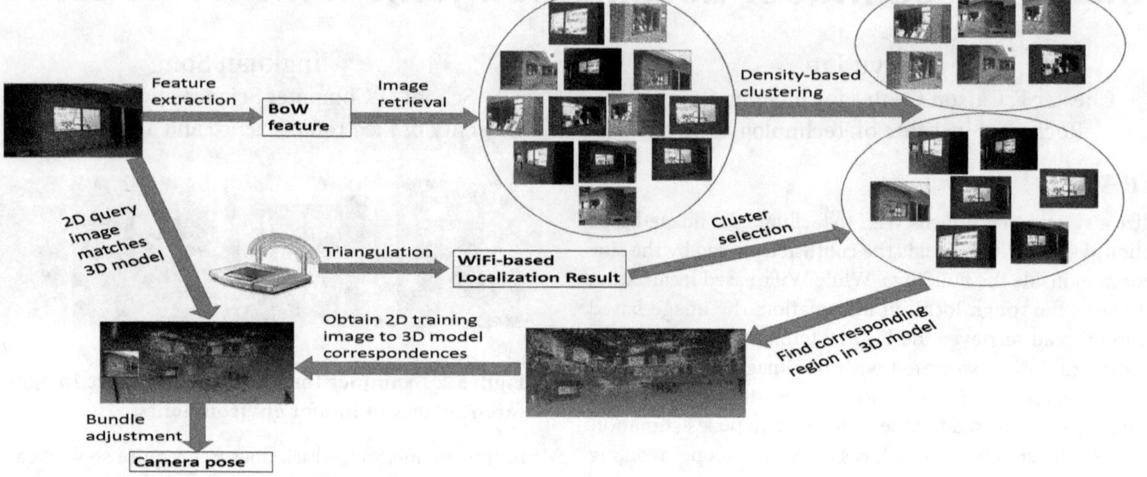

Figure 2: The overall pipeline of our indoor localization system based on WiFi, images and the 3D model. In the WiFi-based localization thread, we first obtain a rough localization result through triangulation as prior positioning knowledge. Simultaneously, bag-of-visual-words features are extracted from images, which are applied to retrieve the best matching images. The returned images are clustered into different groups according to their 3D camera poses by density-based clustering. After selecting the image cluster closest to the WiFi positioning information, the 2D query image matches 2D training images in the cluster through local features which further connect to the 3D model by feature correspondences built in the offline SfM reconstruction step. Through these 2D-to-2D-to-3D correspondences, we estimate the query image camera pose by Bundle Adjustment.

and WiFi signals to realize the localization, taking the advantages of both technologies. In our system, WiFi-based localization and image-based localization are conducted in parallel by two threads. In the WiFi-based localization thread, the mobile phone calculates the rough location through WiFi connection to the Access Points (AP). The WiFi localization is realized by the triangulation method, which we increase the robustness through estimating the mobile phone distance by WiFi signal decaying rate and selecting the best location estimation among multiple triangulation results from different Access Points. In the image-based localization thread, we apply the query image to find the best matching samples in the image database by global features in KD Tree. This step can quickly return the possible locations of the query image, avoiding searching through tens of millions of local descriptors. As all the training images are reconstructed into 3D model through Structure-from-Motion (SfM) reconstruction method, each image in the database is associated with the 3D position in the building. Based on the top retrieved images, we cluster them into several locations according to their position information. These several locations all have the relative high probabilities to be the correct place for the query image due to the similar scene appearance. In this stage, WiFi-based localization can facilitate to distinguish these possible locations and retrieve the image cluster closest to the WiFi positioning result. We match the query image to the training images in the cluster. As the images in the cluster have local feature correspondences to the 3D model, we thus build the 2D (query)-to-2D (training)-to-3D (model) correspondences. Through these correspondences, the exact camera location and orientation information is estimated by Bundle Adjustment [24, 41]. Combining both WiFi and images, we can in the largest extent make use the benefits of both methods to obtain the fast and accurate localization. The overall WiFi-image localization pipeline is illustrated in Fig. 2.

To sum up, the contributions of the paper are as follows: we combine both images and WiFi to achieve accurate localization; the confusion of indoor building appearance existed in image-based localization is avoided through checking WiFi positioning result; we proposed a framework to apply both 2D images and 3D models in different stages to obtain both location and orientation information; the embedding of WiFi in the image-based localization system also facilitates to reduce the search scope of exact local image feature correspondences.

2 RELATED WORK

2.1 Image Retrieval-based Localization

Image-based localization deals with the localization problems by analyzing the images and looking for the matching part in the image database. As GPS signals are usually unavailable inside buildings, images have noticeable benefits over GPS in indoor environment. Robertson et al. [33] developed a system to compute the user query images in an image database with facades views. Shao et al. [36] and Zhang et al. [43] conducted image retrieval on scene images to get the location information in urban environment. Steinhoff et al. [40] used vocabulary tree [31] to retrieve matching scene images in real-time. Lu et al. [28, 29] regarded each viewing direction as a task and applied multi-task learning to retrieve the position and direction information simultaneously. Jacobs et al. [12] realized the coarse goe-localization on the use of a global outdoor web-camera network through calculating the solar zenith angle to the image intensity. Beltran et al. [2] developed a virtual globe tool combining search technologies, geo-referenced media annotations, and visualization techniques to search geographical images and visualize them. Sang et al. [34] cropped the region of interest in the image to retrieve the most closing scene image, which is further extended by retrieving images according to the cropped region's attributes [9]. Ji et al. [13, 14] explored the most discriminative image vocabulary through graph modeling to locate the mobile phones. The above mentioned methods estimate the position information through different image retrieval frameworks. However, orientation information is missed, which is also a key component in localization tasks.

2.2 3D Model-based Localization

SfM methods [5, 10, 39] enable 3D point cloud to be applied in localization tasks to improve the accuracy. Irschara et al. [11] retrieved images with most matching descriptors to the 3D points. Li et al. [20] matched the 3D model to the 2D images through mutual visibility information to find the 3D-to-2D correspondences. Simultaneous Localization and Mapping (SLAM) algorithms [4, 6, 18, 38] build 3D models online and localize the object at the same time. However, SLAM usually accumulates errors in the process of building models, for which it is usually applicable in small scenes. Moreover, SLAM requires strong computational power and extra equipment, such as Lidar, Radar and stereo cameras, not ideal for common indoor localization users. Sattler et al. [35] proposed to match a 2D image directly to a 3D model with the usage of visual words to accelerate the process. Similarly, Liu et al. [22] indexed the 3D model in a visual vocabulary tree and retrieved 3D scenes from the vocabulary tree for the query image.Donoser et al. [8] applied embedded random-ferns to train 3D point classifiers, which builds query image to 3D model correspondences by classifying descriptors to 3D point classes.Lu et al. [25, 26] increased the 3D localization through increasing correct correspondences and applying videos to remove features extracted from foreground. The use of 3D model supports the accurate pose estimation of the query images. A 3D model, however, contains millions of descriptors. Searching through the whole model usually consumes a large amount of time. Various technologies, such as visual words and key frames, are utilized to accelerate the matching process. These methods select matching samples to reduce the search scope to make the localization fast. On the other side, the diminished scope makes the possibility to find the best matching descriptor also decreased, as excluded search region also contains high probability to keep the correct matches to the query image.

2.3 Image-based Indoor Localization

On the application of indoor localization based on images, Kosecka et al. [17] detected edges in the images and matched the edge histograms to the database to find the location. Similar work was conducted by Ravi et al. [32], which used color and shapes in the images to query the indoor images. Kawaji et al. [16] generated the binary code from ASIFT features to query the indoor images database, which used RANSAC [19] to remove outliers. Kinect was also applied to localize the RGB-D image through regression forests [37, 42], which is limited to the usage in small rooms. Lu et al. [27] applied a rough-to-fine strategy to realize a 3D-to-3D localization framework.

Different from previous works which separately applied radio signal and images in the localization task, we simultaneously make use of these different modalities of information to compensate for each otherâĂŹs deficiency. As WiFi receiver and cameras are equipped in robotics or even small mobile phones, we can easily apply WiFi signals and images in our localization tasks in parallel. The usage of images can resolve the WiFi localization issue owing to the unstable signal and the sensitivity to the slight motion of objects. Meanwhile, the application of WiFi can avoid the confusion of similar appearance of indoor decoration. Although WiFi and image-based localization are conducted in parallel, we leverage the WiFi localization to resolve the issues existed in image-based localization, which can provide us the accurate position and orientation information. We introduce our WiFi-based localization method and the approach to improve its robustness in section 3. The WiFi localization outcome is applied to the 3D image-based localization. As the output of entire framework is based on the image-based localization stage, we introduce a novel 2D-to-2D-to-3D localization framework to quickly find the location candidates and improve matching and pose estimation accuracy, which is described in section 4.

3 WIFI-BASED LOCALIZATION

Our localization system starts from two parallel components, which are WiFi-based localization and image-based localization. In this process, WiFi-based localization is the auxiliary thread and image-based localization is the main thread, responsible for the entire system output. As the WiFi localization is applied to enhance the image localization accuracy, we first introduce the WiFi-based localization algorithm, followed by the introduction of applying WiFi-based localization to image-based localization in the next section.

Different from the recent WiFi-based localization methods that reply on nearby people' acoustic ranging [23] and graph matching [21] to improve the localization accuracy, our method puts more focus on the system reliability and robustness, instead of enhancing the WiFi localization accuracy in special cases and assumptions. For this reason, we select the signal triangulation method, a widely used technology in real applications. Conventional triangulation methods utilize the WiFi signals strength received by RSSI as the indication to calculate the distance to the APs. However, the WiFi signal strength varies significantly due to the unstable AP transmission power, which may cause a relatively large variation of the distance estimation. Instead, we propose to apply the signal strength decaying rate to estimate the distance between mobile phone to the APs, which appears to be more stable than the WiFi signal strength. To further increase robustness of the WiFi localization method, we apply multiple triangulation results from different combinations of APs and choose the location with smallest sum of least square distance to others. We introduce details of our WiFi-based localization method in the rest of the section.

Most indoor environments are covered by WiFi signals. Every WiFi access point (AP) maintains a unique MAC address, which can be accessed no matter it is encrypted or not. Based on the MAC address and the received signal strength indicator (RSSI), the mobile phone is able to know the AP location and the distance to the AP based on the signal attenuation model. The RSSI calculation is based on the following equation [7]:

$$RSSI = -(10 \times n)log_{10}D - A \quad (1)$$

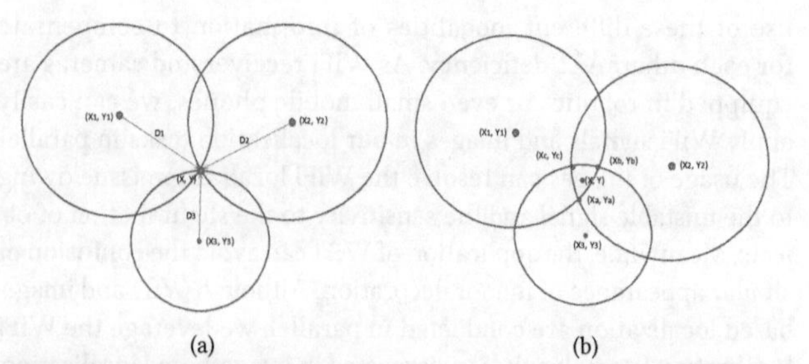

(a) (b)

Figure 3: (a) WiFi signal circles intersect at one point. (b) WiFi signal circles intersect at 3 points in triangulation localization.

where n is the signal propagation exponent constant, and we use the most common value 2 in our setting. A is the reference received signal strength in decibel-milliwatts (dBm), which is the RSSI value when the distance between mobile phone signal receiver and AP transmitter is one meter. D is the distance between the receiver and transmitter. Due to the unstable WiFi signals, the RSSI value varies significantly. However, the signal decaying rate is more related to the distance to the APs, much less dependent on the AP transmission power compared to RSSI absolute values. The signal strength difference between two positions with unit distance maintains relatively consistent even the absolute RSSI value varies significantly in different time. For these reasons, we propose to apply signal decaying rate to estimate the mobile phone distance to the APs instead of the absolute RSSI value. Based on Eq. 1, we can calculate the decaying rate DT as:

$$DT = RSSI' = \frac{-10n}{D * ln10} \tag{2}$$

From Eq. 2, the distance D is calculated as:

$$D = \frac{-10n}{DT * ln10} \tag{3}$$

From Eq. 3, we can get the rough distance to the AP address. The RSSI decaying rate is estimated by the RSSI difference in a distance of 1 meter controlled by the mobile phone embedded IMU. Based on this calculation model change, the variation of distance estimation reduces about 60% by experiments. However, the possible location options with the same distance to a point form a circle. It is still uncertain to localize the mobile phone based on the distance to an AP. The intersection of 3 circles can define a determined point, as illustrated in Fig. 3(a). Assuming the coordinates of the three AP address are (X_1, Y_1), (X_2, Y_2) and (X_3, Y_3) and distances to the corresponding AP address are D_1, D_2 and D_3, the intersection point (X, Y) of the three circles are computed through the following equations:

$$\begin{cases} (X - X_1)^2 + (Y - Y_1)^2 = D_1^2 \\ (X - X_2)^2 + (Y - Y_2)^2 = D_2^2 \\ (X - X_3)^2 + (Y - Y_3)^2 = D_3^2 \end{cases} \tag{4}$$

Ideally, the circles intersect at one point. In reality, the signals are affected by complex circumstances and signal decaying rate does not always maintain the same, which results in the inaccurate estimation of the mobile phone location. Most situations are that every circle pair intersects at two points, as shown in Fig. 3(b). The solution to obtain the intersection point for every two circles are as Eq. 5, Eq. 6 and Eq. 7.

$$\begin{cases} (X_a - X_1)^2 + (Y_a - Y_1)^2 = D_1^2 \\ (X_a - X_2)^2 + (Y_a - Y_2)^2 = D_2^2 \\ (X_a - X_3)^2 + (Y_a - Y_3)^2 \leqslant D_3^2 \end{cases} \tag{5}$$

$$\begin{cases} (X_b - X_1)^2 + (Y_b - Y_1)^2 = D_1^2 \\ (X_b - X_3)^2 + (Y_b - Y_3)^2 = D_3^2 \\ (X_b - X_2)^2 + (Y_b - Y_2)^2 \leqslant D_2^2 \end{cases} \tag{6}$$

$$\begin{cases} (X_c - X_2)^2 + (Y_c - Y_2)^2 = D_2^2 \\ (X_c - X_3)^2 + (Y_c - Y_3)^2 = D_3^2 \\ (X_c - X_1)^2 + (Y_c - Y_1)^2 \leqslant D_1^2 \end{cases} \tag{7}$$

Here, (X_a, Y_a), (X_b, Y_b) and (X_c, Y_c) are the intersection point between every two circles. As every circle pair can intersect at most two points, the last condition of Eq. 5, Eq. 6 and Eq. 7 constrains the expected point to be within the third circle. The mobile phone location is considered as the average value of the three estimated intersection points, as shown in Eq. 8.

$$\begin{cases} X = (X_a + X_b + X_c)/3 \\ Y = (Y_a + Y_b + Y_c)/3 \end{cases} \tag{8}$$

As any change of indoor layout causes the signal distribution variation, especially people walking around, the average mobile phone location can still have errors to the real signal receiver position. In some situations, the affected signal strength can result in the estimated distance circles without overlapping. To further make the WiFi-based localization robust, we select more Access Points to overcome the possible significant alteration of signal decaying rate. In our setting, we choose five APs to estimate the mobile phone position. In such a case, we can have ($C_5^3 = 5!/((5-3)! * 3!) = 10$) localization results. Among these 10 positions, we select the one with the least square distance to other locations as Eq. 9.

$$\underset{X,Y}{arg\,min} \sum_{i=1}^{10} \sqrt{(X - X_i)^2 + (Y - Y_i)^2} \tag{9}$$

Selecting from multiple positions, the one with the smallest distance to other locations in the largest extent ensures the mobile phone is localized around the correct place it appears, reducing the localization error. This step will help to distinguish the returned similar images from different locations of the buildings and find the correct place where the query image is captured.

4 IMAGE-BASED LOCALIZATION

Based on WiFi, we can roughly obtain the desired location as the prior knowledge. However, as WiFi-based localization usually has relatively large error and no orientation information is obtained from WiFi, we make use of images to perform accurate 6 DoF localization. We take 3D models as the reference image database, which are generated from Structure-from-Motion reconstruction. We extract SIFT features from images and match each other to find the image matching trajectory. Through Bundle Adjustment, we can get refined reconstructed 3D points and the camera pose of each image obtained in the reconstruction process.

Local features can usually generate higher image retrieval accuracy than global features. However, searching through the entire 3D model and the 2D image database by local feature would require a large amount of time, especially for the high dimensional SIFT feature. In dealing with this issue, we first search the images through global feature and then refine the result through local features. We cast the SIFT features extracted from images into histogram bins by a 500 dimensional codebook. We then generate the bag-of-visual-word (BoW) global feature for each image. We retrieve the images through BoW features, which would be faster than local features. The top 30 images with the closest distance to the query image are returned. The retrieval is conducted through K-Dimensional Tree (KD Tree) to quickly obtain the approximate nearest neighbor images.

4.1 Location Clustering for Retrieved Images

The top 30 images are associated with the position information, estimated in the SfM reconstruction stage. Based on the returned images, we utilize the WiFi-based localization result to select the images with roughly the same location as the query image. The returned images maintain high probabilities to be captured from different places. We separate the images into different groups based on their associated position coordinates. The groups are identified through the clustering method. As similar appearance may happen in multiple places, the exact cluster number is not identified. To deal with this issue, we cluster the images based on their distribution density. As we do not know exactly the cluster number prior to clustering, we apply Ordering Points to Identify the Clustering Structure (OPTICS) algorithm [1] to cluster the image locations based on the image distribution in the 3D model.In our OPTICS algorithm settings, as every point maintains at least 3 associated descriptors, we set the minimum number of neighbors as 3. The maximum distance for the radius distance is 10 meters according the real-world coordinate baseline. As OPTICS algorithm is relative robust to the parameters, the slight change for the settings does not affect to the clustering result significantly.

Assuming the image coordinate of the retrieved images are (x_1, y_1, z_1), $(x_2, y_2, z_2)...(x_{30}, y_{30}, z_{30})$, the clustering algorithm is shown in Algorithm 1. Algorithm 1 details each step for our clustering method. We calculate the mean position coordinate for each cluster. The image cluster with the closest distance to the WiFi-based localization result will be selected for the exact camera pose estimation. From image coordinate clustering, we can obtain the group of images which are the closest to the place where the query image is captured, describing the same scene. During the clustering process, some isolated images far away from the majority of image distribution are considered as outliers, excluding some false positive samples caused by the use of global features. From the final selected image cluster, we can obtain the region that the query image is located in the 3D model, by which we can estimate the exact camera pose through local feature matching.

4.2 Camera Pose Estimation through 3D Localization

In the image retrieval stage, we obtain the matching images through BoW global features, without building point-to-point correspondences. In order to estimate the camera pose, we need to establish correspondences between 2D images and the 3D model. In the previous work [35], local feature correspondences between 2D image and 3D reconstruction model are built through searching the entire model to find the best matching features, which could consume a relatively long time and generate extensive wrong correspondences. In order to filter out the outliers, RANSAC is required to perform a

Algorithm 1: Algorithm for clustering the image locations

INPUT: $PointSet(x_1, y_1, z_1), (x_2, y_2, z_2)...(x_{30}, y_{30}, z_{30})$
Initialize $MinP = 3$, $MaxR = 10m$.
ACTION:
(1)Create Ordered Queue Q_1 to store the core points and their directly reachable points sorted by ascending order and create Result Queue Q_2 to store the ordered output
(2)For each point P_i in PointSet
(3) Search $MinP$ neighbors $NeighborSet$
(4) Set the Core Distance $CoreDis_i$ for P_i
(5) Push P_i to Q_1
(6) If $CoreDis_i$!= NULL
(7) For each unprocessed point P_j in $NeighborSet$
(8) Dis = max($CoreDis_i$, distance(P_j, P_i))
(9) If $ReachableDis_j$ == NULL
(10) Reachable distance of P_j, $ReachableDis_j = Dis$
(11) Insert P_j to Q_2
(12) Else if $Dis < ReachableDis_j$
(13) $ReachableDis_j = Dis$
(14) For each point P_k in Q_1
(15) Search $MinP$ neighbors for P_k
(16) Set the Core Distance $CoreDis_k$ for P_k
(17) If $CoreDis_k$!= NULL
(18) Repeat Step (7) to (13)
Stop until all points processed Output: Q_2

large number of iterations. In contrast to the previous methods of searching the entire model, we have already obtained the images from the same location as the query image. Taking these images as prior information, we can largely reduce the research scope to maintain a fast matching process.

From the 3D SfM reconstruction model, we have obtained the 3D points and the associated SIFT descriptors. The SIFT descriptors are extracted from the 2D images in the SfM reconstruction stage, which builds 2D-to-3D correspondences offline. Here the 2D-to-3D correspondence represents the 2D training image matching to the 3D model, different from the 2D query image matching to the 3D model. Using the SIFT features extracted in the reconstruction process, each image in the retrieved cluster matches against the query image to build the 2D (query)-to-2D (training) correspondences through local features. Combining with the 2D (training)-to-3D model correspondences, we build 2D (query)-to-2D (training)-to-3D model correspondences for each image in the cluster, as shown in Fig. 4. Thus, we have multiple matching chains between the query image and the 3D model. During 2D-to-2D feature matching, we keep a strict verification step. While the query image matches the training image, a match is passed only when the matching feature distance is less than 0.7 times of the second nearest neighbor distance. This process is also conducted in the opposite direction that the training image matches the testing image. Only when a match passes the ratio test in both directions, we consider it as a solid match and accept the feature correspondence.

As the query image matches the 3D model through multiple paths (multiple cluster images), it could happen that a 3D point corresponds to multiple pixels in the 2D image or a pixel in the 2D query image corresponds to more than one 3D point in the 3D model. In dealing with this issue, we project the 3D point to the query image through the camera pose of the training image in the path. The match with the smallest re-projection error is accepted

Figure 4: The 2D query image matches the 2D training image, which is further connected to the 3D model.

as the unique 2D (query)-to-3D (model) correspondence. After obtaining at least 6 correspondences, we apply 6-point direct linear transformation (DLT) to estimate the query image camera pose. The 6-point DLT algorithm is embedded inside a RANSAC loop to best estimate the transformation matrix. When the transformation matrix estimation converges, we stop RANSAC and further apply local bundle adjustment to refine the camera pose, which provides us the accurate camera position and orientation. As we constrain the bundle adjustment in a small window, Levenberg-Marquardt optimization [15] is applied to obtain the accurate camera pose in contrast to many other SLAM methods that utilize Gauss-Newton algorithm [3] to achieve faster convergence, yet less precise optimization effect. As our 3D model is already built offline as a prior map, our optimization target is the query image camera pose without optimizing the 3D points' coordinates, which differs from typical bundle adjustment tasks. The cost function for our optimization target is described as Eq. 10.

$$D = f(R,T) = \left\| p - \prod(P;R,T) \right\|^2 \tag{10}$$

Here, D represents the distance between the 2D image feature coordinate and the coordinate of the 3D model re-projected to the 2D image. p is the feature pixel coordinate (x, y) and P represents the corresponding 3D point (X, Y, Z). R and T separately mean the rotation and translation matrices. $\prod$ is the matrix product mark. Based on Eq. 10, our objective is to obtain the R and T that minimizes the 3D re-projection error, as Eq. 11.

$$\underset{R;T}{argmin} \left\| p - \prod(P;R,T) \right\|^2 \tag{11}$$

By calculating the gradient of our cost function with respect to (R, T), we obtain the Jacobian matrix as Eq. 12.

$$J = \frac{\partial f}{\partial(R,T)} \tag{12}$$

Based on Levenberg-Marquardt algorithm, the final transformation matrix is estimated by Eq. 13, which iteratively optimizes R and T. This process is repeated between Eq. 10 to Eq. 13 until the re-projection error D less than a defined threshold. λ is the step length parameter defined in Levenberg-Marquardt algorithm.

$$(R,T) \leftarrow (R,T) - (J^T J + \lambda diag(J^T J))^{-1} J^T D \tag{13}$$

Based on the optimized rotation R and translation T matrices, the camera position is calculated as $(-R^{-1} * T)$ and orientation is $(-R^{-1} * [0\ 0\ -1])$.

5 EXPERIMENT RESULTS

We capture both WiFi signals and images for localization. In the WiFi-based localization process, we retrieve the top 5 APs with the strongest RSSI signals to localize the mobile phone. For the image-based localization stage, we extract SIFT features from the images and cast the features into a 500 dimensional BoW. The BoW feature is utilized for image retrieval. The original SIFT features are also stored in the memory for 3D localization. The WiFi-based localization and image retrieval component can be conducted in parallel in two different threads.

5.1 Dataset

As there is no public dataset in indoor environment with both images and WiFi signals, we capture our own dataset with WiFi signals, indoor images and build 3D models. We capture 100 Access Points' MAC addresses and their corresponding physical locations distributed through the building. As the RSSI decaying rate frequently changes with a small range, we sample 100 times of the RSSI decaying rate for each Access Point with the sampling distance of 1 meter estimated by mobile phone embedded IMU. The average value of the 100 times RSSI decaying rate is recorded for the corresponding AP.

We also capture 25,830 images and reconstruct the 3D point cloud of the indoor buildings. For testing, we captured 300 images containing landmark areas and non-landmark areas. The details of the dataset is shown in Table 1.

	Image #	Point #	SIFT descriptor #	Access point #	Query image #
Indoor environment	25,830	4,794,173	24,440,564	100	300

Table 1: Details of our dataset

5.2 Comparison with WiFi-based Localization

The usage of WiFi is to facilitate image-based localization by resolving the appearance confusion issue. A roughly accurate localization result from WiFi is required to distinguish the images retrieved from different locations. To increase the system robustness and avoid the significant signal strength changes, we apply signal decaying rate to compute the distance instead of the absolute RSSI value. The localization error and the estimated distance variance are displayed in Table 2.

Method	Error	Distance variance
Signal decaying rate	9.43	12.62
Absolute RSSI value	14.62	19.75

Table 2: Localization error and distance variance based on signal decaying rate and absolute RSSI value two method.

From Table 2, the signal decaying rate model largely reduces the localization error and distance calculation variance, significantly increasing the reliability of WiFi localization. To further enhance the robustness of the WiFi localization, we make use of 5 APs, which generate 10 triangulation results, to localize the mobile phone by finding the location with the least square distance to other estimated locations. We compare different numbers of APs on the use of WiFi-based localization to check the influence of AP number on the localization accuracy, as Fig. 5.

Based on the increase of AP number, the localization error first reduces, which means more access points can improve the localization accuracy through selecting the triangulation result with the

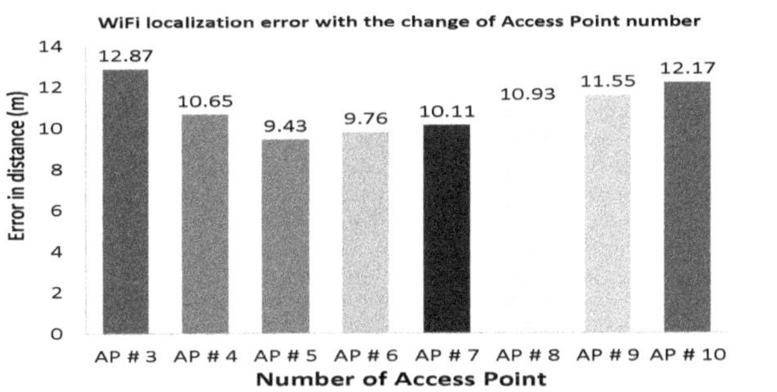

Figure 5: WiFi localization error in meters based on different numbers of Access Points.

one closest to others. However, when further adding access points, the localization error begins to raise again. This is because more access points with weak signals weaken the localization effects. The weak signals generate a relative large error compared with APs with strongest signals, which may move the WiFi localization farther from the ground truth. From test, 5 Access Points provide a best average localization result in our data. At the same time, too many Access Points would largely increase the triangulation times. For example, 6 APs need ($C_6^3 = 6!/((6-3)! * 3!) = 20$) times triangulation and 10 APs require to repeat 120 times of this procedure. For this reason, we choose 5 access points to obtain the WiFi localization.

5.3 Comparison with Image-based Localization

The use of WiFi can help to select the images with similar appearance from different places. We conduct experiments to verify the effectiveness on the usage of WiFi and our proposed localization framework, comparing with other state-of-the-art image-based localization methods. The testing images contain landmark images and images with similar appearance of different places including some extreme difficult cases, such as the plain walls. The comparison result is shown in Fig. 6(b). We can see that our method outperforms other methods, showing that our method takes advantages of both WiFi and images to overcome the difficulties existed in localization tasks. Generally, image-based localization can outperform WiFi and most other signal-based methods. However, due to the similar appearance of buildings, especially in indoor environments, localizing an image in less distinguishable scenes can be difficult. With the leverage of WiFi, this issue can be largely lessened.

We also compare the image registration number with other image-based localization methods. As indicated in [20, 35], images with at least 12 inliers are considered as the registered images. Following this criteria, we count the number of images registered by our method and compare it with other methods, whose result is shown in Fig. 6(a). In this experiment, single WiFi-based localization is not compared as there is no images involved. Compared with other image-based localization algorithms, our method provides a superior performance. This is due to the avoidance of many false positive matches between the query local feature to the 3D points. Other methods contain a significant amount of wrong matches to database images or 3D model, which appear similar to the query image but are not the real correct place. Those outliers cannot fit

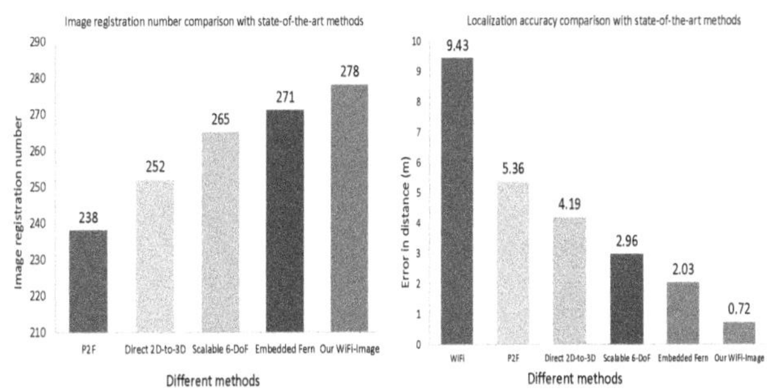

(a) (b)

Figure 6: (a): Comparison in terms of image registration number with other state-of-the-art methods (P2F [20], Direct 2D-to-3D [35], Scalable 6-DoF [30], Embedded Fern [8]). (b): Comparison in terms of accuracy with other state-of-the-art methods (WiFi and other methods in (a)).

RANSAC, resulting in a lower image registration number. At the same time, time consumption for RANSAC loop is also increased due to the repeated attempts of searching inliers. High image registration number also facilitates the accurate transformation matrix calculation, which is critical in camera pose estimation. The reduced search scope enhances the probability of finding the correct correspondences between the query image and the 3D model.

Another advantage of the WiFi usage is that it can help to reduce the searching time in the local feature level, which can involve extensive computation. With the prior location provided by WiFi, we can quickly identify the 3D points matching to the query image, as exhibited in Table 3, which demonstrates the time performance of our method. Though WiFi is still faster than our method slightly, our method outperforms state-of-the-art methods. Benefiting from the reduced search scope for local feature matching by WiFi, our method only makes use of global image feature and the least number of local features to obtain the exact camera pose, which at the same time avoids extensive false positive matches. Time consumption for each component of our system is displayed in Fig. 7.

Method	WiFi	P2F [20]	Direct 2D-to-3D [35]	Scalable 6-DoF [30]	Embedded Fern [8]	Our WiFi-Image localization
Elapsed Time	0.18 (s)	7.83 (s)	6.35 (s)	3.51 (s)	1.46 (s)	0.29 (s)

Table 3: Time performance in localizing an image between our WiFi-Image localization and other state-of-the-art methods.

As Fig. 7 indicates, the 2D-to-2D-to-3D correspondence establishment component consumes very little time, compared with other parts. This is because the application of WiFi avoids the extensive search through the 3D point cloud. Image retrieval and WiFi localization consumes the most computation resources. However, WiFi localization and image retrieval can be conducted in parallel without affecting each other, which makes WiFi and images applicable to achieve high performance simultaneously.

6 CONCLUSION

The combination of WiFi and image can make use of the benefits of both methods. To distinguish the similar decoration of indoor environments, we apply WiFi to facilitate the decision of image-based localization among multiple possible regions. As WiFi signal

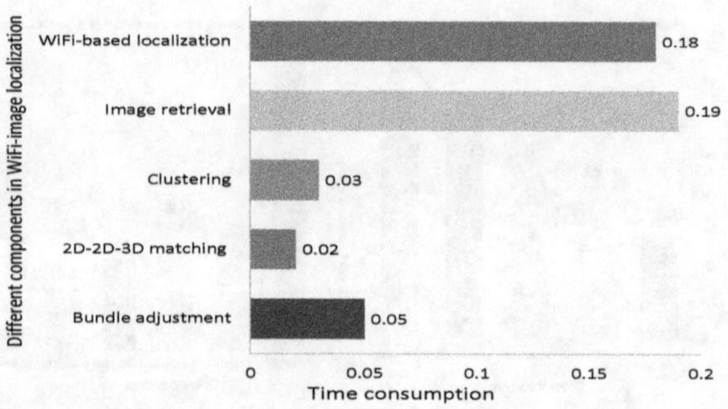

Figure 7: Time consumption for each component in WiFi-image localization.

frequently changes, we utilize the WiFi signal decaying rate instead of the absolute RSSI value to compute the distance. During the image-based localization stage, we quickly retrieve the top matching images through global features under KD-tree. Based on the returned images, we retrieve their locations obtained from offline SfM reconstruction process. The image locations are clustered into several regions through a density-based clustering method. The image cluster closest to the WiFi positioning result is selected for accurate camera pose estimation. The query image matches against the 3D model through the bridge of the images in the selected cluster, so that we target at a small portion of the 3D model to find the 2D (query)-to-3D (model) correspondences for fast and accurate indoor localization.

ACKNOWLEDGEMENT

The authors would like to thank Prof. Chandra Kambhamettu from University of Delaware to provide data for this work.

REFERENCES

[1] Mihael Ankerst, Markus M Breunig, Hans-Peter Kriegel, and Jörg Sander. 1999. OPTICS: ordering points to identify the clustering structure. In *ACM Sigmod Record*, Vol. 28. 49–60.
[2] Arturo Beltran, Carlos Abargues, Carlos Granell, Manuela Núñez, Laura Díaz, and Joaquín Huerta. 2013. A virtual globe tool for searching and visualizing geo-referenced media resources in social networks. *MTA* (2013), 1–25.
[3] Luca Carlone. 2013. A convergence analysis for pose graph optimization via gauss-newton methods. In *ICRA*. 965–972.
[4] Robert Castle, Georg Klein, and David W. Murray. 2008. Video-rate localization in multiple maps for wearable augmented reality. In *ISWC*. 15–22.
[5] David Crandall, Andrew Owens, Noah Snavely, and Dan Huttenlocher. 2011. Discrete-continuous optimization for large-scale structure from motion. In *CVPR*. 3001 –3008.
[6] Mark Cummins and Paul Newman. 2008. FAB-MAP: Probabilistic Localization and Mapping in the Space of Appearance. *IJRR* 27, 6 (2008), 647–665.
[7] Qian Dong and Waltenegus Dargie. 2012. Evaluation of the reliability of RSSI for indoor localization. In *ICWCUCA*. 1–6.
[8] Michael Donoser and Dieter Schmalstieg. 2014. Discriminative Feature-to-Point Matching in Image-Based Localization. In *CVPR*. 516–523.
[9] Quan Fang, Jitao Sang, and Changsheng Xu. 2013. Giant: Geo-informative attributes for location recognition and exploration. In *MM*. 13–22.
[10] Jan-Michael Frahm, Pierre Fite-Georgel, David Gallup, Tim Johnson, Rahul Raguram, Changchang Wu, Yi-Hung Jen, Enrique Dunn, Brian Clipp, Svetlana Lazebnik, and Marc Pollefeys. 2010. Building Rome on a cloudless day. In *ECCV*. 368–381.
[11] Arnold Irschara, Christopher Zach, Jan-Michael Frahm, and Horst Bischof. 2009. From structure-from-motion point clouds to fast location recognition. In *CVPR*. 2599–2606.
[12] Nathan Jacobs, Kylia Miskell, and Robert Pless. 2011. Webcam geo-localization using aggregate light levels. In *WACV*. 132–138.
[13] Rongrong Ji, Ling-Yu Duan, Jie Chen, Hongxun Yao, Junsong Yuan, Yong Rui, and Wen Gao. 2012. Location discriminative vocabulary coding for mobile landmark search. *IJCV* 96, 3 (2012), 290–314.
[14] Rongrong Ji, Xing Xie, Hongxun Yao, and Wei-Ying Ma. 2009. Mining city landmarks from blogs by graph modeling. In *MM*. 105–114.
[15] Christian Kanzow, Nobuo Yamashita, and Masao Fukushima. 2004. Levenberg–Marquardt methods with strong local convergence properties for solving nonlinear equations with convex constraints. *JAMC* 172, 2 (2004), 375–397.
[16] Hisato Kawaji, Koki Hatada, Toshihiko Yamasaki, and Kiyoharu Aizawa. 2010. Image-based indoor positioning system: fast image matching using omnidirectional panoramic images. In *MPVA*. 1–4.
[17] Jana Kosecka, Liang Zhou, Philip Barber, and Zoran Duric. 2003. Qualitative image based localization in indoors environments. In *CVPR*, Vol. 2. II–3.
[18] John J. Leonard and Hugh F. Durrant-Whyte. 1991. Simultaneous map building and localization for an autonomous mobile robot. In *IROS workshop*, Vol. 3. 1442–1447.
[19] Xun Li and Jinling Wang. 2012. Image matching techniques for vision-based indoor navigation systems: performance analysis for 3D map based approach. In *IPIN*. 1–8.
[20] Yunpeng Li, Noah Snavely, and Daniel P. Huttenlocher. 2010. Location recognition using prioritized feature matching. In *ECCV*. 791–804.
[21] Hongbo Liu, Yu Gan, Jie Yang, Simon Sidhom, Yan Wang, Yingying Chen, and Fan Ye. 2012. Push the limit of WiFi based localization for smartphones. In *MobiCom*. 305–316.
[22] Heng Liu, Tao Mei, Jiebo Luo, Houqiang Li, and Shipeng Li. 2012. Finding perfect rendezvous on the go: accurate mobile visual localization and its applications to routing. In *MM*. 9–18.
[23] Hongbo Liu, Jie Yang, Simon Sidhom, Yan Wang, Yingying Chen, and Fan Ye. 2014. Accurate WiFi based localization for smartphones using peer assistance. *TMC* 13, 10 (2014), 2199–2214.
[24] Manolis I.A. Lourakis and Antonis A. Argyros. 2009. SBA: A software package for generic sparse bundle adjustment. *TOMS* 36, 1 (2009), 2.
[25] Guoyu Lu, Vincent Ly, Haoquan Shen, Abhishek Kolagunda, and Chandra Kambhamettu. 2013. Improving Image-Based Localization through Increasing Correct Feature Correspondences. In *International Symposium on Visual Computing (ISVC)*. 312–321.
[26] Guoyu Lu, Yan Yan, Abhishek Kolagunda, and Chandra Kambhamettu. 2016. A fast 3D indoor-localization approach based on video queries. In *MMM*. 218–230.
[27] Guoyu Lu, Yan Yan, Li Ren, Jingkuan Song, Nicu Sebe, and Chandra Kambhamettu. 2015. Localize me anywhere, anytime: a multi-task point-retrieval approach. In *ICCV*. 2434–2442.
[28] Guoyu Lu, Yan Yan, Nicu Sebe, and Chandra Kambhamettu. 2014. Knowing where I am: Exploiting multi-task learning for multi-view indoor image-based localization. In *British Machine Vision Conference (BMVC)*.
[29] Guoyu Lu, Yan Yan, Nicu Sebe, and Chandra Kambhamettu. 2017. Indoor localization via multi-view images and videos. *CVIU* 161 (2017), 145–160.
[30] Sven Middelberg, Torsten Sattler, Ole Untzelmann, and Leif Kobbelt. 2014. Scalable 6-DOF Localization on Mobile Devices. In *ECCV*. 268–283.
[31] David Nister and Henrik Stewenius. 2006. Scalable Recognition with a Vocabulary Tree. In *CVPR*, Vol. 2. 2161–2168.
[32] Nishkam Ravi, Pravin Shankar, Andrew Frankel, Ahmed Elgammal, and Liviu Iftode. 2006. Indoor localization using camera phones. In *WMCSA*. 49.
[33] Duncan P. Robertson and Roberto Cipolla. 2004. An Image-Based System for Urban Navigation. In *BMVC*. 819–828.
[34] Jitao Sang, Tao Mei, Ying-Qing Xu, Chen Zhao, Changsheng Xu, and Shipeng Li. 2013. Interaction design for mobile visual search. *TMM* 15, 7 (2013), 1665–1676.
[35] Torsten Sattler, Bastian Leibe, and Leif Kobbelt. 2011. Fast image-based localization using direct 2D-to-3D matching. In *ICCV*. 667–674.
[36] Hao Shao, Tomáš Svoboda, Tinne Tuytelaars, and Luc Van Gool. 2003. HPAT Indexing for Fast Object/Scene Recognition Based on Local Appearance. In *CIVR*. 71–80.
[37] Jamie Shotton, Ben Glocker, Christopher Zach, Shahram Izadi, Antonio Criminisi, and Andrew Fitzgibbon. 2013. Scene coordinate regression forests for camera relocalization in RGB-D images. In *CVPR*. 2930–2937.
[38] Randall C. Smith and Peter Cheeseman. 1986. On the Representation and Estimation of Spatial Uncertainty. *IJRR* 5, 6 (1986), 56–68.
[39] Noah Snavely, Steven M Seitz, and Richard Szeliski. 2006. Photo tourism: exploring photo collections in 3D. *ToG* 25, 3 (2006), 835–846.
[40] Ulrich Steinhoff, Dušan Omerčević, Roland Perko, Bernt Schiele, and Aleš Leonardis. 2007. How computer vision can help in outdoor positioning. In *AmI*. 124–141.
[41] Bill Triggs, Philip F McLauchlan, Richard I Hartley, and Andrew W. Fitzgibbon. 2000. Bundle adjustment-a modern synthesis. In *International Workshop on Vision Algorithms: Theory and Practice*. 298–372.
[42] Julien Valentin, Matthias Nießner, Jamie Shotton, Andrew Fitzgibbon, Shahram Izadi, and Philip HS Torr. 2015. Exploiting uncertainty in regression forests for accurate camera relocalization. In *CVPR*. 4400–4408.
[43] Wei Zhang and Jana Kosecka. 2006. Image Based Localization in Urban Environments. In *3DPVT*. 33–40.

Compare Stereo Patches Using Atrous Convolutional Neural Networks

Zhiwei Li
Beihang University
Haidian, Beijing Shi, China
pierrelzw@buaa.edu.cn

Lei Yu
Beihang University
Haidian, Beijing Shi, China
yulei@buaa.edu.cn

ABSTRACT

In this work, we address the task of dense stereo matching with Convolutional Neural Networks (CNNs). Particularly, we focus on improving matching cost computation by better aggregating contextual information. Towards this goal, we advocate to use atrous convolution, a powerful tool for dense prediction task that allows us to control the resolution at which feature responses are computed within CNNs and to enlarge the receptive field of the network without losing image resolution and requiring learning extra parameters. Aiming to improve the performance of atrous convolution, we propose different frameworks for further boosting performance. We evaluate our models on KITTI 2015 benchmark, the result shows that we achieve on-par performance with fewer post-processing methods applied.

CCS CONCEPTS

• **Information systems → Image search**;

KEYWORDS

Stereo Matching, Atrous Convolution, Context Aggregation

ACM Reference Format:
Zhiwei Li and Lei Yu. 2018. Compare Stereo Patches Using Atrous Convolutional Neural Networks. In *ICMR '18: 2018 International Conference on Multimedia Retrieval, June 11–14, 2018, Bunkyo, Japan.* ACM, New York, NY, USA, 8 pages. https://doi.org/10.1145/3206025.3206075

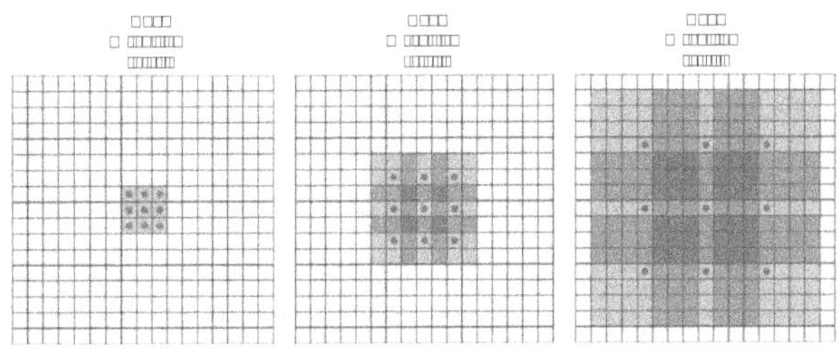

Figure 1: Atrous convolution supports exponential expansion of the receptive field without loss of resolution or coverage[24]. Standard convolution corresponds to atrous convolution with $rate = 1$.

1 INTRODUCTION

The research of depth estimation has always been an active research area in computer vision. It is a core technology in variant fields, such as Robots, Autonomous driving, 3D construction, etc. Active methods, such as Lidar, ToF and structured light have been widely used in many applications to acquire depth map. However, those approaches could be costly (e.g. Laser Lidar) or be very sensitive with environmental factors (e.g. distance, illumination) since they require interference with the estimated object. In contrast, the passive methods are more cost-effective and applicable in a wider range of situations.

A typical passive method is the binocular stereo vision. It is an image-based approach, meaning that the input is only two normal images and the depth map is estimated based on image understanding technologies. To be more exact, given a rectified stereo pair of images, we are interested in computing a dense disparity image of the left view. Two input images are rectified so that their epipolar lines are aligned with image horizontal axis. Thus, for an arbitrary pixel $p = (x, y)$ in left image, its correspondence, can be found at location $(x + d, y)$ in right image. d is what we call the disparity. It allows us to derive the depth z of p by

$$z = \frac{Bf}{d}$$

B is the baseline of the stereo cameras, i.e. the distance between two camera centers, and f is the camera focal length. In short, the above equation says that the depth varies inversely to the disparity. Therefore, the core problem of depth estimation in stereo system can be converted into searching for the accurate dense disparity, or rather finding the most likely matches between pixels in two images.

According to the taxonomy of Scharstein[18], stereo algorithms usually consist of four steps: 1) matching cost computation, 2) cost aggregation, 3) disparity computation, 4) disparity refinement. In recent years, Convolutional Neural Networks (CNNs) have been exploited to learn the matching cost computation[4][21][27][28]. Taking advantage of the large accessible labeled dataset in benchmark like KITTI[14] and Middleburry[17], CNNs-based methods have shown great performance exceeding traditional approaches.

Learning effective deep convolutional network representation usually requires a large receptive field (or "field of view" in [1]) so as to combine more contextual information. To this end, the common way is to conduct downsampling operations. However, it results in reducing image resolution and hence leads to the reduction of detailed spatial information, which is not desired in dense estimation

ICMR '18, June 11–14, 2018, Bunkyo, Japan

ACM ISBN 978-1-4503-5046-4/18/06...$15.00
https://doi.org/10.1145/3206025.3206075

task. Thus, the current algorithms still suffer from ill-posed regions such as repetitive-pattern regions, textureless areas and occlusions.

Atrous convolution, also known as dilated convolution, allows us to enlarge the receptive field of CNNs without losing image resolution and requiring learning extra parameters. Let $F : \mathbb{Z}^2 \quad \mathbb{R}$ be a discrete function. Let $\Omega_r = [\ r, r]^2 \quad \mathbb{Z}^2$ and let $k : \Omega_r \quad \mathbb{R}$ be a discrete filter of size $(2r + 1)^2$. The standard discrete convolution operator   can be defined as

$$(F \quad k)(p) = \sum_{s+t=p} F(s)k(t)$$

Now, we generalize the convolution operator. Let d be the atrous factor and $\ _d$ be defined as

$$(F \quad _d k)(p) = \sum_{s+dt=p} F(s)k(t)$$

We refer to $\ _d$ as an atrous convolution. Specifically, given a 2-dimensional matrix I and a convolution kernel k of size $(2r + 1)^2$, the standard convolution operation at position (p, q) in I can be defined as:

$$C(p, q\ I, k) = \sum_{i=\ r}^{r} \sum_{j=\ r}^{r} I_{p+i,q+j} k_{i,j}$$

therefore, an atrous convolution with $rate = d$ at position (p, q) in I is

$$C_d(p, q\ I, k) = \sum_{i=\ r}^{r} \sum_{j=\ r}^{r} I_{p+di,q+dj} k_{i,j}$$

Figure 1 shows a network that consists of 3 convolution layers with different atrous rates (1, 2, 4). It takes a receptive field of 15x15. In contrast, if the network is a standard convolution network, the size of field of view is decreased to 7x7 with the same parameter size.

In this paper, we present a new architecture for dense stereo matching. To tackle the aforementioned problem (i.e. the con⊠ict between enlarging receptive field and requiring maintaining local variance), we propose to utilize atrous convolution which has shown its effectiveness in Semantic Segmentation[1]. By incorporating atrous convolution, we are able to control the resolution at which features response are computed within CNNs and to enlarge the receptive field of CNNs for better aggregating contextual information.

2 RELATED WORK

2.1 Atrous convolution

Atrous convolution has been proved to perform well in another active dense prediction task - Semantic Segmentation[1][22][24]. However, to our knowledge, there is few work utilizing atrous convolution in stereo dense estimation. Liu *et al.*[11] simply modified parts of layers of MC-CNN by atrous convolution without taking into acount the atrous rates setting and computation efficiency. In contrast, inspired by [1] [2] [24], we dig deeper into atrous convolution for better aggregating context information and eventually generating more accurate disparity images.

2.2 Deep learning for stereo matching

There are amounts of surveys of stereo matching algorithms. In this section, we restrict ourselves mostly to the recent approaches which employed convolutional networks.

According to the recent researches, CNNs can be involved in parts of four steps by casting them as learning problem. There are mainly three classes of CNNs-based approaches for stereo matching: matching cost learning, regularity learning and end-to-end disparity learning[16]. Our work belongs to the first one that employs CNNs for matching cost computation and then conducts a set of post-processing methods to acquire the final disparity image.

Matching cost learning: As the first step of stereo algorithms, matching cost computation aims to offer a similarity measure of two input image patch pairs.

Inspired by CNNs' outperformance in kinds of computer vision tasks as Classification, Object Detection and Semantic Segmentation. Zagoruyko *et al.*[27] proposed several stacked CNNs to learn raw image data from a general similarity function for comparing image patches. Han *et al.*[4] referred to an unified network called "MatchNet". Zontar *et al.*[28] proposed two MC-CNN architectures, of which one was relatively faster than the other, but produced disparity maps that were slightly less accurate. Particularly, they all cast the matching cost computation as a binary classification problem and trained a Siamese network by minimizing a hinge loss considering both positive example and negative example, i.e. the matching patch pairs and no matching ones. In addition, MC-CNN takes a small 9x9 patch without using pooling layer, that helps to avoid the reduction of resolution but restricts the receptive field from increasing.

In contrast to an independent binary classification scheme between image patches, Luo *et al.*[12] proposed to learn a probability distribution over all possible disparities. The matching cost learning network was trained by minimizing the multi-class cross entropy. They proved that the multi-class learning method outperformed binary classification strategy and a large receptive field resulted in a more accurate coarse disparity map. Amit *et al.*[21] exploited Highway Network for matching cost learning and proposed to learn disparity computation instead of using conventional "WTA" strategy.

Due to CNNs' powerful encoding ability, these approaches have made dramatic progress in patch-based stereo matching. However, most of them still suffer from the inherently ill-posed regions, such as object occlusions, repeated patterns and textureless regions. One main reason is the restriction of the small receptive field that leads to the lack of context information.

Regularity learning: In contrast to heuristic methods that smooth and refine the disparity in the o⊠ ine manner, some works imposed smoothness constrains in learning procedure. For example, Guney and Geiger[3] incorporated object knowledge for stereo matching. With the help of techniques of Semantic Segmentation, [10][14] achieved a large gain in accuracy.

End-to-end disparity learning: More recently, inspired by the development of techniques in Semantic Segmentation, end-to-end learning for depth estimation has also been proposed. By carefully designed network, it is possible to incorporate the post processing

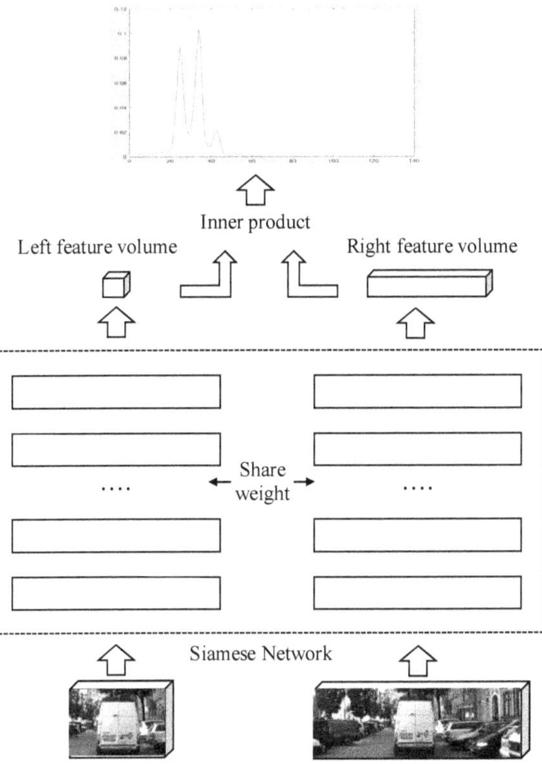

Figure 2: Cost learning networks

steps in learning process and train the whole network in an end-to-end manner[7] [9][13][16][26].

Most of the end-to-end approaches highlight optimization of coarse initial cost volume or disparity image by learning method and carefully design the network to make it end-to-end trainable. However, only little attention is given to the feature extraction from raw image data to obtain more accurate matching cost, which is the basis of stereo algorithms.

Thus, our work focuses on matching cost learning. To this end, we introduce atrous convolution in our networks. Furthermore, we are interested in developing an efficient architecture for stereo matching. Our contributions are: 1) We introduce the atrous convolution into the matching cost learning network. It allows us to enlarge network's field of view and improve the matching cost computation. 2) We propose different rates assignment schemes to better aggregate context information using atrous convolutional networks. 3) We submit the test result on KITTI 2015 benchmark and achieve a comparable result.

3 NETWORK ARCHITECTURE

Multi-class classification scheme for matching cost computation

Inspired by [12] [21], we cast matching cost computation as a multi-class classification problem. As shown in Figure 2, we employ the architecture of [12]. The input are two different-size images and the main part of the model is a Siamese network for feature encoding. The left input patch centers on target pixel and the right input image patch extends over all possible matching positions in right image.

Firstly, the input image patches are respectively processed by two sharing-weight networks to produce two different-size deep net features. Then an inner product computation is applied to measure similarities of left image patch and all potential matching patches in right image. In the end, a Softmax is employed to normalize the similarities so as to output a probability distribution over all possible disparities.

In the training procedure, we address to minimize a weighted cross-entropy that centers the mass around the ground truth y^{GT}, w.r.t the error metric of the data set:

$$loss(y, y^{GT}) = -\sum_{y_i} p(y_i, y^{GT}) log \frac{e^{y_i}}{\sum_j e^{y_j}}$$

where $p(y_i, y^{GT})$ is a smooth target distribution, centered around the ground truth y^{GT}. Since the KITTI dataset utilizes a 3-pixel error metric, we define $p(y_i, y^{GT})$ as follows:

$$p(y_i, y^{GT}) = \begin{cases} \lambda_1, & \text{if } y_i - y^{GT} = 0 \\ \lambda_2, & \text{if } y_i - y^{GT} = 1 \\ \lambda_3, & \text{if } y_i - y^{GT} = 2 \\ 0, & \text{otherwise} \end{cases}$$

while $\lambda_1 = 0.5, \lambda_2 = 0.2, \lambda_3 = 0.05$ in this paper. During testing, the network computes only once the final deep net representation for every pixel i by taking the whole image as input. Then we re-used the previous results for all disparities that involve this location to construct the cost volume. This allows the inference to be run in an efficient way.

Once the cost volume is constructed, a set of optimization steps, such as Cost Aggregation (CA) and Semi-global Matching (SGM), are conducted to aggregating the matching cost. Then a simple "Winner Takes All (WTA)" method is applied to generate the disparity image. In the end, refinement methods, such as interpolation, median filtering or bilateral filtering can be employed to produce the final result.

The raw output of CNNs allows us to construct the coarse cost volume and to compute the disparity image using WTA. In this paper, we refer to this coarse result as "unary result". Further, the final disparity image, produced after applying a set of post optimization steps to coarse cost volume, is referred to "optimized result".

Multi-scale context aggregation by atrous convolution

It is challenging for local match methods to deal with weak-texture and repetitive-pattern regions. Taking account of more contextual information helps to solve this problem. To this end, the straight way is to enlarge the receptive field, which can be implemented by three approaches: 1) increasing convolutional layers 2) using larger convolutional kernel 3) employing subsampling operations such as pooling or striding convolution.

However, the first two methods require a large model with more parameters. The third one leads to the loss of image details and local variance, which impedes the dense prediction task like ours. In contrast, atrous convolution could expand the receptive field without losing image resolution and requiring learning extra parameters.

Layer	Channel	Kernel	Rate	RELU	Receptive Field
1	64	3x3	1	Yes	3x3
2	64	3x3	1	Yes	5x5
3	64	3x3	1	Yes	7x7
4	64	3x3	1	Yes	9x9
5	64	3x3	1	Yes	11x11
6	64	3x3	1	Yes	13x13
7	64	3x3	1	Yes	15x15
8	64	3x3	1	Yes	17x17
9	64	3x3	1	No	19x19

Table 1: The baseline architecture[12]

Layer	Channel	Kernel	Rate	RELU	Receptive Field
1	64	3x3	1	Yes	3x3
2	64	3x3	2	Yes	7x7
3	64	3x3	2	Yes	11x11
4	64	3x3	2	Yes	15x15
5	64	3x3	4	Yes	23x23
6	64	3x3	2	Yes	27x27
7	64	3x3	2	Yes	31x31
8	64	3x3	2	Yes	35x35
9	64	3x3	1	No	37x37

Table 2: Atrous convolutional network atchitecture

Again, in our work, we focus on matching cost learning. Our network is designed to enlarge the field of view and to better aggregate contextual information so as to increase performance of matching cost computation. The baseline model, as shown in Table 1, consists of 9 convolutional layers with 3x3 standard convolution, hence taking a 19x19 receptive field. Every convolution is followed by a batch normalization and a rectified linear unit (RELU). In particular, the RELU in the last layer is removed to avoid losing the negative information. As shown in Table 2, our architecture acquires a larger field of view (37x37), by replacing parts of layers with atrous convolution.

4 SMOOTHING AND REFINEMENT

Simply taking the most confident result does not produce desirable performance, since the matching cost is calculated based on local patches (even we enlarge the receptive field). Post-processing techniques for cost aggregation, smoothing and refinement are still required.

In our work, we employ heuristic post-processing methods (i.e. CA, SGM and Interpolation [6][12][28]). To aggregate the cost volume of neighbor pixels, we first apply a 5x5 average pooling over all cost volume. Then we employ SGM to add smoothness constrains which address to minimize the following function:

$$E(y) = \sum_{i\ N} E_i(y_i) + \sum_{(i,j)\ \mathcal{E}} E_{i,j}(y_i, y_j),$$

where $\mathcal{E}$ is a 4-connected grid and the unary energy term $E_i(y_i)$ is the output of deep CNNs. The pairwise term is defined as follows:

$$E_{i,j}(y_i, y_j) = \begin{cases} 0, & \text{if } y_i = y_j \\ c_1, & \text{if } y_i \quad y_j \ = 1 \\ c_2, & \text{otherwise} \end{cases}$$

c_1 is the penalty when the neighboring disparity pixels differ by one. c_2 is the penalty when the neighboring disparities differ by more than one. As [12][29], we set $c_1 < c_2$ so that the jumps in disparity coincide with edges in the image.

5 EXPERIMENT

We evaluate our convolutional network architectures on KITTI 2015 benchmark[14][15]. Comparisons with baseline work and the state of the art are provided later in this section.

Before training, we apply standard deviation normalization on each image. To initialize the parameters of our network, we employ uniform distribution. As for optimization method, we utilize Adam algorithm[8] and we regulate learning rate during training instead of using default setting, since we find that the default setting does not provide satisfactory result. We initialize learning rate by 0.01, reduce it by a factor of 5 after 24k iterations and then further decrease it by a factor of 5 every 8k iterations. With a batch size of 128, we train the network for 40k iterations using one Nvidia Titan-X GPU, taking roughly 10h for our model of 37x37 receptive field, which we present later in this section.

For post propressing, we rely less on optimization than the baseline [12] (without Slanted Plane method[23]). After the cost volume is constructed, we employ successively a 5x5 average pooling, SGM and another 5x5 average pooling. In the end, we conduct the left-right check and interpolation for refinement.

5.1 Benchmark dataset

KITTI is one of the largest online benchmarks for tasks such as stereo, optical flow, visual Geometry, 3D object detection and 3D tracking. For the task of stereo estimation, the KITTI 2015 provides 200 training images and 200 test images. To evaluate the different models, the 3-pixel error is employed: a pixel is considered to be correctly estimated if the disparity error is <3px or <5%.

5.2 Comparison with baseline

We first compared our proposed atrous convolutional network with baseline model[12]. The comparison was based on KITTI 2015 dataset. We randomly splited the 200 labeled image pairs into training/validation subsets in 80:20 proposition. Since we could not ensure our split was the same as Luo *et al.*[12], we re-implemented their work and compared with the re-implemented result, instead of what was depicted in the paper.

Following [11][24], we first constructed a network where the rates are 1, 1, 1, 2, 4, 8, 1. The 3 first layers employed standard convolution for low-level feature learning. The three middle layers

Models	Kernel	Rates	Unary	Optimized
Baseline-paper(19)	3x3	111-111-111	8.95	4.31
Baseline-paper(37)	5x5	111-111-111	7.13	4.38
Baseline-re-imp(19)	3x3	111-111-111	7.87	3.75
Baseline-re-imp(37)	5x5	111-111-111	7.26	4.29
Our(37)	3x3	111-248-1	6.12	3.68
Our(73)	5x5	111-248-1	**5.23**	**3.82**

Table 3: Comparison of our architectures and baseline models. The table illustrates the non-occluded 3-pixel error on KITTI 2015 validation set. The first column shows the different models where the number between the parentheses is the size of corresponding receptive field. Particularly, we use rates of atrous convolutional networks to represent them. For instance, 111-111-111 indicates a 9-layer network where all convolution are standard convolution. The field of view is 19x19.

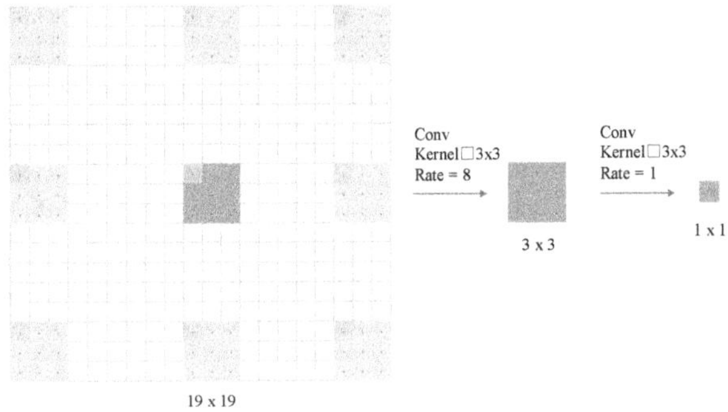

Figure 3: Top-3 layer of our 111-248-1 model. Since we employ convolution without padding, the feature map size is progressively reduced along depth. The penultimate convolution reduces feature map from 21x21 to 3x3 by using only 22.44% pixel of input.

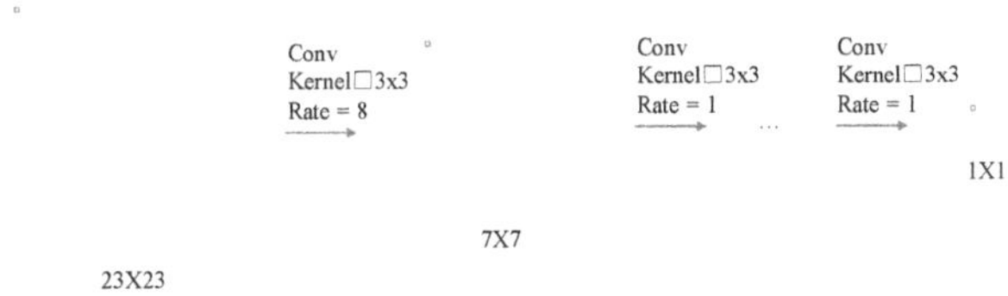

Figure 4: Top-4 layer of our 111-248-111 model. The penultimate convolution reduces feature map from 23x23 to 7x7 by taking account 83.36% field of input.

with progressively increased factors (2, 4, 8) were in charge of aggregating multi-scale contextual information. The last layer utilized standard convolution to ensure that all information of penultimate layer was encoded.

As shown in Table 3, for the network with 3x3 convolution, the receptive field was extended from 19x19 to 37x37 by a lighter network. Further, the raw CNN output result (i.e. unary result) was improved from 7.87% to 6.12% (22.24% improvement). Note that we did not give much attention on finding good combination of coarse output and smoothness. The improvement of optimized result became slighter (from 3.75% to 3.68%, 1.9% improvement). For the network with 5x5 convolution, we could also find that our model benefited from a larger field of view, decreasing the unary error rate by 27.96% (from 7.26% to 5.23%) and the optimized error rate by 10.96% (from 4.29% to 3.82%).

5.3 Comparison between atrous convolutional network architectures

Simply using the common (2, 4, 8) rates setting did not produce expected performance, especially for the optimized result. It could be primarily due to two factors: 1) the gridding effect[22] caused by equal rates or exponential increasing rates in consecutive layer that results in wrong or useless context aggregation. 2) the large proportion of information loss in top layers due to large atrous rate and small feature map size on top layers. More details are shown in Figure3. In penultimate layer, only 22.45% of input pixel participate the last convolution.

Atrous rate assignment

We proposed different atrous convolutional networks with different rates setting to tackle the aforementioned problems. Differing from most atrous CNNs for Semantic Segmentation that exploit ResNet[5] as basic model, we used simple stacked CNNs. In particular, we restricted us on 9-layer convolutional network with 3x3 kernel size. Moreover, we used hierarchical rates setting in consecutive layers to acquire rich hierarchical features. Our proposed architectures are as follows:

111-248-111 model: We first simply added two layers on top of our previous model (111-248-1) to move the large rate convolution backward. In this case, the convolution with $rate = 8$ employs 83.36% pixels of input, as shown in Figure 4.

122-242-221 model: Inspired by[25], we set progressively lower rates on top layers of CNNs to reduce the gridding problem, resulting in the 122-242-221 model.

11-125-125-1 model: Another solution for removing gridding effect is the hybrid dilated convolution (HDC) proposed by [22], which proposed (1, 2, 3), (1, 2, 5) rates relation within a convolutional group (e.g. ResNet block[5]). The goal of HDC is to let the final size of the receptive field fully covers a square region without any holes or missing edges. Motivated by their work, we proposed 11-125-125-1 model.

111-41-41-41 model: As the gridding effect caused by large rate difference in top layers, we therefore proposed to simply insert standard convolution after every atrous convolution operation in order to regularize the small participation problem. The correspondent model is 111-41-41-41.

Table 4 shows the comparison of above atrous convolutional networks's performane on KITTI 2015 validation set. The proposed frameworks variously improved the basic model (111-248-1) and outperformed the baseline model[12]. Moreover, comparing with the baseline, the proposed models took almost the same run time

Models	Kernel	Rates	Unary	Optimized	Inference time(s)	Inference Memory(Mb)
Baseline-re-imp(19)	3x3	111-111-111	7.87	3.75	0.1395	6437
Our(37)	3x3	111-248-1	6.12	3.68	0.1380	6381
Our(37)	3x3	122-242-221	6.20	3.60	0.1396	6601
Our(37)	3x3	111-41-41-41	5.90	3.60	0.1397	7567
Our(39)	3x3	11-125-125-1	**5.45**	**3.38**	0.1389	7623
Our(41)	3x3	111-248-111	5.99	3.45	0.1402	6479

Table 4: Comparison of different atrous convolutional architectures. The table illustrates the non-occluded 3 pixel error, inference time and inference memory on KITTI 2015 validation set.

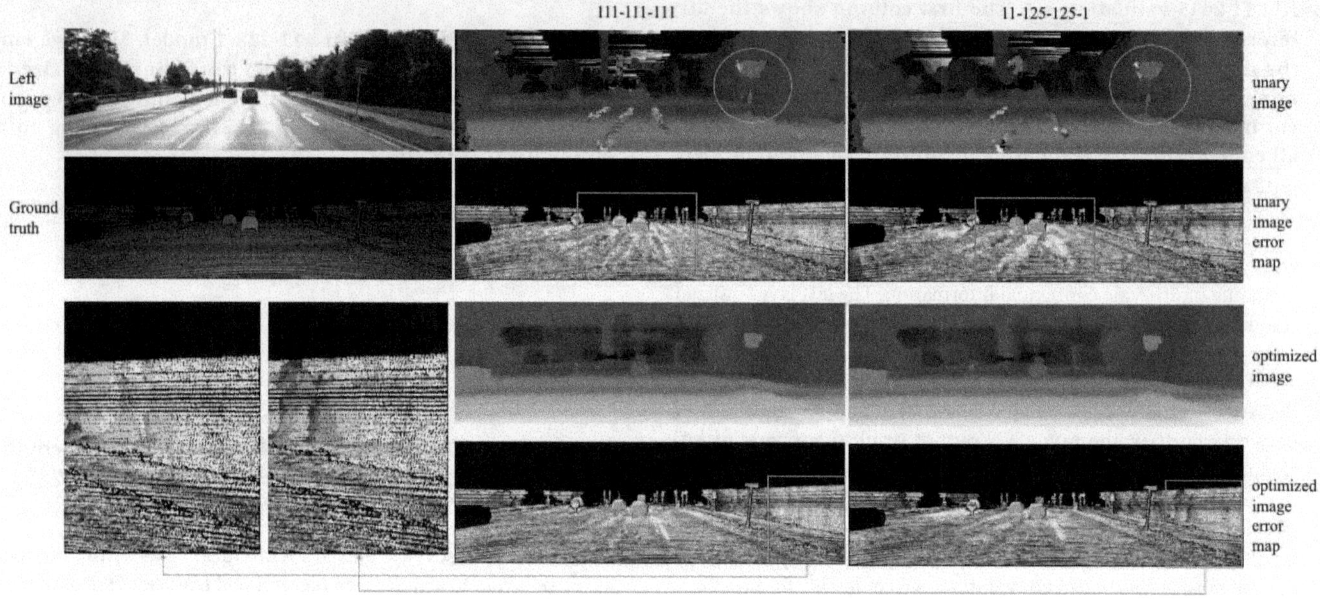

Figure 5: Qualitative result: The error map uses the log-color scale described in [14], depicting correct estimates (<3px or <5% error) in blue and wrong estimates in red color tones. Dark regions in the error images denote the occluded pixels which fall outside the image boundaries.

Models	Kernel	Rates	Unary	Optimized
Our(37)	3x3	122-242-221	6.20	3.60
Our(93)	3x3	124-8‘16’8-421	7.14	4.81
Our(37)	3x3	111-41-41-41	5.90	3.60
Our(61)	3x3	111-81-81-81	**5.55**	3.80
Our(41)	3x3	111-248-111	5.99	**3.45**
Our(93)	3x3	111-248-‘16’11	5.86	3.80

Table 5: Comparison of our architectures with different receptive fields. The table illustrates the non-occluded 3-pixel error on KITTI 2015 validation set. We enlarged receptive field of previous models by using large rates. For instance, 122-242-221 model and 124-8‘16’8-421 model employ the same architecture inspired by [25]. The later takes a larger field of view (93x93) but produces worse performance.

and only a bit more memory in inference procedure. Note that they took nearly equal field of view. Among all proposed models, HDC architecture produced the best performance by acquiring a 5.45% unary error rate and a 3.38% optimized error rate on KITTI 2015 validation dataset.

Further, the qualitative result of 11-125-125-1 model is shown in Figure 5. We observed that our proposed model brought the following improvements: 1) Generating purer unary disparity map since the large receptive field helps to remove isolate prediction, as shown in first row of Figure 5. 2) Improving performance on textureless region and repetitive-pattern region, both in unary result and optimized result, as shown in second and fourth row in Figure 5.

In addition, we found that the post processing was in some way harmful for the prediction. An example is shown in Figure 6. The optimized methods failed in depth discontinuity region, resulting in increasing error rate. In addition, we noticed that our model suffered more when there was a tiny object (the circle regions in the Figure 5) and there was no enough contextual information around the object. However, once there was enough contextual information around pixel, our model could perform better by taking a large receptive field (the rectangle regions in the Figure 5).

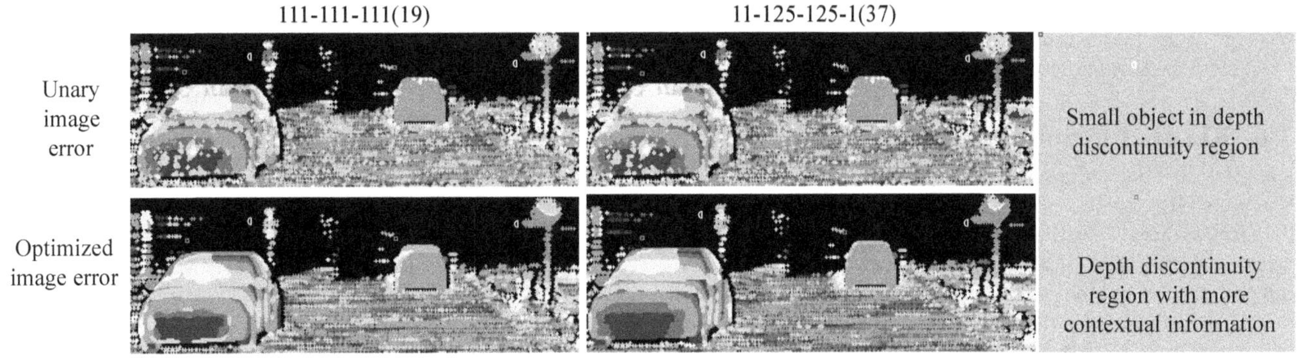

Figure 6: Models' performance in depth discontinuity region, comparing with the baseline, the HDC model performs better on regions where there is more context, but worse on tiny objects.

	All / All			All / Est			Noc / All			Noc / Est			
Error	**D1-bg**	**D1-fg**	**D1-all**	**D1-bg**	**D1-fg**	**D1-all**	**D1-bg**	**D1-fg**	**D1-all**	**D1-bg**	**D1-fg**	**D1-all**	**Runtime**
MC-CNN-acrt[29]	2.89 %	8.88 %	3.89 %	2.89 %	8.88 %	3.88 %	2.48 %	7.64 %	3.33 %	2.48 %	7.64 %	3.33 %	76s
Content-CNN[12]	3.73 %	8.58 %	4.54 %	3.73 %	8.58 %	4.54 %	3.32 %	7.44 %	4.00 %	3.32 %	7.44 %	4.00 %	**0.12s**
L-ResMatch[21]	2.72 %	6.95 %	3.42 %	2.72 %	6.95 %	3.42 %	2.35 %	5.74 %	2.91 %	2.35 %	5.74 %	**2.91** %	48s
CNNF+SGM[30]	2.78 %	7.69 %	3.60 %	2.78 %	7.69 %	3.60 %	2.36 %	6.48 %	3.04 %	2.36 %	6.48 %	3.04 %	71s
Displets v2[3]	3.00 %	5.56 %	3.43 %	3.00 %	5.56 %	3.43 %	2.73 %	4.95 %	3.09 %	2.72 %	4.95 %	3.09 %	265s
PBCP[19]	2.58 %	8.74 %	3.61 %	2.58 %	8.74 %	3.60 %	2.27 %	7.71 %	3.17 %	2.27 %	7.71 %	3.17 %	68s
SGM-Net[20]	2.66 %	8.64 %	3.66 %	2.66 %	8.64 %	3.66 %	2.23 %	7.44 %	3.09 %	2.23 %	7.43 %	3.09 %	67s
our(11-125-125-1)	3.73 %	9.83 %	4.75 %	3.72 %	9.83 %	4.74 %	3.33 %	8.79 %	4.23 %	3.32 %	8.79 %	4.23 %	**0.14s**

Table 6: Comparison with the state of the art that focus on matching cost learning (thus not end-to-end methods) on the test set of KITTI 2015 benchmark.

Figure 7: Qualitative result on KITTI 2015 test set: original left image (left), disparity image (middle), disparity error map (right)

Receptive field

Further, we tested models with larger receptive fields. However, we found that enlarging the receptive field do not always produce better result. Since the layer number of our model is bound to 9, enlarging the field of view requires larger atrous rate. The aforementioned problems could occur again in those models, thus resulting in a relatively worse performance. Finally, the HDC model (11-125-125-1) acquired the best performance on KITTI 2015 validation set.

5.4 KITTI 2015 online test result

We also tested our proposed model on KITTI online benchmark. Using the HDC model, followed by fewer post-processing steps than the baseline[12] (without using the Slanted Plane method), we achieved a comparable result both in efficiency and accuracy. The test performance and comparison with the state of the art are shown in Table 6. Unexpectedly, the baseline performed slightly better for foreground pixel. Note that we tested on totally 200 images online. It is possible that the tiny object, for which our model suffered from accuracy loss after post processing, occupies a larger part of foreground pixels. The qualitative result is shown in Figure 7.

6 CONCLUSIONS

For the task of dense stereo correspondence, it is vital to take account of both the contextual information and the local variance. However, it is difficult for the standard CNNs to balance them. We have proved that the atrous convolution, a powerful tool that allows us to enlarge the receptive field and to extract hierarchical features, could offer a good trade-off between them. Our experiment results have shown that it could help to improve matching cost computation. Further, we investigated that with large field of view, our proposed model suffers less from textureless regions and repetitive areas. Finally, we evaluated our model on KITTI 2015 benchmark and achieved a comparable result both in accuracy and efficiency.

REFERENCES

[1] Liang-Chieh Chen, George Papandreou, Iasonas Kokkinos, Kevin Murphy, and Alan L Yuille. 2018. Deeplab: Semantic image segmentation with deep convolutional nets, atrous convolution, and fully connected crfs. *IEEE transactions on pattern analysis and machine intelligence* 40, 4 (2018), 834–848.

[2] Liang-Chieh Chen, George Papandreou, Florian Schroff, and Hartwig Adam. 2017. Rethinking atrous convolution for semantic image segmentation. *arXiv preprint arXiv:1706.05587* (2017).

[3] Fatma Guney and Andreas Geiger. 2015. Displets: Resolving stereo ambiguities using object knowledge. In *Proceedings of the IEEE Conference on Computer Vision and Pattern Recognition.* 4165–4175.

[4] Xufeng Han, Thomas Leung, Yangqing Jia, Rahul Sukthankar, and Alexander C Berg. 2015. Matchnet: Unifying feature and metric learning for patch-based matching. In *Proceedings of the IEEE Conference on Computer Vision and Pattern Recognition.* 3279–3286.

[5] Kaiming He, Xiangyu Zhang, Shaoqing Ren, and Jian Sun. 2016. Deep residual learning for image recognition. In *Proceedings of the IEEE conference on computer vision and pattern recognition.* 770–778.

[6] Heiko Hirschmuller. 2005. Accurate and efficient stereo processing by semi-global matching and mutual information. In *Computer Vision and Pattern Recognition, 2005. CVPR 2005. IEEE Computer Society Conference on*, Vol. 2. IEEE, 807–814.

[7] Alex Kendall, Hayk Martirosyan, Saumitro Dasgupta, Peter Henry, Ryan Kennedy, Abraham Bachrach, and Adam Bry. 2017. End-to-End Learning of Geometry and Context for Deep Stereo Regression. *arXiv preprint arXiv:1703.04309* (2017).

[8] Diederik P Kingma and Jimmy Ba. 2014. Adam: A method for stochastic optimization. *arXiv preprint arXiv:1412.6980* (2014).

[9] Patrick Knöbelreiter, Christian Reinbacher, Alexander Shekhovtsov, and Thomas Pock. 2016. End-to-End Training of Hybrid CNN-CRF Models for Stereo. *arXiv preprint arXiv:1611.10229* (2016).

[10] Lubor Ladický, Paul Sturgess, Chris Russell, Sunando Sengupta, Yalin Bastanlar, William Clocksin, and Philip HS Torr. 2012. Joint optimization for object class segmentation and dense stereo reconstruction. *International Journal of Computer Vision* 100, 2 (2012), 122–133.

[11] Xiao Liu, Ye Luo, Yu Ye, and Jianwei Lu. 2017. MC-DCNN: Dilated Convolutional Neural Network for Computing Stereo Matching Cost. (2017).

[12] Wenjie Luo, Alexander G Schwing, and Raquel Urtasun. 2016. Efficient deep learning for stereo matching. In *Proceedings of the IEEE Conference on Computer Vision and Pattern Recognition.* 5695–5703.

[13] Nikolaus Mayer, Eddy Ilg, Philipp Hausser, Philipp Fischer, Daniel Cremers, Alexey Dosovitskiy, and Thomas Brox. 2016. A large dataset to train convolutional networks for disparity, optical flow, and scene flow estimation. In *Proceedings of the IEEE Conference on Computer Vision and Pattern Recognition.* 4040–4048.

[14] Moritz Menze and Andreas Geiger. 2015. Object Scene Flow for Autonomous Vehicles. In *Conference on Computer Vision and Pattern Recognition (CVPR).*

[15] Moritz Menze, Christian Heipke, and Andreas Geiger. 2015. Joint 3D Estimation of Vehicles and Scene Flow. In *ISPRS Workshop on Image Sequence Analysis (ISA).*

[16] Jiahao Pang, Wenxiu Sun, JS Ren, Chengxi Yang, and Qiong Yan. 2017. Cascade residual learning: A two-stage convolutional neural network for stereo matching. In *International Conf. on Computer Vision-Workshop on Geometry Meets Deep Learning (ICCVW 2017)*, Vol. 3.

[17] Daniel Scharstein, Heiko Hirschmüller, York Kitajima, Greg Krathwohl, Nera Nešić, Xi Wang, and Porter Westling. 2014. High-resolution stereo datasets with subpixel-accurate ground truth. In *German Conference on Pattern Recognition.* Springer, 31–42.

[18] Daniel Scharstein and Richard Szeliski. 2002. A taxonomy and evaluation of dense two-frame stereo correspondence algorithms. *International journal of computer vision* 47, 1-3 (2002), 7–42.

[19] Akihito Seki and Marc Pollefeys. 2016. Patch Based Confidence Prediction for Dense Disparity Map.. In *BMVC.*

[20] Akihito Seki and Marc Pollefeys. 2017. Sgm-nets: Semi-global matching with neural networks. In *Proceedings of the 2017 IEEE Conference on Computer Vision and Pattern Recognition Workshops (CVPRW), Honolulu, HI, USA.* 21–26.

[21] Amit Shaked and Lior Wolf. 2016. Improved Stereo Matching with Constant Highway Networks and Reflective Confidence Learning. *arXiv preprint arXiv:1701.00165* (2016).

[22] Panqu Wang, Pengfei Chen, Ye Yuan, Ding Liu, Zehua Huang, Xiaodi Hou, and Garrison Cottrell. 2017. Understanding convolution for semantic segmentation. *arXiv preprint arXiv:1702.08502* (2017).

[23] Koichiro Yamaguchi, David McAllester, and Raquel Urtasun. 2014. Efficient joint segmentation, occlusion labeling, stereo and flow estimation. In *European Conference on Computer Vision.* Springer, 756–771.

[24] Fisher Yu and Vladlen Koltun. 2015. Multi-scale context aggregation by dilated convolutions. *arXiv preprint arXiv:1511.07122* (2015).

[25] Fisher Yu, Vladlen Koltun, and Thomas Funkhouser. 2017. Dilated residual networks. In *Computer Vision and Pattern Recognition*, Vol. 1.

[26] Lidong Yu, Yucheng Wang, Yuwei Wu, and Yunde Jia. 2018. Deep Stereo Matching with Explicit Cost Aggregation Sub-Architecture. *arXiv preprint arXiv:1801.04065* (2018).

[27] Sergey Zagoruyko and Nikos Komodakis. 2015. Learning to compare image patches via convolutional neural networks. In *Proceedings of the IEEE Conference on Computer Vision and Pattern Recognition.* 4353–4361.

[28] Jure Zbontar and Yann LeCun. 2015. Computing the stereo matching cost with a convolutional neural network. In *Proceedings of the IEEE Conference on Computer Vision and Pattern Recognition.* 1592–1599.

[29] Jure Zbontar and Yann LeCun. 2016. Stereo matching by training a convolutional neural network to compare image patches. *Journal of Machine Learning Research* 17, 1-32 (2016), 2.

[30] Feihu Zhang and Benjamin W Wah. 2018. Fundamental Principles on Learning New Features for Effective Dense Matching. *IEEE Transactions on Image Processing* 27, 2 (2018), 822–836.

Personal Basketball Coach: Tactic Training through Wireless Virtual Reality

Wan-Lun Tsai
Dept. of Computer Science and Information Engineering, National Cheng Kung University, Taiwan
lookoutking@mislab.csie.ncku.edu.tw

ABSTRACT

In this paper, we present a basketball tactic training framework with the aid of virtual reality (VR) technology to improve the effectiveness and experience of tactic learning. Our proposal is composed of **1)** a wireless VR interaction system with motion capture devices which is applicable in the fast movement basketball running scenario; **2)** a computing server that generates three-dimensional virtual players, defenders, and advantageous tactics guide. By the assistance of our VR training system, the user can vividly experience how the tactics are executed by viewing from the a specific player's viewing direction. Moreover, the basketball tactic movement guidance and virtual defenders are rendered in our VR system to make the users feel like playing in a real basketball game, which improves the efficiency and effectiveness of tactics training.

CCS CONCEPTS

• **Computing methodologies** → **Virtual reality**; • **Human-centered computing** → *User interface programming*;

KEYWORDS

virtual reality, basketball tactics, streaming technology, motion capture, sports, training

ACM Reference Format:
Wan-Lun Tsai. 2018. Personal Basketball Coach: Tactic Training through Wireless Virtual Reality. In *ICMR '18: 2018 International Conference on Multimedia Retrieval, June 11–14, 2018, Yokohama, Japan,* Jennifer B. Sartor, Theo D'Hondt, and Wolfgang De Meuter (Eds.). ACM, New York, NY, USA, 4 pages. https://doi.org/10.1145/3206025.3206084

1 INTRODUCTION

In recent years, virtual reality (VR) technology has been widely applied to sports training. Compared with training in the real world, VR-based training offers a fully controllable environment, allowing feasible training systems to help athletes improve skills for playing in high-pressure situations. For example, in the virtual circumstance, trainees can interact with simulated opponents which are controlled by the coaches. With the tracking of the head mount display (HMD) and trainees' pose, coaches can monitor and analyze players' behavior while training in the designed virtual scenario.

ICMR '18, June 11–14, 2018, Yokohama, Japan

ACM ISBN 978-1-4503-5046-4/18/06...$15.00
https://doi.org/10.1145/3206025.3206084

Tactic training is important for training a basketball team. If players of the basketball team are unfamiliar with target tactic(s), it will be very difficult for them to realize/practice tactic(s) correctly. More importantly, the timing of running, ball-passing, and exact motion of pump fake or cross entry have a great influence on the successful execution of tactics.

This thesis proposes to improve the training effectiveness of conventional basketball tactic training through the use of VR technology. We would like to build a wireless VR interaction system for the fast movement training scenario. Take the advantage of the controllability of the virtual scene, it can provide additional guide, and quickly adapt to various competitive situations. Besides, applying motion sensors during the training procedure can analyze the trainees' body pose and offer correct motion hints (e.g. pump fake or ball-passing).

2 STATE OF THE ART

Previous studies have discussed the applications of using VR technology in sports training. Bideau *et al.* [6] introduced a framework using motion analysis to better understand athlete's performance from a behavioral-neuroscience perspective. Some advantages over video playback training were proposed; however, VR training can provide more immersive experience to the trainees. Moreover, VR training is more systematically controllable and easy for the trainer(s) to analyze the behaviors of the trainees. Miles *et al.*[24] and Klemish *et al.*[16] gave reviews of current approaches and tools that help to train the vision of player(s).

Both psychology and physical skills improvement with highly immersive VR sports training systems have been discussed. There are some researches investigated VR training programs dealing with pressure or anxiety management. Wellner *et al.* [32] explored the influence of virtual audience and opponents during a competitive boat rowing game in a CAVE virtual environment. Stinson *et al.* [29] developed a virtual soccer goalkeeping application in a CAVE-like display system to investigate the feasibility and usefulness of using VR for sport psychology training. Argelaguet *et al.*[4] proposed a framework to design the virtual environment with competitive anxiety and pressure similar to the ones athletes would face in the real world. With this high-fidelity VR systems, realistic 3D environments can induce anxiety, which is a prerequisite for the athletes to prepare for real-world, high-pressure situations.

Simulated VR environment has been widely used in the improvement of physical and perceptual motor skills in sports training. Covaci *et al.* [9] designed a VR system for basketball free-throw training, whereas Hung *et al.* [14] analyzed the movements of the rugby defender under different conditions in CAVE-like VR environment and performed a training for the athletes to identify the optimal receiver to pass the ball to on each play. Kulpa *et al.*

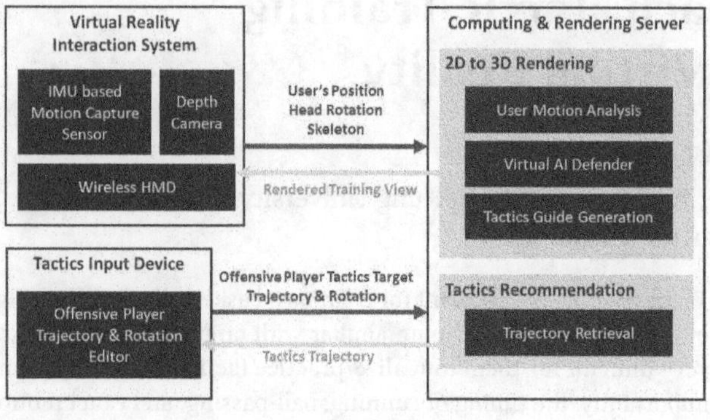

Figure 1: System Framework.

[17] investigated the player performance differences by using VR technology, such as finding the dissimilarity of the reaction time between the beginner and expert in rugby when facing a defender with and without deceptive movements in VR environment.

Some companies, such as StriVR Labs [18] and Eon Sports [28], have recently developed commercial sport-specific training systems. They provide prerecorded 360° videos of baseball, basketball, football, and hockey to simulate real world competition, and utilize HMD to allow the trainees to learn from the same vantage point which they are interested in. In comparison with computer-generated virtual training circumstances, prerecorded real game 360° videos will be limited by the content of record videos since extra information or training situations can not be real-time modified by the trainers.

Motion capture have been widely used in the field of sport training. Various mature techniques have been developed to do human motion tracking and analysis. Field *et al.*[12] gave a review on several major techniques. These approaches such as optical solution with markers[20, 25], markerless image-based method[8, 27], and Inertial Measurement Unit (IMU) sensing are distinct according to different applications. Optical motion capture system has high accuracy but restricts the user to small environment. Additionally, it suffers from motion occlusions and lacks portability to set up multi-camera system. By contrast, IMU-based body motion capture is composed of miniature, portable, and low-cost sensors. It has relatively good accuracy and high capability of capturing the user's movements in a large working space. Some commercial IMU-based motion capture devices, such as Xsens MVN suits[26] and Perception Neuron by Noitom[19] have been produced for orientation-based motion tracking. However, serious drift error[21] would show up over long-term measurements since it integrates noise over time. A couple of previous researches[5, 11] proposed frameworks of fusing depth camera information (such as skeleton information sensed by Microsoft Kinect) and signals acquired by inertial sensors to give more accurate estimations. Also, some kinematic models with biomechanical constraints of the joint[3, 23] were exploited for the sake of improving the accuracy of body segment estimation.

3 PRE-STUDY

To understand the training procedure and the practicability of using conventional physical basketball tactic board (BTB) to convey basketball tactics between the coach and player, we conducted interviews with trainees who have been trained by using conventional physical BTB.

3.1 Design and Procedure

12 subjects (4 females, 8 males), playing basketball for 8 years in average were invited to participate in the face-to-face interviews. The interview started with querying some basic information (gender, years of playing basketball, offensive position). Each interview lasted about 10 minutes and each participant was asked to repeat the tactic immediately after we taught them through a conventional physical BTB. Three kinds of tactics (from entry-level to advanced-level) were taught by a coach and repeated by the participant. Moreover, we inquired participants the following questions : *[Q1] What obstacles did they encounter while being trained with a conventional physical BTB? [Q2] How many times of explanations do you need to understand the advanced-level tactic well? [Q3] What kinds of presentation do you think could help you be familiar with the tactics more easily?*

3.2 Result and Discussion

[Q1] What obstacles did they encounter while being trained with a conventional physical BTB?

Five main comments were proposed by most of the subjects. (1) If the tactic has too many steps, it would be hard for player to remember every detail. (2) It doesn't have any marker on the conventional physical BTB's player for the user to distinguish different offensive positions. For example, number one stands for the point guard player and five for the center position. (3) If the coach moves more than one offensive players on the board at the same time, the trainee would be confused with the running path. (4) While the players are learning tactics, most players will only focus on the movement or offensive action of their own position. Therefore, the way of describing the tactics should differ according to the offensive position. (5) It is difficult for the trainee to learn the timing of running with tactics board, and learning by actually practicing on the court is essential.

[Q2] How many times of explanations do you need to understand the advanced-level tactic well?

Most of the subjects think they could get the key points of a advanced-level tactic after 2 to 3 times of illustrations. Only subject 12 said it takes 5 to 6 times to be familiar with the advanced-level tactic due to the lack of basketball playing experience.

[Q3] In your opinion, what kinds of presentation could help you be familiar with the tactics more easily?

Most common answers are (1) Auxiliary video with proper guidance. (2) Displaying defensive player on the board. (3) Actual practice on the court with enough training players. (4) Visualizing the tactics board by making the player marker more representative.

The participants proposed severals problems, e.g., the uncertainty of running path, the ambiguity of timing for running or ball-passing, and the assistant's lack of proper instructions on teaching the participant with the tactic(s). All of the participants showed incapability to successfully repeat the advanced-level tactic, which requires multiple players to move simultaneously with complexity. However, many subjects argued that watching an understandable tactic video (e.g. recording the tactic execution process performed by real players) or actual practice on the court can greatly improve the training effectiveness.

4 PROPOSED APPROACHES

According to feedbacks from the pre-study, we found that the main problem in recent training scenario using conventional BTB is the limited information expressed by the conventional BTB, which makes it difficult for the trainees to thoroughly understand important aspects, such as the timing of running and confusing running paths for multiple player movements. Also, many subjects stated that actual practice on the court can make them understand the target tactic in a more helpful way. Therefore, we propose a framework that takes the advantage of the high-fidelity in virtual reality to improve the training effectiveness in basketball tactic training even when there are players within a basketball team unfamiliar with the target tactic .

The proposed framework consists of three main components. A tactics input device is required for the user to input target training tactics (section 4.1). To provide a real-time interactive training process, a wireless streaming virtual reality system with human motion tracking technology is presented in section 4.2. Last but not least, a computing and rendering server (section 4.3) is constructed to integrate the information for rendering the VR content and analyzing player motion. Furthermore, tactics recommendation via 2D trajectory retrieval is achieved in the server and the recommendation results will be displayed on the tactic input device.

4.1 Tactics Input

Compared with conventional physical BTB, electronic tactics board can provide more comprehensive assistance for tactic training. On the 2D tactics input device, such as electronic tablet tactic board, users can input players' offensive trajectories and orientations for target tactic. In addition, accuracy of the timing for running and ball-passing is one of the important parts for a successful execution of a basketball tactic. Users are able to modify each player's travel time intuitively, especially when multiple players have to move simultaneously, on the electronic BTB. Take the advantage of memorizing tactics, electronic BTB allows the user to access a target tactic easily and learn it effectively even without a coach.

4.2 Virtual Reality Interaction System

4.2.1 Human Body Motion Capture. Inertial measurement units (IMUs) uses three-axis gyroscopes, three-axis accelerometers and three-axis magnetometers to measure acceleration, angular rate and the magnetic field vector in their own 3D local coordinate system. By integrating the gyroscope's angular velocity data over time, the relative change in angle could be found. The accelerometer data could be integrated once to get velocity and twice to get position information, which could be combined with magnetometers data and integrated angular velocity to estimate the orientation of each body part.

According to [26], some calibration postures must be performed in advance owing to the identification of the sensor-to-body-segment orientations, which makes a major contribution to the quality of IMU-based joint angle measurements and body alignment. The data obtained from different sensors are then fused by sensor fusion algorithms, for example, direct cosine matrix (DCM)[1, 2], to obtain the orientation and relative position. This approach can accurately track person's posture locally but suffers from global drift over time. The drift accumulates due to the integration of data, which makes it impossible to position accurately. To eliminate the effect of drift, low drift data, such as camera capture information, should be used. Microsoft Kinect is a depth camera which consists of an RGB camera, infrared emitter and infrared camera for depth sensing. With the combination of depth information captured by Kinect and orientations captured by IMUs, the interaction system can capture accurate user's full body pose and track the position within the training area.

4.2.2 Wireless Streaming HMD. Free movement is necessary for the trainees to perform tactics in the training area. Streaming technology is the main approach to remove the limitation of transmission cable between computer and the HMD. To offer users fully immersive experiences, low-latency and high-throughput capabilities are needed to handle the demands of VR content and make the human brain perceive the virtual environment as real as possible.

4.3 Computing and Rendering Server

The high performance computing server is in charge of trajectory and motion analysis. Based on the target tactic trajectory obtained from the input device, the computing server establishes three-dimensional virtual training scene with players running on the virtual court. Virtual defenders with artificial intelligence will also be generated to make the training more realistic. In addition, the trainees could compete with defenders having different defensive strengths to make the training more effective.

When the user learns tactics with the virtual reality system, the information such as the user's trajectory, head pose, and skeleton will be sent to the computing server. With the user's interaction data, the server will supply proper tactics guidance to the trainees. In general cases, while the trainee is moving without the ball, he/she should keep the eye on the ball holder. If the user's head pose is not on the right orientation, there will be a guide showing up to lead the user. Besides, offensive aggressiveness and fake move are important parts of a successful tactic execution. Benefited by the IMU-based human motion capture device, user's incorrect movements could be detected by motion analysis. The guidance will give proper motion hints to remind the user to perform fake action or ball-passing. Also, the target trajectory is rendered on the virtual court to show the exact path trainees should go.

Another task achieves on the computing server is trajectory retrieval for tactics recommendation. Many algorithms [22] have been proposed to calculate the similarity between two trajectories, such as Edit distance on real sequences (EDR)[7] and Dynamic Time Warping (DTW)[15]. By applying above similarity evaluation methods between partial trajectories drawn by the user and common tactics stored in the server database, the server could facilitate the user to quickly search for the desired tactic, which is convenient for being used in the time-out(s) of a game.

Figure 2: The recent results. 1. Training Assistant. 2. Streaming frame on the computer and smartphone. 3. User interacting with the proposed system (including Myo, multiple Kinect, and cardboard)

5 RESULTS TO DATE

This section presents a summary of some previous works which have been done or published. 1) We developed a system that combines a tablet-based tactic board application, named 2D-BTB, and a VR experiencing system [30]. Also, an experiment which measures the effectiveness of the system is reported. 2) We proposed a streaming-based virtual reality system [31] that users can have more immersive and realistic experience without the limitation of transmission cable. In this system, we utilize Myo, a wearable armband equipped with eight sEMG sensors and one IMU sensor, to measure the trajectory of hand movements and recognize the hand gestures.

6 CONCLUSION AND PLANNED WORK

We propose a framework of basketball tactics training via VR technology with human tracking, motion capture and streaming techniques. With the help of high-immersive VR interaction system and beneficial training assistants (movement guidance and virtual defender), tactic(s) training can be much more effective.

Future works will direct in the following aspects: **1)** As the high-fidelity simulation is necessary while training in the virtual court, generating smooth animation of virtual player's movement is essential. We will refer to the method presented by Holden *et al.* [10, 13], which can automatically produce high quality virtual character's motions by only inputting planned character trajectories. **2)** A motion capture system fusing IMU sensors and depth cameras will be built to meet the demand of fast movement analysis (e.g. running and jumping).

REFERENCES

[1] 2011. DCM Tutorial An introduction to orientation kinematics. www.starlino.com/dcmtutorial.html.
[2] 2011. Direction Cosine Matrix IMU: Theory. http://gentlenav.googlecode.com/files/DCMDraft2.pdf.
[3] Amin Ahmadi, Francois Destelle, David Monaghan, Kieran Moran, Noel E O'Connor, Luis Unzueta, and Maria Teresa Linaza. 2015. Human gait monitoring using body-worn inertial sensors and kinematic modelling. In *SENSORS, 2015 IEEE*. IEEE, 1–4.
[4] Ferran Argelaguet Sanz, Franck Multon, and Anatole Lécuyer. 2015. A methodology for introducing competitive anxiety and pressure in VR sports training. *Frontiers in Robotics and AI* 2 (2015), 10.
[5] Arash Atrsaei, Hassan Salarieh, and Aria Alasty. 2016. Human Arm Motion Tracking by Orientation-Based Fusion of Inertial Sensors and Kinect Using Unscented Kalman Filter. *Journal of Biomechanical Engineering* 138, 9 (2016), 091005.
[6] Benoit Bideau, Richard Kulpa, Nicolas Vignais, Sébastien Brault, Franck Multon, and Cathy Craig. 2010. Using virtual reality to analyze sports performance. *IEEE Computer Graphics and Applications* 30, 2 (2010), 14–21.
[7] Lei Chen, M Tamer Özsu, and Vincent Oria. 2005. Robust and fast similarity search for moving object trajectories. In *Int'l Conference on Management of Data*. ACM, 491–502.
[8] Lulu Chen, Hong Wei, and James Ferryman. 2013. A survey of human motion analysis using depth imagery. *Pattern Recognition Letters* 34, 15 (2013), 1995–2006.
[9] Alexandra Covaci, Anne-Hélène Olivier, and Franck Multon. 2015. Visual Perspective and Feedback Guidance for VR Free-Throw Training. *IEEE computer graphics and applications* 35, 5 (2015), 55–65.
[10] JUN SAITO DANIEL HOLDEN, TAKU KOMURA. 2017. Phase-Functioned Neural Networks for Character Control. In *Transactions on Graphics*. ACM.
[11] François Destelle, Amin Ahmadi, Noel E O'Connor, Kieran Moran, Anargyros Chatzitofis, Dimitrios Zarpalas, and Petros Daras. 2014. Low-cost accurate skeleton tracking based on fusion of kinect and wearable inertial sensors. In *Signal Processing Conference (EUSIPCO), 2014 Proceedings of the 22nd European*. IEEE, 371–375.
[12] Matthew Field, Zengxi Pan, David Stirling, and Fazel Naghdy. 2011. Human motion capture sensors and analysis in robotics. *Industrial Robot: An International Journal* 38, 2 (2011), 163–171.
[13] Daniel Holden, Jun Saito, and Taku Komura. 2016. A deep learning framework for character motion synthesis and editing. *ACM Transactions on Graphics (TOG)* 35, 4 (2016), 138.
[14] Huang.Y, Churches.L, and Reilly.B. 2015. A case study on virtual reality American football training. In *2015 Virtual Reality Int'l Conference*. ACM, 6.
[15] Eamonn Keogh. 2002. Exact indexing of dynamic time warping. In *28th Int'l conference on Very Large Data Bases*. VLDB Endowment, 406–417.
[16] David Klemish, Benjamin Ramger, Kelly Vittetoe, Jerome P Reiter, Surya T Tokdar, and Lawrence Gregory Appelbaum. 2017. Visual abilities distinguish pitchers from hitters in professional baseball. *Journal of Sports Sciences* (2017), 1–9.
[17] Richard Kulpa, Benoît Bideau, and Sebastien Brault. 2013. Displacements in Virtual Reality for sports performance analysis. In *Human walking in virtual environments*. Springer, 299–318.
[18] StriVR Labs. 2016. STRIVR | Immersive Training Solutions. (n.d.). http://www.strivrlabs.com/
[19] Noitom Ltd. 2017. Perception Neuron MOCAP system. https://neuronmocap.com/
[20] Vicon Motion Systems Ltd. 2016. Vicon Motion Capture. http://www.vicon.com
[21] Henk J Luinge and Peter H Veltink. 2005. Measuring orientation of human body segments using miniature gyroscopes and accelerometers. *Medical and Biological Engineering and computing* 43, 2 (2005), 273–282.
[22] Nehal Magdy, Mahmoud A Sakr, Tamer Mostafa, and Khaled El-Bahnasy. 2015. Review on trajectory similarity measures. In *Intelligent Computing and Information Systems (ICICIS), 2015 IEEE Seventh International Conference on*. IEEE, 613–619.
[23] Markus Miezal, Bertram Taetz, and Gabriele Bleser. 2016. On inertial body tracking in the presence of model calibration errors. *Sensors* 16, 7 (2016), 1132.
[24] Helen C Miles, Serban R Pop, Simon J Watt, Gavin P Lawrence, and Nigel W John. 2012. A review of virtual environments for training in ball sports. *Computers & Graphics* 36, 6 (2012), 714–726.
[25] Natural Point. 2017. OptiTrack Motion Capture. http://optitrack.com/
[26] Daniel Roetenberg, Henk Luinge, and Per Slycke. 2013. Xsens MVN: full 6DOF human motion tracking using miniature inertial sensors. (2013).
[27] Jamie Shotton, Toby Sharp, Alex Kipman, Andrew Fitzgibbon, Mark Finocchio, Andrew Blake, Mat Cook, and Richard Moore. 2013. Real-time human pose recognition in parts from single depth images. *Commun. ACM* 56, 1 (2013), 116–124.
[28] EON Sports. 2016. EON Sports VR. (n.d.). https://eonsportsvr.com/
[29] Cheryl Stinson and Doug A Bowman. 2014. Feasibility of training athletes for high-pressure situations using virtual reality. *IEEE transactions on visualization and computer graphics* 20, 4 (2014), 606–615.
[30] Wan-Lun Tsai, Ming-Fen Chung, Tse-Yu Pan, and Min-Chun Hu. 2017. Train in Virtual Court: Basketball Tactic Training via Virtual Reality. In *Proceedings of the 2017 ACM Workshop on Multimedia-based Educational and Knowledge Technologies for Personalized and Social Online Training*. 3–10.
[31] Wan-Lun Tsai, You-Lun Hsu, Chen-Yu Zhu Chi-Po Lin, Yu-Cheng Chen, and Min-Chun Hu. 2016. Immersive virtual reality with multimodal interaction and streaming technology. In *Int'l Conference on Multimodal Interaction*. ACM, 416.
[32] Mathias Wellner, Roland Sigrist, and Robert Riener. 2010. Virtual competitors influence rowers. *Presence: Teleoperators and Virtual Environments* 19, 4 (2010), 313–330.

Extracting and Using Medical Expert Knowledge to Advance in Video Processing for Gynecologic Endoscopy

Andreas Leibetseder, Klaus Schoeffmann
Institute of Information Technology
Alpen-Adria University, 9020 Klagenfurt Austria
{aleibets|ks}@itec.aau.at

ABSTRACT

Modern day endoscopic technology enables medical staff to conveniently document surgeries via recording raw treatment footage, which can be utilized for planning further proceedings, future case revisitations or even educational purposes. However, the prospect of manually perusing recorded media files constitutes a tedious additional workload on physicians' already packed timetables and therefore ultimately represents a burden rather than a benefit. The aim of this PhD project is to improve upon this situation by closely collaborating with medical experts in order to devise datasets and systems to facilitate semi-automatic post-surgical media processing.

CCS CONCEPTS

• **Applied computing** → **Health care information systems**; • **Human-centered computing** → *User studies*; • **Computing methodologies** → *Neural networks*;

KEYWORDS

endoscopy; gynecology; machine learning; interactive systems

ACM Reference Format:
Andreas Leibetseder, Klaus Schoeffmann. 2018. Extracting and Using Medical Expert Knowledge to Advance in Video Processing for Gynecologic Endoscopy. In *ICMR '18: 2018 International Conference on Multimedia Retrieval, June 11–14, 2018, Yokohama, Japan.* ACM, New York, NY, USA, 4 pages. https://doi.org/10.1145/3206025.3206082

1 MOTIVATION

Endoscopy in this day and age with good reason has become a familiar term: advanced medical technology enables this type of procedure to be applied for *minimally invasive surgery* (MIS) in order to considerably reduce patient recovery rates as well as the trauma inflicted upon them. The procedure is carried out by introducing a camera – the endoscope – together with various instruments into a body via natural apertures or artificially created incisions. Treatments are then applied via observing an external medium: typically a monitor displaying the captured video signal, serving as the "eye of the surgeon". Inherently, this process requires most equipment for recording to already be in place, therefore, it seems reasonable to videotape surgical actions, at the very least in order to retain a legal safeguard for the medical staff. In fact, archiving interventions is already commonly practiced, ever more keeping a fundamental practical benefit in mind: post-procedural documentation.

Documenting surgeries is an established administrative requirement for modern physicians and traditionally it involves creating a written report, containing little expressive media such as a few pictures at the most. Potential purposes of such a custom include briefing patients, devising treatment plans or revisiting particular cases for informational as well as educational purposes. Specifically the latter can be tedious, since on one hand relevant information must be recovered manually and on the other reports might be of poor quality, owing to the fact that physicians' tight schedules simply do not always accommodate thorough documentations.

At first glance, full surgery recordings can at least partially alleviate such problems as they certainly are complete in a sense that no information regarding the conducted procedure is missing. On the downside, manually scanning through the raw media hardly qualifies for an improvement over perusing textual documents and if nothing else merely adds to the on average 8.7 weekly hours medical doctors already spend on administrative duties [32]. Thus, none of these naive approaches, textual- or media-based, are satisfactory solutions for swiftly accessing patient information, which physicians are in dire need of, not least because of the growing amount of patients they are expected to attend [17].

As part of a larger framing project, this PhD proposition is concerned with improving upon above-mentioned deficiencies, specifically targeting the field of *gynecology*. In general, the planned thesis is aimed at both, interactively gathering data through knowledge exchange with medical experts as well as its analysis in order to create media post-processing tools capable of semi-automatic content annotation. In particular, the PhD project aims at improving post-procedural image and video analysis of gynecologic procedures performed via *laparoscopy* – a sub-discipline of endoscopy restricted to the abdominal body region. In order to develop an understanding for involved medical procedures as well as creating extensive ground truth datasets we collaborate with medical experts – more precisely including leading specialists in the field of *endometriosis*, a painful anomaly where uterine-like tissue gathers at anatomical regions it does not belong to [12]. We are intent on (i) gaining insight by gathering knowledge about semantically relevant aspects such as pathology, anatomy as well as surgical actions, (ii) determining significant similarities within the collected data via utilizing state of the art machine learning techniques and (iii) appropriately integrating related findings into media annotation tools improving physicians' patient documentation workflow as well as accelerating case revisitations.

ICMR '18, June 11–14, 2018, Yokohama, Japan

ACM ISBN 978-1-4503-5046-4/18/06...$15.00
https://doi.org/10.1145/3206025.3206082

2 RESEARCH OBJECTIVES

Starting out with limited knowledge about post-surgical procedures involving video analysis, we first address intention (i) by investigating current medical practices and compare methodologies in order to determine possible similarities. Consequently regarding (ii), system prototypes able to capture individual physician behavior as well as post-surgical documentation methods need to be employed in collaborating facilities. Data gathered this way can then be evaluated towards finding similarities between semantic annotations, data correlations among different physicians as well as similar usage patterns. Finally, in (iii) we integrate our findings into semi-automatic content analysis tools and compare their performances appropriately. Considering above basic outlines, we formulate our main topic **T**, specify definition **A** and address concrete research questions **Q1-Q5** during the course of this PhD project:

- **T** Gynecologic image and video post-processing
- **A** A fully documented video collection D includes all semantic annotations deemed relevant by a single physician. Analogously, the overall documented video collections of N physicians are described as $C = \sum_{i=1}^{N} D_i$.
- **Q1** When analyzing documented video collection D in the context of **T**, is it possible to automatically predict scenes relevant for individual physicians with reasonable precision[1]?
- **Q2** When using the entirety of video collections C in the context of **T**, how does the performance of relevance prediction change in comparison to **Q1**?
- **Q3** When reducing a video from collection D exclusively to automatic predictions, are the remaining scenes still sufficiently expressive for case analysis?
- **Q4** How can terminology and models in clinical use efficiently be mapped and integrated into appropriate annotation tools?
- **Q5** When strictly focusing on one specific gynecologic condition, is it possible to automatically determine symptoms and/or stages of progression?

3 RELATED WORK

Numerous scientific communities actively are working on distinct aspects of endoscopic video processing: pre-processing, real-time support and post-procedural applications [22]. Remarkably, the latter area of media post-processing currently is least thoroughly investigated, as opposed to tremendous research targeting similar purposes in the non-medical field [30]. While post-procedural applications can benefit from previously conducted work in other disciplines, it certainly has to be born in mind that recorded data from endoscopic procedures in most cases differs substantially from unrelated domains: the predominantly red-yellowish body-internal tissue, for example, in no way resembles the characteristic green tints of a recorded soccer match.

Improving upon interactive systems for post-procedural video analysis in the endoscopic field to a great extent involves optimizing video management and retrieval capabilities [22]. These aspects can be sub-categorized into compression and storage, retrieval, segmentation as well as summarization tasks. Although the framing project covers a broader range of facets even addressing video storage [21] and quality requirements [23], we specifically situate this work in-between the latter three categories.

The goal of gathering medical expert annotations within video collections in order to facilitate retrieving relevant scenes, i.e. particular image sequences, to the best of our knowledge has not yet been attempted. However, a few tools for enriching endoscopic videos with semantic information can be discovered. Hudelist et al. propose a tool for laparoscopic surgical quality assessment [10] that allows for annotating video sequences using established task groups as well as error definitions for rating apprentice physicians' performances. They furthermore develop another tablet-based application [9], supporting textual and hand-drawn annotations for video frames and sections for the purpose of information sharing among medical staff. Lux et al. follow a similar approach for understanding endoscopic events and provide a mobile tool [5] supporting textual notes, graphical annotations and speech recording. Albisser et al. [1] focus on supporting medical experts by developing a semi-supervised annotation tool that learns from coarsely set video frame annotations. Lastly, Liu et al. present Arthemis [18] for annotating colonoscopy videos according to the *Minimal Standard Terminology* (MST) of the *European Gastrointestinal Society for Endoscopy* (ESGE). With the exception of Lux et al. [5] presenting a conceptual model for endoscopic events, albeit resulting from a single user test, and Albisser et al. developing a machine learning based classifier predicting regions of interest [1], the tools described lack evaluations altogether, especially regarding collections of annotated data.

Segmentation in the context of this PhD project refers to the ability of automatically separating medically relevant video parts from uninteresting ones. Since the content of gynecologic videos is highly complex and changes in surgical procedures can not easily be identified using traditional video segmentation methods, the need for custom, often procedure-specific measures arises. Even otherwise well-researched tasks like simple shot-segmentation, due to the one-shot nature of endoscopic videos, must be regarded from a new angle: Primus et al. perform segmentation [27] by observing changes in motion throughout the progression of a video. They further propose another approach based on the visibility of certain surgical instruments, which works remarkably well for routine interventions like the laparoscopic cholecystectomy [28]. Lastly, various phenomena like for example the emergence of surgical smoke can be leveraged to achieve a reasonable video subdivision [15].

Although above-listed methodologies might be useful for providing a structured video overview and potentially reveal information deemed relevant by physicians, they do not discern between semantic context nor are they able to reasonably utilize documented expert knowledge in order to do so. *Machine learning* (ML) techniques, on the other hand, are perfectly suited for trying to understand such input. ML is already widely utilized in the medical field, in particular *Convolutional Neural Networks* (CNNs) presently yield promising results, as shown in [2, 33]. Nonetheless when again regarding endoscopy, research currently conducted is rather scarce. Häfner et al. use a k-nearest neighbors (k-NN) as well as Bayes classifier to classify colonic mucosa [6] and in [7] automatically detect colon cancer via pit pattern classification. Furthermore, Park et al. [25] learn hierarchical features of colonoscopic images in order to identify polyp regions, achieving an accuracy of 90%. Finally, work in parts related is proposed by Petscharnig et al. [26], who

[1] 'Reasonable precision' is subject to both quantitative evaluations as well as physicians' qualitative judgements.

train a CNN for classifying different types of laparoscopic shots portraying surgical actions and human anatomy.

Following expedient segment indication, video analysis can additionally be optimized by creating a meaningful video summarization, even further alleviating the need for time-consuming manual search and thus allowing for more focused case analyses. This especially becomes relevant for the development of practical tools, as we intend in later phases of this project. One kind of summarization is concerned with determining representative frames, aptly termed *keyframe extraction*. Regarding endoscopy, Lux et al. [20] propose an algorithm generating a single image depicting the essence of a video, which is comprised of representative frames that are determined via k-medoid clustering of color as well as texture features. Furthermore, Schoeffmann et al. [29] use Oriented FAST and Rotated BRIEF (ORB) as a descriptor, while applying an adaptive threshold in order to differentiate between frames. Keyframes extracted by these or similar methods can be visualized by interactive tools such as the one developed by Lokoč et al. [19], enabling dynamic keyframe browsing by hierarchically clustering representative images. Another option for summarizing videos is to simply remove irrelevant parts, which could be easily detectable segments like blurry or out-of-patient shots or more expressive, yet partially non-relevant sequences such as the removal of tissue following a much more significant scene. An elementary approach is presented by Leszczuk et al. [16] in the bronchoscopy domain, which combines manual video tagging with community classification techniques for determining non-relevant frames. As a third and final possibility, merging images can as well be considered a specific form of summarization: Bergen et al. [3] in a recent survey highlight the endoscopic community's prevalent interest in these techniques.

As stated throughout this section, the field of post-surgical video processing in the endoscopic domain currently is scarcely researched, yet considering the rising popularity of MIS ever more scientific interest emerges. This PhD project's contribution should, therefore, be regarded as early work towards semi-automatically finding relevance in this very specific medical domain as well as a continuation to partially related publications, such as [5], [1], [16], and [26].

4 APPROACH

Preparations for addressing research questions **Q1**, **Q2** and **Q4** require collaborative effort in both involved scientific areas: medical experts as well as computer scientists have to agree on how media should semantically be annotated and together develop the best possible preliminary tools to do so. Due to the scarcity of research in endoscopic video annotation, such applications have to be devised, tested and refined incrementally, as to maximize their practical relevance and ensure the usefulness of data resulting from utilizing the tools. For the most part, these steps are realized via in-person meetings for requirement analyses and hands-on evaluations, which yield written agreed upon strategies and requisite functionalities. Once comparable datasets for relevant frames or scenes are created by multiple physicians, the resulting video collections C (cf. Section 2) can be analyzed and evaluated in successive project phases.

Early in the data analysis phase, we aim at inspecting provided documentations for determining methodological correlations as well as differences between individual physicians. Concurrently, since relevant endoscopic scenes are highly complex, as mentioned in Section 3, sophisticated approaches in machine learning need to be employed in order to attempt automatically detecting such scenes. As presently results achieved by taking advantage of Neural Networks (NNs) seem promising, we intend on exploring and improving upon corresponding architectures. Specifically, deep NNs such as Convolutional (CNNs) [13, 31] as well as Recurrent NNs (RNNs) [4] potentially contribute to answering **Q1**, **Q2** and **Q4**. For instance, comparable relevant scenes can contain similar objects, which could be identifiable by delving into deep residual networks [8]. Combining spatial with temporal reasoning [11] might further prove beneficial for improving detection accuracies. Moreover, taking advantage of hand-drawn annotations (**Q4**) possibly allows for automatic detection of salient regions in video frames [24].

Outcomes resulting from evaluations for **Q1** and **Q2** contribute to newly devising prototypes for assessing **Q3**, while analogously we focus on results from evaluating **Q4** for building a prototype that enables the discussion of **Q5**. In utilizing such newly gained insights, besides exploring possibilities for relevance segmentation in the videos, we additionally examine and devise video summarization techniques fitting physicians needs as well as potentially serving further scientific purposes.

5 PROGRESS AND PLANNED SCHEDULE

The project framing this PhD thesis is scheduled over a period of about three years. Thus, this work is scheduled mostly within the corresponding time period with the intention of finishing both project and thesis between mid and late 2019. The first year since joining the project in April 2016 has been spent researching, defining and refining the topic and therefore setting the PhD project's goals. Besides pursuing this fundamental matter, close collaboration with medical experts on endometriosis resulted in a preliminary prototype [14] (see suppl. materials), which enables physicians to graphically as well as textually annotate said condition on selected video frames with a twofold purpose: on one hand surgeons can create more meaningful patient documentation by specifying the endometriosis severity and on the other hand they contribute to creating a proper dataset for discussing **Q5**. Additional prototypes ($P1$) for annotating relevant scenes have as well recently been deployed for our medical collaborators and we are in the process of collecting data for evaluations regarding **Q1**, **Q2** and **Q4**. Depending on the feasibility of analyzing preliminary collected data, we intend on incrementally improving $P1$ until sound studies can be conducted.

During the ongoing data collection phase, we additionally carry out studies based on annotations non-medical experts are able to produce, as to gather insights and prove our concepts. Along these lines, in [15] we investigate the feasibility of detecting the emergence of smoke in endoscopic videos (see suppl. materials), which often indicates a key point in surgical procedures, as it frequently results from critical actions such as burning tissue in order to prevent created wounds from bleeding when severing organs. Hence, indicating scenes containing smoke post-surgery could be a valuable addition to a relevance segmentation system.

Eventually, after sufficient expert-annotated datasets are available, as described above, we focus on evaluations. That is, we agree on a set of sufficiently documented relevant scenes and points of interest, which should be automatically detected with the highest possible accuracies. Exploring different machine learning approaches, we strive for getting a clear understanding of their usefulness on gynecologic events. Furthermore, at this point we cease developing *P*1 prototypes in favor of focusing on prototypes integrating our discoveries (*P*2). Besides providing a proper implementation to physicians, we intend on conducting quantitative and qualitative studies with our project partners as well as potentially interested colleagues of them within the medical community.

6 LIMITATIONS AND RISKS

Since the project is targeted at the very specific field of gynecology, it needs to born in mind that potential findings will almost exclusively contribute to said domain and, while most certainly being inapplicable to traditional surgery, it is even doubtful to employ them in related endoscopic disciplines such as inner intestinal examinations or arthroscopic interventions. This can be attributed to a variety of factors, like for example different endoscope types producing dissimilar video streams, distinct body regions lacking common features or simply applied treatments being unlike one another. Finally, as a consequence of heavily depending on medical expert annotations, the overall progression relies on close collaboration with physicians contributing to datasets that can be evaluated. Due to this restriction combined with the limited time available to these experts, the project might fail to achieve its original goals. The explicit inclusion of specialists should mitigate such risks, however, as a potential alternative strategy, the project could still yield insightful outcomes when further investigating non-expert annotations the remaining team members are able to provide.

ACKNOWLEDGMENTS

This work is supported by Universität Klagenfurt and Lakeside Labs GmbH, Klagenfurt, Austria and funding from the European Regional Development Fund and the Carinthian Economic Promotion Fund (KWF) under grant KWF 20214 u. 3520/26336/38165.

REFERENCES

[1] Z. Albisser, M. Riegler, P. Halvorsen, J. Zhou, C. Griwodz, I. Balasingham, and C. Gurrin. 2015. Expert driven semi-supervised elucidation tool for medical endoscopic videos. In *Proc. of 6th ACM Multimedia Systems Conference.* 73–76.

[2] M. Anthimopoulos, S. Christodoulidis, L. Ebner, A. Christe, and S. Mougiakakou. 2016. Lung Pattern Classification for Interstitial Lung Diseases Using a Deep Convolutional Neural Network. *IEEE TRANSACTIONS ON MEDICAL IMAGING* 35, 5 (2016). DOI: http://dx.doi.org/10.1109/TMI.2016.2535865

[3] T. Bergen and T. Wittenberg. 2016. Stitching and surface reconstruction from endoscopic image sequences: a review of applications and methods. *IEEE journal of biomedical and health informatics* 20, 1 (2016), 304–321.

[4] K. Cho, B. Van Merriënboer, C. Gulcehre, D. Bahdanau, F. Bougares, H. Schwenk, and Y. Bengio. 2014. Learning phrase representations using RNN encoder-decoder for statistical machine translation. *arXiv preprint arXiv:1406.1078* (2014).

[5] M. Guggenberger, M. Riegler, M. Lux, and P. Halvorsen. 2014. Event understanding in endoscopic surgery videos. In *Proc. of 1st ACM Intl. Workshop on Human Centered Event Understanding from Multimedia.* ACM, 17–22.

[6] M. Häfner, A. Gangl, M. Liedlgruber, A. Uhl, A. Vécsei, and F. Wrba. 2009. Combining Gaussian Markov random fields with the discretewavelet transform for endoscopic image classification. In *DSP 2009: 16th Intl. Conference on Digital Signal Processing, Proc.* DOI: http://dx.doi.org/10.1109/ICDSP.2009.5201226

[7] M. Hafner, A. Gangl, M. Liedlgruber, A. Uhl, A. Vecsei, and F. Wrba. 2010. Endoscopic Image Classification Using Edge-Based Features. In *2010 20th Intl. Conference on Pattern Recognition.* IEEE, 2724–2727.

[8] K. He, X. Zhang, S. Ren, and J. Sun. 2016. Deep residual learning for image recognition. In *IEEE Conf. on Computer Vision and Pattern Recognition.* 770–778.

[9] M. A. Hudelist, S. Kletz, and K. Schoeffmann. 2016. A Tablet Annotation Tool for Endoscopic Videos. In *Proc. of 2016 ACM on Multimedia Conference.* 725–727.

[10] M. A. Hudelist, B. Münzer, S. Kletz, K. Schoeffmann, and H. Husslein. 2017. A Tool to Support Surgical Quality Assessment. In *IEEE Proc. of Third Intl. Conference on Multimedia Big Data (BigMM).*

[11] A. Jain, A. R. Zamir, S. Savarese, and A. Saxena. 2016. Structural-RNN: Deep learning on spatio-temporal graphs. In *Proc. of IEEE Conference on Computer Vision and Pattern Recognition.* 5308–5317.

[12] J. Keckstein. 2017. Endometriosis in the Intestinal Tract – Important Facts for Diagnosis and Therapy. *coloproctology* 39, 2 (mar 2017), 121–133.

[13] A. Krizhevsky, I. Sutskever, and G. E. Hinton. 2012. ImageNet Classification with Deep Convolutional Neural Networks. In *Advances in Neural Information Processing Systems 25*, F. Pereira, C. J. C. Burges, L. Bottou, and K. Q. Weinberger (Eds.). Curran Associates, Inc., 1097–1105.

[14] A. Leibetseder, B. Münzer, K. Schoeffmann, and J. Keckstein. 2017. Endometriosis Annotation in Endoscopic Videos. In *2017 IEEE International Symposium on Multimedia (ISM).* 364–365. DOI: http://dx.doi.org/10.1109/ISM.2017.69

[15] A. Leibetseder, M. J. Primus, S. Petscharnig, and K. Schoeffmann. 2017. Real-Time Image-based Smoke Detection in Endoscopic Videos. In *Proc. of Thematic Workshops of ACM Multimedia 2017, Mountain View, CA, USA, October 23 - 27, 2017.* 296–304. DOI: http://dx.doi.org/10.1145/3126686.3126690

[16] M. I Leszczuk and M. Duplaga. 2011. Algorithm for Video Summarization of Bronchoscopy Procedures. *Biomedical engineering online* 10, 1 (2011), 110.

[17] M. Linzer, M. Gerrity, J. A. Douglas, J. E. McMurray, E. S. Williams, and T. R. Konrad. 2002. Physician stress: results from the physician worklife study. *Stress and Health* 18, 1 (2002), 37–42.

[18] D Liu, Y Cao, KH Kim, and S Stanek. 2007. Arthemis: Annotation software in an integrated capturing and analysis system for colonoscopy. *Computer methods and* (2007). DOI: http://dx.doi.org/10.1016/j.cmpb.2007.07.011

[19] J. Lokoč, K. Schoeffmann, and M. del Fabro. 2015. Dynamic hierarchical visualization of keyframes in endoscopic video. In *Intl. Conference on Multimedia Modeling.* Springer, 291–294.

[20] M. Lux, O. Marques, K. Schöffmann, L. Böszörmenyi, and G. Lajtai. 2010. A novel tool for summarization of arthroscopic videos. *Multimedia Tools and Applications* 46, 2-3 (2010), 521–544.

[21] B. Münzer, K. Schoeffmann, and L. Böszörmenyi. 2013. Improving encoding efficiency of endoscopic videos by using circle detection based border overlays. In *Multimedia and Expo Workshops (ICMEW), 2013 IEEE Intl. Conference.* 1–4.

[22] B. Münzer, K. Schoeffmann, and L. Böszörmenyi. 2017. Content-based processing and analysis of endoscopic images and videos: A survey. *Multimedia Tools and Applications* (2017), 1–40.

[23] B. Munzer, K. Schoeffmann, L. Boszormenyi, J.F. Smulders, and J. J. Jakimowicz. 2014. Investigation of the impact of compression on the perceptional quality of laparoscopic videos. In *Computer-Based Medical Systems (CBMS), 2014 IEEE 27th Intl. Symposium on.* IEEE, 153–158.

[24] J. Pan, E. Sayrol, X. Giro-i Nieto, K. McGuinness, and N. E. O'Connor. 2016. Shallow and deep convolutional networks for saliency prediction. In *Proc. of IEEE Conf. on Computer Vision and Pattern Recognition.* 598–606.

[25] S. Y. Park and D. Sargent. 2016. Colonoscopic polyp detection using convolutional neural networks, Georgia D. Tourassi and Samuel G. Armato (Eds.). Intl. Society for Optics and Photonics, 978528. DOI: http://dx.doi.org/10.1117/12.2217148

[26] S. Petscharnig and K. Schöffmann. 2017. Learning laparoscopic video shot classification for gynecological surgery. *Multimedia Tools and Applications* (2017), 1–19. DOI: http://dx.doi.org/10.1007/s11042-017-4699-5

[27] M. J. Primus, K. Schoeffmann, and L. Böszörmenyi. 2013. Segmentation of recorded endoscopic videos by detecting significant motion changes. In *Content-Based Multimedia Indexing (CBMI), 2013 11th Intl. Workshop on.* IEEE, 223–228.

[28] M. J. Primus, K. Schoeffmann, and L. Böszörmenyi. 2016. Temporal segmentation of laparoscopic videos into surgical phases. In *Content-Based Multimedia Indexing (CBMI), 2016 14th Intl. Workshop on.* IEEE, 1–6.

[29] K. Schoeffmann, M. Del Fabro, T. Szkaliczki, L. Böszörmenyi, and J. Keckstein. 2015. Keyframe extraction in endoscopic video. *Multimedia Tools and Applications* 74, 24 (2015), 11187–11206.

[30] K. Schoeffmann, M. A. Hudelist, and J. Huber. 2015. Video interaction tools: a survey of recent work. *ACM Computing Surveys (CSUR)* 48, 1 (2015), 14.

[31] C. Szegedy, W. Liu, Y. Jia, P. Sermanet, S. Reed, D. Anguelov, D. Erhan, V. Vanhoucke, and A. Rabinovich. 2015. Going deeper with convolutions. In *Proc. of IEEE Conference on Computer Vision and Pattern Recognition.* 1–9.

[32] S. Woolhandler and D. U. Himmelstein. 2014. Administrative work consumes one-sixth of US physicians' working hours and lowers their career satisfaction. *Intl. Journal of Health Services* 44, 4 (2014), 635–642.

[33] Z. Yan, Y. Zhan, Z. Peng, S. Liao, Y. Shinagawa, S. Zhang, D. N. Metaxas, and X. S. Zhou. 2016. Multi-Instance Deep Learning: Discover Discriminative Local Anatomies for Bodypart Recognition. *IEEE Transactions on Medical Imaging* 35, 5 (may 2016), 1332–1343.

Temporal Aggregation of Visual Features for Large-Scale Image-to-Video Retrieval

Noa Garcia
Aston University
Birmingham, UK
garciadn@aston.ac.uk

ABSTRACT

In this research we study the specific task of image-to-video retrieval, in which static pictures are used to find a specific timestamp or frame within a collection of videos. The inner temporal structure of video data consists of a sequence of highly correlated images or frames, commonly reproduced at rates of 24 to 30 frames per second. To perform large-scale retrieval, it is necessary to reduce the amount of data to be processed by exploiting the redundancy between these highly correlated images. In this work, we explore several techniques to aggregate visual temporal information from video data based on both standard local features and deep learning representations with the focus on the image-to-video retrieval task.

CCS CONCEPTS

• **Information systems** → **Image search**; **Video search**;

KEYWORDS

Image Retrieval, Video Retrieval, Temporal Aggregation

ACM Reference Format:

Noa Garcia. 2018. Temporal Aggregation of Visual Features for Large-Scale Image-to-Video Retrieval. In *ICMR '18: 2018 International Conference on Multimedia Retrieval, June 11–14, 2018, Yokohama, Japan.* ACM, New York, NY, USA, 4 pages. https://doi.org/10.1145/3206025.3206083

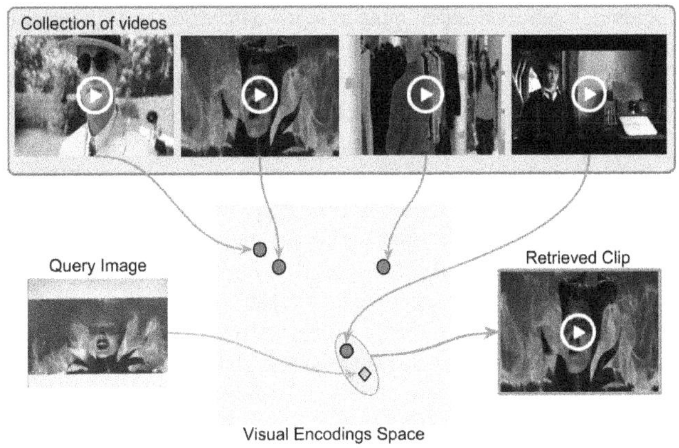

Figure 1: Image-to-video retrieval task. Using visual encodings, videos are indexed in a collection and static images are used as queries to find a specific video clip or timestamp.

1 INTRODUCTION

Billions of images and videos are generated online every day. With this amount of data publicly available, systems to access and manage multimedia content efficiently are crucial. In this context, visual search and retrieval techniques play an important role in the management of multimedia datasets. Visual multimedia retrieval systems index and find visual content in a collection of images or videos by using a query input. These systems may perform several retrieval tasks, depending on the type of data to be processed.

There exists many different kinds of multimedia retrieval tasks. For example, the well-known image retrieval task, in which a query image is used to find a picture within a collection, has been an active field of research in the computer vision community for a long time [24] and only lately, with the introduction of deep learning techniques [6] its performance has been boosted considerably [11]. Other methods for retrieving images from datasets include text-to-image retrieval [23], in which a detailed text description is provided to find the image of interest, and audio-to-image retrieval [12], in which images are retrieved based on descriptive audio tracks. Regarding video, video-to-video retrieval [18], in which video clips are found by providing a relevant video, is widely used for video copy detection, and image-to-video retrieval [4] aims to find a specific frame within a video collection from a static image.

In this work we study the specific task of image-to-video retrieval, which has not been explored as much as other multimedia retrieval tasks. Identifying a certain frame from a collection of videos (Figure 1) is a task with many applications, such as video search [2], video content augmentation [10] or video bookmark [9], among others. In contrast to image-to-image retrieval, image-to-video retrieval is an asymmetric task in which dataset items and query images require different processing algorithms. When only considering their visual content (i.e. ignoring audio tracks and metadata), videos are a sequence of consecutive images, which usually are presented at rates between 24 to 30 frames per second to fake the human brain and simulate temporal movement. This temporal structure implies that frames that are close in time are highly correlated to each other. As a consequence, most of the visual information in a video turns out to be redundant or duplicated. Large-scale image-to-video retrieval systems cannot afford to process and index all the visual data available in videos and thus, summarization methods to reduce the amount of data are required. Temporal aggregation of visual

ICMR '18, June 11–14, 2018, Yokohama, Japan

ACM ISBN 978-1-4503-5046-4/18/06...$15.00
https://doi.org/10.1145/3206025.3206083

features in videos is the technique to summarize redundant visual data in video frames into more compact representations (Figure 2). In this work, we study several temporal aggregation methods to exploit visual redundancy in video data whereas at the same time, meaningful representations for image-to-video retrieval are obtained.

2 RELATED WORK

Early work in image-to-video retrieval [16, 21] was based on applying image retreival techniques to video data. Sivic and Zisserman presented in [21] the well-known bag-of-words (BoW) algorithm by indexing video frames from two movies. Similarly, other work [9, 16] proposed to use BoW with vocabulary trees to index video frames. These methods, however, processed each video frame independently, without considering any temporal correlation between similar frames.

However, to perform large-scale image-to-video retrieval and to exploit temporal redundancy within highly correlated frames, temporal aggregation techniques are needed. Temporal aggregation techniques for image-to-video retrieval can be classified into two different groups: local features-based and global features-based. Local features-based methods [1, 5], extract a set of local features from each frame, typically a few hundred. Each visual feature is tracked along similar frames. Features in the same track are aggregated into a single feature, so the total number of visual features representing each video segment is reduced. For example, in [1] aggregated vectors are obtained by averaging SIFT [15] descriptors within the same track, whereas authors in [5] explore other methods, such as keeping one feature or computing the minimum distance.

On the other hand, global features-based temporal aggregation methods for image-to-video retrieval [4, 25] aim to encode the visual information of a video segment into a single compact vector. Zhu and Satoh [25] aggregate all the SIFT local features in a video clip into a high-dimensional BoW vector. Similarly, Araujo et al. [4] compute compact Fisher Vectors [19] per frame and aggregate them into a single binarized vector per clip.

Previous work in image-to-video retrieval is mostly based on the aggregation of hand-crafted local SIFT features. Considering the outstanding results of deep learning in other retrieval tasks (such as image-to-image [11] or text-to-image retrieval [23]), in this work we explore temporal aggregation methods based on the aggregation of other kind of features, such as local binary features [8] and deep learning visual features [6, 22].

3 PROBLEM FORMULATION

In this section, we formalize the problem of image-to-video retrieval. Considering the inner visual structure of videos, which consist on a set of standard static images known as frames, a shot is defined as a set of consecutive frames that have been captured with the same camera without interruptions.

Let's consider a set of videos $\mathbf{V} = \{\mathbf{V}_i\}_{i \in (0,..,N)}$ of size N, where each video $\mathbf{V}_i$ is at the same time a set of shots $\mathbf{V}_i = \{\mathbf{S}_{i,j}\}_{j \in (0,..,N_{V_i})}$ of size N_{V_i}, and where each shot $\mathbf{S}_{i,j}$ is at the same time a set of frames $\mathbf{S}_{i,j} = \{f_{i,j,k}\}_{k \in (0,..,N_{S_{i,j}})}$ of size $N_{S_{i,j}}$. Note that $f_{i,j,k}$ corresponds to the k-th frame of the j-th shot of the i-th video in the collection. Given a query image q, the goal is

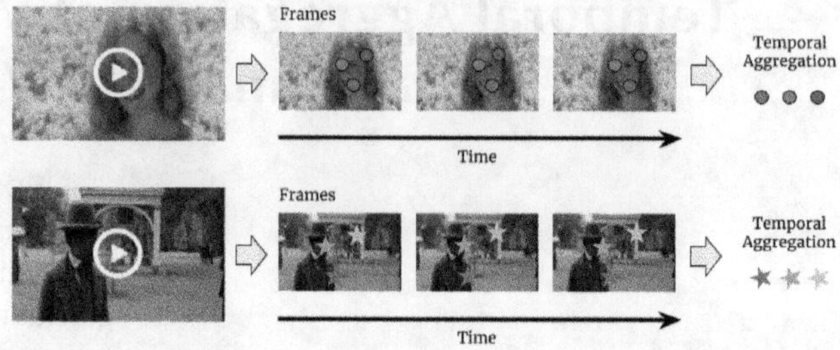

Figure 2: Visual data in video frames is encoded into visual vectors. When frames are very similar, many visual vectors are redundant. By using temporal aggregation methods, compact and meaningful representations are obtained.

to find the most similar frame $\hat{f}$, belonging to the shot $\hat{\mathbf{S}}$, according to a specific metric distance d, such as:

$$\hat{f} = \underset{f_{i,j,k} \in \mathbf{V}}{\arg\min}\, d(\phi(q), \phi(f_{i,j,k})) \tag{1}$$

where $\phi(q)$ and $\phi(f_{i,j,k})$ are the visual representations of q and $f_{i,j,k}$, respectively.

For large-scale datasets, performing a search over all frames within the collection $\mathbf{V}$ is prohibitive. To alleviate the search, two techniques are used. Firstly, the amount of visual features $\phi(f_{i,j,k})$ within a shot $\mathbf{S}_{i,j}$ is reduced by using a temporal aggregation method $\Theta(\cdot)$ over each shot:

$$\Theta(\mathbf{S}_{i,j}) = \Theta(\{\phi(f_{i,j,k})\}) \tag{2}$$

Secondly, taking advantage of the inner visual structure of videos, the search is performed in two stages: shot-level search and frame-level search. In the shot-level search, the shot of interest $\hat{\mathbf{S}}$ is found:

$$\hat{\mathbf{S}} = \underset{\mathbf{S}_{i,j} \in \mathbf{V}}{\arg\min}\, d(\phi(q), \Theta(S_{i,j})) \tag{3}$$

Finally, in the frame-level search, $\hat{f}$ is retrieved from the frames contained in $\hat{S}$:

$$\hat{f} = \underset{f_{i,j,k} \in \hat{\mathbf{S}}}{\arg\min}\, d(\phi(q), \phi(f_{i,j,k})) \tag{4}$$

In the next section, we present two different aggregation methods $\Theta(\cdot)$ to perform image-to-video retrieval for large-scale datasets.

4 OUR APPROACHES

We propose two different models to aggregate temporal redundant visual information from videos:

- Local Binary Temporal Tracking (LBTT)
- Deep Features Temporal Aggregation (DFTA)

4.1 Local Binary Temporal Tracking

LBTT method, which is detailed in [10], is based on the summarization of hand-crafted local binary features.

4.1.1 Image Representation. In LBTT, images are represented by a set of BRIEF [8] features, which encode the pixel intensity value of small image regions into 256-dimensional binary vectors.

4.1.2 Temporal Encoding. Binary features are tracked along time by matching descriptors in consecutive frames. Two descriptors are a match when the Hamming distance between them is below a threshold. Matches that are not spatially close in the pixel space are filtered. The tracking is performed in a bidirectional way so features within a track are unique (i.e. each feature can only be matched with up to two features: one in the previous frame and one in the following frame). To avoid adding noisy features, only stable tracks in time are considered.

The motivation of using binary features as the local descriptor is two-fold. Firstly, Hamming distance for matching binary features is faster to compute than Euclidean distance for matching SIFT vectors. Secondly, we find that binary features are more stable over time than SIFT (Figure 3) and hence, easier to aggregate. We define a *key feature* as the aggregation of all the features in the same track into a single vector. For each track, its key feature is computed by using majorities.

4.1.3 Shot Boundary Detection. Consecutive frames that share visual similarities are grouped into shots. The boundaries of different shots are detected when two consecutive frames have no common tracks. Subsequently, each shot is then represented by a set of key features, similarly to how frames are represented by a set of features.

4.1.4 Retrieval. At query time, BRIEF features are extracted from the query image. To find the most similar shot to the query image, for each query feature a set of nearest neighbour (NN) key features is obtained. Key features are indexed in a kd-tree so that the NN search can be performed faster. Each key feature votes for the shot it belongs to. The set of frames contained in the most voted shot are compared against the input image by brute force, i.e. distances between descriptors in the query image and descriptors in the candidate frames are computed. The frame with minimum distance is retrieved.

4.2 Deep Features Temporal Aggregation

DLTA method is based on the temporal aggregation of deep learning visual features.

4.2.1 Image Representation. In DLTA, the visual content of each frame is encoded in a RMAC [22] image vector. RMAC is a deep global image representation obtained from the last convolutional layer of a convolutional neural network (CNN). When an image is fed into the CNN, the response of each filter of the last convolutional layer is represented by a feature map. RMAC computes local features by max-pooling the activations of different regions in the feature map. Each of these local vectors is independently post-processed with $\ell 2$-normalization, PCA-whitening and $\ell 2$-normalization. Post-processed vectors are summed together and $\ell 2$-normalized one last time to obtain a single vector per image.

4.2.2 Temporal Encoding. By encoding each video segment into a single visual vector, we aim to capture as much visual information as possible whereas at the same time we reduce the amount of redundant data. So far, we study two different approaches to aggregate global RMAC vectors into a video shot representation:

- DLTA-Max: for each dimension, the shot encoding is obtained by computing the frame RMAC maximum value.

$$\Theta(\mathbf{S}_{i,j}) = maxpool(\phi(f_{i,j,k})) \tag{5}$$

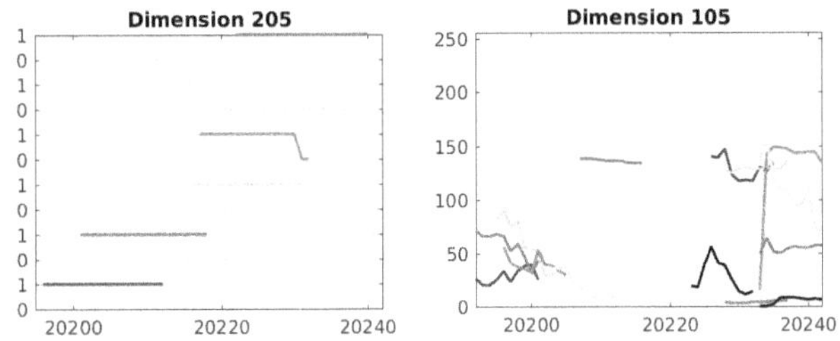

Figure 3: Trajectories of sample tracks along a sequence of frames. Left: Binary features. Right: SIFT features. Binary features are more constant over time than SIFT features.

- DLTA-Mean: the shot encoding is computed as the average of the RMAC features within the shot.

$$\Theta(\mathbf{S}_{i,j}) = \frac{1}{N_{S_{i,j}}} \sum_{k=1}^{N_{S_{i,j}}} \phi(f_{i,j,k}) \tag{6}$$

Shot boundaries are detected using the same algorithm as in §4.1.3.

4.2.3 Retrieval. For each query image, its RMAC vector is obtained. Query vector is matched against the aggregated shot encodings using cosine similarity. The shot encoding with minimum distance to the query is retrieved. Then, frame RMACs within the retrieved shot are matched against the query vector. The most similar frame according to its cosine similarity is retrieved.

5 EXPERIMENTS

5.1 Experimental Details

Dataset. We have created the MoviesDB dataset [10] to evaluate different image-to-video methods. This dataset is a collection of 40 movies with more than 80 hours of video and up to 7 million frames. Query images for retrieval are captured by a webcam while movies are being played on a screen in front of it. The frame number of each captured image is saved in a text file as a ground truth. Movies and queries have different resolutions and aspect ratios. For evaluation, as long as the retrieved frame shares strong similarities with the ground truth frame by matching SURF [7] features, it is consider a *Visual Match*. Performance is measured in terms of accuracy:

$$\text{Acc} = \frac{\text{No. Visual Matches}}{\text{Total No. Queries}} \tag{7}$$

LBTT. All the frames and images are scaled down to 720 pixels in width. When tracking binary features, only matches with a Hamming distance less than 20 and a spatial distance less than 100 pixels are considered. For computing key features, only stable tracks longer than 7 frames are used.

DLTA. Frames are resized to 1024 pixels width. Query images are resized to 960 pixels width. RMAC features are extracted using the end-to-end architecture proposed in [11] with pretrained VGG16 weights [20]. Frames are subsampled and processed at 5 fps. PCA whitening is computed using the movie *American Beauty*, which is not in the MoviesDB dataset.

Table 1: Results in *The Devil Wears Prada* from MovieDB.

	Method	Dim	Memory	N.Features	Acc
Local	IR-BRIEF	256	2.53 GB	85M	0.93
	LBTT	256	61 MB	2M	0.93
Global	IR-FC1	4096	614 MB	39,324	0.63
	IR-FC2	4096	614 MB	39,324	0.42
	IR-RMAC	512	76.8 MB	39,324	0.91
	DLTA-Max	512	3.13 MB	1,602	0.22
	DLTA-Mean	512	3.13 MB	1,602	0.69

5.2 Experimental Results

We evaluate our temporal aggregation methods in a small subset of the MoviesDB dataset. Table 1 shows the results for *The Devil Wears Prada* movie. Our aggregation methods LBTT and DLTA are compared to their corresponding image retrieval versions, IR-BRIEF and IR-RMAC, respectively (i.e. no temporal aggregation is used). IR-FC1 and IR-FC2 are image-retrieval algorithms on top of features from VGG16 network's first and second fully connected layer, respectively, which obtain significantly worst accuracy than IR-RMAC by using 8 times more memory. This indicates that features from fully connected layers may not be good enough for image-to-video retrieval, as suggested by other authors [4]. With respect to our temporal aggregation methods, LBTT achieves comparable accuracy to both IR-BRIEF and IR-RMAC by using significantly less memory. With only 3.13MB of memory, DLTA-Mean performance is slightly worst then IR-RMAC. However, DLTA-Max is clearly not capturing the visual video data according to the needs of the image-to-video retrieval task. Our temporal aggregation methods, are further compared in fours different movies in Table 1, where again, DLTA methods are not able to capture the visual video data as well as LBTT. This may suggest that either representing each shot into a single vector is not enough for image-to-video retrieval or that more complex DLTA methods are needed.

6 CONCLUSIONS AND FUTURE WORK

This research proposes temporal aggregation models of visual features for image-to-video retrieval, in which static pictures are used to find a specific frame in a video a collection. The models presented in this work are based on the aggregation of local binary features and deep learning features. The experiments conducted so far show that methods based on binary features outperform deep learning methods. As a future work, we aim to explore more complex methods to aggregate deep learning features for image-to-video retrieval task. According to other work [4], which successfully aggregates shots into single vectors using SIFT features, we believe that there is still room for improvement in the aggregation of deep learning features. So far, DLTA methods are based on the aggregation of deep features from pre-trained CNN architectures. Re-training and fine-tunning these architectures for the specific retrieval task should lead to better results [11]. As part of our work in progress, we are studying DLTA based in LSTMs [13]. However, it is still an open question whether LSTMs are able to properly encode data for image-to-video retrieval. Other methods to be considered in the future are 3D CNN [14] and temporal autoencoders [17]. We also aim to conduct experiments in the full MoviesDB dataset as well as in other image-to-video retrieval collections (SI2V [2] and VB [3]).

Table 2: Accuracy in The Devil Wears Prada, Groundhog Day, Her and Pirates of the Caribbean movies from MoviesDB.

Method	Movie1	Movie2	Movie3	Movie4
LBTT	0.93	0.97	0.76	0.80
DLTA-Max	0.22	0.16	0.18	0.12
DLTA-Mean	0.69	0.56	0.53	0.47

REFERENCES

[1] Arasanathan Anjulan and Nishan Canagarajah. 2007. Object based video retrieval with local region tracking. *Signal Processing: Image Communication* 22, 7 (2007).

[2] André Araujo, Jason Chaves, David Chen, Roland Angst, and Bernd Girod. 2015. Stanford I2V: a news video dataset for query-by-image experiments. In *ACM Multimedia Systems.*

[3] André Araujo, Jason Chaves, Haricharan Lakshman, Roland Angst, and Bernd Girod. 2016. Large-scale query-by-image video retrieval using bloom filters. *arXiv preprint arXiv:1604.07939* (2016).

[4] Andre Araujo and Bernd Girod. 2017. Large-Scale Video Retrieval Using Image Queries. *IEEE Transactions on Circuits and Systems for Video Technology* (2017).

[5] A Araujo, Mina Makar, Vijay Chandrasekhar, D Chen, S Tsai, Huizhong Chen, Roland Angst, and Bernd Girod. 2014. Efficient video search using image queries. In *ICIP.*

[6] Artem Babenko, Anton Slesarev, Alexandr Chigorin, and Victor Lempitsky. 2014. Neural codes for image retrieval. In *ECCV.*

[7] Herbert Bay, Tinne Tuytelaars, and Luc Van Gool. 2006. SURF : Speeded Up Robust Features. *ECCV* (2006), 404–417.

[8] Michael Calonder, Vincent Lepetit, Christoph Strecha, and Pascal Fua. 2010. Brief: Binary robust independent elementary features. *ECCV* (2010).

[9] David Chen, Ngai-Man Cheung, Sam Tsai, Vijay Chandrasekhar, Gabriel Takacs, Ramakrishna Vedantham, Radek Grzeszczuk, and Bernd Girod. 2010. Dynamic selection of a feature-rich query frame for mobile video retrieval. In *ICIP.*

[10] Noa Garcia and George Vogiatzis. 2017. Dress Like a Star: Retrieving Fashion Products From Videos. In *ICCV Workshops.*

[11] Albert Gordo, Jon Almazan, Jerome Revaud, and Diane Larlus. 2017. End-to-end learning of deep visual representations for image retrieval. *IJCV* 124, 2 (2017).

[12] David Harwath, Antonio Torralba, and James Glass. 2016. Unsupervised learning of spoken language with visual context. In *NIPS.*

[13] Sepp Hochreiter and Jürgen Schmidhuber. 1997. Long short-term memory. *Neural computation* 9, 8 (1997).

[14] Shuiwang Ji, Wei Xu, Ming Yang, and Kai Yu. 2013. 3D convolutional neural networks for human action recognition. *IEEE transactions on pattern analysis and machine intelligence* 35, 1 (2013), 221–231.

[15] David G Lowe. 2004. Distinctive image features from scale-invariant keypoints. *IJCV* 60, 2 (2004).

[16] David Nistér and Henrik Stewénius. 2006. Scalable recognition with a vocabulary tree. *CVPR* (2006).

[17] Viorica Patraucean, Ankur Handa, and Roberto Cipolla. 2015. Spatio-temporal video autoencoder with differentiable memory. *arXiv preprint arXiv:1511.06309* (2015).

[18] Sébastien Poullot, Shunsuke Tsukatani, Anh Phuong Nguyen, Hervé Jégou, and Shin'Ichi Satoh. 2015. Temporal matching kernel with explicit feature maps. In *ACM Multimedia.*

[19] Jorge Sánchez, Florent Perronnin, Thomas Mensink, and Jakob Verbeek. 2013. Image classification with the fisher vector: Theory and practice. *IJCV* 105, 3 (2013).

[20] Karen Simonyan and Andrew Zisserman. 2014. Very deep convolutional networks for large-scale image recognition. *CoRR* (2014).

[21] Josef Sivic and Andrew Zisserman. 2003. Video google: A text retrieval approach to object matching in videos. In *ICCV.*

[22] Giorgos Tolias, Ronan Sicre, and Hervé Jégou. 2016. Particular object retrieval with integral max-pooling of CNN activations. In *ICLR.*

[23] Liwei Wang, Yin Li, and Svetlana Lazebnik. 2016. Learning deep structure-preserving image-text embeddings. In *CVPR.*

[24] Liang Zheng, Yi Yang, and Qi Tian. 2017. SIFT meets CNN: A decade survey of instance retrieval. *TPAMI* (2017).

[25] Cai-Zhi Zhu and Shin'ichi Satoh. 2012. Large vocabulary quantization for searching instances from videos. In *ACM Multimedia Retrieval.*

Tourism Category Classification on Image Sharing Services Through Estimation of Existence of Reliable Results

Naoki Saito†, Takahiro Ogawa†, Satoshi Asamizu‡ and Miki Haseyama†
†Graduate School of Information Science and Technology, Hokkaido University, Sapporo, Hokkaido, Japan
‡National Institute of Technology, Kushiro College, Kushiro, Hokkaido, Japan
{saito,ogawa}@lmd.ist.hokudai.ac.jp,asamizu@kushiro-ct.ac.jp,miki@ist.hokudai.ac.jp

ABSTRACT

A new tourism category classification method through estimation of existence of reliable classification results is presented in this paper. The proposed method obtains two kinds of classification results by applying a convolutional neural network to tourism images and applying a Fuzzy K-nearest neighbor algorithm to geotags attached to the tourism images. Then the proposed method estimates existence of reliable classification results in the above two results. If the reliable result is included, the result is selected as the final classification result. If any reliable result is not included, the final result is obtained by another approach based on a multiple annotator logistic regression model. Consequently, the proposed method enables accurate classification based on the new estimation scheme.

KEYWORDS

Image sharing services, tourism images, tourism category classification.

ACM Reference Format:
Naoki Saito, Takahiro Ogawa, Satoshi Asamizu and Miki Haseyama. 2018. Tourism Category Classification on Image Sharing Services Through Estimation of Existence of Reliable Results. In *ICMR '18: 2018 International Conference on Multimedia Retrieval, June 11–14, 2018, Yokohama, Japan.* Yokohama, Japan , 4 pages. https://doi.org/10.1145/3206025.3206085

1 INTRODUCTION

Tourism industry is important to the economy of all countries. Tourists bring economic effects to a wide range of industries. For expansion of tourism service-related consumption, travel support applications such as travel information recommendation are required. Desired travel information differs according to each tourist, and realization of the personalized recommendation has been expected. Then this approach requires personal trends of tourism spots.

Recently, image sharing services such as Flickr[1] have been utilized for analysis of tourism information since tourists upload a huge number of tourism images to these services. Then, as a preprocessing of the above recommendation, we have proposed tourism category classification using tourism images uploaded to image sharing services for obtaining the trends of tourism spots.

The images uploaded to image sharing services usually include metadata such as textual tags and geotags [12]. Classification methods of such images using multiple features have been proposed in [6, 14, 15]. However, all of the features do not always contribute to improvement of the classification performance. For example, when one user goes sightseeing at the Trocadéro Square in Paris while another user takes a meal at the same location, it becomes difficult to correctly classify their categories. To overcome this problem, we previously proposed a tourism category classification method based on estimation of reliable results in [10]. This method obtains two kinds of classification results based on a Multiple Annotator Logistic Regression (MALR) model [9] using the tourism images and the textual tags and a Fuzzy K-Nearest Neighbor (FK-NN) algorithm [4] using the geotags. Then a reliable classification result is obtained from these two results. This estimation method performs discrimination of the classification method whether decision is correct or not by using Support Vector Machine (SVM) [1] whose input is posterior probability of categories obtained by the MALR model and the FK-NN algorithm. Consequently, we obtain the reliable classification result, and this result is selected as the final classification result of the method. However, when these two kinds of results are both incorrect, incorrect result is output as final classification result since the previous method selects the final result from these two kinds of results. To deal with this problem, we need to consider existence of reliable results in multiple classification results.

In this paper, we propose a new tourism category classification method on image sharing services through estimation of existence of reliable results. The proposed method estimates existence of reliable classification results from two kinds of results obtained by a Convolutional Neural Network (CNN) [5] using tourism images and the FK-NN algorithm using geotags attached to the tourism images. If the reliable result is included in the above two kinds of results, the result is selected as the final classification result. On the other hand, if any reliable result is not included in these results, the final result is obtained by another

[1]https://www.flickr.com/

ICMR '18, June 11–14, 2018, Yokohama, Japan

ACM ISBN 978-1-4503-5046-4/18/06...$15.00
https://doi.org/10.1145/3206025.3206085

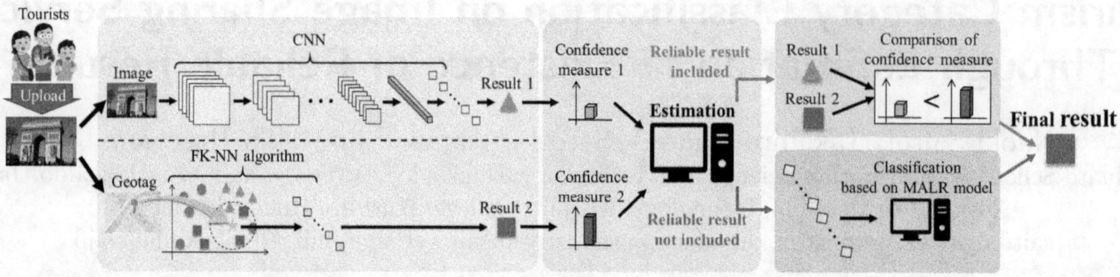

Figure 1: Overview of the proposed method. The proposed method obtains two kinds of classification results utilizing tourism images and geotag. Furthermore, the proposed method estimates the existence of reliable results in these classification results.The final classification results are adaptively decided by the estimation result.

classification approach different from the CNN and the FK-NN algorithm. The above estimation scheme utilizes a confidence measure calculated by using intermediate values from classifiers [13]. Consequently, the estimation in the proposed method solves the problem of the previous method [10].

2 TOURISM CATEGORY CLASSIFICATION METHOD

In this section, we present a tourism category classification method through estimation of existence of reliable results. An overview of the proposed method is shown in Fig. 1. First, the proposed method separately obtains two kinds of classification results based on the CNN using tourism images uploaded to the image sharing services and the FK-NN algorithm using the geotags. Second, the proposed method calculates the confidence measure of these classification results and estimates the existence of reliable results. Finally, the proposed method calculates the final classification result. When the above estimation scheme determines that the classification results include a reliable one, the proposed method selects the result with the higher confidence measure as the final classification result. On the other hand, if reliable results do not exist, the proposed method obtains the final classification result by another classification method based on the MALR model. The proposed method can apply to only images which include the geotag. To apply the proposed method to images that do not include the geotag, this method requires that predicts geotag from these images utilizing geo-coordinate prediction approaches such as an IM2GPS [3].

2.1 Classification Using Tourism Images and Geotags

For classifying tourism images, the proposed method adopts VGG16 [11], which is trained from the IRSVRC2012 dataset[2]. This above VGG16 is composed of 13 convolution layers and three full connect layers. Then we perform its fine-tuning for the tourism category classification by using the tourism images and their categories. This fine-tuning calculates the parameters of the last convolution and full connected layers.

[2]http://www.image-net.org/challenges/LSVRC/2012/

The proposed method classifies the tourism category using tourism images based on the obtained fine-tuned CNN.

Next, the FK-NN algorithm using the geotags are explained. The proposed method calculates the geotag features that are obtained as two-dimensional vectors whose components are the latitude and longitude obtained from the geotags. The FK-NN algorithm calculates membership to each tourism category by using the above geotag features. Then the classification result is obtained as the category that has the maximum membership.

2.2 Estimation Scheme of Existence of Reliable Results

First, the proposed method calculates the confidence measure of these classification results based on [13]. Specifically, our method discriminates whether the classification result is correct or not by SVM whose input is a feature vector that is composed of the membership obtained by the FK-NN algorithm or the output values from the final layer of CNN. Then the probability value is obtained as the confidence measure that represents how confident the classification result is.

The proposed method estimates the existence of the reliable results by utilizing the above confidence measure. Let l^{v} and l^{g} (v and g being visual and geotag features) be tourism categories obtained by the CNN using tourism images and the FK-NN algorithm using geotags, respectively. If l^{v} and l^{g} are the same category, the proposed method calculates the estimation result $t \in \{0, 1\}$ as follows:

$$t = \begin{cases} 1 & \text{if } \frac{C^{\mathrm{v}}+C^{\mathrm{g}}}{2} \geq \mathrm{Th}_1 \\ 0 & \text{otherwise,} \end{cases} \tag{1}$$

where C^{v} and C^{g} are the confidence measure of the classification results obtained by the CNN using tourism images and the FK-NN algorithm using geotags, and Th_1 is a predefined threshold. On the other hand, when l^{v} and l^{g} are different categories, the estimation result t is calculated as follows:

$$t = \begin{cases} 1 & \text{if } |C^{\mathrm{v}} - C^{\mathrm{g}}| \geq \mathrm{Th}_2 \\ 0 & \text{otherwise,} \end{cases} \tag{2}$$

where Th_2 is also a predefined threshold. If $t = 1$, we judge that the reliable result is included in the above classification results, and the classification result that has a higher confidence measure is selected as the final classification result. On the other hand, when $t = 0$, the proposed method judges that any reliable results do not exist in these results, and the final classification result is obtained by another classification scheme, MALR model, whose details are explained below.

2.3 Classification based on MALR model

The MALR model [9] calculates the final classification results utilizing the accuracy of classification results and output values from the final layer of the CNN and the membership of the FK-NN algorithm. The accuracy indicates the classification performance of each classifier, and these output values represent an inclination that classification results are correct or not. Therefore, the MALR model enables classification considering the classification performance and the above inclination. Then the proposed method utilizes this model as a final classification approach. The numbers of tourism images uploaded to the image sharing services are imbalanced in each category. Therefore, the proposed method extends the MALR model is such a may that it can solve the above class imbalance problem based on a class imbalance oriented logistic regression [2].

In the training phase, we separately obtain classification results by applying cross-validation of training samples using the CNN and the FK-NN algorithm. This training phase of the MALR model utilizes only training samples being $t = 0$ in Eq. (1) or (2). Let N_{T} be the number of the above training samples, and $\boldsymbol{z} \in \mathbb{R}^{2J}$ (J being the number of tourism categories) is a feature vector that is composed of output values from the final layer of the CNN and the membership of the FK-NN algorithm. The proposed method performs the classification based on a multi-class logistic regression model as follows:

$$P(j|\boldsymbol{z}, \boldsymbol{W}) = \frac{\exp(\boldsymbol{w}_j^{\top}\boldsymbol{z})}{\sum_{j'=1}^{J}\exp(\boldsymbol{w}_{j'}^{\top}\boldsymbol{z})}, \tag{3}$$

where $\boldsymbol{W} = [\boldsymbol{w}_1, \boldsymbol{w}_2, \cdots, \boldsymbol{w}_J]^{\top}$ ($\boldsymbol{w}_j \in \mathbb{R}^{2J}$ being a weight vector of the j ($= 1, 2, \ldots, J$) th tourism category) is a weight matrix. In the proposed method, the optimal weight matrix $\boldsymbol{W}_{\mathrm{ML}}$ is calculated by solving the following optimization problem:

$$\begin{aligned}\boldsymbol{W}_{\mathrm{ML}} = \arg\max_{\boldsymbol{W}} &\left[\sum_{q=1}^{N_{\mathrm{T}}}\sum_{r\in\{\mathrm{v},\mathrm{g}\}}\left[s_q^r \ln\{\pi^r P(y_q^r|\boldsymbol{z}, \boldsymbol{W})\}\right]\right.\\ &\left.+N_{\mathrm{T}}\cdot\zeta\sum_{j=1}^{J}R_j(\boldsymbol{W}) - \lambda||\boldsymbol{W}||_{\mathrm{F}}^2\right],\end{aligned} \tag{4}$$

where s_q^r ($q = 1, 2, \ldots, N_{\mathrm{T}}$; $r \in \{\mathrm{v}, \mathrm{g}\}$) is defined as follows:

$$s_q^r = \begin{cases}1 & \text{if } y_q^r = g_q\\ 0 & \text{otherwise,}\end{cases} \tag{5}$$

where y_q^r is the category into which the qth training sample is classified based on the feature r. In addition, $\pi^r \in [0, 1]$ is classification accuracy in the above cross-validation using the training feature r, and $\zeta \in [0, 1]$ and λ are trade-off and regularization parameters, respectively. Let L_j be a set of feature vectors of training samples that belong to the jth category. $R_j(\boldsymbol{W})$ in Eq. (4) is defined as follows:

$$R_j(\boldsymbol{W}) = \frac{1}{|L_j|}\sum_{\boldsymbol{z}\in L_j} P(j|\boldsymbol{z}, \boldsymbol{W}), \tag{6}$$

where $|L_j|$ is the number of elements in the set L_j. The proposed method solves the optimization problem defined in Eq. (4) by the quasi Newton method using the Limited memory-Broyden Fletcher Goldfarb Shanno (L-BFGS) method [7].

In the test phase, we classify an input tourism image by the logistic regression model of Eq. (3) based on the optimal weight matrix $\boldsymbol{W}_{\mathrm{ML}}$. We obtain a category $\hat{y}$ of the input tourism image as follows:

$$\hat{y} = \arg\max_{j\in\{1,2,\ldots,J\}} P(j|\hat{\boldsymbol{z}}, \boldsymbol{W}_{\mathrm{ML}}), \tag{7}$$

where $\hat{\boldsymbol{z}}$ is a feature vector calculated from a test sample.

Table 1: Numbers of tourism images in each category.

Tourism category	Number of images
Sights&Landmarks	46,672
Museums	11,891
Nature&Parks	19,592
Concerts&Shows	4,783
Shopping	1,262
Food&Drink	7,988
Zoo&Aquariums	1,942
Event	6,319

3 EXPERIMENTAL RESULTS

In this section, we show experimental results to verify the effectiveness of the proposed method. In this experiment, we conducted the tourism category classification using tourism images uploaded on Flickr. We constructed a dataset including 100,449 tourism images taken in Paris. Specifically, we collected these images of eight categories. These categories and the numbers of tourism images in each category are shown in Table 1. This dataset consists of the tourism images that have textual tags of travel spot names, and these names are included in the top ten spots of each category that were ranked by trip advisor[3].

This experiment compared the performance of our method with those of the following comparative methods.

CM1: The classification result is obtained by the CNN using tourism images.

CM2: The classification result is calculated by the FK-NN algorithm using geotags.

CM3: The classification result is obtained by the MALR model using tourism images and geotags.

CM4: The classification result is calculated by our previous method [10] using tourism images and geotags.

[3] https://www.tripadvisor.co.uk/

Table 2: MCC of the proposed method (PM) and comparative methods.

Tourism category	PM	CM1	CM2	CM3	CM4
Sights&Landmarks	**0.851**	0.703	0.817	0.817	0.833
Museums	**0.894**	0.713	0.869	0.862	0.889
Nature&Parks	**0.807**	0.594	0.791	0.765	0.792
Concerts&Shows	**0.703**	0.553	0.631	0.681	0.681
Shopping	**0.797**	0.463	0.752	0.744	0.761
Food&Drink	**0.888**	0.850	0.780	0.887	0.868
Zoo&Aquariums	**0.985**	0.648	0.984	0.960	0.982
Event	**0.839**	0.736	0.784	0.822	0.831
Average	**0.846**	0.658	0.801	0.817	0.830

The performance of the proposed method and comparative methods were evaluated via five-fold cross-validation. In addition, in order to evaluate the accuracy of the tourism category classification, this experiment utilized Matthews Correlation Coefficient (MCC) [8] shown in the following equation:

$$\mathrm{MCC}=\frac{\mathrm{TP}\times\mathrm{TN}-\mathrm{FP}\times\mathrm{FN}}{\sqrt{(\mathrm{TP}+\mathrm{FP})(\mathrm{TP}+\mathrm{FN})(\mathrm{TN}+\mathrm{FP})(\mathrm{TN}+\mathrm{FN})}}, \qquad (8)$$

where TP, TN, FP, and FN indicate the numbers of True Positive, True Negative, False Positive and False Negative samples, respectively. In addition, the parameter K of the FK-NN algorithm was set to 100, and the thresholds Th_1 and Th_2 were set to 0.6 and 0.8, respectably.

The experimental results are shown in Table 2. We can confirm that the proposed method realizes the most accurate classification. Therefore, the effectiveness of the proposed method is verified. Specifically, when we compare results of the proposed method and CM4, we can confirm that the estimation of existence of the reliable results contributes to improvement in tourism category classification performance. This is because the estimation can accurately determine existence of reliable results in the two kinds of results obtained by the CNN and the FK-NN algorithm. Consequently, this estimation successfully solves the problem in the previous method [10]. From these results, we can confirm that the proposed method realizes successful classification of tourism categories using tourism images uploaded to image sharing services.

4 CONCLUSIONS AND FUTURE WORK

In this paper, we have proposed a tourism category classification method on image sharing services through estimation of existence of reliable results. The proposed method estimates existence of reliable classification results obtained from the two classifiers, the CNN and the FK-NN algorithm. If a reliable result is included, the result is selected as the final classification result. On the other hand, when any reliable result is not included in these results, the final result is obtained by the MALR model. The experimental results show the effectiveness of the proposed method.

In the future, we will tackle realization of a tourism information recommendation based on tourism categories obtained by the proposed method. The above recommendation will utilize a collaborative filtering. Specifically, we will find similar tourists based on tourism categories obtained by the classification method in this paper. Then tourism information will be recommended to tourists based on trends of tourism spots obtained by these similar tourists.

ACKNOWLEDGMENTS

This research was partly supported by the MIC/SCOPE #181601001 , JSPS KAKENHI Grant Number JP17H01744 and Global Station for Big Data and Cybersecurity, a project of Global Institution for Collaborative Research and Education at Hokkaido University.

REFERENCES

[1] Corinna Cortes and Vladimir Vapnik. 1995. Support-vector Networks. *Machine Learning* 20, 3 (Sept. 1995), 273–297.
[2] Yadong Dong, Huaping Guo, Weimei Zhi, and Ming Fan. 2014. Class Imbalance oriented Logistic Regression. In *Proceedings of IEEE International Conference on Cyber-Enabled Distributed Computing and Knowledge Discovery*. IEEE, 187–192.
[3] James Hays and Alexei A Efros. 2008. IM2GPS: estimating geographic information from a single image. In *Computer Vision and Pattern Recognition, 2008. CVPR 2008. IEEE Conference on*. IEEE, 1–8.
[4] James M Keller, Michael R Gray, and James A Givens. 1985. A Fuzzy K-Nearest Neighbor Algorithm. *IEEE Transactions on Systems, Man and Cybernetics* 15, 4 (July 1985), 580–585.
[5] Yann LeCun, Léon Bottou, Yoshua Bengio, and Patrick Haffner. 1998. Gradient-based Learning Applied to Document Recognition. *Proc. IEEE* 86, 11 (Nov. 1998), 2278–2324.
[6] Yunpeng Li, David J Crandall, and Daniel P Huttenlocher. 2009. Landmark classification in large-scale image collections. In *Proceedings of IEEE International Conference on Computer Vision*. IEEE, 1957–1964.
[7] Dong C Liu and Jorge Nocedal. 1989. On the Limited Memory BFGS Method for Large Scale Optimization. *Mathematical Programming* 45, 1-3 (Aug. 1989), 503–528.
[8] Brian W Matthews. 1975. Comparison of the Predicted and Observed Secondary Structure of T4 Phage Lysozyme. *Biochimica et Biophysica Acta (BBA)-Protein Structure* 405, 2 (Oct. 1975), 442–451.
[9] Filipe Rodrigues, Francisco Pereira, and Bernardete Ribeiro. 2013. Learning from Multiple Annotators: Distinguishing Good from Random Labelers. *Pattern Recognition Letters* 34, 12 (Sept. 2013), 1428–1436.
[10] Naoki Saito, Takahiro Ogawa, Satoshi Asamizu, and Miki Haseyama. 2016. A Tourism Category Classification Method Based on Estimation of Reliable Decision. In *Proceedings of the Global Conference on Consumer Electronics*. IEEE, 52–53.
[11] Karen Simonyan and Andrew Zisserman. 2014. Very Deep Convolutional Networks for Large-scale Image Recognition. *arXiv preprint arXiv:1409.1556* (2014).
[12] Evaggelos Spyrou and Phivos Mylonas. 2016. A Survey on Flickr Multimedia Research Challenges. *Engineering Applications of Artificial Intelligence* 51 (May 2016), 71–91.
[13] Toshihiko Yamasaki, Shinnosuke Ohshima, and Kiyoharu Aizawa. 2015. Confidence Analysis for Multi-class Object Recognition Using the Intermediate Values from Machine Learning Algorithm (in Japanese) . *ITE transaction* 69, 8 (Aug. 2015), J257–J260.
[14] Yiyang Yang, Zhiguo Gong, and Leong Hou U. 2015. Identifying Points of Interest Using Heterogeneous Features. *ACM Transactions on Intelligent Systems and Technology* 5, 4 (Jan. 2015), 68:1–68:27.
[15] Lei Zhu, Jialie Shen, Hai Jin, Liang Xie, and Ran Zheng. 2015. Landmark Classification with Hierarchical Multi-modal Exemplar Feature. *IEEE Transactions on Multimedia* 17, 7 (July 2015), 981–993.

Considering Documents in Lifelog Information Retrieval

Rashmi Gupta
(Supervised by Cathal Gurrin, Dublin City University)
Insight Centre for Data Analytics
Dublin, Ireland
rashmi.gupta3@mail.dcu.ie

ABSTRACT

Lifelogging is a research topic that is receiving increasing attention and although lifelog research has progressed in recent years, the concept of what represents a document in lifelog retrieval has not yet been sufficiently explored. Hence, the generation of multimodal lifelog documents is a fundamental concept that must be addressed. In this paper, I introduce my general perspective on generating documents in lifelogging and reflect on learnings from collecting multimodal lifelog data from a number of participants in a study on lifelog data organization. In addition, the main motivation behind document generation is proposed and the challenges faced while collecting data and generating documents are discussed in detail. Finally, a process for organizing the documents in lifelog data retrieval is proposed, which I intend to follow in my PhD research.

CCS CONCEPTS

• **Information systems → Document structure**; **Multimedia and multimodal retrieval**; *Information extraction*;

KEYWORDS

Lifelogging; Lifelog Documents; Information Retrieval; Moment; Activity; Event

ACM Reference Format:
Rashmi Gupta. 2018. Considering Documents in Lifelog Information Retrieval. In *ICMR'18:2018 International Conference on Multimedia Retrieval, June 11–14, 2018, Yokohama, Japan.* ACM, New York, NY, USA, 4 pages. https://doi.org/10.1145/3206025.3206081

1 INTRODUCTION

Lifelogging refers to the process of passively acquiring a rich multimodal record (log) of daily life activities using one, or more wearable devices, typically involving a wearable camera [4]. This data is usually referred to as a lifelog and it offers considerable potential to enhance the life experience of the wearer, offering new sources of information for self-knowledge and insight generation [11]. In order to provide useful and indexable content for a lifelog retrieval system, it is necessary to align and synchronize the streams of multimodal lifelog data and combine them into some form of retrievable units. Heretofore, there has been little consideration of what a document means for lifelog-based retrieval. Hence, in this work, I propose a new unit of retrieval for lifelog data, which is an indexable unit of an individual's life experience called an activity. Since lifelogging is an inherently multimodal data capture activity, such an indexable unit would manifest as a fusion of a number of synchronized lifelog data sources at a given point in time, such as audio, video or images from wearable cameras, readings from biometric sensors, communication records, information creation or access logs, and various other sensor sources. Such a unit would represent a contiguous period of time and would form the basis of a document of life experience data. Providing access to a large number of such documents would produce a lifelog retrieval engine.

Although the concept of a document has not been explored in depth in the research field, the idea of lifelog annotation and search has been receiving increasing research attention, with dedicated workshops and collaborative bench-marking efforts underway [9]. Thus far in lifelog research, the unit of retrieval has been the life event [11], the minute as a time-unit [9], or the individual data points (e.g. image, temperature, location)[7]. The contribution of this paper, and of my proposed PhD research is to consider what exactly is a document for lifelog retrieval and how can such documents be generated from continuous lifelog data streams. It is my conjecture that this is not a simple research question, since there are many different approaches that one can take, which can either generate indexable documents at indexing time or form query-specific units in some post-query process. It is these factors that motivate my PhD research at Dublin City University under the supervision of Cathal Gurrin.

2 HISTORY AND BACKGROUND

Gathering data in lifelogging has long history, Richard Buckminster Fuller's Dymaxion Chronofile, which was started in the late 1920s [13] included a complete record of his personal and business data, thousand of physical papers, thousand of hours of audios and videos, hundreds of models and artifacts, 1400 feet of content and seventeen hundred hours of recordings. In this case the unit of retrieval would not be in question since the Dymaxion Chronofile was essentially a collection of physical documents and and objects. Decades later, in 2009 [16], Gordon Bell and Jim Gammell coined the concept "total capture" of personally relevant information in their seminal lifelogging work called MyLifeBits [7]. All this data was indexed into a database and made available through an interface that allowed for the retrieval of any unit of information based on a user query. This was instantiated as the MyLifeBits [7] framework which was the first true lifelog retrieval engine. However in this work, the retrieval challenge is viewed as a data retrieval challenge, rather than an information retrieval challenge and the unit of retrieval was the individual unit of data stored. It is my conjecture that a

ICMR'18, June 11–14, 2018, Yokohama, Japan

ACM ISBN 978-1-4503-5046-4/18/06...$15.00
https://doi.org/10.1145/3206025.3206081

lifelog retrieval system should support a user by returning a ranked list of life experiences, as opposed to data values, which would be necessary for lifelog retrieval due to the vast volumes of data that will likely be contained in lifelogs.

In terms of fusing lifelog data from multiple sources into meaningful units, heretofore, there have been two approaches. The simple approach taken by the NTCIR12-Lifelog collaborative benchmarking exercise was to define a retrieval unit as one minute long [9]. While this is effective when developing and evaluating multimodal ranking models, it is not going to be an effective process for a user wishing to retrieve a past life experience due to the volume of documents that are likely to be considered potentially relevant for any given user need. Another approach is the idea of event segmentation, which segments the continual lifelog data into a set of discrete events, by identifying changes in a user's environment as an indicator of life event changes. Doherty et al. in 2007, gathered five sources of lifelog data such as audio data via audio recorders, continual capture images, temperature, white-light level and accelerometer sensors to provide a first generation human memory augmentation tool based on indexing events. They found that the fusion of image, light and accelerometer sensor worked well for identifying the event boundaries when lifelogger moves from one location to another while image and light helps to identify the activity performed by the lifelogger within same location. Thus, they automatically segmented this collection of personal data into specific events [6]. In addition, Li et al. in 2013, collected a fusion of multi-sensor data as a document and segmented whole day activities into specific chunks of time periods for lifestyle evaluation and retrieval purposes [17]. These event segmentation approaches typically produced a small number of daily events (typically 30-40). This averages to about 20 minutes per event, which for some use-cases is appropriate, but for many, it is likely to be too large or certainly is unlikely to be flexible enough for use in a lifelog retrieval system.

In parallel to these event segmentation approaches, the first collaborative benchmarking exercises were being prepared and have been released in recent years under the umbrella of NTCIR [10] and ImageCLEF. These activities release test collections that provide researchers with access to archives of anonymised lifelog data with associated real-world information needs of lifeloggers [9]. Such datasets give us an indication of the types of queries that a lifelogger will make against their collection, and help to motivate and guide this research.

Besides test collections, other researchers have considered the reasons for accessing lifelogs. I propose that it is necessary to take a step back and explore the many potential ways that lifelogs can be used by an individual in daily life. Sellen and Whittaker [16] suggested the five R's of memory access as reasons why individuals access their memories. By extrapolating from these 5Rs, I can then identify five reasons why an individual might keep a lifelog, which are *Recalling* and *Recollecting* of the past experience to support memory-augmentation applications, *Reminiscing* about past experiences to support personal wellness, *Reflecting* on past life experiences for self-enhancement and finally *Remembering Intentions* which is a means of context-aware memory-assistance.

3 RESEARCH FOCUS

Specifically in this research, I will be focusing on recalling and recollecting as the most appropriate forms of retrieval from lifelogs. Consequently, it is my conjecture that neither minute-based retrieval or event segmentation are suitable to provide a flexible retrieval system for the user which can address many of the five R's of memory access. Defining the minute as the unit is clearly too small to represent a human activity, whereas defining the unit as an event could result in units of retrieval that are too long to adequately address an information need. For example, consider an event that is a party; there could be many user activities contained in one large event. Consequently, in my research, I am proposing a new concept called an activity, which I propose to be a more suitable unit of retrieval. The activity unit is shorter than an event and more meaningful in terms of user activity than a minute.

4 CONSIDERING ACTIVITIES AS A UNIT OF RETRIEVAL

As introduced above, the main motivation for this work is to identify what a lifelog document should be and how to generate such document units from the continuous streams of lifelog data coming off various sensors and wearable devices. Some research has focused on an activity-based measure as the important or indexable unit. Braber used a person's daily food consumption record and environment quality, personal behaviour and biometric data and individual performance in terms of mental and physical activities as a document segmentation model in order to promote health and wellness [3]. Zhen et al. in 2013, collected a fusion of multi-sensor data as a document and segmented daily activities into specific segments for lifestyle evaluation and retrieval purposes [17]. Such a viewpoint puts the individual at the centre of the segmentation process and it is my belief that an activity-based segmentation at indexing time will be the most appropriate query-agnostic unit for lifelog search and retrieval .

In order to understand the context in which I define different units of retrieval, I present a hierarchical model of lifelog data units: **Item:** Item is defined as the smallest retrievable unit, the atomic unit of data, such as an image, temperature reading, location, etc. It is the unit of retrieval that was favoured in MyLifeBits [7]. **Moment:** Moment is defined as a fixed length temporal unit, which heretofore has been a minute. Consequently, there are 1440 moments in each day and the minute unit is represented by a combination of all the atomic items that take place within that minute. Moments were used as the retrieval unit in the NTCIR Lifelog comparative benchmarking exercises [10]. **Activity:** Activity is defined as an un-interrupted sequential state of the individual in terms of their person or environment or stimuli. The activity is the indexing-time unit of retrieval that we define in this work and propose as the most appropriate indexing time unit. It represents a combination of sequential items whose size is dependent on the activities of the individual. **Event:** Event is combination of moments or activities or experiences developed (up until now) at indexing time and typically an event is a longest unit of which there may be 2-4 in any given hour (based on past research). The event has been considered to be the first unit of retrieval for lifelog data and was employed manually in the initial Sensecam image viewer tool [7] as well as the early

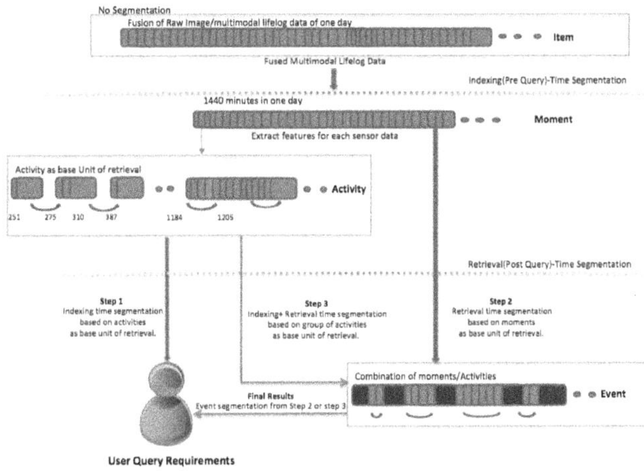

Figure 1: The concept of segmenting one day lifelog visual/sensor archive into events.

work of Doherty et al. in the development of early lifelog search engines [6]. A visualization of numerous different approaches to segmentation of lifelog data is shown in Figure 1. These can be seen as either begin pre-indexing time or post-query time processes. During this research, I intend to explore both pre-indexing and post-query document segmentation (or generation) approaches. In this paper, I report on initial experiments that evaluate the activity-based pre-indexing segmentation (Step 1 in Figure 1). Of course, there are alternative segmentation approaches, such as post-query generation of query-focused temporal segments of lifelog data that are generated in response to a query (Step 2 in Figure 1), or the process of generating events from sequential query-relevant activities in a fused pre/post approach (Step 3 in Figure 1). These alternative approaches will be evaluated over existing datasets in later work.

In terms of activity-based indexing, human activities labeling can range from the broad physical activity measurements (e.g. walking, sitting, running), to detailed activities such as looking, speaking, opening a door, etc. For this work, what I have done is to define a set of sixteen lifestyle activities that are based on, but not the same as Kahenmann's set of the sixteen most enjoyable lifestyle activities [15], which were selected based on personal interview and have been previously used as target activity labels in the SenseSeer smartphone-based lifelogging framework [2]. In this research, activities are defined after examining the long-term lifelogs of two individuals and as such, represent an achievable segmentation target. These sixteen lifestyle activities are detailed in [10] and are designed to explore knowledge mining and visualization of lifelogs.

5 AN APPROACH FOR GENERATING ACTIVITY-BASED LIFELOG DOCUMENTS

Based on my experience of developing and evaluating event-segmentation approaches to lifelog data retrieval, I have created a three-step process for generating activity-based documents for indexing lifelog content. The initial step is to gather sufficient multimodal data from numerous sources, as discussed in [11]. I then propose that these multimodal sources of data are time-aligned, processed to ensure adherence to any legal or ethical data governance expectations (e.g. face blurring or other anonymisation procedures) and then indexable features extracted from the raw lifelog data (e.g. visual concepts from the image content). Following that I propose the fusion of these different data sources into vectors that represent every minute and to simplify the process, the subsequent combination of three minutes into our activity-based segmentation. My proposed process of generating lifelog document is discussed in detail and shown in Figure 2 below.

Data Gathering involves the utilization of multiple sources of unstructured, continuous, raw lifelog data from wearable, fixed and informational (software/online) sensors. Although the data sources are many and varied, I utilize the following sources: **Wearable multimedia information:** Visual and audio data gathered using wearable cameras and microphones, which generates large volumes of content per day (1,500-2,000 images and hours of audio). These give details of the actual human activities and act as reminders for the individual of what they were doing at any point in time. **Human biometrics:** Using a smartwatch we can obtain all-day human biometrics, such as heart rate, calorie burn, and steps, etc. **Human activity:** Logging an individual's physical activities (e.g. walking, driving, running, resting) can be done using wearable devices or smartphone apps , without requiring any user intervention). **Information access:** Using the LoggerMan[12] application, I can collect human-computer interaction data produced during normal computer usage. LoggerMan allows the gathering of a wide range of keyboard, mouse and screen actions, thereby capturing the information creation and consumption activities of the individual.

Following data gathering, I consider the preprocessing of the data that temporally aligns and synchronizes the continual data streams. The multimodal lifelog data gathered by lifeloggers varies in volume, fidelity, accuracy, semantic meaning, and ultimately these vary from one lifelogger to another. Following alignment, it may be necessary to engage in a process of data anonymisation, and many anonymisation techniques can be applied, such as face or tattoo blurring, named identity removal, document/screen blurring from wearable camera data, etc. Finally the preprocessing stage requires feature extraction to convert the raw lifelog data into machine-indexable content. There are many options for selecting

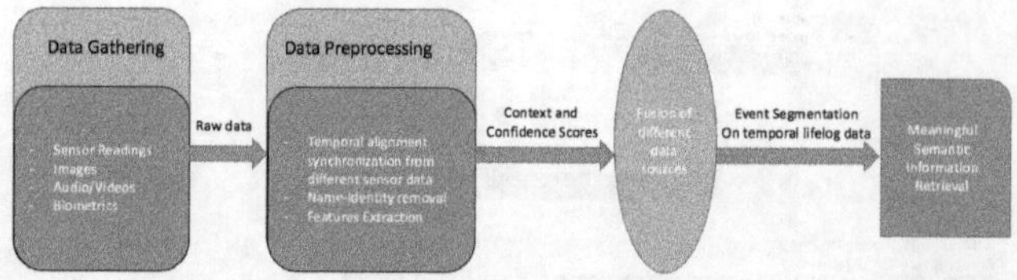

Figure 2: Process of segmenting lifelog data into document units.

sources of visual features for image data, with the most well known being the open-source CAFFE framework[14] that provides a visual annotation of each image from a 1,000 visual feature set.

This data is then fused together to form moments of length one minute before being combined into the indexable activity-based documents by employing a activity recognition algorithm. In my initial work, The two pre-existing segmentation approaches based on MPEG-7 Descriptors implemented by Doherty [5] was re-implemented as a baseline approach and two new approaches (Caffe concepts [14] and Microsoft Computer Vision API image categorization [1]) to segment one day lifelog data into activities were implemented that intend to perform better from baseline approach. Then, euclidean distance measure was implemented to identify the distance between vectors representing the content of every minute. The specific document boundaries were identified using thresholding which was defined based on a manually generated groundtruth by ten users and the average performance of a document segmentation approach using this process was evaluated in terms of precision and recall as shown in Table 1. In results, document segmentation based on image categorization via Computer Vision API approach proved the best approach for document segmentation; for full details see [8].

Event Segmentation Approaches	Threshold Value	Precision	Recall	F1- Score	MCC
Hearst's TexTiling based on MPEG-7 Descriptors	mean(K = 0.5)	20.6	65.4	30.7	6.98
	Kapur	**20.6**	**65.8**	**31.3**	**7.42**
Non TexTiling based on MPEG-7 Descriptors	**mean(K = 0.5)**	**29.5**	**60.6**	**38.7**	**22.0**
	Kapur	29.4	60	38.7	21.43
Caffe Visual Concepts	**0.4**	**70.4**	**72**	**69.3**	**64.3**
	0.5	64.6	76.5	68.5	62.9
	0.6	56.4	80.9	64.8	58.6
	0.7	40.5	88.2	54.2	46
Image categorization via MS Concepts	0.4	78.3	65.5	69.2	65.2
	0.5	77.5	66.2	69.4	65.4
	0.6	77.2	67.2	69.8	61.4
	0.7	**76.2**	**68.3**	**70.1**	**65.7**
Summary Results (Overall Best Approach)	**Threshold Value**	**Precision**	**Recall**	**F1- Score**	**MCC**
MS Concepts	**0.7**	**76.2**	**68.3**	**70.1**	**65.7**
Caffe Concepts	0.4	70.4	72	69.3	64.3
MPEG-7 without TexTiling	mean (K = 0.5)	29.5	60.6	38.7	22.0
MPEG-7 with TexTiling	Kapur	20.6	65.8	31.3	7.42

Table 1: Various Document Segmentation Approaches and found Overall Best Approach.

6 CONCLUSIONS AND FUTURE WORK

In this paper, I motivated the need for generating documents in lifelogging based on activities as a basic unit of retrieval. I identified a taxonomy of lifelog documents from the single data unit to the event. Finally, I proposed a process through-which lifelog documents can be generated.

In future work, I can identify the following tasks that I need to complete: Engage in a larger-scale study on the effectiveness of activity-based segmentation for lifelog retrieval; Develop an approach to query-time document-generation from sequential moments that are highly-ranked in relation to a given information need. This approach will be compared to the activity-based segmentation; Develop a third approach (query-biased combination of highly-ranked activities) to provide a third alternative segmentation approach; Compare the three approaches to segmentation for the processing of known-item lifelog queries.

ACKNOWLEDGMENTS

This publication has emanated from research conducted with the financial support of Science Foundation Ireland (SFI) under grant number SFI/12/RC/2289.

REFERENCES

[1] [n. d.]. Microsoft's Computer Vision API. https://docs.microsoft.com/en-us/azure/cognitive-services/computer-vision/category-taxonomy.

[2] Rami Albatal, Cathal Gurrin, Jiang Zhou, Yang Yang, Denise Carthy, and Na Li. 2013. Senseseer mobile-cloud-based Lifelogging framework. In *ISTAS*. IEEE, 144–146.

[3] Maarten den Braber. 2016. The Emergence of Quantified Self as a Data-driven Movement to Promote Health and Wellness. *Proceedings of the first Workshop on Lifelogging Tools and Applications* (Oct. 2016).

[4] Martin Dodge and Rob Kitchin. 2007. 'Outlines of a world coming into existence': Pervasive computing and the ethics of forgetting. *Environment and Planning B: Planning and Design* 34, 3 (2007), 431–445. https://doi.org/10.1068/b32041t

[5] Aiden R. Doherty and Alan F. Smeaton. [n. d.]. Automatically segmenting lifelog data into events. *9th International Workshop on Image Analysis for Multimedia Interactive Services* (june [n. d.]).

[6] Aiden R. Doherty, Alan F. Smeaton, Keansub Lee, and Danial P.W. Ellis. 2007. Multimodal segmentation of lifelog data. *Large Scale Semantic Access to Content (Text, Image, Video, and Sound)* (june 2007), 21–38.

[7] J. Gemmell, G. Bell, and R. Lueder. 2006. MyLifeBits: a personal database for everything. *Commun. ACM* 49, 1 (2006), 88–95.

[8] Rashmi Gupta and Cathal Gurrin. 2018. Approaches for Event Segmentation of Visual Lifelog Data. *24th International Conference on Advances in Multimedia Modeling, MMM 2018* (2018).

[9] Cathal Gurrin, Hideo Joho, Frank Hopfgartner, Liting Zhou, and Rami Albatal. 2016. NTCIR Lifelog: the first test collection for lifelog research. In *SIGIR'16 - the 39th International ACM SIGIR conference on Research and Development in Information Retrieval*. 705–708.

[10] Cathal Gurrin, Hideo Joho, Frank Hopfgartner, Liting Zhou, Rashmi Gupta, Rami Albatal, and Duc Tien Dang Nguyen. 2017. Overview of NTCIR-13 Lifelog-2 Task. *The Thirteenth NTCIR conference (NTCIR-13)* (dec 2017).

[11] Cathal Gurrin, Alan F. Smeaton, and Aiden R. Doherty. 2014. LifeLogging: Personal Big Data. *Foundations and Trends in Information Retrieval* 8, 1 (2014), 1–125. https://doi.org/10.1561/1500000033

[12] Zaher Hinbarji, Rami Albatal, Noel E. OâĂŹConnor, and Cathal Gurrin. 2016. LoggerMan, a comprehensive logging and visualisation tool to capture computer usage. *22st International Conference on MultiMedia Modelling* (2016), 342–347.

[13] Roberto G. Trujillo Hsiao-yun Chu. 2009. New Views on R. Buckminster Fuller. *New Views on R. Buckminster Fuller* (2009), 6–23.

[14] Yangqing Jia, Evan Shelhamer, Jeff Donahue, Sergey Karayev, Jonathan Long, Ross Girshick, Sergio Guadarrama, and Trevor Darrell. 2014. Caffe: Convolutional Architecture for Fast Feature Embedding. *arXiv preprint arXiv:1408.5093* (2014).

[15] Daniel Kahneman, Alan B. Krueger, David A. Schkade, Norbert Schwarz, and Arthur A. Stone. 2004. A Survey Method for Characterizing Daily Life Experience: The Day Reconstruction Method. *Science* 306 (2004), 1776–1780.

[16] Abigail Sellen and Steve Whittaker. 2010. Beyond total capture: A constructive critique of lifelogging. *Commun. ACM* 53 (may 2010), 70–77.

[17] Li Zhen, Wei Zhiqiang, Jia Wenyan, and Sun Mingui. 2013. Daily Life Event Segmentation for Lifestyle Evaluation Based on Multi-Sensor Data Recorded by a Wearable Device. *Conf Proc IEEE Eng Med Biol Soc* (oct 2013).

VP-ReID: Vehicle and Person Re-Identification System

Longhui Wei, Xiaobin Liu, Jianing Li, Shiliang Zhang
School of Electronic Engineering and Computer Science, Peking University, Beijing 100871, China
{longhuiwei,liu-xb,ljn-vmc,slzhang.jdl}@pku.edu.cn

ABSTRACT

With the capability of locating and tracking specific suspects or vehicles in a large camera network, person Re-Identification (ReID) and vehicle ReID show potential to be a key technology in smart surveillance system. They have been drawing lots of attentions from both academia and industry. To demonstrate our recent research progresses on those two tasks, we develop a robust and efficient person and video ReID system named as VP-ReID. This system is build based on our recent works including Deep Convolutional Neural Network design for discriminative feature extraction, efficient off-line indexing, as well as distance metric optimization for deep feature learning. Constructed upon those algorithms, VP-ReID identifies query vehicle and person efficiently and accurately from a large gallery set.

KEYWORDS

Person Re-Identification, Vehicle Re-Identification

ACM Reference Format:
Longhui Wei, Xiaobin Liu, Jianing Li, Shiliang Zhang. 2018. VP-ReID: Vehicle and Person Re-Identification System. In *ICMR '18: 2018 International Conference on Multimedia Retrieval, June 11–14, 2018, Yokohama, Japan*, Jennifer B. Sartor, Theo D'Hondt, and Wolfgang De Meuter (Eds.). ACM, New York, NY, USA, Article 4, 4 pages. https://doi.org/10.1145/3206025.3206086

1 INTRODUCTION

Person Re-Identification (ReID) [12] and vehicle ReID [4] can be regarded as two special instance retrieval tasks. Both of them target to match images of a given instance, *i.e.*, a person or vehicle from a large-scale surveillance video dataset. With the capability of locating and tracking specific suspects or cars in a large camera network, person and vehicle ReID are important for applications on public security. In recent years, those two tasks have been attracting more and more attentions from both the academia and industry.

Person and vehicle ReID face many challenging issues. For instance, the appearance of a vehicle or person image can be easily affected by various factors like lighting conditions, camera viewpoints, misalignment error in detected bounding boxes, *etc.* They also need to cope with the issue of large intraclass variance and small interclass difference, as well as the massive amount of surveillance data. In recent years, we have conducted many works toward conquering those challenges [2, 5–8, 11–13]. Those research progresses have significantly boosted the performance of person ReID and vehicle ReID. Based on those works, we develop a robust and efficient person and video ReID system named as VP-ReID.

VP-ReID is a web-based demo system composed of two modules, *i.e.*, person ReID module and vehicle ReID module, respectively. Those two models are implemented with different algorithms but has similar idea and user interface. Users can upload and choose a person or vehicle image. The system would return the matched person or vehicle images from a gallery set. Targeting to achieve high accuracy and efficiency, VP-ReID is designed from two aspect, *i.e.*, discriminative descriptor extraction and efficient retrieval strategy, respectively. VP-ReID trains Deep Convolutional Neural Networks (DCNNs) for feature extraction and fuses regional and global descriptors to achieve high discriminative power and robustness. To improve the ReID efficiency, VP-ReID introduces an offline indexing algorithm, which builds the connections among gallery images of the same instance during offline indexing stage. The resulting image connections thus help to improve the online accuracy, recall, and efficiency. There, VP-ReID has the potential to retrieve a given person or vehicle image from a large-scale dataset with high accuracy and efficiency.

Table 1: Comparison on Market1501 in single query mode.

Methods	mAP	Top-1
Spindle [16]	-	76.9
SVDNet [9]	62.1	82.3
PAN [18]	63.4	82.8
DML [15]	68.8	87.7
Proposed Method	**73.9**	**89.9**

2 ALGORITHMS

2.1 Person Re-Identification

The person ReID module is mainly based on our recent work GLAD [12]. It includes the following components for human parts detection, descriptors extraction, and indexing and retrieval, respectively.

Part detection: Human parts convey detailed and distinctive visual cues [5]. We thus detect human parts for feature extraction. Originally detected person bounding boxes are commonly not well-aligned. To overcome the misalignment error, we detect human parts using Deepercut [1], instead of directly dividing images into fixed strips. Deepercut [1] outputs human joint points, based on which, three body regions can be cropped, *i.e.*, the head region, upper-body region, and lower-body region, respectively. Our experiments show coarse part segmentation is robust to pose variations and makes the feature extraction model compact and efficient [12].

Descriptor extraction: The descriptor extraction is conducted by a CNN network composed of four sub-networks, that correspond

ACM ISBN 978-1-4503-5046-4/18/06...$15.00
https://doi.org/10.1145/3206025.3206086

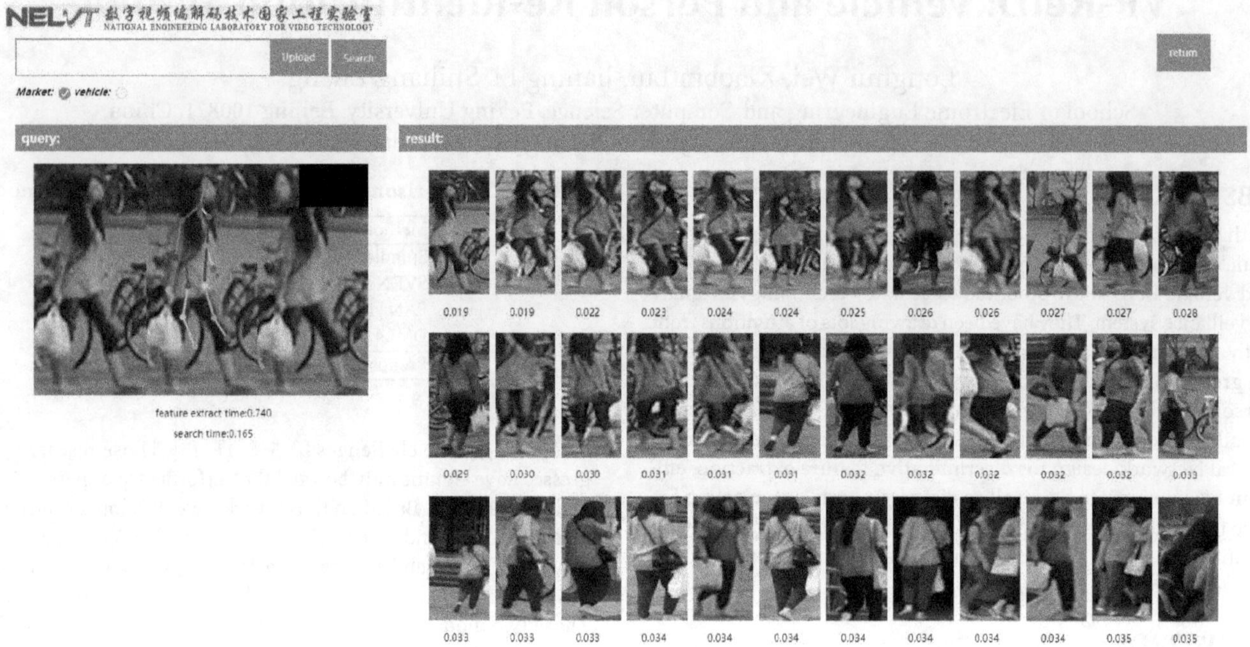

(a) Illustration of person ReID result

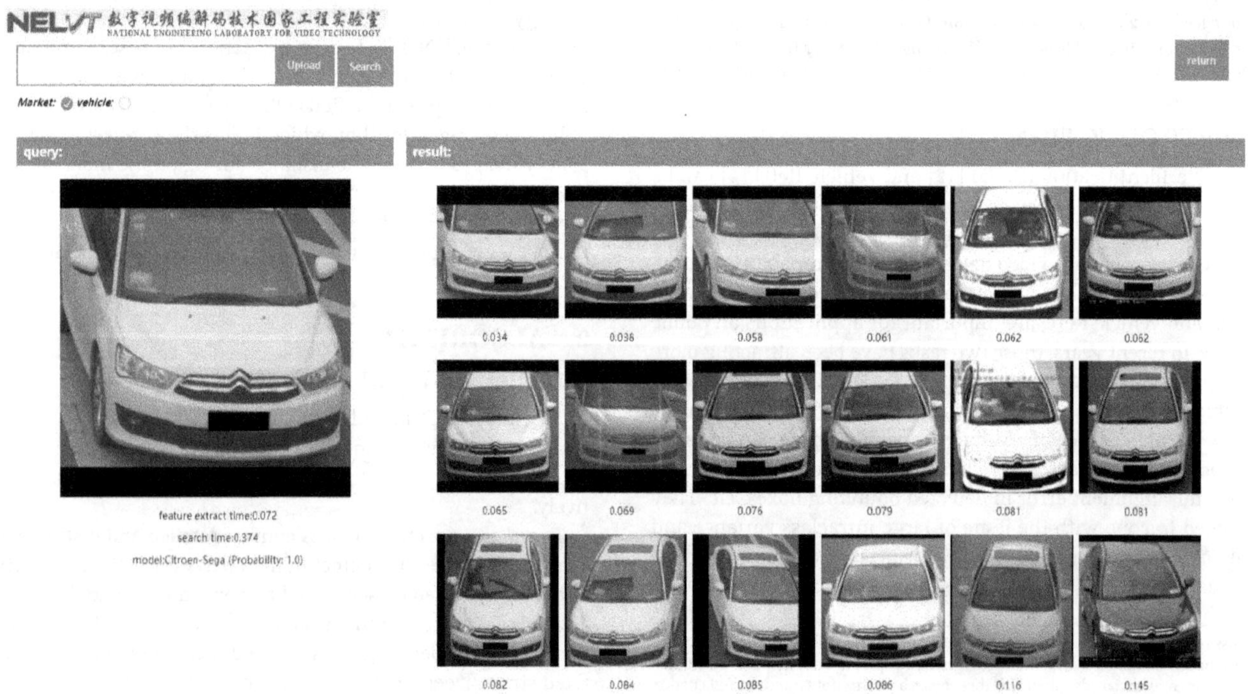

(b) Illustration of vehicle ReID result

Figure 1: Illustration of VP-ReID System.

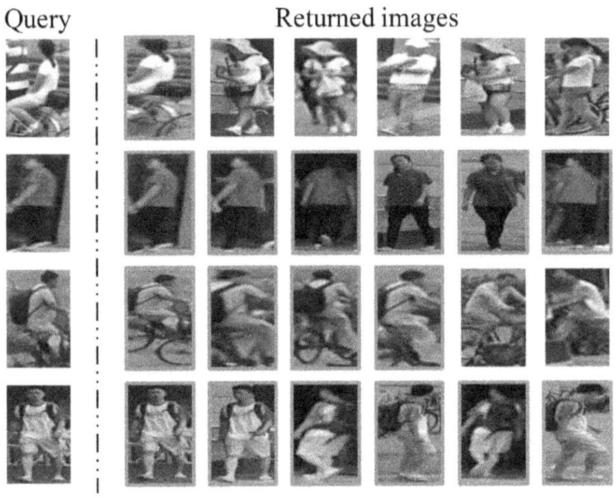

Figure 2: Examples of returned images on *Market1501*. True positives are annotated by green bounding box.

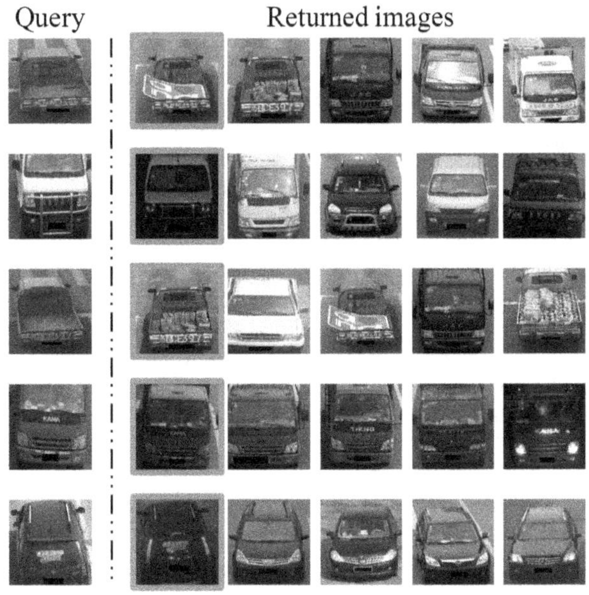

Figure 3: Examples of returned images on *VehicleID*. True positives are annotated by green bounding box. Note that there is only one true positive for each query.

to the global image and the three body regions, respectively. Those sub-networks share parameters in the first several layers, then have their own parameters for feature learning. In the testing stage, the global image and three detected part regions are inputted into those four sub-networks for global and regional feature extraction, respectively. The resulting four descriptors are concatenated as the final descriptor.

Retrieval procedure: To accelerate the retrieval procedure, offline indexing and coarse-to-fine retrieval strategy are utilized. In offline stage, a hierarchical clustering method, *e.g.*, TDC [12], is utilized to group the images belong to the same person together. In online retrieval stage, coarse retrieval are conducted to retrieve the relevant image groups, then fine retrieval is conducted to get a precise image rank list. As shown in our experiments [12], this strategy substantially accelerates the online retrieval without degrading the accuracy.

Performance of Person ReID: We use *Market1501* [17] dataset to evaluate our person Re-ID methods. *Market1501* [3] contains 32,668 images of 1,501 person identities. 12,936 images of 751 identities are selected as training set and others are used for testing. Following previous work [17], we report the Top-1 accuracy and mAP in Table 1. As shown in Table 1, our proposed methods achieve the best performance compared with state-of-the-art methods. Some examples of returned images are shown in Fig. 2

2.2 Vehicle Re-Identification

The vehicle ReID model is mainly based on our recent work RAM [4]. The CNN model has several sub-networks to extract complementary global and local features. A weights prediction sub-network is also designed to predict weights for different features to chase a more reasonable feature fusion. We also propose a new distance loss to accelerate the feature learning procedure. We briefly introduce each component in the following parts.

Global feature extraction: We use two different sub-networks to extract complementary global features, *i.e.*, the CN branch and BN branch, respectively. CN branch uses two Fully Connected (FC) layers to extract a global feature. The BN branch has a similar structure with CN branch, but embeds a Batch Normalization (BN) layer [14] between feature maps and the pooling layer. We observed that BN and CN branches have different focuses on the input image, *e.g.*, local discriminative regions vs. larger contextual regions, respectively [14]. CN and BN branches thus extract different global features.

Regional feature extraction: Regional differences could be important for differentiating similar vehicles sharing the identical model and color. We use regional sub-networks to extract regional features. Regional sub-networks first divide feature maps extracted from global image into overlapped regions. Then regional features are extracted from those regions, respectively. Adjacent regions are set to be overlapped to take alignment error and variations of angle of views into account.

Weights prediction: To chase a more reasonable feature fusion and enhance the feature robustness against vehicle detection errors, viewpoint changes, and other noises, we design a weight prediction sub-network to predict feature weights. During the training stage, weights prediction sub-network takes the global and local features as inputs and outputs feature weights to maximize the vehicle classification accuracy. This sub-network hence dynamically predicts feature weights during the testing stage.

Feature Learning: A new distance loss is proposed to accelerate the procedure of feature learning and network training. Different from the sample-wise triplet loss, it considers samples of the identical vehicle as an image set, then guides the network training procedure to optimize the distance between and within image sets. Specifically, it pulls samples in the same set close to each other and pushes different sets away from each other. It exhibits better efficiency than the commonly used sample-wise triplet loss.

Table 2: Performance comparison on *VehicleID*.

Method	Small		Medium		Large	
	Top-1	Top-5	Top-1	Top-5	Top-1	Top-5
VGG+CCL [3]	0.436	0.642	0.370	0.571	0.329	0.533
Mixed Diff+CCL [3]	0.490	0.735	0.428	0.668	0.382	0.616
OIF$^+$ [10]	-	-	-	-	0.670	0.829
Proposed	**0.771**	**0.928**	**0.727**	**0.892**	**0.700**	**0.871**

Performance of Vehicle ReID: We use *VehicleID* [3] dataset to evaluate our vehicle ReID methods. *VehicleID* [3] contains 221,763 images of 26,267 vehicles. 13,134 vehicles and 110,178 images are selected for training and others are used for testing. Three subsets containing 800, 1,600, and 2,400 vehicles are extracted from the testing set as *small*, *medium*, and *large* sets. Following previous work [3], we report the Top-1 and Top-5 accuracies in Table 2. On the three testsets, proposed methods achieve promising performance compared with other methods. Some examples of returned images are shown in Fig. 3

3 THE VP-REID SYSTEM

VP-ReID is a web-based demo system build with the above two models. It provides two web interfaces: one allows users to upload a person or vehicle image, and another one shows the retrieved person or vehicle images from gallery set. User can choose any returned image as a new query by clicking it.

We show a person ReID result page in Fig. 1-(a). The three images in the left of Fig. 1 are query person image, detected 14 joint points of human body, and the cropped part regions. Under the query, the system shows the feature extraction time and search time, which are computed on a GTX-1080 GPU and an intel i7 CPU. With our off-line indexing strategy, VP-ReID can finish person ReID in a large-scale dataset in real time [12, 13]. The ReID results are shown on the right side of the webpage. The number under each returned image is the feature distance between it and the query. We rank the results by the feature distance.

We also show a vehicle ReID result in Fig. 1-(b). Similar to person ReID, left side of the webpage shows the query image, feature extraction time, and search time. We additionally show the fine-grained category of the query predicted by our model, *i.e.*, the model and maker of query vehicle, as well as the prediction probability. The ReID results are shown on the right side of the webpage, and the feature distance is also shown under each returned image.

4 CONCLUSIONS

This demo presents a robust and efficient person and video ReID system named VP-ReID. VP-ReID is build upon our recent research progresses on person ReID and vehicle ReID [2, 5–8, 11–13]. It consists of two models, *i.e.*, person ReID model and vehicle ReID model, respectively. By learning and fusing complementary regional and global features with multi-branch DCNNs, VP-ReID extracts robust visual descriptors. VP-ReID also optimizes the offline indexing to ensure high online ReID efficiency. Therefore, VP-ReID has the potential to identify a given person or vehicle image from a large-scale dataset with high accuracy and efficiency.

ACKNOWLEDGEMENT

This work is supported by National Science Foundation of China under Grant No. 61572050, 91538111, 61620106009, 61429201, and the National 1000 Youth Talents Plan.

REFERENCES

[1] Eldar Insafutdinov, Leonid Pishchulin, Bjoern Andres, Mykhaylo Andriluka, and Bernt Schiele. 2016. Deepercut: A deeper, stronger, and faster multi-person pose estimation model. In *ECCV*.
[2] Jianing Li, Shiliang Zhang, Jingdong Wang, Wen Gao, and Qi Tian. 2017. LVreID: Person Re-Identification with Long Sequence Videos. *arXiv preprint arXiv:1712.07286* (2017).
[3] Hongye Liu, Yonghong Tian, Yaowei Yang, Lu Pang, and Tiejun Huang. 2016. Deep relative distance learning: Tell the difference between similar vehicles. In *CVPR*.
[4] Xiaobin Liu, Shiliang Zhang, Qingming Huang, and Wen Gao. 2018. RAM: A Region-Aware Deep Model for Vehicle Re-Identification. In *ICME*.
[5] Chi Su, Jianing Li, Shiliang Zhang, Junliang Xing, Wen Gao, and Qi Tian. 2017. Pose-driven Deep Convolutional Model for Person Re-identification. In *ICCV*.
[6] Chi Su, Fan Yang, Shiliang Zhang, Qi Tian, Larry S Davis, and Wen Gao. 2017. Multi-Task Learning with Low Rank Attribute Embedding for Multi-Camera Person Re-identification. *IEEE Transactions on Pattern Analysis and Machine Intelligence* (2017).
[7] Chi Su, Shiliang Zhang, Junliang Xing, Wen Gao, and Qi Tian. 2018. Multi-type attributes driven multi-camera person re-identification. *Pattern Recognition* 75 (2018), 77–89.
[8] Chi Su, Shiliang Zhang, Fan Yang, Guangxiao Zhang, Qi Tian, Wen Gao, and Larry S Davis. 2017. Attributes driven tracklet-to-tracklet person re-identification using latent prototypes space mapping. *Pattern Recognition* 66 (2017), 4–15.
[9] Yifan Sun, Liang Zheng, Weijian Deng, and Shengjin Wang. 2017. SVDNet for Pedestrian Retrieval. In *ICCV*.
[10] Zhongdao Wang, Luming Tang, Xihui Liu, Zhuliang Yao, Shuai Yi, Jing Shao, Junjie Yan, Shengjin Wang, Hongsheng Li, and Xiaogang Wang. 2017. Orientation Invariant Feature Embedding and Spatial Temporal Regularization for Vehicle Re-Identification. In *ICCV*.
[11] Longhui Wei, Shiliang Zhang, Wen Gao, and Qi Tian. 2017. Person Transfer GAN to Bridge Domain Gap for Person Re-Identification. *arXiv preprint arXiv:1711.08565* (2017).
[12] Longhui Wei, Shiliang Zhang, Hantao Yao, Wen Gao, and Qi Tian. 2017. GLAD: Global-Local-Alignment Descriptor for Pedestrian Retrieval. In *ACM MM*.
[13] Hantao Yao, Shiliang Zhang, Dongming Zhang, Yongdong Zhang, Jintao Li, Yu Wang, and Qi Tian. 2017. Large-scale person re-identification as retrieval. In *ICME*.
[14] Hantao Yao, Shiliang Zhang, Yongdong Zhang, Jintao Li, and Qi Tian. 2017. One-Shot Fine-Grained Instance Retrieval. In *ACM Multimedia*.
[15] Ying Zhang, Tao Xiang, Timothy M Hospedales, and Huchuan Lu. 2017. Deep Mutual Learning. *arXiv preprint arXiv:1706.00384* (2017).
[16] Haiyu Zhao, Maoqing Tian, Shuyang Sun, Jing Shao, Junjie Yan, Shuai Yi, Xiaogang Wang, and Xiaoou Tang. 2017. Spindle net: Person re-identification with human body region guided feature decomposition and fusion. In *CVPR*.
[17] Liang Zheng, Liyue Shen, Lu Tian, Shengjin Wang, Jingdong Wang, and Qi Tian. 2015. Scalable person re-identification: A benchmark. In *ICCV*.
[18] Zhedong Zheng, Liang Zheng, and Yi Yang. 2017. Pedestrian Alignment Network for Large-scale Person Re-identification. *arXiv preprint arXiv:1707.00408* (2017).

VisLoiter$^+$: An Entropy Model-Based Loiterer Retrieval System with User-Friendly Interfaces *

Maguell L.T.L. Sandifort[†,‡], Jianquan Liu[‡], Shoji Nishimura[‡], Wolfgang Hürst[†]
[†]Utrecht University, the Netherlands
[‡]Biometrics Research Laboratories, NEC Corporation, Japan

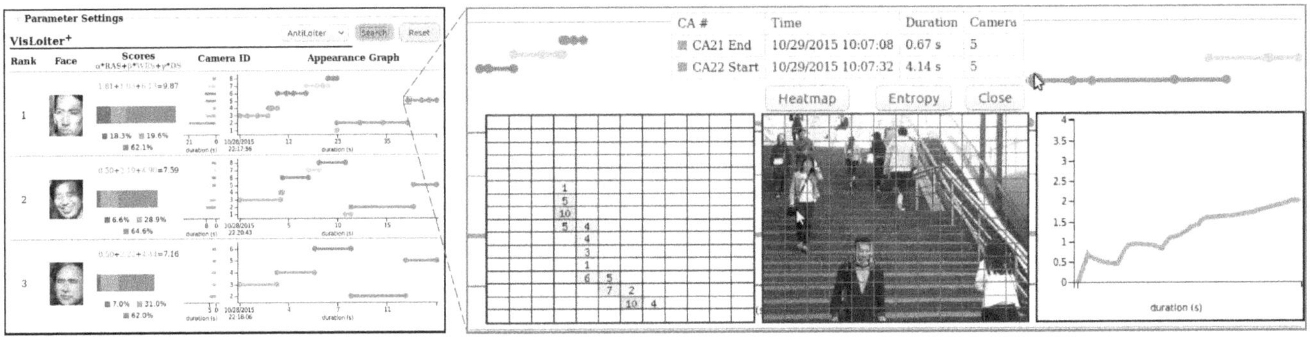

Figure 1: System overview and interfaces of VisLoiter$^+$. (left) A ranked list of loiterer candidates retrieved by VisLoiter$^+$. Each row presents the abstracted information of a person including a face thumbnail, scores for ranking, a histogram of appearance duration w.r.t different cameras, and an appearance graph showing a person's appearance on different cameras. (right) When clicking on the point line of a camera, the person's details will be shown in a popup window. There, the appearance information is summarized; in the middle, a lightweight playback of the video clip of the appearing person is displayed; by clicking on the "Heatmap" button, a grid will be overlaid on the video clip and a heatmap will be attached to show the distribution of features of the candidate; by clicking on the "Entropy" button, an entropy graph will be attached to show the change of entropy w.r.t the heatmap over time.

ABSTRACT

It is very difficult to fully automate the detection of loitering behavior in video surveillance, therefore humans are often required for monitoring. Alternatively, we could provide a list of potential loiterer candidates for a final yes/no judgment of a human operator. Our system, VisLoiter$^+$, realizes this idea with a unique, user-friendly interface and by employing an entropy model for improved loitering analysis. Rather than using only frequency of appearance, we expand the loiter analysis with new methods measuring the amount of person movements across multiple camera views. The interface gives an overview of loiterer candidates to show their behavior at a glance, complemented by a lightweight video playback for further details about why a candidate was selected. We demonstrate that our system outperforms state-of-the-art solutions using real-life data sets.

KEYWORDS

Loiterer Retrieval; Loitering Discovery; Video Surveillance; Entropy Model; Heatmap; Ranking System

ACM Reference Format:
Maguell L.T.L. Sandifort[†,‡], Jianquan Liu[‡], Shoji Nishimura[‡], Wolfgang Hürst[†]. 2018. VisLoiter$^+$: An Entropy Model-Based Loiterer Retrieval System with User-Friendly Interfaces . In *ICMR '18: 2018 International Conference on Multimedia Retrieval, June 11–14, 2018, Yokohama, Japan.* ACM, New York, NY, USA, 4 pages. https://doi.org/10.1145/3206025.3206091

*This work is mainly completed during the period of internship.

ICMR '18, June 11–14, 2018, Yokohama, Japan

ACM ISBN 978-1-4503-5046-4/18/06...$15.00
https://doi.org/10.1145/3206025.3206091

1 INTRODUCTION

Nowadays, most public areas are equipped with a large amount of surveillance cameras to enhance security. One security risk is loitering, i.e., people staying in an area for an extended period of time without a clear goal [10]. Loitering is often followed up by illegal actions such as illegal entry or pickpocketing and is therefore important behavior to detect. However, to do this, the camera footage needs to be viewed by operators. Manually searching through footage of a multi-camera system is time consuming and requires a lot of man power. While there are many automatic loitering detection approaches that do not require an operator [1, 2, 4, 9, 13], they require a threshold to recognize loitering, leading to potential misclassification above or below this threshold line. Research suggests that operators will always be necessary in some form [3]. Therefore a suitable alternative to automated recognition is reducing the workload of operators instead of replacing them by providing an overview list of loiterer candidates. This eases the job of the operators, but still leaves the final yes/no judgment to them.

Liu et al. introduced AntiLoiter [5], which provides such a list of candidates based on the frequency of appearance. This state-of-the-art commercial product extracts identifiable features of people from video frames. After that the features are grouped by similarity to get clusters of features that are of the same person. However, frequency or duration is not the only indicator of loitering behavior. For example, the trajectory information of people is a considerable indicator, but not used in AntiLoiter. They opt to forgo tracking methods due to tracking requiring a continuous view, which is difficult to achieve in crowded scenes or across multiple cameras.

Liu et al. also provided a visualization system for their method named VisLoiter [6] that visualizes the discovery results of loiterer

Table 1: Differences between VisLoiter⁺ and previous versions.

Functionality	VisLoiter⁺	AntiLoiter [5] VisLoiter [6]
List of candidates	✓	✓
Uses duration of appearance	✓	✓
Consider reappearance on cameras	✓	
Consider movement of candidates	✓	
Overview of duration per camera	✓	
Overview of appearances on cameras	✓	
Allow tuning for retrieval ranking	✓	
Allow video playback	✓	✓

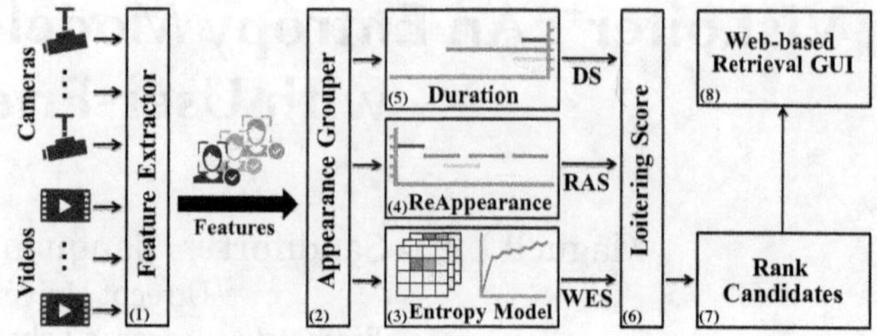

Figure 2: Architecture of VisLoiter⁺.

candidates. For each candidate they then show a chart of appearances. The higher the amount of features, the greater the segment will be. Clicking on one of the appearances plays back the video of those appearance segments. However, as the amount of features scales with the duration, which is already on the x-axis, it does not provide much additional information. Also, the overview does not display which camera view the features were captured from, so operators will have to open the video playback to find this out.

In this paper we propose an improved loiterer retrieval system that builds on the previous versions mentioned above (AntiLoiter [5], VisLoiter [6]). To achieve this goal, we use a new approach [11] that focuses on three aspects of loitering behavior by answering three questions. (1) How irregular is the abstracted movement of a person in a camera or across multiple cameras? (2) How frequent is the same person re-entering the same camera? (3) How abnormal is the duration of a person showing up on the same camera?

Therefore, responding to the three questions, we propose (1) employing an entropy model, which utilizes the more in-depth information that tracking approaches can provide, but without relying on detailed tracking. We map the positions of a person's features to a heatmap and calculate the entropy over it to determine how the person has moved across the camera view. This model serves as an abstraction for tracking methods. In addition, we consider (2) the transition of a person between cameras, as well as (3) the duration of appearance. These three aspects are then combined into a final score, which is used to determine the rank of loitering candidates.

Regarding the functionality and the interface, our new system VisLoiter⁺ provides an overview of the top loitering candidates. In addition, it gives an overview of which cameras candidates have appeared on and what has caused them to have their high loitering score. Additionally, VisLoiter⁺ allows operators to further investigate candidates of choice by showing the appearances of the candidate over time and playing video segments with the candidate in them. The operator can use this information to make the final call on whether or not someone is a loiterer.

Finally, for the purpose of demonstration, we will present a live demo[1] where we highlight our improvements and show the usability of VisLoiter⁺ with user-friendly interfaces. We also show that VisLoiter⁺ can provide additional potential loitering candidates based on their amount of movement and reappearances on the same camera. We summarize our key contributions and differences from previous work in Table 1.

2 NEW APPROACH: VISLOITER⁺

Fig. 2 shows the architecture of VisLoiter⁺. In the *Feature Extractor* (1), any feature extraction method can be used, which groups features from the same person together, such as by means of a similarity function. The metadata of a feature includes: a person identifier, a camera identifier, a timestamp and the position in the camera view. Next the *Appearance Grouper* (2) groups features into Camera Appearances (*CAs*). Each *CA* contains features from one person on one camera. Then we calculate three loitering measures: the Weighted Entropy Score (*WES*) using our *Entropy Model* (3), the *ReAppearance Score* (*RAS*) (4) using the *CAs*, and a *Duration Score* (*DS*) (5). These measures are then weighted and combined into one (6) *Loitering Score* (*LS*) (6). Finally, the candidates are *ranked* by their *LS* (7) and sent, along with their representation data, to the *Web-based GUI* (8), where the operator can check the results.

2.1 Loitering Measures

To determine the likeliness of loitering behavior, we incorporate three different measures [11]: entropy, reappearance and duration. Each of these measures contribute to the final score for retrieval ranking. Why we need to propose these measures is also corresponding to the questions we mentioned in Section 1.

First the metadata of the features are grouped into Camera Appearances (*CAs*). A *CA* starts when a person enters the camera view and ends when they leave. We provide a *CA* timeframe parameter T_{CA}, to determine how much time has to pass for 2 features to be considered in a different camera appearance. The *CAs* are then used to calculate the measures.

(1) Entropy Model. The entropy model determines the amount of movement of a person. We construct a heatmap for each candidate such as shown in Fig. 5. The amount of bins can be specified by the operator. The features of the same person in a *CA* will be mapped to the heatmap based on their position in the camera view. Then we calculate the probability distribution of the bins (p_{b_i}) on the heatmap: each bin gets a value indicating the percentage of total features of the *CA* that are in that bin. With the probability distribution we can calculate the entropy over the heatmap (he_j). Finally, we weight the entropy value of each heatmap by their percentage contribution to the total duration of all their *CAs* and then add them together into the Weighted Entropy Score (*WES*).

$$he_j = -\sum_{i=1}^{n} p_{b_i} \log(p_{b_i}),\ where\ p_{b_i} = \frac{count(b_i)}{count(CA_j)} \tag{1}$$

$$WES = \sum_{j=1}^{m} \left(he_j \frac{Duration(CA_j)}{\sum_{j=1}(Duration(CA_j))} \right) \tag{2}$$

(2) ReAppearance. We define reappearing behavior as a situation where someone leaves a camera view and re-enters it again. To model this we count the amount of *CAs* for each of the cameras a person appears on. The amount of appearances (a_i) is used as an exponent in an exponential function (2^{a_i-1}) to determine the ReAppearance on that camera. Finally, the *RAS* is calculated by adding the ReAppearance values of all the cameras together, divided by the amount of cameras that the person appeared on.

$$RAS = \sum_{i=1}^{n} 2^{a_i-1} / count(CAMERA) \tag{3}$$

[1] https://github.com/ryukenzen/visloiterplus

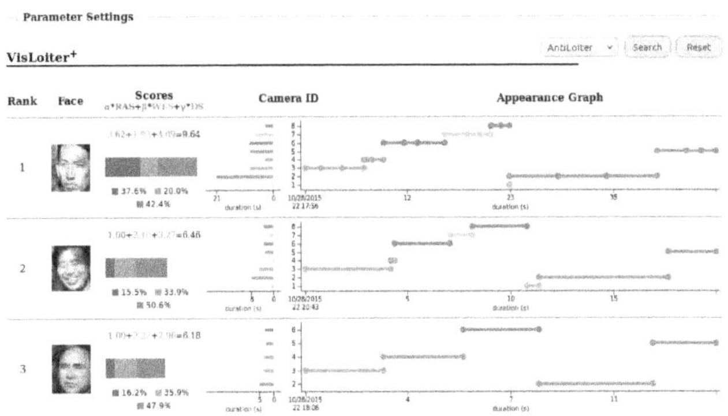

Figure 3: Candidate list overview of VisLoiter⁺.

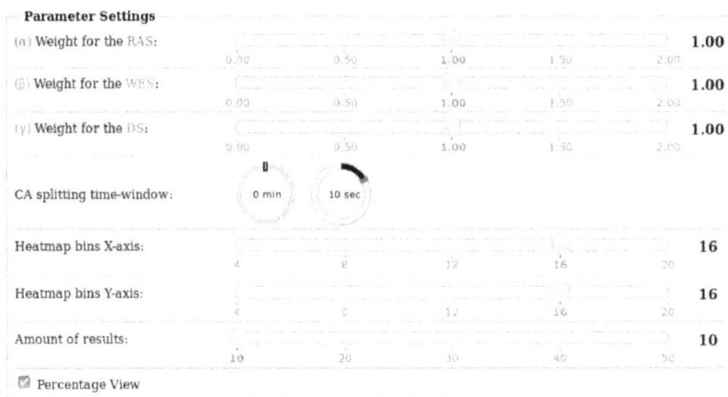

Figure 4: Parameter settings panel of VisLoiter⁺.

(3) Duration. Duration is a general indicator for loitering. The longer someone is in the area, the more likely they are loitering. We calculate the Duration Score (*DS*) of a person by adding the duration of all *CAs*. The duration of a *CA* is the time difference between the first and last timestamp in the *CA*. In the case of *CAs* with overlapping duration intervals, the duration is not added multiple times. As the duration of appearance for each person can vary wildly, we scale down its impact by taking the logarithm over the final duration.

$$DS = \log\left(\sum_{j=1}(Duration(CA_j)) + 1\right) \tag{4}$$

(4) Loitering Score. Finally, to create a ranking measure, we combine the three measures into one Loitering Score (*LS*). Different surveilled scenes can have different loitering behaviors that should be distinguished. Therefore we introduce the weights α, β and γ. With these the operator can tweak the impact of each on the rank of loiterer candidates. We then rank the people appearing in surveilled scenes in descending order of *LS* to create a list of loitering candidates.

$$LS = \alpha RAS + \beta WES + \gamma DS \tag{5}$$

2.2 Implementation

VisLoiter⁺ is implemented as a Browser/Server (B/S) system according to Fig. 2. The client side frontend can be opened on the browser. From here, the user can send requests to the server, after which the results will be displayed. The GUI is constructed using JavaScript, with the D3 [8] and C3 [12] libraries. The server side backend listens for requests. The loitering analysis and search request listener are implemented in C++ and run on a Ubuntu 16.04 machine.

After receiving a search request, the loitering analysis system will go over each person's metadata and calculates the measures for them. After that the list of top candidates, with summary information for each, will be sent to the client in JSON format. The summary information consists of a face image, scores for the different measures and all *CAs* for that person. In addition, the intermediate results of the entropy calculations are stored for heatmap and entropy requests.

Playing back the raw surveillance videos causes heavy network traffic. Therefore we use a lightweight video playback instead. For this playback request the selected *CA* is sent to the server. The video playback script then adds the bounding box of the feature of the person to each of the frames. These frames are then combined into a sequence, which is sent to the client to play back.

The heatmap overlay is handled by the heatmap script. It draws the heatmap grid over the frames provided by the video playback. It also requests the intermediate results from the entropy calculation and constructs a heatmap image to display next to the video playback (see Fig. 5).

Finally, for the entropy over time view, a stepwise entropy request is sent to the loitering analyzer, which returns the entropy for each intermediate addition to the heatmap. This data is then used to plot a chart next to the video playback box to show the change of entropy over time (see Fig. 6).

2.3 Visualization and Usage

In addition to an improved result ranking, our system features a web-based user-friendly interface. It is designed for the operator to make the correct final decisions, by enabling them to adjust parameters and easily review the list of candidates (see Fig. 3).

The top of Fig. 3 shows a collapsible menu for the *parameter settings*, where the operator can adjust the following parameters through a series of slider bars (see Fig. 4):

- The weights α, β and γ for each of the loitering measures. Increasing a weight will make that respective measure contribute more heavily to the *LS*. Higher weights result in a higher overall *LS*, but as the *LS* is a comparative measure, only the ratio between the weights will have an effect on the ordering.
- The time window T_{CA} that affects the length of the *CAs*. Increasing this will give people a higher "grace period" for leaving and re-entering the camera view, which can be helpful if many people walk along the sides of a camera view.
- The dimensions for the heatmap. Using higher dimensions will give more detailed movement information.
- The amount of results, which can be increased at the cost of a longer processing time.

In addition, there is a toggle for the timescale view. By default, the Appearance Graph shows all the *CAs* in sequence, so their relative length can be easily determined. By toggling this option, the *CAs* will be displayed on a linear timescale. This gives the operator a better overview on when a candidate showed up on the cameras.

Pressing the *search button* will send a search request to the server. After the candidate list is determined, they are sent back to the client and will be displayed in the *Candidate List* below. It gives a detailed overview of the top loitering candidates, with the most likely loiterer at the top. Each row of the list contains the loitering overview of a candidate, each in turn providing some valuable information about that person. They are the *Rank, Face Image, Score Overview, Camera Duration Histogram* and *Appearance Graph.*

The operator can quickly go over the face images in case they are looking for a specific person. Looking at the score overview, the operator can immediately see why the candidate has a high *LS* as the respective measure will have the largest bar segment, such

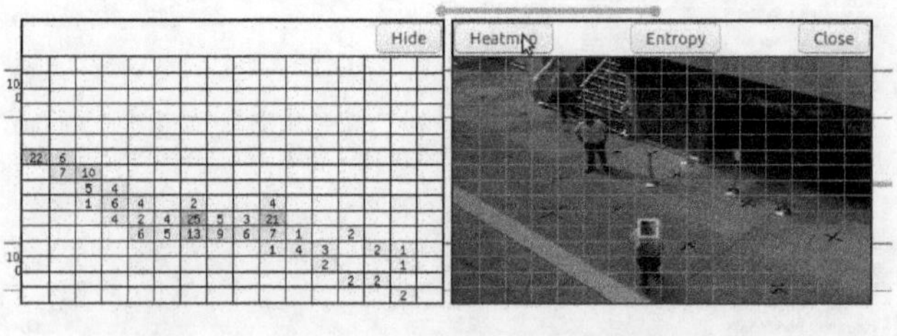

Figure 5: The heatmap view of the video window. It draws the heatmap grid over the video frame and displays the heatmap for the respective Camera Appearance (*CA*) of a person.

as a high reappearance in the same area (*RAS*), moving irregularly (*WES*) or in the area significantly longer than other people (*DS*).

Next is the duration histogram, which shows the total duration of appearance on each camera the candidate has appeared on. This shows which cameras will be most interesting to investigate further. Hovering over each line shows the respective camera's total duration and amount of *CAs*. The duration histogram and appearance graph color of the lines is consistent for each camera. This makes it easy to recognize what *CA* belongs to which camera, and allows a quick comparison between candidates.

Finally, the appearance graph shows all the *CAs* for that candidate. *CAs* are sorted by timestamp and *CAs* with the same camera will be on the same y-level. The appearance graph has two uses. First, it gives the operator a quick overview about the transition of a candidate between cameras and quickly shows if a pedestrian repeatedly entered and exited a camera view. Hovering over a segment will provide the time when the person entered that camera, as well as for how long they were in its view before they left. Second, the operator can click on one of the segments to open a video playback window (in Fig. 5 and Fig. 6), which shows the video footage for the respective *CA* of a person.

In addition to the regular footage, there is also a heatmap overlay and entropy over time view, which can be activated by pressing the respective buttons at the top of the video playback window.

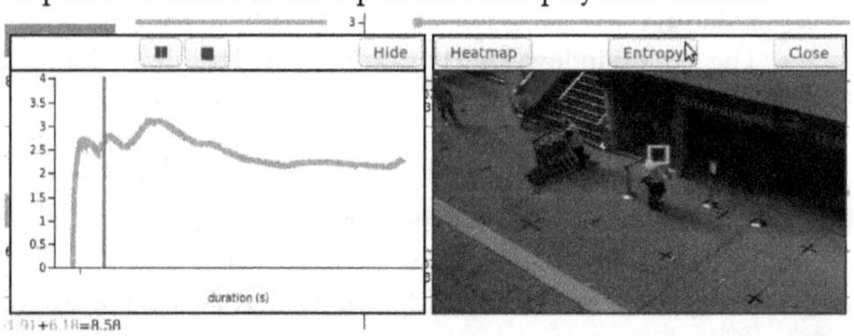

Figure 6: The entropy over time view. Increasing entropy indicates someone moving, while decreasing entropy indicates someone standing still.

The heatmap overlay shows the heatmap grid over the video window. Next to it, it displays the filled heatmap of that person to get a quick idea of how the person moved across the camera view. The heatmap is color coded: the color scale changes from yellow to red, depending on the amount of features in the bin. An example can be seen in Fig. 5. The darker orange spots indicate "walk-stop-walk-stop" behavior.

The entropy over time view shows a graph with the change of entropy score for a candidate plotted over time to get an idea about their movement behavior in the area. If the entropy goes up, the person is moving, if it goes down, the person is standing still and if it stays roughly equal, the person moves in a constrained area. Fig. 6 shows an example of a "walk-stop-change direction" pattern, which can be identified by an upwards trend where the entropy is repeatedly going up and down over time. After the entropy peak, the person stands still, causing the entropy to gradually decrease. Then the person goes back the same way they came, causing the entropy to stagnate. Finally, the operator can pause the footage or go back to the start with the media buttons at the top.

With these features, the operator can further investigate candidates they consider suspicious and then make a final, reliable verdict with their own expert knowledge.

3 DEMO

To highlight our improvements compared to the previous approach, we use the AntiLoiter dataset[2] [5, 7] for an on-site live demo. We show that the ordering of the candidates is different, due to the new measure being used. In addition, we demonstrate the improved overview of the appearances of each candidate. Next, to highlight the effectiveness of the entropy model approach and to show that our system can be used with different feature extraction methods, we use Scenarios 1 and 3 of the PETS dataset[3] as well for the live demo. With this part of the demo we illustrate the differences in heatmaps between walking, waiting and loitering people. We also show what the effect of each of these behaviors has on the entropy that is calculated over time. Finally, we demonstrate the effects of adjusting the parameters, by showing the candidate lists based on the parameters inputted.

4 CONCLUSION

We created an improved loiter retrieval system called VisLoiter$^+$ and highlighted its improvements compared to previous versions. Our new system can reduce the number of missed candidates by considering a person's amount of movement and reappearances, and provides additional information that is helpful for operators in their final judgment.

REFERENCES

[1] Héctor F. Gómez A., Rafael Martínez-Tomás, Susana Arias Tapia, Antonio Fernández-Caballero, Sylvie Ratté, Alexandra González Eras, and Patricia Ludeña González. 2015. Identification of Loitering Human Behaviour in Video Surveillance Environments. In *Proc. of IWINAC*. 516–525.

[2] N. D. Bird, O. Masoud, P. Papanikolopoulos, and A. Isaacs. 2005. Detection of loitering individuals in public transportation areas. *IEEE Tran. on Intelligent Transportation Systems* 6(2) (2005), 167–177.

[3] Helen M Hodgetts, François Vachon, Cindy Chamberland, and Sébastien Tremblay. 2017. See no evil: Cognitive challenges of security surveillance and monitoring. *Journal of Applied Research in Memory and Cognition* 6, 3 (2017), 230–243.

[4] Jong-Gook Ko and Jang-Hee Yoo. 2013. Rectified Trajectory Analysis Based Abnormal Loitering Detection for Video Surveillance. In *Proc. of AIMS*. 289–293.

[5] Jianquan Liu, Shoji Nishimura, and Takuya Araki. 2016. AntiLoiter: A loitering discovery system for longtime videos across multiple surveillance cameras. In *Proc. of ACM Multimedia*. 675–679.

[6] Jianquan Liu, Shoji Nishimura, and Takuya Araki. 2016. VisLoiter: a system to visualize loiterers discovered from surveillance videos. In *Proc. of ACM SIGGRAPH Posters*. 47.

[7] Jianquan Liu, Shoji Nishimura, Takuya Araki, and Yuichi Nakamura. 2017. A Loitering Discovery System Using Efficient Similarity Search Based on Similarity Hierarchy. *IEICE Transactions* 100-A, 2 (2017), 367–375.

[8] Glenn J Myatt and Wayne P Johnson. 2011. *Making Sense of Data III: A practical guide to designing interactive data visualizations*. Vol. 3. John Wiley & Sons.

[9] Yunyoung Nam. 2015. Loitering detection using an associating pedestrian tracker in crowded scenes. *Multimedia Tools Application* 74, 9 (2015), 2939–2961.

[10] Scott A. Richmond and Patric R. Spence. 2013. Loitering. In *Encyclopedia of Street Crime in America*, Jeffrey Ian Ross (Ed.). SAGE Publications, Inc, 240–241.

[11] Maguell L. T. L. Sandifort, Jianquan Liu, Shoji Nishimura, and Wolfgang Hürst. 2018. An Entropy Model for Loiterer Retrieval across Multiple Surveillance Cameras. In *Proc. of ACM ICMR*.

[12] Masayuki Tanaka. 2013. D3-based Reusable Chart Library. c3js.org. (2013).

[13] Thi Thi Zin, Pyke Tin, Takashi Toriu, and Hiromitsu Hama. 2010. A Markov Random Walk Model for Loitering People Detection. In *Sixth International Conference on Intelligent Information Hiding and Multimedia Signal Processing (IIH-MSP)*. 680–683.

[2]https://github.com/ryukenzen/antiloiter/

[3]http://www.cvg.reading.ac.uk/PETS2007/data.html

Automated Scanning and Individual Identification System for Parts without Marking or Tagging

Kengo Makino
NEC Corporation
Kawasaki, Japan
k-makino@mb.jp.nec.com

Wenjie Duan
Delft University of Technology
Delft, Netherlands
W.Duan-1@student.tudelft.nl

Rui Ishiyama
NEC Corporation
Kawasaki, Japan
r-ishiyama@bl.jp.nec.com

Toru Takahashi
NEC Corporation
Kawasaki, Japan
t-takahashi@hg.nec.com

Yuta Kudo
NEC Corporation
Kawasaki, Japan
y-kudo@bc.jp.nec.com

Pieter Jonker
Delft University of Technology
Delft, Netherlands
p.p.jonker@tudelft.nl

ABSTRACT

This paper presents a fully automated system for detecting, classifying, microscopic imaging, and individually identifying multiple parts without ID-marking or tagging. The system is beneficial for product assemblers, who handle multiple types of parts simultaneously. They can ensure traceability quite easily by only placing the parts freely on the system platform. The system captures microscopic images of parts as their "fingerprints," which are matched with pre-registered images in a database to identify an individual part's information such as its serial number. We demonstrate a working prototype and interaction scenario.

CCS CONCEPTS

• **Computing methodologies** → **Object identification**;

KEYWORDS

IoT; Traceability; Image recognition; Individual identification; Classification; Objects localization; Fingerprint of Things

ACM Reference Format:
Kengo Makino, Wenjie Duan, Rui Ishiyama, Toru Takahashi, Yuta Kudo, and Pieter Jonker. 2018. Automated Scanning and Individual Identification System for Parts without Marking or Tagging. In *ICMR '18: 2018 International Conference on Multimedia Retrieval, June 11–14, 2018, Yokohama, Japan.* ACM, New York, NY, USA, 4 pages. https://doi.org/10.1145/3206025.3206088

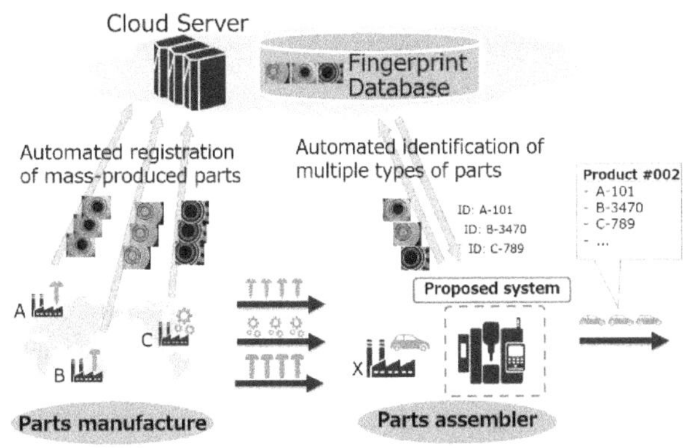

Figure 1: Concept of parts traceability throughout supply chain using the proposed system.

1 INTRODUCTION

Traceability of individual parts is essential for ensuring quality and safety of assembled products. For example, to determine the cause of a product failure, information about the individual parts used in the assembly process must be retrieved. The conventional method for ensuring parts traceability is attaching ID tags such as barcodes, radio frequency ID (RFID) tags, etc. onto the parts and reading them. Marking or tagging makes parts identification accurate and convenient. However, these approach cannot be applied to mass-production use, especially in case of small parts. Since characters, barcodes or tags have to be further smaller as parts become smaller, marking and reading them becomes increasingly difficult thus costly. Therefore, total cost for marking or reading will become prohibitive as the amount of production increase. A fully automated identification system without marking or tagging is demanded for mass-production use.

Some emerging identification techniques have been proposed to enable tag-less identification of objects [1, 3, 8, 12]. These techniques use unique surface patterns naturally formed during the manufacturing process. Bunchanan et al. [3] proposed a document and package identification technique that uses laser speckle patterns. Beekhof et al. [1] proposed a basic framework to identify papers using random microstructures of fibers. Matsumoto et al. [8] proposed a nano-artifact metrics based on the random collapse of resist pillars. Furthermore, a fingerprint-based identification method has been proposed for metal parts that are widely used in industrial products [12]. This method has been applied to ensuring traceability and preventing misuse of parts [11].

Automation is mandatory for use in mass-production. If an operator of a factory line manually places parts under a camera to capture a fingerprint image, the operator must precisely adjust

ICMR '18, June 11–14, 2018, Yokohama, Japan

ACM ISBN 978-1-4503-5046-4/18/06...$15.00
https://doi.org/10.1145/3206025.3206088

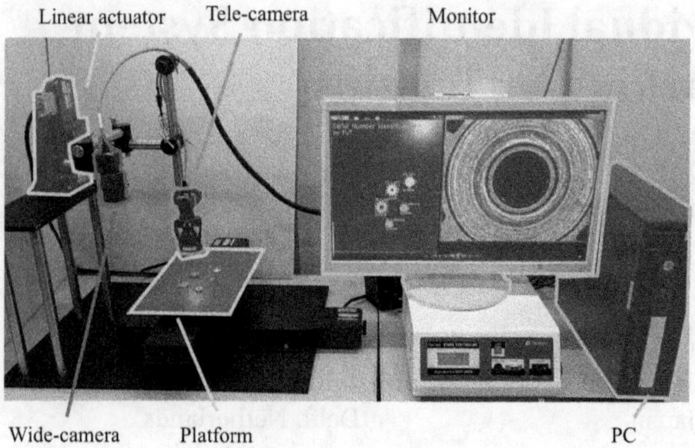

Figure 2: Hardware components of the system.

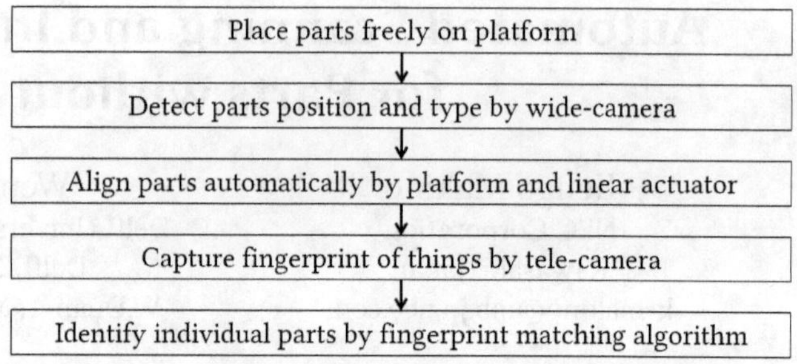

Figure 3: Overview of the proposed system.

the part's position and the camera's focus (we call this process alignment). This is because the microscopic camera's field of view and depth of field are very narrow. Such manual alignment is time consuming and detrimental to assembly efficiency. To use the fingerprint identification in a real assembly process, a fully automated capturing system is needed to solve this problem.

Of the aforementioned tag-less identification methods, only the fingerprint-based identification method [12] has been fully automated. The prototype machine [12] can capture fingerprint images for numerous bolts with automated feeding. It is designed for parts manufacturers to register fingerprints and parts information, as it can handle only a single type of mass-produced parts. It is too limited for assembling, which requires handling multiple part types simultaneously. Developing dedicated hardware for every type of parts is too costly.

This paper proposes a fully automated identification system that can scan and identify multiple types of parts with a single general setup. The proposed system first automatically detects part position and type by using a wide-view camera and adjusts the position of the microscopic camera to capture a fingerprint image. Using the fingerprint image, the proposed system also automatically identifies individuals of those parts. As the operator needs only to freely place parts on the platform of our system, the system ensures traceability without any costly manual operation.

Figure 1 shows the concept of the parts traceability system using our parts identification system. First, fingerprint images of mass-produced parts are registered in the database during the parts' manufacturing processes. When the parts are picked out during the assembly process, fingerprint images of the parts are captured and identified automatically by our proposed system. This enables the parts assembler to identify all constituent parts of any product, thus the traceability is ensured throughout the supply chain.

2 SYSTEM

Our proposed system consists of a platform, a linear actuator, a desktop PC with a display monitor, and two cameras. Figure 2 shows the hardware components of the system. Figure 3 shows the workflow of the system. First, the operator freely places parts on the platform. Then, a wide-view camera (referred to as a wide-camera from here on) detects and classifies the positions and types of the parts. This process will be further described in section 2.1. The other camera equipped with a microscopic lens (referred to as a tele-camera from here on) captures a microscopic image of a part's surface. The platform and tele-camera move simultaneously to align the part and bring it into focus, the details of which will be described in section 2.2. Captured microscopic images are individually unique and considered as parts' "fingerprints," which we will call "fingerprint images" from here on. These fingerprint images will be matched with pre-registered images in a database. The matching process will be further described in section 2.3. The PC processes images from the cameras and controls the movements of the linear actuator and platform. The monitor shows the results of part detection, captured fingerprint images, and individual part IDs to the operator in real-time.

2.1 Detection of Part Position and Type by Wide-camera

The wide-camera monitors the whole platform to detect where parts are placed and classifies part types in real-time. The detected positions and classified types will be used to align the parts with the tele-camera and to capture a fingerprint image.

We use background subtraction, binarization, and morphological operations to extract part regions in a captured image. Then, a contour detection method [10] is used to detect the center position and region of each part. The center position is used to align parts. Lens distortion of the wide-camera is corrected by the camera calibration method [13], so the detected part's position is accurate enough for aligning the part with the tele-camera's view, described in section 2.2.

The detected regions of parts in the image are cropped out before part type is classified. We use the bag of features method [7] and the support vector machine classifier [5]. In the bag of features method, we use the Oriented FAST and Rotated BRIEF (ORB) feature [9] as our feature point detector and descripter.

In our demonstration, the detection and classification results are displayed on the monitor in real-time. Figure 7 (a) shows the interface of the detection mode. The part types are shown in different colors.

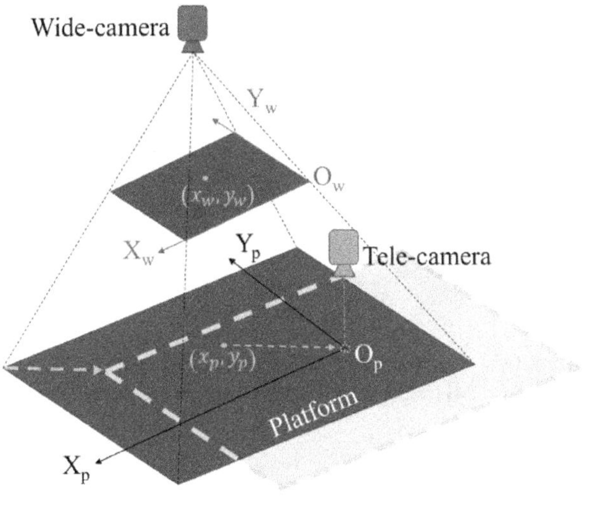

Figure 4: Graph for wide-camera coordinate and platform coordinate. Green point is on platform and is detected by wide-camera at (x_w, y_w). Its relative position to tele-camera is (x_p, y_p). After platform moves to dashed position, green point is aligned with tele-camera.

2.2 Automatic Microscopic Fingerprint Capturing by Tele-camera

After detecting all part positions and types, the system captures fingerprint images. First, the platform automatically moves in the horizontal plane to align parts with the focal position of the tele-camera. This alignment needs to be automated, because the field of view of the tele-camera is very small (about 10 mm × 10 mm). Simultaneously, the tele-camera's height is adjusted by a linear actuator to align the tele-camera's focal distance with the part's top surface.

Let us define two coordinate systems: wide-camera coordinate and platform coordinate, as shown in Figure 4. The wide-camera coordinate is the wide-camera's image coordinate. The platform coordinate indicates a part's relative position to O_p, which is the focal position of the tele-camera on the platform. The origin of the platform coordinate is O_p. Using the methods described in section 2.1, we can obtain the part position in wide-camera coordinate (x_w, y_w). To align the part with the tele-camera, we need the part position in platform coordinate (x_p, y_p). We use a preset 3 × 3 homography matrix H to map a point from (x_w, y_w) to (x_p, y_p) as follows.

$$\begin{bmatrix} x_p \\ y_p \\ 1 \end{bmatrix} = H \begin{bmatrix} x_w \\ y_w \\ 1 \end{bmatrix}, \tag{1}$$

H is calibrated beforehand by using eight points marked on the platform. The eight points' positions in wide-camera coordinates (x_w, y_w) are obtained by detecting the marks in a captured image. Next, we manually control the platform to align the marks with the tele-camera's focal position, where the part is captured at image center. We then read the traveled distances of the platform from the platform's encoder. The distances give us the mark's position in platform coordinates (x_p, y_p). After obtaining 16 coordinates of the 8 marks, we estimate the homography H by minimizing the back-projection error of Equation (1) by using the least squares method [2] and preset the values of H in the system.

Using the homography H, we can calculate a part's relative position to the tele-camera and control the platform to align the part with the focal position of the tele-camera.

The linear actuator adjusts the tele-camera's height in accordance with part type, because the lens of the tele-camera is fixed-focus and its depth of field is very narrow (<1 mm). To capture in-focus fingerprint images for multiple types of parts having different heights, the tele-camera's height needs to be adjusted. The appropriate heights of the tele-camera for all types of the parts are preset. Once a part is in focus, a fingerprint image will be captured as shown in Figure 5.

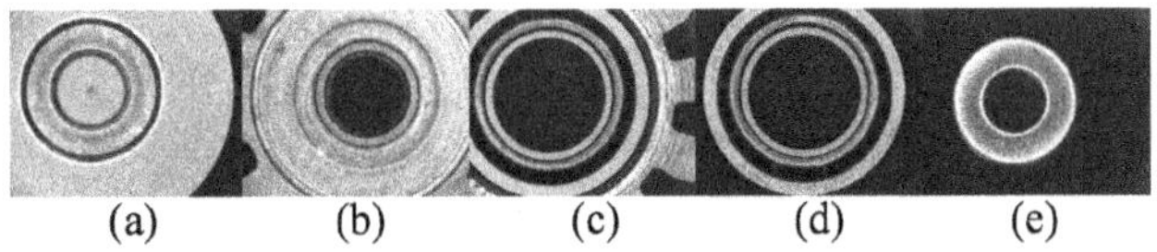

Figure 5: Examples of tested parts' fingerprint images. (a) big bolt; (b) d4.4 gear; (c) d6.4 gear; (d) D13 bearing; (e) washer.

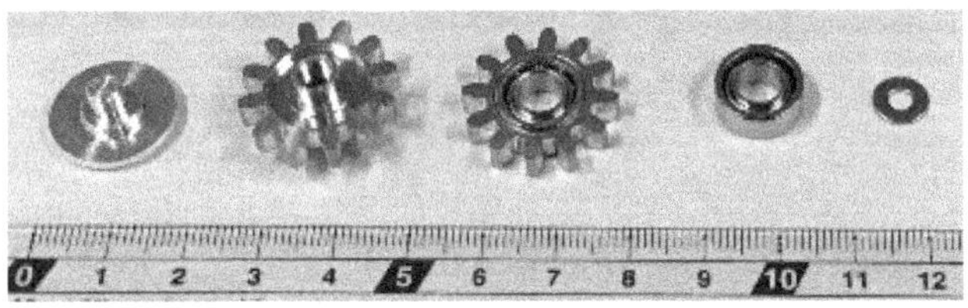

Figure 6: Tested parts types. From left to right are big bolt, d4.4 gear, d6.4 gear, D13 bearing, and washer.

2.3 Fingerprint Matching

A captured fingerprint image is matched with each of the pre-registered images in the database, and the individual identifier of the best matched part is obtained. The identifier specifies the individual part's information such as a serial number, which is displayed on the monitor.

For matching fingerprint images, we use a phase only correlation based image matching algorithm. As the parts are freely placed on the platform, the matching algorithm must be robust to rotations. To achieve such robustness, we use the method using Fourier-Mellin transform to estimate scale and rotation between the matched images [4, 6]. We use the peak correlation value obtained in the estimation as the matching score. The matching scores are calculated between a captured image and all database images, thus the best match is determined in accordance with the highest score. The identifier specifies the individual part's information, which is displayed on the monitor.

3 EXPERIMENTS

We tested our proposed system with 170 individual parts of five different types of mechanical parts. We used 20 big bolts, 10 d4.4

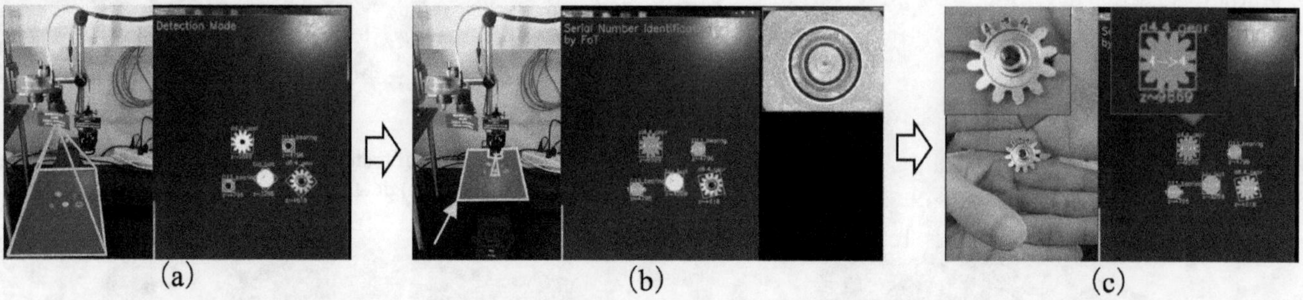

Figure 7: Demonstration of automated individual identification system. (a) Parts are placed freely on platform. (b) Platform moves parts to focal position of tele-camera and capture fingerprint image. (c) All parts are identified, and identification results are checked against ground truth.

gears, 20 d6.4 gears, 20 D13 bearing, and 100 washers. The washer is a steel flat washer that is commonly sold in hardware stores. The other four types of parts are taken from 10 disassembled commonly sold spinner toys. Figure 6 shows how these parts look.

20 images were captured for each of 5 parts types by wide-camera, thus 100 training images in total were used for training the classifier. The 20 images come from the one individual that was randomly chosen. The individual was randomly placed on the platform for 20 times to be captured with different appearances to the wide-camera due to changes of the viewing angle.

In the experiments, 170 individual parts were randomly placed on the platform, and all the parts were correctly detected, classified, and identified. The automated position detection proved sufficiently accurate, and all the five types were classified without error. This enabled us to capture fingerprint images without troublesome misalignment and miss-focus, and all the parts were successfully identified.

4 DEMONSTRATION

At the start of a demonstration, an operator can randomly choose some parts from all the pre-registered parts, which are 170 individuals of five different part types, and freely place them on the platform. The part detection and type classification are processed in real-time, and results are shown on the monitor, as shown in the right half of Figure 7 (a).

On the basis of the detection and classification results, the platform starts to align the parts with the tele-camera's focal position. The tele-camera's height is simultaneously adjusted with the part's surface height, which differs depending on the part type. After each part is aligned with the focal position of the tele-camera, a fingerprint image is captured. A captured fingerprint image is shown at the right side of the interface as shown in the right of Figure 7 (b). Matching runs in a background process, and the identification results are displayed on the monitor immediately. As shown in the center of Figure 7 (b), identified parts are colored and tagged with their individual information. For example, "2->1" indicates the part's own serial number is No. 2 and it is disassembled from assembly spinner No. 1.

After the all chosen parts are identified, the operator can check the identification results against the ground truth of the serial number written on the back side of each part. As shown in Figure 7 (c), the tag of d4.4 gear is "4->4," which is identical to the serial number written on the part.

5 CONCLUSION

We have proposed a fully automated parts identification system that requires neither tagging nor additional operation costs for identification. An operator only needs to freely place parts on the platform, then the system automatically identifies the serial numbers of those parts. Since the system can handle multiple types of parts simultaneously, it helps product assemblers ensure total traceability throughout the supply chain.

The system currently can only capture the parts' top surface that is paralleled to the platform. Detection of orientation of parts' top surface and 6-d alignment with the tele-camera remains as our future works.

REFERENCES

[1] F. Beekhof et al. 2008. Secure surface identification codes. In *Security, Forensics, Steganography, and Watermarking of Multimedia Contents X*, Vol. 6819. International Society for Optics and Photonics, 68190D.

[2] G. Bradski et al. 2008. *Learning OpenCV: Computer vision with the OpenCV library.* " O'Reilly Media, Inc.".

[3] J.D.R. Buchanan et al. 2005. Forgery:'fingerprinting' documents and packaging. *Nature* 436, 7050 (2005), 475.

[4] D. Casasent et al. 1977. New optical transforms for pattern recognition. *Proc. of the IEEE* 65, 1 (Jan. 1977), 77–84.

[5] N. Cristianini et al. 2000. *An introduction to support vector machines and other kernel-based learning methods.* Cambridge university press.

[6] H.T. Ho et al. 2008. Optical flow estimation using Fourier Mellin transform. In *Proc. of the 2008 IEEE Conf. on Computer Vision and Pattern Recognition (CVPR).* IEEE, 1–8.

[7] F-F. Li et al. 2005. A bayesian hierarchical model for learning natural scene categories. In *Proc. of 2005 IEEE Computer Society Conf. on Computer Vision and Pattern Recognition (CVPR)*, Vol. 2. IEEE, 524–531.

[8] T. Matsumoto et al. 2014. Nano-artifact metrics based on random collapse of resist. *Scientific reports* 4 (Aug. 2014), 6142.

[9] E. Rublee et al. 2011. ORB: An efficient alternative to SIFT or SURF. In *Proc. of 2011 Int. Conf. on Computer Vision (ICCV).* IEEE, 2564–2571.

[10] S. Suzuki et al. 1985. Topological structural analysis of digitized binary images by border following. *Computer vision, graphics, and image processing* 30, 1 (Apr. 1985), 32–46.

[11] T. Takahashi et al. 2016. Intelli-Wrench: Smart Navigation Tool for Mechanical Assembly and Maintenance. In *Proc. of the 24th Annual ACM Int. Conf. on Multimedia (ACMMM).* ACM, 752–753.

[12] T. Takahashi et al. 2017. Mass-produced parts traceability system based on automated scanning of "Fingerprint of Things". In *Proc. of Fifteenth IAPR International Conference on Machine Vision Applications (MVA).* IEEE, 202–206.

[13] Z. Zhang. 2000. A flexible new technique for camera calibration. *IEEE Trans. on pattern analysis and machine intelligence (PAMI)* 22, 11 (Nov. 2000), 1330–1334.

Dynamic Construction and Manipulation of Hierarchical Quartic Image Graphs

Nico Hezel
Visual Computing Group
HTW Berlin
Berlin, Germany
hezel@htw-berlin.com

Kai Uwe Barthel
Visual Computing Group
HTW Berlin
Berlin, Germany
barthel@htw-berlin.com

ABSTRACT

Over the last years, we have published papers about intuitive image graph navigation and showed how to build static hierarchical image graphs efficiently. In this paper, we showcase new results and present techniques to dynamically construct and manipulate these kinds of graphs. They connect similar images and perform well in retrieving tasks regardless of the number of nodes. By applying an improved fast self-sorting map algorithm, entire image collections (structured in a graph) can be explored with a user interface resembling common navigation services.

CCS CONCEPTS

• **Theory of computation** → **Dynamic graph algorithms**; • **Human-centered computing** → Visualization techniques;

KEYWORDS

Image Graph; Quartic Graph; Exploration; Dynamic Construction and Manipulation of Graphs; Visualization

ACM Reference Format:

Nico Hezel and Kai Uwe Barthel. 2018. Dynamic Construction and Manipulation of Hierarchical Quartic Image Graphs. In *ICMR '18: 2018 International Conference on Multimedia Retrieval, June 11–14, 2018, Yokohama, Japan.* ACM, New York, NY, USA, 4 pages. https://doi.org/10.1145/3206025.3206093

1 INTRODUCTION

The problem of visualizing and navigating millions of images is very challenging, but has partially been solved by using image graphs [1]. These graphs connect very similar images and allow reaching other related images by traversing the edges. The authors have shown techniques for exploring large data collections with a user interface similar to *Google Maps*. Parts of an image graph were projected onto a regular grid and displayed on the screen. The user can drag and zoom the presented image map to move to other regions of the graph, producing the impression of an infinite 2D map. The underlying structure is a weighted, connected, fixed sized simple regular graph of degree 4. The similarity between two images is stored in the edge connecting them and the overall graph quality is measured by the sum of all edge weights. A novel swapping algorithm changes the connections of a node to more suited ones for a better overall graph quality.

In this paper, we extend the idea by creating and manipulating a dynamic graph. The dynamic nature enables adding and removing nodes at any time without rebuilding the graph from scratch. Our second contribution is a scheme to build hierarchical graph layers dynamically. Additional layers help to summarize lower ones and ensure overview is not lost when navigating through the graph. Combining the two approaches allows generating hierarchical image graphs, which can grow and improve over time. These graphs can be navigated immediately after the initial setup.

2 RELATED WORK

Constructing a similarity graph where similar elements are connected using a metric, is a linear assignment problem and cannot be solved efficiently. There are several approximation methods following similar strategies: computing a similarity matrix W for a dataset X and then sparsifying an adjacency matrix A. The non-zero entities in A decide which elements of X should be connected to each other, using the values of W as the edge weights, to form the final graph G.

Some proposed methods generate graphs with variations of the B-Matching algorithm [2] [3], which itself is a generalized version of the Hungarian algorithm and has a complexity of $O(n^3)$. Another solution adopts the auction algorithm for graph construction [4] and solves the same problem faster, yielding similar connection qualities. The complexity is just $O(n)$. All mentioned techniques try to build a perfect graph in one run, but have no concept for manipulating it afterwards. Furthermore, none of them guarantees a connected graph, making navigation difficult since not all images can be reached. A much simpler and faster approach is using k-nearest neighbor (kNN) graph construction [5], where each node is connected to the ones most similar. On the one hand, the greedy construction process produces irregular, imbalanced and sometimes disconnected graphs; on the other hand, it allows addition and deletion of nodes at any time.

Back in 1972 Toida published a paper [6] describing rules for what he calls V-type and H-type reduction and expansions of quartic graphs. These steps allow addition and subtraction of nodes without changing the regularity and connectivity of a graph. The only disadvantage is, not every node can be removed at any time. While useful for mathematical purposes, it restricts manipulative actions down to cases where a graph is H-type and/or V-type reducible.

ICMR '18, June 11–14, 2018, Yokohama, Japan

ACM ISBN 978-1-4503-5046-4/18/06...$15.00
https://doi.org/10.1145/3206025.3206093

We present a method combining the idea of kNN and Toida by connecting new nodes to the best matching existing ones, guaranteeing graph regularity and connectivity even after adding or removing a node. The graph is built step by step starting from a small initial graph K_5. New nodes replace existing edges with two new edges connecting all three participating nodes. The quality of the rerouted links is sufficient to not destroy the feeling of a well-organized graph and is improved continuously over time with an edge swapping algorithm.

3 MANIPULATING THE GRAPH

In order to reuse the presented navigation concept of [1], the final graph needs to be 4-regular, strict and connected. Otherwise not all images can be reached. An initial graph K_5 (figure 1 left) can be build when at least five images are available. Consider G_4^n to be a quartic graph with n-nodes and x_1 to be one of its vertices. There are four edges connecting x_1 with four different nodes x_2, x_3, x_4, x_5 forming four pairs $\{x_1, x_2\}$, $\{x_1, x_3\}$, $\{x_1, x_4\}$, $\{x_1, x_5\}$. In K_5 or G_4^5 all nodes are connected to all other nodes making it a complete graph. Starting from this base graph, new nodes are added to extend the graph, while reduction becomes possible if more than 5 nodes are present.

Let $\{x\}$ be a subgraph of G_4^n consisting of the node x and $\{z\}$ be a subgraph consisting z. The node x is reachable from node z if there is a set of edges $E_{(z \leftrightarrow x)}$ leading from the subgraph $\{z\}$ to $\{x\}$. For connected graphs, at least one such set exists. Quartic graphs guarantee a minimum of two sets, providing two redundant paths to $\{x\}$. This *reachability rule* assures that at least two edges leaving $\{z\}$ can reach two different incoming connections of $\{x\}$.

Proof: Assume the subgraph $\{x\}$ consists of x and its four edges. These edges represent the four entrances into the subgraph (see figure 1 middle). When increasing the number of nodes in the subgraph, it becomes difficult to know the exact number of entrances. The formula to count all edges in a quartic graph is $k * 4/2$ where k is the number of vertices. Suppose there is only one path into the subgraph, the number of edges inside can be computed by $(k * 4 - 1)/2$. But then it would be necessary to create a $^1/_2$ edge, which is not possible. Therefore, there must be a second entrance into the subgraph. Any subgraph can only have an even amount of entrances. It is not possible to construct a subgraph or a series of subgraphs connected with just one edge into the supergraph. See figure 1 right for an illustration of the problem. Toida [6] states the same fact with his remark "No quartic graph can have a bridge".

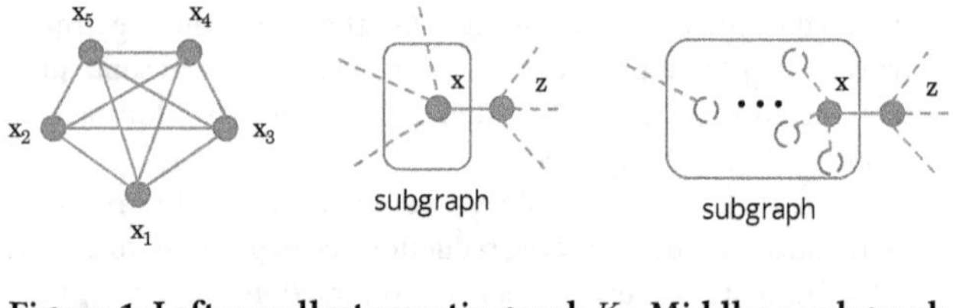

Figure 1: Left: smallest quartic graph K_5. Middle: a subgraph with one vertex. Right: a subgraph with two entrances.

3.1 Extending the graph

There are many ways to extend a graph with a new node x. A naïve version might just remove two edges connecting four distinct nodes x_1, x_2, x_3, x_4 and reconnect them with x. A better strategy is to first perform a search across all nodes in the graph and find the one most similar to x. Remove an edge from the winning node x_1 connecting it to x_2 which is also very similar to x. Afterwards add two edges associating x_1 and x_2 with the new node. Repeating the procedure (looking for x_3 and x_4) increases the number of edges of x by two. None of the chosen nodes should be adjacent to x beforehand. This approach integrates parts of the kNN guidelines and guarantees a connected graph by adding an intermediate node and replacing an existing edge with a pair of edges $\{x, x_1\}$, $\{x, x_2\}$ forming a path from x_1 to x_2 (see figure 2). The quality of the connections is not as good as the ones from kNN, yet at least half of the new edges are connected to the most similar existing nodes and the resulting graph is regular and connected. In theory these steps have a complexity of $O(1)$. Depending on the implementation of the search for good neighbors it can increase to $O(log(n))$.

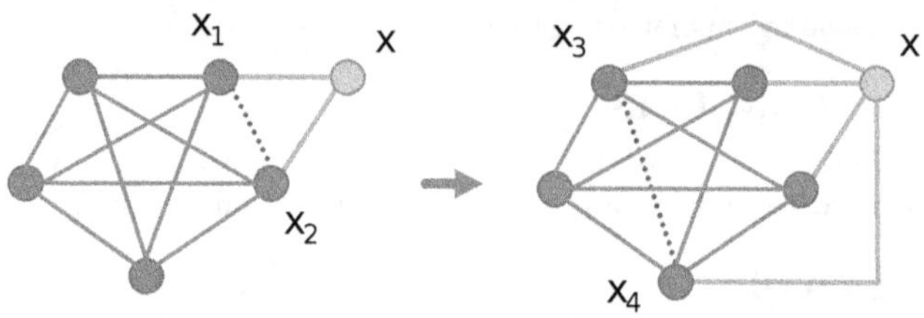

Figure 2: Left: smallest quartic graph K_5. Middle: a subgraph with one vertex. Right: a subgraph with two entrances.

3.2 Reducing the graph

According to Toida a graph G_4^n is V-type reducible if for at least one node x of G_4^n holds: If x is removed from G_4^n, a set of unique edges exists that can be added to the reduced graph to making it 4-regular and connected again. Sometimes up to three sets are feasible; one of them might disconnect the graph while the other two will not. Unfortunately, not every node is removable by this type of reduction at any moment. We provide an easy way to find the bad set of edges and a solution to allow deleting any node without losing connectivity or regularity of the graph.

There is only a limited amount of possible edge configurations around a node. Assume the node x is connected to the nodes a, b, c, d (for an example see figure 3 left) and they are not connected to each other. When removing x, the four other nodes need to be reconnected. The three feasible pairings are $\{a, b\}\&\{c, d\}$ or $\{a, c\}\&\{b, d\}$ or $\{a, d\}\&\{b, c\}$. They all are viable because none of the suggested edges exists yet. Depending on the rest of the graph, one of the pairings might cut the graph in two. Checking the reachability from node a to node b, c, d helps to choose the right set of edges. The following assumptions are true:

If $E_{(a \leftrightarrow b)}$ exist then $E_{(c \leftrightarrow d)}$ exists.
If $E_{(a \leftrightarrow c)}$ exist then $E_{(b \leftrightarrow d)}$ exists.
If $E_{(a \leftrightarrow d)}$ exist then $E_{(b \leftrightarrow c)}$ exists.

These facts are derivable by the *reachability rule.* Consider $E_{(a\leftrightarrow b)}$ exists and suppose x is not removed yet, then there are at least two ways to reach c from x. One via the direct edge $\{x, c\}$ and another one traversing a set of edges from node a, b or d. Now assume x is removed, there is still a path from c to a, b or d. In case $E_{(a\leftrightarrow c)}$ exists, c can reach b because of $E_{(a\leftrightarrow b)}$. As d needs two ways of reachability, it is also connected to any of a, b, c making essentially all nodes reachable among each other. The same constellation arises if $E_{(b\leftrightarrow c)}$ exists. The third possible case is $E_{(c\leftrightarrow d)}$, where only a and b can reach each other, just as c and d can. In all cases c can reach d via path $E_{(c\leftrightarrow d)}$ confirming the assumption: If $E_{(a\leftrightarrow b)}$ exist then $E_{(c\leftrightarrow d)}$ exists.

Checking $E_{(a\leftrightarrow(b\&c\&d))}$ helps finding the best set of edges reconnecting a, b, c and d. In the end, any of these choices may reduce the reachability of nodes between each other, as x is no longer the intermediate router. Adding another path between two already reachable nodes, might destroy the reachability to other nodes and the connectivity of the graph. Therefore, it is necessary to comply with these rules:

If $E_{(a\leftrightarrow b)}$ exist choose $\{a, c\}\&\{b, d\}$ or $\{a, d\}\&\{b, c\}$.
If $E_{(a\leftrightarrow c)}$ exist choose $\{a, b\}\&\{c, d\}$ or $\{a, d\}\&\{b, c\}$.
If $E_{(a\leftrightarrow d)}$ exist choose $\{a, b\}\&\{c, d\}$ or $\{a, c\}\&\{b, d\}$.

The concept of adding any set of edges applies only if none of the containing edges exists separately before. If just two pairings are feasible any of them guarantees a connected graph, because some other desirable edges already exists. This simplifies the process mentioned prior and no reachability test is needed. Using the set $\{a, b\}\&\{c, d\}$ does not work for the graph in figure 3 right, leaving just two remaining reconnection combinations.

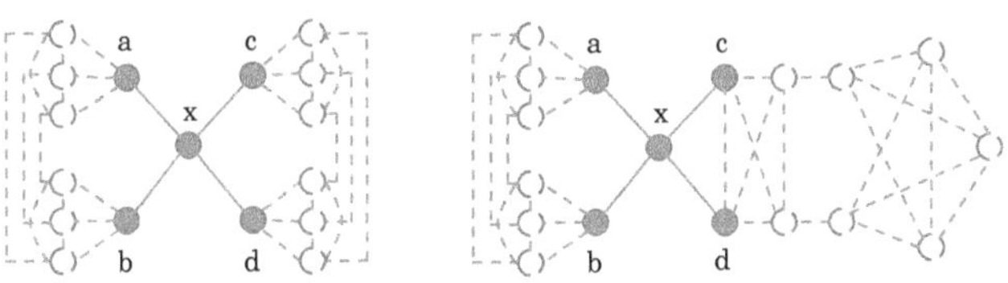

Figure 3: Left: a, b, c, and d are not connected to each other. Right: c and d are connected leaving only two reconnection choices.

Not every node is V-type reducible. In specific configurations, not a single set of edges is feasible (see figure 4). However, no matter what, at least one of the six potential edges does not yet exist. Otherwise the graph would be K_5, being not reducible at all. Adding any of these edges leaves two nodes with just three connections. At the same time completing all edges of a set always results in full reachability among the nodes. Assume the nodes with a missing link are a and b and the edge $\{c, d\}$ already exists (see figure 4 right). To complete the set $\{a, b\}\&\{c, d\}$, add the edge $\{a, b\}$ and remove the edge of c to the node z that is not connected to d yet. Add the edge $\{z, d\}$ and use c as an intermediate node for the extension process of the graph described in 3.1. This assures c is linked to two other very similar nodes and the graph stays connected.

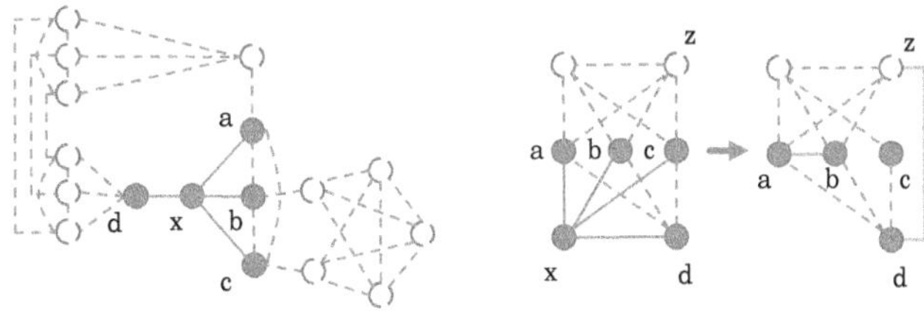

Figure 4: Left: x, a, b, c form a complete subgraph. Right: a, b, c are connected to d. New edges are added between $\{a, b\}$ and $\{d, z\}$. c is used as an intermediate node for graph extension. This special case increases the complexity of the graph reduction scheme from $O(1)$ to $O(log(n))$.

4 DYNAMIC GRAPH HIERARCHY

Browsing several thousand or even millions of images with a graph is difficult. Moving to a specific semantic topic is nearly impossible, as an overview is quickly lost. Constructing hierarchical graph layers can help. Lower layers should connect very similar images, while higher layers should connect less related images. The number of layers and assigned images should change when new images are added to the graph. This dynamic behavior limits rearrangements to those that can be performed in a constant time.

Our proposed scheme is based on a random uniform distribution and gives each image an equal chance to be placed on a higher layer. The size and number of levels are defined by two parameters. The *TopLayerSize* parameter regulates the maximum number of images on the top layer of the graph and a *GrowthFactor* determines the size difference of consecutive layers.

All elements of an initial graph K_5 form the first layer. New nodes are added to this layer. When the lowest layer reaches its maximum size, a new layer is constructed below and filled with the nodes of the entire graph. A node itself can exist on many layers. The chance of a new node to be added to a higher layer is:

$$propability = \frac{(elements\ on\ the\ layer)}{(all\ elements)}$$

The node is also added to all the layers below the identified layer. When a layer is full, a randomly selected node of it is downgraded by one level. This approach fills the higher layers and allows size fluctuation of the bottom layer. Building the hierarchy for 1000 images with 100 nodes at the top layer and a growth factor of 4, would result in three layers containing a maximum of 100, 400 and 1600 images and a distribution of 100, 400, 1000 images. Adding one million nodes to an empty graph on a single core of an E3-1230 v3 takes around 700ms.

Removing a node from the graph would remove it from all layers. A follow up rebalancing process promotes random nodes from deeper layers into a higher layers to fill the resulting holes. In case the lowest and second lowest layer contain the same number of nodes afterwards, the lowest layer is deleted. Most of the time adding or deleting a node from the hierarchy has a complexity of $O(1)$. When the amount of layers changes, $O(n)$ can occur depending on the implementation.

5 DEMO SYSTEM

The dynamic graph construction and navigation algorithms are implemented in an application called *ImageX*. Additional features are analyzing and indexing private images from the hard drive, keyword search capabilities for untagged images and a browsing concept based on *Google Maps* navigation scheme. The application works on all major desktop operating systems and will be available to download for free in June 2018 at www.visual-computing.com. It supports millions of images and only needs a tiny amount of memory due to the 64-byte image descriptors used internally. To run the program, no Internet connection is required, hence privacy issues do not occur as no cloud processing has to be used.

As the program needs to deal with many images and their similarities, we rely on small high-quality image descriptors. These feature vectors are computed with the help of a ResNet152 [7] trained on the entire ImageNet [8] data set. After removing the fully connected layers, the network produces 2048-dimensional activation vectors. Normalizing them and reducing their dimensionality to 64 with a principal component analysis (PCA) still yields excellent retrieval properties [9]. Additional scaling and quantization packs them into 64 bytes. These feature vectors are compared using a SIMD like implementation of the Manhattan distance [10].

The application starts with an empty index. The user can choose directories, which will be monitored. Every image placed in those folders is analyzed and added to the index. After adding 5 entries the initial graph is constructed. From then on, the graph is continuously improved using the edge path-swapping algorithm [1]. In regular intervals, the current state of the graph is copied and transferred to the navigation interface, where the user can explore the indexed images. Any additional image is immediately appended to the graph and extra layers are built if needed. The top layer has a maximum size of 250 places to fill slightly more images than would fit onto one screen and a growing factor of 4 to give the feeling of doubling the images in all four directions.

An internal database stores image descriptors for common keywords. Each keyword is represented by at most 10 descriptors. The underlying images and metadata were collected from Pixabay, a website for royalty-free stock photos. When searching for a keyword, the corresponding feature vectors are compared against all the images of the user. The resulting list is sorted by similarity with the best matching images on top. Several thousand of them are used to create a small image map. This map is organized by an improved version of the self-sorting map algorithm [11]. The arrangement places similar looking images next to each other on a regular 2D grid. Next, hierarchical layers are added to the map forming a pyramid. Starting from the base layer, higher layers are generated pooling the median image of a 2x2 region from the layer below. The median image is determined as the image most similar to the other three in the region.

The pyramid replaces the top layers of the graph and connects its bottom layer with the next highest graph layer. This temporary configuration allows switching between pyramid and graph navigation seamlessly to make the entire image collection accessible after a search request. Furthermore, the best matching private images are displayed on the right. They are clickable and provide fast access to different regions of the pyramid.

The navigation concept of the pyramid or graph is the same and follows the scheme of Google Maps. Dragging the map moves some images out of the viewport and leaves some empty space on the opposite side. These holes are filled with the prearranged images of the pyramid or from the graph, traversing the edges of nearby images to find other images. Zooming out or in, changes the hierarchical level. Lower layers show images with similar content close to each other, while higher layers give an overview about different topics.

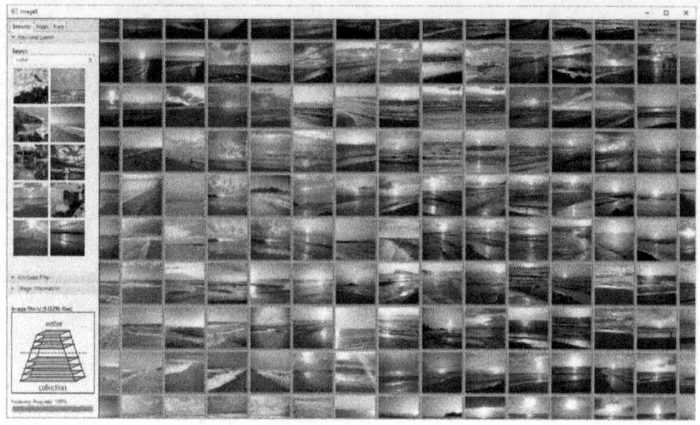

Figure 5: Left: Navigating the keyword search result through the presented image map. Right: Indexing of local images.

REFERENCES

[1] Kai Uwe Barthel, Nico Hezel, and Klaus Jung. 2017. Visually Browsing Millions of Images Using Image Graphs.. In *ICMR*, Bogdan Ionescu, Nicu Sebe, Jiashi Feng, Martha Larson, Rainer Lienhart, and Cees Snoek (Eds.). ACM, 475–479.

[2] Arif M. Khan, Alex Pothen, Md. Mostofa Ali Patwary, Nadathur Rajagopalan Satish, Narayanan Sundaram, Fredrik Manne, Mahantesh Halappanavar, and Pradeep Dubey. 2016. Efficient Approximation Algorithms for Weighted b-Matching. *SIAM J. Scientific Computing* 38, 5 (2016).

[3] Bert C. Huang and Tony Jebara. 2011. Fast b-matching via Sufficient Selection Belief Propagation.. In *AISTATS (JMLR Proceedings)*, Geoffrey J. Gordon, David B. Dunson, and Miroslav DudÃŋk (Eds.), Vol. 15. JMLR.org, 361–369.

[4] Jun Wang and Yinglong Xia. 2012. Fast Graph Construction Using Auction Algorithm.. In *UAI*, Nando de Freitas and Kevin P. Murphy (Eds.). AUAI Press, 873–882.

[5] Cong Fu, Changxu Wang, and Deng Cai. 2017. Fast Approximate Nearest Neighbor Search With Navigating Spreading-out Graphs. *CoRR* abs/1707.00143 (2017).

[6] S Toida. [n. d.]. Construction of quartic graphs. *Journal of Combinatorial Theory, Series B* 16, 2 ([n. d.]), 124 – 133. https://doi.org/10.1016/0095-8956(74)90054-9

[7] Kaiming He, Xiangyu Zhang, Shaoqing Ren, and Jian Sun. 2016. Identity Mappings in Deep Residual Networks.. In *ECCV (4) (Lecture Notes in Computer Science)*, Bastian Leibe, Jiri Matas, Nicu Sebe, and Max Welling (Eds.), Vol. 9908. Springer, 630–645.

[8] Olga Russakovsky, Jia Deng, Hao Su, Jonathan Krause, Sanjeev Satheesh, Sean Ma, Zhiheng Huang, Andrej Karpathy, Aditya Khosla, Michael S. Bernstein, Alexander C. Berg, and Fei-Fei Li. 2015. ImageNet Large Scale Visual Recognition Challenge. *International Journal of Computer Vision* 115, 3 (2015), 211–252.

[9] Artem Babenko, Anton Slesarev, Alexander Chigorin, and Victor S. Lempitsky. 2014. Neural Codes for Image Retrieval.. In *ECCV (1) (Lecture Notes in Computer Science)*, David J. Fleet, TomÃąs Pajdla, Bernt Schiele, and Tinne Tuytelaars (Eds.), Vol. 8689. Springer, 584–599.

[10] Nico Hezel, Kai Uwe Barthel, and Klaus Jung. 2018. ImageX - Explore and Search Local/Private Images.. In *MMM (2) (Lecture Notes in Computer Science)*, Klaus Schoeffmann, Thanarat H. Chalidabhongse, Chong-Wah Ngo, Supavadee Aramvith, Noel E. O'Connor, Yo-Sung Ho, Moncef Gabbouj, and Ahmed Elgammal (Eds.), Vol. 10705. Springer, 372–376.

[11] Grant Strong and Minglun Gong. 2014. Self-Sorting Map: An Efficient Algorithm for Presenting Multimedia Data in Structured Layouts. *IEEE Transactions on Multimedia* 16, 4 (2014), 1045–1058.

WTPlant (What's That Plant?): a Deep Learning System for Identifying Plants in Natural Images

Jonas Krause Gavin Sugita Kyungim Baek Lipyeow Lim
Department of Information and Computer Sciences, University of Hawai'i at Mānoa
1680 East-West Road, Honolulu, HI 96822, U.S.A.
(krausej|gsugita6|kyungim|lipyeow)@hawaii.edu

ABSTRACT

Despite the availability of dozens of plant identification mobile applications, identifying plants from a natural image remains a challenging problem – most of the existing applications do not address the complexity of natural images, the large number of plant species, and the multi-scale nature of natural images. In this technical demonstration, we present the *WTPlant* system for identifying plants in natural images. *WTPlant* is based on deep learning approaches. Specifically, it uses stacked Convolutional Neural Networks for image segmentation, a novel preprocessing stage for multi-scale analyses, and deep convolutional networks to extract the most discriminative features. *WTPlant* employs different classification architectures for plants and flowers, thus enabling plant identification throughout all the seasons. The user interface also shows, in an interactive way, the most representative areas in the image that are used to predict each plant species. The first version of *WTPlant* is trained to classify 100 different plant species present in the campus of the University of Hawai'i at Mānoa. First experiments support the hypothesis that an initial segmentation process helps guide the extraction of representative samples and, consequently, enables Convolutional Neural Networks to better recognize objects of different scales in natural images. Future versions aim to extend the recognizable species to cover the land-based flora of the Hawaiian Islands.

CCS CONCEPTS

• **Computing methodologies** → **Machine learning**; *Artificial intelligence*; Computer vision problems • **Object identification**

KEYWORDS

Image Processing, Deep Learning, Convolutional Neural Network, Plant Taxonomy, Multi-Scale Analysis.

ACM Reference format:

Jonas Krause, Gavin Sugita, Kyungim Baek, Lipyeow Lim. 2018. *WTPlant* (What's That Plant?): a Deep Learning System for Identifying Plants in Natural Images. In *Proceedings of ACM ICMR conference, Yokohama, Japan, June 2018 (ICMR'18)*, 4 pages. DOI: 10.1145/3206025.3206089

ICMR'18, June 11-14, 2018, Yokohama, Japan.

ACM ISBN 978-1-4503-5046-4/18/06...$15.00.
https://doi.org/10.1145/3206025.3206089

1 INTRODUCTION

Plant identification has many important applications ranging from conservation to agriculture. Traditionally, botanists analyze different characteristics (visual and non-visual) of plants to be used as identification factors. However, identifying the species of plants accurately based on visual characteristics requires considerable expertise [1], which is almost impossible for the general public and challenging even for specialists. Previous efforts in using computer vision techniques for automated plant identification from controlled images have shown promising results [2,3,4,5,6]. However, a real-world plant identification application needs to be able to handle natural images, which is a big challenge for automated computer vision systems. Analysis of unconstrained natural images can be extremely difficult due to factors related to background, illumination, occlusions, shadows, and a rich local covariance structure that is usually present in the image. While human visual processing system navigates those factors with ease, an equivalent computational model for plant identification from natural images is still an open problem, the solution of which may have a substantial impact on botanical and agricultural fields.

Machine Learning (ML) approaches have shown promising results in various computer vision problems including the plant identification problem. Most previous efforts have used hand-designed features of leaves, flowers, and fruits [1,2,7,8,9] and are restricted to fairly controlled images with clean backgrounds. Identifying plant species relying on morphological characteristics extracted from well-controlled images is quite different from the noisy natural images that are found in real-world image classification applications.

More recently, Deep Learning (DL) methods have been introduced to this task [3,4,5,6,10,11,12,13,14] driven by the success of the Convolutional Neural Networks (CNNs). The deep convolutional approaches have been a growing trend in the computer vision field demonstrating impressive results in various tasks involving natural images. *WTPlant*, therefore, adopts the deep CNN approach and further extends it with the use of multiple stages or components of deep CNN in its architecture. In contrast to current plant identification methods that use hand-designed features, simple CNN architectures, and pre-trained models, *WTPlant* uses a carefully designed system of CNNs to classify plants and flowers in natural images.

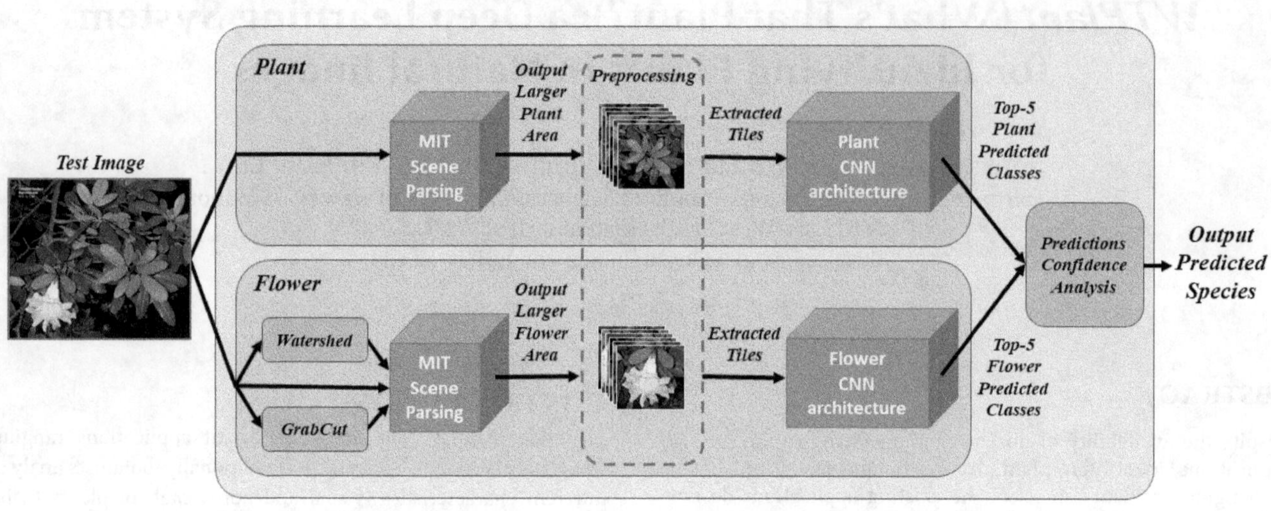

Figure 1: Block diagram of the *WTPlant* system.

The *WTPlant* system of CNNs consists of multiple pipelines and multiple stages of CNN components designed to extract deep discriminatory features. Each pipeline will segment the query image, preprocess the regions of interest into tiles of different sizes and classify the tiles using deep CNNs. The results from each pipeline are then combined to obtain more accurate predictions in a process reminiscent of ensemble techniques. The initial version of *WTPlant* presented here is trained to classify about 100 different plant species found on the campus of the University of Hawai'i (UH) at Mānoa. Preliminary experiments show that the initial segmentation process helps guide the extraction of representative samples and, consequently, enables Convolutional Neural Networks to better recognize objects of different scales in natural images.

In Section 2, we describe *WTPlant* in greater detail by explaining the system capabilities, the innovative preprocessing stage for the multi-scale problem, and the implemented CNN architectures. Section 3 describes how the system can be demonstrated. Section 4 reports initial results and Section 5 concludes the presentation of the system.

2 THE *WTPlant* SYSTEM

By training individual CNN architectures, one for plants and one for flowers, the *WTPlant* system is able to handle natural images with plants only, flowers only, or both together. In the latter case, the system will consolidate the predictions for plant and flower to output the final classification species. This collection of CNNs brings state-of-the-art DL architectures working together to provide the most accurate plant identification system. The accuracy will be measured by counting the correctly classified top-5 plants and flowers versus the incorrect ones during initial experiments. In the first version of *WTPlant* presented at this demo, the system is able to identify the 100 plant species present on the UH Mānoa campus. In future versions, this system will be extended to all plant species in the state of Hawai'i.

Figure 1 presents a block diagram of the *WTPlant* and details the workflow during the classification process of a query (unseen) image. The process begins by replicating the query image to the pipeline for plants and the pipeline for flowers. One of the key problems in computer vision is called scene parsing, i.e., recognizing and segmenting objects in a natural image. We used the MIT Scene Parsing method from Zhou et al. [15] which is a cascade segmentation module based on a CNN architecture with stacked convolutional blocks. MIT Scene Parsing is trained to segment 150 different objects from a scene, including plants and flowers. The *WTPlant* system uses the MIT Scene Parsing to segment and localizes regions potentially containing plants and flowers. For flowers, two pre-segmentation algorithms are used to assist the main segmentation process performed by the MIT Scene Parsing. After segmentation, the largest segmented areas of plant and flower are identified and passed to the preprocessing stage to create multi-position and multi-scale representative tiles. These tiles are individually classified by the CNN architectures that output the prediction results. In the final stage, the predicted classes for plant and flower are analyzed and combined according to the highest prediction values of each of the multi-position and multi-scale tiles. Based on these predicted high-confidence results, the top-5 final plant species are determined.

2.1 Capabilities

2.1.1 Modularity. The collection of CNNs is modularly designed to incorporate auxiliary methods that improve each stage of the system (segmentation, preprocessing, and classification). Moreover, each CNN can be easily upgraded (fine-tuned, retrained, or replaced) and incorporated back into the system. Therefore, new versions of the *WTPlant* system will be more accurate with the addition of new and more powerful CNNs. These new architectures may also be scaled up to a broader range of plant species, covering a wider ecosystem.

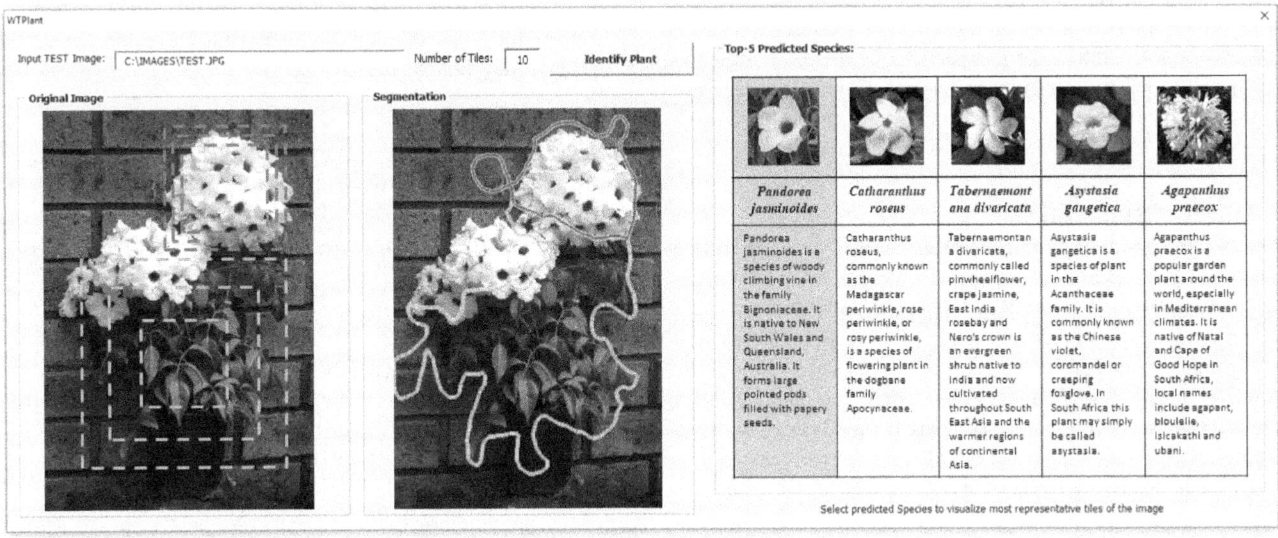

Figure 2: Graphical User Interface (GUI) of the *WTPlant* system.

2.1.2 Pre-Segmentation. Two pre-segmentation methods are incorporated into the *WTPlant* to assist the MIT Scene Parsing on the detection of flowers. They are needed due to the fact that some plant images have small flowers that are not initially captured by the MIT Scene Parsing. Hence, by separating background from the foreground using the Watershed Transform [16] and the GrabCut [17] algorithms the small flowers become more evident for the scene parsing.

2.1.3 Preprocessing. After the segmentation process performed by the MIT Scene Parsing, Regions of Interest (RoI) delimitating the larger plant and flower areas are collected from the inputted image. Searching for the most representative square areas within these RoI, a preprocessing step is implemented to extract multi-position and multi-scale representative tiles from the segmented plant and flower. The novelty of extracting tiles with multi-scale properties and using them to train the CNNs gives this system a better scale generalization capability when compared with common preprocessing methods such as resizing and random crop. Some of the reviewed approaches [6,10,13] suggest that simply downscaling the entire image is good practice. But CNN architectures generally receives small area images and a drastic downscale of a natural image will inevitably result in the loss of valuable information. Therefore, a preprocessing approach is needed to correctly handle the segmented RoI. The proposed method is aligned with previous approaches [3,4,5,14] that divided their analyzed regions into small tiles. However, instead of randomly crop these tiles, *WTPlant* performs a guided tile extraction which collects multi-location and multi-scale representative samples of the plant and flower to be analyzed.

2.1.4 Classification Architectures. The classification engines of this first version of the *WTPlant* system are two *AlexNets* [18], a DL architecture well-studied in the literature. They were both implemented using the *MatConvNet*[1] toolbox, one was trained exclusively for the analysis of plant tiles and the second one focuses on the analysis of flower tiles only. The separation between plants and flowers allows the networks to learn specific filters for each task in order to produce a good analysis of plant leaves and flower petals individually. Furthermore, by training both networks with multi-scale tile samples extracted based on the guided segmentation process, these classification architectures are able to learn and analyze plant images at diverse scales.

2.1.5 Confidence Analysis. The classification engines output the top-5 predictions for each one of the preprocessed tiles. The analysis of the plant tiles is done in parallel of the flower tiles, combining their confidence results to determine the plant species. This strategy covers the seasonality of the flowers and enables the system to work with plant species that are known as non-flowering plants, such as ferns, mosses, and liverworts.

2.2 Graphical User Interface (GUI)

WTPlant user interface was created using MATLAB R2015a and is shown in Figure 2. The MIT Scene Parsing is also implemented using MATLAB, as well as the preprocessing stage and the *MatConvNets*. In the GUI, the user inputs the test image and clicks the "Identify Plant" button. Then the test image will be loaded into the "Original Image" area and the segmentation stage produces the plant and flower RoI. These regions function as a guide to the preprocessing of representative multi-location and multi-scale tiles of the plant. These tiles are then inputted into each trained CNN. After the *WTPlant* analyzes the prediction confidence for each tile, the top-5 results are outputted into the "Top-5 Predicted Species" designated area with a brief description of the plant taxonomy.

2.2.1 User Interaction. The *WTPlant* GUI was designed to be a simple and user-friendly interface with highly interactive

[1] http://www.vlfeat.org/matconvnet/

features. For example, to deeply explore the multi-location and multi-scale properties in high-resolution images, the user can change the number of analyzed tiles (default 10) and expand the analysis to more multi-scale perspectives. In addition, after the top-5 predictions, the user can visualize which extracted tiles were responsible for the top-1 prediction, as demonstrated in Figure 2 where the *Pandora jasminoides* species is predicted.

3 DEMONSTRATION

For this demonstration conference, attendees will have the chance to take live pictures of a small plant and identify its species using the *WTPlant* system. Users will be able to test the system accuracy by taking photos with different angles, illumination, scales, and backgrounds. Numerous test images of other species will also be available during the demonstration. After the plant species analysis, the user will be able to compare the predictions with the ground-truth species and visualize which of the preprocessed tiles were used to determine the correct plant species.

4 RESULTS AND DISCUSSION

Initial experiments showed that the *WTPlant* system was able to detect the presence of **99.3%** of plants in ~17,000 natural images. Using representative tiles extracted from this initial segmentation process, two CNNs were trained and yielded **61.87%** top-1 and **85.25%** top-5 accuracies when plant and flower results are combined. However, species classification accuracy is constantly improving as new CNN architectures are trained and upgraded as classification engines. Furthermore, these experiments aimed to compare our proposed multi-location and multi-scale method with the common resize and random crop approaches during the training and testing of CNNs. As a result, *WTPlant* performed **14.6%** better on the top-1 accuracy when compared with CNNs trained using a naïve resize approach, and **9.1%** better when compared with the random crop approach. A total of 278 unseen natural images with complex backgrounds from 100 different plant species were used to produce these results. *WTPlant* took an average of 20 seconds to analyze each image, which may vary according to its size. These initial results support the hypothesis that a preprocessed stage guided by a segmentation process may help the training of CNNs.

5 CONCLUSION

In this paper, we present the first version of the *WTPlant*, describing its capabilities and functionalities. The modularity of this system allows the incorporation of different CNN architectures and will be upgraded as soon as new networks are trained. The preprocessing stage implemented to collect multi-scale tiles is also an important characteristic of this system, which creates proper scale data for more accurate analysis. The described GUI presents these features and enables the user to easily interact with the system visualizing the most representative analyzed areas. Future work aims to expand current CNN architectures and explore new classification pipelines for fruits and seedlings in natural images.

ACKNOWLEDGMENTS

This research was supported in part by the Brazilian National Council for Scientific and Technological Development (CNPq) under grant number 219438-14.5.

REFERENCES

[1] Jana Wäldchen and Patrick Mäder. Plant Species Identification Using Computer Vision Techniques: A Systematic Literature Review. *Archives of Computational Methods in Engineering*, pages 1-37, 2017.

[2] Neeraj Kumar, Peter N. Belhumeur, Arijit Biswas, David W. Jacobs, W. John Kress, Ida C. Lopez, and João V. B. Soares. LeafSnap: A Computer Vision System for Automatic Plant Species Identification. In *Proceedings of the 12th European Conference on Computer Vision* (ECCV), pages 502-516, Florence, Italy, 2012.

[3] Sue H. Lee, Chee S. Chan, Paul Wilkin, and Paolo Remagnino. Deep-Plant: Plant identification with convolutional neural networks. *ArXiv Preprint*, 2015. arxiv.org/abs/1506.08425.

[4] Michael P. Pound, Jonathan A. Atkinson, Darren M. Wells, Tony P. Pridmore, and Andrew P. French. Deep Learning for Multi-task Plant Phenotyping. *bioRxiv Preprint*, 2017. doi.org/10.1101/204552.

[5] Michael P. Pound, Jonathan A. Atkinson, Alexandra J. Townsend, Michael H. Wilson, Marcus Griffiths, Aaron S. Jackson, Adrian Bulat, Georgios Tzimiropoulos, Darren M. Wells, Erik H. Murchie, Tony P. Pridmore, and Andrew P. French. Deep machine learning provides state-of-the-art performance in image-based plant phenotyping. *GigaScience*, 6(10):1-10, 2017.

[6] Pierre Barré, Ben C. Stöver, Kai F. Müller, and Volker Steinhage. LeafNet: A computer vision system for automatic plant species identification. *Ecological Informatics*, 40:50-56, 2017.

[7] Peter N. Belhumeur, Daozheng Chen, Steven Feiner, David W. Jacobs, W. John Kress, Haibin Ling, Ida Lopez, Ravi Ramamoorthi, Sameer Sheorey, Sean White, and Ling Zhang. Searching the world's herbaria: A system for visual identification of plant species. In *Proceedings of the 10th European Conference on Computer Vision* (ECCV), pages 116-129, 2008.

[8] Guillaume Cerutti, Laure Tougne, Julien Millea, Antoine Vacavant, and Didier Coquin. Understanding leaves in natural images – A model-based approach for tree species identification. In *Computer Vision and Image Understanding*, 117(10):1482-1501, 2013.

[9] Alexis Joly, Hervé Goëau, Pierre Bonnet, Vera Backić, Julien Barbe, Souheil Selmi, Itheri Yahiaoui, Jennifer Carré, Elise Mouysset, Jean-François Molino, Nozha Boujemaa, and Daniel Barthélémy. Interactive plant identification based on social image data. *Ecological Informatics*, 23:22-34, 2014.

[10] Yu Sun, Yuan Liu, Guan Wang, and Haiyan Zhang. Deep Learning for Plant Identification in Natural Environment. *Computational Intelligence and Neuroscience*, 2017. doi.org/10.1155/2017/7361042.

[11] Sarah T. Namin, Mohammad Esmaeilzadeh, and Mohammad Najafi, Tim B. Brown, and Justin O. Borevitz. Deep Phenotyping: Deep Learning For Temporal Phenotype/Genotype Classification. *bioRxiv Preprint*, 2017. doi.org/10.1101/134205

[12] Antoine Affouard, Herve Goeau, Pierre Bonnet, Jean-Christophe Lombardo, and Alexis Joly. Pl@ntnet app in the era of deep learning. In *Proceedings of the 5th International Conference on Learning Representations* (ICLR), pages 1-6, Toulon, France, 2017.

[13] Jordan R. Ubbens and Ian Stavness. Deep Plant Phenomics: A Deep Learning Platform for Complex Plant Phenotyping Tasks. *Frontiers in Plant Science*, 2017. doi.org/10.3389/fpls.2017.01190.

[14] Mario Lasseck. Image-based plant species identification with deep convolutional neural networks. In *Working Notes of Cross Language Evaluation Forum* (CLEF), 2017.

[15] Bolei Zhou, Hang Zhao, Xavier Puig, Sanja Fidler, Adela Barriuso, and Antonio Torralba. Scene Parsing through ADE20K Dataset. In *Proceedings of the IEEE Conference on Computer Vision and Pattern Recognition (CVPR)*, pages 633-641, Honolulu, Hawaii, 2017.

[16] Jos B.T.M. Roerdink and Arnold Meijster. The Watershed Transform: Definitions, Algorithms and Parallelization Strategies. *Fundamenta Informaticae*, 41(1-2):187-228, 2000.

[17] Carsten Rother, Vladimir Kolmogorov, and Andrew Blake. "GrabCut": interactive foreground extraction using iterated graph cuts. *ACM Transactions on Graphics*, 23(3):309-314, 2004.

[18] Alex Krizhevsky, Ilya Sutskever, and Geoffrey E Hinton. Imagenet classification with deep convolutional neural networks. *Advances in Neural Information Processing Systems (NIPS) 25*, pages 1097-1105, Lake Tahoe, Nevada, 2012.

MOOCex: Exploring Educational Video via Recommendation

Matthew Cooper, Jian Zhao, Chidansh Bhatt, David A. Shamma
FX Palo Alto Laboratory
Palo Alto, CA, USA
{cooper,zhao,bhatt}@fxpal.com
aymans@acm.org

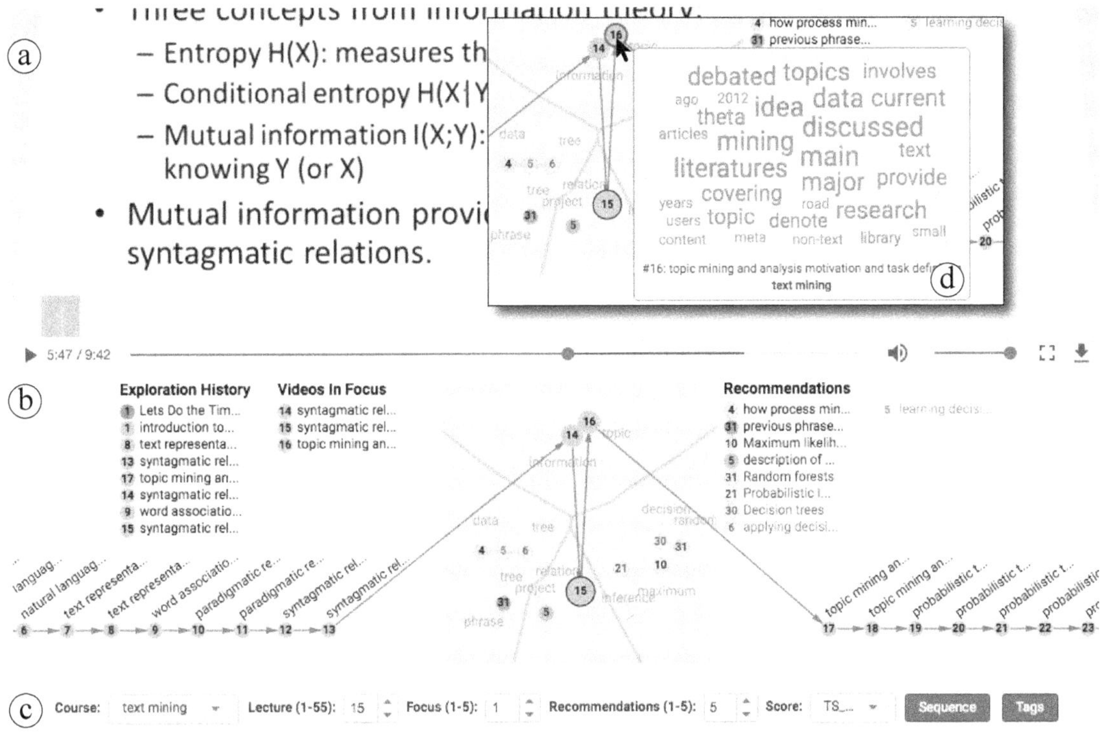

Figure 1: A learner is using MOOCex to explore recommendations for lecture "15" in *Text Mining*. The interface consists of three main components: a) a Video Panel (cropped), b) a Recommendation Panel, and c) a Configuration Panel, d) Hovering over a video initiates a tooltip with a tag cloud to describe the content of the video.

ABSTRACT

Massive Open Online Course (MOOC) platforms have scaled online education to unprecedented enrollments, but remain limited by their predetermined curricula. Increasingly, professionals consume this content to augment or update specific skills rather than complete degree or certification programs. To better address the needs of this emergent user population, we describe a visual recommender system called MOOCex. The system recommends lecture videos *across* multiple courses and content platforms to provide a choice of perspectives on topics of interest. The recommendation engine considers both video content and sequential inter-topic relationships mined from course syllabi. Furthermore, it allows for interactive visual exploration of the semantic space of recommendations within a learner's current context.

CCS CONCEPTS

• **Information systems → Multimedia information systems; Users and interactive retrieval;**

KEYWORDS

educational video recommendation, exploratory visualization

ACM Reference Format:
Matthew Cooper, Jian Zhao, Chidansh Bhatt, David A. Shamma. 2018. MOOCex: Exploring Educational Video via Recommendation . In *ICMR '18: 2018 International Conference on Multimedia Retrieval, June 11–14, 2018, Yokohama, Japan.* ACM, New York, NY, USA, 4 pages. https://doi.org/10.1145/3206025.3206087

ICMR '18, June 11–14, 2018, Yokohama, Japan

ACM ISBN 978-1-4503-5046-4/18/06...$15.00
https://doi.org/10.1145/3206025.3206087

1 INTRODUCTION

Modern online education platforms, such as Coursera, edX, and Udacity, have become popular in recent years. These platforms allow for teaching at a distance and at scale by presenting educational materials as Massive Open Online Courses (MOOCs). A course usually consists of a number of short videos, each targeting specific concepts. To achieve desired learning objectives, instructors commonly order the videos in a syllabus which may also group videos hierarchically into sections. However, the syllabus remains a *one size fits all* approach with a predefined curriculum, which contributes to MOOCs' low retention rates [20, 28].

While these services initially intended to disrupt higher education, more recent studies indicate professionals, rather than students, comprise an increasing proportion of MOOC learners. These "lifelong learners" typically aim to achieve career growth rather than complete degrees or obtain certifications. As a result, they are less likely to adhere to the syllabus [28], and often have varied individual information needs and experience levels. It is critical to offer learners more flexible access to a broader range of content and perspectives (e.g., from multiple courses) [6, 15, 25].

Although the syllabus is rigid, it encodes expert instructors' sequencing of topics to best aid comprehension. Indeed, the sequential character of educational video is an important cue for effectively exploring this content. Platforms such as KhanAcademy [14] provide an interactive knowledge (concept) map to enable more personalized navigation. However, concept maps are not well suited for sequential flow [19] and are neither scalable nor adaptive.

MOOCex aims to help learners effectively access MOOC content across content platforms. We first aggregate MOOC content across multiple courses, introducing the challenge of linking videos in which instructors cover related topics from different perspectives. Additionally, users must select among such related videos to address their information needs. While the course syllabus provides guidance *within* courses, we propose content-based recommendation and interactive visualization to facilitate navigation *across* courses.

MOOCex builds upon advanced data mining techniques, and recommends lectures by considering both videos' topics and sequential inter-topic relationships. MOOCex optionally recommends short sub-sequences of videos within courses, rather than individual videos, to provide additional depth around specific concepts and simplify exploration. Unlike conventional user interfaces for recommendation, i.e., a ranked list or a set of ranked lists, MOOCex supports semantic visualization of recommended videos within users' current learning context, by projecting videos onto a 2D space annotated with topical regions and key phrases. This provides additional dimensions for learners to effectively explore related content and select what to watch next confidently.

2 RELATED WORK

We review related work with a focus on video recommendation techniques as well as visual analytics systems for MOOC content.

2.1 Recommendation

Many approaches to video recommendation are content-based, for example, using features extracted via analysis of text transcripts or video frames. VideoReach implements recommendation by combining unimodal models for textual, visual, and aural information of videos [17]. TalkMiner is an educational video search system using OCR and lexical analysis of text displayed in video frames [1]. Topic modeling, such as Latent Dirichlet Allocation (LDA) [4], has also been applied [29]. However, none of these methods considered the sequential relationships between videos, or the explicit inter-video orderings of course syllabi.

Likewise, applications of sequential pattern mining techniques are generally distinct from video recommendation. Morales et al. [18] facilitates information discovery via educational hypermedia linking based on sequence mining of user logs. Agrawal et al. [2] proposed a system for linking web videos to supplement electronic textbooks, and argued that topic mining alone is insufficient. In other applications, sequential information has been used in recommending music [11], online products [5, 12], and travel itineraries [13].

Sequential organization of topics by experts in course syllabi can provide valuable information for educational content recommendation. However, we face the additional challenge that videos do not overlap across different courses. This contrasts with datasets used in previous user-centered work including, music playlists [11], movies (i.e.Netflix) or e-commerce products (i.e.amazon and [12]). To address this issue, we apply established sequential pattern mining techniques to analyze both global and local patterns in topic transitions exhibited in instructors' syllabi.

2.2 Information visualization

Many techniques have been proposed for visual analysis of data generated by MOOCs, such as user clickstreams and forum discussions [21]. One main topic in this area is to study learner behaviors [7, 24]. In addition, iForum provides another perspective for understanding learners via the analysis of the content and structure of MOOC forum threads [10].

In contrast with systems designed for instructors or analysts, we focus on recommendation and visual exploration of MOOC videos to benefit ordinary learners. One related system is booc.io [23], which allows visual exploration of concept maps of instructional materials and following personalized learning plans. However, this approach is less scalable or flexible because of the required manual creation of the concept maps upfront. Also, they focus on video exploration within a single course whereas we recommend videos sourced across multiple courses.

3 SYSTEM DESCRIPTION

MOOCex consists of two components: a content-based recommendation engine and a visual interface for video playback and semantic exploration (Figure 2).

3.1 Recommendation engine

While syllabi provide learners guidance within courses, we use recommendation to facilitate exploration of a multi-course video collection. We use sequential pattern mining to incorporate sequential information into the recommendation engine.

We assemble content from a number of courses, including videos, available text transcripts, and other meta-data. Generating recommendations across heterogeneous content requires a common data

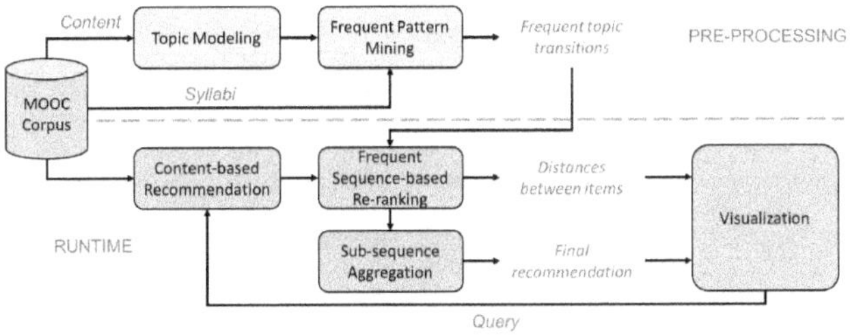

Figure 2: System architecture overview of MOOCex.

representation. Useful visual attributes such as whether the format is a classroom lecture, khan-academy style electronic ink, or slide-based video, etc. are largely captured by associated meta-data. Most platforms provide semantically rich closed caption transcripts enabling the identification of videos' prominent topics. We discover latent topics present across the collection using LDA [4], an established unsupervised topic modeling method.

Sequential pattern mining (SPM) algorithms identify recurrent subsequences within a sequence database. Denote the *topic signature* of the ith video by $V_i = \{k : P^{(i)}(z_k) \geq 0.1\}$ which is the discrete set of topic indices weighted at least 0.1 in the video's topic distribution. We construct an ordered sequence of video topic signatures according to each course's syllabus. These sequences are aggregated into a sequence database. The Top-K non-redundant sequential patterns (TNS) algorithm [9] is applied to detect inter-topic transitions that are *globally* prominent in our database. TNS eliminates rules that are deemed "redundant" (rules that are implied by other rules having the same support and confidence) to capture more varied sequences and automatically fine-tunes the minimum support parameter.

However, our aim is to use the currently watched video to recommend videos covering concepts users are likely to *watch next*, and infrequent topic sets can be overlooked in the global analysis. Sequence mining addresses prediction by discovering rules of the form $X \Rightarrow Y$, where X and Y are two sets of topics. $X \Rightarrow Y$ indicates "topic(s) Y appear in the sequence after topic(s) X". The Top-K sequential pattern mining (TKS) algorithm [8] finds sequential patterns within a given minimum and maximum length such that specified items must appear within a defined allowable gap. For *local* analysis, we collect sequences that include each video's signature. We apply TKS with the constraint that each video's topic set appears within a distance of 3 to 6 in the sequence. We then apply TNS algorithm on these derived sequences to find significant sequential rules within this local data subset. By this design, each video's topic signature is described by sequential rules in the local analysis. Each sequential rule in the local analysis has a corresponding confidence score. This application of sequential pattern mining produces sets of prominent topic transitions describing the sequence database both globally and locally.

The recommendation engine first issues the currently watched video as the query against our baseline content-based recommendation system. This currently uses standard tf/idf vectorspace retrieval [16] based on the video transcripts with ranking according to cosine similarity. To emphasize results that users are more likely to want to watch next, we use a re-ranking method that emphasizes results consistent with topic transitions mined in the analysis of the syllabi. For global analysis, we retrieve N support and confidence score values, $\{(s_n, c_n)\}$ from the mined *global* sequential patterns with antecedent values matching V_q and consequent values matching subsets of V_r. The *GS score* is

$$\mathrm{Sim}_{\mathrm{GS}}(V_q, V_r) = \frac{1}{N}\sum_{n=0}^{N} c_n \frac{|V_r \cap V_q|}{|V_r|} + \frac{s_n}{D_G} \tag{1}$$

D_G is the total number of global sequences. Additionally, we retrieve M additional support and confidence score values from mined *local* sequential patterns with antecedent matching a subset of V_q and consequent matching a subset of V_r. The *LS score* is

$$\mathrm{Sim}_{\mathrm{LS}}(V_q, V_r) = \frac{1}{M}\sum_{m=0}^{M} c_m \frac{|V_r \cap V_q|}{|V_r|} + \frac{s_m}{D_q} \tag{2}$$

D_q is total number of mined local sequences with antecedent matching any subset of V_q. These scores are uniformly fused with a topic similarity score derived from LDA to re-rank the initial pool of recommendations. For additional details, refer to [3].

3.2 Visualization interface

The MOOCex interface consists of three parts. The *Video Panel* is a media player for watching a selected video. The *Recommendation Panel* is where a learner can explore recommended videos and assess relationships between them, to inform their choice of a video to watch next. The *Configuration Panel* allows manipulation of basic parameters controlling the display of recommendations and the specific courses and videos in view.

The Recommendation Panel displays the current video, adjacent videos in its syllabus, and recommendations in a two-dimensional *Exploration Canvas* in the middle. Other videos in the current course appear in order on both sides (Figure 1-b), and are connected with gray arrows to indicate their order in the syllabus. Each video is represented as a circle with a number indicating its position in its course syllabus. Color hues distinguish different courses, and color opacity indicates the rank of that video in the recommendation list (the lighter the color, the lower its rank).

In contrast to ranked result lists, we employ multidimensional scaling (MDS) [26] to position videos on the Exploration Canvas based on their pairwise similarities. In MDS, only the relative distance between items has meaning while the axes do not. Thus, we rotate the layout so that the direction of videos in the current course flows from left to right, aligning naturally with the videos on either side. This rotation eases comprehension of the visualization. Zig-zags in longer video sequences occur, which cannot be completely averted. Because learners often focus on semantics in a local space, they typically do not include many neighboring videos in the Exploration Canvas. To minimize overlap of circles, we later apply a repulsive force between videos to obtain the final layout.

To help learners utilize the MDS layout, we perform an agglomerative clustering [27] of the videos, and split the Exploration Canvas into corresponding regions. Each region exhibits a coherent set of topics. We use the agglomerative approach because it does not require prior specification of the number of clusters. The boundaries of the regions are shown as subtle white polylines, determined by aggregating Voronoi cells of videos in the same cluster.

In addition, we overlay topical keywords extracted from the text transcripts of each video cluster to reveal contextual information of different regions in the MDS projection. To obtain discriminative keywords, we first employ the standard TF-IDF method and then re-weight the keywords based on terms in video titles, because the titles are created by human and provide high quality summarization. Next, we post-process the keywords for the video clusters to remove duplications. These keywords are placed using a force-directed layout, and can be optionally hidden.

To facilitate exploration of videos, the Recommendation Panel displays auxiliary information on both sides (Figure 1-b). Videos that were recently visited and adjacent videos from the current course are shown in two vertical lists on the left. Similarly, recommended videos are shown on the right in a ranked list similar to the traditional approach. Interactive linking of the same video is provided as it is hovered over in the lists or in the Exploration Canvas. Meanwhile, a tooltip pops up showing a set of important keywords extracted from the video transcript and title based on the RAKE algorithm [22] (Figure 1-d). Also, clicking any of the videos selects it as the current video and updates the visualization accordingly. Our goal here is to provide some semantic structure in the information space, allowing everyday users to better understand the MDS layout and confidently select a video to watch next.

4 CONCLUSION

We have demonstrated MOOCex with a corpus of over four thousand videos from 41 MOOCs. MOOCex enables exploration of this content via recommendations that reflect sequential patterns mined from the corresponding course syllabi. The visual interface facilitates assessment of the semantic relationships between videos both within the current video's course and with recommended results from other courses. The prominence of inter-topic sequential information and inter-video semantics in our system empowers users to confidently select a video to watch next.

REFERENCES

[1] John Adcock, Matthew Cooper, Laurent Denoue, Hamed Pirsiavash, and Lawrence A. Rowe. 2010. TalkMiner: A Lecture Webcast Search Engine. In *Proceedings of the ACM International Conference on Multimedia (MM '10)*. 241–250. https://doi.org/10.1145/1873951.1873986

[2] Rakesh Agrawal, Maria Christoforaki, Sreenivas Gollapudi, Anitha Kannan, Krishnaram Kenthapadi, and Adith Swaminathan. 2014. *Mining Videos from the Web for Electronic Textbooks*. Springer International Publishing, 219–234. https://doi.org/10.1007/978-3-319-07248-7_16

[3] Chidansh Bhatt, Matthew Cooper, and Jian Zhao. 2018. SeqSense: Video Recommendation Using Topic Sequence Mining. In *MultiMedia Modeling*, Klaus Schoeffmann, Thanarat H. Chalidabhongse, Chong Wah Ngo, Supavadee Aramvith, Noel E. O'Connor, Yo-Sung Ho, Moncef Gabbouj, and Ahmed Elgammal (Eds.). Springer International Publishing, Cham, 252–263.

[4] David M Blei, Andrew Y Ng, and Michael I Jordan. 2003. Latent dirichlet allocation. *Journal of Machine Learning Research* 3 (2003), 993–1022.

[5] Keunho Choi, Donghee Yoo, Gunwoo Kim, and Yongmoo Suh. 2012. A Hybrid Online-product Recommendation System: Combining Implicit Rating-based Collaborative Filtering and Sequential Pattern Analysis. *Electronic Commerce Research and Applications* 11, 4 (July 2012), 309–317. https://doi.org/10.1016/j.elerap.2012.02.004

[6] Carleton Coffrin, Linda Corrin, Paula de Barba, and Gregor Kennedy. 2014. Visualizing Patterns of Student Engagement and Performance in MOOCs. In *Proceedings of the Fourth International Conference on Learning Analytics And Knowledge (LAK '14)*. 83–92. https://doi.org/10.1145/2567574.2567586

[7] Franck Dernoncourt, Colin Taylor, Una-May O'Reilly, Kayan Veeramachaneni, Sherwin Wu, Chuong Do, and Sherif Halawa. 2013. MoocViz: A Large Scale, Open Access, Collaborative, Data Analytics Platform for MOOCs. In *Proceedings of NIPS Workshop on Data-Driven Education*.

[8] Philippe Fournier-Viger, Antonio Gomariz, Ted Gueniche, Espérance Mwamikazi, and Rincy Thomas. 2013. TKS: Efficient Mining of Top-K Sequential Patterns. In *Advanced Data Mining and Applications*, Hiroshi Motoda, Zhaohui Wu, Longbing Cao, Osmar Zaiane, Min Yao, and Wei Wang (Eds.). Springer Berlin Heidelberg, 109–120. https://doi.org/10.1007/978-3-642-53914-5_10

[9] Philippe Fournier-Viger and Vincent S. Tseng. 2013. TNS: Mining Top-k Non-redundant Sequential Rules. In *Proceedings of the 28th Annual ACM Symposium on Applied Computing (SAC '13)*. 164–166. https://doi.org/10.1145/2480362.2480395

[10] S. Fu, J. Zhao, W. Cui, and H. Qu. 2017. Visual Analysis of MOOC Forums with iForum. *IEEE Transactions on Visualization and Computer Graphics* 23, 1 (Jan 2017), 201–210. https://doi.org/10.1109/TVCG.2016.2598444

[11] Negar Hariri, Bamshad Mobasher, and Robin Burke. 2012. Context-aware Music Recommendation Based on Latenttopic Sequential Patterns. In *Proceedings of ACM Conference on Recommender Systems (RecSys '12)*. 131–138. https://doi.org/10.1145/2365952.2365979

[12] Ruining He, Wang-Cheng Kang, and Julian McAuley. 2017. Translation-based Recommendation. In *Proceedings of the Eleventh ACM Conference on Recommender Systems (RecSys '17)*. ACM, New York, NY, USA, 161–169. https://doi.org/10.1145/3109859.3109882

[13] S. Jiang, X. Qian, T. Mei, and Y. Fu. 2016. Personalized Travel Sequence Recommendation on Multi-Source Big Social Media. *IEEE Transactions on Big Data* 2, 1 (March 2016), 43–56. https://doi.org/10.1109/TBDATA.2016.2541160

[14] KhanAcademy Knowledge Map. Accessed in 2017. https://www.khanacademy.org/exercisedashboard. (Accessed in 2017).

[15] Juho Kim, Philip J. Guo, Daniel T. Seaton, Piotr Mitros, Krzysztof Z. Gajos, and Robert C. Miller. 2014. Understanding In-video Dropouts and Interaction Peaks Inonline Lecture Videos. In *Proceedings of the First ACM Conference on Learning @ Scale Conference (L@S '14)*. 31–40. https://doi.org/10.1145/2556325.2566237

[16] Christopher D. Manning, Prabhakar Raghavan, and Hinrich Schütze. 2008. *Introduction to Information Retrieval*. Cambridge University Press.

[17] Tao Mei, Bo Yang, Xian-Sheng Hua, and Shipeng Li. 2011. Contextual Video Recommendation by Multimodal Relevance and User Feedback. *ACM Transactions on Information Systems* 29, 2, Article 10 (2011), 24 pages. https://doi.org/10.1145/1961209.1961213

[18] C Romero Morales, AR Porras Pérez, S Ventura Soto, C Hervás Martınez, and A Zafra. 2006. Using sequential pattern mining for links recommendation in adaptive hypermedia educational systems. In *Current Developments in Technology Assisted Education*, Vol. 2. 1016–1020.

[19] Joseph D Novak and D Bob Gowin. 1984. *Learning how to learn*. Cambridge University Press.

[20] D.F.O. Onah, J. Sinclair, and R. Boyatt. 2014. Dropout Rates Of Massive Open Online Courses: Behavioural Patterns. In *Proceedings of International Conference on Education and New Learning Technologies*. 5825–5834.

[21] H. Qu and Q. Chen. 2015. Visual Analytics for MOOC Data. *IEEE Computer Graphics and Applications* 35, 6 (Nov 2015), 69–75. https://doi.org/10.1109/MCG.2015.137

[22] Stuart Rose, Dave Engel, Nick Cramer, and Wendy Cowley. 2010. Automatic keyword extraction from individual documents. *Text Mining: Applications and Theory* (2010), 1–20.

[23] M. Schwab, H. Strobelt, J. Tompkin, C. Fredericks, C. Huff, D. Higgins, A. Strezhnev, M. Komisarchik, G. King, and H. Pfister. 2017. booc.io: An Education System with Hierarchical Concept Maps and Dynamic Non-linear Learning Plans. *IEEE Transactions on Visualization and Computer Graphics* 23, 1 (Jan 2017), 571–580. https://doi.org/10.1109/TVCG.2016.2598518

[24] Conglei Shi, Siwei Fu, Qing Chen, and Huamin Qu. 2015. VisMOOC: Visualizing video clickstream data from Massive Open Online Courses. In *Proceedings of IEEE Pacific Visualization Symposium (PacificVis)*. 159–166. https://doi.org/10.1109/PACIFICVIS.2015.7156373

[25] R. Spiro and J. Jehng. 1990. Cognitive flexibility and hypertext: Theory and technology for the nonlinear and multidimensional traversal of complex subject matter. In *Cognition, education and multimedia: Exploring ideas in high technology*, D. Nix and R. Spiro (Eds.). Lawrence Erlbaum.

[26] Warren S. Torgerson. 1952. Multidimensional scaling: I. Theory and method. *Psychometrika* 17, 4 (Dec 1952), 401–419. https://doi.org/10.1007/BF02288916

[27] Ian H. Witten, Eibe Frank, and Mark A. Hall. 2011. *Data Mining: Practical Machine Learning Tools and Techniques* (3rd ed.). Morgan Kaufmann.

[28] Saijing Zheng, Mary Beth Rosson, Patrick C. Shih, and John M. Carroll. 2015. Understanding Student Motivation, Behaviors and Perceptions in MOOCs. In *Proceedings of the ACM Conference on Computer Supported Cooperative Work and Social Computing (CSCW '15)*. 1882–1895. https://doi.org/10.1145/2675133.2675217

[29] Q. Zhu, M. L. Shyu, and H. Wang. 2013. VideoTopic: Content-Based Video Recommendation Using a Topic Model. In *Proceedings of the IEEE International Symposium on Multimedia*. 219–222. https://doi.org/10.1109/ISM.2013.41

Who to Ask: An Intelligent Fashion Consultant

Yangbangyan Jiang
State Key Laboratory of Information Security, Institute of Information Engineering, CAS
School of Cyber Security, University of Chinese Academy of Sciences
Beijing, China
jiangyangbangyan@iie.ac.cn

Qianqian Xu
Key Laboratory of Intelligent Information Processing, Institute of Computing Technology, CAS
Beijing, China
xuqianqian@ict.ac.cn

Xiaochun Cao
State Key Laboratory of Information Security, Institute of Information Engineering, CAS
School of Cyber Security, University of Chinese Academy of Sciences
Beijing, China
caoxiaochun@iie.ac.cn

Qingming Huang*
University of Chinese Academy of Sciences
Institute of Computing Technology, CAS
Beijing, China
qmhuang@ucas.ac.cn

ABSTRACT

Humankind has always been in pursuit of fashion. Nevertheless, people are often troubled by collocating clothes, e.g., tops, bottoms, shoes, and accessories, from numerous fashion items in their closets. Moreover, it may be expensive and inconvenient to employ a fashion stylist. In this paper, we present *Stile*, an end-to-end intelligent fashion consultant system, to generate stylish outfits for given items. Unlike previous systems, our framework considers the global compatibility of fashion items in the outfit and models the dependencies among items in a fixed order via a bidirectional LSTM. Therefore, it can guarantee that items in the same outfit should share a similar style and neither redundant nor missing items exist in the resulting outfit for essential categories. The demonstration shows that our proposed system provides people with a practical and convenient solution to find natural and proper fashion outfits.

KEYWORDS

Outfit recommendation; Deep learning; LSTM

ACM Reference Format:

Yangbangyan Jiang, Qianqian Xu, Xiaochun Cao, and Qingming Huang. 2018. Who to Ask: An Intelligent Fashion Consultant. In *ICMR '18: 2018 International Conference on Multimedia Retrieval, June 11–14, 2018, Yokohama, Japan.* ACM, New York, NY, USA, 4 pages. https://doi.org/10.1145/3206025.3206092

*Corresponding author.

ICMR '18, June 11–14, 2018, Yokohama, Japan

ACM ISBN 978-1-4503-5046-4/18/06...$15.00
https://doi.org/10.1145/3206025.3206092

1 INTRODUCTION

What to wear may be the most troubling question besides *what to eat*. The pursuit of fashion is a nature of human beings. No matter what the occasion is, a decent and stylish costume could make people brilliant, full of confidence and welcomed by others. However, a person always possesses a large number of clothes and accessories in his/her closet, which makes the outfit much difficult to decide since there are too many options for him/her to choose. When we select fashion items for an outfit, a myriad of factors should be taken into account, such as body size, skin color, lifestyle, occupational characteristics, etc. While on the other hand, resorting to a professional fashion consultant is so expensive that people often choose clothing items without professional advice, which may cause improper clothing collocations.

With the help of machine learning, it is possible for everyone to own an intelligent fashion consultant without worrying about *what to wear tomorrow*. Currently, there are many studies on fashion items such as clothing parsing [7], clothing street-shop matching [1, 10], clothing retrieval [8], clothing recommendation [9], etc.

Most existing researches on fashion recommendation focus on predicting whether the candidate items are suitable to build a fashion outfit, or scoring the compatibility of these items. For example, a Siamese network is used to learn the compatibility of a pair of items in [14]. However, unlike global compatibility, pairwise compatibility learning often tends to emphasize a specific part of the items. Moreover, the high computational cost of enumerating all the pairs for a large candidate item set makes this kind of method less practical. Thus some studies on predicting the popularity of an outfit have appeared [6, 11]. These studies address the problem of *consistency* that fashion items in the same outfit should a share similar style. But they could not directly generate outfits. Furthermore, the *completeness* that there are neither redundant or missing items for essential categories in the outfit is somehow ignored (e.g., two pants in an outfit or no shoes but only bottoms in the outfit).

In this demo paper, we propose an end-to-end outfit recommendation system entitled *Stile* along with an efficient implementation.

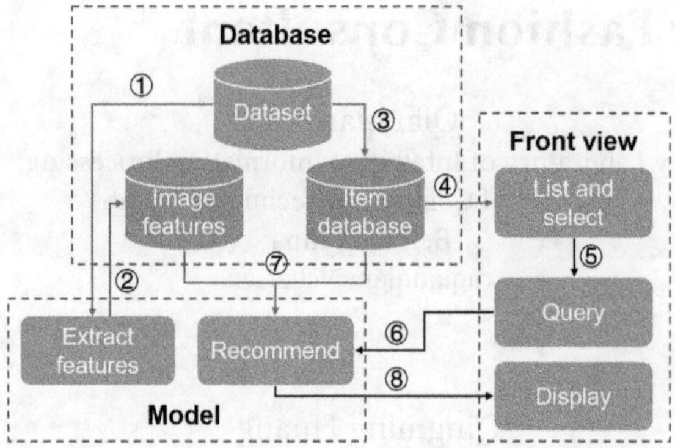

Figure 1: System architecture. Our system is composed of three components: Front view, Database, and Model. It works with following steps: (1) feed the images into the model; (2) extract image features and cache them in the database; (3) store the information of items; (4) provide information of all the items for the front view; (5) take ids of selected item as query; (6) pass the query to the model; (7) parse the query ids to corresponding features using the database; (8) recommend an outfit and return the items to the front view to display.

Different from previous studies [13], our system works as an intelligent fashion consultant and aims at generating an outfit for given items in an end-to-end framework by modeling the global compatibility. Our recommendation method is inspired by [4], where the fashion compatibility is predicted by mining the dependencies among items in a fixed order via deep neural networks. Specifically, the algorithm generates outfit items that maximize the co-occurrence probability of given items and themselves. By fixing the order of item categories in an outfit, some kinds of items, such as *tops, bottoms,* and *shoes,* are generated only once. Accordingly, the property of *completeness* holds. Meanwhile, the global compatibility guarantees the style *consistency* of items. In the system, images of fashion items are fed into a convolutional network to extract the features used for recommendation. One can browse and select the items of interest to their fashion carts. After the query is sent to the back-end recommendation model, the generation result and the query will both be displayed in the user interface.

2 SYSTEM ARCHITECTURE

In this section, we describe the pipeline of our system in detail. First, we introduce the overview of our system and explain the functions of its components. And then we demonstrate the method employed for outfit recommendation.

2.1 Overview

The block diagram of our system architecture is depicted in Figure 1. Our intelligent fashion consultant consists of three components: (i) Front view, which provides a user interface to enable users to browse, select and query the fashion items; (ii) Database, which stores the information of items and also the image features extracted by the network; (iii) Model, which extracts the features for images, receives the query and generates the result of outfit recommendation. Their behaviors are described as follows:

Database. A good database is simple but complete for queries. We store the necessary information of each item, such as *name* and *category*, to support their display in the front view. On the other hand, we should cache the intermediate results of some steps that cost much time but will be frequently used. In our system, we preprocess the outfit dataset to prepare the data used in Model. Useful features for the raw image data are extracted and stored in another file to cache the query for item information.

Front view. This module provides a friendly user interface for interacting with our system. We fetch all the items in the database and list them with their images for users. Users are allowed to browse the detail information for each item and add several items to their outfit carts. After the query items are selected, users can send the query request to our recommendation model, then get and display the results.

Model. As the "intelligence" of the system, this module takes charge of recommending outfit according to the query items. Since we take the raw images of these items as input for this problem, we need to transform the 2-D data into 1-D vectors in a proper way. In our system, we utilize a deep neural network to extract useful image features. When a user sends the selected items to the model, the features of these items are fed into another network to generate a fashion item sequence, which is the recommended result, and then this outfit is returned to the front view.

2.2 Outfit Recommendation

Inspired by [4], we build a similar network to perform the outfit recommendation. By sorting items in a given outfit in terms of their categories (say *top, bottom, bag,* and *accessory*), we could cast outfit recommendation as a sequence learning problem which is well-defined in machine learning community. In fact, the items in an outfit often share similar fashion styles. To find such connections, we can use LSTM [3] to address this problem. This network has a short-term memory of past information that can last for a long period of time. Such long-lasting memory enables LSTM to utilize more information to exploit the latent relationship between the current item and all the past items. On the other hand, to make the learning more flexible and complete, it is desired to learn the relationship between the current item and future items. Bidirectional LSTM (Bi-LSTM) [2] allows us to model the connection among current item, past items, and future items at the same time through a forward and a backward LSTM. Therefore, we choose Bi-LSTM to perform outfit generation. Given a query item, we can predict all the items before and after it by the bidirectional connections.

Before using LSTM to generate the item sequence, we should map the 2-D images into 1-D vectors to match the input format of LSTM. It is significant to find a proper way to conduct the transformation and get compact and useful feature vectors. Recently, convolutional neural networks (CNNs) have been proven to be successful in the field of image processing and computer vision [5, 12]. On account of its powerful feature representation ability, we obtain the representation by an Inception-v3 model [12], in our system.

Given an item feature sequence of an outfit $S = \{\mathbf{x}_t\}_{t=1}^{m}$, for t-th item $\mathbf{x}_t$, we use the forward LSTM to predict the next item

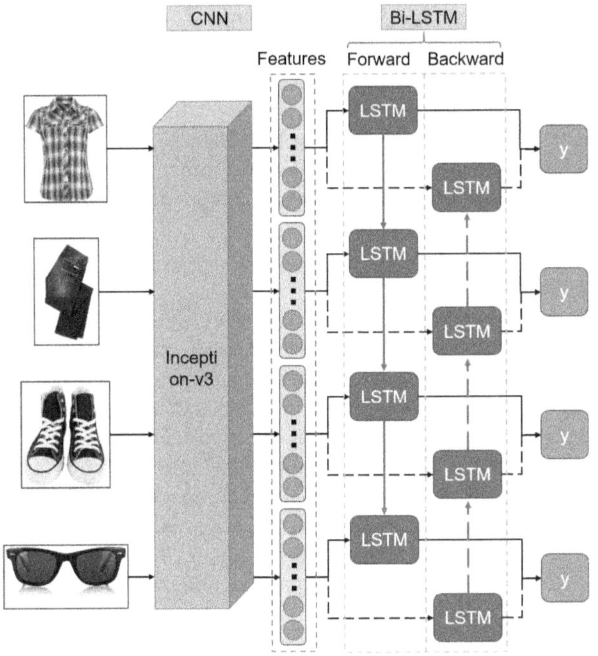

Figure 2: Network architecture. We use an Inception-v3 convolutional network to obtain image feature vectors and then feed them into a bidirectional LSTM to generate the outfit item sequence. The forward LSTM learns from the past information and the backward one learns from the future.

$\mathbf{x}_{t+1}$ based on previous items $\{\mathbf{x}_i\}_{i=1}^{t}$ and the backward LSTM to conduct the prediction in the reverse order. Two zero vectors $\mathbf{x}_0$ and $\mathbf{x}_{m+1}$ are added to the sequence as the stopping mark of prediction for the backward and forward LSTM, respectively. Consequently, the sequence used as input for Bi-LSTM should be denoted as $\tilde{S} = \{\mathbf{x}_t\}_{t=0}^{m+1}$. We can predict an item by choosing the item with the highest occurrence probability given all previous items. Let θ_f denote the parameter of the forward LSTM and θ_b denote that of the backward LSTM. Then we can formulate the loss function for the forward LSTM as follows:

$$L_{\text{fw}}(\tilde{S};\theta_f) = -\frac{1}{m}\sum_{t=1}^{m} \log P(\mathbf{x}_{t+1}|\mathbf{x}_1, \mathbf{x}_2, \cdots, \mathbf{x}_t; \theta_f) \quad (1)$$

and that for the backward LSTM as follows:

$$L_{\text{bw}}(\tilde{S};\theta_b) = -\frac{1}{m}\sum_{t=m-1}^{0} \log P(\mathbf{x}_t|\mathbf{x}_m, \mathbf{x}_{m-1}, \cdots, \mathbf{x}_{t+1}; \theta_b) \quad (2)$$

Here the probability of the next item conditioned on all previously known items can be calculated using softmax function:

$$P(\mathbf{x}_{t+1}|\mathbf{x}_1, \mathbf{x}_2, \cdots, \mathbf{x}_t; \theta_f) = \frac{\exp(\mathbf{h}_t \mathbf{x}_{t+1})}{\sum_{\mathbf{x}\in\mathcal{X}_C} \exp(\mathbf{h}_t \mathbf{x})} \quad (3)$$

and

$$P(\mathbf{x}_t|\mathbf{x}_m, \mathbf{x}_{m-1}, \cdots, \mathbf{x}_{t+1}; \theta_b) = \frac{\exp(\tilde{\mathbf{h}}_{t+1} \mathbf{x}_t)}{\sum_{\mathbf{x}\in\mathcal{X}_C} \exp(\tilde{\mathbf{h}}_{t+1} \mathbf{x})} \quad (4)$$

where $\mathbf{h}$ and $\tilde{\mathbf{h}}$ are the hidden state of the forward and backward LSTM respectively, and $\mathcal{X}_C$ denotes the candidate item set.

The whole network architecture is depicted in Figure 2. We first transform the images into feature representations by various operations in CNN. Then these features are fed into the Bi-LSTM, where the forward LSTM learns from the past information and the backward LSTM learns from the future one, to refine their relationships out of all the information.

Outfit generation is performed by the following steps. First, we take the first query item as input and run the Bi-LSTM in both directions to generate an initial item set. When there are more than one items, we locate the position of the second query item in the initial set by finding its nearest neighbor and then replace that item with it. If the second item is not adjacent to the first one, to fill the blank positions between them, we choose the item maximizing the sum of the co-occurrence probability of current items given items before and after the blank. After that, we can run the backward and forward inference for the start and end items respectively to generate a new outfit. This procedure is repeated for the rest query items. Note that the step of filling blank positions between two query items guarantees the compatibility of the outfit subsequence, consequently the global compatibility of the result.

3 USER INTERFACE

3.1 Dataset

We use the dataset collected from Polyvore (polyvore.com), a fashion website providing the outfits created by users [4]. The Polyvore dataset contains 21,889 outfits and 164,379 items. Each outfit consists of up to 8 fashion items with distinct categories such as *Coats, Pants, Hats.* The order of items in each outfit is fixed to *tops, bottoms, shoes,* and *accessories.* Specifically, for accessories, the order is usually like handbags, hats, glasses, watches, necklaces, earrings, etc. This property allows the Bi-LSTM to learn the relationship between the items in an outfit.

3.2 Implementation

We build the system as a web application using Flask, a flexible microframework written in Python that makes the development easier. The items in the Polyvore dataset are recorded in an SQLite database. We also store the path of the images instead of the raw data to keep the database simple and fast to query. The bidirectional LSTM is implemented using TensorFlow.

The user interface is shown in Figure 3a. When the web application is started up, we load all the databases and initialize the network model for prediction. All the items in the database are listed with images like Figure 3a. Users can browse the detail information for each item by clicking its name or image. A fashion cart is provided for each user to pick their preferable items. From the cart interface, users can send the query request into our recommendation model by clicking the "add" button. Then our model is inferencing on the server. The result is returned to the Front view and displayed like Figure 3b. For example, we add a *luxury classic t-shirt* into our cart, and the corresponding recommendation items include jeans, blouse, sunglasses, and boots. When another item is added to the query, we get a different result in Figure 3c.

(a) List all the items.

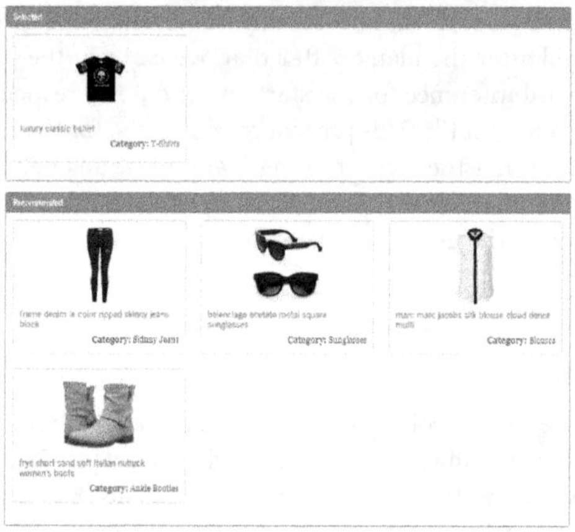

(b) Display the result for a single query item.

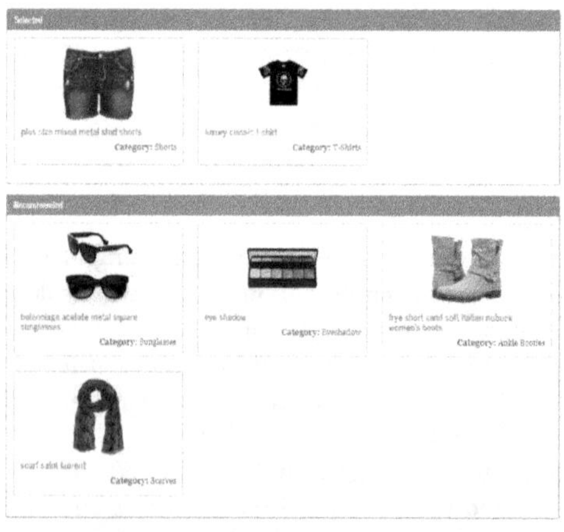

(c) Display the result for a list of query items.

Figure 3: Demonstration Results.

4 CONCLUSION

In this demo paper, we propose an end-to-end intelligent fashion consultant system. It takes images of query items as input and generates a recommended item sequence, which provides a solution to the question *what to wear*. Our system composes of a well-designed front view, a complete database, and a recommendation model based on a bidirectional LSTM. By sorting the items by categories, we turn outfit recommendation into a sequence prediction problem. Then the Bi-LSTM can capture and utilize the style similarity of all the items to generate the result. Therefore, the style *consistency* of items in the same outfit and the *completeness* of an outfit can be preserved simultaneously. Furthermore, other functions like personal closets, clothing parsing, and street-shop matching could be unified into this framework.

ACKNOWLEDGMENTS

The research of Yangbangyan Jiang and Xiaochun Cao was supported by National Key Research and Development Plan (No.2016YFC0801004), National Natural Science Foundation of China (No.U1636214, 61733007). The research of Qianqian Xu was supported in part by National Natural Science Foundation of China (No.61672514), Beijing Natural Science Foundation (No.4182079), Youth Innovation Promotion Association CAS, and CCF-Tencent Open Research Fund. The research of Qingming Huang was supported in part by National Natural Science Foundation of China: 61650202 and 61332016, in part by Key Research Program of Frontier Sciences, CAS: QYZDJ-SSW-SYS013.

REFERENCES

[1] Zhiqi Cheng, Xiao Wu, Yang Liu, and Xiansheng Hua. 2017. Video2Shop: Exact Matching Clothes in Videos to Online Shopping Images. In *IEEE Conference on Computer Vision and Pattern Recognition*. 4169–4177.

[2] Alex Graves, Navdeep Jaitly, and Abdel-rahman Mohamed. 2013. Hybrid speech recognition with Deep Bidirectional LSTM. In *IEEE Workshop on Automatic Speech Recognition and Understanding*. 273–278.

[3] Alex Graves, Abdel-rahman Mohamed, and Geoffrey E. Hinton. 2013. Speech recognition with deep recurrent neural networks. In *IEEE International Conference on Acoustics, Speech and Signal Processing*. 6645–6649.

[4] Xintong Han, Zuxuan Wu, Yu-Gang Jiang, and Larry S. Davis. 2017. Learning Fashion Compatibility with Bidirectional LSTMs. In *ACM Multimedia Conference*. 1078–1086.

[5] Kaiming He, Xiangyu Zhang, Shaoqing Ren, and Jian Sun. 2016. Deep Residual Learning for Image Recognition. In *IEEE Conference on Computer Vision and Pattern Recognition*. 770–778.

[6] Yuncheng Li, Liangliang Cao, Jiang Zhu, and Jiebo Luo. 2017. Mining Fashion Outfit Composition Using an End-to-End Deep Learning Approach on Set Data. *IEEE Transactions on Multimedia* 19, 8 (2017), 1946–1955.

[7] Xiaodan Liang, Liang Lin, Wei Yang, Ping Luo, Junshi Huang, and Shuicheng Yan. 2016. Clothes Co-Parsing Via Joint Image Segmentation and Labeling With Application to Clothing Retrieval. *IEEE Transactions on Multimedia* 18, 6 (2016), 1175–1186.

[8] Kevin Lin, Huei-Fang Yang, Kuan-Hsien Liu, Jen-Hao Hsiao, and Chu-Song Chen. 2015. Rapid Clothing Retrieval via Deep Learning of Binary Codes and Hierarchical Search. In *ACM International Conference on Multimedia Retrieval*. 499–502.

[9] Si Liu, Jiashi Feng, Zheng Song, Tianzhu Zhang, Hanqing Lu, Changsheng Xu, and Shuicheng Yan. 2012. Hi, magic closet, tell me what to wear!. In *ACM Multimedia Conference*. 619–628.

[10] Si Liu, Zheng Song, Guangcan Liu, Changsheng Xu, Hanqing Lu, and Shuicheng Yan. 2012. Street-to-shop: Cross-scenario clothing retrieval via parts alignment and auxiliary set. In *IEEE Conference on Computer Vision and Pattern Recognition*. 3330–3337.

[11] Edgar Simo-Serra, Sanja Fidler, Francesc Moreno-Noguer, and Raquel Urtasun. 2015. Neuroaesthetics in fashion: Modeling the perception of fashionability. In *IEEE Conference on Computer Vision and Pattern Recognition*. 869–877.

[12] Christian Szegedy, Vincent Vanhoucke, Sergey Ioffe, Jonathon Shlens, and Zbigniew Wojna. 2016. Rethinking the Inception Architecture for Computer Vision. In *IEEE Conference on Computer Vision and Pattern Recognition*. 2818–2826.

[13] Pongsate Tangseng, Kota Yamaguchi, and Takayuki Okatani. 2017. Recommending Outfits from Personal Closet. In *IEEE International Conference on Computer Vision Workshops*. 2275–2279.

[14] Andreas Veit, Balazs Kovacs, Sean Bell, Julian McAuley, Kavita Bala, and Serge Belongie. 2015. Learning visual clothing style with heterogeneous dyadic co-occurrences. In *IEEE International Conference on Computer Vision*. 4642–4650.

A Simple Score Following System for Music Ensembles Using Chroma and Dynamic Time Warping

Po-Wen Chou Fu-Neng Lin Keh-Ning Chang Herng-Yow Chen
Department of Computer Science and Information Engineering, National Chi Nan University, Taiwan
E-mail:{ s103321535, s102321902, klim, hychen}@ncnu.edu.tw

ABSTRACT

It [1] is disruptive for instrumentalists to turn the page of music sheet when they are playing instruments. The purpose of this study is to investigate how real-time music score alignment can serve as a tool for a computer-assisted page turner. We proposed a simple system which can be set up easily and quickly for use to solve the problem. The framework of the system has two parts: off-line preprocessing stage and online alignment stage. In the first stage, the system extracts chroma feature vectors from the reference recording. In the second stage, the system receives audio signals of live performance and extracts chroma feature vectors from them. Finally, the system uses Dynamic Time Warping (DTW) to find an alignment between those two sets of chroma feature vectors to mark the current measure of the score. The prototype system was evaluated by musicians in different music ensembles like string quartet and orchestra. Most musicians agreed that the system is helpful and can indicate the current measure of a live performance correctly. Some musicians, however, disagreed that the system turned the page at right time. The user survey showed that the best timing for page turning is user-dependent because it is highly to do with musicians' sight reading skills and speed.

CCS CONCEPTS

• **Computer systems organization → Embedded systems**; *Redundancy*; Robotics • **Networks** → Network reliability

KEYWORDS

Score following; chroma; dynamic time warping

ACM Reference Format:
Po-Wen Chou, Fu-Neng Lin, Keh-Ning Chang, and Herng-Yow Chen. 2018. A Simple Score Following System for Music Ensembles Using Chroma and Dynamic Time Warping. In *ICMR '18: 2018 International Conference on Multimedia Retrieval, June 11–14, 2018, Yokohama, Japan.* ACM, New York, NY, USA, 4 pages. https://doi.org/10.1145/3206025.3206090

*Produces the permission block, and copyright information
†The full version of the author's guide is available as acmart.pdf document
[1]It is a datatype.

ICMR '18, June 11–14, 2018, Yokohama, Japan

ACM ISBN 978-1-4503-5046-4/18/06...$15.00
https://doi.org/10.1145/3206025.3206090

1 INTRODUCTION

Music ensembles connect musicians and audiences together mentally and emotionally. Consider instrumentalists whose hands are already busy playing, it is disruptive for them to turn the page of music sheet. In a symphony orchestra, two musicians usually share one music stand. The junior person on the inside of stand is responsible for page turning. We try to solve the above problem by a score following system. Score following is a technique that can track live performance and point out the current playing notes on the score. It was first presented at ICMC in 1984 by Roger Dannenberg [1]. Typical application of score following is to provide a real-time musical accompaniment for a live soloist [2]. Another example, the Orchestral Performance Companion [3], employs score following to provide an automated personal guide that presents time-relevant annotations and contextual information on a hand-held device. In this paper, we focus on the application of score following about automatic page turning.

A musical ensemble is a group of people who perform instrumental and/or vocal music. Our system not only turns pages for a single instrumentalist but also turns pages for all musicians of an ensemble. One part of this system is located on the conductor side to track the performance of an ensemble. After analyzing the audio signals, synchronizing events are sent to the other part of the system that is located on instrumentalist. Through the events, all members of the ensemble including the conductor know where the current playing measure is and the system can turn the pages automatically.

2 RELATED WORK

2.1 Chroma Feature

The audio signals of music performances can be classified as monophonic and polyphonic. Monophonic audio signals can be reliably transcribed by mature single-pitch detection techniques. Polyphonic pitch estimation remains an open area of research [4].

The audio signals of music ensembles is a polyphonic problem. The method of pitch detection technique is not suitable in this case. Chroma vector is a 12-dimensional vector, each of whose elements is total power of the frequencies corresponding to one note in all octaves [5]. Using Chroma feature can ignore the difference of octaves, so the researchers adopted the chroma feature of audio signals to overcome the polyphonic problem.

2.2 Dynamic Time Warping

Audio-score alignment is the problem of aligning (synchronizing) a music audio performance with its score [6]. In this paper, the researchers use the recording of music performance as reference, and compare the audio signals of live performance with it. The problem is defined as audio to audio alignment case.

Two methods well known in speech recognition have been extensively used in the literature: statistical approaches (e.g. HMMs), and dynamic time warping (DTW) [7]. We adopted dynamic time warping (DTW) to align score in this system.

The Dynamic Time Warping algorithm (DTW) is a well-known algorithm in many areas. While first introduced in 60s [8] and extensively explored in 80s by application to the speech recognition [9]. It is currently used in many areas, especially in music and signal processing. The DTW algorithm can find the similarity of two time series. In order to align two sequences, Figure 1 shows how the DTW algorithm works. We use Euclidean distance to calculate the similarity between two sequences to find the minimum path in DTW matrix.

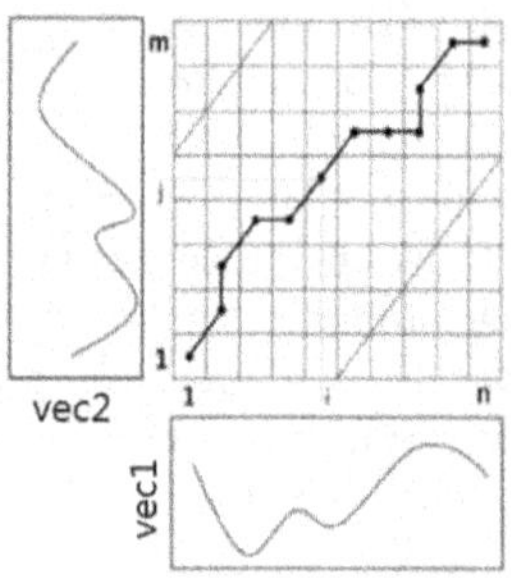

Figure 1: Finding the best path in DTW matrix.

The warping path has more than one pattern to be chosen. Figure 2(a) shows the classic path pattern. If adjusting the path weight, we could obtain a different result in DTW matrix. The researches adopted the path pattern in Figure 2(b) to calculate the minimum distance, because the algorithm can skip the wrong point and save the calculating time.

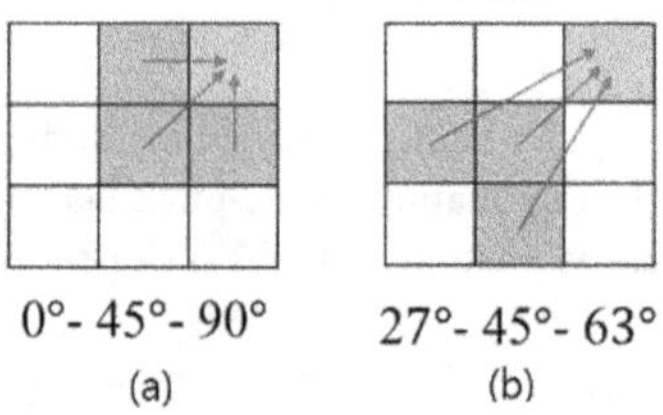

Figure 2: The step patterns of DTW.

3 IMPLEMENTATION

The proposed framework for audio-to-score alignment is presented in Figure 3. As can be seen, the framework has two stages. First, the chroma vectors of reference recording need to be computed beforehand and the measure numbers of score must be marked in the preprocessing stage. Then the DTW function will work to align audio to score in the alignment stage. As shown in Figure 4, we use iPad Pro as server, and iPads as clients. The protocol of the system is Bluetooth, so our system can be set up easily and quickly for use in practice.

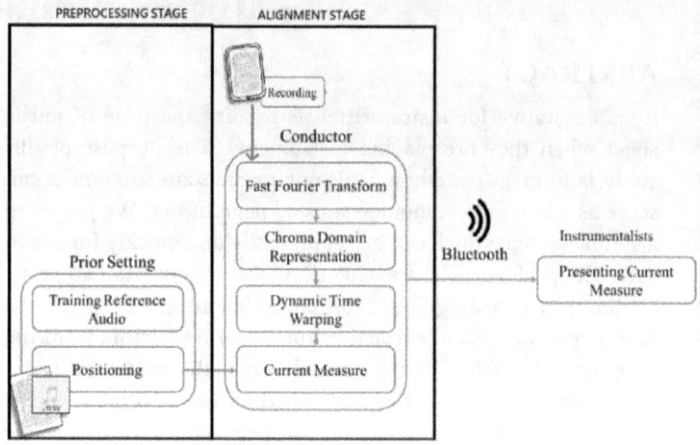

Figure 3: Block diagram of the proposed system.

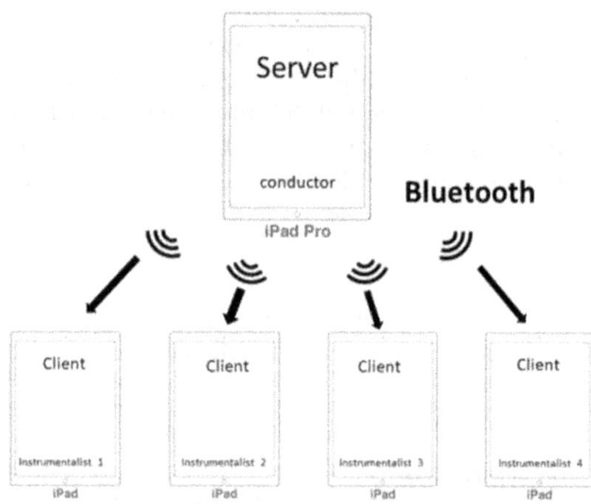

Figure 4: Actual layout of the proposed system.

3.1 Preprocessing Stage

There are two important things to do in this stage. One is to transform the reference recording into sequences of chroma feature vectors. The other is to mark the measure position of the score image which will be used in next stage.

3.1.1 Transform the reference recording to chroma. First of all, the researchers choose the reference recording with wave format and input it into this system. Second, this system will play reference recording to get chroma features of each frame. Finally, we save whole chroma features in this system to be compared in alignment stage.

3.1.2 Mark the position of measure number. The researchers need to manually mark the measure to record its position (i.e. (x,

y) coordination in this JPEG score image). We coordinate the consistency between conductor's score and instrumentalist's score by the above method.

3.1.3 Decide the frame size of one measure. After marking the measure position of score, the researchers calculate the chroma feature quantity of each measure, as shown in Figure 5. In general case, there are no big change of tempo in a piece. We use the result from all chroma features divided by number of total measures. Then we can get the number of chroma features per measure. If first measure is incomplete measure of a piece, we would use the result from all chroma features divided by number of beats. Finally, the researchers can get the correct chroma features per measure by above method.

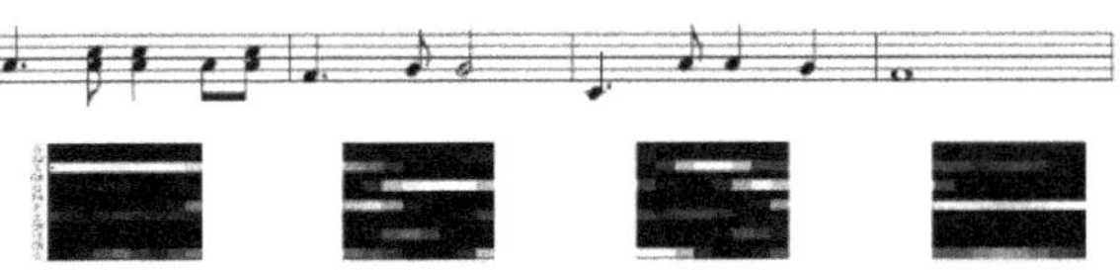

Figure 5: Get the chroma feature quantity of each measure.

3.2 Alignment Stage

This system uses tablet (iPad Pro) microphone to record the music audio signals. We set the sampling frequency of recording by 44.1 kHz, window size is 4096 points and frame size is 1024 points. This system obtains the chroma features about 43 frames per second. In order to compare the live performance features with the reference ones, two cases in alignment stage described below.

Case 1: The first measure alignment method. For the first measure, the system matches the input chroma features with the reference ones within a two-consecutive-measure window (i.e., the present and the next), as shown in Figure 6. The researchers decide the correct measure by the most similar result from two comparisons. If the result is first measure, the arrow would indicate the second measure. If the result is second measure, the arrow would indicate the third measure, and so on.

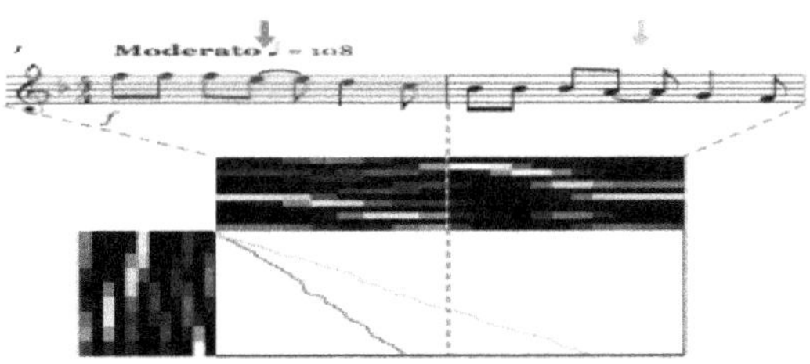

Figure 6: Example of the first measure alignment.

Case 2: The normal measures alignment method. Except for the first measure, the system matches the input chroma features with the reference ones within a three-consecutive-measure window (i.e., the previous, the present and the next), as shown in Figure 7. The method to decide the correct measure is the same as Case 1.

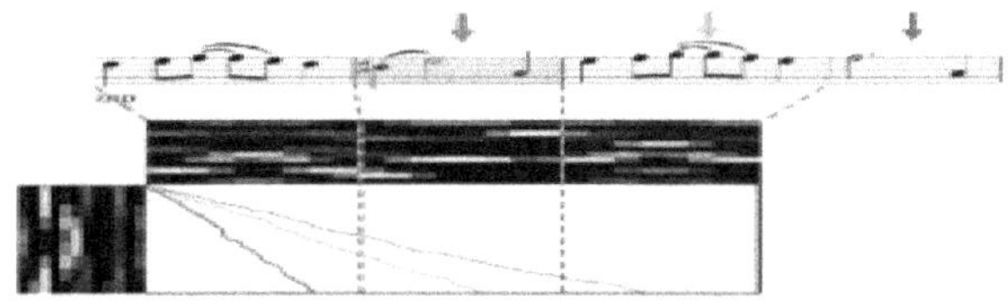

Figure 7: Example of the normal measure alignment.

In addition, the arrow of this system won't move when the similarity value is below the threshold. When the arrow indicates the last measure, the system will stop receiving audio signals to express the end of the piece.

3.3 System Interface

This system was developed in iOS by Swift language. There are two parts in it. The server is in conductor's tablet, and the clients are in different instrumentalists' tablets. The main function of server is to align and show score; the clients only show individual instrument score. Figure 8 shows the actual layout of the system. You can find the demo video of this system at this link: https://youtu.be/qpnIF68g7Vg

Figure 8: The capture picture of actual performance.

3.3.1 Conductor tablet. The conductor can choose the piece in music list, and then touches the "Start" button to start. This system has the function of error control. If all musicians of the ensemble play wrong note or that any noise interferes the system, the conductor can indicate the correct measure directly or turn page manually by turn off "Score Following" button.

3.3.2 Instrumentalist tablet. The connection status is shown in the upper left corner. The instrumentalist can decide the using of arrow on the score by "Arrow" button.

This system has the function to select different instrument score by instrumentalist. It is convenient to use in actual conditions.

4 EVALUATION

In order to evaluate the functions of this system, the researchers invited two ensembles including 9 subjects to test this system and give us some feedback, as shown in Table 1. All the subjects must have some ensemble experience.

Table 1: The piece name and instruments of each ensemble

ID	Piece Name	Instruments
ensemble1	Mellow Cellos Tango	violin1, violin2, cello
ensemble2	Taiwanese Folk Song	trumpet, trombone, tuba, flute, drum french horn

According to Figure 9, most users agreed that this system can determine the current measure and the reaction of score following is fast. But most users neither agreed nor disagreed that this system can turn the page in correct time. To explore the reason for this result, we consulted two conductors to know when to turn the page is best. One conductor said that he likes to turn the page before two measures. The other conductor said that she likes to turn the page at last measure. Because everyone has different habit, it doesn't have standard of correct time for page turning.

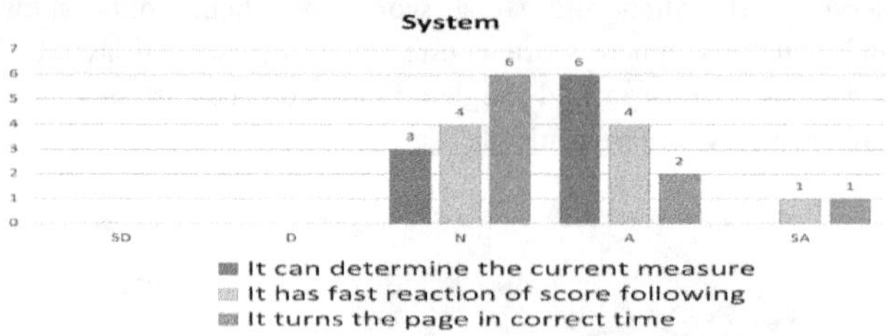

Figure 9: Survey result about functions of this system.

According to Figure 10, most users agreed that the arrow couldn't affect their reading on score. If the arrow affects users, they can disable it by themselves. But still two users disagreed this design. Our arrow is a red solid circle and shows on the current measure, so we guessed that they don't like this design. The vast majority of users agreed that it is useful to correct the measure by themselves.

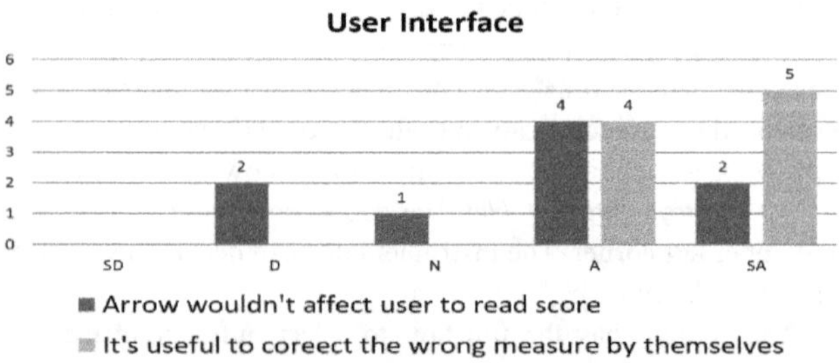

Figure 10: Survey result about user interface of this system.

According to Figure 11, most users agreed that our system can replace paper music score, but two users disagreed. The researchers guessed that it could be the device problem like running down of battery; failure of tablet, or reflection of tablet screen. Paper music score is more stable than device. Most users agreed this system is convenient to use. Our system has not complicated interface design, so most users agreed that it is useful for instrumentalist to use in an ensemble.

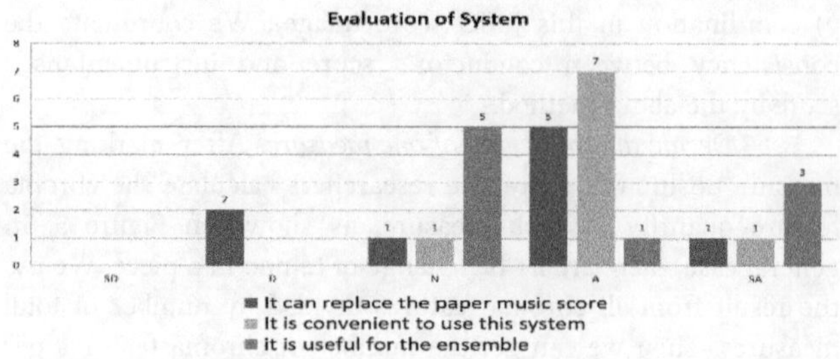

Figure 11: Survey result about evaluation of this system.

5 CONCLUSION AND FUTURE WORK

5.1 Conclusion

The researchers developed a simple score following system for music ensembles. This system could highlight present measure of live performance and turn the page automatically. We designed the simple user interface for music ensembles to use. After evaluating, we found that this system is not suitable for music performance which has various tempos. If there is more than one speed in the piece or the conductor changes the speed of piece partly, the system won't work well. The system could not indicate the correct measure because it can't distribute average features to each measure in different tempos of one piece.

5.2 Future Work

This system can't deal with the performance of different tempos. Maybe we can adopt beat tracking algorithm to improve the score following system. Because this system uses picture file of music score, the method of using MIDI file or MusicXML to improve the convenience of preprocessing work is perhaps better. It is useful to design the function which can let conductor or instrumentalist annotate something on the score. These factors should be considered for system design in the future.

REFERENCES

[1] Dannenberg, R. B. (1984, October). An on-line algorithm for real-time accompaniment. In ICMC (Vol. 84, pp. 193-198).

[2] Raphael, C. (2002). A Bayesian network for real-time musical accompaniment. In Advances in Neural Information Processing Systems (pp. 1433-1439).

[3] Prockup, M., Grunberg, D., Hrybyk, A., & Kim, Y. E. (2013). Orchestral performance companion: Using real-time audio to score alignment. IEEE MultiMedia, 20(2), 52-60.

[4] Zhiyao, D., & Pardo, B(2011). A state space model for online polyphonic audio-score alignment. In International Conference on Acoustics, Speech and Signal Processing (ICASSP) (pp. 22-27).

[5] Fujishima, T. (1999, October). Realtime Chord Recognition of Musical Sound: a System Using Common Lisp Music. In ICMC (pp. 464-467).

[6] Dannenberg, R. B., & Raphael, C. (2006). Music score alignment and computer accompaniment. Communications of the ACM, 49(8), 38-43.

[7] Carabias-Orti, J. J., Rodríguez-Serrano, F. J., Vera-Candeas, P., Ruiz-Reyes, N., & Cañadas-Quesada, F. J. (2015). An Audio to Score Alignment Framework Using Spectral Factorization and Dynamic Time Warping. In ISMIR (pp. 742-748).

[8] Bellman, R., & Kalaba, R. (1959). On adaptive control processes. IRE Transactions on Automatic Control, 4(2), 1-9.

[9] Myers, C., Rabiner, L., & Rosenberg, A. (1980). Performance tradeoffs in dynamic time warping algorithms for isolated word recognition. IEEE Transactions on Acoustics, Speech, and Signal Processing, 28(6), 623-635.

Author Index

www.ingramcontent.com/pod-product-compliance
Lightning Source LLC
LaVergne TN
LVHW082018200926
848481LV00010B/2880